THE OXFORD POPULAR DICTIONARY & THESAURUS

Prepared by

SARA HAWKER *and* JOYCE M HAWKINS

·PARRAGON·

Based on The Oxford Minidictionary, 3rd Edition © *Oxford University Press 1991, and* The Oxford Minireference Thesaurus © *Alan Spooner 1992. This abridged edition published 1995 as* The Oxford Popular Dictionary & Thesaurus *by Parragon Book Services and Magpie Books Ltd, an imprint of Robinson Publishing Ltd., by arrangement with Oxford University Press*

ISBN 0 7525-0027-9

Printed and Bound in the U.K.

ABBREVIATIONS

a. adjective
abbr. abbreviation
adjs. adjectives
adv. adverb
advs. adverbs
Amer. American
attrib. attributively
Austr. Australian
colloq. colloquial
conj. conjunction
Dec. December
derog. derogatory
esp. especially
fem. feminine
Fr. French
inf. informal
int. interjection
Ir. Irish
Jan. January
Lat. Latin
joc. jocularly
n. noun
N. Engl. Northern England
n.fem noun feminine
Nov. November
ns. nouns
orig. originally
opp. opposite
[P.] proprietary term
pl. plural
poet. poetic
poss. possessive
pref. prefix
prep. preposition
preps. prepositions
pron. pronoun
rel.pron. relative pronoun
S. Afr. South African
Sc. Scottish
Sept. September
sing. singular
sl. slang
U.S. United States
usu. usually
v. verb
v.aux. auxiliary verb

Abbreviations that are in general use (such as ft., R.C.) appear in the dictionary itself.

Proprietary Terms

This dictionary includes some words which are, or are asserted to be, proprietary terms or trade marks. Their inclusion does not mean that they have acquired for legal purposes a non-proprietary or general significance, nor is any other judgement implied concerning their legal status. In cases where the editor has some evidence that a word is used as a proprietary name or trade mark this is indicated by the letter [P.], but no judgement concerning the legal status of such words is made or implied thereby.

PRONUNCIATION

This dictionary uses a simple respelling system to show how words are pronounced. The following symbols are used:

a, á,	*as in*	**pat** /pat, **pattern** /páttern
aa, aá	*as in*	**palm** /paam/, **rather** /raáther/
air, áir	*as in*	**fair** /fair/, **fairy** /fáiri/
aw, áw	*as in*	**law** /law/, **caught** /kawt/, **caution** /kawsh'n/
awr, áwr	*as in*	**warm** /wawrm/, **warning** /wáwrning/
ay, áy	*as in*	**gauge** /gayj/, **daily** /dáyli
ch	*as in*	**church** /church/, **cello** /chéllo
e, é	*as in*	**said** /sed/, **jealous** /jélləss/
ee, eé	*as in*	**feet** /feet/, **recent** /reéss'nt/
er, ér	*as in*	**fern** /fern/, **early** /érli/
érr	*as in*	**ferry** /férri/, **burial** /bérrial/
ə	*as in*	**along** /əlóng/, **pollen** /póllən/, **lemon** /lémmən/, **serious** /seériəss/
g	*as in*	**get** /get/
i, í	*as in*	**pin** /pin/, **women** /wímmin/
ī, ī́	*as in*	**time** /tīme/, **writing** /rī́ting/
īr, ī́r	*as in*	**fire** /fīre/, **choir** /kwīr/, **desire** /dizī́r/
irr	*as in*	**lyrics** /lirriks/
j	*as in*	**judge** /juj/
kh	*as in*	**loch** /lokh/
N	*as in*	**en route** /oN rōōt/
ng	*as in*	**sing** /sing/, **sink** /singk/
ngg	*as in*	**single** /singg'l/, **anger** /ánggər/
o, ó	*as in*	**rob** /rob/, **robin** /róbbin/
ō, ṓ	*as in*	**boat** /bōt/, **motion** /mṓsh'n/
ö, ö́	*as in*	**colonel** /kö́n'l/
oo	*as in*	**unite** /yoonī́t
oŏ, oŏ́	*as in*	**wood** /woŏd/, **football** /foŏ́tbawl/
ōō, ōṓ	*as in*	**food** /fōōd/, **music** /myōṓzik/
oor, oór	*as in*	**cure** /kyoor/, **jury** /joóri/
or, ór	*as in*	**door** /dor/, **corner** /kórnər/
ow, ów	*as in*	**mouse** /mowss/, **coward** /kóward/
oy, óy	*as in*	**boy** /boy/, **noisy** /nóyzi/
r, rr	*as in*	**run** /run/, **fur** /fur/, **spirit** /spirrit/
sh	*as in*	**shut** /shut/
th	*as in*	**thin** /thin, **truth** /trōōth/
th	*as in*	**then** /then/, **mother** /múthər/
u, ú	*as in*	**cut** /kut/, **money** /múnni/
ur, úr	*as in*	**curl** /kurl/, **journey** /júrni/
úrr	*as in*	**hurry** /húrri/
y	*as in*	**yet** /yet/, **million** /milyən/
zh	*as in*	**measure** /mézhər/, **vision** /vizh'n/

Consonants

The consonants *b, d, f, h, k, l, m, n, p, s, t, v, w, z,* are pronounced in the usual way. A doubled consonant indicates that the preceding vowel is short, as in **robin** /róbbin/.

Stress

The mark ´ that appears over the vowel symbol in words of more than one syllable indicates the part of the word which carries the stress.

THE OXFORD POPULAR DICTIONARY

A

a *a.* one, any; in, to, or for each.
aback *adv.* **taken aback** disconcerted.
abacus *n.* (*pl.* **-cuses**) frame with balls sliding on rods, used for counting.
abandon *v.* leave without intending to return; give up. — *n.* careless freedom of manner. **abandonment** *n.*
abandoned *a.* (of manner etc.) showing abandon, depraved.
abase *v.* humiliate, degrade. **abasement** *n.*
abashed *a.* embarrassed, ashamed.
abate *v.* make or become less intense. **abatement** *n.*
abattoir /ábbətwaar/ *n.* slaughterhouse.
abbey *n.* building occupied by a community of monks or nuns; church belonging to this.
abbot *n.* head of a community of monks. **abbess** *n.fem.*
abbreviate *v.* shorten.
abbreviation *n.* shortened form of word(s).
ABC *n.* alphabet; alphabetical guide; rudiments (of a subject).
abdicate *v.* renounce the throne. **abdication** *n.*
abdomen *n.* part of the body containing the digestive organs. **abdominal** *a.*
abduct *v.* kidnap. **abduction** *n.*, **abductor** *n.*
aberrant *a.* showing aberration. **aberrance** *n.*
aberration *n.* deviation from what is normal; distortion.
abet *v.* (**abetted**) encourage or assist in wrongdoing. **abettor** *n.*
abeyance *n.* **in abeyance** not being used for a time.
abhor *v.* (**abhorred**) detest. **abhorrence** *n.*
abhorrent *a.* detestable.
abide *v.* tolerate. **abide by** keep (a promise); accept (consequences etc.).
abiding *a.* lasting, permanent.
ability *n.* power to do something; cleverness.
abject *a.* wretched; lacking pride. **abjectly** *adv.*
ablaze *a.* blazing.
able *a.* having power or ability. **ably** *adv.*
ablutions *n.pl.* process of washing oneself.
abnegate *v.* renounce.
abnormal *a.* not normal. **abnormally** *adv.*, **abnormality** *n.*
aboard *adv.* & *prep.* on board.
abode *n.* home, dwelling place.
abolish *v.* put an end to. **abolition** *n.*
abominable *a.* very bad or unpleasant. **abominably** *adv.*
abominate *v.* detest. **abomination** *n.*
aboriginal *a.* existing in a country from its earliest times.
aborigine /ábbərijini/ *n.* aboriginal inhabitant.
abort *v.* (cause to) expel a foetus prematurely; end prematurely and unsuccessfully.
abortion *n.* premature expulsion of a foetus from the womb; operation to cause this.
abortionist *n.* person who performs abortions.
abortive *a.* unsuccessful; causing an abortion. **abortively** *adv.*
abound *v.* be plentiful.
about *adv.* & *prep.* near; here and there; in circulation; approximately; in connection with; so as to face in the opposite direction. **about-face, about-turn** *ns.* reversal of direction or policy. **be about to** be on the point of (doing).
above *adv.* & *prep.* at or to a higher point (than); beyond the level or understanding of. **above board** without deception.
abracadabra *n.* magic formula.
abrasion *n.* rubbing or scraping away; injury caused by this.
abrasive *a.* causing abrasion; harsh. — *n.* substance used for grinding or polishing surfaces.
abreast *adv.* side by side.
abridge *v.* shorten by using fewer words. **abridgement** *n.*
abroad *adv.* away from one's home country.
abrogate *v.* repeal, cancel. **abrogation** *n.*
abrupt *a.* sudden; curt; steep. **abruptly** *adv.*, **abruptness** *n.*
abscess *n.* collection of pus formed in the body.
abscond *v.* go away secretly or illegally.
abseil *v.* descend by using a rope fixed at a higher point.
absence *n.* being absent; lack.
absent [1] /ábs'nt/ *a.* not present; lacking, non-existent. **absent-minded** *a.* with one's mind on other things; forgetful.
absent [2] /əbsént/ *v.* **absent oneself** stay away.

absentee *n.* person who is absent from work etc. **absenteeism** *n.*
absinthe *n.* a green liqueur.
absolute *a.* complete; unrestricted. **absolutely** *adv.*
absolution *n.* priest's formal declaration of forgiveness of sins.
absolutism *n.* principle of government with unrestricted powers. **absolutist** *n.*
absolve *v.* clear of blame or guilt.
absorb *v.* take in, combine into itself or oneself; occupy the attention or interest of. **absorption** *n.*, **absorptive** *a.*
absorbent *a.* able to absorb moisture etc.
abstain *v.* refrain, esp. from drinking alcohol; decide not to use one's vote. **abstainer** *n.*, **abstention** *n.*
abstemious *a.* not self-indulgent. **abstemiously** *adv.*, **abstemiousness** *n.*
abstinence *n.* abstaining esp. from food or alcohol.
abstract *a.* /ábstrakt/ having no material existence; theoretical; (of art) not representing things pictorially. — *n.* /ábstrakt/ abstract quality or idea; summary; piece of abstract art. — *v.* /əbstrákt/ take out, remove; make a summary of. **abstraction** *n.*
abstruse *a.* hard to understand, profound.
absurd *a.* not in accordance with common sense, ridiculous. **absurdly** *adv.*, **absurdity** *n.*
abundant *a.* plentiful; having plenty of something. **abundantly** *adv.*, **abundance** *n.*
abuse *v.* /əbyōōz/ ill-treat; attack with abusive language. — *n.* /əbyōōss/ ill-treatment; abusive language.
abusive *a.* using harsh words or insults. **abusively** *adv.*
abut *v.* **(abutted)** border (upon), end or lean (against); have a common boundary.
abysmal *a.* very bad.
abyss *n.* bottomless chasm.
acacia /əkáyshə/ *n.* a kind of flowering tree or shrub.
academic *a.* of a college or university; scholarly; of theoretical interest only. — *n.* academic person. **academically** *adv.*
academician *n.* member of an Academy.
Academy *n.* society of scholars or artists.
academy *n.* school, esp. for specialized training.
acanthus *n.* plant with large thistle-like leaves.
accede /akséed/ *v.* agree (to).
accelerate *v.* increase the speed (of). **acceleration** *n.*
accelerator *n.* pedal on a vehicle for increasing speed.
accent *n.* /áks'nt/ mark showing how a vowel is pronounced; particular regional, national, or other way of pronouncing words; emphasis on a word. — *v.* /aksént/ pronounce with an accent; emphasize.
accentuate *v.* emphasize; make prominent. **accentuation** *n.*
accept *v.* say yes (to); take as true. **acceptance** *n.*
acceptable *a.* worth accepting; tolerable. **acceptably** *adv.*, **acceptability** *n.*
access *n.* way in; right to enter; right to visit.
accessible *a.* able to be reached or obtained. **accessibly** *adv.*, **accessibility** *n.*
accessory *a.* additional. — *n.* additional fitment; person who helps in a crime.
accident *n.* unexpected event, esp. one causing damage; chance.
accidental *a.* happening by accident. **accidentally** *adv.*
acclaim *v.* welcome or applaud enthusiastically. — *n.* shout of welcome, applause. **acclamation** *n.*
acclimatize *v.* make or become used to a new climate. **acclimatization** *n.*
accolade *n.* bestowal of a knighthood or other honour; praise.
accommodate *v.* provide lodging or room for; adapt to.
accommodating *a.* willing to do as asked.
accommodation *n.* place to live.
accompany *v.* go with; play an instrumental part supporting (singer(s) or an instrument). **accompaniment** *n.*, **accompanist** *n.*
accomplice *n.* partner in crime.
accomplish *v.* succeed in doing or achieving.
accomplished *a.* skilled; having many accomplishments.
accomplishment *n.* useful ability.
accord *v.* be consistent. — *n.* consent, agreement. **of one's own accord** without being asked.
accordance *n.* conformity.
according *adv.* **according to** as stated by; in proportion to. **accordingly** *adv.*
accordion *n.* portable musical instrument with bellows and a keyboard.
accost *v.* approach and speak to.
account *n.* statement of money paid or owed; credit arrangement with a bank or firm; description, report. — *v.* **account for** give a reckoning of; explain; kill, overcome. **on account of** because of.
accountable *a.* obliged to account for one's actions. **accountability** *n.*
accountant *n.* person who keeps or

inspects business accounts. **accountancy** *n.*

accoutrements /əkōōtrəmənts/ *n.pl.* equipment, trappings.

accretion *n.* growth; matter added.

accrue *v.* accumulate. **accrual** *n.*

accumulate *v.* acquire more and more of; increase in amount. **accumulation** *n.*

accumulator *n.* rechargeable electric battery; bet on a series of events with winnings restaked.

accurate *a.* free from error. **accurately** *adv.*, **accuracy** *n.*

accuse *v.* lay the blame for a crime or fault on. **accusation** *n.*, **accuser** *n.*

accustom *v.* make used (to).

ace *n.* playing card with one spot; expert; unreturnable stroke in tennis.

acerbity *n.* sharpness of manner.

acetate *n.* synthetic textile fibre.

acetic acid ethanoic acid, essential ingredient of vinegar.

acetone *n.* colourless liquid used as a solvent.

acetylene *n.* colourless gas burning with a bright flame.

ache *n.* dull continuous pain. — *v.* suffer an ache. **achy** *a.*

achieve *v.* accomplish; reach or gain by effort. **achievable** *a.*, **achievement** *n.*, **achiever** *n.*

Achilles heel vulnerable point. **Achilles tendon** tendon attaching the calf muscles to the heel.

acid *a.* sour. — *n.* any of a class of substances that contain hydrogen and neutralize alkalis. **acidly** *adv.*, **acidity** *n.*

acknowledge *v.* admit the truth of; confirm receipt of. **acknowledgement** *n.*

acme /ákmi/ *n.* peak (of perfection).

acne /ákni/ *n.* eruption of pimples.

acolyte *n.* person assisting a priest in a church service.

acorn *n.* oval nut of the oak tree.

acoustic *a.* of sound. **acoustics** *n.pl.* qualities of a room that affect the way sound carries in it.

acquaint *v.* make known to. **be acquainted with** know slightly.

acquaintance *n.* slight knowledge; person one knows slightly.

acquiesce *v.* assent. **acquiescent** *a.*, **acquiescence** *n.*

acquire *v.* get possession of.

acquisition *n.* acquiring; thing acquired.

acquisitive *a.* eager to acquire things. **acquisitiveness** *n.*

acquit *v.* (**acquitted**) declare to be not guilty. **acquittal** *n.*

acre *n.* measure of land, 4,840 sq. yds (0.405 hectares).

acreage /áykərij/ *n.* number of acres.

acrid *a.* bitter.

acrimonious *a.* angry and bitter. **acrimony** *n.*

acrobat *n.* performer of acrobatics.

acrobatic *a.* involving spectacular gymnastic feats. **acrobatics** *n.pl.* acrobatic feats.

acronym *n.* word formed from the initial letters of others.

acropolis *n.* upper fortified part of an ancient Greek city.

across *prep.* & *adv.* from side to side (of); on the other side (of).

acrostic *n.* poem in which the first and/or last letters of lines form word(s).

acrylic *a.* & *n.* (synthetic fibre) made from an organic substance.

act *n.* thing done; law made by parliament; section of a play; item in a circus or variety show. — *v.* perform actions, behave; play the part of; be an actor.

action *n.* process of doing something or functioning; thing done; lawsuit; battle.

actionable *a.* giving cause for a lawsuit.

activate *v.* make active. **activation** *n.*, **activator** *n.*

active *a.* doing things; energetic. **actively** *adv.*

activist *n.* person adopting a policy of vigorous action in politics etc. **activism** *n.*

activity *n.* action, occupation.

actor *n.* performer in stage play(s) or film(s). **actress** *n.fem.*

actual *a.* existing in fact, current.

actuality *n.* reality.

actually *adv.* in fact, really.

actuary *n.* insurance expert who calculates risks and premiums. **actuarial** *a.*

actuate *v.* activate; be a motive for. **actuation** *n.*

acumen *n.* shrewdness.

acupressure *n.* pressing the body at specific points to relieve pain. **acupressurist** *n.*

acupuncture *n.* pricking the body with needles to relieve pain. **acupuncturist** *n.*

acute *a.* sharp; intense, (of illness) severe for a time; quick at understanding. **acute accent** the accent ´. **acutely** *adv.*, **acuteness** *n.*

adamant *a.* not yielding to requests.

Adam's apple prominent cartilage at the front of the neck.

adapt *v.* make or become suitable for new use or conditions. **adaptation** *n.*, **adaptor** *n.*

adaptable *a.* able to be adapted or to adapt oneself. **adaptability** *n.*

add *v.* join as an increase or supplement; say further; put together to get a total.

addendum *n.* (*pl.* **-da**) section added to a book.
adder *n.* small poisonous snake.
addict *n.* one who is addicted, esp. to drug(s).
addicted *a.* doing or using something as a habit or compulsively. **addiction** *n.*, **addictive** *a.*
addition *n.* adding; thing added.
additional *a.* added, extra. **additionally** *adv.*
additive *n.* substance added.
addle *v.* make (an egg) rotten; become rotten; muddle, confuse.
address *n.* particulars of where a person lives or where mail should be delivered; a speech. — *v.* write the address on; speak to; apply (oneself) to a task.
addressee *n.* person to whom a letter etc. is addressed.
adduce *v.* cite as proof.
adenoids *n.pl.* enlarged tissue at the back of the throat. **adenoidal** *a.*
adept *a.* & *n.* very skilful (person).
adequate *a.* enough; satisfactory but not excellent. **adequately** *adv.*, **adequacy** *n.*
adhere *v.* stick; continue to give one's support. **adherence** *n.*, **adherent** *a.* & *n.*
adhesion *n.* process or fact of sticking to something.
adhesive *a.* sticking, sticky.
ad hoc for a specific purpose.
adieu /ədyōō/ *int.* & *n.* goodbye.
ad infinitum for ever.
adjacent *a.* lying near; adjoining.
adjective *n.* descriptive word. **adjectival** *a.*
adjourn *v.* move (a meeting etc.) to another place or time. **adjournment** *n.*
adjudge *v.* decide judicially.
adjudicate *v.* act as judge (of); adjudge. **adjudication** *n.*, **adjudicator** *n.*
adjunct *n.* thing that is subordinate to another.
adjure *v.* command or urge strongly.
adjust *v.* alter slightly so as to be correct or in the proper position; adapt (oneself) to new conditions. **adjustable** *a.*, **adjustment** *n.*
adjutant *n.* army officer assisting in administrative work.
ad lib as one pleases; (*colloq.*) improvise(d).
administer *v.* manage (business affairs); give or hand out.
administrate *v.* act as manager (of). **administrator** *n.*
administration *n.* administering; management of public or business affairs. **administrative** *a.*
admirable *a.* worthy of admiration. **admirably** *adv.*
admiral *n.* naval officer of the highest rank.
admire *v.* regard with pleasure; think highly of. **admiration** *n.*
admissible *a.* able to be admitted or allowed. **admissibility** *n.*
admission *n.* admitting; statement admitting something.
admit *v.* (**admitted**) allow to enter; accept as valid; state reluctantly.
admittance *n.* admitting, esp. to a private place.
admittedly *adv.* as an acknowledged fact.
admixture *n.* thing added as an ingredient; adding of this.
admonish *v.* exhort; reprove. **admonition** *n.*
ad nauseam to a sickening extent.
ado *n.* fuss, trouble.
adobe /ədōbi/ *n.* sun-dried brick.
adolescent *a.* & *n.* (person) between childhood and maturity. **adolescence** *n.*
adopt *v.* take as one's own; accept responsibility for maintenance of; accept, approve (a report etc.). **adoption** *n.*
adorable *a.* very lovable.
adore *v.* love deeply. **adoration** *n.*
adorn *v.* decorate with ornaments; be an ornament to. **adornment** *n.*
adrenal /ədreen'l/ *a.* close to the kidneys.
adrenalin /ədrénnəlin/ *n.* stimulant hormone produced by the adrenal glands.
adrift *a.* & *adv.* drifting; loose.
adroit *a.* skilful, ingenious.
adsorb *v.* attract and hold (a gas or liquid) to a surface.
adulation *n.* excessive flattery.
adult *a.* & *n.* fully grown (person etc.). **adulthood** *n.*
adulterate *v.* make impure by adding substance(s). **adulteration** *n.*
adulterer *n.* person who commits adultery. **adulteress** *n.fem.*
adultery *n.* sexual infidelity to one's wife or husband. **adulterous** *a.*
advance *v.* move or put forward; lend (money). — *n.* forward movement; progress; increase in price; loan; attempt to establish a friendly relationship. **advancement** *n.*
advanced *a.* far on in time or progress etc.; not elementary.
advantage *n.* favourable circumstance; benefit. **take advantage of** make use of; exploit.
advantageous *a.* profitable, beneficial.
Advent *n.* season before Christmas. **advent** *n.* arrival.

adventure *n.* exciting or dangerous experience. **adventurer** *n.*, **adventuress** *n.*, **adventurous** *a.*

adverb *n.* word qualifying a verb, adjective, or other adverb. **adverbial** *a.*, **adverbially** *adv.*

adversary *n.* opponent, enemy. **adversarial** *a.*

adverse *a.* unfavourable, bringing harm. **adversely** *adv.*, **adversity** *n.*

advertise *v.* make publicly known, esp. to encourage sales.

advertisement *n.* advertising; public notice about something.

advice *n.* opinion given about what should be done.

advisable *a.* worth recommending as a course of action. **advisability** *n.*

advise *v.* give advice to; recommend; inform. **adviser** *n.*

advisory *a.* giving advice.

advocacy *n.* speaking in support.

advocate *n.* /ádvəkət/ person who speaks in court on behalf of another. — *v.* /ádvəkayt/ recommend.

aegis /éejiss/ *n.* protection, sponsorship.

aeon /ée-on/ *n.* immense time.

aerate *v.* expose to the action of air; add carbon dioxide to.

aerial *a.* of or like air; existing or moving in the air; by or from aircraft. — *n.* wire for transmitting or receiving radio waves. **aerially** *adv.*

aerobatics *n.pl.* spectacular feats by aircraft in flight. **aerobatic** *a.*

aerobics *n.pl.* vigorous exercises designed to increase oxygen intake. **aerobic** *a.*

aerodynamic *a.* of the airflow round solid objects moving through air. **aerodynamics** *n.* study of this. **aerodynamically** *adv.*

aerofoil *n.* aircraft wing, fin, or tailplane giving lift in flight.

aeronautics *n.* study of the flight of aircraft. **aeronautical** *a.*

aeroplane *n.* power-driven aircraft with wings.

aerosol *n.* container holding a substance for release as a fine spray.

aerospace *n.* earth's atmosphere and space beyond this.

aesthete /éess-theet/ *n.* person claiming to understand and appreciate beauty, esp. in the arts.

aesthetic /eess-théttik/ *a.* of or showing appreciation of beauty; artistic, tasteful. **aesthetically** *adv.*

aetiology /eetióllәji/ *n.* study of causes, esp. of disease.

affable *a.* polite and friendly. **affably** *adv.*, **affability** *n.*

affair *n.* thing to be done; business; temporary sexual relationship.

affect *v.* pretend to have or feel or be; have an effect on.

affectation *n.* pretence, esp. in behaviour.

affected *a.* full of affectation.

affection *n.* love, liking.

affectionate *a.* loving. **affectionately** *adv.*

affidavit *n.* written statement sworn on oath to be true.

affiliate *v.* connect as a subordinate member or branch. **affiliation** *n.*

affinity *n.* close resemblance or attraction.

affirm *v.* state as a fact; declare formally and solemnly instead of on oath. **affirmation** *n.*

affirmative *a.* & *n.* saying 'yes'. **affirmatively** *adv.*

affix *v.* /əfiks/ attach; add (a signature etc.). — *n.* /áffiks/ thing affixed; prefix, suffix.

afflict *v.* distress physically or mentally.

affliction *n.* distress.

affluence *n.* wealth. **affluent** *a.*

afford *v.* have enough money or time for.

afforest *v.* convert into forest; plant with trees. **afforestation** *n.*

affray *n.* public fight or riot.

affront *v.* & *n.* insult.

afloat *adv.* & *a.* floating; on the sea.

afoot *adv.* & *a.* going on.

aforesaid *a.* mentioned previously.

afraid *a.* frightened; regretful.

afresh *adv.* anew, with a fresh start.

Afrikaans *n.* language of South Africa, developed from Dutch.

Afrikaner *n.* Afrikaans-speaking White person in South Africa.

aft *adv.* at or towards the rear of a ship or aircraft.

after *prep.*, *adv.*, & *a.* behind; later (than); in pursuit of; concerning; according to. — *conj.* at a time later than. **after-effect** *n.* effect persisting after its cause has gone.

afterbirth *n.* placenta discharged from the womb after childbirth.

aftermath *n.* after-effects.

afternoon *n.* time between morning and about 6 p.m. or sunset.

afterthought *n.* thing thought of or added later.

afterwards *adv.* at a later time.

again *adv.* another time, once more; besides.

against *prep.* in opposition or contrast to; in preparation or return for; into collision or contact with.

age *n.* length of life or existence; later part of life; historical period; (*colloq.*, usu. *pl.*)

very long time. — *v.* (**ageing**) grow old, show signs of age; cause to do this.
aged *a.* /ayjd/ of the age of; /áyjid/ old.
ageism *n.* prejudice on grounds of age.
ageless *a.* not growing old; not seeming old.
agency *n.* business or office of an agent; means of action by which something is done.
agenda *n.* list of things to be dealt with, esp. at a meeting.
agent *n.* person who does something, esp. on behalf of another; thing producing an effect.
agent provocateur /aázhoN prəvókkətőr/ person employed to tempt suspected offenders into overt action.
aggrandize *v.* make seem greater. **aggrandizement** *n.*
aggravate *v.* make worse; (*colloq.*) annoy. **aggravation** *n.*
aggregate *a.* /ágrigət/ combined, total. — *n.* /ágrigət/ collected mass; broken stone etc. used in making concrete. — *v.* /ágrigayt/ collect into an aggregate, unite; (*colloq.*) amount to. **aggregation** *n.*
aggression *n.* unprovoked attacking; hostile act(s) or behaviour.
aggressive *a.* showing aggression; forceful. **aggressively** *adv.*
aggressor *n.* one who begins hostilities.
aggrieved *a.* having a grievance.
aghast *a.* filled with horror.
agile *a.* nimble, quick-moving. **agility** *n.*
agitate *v.* shake briskly; cause anxiety to; stir up concern. **agitation** *n.*, **agitator** *n.*
agnostic *a.* & *n.* (person) holding that nothing can be known about the existence of God. **agnosticism** *n.*
ago *adv.* in the past.
agog *a.* eager, expectant.
agonize *v.* cause agony to; suffer agony, worry intensely.
agony *n.* extreme suffering.
agoraphobia *n.* abnormal fear of crossing open spaces.
agrarian *a.* of land or agriculture.
agree *v.* approve as correct or acceptable; hold or reach a similar opinion. **agree with** suit the health or digestion of.
agreeable *a.* pleasing; willing to agree. **agreeably** *adv.*
agreement *n.* agreeing; arrangement agreed between people.
agriculture *n.* large-scale cultivation of land. **agricultural** *a.*
agronomy *n.* soil management and crop production.
aground *adv.* & *a.* (of a ship) on the bottom in shallow water.
ahead *adv.* further forward in position or time.
ahoy *int.* seaman's shout to call attention.
aid *v.* & *n.* help.
aide *n.* aide-de-camp; assistant.
aide-de-camp *n.* officer assisting a senior officer.
Aids *or* **AIDS** *abbr.* acquired immune deficiency syndrome, a condition that breaks down a person's natural defences against illness.
ail *v.* make or become ill.
aileron *n.* hinged flap on an aircraft wing.
ailment *n.* slight illness.
aim *v.* point, send, or direct towards a target. — *n.* aiming; intention.
aimless *a.* without a purpose. **aimlessly** *adv.*, **aimlessness** *n.*
air *n.* mixture of oxygen, nitrogen, etc., surrounding the earth; atmosphere overhead; light wind; impression given; melody. — *v.* expose to air; dry off; express publicly. **air-bed** *n.* inflatable mattress. **airbrick** *n.* perforated brick for ventilation. **air-conditioned** *a.* supplied with **air-conditioning**, system controlling the humidity and temperature of air. **air force** branch of the armed forces using aircraft. **air raid** attack by aircraft dropping bombs. **on the air** broadcast (-ing) by radio or television.
airborne *a.* carried by air or aircraft; (of aircraft) in flight.
aircraft *n.* machine capable of flight in air.
airfield *n.* area with runways etc. for aircraft.
airgun *n.* gun with a missile propelled by compressed air.
airlift *n.* large-scale transport of supplies by aircraft. — *v.* transport thus.
airline *n.* company providing air transport service.
airliner *n.* passenger aircraft.
airlock *n.* stoppage of the flow in a pipe, caused by an air-bubble; airtight compartment giving access to a pressurized chamber.
airmail *n.* mail carried by aircraft. — *v.* send by airmail.
airman *n.* (*pl.* **-men**) member of an air force, esp. below the rank of officer.
airport *n.* airfield with facilities for passengers and goods.
airship *n.* power-driven lighter-than-air aircraft.
airstrip *n.* strip of ground for take-off and landing of aircraft.
airtight *a.* not allowing air to enter or escape.
airworthy *a.* (of aircraft) fit to fly.
airy *a.* (**-ier, -iest**) well-ventilated; light as

air; careless and light-hearted. **airily** *adv.*, **airiness** *n.*

aisle /īl/ *n.* side part of a church; gangway between rows of seats.

ajar *adv.* & *a.* slightly open.

akimbo *adv.* with hands on hips and elbows pointed outwards.

akin *a.* related, similar.

alabaster *n.* translucent usu. white form of gypsum.

à la carte (of a meal) ordered as separate items from a menu.

alacrity *n.* eager readiness.

alarm *n.* warning sound or signal; fear caused by expectation of danger. — *v.* cause alarm to.

alarmist *n.* person who raises unnecessary or excessive alarm.

alas *int.* exclamation of sorrow.

albatross *n.* seabird with long wings.

albino *n.* (*pl.* **-os**) person or animal with no natural colouring matter in the hair or skin.

album *n.* blank book for holding photographs, stamps, etc.; set of recordings.

albumen *n.* white of egg.

albumin *n.* protein found in egg white, milk, blood, etc.

alchemy *n.* medieval form of chemistry, seeking to turn other metals into gold. **alchemist** *n.*

alcohol *n.* colourless inflammable liquid, intoxicant in wine, beer, etc.; liquor containing this.

alcoholic *a.* of alcohol. — *n.* person addicted to continual drinking of alcohol. **alcoholism** *n.*

alcove *n.* recess in a wall or room.

alder *n.* tree related to birch.

ale *n.* beer.

alert *a.* watchful, observant. — *v.* rouse to be alert.

alfresco *adv.* & *a.* in the open air.

alga *n.* (*pl.* **-gae**) water plant with no true stems or leaves.

algebra *n.* branch of mathematics using letters etc. to represent quantities. **algebraic** *a.*, **algebraically** *adv.*

algorithm *n.* step by step procedure for calculation.

alias *n.* (*pl.* **-ases**) false name. — *adv.* also called.

alibi *n.* evidence that an accused person was elsewhere when a crime was committed; (*loosely*) excuse.

alien *n.* person who is not a citizen of the country where he or she lives; a being from another world. — *a.* foreign; unfamiliar.

alienate *v.* cause to become unfriendly. **alienation** *n.*

alight [1] *v.* get down from (a vehicle etc.); descend and settle.

alight [2] *a.* on fire.

align *v.* place or bring into line; join as an ally. **alignment** *n.*

alike *a.* like one another. — *adv.* in the same way.

alimentary *a.* of nourishment.

alive *a.* living; alert; lively.

alkali *n.* (*pl.* **-is**) any of a class of substances that neutralize acids. **alkaline** *a.*

alkaloid *n.* a kind of organic compound containing nitrogen.

all *a.* whole amount or number or extent of. — *n.* all those concerned. **all but** almost. **all-clear** *n.* signal that danger is over. **all in** exhausted; including everything. **all out** using maximum effort. **all right** satisfactory, satisfactorily; in good condition.

allay *v.* lessen (fears).

allegation *n.* thing alleged.

allege *v.* declare without proof.

allegedly *adv.* according to allegation.

allegiance *n.* support given to a government, sovereign, or cause.

allegory *n.* story symbolizing an underlying meaning. **allegorical** *a.*, **allegorically** *adv.*

allegro *adv.* & *n.* (passage to be played) briskly.

allergen *n.* substance causing an allergic reaction.

allergic *a.* having or caused by an allergy; having a strong dislike.

allergy *n.* condition causing an unfavourable reaction to certain foods, pollens, etc.

alleviate *v.* lessen (pain or distress). **alleviation** *n.*

alley *n.* narrow street; long enclosure for tenpin bowling.

alliance *n.* association formed for mutual benefit.

allied *a.* of an alliance; similar.

alligator *n.* reptile of the crocodile family.

alliteration *n.* occurrence of the same sound at the start of words. **alliterative** *a.*

allocate *v.* allot. **allocation** *n.*

allot *v.* (**allotted**) distribute officially, give as a share.

allotment *n.* share allotted; small area of land for cultivation.

allow *v.* permit; give a limited quantity or sum; add or deduct in estimating; admit, agree.

allowance *n.* allowing; amount or sum allowed. **make allowances for** be lenient towards or because of.

alloy *n.* mixture of metals. — *v.* mix (with

another metal); spoil or weaken (pleasure etc.).

allude *v.* refer briefly or indirectly.

allure *v.* entice, attract. — *n.* attractiveness.

allusion *n.* statement alluding to something. **allusive** *a.*

alluvium *n.* deposit left by a flood. **alluvial** *a.*

ally *n.* /állī/ country or person in alliance with another. — *v.* /əlī/ join as an ally.

almanac *n.* calendar with astronomical or other data.

almighty *a.* all-powerful; (*colloq.*) very great.

almond *n.* kernel of a fruit related to the peach; tree bearing this.

almost *adv.* very little short of, as the nearest thing to.

alms *n.* money given to the poor.

almshouse *n.* house built by charity for poor elderly people.

aloe *n.* plant with bitter juice.

aloft *adv.* high up; upwards.

alone *a.* not with others; without company or help. — *adv.* only.

along *adv.* through part or all of a thing's length; onward; in company with others. — *prep.* beside the length of.

alongside *adv.* close to the side of a ship or wharf etc.

aloof *adv.* apart. — *a.* showing no interest, unfriendly.

aloud *adv.* in a voice that can be heard, not in a whisper.

alpaca *n.* llama with long wool; its wool; cloth made from this.

alpha *n.* first letter of the Greek alphabet, = a.

alphabet *n.* letters used in writing a language. **alphabetical** *a.*, **alphabetically** *adv.*

alphabetize *v.* put into alphabetical order. **alphabetization** *n.*

alpine *a.* of high mountains. — *n.* plant growing on mountains or in rock gardens.

already *adv.* before this time; as early as this.

Alsatian *n.* dog of a large strong smooth-haired breed.

also *adv.* in addition, besides.

altar *n.* table used in religious service.

alter *v.* make or become different. **alteration** *n.*

altercation *n.* noisy dispute.

alternate *a.* /awltérnət/ first one then the other successively. — *v.* /áwltərnayt/ place or occur alternately. **alternately** *adv.*, **alternation** *n.*

alternative *a.* usable instead of another; different, unconventional. — *n.* alternative thing. **alternatively** *adv.*

although *conj.* though.

altimeter *n.* instrument in an aircraft showing altitude.

altitude *n.* height above sea level or above the horizon.

alto *n.* (*pl.* **-os**) highest adult male voice; musical instrument with the second-highest pitch in its group.

altogether *adv.* entirely; on the whole.

altruism *n.* unselfishness.

altruist *n.* unselfish person. **altruistic** *a.*, **altruistically** *adv.*

aluminium *n.* lightweight silvery metal.

always *adv.* at all times; whatever the circumstances.

alyssum *n.* plant with small yellow or white flowers.

a.m. *abbr.* (Latin *ante meridiem*) before noon.

amalgam *n.* alloy of mercury; soft pliable mixture.

amalgamate *v.* mix, combine. **amalgamation** *n.*

amaryllis *n.* lily-like plant.

amass *v.* heap up, collect.

amateur *n.* person who does something as a pastime not as a profession.

amateurish *a.* lacking professional skill.

amatory *a.* of or showing love.

amaze *v.* overwhelm with wonder. **amazement** *n.*

amazon *n.* fierce strong woman.

ambassador *n.* diplomat representing his or her country abroad.

amber *n.* hardened brownish-yellow resin; its colour.

ambergris *n.* waxy substance found in tropical seas, used in perfume manufacture.

ambidextrous *a.* able to use either hand equally well.

ambience *n.* surroundings.

ambiguous *a.* having two or more possible meanings. **ambiguously** *adv.*, **ambiguity** *n.*

ambit *n.* bounds, scope.

ambition *n.* strong desire to achieve something.

ambitious *a.* full of ambition. **ambitiously** *adv.*

ambivalent *a.* with mixed feelings towards something. **ambivalence** *n.*, **ambivalently** *adv.*

amble *v.* & *n.* walk at a leisurely pace. **ambler** *n.*

ambrosia *n.* something delicious.

ambulance *n.* vehicle equipped to carry sick or injured persons.

ambuscade *v.* & *n.* ambush.

ambush *n.* troops etc. lying concealed to make a surprise attack; this attack. — *v.* attack thus.
ameliorate *v.* make or become better. **amelioration** *n.*
amenable *a.* responsive. **amenably** *adv.*, **amenability** *n.*
amend *v.* make minor alteration(s) in. **make amends** compensate for something. **amendment** *n.*
amenity *n.* pleasant feature of a place.
American *a.* of America; of the USA. — *n.* American person.
Americanism *n.* American word or phrase.
Americanize *v.* make American in character. **Americanization** *n.*
amethyst *n.* precious stone, purple or violet quartz; its colour.
amiable *a.* likeable; friendly. **amiably** *adv.*, **amiability** *n.*
amicable *a.* friendly. **amicably** *adv.*
amid, amidst *preps.* in the middle of, during.
amino acid organic acid found in proteins.
amiss *a.* & *adv.* wrong(ly), badly.
ammonia *n.* strong-smelling gas; solution of this in water.
ammonite *n.* fossil of a spiral shell.
ammunition *n.* bullets, shells, etc.
amnesia *n.* loss of memory. **amnesiac** *a.* & *n.*
amnesty *n.* general pardon.
amniotic fluid fluid surrounding the foetus in the womb.
amoeba /əmeébə/ *n.* (*pl.* **-bae** *or* **-bas**) simple microscopic organism changing shape constantly.
amok *adv.* **run amok** be out of control and do much damage.
among, amongst *preps.* surrounded by; in the number of; between.
amoral *a.* not based on moral standards.
amorous *a.* showing sexual love.
amorphous *a.* shapeless.
amortize *v.* pay off (a debt) gradually. **amortization** *n.*
amount *n.* total of anything; quantity. — *v.* **amount to** add up to; be equivalent to.
ampere *n.* unit of electric current.
ampersand *n.* the sign & (= and).
amphetamine *n.* stimulant drug.
amphibian *n.* animal with an aquatic larval and air-breathing adult stage; amphibious vehicle.
amphibious *a.* able to live or operate both on land and in water.
amphitheatre *n.* semicircular unroofed building with tiers of seats round a central arena.
ample *a.* plentiful, quite enough; large. **amply** *adv.*
amplify *v.* increase the strength of, make louder; add details to (a statement). **amplification** *n.*, **amplifier** *n.*
amplitude *n.* breadth; abundance.
amputate *v.* cut off by surgical operation. **amputation** *n.*
amulet *n.* thing worn as a charm against evil.
amuse *v.* cause to laugh or smile; make time pass pleasantly for. **amusement** *n.*, **amusing** *a.*
an *a.* form of *a* used before vowel sounds other than long 'u'.
anachronism *n.* thing that does not belong in the period in which it is placed. **anachronistic** *a.*
anaemia /əneémiə/ *n.* lack of haemoglobin in blood.
anaemic /əneémik/ *a.* suffering from anaemia; lacking strong colour or characteristics.
anaesthesia /ánniss-theéziə/ *n.* loss of sensation, esp. induced by anaesthetics.
anaesthetic /ánniss-théttik/ *a.* & *n.* (substance) causing loss of sensation.
anaesthetist /əneéss-thətist/ *n.* person who administers anaesthetics.
anagram *n.* word formed from the rearranged letters of another.
anal *a.* of the anus.
analgesic *a.* & *n.* (drug) relieving pain. **analgesia** *n.*
analogous *a.* similar in certain respects.
analogue *n.* analogous thing.
analogy *n.* partial likeness between things.
analyse *v.* make an analysis of; psychoanalyse. **analyst** *n.*
analysis *n.* (*pl.* **-lyses**) detailed examination or study of something.
analytic, analytical *adjs.* of or using analysis. **analytically** *adv.*
anarchist *n.* person who believes that government is undesirable and should be abolished. **anarchism** *n.*
anarchy *n.* total lack of organized control; lawlessness. **anarchical** *a.*, **anarchically** *adv.*
anathema /ənáthəmə/ *n.* formal curse; detested thing.
anathematize *v.* put under an anathema.
anatomist *n.* expert in anatomy.
anatomize *v.* examine the anatomy or structure of.
anatomy *n.* bodily structure; study of this. **anatomical** *a.*, **anatomically** *adv.*
ancestor *n.* person from whom one's father or mother is descended. **ancestral** *a.*, **ancestress** *n.fem.*
ancestry *n.* line of ancestors.

anchor *n.* heavy metal structure for mooring a ship to the sea bottom. — *v.* moor with an anchor; fix firmly.

anchorage *n.* place where ships may anchor; lying at anchor.

anchovy *n.* small tasty fish.

ancient *a.* very old.

ancillary *a.* helping in a subsidiary way.

and *conj.* connecting words, phrases, or sentences.

anecdote *n.* short amusing or interesting true story.

anemone *n.* plant with white, red, or purple flowers.

aneurysm *n.* excessive swelling of an artery.

anew *adv.* again; in a new way.

angel *n.* messenger of God; kind person. **angelic** *a.*

angelica *n.* candied stalks of a fragrant plant; this plant.

anger *n.* extreme displeasure. — *v.* make angry.

angina *n.* constricting pain. **angina pectoris** sharp pain in the chest.

angle [1] *n.* space between two lines or surfaces that meet; point of view. — *v.* place obliquely; present from a particular point of view.

angle [2] *v.* fish with hook and bait; try to obtain by hinting. **angler** *n.*

Anglican *a.* & *n.* (member) of the Church of England. **Anglicanism** *n.*

Anglicism *n.* English idiom.

anglicize *v.* make English in character. **anglicization** *n.*

Anglo- *pref.* English, British.

Anglo-Saxon *n.* & *a.* (of) English person or language before the Norman Conquest; (of) person of English descent.

angora *n.* long-haired variety of cat, goat, or rabbit; yarn or fabric made from the hair of such goats or rabbits.

angostura *n.* aromatic bitter bark of a South American tree.

angry *a.* **(-ier, -iest)** feeling or showing anger. **angrily** *adv.*

angstrom *n.* unit of measurement for wavelengths.

anguish *n.* severe physical or mental pain. **anguished** *a.*

angular *a.* having angles or sharp corners; forming an angle.

aniline *n.* oily liquid used in making dyes and plastics.

animal *n.* & *a.* (of) a living thing that can move voluntarily.

animate *a.* /ánnimət/ living. — *v.* /ánnimayt/ give life or movement to. **animation** *n.*, **animator** *n.*

animosity *n.* hostility.

animus *n.* animosity.

aniseed *n.* fragrant seed of a plant **(anise)**, used for flavouring.

ankle *n.* joint connecting the foot with the leg; part of the leg below the calf.

anklet *n.* chain or band worn round the ankle.

annals *n.pl.* narrative of events year by year; historical records.

anneal *v.* toughen (metal or glass) by heat and slow cooling.

annex *v.* take possession of; add as a subordinate part. **annexation** *n.*

annexe *n.* additional building.

annihilate *v.* destroy completely. **annihilation** *n.*

anniversary *n.* yearly return of the date of an event.

annotate *v.* add explanatory notes to. **annotation** *n.*

announce *v.* make known publicly; make known the presence or arrival of. **announcement** *n.*

announcer *n.* person who announces items in a broadcast.

annoy *v.* cause slight anger to; be troublesome to. **annoyance** *n.*

annoyed *a.* slightly angry.

annual *a.* yearly. — *n.* plant that lives for one year or one season; book published in yearly issues. **annually** *adv.*

annuity *n.* yearly allowance provided by an investment.

annul *v.* **(annulled)** make null and void. **annulment** *n.*

annular *a.* ring-shaped.

Annunciation *n.* announcement by the angel Gabriel to the Virgin Mary that she was to be the mother of Christ.

anode *n.* electrode by which current enters a device.

anodize *v.* coat (metal) with a protective layer by electrolysis.

anodyne *n.* something that relieves pain or distress.

anoint *v.* apply ointment or oil etc. to, esp. in religious consecration.

anomaly *n.* something irregular or inconsistent. **anomalous** *a.*

anon *adv.* (*old use*) soon.

anon. *abbr.* anonymous.

anonymous *a.* of unknown or undisclosed name or authorship. **anonymously** *adv.*, **anonymity** *n.*

anorak *n.* waterproof jacket with hood attached.

anorexia *n.* reluctance to eat. **anorexic** *a.* & *n.*

another *a.* one more; a different; any other. — *pron.* another one.

answer *n.* thing said, written, needed, or

done to deal with a question, problem, etc.; figure etc. produced by calculation. — *v.* make or be an answer (to); act in response to; take responsibility; correspond (to a description).

answerable *a.* having to account for something.

ant *n.* small insect that lives in highly organized groups.

antacid *n.* & *a.* (substance) preventing or correcting acidity.

antagonism *n.* active opposition, hostility. **antagonistic** *a.*

antagonist *n.* opponent.

antagonize *v.* rouse antagonism in.

Antarctic *a.* & *n.* (of) regions round the South Pole.

ante *n.* stake put up by a poker-player before drawing new cards.

ante- *pref.* before.

anteater *n.* mammal that eats ants.

antecedent *n.* preceding thing or circumstance. — *a.* previous.

antedate *v.* put an earlier date on; precede in time.

antediluvian *a.* of the time before Noah's Flood; antiquated.

antelope *n.* animal resembling a deer.

antenatal *a.* before birth; of or during pregnancy.

antenna *n.* (*pl.* **-ae**) insect's feeler; (*US*, *pl.* **-as**) radio or TV aerial.

anterior *a.* coming before in position or time.

ante-room *n.* room leading to a more important one.

anthem *n.* piece of music to be sung in a religious service.

anther *n.* part of a flower's stamen containing pollen.

anthology *n.* collection of passages from literature, esp. poems.

anthracite *n.* form of coal burning with little flame or smoke.

anthrax *n.* disease of sheep and cattle, transmissible to people.

anthropoid *a.* & *n.* human-like (ape).

anthropology *n.* study of the origin and customs of mankind. **anthropological** *a.*, **anthropologist** *n.*

anthropomorphic *a.* attributing human form to a god or animal. **anthropomorphism** *n.*

anti- *pref.* opposed to; counteracting. **anti-aircraft** *a.* used against enemy aircraft.

antibiotic *n.* substance that destroys bacteria.

antibody *n.* protein formed in the blood in reaction to a substance which it then destroys.

antics *n.pl.* absurd behaviour.

anticipate *v.* deal with or use in advance; look forward to; expect. **anticipation** *n.*

anticlimax *n.* dull ending where a climax was expected.

anticlockwise *a.* & *adv.* in the direction opposite to clockwise.

anticyclone *n.* outward flow of air from an area of high pressure, producing fine weather.

antidote *n.* substance that counteracts the effects of poison.

antifreeze *n.* substance added to water to prevent freezing.

antigen *n.* foreign substance stimulating the production of antibodies.

antihistamine *n.* substance counteracting the effect of histamine.

antimacassar *n.* protective covering for a chair-back.

antimony *n.* brittle silvery metallic element.

antipathy *n.* strong dislike.

antiperspirant *n.* substance that prevents or reduces sweating.

antipodes /antippədeez/ *n.pl.* places on opposite sides of the earth, esp. Australia and New Zealand (opposite Europe).

antiquarian *a.* of the study of antiques. — *n.* person who studies antiques.

antiquated *a.* very old; very old-fashioned.

antique *a.* belonging to the distant past. — *n.* antique interesting or valuable object.

antiquity *n.* ancient times; object dating from ancient times.

antirrhinum *n.* snapdragon.

anti-Semitic *a.* hostile to Jews.

antiseptic *a.* & *n.* (substance) preventing things from becoming septic. **antiseptically** *adv.*

antisocial *a.* destructive or hostile to other members of society.

antistatic *a.* counteracting the effects of static electricity.

antithesis *n.* (*pl.* **-eses**) opposite; contrast. **antithetical** *a.*

antitoxin *n.* substance that neutralizes a toxin. **antitoxic** *a.*

antivivisectionist *n.* person opposed to making experiments on live animals.

antler *n.* branched horn of a deer.

antonym *n.* word opposite to another in meaning.

anus *n.* opening at the excretory end of the alimentary canal.

anvil *n.* iron block on which a smith hammers metal into shape.

anxiety *n.* state of being anxious.

anxious *a.* troubled and uneasy in mind; eager. **anxiously** *adv.*

any *a.* one or some from a quantity; every.
anybody *n.* & *pron.* any person.
anyhow *adv.* anyway; not in an orderly manner.
anyone *n.* & *pron.* anybody.
anything *n.* & *pron.* any item.
anyway *adv.* in any case.
anywhere *adv.* & *pron.* (in or to) any place.
aorta *n.* main artery carrying blood from the heart.
apart *adv.* separately, so as to become separated; to or at a distance; into pieces.
apartheid /əpaártayt/ *n.* former policy of racial segregation in South Africa.
apartment *n.* set of rooms; (*US*) flat.
apathy *n.* lack of interest or concern. **apathetic** *a.*
ape *n.* tailless monkey. — *v.* imitate, mimic.
aperitif *n.* alcoholic drink taken as an appetizer.
aperture *n.* opening, esp. one that admits light.
apex *n.* tip, highest point; pointed end.
aphid *n.* small insect destructive to plants.
aphorism *n.* pithy saying.
aphrodisiac *a.* & *n.* (substance) arousing sexual desire.
apiary *n.* place where bees are kept. **apiarist** *n.*
apiece *adv.* to or for or by each.
aplomb /əplóm/ *n.* dignity and confidence.
apocalyptic *a.* prophesying great and dramatic events like those in the **Apocalypse** (last book of the New Testament).
Apocrypha *n.pl.* books of the Old Testament not accepted as part of the Hebrew scriptures.
apocryphal *a.* untrue, invented.
apogee *n.* point in the moon's orbit furthest from the earth.
apologetic *a.* making an apology. **apologetically** *adv.*
apologize *v.* make an apology.
apology *n.* statement of regret for having done wrong or hurt; explanation of one's beliefs.
apoplectic *a.* of or liable to suffer apoplexy; liable to fits of red-faced rage.
apoplexy *n.* a stroke; sudden loss of ability to feel and move, caused by rupture or blockage of the brain artery.
apostasy *n.* abandonment of one's former religious belief.
apostate *n.* person who is guilty of apostasy.
Apostle *n.* any of the twelve men sent forth by Christ to preach the gospel. **apostolic** *a.*
apostrophe /əpóstrəfi/ *n.* the sign ' used to show the possessive case or omission of a letter.
apothecary *n.* (*old use*) pharmaceutical chemist.
appal *v.* (**appalled**) fill with horror or dismay. **appalling** *a.*
apparatus *n.* equipment for scientific or other work.
apparel *n.* clothing.
apparent *a.* clearly seen or understood; seeming but not real. **apparently** *adv.*
apparition *n.* thing appearing, esp. of a startling or remarkable kind; ghost.
appeal *v.* make an earnest or formal request; refer to a higher court; seem attractive. — *n.* act of appealing; attractiveness.
appear *v.* be or become visible; seem. **appearance** *n.*
appease *v.* soothe or conciliate, esp. by giving what was asked. **appeasement** *n.*
appellant *n.* person who appeals to a higher court.
append *v.* add at the end.
appendage *n.* thing appended.
appendicitis *n.* inflammation of the intestinal appendix.
appendix *n.* (*pl.* **-ices**) section at the end of a book, giving extra information; (*pl.* **-ixes**) small blind tube of tissue attached to the intestine.
appertain *v.* be relevant.
appetite *n.* desire, esp. for food.
appetizer *n.* thing eaten or drunk to stimulate the appetite.
appetizing *a.* stimulating the appetite.
applaud *v.* express approval (of), esp. by clapping; praise. **applause** *n.*
apple *n.* fruit with firm flesh.
appliance *n.* device, instrument.
applicable *a.* appropriate; relevant. **applicability** *n.*
applicant *n.* person who applies for a job.
application *n.* thing applied; process or capability of working hard.
applied *a.* put to practical use.
appliqué /apleékay/ *n.* piece of fabric attached ornamentally.
apply *v.* make a formal request; bring into use or action; be relevant. **apply oneself** give one's attention and energy.
appoint *v.* choose (a person) for a job, committee, etc.
appointee *n.* person appointed.
appointment *n.* arrangement to meet or visit at a specified time; job.
apportion *v.* divide into shares.
apposite *a.* appropriate.

apposition *n.* relationship of words that are syntactically parallel.
appraise *v.* estimate the value or quality of. **appraisal** *n.*
appreciable *a.* perceptible; considerable. **appreciably** *adv.*
appreciate *v.* enjoy intelligently; understand; increase in value. **appreciation** *n.*, **appreciative** *a.*
apprehend *v.* seize, arrest; grasp the meaning of; expect with fear or anxiety. **apprehension** *n.*
apprehensive *a.* feeling apprehension, anxious. **apprehensively** *adv.*
apprentice *n.* person learning a craft. **apprenticeship** *n.*
apprise *v.* inform.
approach *v.* come nearer (to); set about doing; go to with a request or offer. — *n.* approaching; way or means of this.
approachable *a.* easy to talk to.
approbation *n.* approval.
appropriate *a.* /əprṓpriət/ suitable, proper — *v.* /əprṓpriayt/ take and use; set aside for a special purpose. **appropriately** *adv.*, **appropriation** *n.*
approval *n.* approving. **on approval** (of goods) supplied without obligation to buy if not satisfactory.
approve *v.* say that (a thing) is good or suitable; agree to.
approximate *a.* /əprόksimət/ almost but not quite exact. — *v.* /əprόksimayt/ be almost the same; make approximate. **approximately** *adv.*, **approximation** *n.*
après-ski /áprayskeé/ *a.* & *n.* (of or for) the evening period of relaxation and partying after skiing.
apricot *n.* stone fruit related to the peach; its orange-pink colour.
apron *n.* garment worn over the front of the body to protect clothes.
apropos /áprəpṓ/ *adv.* concerning.
apse *n.* recess with an arched or domed roof in a church.
apt *a.* suitable; having a certain tendency; quick at learning. **aptly** *adv.*, **aptness** *n.*
aptitude *n.* natural ability.
aqualung *n.* portable underwater breathing-apparatus.
aquamarine *n.* bluish-green beryl; its colour.
aquarium *n.* (*pl.* **-ums**) tank for keeping living fish etc.; building containing such tanks.
aquatic *a.* living in or near water; taking place in or on water.
aquatint *n.* a kind of etching.
aqueduct *n.* artificial channel on a raised structure, carrying water across country.
aqueous /áykwiəss/ *a.* of or like water.
aquifer *n.* water-bearing rock or soil.
aquiline *a.* like an eagle; (of a nose) hooked.
Arab *n.* & *a.* (member) of a Semitic people of the Middle East.
arabesque *n.* dancer's posture with the body bent forward and leg and arm extended in line; decoration with intertwined lines etc.
Arabian *a.* of Arabia.
Arabic *a.* & *n.* (of) the language of the Arabs. **arabic numerals** the symbols 1, 2, 3, etc.
arable *a.* & *n.* (land) suitable for growing crops.
arachnid *n.* member of the class to which spiders belong.
arachnophobia *n.* fear of spiders.
arbiter *n.* person with power to decide what shall be done or accepted; arbitrator.
arbitrary *a.* based on random choice. **arbitrarily** *adv.*
arbitrate *v.* act as arbitrator. **arbitration** *n.*
arbitrator *n.* impartial person chosen to settle a dispute.
arboreal *a.* of or living in trees.
arboretum *n.* place where trees are grown for study and display.
arbour *n.* shady shelter under trees or a framework with climbing plants.
arc *n.* part of a curve; luminous electric current crossing a gap between terminals.
arcade *n.* covered walk between shops; place with pin-tables, gambling machines, etc.
arcane *a.* mysterious.
arch [1] *n.* curved structure, esp. as a support. — *v.* form into an arch. **archway** *n.*
arch [2] *a.* consciously or affectedly playful. **archly** *adv.*, **archness** *n.*
archaeology *n.* study of civilizations through their remains. **archaeological** *a.*, **archaeologist** *n.*
archaic *a.* belonging to former or ancient times.
archaism *n.* (use of) an archaic word or phrase.
archangel *n.* angel of the highest rank.
archbishop *n.* chief bishop.
archdeacon *n.* priest ranking next below bishop.
archer *n.* person who shoots with bow and arrows. **archery** *n.* sport of shooting in this way.
archetype /aárkitīp/ *n.* prototype; typical specimen. **archetypal** *a.*

archipelago *n.* (*pl.* **-os**) group of islands; sea round this.
architect *n.* designer of buildings.
architecture *n.* designing of buildings; style of building(s). **architectural** *a.*
architrave *n.* moulded frame round a doorway or window.
archive /aarkīv/ *n.* (usu. *pl.*) historical documents.
archivist /aarkivist/ *n.* person trained to deal with archives.
archway *n.* arched entrance or passage.
Arctic *a.* & *n.* (of) regions round the North Pole; very cold.
ardent *a.* full of ardour, enthusiastic. **ardently** *adv.*
ardour *n.* great warmth of feeling, enthusiasm.
arduous *a.* needing much effort.
area *n.* extent or measure of a surface; region; range of a subject etc.; sunken courtyard.
arena *n.* level area in the centre of an amphitheatre or sports stadium; scene of conflict.
argon *n.* an inert gas.
argot /aargō/ *n.* jargon.
arguable *a.* able to be asserted; not certain. **arguably** *adv.*
argue *v.* express disagreement; exchange angry words; give as reason(s).
argument *n.* discussion involving disagreement, quarrel; reason put forward; chain of reasoning.
argumentative *a.* fond of arguing.
aria *n.* solo in opera.
arid *a.* dry, parched. **aridly** *adv.*, **aridity** *n.*
arise *v.* (**arose, arisen**) come into existence or to people's notice; (*old use*) rise.
aristocracy *n.* hereditary upper classes. **aristocratic** *a.*
aristocrat *n.* member of the aristocracy.
arithmetic *n.* calculating by means of numbers.
ark *n.* Noah's boat in which he and his family and animals were saved from the Flood; wooden chest in which the writings of Jewish Law were kept.
arm [1] *n.* upper limb of the human body; raised side part of a chair.
arm [2] *v.* equip with weapons; make (a bomb) ready to explode. — *n.pl.* weapons.
armada *n.* fleet of warships.
armadillo *n.* burrowing animal of South America with a body encased in bony plates.
Armageddon *n.* final disastrous conflict.
armament *n.* military weapons; process of equipping for war.
armature *n.* wire-wound core of a dynamo.
armchair *n.* chair with raised sides.
armistice *n.* agreement to stop fighting temporarily.
armlet *n.* band worn round an arm or sleeve.
armour *n.* protective metal covering, esp. that formerly worn in fighting.
armoured *a.* protected by armour.
armourer *n.* maker, repairer, or keeper of weapons.
armoury *n.* place where weapons are kept.
armpit *n.* hollow under the arm at the shoulder.
army *n.* organized force for fighting on land; vast group.
aroma *n.* smell, esp. a pleasant one. **aromatic** *a.*
aromatherapy *n.* use of fragrant oils etc. in massage.
arose *see* **arise**.
around *adv.* & *prep.* all round, on every side (of); (*US*) approximately.
arouse *v.* rouse.
arpeggio *n.* (*pl.* **-os**) notes of a musical chord played in succession.
arraign *v.* indict, accuse; find fault with. **arraignment** *n.*
arrange *v.* put into order; form plans, settle the details of; adapt. **arrangement** *n.*
arrant *a.* downright. **arrantly** *adv.*
array *v.* arrange in order; adorn. — *n.* imposing series, display.
arrears *n.pl.* money owed and overdue for repayment; work overdue for being finished.
arrest *v.* stop (a movement or moving thing); seize by authority of law. — *n.* legal seizure of an offender.
arrival *n.* arriving; person or thing that has arrived.
arrive *v.* reach the end of a journey; (of time) come; be recognized as having achieved success.
arrogant *a.* proud and overbearing. **arrogantly** *adv.*, **arrogance** *n.*
arrow *n.* straight shaft with a sharp point, shot from a bow; line with a V at the end, indicating direction.
arrowroot *n.* edible starch made from the root of a West Indian plant.
arsenal *n.* place where weapons are stored or made.
arsenic *n.* semi-metallic element; strongly poisonous compound of this. **arsenical** *a.*
arson *n.* intentional and unlawful setting on fire of a building.
art *n.* production of something beautiful; paintings and sculptures; (*pl.*) subjects other than sciences, requiring sensitive

understanding rather than use of measurement; (*pl.*) creative activities (e.g. painting, music, writing).

artefact *n.* man-made object; simple prehistoric tool or weapon.

arterial *a.* of an artery. **arterial road** main trunk road.

artery *n.* large blood vessel conveying blood away from the heart.

artesian well a well that is bored vertically into oblique strata so that water rises naturally with little or no pumping.

artful *a.* crafty. **artfully** *adv.*

arthritis *n.* condition in which there is pain and stiffness in the joints. **arthritic** *a.*

arthropod *n.* animal with a segmented body and jointed limbs (e.g. an insect or crustacean).

artichoke *n.* plant with a flower of leaf-like scales used as a vegetable. **Jerusalem artichoke** sunflower with an edible root.

article *n.* particular or separate thing; piece of writing in a newspaper etc.; clause in an agreement. **definite article** the word 'the'. **indefinite article** 'a' or 'an'.

articulate *a.* /aartíkyoolət/ spoken distinctly; able to express ideas clearly. — *v.* /aartíkyoolayt/ say or speak distinctly; form a joint, connect by joints. **articulated lorry** one with sections connected by a flexible joint. **articulation** *n.*

artifice *n.* trickery; device.

artificial *a.* not originating naturally; man-made. **artificially** *adv.*, **artificiality** *n.*

artillery *n.* large guns used in fighting on land; branch of an army using these.

artisan *n.* skilled workman.

artist *n.* person who produces works of art, esp. paintings; one who does something with exceptional skill; professional entertainer. **artistry** *n.*

artiste /aarteést/ *n.* professional entertainer.

artistic *a.* of art or artists; showing or done with good taste. **artistically** *adv.*

artless *a.* free from artfulness, simple and natural. **artlessly** *adv.*, **artlessness** *n.*

arty *a.* (**-ier**, **-iest**) (*colloq.*) with an exaggerated or affected display of artistic style or interests.

as *adv.* & *conj.* in the same degree, similarly; in the form or function of; while, when; because. **as for, as to** with regard to. **as well** in addition.

asbestos *n.* soft fibrous mineral substance; fireproof material made from this.

asbestosis *n.* lung disease caused by inhaling asbestos particles.

ascend *v.* go or come up.

ascendant *a.* rising. **in the ascendant** rising in power or influence.

ascension *n.* ascent, esp. (**Ascension**) that of Christ to heaven.

ascent *n.* ascending; way up.

ascertain *v.* find out by enquiring. **ascertainable** *a.*

ascetic *a.* not allowing oneself pleasures and luxuries. — *n.* person who is ascetic. **asceticism** *n.*

ascorbic acid vitamin C.

ascribe *v.* attribute. **ascription** *n.*

asepsis *n.* aseptic condition.

aseptic *a.* free from harmful bacteria. **aseptically** *adv.*

asexual *a.* without sex. **asexually** *adv.*

ash [1] *n.* tree with silver-grey bark.

ash [2] *n.* powder that remains after something has burnt.

ashamed *a.* feeling shame.

ashen *a.* pale as ashes; grey.

ashlar *n.* square-cut stones; masonry made of this.

ashore *adv.* to or on shore.

ashram *n.* (orig. in India) retreat for religious meditation.

ashy *a.* (**-ier**, **-iest**) ashen; covered with ash.

Asian *a.* of Asia or its people. — *n.* Asian person.

Asiatic *a.* of Asia.

aside *adv.* to or on one side, away from the main part or group. — *n.* words spoken so that only certain people will hear.

asinine /ássinīn/ *a.* silly.

ask *v.* call for an answer to or about; address a question to; seek to obtain; invite.

askance *adv.* **look askance at** look at with distrust or displeasure.

askew *adv.* & *a.* crooked(ly).

asleep *adv.* & *a.* in or into a state of sleep.

asp *n.* small poisonous snake.

asparagus *n.* plant whose shoots are used as a vegetable.

aspect *n.* look or appearance; feature of a complex matter; direction a thing faces.

aspen *n.* a kind of poplar tree.

asperity *n.* harshness.

aspersion *n.* derogatory remark.

asphalt *n.* black substance like coal tar; mixture of this with gravel etc. for paving.

asphyxia *n.* suffocation.

asphyxiate *v.* suffocate. **asphyxiation** *n.*

aspic *n.* savoury jelly for coating cooked meat, eggs, etc.

aspidistra *n.* ornamental plant with broad tapering leaves.

aspirant *n.* person who aspires to something.

aspirate *n.* /áspirət/ sound of h. — *v.* /áspiráyt/ pronounce with an h.

aspiration *n.* aspirating; earnest desire or ambition.

aspire *v.* feel an earnest ambition.

aspirin *n.* drug that relieves pain and reduces fever; tablet of this.

ass *n.* donkey; stupid person.

assail *v.* attack violently.

assailant *n.* attacker.

assassin *n.* person who assassinates another.

assassinate *v.* kill (an important person) by violent means. **assassination** *n.*

assault *n.* & *v.* attack.

assay *n.* test of metal for quality. — *v.* make an assay of.

assemble *v.* bring or come together; put or fit together.

assembly *n.* assembled group.

assent *v.* consent; express agreement. — *n.* consent, permission.

assert *v.* state, declare to be true; use (power etc.) effectively. **assertion** *n.*, **assertive** *a.*, **assertiveness** *n.*

assess *v.* decide the amount or value of; estimate the worth or likelihood of. **assessment** *n.*, **assessor** *n.*

asset *n.* property with money value; useful quality, person or thing having this.

assiduous *a.* diligent and persevering. **assiduously** *adv.*, **assiduousness** *n.*, **assiduity** *n.*

assign *v.* allot; designate to perform a task.

assignation *n.* arrangement to meet.

assignment *n.* task assigned.

assimilate *v.* absorb or be absorbed into the body or a group etc., or into the mind as knowledge. **assimilation** *n.*

assist *v.* help. **assistance** *n.*

assistant *n.* helper; person who serves customers in a shop. — *a.* assisting, esp. as a subordinate.

associate *v.* /əsṓshiayt/ join as a companion or supporter; mix socially; connect in one's mind. — *n.* /əsṓshiət/ companion, partner; subordinate member.

association *n.* associating; group organized for a common purpose; connection between ideas.

assonance *n.* resemblance of sound in syllables; rhyme of vowel sounds. **assonant** *a.*

assorted *a.* of different sorts.

assortment *n.* collection composed of several sorts.

assuage /əswáyj/ *v.* soothe, allay.

assume *v.* take as true, without proof; take or put upon oneself.

assumption *n.* assuming; thing assumed to be true.

assurance *n.* positive assertion; self-confidence; life insurance.

assure *v.* tell confidently, promise.

assured *a.* sure, confident; insured.

assuredly *adv.* certainly.

aster *n.* garden plant with daisy-like flowers.

asterisk *n.* star-shaped symbol *.

astern *adv.* at or towards the stern; backwards.

asteroid *n.* any of the tiny planets revolving round the sun.

asthma /ásmə/ *n.* chronic condition causing difficulty in breathing. **asthmatic** *a.* & *n.*

astigmatism *n.* defect in an eye, preventing proper focusing. **astigmatic** *a.*

astonish *v.* surprise very greatly. **astonishment** *n.*

astound *v.* shock with surprise.

astrakhan *n.* dark curly fleece of lambs from Russia.

astray *adv.* & *a.* away from the proper path.

astride *adv.* with legs wide apart; with one leg on each side.

astringent *a.* causing tissue to contract; harsh, severe. — *n.* astringent substance. **astringency** *n.*, **astringently** *adv.*

astrology *n.* study of the supposed influence of stars on human affairs. **astrologer** *n.*, **astrological** *a.*

astronaut *n.* person trained to travel in a spacecraft.

astronautics *n.* study of space travel and its technology.

astronomer *n.* person skilled in astronomy.

astronomical *a.* of astronomy; enormous in amount. **astronomically** *adv.*

astronomy *n.* study of stars and planets and their movements.

astute *a.* shrewd, quick at seeing how to gain an advantage. **astutely** *adv.*, **astuteness** *n.*

asunder *adv.* apart, into pieces.

asylum *n.* refuge; (*old use*) mental institution.

asymmetrical *a.* not symmetrical. **asymmetrically** *adv.*, **asymmetry** *n.*

at *prep.* having as position, time of day, condition, or price.

atavism *n.* resemblance to remote ancestors. **atavistic** *a.*

ate *see* **eat**.

atheist *n.* person who does not believe in God. **atheism** *n.*

athlete *n.* person who is good at athletics.
athletic *a.* of athletes; muscular and physically active. **athletically** *adv.*, **athleticism** *n.*
athletics *n.pl.* or *sing.* sports, esp. running, jumping, and throwing.
atlas *n.* book of maps.
atmosphere *n.* mixture of gases surrounding a planet; air in any place; feeling conveyed by an environment or group; unit of pressure. **atmospheric** *a.*
atoll *n.* ring-shaped coral reef enclosing a lagoon.
atom *n.* smallest particle of a chemical element; very small quantity or thing.
atomic *a.* of atom(s). **atomic bomb** bomb deriving its power from atomic energy. **atomic energy** that obtained from nuclear fission.
atomize *v.* reduce to atoms or fine particles. **atomization** *n.*, **atomizer** *n.*
atonal /áytṓn'l/ *a.* (of music) not written in any key. **atonality** *n.*
atone *v.* make amends for an error or deficiency. **atonement** *n.*
atrocious *a.* extremely wicked; very bad. **atrociously** *adv.*
atrocity *n.* wickedness; cruel act.
atrophy *n.* wasting away through lack of nourishment or use. — *v.* cause atrophy in; suffer atrophy.
attach *v.* fix to something else; join; attribute, be attributable. **attached** *a.* bound by affection or loyalty. **attachment** *n.*
attaché *n.* person attached to an ambassador's staff. **attaché case** small rectangular case for carrying documents.
attack *n.* violent attempt to hurt or defeat; strong criticism; sudden onset of illness. — *v.* make an attack (on). **attacker** *n.*
attain *v.* achieve. **attainable** *a.*, **attainment** *n.*
attempt *v.* make an effort to do. — *n.* such an effort.
attend *v.* give attention to; be present at. **attendance** *n.*
attendant *a.* accompanying. — *n.* person present to provide service.
attention *n.* applying one's mind; consideration, care; erect attitude in military drill.
attentive *a.* giving attention. **attentively** *adv.*, **attentiveness** *n.*
attenuate *v.* make slender, thin, or weaker. **attenuation** *n.*
attest *v.* provide proof of; declare true or genuine. **attestation** *n.*
attic *n.* room in the top storey of a house.
attire *n.* clothes. — *v.* clothe.
attitude *n.* position of the body; way of thinking or behaving.
attorney *n.* (*US*) lawyer.
attract *v.* draw towards itself by unseen force; arouse the interest or pleasure of. **attraction** *n.*
attractive *a.* attracting; pleasing in appearance. **attractively** *adv.*, **attractiveness** *n.*
attribute ¹ /ətríbyōōt/ *v.* **attribute to** regard as belonging to or caused by. **attributable** *a.*, **attribution** *n.*
attribute ² /átribyōōt/ *n.* characteristic quality.
attrition *n.* wearing away.
attune *v.* adapt; tune.
atypical *a.* not typical. **atypically** *adv.*
aubergine /ṓbərzheen/ *n.* deep-purple vegetable; its colour.
aubrietia *n.* perennial rock-plant flowering in spring.
auburn *a.* (of hair) reddish-brown.
auction *n.* public sale where articles are sold to the highest bidder. — *v.* sell by auction.
auctioneer *n.* person who conducts an auction.
audacious *a.* bold, daring. **audaciously** *adv.*, **audacity** *n.*
audible *a.* loud enough to be heard. **audibly** *adv.*
audience *n.* group of listeners or spectators; formal interview.
audio *n.* sound reproduced mechanically; its reproduction. **audio-visual** *a.* using both sight and sound.
audit *n.* official examination of accounts. — *v.* make an audit of.
audition *n.* test of a prospective performer's ability. — *v.* test or be tested in an audition.
auditor *n.* one who audits accounts.
auditorium *n.* part of a building where the audience sits.
auditory *a.* of hearing.
augment *v.* increase. **augmentation** *n.*, **augmentative** *a.*
augur *v.* bode.
augury *n.* divination; omen.
august *a.* majestic.
auk *n.* northern seabird.
aunt *n.* sister or sister-in-law of one's father or mother.
au pair young person (esp. a woman) from overseas helping with housework in return for board and lodging.
aura *n.* atmosphere surrounding a person or thing.
aural *a.* of the ear. **aurally** *adv.*

aureole *n.* halo.
auscultation *n.* listening to the sound of the heart for diagnosis.
auspice *n.* omen; (*pl.*) patronage.
auspicious *a.* showing signs that promise success. **auspiciously** *adv.*, **auspiciousness** *n.*
austere *a.* severely simple and plain. **austerity** *n.*
Australasian *a.* & *n.* (native or inhabitant) of Australia, New Zealand, and neighbouring islands.
Australian *a.* & *n.* (native or inhabitant) of Australia.
authentic *a.* genuine, known to be true. **authentically** *adv.*, **authenticity** *n.*
authenticate *v.* prove the truth or authenticity of. **authentication** *n.*
author *n.* writer of a book etc.; originator. **authorship** *n.*
authoritarian *a.* favouring complete obedience to authority. **authoritarianism** *n.*
authoritative *a.* having or using authority. **authoritatively** *adv.*
authority *n.* power to enforce obedience; person(s) with this; person with specialized knowledge.
authorize *v.* give permission for. **authorization** *n.*
autistic *a.* suffering from a mental disorder that prevents proper response to one's environment. **autism** *n.* this disorder.
auto- *pref.* self-.
autobiography *n.* story of a person's life written by that person. **autobiographical** *a.*
autocracy *n.* despotism.
autocrat *n.* person with unrestricted power. **autocratic** *a.*, **autocratically** *adv.*
autocross *n.* motor racing on dirt tracks.
autograph *n.* person's signature. — *v.* write one's name in or on.
automate *v.* control by automation.
automatic *a.* mechanical, self-regulating; done without thinking. — *n.* automatic machine or firearm. **automatically** *adv.*
automation *n.* use of automatic equipment in industry.
automaton *n.* (*pl.* **-tons, -ta**) robot.
automobile *n.* (*US*) car.
automotive *a.* concerned with motor vehicles.
autonomous *a.* self-governing. **autonomy** *n.* self-government.
autopilot *n.* device for keeping an aircraft on a set course automatically.
autopsy *n.* post-mortem.
autumn *n.* season between summer and winter. **autumnal** *a.*
auxiliary *a.* giving help or support. *n.* helper. **auxiliary verb** one used in forming tenses of other verbs.
avail *v.* be of use or help (to). — *n.* effectiveness, advantage. **avail oneself of** make use of.
available *a.* ready to be used; obtainable. **availability** *n.*
avalanche *n.* mass of snow pouring down a mountain.
avant-garde /ávvoN-gaård/ *n.* group of innovators. — *a.* progressive.
avarice *n.* greed for gain. **avaricious** *a.*, **avariciously** *adv.*
avenge *v.* take vengeance for. **avenger** *n.*
avenue *n.* wide street or road; way of approach.
average *n.* value arrived at by adding several quantities together and dividing by the number of these; standard regarded as usual. — *a.* found by making an average; of ordinary standard.
averse *a.* unwilling, disinclined.
aversion *n.* strong dislike.
avert *v.* turn away; ward off.
aviary *n.* large cage or building for keeping birds.
aviation *n.* flying an aircraft.
avid *a.* eager, greedy. **avidly** *adv.*, **avidity** *n.*
avocado *n.* (*pl.* **-os**) pear-shaped tropical fruit.
avocet *n.* wading bird with a long upturned bill.
avoid *v.* keep oneself away from; refrain from. **avoidable** *a.*, **avoidance** *n.*
avow *v.* declare. **avowal** *n.*
avuncular *a.* of or like a kindly uncle.
await *v.* wait for.
awake *v.* (**awoke, awoken**) wake. — *a.* not asleep; alert.
awaken *v.* awake.
award *v.* give by official decision as a prize or penalty. — *n.* thing awarded.
aware *a.* having knowledge or realization. **awareness** *n.*
awash *a.* washed over by water.
away *adv.* to or at a distance; into nonexistence; persistently. — *a.* played on an opponent's ground.
awe *n.* respect combined with fear or wonder. — *v.* fill with awe.
aweigh *adv.* (of anchor) raised just clear of the sea bottom.
awesome *a.* causing awe.
awful *a.* extremely bad or unpleasant; (*colloq.*) very great. **awfully** *adv.*
awhile *adv.* for a short time.
awkward *a.* difficult to use or handle; clumsy, having little skill; inconvenient; embarrassed. **awkwardly** *adv.*, **awkwardness** *n.*

awning *n.* roof-like canvas shelter.

awoke, awoken *see* **awake**.

awry /ərī/ *adv.* & *a.* twisted to one side; amiss.

axe *n.* chopping tool. — *v.* (**axing**) remove by abolishing or dismissing.

axiom *n.* accepted general truth or principle. **axiomatic** *a.*

axis *n.* (*pl.* **axes**) line through the centre of an object, round which it rotates if spinning. **axial** *a.*

axle *n.* rod on which wheels turn.

ay *adv.* & *n.* (*pl.* **ayes**) aye.

ayatollah *n.* Muslim religious leader in Iran.

aye [1] *adv.* yes. — *n.* vote in favour of a proposal.

aye [2] *adv.* (*old use*) always.

azalea *n.* shrub-like flowering plant.

Aztec *n.* member of a former Indian people of Mexico.

azure *a.* & *n.* sky-blue.

B

baa *n.* & *v.* bleat.

babble *v.* chatter indistinctly or foolishly; (of a stream) murmur. — *n.* babbling talk or sound.

babe *n.* baby.

babel *n.* confused noise.

baboon *n.* a kind of large monkey.

baby *n.* very young child or animal; (*US sl.*) person, esp. a man's girlfriend. **baby-sit** *v.* act as **babysitter**, person employed to look after a child while its parents are out. **babyish** *a.*

baccarat /bákkəraa/ *n.* gambling card game.

bachelor *n.* unmarried man; person with university degree.

bacillus *n.* (*pl.* **-li**) rod-like bacterium.

back *n.* surface or part furthest from the front; rear part of the human body from shoulders to hips; corresponding part of an animal's body; defensive player positioned near the goal in football etc. — *a.* situated behind; of or for past time. — *adv.* at or towards the rear; in or into a previous time, position, or state; in return. — *v.* move backwards; help, support; lay a bet on. **back down** withdraw a claim or argument. **back-pedal** *v.* reverse one's previous action or opinion. **back seat** inferior position or status. **back up** support. **backer** *n.*

backache *n.* pain in one's back.

backbencher *n.* MP not entitled to sit on the front benches.

backbiting *n.* spiteful talk.

backbone *n.* column of small bones down the centre of the back.

backchat *n.* answering back.

backcloth *n.* painted cloth at the back of a stage or scene.

backdate *v.* regard as valid from an earlier date.

backdrop *n.* backcloth; background.

backfire *v.* make an explosion in an exhaust pipe; produce an undesired effect.

backgammon *n.* game played on a board with draughts and dice.

background *n.* back part of a scene or picture; conditions surrounding something.

backhand *n.* backhanded stroke.

backhanded *a.* performed with the back of the hand turned forwards; said with underlying sarcasm.

backhander *n.* backhanded stroke; (*sl.*) bribe, reward for services.

backlash *n.* violent hostile reaction.

backlog *n.* arrears of work.

backpack *n.* rucksack.

backside *n.* (*colloq.*) buttocks.

backslide *v.* slip back from good behaviour into bad.

backstage *a.* & *adv.* behind a theatre stage.

backstroke *n.* stroke used in swimming on one's back.

backtrack *v.* retrace one's route; reverse one's opinion.

backward *a.* directed backwards; having made less than normal progress; diffident. — *adv.* backwards.

backwards *adv.* towards the back; with the back foremost.

backwash *n.* receding waves created by a ship etc.; reaction.

backwater *n.* stagnant water joining a stream; place unaffected by new ideas or progress.

backwoods *n.pl.* remote region.

backyard *n.* yard behind a house; area near where one lives.

bacon *n.* salted or smoked meat from a pig.

bacteriology *n.* study of bacteria. **bacteriological** *a.*, **bacteriologist** *n.*

bacterium *n.* (*pl.* **-ia**) microscopic organism. **bacterial** *a.*

bad *a.* (**worse, worst**) having undesirable qualities; wicked, evil; harmful; decayed. **badly** *adv.*, **badness** *n.*

bade *see* **bid** [2].

badge *n.* thing worn to show membership, rank, etc.

badger *n.* burrowing animal. — *v.* pester.

badminton *n.* game like tennis, played with a shuttlecock.

baffle *v.* be too difficult for; frustrate. **bafflement** *n.*

bag *n.* flexible container; handbag; (*pl.*, *colloq.*) large amount. — *v.* (**bagged**) (*colloq.*) take for oneself.

baggage *n.* luggage.

baggy *a.* (**-ier, -iest**) hanging in loose folds.

bagpipes *n.pl.* wind instrument with air stored in a bag and pressed out through pipes.

bail [1] *n.* money pledged as security that an accused person will return for trial. — *v.* **bail out** obtain or allow the release of (a person) on bail; relieve by financial help.

bail [2] *n.* each of two crosspieces resting on the stumps in cricket.
bail [3] *v.* scoop water out of. See also **bale**.
bailey *n.* outer wall of a castle.
bailiff *n.* law officer empowered to seize goods for non-payment of fines or debts.
bailiwick *n.* area of authority.
bait *n.* food etc. placed to attract prey, esp. fish. — *v.* place bait on or in; torment by jeers.
baize *n.* thick woollen green cloth used for covering billiard tables.
bake *v.* cook or harden by dry heat.
baker *n.* person who bakes and sells bread.
bakery *n.* place where bread is baked for sale.
baking powder mixture used to make cakes rise.
Balaclava (helmet) woollen cap covering the head and neck.
balalaika *n.* Russian guitar-like instrument with a triangular body.
balance *n.* weighing apparatus; regulating apparatus of a clock; even distribution of weight or amount; difference between credits and debits; remainder. — *v.* consider by comparing; be, put, or keep in a state of balance.
balcony *n.* projecting platform with a rail or parapet; upper floor of seats in a theatre etc.
bald *a.* with scalp wholly or partly hairless; without details; (of tyres) with the tread worn away. **baldly** *adv.*, **baldness** *n.*
balderdash *n.* nonsense.
balding *a.* becoming bald.
bale *n.* large bound bundle of straw etc.; large package of goods. — *v.* make into a bale or bales. **bale out** make an emergency parachute jump from an aircraft etc. See also **bail** [3].
baleful *a.* menacing, destructive. **balefully** *adv.*
balk *v.* shirk; frustrate. — *n.* hindrance.
ball [1] *n.* spherical object used in games; rounded part or mass; single delivery of a ball by a bowler. **ball-bearing** *n.* bearing using small steel balls; one such ball. **ballpoint** *n.* pen with a tiny ball as its writing-point.
ball [2] *n.* social assembly for dancing.
ballad *n.* song telling a story.
ballade /balaád/ *n.* short lyrical piece of music.
ballast *n.* heavy material placed in a ship's hold to steady it.
ballcock *n.* device with a floating ball controlling the water level in a cistern.
ballerina *n.* female ballet dancer.
ballet *n.* performance of dancing and mime to music.
ballistics *n.pl.* study of projectiles. **ballistic** *a.*
balloon *n.* bag inflated with air or lighter gas. — *v.* swell like this.
ballot *n.* vote recorded on a slip of paper; voting by this. — *v.* **(balloted)** (cause to) vote by ballot.
ballroom *n.* large room where dances are held.
ballyhoo *n.* fuss; extravagant publicity.
balm *n.* soothing influence; fragrant herb; (*old use*) ointment.
balmy *a.* **(-ier, -iest)** fragrant; (of air) soft and warm.
balsa *n.* tropical American tree; its lightweight wood.
balsam *n.* soothing oil; a kind of flowering plant.
baluster *n.* short stone pillar in a balustrade.
balustrade *n.* row of short pillars supporting a rail or coping.
bamboo *n.* giant tropical grass with hollow stems.
bamboozle *v.* (*colloq.*) mystify, trick.
ban *v.* **(banned)** forbid officially. — *n.* order banning something.
banal *a.* commonplace, uninteresting. **banality** *n.*
banana *n.* finger-shaped fruit; tropical tree bearing this.
band *n.* strip, hoop, loop; range of values or wavelengths; organized group of people; set of musicians, esp. one playing wind or percussion instruments. **bandmaster** *n.*, **bandsman** *n.*
bandage *n.* strip of material for binding a wound. — *v.* bind with this.
bandit *n.* member of a band of robbers.
bandstand *n.* covered outdoor platform for a band playing music.
bandwagon *n.* **climb on the bandwagon** join a movement heading for success.
bandy [1] *v.* pass to and fro.
bandy [2] *a.* **(-ier, -iest)** curving apart at the knees.
bane *n.* cause of trouble or anxiety. **baneful** *a.*, **banefully** *adv.*
bang *n.* noise of or like an explosion; sharp blow. — *v.* make this noise; strike; shut noisily. — *adv.* abruptly; exactly.
banger *n.* firework that explodes noisily; (*sl.*) noisy old car; (*sl.*) sausage.
bangle *n.* bracelet of rigid material.
banish *v.* condemn to exile; dismiss from one's presence or thoughts. **banishment** *n.*
banisters *n.pl.* uprights and handrail of a staircase.
banjo *n.* guitar-like musical instrument with a circular body.

bank [1] *n.* slope, esp. at the side of a river; raised mass of earth etc.; row of lights, switches, etc. — *v.* build up into a bank; tilt sideways in rounding a curve.
bank [2] *n.* establishment for safe keeping of money; place storing a reserve supply. — *v.* place money in a bank; base one's hopes.
banknote *n.* printed strip of paper issued by a bank as currency.
bankrupt *a.* unable to pay one's debts. — *n.* bankrupt person. — *v.* make bankrupt. **bankruptcy** *n.*
banner *n.* kind of flag.
banns *n.pl.* announcement in church about a forthcoming marriage.
banquet *n.* elaborate ceremonial public meal. **banqueting** *n.* taking part in a banquet.
banquette *n.* long upholstered seat attached to a wall.
banshee *n.* (*Ir.* & *Sc.*) spirit whose wail is said to foretell a death.
bantam *n.* small kind of fowl.
banter *n.* good-humoured joking. — *v.* joke thus.
Bantu *a.* & *n.* (*pl.* **-u** *or* **-us**) (member) of a group of African Negroid peoples.
bap *n.* large soft bread roll.
baptism *n.* religious rite of sprinkling with water as a sign of purification, usu. with name-giving. **baptismal** *a.*
Baptist *n.* member of a Protestant sect believing that baptism should be by immersion.
baptistery *n.* place where baptism is performed.
baptize *v.* perform baptism on; name, nickname.
bar [1] *n.* long piece of solid material; strip; barrier; counter where alcohol or refreshments are served, room containing this; vertical line dividing music into units, this unit; barristers, their profession. — *v.* (**barred**) fasten or keep in or out with bar(s); obstruct; prohibit. — *prep.* except.
bar [2] *n.* unit of atmospheric pressure.
barb *n.* backward-pointing part of an arrow; wounding remark.
barbarian *n.* uncivilized person.
barbaric *a.* suitable for barbarians, rough and wild.
barbarity *n.* savage cruelty.
barbarous *a.* uncivilized, cruel. **barbarously** *adv.*, **barbarism** *n.*
barbecue *n.* frame for grilling food above an open fire; this food; open-air party where such food is served. — *v.* cook on a barbecue.
barbed *a.* having barbs. **barbed wire** wire with many sharp points.
barber *n.* men's hairdresser.
barbican *n.* outer defence to a city or castle; double tower over a gate or bridge.
barbiturate *n.* sedative drug.
bar code pattern of printed stripes as a machine-readable code identifying a commodity, its price, etc.
bard *n.* Celtic minstrel; poet. **bardic** *a.*
bare *a.* not clothed or covered; not adorned; scanty. — *v.* reveal. **barely** *adv.*
bareback *adv.* on horseback without a saddle.
barefaced *a.* shameless, undisguised.
bargain *n.* agreement with obligations on both sides; thing obtained cheaply. — *v.* discuss the terms of an agreement; expect.
barge *n.* large flat-bottomed boat used on rivers and canals. — *v.* move clumsily. **barge in** intrude.
baritone *n.* male voice between tenor and bass.
barium *n.* white metallic element.
bark [1] *n.* outer layer of a tree. — *v.* scrape skin off accidentally.
bark [2] *n.* sharp harsh sound made by a dog. — *v.* make this sound; utter in a sharp commanding voice.
barley *n.* a kind of cereal plant; its grain. **barley sugar** sweet made of boiled sugar. **barley water** drink made from pearl barley.
barmaid *n.* female attendant at a bar serving alcohol.
barman *n.* (*pl.* **-men**) male attendant at a bar serving alcohol.
barmy *a.* (**-ier, -iest**) (*sl.*) crazy.
barn *n.* simple roofed farm building for storing grain or hay etc.
barnacle *n.* shellfish that attaches itself to objects under water.
barometer *n.* instrument measuring atmospheric pressure, used in forecasting weather. **barometric** *a.*
baron *n.* member of the lowest rank of nobility. **baroness** *n.fem.*, **baronial** *a.*
baronet *n.* hereditary title; man holding this. **baronetcy** *n.*
baroque /bərók/ *a.* of the ornate architectural style of the 17th–18th centuries. — *n.* this style.
barque *n.* sailing ship.
barrack *v.* shout protests; jeer at.
barracks *n.pl.* building(s) for soldiers to live in.
barracuda *n.* large voracious West Indian fish.
barrage *n.* heavy bombardment; artificial barrier.

barrel *n.* large round container with flat ends; tube-like part esp. of a gun. **barrel organ** mechanical instrument producing music by a pin-studded cylinder acting on pipes or keys.

barren *a.* not fertile, unable to bear fruit. **barrenness** *n.*

barricade *n.* barrier. — *v.* block or defend with a barricade.

barrier *n.* thing that prevents or controls advance or access.

barrister *n.* lawyer representing clients in court.

barrow ¹ *n.* wheelbarrow; cart pushed or pulled by hand.

barrow ² *n.* prehistoric burial mound.

barter *n.* & *v.* trade by exchange of goods for other goods.

basalt /bássawlt/ *n.* dark rock of volcanic origin.

base *n.* lowest part; part on which a thing rests or is supported; basis; headquarters; substance capable of combining with an acid to form a salt; each of four stations to be reached by a batter in baseball. — *v.* use as a base or foundation or evidence for a forecast. — *a.* dishonourable; of inferior value.

baseball *n.* American team game played with bat and ball, in which the batter has to hit the ball and run round a circuit.

baseless *a.* without foundation. **baselessly** *adv.*

basement *n.* storey below ground level.

bash *v.* strike violently; attack. — *n.* violent blow or knock.

bashful *a.* shy and self-conscious. **bashfully** *adv.*, **bashfulness** *n.*

basic *a.* forming a basis; fundamental. **basically** *adv.*

basil *n.* sweet-smelling herb.

basilica *n.* oblong hall or church with an apse at one end.

basilisk *n.* American lizard; mythical reptile said to cause death by its glance or breath.

basin *n.* deep open container for liquids; washbasin; sunken place, area drained by a river. **basinful** *n.* (*pl.* **-fuls**)

basis *n.* (*pl.* **bases**) foundation or support; main principle.

bask *v.* sit or lie comfortably exposed to pleasant warmth.

basket *n.* container for holding or carrying things, made of interwoven cane or wire.

basketball *n.* team game in which the aim is to throw the ball through a high hoop or 'basket'.

basketwork *n.* material woven in the style of a basket.

Basque *n.* & *a.* (member) of a people living in the western Pyrenees; (of) their language.

bas-relief *n.* sculpture or carving in low relief.

bass ¹ /bass/ *n.* (*pl.* **bass**) fish of the perch family.

bass ² /bayss/ *a.* deep-sounding, of the lowest pitch in music. — *n.* (*pl.* **basses**) lowest male voice; bass pitch; double bass.

basset *n.* short-legged hound.

bassoon *n.* woodwind instrument with a deep tone.

bast *n.* inner bark of the lime tree; similar fibre.

bastard *n.* illegitimate child; (*sl.*) unpleasant or difficult person or thing. **bastardy** *n.*

baste ¹ *v.* sew together temporarily with loose stitches.

baste ² *v.* moisten with fat during cooking; thrash.

bastion *n.* projecting part of a fortified place; stronghold.

bat ¹ *n.* wooden implement for striking a ball in games; batsman. — *v.* (**batted**) perform or strike with the bat in cricket etc.

bat ² *n.* flying animal with a mouse-like body.

batch *n.* set of people or things dealt with as a group.

bated *a.* **with bated breath** with breath held anxiously.

bath *n.* washing (of the whole body) by immersion; container used for this. — *v.* wash in a bath.

bathe *v.* immerse in liquid; swim for pleasure. — *n.* swim. **bather** *n.*

bathos *n.* anticlimax, descent from an important thing to a trivial one.

bathroom *n.* room containing a bath.

batik *n.* method of printing designs on textiles by waxing parts not to be dyed; fabric printed thus.

batman *n.* soldier acting as an officer's personal servant.

baton *n.* short stick, esp. used by a conductor.

batrachian /bətráykiən/ *n.* amphibian that discards gills and tail when fully developed.

batsman *n.* player batting in cricket.

battalion *n.* army unit of several companies.

batten ¹ *n.* bar of wood or metal, esp. holding something in place. — *v.* fasten with batten(s).

batten ² *v.* **batten on** thrive at another's expense.

batter ¹ *v.* hit hard and often. — *n.* beaten

mixture of flour, eggs, and milk, used in cooking.

batter [2] *n.* player batting in baseball.

battering ram iron-headed beam formerly used in war for breaking through walls or gates.

battery *n.* group of big guns; artillery unit; set of similar or connected units of equipment, poultry cages, etc.; electric cell(s) supplying current; unlawful blow or touch.

battle *n.* fight between large organized forces; contest. — *v.* engage in battle, struggle.

battleaxe *n.* heavy axe used as a weapon in ancient times; (*colloq.*) formidable woman.

battlefield *n.* scene of battle.

battlements *n.pl.* parapet with gaps for firing from.

battleship *n.* warship of the most heavily armed kind.

batty *a.* (**-ier, -iest**) (*sl.*) crazy.

bauble *n.* valueless ornament.

baulk *n.* starting-area on a billiard table.

bauxite *n.* mineral from which aluminium is obtained.

bawdy *a.* (**-ier, -iest**) humorously indecent. **bawdiness** *n.*

bawl *v.* shout; weep noisily. **bawl out** (*colloq.*) reprimand.

bay [1] *n.* a kind of laurel.

bay [2] *n.* part of a sea or lake within a wide curve of the shore.

bay [3] *n.* recess, compartment. **bay window** one projecting from an outside wall.

bay [4] *n.* deep cry of a large dog or of hounds. — *v.* make this sound. **at bay** forced to face attackers.

bay [5] *a.* & *n.* reddish-brown (horse).

bayonet *n.* stabbing blade fixed to the muzzle of a rifle.

bazaar *n.* series of shops or stalls in an Oriental market; sale of goods to raise funds.

bazooka *n.* portable weapon for firing anti-tank rockets.

be *v.* exist, occur; have a certain position or quality or condition. — *v.aux.* (used to form tenses of other verbs).

beach *n.* shore between high and low water marks. — *v.* bring on shore from water.

beachcomber *n.* person who salvages things on a beach.

beachhead *n.* fortified position set up on a beach by an invading army.

beacon *n.* signal fire on a hill.

bead *n.* small shaped piece of hard material pierced for threading with others on a string; drop or bubble of liquid.

beading *n.* strip of trimming for wood.

beadle *n.* (formerly) minor parish official.

beady *a.* (**-ier, -iest**) (of eyes) small and bright.

beagle *n.* small hound used for hunting hares.

beak *n.* bird's horny projecting jaws; any similar projection; (*sl.*) magistrate.

beaker *n.* tall drinking-cup.

beam *n.* long piece of timber or metal carrying the weight of part of a building; ship's breadth; ray of light or other radiation; bright look, smile. — *v.* send out light etc.; look or smile radiantly.

bean *n.* plant with kidney-shaped seeds in long pods; seed of this or of coffee.

bear [1] *n.* large heavy animal with thick fur; child's toy like this.

bear [2] *v.* (**bore, borne**) carry, support; have in one's heart or mind; endure; be fit for; produce, give birth to; take (a specified direction); exert pressure.

bearable *a.* endurable.

beard *n.* hair on and round a man's chin. — *v.* confront boldly.

bearing *n.* deportment, behaviour; relevance; compass direction; device reducing friction where a part turns.

bearskin *n.* guardsman's tall furry cap.

beast *n.* large four-footed animal; unpleasant person or thing.

beastly *a.* (**-ier, -iest**) (*colloq.*) very unpleasant. **beastliness** *n.*

beat *v.* (**beat, beaten**) hit repeatedly; mix vigorously; (of the heart) pump rhythmically; do better than, defeat. — *n.* regular repeated stroke; recurring emphasis marking rhythm; appointed course of a policeman or sentinel. **beat up** assault violently.

beatific *a.* showing great happiness. **beatifically** *adv.*

beatify *v.* (*RC Church*) declare blessed, as first step in canonization. **beatification** *n.*

beatitude *n.* blessedness.

beauteous *a.* (*poetic*) beautiful.

beautician *n.* person whose job is to give beautifying treatment.

beautiful *a.* having beauty; very satisfactory. **beautifully** *adv.*

beautify *v.* make beautiful. **beautification** *n.*

beauty *n.* combination of qualities giving pleasure to the sight or other senses or to the mind; beautiful person or thing.

beaver *n.* small amphibious rodent. — *v.* work hard.

becalmed *a.* unable to move because there is no wind.

because *conj.* for the reason that. — *adv.* **because of** by reason of.
beck [1] *n.* **at the beck and call of** ready and waiting to obey.
beck [2] *n.* mountain stream.
beckon *v.* summon by a gesture.
become *v.* **(became, become)** come or grow to be, begin to be; give a pleasing appearance or effect upon; befit.
bed *n.* thing to sleep or rest on; framework with a mattress and coverings; flat base, foundation; bottom of a sea or river etc.; layer; garden plot.
bedbug *n.* bug infesting beds.
bedclothes *n.pl.* sheets, blankets, etc.
bedding *n.* beds and bedclothes.
bedevil *v.* **(bedevilled)** afflict with difficulties.
bedfellow *n.* person sharing one's bed; associate.
bedlam *n.* scene of uproar.
Bedouin /bédoo-in/ *n.* (*pl.* **Bedouin**) member of an Arab people living in tents in the desert.
bedpan *n.* pan for use as a lavatory by a person confined to bed.
bedraggled *a.* limp and untidy.
bedridden *a.* permanently confined to bed through illness.
bedrock *n.* solid rock beneath loose soil; basic facts.
bedroom *n.* room for sleeping in.
bedside *n.* position by a bed.
bedsitting room room used for both living and sleeping in. **bedsitter** *n.*
bedsore *n.* sore developed by lying in bed for a long time.
bedspread *n.* covering spread over a bed during the day.
bedstead *n.* framework of a bed.
bee *n.* insect that produces honey.
beech *n.* tree with smooth bark and glossy leaves.
beef *n.* meat from ox, bull, or cow; muscular strength; (*sl.*) grumble. — *v.* (*sl.*) grumble.
beefburger *n.* hamburger.
beefeater *n.* warder in the Tower of London, wearing Tudor dress.
beefy *a.* **(-ier, -iest)** having a solid muscular body.
beehive *n.* structure in which bees live.
beeline *n.* **make a beeline for** go straight or rapidly towards.
beep *n.* & *v.* bleep. **beeper** *n.*
beer *n.* alcoholic drink made from malt and hops. **beery** *a.*
beeswax *n.* yellow substance secreted by bees, used as polish.
beet *n.* plant with a fleshy root used as a vegetable or for making sugar; beetroot.
beetle [1] *n.* insect with hard wing-covers.
beetle [2] *n.* tool for ramming or crushing things.
beetle [3] *v.* overhang, project.
beetroot *n.* root of beet as a vegetable.
befall *v.* **(befell, befallen)** happen; happen to.
befit *v.* **(befitted)** be suitable for.
before *adv.*, *prep.*, & *conj.* at an earlier time (than); ahead, in front of; in preference to.
beforehand *adv.* in advance.
befriend *v.* show kindness towards.
beg *v.* **(begged)** ask for as a gift or charity; request earnestly or humbly; (of a dog) sit up expectantly with forepaws off the ground.
beggar *n.* person who lives by begging. — *v.* reduce to poverty. **beggary** *n.*
beggarly *a.* mean and insufficient.
begin *v.* **(began, begun, beginning)** perform the first or earliest part of (an activity); be the first to do a thing; come into existence.
beginner *n.* person just beginning to learn a skill.
beginning *n.* first part; starting point, source or origin.
begonia *n.* garden plant with bright leaves and flowers.
begrudge *v.* be unwilling to give or allow.
beguile *v.* deceive; entertain pleasantly.
begum *n.* title of a Muslim married woman in India and Pakistan.
behalf *n.* **on behalf of** as the representative of.
behave *v.* act or react in a specified way; (also **behave oneself**) show good manners.
behaviour *n.* way of behaving.
behead *v.* cut the head off.
beheld *see* **behold**.
behind *adv.* & *prep.* in or to the rear (of); in arrears; remaining after others' departure. — *n.* buttocks.
behold *v.* **(beheld)** (*old use*) see, observe. **beholder** *n.*
beholden *a.* owing thanks.
behove *v.* be incumbent on.
beige *a.* & *n.* light fawn (colour).
being *n.* existence; thing that exists and has life, person.
belabour *v.* beat; attack.
belated *a.* coming very late or too late. **belatedly** *adv.*
belch *v.* send out wind noisily from the stomach through the mouth. — *n.* act or sound of belching.
beleaguer *v.* besiege.
belfry *n.* bell tower; space for bells in a tower.

belie *v.* contradict, fail to confirm.

belief *n.* believing; thing believed.

believe *v.* accept as true or as speaking truth; think, suppose. **believe in** have faith in the existence of; feel sure of the worth of. **believer** *n.*

belittle *v.* disparage.

bell *n.* cup-shaped metal instrument that makes a ringing sound when struck; its sound.

belle *n.* beautiful woman.

belles-lettres /bel-létrə/ *n.pl.* literary studies.

bellicose *a.* eager to fight.

belligerent *a.* & *n.* (person or country) waging war; aggressive. **belligerently** *adv.*, **belligerence** *n.*

bellow *n.* loud deep sound made by a bull; deep shout. — *v.* make this sound.

bellows *n.pl.* apparatus for driving air into something.

belly *n.* abdomen; stomach.

bellyful *n.* (*colloq.*) as much as one wants or rather more.

belong *v.* be rightly assigned as property, part, duty, etc.; have a rightful place; (with *to*) be a member of.

belongings *n.pl.* personal possessions.

beloved *a.* & *n.* dearly loved (person).

below *adv.* & *prep.* at or to a lower position or amount (than).

belt *n.* strip of cloth or leather etc., worn round the waist; long narrow region. — *v.* put a belt round; (*sl.*) hit; (*sl.*) rush.

bemoan *v.* complain about.

bemused *a.* bewildered; lost in thought. **bemusement** *n.*

bench *n.* long seat of wood or stone; long working-table; judges or magistrates hearing a case.

benchmark *n.* surveyor's fixed point; point of reference.

bend *v.* (**bent**) make or become curved; turn downwards, stoop; turn in a new direction. — *n.* curve, turn.

bender *n.* (*sl.*) drinking spree.

beneath *adv.* & *prep.* below, underneath; not worthy of.

benediction *n.* spoken blessing.

benefactor *n.* one who gives financial or other help. **benefaction** *n.*, **benefactress** *n.fem.*

beneficent *a.* doing good; actively kind. **beneficence** *n.*

beneficial *a.* having a helpful or useful effect. **beneficially** *adv.*

beneficiary *n.* one who receives a benefit or legacy.

benefit *n.* something helpful or favourable or profitable. — *v.* (**benefited, benefiting**) do good to; receive benefit.

benevolent *a.* kindly and helpful. **benevolently** *adv.*, **benevolence** *n.*

benighted *a.* in darkness; ignorant.

benign *a.* kindly; mild and gentle; not malignant. **benignly** *adv.*

bent *see* **bend**. — *n.* natural skill or liking. — *a.* **bent on** seeking or determined to do.

benzene *n.* liquid obtained from petroleum and coal tar, used as a solvent, fuel, etc.

benzine *n.* liquid mixture of hydrocarbons used in dry-cleaning.

benzol *n.* (unrefined) benzene.

bequeath *v.* leave as a legacy.

bequest *n.* legacy.

berate *v.* scold.

bereave *v.* deprive, esp. of a relative, by death. **bereavement** *n.*

bereft *a.* deprived.

beret /bérray/ *n.* round flat cap with no peak.

beriberi *n.* disease caused by lack of vitamin B.

berry *n.* small round juicy fruit with no stone.

berserk *a.* **go berserk** go into an uncontrollable destructive rage.

berth *n.* bunk or sleeping place in a ship or train; place for a ship to tie up at a wharf. — *v.* moor at a berth. **give a wide berth to** keep a safe distance from.

beryl *n.* transparent green gem.

beseech *v.* (**besought**) implore.

beset *v.* (**beset, besetting**) hem in, surround; habitually affect or trouble.

beside *prep.* at the side of, close to; compared with. **be beside oneself** be at the end of one's self-control. **beside the point** irrelevant.

besides *prep.* in addition to, other than. — *adv.* also.

besiege *v.* lay siege to.

besotted *a.* infatuated.

besought *see* **beseech**.

bespeak *v.* (**bespoke, bespoken**) engage beforehand; be evidence of.

bespoke *a.* (of clothes) made to a customer's order.

best *a.* of the most excellent kind. — *adv.* in the best way; most usefully. — *n.* best thing; victory. **best man** bridegroom's chief attendant. **best part of** most of.

bestial *a.* of or like a beast, savage. **bestiality** *n.*

bestir *v.* (**bestirred**) **bestir oneself** exert oneself.

bestow *v.* confer as a gift. **bestowal** *n.*

bestride *v.* (**bestrode**) stand astride over.

bet *n.* pledge that will be forfeited if one's

forecast is wrong. — *v.* (**bet** *or* **betted**) make a bet; (*colloq.*) predict.
beta *n.* second letter of the Greek alphabet, = b.
betake *v.* (**betook, betaken**) **betake oneself** go.
betide *v.* happen to.
betimes *adv.* in good time, early.
betoken *v.* be a sign of.
betray *v.* hand over disloyally to an enemy. **betrayal** *n.*, **betrayer** *n.*
betroth *v.* cause to be engaged to marry. **betrothal** *n.*
better [1] *a.* of a more excellent kind; recovered from illness. — *adv.* in a better manner; more usefully. — *v.* improve; do better than. **better part** more than half. **get the better of** overcome; outwit.
better [2] *n.* person who bets.
betting shop bookmaker's office.
between *prep.* in the space, time, or quality bounded by (two limits); separating; to and from; connecting; shared by. — *adv.* between points or limits etc.
bevel *n.* sloping edge. — *v.* (**bevelled**) give a sloping edge to.
beverage *n.* any drink.
bevy *n.* company, large group.
bewail *v.* wail over.
beware *v.* be on one's guard.
bewilder *v.* puzzle, confuse. **bewilderment** *n.*
bewitch *v.* put under a magic spell; delight very much.
beyond *adv.* & *prep.* at or to the further side (of); outside the range of.
biannual *a.* happening twice a year. **biannually** *adv.*
bias *n.* influence favouring one of a group unfairly; tendency of a bowl to swerve because of its lopsided form. — *v.* (**biased**) give a bias to, influence.
bib *n.* covering put under a young child's chin to protect its clothes while feeding.
Bible *n.* Christian or Jewish scripture.
biblical *a.* of or in the Bible.
bibliography *n.* list of books about a subject or by a specified author. **bibliographer** *n.*, **bibliographical** *a.*
bibliophile *n.* book-lover.
bibulous *a.* fond of drinking.
bicentenary *n.* 200th anniversary.
bicentennial *a.* happening every 200 years. — *n.* bicentenary.
biceps *n.* large muscle at the front of the upper arm.
bicker *v.* quarrel constantly about unimportant things.
bicycle *n.* two-wheeled vehicle driven by pedals. — *v.* ride a bicycle.
bid [1] *n.* offer of a price, esp. at an auction; statement of the number of tricks a player proposes to win in a card game; attempt. — *v.* (**bid, bidding**) make a bid (of), offer. **bidder** *n.*
bid [2] *v.* (**bid** or **bade, bidden, bidding**) command; say as a greeting.
biddable *a.* willing to obey.
bide *v.* await (one's time).
bidet /beeday/ *n.* low washbasin that one can sit astride to wash the genital and anal regions.
biennial *a.* lasting for two years; happening every second year. — *n.* plant that flowers and dies in its second year. **biennially** *adv.*
bier /beer/ *n.* movable stand for a coffin.
biff *v.* & *n.* (*sl.*) hit.
bifocals *n.pl.* spectacles with lenses that have two segments, assisting both distant and close focusing.
bifurcate *v.* fork. **bifurcation** *n.*
big *a.* (**bigger, biggest**) large in size, amount, or intensity.
bigamy *n.* crime of going through a form of marriage while a previous marriage is still valid. **bigamist** *a.*, **bigamous** *a.*
bigot *n.* person who is prejudiced and is intolerant towards those who disagree. **bigoted** *a.*, **bigotry** *n.*
bike *n.* (*colloq.*) bicycle, motor cycle. — *v.* (*colloq.*) ride a bicycle or motor cycle. **biker** *n.*
bikini *n.* (*pl.* **-is**) woman's scanty two-piece beach garment.
bilateral *a.* having two sides; existing between two groups. **bilaterally** *adv.*
bilberry *n.* small round dark blue fruit; shrub producing this.
bile *n.* bitter yellowish liquid produced by the liver.
bilge *n.* ship's bottom; water collecting there; (*sl.*) worthless talk.
bilharzia *n.* disease caused by a tropical parasitic flatworm.
bilingual *a.* written in or able to speak two languages.
bilious *a.* sick, esp. from trouble with bile or liver. **biliousness** *n.*
bilk *v.* defraud of payment.
bill [1] *n.* written statement of charges to be paid; poster; programme; certificate; draft of a proposed law; (*US*) banknote.
bill [2] *n.* bird's beak. — *v.* **bill and coo** exchange caresses.
billabong *n.* (*Austr.*) backwater.
billet *n.* lodging for troops. — *v.* (**billeted**) place in a billet.
billhook *n.* pruning-instrument with a concave edge.
billiards *n.* game played with cues and three balls on a table.

billion *n.* one thousand million.
billow *n.* great wave. — *v.* rise or move like waves; swell out.
bimbo *n.* (*pl.* **-os**) (*sl.*) person; (empty-headed) young woman.
bin *n.* large rigid container or receptacle.
binary *a.* of two. **binary digit** either of two digits (0 and 1) used in the **binary scale**, system of numbers using only these.
bind *v.* (**bound**) tie, fasten together; cover the edge of so as to strengthen or decorate; fasten into a cover; place under an obligation or legal agreement. — *n.* (*sl.*) bore, nuisance.
binding *n.* book cover; braid etc. used to bind an edge.
bindweed *n.* wild convolvulus.
bine *n.* flexible stem of a climbing plant, esp. the hop.
binge *n.* (*sl.*) spree, eating and drinking and making merry.
bingo *n.* gambling game using cards marked with numbered squares.
binocular *a.* using two eyes.
binoculars *n.pl.* instrument with lenses for both eyes, making distant objects seem larger.
binomial *a.*& *n.* (expression or name) consisting of two terms.
biochemistry *n.* chemistry of living organisms. **biochemical** *a.*, **biochemist** *n.*
biodegradable *a.* able to be decomposed by bacteria.
biographer *n.* writer of a biography.
biography *n.* story of a person's life. **biographical** *a.*
biology *n.* study of the life and structure of living things. **biological** *a.*, **biologist** *n.*
bionic *a.* (of a person or faculties) operated electronically.
biopsy *n.* examination of tissue cut from a living body.
biorhythm *n.* any of the recurring cycles of activity in a person's life.
bipartite *a.* consisting of two parts; involving two groups.
biped *n.* two-footed animal such as man.
biplane *n.* aeroplane with two pairs of wings.
birch *n.* tree with smooth bark.
bird *n.* feathered animal.
birth *n.* emergence of young from the mother's body; parentage. **birth control** prevention of unwanted pregnancy.
birthday *n.* anniversary of the day of one's birth.
birthmark *n.* unusual coloured mark on the skin at birth.
birthright *n.* thing that is one's right through being born into a certain family or country.
biscuit *n.* small flat thin piece of pastry baked crisp.
bisect *v.* divide into two equal parts. **bisection** *n.*, **bisector** *n.*
bisexual *a.* sexually attracted to members of both sexes. **bisexuality** *n.*
bishop *n.* clergyman of high rank; mitre-shaped chess piece.
bishopric *n.* diocese of a bishop.
bismuth *n.* metallic element; compound of this used in medicines.
bison *n.* (*pl.* **bison**) wild ox; buffalo.
bistro *n.* (*pl.* **-os**) small bar or restaurant.
bit [1] *n.* small piece or quantity; short time or distance; mouthpiece of a bridle; part of a tool that cuts or bores or grips when twisted.
bit [2] *n.* (in computers) binary digit.
bit [3] *see* **bite**.
bitch *n.* female dog; (*colloq.*) spiteful woman, difficult thing. — *v.* (*colloq.*) speak spitefully or sourly. **bitchy** *a.*, **bitchiness** *n.*
bite *v.* (**bit, bitten**) cut with the teeth; penetrate; grip or act effectively. — *n.* act of biting; wound made by this; small meal.
biting *a.* causing a smarting pain; sharply critical.
bitter *a.* tasting sharp, not sweet or mild; with mental pain or resentment; piercingly cold. — *n.* bitter beer. **bitterly** *adv.*, **bitterness** *n.*
bittern *n.* a kind of marsh bird.
bitty *a.* (**-ier, -iest**) made up of unrelated bits. **bittiness** *n.*
bitumen *n.* black substance made from petroleum. **bituminous** *a.*
bivalve *n.* shellfish with a hinged double shell.
bivouac *n.* temporary camp without tents or other cover. — *v.* (**bivouacked**) camp thus.
bizarre *a.* strikingly odd in appearance or effect.
blab *v.* (**blabbed**) talk indiscreetly. **blabber** *n.*
black *a.* of the very darkest colour, like coal or soot; having a black skin; dismal, gloomy; hostile; evil. — *n.* black colour or thing; **Black** Negro. **black eye** bruised eye. **black hole** region in outer space from which matter and radiation cannot escape. **blacklist** *n.* list of persons who are disapproved of. **black market** illegal buying and selling. **black out** cover windows so that no light can penetrate. **black pudding** sausage of blood and suet. **black sheep** scoundrel. **in the black** with a credit balance, not in debt.
blackberry *n.* bramble; its edible dark berry.

blackbird *n.* European songbird, male of which is black.
blackboard *n.* board for writing on with chalk in front of a class.
blacken *v.* make or become black; say evil things about.
blackguard /blággaard/ *n.* scoundrel. **blackguardly** *adv.*
blackhead *n.* small dark lump blocking a pore in the skin.
blackleg *n.* person who works while fellow workers are on strike.
blackmail *v.* demand payment or action from (a person) by threats. — *n.* money demanded thus. **blackmailer** *n.*
blackout *n.* temporary loss of consciousness or memory.
blacksmith *n.* smith who works in iron.
blackthorn *n.* thorny shrub bearing white flowers and sloes.
bladder *n.* sac in which urine collects in the body; inflatable bag.
blade *n.* flattened cutting part of a knife or sword; flat part of an oar or propeller; flat narrow leaf of grass; broad bone.
blame *v.* hold responsible for a fault. — *n.* responsibility for a fault.
blameless *a.* not subject to blame.
blameworthy *a.* deserving blame.
blanch *v.* make or become white or pale.
blancmange /bləmónj/ *n.* flavoured jelly-like pudding.
bland *a.* mild; gentle and casual, not irritating or stimulating. **blandly** *adv.*
blandishments *n.pl.* flattering or coaxing words.
blank *a.* not written or printed on; without interest or expression. — *n.* blank space; cartridge containing no bullet. **blank cheque** one with the amount left blank for the payee to fill in. **blank verse** verse without rhyme.
blanket *n.* warm covering made of woollen or similar material; thick covering mass.
blare *v.* sound loudly and harshly. — *n.* this sound.
blarney *n.* smooth talk that flatters and deceives.
blasé /blaázay/ *a.* bored or unimpressed by things.
blaspheme *v.* utter blasphemies (about). **blasphemer** *n.*
blasphemy *n.* irreverent talk about sacred things. **blasphemous** *a.*, **blasphemously** *adv.*
blast *n.* strong gust; wave of air from an explosion; sound of a wind instrument or whistle; severe reprimand. — *v.* blow up with explosives; cause to wither, destroy; (*colloq.*) reprimand severely. **blast off** be launched by firing of rockets.
blatant *a.* very obvious; shameless. **blatantly** *adv.*
blaze [1] *n.* bright flame or fire; bright light or display; outburst. — *v.* burn or shine brightly.
blaze [2] *n.* white mark on an animal's face; mark chipped in the bark of a tree to mark a route. **blaze a trail** make such marks; pioneer.
blazer *n.* loose-fitting jacket, esp. in the colours or bearing the badge of a school, team, etc.
blazon *n.* heraldic shield, coat of arms. — *v.* proclaim; ornament with heraldic or other devices.
bleach *v.* whiten by sunlight or chemicals. — *n.* bleaching substance or process.
bleak *a.* cold and cheerless. **bleakly** *adv.*, **bleakness** *n.*
bleary *a.* (**-ier**, **-iest**) (of eyes) watery and seeing indistinctly. **blearily** *adv.*, **bleariness** *n.*
bleat *n.* cry of a sheep or goat. — *v.* utter this cry; speak or say plaintively.
bleed *v.* (**bled**) leak blood or other fluid; draw blood or fluid from; extort money from.
bleep *n.* short high-pitched sound. — *v.* make this sound. **bleeper** *n.*
blemish *n.* flaw or defect that spoils the perfection of a thing. — *v.* spoil with a blemish.
blench *v.* flinch.
blend *v.* mix into a harmonious compound. — *n.* mixture. **blender** *n.*
blenny *n.* sea fish with spiny fins.
bless *v.* call God's favour upon; make sacred or holy; praise (God). **be blessed with** be fortunate in having.
blessed *a.* holy, sacred; in paradise; (*colloq.*) damned. **blessedly** *adv.*, **blessedness** *n.*
blessing *n.* God's favour; prayer for this; something one is glad of.
blight *n.* disease or fungus that withers plants; malignant influence. — *v.* affect with blight; spoil.
blind *a.* without sight; without foresight or understanding or adequate information; (in cookery) without filling. — *v.* make blind; take away power of judgement from. — *n.* screen, esp. on a roller, for a window; pretext. **blindly** *adv.*, **blindness** *n.*
blindfold *n.* cloth used to cover the eyes and block the sight. — *v.* cover the eyes of (a person) thus.
blink *v.* open and shut one's eyes rapidly; shine unsteadily. — *n.* act of blinking; quick gleam.
blinker *n.* leather piece fixed to a bridle

to prevent a horse from seeing sideways. — *v.* obstruct the sight or understanding of.

blip *n.* quick sound or movement; small image on a radar screen.

bliss *n.* perfect happiness. **blissful** *a.*, **blissfully** *adv.*

blister *n.* bubble-like swelling on skin; raised swelling on a surface. — *v.* cause blister(s) on; be affected with blister(s).

blithe *a.* casual and carefree. **blithely** *adv.*

blitz *n.* violent attack, esp. from aircraft. — *v.* attack in a blitz.

blizzard *n.* severe snowstorm.

bloat *v.* swell with fat, gas, or liquid.

bloater *n.* salted smoked herring.

blob *n.* drop of liquid; round mass.

bloc *n.* group of parties or countries who combine for a purpose.

block *n.* solid piece of hard substance; log of wood; (*sl.*) head; pulley(s) mounted in a case; compact mass of buildings; large building divided into flats or offices; large quantity treated as a unit; pad of paper for drawing or writing on; obstruction. — *v.* obstruct, prevent the movement or use of. **block letters** plain capital letters.

blockade *n.* blocking of access to a place, to prevent entry of goods. — *v.* set up a blockade of.

blockage *n.* blocking; thing that blocks.

blockhead *n.* stupid person.

bloke *n.* (*sl.*) man.

blond *a.* & *n.* fair-haired (man).

blonde *a.* & *n.* fair-haired (woman).

blood *n.* red liquid circulating in the bodies of animals; temper, courage; race, descent, parentage; kindred. — *v.* give a first taste of blood to (a hound); initiate (a person). **blood-curdling** *a.* horrifying. **blood sports** sports involving killing. **blood vessel** tubular structure conveying blood within the body.

bloodhound *n.* large keen-scented dog, formerly used in tracking.

bloodless *a.* without bloodshed. **bloodlessly** *adv.*

bloodshed *n.* killing or wounding.

bloodshot *a.* (of eyes) red from dilated veins.

bloodstock *n.* thoroughbred horses.

bloodstream *n.* blood circulating in the body.

bloodsucker *n.* creature that sucks blood; person who extorts money.

bloodthirsty *a.* eager for bloodshed.

bloody *a.* (**-ier**, **-iest**) bloodstained; with much bloodshed; cursed. — *adv.* (*sl.*) extremely. — *v.* stain with blood. **bloody-minded** *a.* (*colloq.*) deliberately uncooperative.

bloom *n.* flower; beauty, perfection. — *v.* bear flowers; be in full beauty.

blossom *n.* flower(s), esp. of a fruit tree. — *v.* open into flowers; develop and flourish.

blot *n.* spot of ink etc.; something ugly or disgraceful. — *v.* (**blotted**) make blot(s) on.

blotch *n.* large irregular mark. **blotchy** *a.*

blouse *n.* shirt-like garment worn by women.

blow [1] *v.* (**blew, blown**) send out a current of air or breath; move or flow as a current of air does; move, shape, or sound by this; puff and pant; (of a fuse) melt; break with explosives. — *n.* blowing. **blow-out** *n.* burst tyre; melted fuse. **blow up** explode, shatter by an explosion; inflate; exaggerate; enlarge (a photograph); lose one's temper; reprimand severely.

blow [2] *n.* hard stroke with a hand, tool, or weapon; shock, disaster.

blowfly *n.* fly that lays its eggs on meat.

blowlamp *n.* portable burner for directing a very hot flame.

blowpipe *n.* tube through which air etc. is blown, e.g. to heat a flame or send out a missile.

blowy *a.* (**-ier, -iest**) windy.

blowzy *a.* (**-ier, -iest**) red-faced and coarse-looking.

blub *v.* (**blubbed**) (*sl.*) weep.

blubber [1] *n.* whale fat.

blubber [2] *v.* weep noisily.

bludgeon *n.* heavy stick used as a weapon. — *v.* strike with a bludgeon; compel forcefully.

blue *a.* of a colour like the cloudless sky; unhappy; indecent. — *n.* blue colour or thing; (*pl.*) melancholy jazz melodies, state of depression. **blue-blooded** *a.* of aristocratic descent. **out of the blue** unexpectedly.

bluebell *n.* plant with blue bell-shaped flowers.

blueberry *n.* edible blue berry; shrub bearing this.

bluebottle *n.* large bluish fly.

blueprint *n.* blue photographic print of building plans; detailed scheme.

bluff [1] *a.* with a broad steep front; abrupt, frank, and hearty. — *n.* bluff cliff etc.

bluff [2] *v.* deceive by a pretence. — *n.* bluffing.

bluish *a.* rather blue.

blunder *v.* move clumsily and uncertainly; make a bad mistake. — *n.* bad mistake.

blunderbuss *n.* old type of gun firing many balls at one shot.

blunt *a.* without a sharp edge or point; speaking or expressed plainly. — *v.*

make or become blunt. **bluntly** *adv.*, **bluntness** *n.*

blur *n.* smear; indistinct appearance. — *v.* (**blurred**) smear; make or become indistinct.

blurb *n.* written description praising something.

blurt *v.* utter abruptly or tactlessly.

blush *v.* become red-faced from shame or embarrassment. — *n.* blushing; pink tinge.

blusher *n.* rouge.

bluster *v.* blow in gusts; talk aggressively, with empty threats. — *n.* blustering talk. **blustery** *a.*

BMX *n.* bicycle racing on a dirt track; bicycle for this.

boa /bṓə/ *n.* large South American snake that crushes its prey.

boar *n.* male pig.

board *n.* long piece of sawn wood; flat piece of wood or stiff material; daily meals supplied in return for payment or services; committee. — *v.* cover or block with boards; enter (a ship, aircraft, or vehicle); provide with or receive meals and accommodation for payment. **on board** on or in a ship, aircraft, or vehicle.

boarder *n.* person who boards with someone; resident pupil.

boarding house, boarding school one taking boarders.

boardroom *n.* room where a board of directors meets.

boast *v.* speak with great pride, trying to impress people; be the proud possessor of. — *n.* boastful statement; thing one is proud of. **boaster** *n.*

boastful *a.* boasting frequently. **boastfully** *adv.*, **boastfulness** *n.*

boat *n.* vessel for travelling on water.

boater *n.* flat-topped straw hat.

boathouse *n.* shed at the water's edge for boats.

boating *n.* going out in a rowing-boat for pleasure.

boatman *n.* (*pl.* **-men**) man who rows or sails or rents out boats.

boatswain /bṓs'n/ *n.* ship's officer in charge of rigging, boats, etc.

bob *v.* (**bobbed**) move quickly up and down; cut (hair) short to hang loosely. — *n.* bobbing movement; bobbed hair.

bobbin *n.* small spool holding thread or wire in a machine.

bobble *n.* small woolly ball as an ornament.

bobsleigh *n.* sledge with two sets of runners in tandem.

bode *v.* be a sign of, promise.

bodice *n.* part of a dress from shoulder to waist; undergarment for this part of the body.

bodily *a.* of the human body or physical nature. — *adv.* in person, physically; as a whole.

body *n.* structure of bones and flesh etc. of man or animal; corpse; main part; group regarded as a unit; separate piece of matter; strong texture or quality. **body-blow** *n.* severe blow.

bodyguard *n.* escort or personal guard of an important person.

bodysuit *n.* close-fitting garment for the whole body worn by women esp. for sports.

Boer /bṓər/ *n.* Afrikaner.

boffin *n.* (*colloq.*) person engaged in technical research.

bog *n.* permanently wet spongy ground. — *v.* (**bogged**) make or become stuck and unable to progress. **bogginess** *n.*, **boggy** *a.*

bogey *n.* thing causing fear.

boggle *v.* be bewildered.

bogie *n.* undercarriage on wheels, pivoted at each end.

bogus *a.* false.

bohemian *a.* socially unconventional.

boil [1] *n.* inflamed swelling producing pus.

boil [2] *v.* bubble up with heat; heat so that liquid does this.

boiler *n.* container in which water is heated. **boiler suit** one-piece suit for rough work.

boisterous *a.* windy; noisy and cheerful. **boisterously** *adv.*

bold *a.* confident and courageous; (of colours) strong and vivid. **boldly** *adv.*, **boldness** *n.*

bole *n.* trunk of a tree.

bolero *n.* Spanish dance; woman's short jacket with no fastening.

boll *n.* round seed vessel of cotton, flax, etc.

bollard *n.* short thick post.

boloney *n.* (*sl.*) nonsense.

bolster *n.* long pad placed under a pillow. — *v.* support, prop.

bolt *n.* sliding bar for fastening a door; strong metal pin; sliding part of a rifle-breech; shaft of lightning; roll of cloth; arrow from a crossbow. — *v.* fasten with bolt(s); run away; gulp (food) hastily. **bolt-hole** *n.* place into which one can escape.

bomb *n.* case of explosive or incendiary material to be set off by impact or a timing device. — *v.* attack with bombs.

bombard *v.* attack with artillery; attack with questions etc. **bombardment** *n.*

bombardier *n.* artillery NCO.
bombastic *a.* using pompous words.
bomber *n.* aircraft that carries and drops bombs; person who throws or places bombs.
bombshell *n.* great shock.
bona fide /bŏnə fīdi/ genuine.
bona fides honest intention, sincerity.
bonanza *n.* sudden great wealth or luck.
bond *n.* thing that unites or restrains; binding agreement; document issued by a government or public company acknowledging that money has been lent to it and will be repaid with interest; emotional link; high-quality writing paper. — *v.* unite with a bond. **in bond** stored in a Customs warehouse until duties are paid.
bondage *n.* slavery, captivity.
bone *n.* each of the hard parts making up the vertebrate skeleton. — *v.* remove bones from. **bone china** made of clay and bone ash.
bonehead *n.* (*sl.*) stupid person.
bonfire *n.* fire built in the open air.
bongo *n.* each of a pair of small drums played with the fingers.
bonhomie /bónnomeé/ *n.* geniality.
bonk *v.* make an abrupt thudding sound; bump; (*sl.*) have sexual intercourse (with). — *n.* thudding sound.
bonnet *n.* hat with strings that tie under the chin; Scottish headgear; hinged cover over the engine of a motor vehicle.
bonny *a.* **(-ier, -iest)** healthy-looking; (*Sc.*) good-looking.
bonsai *n.* miniature tree or shrub; art of growing these.
bonus *n.* extra payment or benefit.
bony *a.* **(-ier, -iest)** like bones; having bones with little flesh.
boo *int.* exclamation of disapproval. — *v.* shout 'boo' (at).
boob *n.* & *v.* (*sl.*) blunder.
booby *n.* foolish person. **booby prize** one given as a joke to the competitor with the lowest score. **booby trap** hidden trap rigged up as a practical joke; hidden bomb.
boogie *n.* jazz piano music with a persistent bass rhythm. — *v.* dance to this.
book *n.* set of sheets of paper bound in a cover; literary work filling this; main division of a literary work; record of bets made. — *v.* enter in a book or list; reserve; buy a ticket in advance.
bookcase *n.* piece of furniture with shelves for books.
bookie *n.* (*colloq.*) bookmaker.
bookkeeping *n.* systematic recording of business transactions.
booklet *n.* small thin book.
bookmaker *n.* person whose business is the taking of bets.
bookmark *n.* strip of paper etc. to mark a place in a book.
bookworm *n.* grub that eats holes in books; person fond of reading.
boom [1] *v.* make a deep resonant sound; have a period of prosperity. — *n.* booming sound; prosperity.
boom [2] *n.* long pole; floating barrier.
boomerang *n.* Australian missile of curved wood that can be thrown so as to return to the thrower.
boon [1] *n.* benefit.
boon [2] *a.* **boon companion** pleasant companion.
boor *n.* ill-mannered person. **boorish** *a.*, **boorishness** *n.*
boost *v.* push upwards; increase the strength or reputation of. — *n.* upward thrust; increase. **booster** *n.*
boot *n.* sturdy shoe covering both foot and ankle; luggage compartment in a car; (*sl.*) dismissal. — *v.* kick.
bootee *n.* baby's woollen boot.
booth *n.* small shelter.
bootleg *a.* smuggled, illicit. **bootlegger** *n.*, **bootlegging** *n.*
booty *n.* loot.
booze (*colloq.*) *v.* drink alcohol. — *n.* alcoholic drink; drinking spree. **boozer** *n.*, **boozy** *a.*
borage *n.* blue-flowered plant.
borax *n.* compound of boron used in detergents.
border *n.* edge, boundary; flower bed round part of a garden. — *v.* put or be a border to. **border on** come close to being.
borderline *n.* line of demarcation.
bore [1] *see* **bear** [2].
bore [2] *v.* make (a hole) with a revolving tool. — *n.* hole bored; hollow inside of a cylinder; its diameter.
bore [3] *v.* weary by dullness. — *n.* boring person or thing. **boredom** *n.*
bore [4] *n.* tidal wave in an estuary.
born *a.* brought forth by birth; having a specified natural quality. **born-again** *a.* reconverted to religion.
borne *see* **bear** [2].
boron *n.* chemical element very resistant to high temperatures.
borough *n.* town or district with rights of local government.
borrow *v.* get temporary use of (a thing or money). **borrower** *n.*
Borstal *n.* former name of an institution for young offenders.
borzoi *n.* Russian wolfhound.

bosom *n.* breast. **bosom friend** very dear friend.

boss [1] *n.* (*colloq.*) master, manager, overseer. — *v.* (*colloq.*) be the boss of; give orders to.

boss [2] *n.* projecting knob.

bossy *a.* (**-ier, -iest**) fond of giving orders to people. **bossily** *adv.*, **bossiness** *n.*

botany *n.* study of plants. **botanical** *a.*, **botanist** *n.*

botch *v.* spoil by poor work.

both *a.*, *pron.*, & *adv.* the two.

bother *v.* cause trouble, worry, or annoyance to; pester; take trouble, feel concern. — *n.* worry, minor trouble. **bothersome** *a.*

bottle *n.* narrow-necked glass or plastic container for liquid. — *v.* store in bottles; preserve in jars.

bottleneck *n.* narrow place where traffic cannot flow freely; obstruction to an even flow of work etc.

bottom *n.* lowest part or place; buttocks; ground under a stretch of water. — *a.* lowest in position, rank, or degree.

bottomless *a.* extremely deep.

botulism *n.* poisoning by bacteria in food.

bougainvillaea *n.* tropical shrub with red or purple bracts.

bough *n.* large branch coming from the trunk of a tree.

bought *see* **buy**.

boulder *n.* large rounded stone.

boulevard *n.* wide street.

bounce *v.* rebound; (*sl.*, of a cheque) be sent back by a bank as worthless; move in a lively manner. — *n.* bouncing movement or power; liveliness.

bouncer *n.* (*sl.*) person employed to eject troublemakers.

bound [1] *v.* limit, be a boundary of. — *n.* (usu. *pl.*) limit. **out of bounds** beyond the permitted area.

bound [2] *v.* run with a jumping movement. — *n.* bounding movement.

bound [3] *see* **bind**. — *a.* obstructed by a specified thing (*snow-bound*). **bound to** certain to.

bound [4] *a.* going in a specified direction.

boundary *n.* line that marks a limit; hit to the boundary in cricket.

bounden *a.* **bounden duty** duty dictated by conscience.

boundless *a.* without limits.

bountiful *a.* giving generously; abundant. **bountifully** *adv.*

bounty *n.* generosity; generous gift. **bounteous** *a.*

bouquet /bookáy/ *n.* bunch of flowers; perfume of wine.

bouquet garni /bookáy gaárni/ bunch of herbs for flavouring.

bourbon /búrb'n/ *n.* whisky made mainly from maize.

bourgeois /boórzhwaá/ *a.* urban middle-class.

bourgeoisie /boórzhwaazeé/ *n.* bourgeois society.

bout *n.* period of exercise or work or illness; boxing contest.

boutique *n.* small shop selling fashionable clothes etc.

bovine *a.* of oxen; dull and stupid.

bow [1] /bō/ *n.* weapon for shooting arrows; rod with horsehair stretched between its ends, for playing a violin etc.; knot with loops in a ribbon or string.

bow [2] /bow/ *n.* bending of the head or body in greeting, respect, etc. — *v.* bend thus; bend downwards under weight; submit.

bow [3] /bow/ *n.* front end of a boat or ship; oarsman nearest the bow.

bowdlerize *v.* expurgate. **bowdlerization** *n.*

bowel *n.* intestine; (*pl.*) intestines, innermost parts.

bower *n.* leafy shelter.

bowie knife hunting knife with a long curved blade.

bowl [1] *n.* basin; hollow rounded part of a spoon etc.

bowl [2] *n.* heavy ball weighted to roll in a curve; (*pl.*) game played with such balls; ball used in skittles. — *v.* send rolling along the ground; go fast and smoothly; send a ball to a batsman, dismiss by knocking bails off with this. **bowl over** knock down; overwhelm with surprise or emotion.

bowler [1] *n.* person who bowls in cricket; one who plays at bowls.

bowler [2] *n.* **bowler hat** hard felt hat with a rounded top.

bowling *n.* playing bowls or skittles or a similar game.

box [1] *n.* container or receptacle with a flat base; numbered receptacle at a newspaper office for holding replies to an advertisement; compartment in a theatre, stable, etc.; small shelter. — *v.* put into a box. **box office** office for booking seats at a theatre etc. **boxroom** *n.* room for storing empty boxes etc.

box [2] *v.* fight with fists as a sport, usu. in padded gloves. — *n.* slap. **boxing** *n.*

box [3] *n.* small evergreen shrub; its wood. **boxwood** *n.*

boxer *n.* person who engages in the sport of boxing; dog of a breed resembling a bulldog.

boy *n.* male child. **boyfriend** *n.* person's regular male companion or lover. **boyhood** *n.*, **boyish** *a.*
boycott *v.* refuse to deal with or trade with. — *n.* boycotting.
bra *n.* woman's undergarment worn to support the breasts.
brace *n.* device that holds things together or in position; pair; (*pl.*) straps to keep trousers up, passing over the shoulders. — *v.* give support or firmness to.
bracelet *n.* ornamental band worn on the arm.
bracing *a.* invigorating.
bracken *n.* large fern that grows on waste land; mass of such ferns.
bracket *n.* projecting support; any of the marks used in pairs for enclosing words or figures, (), [], {}. — *v.* enclose by brackets; put together as similar.
brackish *a.* slightly salt.
bract *n.* leaf-like part of a plant.
brag *v.* (**bragged**) boast.
braggart *n.* person who brags.
brahmin *n.* member of the Hindu priestly caste.
braid *n.* woven ornamental trimming; plait of hair. — *v.* trim with braid; plait.
Braille *n.* system of representing letters etc. by raised dots which blind people read by touch.
brain *n.* mass of soft grey matter in the skull, centre of the nervous system in animals; (also *pl.*) mind, intelligence.
brainchild *n.* person's invention or plan.
brainstorm *n.* violent mental disturbance; (*US*) bright idea.
brainwash *v.* force (a person) to change their views by subjecting them to great mental pressure.
brainwave *n.* bright idea.
brainy *a.* (**-ier, -iest**) clever.
braise *v.* cook slowly with little liquid in a closed container.
brake *n.* device for reducing speed or stopping motion. — *v.* slow by use of this.
bramble *n.* shrub with long prickly shoots, blackberry.
bran *n.* ground inner husks of grain, sifted from flour.
branch *n.* arm-like part of a tree; similar part of a road, river, etc.; subdivision of a subject; local shop or office belonging to a large organization. — *v.* send out or divide into branches.
brand *n.* goods of a particular make; mark of identification made with hot metal. — *v.* mark with a brand. **brand new** new, unused.
brandish *v.* wave, flourish.
brandy *n.* strong alcoholic spirit distilled from wine or fermented fruit juice.
brash *a.* vulgarly self-assertive. **brashly** *adv.*, **brashness** *n.*
brass *n.* yellow alloy of copper and zinc; musical wind instruments made of this. — *a.* made of brass.
brasserie *n.* restaurant (orig. one serving beer with food).
brassière /brázziər/ *n.* bra.
brassy *a.* (**-ier, -iest**) like brass; bold and vulgar. **brassiness** *n.*
brat *n.* (*derog.*) child.
bravado *n.* show of boldness.
brave *a.* able to face and endure danger or pain; spectacular. — *v.* face and endure bravely. **bravely** *adv.*, **bravery** *n.*
bravo *int.* well done!
brawl *n.* noisy quarrel or fight. — *v.* take part in a brawl.
brawn *n.* muscular strength; pressed meat from a pig's or calf's head.
brawny *a.* (**-ier, -iest**) muscular.
bray *n.* donkey's cry; similar sound. — *v.* make this cry or sound.
braze *v.* solder with an alloy of brass.
brazen *a.* like or made of brass; shameless, impudent. — *v.* **brazen it out** behave (after doing wrong) as if one has no need to be ashamed. **brazenly** *adv.*
brazier *n.* basket-like stand for holding burning coals.
breach *n.* breaking or neglect of a rule or contract; estrangement; broken place, gap. — *v.* break through, make a breach in.
bread *n.* food made of baked dough of flour and liquid, usu. leavened by yeast. **breadfruit** *n.* tropical fruit with bread-like pulp. **breadwinner** *n.* member of a family who earns money to support the other(s).
breadline *n.* **on the breadline** living in extreme poverty.
breadth *n.* width, broadness.
break *v.* (**broke, broken**) divide or separate otherwise than by cutting; fall into pieces; damage; become unusable; fail to keep (a promise or law); make or become discontinuous; make a way suddenly or violently; appear suddenly; reveal (news); surpass (a record); (of a ball) change direction after touching the ground. — *n.* breaking; sudden dash; gap; interval; points scored continuously in snooker; (*colloq.*) opportunity, piece of luck. **break down** fail, collapse; give way to emotion; analyse. **break even** make gains and losses that balance exactly.
breakable *a.* able to be broken.
breakage *n.* breaking.

breakdown *n.* mechanical failure; collapse of health or mental stability; analysis.

breaker *n.* heavy ocean wave that breaks on a coast.

breakfast *n.* first meal of the day. — *v.* eat breakfast.

breakneck *a.* dangerously fast.

breakthrough *n.* breaking through; major advance in knowledge or negotiation.

breakwater *n.* wall built out into the sea to break the force of waves.

bream *n.* fish of the carp family.

breast *n.* upper front part of the body; either of the two milk-producing organs on a woman's chest. **breast-stroke** *n.* swimming stroke performed face downwards.

breastbone *n.* bone down the upper front of the body.

breath *n.* air drawn into and sent out of the lungs in breathing; breathing in; gentle blowing. **out of breath** panting after exercise. **under one's breath** in a whisper. **breathy** *a.*

breathalyse *v.* test by a breathalyser.

breathalyser *n.* device measuring the alcohol in a person's breath.

breathe *v.* draw (air) into the lungs and send it out again; utter.

breather *n.* pause for rest; short period in fresh air.

breathless *a.* out of breath.

breathtaking *a.* amazing.

bred *see* **breed**.

breech *n.* buttocks; back part of a gun barrel, where it opens.

breeches *n.pl.* (*old use*) trousers reaching to just below the knees.

breed *v.* **(bred)** produce offspring; train, bring up; give rise to. — *n.* variety of animals etc. within a species; sort. **breeder** *n.*

breeding *n.* good manners resulting from training or background.

breeze *n.* light wind. **breezy** *a.*

breeze-blocks *n.pl.* lightweight building blocks.

brethren *n.pl.* (*old use*) brothers.

Breton *a.* & *n.* (native) of Brittany.

breve *n.* mark (˘) over a short vowel; (in music) long note.

breviary *n.* book of prayers to be said by RC priests.

brevity *n.* briefness.

brew *v.* make (beer) by boiling and fermentation; make (tea) by infusion; bring about, develop. — *n.* liquid or amount brewed.

brewer *n.* person whose trade is brewing beer.

brewery *n.* building where beer is brewed commercially.

briar *n.* = **brier**.

bribe *n.* thing offered to influence a person to act in favour of the giver. — *v.* persuade by this. **bribery** *n.*

bric-à-brac *n.* odd items of ornaments, furniture, etc.

brick *n.* block of baked or dried clay used to build walls; rectangular block. — *v.* block with a brick structure. **brick-red** *a.* reddish.

brickbat *n.* missile hurled at someone; criticism.

bricklayer *n.* workman who builds with bricks.

bridal *a.* of a bride or wedding.

bride *n.* woman on her wedding day or when newly married.

bridegroom *n.* man on his wedding day or when newly married.

bridesmaid *n.* girl or unmarried woman attending a bride.

bridge ¹ *n.* structure providing a way across or joining something; captain's platform on a ship; bony upper part of the nose. — *v.* make or be a bridge over, span as if with a bridge.

bridge ² *n.* card game developed from whist.

bridgehead *n.* fortified area established in enemy territory, esp. on the far side of a river.

bridle *n.* harness on a horse's head. — *v.* put a bridle on; restrain; draw up one's head in pride or scorn. **bridle path** path suitable for horse-riding.

brief ¹ *a.* lasting only for a short time; concise; short. **briefly** *adv.*, **briefness** *n.*

brief ² *n.* set of instructions and information, esp. to a barrister about a case. — *v.* employ (a barrister); inform or instruct in advance.

briefcase *n.* case for carrying documents.

briefs *n.pl.* very short pants or knickers.

brier *n.* thorny bush, wild rose.

brigade *n.* army unit forming part of a division.

brigadier *n.* officer commanding a brigade or of similar status.

brigand *n.* member of a band of robbers.

bright *a.* giving out or reflecting much light, shining; cheerful; quick-witted, clever. **brightly** *adv.*, **brightness** *n.*

brighten *v.* make or become brighter.

brilliant *a.* very bright, sparkling; very clever. — *n.* cut diamond with many facets. **brilliantly** *adv.*, **brilliance** *n.*

brim *n.* edge of a cup or hollow; projecting edge of a hat. — *v.* **(brimmed)** be full to the brim.

brimstone *n.* (*old use*) sulphur.
brindled *a.* brown with streaks of another colour.
brine *n.* salt water; sea water.
bring *v.* (**brought**) convey; cause to come. **bring about** cause to happen. **bring off** do successfully. **bring out** show clearly; publish. **bring up** look after and train (growing children).
brink *n.* edge of a steep place or of a stretch of water; point just before a change.
brinkmanship *n.* policy of pursuing a dangerous course to the brink of catastrophe.
briny *a.* of brine or sea water.
briquette *n.* block of compressed coal dust.
brisk *a.* lively, moving quickly. **briskly** *adv.*
brisket *n.* joint of beef from the breast.
bristle *n.* short stiff hair; one of the stiff pieces of hair or wire in a brush. — *v.* raise bristles in anger or fear; show indignation; be thickly set with bristles.
Britannic *a.* of Britain.
British *a.* of Britain or its people.
Briton *n.* British person.
brittle *a.* hard but easily broken. **brittleness** *n.*
broach *v.* open and start using; begin discussion of.
broad *a.* large across, wide; full and complete; in general terms; (of humour) rather coarse. **broad bean** edible bean with flat seeds. **broad-minded** *a.* having tolerant views. **broadly** *adv.*
broadcast *v.* (**broadcast**) send out by radio or television; make generally known; sow (seed) by scattering. — *n.* broadcast programme. **broadcaster** *n.*
broaden *v.* make or become broader.
broadside *n.* firing of all guns on one side of a ship.
brocade *n.* fabric woven with raised patterns.
broccoli *n.* (*pl.* **-li**) hardy kind of cauliflower.
brochure /brŏshər/ *n.* booklet or leaflet giving information.
brogue *n.* strong shoe with ornamental perforated bands; dialectal esp. Irish accent.
broil *v.* grill; make or become very hot.
broiler *n.* chicken suitable for broiling.
broke *see* **break**. *a.* (*sl.*) having spent all one's money; bankrupt.
broken *see* **break**. *a.* **broken English** English spoken imperfectly by a foreigner. **broken-hearted** *a.* crushed by grief.
broker *n.* agent who buys and sells on behalf of others.
bromide *n.* chemical compound used to calm nerves.
bromine *n.* poisonous liquid element.
bronchial *a.* of the branched tubes into which the windpipe divides.
bronchitis *n.* inflammation of the bronchial tubes.
bronco *n.* (*pl.* **-os**) wild or half-tamed horse of western North America.
brontosaurus *n.* large plant-eating dinosaur.
bronze *n.* brown alloy of copper and tin; thing made of this; its colour. — *v.* make or become suntanned.
brooch /brōch/ *n.* ornamental hinged pin fastened with a clasp.
brood *n.* young produced at one hatching or birth. — *v.* sit on (eggs) and hatch them; think long and deeply.
broody *a.* (of a hen) wanting to brood; thoughtful and depressed.
brook [1] *n.* small stream.
brook [2] *v.* tolerate, allow.
broom *n.* long-handled brush for sweeping floors; shrub with white, yellow, or red flowers.
broomstick *n.* broom-handle.
broth *n.* thin meat or fish soup.
brothel *n.* house where women work as prostitutes.
brother *n.* son of the same parents as another person; man who is a fellow member of a group, trade union, or Church; monk who is not a priest. **brother-in-law** *n.* (*pl.* **brothers-in-law**) brother of one's husband or wife; husband of one's sister. **brotherly** *a.*
brotherhood *n.* relationship of brothers; comradeship.
brought *see* **bring**.
brow *n.* eyebrow; forehead; projecting or overhanging part.
browbeat *v.* (**-beat, -beaten**) intimidate.
brown *a.* of a colour between orange and black. — *v.* make or become brown. **browned off** (*sl.*) bored, fed up.
browse *v.* feed on leaves or grass; read or look around casually.
bruise *n.* injury that discolours skin without breaking it. — *v.* cause bruise(s) on.
bruiser *n.* tough brutal person.
brunch *n.* meal combining breakfast and lunch.
brunette *n.* woman with brown hair.
brunt *n.* chief stress or strain.
brush *n.* implement with bristles; fox's tail; skirmish; brushing; undergrowth. — *v.* use a brush on; touch lightly in passing. **brush off** reject curtly; snub. **brush up** smarten; study and revive one's knowledge of.

brushwood *n.* undergrowth; cut or broken twigs.
brusque /broōsk/ *a.* curt and offhand. **brusquely** *adv.*
Brussels sprout edible bud of a kind of cabbage.
brutal *a.* cruel, without mercy. **brutally** *adv.*, **brutality** *n.*
brutalize *v.* make brutal; treat brutally. **brutalization** *n.*
brute *n.* animal other than man; brutal person; (*colloq.*) unpleasant person or thing. — *a.* unable to reason; unreasoning. **brutish** *a.*
bryony *n.* climbing hedge-plant.
BSE *abbr.* bovine spongiform encephalopathy (disease of cattle).
Bt. *abbr.* Baronet.
bubble *n.* thin ball of liquid enclosing air or gas; air-filled cavity. — *v.* rise in bubbles; show great liveliness. **bubbly** *a.*
bubonic *a.* (of plague) characterized by swellings (**buboes**).
buccaneer *n.* pirate; adventurer.
buck [1] *n.* male of deer, hare, or rabbit. — *v.* (of a horse) jump with the back arched. **buck up** (*sl.*) make haste; make or become more cheerful.
buck [2] *n.* article placed before the dealer in a game of poker. **pass the buck** shift the responsibility (and possible blame).
buck [3] *n.* (*US* & *Austr. sl.*) dollar.
bucket *n.* open container with a handle, for carrying or holding liquid. — *v.* pour heavily.
buckle *n.* device through which a belt or strap is threaded to secure it. — *v.* fasten with a buckle; crumple under pressure. **buckle down to** set about doing.
buckwheat *n.* cereal plant; its seed.
bucolic *a.* rustic.
bud *n.* leaf or flower not fully open. — *v.* (**budded**) put forth buds; begin to develop.
Buddhism *n.* Asian religion based on the teachings of Buddha. **Buddhist** *a.* & *n.*
buddleia *n.* tree or shrub with purple or yellow flowers.
buddy *n.* (*colloq.*) friend.
budge *v.* move slightly.
budgerigar *n.* a kind of Australian parakeet.
budget *n.* plan of income and expenditure; amount allowed. — *v.* (**budgeted**) allow or arrange in a budget.
buff *n.* fawn colour; bare skin; (*US colloq.*) enthusiast. — *v.* polish with soft material.
buffalo *n.* (*pl.* **-oes** *or* **-o**) a kind of ox.
buffer *n.* thing that lessens the effect of impact; (*sl.*) man. — *v.* act as a buffer to.
buffet [1] /booffay/ *n.* counter where food and drink are served; meal where guests serve themselves.
buffet [2] /búffit/ *n.* blow, esp. with a hand. — *v.* (**buffeted**) deal blows to.
buffoon *n.* person who plays the fool. **buffoonery** *n.*
bug *n.* small unpleasant insect; (*sl.*) microbe; (*sl.*) secret microphone; (*sl.*) defect. — *v.* (**bugged**) (*sl.*) install a secret microphone in; (*US sl.*) annoy.
bugbear *n.* thing feared or disliked.
buggy *n.* light carriage; small sturdy vehicle.
bugle *n.* brass instrument like a small trumpet. **bugler** *n.*
build *v.* (**built**) construct by putting parts or material together. — *n.* bodily shape. **build up** establish gradually; increase. **build-up** *n.* this process. **builder** *n.*
building *n.* house or similar structure. **building society** organization that accepts deposits of money and lends to people buying houses.
built *see* **build**. **built-in** *a.* forming part of a structure. **built-up** *a.* covered with buildings.
bulb *n.* rounded base of the stem of certain plants; thing (esp. an electric lamp) shaped like this. **bulbous** *a.*
bulge *n.* rounded swelling. — *v.* form a bulge, swell.
bulk *n.* size; mass; greater part; bulky thing. — *v.* increase the size or thickness of.
bulkhead *n.* partition in a ship etc.
bulky *a.* (**-ier, -iest**) taking up much space.
bull [1] *n.* male of ox, whale, elephant, etc.; bull's-eye of a target. **bull's-eye** *n.* centre of a target; hard round peppermint sweet. **bull terrier** terrier resembling a bulldog.
bull [2] *n.* pope's official edict.
bull [3] *n.* (*sl.*) absurd statement; unnecessary routine tasks.
bulldog *n.* powerful dog with a short thick neck.
bulldozer *n.* powerful tractor with a device for clearing ground.
bullet *n.* small missile fired from a rifle or revolver.
bulletin *n.* short official statement of news.
bullfight *n.* sport of baiting and killing bulls as an entertainment.
bullfinch *n.* songbird with a strong beak and pinkish breast.
bullion *n.* gold or silver in bulk or bars, before manufacture.
bullock *n.* castrated bull.
bully [1] *n.* one who uses his strength or power to hurt or intimidate others. — *v.* behave as a bully towards.

bully [2] *v.* **bully off** put the ball into play in hockey by two opponents striking sticks together.
bulrush *n.* a kind of tall rush.
bulwark *n.* wall of earth built as a defence; ship's side above the deck.
bum [1] *n.* (*sl.*) buttocks.
bum [2] *n.* (*US sl.*) beggar, loafer.
bumble *v.* move or act in a blundering way. **bumbler** *n.*
bumble-bee *n.* large bee.
bump *v.* knock with a dull-sounding blow; travel with a jolting movement. — *n.* bumping sound or knock; swelling, esp. left by a blow. **bumpy** *a.*
bumper *n.* something unusually large; horizontal bar at the front and back of a motor vehicle to lessen the effect of collision; brim-full glass.
bumpkin *n.* country person with awkward manners.
bumptious *a.* conceited.
bun *n.* small round sweet cake; hair twisted into a bun shape at the back of the head.
bunch *n.* cluster; number of small things fastened together. — *v.* make into bunch(es); form a group.
bundle *n.* collection of things loosely fastened or wrapped together. — *v.* make into a bundle; push hurriedly.
bung *n.* stopper for the hole in a barrel or jar. — *v.* (*sl.*) throw.
bungalow *n.* one-storeyed house.
bungle *v.* spoil by lack of skill, mismanage. — *n.* bungled attempt. **bungler** *n.*
bunion *n.* swelling at the base of the big toe, with thickened skin.
bunk [1] *n.* shelf-like bed.
bunk [2] *n.* **do a bunk** (*sl.*) run away.
bunker *n.* container for fuel; sandy hollow forming a hazard on a golf course; reinforced underground shelter.
bunkum *n.* nonsense, humbug.
Bunsen burner device burning mixed air and gas in a single very hot flame.
bunting [1] *n.* bird related to the finches.
bunting [2] *n.* decorative flags.
buoy /boy/ *n.* anchored floating object serving as a navigation mark. — *v.* **buoy up** keep afloat; sustain, hearten.
buoyant /bóyənt/ *a.* able to float; cheerful. **buoyancy** *n.*
bur *n.* plant's seed case that clings to clothing etc.
burble *v.* make a gentle murmuring sound; speak lengthily.
burden *n.* thing carried; heavy load or obligation; trouble. — *v.* put a burden on.
bureau *n.* /byoórō/ (*pl.* **-eaux**) writing desk with drawers; office, department.
bureaucracy /byoorókrəsi/ *n.* government by unelected officials; excessive administration. **bureaucratic** *a.*
bureaucrat *n.* government official.
burgeon *v.* begin to grow rapidly.
burglar *n.* person who breaks into a building, esp. in order to steal. **burglary** *n.*
burgle *v.* rob as a burglar.
burial *n.* burying.
burlesque *n.* mocking imitation. — *v.* imitate mockingly.
burly *a.* (**-ier, -iest**) with a strong heavy body. **burliness** *n.*
burn [1] *v.* (**burned** or **burnt**) be on fire; damage, destroy, or mark by fire, heat, or acid; use as fuel; produce heat or light; feel a sensation (as) of heat. — *n.* mark or sore made by burning.
burn [2] *n.* (*Sc.*) brook.
burner *n.* part that shapes the flame in a lamp or cooker etc.
burning *a.* intense; hotly discussed.
burnish *v.* polish by rubbing.
burnt *see* **burn** [1].
burp *n.* & *v.* (*colloq.*) belch.
burr *n.* whirring sound; rough pronunciation of 'r'; country accent using this.
burrow *n.* hole dug by a fox or rabbit as a dwelling. — *v.* dig a burrow, tunnel; form by tunnelling; search deeply, delve.
bursar *n.* person who manages the finances and other business of a college.
bursary *n.* scholarship or grant given to a student; bursar's office.
burst *v.* (**burst**) force or be forced open; fly violently apart; begin or appear or come suddenly. — *n.* bursting; outbreak; brief violent effort, spurt.
bury *v.* place (a dead body) in the earth or a tomb; put or hide underground; cover up; involve (oneself) deeply.
bus *n.* (*pl.* **buses**) long-bodied passenger vehicle. — *v.* (**bussed**) travel by bus; transport by bus.
bush [1] *n.* shrub; thick growth; wild uncultivated land.
bush [2] *n.* perforated plug; metal-lined hole.
bushy *a.* (**-ier, -iest**) covered with bushes; growing thickly.
business *n.* occupation, trade; task, duty; thing to be dealt with; buying and selling, trade; commercial establishment.
businesslike *a.* practical, systematic.
businessman *n.* (*pl.* **-men**) man engaged in trade or commerce. **businesswoman** *n.fem.* (*pl.* **-women**)
busk *v.* perform as a busker.
busker *n.* entertainer performing in the street.

bust [1] *n.* sculptured head, shoulders, and chest; bosom.

bust [2] *v.* (**busted** *or* **bust**) (*sl.*) burst, break. **bust-up** *n.* (*sl.*) quarrel. **go bust** (*sl.*) become bankrupt.

bustier /bústiay/ *n.* strapless usu. boned bodice.

bustle [1] *v.* make a show of activity or hurry. — *n.* excited activity.

bustle [2] *n.* (*old use*) padding to puff out the top of a skirt at the back.

busy *a.* (**-ier**, **-iest**) working, occupied; having much to do; full of activity. **busily** *adv.*

busybody *n.* meddlesome person.

but *adv.* only. — *prep.* & *conj.* however; except.

butane *n.* inflammable liquid used as fuel.

butch *n.* (*sl.*) strongly masculine.

butcher *n.* person who cuts up and sells animal flesh for food; one who butchers people. — *v.* kill needlessly or brutally. **butchery** *n.*

butler *n.* chief manservant, in charge of the wine cellar.

butt [1] *n.* large cask or barrel.

butt [2] *n.* thicker end of a tool or weapon; short remnant, stub.

butt [3] *n.* mound behind a target, (*pl.*) shooting range; target for ridicule or teasing.

butt [4] *v.* push with the head; meet or place edge to edge. **butt in** interrupt; meddle.

butter *n.* fatty food substance made from cream. — *v.* spread with butter. **butter up** flatter.

buttercup *n.* wild plant with yellow cup-shaped flowers.

butterfly *n.* insect with four large often brightly coloured wings; swimming stroke with both arms lifted at the same time.

buttermilk *n.* liquid left after butter is churned from milk.

butterscotch *n.* hard toffee-like sweet.

buttock *n.* either of the two fleshy rounded parts at the lower end of the back of the body.

button *n.* disc or knob sewn to a garment as a fastener or ornament; small rounded object; knob etc. pressed to operate a device. — *v.* fasten with button(s).

buttonhole *n.* slit through which a button is passed to fasten clothing; flower worn in the buttonhole of a lapel. — *v.* accost and talk to.

buttress *n.* support built against a wall; thing that supports. — *v.* reinforce, prop up.

buxom *a.* plump and healthy.

buy *v.* (**bought**) obtain in exchange for money. — *n.* purchase. **buyer** *n.*

buzz *n.* vibrating humming sound; rumour; thrill. — *v.* make or be filled with a buzz; go about busily; threaten (an aircraft) by flying close to it. **buzzword** *n.* (*sl.*) fashionable jargon.

buzzard *n.* a kind of hawk.

buzzer *n.* device that produces a buzzing sound as a signal.

by *prep.* & *adv.* near, beside, in reserve; along, via, past; during; through the agency or means of; not later than. **by and by** before long. **by and large** on the whole. **by-election** *n.* election of an MP to replace one who has died or resigned. **by-law** *n.* regulation made by a local authority or corporation. **by oneself** alone, without help. **by-product** *n.* thing produced while making something else.

bye *n.* run scored from a ball not hit by the batsman; having no opponent for one round of a tournament.

bygone *a.* belonging to the past.

bygones *n.pl.* bygone things.

bypass *n.* road taking traffic round a town. — *v.* provide with a bypass; use a bypass round; avoid.

byre *n.* cowshed.

byroad *n.* minor road.

bystander *n.* person standing near when something happens.

byte *n.* (in computers) group of bits.

byway *n.* minor road.

byword *n.* notable example; familiar saying.

Byzantine *a.* of Byzantium; complicated, underhand.

C

C *abbr.* Celsius; centigrade.
cab *n.* taxi; compartment for the driver of a train, lorry, etc.
cabaret /kábbəray/ *n.* entertainment provided in a nightclub etc.
cabbage *n.* vegetable with a round head of green or purple leaves.
cabby *n.* (*colloq.*) taxi driver.
caber *n.* trimmed tree trunk.
cabin *n.* small hut; compartment in a ship or aircraft.
cabinet *n.* cupboard with drawers or shelves; **Cabinet** central group of government, formed from the most important ministers.
cable *n.* thick rope of fibre or wire; set of insulated wires for carrying electricity or signals. **cable car** car of a **cable railway** drawn on an endless cable by a stationary engine. **cable television** transmission by cable to subscribers.
cacao *n.* seed from which cocoa and chocolate are made; tree producing this.
cache /kash/ *n.* hiding place for treasure or stores; things in this. — *v.* put into a cache.
cachet /káshay/ *n.* prestige; distinctive mark or characteristic.
cackle *n.* clucking of hens; chattering talk; loud silly laugh. — *v.* utter a cackle.
cacophony *n.* harsh discordant sound. **cacophonous** *a.*
cactus *n.* (*pl.* **-ti** *or* **-tuses**) fleshy plant, often with prickles, from a hot dry climate.
cadaver *n.* corpse.
cadaverous *a.* gaunt and pale.
caddie *n.* golfer's attendant carrying clubs. — *v.* act as caddie.
caddis-fly *n.* four-winged insect living near water.
caddy *n.* small box for tea.
cadence *n.* rhythm in sound; rise and fall of the voice in speech; end of a musical phrase.
cadenza *n.* elaborate passage for a solo instrument or singer.
cadet *n.* young person being trained for service in the armed forces or police.
cadge *v.* ask for as a gift, beg.
cadmium *n.* metallic element.
cadre *n.* small group forming a nucleus that can be expanded.
caecum /seekəm/ *n.* (*pl.* **-ca**) blind tube at the first part of the large intestine.
Caesarean section operation to deliver a child by an incision through the walls of the mother's abdomen and womb.
café *n.* shop selling refreshments, informal restaurant.
cafeteria *n.* self-service restaurant.
caffeine *n.* stimulant found in tea and coffee.
caftan *n.* long loose robe or dress.
cage *n.* enclosure of wire or with bars, esp. for birds or animals.
cagey *a.* (**-ier, -iest**) (*colloq.*) secretive; shrewd; wary. **cagily** *adv.*, **caginess** *n.*
cagoule *n.* light hooded waterproof jacket.
cahoots *n.* (*sl.*) partnership.
cairn *n.* mound of stones as a memorial or landmark. **cairn terrier** small shaggy short-legged terrier.
caisson *n.* watertight chamber used in underwater construction work.
cajole *v.* coax. **cajolery** *n.*
cake *n.* baked sweet bread-like food; small flattened mass.
calamine *n.* lotion containing zinc carbonate.
calamity *n.* disaster. **calamitous** *a.*, **calamitously** *adv.*
calcify *v.* harden by a deposit of calcium salts. **calcification** *n.*
calcium *n.* whitish metallic element.
calculate *v.* reckon mathematically; estimate; plan deliberately. **calculation** *n.*
calculator *n.* electronic device for making calculations.
calculus *n.* (*pl.* **-li**) method of calculating in mathematics; stone formed in the body.
Caledonian *a.* of Scotland. — *n.* Scottish person.
calendar *n.* chart showing dates of days of the year.
calender *n.* machine for smoothing paper.
calf [1] *n.* (*pl.* **calves**) young of cattle, also of elephant, whale, and seal.
calf [2] *n.* (*pl.* **calves**) fleshy part of the human leg below the knee.
calibrate *v.* mark or correct the units of measurement on (a gauge); find the calibre of. **calibration** *n.*
calibre *n.* diameter of a gun or tube or bullet; level of ability or importance.
calico *n.* a kind of cotton cloth.
caliph *n.* (formerly) Muslim ruler.
call *v.* shout to attract attention; utter a characteristic cry; summon; command,

invite; rouse from sleep; communicate (with) by telephone or radio; name; describe or address as; make a brief visit. — *n.* shout; bird's cry; vocation; invitation, demand; need; telephone communication; short visit. **call box** telephone kiosk. **call off** cancel. **caller** *n.*

calligraphy *n.* (beautiful) handwriting. **calligraphic** *a.*

calliper *n.* splint for a weak leg.

callisthenics *n.pl.* exercises to develop strength and grace.

callous *a.* feeling no pity or sympathy. **callously** *adv.*, **callousness** *n.*

callow *a.* immature and inexperienced.

callus *n.* patch of hardened skin.

calm *a.* still, not windy; not excited or agitated. — *n.* calm condition. — *v.* make calm. **calmly** *adv.*, **calmness** *n.*

calorie *n.* unit of heat; unit of the energy-producing value of food.

calorific *a.* heat-producing.

calumniate *v.* slander. **calumniation** *n.*

calumny *n.* slander.

calve *v.* give birth to a calf.

Calvinism *n.* teachings of the Protestant reformer John Calvin or his followers. **Calvinist** *n.*

calypso *n.* topical West Indian song.

calyx *n.* ring of sepals covering a flower bud.

cam *n.* device changing rotary to to-and-fro motion. **camshaft** *n.*

camaraderie *n.* comradeship.

camber *n.* slight convex curve given to a surface esp. of a road.

cambric *n.* thin linen or cotton cloth.

camcorder *n.* combined video and sound recorder.

came *see* **come**.

camel *n.* quadruped with one hump or two; fawn colour.

camellia *n.* evergreen flowering shrub.

cameo *n.* stone in a ring or brooch with coloured layers carved in a raised design; small part in a play or film taken by a famous actor or actress.

camera *n.* apparatus for taking photographs or film pictures. **in camera** in private. **cameraman** *n.*

camiknickers *n.pl.* woman's undergarment combining camisole and knickers.

camisole *n.* woman's cotton bodice-like garment or undergarment.

camomile *n.* aromatic herb.

camouflage *n.* disguise, concealment, by colouring or covering. — *v.* disguise or conceal thus.

camp ¹ *n.* temporary accommodation in tents; place where troops are lodged or trained; fortified site. — *v.* encamp, be in a camp. **camp bed** portable folding bed. **camper** *n.*

camp ² *a.* affected, exaggerated; homosexual. — *n.* camp behaviour. — *v.* act or behave in a camp way.

campaign *n.* series of military operations; organized course of action. — *v.* conduct or take part in a campaign. **campaigner** *n.*

campanology *n.* study of bells, bell-ringing. **campanologist** *n.*

campanula *n.* plant with bell-shaped flowers.

camphor *n.* strong-smelling white substance used in medicine and moth-balls. **camphorated** *a.*

campion *n.* wild plant with pink or white flowers.

campus *n.* (*pl.* **-puses**) grounds of a university or college.

can ¹ *n.* container in which food etc. is sealed and preserved. — *v.* (**canned**) put or preserve in a can.

can ² *v.aux.* is or are able or allowed to.

Canadian *a.* & *n.* (native, inhabitant) of Canada.

canal *n.* artificial watercourse; duct.

canalize *v.* convert into a canal; channel. **canalization** *n.*

canapé /kánnəpi/ *n.* small piece of bread etc. with savoury topping.

canary *n.* small yellow songbird.

cancan *n.* lively high-kicking dance performed by women.

cancel *v.* (**cancelled**) declare that (something arranged) will not take place; order to be discontinued; cross out; neutralize. **cancellation** *n.*

cancer *n.* malignant tumour; spreading evil. **cancerous** *a.*

candela *n.* unit of luminous intensity.

candelabrum *n.* (*pl.* **-bra**) large branched candlestick or stand for a lamp.

candid *a.* frank. **candidly** *adv.*, **candidness** *n.*

candidate *n.* person applying for a job or taking an examination. **candidacy** *n.*, **candidature** *n.*

candied *a.* encrusted or preserved in sugar.

candle *n.* stick of wax enclosing a wick which is burnt to give light.

candlestick *n.* holder for a candle.

candlewick *n.* fabric with a tufted pattern.

candour *n.* frankness.

candy *n.* (*US*) sweets, a sweet.

candyfloss *n.* fluffy mass of spun sugar.

candy stripe alternate stripes of white and colour.

candytuft *n.* garden plant with flowers in flat clusters.

cane *n.* stem of a tall reed or grass or slender palm; light walking stick.

canine /káynīn/ *a.* of dog(s). — *n.* a **canine tooth**, a pointed tooth between incisors and molars.

canister *n.* small metal container.

canker *n.* disease of animals or plants; influence that corrupts.

cannabis *n.* hemp plant; drug made from this.

canned *see* **can** [1].

cannibal *n.* person who eats human flesh. **cannibalism** *n.*

cannibalize *v.* use parts from (a machine) to repair another. **cannibalization** *n.*

cannon *n.* large gun; hitting of two balls in one shot in billiards. — *v.* bump heavily (into).

cannonade *n.* continuous gunfire. — *v.* bombard with this.

cannot negative form of **can** [2].

canny *a.* (**-ier, -iest**) shrewd. **cannily** *adv.*

canoe *n.* light boat propelled by paddle(s). — *v.* go in a canoe. **canoeist** *n.*

canon *n.* member of cathedral clergy; general rule or principle; set of writings accepted as genuine. **canonical** *a.*

canonize *v.* declare officially to be a saint. **canonization** *n.*

canopy *n.* covering hung up over a throne, bed, person, etc.

cant *n.* insincere talk; jargon.

cantaloup *n.* small ribbed melon.

cantankerous *a.* perverse, peevish. **cantankerously** *adv.*

cantata *n.* choral composition.

canteen *n.* restaurant for employees; case of cutlery.

canter *n.* gentle gallop. — *v.* go at a canter.

cantilever *n.* projecting beam or girder supporting a structure.

canto *n.* division of a long poem.

canton *n.* division of Switzerland.

canvas *n.* strong coarse cloth; a painting on this.

canvass *v.* ask for political support; propose (a plan).

canyon *n.* deep gorge.

cap *n.* soft brimless hat, often with a peak; headdress worn as part of a uniform; cover or top; explosive device for a toy pistol. — *v.* (**capped**) put a cap on; form the top of; surpass.

capable *a.* having a certain ability or capacity; competent. **capably** *adv.*, **capability** *n.*

capacious *a.* roomy.

capacitance *n.* ability to store an electric charge.

capacitor *n.* device storing a charge of electricity.

capacity *n.* ability to contain or accommodate; amount that can be contained or produced; mental power; function or character.

cape [1] *n.* cloak; short similar part.

cape [2] *n.* coastal promontory.

caper [1] *v.* move friskily. — *n.* frisky movement; (*sl.*) activity.

caper [2] *n.* bramble-like shrub; one of its buds, pickled for use in sauces.

capercaillie *n.* (also **capercailzie**) largest kind of grouse.

capillary *n.* very fine hair-like tube or blood vessel.

capital *a.* chief, very important; involving the death penalty; (of a letter of the alphabet) of the kind used to begin a name or sentence. — *n.* chief town of a country etc.; capital letter; money with which a business is started; top part of a pillar.

capitalism *n.* system in which trade and industry are controlled by private owners.

capitalist *n.* person who has money invested in businesses.

capitalize *v.* convert into or provide with capital; write as or with a capital letter. **capitalize on** make advantageous use of. **capitalization** *n.*

capitulate *v.* surrender, yield. **capitulation** *n.*

caprice /kəpreéss/ *n.* whim; piece of music in a lively fanciful style.

capricious *a.* guided by caprice, impulsive; unpredictable. **capriciously** *adv.*, **capriciousness** *n.*

capsicum *n.* tropical plant with pungent seeds.

capsize *v.* overturn.

capstan *n.* revolving post or spindle on which a cable etc. winds.

capsule *n.* (gelatine case enclosing) medicine for swallowing; detachable compartment of a spacecraft; plant's seed case.

captain *n.* leader of a group or sports team; person commanding a ship or civil aircraft; naval officer next below rear admiral; army officer next below major. — *v.* be captain of. **captaincy** *n.*

caption *n.* short title or heading; explanation on an illustration.

captious *a.* fond of finding fault, esp. about trivial matters.

captivate *v.* capture the fancy of, charm. **captivation** *n.*

captive *a.* taken prisoner, unable to escape. — *n.* captive person or animal. **captivity** *n.*

captor *n.* one who takes a captive.

capture *v.* take prisoner; take or obtain by

force or skill; cause (data) to be stored in a computer. — *n.* capturing.

car *n.* private motor vehicle for a small number of passengers; compartment in a cable railway, lift, etc.

carafe /kəráf/ *n.* glass bottle for serving wine or water.

caramel *n.* brown syrup made from heated sugar; toffee tasting like this.

caramelize *v.* become caramel. **caramelization** *n.*

carapace *n.* upper shell of a tortoise.

carat *n.* unit of purity of gold.

caravan *n.* dwelling on wheels, able to be towed by a horse or car; company travelling together across desert. **caravanning** *n.*

caraway *n.* (plant with) spicy seeds used for flavouring cakes.

carbine *n.* automatic rifle.

carbohydrate *n.* energy-producing compound (e.g. starch) in food.

carbolic *n.* a kind of disinfectant.

carbon *n.* non-metallic element occurring as diamond, graphite, and charcoal, and in all living matter. **carbon copy** copy made with carbon paper; exact copy. **carbon paper** paper coated with pigment for making a copy as something is typed or written.

carbonate *n.* compound releasing carbon dioxide when mixed with acid. — *v.* impregnate with carbon dioxide.

carboniferous *a.* producing coal.

carborundum *n.* compound of carbon and silicon used for grinding and polishing things.

carbuncle *n.* severe abscess; garnet cut in a round knob shape.

carburettor *n.* apparatus mixing air and petrol in a motor engine.

carcass *n.* dead body of an animal.

carcinogen *n.* cancer-producing substance. **carcinogenic** *a.*

carcinoma *n.* cancerous tumour.

card ¹ *n.* piece of cardboard or thick paper; this printed with a greeting or invitation; postcard; playing card; credit card; (*pl.*, *colloq.*) employee's official documents, held by his employer. **card-sharper** *n.* professional swindler at card games.

card ² *v.* clean or comb (wool) with a wire brush or toothed instrument. **carder** *n.*

cardboard *n.* stiff substance made by pasting together sheets of paper.

cardiac *a.* of the heart.

cardigan *n.* knitted jacket.

cardinal *a.* chief, most important. — *n.* prince of the RC Church. **cardinal numbers** whole numbers 1, 2, 3, etc.

cardiogram *n.* record of heart movements. **cardiograph** *n.* instrument producing this.

cardiology *n.* study of diseases of the heart. **cardiological** *a.*, **cardiologist** *n.*

cardphone *n.* public telephone operated by a plastic machine-readable card.

care *n.* serious attention and thought; caution to avoid damage or loss; protection; worry, anxiety. — *v.* feel concern, interest, affection, or liking.

careen *v.* tilt or keel over.

career *n.* way of making one's living, profession; course through life; swift course. — *v.* go swiftly or wildly.

careerist *n.* person intent on advancement in a career.

carefree *a.* light-hearted through being free from anxieties.

careful *a.* acting or done with care. **carefully** *adv.*

careless *a.* not careful. **carelessly** *adv.*, **carelessness** *n.*

carer *n.* person who looks after a sick or disabled person at home.

caress *n.* loving touch, kiss. — *v.* give a caress to.

caret *n.* omission mark.

caretaker *n.* person employed to look after a building.

careworn *a.* showing signs of prolonged worry.

cargo *n.* (*pl.* **-oes**) goods carried by ship or aircraft.

Caribbean *a.* of the West Indies or their inhabitants.

caribou *n.* North American reindeer.

caricature *n.* exaggerated portrayal of a person for comic effect. — *v.* make a caricature of.

caries *n.* decay of tooth or bone.

carillon /kərílyən/ *n.* set of bells sounded mechanically; tune played on these.

Carmelite *n.* member of an order of white-cloaked friars or nuns.

carmine *a.* & *n.* vivid crimson.

carnage *n.* great slaughter.

carnal *a.* of the body or flesh, not spiritual. **carnally** *adv.*

carnation *n.* cultivated clove-scented pink.

carnet /kaárnay/ *n.* permit.

carnival *n.* public festivities, usu. with a procession.

carnivore *n.* carnivorous animal.

carnivorous *a.* feeding on flesh.

carol *n.* Christmas hymn. — *v.* **(carolled)** sing carols; sing joyfully.

carotid *a.* & *n.* (artery) carrying blood to the head.

carouse *v.* drink and be merry. **carousal** *n.*, **carouser** *n.*

carousel *n.* (*US*) merry-go-round; rotating conveyor.

carp [1] *n.* freshwater fish.

carp [2] *v.* keep finding fault.

carpenter *n.* person who makes or repairs wooden objects and structures. **carpentry** *n.*

carpet *n.* textile fabric for covering a floor. — *v.* **(carpeted)** cover with a carpet; reprimand. **on the carpet** (*colloq.*) being reprimanded.

carport *n.* roofed open-sided shelter for a car.

carpus *n.* set of small bones forming the wrist joint.

carriage *n.* wheeled vehicle or support; moving part; conveying of goods etc., cost of this. **carriage clock** small portable clock with a handle on top.

carriageway *n.* that part of the road on which vehicles travel.

carrier *n.* person or thing carrying something; paper or plastic bag with handles, for holding shopping.

carrion *n.* dead decaying flesh.

carrot *n.* tapering orange-red root vegetable; incentive.

carry *v.* transport, convey; support; be the bearer of; involve, entail; take (a process etc.) to a specified point; get the support of; win acceptance for (a motion etc.); stock (goods for sale); be audible at a distance. **carry on** continue; (*colloq.*) behave excitedly. **carry out** put into practice.

cart *n.* wheeled structure for carrying loads. — *v.* carry, transport. **carthorse** *n.* horse of heavy build.

carte blanche /kaart blónsh/ full power to do as one thinks best.

cartel *n.* manufacturer's or producer's union to control prices.

cartilage *n.* firm elastic tissue in skeletons of vertebrates, gristle.

cartography *n.* map-drawing. **cartographer** *n.*, **cartographic** *a.*

carton *n.* cardboard or plastic container.

cartoon *n.* humorous drawing; film consisting of an animated sequence of drawings; sketch for a painting. **cartoonist** *n.*

cartridge *n.* case containing explosive for firearms; sealed cassette. **cartridge paper** thick strong paper.

cartwheel *n.* handspring with limbs spread like spokes of a wheel.

carve *v.* make or inscribe or decorate by cutting; cut (meat) into slices for eating.

carvel-built *a.* made with planks flush with the side.

caryatid *n.* supporting pillar sculpted as a female figure.

Casanova *n.* man noted for his love affairs.

cascade *n.* waterfall; thing falling or hanging like this. — *v.* fall thus.

cascara *n.* a purgative tree-bark.

case [1] *n.* instance of a thing's occurring; situation; lawsuit; set of facts or arguments supporting something. **in case** lest.

case [2] *n.* container or protective covering; this with its contents; suitcase. — *v.* enclose in a case; (*sl.*) examine (a building etc.) in preparation for a crime.

casement *n.* window opening on vertical hinges.

cash *n.* money in the form of coins or banknotes. — *v.* give or obtain cash for (a cheque etc.). **cash in (on)** get profit or advantage (from).

cash card plastic card with magnetic code for drawing money from a machine.

cashew *n.* a kind of edible nut.

cashier [1] *n.* person employed to receive money.

cashier [2] *v.* dismiss from military service in disgrace.

cashmere *n.* very fine soft wool; fabric made from this.

cashpoint *n.* machine dispensing cash.

casino *n.* (*pl.* **-os**) public building or room for gambling.

cask *n.* barrel for liquids.

casket *n.* small usu. ornamental box for valuables; (*US*) coffin.

cassava *n.* tropical plant; flour made from its roots.

casserole *n.* covered dish in which meat etc. is cooked and served; food cooked in this. — *v.* cook in a casserole.

cassette *n.* small case containing a reel of film or magnetic tape.

cassock *n.* long robe worn by clergy and choristers.

cassowary *n.* large flightless bird related to the emu.

cast *v.* **(cast)** throw; shed; direct (a glance); register (one's vote); shape (molten metal) in a mould; calculate; select actors for a play or film, assign a role to. — *n.* throw of dice, fishing line, etc.; moulded mass of solidified material; set of actors in a play etc.; type, quality; slight squint. **cast-iron** *a.* very strong. **cast-off** *a.* & *n.* discarded (thing).

castanets *n.pl.* pair of shell-shaped pieces of wood clicked in the hand to accompany dancing.

castaway *n.* shipwrecked person.

caste *n.* exclusive social class, esp. in the Hindu system.

castigate *v.* punish or rebuke or criticize severely. **castigation** *n.*

casting vote deciding vote when those on each side are equal.

castle *n.* large fortified residence.

castor *n.* small swivelling wheel on a leg of furniture; small container with a perforated top for sprinkling sugar etc.

castor oil purgative and lubricant oil from seeds of a tropical plant.

castrate *v.* remove the testicles of. **castration** *n.*

casual *a.* happening by chance; not serious or formal or methodical; not permanent. **casually** *adv.*, **casualness** *n.*

casualty *n.* person killed or injured; thing lost or destroyed.

casuist *n.* theologian who studies moral problems; sophist, quibbler. **casuistic** *a.*, **casuistry** *n.*

cat *n.* small furry domesticated animal; wild animal related to this; whip with knotted lashes. **cat's cradle** child's game with string. **cat's-paw** *n.* person used as a tool by another.

cataclysm *n.* violent upheaval or disaster. **cataclysmic** *a.*

catacomb /káttəkōōm/ *n.* underground gallery with recesses for tombs.

catafalque *n.* platform for the coffin of a distinguished person before or during a funeral.

catalepsy *n.* seizure or trance with rigidity of the body. **cataleptic** *a.*

catalogue *n.* systematic list of items. — *v.* list in a catalogue.

catalyse *v.* subject to the action of a catalyst. **catalysis** *n.*

catalyst *n.* substance that aids a chemical reaction while remaining unchanged.

catamaran *n.* boat with twin hulls.

catapult *n.* device with elastic for shooting small stones. — *v.* hurl from or as if from a catapult.

cataract *n.* large waterfall; opaque area clouding the lens of the eye.

catarrh *n.* inflammation of mucous membrane, esp. of the nose, with a watery discharge.

catastrophe /kətástrəfi/ *n.* sudden great disaster. **catastrophic** *a.*, **catastrophically** *adv.*

catcall *n.* whistle of disapproval.

catch *v.* **(caught)** capture, seize; detect; surprise, trick; overtake; be in time for; grasp and hold; become infected with; hit. — *n.* act of catching; thing caught or worth catching; concealed difficulty; fastener. **catch on** (*colloq.*) become popular; understand what is meant. **catch out** detect in a mistake etc. **catchphrase** *n.* phrase in frequent current use, slogan. **catch-22** *n.* dilemma where the victim is bound to suffer. **catch up** come abreast with; do arrears of work.

catching *a.* infectious.

catchment area area from which rainfall drains into a river; area from which a hospital draws patients or a school draws pupils.

catchword *n.* catchphrase.

catchy *a.* **(-ier, -iest)** (of a tune) pleasant and easy to remember.

catechism *n.* series of questions and answers.

catechize *v.* put a series of questions to.

categorical *a.* unconditional, absolute. **categorically** *adv.*

categorize *v.* place in a category. **categorization** *n.*

category *n.* class of things.

cater *v.* supply food; provide what is needed or wanted. **caterer** *n.*

caterpillar *n.* larva of butterfly or moth. **Caterpillar track** [P.] steel band with treads, passing round a vehicle's wheels.

caterwaul *v.* make a cat's howling cry.

catgut *n.* gut as thread.

catharsis *n.* purgation; emotional release. **cathartic** *a.*

cathedral *n.* principal church of a diocese.

Catherine wheel rotating firework.

catheter *n.* tube inserted into the bladder to extract urine.

cathode *n.* electrode by which current leaves a device. **cathode ray** beam of electrons from the cathode of a vacuum tube.

catholic *a.* universal; of all Churches or all Christians. **Catholic** *a.* & *n.* Roman Catholic.

catholicism *n.* being catholic; adherence to the Catholic Church.

cation *n.* positively charged ion.

catkin *n.* hanging flower of willow, hazel, etc.

catmint *n.* strong-smelling plant attractive to cats.

catnap *n.* short nap.

catnip *n.* catmint.

Catseye *n.* [P.] reflector stud on a road.

cattle *n.pl.* large animals with horns and cloven hoofs.

catty *a.* **(-ier, -iest)** slightly spiteful. **cattily** *adv.*, **cattiness** *n.*

catwalk *n.* narrow strip for walking on as pathway or platform.

caucus *n.* (often *derog.*) local committee of a political party; (*US*) meeting of party leaders.

caught *see* **catch**.

cauldron *n.* large deep pot for boiling things in.

cauliflower *n.* cabbage with a white flower head.

caulk *v.* stop up (a ship's seams) with waterproof material.

causal *a.* of or forming a cause; of cause and effect. **causality** *n.*

causation *n.* causality.

cause *n.* what produces an effect; reason or motive for action; lawsuit; principle supported. — *v.* be the cause of, make happen.

causeway *n.* raised road across low or wet ground.

caustic *a.* burning by chemical action; sarcastic. — *n.* caustic substance. **caustically** *adv.*

cauterize *v.* burn (tissue) to destroy infection or stop bleeding. **cauterization** *n.*

caution *n.* avoidance of rashness; warning. — *v.* warn; reprimand.

cautionary *a.* conveying a warning.

cautious *a.* having or showing caution. **cautiously** *adv.*

cavalcade *n.* procession.

Cavalier *n.* supporter of Charles I in the English Civil War.

cavalier *a.* arrogant, offhand.

cavalry *n.* troops who fight on horseback.

cave *n.* natural hollow. — *v.* **cave in** collapse; yield.

caveat /kávviat/ *n.* warning.

caveman *n.* person of prehistoric times living in a cave.

cavern *n.* large cave; hollow part.

cavernous *a.* like a cavern.

caviar *n.* pickled roe of sturgeon or other large fish.

cavil *v.* (**cavilled**) raise petty objections. — *n.* petty objection.

caving *n.* sport of exploring caves.

cavity *n.* hollow within a solid body.

cavort *v.* caper excitedly.

cavy *n.* small rodent of the kind that includes guinea pigs.

caw *n.* harsh cry of a rook etc. — *v.* utter a caw.

cayenne *n.* hot red pepper.

cayman *n.* South American alligator.

CB *abbr.* citizens' band.

cc *abbr.* cubic centimetre(s).

CD *abbr.* compact disc.

cease *v.* come to an end, discontinue, stop. **ceasefire** *n.* signal to stop firing guns.

ceaseless *a.* not ceasing.

cedar *n.* evergreen tree; its hard fragrant wood.

cede *v.* surrender (territory etc.).

cedilla *n.* mark written under c (ç) pronounced as s.

ceilidh /káyli/ *n.* (*Sc.* & *Ir.*) informal gathering for music and dancing.

ceiling *n.* surface of the top of a room; upper limit or level.

celandine *n.* small wild plant with yellow flowers.

celebrate *v.* mark or honour with festivities. **celebration** *n.*

celebrated *a.* famous.

celebrity *n.* famous person; fame.

celeriac *n.* celery with a turnip-like root.

celerity *n.* swiftness.

celery *n.* plant with edible crisp juicy stems.

celestial *a.* of the sky; of heaven.

celibate *a.* abstaining from sexual intercourse. **celibacy** *n.*

cell *n.* small room for a monk or prisoner; compartment in a honeycomb; device for producing electric current chemically; microscopic unit of living matter; small group as a nucleus of political activities.

cellar *n.* underground room; stock of wine.

cello /chéllō/ *n.* bass instrument of the violin family. **cellist** *n.*

Cellophane *n.* [P.] thin transparent wrapping material.

celluloid *n.* plastic made from cellulose nitrate and camphor.

cellulose *n.* substance in plant tissues used in making plastics.

Celsius *a.* of a centigrade scale with 0° as the freezing point and 100° as the boiling point of water.

Celt *n.* member of an ancient European people or their descendants. **Celtic** *a.*

cement *n.* substance of lime and clay setting like stone; adhesive; substance for filling cavities in teeth. — *v.* join with cement; unite firmly.

cemetery *n.* burial ground other than a churchyard.

cenotaph *n.* tomb-like monument to persons buried elsewhere.

censer *n.* container for burning incense.

censor *n.* person authorized to examine letters, books, films, etc., and remove or ban anything regarded as harmful. — *v.* remove or ban thus. **censorship** *n.*

censorious *a.* severely critical.

censure *n.* severe criticism and rebuke. — *v.* criticize and rebuke severely.

census *n.* official counting of population.

cent *n.* 100th part of a dollar or other currency; coin worth this.

centaur *n.* mythical creature half man, half horse.

centenarian *n.* person 100 years old or more.

centenary *n.* 100th anniversary.
centennial *a.* of a centenary. — *n.* (*US*) centenary.
centigrade *a.* using a temperature scale of 100°; = Celsius.
centigram *n.* 100th of a gram.
centilitre *n.* 100th of a litre.
centimetre *n.* 100th of a metre.
centipede *n.* small crawling creature with many legs.
central *a.* of, at, or forming a centre; most important. **central heating** heating of a building from one source. **centrally** *adv.*, **centrality** *n.*
centralize *v.* bring under the control of a central authority. **centralization** *n.*
centre *n.* middle point or part. — *v.* (**centred, centring**) place in or at a centre.
centrifugal *a.* moving away from the centre.
centrifuge *n.* machine using centrifugal force for separating substances.
centripetal *a.* moving towards the centre.
centurion *n.* commander in the ancient Roman army.
century *n.* period of 100 years; 100 runs at cricket.
cephalic *a.* of the head.
cephalopod *n.* mollusc with tentacles (e.g. an octopus).
ceramic *a.* of pottery or a similar substance. **ceramics** *n.* art of making pottery.
cereal *n.* grass plant with edible grain; this grain, breakfast food made from it.
cerebral *a.* of the brain; intellectual. **cerebrally** *adv.*
cerebrum *n.* main part of the brain.
ceremonial *a.* of or used in ceremonies, formal. — *n.* ceremony; rules for this. **ceremonially** *adv.*
ceremonious *a.* full of ceremony. **ceremoniously** *adv.*
ceremony *n.* set of formal acts.
cerise /səréez/ *a.* & *n.* light red.
certain *a.* feeling sure; believed firmly; specific but not named; some.
certainly *adv.* without doubt; yes.
certainty *n.* being certain; thing that is certain.
certifiable *a.* able to be certified; (*sl.*) mad. **certifiably** *adv.*
certificate *n.* official document attesting certain facts.
certify *v.* declare formally.
certitude *n.* feeling of certainty.
cerulean *a.* sky-blue.
cervix *n.* neck; neck-like structure, esp. of the womb. **cervical** *a.*
cessation *n.* ceasing.
cesspit, cesspool *ns.* covered pit to receive liquid waste or sewage.
cetacean /sitáysh'n/ *a.* & *n.* (member) of the whale family.
cf. *abbr.* compare.
CFC *abbr.* chlorofluorocarbon, gaseous compound that harms the earth's atmosphere.
chafe *v.* warm by rubbing; make or become sore by rubbing; become irritated or impatient.
chafer *n.* large beetle.
chaff *n.* corn husks separated from seed; chopped hay and straw; banter. — *v.* banter, tease.
chaffinch *n.* European finch.
chafing dish heated pan for keeping food warm at the table.
chagrin *n.* annoyance and embarrassment.
chain *n.* series of connected metal links; connected series or sequence. — *v.* fasten with chain(s). **chain reaction** change causing further changes.
chair *n.* movable seat, with a back, for one person; (position of) chairman; position of a professor. — *v.* act as chairman of. **chairlift** *n.* series of chairs on a cable for carrying people up a mountain.
chairman *n.* (*pl.* **-men**) person who presides over a meeting or committee. **chairwoman** *n.fem.* (*pl.* **-women**), **chairperson** *n.*
chaise longue /sháyz lóngg/ chair with a very long seat to support a sitter's legs.
chalcedony *n.* type of quartz.
chalet /shállay/ *n.* Swiss hut or cottage; small villa; small hut in a holiday camp etc.
chalice *n.* large goblet.
chalk *n.* white soft limestone; piece of this or similar coloured substance used for drawing. **chalky** *a.*
challenge *n.* call to try one's skill or strength; demand to respond or identify oneself; formal objection; demanding task. — *v.* make a challenge to; question the truth or rightness of. **challenger** *n.*
chamber *n.* hall used for meetings of an assembly; (*old use*) room, bedroom; (*pl.*) set of rooms; cavity or compartment. **chamber music** music for performance in a room rather than a hall. **chamber pot** bedroom receptacle for urine.
chamberlain *n.* official managing a sovereign's or noble's household.
chambermaid *n.* woman cleaner of hotel bedrooms.
chameleon /kəmméeliən/ *n.* small lizard that changes colour according to its surroundings.
chamfer *v.* (**chamfered**) bevel the edge of.

chamois *n.* /shámwaa/ small mountain antelope; /shámmi/ a kind of soft leather.

champ *v.* munch noisily, make a chewing action; show impatience.

champagne *n.* sparkling white wine; its pale straw colour.

champion *n.* person or thing that defeats all others in a competition; person who fights or speaks in support of another or of a cause. — *v.* support as champion. **championship** *n.*

chance *n.* way things happen through no known cause or agency, luck; likelihood; opportunity. — *a.* happening by chance. — *v.* happen; risk.

chancel *n.* part of a church near the altar.

chancellor *n.* government minister in charge of the nation's budget; State or law official of various other kinds; non-resident head of a university. **chancellorship** *n.*

Chancery *n.* division of the High Court of Justice.

chancy *a.* (**-ier, -iest**) risky, uncertain.

chandelier *n.* hanging support for several lights.

chandler *n.* dealer in ropes, canvas, etc., for ships.

change *v.* make or become different; exchange, substitute; put fresh clothes or coverings on; go from one of two (sides, trains, etc.) to another; get or give small money or different currency for. — *n.* changing; money in small units or returned as balance.

changeling *n.* child or thing believed to have been substituted secretly for another.

channel *n.* stretch of water connecting two seas; passage for water; medium of communication; band of broadcasting frequencies. — *v.* (**channelled**) direct through a channel.

chant *n.* melody for psalms; monotonous singing; rhythmic shout. — *v.* sing, esp. to a chant; shout rhythmically.

chantry *n.* chapel founded for priests to sing masses for the founder's soul.

chaos *n.* great disorder. **chaotic** *a.*, **chaotically** *adv.*

chap ¹ *n.* (*colloq.*) man.

chap ² *n.* crack in skin. — *v.* (**chapped**) cause chaps in; suffer chaps.

chaparral *n.* (*US*) dense tangled brushwood.

chapatti *n.* (*pl.* **-is**) small flat cake of unleavened bread.

chapel *n.* place used for Christian worship, other than a cathedral or parish church; place with a separate altar within a church.

chaperon *n.* older woman looking after a young unmarried woman on social occasions. — *v.* act as chaperon to.

chaplain *n.* clergyman of an institution, private chapel, ship, regiment, etc. **chaplaincy** *n.*

chapter *n.* division of a book; canons of a cathedral.

char ¹ *n.* charwoman.

char ² *v.* (**charred**) make or become black by burning.

character *n.* qualities making a person or thing what he, she, or it is; moral strength; notable or eccentric person; person in a novel or play etc.; reputation; biological characteristic; letter or sign used in writing, printing, etc.

characteristic *a.* & *n.* (feature) forming part of the character of a person or thing. **characteristically** *adv.*

characterize *v.* describe the character of; be a characteristic of. **characterization** *n.*

charade /shəraád/ *n.* scene acted as a clue to a word in the game of **charades**; absurd pretence.

charcoal *n.* black substance made by burning wood slowly.

charge *n.* price asked for goods or services; quantity of explosive; electricity contained in a substance; task, duty; custody; person or thing entrusted; accusation; rushing attack; heraldic device. — *v.* ask as a price or from (a person); record as a debt; load or fill with explosive; give an electric charge to; give as a task or duty, entrust; accuse formally; rush forward in attack. **charge card** a kind of credit card. **in charge** in command. **take charge** take control.

chargé d'affaires (*pl.* **-gés**) ambassador's deputy.

chariot *n.* two-wheeled horse-drawn vehicle used in ancient times in battle and in racing.

charioteer *n.* driver of a chariot.

charisma /kərízmə/ *n.* power to inspire devotion and enthusiasm.

charismatic *a.* having charisma; (of worship) characterized by spontaneity. **charismatically** *adv.*

charitable *a.* full of charity; of or belonging to charities. **charitably** *adv.*

charity *n.* loving kindness; unwillingness to think badly of others; institution or fund for helping the needy, help so given.

charlady *n.* charwoman.

charlatan *n.* person falsely claiming to be an expert.

charlotte *n.* pudding of cooked fruit with breadcrumbs.
charm *n.* attractiveness, power of arousing love or admiration; act, object, or words believed to have magic power; small ornament worn on a bracelet etc. — *v.* give pleasure to; influence by personal charm; influence as if by magic. **charmer** *n.*
charming *a.* delightful.
charnel house place containing corpses or bones.
chart *n.* map for navigators; table, diagram, or outline map; list of recordings that are currently most popular. — *v.* make a chart of.
charter *n.* official document granting rights; chartering of aircraft etc. — *v.* grant a charter to; let or hire (an aircraft, ship, or vehicle). **chartered accountant** one qualified according to the rules of an association holding a royal charter.
chartreuse /shaartrűz/ *n.* fragrant green or yellow liqueur.
charwoman *n.* (*pl.* **-women**) woman employed to clean a house etc.
chary *a.* (**-ier, -iest**) cautious. **charily** *adv.*, **chariness** *n.*
chase *v.* go quickly after in order to capture, overtake, or drive away. — *n.* chasing, pursuit; hunting; steeplechase.
chasm *n.* deep cleft.
chassis /shássi/ *n.* (*pl.* **chassis**) baseframe of a vehicle.
chaste *a.* virgin, celibate; sexually pure; simple in style, not ornate. **chastely** *adv.*
chasten *v.* discipline by punishment; subdue the pride of.
chastise *v.* punish, esp. by beating. **chastisement** *n.*
chastity *n.* being chaste.
chat *n.* informal conversation. — *v.* (**chatted**) have a chat.
chateau *n.* (*pl.* **-eaux**) French castle or large country house.
chatelaine *n.* mistress of a large house.
chattel *n.* movable possession.
chatter *v.* talk quickly and continuously about unimportant matters; (of teeth) rattle together. — *n.* chattering talk. **chatterer** *n.*
chatterbox *n.* talkative person.
chatty *a.* (**-ier, -iest**) fond of chatting; resembling chat. **chattily** *adv.*, **chattiness** *n.*
chauffeur *n.* person employed to drive a car. **chauffeuse** *n.fem.*
chauvinism *n.* exaggerated patriotism. **male chauvinism** prejudiced belief in male superiority over women. **chauvinist** *n.*, **chauvinistic** *a.*
cheap *a.* low in cost or value; poor in quality. **cheaply** *adv.*, **cheapness** *n.*
cheapen *v.* make or become cheap; degrade.
cheat *v.* act dishonestly or unfairly to win profit or advantage; trick, deprive by deceit. — *n.* person who cheats; deception.
check [1] *v.* test or examine, inspect; stop, slow the motion (of). — *n.* inspection; pause; restraint; exposure of a chess king to capture; bill in a restaurant; (*US*) cheque. **check in** register on arrival. **check out** register on departure or dispatch. **check-out** *n.* desk where goods are paid for in a supermarket. **checker** *n.*
check [2] *n.* pattern of squares or crossing lines. **checked** *a.*
checkmate *n.* situation in chess where capture of a king is inevitable; complete defeat, deadlock. — *v.* put into checkmate; defeat, foil.
cheek *n.* side of the face below the eye; impudent speech, arrogance. — *v.* speak cheekily to. **cheek by jowl** close together.
cheeky *a.* (**-ier, -iest**) showing cheerful lack of respect. **cheekily** *adv.*
cheep *n.* weak shrill cry like that of a young bird. — *v.* make this cry.
cheer *n.* shout of applause; cheerfulness. — *v.* utter a cheer, applaud with a cheer; gladden. **cheer up** make or become more cheerful.
cheerful *a.* happy, contented; pleasantly bright. **cheerfully** *adv.*, **cheerfulness** *n.*
cheerless *a.* gloomy, dreary.
cheery *a.* (**-ier, -iest**) cheerful. **cheerily** *adv.*, **cheeriness** *n.*
cheese *n.* food made from pressed milk curds. **cheese-paring** *a.* stingy, (*n.*) stinginess.
cheeseburger *n.* hamburger with cheese on it.
cheesecake *n.* open tart filled with sweetened curds; (*sl.*) display of a woman's shapely body.
cheesecloth *n.* thin loosely-woven cotton fabric.
cheetah *n.* a kind of leopard.
chef *n.* professional cook.
chef-d'œuvre /shaydűvrə/ *n.* (*pl.* ***chefs-d'œuvre***) masterpiece.
chemical *a.* of or made by chemistry. — *n.* substance obtained by or used in a chemical process. **chemically** *adv.*
chemise *n.* woman's loose-fitting undergarment or dress.
chemist *n.* person skilled in chemistry; dealer in medicinal drugs.
chemistry *n.* study of substances and their

reactions; structure and properties of a substance.

chemotherapy *n.* treatment of disease by drugs etc.

chenille *n.* fabric with a velvety pile.

cheque *n.* written order to a bank to pay out money from an account; printed form for this. **cheque card** card guaranteeing payment of cheques.

chequer *n.* pattern of squares, esp. of alternating colours.

chequered *a.* marked with a chequer pattern; having frequent changes of fortune.

cherish *v.* take loving care of; be fond of; cling to (hopes etc.).

cheroot *n.* cigar with both ends open.

cherry *n.* small soft round fruit with a stone; tree bearing this or grown for its ornamental flowers; deep red.

cherub *n.* angelic being (*pl.* **cherubim**); (in art) chubby infant with wings; angelic child. **cherubic** *a.*

chervil *n.* herb with aniseed flavour.

chess *n.* game for two players using 32 **chessmen** on a chequered board with 64 squares.

chest *n.* large strong box; upper front surface of the body. **chest of drawers** piece of furniture with drawers for clothes etc.

chesterfield *n.* sofa with a padded back, seat, and ends.

chestnut *n.* tree with a hard brown nut; this nut; reddish-brown, horse of this colour; old joke or anecdote.

chevron *n.* V-shaped symbol.

chew *v.* work or grind between the teeth; make this movement.

chewing gum flavoured gum used for prolonged chewing.

chewy *a.* (**-ier**, **-iest**) suitable for chewing. **chewiness** *n.*

chiaroscuro /kiaároskoórō/ *n.* light and shade effects; use of contrast.

chic *a.* stylish and elegant. — *n.* stylishness, elegance.

chicane /shikáyn/ *n.* barriers on a motor racing course.

chicanery *n.* trickery.

chick *n.* newly hatched young bird.

chicken *n.* young domestic fowl; its flesh as food. — *a.* (*sl.*) cowardly. — *v.* **chicken out** (*sl.*) withdraw through cowardice. **chicken feed** (*colloq.*) trifling amount of money. **chickenpox** *n.* disease with a rash of small red blisters.

chicory *n.* blue-flowered plant used for salad.

chide *v.* (**chided** or **chid**, **chidden**) (*old use*) rebuke.

chief *n.* leader, ruler; person with the highest rank. — *a.* highest in rank; most important.

chiefly *adv.* mainly.

chieftain *n.* chief of a clan or tribe.

chiffon *n.* thin almost transparent fabric.

chignon /sheényoN/ *n.* coil of hair worn at the back of the head.

chihuahua /chiwaáwə/ *n.* very small smooth-haired dog.

chilblain *n.* painful swelling caused by exposure to cold.

child *n.* (*pl.* **children**) young human being; son or daughter. **childhood** *n.*

childbirth *n.* process of giving birth to a child.

childish *a.* like a child, unsuitable for a grown person.

childless *a.* having no children.

childlike *a.* simple and innocent.

chill *n.* unpleasant coldness; illness with feverish shivering. — *a.* chilly. — *v.* make or become chilly; preserve at a low temperature without freezing.

chilli *n.* (*pl.* **-ies**) dried pod of red pepper.

chilly *a.* (**-ier**, **-iest**) rather cold; unfriendly in manner.

chime *n.* tuned set of bells; series of notes from these. — *v.* ring as a chime. **chime in** put in a remark.

chimera /kīmeérə/ *n.* legendary monster with a lion's head, goat's body, and serpent's tail; hybrid thing.

chimney *n.* (*pl.* **-eys**) structure for carrying off smoke or gases. **chimney pot** pipe on top of a chimney.

chimpanzee *n.* African ape.

chin *n.* front of the lower jaw.

china *n.* fine earthenware, porcelain; things made of this.

chinchilla *n.* small squirrel-like South American animal; its grey fur.

chine *n.* animal's backbone; ravine in southern England. — *v.* cut or slit (meat) along the chine.

Chinese *a.* & *n.* (native, language) of China.

chink [1] *n.* narrow opening, slit.

chink [2] *n.* sound of glasses or coins striking together. — *v.* make this sound.

chintz *n.* glazed cotton cloth used for furnishings.

chip *n.* small piece cut or broken off something hard; fried oblong strip of potato; counter used in gambling. — *v.* (**chipped**) break or cut the edge or surface of; shape thus. **chip in** (*colloq.*) interrupt; contribute money.

chipboard *n.* board made of compressed wood chips.

chipmunk *n.* striped squirrel-like animal of North America.

chipolata *n.* small sausage.
chiropody /kiróppədi/ *n.* treatment of minor ailments of the feet. **chiropodist** *n.*
chiropractic /kī́rōpráktik/ *n.* treatment of physical disorders by manipulation of the spinal column. **chiropractor** *n.*
chirp *n.* short sharp sound made by a small bird or grasshopper. — *v.* make this sound.
chirpy *a.* (**-ier, -iest**) lively and cheerful.
chisel *n.* tool with a sharp bevelled end for shaping wood or stone etc. — *v.* (**chiselled**) cut with this.
chit [1] *n.* young child.
chit [2] *n.* short written note.
chivalry *n.* courtesy and considerate behaviour, inclination to help weaker persons. **chivalrous** *a.*
chive *n.* small herb with onion-flavoured leaves.
chivvy *v.* (*colloq.*) urge to hurry.
chloride *n.* compound of chlorine and another element.
chlorinate *v.* treat or sterilize with chlorine. **chlorination** *n.*
chlorine *n.* chemical element, heavy yellowish-green gas.
chloroform *n.* liquid giving off vapour that causes unconsciousness when inhaled.
chlorophyll *n.* green colouring matter in plants.
choc *n.* (*colloq.*) chocolate. **choc ice** bar of ice cream coated with chocolate.
chock *n.* block or wedge for preventing something from moving. — *v.* wedge with chock(s). **chock-a-block** *a.* & *adv.* crammed, crowded together.
chocolate *n.* edible substance made from cacao seeds; sweet made or coated with this, drink made with this; dark brown colour.
choice *n.* choosing, right of choosing; variety from which to choose; person or thing chosen. — *a.* of especially good quality. **choicely** *adv.*
choir *n.* organized band of singers, esp. in church; part of a church where these sit, chancel.
choirboy *n.* boy singer in a church choir.
choke *v.* stop (a person) breathing by squeezing or blocking the windpipe; be unable to breathe; clog, smother. — *n.* valve controlling the flow of air into a petrol engine.
choker *n.* close-fitting necklace.
cholera *n.* serious often fatal disease caused by bacteria.
choleric *a.* easily angered.
cholesterol *n.* fatty animal substance thought to cause hardening of arteries.
choose *v.* (**chose, chosen**) select out of a number of things; decide (on), prefer.
choosy *a.* (**-ier, -iest**) (*colloq.*) careful in choosing, hard to please. **choosiness** *n.*
chop *v.* (**chopped**) cut by a blow with an axe or knife; hit with a short downward movement. — *n.* chopping stroke; thick slice of meat, usu. including a rib.
chopper *n.* chopping tool; (*colloq.*) helicopter.
choppy *a.* (**-ier, -iest**) full of short broken waves; jerky.
chopstick *n.* each of a pair of sticks used in China, Japan, etc., to lift food to the mouth.
chop suey Chinese dish of meat or fish fried with vegetables.
choral *a.* for or sung by a chorus.
chorale *n.* choral composition using the words of a hymn.
chord [1] *n.* string of a harp etc.; straight line joining two points on a curve.
chord [2] *n.* combination of notes sounded together.
chore *n.* routine task.
choreography *n.* composition of stage dances. **choreographer** *n.*, **choreographic** *a.*
chorister *n.* member of a choir.
chortle *n.* loud chuckle. — *v.* utter a chortle.
chorus *n.* group of singers; thing spoken or sung by many together; refrain of a song; group of singing dancers in a musical comedy etc. — *v.* say as a group.
chose, chosen *see* **choose**.
choux pastry /shōō/ light pastry for making small cakes.
chow *n.* long-haired dog of a Chinese breed; (*sl.*) food.
chowder *n.* stew of shellfish with bacon and onions etc.
chow mein Chinese dish of fried noodles and shredded meat etc.
christen *v.* admit to the Christian Church by baptism; name.
Christendom *n.* all Christians or Christian countries.
Christian *a.* of or believing in Christianity; kindly, humane. — *n.* believer in Christianity. **Christian name** personal name given at a christening. **Christian Science** religious system by which health and healing are sought by Christian faith, without medical treatment.
Christianity *n.* religion based on the teachings of Christ.
Christmas *n.* festival (25 Dec.) commemorating Christ's birth. **Christmas tree** evergreen or artificial tree decorated at Christmas.

chromatic *a.* of colour, in colours. **chromatic scale** music scale proceeding by semitones. **chromatically** *adv.*

chromatography *n.* separation of substances by slow passage through an adsorbing material.

chrome *n.* chromium; yellow pigment from a compound of this.

chromium *n.* metallic element that does not rust.

chromosome *n.* thread-like structure carrying genes in animal and plant cells.

chronic *a.* constantly present or recurring; having a chronic disease or habit; (*colloq.*) bad. **chronically** *adv.*

chronicle *n.* record of events. — *v.* record in a chronicle. **chronicler** *n.*

chronological *a.* arranged in the order in which things occurred. **chronologically** *adv.*

chronology *n.* arrangement of events in order of occurrence.

chronometer *n.* time-measuring instrument, esp. one unaffected by temperature changes.

chrysalis *n.* form of an insect in the stage between grub and adult insect; case enclosing it.

chrysanthemum *n.* garden plant flowering in autumn.

chub *n.* river fish.

chubby *a.* (**-ier, -iest**) round and plump. **chubbiness** *n.*

chuck [1] *v.* (*colloq.*) throw carelessly or casually.

chuck [2] *n.* part of a lathe holding the drill; part of a drill holding the bit; cut of beef from neck to ribs.

chuckle *n.* quiet laugh. — *v.* utter a chuckle.

chug *v.* (**chugged**) make or move with a dull short repeated sound. — *n.* this sound.

chukka *n.* period of play in a polo game.

chum *n.* (*colloq.*) close friend. **chummy** *a.* & *n.*

chump *n.* (*sl.*) head; foolish person. **chump chop** chop from the thick end of a loin of mutton.

chunk *n.* thick piece; substantial amount.

chunky *a.* (**-ier, -iest**) short and thick; in chunks, containing chunks. **chunkiness** *n.*

church *n.* building for public Christian worship; religious service in this; **the Church** Christians collectively; particular group of these.

churchwarden *n.* parish representative, assisting with church business.

churchyard *n.* enclosed land round a church, used for burials.

churlish *a.* ill-mannered, surly. **churlishly** *adv.*

churn *n.* machine in which milk is beaten to make butter; very large milk can. — *v.* beat (milk) or make (butter) in a churn; stir or swirl violently. **churn out** produce rapidly.

chute *n.* sloping channel down which things can be slid or dropped.

chutney *n.* (*pl.* **-eys**) seasoned mixture of fruit, vinegar, spices, etc., eaten with meat or cheese.

cicada *n.* chirping insect resembling a grasshopper.

cicatrice *n.* scar.

cider *n.* fermented drink made from apples.

cigar *n.* roll of tobacco leaf for smoking.

cigarette *n.* roll of shredded tobacco in thin paper for smoking.

cinch *n.* (*colloq.*) certainty, easy task.

cinder *n.* piece of partly burnt coal or wood.

cine-camera *n.* cinematographic camera.

cinema *n.* theatre where films are shown; films as an art form or industry.

cinematography *n.* process of making and projecting moving pictures. **cinematographic** *a.*

cinnamon *n.* spice made from the bark of a south-east Asian tree.

cipher *n.* symbol 0 representing nought or zero; numeral; person of no importance; system of letters or numbers used to represent others for secrecy.

circa *prep.* about.

circle *n.* perfectly round plane figure; curved tier of seats at a theatre etc.; group with similar interests. — *v.* move in a circle; form a circle round.

circlet *n.* small circle; circular band worn as an ornament.

circuit *n.* line, route, or distance round a place; path of an electric current.

circuitous *a.* roundabout, indirect. **circuitously** *adv.*

circuitry *n.* circuits.

circular *a.* shaped like or moving round a circle. — *n.* letter or leaflet sent to a circle of people. **circularity** *n.*

circulate *v.* go or send round.

circulation *n.* circulating; movement of blood round the body; number of copies sold, esp. of a newspaper.

circumcise *v.* cut off the foreskin of. **circumcision** *n.*

circumference *n.* boundary of a circle, distance round this.

circumflex accent the accent ˆ.

circumlocution *n.* roundabout, verbose, or evasive expression. **circumlocutory** *a.*

circumnavigate *v.* sail completely round. **circumnavigation** *n.*, **circumnavigator** *n.*
circumscribe *v.* draw a line round; restrict.
circumspect *a.* cautious and watchful, wary. **circumspection** *n.*, **circumspectly** *adv.*
circumstance *n.* occurrence or fact.
circumstantial *a.* detailed; consisting of facts that suggest something but do not prove it.
circumvent *v.* evade (a difficulty etc.). **circumvention** *n.*
circus *n.* travelling show with performing animals, acrobats, etc.
cirrhosis /sirōsiss/ *n.* disease of the liver.
cirrus *n.* (*pl.* **cirri**) high wispy white cloud.
cistern *n.* tank for storing water.
citadel *n.* fortress overlooking a city.
cite *v.* quote or mention as an example etc. **citation** *n.*
citizen *n.* inhabitant of a city; person with full rights in a country. **citizenship** *n.*
citric acid acid in the juice of lemons, limes, etc.
citrus *n.* tree of a group including lemon, orange, etc.
city *n.* important town; town with special rights given by charter.
civet *n.* cat-like animal of central Africa; musky substance obtained from its glands.
civic *a.* of a city or citizenship.
civil *a.* of citizens; not of the armed forces or the Church; polite and obliging. **civil engineering** designing and construction of roads, bridges, etc. **Civil List** annual allowance for the sovereign's household expenses. **civil servant** employee of the **civil service,** government departments other than the armed forces. **civil war** war between citizens of the same country. **civilly** *adv.*
civilian *n.* & *a.* (of) person(s) not in the armed forces.
civility *n.* politeness.
civilization *n.* making or becoming civillized; stage in the evolution of society; civilized conditions.
civilize *v.* cause to improve to a developed stage of society; improve the behaviour of.
clack *n.* short sharp sound; noise of chatter. — *v.* make this sound.
clad *a.* clothed.
cladding *n.* boards or metal plates as a protective covering.
claim *v.* demand as one's right; assert. *n.* demand; assertion; right or title.
claimant *n.* person making a claim.
clairvoyance *n.* power of seeing the future. **clairvoyant** *n.* person thought to have this power.
clam *n.* shellfish with a hinged shell. — *v.* **(clammed) clam up** (*colloq.*) refuse to talk.
clamber *v.* climb with difficulty.
clammy *a.* (**-ier, -iest**) unpleasantly moist and sticky.
clamour *n.* loud confused noise; loud protest etc. **clamorous** *a.*
clamp *n.* device for holding things tightly; device for immobilizing an illegally parked car. — *v.* grip with a clamp, fix firmly; immoblize an illegally parked car with a clamp. **clamp down on** become firmer about, put a stop to.
clan *n.* group of families with a common ancestor. **clannish** *a.*
clandestine *a.* kept secret, done secretly.
clang *n.* loud ringing sound. — *v.* make this sound.
clanger *n.* (*sl.*) blunder.
clangour *n.* clanging noise.
clank *n.* sound like metal striking metal. — *v.* make or cause to make this sound.
clap *v.* (**clapped**) strike the palms loudly together, esp. in applause; strike or put quickly or vigorously. — *n.* act or sound of clapping; sharp noise of thunder. **clapped out** (*sl.*) worn out.
clapper *n.* tongue or striker of a bell.
clapperboard *n.* device in film-making for making a sharp clap for synchronizing picture and sound at the start of a scene.
claptrap *n.* insincere talk.
claret *n.* a dry red wine.
clarify *v.* make or become clear. **clarification** *n.*
clarinet *n.* woodwind instrument with finger-holes and keys. **clarinettist** *n.* its player.
clarion *a.* loud, rousing.
clarity *n.* clearness.
clash *n.* conflict; discordant sounds or colours. — *v.* make clash; conflict.
clasp *n.* device for fastening things, with interlocking parts; grasp, handshake. — *v.* fasten, join with a clasp; grasp, embrace closely.
class *n.* set of people or things with characteristics in common; standard of quality; rank of society; set of students taught together. — *v.* place in a class.
classic *a.* of recognized high quality; typical; simple in style. — *n.* classic author or work etc.; (*pl.*) study of ancient Greek and Roman literature, history, etc. **classicism** *n.*, **classicist** *n.*
classical *a.* classic; of the ancient Greeks

and Romans; traditional and standard. **classically** *adv.*

classifiable *a.* able to be classified.

classify *v.* arrange systematically, class; designate as officially secret. **classification** *n.*

classless *a.* without distinctions of social class. **classlessness** *n.*

classroom *n.* room where a class of students is taught.

classy *a.* (*colloq.*) of high quality.

clatter *n.* rattling sound. — *v.* make this sound.

clause *n.* single part in a treaty, law, or contract; distinct part of a sentence, with its own verb.

claustrophobia *n.* abnormal fear of being in an enclosed space. **claustrophobic** *a.*

clavichord *n.* early small keyboard instrument.

claw *n.* pointed nail on an animal's or bird's foot; claw-like device for grappling or holding things. — *v.* scratch or pull with a claw or hand.

clay *n.* stiff sticky earth, used for making bricks and pottery. **clay pigeon** breakable disc thrown up as a target for shooting. **clayey** *a.*

claymore *n.* Scottish two-edged broadsword.

clean *a.* free from dirt or impurities; not soiled or used. — *v.* make clean. **cleaner** *n.*, **cleanly** *adv.*

cleanly /klénli/ *a.* attentive to cleanness. **cleanliness** *n.*

cleanse /klenz/ *v.* make clean. **cleanser** *n.*

clear *a.* transparent; free from doubt, difficulties, obstacles, etc.; easily seen or heard or understood. — *v.* make or become clear; prove innocent; get past or over; make as net profit. **clear off** (*colloq.*) go away. **clear out** empty; remove; (*colloq.*) go away. **clearly** *adv.*

clearance *n.* clearing; permission; space allowed for one object to pass another.

clearing *n.* space cleared of trees in a forest.

clearway *n.* road where vehicles must not stop.

cleat *n.* projecting piece for fastening ropes to.

cleavage *n.* split, separation; hollow between full breasts.

cleave *v.* (**cleaved**, **clove**, or **cleft**; **cloven** *or* **cleft**) split.

cleaver *n.* butcher's chopper.

clef *n.* symbol on a stave in music, showing the pitch of notes.

cleft *a.* split. *n.* split, cleavage.

clematis *n.* climbing plant with showy flowers.

clemency *n.* mildness, esp. of weather; mercy. **clement** *a.*

clementine *n.* a kind of small orange.

clench *v.* close (teeth or fingers) tightly.

clerestory *n.* upper row of windows in a large church.

clergy *n.* persons ordained for religious duties. **clergyman** *n.* (*pl.* **-men**).

cleric *n.* member of the clergy.

clerical *a.* of clerks; of clergy.

clerk *n.* person employed to do written work in an office.

clever *a.* quick at learning and understanding things; showing skill. **cleverly** *adv.*, **cleverness** *n.*

cliché /kleéshay/ *n.* hackneyed phrase or idea.

click *n.* short sharp sound. — *v.* make or cause to make a click; (*sl.*) be a success, be understood.

client *n.* person using the services of a professional person; customer.

clientele /kleé-ontél/ *n.* clients.

cliff *n.* steep rock face, esp. on a coast. **cliffhanger** *n.* story or contest full of suspense.

climacteric *n.* period of life when physical powers begin to decline.

climate *n.* regular weather conditions of an area.

climax *n.* point of greatest interest or intensity.

climb *v.* go up or over. — *n.* ascent made by climbing. **climber** *n.*

clime *n.* climate, region.

clinch *v.* fasten securely; settle conclusively; (of boxers) hold on to each other. — *n.* clinching. **clincher** *n.*

cling *v.* (**clung**) hold on tightly; stick. **cling film** thin polythene wrapping.

clinic *n.* place or session at which medical treatment is given to visiting persons; private or specialized hospital.

clinical *a.* of or used in treatment of patients. **clinically** *adv.*

clink *n.* thin sharp sound. — *v.* make this sound.

clinker *n.* fused coal ash.

clip [1] *n.* device for holding things tightly or together. — *v.* (**clipped**) fix or fasten with clip(s).

clip [2] *v.* (**clipped**) cut with shears or scissors; (*colloq.*) hit sharply. — *n.* act of clipping; piece clipped from something; (*colloq.*) sharp blow.

clipper *n.* fast sailing ship; (*pl.*) instrument for clipping things.

clipping *n.* piece clipped off; newspaper cutting.

clique /kleek/ *n.* small exclusive group.

clitoris *n.* small erectile part of female genitals.

cloak *n.* loose sleeveless outer garment. — *v.* cover, conceal.

cloakroom *n.* room where outer garments can be left, often containing a lavatory.

clobber *n.* (*sl.*) equipment; belongings. — *v.* (*sl.*) hit hard; defeat heavily.

cloche *n.* translucent cover for protecting plants.

clock *n.* instrument indicating time. **clock in** *or* **on, out** *or* **off** register one's time of arrival or departure. **clock up** achieve.

clockwise *adv.* & *a.* moving in the direction of the hands of a clock.

clockwork *n.* mechanism with wheels and springs.

clod *n.* lump of earth.

clog *n.* wooden-soled shoe. — *v.* (**clogged**) cause an obstruction in; become blocked.

cloister *n.* covered walk along the side of a church etc.; life in a monastery or convent.

cloistered *a.* shut away, secluded.

clone *n.* group of plants or organisms produced asexually from one ancestor. — *v.* grow thus.

close [1] /klōss/ *a.* near; near together; dear to each other; dense; concentrated; secretive; stingy; stuffy. — *adv.* closely; in a near position. — *n.* street closed at one end; grounds round a cathedral or abbey. **close-up** *n.* photograph etc. showing a subject as at close range. **closely** *adv.*, **closeness** *n.*

close [2] /klōz/ *v.* shut; bring or come to an end; come nearer together. — *n.* conclusion, end.

closet *n.* (*US*) cupboard; store room. — *v.* (**closeted**) shut away in private conference or study.

closure *n.* closing, closed condition.

clot *n.* thickened mass of liquid; (*sl.*) stupid person. — *v.* (**clotted**) form clot(s).

cloth *n.* woven or felted material; piece of this; tablecloth.

clothe *v.* put clothes on, provide with clothes.

clothes *n.pl.* things worn to cover the body.

clothier *n.* person who deals in cloth and men's clothes.

clothing *n.* clothes for the body.

cloud *n.* visible mass of watery vapour floating in the sky; mass of smoke or dust. — *v.* become covered with clouds or gloom.

cloudburst *n.* violent storm of rain.

cloudy *a.* (**-ier, -iest**) covered with clouds; (of liquid) not transparent. **cloudiness** *n.*

clout *n.* blow; (*colloq.*) power of effective action. — *v.* hit.

clove [1] *n.* dried bud of a tropical tree, used as spice.

clove [2] *n.* one division of a compound bulb such as garlic.

clove [3], **cloven** *see* **cleave** [1]. — *a.* **clove hitch** knot used to fasten a rope round a pole etc. **cloven hoof** divided hoof like that of sheep, cows, etc.

clover *n.* plant with three-lobed leaves. **in clover** in luxury.

clown *n.* person who does comical tricks. — *v.* perform or behave as a clown.

cloy *v.* sicken by glutting with sweetness or pleasure.

club *n.* heavy stick used as a weapon; stick with a wooden or metal head, used in golf; playing card of the suit marked with black clover leaves; group who meet for social or sporting purposes, their premises; organization offering benefit to subscribers. — *v.* (**clubbed**) strike with a club. **club together** join in subscribing.

cluck *n.* throaty cry of hen. — *v.* utter a cluck.

clue *n.* fact or idea giving a guide to the solution of a problem.

clump *n.* cluster, mass. — *v.* tread heavily; form into a clump.

clumsy *a.* (**-ier, -iest**) large and ungraceful. **clumsily** *adv.*, **clumsiness** *n.*

clung *see* **cling**.

cluster *n.* small close group. — *v.* form a cluster.

clutch [1] *v.* grasp tightly. — *n.* tight grasp; device for connecting and disconnecting moving parts.

clutch [2] *n.* set of eggs for hatching; chickens hatched from these.

clutter *n.* things lying about untidily. — *v.* fill with clutter.

Co. *abbr.* Company; County.

c/o *abbr.* care of.

co- *pref.* joint, jointly.

coach *n.* long-distance bus; large horse-drawn carriage; private tutor; instructor in sports. — *v.* train, teach.

coagulate *v.* change from liquid to semi-solid, clot. **coagulant** *n.*, **coagulation** *n.*

coal *n.* hard black mineral used for burning as fuel.

coalesce *v.* combine. **coalescence** *n.*

coalfield *n.* area where coal occurs.

coalition *n.* union, esp. temporary union of political parties.

coarse *a.* composed of large particles; rough in texture; rough or crude in manner, vulgar. **coarse fish** freshwater fish other than salmon and trout. **coarsely** *adv.*, **coarseness** *n.*

coarsen *v.* make or become coarse.

coast *n.* seashore and land near it. — *v.* sail along a coast; ride a bicycle or drive a motor vehicle without using power. **coastal** *a.*

coaster *n.* ship trading along a coast; mat for a glass.

coastguard *n.* officer of an organization that keeps watch on the coast.

coat *n.* outdoor garment with sleeves; fur or hair covering an animal's body; covering layer. — *v.* cover with a layer. **coat of arms** design on a shield as the emblem of a family or institution.

coating *n.* covering layer.

coax *v.* persuade gently; manipulate carefully or slowly.

coaxial *a.* (of cable) containing two conductors, one surrounding but insulated from the other.

cob *n.* sturdy short-legged horse; a kind of hazelnut; stalk of an ear of maize; small round loaf.

cobalt *n.* metallic element; deep-blue pigment made from it.

cobber *n.* (*Austr.* & *NZ colloq.*) friend, mate.

cobble [1] *n.* rounded stone formerly used for paving roads.

cobble [2] *v.* mend roughly.

cobbler *n.* (*old use*) shoe-mender.

cobra *n.* poisonous snake of India and Africa.

cobweb *n.* network spun by a spider.

cocaine *n.* drug used illegally as a stimulant.

coccyx /kóksiks/ *n.* bone at the base of the spinal column.

cochineal *n.* red colouring matter used in food.

cock *n.* male bird; tap or valve controlling a flow. — *v.* tilt or turn upwards; set (a gun) for firing. **cock-a-hoop** *a.* pleased and triumphant. **cock-eyed** *a.* (*sl.*) askew; absurd.

cockade *n.* rosette worn on a hat as a badge.

cockatoo *n.* crested parrot.

cockatrice *n.* basilisk; fabled cock with a serpent's tail.

cocker *n.* breed of spaniel.

cockerel *n.* young male fowl.

cockle *n.* edible shellfish.

cockney *n.* native or dialect of the East End of London.

cockpit *n.* compartment for the pilot in a plane, or for the driver in a racing car; pit for cockfighting.

cockroach *n.* beetle-like insect.

cockscomb *n.* cock's crest.

cocksure *a.* very self-confident.

cocktail *n.* mixed alcoholic drink. **fruit cocktail** mixed chopped fruit.

cocky *a.* (**-ier, -iest**) conceited and arrogant. **cockily** *adv.*

cocoa *n.* powder of crushed cacao seeds; drink made from this.

coconut *n.* nut of a tropical palm; its edible lining.

cocoon *n.* silky sheath round a chrysalis; protective wrapping.

cod *n.* large edible sea fish.

coda *n.* final part of a musical composition.

coddle *v.* cherish and protect.

code *n.* set of laws, rules, or signals; word or phrase used to represent a message for secrecy; cipher.

codeine *n.* substance made from opium, used to relieve pain.

codicil *n.* appendix to a will.

codify *v.* arrange (laws etc.) into a code. **codification** *n.*

coeducation *n.* education of boys and girls in the same classes. **coeducational** *a.*

coefficient *n.* multiplier; mathematical factor.

coelacanth /seéləkanth/ *n.* a kind of fish extinct except for one species.

coeliac disease /seéliak/ disease causing inability to digest gluten.

coerce *v.* compel by threats or force. **coercion** *n.*, **coercive** *a.*

coeval *a.* of the same age or epoch.

coexist *v.* exist together, esp. harmoniously. **coexistence** *n.*, **coexistent** *a.*

coffee *n.* bean-like seeds of a tropical shrub, roasted and ground for making a drink; this drink; light-brown colour. **coffee table** small low table.

coffer *n.* large strong box for holding money and valuables; (*pl.*) financial resources. **coffer-dam** *n.* enclosure pumped dry to enable construction work to be done within it.

coffin *n.* box in which a corpse is placed for burial or cremation.

cog *n.* one of a series of projections on the edge of a wheel, engaging with those of another.

cogent *a.* convincing. **cogently** *adv.*, **cogency** *n.*

cogitate *v.* think deeply. **cogitation** *n.*

cognac *n.* French brandy.

cognate *a.* akin, related. — *n.* relative; cognate word.

cognition *n.* knowing, perceiving. **cognitive** *a.*

cognizant *a.* aware, having knowledge. **cognizance** *n.*

cohabit *v.* live together as man and wife. **cohabitation** *n.*

cohere *v.* stick together.

coherent *a.* cohering; connected logically, not rambling. **coherently** *adv.*, **coherence** *n.*

cohesion *n.* tendency to cohere.

cohesive *a.* cohering.

cohort *n.* tenth part of a Roman legion.

coiffure /kwaafyoór/ *n.* hairstyle.

coil *v.* wind into rings or a spiral. — *n.* something coiled; one ring or turn in this.

coin *n.* piece of metal money. — *v.* make (coins) by stamping metal; get (money) in large quantities as profit; invent (a word or phrase). **coiner** *n.*

coinage *n.* coining; coins, system of these; coined word or phrase.

coincide *v.* occupy the same portion of time or space; be in agreement or identical.

coincidence *n.* coinciding; remarkable occurrence of similar events at the same time by chance. **coincidental** *a.*, **coincidentally** *adv.*

coition *n.* sexual intercourse.

coitus *n.* coition.

coke [1] *n.* solid substance left after gas and tar have been extracted from coal, used as fuel.

coke [2] *n.* (*sl.*) cocaine.

col *n.* depression in a range of mountains.

colander *n.* bowl-shaped perforated vessel for draining food.

cold *a.* at or having a low temperature; not affectionate, not enthusiastic. — *n.* low temperature; cold condition; illness causing catarrh and sneezing. **cold-blooded** *a.* having a blood temperature varying with that of the surroundings; unfeeling, ruthless. **cold feet** fear. **cold-shoulder** *v.* treat with deliberate unfriendliness. **coldly** *adv.*, **coldness** *n.*

coleslaw *n.* salad of shredded raw cabbage coated in dressing.

colic *n.* severe abdominal pain.

colitis *n.* inflammation of the colon.

collaborate *v.* work in partnership. **collaboration** *n.*, **collaborator** *n.*, **collaborative** *a.*

collage /kóllaazh/ *n.* artistic composition in which objects are glued to a backing to form a picture.

collapse *v.* fall down suddenly; lose strength suddenly; fold. — *n.* collapsing; breakdown.

collapsible *a.* made so as to fold up.

collar *n.* band round the neck of a garment; band holding part of a machine; cut of bacon from near the head. — *v.* (*colloq.*) seize, take for oneself.

collate *v.* compare in detail; collect and arrange systematically. **collator** *n.*

collateral *a.* parallel; additional but subordinate. — *n.* additional security pledged. **collaterally** *adv.*

collation *n.* collating; light meal.

colleague *n.* fellow worker esp. in a business or profession.

collect *v.* bring or come together; obtain specimens of, esp. as a hobby; fetch.

collected *a.* calm and controlled.

collection *n.* collecting; objects or money collected.

collective *a.* of or denoting a group taken or working as a unit. **collective noun** noun (singular in form) denoting a group (e.g. *army*, *herd*). **collectively** *adv.*

collector *n.* one who collects things.

colleen *n.* (*Ir.*) girl.

college *n.* educational establishment for higher or professional education; organized body of professional people. **collegiate** *a.*

collide *v.* come into collision.

collie *n.* dog with a pointed muzzle and shaggy hair.

colliery *n.* coal mine.

collision *n.* violent striking of one thing against another.

collocate *v.* place (words) together. **collocation** *n.*

colloquial *a.* suitable for informal speech or writing. **colloquially** *adv.*, **colloquialism** *n.*

collusion *n.* agreement made for a deceitful or fraudulent purpose.

colon [1] *n.* lower part of the large intestine. **colonic** *a.*

colon [2] *n.* punctuation mark :.

colonel /kön'l/ *n.* army officer next below brigadier.

colonial *a.* of a colony or colonies. — *n.* inhabitant of a colony.

colonialism *n.* policy of acquiring or maintaining colonies.

colonize *v.* establish a colony in. **colonization** *n.*, **colonist** *n.*

colonnade *n.* row of columns.

colony *n.* settlement or settlers in new territory, remaining subject to the parent State; people of one nationality or occupation living in a particular area; birds congregated similarly.

colophon *n.* publisher's device, esp. tailpiece.

coloration *n.* colouring.

colossal *a.* immense. **colossally** *adv.*

colossus *n.* (*pl.* **colossi**) immense statue.

colostomy *n.* opening made surgically in the surface of the abdomen, through which the bowel can empty.

colour *n.* sensation produced by rays of light of particular wavelengths; pigment, paint; (usu. *pl.*) flag of a ship or regiment. — *v.* put colour on; paint, stain, dye; blush; give a special character or bias to. **colour-blind** *a.* unable to distinguish between certain colours.

colourant *n.* colouring matter.

colourful *a.* full of colour; with vivid details. **colourfully** *adv.*

colourless *a.* without colour; lacking vividness.

colt *n.* young male horse.

coltsfoot *n.* wild plant with yellow flowers.

columbine *n.* garden flower with pointed projections on its petals.

column *n.* round pillar; thing shaped like this; vertical division of a page, printed matter in this; long narrow formation of troops, vehicles, etc.

columnist *n.* journalist who regularly writes a column of comments.

coma *n.* deep unconsciousness.

comatose *a.* in a coma; drowsy.

comb *n.* toothed strip of stiff material for tidying hair; fowl's fleshy crest; honeycomb. — *v.* tidy with a comb; search thoroughly.

combat *n.* battle, contest. — *v.* **(combated)** counter. **combative** *a.*

combatant *a.* & *n.* (person or nation) engaged in fighting.

combination *n.* combining; set of people or things combined; (*pl.*) undergarment covering body and legs. **combination lock** lock controlled by a series of positions of dial(s).

combine [1] /kəmbīn/ *v.* join into a group or set or mixture.

combine [2] /kómbīn/ *n.* combination of people or firms acting together.

combustible *a.* capable of catching fire.

combustion *n.* burning; process in which substances combine with oxygen and produce heat.

come *v.* **(came, come)** move towards the speaker or a place or point; arrive; occur. **come about** happen. **come across** meet or find unexpectedly. **come-back** *n.* return to a former successful position; retort. **come by** obtain. **come-down** *n.* fall in status. **come into** inherit. **come off** be successful. **come out** become visible; emerge. **come round** recover from fainting; be converted to the speaker's opinion. **come to** regain consciousness. **come up** arise for discussion.

comedian *n.* humorous entertainer or actor. **comedienne** *n.fem.*

comedy *n.* light amusing drama.

comely *a.* **(-ier, -iest)** (*old use*) good-looking. **comeliness** *n.*

comestibles *n.pl.* things to eat.

comet *n.* heavenly body with a luminous 'tail'.

comfort *n.* state of ease and contentment; relief of suffering or grief; person or thing giving this. — *v.* give comfort to. **comforter** *n.*

comfortable *a.* providing or having ease and contentment; not close or restricted. **comfortably** *adv.*

comic *a.* causing amusement; of comedy. — *n.* comedian; children's periodical with a series of strip cartoons. **comical** *a.*, **comically** *adv.*

comma *n.* punctuation mark , .

command *n.* statement, given with authority, that an action must be performed; tenure of authority; mastery; forces or district under a commander. — *v.* give a command to; have authority over.

commandant *n.* officer in command of a fortress etc.

commandeer *v.* seize for use.

commander *n.* person in command; naval officer next below captain; police officer next below commissioner.

commandment *n.* one of ten God-given rules for living.

commando *n.* member of a military unit specially trained for making raids and assaults.

commemorate *v.* keep in the memory by a celebration or memorial. **commemoration** *n.*, **commemorative** *a.*

commence *v.* begin. **commencement** *n.*

commend *v.* praise; entrust. **commendation** *n.*

commendable *a.* worthy of praise. **commendably** *adv.*

commensurable *a.* measurable by the same standard. **commensurably** *adv.*, **commensurability** *n.*

commensurate *a.* of the same size; proportionate.

comment *n.* opinion given; explanatory note. — *v.* make comment(s) on.

commentary *n.* series of comments.

commentate *v.* act as commentator.

commentator *n.* person who writes or speaks a commentary.

commerce *n.* all forms of trade and services (e.g. banking, insurance).

commercial *a.* of, engaged in, or financed by commerce. **commercially** *adv.*

commercialize *v.* make commercial; make profitable. **commercialization** *n.*

commingle *v.* mix.

commiserate *v.* express pity for; sympathize. **commiseration** *n.*

commission *n.* committing; giving of authority to perform a task; task given; body of people given such authority; warrant conferring authority on an officer in the armed forces; payment to an agent selling goods or services. — *v.* give commission to; place an order for. **in commission** ready for service. **out of commission** not in working order.

commissionaire *n.* uniformed attendant at the door of a theatre, business premises, etc.

commissioner *n.* member of a commission; head of Scotland Yard; government official in charge of a district abroad.

commit *v.* (**committed**) do, perform; entrust, consign; pledge to a course of action. **committal** *n.*

commitment *n.* committing; obligation or pledge, state of being involved in this.

committee *n.* group of people appointed to attend to special business or manage the affairs of a club etc.

commode *n.* chest of drawers; chamber pot in a chair or box.

commodious *a.* roomy.

commodity *n.* article of trade, product.

commodore *n.* naval officer next below rear admiral; president of a yacht club.

common *a.* of or affecting all; occurring often; ordinary; of inferior quality. — *n.* area of unfenced grassland for all to use; (*pl.*) common people. **common law** unwritten law based on custom and former court decisions. **common room** room shared by students or teachers for social purposes. **common sense** normal good sense in practical matters. **common time** 4 crotchets in the bar in music.

commoner *n.* one of the common people, not a noble.

commonly *adv.* usually, frequently.

commonplace *a.* ordinary; lacking originality.

commonwealth *n.* independent State; federation of States.

commotion *n.* fuss and disturbance.

communal *a.* shared among a group. **communally** *adv.*

commune [1] /kəmyo͞on/ *v.* communicate mentally or spiritually.

commune [2] /kómyo͞on/ *n.* group (not all of one family) sharing accommodation and goods; district of local government in France etc.

communicable *a.* able to be communicated.

communicant *n.* person who receives Holy Communion; one who communicates information.

communicate *v.* make known; transmit; pass news and information to and fro; have or be a means of access. **communicator** *n.*

communication *n.* communicating; letter or message; means of access.

communicative *a.* talkative, willing to give information.

communion *n.* fellowship; social dealings; branch of the Christian Church; **(Holy) Communion** sacrament in which bread and wine are consumed.

communiqué /kəmyo͞onikay/ *n.* official report; agreed statement.

communism *n.* social system based on common ownership of property, means of production, etc.; political doctrine or movement seeking a form of this. **communist** *n.*

community *n.* body of people living in one district or having common interests or origins.

commutable *a.* exchangeable.

commute *v.* exchange for something else; travel regularly by train or bus to and from one's work. **commuter** *n.*

compact [1] /kómpakt/ *n.* pact, contract.

compact [2] *a.* /kəmpákt/ closely or neatly packed together; concise. — *v.* /kəmpákt/ make compact. — *n.* /kómpakt/ small flat case for face powder. **compact disc** small disc from which sound etc. is reproduced by laser action.

companion *n.* one who accompanies another; thing that matches or accompanies another. **companionway** *n.* staircase from a ship's deck to cabins etc. **companionship** *n.*

companionable *a.* sociable.

company *n.* being with another or others; people assembled; guests; associate(s); people working together or united for business purposes, firm; subdivision of an infantry battalion.

comparable *a.* suitable to be compared, similar. **comparability** *n.*, **comparably** *adv.*

comparative *a.* involving comparison; of the grammatical form expressing 'more'. — *n.* comparative form of a word. **comparatively** *adv.*

compare *v.* estimate the similarity of; liken, declare to be similar; be worthy of comparison.

comparison *n.* comparing.

compartment *n.* partitioned space. **compartmental** *a.*

compass *n.* device showing the direction of the magnetic or true north; range, scope; (*pl.*) hinged instrument for drawing circles. — *v.* encompass.

compassion *n.* feeling of pity. **compassionate** *a.*, **compassionately** *adv.*

compatible *a.* able to exist or be used together; consistent. **compatibly** *adv.*, **compatibility** *n.*

compatriot *n.* fellow countryman.

compel *v.* **(compelled)** force; arouse (a feeling) irresistibly.

compendious *a.* giving much information concisely.

compendium *n.* (*pl.* **-dia** *or* **-s**) summary; collection of information etc.

compensate *v.* make payment to (a person) in return for loss or damage; counterbalance. **compensation** *n.*, **compensatory** *a.*

compère *n.* person who introduces performers in a variety show. — *v.* act as compère to.

compete *v.* take part in a competition or other contest.

competence *n.* ability, authority.

competent *a.* having ability or authority to do what is required; adequate. **competently** *adv.*

competition *n.* friendly contest; competing; those who compete.

competitive *a.* involving competition. **competitively** *adv.*, **competitiveness** *n.*

competitor *n.* one who competes.

compile *v.* collect and arrange into a list or book; make (a book) thus. **compilation** *n.*, **compiler** *n.*

complacent *a.* self-satisfied. **complacently** *adv.*, **complacency** *n.*

complain *v.* say one is dissatisfied; say one is suffering from pain. **complainant** *n.*

complaint *n.* statement that one is dissatisfied; illness.

complaisant *a.* willing to please others. **complaisance** *n.*

complement *n.* that which completes or fills something. — *v.* form a complement to. **complementary** *a.*

complete *a.* having all its parts; finished; thorough, in every way. — *v.* make complete; fill in (a form etc.). **completely** *adv.*, **completeness** *n.*, **completion** *n.*

complex *a.* made up of many parts. — *n.* complex whole; set of feelings that influence behaviour; set of buildings. **complexity** *n.*

complexion *n.* colour and texture of the skin of the face; general character of things.

compliant *a.* complying, obedient. **compliance** *n.*

complicate *v.* make complicated. **complicated** *a.* complex and difficult. **complication** *n.*

complicity *n.* involvement in wrongdoing.

compliment *n.* polite expression of praise. — *v.* pay compliment to.

complimentary *a.* expressing a compliment; free of charge.

comply *v.* **comply with** act in accordance with (a request).

component *n.* one of the parts of which a thing is composed.

comport *v.* agree, accord. **comport oneself** behave.

compose *v.* create in music or literature; arrange in good order; calm. **composer** *n.*

composite *a.* made up of parts.

composition *n.* composing; thing composed; compound artificial substance.

compositor *n.* typesetter.

compos mentis sane.

compost *n.* decayed matter used as a fertilizer; mixture of soil or peat for growing seedlings etc.

composure *n.* calmness.

compote *n.* fruit in syrup.

compound ¹ /kómpownd/ *a.* made up of two or more ingredients. — *n.* compound substance.

compound ² /kəmpównd/ *v.* combine; add to; settle by agreement.

comprehend *v.* understand; include.

comprehensible *a.* intelligible. **comprehensibly** *adv.*, **comprehensibility** *n.*

comprehension *n.* understanding.

comprehensive *a.* including much or all. — *n.* comprehensive school. **comprehensive school** one providing secondary education for children of all abilities. **comprehensively** *adv.*, **comprehensiveness** *n.*

compress *v.* /kəmpréss/ squeeze, force into less space. — *n.* /kómpress/ pad to stop bleeding or to cool inflammation. **compression** *n.*, **compressor** *n.*

comprise *v.* include; consist of; form, make up.

compromise *n.* settlement reached by concessions on each side. — *v.* make a settlement thus; expose to suspicion.

compulsion *n.* compelling, being compelled; irresistible urge. **compulsive** *a.*, **compulsively** *adv.*

compulsory *a.* that must be done, required. **compulsorily** *adv.*

compunction *n.* regret, scruple.

compute *v.* calculate; use a computer. **computation** *n.*

computer *n.* electronic apparatus for analysing or storing data, making calculations, etc.

computerize *v.* equip with or perform

or operate by computer. **computerization** *n.*

comrade *n.* companion, associate. **comradeship** *n.*

con [1] *v.* **(conned)** (*colloq.*) persuade or swindle after winning confidence. — *n.* (*sl.*) confidence trick.

con [2] *v.* **(conned)** direct the steering of (a ship).

con [3] *see* **pro and con**.

concatenation *n.* combination.

concave *a.* curved like the inner surface of a ball.

conceal *v.* hide, keep secret. **concealment** *n.*

concede *v.* admit to be true; grant (a privilege etc.); admit defeat in (a contest).

conceit *n.* too much pride in oneself. **conceited** *a.*

conceivable *a.* able to be imagined or believed true. **conceivably** *adv.*

conceive *v.* become pregnant; form (an idea etc.) in the mind.

concentrate *v.* employ all one's thought or effort; bring or come together; make less dilute. — *n.* concentrated substance.

concentration *n.* concentrating; concentrated thing. **concentration camp** camp for political prisoners in Nazi Germany.

concentric *a.* having the same centre. **concentrically** *adv.*

concept *n.* idea, general notion.

conception *n.* conceiving; idea.

conceptual *a.* of concepts.

conceptualize *v.* form a concept of. **conceptualization** *n.*

concern *v.* be relevant or important to; involve. — *n.* thing that concerns one; anxiety; business.

concerned *a.* anxious.

concerning *prep.* with reference to.

concert *n.* musical entertainment.

concerted *a.* done in combination.

concertina *n.* portable musical instrument with bellows and keys.

concerto /kəncháirtō/ *n.* musical composition for solo instrument and orchestra.

concession *n.* conceding; thing conceded; special privilege; right granted.

conch *n.* spiral shell.

conciliate *v.* soothe the hostility of; reconcile. **conciliation** *n.*, **conciliatory** *a.*

concise *a.* brief and comprehensive. **concisely** *adv.*, **conciseness** *n.*

conclude *v.* end; settle finally; reach an opinion by reasoning.

conclusion *n.* concluding; ending; opinion reached.

conclusive *a.* ending doubt, convincing. **conclusively** *adv.*

concoct *v.* prepare from ingredients; invent. **concoction** *n.*

concomitant *a.* accompanying.

concord *n.* agreement, harmony.

concordance *n.* agreement; index of words.

concordant *a.* being in concord.

concourse *n.* crowd, gathering; open area at a railway terminus etc.

concrete *n.* mixture of gravel and cement etc. used for building. — *a.* existing in material form; definite. — *v.* cover with or embed in concrete; solidify.

concretion *n.* solidified mass.

concubine *n.* (*old use*) woman who lives with a man as his wife.

concur *v.* **(concurred)** agree in opinion; happen together, coincide. **concurrence** *n.*, **concurrent** *a.*, **concurrently** *adv.*

concuss *v.* affect with concussion.

concussion *n.* injury to the brain caused by a hard blow.

condemn *v.* express strong disapproval of; convict; sentence; doom; declare unfit for use. **condemnation** *n.*

condense *v.* make denser or briefer; change from gas or vapour to liquid. **condensation** *n.*

condescend *v.* consent to do something less dignified or fitting than is usual. **condescension** *n.*

condiment *n.* seasoning for food.

condition *n.* thing that must exist if something else is to exist or occur; state of being; (*pl.*) circumstances. — *v.* bring to the desired condition; have a strong effect on; accustom. **conditioner** *n.*

conditional *a.* subject to specified conditions. **conditionally** *adv.*

condole *v.* express sympathy. **condolence** *n.*

condom *n.* contraceptive sheath.

condone *v.* forgive or overlook (a fault etc.).

conduce *v.* help to cause or produce. **conducive** *a.*

conduct *v.* /kəndúkt/ lead, guide; be the conductor of; manage; transmit (heat or electricity). — *n.* /kóndukt/ behaviour; way of conducting business etc.

conduction *n.* conducting of heat or electricity. **conductive** *a.*, **conductivity** *n.*

conductor *n.* person who controls an orchestra's or choir's performance; thing that conducts heat or electricity.

conduit *n.* pipe or channel for liquid; tube protecting wires.

cone *n.* tapering object with a circular base; cone-shaped thing; dry scaly fruit of pine or fir.

confection *n.* prepared dish or delicacy.
confectioner *n.* maker or seller of confectionery.
confectionery *n.* sweets, cakes, and pastries.
confederacy *n.* league of States.
confederate *a.* joined by treaty or agreement. — *n.* member of a confederacy; accomplice.
confederation *n.* union of States or people or organizations.
confer *v.* (**conferred**) grant; hold a discussion. **conferment** *n.*
conference *n.* meeting for discussion.
confess *v.* acknowledge, admit; declare one's sins to a priest.
confession *n.* acknowledgement of a fact, sin, guilt, etc.; statement of one's principles.
confessional *n.* enclosed stall in a church for hearing confessions.
confessor *n.* priest who hears confessions and gives counsel.
confetti *n.* bits of coloured paper thrown at a bride and bridegroom.
confidant *n.* person one confides in. **confidante** *n.fem.*
confide *v.* tell or talk confidentially; entrust.
confidence *n.* firm trust; feeling of certainty, boldness; thing told confidentially. **confidence trick** swindle worked by gaining a person's trust.
confident *a.* feeling confidence. **confidently** *adv.*
confidential *a.* to be kept secret; entrusted with secrets. **confidentially** *adv.*, **confidentiality** *n.*
configuration *n.* shape, outline.
confine *v.* keep within limits; keep shut up.
confinement *n.* confining, being confined; time of childbirth.
confines *n.pl.* boundaries.
confirm *v.* make firmer or definite; corroborate. **confirmatory** *a.*
confirmation *n.* confirming; thing that confirms.
confiscate *v.* take or seize by authority. **confiscation** *n.*
conflagration *n.* great fire.
conflate *v.* blend or fuse together. **conflation** *n.*
conflict *n.* /kónflikt/ fight, struggle; disagreement. — *v.* /kənflikt/ have a conflict.
confluence *n.* place where two rivers unite. **confluent** *a.*
conform *v.* make similar; act or be in accordance, keep to rules or custom. **conformity** *n.*
conformable *a.* consistent; adaptable. **conformably** *adv.*
conformist *n.* person who conforms to rules or custom. **conformism** *n.*
confound *v.* astonish and perplex; confuse.
confront *v.* be or come or bring face to face with; face boldly. **confrontation** *n.*
confuse *v.* throw into disorder; make unclear; bewilder; destroy the composure of. **confusion** *n.*
confute *v.* prove wrong. **confutation** *n.*
conga *n.* dance in which people form a long winding line.
congeal *v.* coagulate, solidify.
congenial *a.* pleasant, agreeable to oneself. **congenially** *adv.*
congenital *a.* being so from birth. **congenitally** *adv.*
conger *n.* large sea eel.
congest *v.* make abnormally full. **congestion** *n.*
conglomerate *a.* /kənglómmərət/ gathered into a mass. — *n.* /kənglómmərət/ coherent mass. — *v.* /kənglómmərayt/ collect into a coherent mass. **conglomeration** *n.*
congratulate *v.* tell (a person) that one admires his or her success. **congratulation** *n.*, **congratulatory** *a.*
congregate *v.* flock together.
congregation *n.* people assembled at a church service.
congress *n.* formal meeting of delegates for discussion. **Congress** law-making assembly, esp. of the USA. **congressional** *a.*
congruent *a.* suitable, consistent; having exactly the same shape and size. **congruence** *n.*
conic *a.* of a cone.
conical *a.* cone-shaped.
conifer *n.* tree bearing cones. **coniferous** *a.*
conjecture *n.* & *v.* guess.
conjugal *a.* of marriage.
conjunction *n.* word such as 'and' or 'or' that connects others.
conjunctivitis *n.* inflammation of the membrane (**conjunctiva**) connecting eyeball and eyelid.
conjure *v.* do sleight-of-hand tricks. **conjuror** *n.*
conk *n.* (*sl.*) nose, head. — *v.* (*sl.*) hit. **conk out** (*sl.*) break down.
connect *v.* join, be joined; associate mentally; (of a train, coach, or flight) arrive so that passengers are in time to catch another. **connection** *n.*, **connective** *a.*

connive *v.* **connive at** tacitly consent to. **connivance** *n.*
connoisseur /kònnəsór/ *n.* person with expert understanding esp. of artistic subjects.
connote *v.* imply in addition to its basic meaning. **connotation** *n.*
conquer *v.* overcome in war or by effort. **conqueror** *n.*
conquest *n.* conquering; thing won by conquering.
conscience *n.* person's sense of right and wrong; feeling of remorse.
conscientious *a.* showing careful attention. **conscientiously** *adv.*, **conscientiousness** *n.*
conscious *a.* with mental faculties awake; aware; intentional. **consciously** *adv.*, **consciousness** *n.*
conscript *v.* /kənskrípt/ summon for compulsory military service. — *n.* /kónskript/ conscripted person. **conscription** *n.*
consecrate *v.* make sacred; dedicate to the service of God. **consecration** *n.*
consecutive *a.* following continuously. **consecutively** *adv.*
consensus *n.* general agreement.
consent *v.* say one is willing to do or allow what is asked. — *n.* willingness; permission.
consequence *n.* result; importance.
consequent *a.* resulting.
consequential *a.* consequent; self-important. **consequentially** *adv.*
consequently *adv.* as a result.
conservancy *n.* commission controlling a river etc.
conservation *n.* conserving.
conservationist *n.* one who seeks to preserve the natural environment.
conservative *a.* opposed to change; (of an estimate) purposely low. — *n.* conservative person. **conservatively** *adv.*, **conservatism** *n.*
conservatory *n.* greenhouse built on to a house.
conserve [1] /kənsérv/ *v.* keep from harm, decay, or loss.
conserve [2] /kónserv/ *n.* jam made from fresh fruit and sugar.
consider *v.* think about, esp. in order to decide; allow for; be of the opinion.
considerable *a.* fairly great in amount or importance. **considerably** *adv.*
considerate *a.* careful not to hurt or inconvenience others. **considerately** *adv.*
consideration *n.* careful thought; being considerate; fact that must be kept in mind; payment given as a reward.
considering *prep.* taking into account.
consign *v.* deposit, entrust; send (goods etc.).
consignee *n.* person to whom goods are sent.
consignment *n.* consigning; batch of goods.
consist *v.* **consist of** be composed of.
consistency *n.* being consistent; degree of thickness or solidity.
consistent *a.* unchanging; not contradictory. **consistently** *adv.*
consolation *n.* consoling; thing that consoles.
console [1] /kənsṓl/ *v.* comfort in time of sorrow.
console [2] /kónsōl/ *n.* bracket supporting a shelf; frame or panel holding the controls of equipment.
consolidate *v.* combine; make or become secure and strong. **consolidation** *n.*
consommé /kənsómmay/ *n.* clear soup.
consonant *n.* letter other than a vowel; sound it represents. — *a.* consistent, harmonious.
consort *n.* /kónsort/ husband or wife, esp. of a monarch. — *v.* /kənsórt/ keep company.
consortium *n.* (*pl.* **-tia**) combination of firms acting together.
conspectus *n.* general view.
conspicuous *a.* easily seen, attracting attention. **conspicuously** *adv.*
conspiracy *n.* conspiring; plan made by conspiring.
conspirator *n.* one who conspires. **conspiratorial** *a.*, **conspiratorially** *adv.*
conspire *v.* plan secretly against others; (of events) seem to combine.
constable *n.* policeman or policewoman of the lowest rank.
constabulary *n.* police force.
constancy *n.* quality of being unchanging; faithfulness.
constant *a.* continuous; occurring repeatedly; unchanging; faithful. — *n.* unvarying quantity. **constantly** *adv.*
constellation *n.* group of stars.
consternation *n.* great surprise and anxiety or dismay.
constipation *n.* difficulty in emptying the bowels.
constituency *n.* body of voters who elect a representative; area represented thus.
constituent *a.* forming part of a whole. — *n.* constituent part; member of a constituency.
constitute *v.* be the parts of.
constitution *n.* principles by which a State is organized; bodily condition.
constitutional *a.* in accordance with a constitution. — *n.* walk as exercise.

constrain *v.* compel, oblige.
constraint *n.* constraining; restriction; strained manner.
constrict *v.* tighten, make narrower, squeeze. **constriction** *n.*
construct *v.* make by placing parts together. **constructor** *n.*
construction *n.* constructing; thing constructed; words put together to form a phrase; interpretation.
constructive *a.* constructing; making useful suggestions. **constructively** *adv.*
construe *v.* interpret; analyse word for word.
consul *n.* official representative of a State in a foreign city. **consular** *a.*
consulate *n.* consul's position or premises.
consult *v.* seek information or advice from. **consultation** *n.*
consultant *n.* specialist consulted for professional advice. **consultancy** *n.*
consultative *a.* of or for consultation; advisory.
consume *v.* use up; eat or drink up; destroy (by fire).
consumer *n.* person who buys or uses goods or services.
consummate *v.* accomplish, complete (esp. marriage by sexual intercourse). **consummation** *n.*
consumption *n.* consuming; (*old use*) tuberculosis.
consumptive *a.* & *n.* (person) suffering from tuberculosis.
contact *n.* touching, meeting, communicating; electrical connection; one who may be contacted for information or help. — *v.* get in touch with. **contact lens** very small lens worn in the eye.
contagion *n.* spreading of disease by contact. **contagious** *a.*
contain *v.* have within itself; include; control, restrain.
container *n.* receptacle, esp. of standard design to transport goods.
containerize *v.* use containers for transporting (goods). **containerization** *n.*
containment *n.* prevention of hostile expansion.
contaminate *v.* pollute. **contamination** *n.*
contemplate *v.* gaze at; consider as a possibility, intend; meditate. **contemplation** *n.*
contemplative *a.* meditative; of religious meditation.
contemporaneous *a.* existing or occurring at the same time.
contemporary *a.* of the same period or age; modern in style. *n.* person of the same age.
contempt *n.* despising, being despised; disrespect.
contemptible *a.* deserving contempt.
contemptuous *a.* showing contempt. **contemptuously** *adv.*
contend *v.* strive, compete; assert. **contender** *n.*
content [1] /kəntént/ *a.* satisfied with what one has. — *n.* being content. — *v.* make content. **contented** *a.*, **contentment** *n.*
content [2] /kóntent/ *n.* what is contained in something.
contention *n.* contending; assertion made in argument.
contentious *a.* quarrelsome; likely to cause contention.
contest *v.* /kəntést/ compete for or in; dispute. — *n.* /kóntest/ struggle for victory; competition. **contestant** *n.*
context *n.* what precedes or follows a word or statement and fixes its meaning; circumstances. **contextual** *a.*
contiguous *a.* adjacent, touching.
continent *n.* one of the main land masses of the earth. **continental** *a.*
contingency *n.* something unforeseen; thing that may occur.
contingent *a.* happening by chance; possible but not certain; conditional. — *n.* body of troops contributed to a larger group.
continual *a.* never ending. **continually** *adv.*
continuance *n.* continuing.
continue *v.* not cease; remain in a place or condition; resume. **continuation** *n.*
continuous *a.* without interval. **continuously** *adv.*, **continuity** *n.*
continuum *n.* (*pl.* **-tinua**) continuous thing.
contort *v.* force or twist out of normal shape. **contortion** *n.*
contortionist *n.* performer who can twist his or her body dramatically.
contour *n.* outline; line on a map showing height above sea level.
contra- *pref.* against.
contraband *n.* smuggled goods.
contraception *n.* prevention of conception, birth control.
contraceptive *a.* & *n.* (drug or device) preventing conception.
contract *n.* /kóntrakt/ formal agreement. — *v.* /kəntrákt/ make a contract; arrange (work) to be done by contract; catch (an illness); make or become smaller or shorter. **contraction** *n.*, **contractor** *n.*, **contractual** *a.*
contradict *v.* say that (a statement) is untrue or (a person) is wrong; be contrary to. **contradiction** *n.*, **contradictory** *a.*

contraflow *n.* flow (esp. of traffic) in a direction opposite to and alongside the usual flow.
contralto *n.* lowest female voice.
contraption *n.* (*colloq.*) strange device or machine.
contrapuntal *a.* of or in counterpoint.
contrariwise *adv.* on the other hand; in the opposite way.
contrary [1] /kóntrəri/ *a.* opposite in nature or tendency or direction. — *n.* the opposite. — *adv.* in opposition. **on the contrary** as the opposite of what was just stated.
contrary [2] /kəntráiri/ *a.* perverse. **contrarily** *adv.*, **contrariness** *n.*
contrast *n.* /kóntraast/ difference shown by comparison. — *v.* /kəntraást/ show contrast; compare so as to do this.
contravene *v.* break (a rule etc.). **contravention** *n.*
contretemps /káwntrətoN/ *n.* unfortunate happening.
contribute *v.* give to a common fund or effort; help to bring about. **contribution** *n.*, **contributor** *n.*, **contributory** *a.*
contrite *a.* penitent; sorry. **contritely** *adv.*, **contrition** *n.*
contrivance *n.* contriving; contrived thing, device.
contrive *v.* plan, make, or do something resourcefully.
control *n.* power to give orders or restrain something; means of restraining or regulating; check. — *v.* (**controlled**) have control of; regulate; restrain.
controversial *a.* causing controversy. **controversially** *adv.*
controversy *n.* prolonged dispute.
controvert *v.* deny the truth of. **controvertible** *a.*
contusion *n.* bruise.
conundrum *n.* riddle, puzzle.
conurbation *n.* large urban area formed where towns have spread and merged.
convalesce *v.* regain health after illness. **convalescence** *n.*, **convalescent** *a.* & *n.*
convection *n.* transmission of heat within a liquid or gas by movement of heated particles.
convene *v.* assemble. **convener** *n.*
convenience *n.* being convenient; convenient thing; lavatory.
convenient *a.* easy to use or deal with; with easy access. **conveniently** *adv.*
convent *n.* residence of a community of nuns.
convention *n.* accepted custom; assembly; formal agreement. **conventional** *a.*, **conventionally** *adv.*
converge *v.* come to or towards the same point. **convergence** *n.*, **convergent** *a.*
conversant *a.* **conversant with** having knowledge of.
conversation *n.* informal talk between people. **conversational** *a.*, **conversationally** *adv.*
converse [1] *v.* /kənvérss/ hold a conversation. — *n.* /kónverss/ (*old use*) conversation.
converse [2] /kónverss/ *a.* opposite, contrary. — *n.* converse idea or statement. **conversely** *adv.*
convert *v.* /kənvért/ change from one form or use to another; cause to change an attitude or belief. — *n.* /kónvert/ person converted, esp. to a religious faith. **conversion** *n.*
convertible *a.* able to be converted. — *n.* car with a folding or detachable roof.
convex *a.* curved like the outer surface of a ball. **convexity** *n.*
convey *v.* carry, transport, transmit; communicate as an idea.
conveyance *n.* conveying; means of transport, vehicle.
conveyancing *n.* business of transferring legal ownership of land.
conveyor *n.* person or thing that conveys; continuous moving belt conveying objects.
convict *v.* /kənvíkt/ prove or declare guilty. — *n.* /kónvikt/ convicted person in prison.
conviction *n.* convicting; firm opinion. **carry conviction** be convincing.
convince *v.* make (a person) feel certain that something is true.
convivial *a.* sociable and lively.
convocation *n.* convoking; assembly convoked.
convoke *v.* summon to assemble.
convoluted *a.* coiled, twisted.
convolution *n.* coil, twist.
convolvulus *n.* twining plant with trumpet-shaped flowers.
convoy *n.* ships or vehicles travelling under escort or together.
convulse *v.* cause violent movement or a fit of laughter in.
convulsion *n.* violent involuntary movement of the body; upheaval. **convulsive** *a.*
coo *v.* make a soft murmuring sound like a dove. — *n.* this sound.
cook *v.* prepare (food) by heating; undergo this process; (*sl.*) falsify (accounts etc.). — *n.* person who cooks, esp. as a job. **cook up** (*sl.*) concoct.
cooker *n.* stove for cooking food.
cookery *n.* art and practice of cooking.

cookie *n.* (*US*) sweet biscuit.

cool *a.* fairly cold; calm, unexcited; not enthusiastic. — *n.* coolness; (*sl.*) calmness. — *v.* make or become cool. **coolly** *adv.*, **coolness** *n.*

coolant *n.* fluid for cooling machinery.

coolie *n.* (*old use*) native labourer in eastern countries.

coomb /ko͞om/ *n.* valley.

coop *n.* cage for poultry. — *v.* confine, shut in.

co-op *n.* (*colloq.*) cooperative society; shop run by this.

cooper *n.* person who makes or repairs casks and barrels.

cooperate *v.* work or act together. **cooperation** *n.*

cooperative *a.* cooperating; willing to help; based on economic cooperation. — *n.* farm or firm etc. run on this basis.

co-opt *v.* appoint to a committee by invitation of existing members, not election.

coordinate [1] /kō-órdinət/ *a.* equal in importance. — *n.* any of the magnitudes used to give the position of a point.

coordinate [2] /kō-órdinayt/ *v.* bring into a proper relation; cause to function together efficiently. **coordination** *n.*, **coordinator** *n.*

coot *n.* a kind of waterbird.

cop *n.* (*sl.*) police officer; capture. — *v.* (**copped**) (*sl.*) catch.

cope *v.* (*colloq.*) manage successfully. **cope with** deal successfully with.

copier *n.* copying machine.

coping *n.* sloping top row of masonry in a wall.

copious *a.* plentiful. **copiously** *adv.*

copper [1] *n.* reddish-brown metallic element; coin containing this; its colour. — *a.* made of copper.

copper [2] *n.* (*sl.*) policeman.

coppice, copse *ns.* group of small trees and undergrowth.

Coptic *a.* of the Egyptian branch of the Christian Church.

copula *n.* the verb *be*.

copulate *v.* come together sexually; have sex. **copulation** *n.*, **copulatory** *a.*

copy *n.* thing made to look like another; specimen of a book etc. — *v.* make a copy of; imitate.

copyright *n.* sole right to publish a work. *v.* secure copyright for.

coquette *n.* woman who flirts. **coquettish** *a.*, **coquetry** *n.*

coracle *n.* small wicker boat.

coral *n.* hard red, pink, or white substance built by tiny sea creatures; reddish-pink colour.

cor anglais /kór ónglay/ woodwind instrument like the oboe but lower in pitch.

corbel *n.* stone or wooden support projecting from a wall.

cord *n.* long thin flexible material made from twisted strands; piece of this; corduroy.

cordial *a.* warm and friendly. — *n.* fruit-flavoured essence diluted to make a drink. **cordially** *adv.*

cordon *n.* line of police, soldiers, etc., enclosing something; fruit tree pruned to grow as a single stem. — *v.* enclose by a cordon.

cordon bleu /kórdon blû/ of the greatest excellence in cookery.

corduroy *n.* cloth with velvety ridges.

core *n.* central or most important part; horny central part of an apple etc., containing seeds. — *v.* remove the core from.

co-respondent *n.* person with whom the respondent in a divorce suit is said to have committed adultery.

corgi *n.* dog of a small Welsh breed with short legs.

coriander *n.* plant with seeds used for flavouring.

cork *n.* light tough bark of a South European oak; piece of this used as a float; bottle stopper. — *v.* stop up with a cork.

corkage *n.* restaurant's charge for serving wine.

corkscrew *n.* tool for extracting corks from bottles; spiral thing.

corm *n.* bulb-like underground stem from which buds grow.

cormorant *n.* large black seabird.

corn [1] *n.* wheat, oats, or maize; its grain; (*sl.*) something corny.

corn [2] *n.* small area of horny hardened skin, esp. on the foot.

corncrake *n.* bird with a harsh cry.

cornea *n.* transparent outer covering of the eyeball. **corneal** *a.*

cornelian *n.* reddish or white semi-precious stone.

corner *n.* angle or area where two lines, sides, or streets meet; free kick or hit from the corner of the field in football or hockey. — *v.* drive into a position from which there is no escape; drive fast round a corner; obtain a monopoly of.

cornerstone *n.* basis; vital foundation.

cornet *n.* brass instrument like a small trumpet; cone-shaped wafer holding ice cream.

cornflour *n.* flour made from maize.

cornflower *n.* plant (esp. blue-flowered) that grows among corn.

cornice *n.* ornamental moulding round the top of an indoor wall.
Cornish *a.* of Cornwall. — *n.* extinct Celtic language of Cornwall.
cornucopia *n.* horn-shaped container overflowing with fruit and flowers, symbol of abundance.
corny *a.* (**-ier**, **-iest**) (*colloq.*) hackneyed.
corollary *n.* proposition that follows logically from another.
corona *n.* (*pl.* **-nae**) ring of light round something.
coronary *n.* one of the arteries supplying blood to the heart; thrombosis in this.
coronation *n.* ceremony of crowning a monarch or consort.
coroner *n.* officer holding inquests.
coronet *n.* small crown.
corporal [1] /kórprəl/ *n.* non-commissioned officer next below sergeant.
corporal [2] /kórpərəl/ *a.* of the body. **corporal punishment** whipping or beating.
corporate *a.* shared by members of a group; united in a group.
corporation *n.* group in business or elected to govern a town.
corporeal *a.* having a body, tangible. **corporeally** *adv.*
corps /kor/ *n.* military unit; organized body of people.
corpse *n.* dead body.
corpulent *a.* having a bulky body, fat. **corpulence** *n.*
corpus *n.* (*pl.* **corpora**) set of writings.
corpuscle *n.* blood cell.
corral *n.* (*US*) enclosure for cattle. — *v.* (**coralled**) put or keep in a corral.
correct *a.* true, accurate; in accordance with an approved way of behaving or working. — *v.* make correct; mark errors in; reprove; punish. **correctly** *adv.*, **correctness** *n.*
correction *n.* correcting; alteration correcting something.
corrective *a.* & *n.* (thing) correcting what is bad or harmful.
correlate *v.* compare or connect or be connected systematically. **correlation** *n.*
correspond *v.* be similar or equivalent or in harmony; write letters to each other.
correspondence *n.* similarity; writing letters; letters written.
correspondent *n.* person who writes letters; person employed by a newspaper or TV news station to gather news and send reports.
corridor *n.* passage in a building or train; strip of territory giving access to somewhere.
corroborate *v.* get or give supporting evidence. **corroboration** *n.*, **corroborative** *a.*
corrode *v.* destroy (metal etc.) gradually by chemical action. **corrosion** *n.*, **corrosive** *a.*
corrugated *a.* shaped into alternate ridges and grooves. **corrugation** *n.*
corrupt *a.* dishonest, accepting bribes; immoral, wicked; decaying. — *v.* make corrupt; spoil, taint. **corruption** *n.*
corsage /korsaázh/ *n.* (*US*) flowers worn by a woman.
corset *n.* close-fitting undergarment worn to shape or support the body.
cortège /kortáyzh/ *n.* funeral procession.
cortex *n.* (*pl.* **-ices**) outer part of the brain.
cortisone *n.* hormone produced by adrenal glands or synthetically.
corvette *n.* small fast gunboat.
cos [1] *n.* long-leaved lettuce.
cos [2] *abbr.* cosine.
cosh *n.* weighted weapon for hitting people. — *v.* hit with a cosh.
cosine *n.* sine of the complement of a given angle.
cosmetic *n.* substance for beautifying the complexion etc. — *a.* improving the appearance.
cosmic *a.* of the universe. **cosmic rays** radiation from outer space.
cosmogony *n.* (theory of) the origin of the universe.
cosmology *n.* science or theory of the universe. **cosmological** *a.*
cosmopolitan *a.* of or from all parts of the world; free from national prejudices. — *n.* cosmopolitan person.
cosmos *n.* universe.
Cossack *n.* & *a.* (member) of a people of South Russia, famous as horsemen.
cost *v.* (**cost**) have as its price; involve the sacrifice or loss of; (**costed**) estimate the cost of. — *n.* what a thing costs.
costermonger *n.* (*old use*) person selling fruit etc. from a barrow in the street.
costly *a.* (**-ier**, **-iest**) expensive.
costume *n.* style of clothes, esp. that of a historical period; garment(s) for a specified activity.
cosy *a.* (**-ier**, **-iest**) warm and comfortable. — *n.* cover to keep a teapot hot. **cosily** *adv.*, **cosiness** *n.*
cot *n.* child's bed with high sides. **cot death** unexplained death of a sleeping baby.
coterie *n.* select group.
cotoneaster /kətṓniástər/ *n.* shrub or tree with red berries.
cottage *n.* small simple house in the country. **cottage cheese** that made

from curds without pressing. **cottage pie** dish of minced meat topped with mashed potato.

cotton *n.* soft white substance round the seeds of a tropical plant; this plant; thread or fabric made from cotton. — *v.* **cotton on** (*sl.*) understand. **cotton wool** raw cotton prepared as wadding.

couch *n.* long piece of furniture for lying or sitting on, usu. with a headrest at one end. — *v.* express in a specified way.

couch grass weed with long creeping roots.

cougar /ko͞ogər/ *n.* (*US*) puma.

cough *v.* expel air etc. from lungs with a sudden sharp sound. — *n.* act or sound of coughing; illness causing coughing.

could *see* **can** ²; feel inclined to.

coulomb /ko͞olom/ *n.* unit of electric charge.

council *n.* assembly to govern a town or advise on or organize something.

councillor *n.* member of a council.

counsel *n.* advice, suggestions; barrister(s). — *v.* (**counselled**) advise. **counsellor** *n.*

count ¹ *v.* find the total of; say numbers in order; include or be included in a reckoning; be important; regard as. — *n.* counting, number reached by this; point being considered. **count on** rely on; expect confidently.

count ² *n.* foreign nobleman.

countdown *n.* counting seconds backwards to zero.

countenance *n.* face; expression; approval. — *v.* give approval to.

counter ¹ *n.* flat-topped fitment over which goods are sold or business transacted with customers; small disc used in board games.

counter ² *adv.* in the opposite direction. — *a.* opposed. — *v.* take opposing action against.

counter- *pref.* rival; retaliatory; reversed; opposite.

counteract *v.* reduce or prevent the effects of. **counteraction** *n.*

counter-attack *n.* & *v.* attack in reply to an opponent's attack.

counterbalance *n.* weight or influence balancing another. — *v.* act as a counterbalance to.

counterblast *n.* powerful retort.

counterfeit *a.*, *n.*, & *v.* fake.

counterfoil *n.* section of a cheque or receipt kept as a record.

countermand *v.* cancel.

counterpane *n.* bedspread.

counterpart *n.* person or thing corresponding to another.

counterpoint *n.* method of combining melodies.

counter-productive *a.* having the opposite of the desired effect.

countersign *n.* password. — *v.* add a confirming signature to.

countersink *v.* (**-sunk**) sink (a screwhead) into a shaped cavity so that the surface is level.

counter-tenor *n.* male alto.

countervail *v.* avail against.

countess *n.* count's or earl's wife or widow; woman with the rank of count or earl.

countless *a.* too many to be counted.

countrified *a.* like the countryside or country life.

country *n.* nation's or State's land; people of this; State of which one is a member; region; land consisting of fields etc. with few buildings.

countryman *n.* (*pl.* **-men**) man living in the country; man of one's own country. **countrywoman** *n.fem.*

countryside *n.* rural district.

county *n.* major administrative division of a country; families of high social class long established in a county.

coup /ko͞o/ *n.* sudden action taken to obtain power etc.

coup de grâce /ko͞o də graáss/ finishing stroke.

coup d'état /ko͞o daytaá/ sudden overthrow of a government by force or illegal means.

couple *n.* two people or things; married or engaged pair. — *v.* fasten or link together; copulate.

couplet *n.* two successive rhyming lines of verse.

coupling *n.* connecting device.

coupon *n.* form or ticket entitling the holder to something; entry form for a football pool.

courage *n.* ability to control fear when facing danger or pain. **courageous** *a.*, **courageously** *adv.*

courgette *n.* a kind of small vegetable marrow.

courier *n.* messenger carrying documents; person employed to guide and assist tourists.

course *n.* onward progress; direction taken or intended; series of lessons or treatments; area on which golf is played or a race takes place; layer of stone etc. in a building; one part of a meal. — *v.* move or flow freely. **of course** without doubt.

court *n.* courtyard; area where tennis,

squash, etc., are played; sovereign's establishment with attendants; room or building where legal cases are heard or judged. — *v.* try to win the favour or support or love of; invite (danger etc.). **court martial** court trying offences against military law; trial by this. **court-martial** *v.* (**-martialled**) try by court martial.

courteous *a.* polite. **courteously** *adv.*, **courteousness** *n.*

courtesan *n.* (*old use*) prostitute with high-class clients.

courtesy *n.* courteous behaviour or act.

courtier *n.* (*old use*) one of a sovereign's companions at court.

courtly *a.* dignified and polite.

courtship *n.* courting, esp. of an intended wife or mate.

courtyard *n.* space enclosed by walls or buildings.

cousin *n.* (also **first cousin**) child of one's uncle or aunt. **second cousin** child of one's parent's cousin.

couture *n.* design and making of fashionable clothes.

couturier /kootyoóriay/ *n.* designer of fashionable clothes.

cove *n.* small bay.

coven *n.* assembly of witches.

covenant *n.* formal agreement, contract. — *v.* make a covenant.

cover *v.* place or be or spread over; conceal or protect thus; travel over (a distance); protect by insurance or a guarantee; be enough to pay for; deal with (a subject etc.); report for a newspaper etc. — *n.* thing that covers; wrapper, envelope, binding of a book; screen, shelter, protection; place laid at a meal. **cover up** conceal (a thing or fact). **cover-up** *n.*

coverage *n.* process of covering; area or risk etc. covered.

coverlet *n.* cover lying over other bedclothes.

covert *n.* thick undergrowth where animals hide. — *a.* concealed, done secretly. **covertly** *adv.*

covet *v.* (**coveted**) desire (a thing belonging to another person). **covetous** *a.*

covey *n.* group of partridges.

cow ¹ *n.* fully grown female of cattle or other large animals.

cow ² *v.* intimidate.

coward *n.* person who lacks courage. **cowardly** *a.*

cowardice *n.* lack of courage.

cowboy *n.* man in charge of cattle on a ranch; (*colloq.*) person with reckless methods in business.

cower *v.* crouch or shrink in fear.

cowl *n.* monk's hood or hooded robe; hood-shaped covering.

cowling *n.* removable metal cover on an engine.

cowrie *n.* a kind of seashell.

cowslip *n.* wild plant with small fragrant yellow flowers.

cox *n.* coxswain. — *v.* act as cox of (a racing boat).

coxswain /kóks'n/ *n.* steersman.

coy *a.* pretending to be shy or embarrassed. **coyly** *adv.*

coyote /koyōti/ *n.* prairie wolf.

coypu *n.* beaver-like water animal.

crab *n.* ten-legged shellfish. **crab apple** a kind of small sour apple.

crabbed *a.* bad-tempered; (of handwriting) hard to read.

crabby *a.* bad-tempered; sour.

crack *n.* sudden sharp noise; sharp blow; line where a thing is broken but not separated; (*sl.*) joke. — *a.* (*colloq.*) first-rate. — *v.* make or cause to make the sound of a crack; break without parting completely; knock sharply; find a solution to (a problem); tell (a joke); (of the voice) become harsh; give way under strain. **crack-brained** *a.* (*colloq.*) crazy. **crack down on** (*colloq.*) take severe measures against. **crack up** (*colloq.*) have a physical or mental breakdown; praise.

crackdown *n.* (*colloq.*) severe measures against something.

cracker *n.* small explosive firework; toy paper tube made to give an explosive crack when pulled apart; thin dry biscuit.

crackers *a.* (*sl.*) crazy.

crackle *v.* make or cause to make a series of light cracking sounds. — *n.* these sounds.

crackling *n.* crisp skin on roast pork.

crackpot *n.* (*sl.*) eccentric person. — *a.* (*sl.*) crazy; unworkable.

cradle *n.* baby's bed usu. on rockers; place where something originates; supporting structure. — *v.* hold or support gently.

craft *n.* skill, technique; occupation requiring this; cunning, deceit; (*pl.* **craft**) ship or boat.

craftsman *n.* (*pl.* **-men**) workman skilled in a craft. **craftswoman** *n.fem.* (*pl.* **-women**), **craftsmanship** *n.*

crafty *a.* (**-ier, -iest**) cunning, using underhand methods. **craftily** *adv.*, **craftiness** *n.*

crag *n.* steep or rugged rock.

craggy *a.* (**-ier, -iest**) rugged.

cram *v.* (**crammed**) force into too small a space; overfill thus; study intensively for an examination. **crammer** *n.*

cramp *n.* painful involuntary tightening

of a muscle; metal bar with bent ends for holding masonry together. — *v.* keep within too narrow limits.

crampon *n.* spiked plate worn on boots for climbing on ice.

cranberry *n.* small red acid berry; shrub bearing this.

crane *n.* large wading bird; apparatus for lifting and moving heavy objects. — *v.* stretch (one's neck) to see something. **crane-fly** *n.* long-legged flying insect.

crank [1] *n.* L-shaped part for converting to-and-fro into circular motion. — *v.* turn with a crank. **crankshaft** *n.* shaft turned thus.

crank [2] *n.* person with very strange ideas. **cranky** *a.*

cranny *n.* crevice.

craps *n.pl.* (*US*) gambling game played with a pair of dice.

crash *n.* loud noise of breakage; violent collision; financial collapse. — *v.* make a crash; move with a crash; be or cause to be involved in a crash; (*colloq.*) gatecrash. — *a.* involving intense effort to achieve something rapidly. **crash helmet** padded helmet worn to protect the head in a crash. **crash-land** *v.* land (an aircraft) in emergency, causing damage.

crass *a.* very stupid; insensitive.

crate *n.* packing-case made of wooden slats; (*sl.*) old aircraft or car. — *v.* pack in crate(s).

crater *n.* bowl-shaped cavity.

cravat *n.* short scarf; necktie.

crave *v.* feel an intense longing (for); ask earnestly for.

craven *a.* cowardly.

craving *n.* intense longing.

craw *n.* bird's crop.

crawfish *n.* large spiny sea lobster.

crawl *v.* move on hands and knees or with the body on the ground; move very slowly; (*colloq.*) seek favour by servile behaviour. — *n.* crawling movement or pace; overarm swimming stroke. **crawler** *n.*

crayfish *n.* freshwater shellfish like a small lobster; crawfish.

crayon *n.* stick of coloured wax etc. — *v.* draw or colour with crayon(s).

craze *n.* temporary enthusiasm.

crazy *a.* (**-ier, -iest**) insane; very foolish; (*colloq.*) madly eager. **crazy paving** paving made of irregular pieces. **crazily** *adv.*, **craziness** *n.*

creak *n.* harsh squeak. — *v.* make this sound. **creaky** *a.*

cream *n.* fatty part of milk; its colour, yellowish-white; cream-like substance; best part. — *a.* cream-coloured. — *v.* remove the cream from; beat to a creamy consistency. **cream cheese** soft rich cheese. **cream cracker** crisp unsweetened biscuit. **creamy** *a.*

crease *n.* line made by crushing or pressing; line marking the limit of the bowler's or batsman's position in cricket. — *v.* make a crease in; develop creases.

create *v.* bring into existence; produce by what one does; give a new rank to; (*sl.*) make a fuss. **creation** *n.*, **creative** *a.*, **creativity** *n.*, **creator** *n.*

creature *n.* animal, person.

crèche /kresh/ *n.* day nursery.

credence *n.* belief.

credentials *n.pl.* documents showing that a person is who or what he or she claims to be.

credible *a.* believable. **credibly** *adv.*, **credibility** *n.*

credit *n.* belief that a thing is true; honour for an achievement; system of allowing payment to be deferred; sum at a person's disposal in a bank; entry in an account for a sum received; acknowledgement in a book or film. — *v.* (**credited**) believe; attribute; enter as credit. **credit card** plastic card containing machine-readable magnetic code enabling the holder to make purchases on credit.

creditable *a.* deserving praise. **creditably** *adv.*

creditor *n.* person to whom money is owed.

credulous *a.* too ready to believe things. **credulity** *n.*

creed *n.* set of beliefs or principles.

creek *n.* narrow inlet of water, esp. on a coast; (*US*) tributary.

creep *v.* (**crept**) move with the body close to the ground; move timidly, slowly, or stealthily; develop gradually; (of a plant) grow along the ground or a wall etc.; feel creepy. — *n.* creeping; (*sl.*) unpleasant person; (*pl.*) nervous sensation.

creepy *a.* (**-ier, -iest**) causing an unpleasant shivering sensation.

cremate *v.* burn (a corpse) to ashes. **cremation** *n.*

crematorium *n.* (*pl.* **-ia**) place where corpses are cremated.

crème de menthe /krem də mónth/ peppermint-flavoured liqueur.

crenellated *a.* having battlements.

Creole *n.* descendant of European settlers in the West Indies or South America; their dialect; hybrid language.

creosote *n.* brown oily liquid distilled from coal tar, used as a preservative for wood.

crêpe /krayp/ *n.* fabric with a wrinkled surface.
crept *see* **creep**.
crepuscular *a.* active at twilight.
crescendo /krishéndō/ *adv.* & *n.* (*pl.* **-os**) increasing in loudness.
crescent *n.* narrow curved shape tapering to a point at each end; curved street of houses.
cress *n.* plant with hot-tasting leaves used in salads.
crest *n.* tuft or outgrowth on a bird's or animal's head; plume on a helmet; top of a slope or hill, white top of a large wave; design above a shield on a coat of arms.
crestfallen *a.* disappointed at failure.
cretaceous *a.* chalky.
cretin *n.* (*offensive*) person who is deformed and mentally defective. **cretinous** *a.*
crevasse *n.* deep open crack esp. in a glacier.
crevice *n.* narrow gap in a surface.
crew [1] *see* **crow**.
crew [2] *n.* people working a ship or aircraft; group working together; gang. **crew-cut** *n.* man's closely cropped haircut.
crib *n.* rack for fodder; model of the manger scene at Bethlehem; cot; (*colloq.*) translation for students' use. — *v.* (**cribbed**) copy unfairly.
cribbage *n.* a card game.
crick *n.* painful stiffness in the neck or back.
cricket [1] *n.* outdoor game for two teams of 11 players with ball, bats, and wickets. **cricketer** *n.*
cricket [2] *n.* brown insect resembling a grasshopper.
crime *n.* serious offence, act that breaks a law; illegal acts.
criminal *n.* person guilty of a crime. — *a.* of or involving crime. **criminally** *adv.*, **criminality** *n.*
criminology *n.* study of crime. **criminologist** *n.*
crimp *v.* press into ridges.
crimson *a.* & *n.* deep red.
cringe *v.* cower; behave obsequiously.
crinkle *n.* & *v.* wrinkle.
crinoline *n.* light framework formerly worn to make a long skirt stand out.
cripple *n.* lame person. — *v.* make lame; weaken seriously.
crisis *n.* (*pl.* **crises**) decisive moment; time of acute difficulty.
crisp *a.* brittle; slightly stiff; cold and bracing; brisk and decisive. — *n.* thin slice of potato fried crisp. **crisply** *adv.*, **crispness** *n.*, **crispy** *a.*
criss-cross *n.* pattern of crossing lines. — *a.* & *adv.* in this pattern. — *v.* mark, form, or move thus, intersect.
criterion *n.* (*pl.* **-ia**) standard of judgement.
critic *n.* person who points out faults; one skilled in criticism.
critical *a.* looking for faults; expressing criticism; of or at a crisis. **critically** *adv.*
criticism *n.* pointing out of faults; judging of merit, esp. of literary or artistic work.
criticize *v.* express criticism of.
critique *n.* critical essay.
croak *n.* deep hoarse cry or sound like that of a frog. — *v.* utter or speak with a croak; (*sl.*) die, kill.
crochet /krṓshay/ *n.* handiwork done with a thread and a hooked needle. — *v.* make by or do such work.
crock [1] *n.* earthenware pot; broken piece of this.
crock [2] *n.* (*colloq.*) person who is disabled or ill; worn-out vehicle etc.
crockery *n.* household china.
crocodile *n.* large amphibious tropical reptile. **crocodile tears** pretence of sorrow.
crocus *n.* (*pl.* **-uses**) spring-flowering plant growing from a corm.
croft *n.* small rented farm in Scotland.
crofter *n.* tenant of a croft.
croissant /krwússon/ *n.* rich crescent-shaped roll.
crone *n.* withered old woman.
crony *n.* close friend or companion.
crook *n.* hooked stick; bent thing; (*colloq.*) criminal. — *v.* bend.
crooked *a.* not straight; dishonest. **crookedly** *adv.*
croon *v.* sing softly. **crooner** *n.*
crop *n.* batch of plants grown for their produce; harvest from this; group or amount produced at one time; pouch in a bird's gullet where food is broken up for digestion; whip-handle; very short haircut. — *v.* (**cropped**) cut or bite off; produce or gather as harvest. **crop up** occur unexpectedly.
cropper *n.* (*sl.*) heavy fall.
croquet /krṓkay/ *n.* game played on a lawn with balls and mallets.
croquette /krəkét/ *n.* fried ball or roll of potato, meat, or fish.
cross *n.* mark made by drawing one line across another; thing shaped like this; stake with a transverse bar used in crucifixion; affliction to be borne with Christian patience; hybrid animal or plant; mixture of or compromise between two things; crossing shot in football etc. — *v.* go or extend across; draw line(s) across, mark (a cheque) thus so that it must be paid into a bank; oppose the wishes of; cause to interbreed. — *a.*

passing from side to side; reciprocal; showing bad temper. **at cross purposes** misunderstanding or conflicting. **crossly** *adv.*, **crossness** *n.*

crossbar *n.* horizontal bar.

crossbow *n.* mechanical bow fixed across a wooden stock.

cross-bred *a.* produced by interbreeding. **cross-breed** *n.* cross-bred animal. **cross-breeding** *n.*

cross-check *v.* check again by a different method.

cross-examine *v.* cross-question, esp. in a law court. **cross-examination** *n.*

cross-eyed *a.* squinting.

crossfire *n.* gunfire crossing another line of fire.

crossing *n.* journey across water; place where things cross; place for pedestrians to cross a road.

crosspatch *n.* (*colloq.*) bad-tempered person.

cross-ply *a.* (of a tyre) having fabric layers with cords lying crosswise.

cross-reference *n.* reference to another place in the same book.

crossroads *n.* place where roads intersect.

cross-section *n.* diagram showing internal structure; representative sample.

crosswise *adv.* in the form of a cross.

crossword *n.* puzzle in which intersecting words have to be inserted into a diagram.

crotch *n.* place where things fork, esp. where legs join the trunk.

crotchet *n.* note in music, half a minim.

crotchety *a.* peevish. **crotchetiness** *n.*

crouch *v.* stoop low with legs tightly bent. — *n.* this position.

croupier /kroo͞piər/ *n.* person who rakes in stakes and pays out winnings at a gaming table.

croûton /kroo͞ton/ *n.* small piece of fried or toasted bread.

crow *n.* large black bird; crowing cry or sound. — *v.* utter a cock's cry (**crew**); exult.

crowbar *n.* bar of iron, usually with a bent end, used as a lever.

crowd *n.* large group. — *v.* come together in a crowd; fill or occupy fully.

crown *n.* monarch's ceremonial headdress, usu. a circlet of gold; top part of a head, hat, or arched thing. **the Crown** supreme governing power in a monarchy. — *v.* place a crown on; form or cover the top part of; be a climax to; (*sl.*) hit on the head. **Crown prince** *or* **princess** heir to a throne.

crucial *a.* very important, decisive. **crucially** *adv.*

crucible *n.* pot in which metals are melted.

crucifix *n.* model of the Cross or of Christ on this.

crucifixion *n.* crucifying; **the Crucifixion** that of Christ.

cruciform *a.* cross-shaped.

crucify *v.* put to death by nailing or binding to a transverse bar; cause extreme pain to.

crude *a.* in a natural or raw state; not well finished: lacking good manners, vulgar. **crudely** *adv.*, **crudity** *n.*

cruel *a.* (**crueller, cruellest**) feeling pleasure in another's suffering; hard-hearted; causing suffering. **cruelly** *adv.*, **cruelty** *n.*

cruet *n.* set of containers for oil, vinegar, and salt at the table.

cruise *v.* sail for pleasure or on patrol; travel at a moderate economical speed. — *n.* cruising voyage.

cruiser *n.* fast warship; motor boat with a cabin.

crumb *n.* small fragment of bread etc.

crumble *v.* break into small fragments. — *n.* pudding of fruit with crumbly topping.

crumbly *a.* easily crumbled.

crummy *a.* (**-ier, -iest**) (*sl.*) dirty, squalid; inferior.

crumpet *n.* flat soft yeast cake eaten toasted.

crumple *v.* crush or become crushed into creases; collapse.

crunch *v.* crush noisily with the teeth; make this sound. — *n.* sound of crunching; decisive event.

crunchy *a.* able to be crunched.

crupper *n.* strap looped under a horse's tail from the saddle.

crusade *n.* medieval Christian military expedition to recover the Holy Land from Muslims; campaign against an evil. — *v.* take part in a crusade. **crusader** *n.*

crush *v.* press so as to break or injure or wrinkle; pound into fragments; defeat or subdue completely. — *n.* crowded mass of people; (*colloq.*) infatuation.

crust *n.* hard outer layer, esp. of bread.

crustacean *n.* animal with a hard shell (e.g. lobster).

crusty *a.* (**-ier, -iest**) with a crisp crust; having a harsh manner.

crutch *n.* support for a lame person; crotch.

crux *n.* (*pl.* **cruces**) vital part of a problem; difficult point.

cry *n.* loud wordless sound uttered; appeal; rallying call; spell of weeping. — *v.* shed tears; call loudly; appeal for help.

cryogenics *n.* branch of physics dealing

with very low temperatures. **cryogenic** *a.*

crypt *n.* room below the floor of a church.

cryptic *a.* concealing its meaning in a puzzling way.

cryptogram *n.* thing written in cipher.

cryptography *n.* study of ciphers. **cryptographer** *n.*

crystal *a.* glass-like mineral; high-quality glass; symmetrical piece of a solidified substance.

crystalline *a.* like or made of crystal; clear.

crystallize *v.* form into crystals; make or become definite in form. **crystallization** *n.*

cub *n.* young of certain animals.

cubby hole small compartment.

cube *n.* solid object with six equal square sides; product of a number multiplied by itself twice. **cube root** number which produces a given number when cubed.

cubic *a.* of three dimensions.

cubicle *n.* small division of a large room, screened for privacy.

cubism *n.* style of painting in which objects are shown as geometrical shapes. **cubist** *n.*

cuckold *n.* man whose wife commits adultery. — *v.* make a cuckold of.

cuckoo *n.* bird with a call that is like its name.

cucumber *n.* long green-skinned fruit eaten as salad.

cud *n.* food that cattle bring back from the stomach into the mouth and chew again.

cuddle *v.* hug lovingly; nestle. — *n.* gentle hug. **cuddlesome, cuddly** *adjs.* pleasant to cuddle.

cudgel *n.* short thick stick used as a weapon. — *v.* **(cudgelled)** beat with a cudgel.

cue [1] *n.* & *v.* **(cueing)** signal to do something.

cue [2] *n.* long rod for striking balls in billiards etc. — *v.* strike with a cue.

cuff *n.* band of cloth round the edge of a sleeve; blow with the open hand. — *v.* strike with the open hand. **cuff link** device of two linked discs etc. to hold cuff edges together.

cuisine /kwizeén/ *n.* style of cooking.

cul-de-sac *n.* (*pl.* **culs-de-sac**) street closed at one end.

culinary *a.* of, for, or used in cooking.

cull *v.* pick (flowers); select; select and kill (surplus animals).

culminate *v.* reach its highest point or degree. **culmination** *n.*

culottes *n.pl.* women's trousers styled to resemble a skirt.

culpable *a.* deserving blame. **culpably** *adv.*, **culpability** *n.*

culprit *n.* person who has committed a slight offence.

cult *n.* system of religious worship; excessive admiration of a person or thing.

cultivate *v.* prepare and use (land) for crops; produce (crops) by tending them; develop by practice; further one's acquaintance with (a person). **cultivation** *n.*, **cultivator** *n.*

culture *n.* developed understanding of literature, art, music, etc.; type of civilization; artificial rearing of bacteria; bacteria grown for study. — *v.* grow in artificial conditions. **cultural** *a.*, **culturally** *adv.*

culvert *n.* drain under a road.

cumbersome *a.* clumsy to carry or use.

cumin *n.* plant with aromatic seed.

cummerbund *n.* sash for the waist.

cumulative *a.* increasing by additions. **cumulatively** *adv.*

cumulus *n.* (*pl.* **-li**) cloud in heaped-up rounded masses.

cuneiform *n.* ancient writing done in wedge-shaped strokes cut into stone etc.

cunning *a.* skilled at deception, crafty; ingenious. — *n.* craftiness, ingenuity. **cunningly** *adv.*

cup *n.* drinking vessel usu. with a handle at the side; prize; wine or fruit juice with added flavourings. — *v.* **(cupped)** form into a cup-like shape. **cupful** *n.* (*pl.* **cupfuls**).

cupboard *n.* recess or piece of furniture with a door, in which things may be stored.

cupidity *n.* greed for gain.

cupola *n.* small dome.

cupreous *a.* of or like copper.

cur *n.* worthless dog.

curacy *n.* position of curate.

curare /kyooraári/ *n.* vegetable poison that induces paralysis.

curate *n.* member of the clergy who assists a parish priest.

curator *n.* person in charge of a museum or other collection.

curb *n.* means of restraint. — *v.* restrain.

curds *n.pl.* thick soft substance formed when milk turns sour.

curdle *v.* form or cause to form curds.

cure *v.* restore to health; get rid of (a disease or trouble etc.); preserve by salting, drying, etc. — *n.* curing; substance or treatment that cures disease etc.

curette *n.* surgical scraping instrument. **curettage** *n.*

curfew *n.* signal or time after which people must stay indoors.
curio *n.* (*pl.* **-os**) unusual and therefore interesting object.
curiosity *n.* desire to find out and know things; curio.
curious *a.* eager to learn or know something; strange, unusual. **curiously** *adv.*, **curiousness** *n.*
curl *v.* curve, esp. in a spiral shape or course. — *n.* curled thing or shape; coiled lock of hair.
curler *n.* device for curling hair.
curlew *n.* wading bird with a long curved bill.
curling *n.* game like bowls played on ice.
curly *a.* (**-ier, -iest**) full of curls.
curmudgeon *n.* bad-tempered old man.
currant *n.* dried grape used in cookery; small round edible berry, shrub producing this.
currency *n.* money in use; state of being widely known.
current *a.* belonging to the present time; in general use. — *n.* body of water or air moving in one direction; flow of electricity. **currently** *adv.*
curriculum *n.* (*pl.* **-la**) course of study. **curriculum vitae** brief account of one's career.
curry [1] *n.* seasoning made with hot-tasting spices; dish flavoured with this.
curry [2] *v.* groom (a horse) with a **curry-comb**, a pad with rubber or plastic projections. **curry favour** win favour by flattery.
curse *n.* call for evil to come on a person or thing; a great evil; violent exclamation of anger. — *v.* utter a curse (against); afflict. **cursed** *a.*
cursive *a.* & *n.* (writing) done with joined letters.
cursor *n.* movable indicator on a VDU screen.
cursory *a.* hasty and not thorough. **cursorily** *adv.*
curt *a.* noticeably or rudely brief. **curtly** *adv.*, **curtness** *n.*
curtail *v.* cut short, reduce. **curtailment** *n.*
curtain *n.* piece of cloth hung as a screen, esp. at a window.
curtsy *n.* movement of respect made by bending the knees. — *v.* make a curtsy.
curvaceous *a.* (*colloq.*) having a shapely curved figure.
curvature *n.* curving; curved form.
curve *n.* line or surface with no part straight or flat. — *v.* form (into) a curve.
cushion *n.* stuffed bag used as a pad, esp. for leaning against; padded part; body of air supporting a hovercraft. — *v.* protect with a pad; lessen the impact of.
cushy *a.* (**-ier, -iest**) (*colloq.*) pleasant and easy.
cusp *n.* pointed part where curves meet.
cuss *n.* (*colloq.*) curse; perverse person. **cussed** *a.* perverse.
custard *n.* sauce made with milk and eggs or flavoured cornflour.
custodian *n.* guardian, keeper.
custody *n.* imprisonment.
custom *n.* usual way of behaving or acting; regular dealing by customer(s); (*pl.*) duty on imported goods.
customary *a.* usual. **customarily** *adv.*
customer *n.* person buying goods or services from a shop etc.
cut *v.* (**cut, cutting**) divide, wound, or shape by pressure of a sharp edge; reduce; intersect; divide (a pack of cards); have (a tooth) coming through the gum. — *n.* wound or mark made by a sharp edge; piece cut off; style of cutting; hurtful remark; reduction; (*sl.*) share.
cute *a.* (*colloq.*) sharp-witted; ingenious; (*US*) pleasing, quaint. **cutely** *adv.*, **cuteness** *n.*
cuticle *n.* skin at the base of a nail.
cutlass *n.* short curved sword.
cutler *n.* maker of cutlery.
cutlery *n.* table knives, forks, and spoons.
cutlet *n.* neck-chop; mince cooked in this shape; thin piece of veal.
cut-throat *a.* merciless. — *n.* murderer.
cutting *a.* (of remarks) hurtful. — *n.* passage cut through high ground for a railway etc.; piece of a plant for replanting.
cuttlefish *n.* sea creature that ejects black fluid when attacked.
cyanide *n.* a strong poison.
cybernetics *n.* science of systems of control and communication in animals and machines.
cyclamen *n.* plant with petals that turn back.
cycle *n.* recurring series of events; bicycle, motor cycle. — *v.* ride a bicycle. **cyclist** *n.*
cyclic, cyclical *adjs.* happening in cycles. **cyclically** *adv.*
cyclone *n.* violent wind rotating round a central area. **cyclonic** *a.*
cyclotron *n.* apparatus for accelerating charged particles in a spiral path.
cygnet *n.* young swan.
cylinder *n.* object with straight sides and circular ends. **cylindrical** *a.*, **cylindrically** *adv.*
cymbal *n.* brass plate struck with another or with a stick as a percussion instrument.

cynic *n.* person who believes people's motives are usually bad or selfish. **cynical** *a.*, **cynically** *adv.*, **cynicism** *n.*

cypress *n.* evergreen tree with dark feathery leaves.

cyst *n.* sac of fluid or soft matter on or in the body.

cystic *a.* of the bladder or gall-bladder. **cystic fibrosis** disease affecting the exocrine glands, usu. resulting in respiratory infections.

cystitis *n.* inflammation of the bladder.

cytology *n.* study of biological cells. **cytological** *a.*

D

dab [1] *n.* quick light blow or pressure. — *v.* (**dabbed**) strike or press lightly or feebly.

dab [2] *n.* a kind of small flatfish.

dabble *v.* splash about gently or playfully; work at something in an amateur way.

dace *n.* (*pl.* **dace**) small freshwater fish.

dachshund *n.* small dog with a long body and short legs.

dad *n.* (*colloq.*) father.

daddy *n.* (*children's use*) father.

daddy-long-legs *n.* crane-fly.

daffodil *n.* yellow flower with a trumpet-shaped central part.

daft *a.* silly, crazy.

dagger *n.* short pointed two-edged weapon used for stabbing.

dago *n.* (*pl.* **-oes**) (*sl., offensive*) person from southern Europe.

dahlia *n.* garden plant with bright flowers.

daily *a.* happening or appearing on every day or every weekday. — *adv.* once a day. — *n.* daily newspaper; (*colloq.*) charwoman.

dainty *a.* (**-ier, -iest**) small and pretty; fastidious. **daintily** *adv.*, **daintiness** *n.*

daiquiri /dákkəri/ *n.* cocktail of rum and lime juice.

dairy *n.* place where milk and its products are processed or sold.

dais /dáyiss/ *n.* low platform, esp. at the end of a hall.

daisy *n.* flower with many petal-like rays. **daisy wheel** printing device with radiating spokes.

dale *n.* valley.

dally *v.* idle, dawdle; flirt. **dalliance** *n.*

Dalmatian *n.* large white dog with dark spots.

dam [1] *n.* barrier built across a river to hold back water. — *v.* (**dammed**) hold back with a dam; obstruct (a flow).

dam [2] *n.* mother of an animal.

damage *n.* something done that reduces the value or usefulness of the thing affected or spoils its appearance; (*pl.*) money as compensation for injury. — *v.* cause damage to.

damask *n.* fabric woven with a pattern visible on either side.

dame *n.* (*US sl.*) woman; **Dame** title of a woman with an order of knighthood.

damn /dam/ *v.* condemn to hell; condemn as a failure; swear at. — *int.* & *n.* uttered curse. — *a.* & *adv.* damned.

damnable *a.* hateful, annoying. **damnably** *adv.*

damnation *n.* eternal punishment in hell. — *int.* exclamation of annoyance.

damp *n.* moisture. — *a.* slightly wet. — *v.* make damp; discourage; stop the vibration of. **dampness** *n.*

dampen *v.* make or become damp.

damper *n.* plate controlling the draught in a flue; depressing influence; pad that damps the vibration of a piano string.

damsel *n.* (*old use*) young woman.

damson *n.* small purple plum.

dance *v.* move with rhythmical steps and gestures, usu. to music; move in a quick or lively way. — *n.* piece of dancing, music for this; social gathering for dancing. **dance attendance on** follow about and help dutifully. **dancer** *n.*

dandelion *n.* wild plant with bright yellow flowers.

dandified *a.* like a dandy.

dandle *v.* dance or nurse (a child) in one's arms.

dandruff *n.* scurf from the scalp.

dandy *n.* man who pays excessive attention to his appearance. **dandyism** *n.*

Dane *n.* native or inhabitant of Denmark.

danger *n.* likelihood of harm or death; thing causing this.

dangerous *a.* causing danger, not safe. **dangerously** *adv.*

dangle *v.* hang or swing loosely; hold out temptingly. **dangler** *n.*, **dangly** *a.*

Danish *a.* & *n.* (language) of Denmark.

dank *a.* damp and cold. **dankly** *adv.*, **dankness** *n.*

dapper *a.* neat and smart.

dapple *v.* mark with patches of colour or shade. **dapple-grey** *a.* grey with darker markings.

dare *v.* be bold enough (to do something); challenge to do something risky. — *n.* this challenge.

daredevil *a.* & *n.* recklessly daring (person).

daring *a.* bold. — *n.* boldness.

dark *a.* with little or no light; closer to black than to white; having dark hair or skin; gloomy; secret; mysterious. — *n.* absence of light; time of darkness, night. **dark horse** competitor of whom little is known. **darkroom** *n.* darkened room for processing photographs. **darkly** *adv.*, **darkness** *n.*

darken *v.* make or become dark.

darling *n.* & *a.* loved or lovable (person or thing); favourite.

darn *v.* mend by weaving thread across a hole. — *n.* place darned.

dart *n.* small pointed missile, esp. for throwing at the target in the game of **darts**; darting movement; tapering tuck. — *v.* run suddenly; send out (a glance etc.) rapidly. **darter** *n.*

dartboard *n.* target in the game of darts.

dash *v.* run rapidly, rush; knock or throw forcefully against something; destroy (hopes). — *n.* rapid run, rush; small amount of liquid or flavouring added; dashboard; vigour; punctuation mark — showing a break in the sense.

dashboard *n.* instrument panel of a motor vehicle.

dashing *a.* spirited, showy.

dastardly *a.* contemptible.

data *n.pl.* facts on which a decision is to be based; facts to be processed by computer.

data bank large store of computerized data.

database *n.* organized store of computerized data.

date [1] *n.* day, month, or year of a thing's occurrence; period to which a thing belongs; (*colloq.*) appointment to meet socially; (*colloq.*) person to be met thus. — *v.* mark with a date; assign a date to; originate from a particular date; become out of date; (*colloq.*) make a social appointment (with). **to date** until now.

date [2] *n.* small brown edible fruit. **date palm** tree bearing this.

datum *n.* (*pl.* **data**) item of data.

daub *v.* smear roughly. — *n.* clumsily painted picture; smear.

daughter *n.* female in relation to her parents. **daughter-in-law** *n.* (*pl.* **daughters-in-law**) son's wife.

daunt *v.* dismay or discourage.

dauntless *a.* brave, not daunted.

dauphin *n.* title of the eldest son of former kings of France.

davit *n.* small crane on a ship.

dawdle *v.* walk slowly and idly, take one's time. **dawdler** *n.*

dawn *n.* first light of day; beginning. — *v.* begin to grow light; become apparent. **dawning** *n.*

day *n.* time while the sun is above the horizon; period of 24 hours; hours given to work during a day; specified day; time, period.

daybreak *n.* first light of day.

daydream *n.* pleasant idle thoughts. — *v.* have daydreams.

daze *v.* cause to feel stunned or bewildered. — *n.* dazed state.

dazzle *v.* blind temporarily with bright light; impress with splendour. **dazzlement** *n.*

de- *pref.* implying removal or reversal.

deacon *n.* member of the clergy ranking below priest; layman attending to church business in Nonconformist churches.

dead *a.* no longer alive; no longer used; without brightness or resonance or warmth; dull; exact. — *adv.* completely, exactly. **dead beat** tired out. **dead end** road closed at one end. **dead heat** race in which two or more competitors finish exactly even. **dead letter** law or rule no longer observed.

deaden *v.* deprive of or lose vitality, loudness, feeling, etc.

deadline *n.* time limit.

deadlock *n.* state when no progress can be made. — *v.* reach this.

deadly *a.* (**-ier, -iest**) causing death or serious damage; death-like; very dreary. — *adv.* as if dead; extremely. **deadly nightshade** plant with poisonous black berries. **deadliness** *n.*

deadpan *a.* expressionless.

deaf *a.* wholly or partly unable to hear; refusing to listen. **deafness** *n.*

deafen *v.* make unable to hear by a very loud noise.

deal [1] *n.* fir or pine timber.

deal [2] *v.* (**dealt**) distribute; hand out (cards) to players in a card game; give, inflict; do business; trade. — *n.* player's turn to deal; business transaction; (*colloq.*) large amount. **deal with** take action about; be about or concerned with.

dealer *n.* person who deals; trader.

dean *n.* clergyman who is head of a cathedral chapter; university official.

deanery *n.* dean's position or residence.

dear *a.* much loved, cherished; expensive. — *n.* dear person. — *int.* exclamation of surprise or distress. **dearly** *adv.*, **dearness** *n.*

dearth *n.* scarcity, lack.

death *n.* process of dying, end of life; state of being dead; ending; destruction. **death duty** tax levied on property after the owner's death. **death trap** very dangerous place. **death-watch beetle** beetle whose larvae bore into wood and make a ticking sound.

deathly *a.* (**-ier, -iest**) like death.

debacle /daybaak'l/ *n.* general collapse.

debar *v.* (**debarred**) exclude.

debase *v.* lower in quality or value. **debasement** *n.*

debatable *a.* questionable.
debate *n.* formal discussion. — *v.* hold a debate about, consider.
debauchery over-indulgence in harmful or immoral pleasures.
debilitate *v.* weaken. **debilitation** *n.*
debility *n.* weakness of health.
debit *n.* entry in an account for a sum owing. — *v.* (**debited**) enter as a debit, charge. **direct debit** instruction allowing an organization to take regular payments from one's bank account.
debonair *a.* having a carefree self-confident manner.
debouch *v.* come out from a narrow into an open area.
debrief *v.* question to obtain facts about a completed mission.
debris /débree/ *n.* scattered broken pieces or rubbish.
debt /det/ *n.* something owed. **in debt** owing something.
debtor *n.* person who owes money.
debug *v.* (**debugged**) remove bugs from.
debunk *v.* (*colloq.*) show up as exaggerated or false.
debut /dáy-byoo/ *n.* first public appearance.
deca- *pref.* ten.
decade *n.* ten-year period.
decadent *a.* in a state of moral deterioration. **decadence** *n.*
decaffeinated *a.* with caffeine removed or reduced.
decagon *n.* geometric figure with ten sides. **decagonal** *a.*
Decalogue *n.* the Ten Commandments.
decamp *v.* go away suddenly or secretly.
decant *v.* pour (liquid) into another container, leaving sediment behind.
decanter *n.* bottle into which wine may be decanted before serving.
decapitate *v.* behead. **decapitation** *n.*
decarbonize *v.* remove carbon deposit from (an engine). **decarbonization** *n.*
decathlon *n.* athletic contest involving ten events.
decay *v.* rot; lose quality or strength. — *n.* decaying, rot.
decease *n.* death.
deceased *a.* dead.
deceit *n.* deceiving, deception.
deceitful *a.* intending to deceive. **deceitfully** *adv.*
deceive *v.* cause to believe something that is not true; be sexually unfaithful to. **deceiver** *n.*
decelerate *v.* reduce the speed (of). **deceleration** *n.*
decennial *a.* happening every tenth year; lasting ten years. **decennially** *adv.*
decent *a.* conforming to accepted standards of what is proper; respectable; (*colloq.*) kind, obliging. **decently** *adv.*, **decency** *n.*
decentralize *v.* transfer from central to local control. **decentralization** *n.*
deception *n.* deceiving; a trick.
deceptive *a.* deceiving; misleading. **deceptively** *adv.*
deci- *pref.* one-tenth.
decibel *n.* unit for measuring the relative loudness of sound.
decide *v.* make up one's mind; settle a contest or argument.
decided *a.* having firm opinions; clear, definite. **decidedly** *adv.*
deciduous *a.* shedding its leaves annually.
decimal *a.* reckoned in tens or tenths. — *n.* decimal fraction. **decimal currency** that with each unit 10 or 100 times the value of the one next below it. **decimal fraction** fraction based on powers of ten, shown as figures after a dot. **decimal point** this dot.
decimalize *v.* convert into a decimal. **decimalization** *n.*
decimate *v.* destroy one-tenth of; (*loosely*) destroy a large proportion of. **decimation** *n.*
decipher *v.* make out the meaning of (code, bad handwriting). **decipherment** *n.*
decision *n.* deciding, judgement so reached; ability to decide.
decisive *a.* conclusive; showing decision and firmness. **decisively** *adv.*, **decisiveness** *n.*
deck [1] *n.* floor or storey of a ship or bus. **deckchair** *n.* folding canvas chair.
deck [2] *v.* decorate, dress up.
declaim *v.* speak or say impressively. **declamation** *n.*, **declamatory** *a.*
declare *v.* announce openly or formally; state firmly. **declaration** *n.*, **declaratory** *a.*
declassify *v.* cease to classify as officially secret. **declassification** *n.*
decline *v.* refuse; slope downwards; decrease, lose strength or vigour. — *n.* gradual decrease or loss of strength.
declivity *n.* downward slope.
declutch *v.* disengage the clutch of a motor.
decoct *v.* make a decoction of.
decoction *n.* boiling to extract essence; the essence itself.
decode *v.* put (a coded message) into plain language; make (an electronic signal) intelligible. **decoder** *n.*
decoke *v.* (*colloq.*) decarbonize. — *n.* (*colloq.*) decarbonization.

decompose *v.* (cause to) rot or decay. **decomposition** *n.*

decompress *v.* release from compression; reduce air pressure in. **decompression** *n.*

decongestant *n.* medicinal substance that relieves congestion.

decontaminate *v.* rid of contamination. **decontamination** *n.*

decor *n.* style of decoration used in a room.

decorate *v.* make look attractive by adding objects or details; paint or paper the walls of; confer a medal or award on. **decoration** *n.*

decorative *a.* ornamental. **decoratively** *adv.*

decorator *n.* person who paints and papers rooms etc. professionally.

decorous *a.* polite and well-behaved, decent. **decorously** *adv.*

decorum *n.* correctness and dignity of behaviour.

decoy *n.* person or animal used to lure others into danger. — *v.* lure by a decoy.

decrease *v.* make or become smaller or fewer. — *n.* decreasing; amount of this.

decree *n.* order given by a government or other authority. — *v.* (**decreed**) order by decree.

decrepit *a.* made weak by age or use; dilapidated. **decrepitude** *n.*

decry *v.* disparage.

dedicate *v.* devote to a person, use, or cause. **dedication** *n.*

deduce *v.* arrive at (knowledge) by reasoning. **deducible** *a.*

deduct *v.* subtract.

deduction *n.* deducting; thing deducted; deducing; conclusion deduced.

deductive *a.* based on reasoning.

deed *n.* thing done, act; legal document.

deem *v.* consider to be.

deep *a.* going or situated far down or in; intense; low-pitched; absorbed; profound. **deeply** *adv.*, **deepness** *n.*

deepen *v.* make or become deeper.

deer *n.* (*pl.* **deer**) hoofed animal, male of which usu. has antlers.

deerstalker *n.* cloth cap with a peak in front and at the back.

deface *v.* spoil or damage the surface of. **defacement** *n.*

de facto existing in fact.

defamatory *a.* defaming.

defame *v.* attack the good reputation of. **defamation** *n.*

default *v.* fail to fulfil one's obligations or to appear. — *n.* this failure. **defaulter** *n.*

defeat *v.* win victory over; cause to fail. — *n.* defeating; being defeated.

defeatist *n.* person who pessimistically expects or accepts defeat. **defeatism** *n.*

defecate *v.* discharge faeces from the body. **defecation** *n.*

defect [1] /deéfekt/ *n.* deficiency, imperfection.

defect [2] /difékt/ *v.* desert one's country or cause. **defection** *n.*, **defector** *n.*

defective *a.* having defect(s); incomplete. **defectively** *adv.*, **defectiveness** *n.*

defence *n.* defending; protection; arguments against an accusation.

defenceless *a.* having no defences. **defencelessness** *n.*

defend *v.* protect from attack; uphold by argument; represent (the defendant). **defender** *n.*

defendant *n.* person accused or sued in a lawsuit.

defensible *a.* able to be defended. **defensibility** *n.*, **defensibly** *adv.*

defensive *a.* intended for defence; in an attitude of defence. **defensively** *adv.*, **defensiveness** *n.*

defer [1] *v.* (**deferred**) postpone. **deferment** *n.*, **deferral** *n.*

defer [2] *v.* (**deferred**) yield to a person's wishes or authority.

deference *n.* polite respect. **deferential** *a.*, **deferentially** *adv.*

defiance *n.* defying; open disobedience. **defiant** *a.*, **defiantly** *adv.*

deficiency *n.* lack, shortage; thing or amount lacking.

deficient *a.* not having enough; insufficient, lacking.

deficit *n.* amount by which a total falls short of what is required.

defile [1] *v.* make dirty, pollute.

defile [2] *n.* narrow pass or gorge.

define *v.* state or explain precisely; mark the boundary of.

definite *a.* unmistakable, clearly defined; certain. **definitely** *adv.*

definition *n.* statement of precise meaning; making or being distinct, clearness of outline.

definitive *a.* finally fixing or settling something; most authoritative. **definitively** *adv.*

deflate *v.* (cause to) collapse through release of air. **deflation** *n.*

deflect *v.* turn aside. **deflection** *n.*, **deflector** *n.*

defoliate *v.* remove the leaves of. **defoliant** *n.*, **defoliation** *n.*

deforest *v.* clear of trees. **deforestation** *n.*

deform *v.* spoil the shape of. **deformation** *n.*

deformity *n.* abnormality of shape, esp. of a part of the body.

defraud *v.* deprive by fraud.

defray *v.* provide money to pay (costs). **defrayal** *n.*

defrost *v.* thaw.

deft *a.* skilful, handling things neatly. **deftly** *adv.*

defunct *a.* dead; no longer existing or functioning.

defuse *v.* remove the fuse from (an explosive); reduce the dangerous tension in (a situation).

defy *v.* resist; refuse to obey; challenge to do something.

degenerate *v.* /dijénnərayt/ become worse. — *a.* /dijénnərət/ having degenerated. **degeneration** *n.*, **degeneracy** *n.*

degrade *v.* reduce to a lower rank; humiliate; decompose. **degradation** *n.*

degree *n.* stage in a series or of intensity; academic award for proficiency; unit of measurement for angles or temperature.

dehumanize *v.* remove human qualities from; make impersonal. **dehumanization** *n.*

dehydrate *v.* dry; lose moisture. **dehydration** *n.*, **dehydrator** *n.*

de-ice *v.* free from ice. **de-icer** *n.*

deify *v.* treat as a god. **deification** *n.*

deign *v.* condescend.

deity *n.* god, goddess.

déjà vu /dáyzhaa vóō/ feeling of having experienced the present situation before.

dejected *a.* in low spirits.

dejection *n.* lowness of spirits.

delay *v.* make or be late; postpone. — *n.* delaying.

delectable *a.* delightful. **delectably** *adv.*

delectation *n.* enjoyment.

delegate *n.* /délligət/ representative. — *v.* /délligayt/ entrust (a task or power) to an agent.

delegation *n.* delegating; group of representatives.

delete *v.* strike out (a word etc.). **deletion** *n.*

deleterious *a.* harmful.

deliberate [1] /dilíbbərət/ *a.* intentional; slow and careful. **deliberately** *adv.*

deliberate [2] /dilíbbərayt/ *v.* think over or discuss carefully.

deliberation *n.* deliberating; being deliberate.

delicacy *n.* being delicate; choice food.

delicate *a.* exquisite; not robust or strong; requiring or using tact. **delicately** *adv.*

delicatessen *n.* shop selling prepared delicacies.

delicious *a.* delightful, esp. to taste or smell. **deliciously** *adv.*

delight *n.* great pleasure; thing giving this. — *v.* please greatly; feel delight. **delightful** *a.*, **delightfully** *adv.*

delimit *v.* determine the limits or boundaries of. **delimitation** *n.*

delineate *v.* outline. **delineation** *n.*, **delineator** *n.*

delinquent *a.* & *n.* (person) guilty of persistent law-breaking. **delinquency** *n.*

delirium *n.* disordered state of mind, esp. during fever; wild excitement. **delirious** *a.*, **deliriously** *adv.*

deliver *v.* take to an addressee or purchaser; hand over; utter; aim (a blow or attack); rescue, set free; assist in the birth (of). **deliverer** *n.*, **delivery** *n.*

deliverance *n.* rescue, freeing.

dell *n.* small wooded hollow.

delphinium *n.* tall garden plant with usu. blue flowers.

delta *n.* fourth letter of the Greek alphabet, = d; triangular patch of alluvial land at the mouth of a river.

delude *v.* deceive.

deluge *n.* & *v.* flood.

delusion *n.* false belief or impression. **delusional** *a.*

delusive *a.* deceptive, raising false hopes. **delusively** *adv.*, **delusiveness** *n.*

de luxe of superior quality; luxurious.

delve *v.* search deeply.

demagogue *n.* person who wins support by appealing to popular feelings and prejudices. **demagogic** *a.*, **demagogy** *n.*

demand *n.* firm or official request; customers' desire for goods or services; claim. — *v.* make a demand for; need.

demanding *a.* making many demands; requiring great skill or effort.

demarcation *n.* marking of a boundary or limits, esp. of work for different trades.

demean *v.* lower the dignity of.

demeanour *n.* way a person behaves.

demented *a.* driven mad, crazy.

dementia *n.* a type of insanity.

demerara *n.* brown raw cane sugar.

demi- *pref.* half.

demilitarize *v.* remove military forces from. **demilitarization** *n.*

demise *n.* death.

demisemiquaver *n.* note equal to half a semiquaver.

demist *v.* clear mist from (a windscreen etc.). **demister** *n.*

demob *v.* (**demobbed**) (*colloq.*) demobilize. — *n.* (*colloq.*) demobilization.

demobilize *v.* release from military service. **demobilization** *n.*

democracy *n.* government by all the people, usu. through elected representatives; country governed in this way.

democrat *n.* person favouring democracy.
democratic *a.* of or according to democracy. **democratically** *adv.*
demography *n.* statistical study of human populations. **demographic** *a.*
demolish *v.* pull or knock down; destroy. **demolition** *n.*
demon *n.* devil, evil spirit; cruel or forceful person. **demonic** *a.*, **demoniac** *a.*, **demoniacal** *a.*
demonstrable *a.* able to be demonstrated. **demonstrability** *n.*, **demonstrably** *adv.*
demonstrate *v.* show evidence of, prove; show the working of; take part in a public protest. **demonstration** *n.*, **demonstrator** *n.*
demonstrative *a.* showing, proving; showing one's feelings. **demonstratively** *adv.*
demoralize *v.* dishearten. **demoralization** *n.*
demote *v.* reduce to a lower rank or category. **demotion** *n.*
demur *v.* (**demurred**) raise objections. — *n.* objection raised.
demure *a.* quiet and serious or pretending to be so. **demurely** *adv.*, **demureness** *n.*
den *n.* wild animal's lair; person's small private room.
denationalize *v.* privatize. **denationalization** *n.*
denature *v.* change the properties of; make (alcohol) unfit for drinking.
deniable *a.* able to be denied.
denial *n.* denying; statement that a thing is not true.
denier /dényər/ *n.* unit of weight by which the fineness of yarn is measured.
denigrate *v.* blacken the reputation of. **denigration** *n.*
denim *n.* strong twilled fabric; (*pl.*) trousers made of this.
denizen *n.* person or plant living in a specified place.
denominate *v.* name; describe as.
denomination *n.* name, title; specified Church or sect; class of units of measurement or money. **denominational** *a.*
denominator *n.* number below the line in a vulgar fraction.
denote *v.* be the sign, symbol, or name of; indicate. **denotation** *n.*
denouement /daynoomon/ *n.* final outcome of a play or story.
denounce *v.* speak against; inform against.
dense *a.* thick; closely massed; stupid. **densely** *adv.*, **denseness** *n.*
density *n.* denseness; relation of weight to volume.

dent *n.* hollow left by a blow or pressure. — *v.* make or become dented.
dental *a.* of or for teeth; of dentistry.
dentifrice *n.* substance for cleaning teeth.
dentist *n.* person qualified to treat decay and malformations of teeth.
dentistry *n.* dentist's work.
denture *n.* set of artificial teeth.
denude *v.* strip of covering or property. **denudation** *n.*
denunciation *n.* denouncing; a public condemnation.
deny *v.* say that (a thing) is untrue or does not exist; disown; prevent from having.
deodorant *n.* substance that removes or conceals unwanted odours. — *a.* deodorizing.
deodorize *v.* destroy the odour of. **deodorization** *n.*
depart *v.* go away, leave.
department *n.* section of an organization. **department store** large shop selling many kinds of goods. **departmental** *a.*
departure *n.* departing; setting out on a new course of action.
depend *v.* **depend on** be determined by; be unable to do without; trust confidently.
dependable *a.* reliable.
dependant *n.* one who depends on another for support.
dependence *n.* depending.
dependency *n.* dependent State.
dependent *a.* depending; controlled by another.
depict *v.* represent in a picture or in words. **depiction** *n.*
depilatory *a.* & *n.* (substance) removing hair.
deplete *v.* reduce by using quantities of. **depletion** *n.*
deplorable *a.* regrettable; very bad. **deplorably** *adv.*
deplore *v.* find or call deplorable.
deploy *v.* spread out, organize for effective use. **deployment** *n.*
depopulate *v.* reduce the population of. **depopulation** *n.*
deport *v.* remove (a person) from a country. **deportation** *n.*
deportment *n.* behaviour, bearing.
depose *v.* remove from power.
deposit *v.* (**deposited**) put down; leave as a layer of matter; entrust for safe keeping; pay as a deposit. — *n.* something deposited; sum entrusted or left as guarantee. **depositor** *n.*
deposition *n.* deposing; depositing; sworn statement.

depository *n.* storehouse.

depot /déppō/ *n.* storage area, esp. for vehicles; (*US*) bus or railway station.

deprave *v.* make morally bad, corrupt.

depravity *n.* moral corruption, wickedness.

deprecate *v.* express disapproval of; disclaim politely. **deprecation** *n.*, **deprecatory** *a.*

depreciate *v.* make or become lower in value. **depreciation** *n.*

depredation *n.* plundering, destruction.

depress *v.* press down; reduce (trade etc.); make sad. **depressant** *a.* & *n.*

depression *n.* pressing down; state of sadness; long period of inactivity in trading; area of low atmospheric pressure; sunken place. **depressive** *a.*

deprive *v.* prevent from using or enjoying something. **deprivation** *n.*

depth *n.* deepness, measure of this; deepest or most central part. **depth charge** bomb that will explode under water. **in depth** thoroughly. **out of one's depth** in water too deep to stand in.

deputation *n.* body of people sent to represent others.

depute *v.* appoint to act as one's representative.

deputize *v.* act as deputy.

deputy *n.* person appointed to act as a substitute or representative.

derail *v.* cause (a train) to leave the rails. **derailment** *n.*

derange *v.* disrupt; make insane. **derangement** *n.*

derelict *a.* left to fall into ruin.

dereliction *n.* abandonment; neglect (of duty).

deride *v.* scoff at.

derision *n.* scorn, ridicule.

derisive *a.* scornful, showing derision. **derisively** *adv.*

derisory *a.* showing derision; deserving derision.

derivative *a.* & *n.* derived (thing).

derive *v.* obtain from a source; have its origin. **derivation** *n.*

dermatitis *n.* inflammation of the skin.

dermatology *n.* study of the skin and its diseases. **dermatologist** *n.*

derogatory *a.* disparaging.

derrick *n.* crane with pivoted arm; framework over an oil well etc.

derv *n.* fuel for diesel engines.

dervish *n.* member of a Muslim religious order known for their whirling dance.

desalinate *v.* remove salt from (esp. sea water). **desalination** *n.*

descant *n.* treble accompaniment to a main melody.

descend *v.* go or come down; stoop to unworthy behaviour. **be descended from** have as one's ancestor(s).

descendant *n.* person descended from another.

descent *n.* descending; downward route or slope; lineage.

describe *v.* give a description of; mark the outline of.

description *n.* statement of what a person or thing is like; sort.

descriptive *a.* describing.

descry *v.* catch sight of, discern.

desecrate *v.* treat (a sacred thing) irreverently. **desecration** *n.*, **desecrator** *n.*

desegregate *v.* abolish segregation in or of. **desegregation** *n.*

deselect *v.* reject (an already selected candidate). **deselection** *n.*

desert [1] /dézzert/ *n.* & *a.* barren uninhabited often sandy (area).

desert [2] /dizért/ *v.* abandon; leave one's service in the armed forces without permission. **deserter** *n.*, **desertion** *n.*

deserts *n.pl.* what one deserves.

deserve *v.* be worthy of or entitled to. **deservedly** *adv.*

desiccate *v.* dry out moisture from. **desiccation** *n.*

design *n.* drawing that shows how a thing is to be made; general form or arrangement; lines or shapes forming a decoration; mental plan. — *v.* prepare a design for; plan, intend. **designedly** *adv.*, **designer** *n.*

designate *a.* /dézzignət/ appointed but not yet installed. — *v.* /dézzignayt/ name as; specify; appoint to a position. **designation** *n.*

designing *a.* scheming.

desirable *a.* arousing desire, worth desiring. **desirability** *n.*

desire *n.* feeling of wanting something strongly; thing desired. — *v.* feel a desire for.

desirous *a.* desiring.

desist *v.* cease.

desk *n.* piece of furniture for reading or writing at; counter; section of a newspaper office etc.

desolate *a.* lonely; deserted, uninhabited. **desolated** *a.* feeling very distressed. **desolation** *n.*

despair *n.* complete lack of hope. — *v.* feel despair.

desperado *n.* (*pl.* **-oes**) reckless criminal.

desperate *a.* reckless through despair. **desperately** *adv.*, **desperation** *n.*

despicable *a.* contemptible. **despicably** *adv.*

despise *v.* regard as worthless.

despite *prep.* in spite of.

despoil *v.* plunder. **despoilment** *n.*, **despoliation** *n.*

despondent *a.* dejected. **despondently** *adv.*, **despondency** *n.*

despot *n.* dictator. **despotic** *a.*, **despotically** *adv.*, **despotism** *n.*

dessert *n.* sweet course of a meal. **dessertspoon** *n.* medium-sized spoon for eating puddings etc.

destination *n.* place to which a person or thing is going.

destine *v.* settle the future of, set apart for a purpose.

destiny *n.* fate; one's future destined by fate.

destitute *a.* extremely poor; without means to live. **destitution** *n.*

destroy *v.* pull or break down; ruin; kill (an animal). **destruction** *n.*, **destructive** *a.*

destroyer *n.* one who destroys; fast warship.

destruct *v.* (*US*) destroy deliberately.

destructible *a.* able to be destroyed.

desultory *a.* going from one subject to another, not systematic. **desultorily** *adv.*

detach *v.* release or separate. **detachable** *a.*

detached *a.* not joined to another; free from bias or emotion.

detachment *n.* detaching; being detached; military group.

detail *n.* small fact or item; such items collectively; small military detachment. —*v.* relate in detail; assign to special duty.

detain *v.* keep in confinement; cause delay to. **detainment** *n.*

detainee *n.* person detained in custody.

detect *v.* discover the presence of. **detection** *n.*, **detector** *n.*

detective *n.* person whose job is to investigate crimes.

détente /daytóɴt/ *n.* easing of tension between States.

detention *n.* detaining; imprisonment.

deter *v.* (**deterred**) discourage from action. **determent** *n.*

detergent *a.* & *n.* cleansing (substance, esp. other than soap).

deteriorate *v.* become worse. **deterioration** *n.*

determination *n.* firmness of purpose; process of deciding.

determine *v.* decide; calculate precisely; resolve firmly.

determined *a.* full of determination.

deterrent *n.* thing that deters. **deterrence** *n.*

detest *v.* dislike intensely. **detestable** *a.*, **detestation** *n.*

dethrone *v.* remove from a throne. **dethronement** *n.*

detonate *v.* explode. **detonation** *n.*, **detonator** *n.*

detour *n.* deviation from a direct or intended course.

detract *v.* **detract from** reduce the credit that is due to; lessen. **detraction** *n.*

detractor *n.* person who criticizes a thing unfavourably.

detriment *n.* harm. **detrimental** *a.*, **detrimentally** *adv.*

deuterium *n.* heavy form of hydrogen.

Deutschmark /dóychmaark/ *n.* unit of money in Germany.

devalue *v.* reduce the value of. **devaluation** *n.*

devastate *v.* cause great destruction to. **devastation** *n.*

devastating *a.* overwhelming.

develop *v.* (**developed**) make or become larger or more mature or organized; bring or come into existence; make usable or profitable, build on (land); treat (a film) so as to make a picture visible. **developer** *n.*, **development** *n.*

deviant *a.* & *n.* (person or thing) deviating from normal behaviour.

deviate *v.* turn aside from a course of action, truth, etc. **deviation** *n.*

device *n.* thing made or used for a purpose; scheme.

devil *n.* evil spirit (**the Devil** supreme spirit of evil); cruel or annoying person; person of mischievous energy or cleverness; (*colloq.*) difficult person or problem. **devil's advocate** person who tests a proposition by arguing against it. **devilish** *a.*

devilled *a.* cooked with hot spices.

devilment *n.* mischief.

devilry *n.* wickedness; devilment.

devious *a.* indirect; underhand. **deviously** *adv.*, **deviousness** *n.*

devise *v.* plan; invent. **devisor** *n.*

devoid *a.* **devoid of** lacking, free from.

devolution *n.* devolving; delegation of power from central to local administration.

devolve *v.* pass or be passed to a deputy or successor.

devote *v.* give or use for a particular purpose.

devoted *a.* showing devotion.

devotee *n.* enthusiast.

devotion *n.* great love or loyalty; zeal; worship; (esp. *pl.*) prayer(s).

devotional *a.* used in worship.

devour *v.* eat hungrily or greedily; consume; take in avidly. **devourer** *n.*

devout *a.* earnestly religious; earnest, sincere. **devoutly** *adv.*

dew *n.* drops of condensed moisture on a surface.

dewclaw *n.* small claw on the inner side of a dog's leg.

dewlap *n.* fold of loose skin at the throat of cattle etc.

dexterity *n.* skill.

dexterous *a.* (also **dextrous**) skilful. **dexterously** *adv.*

diabetes *n.* disease in which sugar and starch are not properly absorbed by the body. **diabetic** *a.* & *n.*

diabolic *a.* of the Devil.

diabolical *a.* very cruel, wicked, or cunning. **diabolically** *adv.*

diabolism *n.* worship of the Devil.

diaconate *n.* office of deacon; body of deacons. **diaconal** *a.*

diadem *n.* crown.

diagnose *v.* make a diagnosis of.

diagnosis *n.* (*pl.* **-oses**) identification of a disease or condition after observing its signs. **diagnostic** *a.*, **diagnostician** *n.*

diagonal *a.* & *n.* (line) crossing from corner to corner. **diagonally** *adv.*

diagram *n.* drawing that shows the parts or operation of something. **diagrammatic** *a.*, **diagrammatically** *adv.*

dial *n.* face of a clock or watch; similar plate or disc with a movable pointer; movable disc manipulated to connect one telephone with another. — *v.* **(dialled)** select or operate by using a dial or numbered buttons.

dialect *n.* local form of a language. **dialectal** *a.*

dialectic *n.* investigation of truths in philosophy etc. by systematic reasoning. **dialectical** *a.*

dialogue *n.* talk between people.

dialysis *n.* purification of blood by causing it to flow through a suitable membrane.

diamanté /diəmóntay/ *a.* decorated with artificial jewels.

diameter *n.* straight line from side to side through the centre of a circle or sphere; its length.

diametrical *a.* of or along a diameter; (of opposition) direct. **diametrically** *adv.*

diamond *n.* very hard brilliant precious stone; four-sided figure with equal sides and with angles that are not right angles; playing card marked with such shapes. **diamond wedding** 60th anniversary.

diaper *n.* (*US*) baby's nappy.

diaphanous *a.* almost transparent. **diaphanously** *adv.*

diaphragm /dī́əfram/ *n.* a muscular partition between chest and abdomen; contraceptive cap fitting over the cervix.

diarrhoea /dīəréeə/ *n.* condition with frequent fluid faeces.

diary *n.* daily record of events; book for noting these. **diarist** *n.*

diatribe *n.* violent verbal attack.

dibber *n.* tool to make holes in ground for young plants.

dice *n.* (*pl.* **dice**) small cube marked on each side with 1–6 spots, used in games of chance. — *v.* cut into small cubes. **dice with death** take great risks.

dicey *a.* **(-ier, -iest)** (*sl.*) risky; unreliable.

dichotomy /dīkóttəmi/ *n.* division into two parts or kinds.

dicky *a.* **(-ier, -iest)** (*sl.*) shaky, unsound.

dictate *v.* say (words) aloud to be written or recorded; state or order authoritatively; give orders officiously. **dictation** *n.*

dictates *n.pl.* commands.

dictator *n.* ruler with unrestricted authority; domineering person. **dictatorship** *n.*

dictatorial *a.* of or like a dictator. **dictatorially** *adv.*

diction *n.* manner of uttering or pronouncing words.

dictionary *n.* book that lists and explains the words of a language or the topics of a subject.

dictum *n.* (*pl.* **-ta**) formal saying.

did *see* **do**.

didactic *a.* meant or meaning to instruct. **didactically** *adv.*

die [1] *v.* **(dying)** cease to be alive; cease to exist or function; fade away. **be dying to** *or* **for** feel an intense longing to or for.

die [2] *n.* device that stamps a design or that cuts or moulds material into shape.

diehard *n.* very conservative or stubborn person.

diesel *n.* diesel engine; vehicle driven by this. **diesel-electric** *a.* using an electric generator driven by a diesel engine. **diesel engine** oil-burning engine in which ignition is produced by the heat of compressed air.

diet [1] *n.* usual food; restricted selection of food. — *v.* limit one's diet. **dietary** *a.*, **dieter** *n.*

diet [2] *n.* congress, parliamentary assembly in certain countries.

dietetic *a.* of diet and nutrition. **dietetics** *n.* study of diet and nutrition.

dietitian *n.* expert in dietetics.

differ *v.* be unlike; disagree.

difference *n.* being different; amount of this; remainder after subtraction; disagreement.
different *a.* not the same; separate; unusual. **differently** *adv.*
differential *a.* of, showing, or depending on a difference. — *n.* agreed difference in wage-rates; arrangement of gears allowing a vehicle's wheels to revolve at different speeds when cornering.
differentiate *v.* be a difference between; distinguish between; develop differences. **differentiation** *n.*
difficult *a.* needing much effort or skill to do, deal with, or understand; troublesome. **difficulty** *n.*
diffident *a.* lacking self-confidence. **diffidently** *adv.*, **diffidence** *n.*
diffract *v.* break up a beam of light into a series of coloured or dark-and-light bands. **diffraction** *n.*, **diffractive** *a.*
diffuse *a.* /difyo͞oss/ not concentrated. — *v.* /difyo͞oz/ spread widely or thinly. **diffusely** *adv.*, **diffuser** *n.*, **diffusion** *n.*, **diffusive** *a.* **diffusible** *a.*
dig *v.* (**dug, digging**) break up and move soil; make (a way or hole) thus; excavate; find by investigation; poke. — *n.* excavation; poke; cutting remark; (*pl.*, *colloq.*) lodgings.
digest *v.* /dījést/ break down (food) in the body; absorb into the mind. — *n.* /dī́jest/ methodical summary. **digester** *n.*
digestible *a.* able to be digested. **digestibility** *n.*
digestion *n.* process or power of digesting food.
digestive *a.* of or aiding digestion. **digesttive biscuit** wholemeal biscuit.
digger *n.* one who digs; mechanical excavator.
digit *n.* any numeral from 0 to 9; finger or toe.
digital *a.* of or using digits. **digital clock** one that shows the time as a row of figures. **digitally** *adv.*
digitalis *n.* heart stimulant prepared from foxglove leaves.
dignified *a.* showing dignity.
dignify *v.* give dignity to.
dignitary *n.* person holding high rank or position.
dignity *n.* calm and serious manner; high rank or position.
digress *v.* depart from the main subject temporarily. **digression** *n.*, **digressive** *a.*
dike *n.* = dyke.
dilapidated *a.* in disrepair.
dilapidation *n.* dilapidated state.
dilate *v.* make or become wider. **dilation, dilatation** *ns.*, **dilator** *n.*
dilatory /dillətəri/ *a.* delaying, not prompt. **dilatorily** *adv.*, **dilatoriness** *n.*
dilemma *n.* situation in which a choice must be made between unwelcome alternatives.
dilettante /dillitánti/ *n.* person who dabbles in a subject for pleasure.
diligent *a.* working or done with care and effort. **diligently** *adv.*, **diligence** *n.*
dill *n.* herb with spicy seeds.
dilly-dally *v.* (*colloq.*) dawdle; waste time by indecision.
dilute *v.* reduce the strength of (fluid) by adding water etc.; reduce the forcefulness of. **diluter** *n.*, **dilution** *n.*
dim *a.* (**dimmer, dimmest**) lit faintly; indistinct; (*colloq.*) stupid. — *v.* (**dimmed**) make or become dim. **dimly** *adv.*, **dimness** *n.*
dime *n.* 10-cent coin of the USA.
dimension *n.* measurable extent; scope. **dimensional** *a.*
diminish *v.* make or become less.
diminuendo *adv.* & *n.* (*pl.* **-os**) decreasing in loudness.
diminution *n.* decrease.
diminutive *a.* tiny. — *n.* affectionate form of a name.
dimple *n.* small dent, esp. in the skin. — *v.* show dimple(s); produce dimples in.
din *n.* loud annoying noise. — *v.* (**dinned**) force (information) into a person by constant repetition.
dinar /deénaar/ *n.* unit of money in some Balkan and Middle Eastern countries.
dine *v.* eat dinner. **diner** *n.*
ding-dong *n.* sound of clapper bell(s). — *a.* & *adv.* with vigorous action between contestants.
dinghy *n.* small open boat or inflatable rubber boat.
dingle *n.* deep dell.
dingo *n.* (*pl.* **-oes**) Australian wild dog.
dingy *a.* (**-ier, -iest**) dirty-looking. **dingily** *adv.*, **dinginess** *n.*
dining room room in which meals are eaten.
dinky *a.* (**-ier, -iest**) (*colloq.*) attractively small and neat.
dinner *n.* chief meal of the day; formal evening meal. **dinner jacket** man's usu. black jacket for evening wear.
dinosaur *n.* prehistoric reptile.
dint *n.* dent. **by dint of** by means of.
diocese *n.* district under the care of a bishop. **diocesan** *a.*
diode *n.* thermionic valve with two electrodes; semiconductor rectifier with two terminals.

dioptre /dīóptə/ *n.* unit of refractive power of a lens.
dioxide *n.* oxide with two atoms of oxygen to one of a metal or other element.
dip *v.* **(dipped)** plunge briefly into liquid; lower, go downwards. — *n.* dipping; short bathe; liquid or mixture into which something is dipped; downward slope. **dip into** read briefly from (a book).
diphtheria *n.* infectious disease with inflammation of the throat.
diphthong *n.* compound vowel sound (as *ou* in *loud*).
diploma *n.* certificate awarded on completion of a course of study.
diplomacy *n.* handling of international relations; tact.
diplomat *n.* member of the diplomatic service; tactful person.
diplomatic *a.* of or engaged in diplomacy; tactful. **diplomatically** *adv.*
dipper *n.* diving bird; ladle.
dipsomania *n.* uncontrollable craving for alcohol. **dipsomaniac** *n.*
diptych /diptik/ *n.* pair of pictures on two panels hinged together.
dire *a.* dreadful; ominous; extreme and urgent. **direly** *adv.*, **direness** *n.*
direct *a.* straight, not roundabout; with nothing or no one between; straightforward, frank. — *adv.* by a direct route. — *v.* tell how to do something or reach a place; address (a letter etc.); guide; control; command. **directness** *n.*
direction *n.* directing; line along which a thing moves or faces; instruction. **directional** *a.*
directive *n.* general instruction issued by authority.
directly *adv.* in a direct line or manner; very soon. — *conj.* as soon as.
director *n.* supervisor; member of a board directing a business; one who supervises acting and filming. **directorship** *n.*
directorate *n.* office of director; board of directors.
directory *n.* list of telephone subscribers, members, etc.
dirge *n.* song of mourning.
dirigible *n.* airship.
dirk *n.* a kind of dagger.
dirndl *n.* full gathered skirt.
dirt *n.* unclean matter; soil; foul words, scandal.
dirty *a.* **(-ier, -iest)** soiled, not clean; producing pollution; dishonourable; obscene. — *v.* make or become dirty. **dirtily** *adv.*, **dirtiness** *n.*
disability *n.* thing that disables.
disable *v.* deprive of some ability, make unfit. **disabled** *a.* having a physical disability. **disablement** *n.*
disabuse *v.* disillusion.
disadvantage *n.* unfavourable condition. **disadvantaged** *a.*, **disadvantageous** *a.*
disaffected *a.* discontented, no longer feeling loyalty. **disaffection** *n.*
disagree *v.* have a different opinion; fail to agree; quarrel. **disagreement** *n.*
disagreeable *a.* unpleasant; bad-tempered. **disagreeably** *adv.*
disallow *v.* refuse to sanction.
disappear *v.* pass from sight or existence. **disappearance** *n.*
disappoint *v.* fail to do what was desired or expected. **disappointment** *n.*
disapprobation *n.* disapproval.
disapprove *v.* consider bad or immoral. **disapproval** *n.*
disarm *v.* deprive of weapon(s); reduce armed forces; make less hostile.
disarmament *n.* reduction of a country's forces or weapons.
disarrange *v.* put into disorder. **disarrangement** *n.*
disarray *n.* & *v.* disorder.
disaster *n.* sudden great misfortune; great failure. **disastrous** *a.*, **disastrously** *adv.*
disavow *v.* disclaim. **disavowal** *n.*
disband *v.* separate, disperse.
disbelieve *v.* refuse or be unable to believe. **disbelief** *n.*
disburse *v.* pay out (money). **disbursement** *n.*
disc *n.* thin circular plate or layer; record bearing recorded sound; magnetic disk (see *magnetic*). **disc jockey** compère of a disco or broadcast of recorded pop music.
discard *v.* /diskaárd/ reject as useless or unwanted. — *n.* /diskaard/ discarded thing.
discern *v.* perceive with the mind or senses. **discernment** *n.*
discernible *a.* able to be discerned. **discernibly** *adv.*
discerning *a.* perceptive, showing sensitive understanding.
discharge *v.* send or flow out; release; dismiss; pay (a debt), perform (a duty etc.). — *n.* discharging; substance discharged.
disciple *n.* one of the original followers of Christ; person accepting the teachings of another.
disciplinarian *n.* person who enforces strict discipline.
disciplinary *a.* of or for discipline.
discipline *n.* orderly or controlled behaviour; training or control producing this;

branch of learning. — *v.* train to be orderly; punish.

disclaim *v.* disown.

disclaimer *n.* statement disclaiming something.

disclose *v.* reveal. **disclosure** *n.*

disco *n.* (*pl.* **-os**) place where recorded music is played for dancing; equipment for playing this.

discolour *v.* change in colour; stain. **discoloration** *n.*

discomfit *v.* (**discomfited**) disconcert. **discomfiture** *n.*

discomfort *n.* being uncomfortable; thing causing this.

discommode *v.* inconvenience.

disconcert *v.* upset the self-confidence of, fluster.

disconnect *v.* break the connection of; cut off power supply of. **disconnection** *n.*

disconsolate *a.* unhappy, disappointed. **disconsolately** *adv.*

discontent *n.* dissatisfaction. **discontented** *a.*

discontinue *v.* put an end to; cease. **discontinuance** *n.*

discontinuous *a.* not continuous. **discontinuity** *n.*

discord *n.* disagreement, quarrelling; harsh sound. **discordance** *n.*, **discordant** *a.*

discount *n.* /diskownt/ amount of money taken off the full price. — *v.* /diskównt/ disregard partly or wholly.

discourage *v.* dishearten; dissuade (from). **discouragement** *n.*

discourse *n.* /diskorss/ conversation, lecture; treatise. — *v.* /diskórss/ utter or write a discourse.

discourteous *a.* lacking courtesy. **discourteously** *adv.*, **discourtesy** *n.*

discover *v.* obtain sight or knowledge of. **discovery** *n.*

discredit *v.* (**discredited**) damage the reputation of; cause to be disbelieved. — *n.* (thing causing) damage to a reputation.

discreditable *a.* bringing discredit.

discreet *a.* prudent; not giving away secrets; unobtrusive. **discreetly** *adv.*

discrepancy *n.* failure to tally.

discrete *a.* separate, not continuous. **discretely** *adv.*

discretion *n.* being discreet; freedom to decide something.

discretionary *a.* done or used at a person's discretion.

discriminate *v.* make a distinction (between). **discriminate against** treat unfairly. **discriminating** *a.* having good judgement. **discrimination** *n.*, **discriminatory** *a.*

discursive *a.* rambling, not keeping to the main subject.

discus *n.* heavy disc thrown in contests of strength.

discuss *v.* examine by argument, talk or write about. **discussion** *n.*

disdain *v.* & *n.* scorn. **disdainful** *a.*, **disdainfully** *adv.*

disease *n.* unhealthy condition; specific illness. **diseased** *a.*

disembark *v.* put or go ashore. **disembarkation** *n.*

disembodied *a.* (of a voice) apparently not produced by anyone.

disembowel *v.* (**disembowelled**) take out the bowels of. **disembowelment** *n.*

disenchant *v.* free from enchantment, disillusion. **disenchantment** *n.*

disenfranchise *v.* deprive of the right to vote. **disenfranchisement** *n.*

disengage *v.* separate; detach. **disengagement** *n.*

disentangle *v.* free from tangles or confusion; separate. **disentanglement** *n.*

disfavour *n.* dislike, disapproval.

disfigure *v.* spoil the appearance of. **disfigurement** *n.*

disgorge *v.* eject, pour forth. **disgorgement** *n.*

disgrace *n.* (thing causing) loss of respect. — *v.* bring disgrace upon. **disgraceful** *a.*, **disgracefully** *adv.*

disgruntled *a.* discontented, resentful. **disgruntlement** *n.*

disguise *v.* conceal the identity of. — *n.* disguising, disguised condition; thing that disguises.

disgust *n.* strong dislike. — *v.* cause disgust in. **disgusting** *a.*

dish *n.* shallow bowl, esp. for food; food prepared for the table. — *v.* **dish out** (*colloq.*) distribute. **dish up** serve out food.

disharmony *n.* lack of harmony.

dishearten *v.* cause to lose hope or confidence.

dished *a.* concave.

dishevelled *a.* ruffled and untidy. **dishevelment** *n.*

dishonest *a.* not honest. **dishonestly** *adv.*, **dishonesty** *n.*

dishonour *v.* & *n.* disgrace.

dishonourable *a.* not honourable, shameful. **dishonourably** *adv.*

disillusion *v.* free from pleasant but mistaken beliefs. **disillusionment** *n.*

disincentive *n.* thing that discourages an action or effort.

disinclination *n.* unwillingness.

disincline *v.* cause to feel reluctant or unwilling.
disinfect *v.* cleanse by destroying harmful bacteria. **disinfection** *n.*
disinfectant *n.* substance used for disinfecting things.
disinformation *n.* deliberately misleading information.
disingenuous *a.* insincere.
disinherit *v.* reject from being one's heir. **disinheritance** *n.*
disintegrate *v.* break into small pieces. **disintegration** *n.*
disinter *v.* (**disinterred**) dig up, unearth. **disinterment** *n.*
disinterested *a.* unbiased.
disjointed *a.* lacking orderly connection.
disk *n.* = disc; = magnetic disk (see *magnetic*).
dislike *n.* feeling of not liking something. — *v.* feel dislike for.
dislocate *v.* displace from its position; disrupt. **dislocation** *n.*
dislodge *v.* move or force from an established position.
disloyal *a.* not loyal. **disloyally** *adv.*, **disloyalty** *n.*
dismal *a.* gloomy; (*colloq.*) feeble. **dismally** *adv.*
dismantle *v.* take to pieces.
dismay *n.* feeling of surprise and discouragement. — *v.* cause dismay to.
dismember *v.* remove the limbs of; split into pieces. **dismemberment** *n.*
dismiss *v.* send away from one's presence or employment; reject. **dismissal** *n.*, **dismissive** *a.*
dismount *v.* get off a thing on which one is riding.
disobedient *a.* not obedient. **disobediently** *adv.*, **disobedience** *n.*
disobey *v.* disregard orders.
disoblige *v.* fail to help or oblige. **disobliging** *a.*
disorder *n.* lack of order or of discipline; ailment. — *v.* throw into disorder; upset. **disorderly** *a.*, **disorderliness** *n.*
disorganize *v.* upset the orderly arrangement of. **disorganization** *n.*
disorientate *v.* cause (a person) to lose his or her sense of direction. **disorientation** *n.*
disown *v.* refuse to acknowledge; reject all connection with.
disparage *v.* speak slightingly of. **disparagement** *n.*
disparate *a.* different in kind. **disparately** *adv.*
disparity *n.* inequality, difference.
dispassionate *a.* not emotional; impartial. **dispassionately** *adv.*
dispatch *v.* send off to a destination or for a purpose; kill; complete (a task) quickly. — *n.* dispatching; promptness; official message; news report. **dispatch box** container for carrying official documents. **dispatch rider** messenger who travels by motor cycle.
dispel *v.* (**dispelled**) drive away; disperse. **dispeller** *n.*
dispensable *a.* not essential.
dispensary *n.* place where medicines are dispensed.
dispensation *n.* dispensing; distributing; exemption.
dispense *v.* deal out; prepare and give out (medicine etc.). **dispense with** do without; make unnecessary. **dispenser** *n.*
disperse *v.* go or send in different directions, scatter. **dispersal** *n.*, **dispersion** *n.*
dispirited *a.* dejected. **dispiriting** *a.*
displace *v.* shift; take the place of; oust. **displacement** *n.*
display *v.* show, arrange conspicuously. — *n.* displaying; thing(s) displayed. **displayer** *n.*
displease *v.* irritate; annoy.
displeasure *n.* disapproval.
disport *v.* **disport oneself** frolic.
disposable *a.* at one's disposal; designed to be thrown away after use. **disposability** *n.*
disposal *n.* disposing. **at one's disposal** available for one's use.
dispose *v.* place, arrange; make willing or ready to do something. **dispose of** get rid of; finish off. **be well disposed** be friendly or favourable.
disposition *n.* arrangement; person's character; tendency.
dispossess *v.* deprive of the possession of. **dispossession** *n.*
disproportionate *a.* relatively too large or too small. **disproportionately** *adv.*
disprove *v.* show to be wrong.
disputable *a.* questionable. **disputably** *adv.*
disputant *n.* person engaged in a dispute.
disputation *n.* argument, debate.
disputatious *a.* fond of arguing.
dispute *v.* argue, debate; quarrel; question the validity of. — *n.* debate; quarrel.
disqualify *v.* make ineligible or unsuitable. **disqualification** *n.*
disquiet *n.* uneasiness, anxiety. — *v.* cause disquiet to.
disregard *v.* pay no attention to. — *n.* lack of attention.
disrepair *n.* bad condition caused by lack of repair.

disreputable *a.* not respectable. **disreputably** *adv.*
disrepute *n.* discredit.
disrespect *n.* lack of respect. **disrespectful** *a.*, **disrespectfully** *adv.*
disrobe *v.* undress.
disrupt *v.* cause to break up; interrupt the flow or continuity of. **disruption** *n.*, **disruptive** *a.*
dissatisfaction *n.* lack of satisfaction or of contentment.
dissatisfied *a.* not satisfied.
dissect *v.* cut apart so as to examine the internal structure. **dissection** *n.*, **dissector** *n.*
dissemble *v.* conceal (feelings). **dissemblance** *n.*
disseminate *v.* spread widely. **dissemination** *n.*
dissension *n.* disagreement that gives rise to strife.
dissent *v.* have a different opinion. — *n.* difference in opinion. **dissenter** *n.*, **dissentient** *a.* & *n.*
dissertation *n.* detailed discourse.
disservice *n.* unhelpful or harmful action.
dissident *a.* disagreeing. — *n.* person who disagrees, esp. with the authorities. **dissidence** *n.*
dissimilar *a.* unlike. **dissimilarity** *n.*, **dissimilitude** *n.*
dissimulate *v.* dissemble. **dissimulation** *n.*
dissipate *v.* fritter away. **dissipated** *a.* living a dissolute life. **dissipation** *n.*
dissociate *v.* regard as separate; declare to be unconnected. **dissociation** *n.*
dissolute *a.* lacking moral restraint or self-discipline.
dissolution *n.* dissolving of an assembly or partnership.
dissolve *v.* make or become liquid or dispersed in liquid; disappear gradually; disperse (an assembly); end (a partnership, esp. marriage).
dissonant *a.* discordant. **dissonance** *n.*, **dissonantly** *adv.*
dissuade *v.* persuade against a course of action. **dissuasion** *n.*
distaff *n.* cleft stick holding wool etc. in spinning. **distaff side** maternal side; female lineage.
distance *n.* length of space between two points; distant part; remoteness. — *v.* separate.
distant *a.* at a specified or considerable distance away; aloof. **distantly** *adv.*
distaste *n.* dislike, disapproval.
distasteful *a.* arousing distaste. **distastefully** *adv.*
distemper *n.* disease of dogs; paint for use on walls. — *v.* paint with distemper.
distend *v.* swell from pressure within. **distension** *n.*
distil *v.* (**distilled**) treat or make by distillation; undergo distillation.
distillation *n.* process of vaporizing and condensing a liquid so as to purify it or to extract elements; something distilled.
distiller *n.* one who makes alcoholic liquor by distillation.
distillery *n.* place where alcohol is distilled.
distinct *a.* clearly perceptible; different in kind. **distinctly** *adv.*
distinction *n.* distinguishing; difference; thing that differentiates; mark of honour; excellence.
distinctive *a.* distinguishing, characteristic. **distinctively** *adv.*
distinguish *v.* be or see a difference between; discern; make notable. **distinguishable** *a.*
distinguished *a.* having distinction; famous for great achievements.
distort *v.* pull out of shape; misrepresent. **distortion** *n.*
distract *v.* draw away the attention of.
distracted *a.* distraught.
distraction *n.* distracting; thing that distracts; entertainment; distraught state.
distraught *a.* nearly crazy with grief or worry.
distress *n.* suffering, unhappiness. — *v.* cause distress to. **in distress** in danger and needing help.
distribute *v.* divide and share out; scatter, place at different points. **distribution** *n.*
distributor *n.* one who distributes; device for passing electric current to sparking plugs.
district *n.* part (of a country, county, or city) with a particular feature or regarded as a unit.
distrust *n.* lack of trust, suspicion. — *v.* feel distrust in. **distrustful** *a.*, **distrustfully** *adv.*
disturb *v.* break the quiet or rest or calm of; cause to move from a settled position. **disturbance** *n.*
disturbed *a.* mentally or emotionally unstable or abnormal.
disuse *n.* state of not being used.
disused *a.* no longer used.
ditch *n.* long narrow trench for drainage. — *v.* make or repair ditches; (*sl.*) abandon.
dither *v.* hesitate indecisively.
ditto *n.* (in lists) the same again.
ditty *n.* short simple song.

diuretic *a.* & *n.* (substance) causing more urine to be excreted.

diurnal *a.* of or in the day.

divan *n.* couch without back or arms; bed resembling this.

dive *v.* plunge head first into water; plunge or move quickly downwards; go under water; rush headlong. — *n.* diving; sharp downward movement or fall; (*sl.*) disreputable place.

diver *n.* one who dives; person who works underwater.

diverge *v.* separate and go in different directions; depart from a path etc. **divergence** *n.*, **divergent** *a.*

diverse *a.* of differing kinds.

diversify *v.* introduce variety into; vary. **diversification** *n.*

diversion *n.* diverting; thing that diverts attention; entertainment; route round a closed road.

diversity *n.* variety.

divert *v.* turn from a course or route; entertain, amuse.

divest *v.* **divest of** strip of.

divide *v.* separate into parts or from something else; cause to disagree; find how many times one number contains another; be able to be divided. — *n.* dividing line.

dividend *n.* share of profits payable; benefit from an action.

divider *n.* thing that divides; (*pl.*) measuring compasses.

divination *n.* divining.

divine *a.* of, from, or like God or a god; (*colloq.*) excellent, beautiful. — *v.* discover by intuition or magic. **divinely** *adv.*, **diviner** *n.*

divining rod dowser's stick.

divinity *n.* being divine; god.

divisible *a.* able to be divided. **divisibility** *n.*

division *n.* dividing; dividing line, partition; one of the parts into which a thing is divided. **divisional** *a.*

divisive *a.* tending to cause disagreement.

divisor *n.* number by which another is to be divided.

divorce *n.* legal termination of a marriage; separation. — *v.* end the marriage of (a person) by divorce; separate.

divorcee *n.* divorced person.

divulge *v.* reveal (information).

Diwali *n.* Hindu festival at which lamps are lit, held between September and November.

dizzy *a.* (**-ier**, **-iest**) giddy, feeling confused; causing giddiness. **dizzily** *adv.*, **dizziness** *n.*

djellaba /jélləbə/ *n.* Arab cloak.

do *v.* (**did, done**) perform, complete; deal with; act, proceed; fare; be suitable; suffice. — *v.aux.* (used to form present or past tense, for emphasis, or to avoid repeating a verb just used.) *n.* (*pl.* **dos** *or* **do's**) entertainment, party. **do away with** abolish, get rid of. **do down** (*colloq.*) swindle. **do for** (*colloq.*) ruin, destroy. **do-gooder** *n.* well-meaning but unrealistic promoter of social work or reform. **do in** (*sl.*) ruin, kill; tire out. **do out** clean, redecorate. **do up** fasten, wrap; repair, redecorate. **do with** tolerate; need, want. **do without** manage without.

Dobermann pinscher dog of a large smooth-coated breed.

docile *a.* willing to obey. **docilely** *adv.*, **docility** *n.*

dock [1] *n.* enclosed body of water where ships are loaded, unloaded, or repaired. — *v.* bring or come into dock; connect (spacecraft) in space, be joined thus.

dock [2] *n.* enclosure for the prisoner in a criminal court.

dock [3] *v.* cut short; reduce, take away part of.

dock [4] *n.* weed with broad leaves.

docker *n.* labourer who loads and unloads ships in a dockyard.

docket *n.* document listing goods delivered; voucher. — *v.* (**docketed**) label with a docket.

dockyard *n.* area and buildings round a shipping dock.

doctor *n.* person qualified to give medical treatment; person holding a doctorate. — *v.* treat medically; castrate; patch up; tamper with, falsify.

doctorate *n.* highest degree at a university.

doctrinaire *a.* applying theories or principles rigidly.

doctrine *n.* principle(s) of a religious, political, or other group. **doctrinal** *a.*

document *n.* piece of paper giving information or evidence. — *v.* provide or prove with documents. **documentation** *n.*

documentary *a.* consisting of documents; giving a factual report. — *n.* documentary film.

dodder *v.* totter because of age or frailty. **dodderer** *n.*, **doddery** *a.*

dodge *v.* move quickly to one side so as to avoid (a thing); evade. — *n.* dodging movement; (*colloq.*) clever trick, ingenious action. **dodger** *n.*

dodgem *n.* one of the small cars in an enclosure at a funfair, driven so as to bump or dodge others.

dodo *n.* (*pl.* **-os**) large extinct bird.

doe *n.* female of deer, hare, or rabbit.

doff *v.* take off (one's hat).
dog *n.* four-legged carnivorous wild or domesticated animal; male of this or of fox or wolf; (*pl.*) greyhound racing. — *v.* (**dogged**) follow persistently. **dog collar** (*colloq.*) clerical collar fastening at the back of the neck. **dog-eared** *a.* with page-corners crumpled through use.
dog cart two-wheeled cart with back-to-back seats.
dogfish *n.* a kind of small shark.
dogged *a.* determined. **doggedly** *adv.*
doggerel *n.* bad verse.
doggo *adv.* **lie doggo** (*sl.*) remain motionless or making no sign.
doggy *a.* & *n.* (of) a dog. **doggy bag** bag for carrying away leftovers.
dogma *n.* doctrine(s) put forward by authority.
dogmatic *a.* of or like dogmas; stating things in an authoritative way. **dogmatically** *adv.*
dog rose wild hedge-rose.
dogsbody *n.* (*colloq.*) drudge.
dogwood *n.* shrub with dark-red branches and whitish flowers.
doh *n.* name for the keynote of a scale in music, or the note C.
doily *n.* small ornamental mat.
doldrums *n.pl.* equatorial regions with little or no wind. **in the doldrums** in low spirits.
dole *v.* distribute. — *n.* (*colloq.*) unemployment benefit.
doleful *a.* mournful. **dolefully** *adv.*, **dolefulness** *n.*
doll *n.* small model of a human figure, esp. as a child's toy.
dollar *n.* unit of money in the USA and various other countries.
dollop *n.* (*colloq.*) mass of a soft substance.
dolly *n.* (*children's use*) doll; movable platform for a cine camera.
dolman sleeve tapering sleeve cut in one piece with the body of a garment.
dolmen *n.* megalithic structure of a large flat stone laid on two upright ones.
dolomite *n.* a type of limestone rock. **dolomitic** *a.*
dolour *n.* sorrow. **dolorous** *a.*
dolphin *n.* sea animal like a large porpoise, with a beak-like snout.
dolt *n.* stupid person. **doltish** *a.*
domain *n.* area under a person's control; field of activity.
dome *n.* rounded roof with a circular base; thing shaped like this. **domed** *a.*
domestic *a.* of home or household; of one's own country; domesticated. — *n.* servant in a household. **domestically** *adv.*
domesticate *v.* train (an animal) to live with humans; accustom to household work and home life. **domestication** *n.*
domesticity *n.* domestic life.
domicile *n.* place of residence. **domiciliary** *a.*
dominant *a.* dominating. **dominance** *n.*
dominate *v.* have a commanding influence over; be the most influential or conspicuous person or thing; tower over. **domination** *n.*
domineer *v.* behave forcefully, making others obey.
dominion *n.* authority to rule, control; ruler's territory.
domino *n.* (*pl.* **-oes**) small oblong piece marked with pips, used in the game of **dominoes**.
don [1] *v.* (**donned**) put on.
don [2] *n.* head, fellow, or tutor of a college. **donnish** *a.*
donate *v.* give as a donation.
donation *n.* gift (esp. of money) to a fund or institution.
done *see* **do**. — *a.* (*colloq.*) socially acceptable.
donkey *n.* animal of the horse family, with long ears. **donkey jacket** thick weather-proof jacket. **donkey's years** (*colloq.*) a very long time. **donkey work** drudgery.
donor *n.* one who gives or donates something.
doodle *v.* scribble idly. — *n.* drawing or marks made thus.
doom *n.* grim fate; death or ruin. — *v.* destine to a grim fate.
doomsday *n.* day of the Last Judgement.
door *n.* hinged, sliding, or revolving barrier closing an opening; doorway.
doorway *n.* opening filled by a door.
dope *n.* (*sl.*) drug; information; stupid person. — *v.* (*sl.*) drug.
dopey *a.* half asleep, stupid.
dormant *a.* sleeping; temporarily inactive. **dormancy** *n.*
dormer *n.* upright window under a small gable on a sloping roof.
dormitory *n.* room with several beds, esp. in a school. **dormitory town** one from which most residents travel to work elsewhere.
dormouse *n.* (*pl.* **-mice**) mouse-like animal that hibernates.
dorsal *a.* of or on the back.
dory *n.* edible sea fish.
dosage *n.* size of a dose.
dose *n.* amount of medicine to be taken at one time; amount of radiation received. — *v.* give dose(s) of medicine to.
doss *v.* (*sl.*) sleep in a doss-house or on a

makeshift bed etc. **doss-house** *n.* cheap hostel. **dosser** *n.*

dossier *n.* set of documents about a person or event.

dot *n.* small round mark. — *v.* **(dotted)** mark with dot(s); scatter here and there; (*sl.*) hit. **on the dot** exactly on time.

dotage *n.* senility.

dote *v.* **dote on** feel great fondness for. **doting** *a.*

dotty *a.* **(-ier, -iest)** (*colloq.*) feeble-minded; eccentric; silly. **dottily** *adv.*, **dottiness** *n.*

double *a.* consisting of two things or parts; twice as much or as many; designed for two persons or things. — *adv.* twice as much; in twos. — *n.* double quantity or thing; person or thing very like another; (*pl.*) game with two players on each side. — *v.* make or become twice as much or as many; fold in two; turn back sharply; act two parts; have two uses. **at the double** running, hurrying. **double bass** lowest-pitched instrument of the violin family. **double-breasted** *a.* (of a coat) with fronts overlapping. **double chin** chin with a roll of fat below. **double cream** thick cream. **double-cross** *v.* cheat, deceive. **double-dealing** *n.* deceit, esp. in business. **double-decker** *n.* bus with two decks. **double Dutch** gibberish. **double figures** numbers from 10 to 99. **double glazing** two sheets of glass in a window. **double take** delayed reaction just after one's first reaction. **double-talk** *n.* talk with deliberately ambiguous meaning. **doubly** *adv.*

double entendre /dŏŏb'l aantaándrə/ phrase with two meanings, one of which is usu. indecent.

doublet *n.* each of a pair of similar things; (*old use*) man's close-fitting jacket.

doubt *n.* feeling of uncertainty or disbelief; being undecided. — *v.* feel doubt about, hesitate to believe. **doubter** *n.*

doubtful *a.* feeling or causing doubt; unlikely. **doubtfully** *adv.*

doubtless *a.* certainly.

douche /dōōsh/ *n.* jet of water applied to the body; device for applying this. — *v.* use a douche (on).

dough /dō/ *n.* thick mixture of flour etc. and liquid, for baking; (*sl.*) money. **doughy** *a.*

doughnut /dōnut/ *n.* small cake of fried sweetened dough.

dour /door/ *a.* stern, gloomy-looking. **dourly** *adv.*, **dourness** *n.*

douse /dowss/ *v.* extinguish (a light); throw water on, put into water.

dove *n.* bird with a thick body and short legs; person favouring negotiation rather than violence.

dovecot, dovecote *ns.* shelter for domesticated pigeons.

dovetail *n.* wedge-shaped joint interlocking two pieces of wood. — *v.* combine neatly.

dowager *n.* woman holding a title or property from her dead husband.

dowdy *a.* **(-ier, -iest)** dull, not stylish; dressed in dowdy clothes. **dowdily** *adv.*, **dowdiness** *n.*

dowel *n.* headless wooden or metal pin holding pieces of wood or stone together. **dowelling** *n.* rod for cutting into dowels.

down [1] *n.* area of open undulating land, esp. (*pl.*) chalk uplands.

down [2] *n.* very fine soft furry feathers or short hairs.

down [3] *adv.* to, in, or at a lower place or state etc.; to a smaller size; from an earlier to a later time; recorded in writing; to the source or place where a thing is; as (partial) payment at the time of purchase. — *prep.* downwards along or through or into; at a lower part of. — *a.* directed downwards; travelling away from a central place. — *v.* (*colloq.*) knock or bring or put down; swallow. **down-and-out** *a.* & *n.* destitute (person). **have a down on** (*colloq.*) show hostility towards. **down-to-earth** *a.* sensible and practical. **down under** in the antipodes, esp. Australia.

downcast *a.* dejected; (of eyes) looking downwards.

downfall *n.* fall from prosperity or power; thing causing this.

downgrade *v.* reduce to a lower grade.

downhearted *a.* in low spirits.

downhill *a.* & *adv.* going or sloping downwards.

downpour *n.* great fall of rain.

downright *a.* frank, straightforward; thorough. — *adv.* thoroughly.

Down's syndrome abnormal congenital condition causing a broad face and learning difficulties.

downstairs *adv.* & *a.* to or on a lower floor.

downstream *a.* & *adv.* in the direction in which a stream flows.

downtrodden *a.* oppressed.

downward *a.* moving or leading down. — *adv.* downwards.

downwards *adv.* towards a lower place etc.

downy *a.* **(-ier, -iest)** of, like, or covered with soft down.

dowry *n.* property or money brought by a bride to her husband.

dowse /dowz/ *v.* search for underground

water or minerals by using a stick which dips when these are present. **dowser** *n.*

doxology *n.* formula of praise to God.

doyen *n.* senior member of a staff or profession. **doyenne** *n.fem.*

doze *v.* sleep lightly. — *n.* short light sleep.

dozen *n.* set of twelve; (*pl.*, *colloq.*) very many.

Dr *abbr.* Doctor; debtor.

drab *a.* dull, uninteresting.

drachm /dram/ *n.* one-eighth of an ounce or of a fluid ounce.

drachma *n.* (*pl.* **-as** *or* **-ae**) unit of money in Greece.

draconian *a.* (of laws) harsh.

draft [1] *n.* preliminary written version; written order to a bank to pay money; (*US*) conscription. — *v.* prepare a draft of; (*US*) conscript.

draft [2] *n.* (*US*) draught.

drag *v.* (**dragged**) pull along; trail on the ground; bring or proceed with effort; search (water) with nets or hooks. — *n.* thing that slows progress; (*sl.*) draw at a cigarette; (*sl.*) women's clothes worn by men. **dragnet** net for dragging water. **drag race** acceleration race between cars over a short distance.

dragon *n.* mythical reptile able to breathe out fire; fierce person.

dragonfly *n.* long-bodied insect with gauzy wings.

dragoon *n.* cavalryman or (formerly) mounted infantryman. — *v.* force into action.

drain *v.* draw off (liquid) by channels or pipes etc.; flow away; deprive gradually of (strength or resources); drink all of. — *n.* channel or pipe carrying away water or sewage; thing that drains one's strength etc.

drainage *n.* draining; system of drains; what is drained off.

drake *n.* male duck.

dram *n.* drachm; small drink of spirits.

drama *n.* play(s) for acting on the stage or broadcasting; dramatic quality or series of events.

dramatic *a.* of drama; exciting, impressive. **dramatically** *adv.*

dramatist *n.* writer of plays.

dramatize *v.* make into a drama. **dramatization** *n.*

drank *see* **drink**.

drape *v.* cover or arrange loosely. — *n.* (*US*) curtain.

drastic *a.* having a strong or violent effect. **drastically** *adv.*

draught *n.* current of air; pulling; depth of water needed to float a ship; amount of liquid swallowed at one time; (*pl.*) game played with 24 round pieces on a chessboard. **draught beer** beer drawn from a cask.

draughtsman *n.* (*pl.* **-men**) one who draws plans or sketches.

draughty *a.* (**-ier**, **-iest**) letting in sharp currents of air. **draughtily** *adv.*, **draughtiness** *n.*

draw *v.* (**drew, drawn**) pull; attract; take in (breath etc.); take from or out; obtain by a lottery; finish a contest with scores equal; require (a specified depth) in which to float; produce (a picture or diagram) by making marks; promote or allow a draught of air (in); make one's way, come; infuse. — *n.* act of drawing; thing that draws custom or attention; drawing of lots; drawn game. **draw in** (of days) become shorter. **draw out** prolong; (of days) become longer. **drawstring** *n.* string that can be pulled to tighten an opening. **draw the line at** refuse to do or tolerate. **draw up** halt; compose (a contract etc.); make (oneself) stiffly erect.

drawback *n.* disadvantage.

drawbridge *n.* bridge over a moat, hinged for raising.

drawer *n.* person who draws; one who writes a cheque; horizontal sliding compartment; (*pl.*) knickers, underpants.

drawing *n.* picture made with a pencil or pen. **drawing-pin** *n.* pin for fastening paper to a surface. **drawing room** formal sitting room.

drawl *v.* speak lazily or with drawn-out vowel sounds. — *n.* drawling manner of speaking.

drawn *see* **draw**. — *a.* looking strained from tiredness or worry.

dread *n.* great fear. — *v.* fear greatly. — *a.* dreaded.

dreadful *a.* very bad. **dreadfully** *adv.*

dream *n.* series of pictures or events in a sleeping person's mind; fantasy. — *v.* (**dreamed** *or* **dreamt**) have dream(s); have an ambition; think of as a possibility. **dream up** imagine; invent. **dreamer** *n.*, **dreamless** *a.*

dreamy *a.* (**-ier**, **-iest**) daydreaming. **dreamily** *adv.*, **dreaminess** *n.*

dreary *a.* (**-ier**, **-iest**) dull, boring; gloomy. **drearily** *adv.*, **dreariness** *n.*

dredge [1] *v.* remove (silt) from (a river or channel). **dredger** [1] *n.* boat that dredges.

dredge [2] *v.* sprinkle with flour or sugar. **dredger** [2] *n.* container with perforated lid for dredging.

dregs *n.pl.* sediment at the bottom of liquid; worst and useless part.

drench *v.* wet all through.

dress *n.* outer clothing; woman's or girl's garment with a bodice and skirt. — *v.* put clothes on; clothe oneself; arrange, decorate, trim; put a dressing on. **dress circle** first gallery in a theatre. **dress rehearsal** final one, in costume. **dress shirt** shirt for wearing with evening dress.

dressage /dréssazh/ *n.* management of a horse to show its obedience and deportment.

dresser [1] *n.* one who dresses a person or thing.

dresser [2] *n.* kitchen sideboard with shelves for dishes etc.

dressing *n.* sauce for food; fertilizer etc. spread over land; bandage or ointment etc. for a wound. **dressing down** scolding. **dressing gown** loose robe worn when one is not fully dressed. **dressing table** table with a mirror, for use while dressing.

dressmaker *n.* woman who makes women's clothes. **dressmaking** *n.*

dressy *a.* (**-ier, -iest**) wearing stylish clothes; elegant, elaborate.

drew *see* **draw**.

drey *n.* squirrel's nest.

dribble *v.* have saliva flowing from the mouth; flow or let flow in drops; (in football etc.) move the ball forward with slight touches. — *n.* act or flow of dribbling.

dried *a.* (of food) preserved by removal of moisture.

drift *v.* be carried by a current of water or air; go casually or aimlessly. — *n.* drifting movement; mass of snow piled up by the wind; general meaning of a speech etc.

drifter *n.* aimless person.

driftwood *n.* wood floating on the sea or washed ashore.

drill [1] *n.* tool or machine for boring holes or sinking wells; training; (*colloq.*) routine procedure. — *v.* use a drill, make (a hole) with a drill; train, be trained.

drill [2] *n.* strong twilled fabric.

drily *adv.* in a dry way.

drink *v.* (**drank, drunk**) swallow (liquid); take alcoholic drink, esp. in excess; pledge good wishes (to) by drinking. — *n.* liquid for drinking; alcoholic liquors. **drink in** watch or listen to eagerly. **drinker** *n.*

drip *v.* (**dripped**) fall or let fall in drops. — *n.* liquid falling in drops; sound of this; device administering a liquid at a very slow rate, esp. intravenously. **drip-dry** *v.* & *a.* (able to) dry easily without ironing. **drip-feed** *n.* & *v.* feed(ing) by a drip.

dripping *n.* fat melted from roast meat.

drive *v.* (**drove, driven**) send or urge onwards; propel; operate (a vehicle) and direct its course; travel or convey in a private vehicle; cause, compel; make (a bargain). — *n.* journey in a private vehicle; transmission of power to machinery; energy, urge; organized effort; track for a car, leading to a private house. **drive at** intend to convey as a meaning. **drive-in** *a.* (of a cinema etc.) able to be used without getting out of one's car.

drivel *n.* silly talk, nonsense.

driver *n.* person who drives; golf club for driving from a tee.

drizzle *n.* & *v.* rain in very fine drops.

droll *a.* amusing in an odd way. **drolly** *adv.*, **drollery** *n.*

dromedary *n.* camel with one hump, bred for riding.

drone *n.* male bee; deep humming sound. — *v.* make this sound; speak monotonously.

drool *v.* slaver, dribble; show gushing appreciation.

droop *v.* bend or hang down limply. — *n.* drooping attitude. **droopy** *a.*

drop *n.* small rounded mass of liquid; (*pl.*) medicine measured by drops; very small quantity; fall; steep descent, distance of this. — *v.* (**dropped**) fall; shed, let fall; make or become lower; utter casually; omit; reject, give up. **drop in** pay a casual visit. **drop off** fall asleep. **drop out** cease to participate. **drop-out** *n.* one who drops out from a course of study or from conventional society.

droplet *n.* small drop of liquid.

dropper *n.* device for releasing liquid in drops.

droppings *n.pl.* animal dung.

dropsy *n.* disease in which fluid collects in the body. **dropsical** *a.*

dross *n.* scum on molten metal; impurities, rubbish.

drought *n.* long spell of dry weather.

drove *see* **drive**. — *n.* moving herd or flock or crowd.

drover *n.* person who drives cattle.

drown *v.* kill or be killed by suffocating in water or other liquid; flood, drench; deaden (grief etc.) with drink; overpower (sound) with greater loudness.

drowse *v.* be lightly asleep. **drowsy** *a.*, **drowsily** *adv.*, **drowsiness** *n.*

drudge *n.* person who does laborious or menial work. — *v.* do such work. **drudgery** *n.*

drug *n.* substance used in medicine or as a stimulant or narcotic. — *v.* (**drugged**) add or give a drug to.

drugstore *n.* (*US*) chemist's shop also selling various goods.

Druid *n.* priest of an ancient Celtic religion. **Druidical** *a.*

drum *n.* percussion instrument, a round frame with skin etc. stretched across; cylindrical object; eardrum. — *v.* (**drummed**) tap continually; din. **drum up** obtain by vigorous effort.

drummer *n.* person who plays drum(s).

drumstick *n.* stick for beating a drum; lower part of a cooked fowl's leg.

drunk *see* **drink**. — *a.* excited or stupefied by alcoholic drink. — *n.* drunken person.

drunkard *n.* person who is often drunk.

drunken *a.* intoxicated, often in this condition. **drunkenly** *adv.*, **drunkenness** *n.*

dry *a.* (**drier, driest**) without water, moisture, or rainfall; thirsty; uninteresting; not allowing the sale of alcohol; expressed with pretended seriousness; (of wine) not sweet. — *v.* make or become dry; preserve (food) by removing its moisture. **dry-clean** *v.* clean by solvent that evaporates quickly. **dry rot** decay of wood that is not ventilated. **dry run** (*colloq.*) dummy run. **dry up** dry washed dishes; (*colloq.*) cease talking. **dryness** *n.*

dryad *n.* wood nymph.

dual *a.* composed of two parts, double. **dual carriageway** road with a dividing strip between traffic travelling in opposite directions. **duality** *n.*

dub [1] *v.* (**dubbed**) give a nickname to.

dub [2] *v.* (**dubbed**) replace the soundtrack of a film.

dubbin *n.* thick grease for softening and waterproofing leather.

dubiety *n.* feeling of doubt.

dubious *a.* doubtful. **dubiously** *adv.*

ducal *a.* of a duke.

ducat *n.* former gold coin of various European countries.

duchess *n.* duke's wife or widow; woman with the rank of duke.

duchy *n.* territory of a duke.

duck *n.* swimming bird of various kinds; female of this; batsman's score of 0; ducking movement. — *v.* push (a person) or dip one's head under water; bob down, esp. to avoid being seen or hit; dodge (a task etc.).

duckboards *n.pl.* boards forming a narrow path.

duckling *n.* young duck.

duct *n.* channel or tube conveying liquid or air. **ductless** *a.*

ductile *a.* (of metal) able to be drawn into fine strands.

dud *n.* & *a.* (*sl.*) (thing) that is counterfeit or fails to work.

dude *n.* (*US*) dandy. **dude ranch** ranch used as a holiday centre.

dudgeon *n.* indignation.

due *a.* owed; payable immediately; merited; scheduled to do something or to arrive. — *adv.* exactly. — *n.* a person's right, what is owed to him or her; (*pl.*) fees. **be due to** be attributable to.

duel *n.* fight or contest between two persons or sides. **duelling** *n.*, **duellist** *n.*

duenna *n.* chaperon.

duet *n.* musical composition for two performers.

duff *a.* (*sl.*) dud.

duffer *n.* inefficient or stupid person.

duffle-coat *n.* heavy woollen coat with a hood.

dug [1] *see* **dig**. **dugout** *n.* underground shelter; canoe made from a hollowed tree trunk.

dug [2] *n.* udder, teat.

dugong *n.* Asian sea mammal.

duke *n.* nobleman of the highest hereditary rank; ruler of certain small States. **dukedom** *n.*

dulcet *a.* sounding sweet.

dulcimer *n.* musical instrument with strings struck by two hammers.

dull *a.* not bright; stupid; boring; not sharp; not resonant. — *v.* make or become dull. **dully** *adv.*, **dullness** *n.*

dullard *n.* stupid person.

duly *adv.* in a suitable way.

dumb *a.* unable to speak; silent; (*colloq.*) stupid. **dumb-bell** *n.* short bar with weighted ends, lifted to exercise muscles. **dumbly** *adv.*, **dumbness** *n.*

dumbfound *v.* astonish.

dumdum bullet soft-nosed bullet that expands on impact.

dummy *n.* sham article; model of the human figure, used to display clothes; rubber teat for a baby to suck. — *a.* sham. **dummy run** trial attempt; rehearsal.

dump *v.* deposit as rubbish; put down carelessly; sell abroad at a lower price. — *n.* rubbish heap; temporary store; (*colloq.*) dull place.

dumpling *n.* ball of dough cooked in stew or with fruit inside.

dun *a.* & *n.* greyish-brown.

dunce *n.* person slow at learning.

dune *n.* mound of drifted sand.

dung *n.* animal excrement.

dungarees *n.pl.* overalls of coarse cotton cloth.

dungeon *n.* strong underground cell for prisoners.

dunk *v.* dip into liquid.

duo *n.* (*pl.* **-os**) pair of performers.

duodecimal *a.* reckoned in twelves or twelfths.
duodenum *n.* part of the intestine next to the stomach. **duodenal** *a.*
dupe *v.* deceive, trick. — *n.* duped person.
duple *a.* having two parts; (in music) having two beats to the bar.
duplex *a.* having two elements.
duplicate *n.* /dyōōplikət/ exact copy. — *a.* /dyōōplikət/ exactly like another. — *v.* /dyōōplikayt/ make or be a duplicate; do twice. **duplication** *n.*
duplicity *n.* deceitfulness.
durable *a.* likely to last. **durables** *n.pl.* durable goods. **durably** *adv.*, **durability** *n.*
duration *n.* time during which a thing continues.
duress *n.* use of force or threats.
during *prep.* throughout; at a point in the continuance of.
dusk *n.* darker stage of twilight.
dusky *a.* (**-ier**, **-iest**) shadowy; dark-coloured. **duskiness** *n.*
dust *n.* fine particles of earth or other matter. — *v.* sprinkle with dust or powder; clear of dust by wiping, clean a room etc. thus. **dust bowl** area denuded of vegetation and reduced to desert. **dust cover**, **dust jacket** paper jacket on a book.
dustbin *n.* bin for household rubbish.
duster *n.* cloth for dusting things.
dustman *n.* (*pl.* **-men**) person employed to empty dustbins.
dustpan *n.* container into which dust is brushed from a floor.
dusty *a.* (**-ier**, **-iest**) like dust; covered with dust. **dustiness** *n.*
Dutch *a.* & *n.* (language) of the Netherlands. **Dutch courage** that obtained by drinking alcohol. **go Dutch** share expenses on an outing. **Dutchman** *n.* (*pl.* **-men**), **Dutchwoman** *n.fem.* (*pl.* **-women**).
dutiable *a.* on which customs or other duties must be paid.
dutiful *a.* doing one's duty, showing due obedience. **dutifully** *adv.*
duty *n.* moral or legal obligation; tax on goods or imports. **on duty** at work.
duvet /dōōvay/ *n.* thick soft quilt used as bedclothes.
dwarf *n.* (*pl.* **-fs**) person or thing much below the usual size; (in fairy tales) small being with magic powers. — *a.* very small. — *v.* stunt; make seem small.
dwell *v.* (**dwelt**) live as an inhabitant. **dwell on** write or speak or think lengthily about. **dweller** *n.*
dwelling *n.* house etc. to live in.
dwindle *v.* become less or smaller.
dye *v.* (**dyeing**) colour, esp. by dipping in liquid. — *n.* substance used for dyeing things; colour given by dyeing. **dyer** *n.*
dying *see* **die** [1].
dyke *n.* wall or embankment to prevent flooding; drainage ditch.
dynamic *a.* of force producing motion; energetic, forceful. **dynamically** *adv.*
dynamics *n.* branch of physics dealing with matter in motion.
dynamism *n.* energizing power.
dynamite *n.* powerful explosive made of nitroglycerine. — *v.* fit or blow up with dynamite.
dynamo *n.* (*pl.* **-os**) small generator producing electric current.
dynasty *n.* line of hereditary rulers. **dynastic** *a.*
dysentery *n.* disease causing severe diarrhoea.
dysfunction *n.* malfunction.
dyslexia *n.* condition causing difficulty in reading and spelling. **dyslexic** *a.* & *n.*
dyspepsia *n.* indigestion. **dyspeptic** *a.* & *n.*
dystrophy *n.* progressive weakness of muscles.

E

E. *abbr.* east; eastern.

each *a.* & *pron.* every one of two or more.

eager *a.* full of desire, enthusiastic. **eagerly** *adv.*, **eagerness** *n.*

eagle *n.* large bird of prey.

ear [1] *n.* organ of hearing; external part of this; ability to distinguish sounds accurately. **eardrum** *n.* membrane inside the ear, vibrating when sound waves strike it.

ear [2] *n.* seed-bearing part of corn.

earl *n.* British nobleman ranking between marquess and viscount. **earldom** *n.*

early *a.* (**-ier**, **-iest**) *a.* & *adv.* before the usual or expected time; not far on in development or in a series.

earmark *n.* distinguishing mark. — *v.* put such mark on; set aside for a particular purpose.

earn *v.* get or deserve for work or merit; (of money) gain as interest.

earnest *a.* showing serious feeling or intention. **in earnest** seriously. **earnestly** *adv.*, **earnestness** *n.*

earshot *n.* range of hearing.

earth *n.* the planet we live on; its surface, dry land; soil; fox's den; connection of an electrical circuit to ground. — *v.* connect an electrical circuit to earth. **run to earth** find after a long search.

earthen *a.* made of earth or of baked clay.

earthenware *n.* pottery made of coarse baked clay.

earthly *a.* of this earth, of man's life on it.

earthquake *n.* violent movement of part of the earth's crust.

earthwork *n.* bank built of earth.

earthworm *n.* worm living in the soil.

earthy *a.* like earth or soil; (of humour etc.) gross, coarse.

earwig *n.* small insect with pincers at the end of its body.

ease *n.* freedom from pain, worry, or effort; leisure. — *v.* relieve from pain etc.; make or become less tight or severe; move gently or gradually.

easel *n.* frame to support a painting or blackboard etc.

east *n.* point on the horizon where the sun rises; direction in which this lies; eastern part. — *a.* in the east; (of wind) from the east. — *adv.* towards the east.

Easter *n.* festival commemorating Christ's resurrection. **Easter egg** chocolate egg given at Easter.

easterly *a.* towards or blowing from the east.

eastern *a.* of or in the east.

easternmost *a.* furthest east.

eastward *a.* towards the east. **eastwards** *adv.*

easy *a.* (**-ier**, **-iest**) done or got without great effort; free from pain, trouble, or anxiety. — *adv.* in an easy way. **easy chair** large comfortable chair. **easily** *adv.*, **easiness** *n.*

easygoing *a.* relaxed in manner, not strict.

eat *v.* (**ate**, **eaten**) chew and swallow (food); have a meal; destroy gradually. **eater** *n.*

eatables *n.pl.* food.

eau-de-Cologne /ődəkəlőn/ *n.* a delicate perfume.

eaves *n.pl.* overhanging edge of a roof.

eavesdrop *v.* (**-dropped**) listen secretly to a private conversation. **eavesdropper** *n.*

ebb *n.* outward movement of the tide, away from the land; decline. — *v.* flow away; decline.

ebony *n.* hard black wood of a tropical tree. — *a.* black as ebony.

ebullient *a.* full of high spirits. **ebulliently** *adv.*, **ebullience** *n.*

EC *abbr.* European Community; European Commission.

eccentric *a.* unconventional; not concentric; (of an orbit or wheel) not circular. — *n.* eccentric person. **eccentrically** *adv.*, **eccentricity** *n.*

ecclesiastical *a.* of the Church or clergy.

echelon /éshəlon/ *n.* staggered formation of troops etc.; level of rank or authority.

echo *n.* (*pl.* **-oes**) repetition of sound by reflection of sound waves; close imitation. — *v.* (**echoed**, **echoing**) repeat by an echo; imitate.

éclair *n.* finger-shaped cake with cream filling.

eclectic *a.* choosing or accepting from various sources.

eclipse *n.* blocking of light from one heavenly body by another; loss of brilliance or power etc. — *v.* cause an eclipse of; outshine.

ecliptic *n.* sun's apparent path.

eclogue *n.* short pastoral poem.

ecology *n.* (study of) relationships of living things to their environment; protection of the natural environment.

ecological *a.*, **ecologically** *adv.*, **ecologist** *n.*

economic *a.* of economics; enough to give a good return for money or effort outlaid. **economics** *n.* science of the production and use of goods or services; (as *pl.*) financial aspects.

economical *a.* thrifty, avoiding waste. **economically** *adv.*

economist *n.* expert in economics.

economize *v.* use or spend less.

economy *n.* being economical; community's system of using its resources to produce wealth; state of a country's prosperity.

ecstasy *n.* intense delight. **ecstatic** *a.*, **ecstatically** *adv.*

ecu /ékyoo/ *abbr.* European currency unit.

ecumenical *a.* of the whole Christian Church; seeking world-wide Christian unity.

eczema *n.* skin disease causing scaly itching patches.

eddy *n.* swirling patch of water or air etc. — *v.* swirl in eddies.

edelweiss /áyd'lvīss/ *n.* alpine plant with woolly white bracts.

edge *n.* sharpened side of a blade; sharpness; rim, narrow surface of a thin or flat object; outer limit of an area. — *v.* border; move gradually.

edgeways, edgewise *advs.* with the edge forwards or outwards.

edging *n.* something placed round an edge to define or decorate it.

edgy *a.* (**-ier, -iest**) tense and irritable. **edgily** *adv.*, **edginess** *n.*

edible *a.* suitable for eating. **edibility** *n.*

edict /eédikt/ *n.* order proclaimed by authority.

edifice *n.* large building.

edify *v.* be an uplifting influence on the mind of. **edification** *n.*

edit *v.* (**edited**) prepare for publication; prepare (a film) by arranging sections in sequence.

edition *n.* form in which something is published; number of objects issued at one time.

editor *n.* person responsible for the contents of a newspaper etc. or a section of this; one who edits.

editorial *a.* of an editor. — *n.* newspaper article giving the editor's comments.

educate *v.* train the mind and abilities of; provide such training for. **education** *n.*, **educational** *a.*

Edwardian *a.* of the reign of Edward VII (1901–10).

EEC *abbr.* European Economic Community.

eel *n.* snake-like fish.

eerie *a.* (**-ier, -iest**) mysterious and frightening. **eerily** *adv.*, **eeriness** *n.*

efface *v.* rub out, obliterate; make inconspicuous. **effacement** *n.*

effect *n.* change produced by an action or cause; impression; state of being operative; (*pl.*) property. — *v.* cause to occur.

effective *a.* producing an effect; striking; operative. **effectively** *adv.*, **effectiveness** *n.*

effectual *a.* answering its purpose. **effectually** *adv.*

effeminate *a.* not manly, womanish. **effeminacy** *n.*, **effeminately** *adv.*

effervesce *v.* give off bubbles. **effervescence** *n.*, **effervescent** *a.*

effete *a.* having lost its vitality. **effeteness** *n.*

efficacious *a.* producing the desired result. **efficaciously** *adv.*, **efficacy** *n.*

efficient *a.* producing results with little waste of effort. **efficiently** *adv.*, **efficiency** *n.*

effigy *n.* model of person.

effloresce *v.* flower. **efflorescence** *n.*

effluent *n.* outflow, sewage.

effluvium *n.* (*pl.* **-ia**) outflow, esp. unpleasant or harmful.

effort *n.* use of energy; attempt. **effortless** *a.*

effrontery *n.* bold insolence.

effusion *n.* outpouring.

effusive *a.* expressing emotion in an unrestrained way. **effusively** *adv.*, **effusiveness** *n.*

e.g. *abbr.* (Latin *exempli gratia*) for example.

egalitarian *a.* & *n.* (person) holding the principle of equal rights for all. **egalitarianism** *n.*

egg[1] *n.* hard-shelled oval body produced by the female of birds, esp. that of the domestic hen; ovum. **eggshell** *n.*

egg[2] *v.* **egg on** (*colloq.*) urge on.

eggplant *n.* aubergine.

ego *n.* self; self-esteem.

egocentric *a.* self-centred.

egoism *n.* self-centredness.

egoist *n.* self-centred person. **egoistic** *a.*

egotism *n.* practice of talking too much about oneself, conceit.

egotist *n.* conceited person. **egotistic** *a.*, **egotistical** *a.*

egregious /igreéjəss/ *a.* shocking; (*old use*) remarkable.

egress *n.* departure; way out.

egret *n.* a kind of heron.

Egyptian *a.* & *n.* (native) of Egypt.

Egyptology *n.* study of Egyptian antiquities. **Egyptologist** *n.*

eider *n.* northern species of duck.
eiderdown *n.* quilt stuffed with soft material.
eight *a.* & *n.* one more than seven (8, VIII). **eighth** *a.* & *n.*
eighteen *a.* & *n.* one more than seventeen (18, XVIII). **eighteenth** *a.* & *n.*
eighty *a.* & *n.* ten times eight (80, LXXX). **eightieth** *a.* & *n.*
either *a.* & *pron.* one or other of two; each of two. — *adv.* & *conj.* as the first alternative; likewise.
ejaculate *v.* utter suddenly; eject (semen). **ejaculation** *n.*
eject *v.* send out forcefully. **ejection** *n.*, **ejector** *n.*
eke *v.* **eke out** supplement; make (a living) laboriously.
elaborate *a.* /ilábbərət/ with many parts or details. — *v.* /ilábbərayt/ add detail to. **elaborately** *adv.*, **elaboration** *n.*
élan /aylóɴ/ *n.* vivacity, vigour.
eland /eélənd/ *n.* large African antelope.
elapse *v.* (of time) pass away.
elastic *a.* going back to its original length or shape after being stretched or squeezed; adaptable. — *n.* cord or material made elastic by interweaving strands of rubber etc. **elasticity** *n.*
elate *v.* cause to feel very pleased or proud. **elated** *a.*, **elation** *n.*
elbow *n.* joint between the forearm and upper arm; part of a sleeve covering this; sharp bend. — *v.* thrust with one's elbow. **elbow grease** (*joc.*) vigorous polishing. **elbow room** enough space to move or work in.
elder [1] *a.* older. — *n.* older person; official in certain Churches.
elder [2] *n.* tree with dark berries. **elderberry** *n.* its berry.
elderly *a.* old.
eldest *a.* oldest; first-born.
elect *v.* choose by vote; choose as a course. — *a.* chosen.
election *n.* electing; process of electing representative(s).
electioneer *v.* busy oneself in an election campaign.
elective *a.* chosen by election; entitled to elect; optional.
elector *n.* person entitled to vote in an election. **electoral** *a.*
electorate *n.* body of electors.
electric *a.* of, producing, or worked by electricity.
electrical *a.* of electricity. **electrically** *adv.*
electrician *n.* person whose job is to deal with electrical equipment.
electricity *n.* form of energy occurring in certain particles; supply of electric current.
electrics *n.pl.* electrical fittings.
electrify *v.* charge with electricity; convert to the use of electric power. **electrification** *n.*
electrocardiogram *n.* record of the electric current generated by heartbeats.
electrocute *v.* kill by electricity. **electrocution** *n.*
electrode *n.* solid conductor through which electricity enters or leaves a vacuum tube etc.
electroencephalogram *n.* record of the electrical activity of the brain.
electrolyte *n.* solution that conducts electric current.
electromagnet *n.* magnet consisting of a metal core magnetized by a current-carrying coil round it.
electromagnetic *a.* having both electrical and magnetic properties. **electromagnetism** *n.*, **electromagnetically** *adv.*
electron *n.* particle with a negative electric charge. **electron microscope** very powerful one using a focused beam of electrons instead of light.
electronic *a.* produced or worked by a flow of electrons; of electronics. **electronically** *adv.*
electronics *n.* use of electronic devices; (as *pl.*) electronic circuits.
elegant *a.* tasteful and dignified. **elegantly** *adv.*, **elegance** *n.*
elegy *n.* sorrowful or serious poem. **elegiac** *a.*
element *n.* component part; substance that cannot be broken down into other substances; suitable or satisfying environment; trace; wire that gives out heat in an electrical appliance; (*pl.*) atmospheric forces, basic principles. **elemental** *a.*
elementary *a.* dealing with the simplest facts of a subject.
elephant *n.* very large animal with a trunk and ivory tusks.
elephantine *a.* of or like elephants; very large, clumsy.
elevate *v.* raise to a higher position or level.
elevation *n.* elevating; altitude; hill; drawing showing one side of a structure.
elevator *n.* thing that hoists something; (*US*) lift.
eleven *a.* & *n.* one more than ten (11, XI). **eleventh** *a.* & *n.*
elevenses *n.* mid-morning snack.
elf *n.* (*pl.* **elves**) imaginary small being with magic powers. **elfin** *a.*
elicit *v.* draw out.

eligible *a.* qualified to be chosen or allowed something. **eligibility** *n.*
eliminate *v.* get rid of; exclude. **elimination** *n.*, **eliminator** *n.*
elite /ayleét/ *n.* group regarded as superior and favoured.
elitism /ayleétiz'm/ *n.* favouring of or dominance by a selected group. **elitist** *n.*
elixir *n.* fragrant liquid used as medicine or flavouring.
Elizabethan *a.* of Elizabeth I's reign (1558–1603).
elk *n.* large deer.
ellipse *n.* regular oval.
ellipsis *n.* (*pl.* **-pses**) omission of words.
elliptical *a.* shaped like an ellipse; having omissions. **elliptically** *adv.*
elm *n.* tree with rough serrated leaves; its wood.
elocution *n.* style or art of speaking. **elocutionary** *a.*
elongate *v.* lengthen.
elope *v.* run away secretly with a lover. **elopement** *n.*
eloquence *n.* fluent speaking. **eloquent** *a.*, **eloquently** *adv.*
else *adv.* besides; otherwise.
elsewhere *adv.* somewhere else.
elucidate *v.* throw light on, explain. **elucidation** *n.*
elude *v.* escape skilfully from; avoid; escape the memory or understanding of. **elusion** *n.*
elusive *a.* eluding, escaping.
elver *n.* young eel.
emaciated *a.* thin from illness or starvation. **emaciation** *n.*
emanate *v.* issue, originate from a source. **emanation** *n.*
emancipate *v.* liberate, free from restraint. **emancipation** *n.*
emasculate *v.* deprive of force, weaken. **emasculation** *n.*
embalm *v.* preserve (a corpse) by using spices or chemicals. **embalmment** *n.*
embankment *n.* bank or stone structure to keep a river from spreading or to carry a railway.
embargo *n.* (*pl.* **-oes**) order forbidding commerce or other activity.
embark *v.* board a ship; begin an undertaking. **embarkation** *n.*
embarrass *v.* cause to feel awkward or ashamed. **embarrassment** *n.*
embassy *n.* ambassador and staff; their headquarters.
embed *v.* (**embedded**) fix firmly in a surrounding mass.
embellish *v.* ornament; improve (a story) with invented details. **embellishment** *n.*
embers *n.pl.* small pieces of live coal or wood in a dying fire.
embezzle *v.* take (money etc.) fraudulently for one's own use. **embezzlement** *n.*, **embezzler** *n.*
embitter *v.* rouse bitter feelings in. **embitterment** *n.*
emblem *n.* symbol, design used as a badge etc.
emblematic *a.* serving as an emblem. **emblematically** *adv.*
embody *v.* express (principles or ideas) in visible form; incorporate. **embodiment** *n.*
embolden *v.* make bold, encourage.
embolism *n.* obstruction of a blood vessel by a clot or air-bubble.
emboss *v.* decorate by a raised design; mould in relief.
embrace *v.* hold closely and lovingly, hold each other thus; accept, adopt; include. — *n.* act of embracing, hug.
embrocation *n.* liquid for rubbing on the body to relieve aches.
embroider *v.* ornament with needlework; embellish (a story). **embroidery** *n.*
embroil *v.* involve in an argument or quarrel etc.
embryo *n.* (*pl.* **-os**) animal developing in a womb or egg. **embryonic** *a.*
embryology *n.* study of embryos.
emend *v.* alter to remove errors. **emendation** *n.*, **emendatory** *a.*
emerald *n.* bright green precious stone; its colour.
emerge *v.* come up or out into view; become known. **emergence** *n.*, **emergent** *a.*
emergency *n.* serious situation needing prompt attention.
emery *n.* coarse abrasive. **emery board** strip of cardboard coated with emery, used for filing the nails.
emetic *n.* medicine used to cause vomiting.
emigrate *v.* leave one country and go to settle in another. **emigration** *n.*, **emigrant** *n.*
eminence *n.* state of being eminent; piece of rising ground.
eminent *a.* famous, distinguished. **eminently** *adv.*
emir /emeér/ *n.* Muslim ruler. **emirate** *n.* his territory.
emissary *n.* person sent to conduct negotiations.
emit *v.* (**emitted**) send out (light, heat, fumes, etc.); utter. **emission** *n.*, **emitter** *n.*
emollient *a.* softening, soothing. — *n.* emollient substance.

emolument *n.* fee; salary.
emotion *n.* intense mental feeling.
emotional *a.* of emotion(s); showing great emotion. **emotionally** *adv.*, **emotionalism** *n.*
emotive *a.* rousing emotion.
empathize *v.* show empathy; treat with empathy.
empathy *n.* ability to identify oneself mentally with, and so understand, a person or thing.
emperor *n.* male ruler of an empire.
emphasis *n.* (*pl.* **-ases**) special importance; vigour of expression etc.; stress on a sound or word.
emphasize *v.* lay emphasis on.
emphatic *a.* using or showing emphasis. **emphatically** *adv.*
emphysema *n.* abnormal distension of body tissue with air.
empire *n.* group of countries ruled by a supreme authority; large organization controlled by one person or group.
empirical *a.* based on observation or experiment, not on theory. **empirically** *adv.*, **empiricism** *n.*, **empiricist** *n.*
emplacement *n.* place or platform for a gun or battery of guns.
employ *v.* give work to; use the services of; make use of. **employment** *n.*, **employer** *n.*
employee *n.* person employed by another in return for wages.
empower *v.* authorize, enable.
empress *n.* female ruler of an empire; wife of an emperor.
empty *a.* (**-ier, -iest**) containing nothing; without occupant(s); idle; meaningless. — *v.* make or become empty. **emptiness** *n.*
emu *n.* large Australian bird resembling an ostrich.
emulate *v.* try to do as well as. **emulation** *n.*, **emulator** *n.*
emulsify *v.* convert or be converted into emulsion. **emulsification** *n.*, **emulsifier** *n.*
emulsion *n.* creamy liquid; light-sensitive coating on photographic film.
enable *v.* give the means or authority to do something.
enact *v.* make into a law; perform (a play etc.). **enactment** *n.*
enamel *n.* glass-like coating for metal or pottery; glossy paint; hard outer covering of teeth. — *v.* (**enamelled**) coat with enamel.
enamoured *a.* fond.
en bloc /ON blók/ all together.
encamp *v.* settle in a camp.
encampment *n.* camp.
encapsulate *v.* enclose (as) in a capsule; summarize. **encapsulation** *n.*
encase *v.* enclose in a case.
encephalitis *n.* inflammation of the brain.
enchant *v.* bewitch. **enchanter** *n.*, **enchantment** *n.*, **enchantress** *n.fem.*
encircle *v.* surround. **encirclement** *n.*
enclave *n.* small territory wholly within the boundaries of another.
enclose *v.* shut in on all sides, seclude; include with other contents.
enclosure *n.* enclosing; enclosed area; thing enclosed.
encompass *v.* encircle; include.
encore *n.* a (call for) repetition of a performance. — *int.* this call.
encounter *v.* meet by chance; be faced with. — *n.* chance meeting; battle.
encourage *v.* give hope or confidence or stimulus to; urge. **encouragement** *n.*
encroach *v.* intrude on someone's territory or rights. **encroachment** *n.*
encrust *v.* cover with a crust of hard material. **encrustation** *n.*
encumber *v.* be a burden to, hamper. **encumbrance** *n.*
encyclical *n.* pope's letter for circulation to churches.
encyclopaedia *n.* book of information on many subjects. **encyclopaedic** *a.*
end *n.* limit; furthest point or part; final part; destruction, death; purpose. — *v.* bring or come to an end. **make ends meet** keep expenditure within income.
endanger *v.* cause danger to.
endear *v.* cause to be loved.
endearment *n.* word(s) expressing love.
endeavour *v.* & *n.* attempt.
endemic *a.* commonly found in a specified area or people.
ending *n.* final part.
endive *n.* curly-leaved plant used in salads; (*US*) chicory.
endless *a.* without end, continual. **endlessly** *adv.*
endocrine gland gland secreting hormones into the blood.
endorse *v.* sign the back of (a cheque); note an offence on (a driving licence etc.); declare approval of. **endorsement** *n.*
endow *v.* provide with a permanent income. **endowment** *n.*
endurance *n.* power of enduring.
endure *v.* experience and survive (pain or hardship); tolerate; last. **endurable** *a.*
enema *n.* liquid injected into the rectum.
enemy *n.* one who is hostile to and seeks to harm another.
energetic *a.* full of energy; done with energy. **energetically** *adv.*

energize *v.* give energy to; cause electricity to flow into.

energy *n.* capacity for vigorous activity; ability of matter or radiation to do work; oil etc. as fuel.

enervate *v.* cause to lose vitality. **enervation** *n.*

enfant terrible /ónfon tereébla/ person whose behaviour is embarrassing or irresponsible.

enfeeble *v.* make feeble. **enfeeblement** *n.*

enfold *v.* wrap up; clasp.

enforce *v.* compel obedience to. **enforceable** *a.*, **enforcement** *n.*

enfranchise *v.* give the right to vote. **enfranchisement** *n.*

engage *v.* employ (a person); reserve; occupy the attention of; begin a battle with; interlock.

engaged *a.* having promised to marry a specified person; occupied; in use.

engagement *n.* engaging something; promise to marry a specified person; appointment; battle.

engaging *a.* attractive.

engender *v.* give rise to.

engine *n.* machine using fuel and supplying power; railway locomotive.

engineer *n.* person skilled in engineering; one in charge of machines and engines. — *v.* contrive; bring about.

engineering *n.* application of science for the design and building of machines and structures.

English *a.* & *n.* (language) of England. **Englishman** *n.* (*pl.* **-men**), **Englishwoman** *n.* (*pl.* **-women**).

engrave *v.* cut (a design) into a hard surface; ornament thus. **engraver** *n.*

engraving *n.* print made from an engraved metal plate.

engross *v.* occupy fully by absorbing the attention. **engrossment** *n.*

engulf *v.* swamp.

enhance *v.* increase the quality or power etc. of. **enhancement** *n.*

enigma *n.* mysterious person or thing. **enigmatic** *a.*, **enigmatically** *adv.*

enjoy *v.* get pleasure from; have as an advantage or benefit. **enjoyable** *a.* **enjoyment** *n.*

enlarge *v.* make or become larger. **enlarge upon** say more about. **enlargement** *n.*, **enlarger** *n.*

enlighten *v.* inform; free from ignorance. **enlightenment** *n.*

enlist *v.* enrol for military service; get the support of. **enlistment** *n.*

enliven *v.* make more lively. **enlivenment** *n.*

en masse /on máss/ all together.

enmesh *v.* entangle.

enmity *n.* hostility; hatred.

ennoble *v.* make noble. **ennoblement** *n.*

ennui /onweé/ *n.* boredom.

enormity *n.* great wickedness.

enormous *a.* very large.

enough *a.*, *adv.*, & *n.* as much or as many as necessary.

enquire *v.* ask. **enquiry** *n.*

enrage *v.* make furious.

enrapture *v.* delight intensely.

enrich *v.* make richer. **enrichment** *n.*

enrol *v.* (**enrolled**) admit as or become a member. **enrolment** *n.*

en route /on root/ on the way.

ensconce *v.* establish securely or comfortably.

ensemble /onsómb'l/ *n.* thing viewed as a whole; set of performers; outfit.

enshrine *v.* set in a shrine. **enshrinement** *n.*

ensign *n.* military or naval flag.

enslave *v.* make slave(s) of. **enslavement** *n.*

ensnare *v.* snare; trap.

ensue *v.* happen afterwards or as a result.

en suite /on sweét/ forming a unit.

ensure *v.* make safe or certain.

entail *v.* make necessary.

entangle *v.* tangle; entwine and trap. **entanglement** *n.*

entente *n.* /ontónt/ friendly understanding between countries.

enter *v.* go or come in or into; put on a list or into a record etc.; register as a competitor.

enteritis *n.* inflammation of the intestines.

enterprise *n.* bold undertaking; initiative; business activity.

enterprising *a.* full of initiative.

entertain *v.* amuse, occupy pleasantly; receive with hospitality; consider favourably. **entertainer** *n.*, **entertainment** *n.*

enthral *v.* (**enthralled**) hold spellbound. **enthralment** *n.*

enthrone *v.* place on a throne. **enthronement** *n.*

enthuse *v.* fill with or show enthusiasm.

enthusiasm *n.* eager liking or interest. **enthusiastic** *a.*, **enthusiastically** *adv.*

enthusiast *n.* person who is full of enthusiasm for something.

entice *v.* attract by offering something pleasant. **enticement** *n.*

entire *a.* complete. **entirely** *adv.*

entirety *n.* **in its entirety** as a whole.

entitle *v.* give a title to (a book etc.); give (a person) a right or claim. **entitlement** *n.*

entity *n.* a separate thing.
entomology *n.* study of insects. **entomological** *a.*, **entomologist** *n.*
entourage /óntooraázh/ *n.* people accompanying an important person.
entrails *n.pl.* intestines.
entrance [1] /éntrənss/ *n.* entering; door or passage by which one enters; right of admission, fee for this.
entrance [2] /intraánss/ *v.* fill with intense delight.
entreat *v.* request earnestly or emotionally. **entreaty** *n.*
entrench *v.* establish firmly. **entrenchment** *n.*
entrepreneur *n.* person who organizes a commercial undertaking, esp. involving risk. **entrepreneurial** *a.*
entrust *v.* give as a responsibility, place in a person's care.
entry *n.* entering; entrance; item entered in a list etc. or for a competition.
entwine *v.* twine round.
enumerate *v.* mention (items) one by one. **enumeration** *n.*
enunciate *v.* pronounce; state clearly. **enunciation** *n.*
envelop *v.* (**enveloped**) wrap, cover on all sides. **envelopment** *n.*
envelope *n.* folded gummed cover for a letter.
enviable *a.* desirable enough to arouse envy. **enviably** *adv.*
envious *a.* full of envy. **enviously** *adv.*
environment *n.* surroundings; natural world. **environmental** *a.*, **environmentally** *adv.*
environmentalist *a.* & *n.* (person) seeking to protect the natural environment.
environs *n.pl.* surrounding districts, esp. of a town.
envisage *v.* imagine; foresee.
envoy *n.* messenger, esp. to a foreign government.
envy *n.* discontent aroused by another's possessions or success; object of this. — *v.* feel envy of.
enzyme *n.* protein formed in living cells (or produced synthetically) and assisting chemical processes.
epaulette *n.* ornamental shoulder-piece.
ephemeral *a.* lasting only a short time. **ephemerally** *adv.*
epic *n.* long poem, story, or film about heroic deeds or history. — *a.* of or like an epic.
epicentre *n.* point where an earthquake reaches the earth's surface.
epicure *n.* person who enjoys delicate food and drink. **epicurean** *a.* & *n.*, **epicureanism** *n.*
epidemic *n.* outbreak of a disease etc. spreading through a community.
epidermis *n.* outer layer of the skin.
epidural *n.* spinal anaesthetic affecting the lower part of the body.
epiglottis *n.* cartilage that covers the larynx in swallowing.
epigram *n.* short witty saying. **epigrammatic** *a.*
epilepsy *n.* disorder of the nervous system, causing fits. **epileptic** *a.* & *n.*
epilogue *n.* short concluding section.
episcopal *a.* of or governed by bishop(s).
episcopalian *a.* & *n.* (member) of an episcopal church.
episode *n.* event forming one part of a sequence; one part of a serial. **episodic** *a.*, **episodically** *adv.*
epistle *n.* letter. **epistolary** *a.*
epitaph *n.* words inscribed on a tomb or describing a dead person.
epithet *n.* descriptive word(s).
epitome /ipíttəmi/ *n.* a perfect model or example.
epitomize *v.* be an epitome of. **epitomization** *n.*
epoch /éepok/ *n.* particular period.
eponymous *a.* after whom something is named.
equable *a.* free from extremes; even-tempered. **equably** *adv.*
equal *a.* same in size, amount, value, etc.; having the same rights or status. — *n.* person or thing equal to another. — *v.* (**equalled**) be the same in size etc. as; do something equal to. **equally** *adv.*, **equality** *n.*
equalize *v.* make or become equal; equal an opponent's score. **equalization** *n.*
equalizer *n.* equalizing goal etc.
equanimity *n.* calmness of mind or temper.
equate *v.* consider to be equal or equivalent.
equation *n.* mathematical statement that two expressions are equal.
equator *n.* imaginary line round the earth at an equal distance from the North and South Poles. **equatorial** *a.*
equestrian *a.* of horse-riding; on horseback.
equidistant *a.* at an equal distance.
equilateral *a.* having all sides equal.
equilibrium *n.* state of balance.
equine /ékwīn/ *a.* of or like a horse.
equinox *n.* time of year when night and day are of equal length. **equinoctial** *a.*
equip *v.* (**equipped**) supply with what is needed.
equipment *n.* equipping; tools or outfit etc. needed for a job or expedition.

equipoise *n.* equilibrium.
equitable *a.* fair and just. **equitably** *adv.*
equitation *n.* horse-riding.
equity *n.* fairness, impartiality; (*pl.*) stocks and shares not bearing fixed interest.
equivalent *a.* equal in amount, value, or meaning etc. — *n.* equivalent thing. **equivalence** *n.*
equivocal *a.* ambiguous; questionable. **equivocally** *adv.*
equivocate *v.* use words ambiguously. **equivocation** *n.*
era *n.* period of history.
eradicate *v.* wipe out. **eradication** *n.*
erase *v.* rub out. **eraser** *n.*, **erasure** *n.*
erect *a.* upright; rigid from sexual excitement. — *v.* set up, build.
erection *n.* erecting; becoming erect; thing erected, building.
ergonomics *n.* study of work and its environment in order to improve efficiency. **ergonomic** *a.*, **ergonomically** *adv.*
ermine *n.* stoat; its white winter fur.
erode *v.* wear away gradually. **erosion** *n.*, **erosive** *a.*
erogenous *a.* arousing sexual excitement.
erotic *a.* of or arousing sexual desire. **erotically** *adv.*, **eroticism** *n.*
err *v.* **(erred)** make a mistake; be incorrect; sin.
errand *n.* short journey to take or fetch something; its purpose.
errant *a.* misbehaving.
erratic *a.* irregular, uneven. **erratically** *adv.*
erroneous *a.* incorrect. **erroneously** *adv.*
error *n.* mistake; being wrong; amount of inaccuracy.
erstwhile *a.* former.
erudite *a.* learned. **erudition** *n.*
erupt *v.* break out or through; eject lava. **eruption** *n.*
escalate *v.* increase in intensity or extent. **escalation** *n.*
escalator *n.* moving staircase.
escalope *n.* slice of boneless meat, esp. veal.
escapade *n.* piece of reckless or mischievous conduct.
escape *v.* get free; get out of its container; avoid; be forgotten or unnoticed by. — *n.* act or means of escaping.
escapee *n.* one who escapes.
escapism *n.* escape from the realities of life. **escapist** *n.* & *a.*
escapologist *n.* person who entertains by escaping from confinement.
escarpment *n.* steep slope at the edge of a plateau etc.
eschew *v.* abstain from.
escort *n.* /éskort/ person(s) or vehicle(s) accompanying another as a protection or honour; person accompanying a person of the opposite sex socially. — *v.* /iskórt/ act as escort to.
escudo *n.* (*pl.* **-os**) unit of money in Portugal.
Eskimo *n.* (*pl.* **-os** *or* **-o**) member or language of a people living in Arctic regions.
esoteric *a.* intended only for people with special knowledge or interest.
espadrille *n.* canvas shoe with a sole of plaited fibre.
espalier *n.* trellis; shrub or tree trained on this.
esparto *n.* a kind of grass used in making paper.
especial *a.* special, outstanding. **especially** *adv.*
espionage *n.* spying.
esplanade *n.* promenade.
espouse *v.* support (a cause); marry. **espousal** *n.*
espresso *n.* (*pl.* **-os**) coffee made by forcing steam through powdered coffee beans.
esprit de corps /espreé də kór/ loyalty uniting a group.
espy *v.* catch sight of.
Esq. *abbr.* Esquire, courtesy title placed after a man's surname.
essay *n.* /éssay/ short literary composition in prose. — *v.* /esáy/ attempt.
essence *n.* indispensable quality or element; concentrated extract.
essential *a.* unable to be dispensed with; fundamental. — *n.* essential thing. **essentially** *adv.*
establish *v.* set up; settle; cause to be accepted; prove.
establishment *n.* establishing; staff of employees; firm or institution; **the Establishment** people established in authority.
estate *n.* landed property; residential or industrial district planned as a unit; property left at one's death. **estate car** car that can carry passengers and goods in one compartment.
esteem *v.* think highly of. — *n.* favourable opinion, respect.
estimable *a.* worthy of esteem.
estimate *n.* /éstimət/ judgement of a thing's approximate value, amount, cost, etc. — *v.* /éstimayt/ form an estimate of. **estimation** *n.*
estrange *v.* cause to be no longer friendly or loving. **estrangement** *n.*
estuary *n.* mouth of a large river, affected by tides. **estuarine** *a.*
etc. *abbr.* = **et cetera** and other things of the same kind.

etch *v.* engrave with acids. **etcher** *n.*, **etching** *n.*

eternal *a.* existing always; unchanging. **eternally** *adv.*

eternity *n.* infinite time; endless period of life after death. **eternity ring** jewelled finger ring symbolizing eternal love.

ether *n.* upper air; liquid used as an anaesthetic and solvent.

ethereal *a.* light and delicate; heavenly. **ethereally** *adv.*, **ethereality** *n.*

ethic *n.* moral principle; (as *pl.*) moral philosophy.

ethical *a.* of ethics; morally correct, honourable. **ethically** *adv.*

ethnic *a.* of a group sharing a common origin, culture, or language. **ethnically** *adv.*, **ethnicity** *n.*

ethnology *n.* study of human races and their characteristics. **ethnological** *a.*, **ethnologist** *n.*

ethos /eéthoss/ *n.* characteristic spirit and beliefs.

etiolate /eétiōlayt/ *v.* make pale through lack of light. **etiolation** *n.*

etiquette *n.* rules of correct behaviour.

etymology *n.* account of a word's origin and development. **etymological** *a.*, **etymologically** *adv.*, **etymologist** *n.*

eucalypt, eucalyptus *ns.* evergreen tree with leaves that yield a strong-smelling oil.

Eucharist *n.* Christian sacrament in which bread and wine are consumed; this bread and wine. **Eucharistic** *a.*

eugenics *n.* science of improving the human race by breeding.

eulogy *n.* piece of spoken or written praise. **eulogistic** *a.*, **eulogize** *v.*

eunuch *n.* castrated man.

euphemism *n.* mild word(s) substituted for improper or blunt one(s). **euphemistic** *a.*, **euphemistically** *adv.*

euphonium *n.* tenor tuba.

euphony *n.* pleasantness of sounds, esp. in words.

euphoria *n.* feeling of happiness. **euphoric** *a.*, **euphorically** *adv.*

Eurasian *a.* of Europe and Asia; of mixed European and Asian parentage. — *n.* Eurasian person.

eureka *int.* I have found it! (announcing a discovery etc.).

Euro- *pref.* European.

European *a.* of Europe or its people. — *n.* European person.

Eustachian tube /yo͞ostáysh'n/ passage between the ear and the throat.

euthanasia *n.* bringing about an easy death, esp. to end suffering.

evacuate *v.* send away from a dangerous place; empty. **evacuation** *n.*

evacuee *n.* evacuated person.

evade *v.* avoid by cleverness or trickery.

evaluate *v.* find out or state the value of; assess. **evaluation** *n.*

evangelical *a.* of or preaching the gospel. **evangelicalism** *n.*

evangelist *n.* author of a Gospel; person who preaches the gospel. **evangelism** *n.*, **evangelistic** *a.*

evaporate *v.* turn into vapour; cease to exist. **evaporation** *n.*

evasion *n.* evading; evasive answer or excuse.

evasive *a.* evading; not frank. **evasively** *adv.*, **evasiveness** *n.*

eve *n.* evening, day, or time just before a special event.

even *a.* level, smooth; uniform; calm; equal; exactly divisible by two. — *v.* make or become even. — *adv.* (used for emphasis or in comparing things). **evenly** *adv.*, **evenness** *n.*

evening *n.* latter part of the day, before nightfall.

event *n.* something that happens, esp. something important; item in a sports programme.

eventful *a.* full of incidents.

eventual *a.* coming at last, ultimate. **eventually** *adv.*

eventuality *n.* possible event.

ever *adv.* always; at any time.

evergreen *a.* having green leaves throughout the year. — *n.* evergreen tree or shrub.

everlasting *a.* lasting for ever or for a very long time.

evermore *adv.* for ever, always.

every *a.* each one without exception; each in a series; all possible.

everybody *pron.* every person.

everyday *a.* worn or used on ordinary days; ordinary.

everyone *pron.* everybody.

everything *pron.* all things; all that is important.

everywhere *adv.* in every place.

evict *v.* expel (a tenant) by legal process. **eviction** *n.*, **evictor** *n.*

evidence *n.* anything that gives reason for believing something; statements made in a law court to support a case. — *v.* be evidence of. **be in evidence** be conspicuous. **evidential** *a.*

evident *a.* obvious to the eye or mind. **evidently** *adv.*

evil *a.* morally bad; harmful; very unpleasant. — *n.* evil thing, sin, harm. **evilly** *adv.*, **evildoer** *n.*

evince *v.* show, indicate.
eviscerate *v.* disembowel. **evisceration** *n.*
evoke *v.* bring to one's mind. **evocation** *n.*, **evocative** *a.*
evolution *n.* process of developing into a different form; origination of living things by such development. **evolutionary** *a.*
evolve *v.* develop or work out gradually. **evolvement** *n.*
ewe *n.* female sheep.
ewer *n.* pitcher, water jug.
ex- *pref.* former.
exacerbate /igzássərbayt/ *v.* make worse; irritate. **exacerbation** *n.*
exact [1] *a.* accurate; giving all details. **exactness** *n.*
exact [2] *v.* insist on and obtain. **exaction** *n.*
exacting *a.* making great demands, requiring great effort.
exactly *adv.* in an exact manner; quite so, as you say.
exaggerate *v.* make seem greater than it really is. **exaggeration** *n.*, **exaggerator** *n.*
exalt *v.* raise in rank; praise highly; make joyful. **exaltation** *n.*
exam *n.* (*colloq.*) examination.
examination *n.* examining; formal test of knowledge or ability.
examine *v.* look at closely; question formally. **examiner** *n.*
examinee *n.* person being tested in an examination.
example *n.* fact illustrating a general rule; typical specimen; person or thing worthy of imitation. **make an example of** punish as a warning to others.
exasperate *v.* annoy greatly. **exasperation** *n.*
excavate *v.* make (a hole) by digging, dig out; reveal by digging. **excavation** *n.*, **excavator** *n.*
exceed *v.* be greater than; go beyond the limit of.
exceedingly *adv.* very.
excel *v.* (**excelled**) be or do better than; be very good at something.
excellent *a.* extremely good. **excellently** *adv.*, **excellence** *n.*
except *prep.* not including. — *v.* exclude from a statement etc.
excepting *prep.* except.
exception *n.* excepting; thing that does not follow the general rule. **take exception to** object to.
exceptionable *a.* offensive.
exceptional *a.* very unusual; outstandingly good. **exceptionally** *adv.*
excerpt *n.* extract from a book, film, etc.
excess *n.* exceeding of due limits; amount by which one quantity etc. exceeds another. — *a.* exceeding a limit.
excessive *a.* too much. **excessively** *adv.*
exchange *v.* give or receive in place of another thing. — *n.* exchanging; price at which one currency is exchanged for another; place where merchants, brokers, or dealers assemble to do business; centre where telephone lines are connected. **exchangeable** *a.*
excise [1] /éksīz/ *n.* duty or tax on certain goods and licences.
excise [2] /iksīz/ *v.* cut out or away. **excision** *n.*
excitable *a.* easily excited. **excitably** *adv.*, **excitability** *n.*
excitation *n.* exciting, arousing; stimulation.
excite *v.* rouse the emotions of, make eager; cause (a feeling or reaction). **excitement** *n.*
exclaim *v.* cry out or utter suddenly.
exclamation *n.* exclaiming; word(s) exclaimed. **exclamation mark** punctuation mark ! placed after an exclamation. **exclamatory** *a.*
exclude *v.* keep out from a place or group or privilege etc.; omit, ignore as irrelevant; make impossible. **exclusion** *n.*
exclusive *a.* excluding others; catering only for the wealthy; not obtainable elsewhere. **exclusive of** not including. **exclusively** *adv.*, **exclusiveness** *n.*
excommunicate *v.* cut off from a Church or its sacraments. **excommunication** *n.*
excoriate *v.* strip skin from; criticize severely. **excoriation** *n.*
excrement *n.* faeces.
excrescence *n.* outgrowth on an animal or plant.
excreta *n.pl.* matter (esp. faeces) excreted from the body.
excrete *v.* expel (waste matter) from the body or tissues. **excretion** *n.*, **excretory** *a.*
excruciating *a.* intensely painful.
excursion *n.* short trip or outing, returning to the starting point.
excusable *a.* able to be excused. **excusably** *adv.*
excuse *v.* /ikskyōōz/ pardon (a person); overlook (a fault); justify; exempt. — *n.* /ikskyōōss/ reason put forward to justify a fault etc.
ex-directory *a.* deliberately not listed in a telephone directory.
execrable *a.* abominable. **execrably** *adv.*
execrate *v.* express loathing for; utter curses. **execration** *n.*
execute *v.* carry out (an order); produce (a

work of art); put (a condemned person) to death. **execution** *n.*

executioner *n.* one who executes condemned person(s).

executive *n.* person or group with managerial powers, or with authority to put government decisions into effect. — *a.* having such power or authority.

executor *n.* person appointed to carry out the terms of one's will. **executrix** *n.fem.*

exemplary *a.* fit to be imitated; serving as a warning to others.

exemplify *v.* serve as an example of. **exemplification** *n.*

exempt *a.* free from a customary obligation or payment etc. — *v.* make exempt. **exemption** *n.*

exercise *n.* use of one's powers or rights; activity, esp. designed to train the body or mind. — *v.* use (powers etc.); (cause to) take exercise. **exercise book** book for writing in.

exert *v.* bring into use. **exert oneself** make an effort.

exertion *n.* exerting; great effort.

exeunt /éksiunt/ (*stage direction*) they leave the stage.

exfoliate *v.* come off in scales or layers. **exfoliation** *n.*

ex gratia /eks gráyshə/ done or given as a concession, without legal obligation.

exhale *v.* breathe out; give off in vapour. **exhalation** *n.*

exhaust *v.* use up completely; tire out. — *n.* waste gases from an engine etc.; device through which they are expelled. **exhaustible** *a.*

exhaustion *n.* exhausting; being tired out.

exhaustive *a.* thorough; comprehensive. **exhaustively** *adv.*

exhibit *v.* display, present for the public to see. — *n.* thing exhibited. **exhibitor** *n.*

exhibition *n.* exhibiting; public display.

exhibitionism *n.* tendency to behave in a way designed to attract attention. **exhibitionist** *n.*

exhilarate *v.* make joyful or lively. **exhilaration** *n.*

exhort *v.* urge or advise earnestly. **exhortation** *n.*, **exhortative** *a.*

exhume *v.* dig up (a buried corpse). **exhumation** *n.*

exigency, exigence *ns.* urgent need; emergency.

exigent *a.* urgent; requiring much, exacting.

exiguous *a.* very small. **exiguously** *adv.*, **exiguousness** *n.*

exile *n.* banishment or long absence from one's country or home, esp. as a punishment; exiled person. — *v.* send into exile.

exist *v.* have being; be real; maintain life. **existence** *n.*, **existent** *a.*

existentialism *n.* philosophical theory emphasizing that man is free to choose his actions. **existentialist** *n.*

exit (*stage direction*) he or she leaves the stage. — *n.* departure from a stage or place; way out.

exodus *n.* departure of many people.

ex officio /éks əfishiō/ because of one's official position.

exonerate *v.* declare or show to be blameless. **exoneration** *n.*

exorbitant *a.* (of a price or demand) much too great. **exorbitantly** *adv.*, **exorbitance** *n.*

exorcize *v.* drive out (an evil spirit) by prayer; free (a person or place) of an evil spirit. **exorcism** *n.*, **exorcist** *n.*

exotic *a.* brought from abroad; colourful, unusual. **exotically** *adv.*

expand *v.* make or become larger; spread out; give a fuller account of; become genial. **expandable** *a.*, **expander** *n.*, **expansion** *n.*

expanse *n.* wide area or extent.

expansive *a.* able to expand; genial, communicative. **expansiveness** *n.*

expatiate /ikspáyshiayt/ *v.* speak or write at length about a subject.

expatriate *a.* living abroad. — *n.* expatriate person.

expect *v.* believe that (a person or thing) will come or (a thing) will happen; be confident of receiving; think, suppose.

expectant *a.* filled with expectation. **expectant mother** pregnant woman. **expectantly** *adv.*, **expectancy** *n.*

expectation *n.* expecting; thing expected; probability.

expectorant *n.* medicine for causing a person to expectorate.

expectorate *v.* cough and spit phlegm; spit. **expectoration** *n.*

expedient *a.* advantageous rather than right or just. **expediency** *n.*

expedite *v.* help or hurry the progress of.

expedition *n.* journey for a purpose; people and equipment for this. **expeditionary** *a.*

expeditious *a.* speedy and efficient. **expeditiously** *adv.*

expel *v.* (**expelled**) send or drive out; compel to leave.

expend *v.* spend; use up.

expendable *a.* able to be expended; not worth saving.

expenditure *n.* expending of money etc.; amount expended.

expense *n.* cost; cause of spending money; (*pl.*) reimbursement.
expensive *a.* involving great expenditure; costing or charging more than average. **expensively** *adv.*, **expensiveness** *n.*
experience *n.* observation of fact(s) or event(s), practice in doing something; knowledge or skill gained by this. — *v.* feel or have an experience of.
experienced *a.* having had much experience.
experiment *n.* & *v.* test to find out or prove something; trial of something new. **experimentation** *n.*
experimental *a.* of or used in experiments; still being tested. **experimentally** *adv.*
expert *n.* person with great knowledge or skill in a particular thing. — *a.* having great knowledge or skill. **expertly** *adv.*
expertise *n.* expert knowledge or skill.
expiate *v.* make amends for. **expiation** *n.*, **expiatory** *a.*
expire *v.* breathe out (air); die; cease to be valid. **expiration** *n.*
expiry *n.* termination of validity.
explain *v.* make clear, show the meaning of; account for. **explanation** *n.*, **explanatory** *a.*
expletive *n.* violent exclamation, oath.
explicable *a.* able to be explained. **explicability** *n.*
explicit *a.* stated plainly. **explicitly** *adv.*, **explicitness** *n.*
explode *v.* (cause to) expand and break with a loud noise; show sudden violent emotion; increase suddenly. **explosion** *n.*
exploit *n.* /éksployt/ notable deed. — *v.* /iksplóyt/ make good use of; use selfishly. **exploitable** *a.*, **exploitation** *n.*, **exploiter** *n.*
explore *v.* travel into (a country etc.) in order to learn about it; examine. **exploration** *n.*, **exploratory** *a.*, **explorer** *n.*
explosive *a.* & *n.* (substance) able or liable to explode.
exponent *n.* one who favours a specified theory etc.
export *v.* /ekspórt/ send (goods etc.) to another country for sale. — *n.* /éksport/ exporting; thing exported. **exportation** *n.*, **exporter** *n.*
expose *v.* leave uncovered or unprotected; subject to a risk etc.; allow light to reach (film etc.); reveal. **exposure** *n.*
exposé /ekspṓzay/ *n.* statement of facts; disclosure.
exposition *n.* expounding; explanation; large exhibition.
expostulate *v.* protest, remonstrate. **expostulation** *n.*, **expostulatory** *a.*
expound *v.* explain in detail.
express *a.* definitely stated; travelling rapidly, designed for high speed. — *adv.* at high speed. — *n.* fast train or bus making few or no stops. — *v.* make (feelings or qualities) known; put into words; represent by symbols; press or squeeze out. **expressible** *a.*
expression *n.* expressing; word or phrase; look or manner that expresses feeling.
expressionism *n.* style of art seeking to express feelings rather than represent objects realistically. **expressionist** *n.*
expressive *a.* expressing something; full of expression. **expressively** *adv.*
expressly *adv.* explicitly; for a particular purpose.
expropriate *v.* seize (property); dispossess. **expropriation** *n.*
expulsion *n.* expelling; being expelled. **expulsive** *a.*
expunge *v.* wipe out.
expurgate *v.* remove (objectionable matter) from (a book etc.). **expurgation** *n.*, **expurgator** *n.*, **expurgatory** *a.*
exquisite *a.* having exceptional beauty; acute, keenly felt. **exquisitely** *adv.*
extant *a.* still existing.
extemporize *v.* speak, perform, or produce without preparation. **extemporary** *a.*, **extemporization** *n.*
extend *v.* make longer; stretch; reach; enlarge; offer.
extendible, extensible *adjs.* able to be extended.
extension *n.* extending; extent; additional part or period; subsidiary telephone, its number.
extensive *a.* large in area or scope. **extensively** *adv.*
extensor *n.* muscle that extends a part of the body.
extent *n.* space over which a thing extends; scope; large area.
extenuate *v.* make (an offence) seem less great by providing a partial excuse. **extenuation** *n.*
exterior *a.* on or coming from the outside. — *n.* exterior surface or appearance.
exterminate *v.* destroy all members or examples of. **extermination** *n.*, **exterminator** *n.*
external *a.* of or on the outside. **externally** *adv.*
extinct *a.* no longer burning or active or existing in living form.
extinction *n.* extinguishing; making or becoming extinct.

extinguish *v.* put out (a light or flame); end the existence of.

extinguisher *n.* device for discharging liquid chemicals or foam to extinguish a fire.

extirpate *v.* root out, destroy. **extirpation** *n.*

extol *v.* **(extolled)** praise enthusiastically.

extort *v.* obtain by force or threats. **extortion** *n.*, **extortioner** *n.*

extortionate *a.* excessively high in price, exorbitant. **extortionately** *adv.*

extra *a.* additional, more than is usual or expected. —*adv.* more than usually; in addition. —*n.* extra thing; person employed as one of a crowd in a film.

extra- *pref.* outside, beyond.

extract *v.* /ikstrákt/ take out or obtain by force or effort; obtain by suction or pressure or chemical treatment. —*n.* /ékstrakt/ substance extracted from another; passage from a book, play, film, or music. **extractor** *n.*

extraction *n.* extracting; lineage.

extradite *v.* hand over (an accused person) for trial in the country where a crime was committed. **extradition** *n.*

extramarital *a.* of sexual relationships outside marriage.

extramural *a.* for students who are not members of a university.

extraneous *a.* of external origin; not relevant. **extraneously** *adv.*

extraordinary *a.* remarkable; beyond what is usual. **extraordinarily** *adv.*

extrapolate *v.* estimate on the basis of available data. **extrapolation** *n.*

extrasensory *a.* achieved by some means other than the known senses.

extraterrestrial *a.* of or from outside the earth or its atmosphere.

extravagant *a.* spending or using excessively; going beyond what is reasonable. **extravagantly** *adv.*, **extravagance** *n.*

extravaganza *n.* lavish spectacular display or entertainment.

extreme *a.* very great or intense; at the end(s), outermost; going to great lengths in actions or views. —*n.* end; extreme degree or act or condition. **extremely** *adv.*

extremist *n.* person holding extreme views. **extremism** *n.*

extremity *n.* extreme point; extreme degree of need or danger; (*pl.*) hands and feet.

extricable *a.* able to be extricated.

extricate *v.* free from an entanglement or difficulty. **extrication** *n.*

extrinsic *a.* not intrinsic; extraneous. **extrinsically** *adv.*

extrovert *n.* lively sociable person. **extroversion** *n.*

extrude *v.* thrust or squeeze out. **extrusion** *n.*, **extrusive** *a.*

exuberant *a.* full of high spirits; growing profusely. **exuberantly** *adv.*, **exuberance** *n.*

exude *v.* ooze; give off like sweat or a smell. **exudation** *n.*

exult *v.* rejoice greatly. **exultant** *a.* exulting. **exultation** *n.*

eye *n.* organ of sight; iris of this; region round it; power of seeing; thing like an eye, spot, hole. —*v.* **(eyed, eyeing)** look at, watch. **eye-opener** *n.* thing that brings enlightenment or great surprise. **eye-shade** *n.* device to protect the eyes from strong light. **eye-shadow** *n.* cosmetic applied to the skin round the eyes. **eye-tooth** *n.* canine tooth in the upper jaw, below the eye.

eyeball *n.* whole of the eye within the eyelids.

eyebrow *n.* fringe of hair on the ridge above the eye socket.

eyelash *n.* one of the hairs fringing the eyelids.

eyelet *n.* small hole; ring strengthening this.

eyelid *n.* either of the two folds of skin that can be moved together to cover the eye.

eyepiece *n.* lens(es) to which the eye is applied in a telescope or microscope etc.

eyesight *n.* ability to see; range of vision.

eyesore *n.* ugly object.

eyewitness *n.* person who actually saw something happen.

eyrie /íri/ *n.* eagle's nest; house etc. perched high up.

F

F *abbr.* Fahrenheit.

fable *n.* story not based on fact, often with a moral. **fabled** *a.*

fabric *n.* cloth or knitted material; walls etc. of a building.

fabricate *v.* construct, manufacture; invent (a story etc.). **fabrication** *n.*, **fabricator** *n.*

fabulous *a.* incredibly great; marvellous. **fabulously** *adv.*

façade /fəsaád/ *n.* front of a building; outward appearance.

face *n.* front of the head; expression shown by its features; grimace; outward aspect; front or main side; dial of a clock; coal-face. — *v.* have or turn the face towards; meet firmly; put a facing on. **face flannel** cloth for washing one's face. **facelift** *n.* operation for tightening the skin of the face; alteration that improves the appearance.

faceless *a.* without identity; purposely not identifiable.

facet *n.* one of many sides of a cut stone or jewel; one aspect.

facetious *a.* intended or intending to be amusing. **facetiously** *adv.*, **facetiousness** *n.*

facia /fáyshə/ *n.* dashboard; name-plate over a shop front.

facial *a.* of the face. — *n.* beauty treatment for the face.

facile /fássīl/ *a.* done or doing something easily; superficial.

facilitate *v.* make easy or easier. **facilitation** *n.*

facility *n.* absence of difficulty; means for doing something.

facing *n.* covering made of different material.

facsimile *n.* a reproduction of a document etc.

fact *n.* thing known to have happened or to be true or to exist.

faction *n.* small united group within a larger one.

factitious *a.* made for a special purpose; artificial.

factor *n.* circumstance that contributes towards a result; number by which a given number can be divided exactly.

factory *n.* building(s) in which goods are manufactured.

factotum *n.* servant or assistant doing all kinds of work.

factual *a.* based on or containing facts. **factually** *adv.*

faculty *n.* any of the powers of the body or mind; department teaching a specified subject in a university or college.

fad *n.* craze, whim.

faddy *a.* having petty likes and dislikes, esp. about food.

fade *v.* (cause to) lose colour, freshness, or vigour; disappear gradually.

faeces /feésseez/ *n.pl.* waste matter discharged from the bowels. **faecal** *a.*

fag *v.* (**fagged**) toil; make tired. — *n.* (*colloq.*) tiring work, drudgery.

fagged *a.* tired.

faggot *n.* tied bundle of sticks or twigs; ball of chopped seasoned liver, baked or fried.

Fahrenheit *a.* of a temperature scale with the freezing point of water at 32° and boiling point at 212°.

faience /fīoNss/ *n.* painted glazed earthenware.

fail *v.* be unsuccessful; become weak, cease functioning; neglect or be unable; disappoint; become bankrupt; declare to be unsuccessful. — *n.* failure.

failing *n.* weakness or fault. — *prep.* in default of.

failure *n.* failing, lack of success; person or thing that fails.

faint *a.* indistinct; not intense; weak, feeble; about to faint. — *v.* collapse unconscious. — *n.* act or state of fainting. **faint-hearted** *a.* timid. **faintly** *adv.*, **faintness** *n.*

fair [1] *n.* funfair; gathering for a sale of goods, often with entertainments; exhibition of commercial goods. **fairground** *n.* open space where a fair is held.

fair [2] *a.* light in colour, having light-coloured hair; (of weather) fine, (of wind) favourable; just, unbiased; of moderate quality or amount. — *adv.* fairly.

fairing *n.* streamlining structure.

fairy *n.* imaginary small being with magical powers. **fairy godmother** benefactress. **fairy lights** strings of small coloured lights used as decorations. **fairy story, fairy tale** tale about fairies or magic; falsehood.

fairyland *n.* world of fairies; very beautiful place.

fait accompli /fáyt əkómplee/ thing already done and not reversible.

faith *n.* reliance, trust; belief in religious doctrine; loyalty, sincerity. **faith healing** cure etc. dependent on faith. **faith healer**.
faithful *a.* loyal, trustworthy; true, accurate. **faithfully** *adv.*, **faithfulness** *n.*
faithless *a.* disloyal.
fake *n.* a person or thing that is not genuine. — *a.* faked. — *v.* make an imitation of; pretend. **faker** *n.*
fakir /fáykeer/ *n.* Muslim or Hindu religious mendicant or ascetic.
falcon *n.* a kind of small hawk. **falconry** *n.* breeding and training of hawks. **falconer** *n.*
fall *v.* (**fell, fallen**) come or go down freely; lose one's position or office; decrease; die in battle; pass into a specified state; occur; (of the face) show dismay; be captured or conquered. — *n.* falling; amount of this; (*US*) autumn; (*pl.*) waterfall. **fall back on** have recourse to. **fall for** (*colloq.*) fall in love with; be deceived by. **fall out** quarrel; happen. **fallout** *n.* airborne radioactive debris. **fall short** be inadequate. **fall through** (of a plan) fail to be achieved.
fallacy *n.* false belief or reasoning. **fallacious** *a.*
fallible *a.* liable to make mistakes. **fallibility** *n.*
Fallopian tube either of the two tubes from the ovary to the womb.
fallow [1] *a.* (of land) left unplanted for a time. — *n.* such land.
fallow [2] *a.* **fallow deer** reddish-brown deer with white spots.
false *a.* incorrect; deceitful, unfaithful; not genuine, sham. **falsely** *adv.*, **falseness** *n.*
falsehood *n.* lie(s).
falsetto *n.* (*pl.* **-os**) voice above one's natural range.
falsify *v.* alter fraudulently; misrepresent. **falsification** *n.*
falsity *n.* falseness; falsehood.
falter *v.* go or function unsteadily; become weaker; speak hesitantly.
fame *n.* condition of being known to many people; good reputation.
familial *a.* of a family.
familiar *a.* well known; well acquainted; too informal. **familiarly** *adv.*, **familiarity** *n.*
familiarize *v.* make familiar. **familiarization** *n.*
family *n.* parents and their children; a person's children; set of relatives; group of related plants, animals, or things.
famine *n.* extreme scarcity (esp. of food) in a region.
famished *a.* extremely hungry.
famous *a.* known to very many people. **famously** *adv.*
fan [1] *n.* hand-held or mechanical device to create a current of air. — *v.* (**fanned**) cool with a fan; spread from a central point. **fan belt** belt driving a fan that cools a car engine.
fan [2] *n.* enthusiastic admirer or supporter. **fan mail** letters from fans.
fanatic *n.* person filled with excessive enthusiasm for something. **fanatical** *a.*, **fanatically** *adv.*, **fanaticism** *n.*
fanciful *a.* imaginative; imaginary. **fancifully** *adv.*
fancy *n.* imagination; thing imagined, unfounded idea; desire; liking. — *a.* ornamental, elaborate. — *v.* imagine; suppose; (*colloq.*) like, find attractive. **fancy dress** costume representing an animal, historical character, etc., worn for a party.
fandango *n.* (*pl.* **-oes**) lively Spanish dance.
fanfare *n.* short showy or ceremonious sounding of trumpets.
fang *n.* long sharp tooth; snake's tooth that injects venom.
fanlight *n.* small window above a door or larger window.
fantasia *n.* imaginative musical or other composition.
fantasize *v.* daydream.
fantastic *a.* absurdly fanciful; (*colloq.*) excellent. **fantastically** *adv.*
fantasy *n.* imagination; thing(s) imagined; fanciful design.
far *adv.* at or to or by a great distance. — *a.* distant, remote. **Far East** countries of east and south-east Asia. **far-fetched** *a.* not obvious, very unlikely.
farad *n.* unit of capacitance.
farce *n.* light comedy; absurd and useless proceedings, pretence. **farcical** *a.*, **farcically** *adv.*
fare *n.* price charged for a passenger to travel; passenger paying this; food provided. — *v.* get on or be treated (well, badly, etc.).
farewell *int.* & *n.* goodbye.
farinaceous *a.* starchy.
farm *n.* unit of land used for raising crops or livestock. — *v.* grow crops, raise livestock; use (land) for this. **farmer** *n.*
farmhouse *n.* farmer's house.
farmstead *n.* farm and its buildings.
farmyard *n.* enclosed area round farm buildings.
farrago /fəraágō/ *n.* (*pl.* **-os**) hotchpotch.
farrier *n.* smith who shoes horses.
farrow *v.* give birth to young pigs. — *n.* farrowing; litter of pigs.

farther *adv.* & *a.* at or to a greater distance, more remote.

farthest *adv.* & *a.* at or to the greatest distance, most remote.

fascinate *v.* attract and hold the interest of; charm greatly; make (a victim) powerless by a fixed look. **fascination** *n.*

fascism /fashiz'm/ *n.* system of extreme right-wing dictatorship. **fascist** *n.*

fashion *n.* manner or way of doing something; style popular at a given time. — *v.* shape, make.

fashionable *a.* in or using a currently popular style; used by stylish people. **fashionably** *adv.*

fast [1] *a.* moving or done quickly; allowing quick movement; showing a time ahead of the correct one; firmly fixed. — *adv.* quickly; firmly, tightly.

fast [2] *v.* go without food. — *n.* fasting; period appointed for this.

fasten *v.* fix firmly, tie or join together; become fastened.

fastener, fastening *ns.* device used for fastening something.

fastidious *a.* choosing only what is good; easily disgusted. **fastidiously** *adv.*, **fastidiousness** *n.*

fastness *n.* stronghold, fortress.

fat *n.* white or yellow substance found in animal bodies and certain seeds. — *a.* (**fatter, fattest**) excessively plump; containing much fat; fattened; thick; profitable. **fatness** *n.*, **fatty** *a.*

fatal *a.* causing or ending in death or disaster; fateful. **fatally** *adv.*

fatalist *n.* person who submits to what happens, regarding it as inevitable. **fatalism** *n.*, **fatalistic** *a.*, **fatalistically** *adv.*

fatality *n.* death caused by accident or in war etc.

fate *n.* power thought to control all events; person's destiny.

fated *a.* destined by fate; doomed.

fateful *a.* bringing great usu. unpleasant events. **fatefully** *adv.*

father *n.* male parent or ancestor; founder, originator; title of certain priests. — *v.* beget; originate. **father-in-law** *n.* (*pl.* **fathers-in-law**) father of one's wife or husband. **fatherhood** *n.*, **fatherly** *a.*

fatherland *n.* one's native country.

fatherless *a.* without a living or known father.

fathom *n.* measure (1.82 m) of the depth of water. — *v.* understand. **fathomable** *a.*

fatigue *n.* tiredness; weakness in metal etc., caused by stress; soldier's non-military task. — *v.* cause fatigue to.

fatstock *n.* livestock fattened for slaughter as food.

fatten *v.* make or become fat.

fatuous *a.* foolish, silly. **fatuously** *adv.*, **fatuousness** *n.*

faucet *n.* tap.

fault *n.* defect, imperfection; offence; responsibility for something wrong; break in layers of rock. — *v.* find fault(s) in; make imperfect. **at fault** responsible for a mistake etc. **faultless** *a.*, **faulty** *a.*

faun *n.* Latin rural deity with a goat's legs and horns.

fauna *n.pl.* animals of an area or period.

faux pas /fō paá/ (*pl.* **faux pas** /paás/) embarrassing blunder.

favour *n.* liking, approval; kindly or helpful act beyond what is due; favouritism. — *v.* regard or treat with favour; oblige; resemble (one parent etc.).

favourable *a.* giving or showing approval; pleasing, satisfactory; advantageous. **favourably** *adv.*

favourite *a.* liked above others. — *n.* favoured person or thing; competitor expected to win.

favouritism *n.* unfair favouring of one at the expense of others.

fawn [1] *n.* a deer in its first year; light yellowish brown. — *a.* fawn-coloured.

fawn [2] *v.* (of a dog) show affection; try to win favour by obsequiousness.

fax *n.* facsimile transmission by electronic scanning; document produced thus. — *v.* transmit by this process.

fear *n.* unpleasant sensation caused by nearness of danger or pain. — *v.* feel fear of; be afraid.

fearful *a.* terrible; feeling fear; (*colloq.*) extreme. **fearfully** *adv.*

fearless *a.* feeling no fear. **fearlessly** *adv.*, **fearlessness** *n.*

fearsome *a.* frightening, alarming.

feasible *a.* able to be done; plausible. **feasibly** *adv.*; **feasibility** *n.*

feast *n.* large elaborate meal; joyful festival; treat. — *v.* eat heartily; give a feast to.

feat *n.* remarkable achievement.

feather *n.* each of the structures with a central shaft and fringe of fine strands, growing from a bird's skin. — *v.* cover or fit with feathers; turn (an oar-blade etc.) to pass through the air edgeways. **feather-bed** *v.* make things financially easy for. **feather one's nest** enrich oneself. **feathery** *a.*

featherweight *n.* very lightweight thing or person.

feature *n.* one of the named parts of the face; noticeable quality; prominent article in a newspaper etc.; full-length cinema film. — *v.* give prominence to; be a feature of or in.

febrile /féebrīl/ *a.* of fever.

feckless *a.* incompetent and irresponsible. **fecklessness** *n.*

fecund *a.* fertile. **fecundity** *n.*

fed *see* **feed**. — *a.* **fed up** (*colloq.*) discontented, displeased.

federal *a.* of a system in which States unite under a central authority but are independent in internal affairs. **federalism** *n.*, **federalist** *n.*, **federally** *adv.*

federate *v.* /féddərayt/ unite on a federal basis or for a common purpose. — *a.* /féddərət/ united thus. **federative** *a.*

federation *n.* federating; federated society or group of States.

fee *n.* sum payable for professional services, or for a privilege.

feeble *a.* weak; ineffective. **feebly** *adv.*, **feebleness** *n.*

feed *v.* **(fed)** give food to; give as food; (of animals) take food; nourish; supply. — *n.* meal; food for animals.

feedback *n.* return of part of a system's output to its source; return of information about a product etc. to its supplier.

feeder *n.* one that feeds; baby's feeding bottle; feeding apparatus in a machine; road or railway line linking outlying areas to a central system.

feel *v.* **(felt)** explore or perceive by touch; be conscious of (being); give a sensation; have a vague conviction or impression; have as an opinion. — *n.* sense of touch; act of feeling; sensation produced by a thing touched. **feel like** be in the mood for.

feeler *n.* long slender organ of touch in certain animals; tentative suggestion.

feeling *n.* power to feel things; mental or physical awareness; (*pl.*) emotional susceptibilities; opinion or belief not based on reasoning; sympathy.

feet *see* **foot**.

feign /fayn/ *v.* pretend.

feint /faynt/ *n.* sham attack made to divert attention. — *v.* make a feint. — *a.* (of ruled lines) faint.

feldspar *n.* white or red mineral containing silicates.

felicitate *v.* congratulate. **felicitation** *n.*

felicitous *a.* well-chosen, apt. **felicitously** *adv.*, **felicitousness** *n.*

felicity *n.* happiness; pleasing manner or style.

feline *a.* of cats, cat-like. — *n.* animal of the cat family.

fell [1] *n.* stretch of moor or hilly land, especially in north England.

fell [2] *v.* strike or cut down.

fell [3] *see* **fall**.

fellow *n.* associate, comrade; (*colloq.*) man, boy; thing like another; member of a learned society or governing body of a college.

fellowship *n.* friendly association with others; society, membership of this; position of a college fellow.

felt [1] *n.* cloth made by matting and pressing fibres. — *v.* make or become matted; cover with felt.

felt [2] *see* **feel**.

female *a.* of the sex that can bear offspring or produce eggs; (of plants) fruit-bearing; (of a socket etc.) hollow. — *n.* female animal or plant.

feminine *a.* of, like, or traditionally considered suitable for women; of the grammatical form suitable for names of females. — *n.* feminine word. **femininity** *n.*

feminist *n.* supporter of women's claims to be given rights equal to those of men. **feminism** *n.*

femur *n.* thigh-bone. **femoral** *a.*

fen *n.* low-lying marshy or flooded tract of land. **fenny** *a.*

fence *n.* barrier round the boundary of a field or garden etc. — *v.* surround with a fence; engage in the sport of fencing. **fencer** *n.*

fencing *n.* fences, their material; sport of fighting with foils.

fend *v.* **fend for** provide a livelihood for, look after. **fend off** ward off.

fender *n.* low frame bordering a fireplace; pad hung over a moored vessel's side to prevent bumping.

feral *a.* wild.

ferment *v.* undergo fermentation; cause fermentation in; seethe with excitement.

fermentation *n.* chemical change caused by an organic substance, producing effervescence and heat.

fern *n.* flowerless plant with feathery green leaves. **ferny** *a.*

ferocious *a.* fierce, savage. **ferociously** *adv.*, **ferocity** *n.*

ferret *n.* small animal of the weasel family. — *v.* **(ferreted)** search, rummage. **ferret out** discover by searching. **ferrety** *a.*

ferric, ferrous *adjs.* of or containing iron.

ferroconcrete *n.* reinforced concrete.

ferrule *n.* metal ring or cap on the end of a stick or tube.

ferry *v.* convey in a boat across water; transport. — *n.* boat used for ferrying; place where it operates; service it provides.

fertile *a.* able to produce vegetation, fruit, or young; capable of developing into a new plant or animal; inventive. **fertility** *n.*

fertilize *v.* make fertile; introduce pollen or sperm into. **fertilization** *n.*

fertilizer *n.* material added to soil to make it more fertile.

fervent *a.* showing fervour. **fervently** *adv.*, **fervency** *n.*

fervid *a.* fervent. **fervidly** *adv.*

fervour *n.* intensity of feeling.

fester *v.* make or become septic; cause continuing resentment.

festival *n.* day or period of celebration; series of performances of music or drama etc.

festive *a.* of or suitable for a festival, gaily decorated. **festively** *adv.*, **festiveness** *n.*

festivity *n.* festive proceedings.

festoon *n.* hanging chain of flowers or ribbons etc. — *v.* decorate with hanging ornaments.

fetch *v.* go for and bring back; cause to come out; be sold for (a price).

fête /fayt/ *n.* festival; outdoor entertainment or sale, esp. in aid of charity. — *v.* entertain in celebration of an achievement.

fetid *a.* stinking.

fetish *n.* object worshipped as having magical powers; thing given excessive respect.

fetter *n.* & *v.* shackle.

feud *n.* lasting hostility. — *v.* conduct a feud.

feudal *a.* of or like the feudal system. **feudal system** medieval system of holding land by giving one's services to the owner. **feudalism** *n.*, **feudalistic** *a.*

fever *n.* abnormally high body temperature; disease causing it; nervous excitement. **fevered** *a.*, **feverish** *a.*, **feverishly** *adv.*

few *a.* & *n.* not many. **a few** some. **quite a few** (*colloq.*) a fairly large number.

fey *a.* strange, other-worldly; clairvoyant. **feyness** *n.*

fez *n.* (*pl.* **fezzes**) Muslim man's high flat-topped red cap.

fiancé *n.*, **fiancée** *n.fem.* person one is engaged to marry.

fiasco *n.* (*pl.* **-os**) ludicrous failure.

fib *n.* unimportant lie. **fibbing** *n.* telling fibs. **fibber** *n.*

fibre *n.* thread-like strand; substance formed of fibres; fibrous matter in food; strength of character. **fibre optics** transmission of information by infra-red signals along thin glass fibres. **fibrous** *a.*

fibreglass *n.* material made of or containing glass fibres.

fibroid *a.* consisting of fibrous tissue. — *n.* benign fibroid tumour.

fibrositis *n.* rheumatic pain in tissue other than bones and joints.

fibula *n.* (*pl.* **-lae**) bone on the outer side of the shin.

fiche /feesh/ *n.* microfiche.

fickle *a.* often changing, not loyal. **fickleness** *n.*

fiction *n.* invented story; class of literature consisting of books containing such stories. **fictional** *a.*

fictitious *a.* imaginary, not true.

fiddle *n.* (*colloq.*) violin; (*sl.*) swindle. — *v.* fidget with something; (*sl.*) cheat, falsify; (*colloq.*) play the violin. **fiddler** *n.*

fiddlesticks *n.* nonsense.

fiddly *a.* (**-ier**, **-iest**) (*colloq.*) awkward to do or use.

fidelity *n.* faithfulness, loyalty; accuracy.

fidget *v.* (**fidgeted**) make small restless movements; make or be uneasy. — *n.* one who fidgets; (in *pl.*) restless mood. **fidgety** *a.*

fiduciary *a.* held or given etc. in trust. — *n.* trustee.

fief *n.* land held under the feudal system; domain.

field *n.* piece of open ground, esp. for pasture or cultivation; sports ground; area rich in a natural product; sphere of action or interest; all competitors in a race or contest; (in computers) part of a record. — *v.* be a fielder, stop and return (a ball); put (a team) into a contest. **field day** day of much activity. **field events** athletic contests other than races. **field glasses** binoculars. **Field Marshal** army officer of the highest rank.

fielder *n.* person who fields a ball; member of the side not batting.

fieldwork *n.* practical work done by surveyors, social workers, etc. **fieldworker** *n.*

fiend /feend/ *n.* evil spirit; wicked, mischievous, or annoying person; devotee. **fiendish** *a.*

fierce *a.* violent in manner or action; eager, intense. **fiercely** *adv.*, **fierceness** *n.*

fiery *a.* (**-ier**, **-iest**) consisting of or like fire; intense, spirited. **fierily** *adv.*, **fieriness** *n.*

fiesta *n.* festival in Spanish-speaking countries.

fife *n.* small shrill flute.

fifteen *a.* & *n.* one more than fourteen (15, XV). **fifteenth** *a.* & *n.*

fifth *a.* & *n.* next after fourth. **fifthly** *adv.*

fifty *a.* & *n.* five times ten (50, L). **fifty-fifty** *a.* & *adv.* half-and-half, equally. **fiftieth** *a.* & *n.*

fig *n.* tree with broad leaves and soft pear-shaped fruit; this fruit.

fight *v.* (**fought**) struggle against, esp. in physical combat or war; contend; strive to obtain or accomplish something or to overcome. — *n.* fighting; battle, contest, struggle; boxing match.

fighter *n.* one who fights; aircraft designed for attacking others.

figment *n.* thing that does not exist except in the imagination.

figurative *a.* metaphorical. **figuratively** *adv.*

figure *n.* written symbol of a number; bodily shape; representation of a person or animal; value, amount of money; (*pl.*) arithmetic; diagram; geometric shape. — *v.* appear or be mentioned; form part of a plan etc.; work out by arithmetic or logic. **figurehead** *n.* carved image at the prow of a ship; leader with only nominal power. **figure of speech** word(s) used for effect and not literally.

figured *a.* with a woven pattern.

figurine *n.* statuette.

filament *n.* strand; fine wire giving off light in an electric lamp.

filbert *n.* nut of cultivated hazel.

filch *v.* pilfer, steal.

file¹ *n.* tool with a rough surface for smoothing things. — *v.* shape or smooth with a file.

file² *n.* cover or box etc. for keeping documents; its contents; set of data in a computer; line of people or things one behind another. — *v.* place in a file; place on record; march in a file.

filial *a.* of or due from a son or daughter. **filially** *adv.*

filigree *n.* lace-like work in metal.

filings *n.pl.* particles filed off.

fill *v.* make or become full; block; occupy; appoint to (a vacant post). — *n.* enough to fill a thing; enough to satisfy a person's appetite or desire. **fill in** complete; act as substitute. **fill out** enlarge; become enlarged or plumper. **fill up** fill completely.

filler *n.* thing or material used to fill a gap or increase bulk.

fillet *n.* piece of boneless meat or fish. — *v.* (**filleted**) remove bones from.

filling *n.* substance used to fill a cavity etc. **filling station** place selling petrol to motorists.

filly *n.* young female horse.

film *n.* thin layer; sheet or rolled strip of light-sensitive material for taking photographs; motion picture. — *v.* make a film of; cover or become covered with a thin layer. **filmstrip** *n.* series of transparencies in a strip for projection.

filmy *a.* (**-ier, -iest**) thin and almost transparent.

filter *n.* device or substance for holding back impurities in liquid or gas passing through it; screen for absorbing or modifying light or electrical or sound waves; arrangement for filtering traffic. — *v.* pass through a filter, remove impurities thus; pass gradually in or out; (of traffic) be allowed to pass while other traffic is held up.

filth *n.* disgusting dirt; obscenity. **filthy** *a.*, **filthily** *adv.*, **filthiness** *n.*

filtrate *n.* filtered liquid. — *v.* filter. **filtration** *n.*

fin *n.* thin projection from a fish's body, used for propelling and steering itself; similar projection to improve the stability of aircraft etc.

final *a.* at the end, coming last; conclusive. — *n.* last contest in a series; last edition of a day's newspaper; (*pl.*) final examinations. **finally** *adv.*

finale /finaáli/ *n.* final section of a drama or musical composition.

finalist *n.* competitor in a final.

finality *n.* quality or fact of being final.

finalize *v.* bring to an end; put in final form. **finalization** *n.*

finance *n.* management of money; money resources. — *v.* provide money for. **financial** *a.*, **financially** *adv.*

financier *n.* person engaged in financing businesses.

finch *n.* a kind of small bird.

find *v.* (**found**) discover; obtain; supply; (of a jury etc.) decide and declare. — *n.* discovery; thing found. **find out** get information about; detect, discover. **finder** *n.*

fine¹ *n.* sum of money to be paid as a penalty. — *v.* punish by a fine.

fine² *a.* of high quality or merit; bright, free from rain; slender, in small particles; delicate, subtle; excellent. — *adv.* finely. **finely** *adv.*, **fineness** *n.*

finery *n.* showy clothes etc.

finesse *n.* delicate manipulation; tact.

finger *n.* each of the five parts extending from each hand; any of these other than the thumb; finger-like object or part; measure (about 20 mm) of alcohol in a glass. — *v.* touch or feel with the fingers. **finger-stall** *n.* sheath to cover an injured finger.

fingerprint *n.* impression of ridges on the pad of a finger.

finial *n.* ornament at the apex of a gable, pinnacle, etc.

finish *v.* bring or come to an end, complete; reach the end of a task or race etc.; consume all of; put final touches to. — *n.* last stage; point where a race etc. ends; completed state. **finisher** *n.*

finite *a.* limited.

fiord /fyord/ *n.* narrow inlet of the sea between cliffs esp. in Norway.

fir *n.* evergreen cone-bearing tree.

fire *n.* combustion; flame; burning fuel; heating device with a flame or glow; destructive burning; firing of guns; angry or excited feeling. — *v.* send a bullet or shell from (a gun), detonate; discharge (a missile); dismiss from a job; set fire to; catch fire; bake (pottery etc.); excite. **fire brigade** organized body of people employed to extinguish fires. **fire engine** vehicle with equipment for putting out fires. **fire escape** special staircase or apparatus for escape from a burning building.

firearm *n.* gun, pistol, etc.

firebreak *n.* open space as an obstacle to the spread of fire.

firedamp *n.* explosive mixture of methane and air in mines.

firefly *n.* phosphorescent beetle.

fireman *n.* (*pl.* **-men**) member of a fire brigade.

fireplace *n.* recess with a chimney for a domestic fire.

fireside *n.* space round a fireplace; this as the centre of a home.

firework *n.* device containing chemicals that burn or explode spectacularly.

firing squad group detailed to shoot a condemned man.

firm [1] *n.* business company.

firm [2] *a.* not yielding when pressed or pushed; steady, not shaking; securely established; resolute. — *adv.* firmly. — *v.* make or become firm.

firmament *n.* sky with its clouds and stars, regarded as a vault.

first *a.* coming before all others in time or order or importance. — *n.* first thing or occurrence; first day of a month. — *adv.* before all others or another. **at first** at the beginning. **first aid** treatment given for an injury etc. before a doctor arrives. **first-class** *a.* & *adv.* of the best quality; in the best category of accommodation. **first cousin** (*see* **cousin**). **first name** personal name. **first-rate** *a.* excellent.

firstly *adv.* first.

firth *n.* estuary or narrow inlet of the sea in Scotland.

fiscal *a.* of public revenue.

fish *n.* (*pl.* usu. **fish**) cold-blooded vertebrate living wholly in water; its flesh as food. — *v.* try to catch fish (from); make a search by reaching into something.

fishery *n.* area of sea where fishing is done; business of fishing.

fishmeal *n.* dried ground fish used as a fertilizer.

fishmonger *n.* shopkeeper who sells fish.

fishy *a.* (**-ier, -iest**) like fish; causing disbelief or suspicion.

fissile *a.* tending to split; capable of undergoing nuclear fission.

fission *n.* splitting (esp. of an atomic nucleus, with release of energy).

fissure *n.* cleft.

fist *n.* hand when tightly closed.

fisticuffs *n.* fighting with fists.

fistula *n.* pipe-like ulcer; pipe-like passage in the body.

fit [1] *n.* sudden attack of illness or its symptoms, or of convulsions or loss of consciousness; short period of a feeling or activity.

fit [2] *a.* (**fitter, fittest**) suitable; right and proper; in good health. — *v.* (**fitted**) be or adjust to be the right shape and size for; put into place; make or be suitable or competent. — *n.* way a thing fits. **fitly** *adv.*, **fitness** *n.*

fitful *a.* occurring in short periods not steadily. **fitfully** *adv.*

fitment *n.* piece of fixed furniture.

fitter *n.* person who supervises the fitting of clothes; mechanic.

fitting *a.* right and proper.

fittings *n.pl.* fixtures and fitments.

five *a.* & *n.* one more than four (5, V).

fiver *n.* (*colloq.*) £5; five-pound note.

fix *v.* make firm, stable, or permanent; direct steadily; establish, specify; repair; (*colloq.*) deal with or arrange. — *n.* awkward situation; position determined by taking bearings. **fix up** organize; provide for. **fixer** *n.*

fixated *a.* having an obsession.

fixation *n.* fixing; obsession.

fixative *n.* & *a.* (substance) for keeping things in position, or preventing fading or evaporation.

fixedly *adv.* intently.

fixity *n.* fixed state, stability, permanence.

fixture *n.* thing fixed in position; firmly established person or thing.

fizz *v.* hiss or splutter, esp. when gas escapes in bubbles from a liquid. — *n.* this sound; fizzing drink. **fizziness** *n.*, **fizzy** *a.*

fizzle *v.* fizz feebly. **fizzle out** end feebly or unsuccessfully.

flab *n.* (*colloq.*) flabbiness, fat.

flabbergast *v.* (*colloq.*) astound.

flabby *a.* (**-ier, -iest**) fat and limp, not firm. **flabbiness** *n.*

flaccid *a.* hanging loose or wrinkled, not firm. **flaccidly** *adv.*, **flaccidity** *n.*

flag [1] *n.* piece of cloth attached by one edge to a staff or rope, used as a signal or symbol; similarly shaped device. — *v.* (**flagged**) mark or signal (as) with a flag. **flag day** day on which small emblems are sold for a charity.

flag [2] *v.* (**flagged**) droop; lose vigour.

flagellate *v.* whip, flog. **flagellant** *n.*, **flagellation** *n.*

flageolet *n.* small wind instrument.

flagged *a.* paved with flagstones.

flagon *n.* large bottle for wine or cider; vessel with a handle, lip, and lid for serving wine.

flagrant /fláygrənt/ *a.* (of an offence or offender) very bad and obvious. **flagrantly** *adv.*

flagship *n.* admiral's ship; principal vessel, shop, product, etc.

flagstone *n.* large paving-stone.

flail *n.* implement formerly used for threshing grain. — *v.* thrash or swing about wildly.

flair *n.* natural ability.

flak *n.* anti-aircraft shells; (*colloq.*) barrage of criticism.

flake *n.* small thin piece. — *v.* come off in flakes. **flake out** (*colloq.*) faint, fall asleep from exhaustion. **flaky** *a.*, **flakiness** *n.*

flamboyant *a.* showy in appearance or manner. **flamboyantly** *adv.*, **flamboyance** *n.*

flame *n.* bright tongue-shaped portion of gas burning visibly. — *v.* burn with flames; become bright red. **old flame** (*colloq.*) former sweetheart.

flamenco *n.* (*pl.* **-os**) Spanish style of singing and dancing.

flamingo *n.* (*pl.* **-os**) wading bird with long legs and pink feathers.

flammable *a.* able to be set on fire. **flammability** *n.*

flan *n.* open pastry or sponge case with filling.

flange *n.* projecting rim. **flanged** *a.*

flank *n.* side, esp. of the body between ribs and hip. — *v.* place or be at the side of.

flannel *n.* woollen fabric; face-flannel; (*pl.*) trousers of flannel; (*sl.*) nonsense, flattery. — *v.* (**flannelled**) (*sl.*) flatter.

flannelette *n.* cotton fabric made to look and feel like flannel.

flap *v.* (**flapped**) sway or move up and down with a sharp sound; (*colloq.*) show agitation. — *n.* act or sound of flapping; hanging or hinged piece; (*colloq.*) agitation.

flare *v.* blaze suddenly; burst into activity or anger; widen outwards. — *n.* sudden blaze; device producing flame as a signal or illumination; flared shape. **flare off** burn off (unwanted gas).

flash *v.* give out a sudden bright light; show suddenly or ostentatiously; come suddenly into sight or mind; move rapidly; cause to shine briefly. — *n.* sudden burst of flame or light; sudden show of wit or feeling; very brief time; brief news item; device producing a brief bright light in photography. — *a.* (*colloq.*) flashy. **flash flood** sudden destructive flood.

flashback *n.* change of scene in a story or film to an earlier period.

flashing *n.* strip of metal covering a joint in a roof etc.

flashlight *n.* electric torch.

flashpoint *n.* temperature at which a vapour ignites.

flashy *a.* (**-ier, -iest**) showy, gaudy. **flashily** *adv.*, **flashiness** *n.*

flask *n.* narrow-necked bottle; vacuum flask.

flat *a.* (**flatter, flattest**) horizontal, level; lying at full length; absolute; monotonous; dejected; having lost effervescence or power to generate electric current; below the correct pitch in music. — *adv.* in a flat manner; (*colloq.*) exactly. — *n.* flat surface, level ground; set of rooms on one floor, used as a residence; (sign indicating) music note lowered by a semitone. **flatfish** *n.* fish with a flattened body, swimming on its side. **flat out** at top speed; with maximum effort.

flatlet *n.* small flat.

flatten *v.* make or become flat.

flatter *v.* compliment insincerely; exaggerate the good looks of. **flatterer** *n.*, **flattery** *n.*

flatulent *a.* causing or suffering from formation of gas in the digestive tract. **flatulence** *n.*

flaunt *v.* display proudly or ostentatiously.

flautist *n.* flute-player.

flavour *n.* distinctive taste; special characteristic. — *v.* give flavour to.

flavouring *n.* substance used to give flavour to food.

flaw *n.* imperfection. — *v.* spoil with a flaw. **flawless** *a.*

flax *n.* blue-flowered plant; textile fibre from its stem.

flaxen *a.* made of flax; pale yellow like dressed flax.

flay *v.* strip off the skin or hide of; criticize severely.

flea *n.* small jumping blood-sucking

insect. **flea market** market for second-hand goods.

fleck *n.* very small mark; speck. — *v.* mark with flecks.

fled *see* **flee**.

fledged *a.* (of a young bird) with fully grown wing-feathers, able to fly; (of a person) fully trained.

fledgeling *n.* bird just fledged.

flee *v.* (**fled**) run or hurry away (from).

fleece *n.* sheep's woolly hair. — *v.* rob by trickery. **fleecy** *a.*

fleet [1] *n.* navy; ships sailing together; vehicles or aircraft under one command or ownership.

fleet [2] *a.* moving swiftly, nimble. **fleetly** *adv.*, **fleetness** *n.*

fleeting *a.* passing quickly, brief.

flesh *n.* soft substance of animal bodies; body as opposed to mind or soul; pulpy part of fruits and vegetables. **flesh and blood** human nature; one's relatives. **flesh wound** wound not reaching a vital organ.

fleshy (**-ier, -iest**) *a.* of or like flesh; having much flesh, plump, pulpy.

flew *see* **fly** [2].

flex [1] *v.* bend; move (a muscle) so that it bends a joint. **flexion** *n.*

flex [2] *n.* flexible insulated wire for carrying electric current.

flexible *a.* able to bend easily; adaptable, able to be changed. **flexibly** *adv.*, **flexibility** *n.*

flexitime *n.* system of flexible working hours.

flick *n.* quick light blow or stroke. — *v.* move or strike or remove with a flick. **flick knife** knife with a blade that springs out.

flicker *v.* burn or shine unsteadily; occur briefly; quiver. — *n.* flickering light or movement; brief occurrence.

flier *n.* = flyer.

flight [1] *n.* flying; movement or path of a thing through the air; journey by air; birds or aircraft flying together; series of stairs; feathers etc. on a dart or arrow. **flight deck** cockpit of a large aircraft; deck of an aircraft carrier. **flight recorder** electronic device in an aircraft recording details of its flight.

flight [2] *n.* fleeing.

flightless *a.* unable to fly.

flighty *a.* (**-ier, -iest**) frivolous. **flightily** *adv.*, **flightiness** *n.*

flimsy *a.* (**-ier, -iest**) light and thin; fragile; unconvincing. **flimsily** *adv.*, **flimsiness** *n.*

flinch *v.* draw back in fear, wince; shrink from, avoid.

fling *v.* (**flung**) move or throw violently or hurriedly. — *n.* spell of indulgence in pleasure.

flint *n.* very hard stone; piece of hard alloy producing sparks when struck.

flip *v.* (**flipped**) flick; toss with a sharp movement. — *n.* action of flipping; (*colloq.*) short flight, quick tour. — *a.* (*colloq.*) glib, flippant.

flippant *a.* not showing proper seriousness. **flippantly** *adv.*, **flippancy** *n.*

flipper *n.* sea animal's limb used in swimming; large flat rubber attachment to the foot for underwater swimming.

flirt *v.* pretend lightheartedly to court a person; toy. — *n.* person who flirts. **flirtation** *n.*

flirtatious *a.* flirting; fond of flirting. **flirtatiously** *adv.*

flit *v.* (**flitted**) fly or move lightly and quickly; decamp stealthily. — *n.* act of flitting.

flitter *v.* flit about.

float *v.* rest or drift on the surface of liquid; have or allow (currency) to have a variable rate of exchange; start (a company or scheme). — *n.* thing designed to float on liquid; money for minor expenditure or giving change.

flocculent *a.* like tufts of wool.

flock [1] *n.* number of animals or birds together; large number of people, congregation. — *v.* gather or go in a flock.

flock [2] *n.* tuft of wool or cotton; wool or cotton waste as stuffing.

floe *n.* sheet of floating ice.

flog *v.* (**flogged**) beat severely; (*sl.*) sell. **flogging** *n.*

flood *n.* overflow of water on a place usually dry; great outpouring; inflow of the tide. — *v.* cover or fill with a flood; overflow; come in great quantities.

floodlight *n.* lamp producing a broad bright beam. — *v.* (**floodlit**) illuminate with this.

floor *n.* lower surface of a room; right to speak in an assembly; storey. — *v.* provide with a floor; knock down; baffle. **floor show** cabaret.

flooring *n.* material for a floor.

flop *v.* (**flopped**) hang or fall heavily and loosely; (*sl.*) be a failure. — *n.* flopping movement or sound; (*sl.*) failure.

floppy *a.* (**-ier, -iest**) tending to flop. **floppy disk** flexible disk for storing machine-readable data.

flora *n.* plants of an area or period.

floral *a.* of flowers.

floret *n.* each of the small flowers of a composite flower.

florid *a.* ornate; ruddy. **floridity** *n.*

florist *n.* person who sells or grows flowers as a business.

flotation *n.* floating, esp. of a commercial venture.

flotilla *n.* small fleet; fleet of small ships.

flotsam *n.* floating wreckage. **flotsam and jetsam** odds and ends.

flounce [1] *v.* go in an impatient annoyed manner. — *n.* flouncing movement.

flounce [2] *n.* deep frill attached by its upper edge. **flounced** *a.*

flounder [1] *n.* small flatfish.

flounder [2] *v.* move clumsily, as in mud; become confused when trying to do something.

flour *n.* fine powder made from grain, used in cooking. — *v.* cover with flour. **floury** *a.*

flourish *v.* grow vigorously; prosper, be successful; wave dramatically. — *n.* dramatic gesture; ornamental curve; fanfare.

flout *v.* disobey openly.

flow *v.* glide along as a stream; proceed evenly; hang loosely; gush out. — *n.* flowing movement or mass; amount flowing; inflow of the tide. **flow chart** diagram showing a sequence of processes.

flower *n.* part of a plant where fruit or seed develops; plant grown for this; best part. — *v.* produce flowers.

flowered *a.* ornamented with a design of flowers.

flowery *a.* full of flowers; full of ornamental phrases.

flown *see* **fly** [2].

flu *n.* (*colloq.*) influenza.

fluctuate *v.* vary irregularly. **fluctuation** *n.*

flue *n.* smoke-duct in a chimney; channel for conveying heat.

fluent *a.* speaking or spoken smoothly and readily. **fluently** *adv.*, **fluency** *n.*

fluff *n.* soft mass of fibres or down. — *v.* shake into a soft mass; (*sl.*) bungle. **fluffy** *a.*, **fluffiness** *n.*

fluid *a.* consisting of particles that move freely among themselves; not stable. — *n.* fluid substance. **fluidity** *n.*

fluke [1] *n.* success due to luck.

fluke [2] *n.* barbed arm of an anchor etc.; lobe of a whale's tail.

flummox *v.* (*colloq.*) baffle.

flung *see* **fling**.

fluoresce *v.* be or become fluorescent.

fluorescent *a.* taking in radiations and sending them out as light. **fluorescence** *n.*

fluoridate *v.* add fluoride to (a water supply). **fluoridation** *n.*

fluoride *n.* compound of fluorine with metal.

fluorine *n.* pungent corrosive gas.

fluorspar *n.* calcium fluoride as a mineral.

flurry *n.* short rush of wind, rain, or snow; commotion; nervous agitation. — *v.* fluster.

flush [1] *v.* become red in the face; cleanse or dispose of with a flow of water. — *n.* blush; rush of emotion; rush of water. — *a.* level, in the same plane; (*colloq.*) well supplied with money.

flush [2] *v.* drive out from cover.

fluster *v.* make nervous or confused. — *n.* flustered state.

flute *n.* wind instrument, pipe with a mouth-hole at the side; ornamental groove.

flutter *v.* move wings hurriedly; wave or flap quickly; (of the heart) beat irregularly. — *n.* fluttering movement or beat; nervous excitement; stir.

fluvial *a.* of or found in rivers.

flux *n.* flow; continuous succession of changes; substance mixed with metal etc. to assist fusion.

fly [1] *n.* two-winged insect. **fly-blown** *a.* tainted by flies' eggs.

fly [2] *v.* **(flew, flown)** move through the air on wings or in an aircraft; control the flight of; display (a flag); go quickly; flee. — *n.* flying; (*pl.*) fastening down the front of trousers. **fly-post** *v.* display (posters etc.) in unauthorized places. **fly-tip** *v.* dump (waste) illegally.

flyer *n.* one that flies; airman; fast animal or vehicle.

flying *a.* able to fly. **flying buttress** one based on separate structure, usu. forming an arch. **flying colours** great credit. **flying fox** fruit-eating bat. **flying saucer** unidentified object reported as seen in the sky.

flyleaf *n.* blank leaf at the beginning or end of a book.

flyover *n.* bridge carrying one road or railway over another.

flywheel *n.* heavy wheel revolving on a shaft to regulate machinery.

foal *n.* young of the horse. — *v.* give birth to a foal.

foam *n.* collection of small bubbles; spongy rubber or plastic. — *v.* form foam. **foamy** *a.*

fob *v.* **(fobbed) fob off** palm off; get (a person) to accept something inferior.

focal *a.* of or at a focus.

fo'c's'le /fōks'l/ *n.* forecastle.

focus *n.* (*pl.* **-cuses** *or* **-ci)** point where rays meet; distance at which an object is most clearly seen; adjustment on a lens to produce a clear image; centre of activity or interest. — *v.* **(focused)**

adjust the focus of; bring into focus; concentrate.

fodder *n.* food for animals.

foe *n.* enemy.

foetus /feetəss/ *n.* (*pl.* **-tuses**) developed embryo in a womb or egg. **foetal** *a.*

fog *n.* thick mist. — *v.* (**fogged**) cover or become covered with fog or condensed vapour. **foghorn** *n.* sounding-instrument for warning ships in fog. **foggy** *a.*, **fogginess** *n.*

fogy *n.* (*pl.* **-gies**) person with old-fashioned ideas.

foible *n.* harmless peculiarity in a person's character.

foil [1] *n.* paper-thin sheet of metal; person or thing emphasizing another's qualities by contrast.

foil [2] *v.* thwart, frustrate.

foil [3] *n.* long thin sword with a button on the point.

foist *v.* cause a person to accept (an inferior or unwelcome thing).

fold [1] *v.* bend so that one part lies on another; clasp; envelop; cease to function. — *n.* folded part; line or hollow made by folding.

fold [2] *n.* enclosure for sheep. — *v.* enclose (sheep) in a fold.

folder *n.* folding cover for loose papers; leaflet.

foliage *n.* leaves.

foliate *v.* split into thin layers. **foliation** *n.*

folk *n.* people; one's relatives. **folk dance, folk song** etc., dance, song, etc., in the traditional style of a country. **folky** *a.*

folklore *n.* traditional beliefs and tales of a community.

folksy *a.* informal and friendly.

follicle *n.* very small cavity containing a hair-root. **follicular** *a.*

follow *v.* go or come after; go along (a road etc.); accept the ideas of; take an interest in the progress of; grasp the meaning of; be a natural consequence of. **follow suit** follow a person's example. **follow up** pursue; supplement. **follow-up** *n.* this process. **follower** *n.*

following *n.* body of believers or supporters. — *a.* now to be mentioned. — *prep.* as a sequel to.

folly *n.* foolishness, foolish act; ornamental building.

foment *v.* stir up (trouble). **fomentation** *n.*

fond *a.* affectionate; doting; (of hope) unlikely to be fulfilled. **fondly** *adv.*, **fondness** *n.*

fondant *n.* soft sugary sweet.

fondle *v.* handle lovingly.

fondue *n.* dish of flavoured melted cheese.

font *n.* basin in a church, holding water for baptism.

fontanelle *n.* soft spot where the bones of an infant's skull have not yet grown together.

food *n.* substance (esp. solid) that can be taken into the body of an animal or plant to maintain its life.

foodstuff *n.* substance used as food.

fool *n.* foolish person; creamy fruit-flavoured pudding. — *v.* joke, tease; play about idly; trick.

foolery *n.* foolish acts.

foolhardy *a.* taking foolish risks.

foolish *a.* lacking good sense or judgement; ridiculous. **foolishly** *adv.*, **foolishness** *n.*

foolproof *a.* simple and easy to use, unable to go wrong.

foot *n.* (*pl.* **feet**) part of the leg below the ankle; lower part or end; measure of length, = 12 inches (30.48 cm); unit of rhythm in verse. — *v.* walk; be the one to pay (a bill). **foot-and-mouth disease** contagious virus disease of cattle.

football *n.* large round or elliptical inflated ball; game played with this. **football pool** form of gambling on the results of football matches. **footballer** *n.*

footfall *n.* sound of footsteps.

foothills *n.pl.* low hills near the bottom of a mountain or range.

foothold *n.* place just wide enough for one's foot; small but secure position gained.

footing *n.* foothold; balance; status, conditions.

footlights *n.pl.* row of lights along the front of a stage floor.

footling *a.* (*sl.*) trivial.

footloose *a.* independent, without responsibilities.

footman *n.* (*pl.* **-men**) manservant, usu. in livery.

footnote *n.* note printed at the bottom of a page.

footpath *n.* path for pedestrians, pavement.

footprint *n.* impression left by a foot or shoe.

footsore *a.* with feet sore from walking.

footstep *n.* step; sound of this.

footwork *n.* manner of moving or using the feet in sports etc.

fop *n.* dandy.

for *prep.* in place of; as the price or penalty of; in defence or favour of; with a view to; in the direction of; intended to be received or used by; because of; during. — *conj.* because.

forage *v.* go searching; rummage. — *n.* foraging; food for horses and cattle.

foray *n.* sudden attack, raid. — *v.* make a foray.

forbade *see* **forbid**.

forbear *v.* (**forbore, forborne**) refrain (from).

forbearance *n.* patience, tolerance.

forbearing *a.* patient, tolerant.

forbid *v.* (**forbade, forbidden**) order not to; refuse to allow.

forbidding *a.* having an uninviting appearance, stern.

force *n.* strength; intense effort; influence tending to cause movement; body of troops or police; organized or available group; compulsion; effectiveness. — *v.* use force upon, esp. in order to get or do something; break open by force; strain to the utmost, overstrain; impose; produce by effort.

forceful *a.* powerful and vigorous. **forcefully** *adv.*, **forcefulness** *n.*

forceps *n.* (*pl.* **forceps**) pincers used in surgery etc.

forcible *a.* done by force. **forcibly** *adv.*

ford *n.* shallow place where a stream may be crossed by wading or driving through. — *v.* cross thus.

fore *a.* & *adv.* in, at, or towards the front. — *n.* fore part. **to the fore** in front, conspicuous.

forearm [1] *n.* arm from the elbow downwards.

forearm [2] *v.* arm or prepare in advance against possible danger.

forebears *n.pl.* ancestors.

foreboding *n.* feeling that trouble is coming.

forecast *v.* (**forecast**) tell in advance (what is likely to happen). — *n.* statement that does this. **forecaster** *n.*

forecastle /fōks'l/ *n.* forward part of certain ships.

foreclose *v.* take possession of property when a loan secured on it is not duly repaid. **foreclosure** *n.*

forecourt *n.* enclosed space in front of a building.

forefathers *n.pl.* ancestors.

forefinger *n.* finger next to the thumb.

forefoot *n.* (*pl.* **-feet**) animal's front foot.

forefront *n.* the very front.

foregoing *a.* preceding.

foregone *a.* **foregone conclusion** predictable result.

foreground *n.* part of a scene etc. that is nearest to the observer.

forehand *n.* stroke played with the palm of the hand turned forwards. — *a.* of or made with this stroke. **forehanded** *a.*

forehead *n.* part of the face above the eyes.

foreign *a.* of, from, or dealing with a country that is not one's own; not belonging naturally.

foreigner *n.* person born in or coming from another country.

foreknowledge *n.* knowledge of a thing before it occurs.

foreleg *n.* animal's front leg.

forelock *n.* lock of hair just above the forehead.

foreman *n.* (*pl.* **-men**) worker superintending others; president and spokesman of a jury. **forewoman** *n.fem.*

foremost *a.* most advanced in position or rank; most important. — *adv.* in the foremost position.

forename *n.* first name.

forensic *a.* of or used in law courts. **forensic medicine** medical knowledge used in police investigations etc.

foreplay *n.* stimulation preceding sexual intercourse.

forerunner *n.* person or thing that comes in advance of another which it foreshadows.

foresee *v.* (**foresaw, foreseen**) be aware of or realize beforehand. **foreseeable** *a.*

foreshadow *v.* be an advance sign of (a future event etc.).

foreshore *n.* shore that the tide flows over.

foreshorten *v.* show or portray with apparent shortening giving an effect of distance.

foresight *n.* ability to foresee and prepare for future needs.

foreskin *n.* loose skin at the end of the penis.

forest *n.* trees and undergrowth covering a large area.

forestall *v.* prevent or foil by taking action first.

forestry *n.* science of planting and caring for forests.

foretaste *n.* experience in advance of what is to come.

foretell *v.* (**foretold**) forecast.

forethought *n.* careful thought and planning for the future.

forewarn *v.* warn beforehand.

foreword *n.* introductory remarks at the beginning of a book.

forfeit *n.* thing that has to be paid or given up as a penalty. — *v.* give or lose as a forfeit. — *a.* forfeited. **forfeiture** *n.*

forgather *v.* assemble.

forgave *see* **forgive**.

forge [1] *v.* advance by effort.

forge [2] *n.* blacksmith's workshop; furnace

where metal is heated. — *v.* shape (metal) by heating and hammering; make a fraudulent copy of. **forger** *n.*

forgery *n.* forging; thing forged.

forget *v.* (**forgot, forgotten**) cease to remember or think about. **forget-me-not** *n.* plant with small blue flowers.

forgetful *a.* tending to forget. **forgetfully** *adv.*, **forgetfulness** *n.*

forgive *v.* (**forgave, forgiven**) cease to feel angry or bitter towards or about. **forgivable** *a.*, **forgiveness** *n.*

forgo *v.* (**forwent, forgone**) give up, go without.

fork *n.* pronged instrument or tool; thing or part divided like this; each of its divisions. — *v.* lift or dig with a fork; separate into two branches; follow one of these branches. **fork-lift truck** truck with a forked device for lifting and carrying loads.

forlorn *a.* left alone and unhappy. **forlorn hope** the only faint hope left. **forlornly** *adv.*

form *n.* shape, appearance; way in which a thing exists; school class; etiquette; document with blank spaces for details; bench. — *v.* shape, produce; bring into existence, constitute; take shape; develop.

formal *a.* conforming to accepted rules or customs; of form; regular in design. **formally** *adv.*

formaldehyde *n.* colourless gas used in solution as a preservative and disinfectant.

formality *n.* being formal; formal act, esp. one required by rules.

formalize *v.* make formal or official. **formalization** *n.*

format *n.* shape and size of a book etc.; style of arrangement. — *v.* (**formatted**) arrange in a format.

formation *n.* forming; thing formed; particular arrangement.

formative *a.* forming; of formation.

former *a.* of an earlier period; mentioned first of two.

formerly *adv.* in former times.

formidable *a.* inspiring fear or awe; difficult to do. **formidably** *adv.*

formula *n.* (*pl.* **-ae** *or* **-as**) symbols showing chemical constituents or a mathematical statement; fixed series of words for use on social or ceremonial occasions; list of ingredients; classification of a racing car. **formulaic** *a.*

formulate *v.* express systematically. **formulation** *n.*

fornicate *v.* have sexual intercourse while unmarried. **fornication** *n.*, **fornicator** *n.*

forsake *v.* (**forsook, forsaken**) withdraw one's help or companionship etc. from.

fort *n.* fortified place or building.

forth *adv.* out; onwards. **back and forth** to and fro.

forthcoming *a.* about to occur or appear; communicative.

forthright *a.* frank, outspoken.

forthwith *adv.* immediately.

fortification *n.* fortifying; defensive wall or building etc.

fortify *v.* strengthen against attack; increase the vigour of.

fortitude *n.* courage in bearing pain or trouble.

fortnight *n.* period of two weeks.

fortnightly *a.* & *adv.* (happening or appearing) once a fortnight.

fortress *n.* fortified building or town.

fortuitous *a.* happening by chance. **fortuitously** *adv.*

fortunate *a.* lucky. **fortunately** *adv.*

fortune *n.* chance as a power in mankind's affairs; destiny; prosperity, success; much wealth. **fortune-teller** *n.* person who claims to foretell future events in people's lives.

forty *a.* & *n.* four times ten (40, XL). **fortieth** *a.* & *n.*

forum *n.* place or meeting where a public discussion is held.

forward *a.* directed towards the front or its line of motion; having made more than normal progress; presumptuous. — *n.* attacking player in football or hockey. — *adv.* forwards; towards the future; in advance, ahead. — *v.* send on (a letter, goods) to a final destination; advance (interests). **forwardness** *n.*

forwards *adv.* towards the front; with forward motion; so as to make progress; with the front foremost.

fossil *n.* hardened remains or traces of a prehistoric animal or plant. — *a.* of or like a fossil; (of fuel) extracted from the ground.

fossilize *v.* turn or be turned into a fossil. **fossilization** *n.*

foster *v.* promote the growth of; rear (a child that is not one's own). **foster-child** *n.* child reared thus. **foster home** home in which a foster-child is reared. **foster-parent** *n.* person who fosters a child.

fought *see* **fight**.

foul *a.* causing disgust; against the rules of a game. — *adv.* unfairly. — *n.* action that breaks rules. — *v.* make or become foul; entangle or collide with; obstruct; commit a foul against. **foul-mouthed** *a.* using foul language. **foully** *adv.*, **foulness** *n.*

found [1] *see* **find**.

found [2] *v.* establish (an institution etc.); base. **founder** [1] *n.*

found [3] *v.* melt or mould (metal or glass); make (an object) in this way. **founder** [2] *n.*

foundation *n.* founding; institution or fund founded; base, first layer; underlying principle.

founder [1, 2] *see* **found** [2, 3].

founder [3] *v.* stumble or fall; (of a ship) sink; fail completely.

foundling *n.* deserted child of unknown parents.

foundry *n.* workshop where metal or glass founding is done.

fount *n.* fountain, source; one size and style of printing type.

fountain *n.* spring or jet of water; structure provided for this; source. **fountainhead** *n.* source. **fountain pen** pen that can be filled with a supply of ink.

four *a.* & *n.* one more than three (4, IV). **four-poster** *n.* bed with four posts that support a canopy. **four-wheel drive** motive power acting on all four wheels of a vehicle.

fourfold *a.* & *adv.* four times as much or as many.

foursome *n.* party of four people.

fourteen *a.* & *n.* one more than thirteen (14, XIV). **fourteenth** *a.* & *n.*

fourth *a.* next after the third. — *n.* fourth thing, class, etc.; quarter. **fourthly** *adv.*

fowl *n.* kind of bird kept to supply eggs and flesh for food.

fox *n.* wild animal of the dog family with a bushy tail; its fur; crafty person. — *v.* deceive or puzzle by acting craftily.

foxglove *n.* tall plant with flowers like glove-fingers.

foxhole *n.* small trench as a military shelter.

foxtrot *n.* dance with slow and quick steps; music for this.

foyer /fóyay/ *n.* entrance hall of a theatre, cinema, or hotel.

fracas /frákkaa/ *n.* (*pl.* **-cas**) noisy quarrel or disturbance.

fraction *n.* number that is not a whole number; small part or amount. **fractional** *a.*, **fractionally** *adv.*

fractious *a.* irritable, peevish. **fractiously** *adv.*, **fractiousness** *n.*

fracture *n.* break, esp. of bone. — *v.* break.

fragile *a.* easily broken or damaged; not strong. **fragility** *n.*

fragment *n.* /frágmənt/ piece broken off something; isolated part. — *v.* /fragmént/ break into fragments. **fragmentation** *n.*

fragmentary *a.* consisting of fragments.

fragrant *a.* having a pleasant smell. **fragrance** *n.*

frail *a.* not strong; physically weak. **frailty** *n.*

frame *n.* rigid structure supporting other parts; open case or border enclosing a picture or pane of glass etc.; single exposure on cine film. — *v.* put or form a frame round; construct; (*sl.*) arrange false evidence against. **frame of mind** temporary state of mind.

framework *n.* supporting frame.

franc *n.* unit of money in France, Belgium, and Switzerland.

franchise *n.* right to vote in public elections; authorization to sell a company's goods or services in a certain area. — *v.* grant a franchise to.

Franco- *pref.* French.

frank [1] *a.* showing one's thoughts and feelings unmistakably. **frankly** *adv.*, **frankness** *n.*

frank [2] *v.* mark (a letter etc.) to show that postage has been paid.

frankfurter *n.* smoked sausage.

frankincense *n.* sweet-smelling gum burnt as incense.

frantic *a.* wildly excited or agitated. **frantically** *adv.*

fraternal *a.* of a brother or brothers. **fraternally** *adv.*

fraternity *n.* brotherhood.

fraternize *v.* associate with others in a friendly way. **fraternization** *n.*

fratricide *n.* killing or killer of own brother or sister etc. **fratricidal** *a.*

fraud *n.* criminal deception; dishonest trick; person carrying this out. **fraudulence** *n.*, **fraudulent** *a.*, **fraudulently** *adv.*

fraught *a.* (*colloq.*) causing or suffering anxiety. **fraught with** filled with, involving.

fray [1] *n.* fight, conflict.

fray [2] *v.* make or become worn so that there are loose threads; strain (nerves or temper).

frazzle *n.* exhausted state.

freak *n.* abnormal person or thing. — *v.* **freak out** (*colloq.*) (cause to) hallucinate or become wildly excited. **freakish** *a.*, **freaky** *a.*

freckle *n.* light brown spot on the skin. — *v.* spot or become spotted with freckles. **freckled** *a.*

free *a.* (**freer**, **freest**) not in the power of another, not a slave; having freedom; not fixed; without, not subject to; without charge; not occupied, not in use; lavish. — *v.* (**freed**) make free; rid of; clear, disentangle. **free fall** unrestricted fall under the force of gravity. **free from** not containing. **free hand** right of taking what action one chooses. **free-hand** *a.* (of drawing) done without ruler or compasses etc. **free house** inn or public house not controlled by one brewery. **freelance** *a.* & *n.* (person) selling services to various employers. **free-range** *a.* (of hens) allowed to range freely in search of food; (of eggs) from such hens. **freewheel** *v.* ride a bicycle without pedalling.

freedom *n.* being free; independence; frankness; unrestricted use; honorary citizenship.

freehold *n.* holding of land or a house etc. in absolute ownership. — *a.* owned thus. **freeholder** *n.*

Freemason *n.* member of a fraternity with elaborate ritual and secret signs. **Freemasonry** *n.* their system and institutions.

freemasonry *n.* sympathy and mutual help between people of similar interests.

freesia *n.* a kind of fragrant flower.

freeze *v.* (**froze, frozen**) change from liquid to solid by extreme cold; be so cold that water turns to ice; chill or be chilled by extreme cold or fear; preserve by refrigeration; make (assets) unable to be realized; hold (prices or wages) at a fixed level; stop, stand very still. — *n.* period of freezing weather; freezing of prices etc. **freeze-dry** *v.* freeze and dry by evaporation of ice in a vacuum.

freezer *n.* refrigerated container for preserving and storing food.

freight *n.* cargo; transport of goods. — *v.* load with freight; transport as freight.

freighter *n.* ship or aircraft carrying mainly freight.

freightliner *n.* train carrying goods in containers.

French *a.* & *n.* (language) of France. **French horn** brass wind instrument with a coiled tube. **French-polish** *v.* polish (wood) with shellac polish. **French window** one reaching to the ground, used also as a door. **Frenchman** *n.* (*pl.* **-men**), **Frenchwoman** *n.* (*pl.* **-women**).

frenetic *a.* in a state of frenzy. **frenetically** *adv.*

frenzy *n.* violent excitement or agitation. **frenzied** *a.*

frequency *n.* frequent occurrence; rate of repetition; number of cycles of a carrier wave per second, band or group of these.

frequent [1] /freékwənt/ *a.* happening or appearing often. **frequently** *adv.*

frequent [2] /frikwént/ *v.* go frequently to, be often in (a place).

fresco *n.* (*pl.* **-os**) picture painted on a wall or ceiling before the plaster is dry.

fresh *a.* new, not stale or faded; not preserved by tinning or freezing etc.; not salty; refreshing; vigorous. **freshly** *adv.*, **freshness** *n.*

freshen *v.* make or become fresh. **freshener** *n.*

freshman *n.* (*pl.* **-men**) first-year university student.

fret [1] *v.* (**fretted**) worry; vex; show anxiety.

fret [2] *n.* each of the ridges on the fingerboard of a guitar etc.

fretful *a.* constantly worrying or crying. **fretfully** *adv.*

fretsaw *n.* very narrow saw used for fretwork.

fretwork *n.* woodwork cut in decorative patterns.

friable *a.* easily crumbled. **friability** *n.*

friar *n.* member of certain religious orders of men.

friary *n.* monastery of friars.

fricassee *n.* dish of pieces of meat served in a thick sauce. — *v.* make a fricassee of.

friction *n.* rubbing; resistance of one surface to another that moves over it; conflict of people who disagree. **frictional** *a.*

fridge *n.* (*colloq.*) refrigerator.

fried *see* **fry** [1].

friend *n.* person (other than a relative or lover) with whom one is on terms of mutual affection; helper, sympathizer. **friendship** *n.*

friendly *a.* (**-ier, -iest**) like a friend; favourable. **friendliness** *n.*

frieze *n.* band of decoration round the top of a wall.

frigate *n.* small fast naval ship.

fright *n.* sudden great fear; ridiculous-looking person or thing.

frighten *v.* cause fright to; feel fright; drive or compel by fright.

frightened *a.* afraid.

frightful *a.* causing horror; ugly; (*colloq.*) extremely great or bad. **frightfully** *adv.*, **frightfulness** *n.*

frigid *a.* intensely cold; very cold in manner; unresponsive sexually. **frigidly** *adv.*, **frigidity** *n.*

frill *n.* gathered or pleated strip of trimming attached at one edge; unnecessary extra. **frilled** *a.*, **frilly** *a.*

fringe *n.* ornamental edging of hanging threads or cords; front hair cut short to hang over the forehead; edge of an area or group etc. — *v.* edge. **fringe benefit** one provided by an employer in addition to wages.

frippery *n.* showy unnecessary finery or ornament.

frisk *v.* leap or skip playfully; (*sl.*) pass hands over (a person) to search for concealed weapons etc. — *n.* playful leap or skip.

frisky *a.* (**-ier, -iest**) lively, playful. **friskily** *adv.*, **friskiness** *n.*

fritter [1] *n.* fried batter-coated slice of fruit or meat etc.

fritter [2] *v.* waste little by little on trivial things.

frivolous *a.* lacking a serious purpose, pleasure-loving. **frivolously** *adv.*, **frivolity** *n.*

frizz *v.* curl into a wiry mass. **frizzy** *a.*, **frizziness** *n.*

frizzle *v.* fry crisp.

fro *see* **to and fro**.

frock *n.* woman's or girl's dress. **frock-coat** *n.* man's long-skirted coat not cut away in front.

frog *n.* small amphibian with long web-footed hind legs. **frog in one's throat** hoarseness.

frogman *n.* (*pl.* **-men**) swimmer with a rubber suit and oxygen supply for use under water.

frogmarch *v.* hustle (a person) forcibly, holding the arms.

frolic *v.* (**frolicked**) play about in a lively way. — *n.* such play.

from *prep.* having as the starting point, source, or cause; as separated, distinguished, or unlike. **from time to time** at intervals of time.

frond *n.* leaf-like part of a fern or palm tree etc.

front *n.* side or part normally nearer or towards the spectator or line of motion; battle line; outward appearance; cover for secret activities; promenade of a seaside resort; boundary between warm and cold air-masses. — *a.* of or at the front. — *v.* face, have the front towards; (*sl.*) serve as a cover for secret activities. **front runner** leading contestant. **in front** at the front.

frontage *n.* front of a building; land bordering this.

frontal *a.* of or on the front.

frontier *n.* boundary between countries.

frontispiece *n.* illustration opposite the title-page of a book.

frost *n.* freezing weather condition; white frozen dew or vapour. — *v.* injure with frost; cover with frost or frosting; make (glass) opaque by roughening its surface.

frostbite *n.* injury to body tissue from freezing. **frostbitten** *a.*, **frosty** *a.*

frosting *n.* sugar icing.

froth *n.* & *v.* foam. **frothy** *a.*, **frothiness** *n.*

frown *v.* wrinkle one's brow in thought or disapproval. — *n.* frowning movement or look. **frown on** disapprove of.

frowzy *a.* (**-ier, -iest**) fusty; dingy. **frowziness** *n.*

froze, frozen *see* **freeze**.

frugal *a.* careful and economical; scanty, costing little. **frugally** *adv.*, **frugality** *n.*

fruit *n.* seed-containing part of a plant; this used as food; (usu. *pl.*) product of labour. — *v.* produce or allow to produce fruit. **fruit machine** coin-operated gambling machine.

fruiterer *n.* shopkeeper selling fruit.

fruitful *a.* producing much fruit or good results. **fruitfully** *adv.*, **fruitfulness** *n.*

fruition /froo̅-ish'n/ *n.* fulfilment of hopes; results of work.

fruitless *a.* producing little or no result. **fruitlessly** *adv.*, **fruitlessness** *n.*

fruity *a.* (**-ier, -iest**) like fruit in smell or taste. **fruitiness** *n.*

frump *n.* dowdy woman. **frumpish** *a.*, **frumpy** *a.*

frustrate *v.* prevent from achieving something or from being achieved. **frustration** *n.*

fry [1] *v.* (**fried**) cook or be cooked in very hot fat.

fry [2] *n.* (*pl.* **fry**) young fish. **small fry** people of little importance.

ft *abbr.* foot or feet (as a measure).

fuchsia /fyo͞oshə/ *n.* ornamental shrub with drooping flowers.

fuddle *v.* stupefy, esp. with drink.

fuddy-duddy *a.* & *n.* (*sl.*) (person who is) out of date and unable to accept new ideas.

fudge *n.* soft sweet made of milk, sugar, and butter. — *v.* put together in a makeshift or dishonest way, fake.

fuel *n.* material burnt as a source of energy; thing that increases anger etc. — *v.* (**fuelled**) supply with fuel.

fug *n.* stuffy atmosphere in a room etc. **fuggy** *a.*, **fugginess** *n.*

fugitive *n.* person who is fleeing or escaping. — *a.* fleeing.

fulcrum *n.* (*pl.* **-cra**) point of support on which a lever pivots.

fulfil *v.* (**fulfilled**) accomplish, carry out (a task); satisfy, do what is required by (a contract etc.). **fulfil oneself** develop and use one's abilities fully. **fulfilment** *n.*

full *a.* holding or having as much as is possible; copious; complete; plump; made with material hanging in folds; (of tone) deep and mellow. — *adv.* completely; exactly. **full-blooded** *a.* vigorous, hearty. **full-blown** *a.* fully developed. **full**

moon moon with the whole disc illuminated. **full-scale** *a.* of actual size, not reduced. **full stop** dot used as a punctuation mark at the end of a sentence or abbreviation; complete stop. **fully** *adv.*, **fullness** *n.*

fulminate *v.* protest loudly and bitterly. **fulmination** *n.*

fulsome *a.* praising excessively and sickeningly. **fulsomeness** *n.*

fumble *v.* touch or handle (a thing) awkwardly; grope about.

fume *n.* pungent smoke or vapour. — *v.* emit fumes; seethe with anger; subject to fumes.

fumigate *v.* disinfect by fumes. **fumigation** *n.*, **fumigator** *n.*

fun *n.* light-hearted amusement; source of this. **funfair** *n.* fair consisting of amusements and sideshows. **make fun of** cause people to laugh at.

function *n.* special activity or purpose of a person or thing; important ceremony; (in mathematics) quantity whose value depends on varying values of others. — *v.* perform a function; be in action.

functional *a.* of function(s); practical, not decorative; able to function. **functionally** *adv.*

fund *n.* sum of money for a special purpose; stock, supply; (*pl.*) money resources. — *v.* provide with money.

fundamental *a.* basic; essential. — *n.* fundamental fact or principle. **fundamentally** *adv.*

fundamentalist *n.* person who upholds a strict or literal interpretation of traditional religious beliefs. **fundamentalism** *n.*

funeral *n.* ceremony of burial or cremation; procession to this.

funerary *a.* of or used for a burial or funeral.

funereal *a.* suitable for a funeral, dismal, dark.

fungicide *n.* substance that kills fungus. **fungicidal** *a.*

fungus *n.* (*pl.* **-gi**) plant without green colouring matter (e.g. mushroom, mould). **fungal** *a.*, **fungous** *a.*

funnel *n.* tube with a wide top for pouring liquid into small openings; chimney on a steam engine or ship. — *v.* (**funnelled**) move through a narrowing space.

funny *a.* (**-ier, -iest**) causing amusement; puzzling, odd. **funny bone** part of the elbow where a very sensitive nerve passes. **funnily** *adv.*

fur *n.* short fine hair of certain animals; skin with this used for clothing; coating, incrustation. — *v.* (**furred**) cover or become covered with fur.

furbish *v.* clean up; renovate.

furious *a.* full of anger; violent, intense. **furiously** *adv.*

furl *v.* roll up and fasten.

furlong *n.* one-eighth of a mile.

furnace *n.* enclosed fireplace for intense heating or smelting.

furnish *v.* equip with furniture; provide, supply. **furnishings** *n.pl.* furniture and fitments etc.

furniture *n.* movable articles (e.g. chairs, beds) for use in a room.

furore /fyooróri/ *n.* uproar of enthusiastic admiration or fury.

furrier *n.* person who deals in furs or fur clothes.

furrow *n.* long cut in the ground; groove. — *v.* make furrows in.

furry *a.* (**-ier, -iest**) like fur; covered with fur. **furriness** *n.*

further *adv.* & *a.* more distant; to a greater extent; additional(ly). — *v.* help the progress of. **further education** that provided for persons above school age. **furtherance** *n.*

furthermore *adv.* moreover.

furthest *a.* most distant. — *adv.* at or to the greatest distance.

furtive *a.* sly, stealthy. **furtively** *adv.*, **furtiveness** *n.*

fury *n.* wild anger, rage; violence.

furze *n.* gorse.

fuse [1] *v.* blend (metals etc.), become blended; unite; fit with a fuse; stop functioning through melting of a fuse. — *n.* strip of wire placed in an electric circuit to melt and interrupt the current when the circuit is overloaded.

fuse [2] *n.* length of easily burnt material for igniting a bomb or explosive. — *v.* fit a fuse to.

fuselage *n.* body of an aeroplane.

fusible *a.* able to be fused. **fusibility** *n.*

fusion *n.* fusing; union of atomic nuclei, with release of energy.

fuss *n.* unnecessary excitement or activity; vigorous protest. — *v.* make a fuss; agitate.

fussy *a.* (**-ier, -iest**) often fussing; fastidious; with much unnecessary detail or decoration. **fussily** *adv.*, **fussiness** *n.*

fusty *a.* (**-ier, -iest**) smelling stale and stuffy. **fustiness** *n.*

futile *a.* producing no result. **futilely** *adv.*, **futility** *n.*

futon /fōōton/ *n.* light orig. Japanese kind of mattress.

future *a.* belonging to the time after the present. — *n.* future time, events, or condition; prospect of success etc. **in future** from now on.

futuristic *a.* looking suitable for the distant future, not traditional. **futuristically** *adv.*

fuzz *n.* fluff, fluffy or frizzy thing.

fuzzy *a.* (**-ier**, **-iest**) like or covered with fuzz; blurred, indistinct. **fuzzily** *adv.*, **fuzziness** *n.*

G

g *abbr.* gram(s).

gabardine *n.* strong twilled fabric.

gabble *v.* talk quickly and indistinctly. — *n.* gabbled talk.

gable *n.* triangular part of a wall, between sloping roofs. **gabled** *a.*

gad *v.* (**gadded**) **gad about** travel constantly for pleasure.

gadabout *n.* person who gads about.

gadfly *n.* fly that bites cattle.

gadget *n.* small mechanical device or tool. **gadgetry** *n.* gadgets.

Gaelic /gáylik/ *n.* Celtic language of Scots or Irish.

gaff *n.* stick with a hook for landing large fish. — *v.* seize with a gaff.

gaffe *n.* blunder.

gaffer *n.* (*colloq.*) elderly man; boss, foreman.

gag *n.* thing put in or over a person's mouth to silence them; surgical device to hold the mouth open; joke. — *v.* (**gagged**) put a gag on; deprive of freedom of speech; tell jokes; retch.

gaggle *n.* flock (of geese); disorderly group.

gaiety *n.* cheerfulness, bright appearance; merrymaking.

gaily *adv.* with gaiety.

gain *v.* obtain, secure; acquire gradually; profit; get nearer in pursuit; reach; (of a clock) become fast. — *n.* increase in wealth or value.

gainful *a.* profitable. **gainfully** *adv.*

gainsay *v.* (**gainsaid**) (*formal*) deny, contradict.

gait *n.* manner of walking or running.

gaiter *n.* cloth or leather covering for the lower part of the leg.

gala /gaàlə/ *n.* festive occasion; fête.

galaxy *n.* system of stars; brilliant company. **galactic** *a.*

gale *n.* very strong wind; noisy outburst.

gall [1] *n.* bile; bitterness of feeling; (*sl.*) impudence. **gall bladder** organ storing bile.

gall [2] *n.* sore made by rubbing. — *v.* rub and make sore; vex.

gall [3] *n.* abnormal growth on a plant, esp. on an oak tree.

gallant *a.* brave, chivalrous; attentive to women. — *n.* ladies' man. **gallantly** *adv.*, **gallantry** *n.*

galleon *n.* large Spanish sailing ship in the 15th–17th centuries.

gallery *n.* balcony in a hall or theatre etc.; long room or passage, esp. used for special purpose; room or building for showing works of art.

galley *n.* (*pl.* **-eys**) ancient ship, esp. propelled by oars; kitchen in a ship or aircraft; oblong tray holding type for printing; (also **galley proof**) printer's proof in a long narrow form.

Gallic *a.* of ancient Gaul; French.

gallon *n.* measure for liquids, = 4 quarts (4.546 litres).

gallop *n.* horse's fastest pace; ride at this. — *v.* (**galloped**) go or ride at a gallop; progress rapidly.

gallows *n.* framework with a noose for hanging criminals.

gallstone *n.* small hard mass formed in the gall bladder.

galore *adv.* in plenty.

galosh *n.* rubber overshoe.

galvanize *v.* stimulate into activity; coat with zinc. **galvanization** *n.*

gambit *n.* opening move.

gamble *v.* play games of chance for money; risk in hope of gain. — *n.* gambling; risky undertaking. **gambler** *n.*

gambol *v.* (**gambolled**) jump about in play. — *n.* gambolling movement.

game [1] *n.* play or sport, esp. with rules; section of this as a scoring unit; scheme; wild animals hunted for sport or food; their flesh as food. — *v.* gamble for money stakes. — *a.* brave; willing. **gamely** *adv.*, **gameness** *n.*

game [2] *a.* lame.

gamekeeper *n.* person employed to protect and breed game.

gamesmanship *n.* art of winning games by upsetting the confidence of one's opponent.

gamete *n.* sexual cell.

gamine *n.* girl with mischievous charm.

gamma *n.* third letter of the Greek alphabet, = g.

gammon *n.* cured or smoked ham.

gammy *a.* (*sl.*) = game [2].

gamut *n.* whole range of musical notes; whole series or scope.

gamy *a.* smelling or tasting like high game. **gaminess** *n.*

gander *n.* male goose.

gang *n.* group of people working or going about together. — *v.* **gang up** combine in a gang.

gangling *a.* tall and awkward.
ganglion *n.* (*pl.* **-ia**) group of nerve cells; cyst on a tendon.
gangplank *n.* plank placed for walking into or out of a boat.
gangrene *n.* decay of body tissue. **gangrenous** *a.*
gangster *n.* member of a gang of violent criminals.
gangway *n.* gap left for people to pass, esp. between rows of seats; passageway, esp. on a ship; movable bridge from a ship to land.
gannet *n.* large seabird.
gantry *n.* overhead bridge-like framework supporting railway signals or a travelling crane etc.
gaol *n.* = jail. **gaoler** *n.*
gap *n.* opening, space, interval; deficiency; wide difference.
gape *v.* open the mouth wide; stare in surprise; be wide open. — *n.* yawn; stare.
garage *n.* building for storing motor vehicle(s); commercial establishment for refuelling or repairing motor vehicles. — *v.* put or keep in a garage.
garb *n.* clothing. — *v.* clothe.
garbage *n.* domestic rubbish.
garble *v.* distort or confuse (a message or story etc.).
garden *n.* piece of cultivated ground, esp. attached to a house; (*pl.*) ornamental public grounds. — *v.* tend a garden. **gardener** *n.*
gardenia *n.* fragrant white or yellow flower; shrub bearing this.
gargantuan *a.* gigantic.
gargle *v.* wash the inside of the throat with liquid held there by the breath. — *n.* liquid for this.
gargoyle *n.* grotesque carved face or figure on a building.
garish *a.* gaudy. **garishly** *adv.*, **garishness** *n.*
garland *n.* wreath of flowers etc. as a decoration. — *v.* deck with garland(s).
garlic *n.* onion-like plant. **garlicky** *a.*
garment *n.* article of clothing.
garner *v.* store up, collect.
garnet *n.* red semiprecious stone.
garnish *v.* decorate (esp. food). — *n.* thing used for garnishing.
garret *n.* attic, esp. a poor one.
garrison *n.* troops stationed in a town or fort; building they occupy. — *v.* occupy thus.
garrotte *n.* cord, wire, or a metal collar used to strangle a victim. — *v.* strangle or (in Spain) execute with this.
garrulous *a.* talkative. **garrulously** *adv.*, **garrulousness** *n.*
garter *n.* band worn round the leg to keep a stocking up.
gas *n.* (*pl.* **gases**) substance with particles that can move freely; such a substance used as a fuel or anaesthetic; (*colloq.*) empty talk; (*US*) petrol. — *v.* (**gassed**) kill or overcome by poisonous gas; (*colloq.*) talk lengthily. **gas chamber** room that can be filled with poisonous gas to kill animals or prisoners. **gas mask** device worn over face as a protection against poisonous gas. **gassy** *a.*
gaseous *a.* of or like a gas.
gash *n.* long deep cut. — *v.* make a gash in.
gasify *v.* convert or be converted into gas. **gasification** *n.*
gasket *n.* piece of rubber etc. sealing a joint between metal surfaces.
gasoline *n.* (*US*) petrol.
gasp *v.* draw breath in sharply; speak breathlessly. — *n.* breath drawn in thus.
gastric *a.* of the stomach.
gastropod *n.* mollusc, such as a snail, that moves by means of a ventral organ.
gate *n.* hinged movable barrier in a wall or fence etc.; gateway; number of spectators paying to attend a sporting event, amount of money taken.
gateau /gáttō/ *n.* (*pl.* **-eaux**) large rich cream cake.
gatecrash *v.* go to (a private party) uninvited. **gatecrasher** *n.*
gateway *n.* opening or structure framing a gate; entrance.
gather *v.* bring or come together; collect; obtain gradually; understand, conclude; draw together in folds.
gathering *n.* people assembled.
gauche /gōsh/ *a.* socially awkward. **gaucherie** *n.*
gaucho /gówchō/ *n.* (*pl.* **-os**) South American cowboy.
gaudy *a.* (**-ier**, **-iest**) showy or bright in a tasteless way. **gaudily** *adv.*, **gaudiness** *n.*
gauge /gayj/ *n.* standard measure esp. of contents or thickness; device for measuring things; distance between pairs of rails or wheels. — *v.* measure; estimate.
gaunt *a.* lean and haggard; grim, desolate. **gauntness** *n.*
gauntlet [1] *n.* glove with a long wide cuff; this cuff.
gauntlet [2] *n.* **run the gauntlet** be exposed to continuous criticism or risk.
gauze *n.* thin transparent fabric; fine wire mesh. **gauzy** *a.*
gave *see* **give**.
gavel *n.* mallet used by an auctioneer

or chairman etc. to call for attention or order.

gawky *a.* (**-ier**, **-iest**) awkward and ungainly. **gawkiness** *n.*

gay *a.* happy and full of fun; brightly coloured; homosexual. — *n.* homosexual person. **gayness** *n.*

gaze *v.* look long and steadily. — *n.* long steady look.

gazebo /gəzeébō/ *n.* (*pl.* **-os**) turret or summer house with a wide view.

gazelle *n.* small antelope.

gazette *n.* title of certain newspapers or of official journals containing public notices.

gazetteer *n.* index of places, rivers, mountains, etc.

gazump *v.* disappoint (an intended house buyer) by raising the price agreed.

GB *abbr.* Great Britain.

gear *n.* equipment; apparatus; set of toothed wheels working together in machinery. — *v.* provide with gear(s); adapt (to a purpose). **in gear** with gear mechanism engaged.

gearbox, gearcase *ns.* case enclosing gear mechanism.

gecko *n.* (*pl.* **-os**) tropical lizard.

geese *see* **goose**.

Geiger counter /gígər/ device for detecting and measuring radioactivity.

geisha /gáyshə/ *n.* Japanese woman trained to entertain men.

gel *n.* jelly-like substance.

gelatine *n.* clear substance made by boiling bones. **gelatinous** *a.*

geld *v.* castrate, spay.

gelding *n.* gelded horse.

gelignite *n.* explosive containing nitroglycerine.

gem *n.* precious stone; thing of great beauty or excellence.

gender *n.* one's sex; grammatical classification corresponding roughly to sex.

gene *n.* one of the factors controlling heredity.

genealogy *n.* list of ancestors; study of family pedigrees. **genealogical** *a.*, **genealogist** *n.*

genera *see* **genus**.

general *a.* of or involving all or most parts, things, or people; not detailed or specific; (in titles) chief. — *n.* army officer next below field marshal. **general election** election of parliamentary representatives from the whole country. **general practitioner** community doctor treating cases of all kinds. **in general** usually; for the most part. **generally** *adv.*

generality *n.* being general; general statement without details.

generalize *v.* draw a general conclusion; speak in general terms. **generalization** *n.*

generate *v.* bring into existence, produce.

generation *n.* generating; single stage in descent or pedigree; all persons born at about the same time; period of about 30 years.

generator *n.* machine converting mechanical energy into electricity.

generic *a.* of a whole genus or group. **generically** *adv.*

generous *a.* giving or given freely; not small-minded. **generously** *adv.*, **generosity** *n.*

genesis *n.* origin.

genetic *a.* of genes or genetics. **genetically** *adv.*

genetics *n.* science of heredity.

genial *a.* kindly and cheerful. **genially** *adv.*, **geniality** *n.*

genie *n.* (*pl.* **genii**) spirit or goblin in Arabian tales.

genital *a.* of animal reproduction; of genitals. **genitals** *n.pl.* external sex organs.

genius *n.* (*pl.* **-uses**) exceptionally great natural ability; person having this.

genocide *n.* deliberate extermination of a race of people.

genre /zhóNrə/ *n.* kind, esp. of art or literature.

genteel *a.* affectedly polite and refined. **genteelly** *adv.*

gentian /jénsh'n/ *n.* alpine plant with usu. deep-blue flowers.

gentile *n.* non-Jewish person.

gentility *n.* good manners and elegance.

gentle *a.* mild, moderate, not rough or severe. — *v.* coax. — *n.* maggot used as bait. **gently** *adv.*, **gentleness** *n.*

gentleman *n.* (*pl.* **-men**) man, esp. of good social position; well-mannered man. **gentlemanly** *a.*

gentrify *v.* alter (an area) socially by arrival of middle-class residents. **gentrification** *n.*

gentry *n.pl.* people ranking next below nobility; (*derog.*) people.

genuflect *v.* bend the knee and lower the body, esp. in worship. **genuflection** *n.*

genuine *a.* really what it is said to be. **genuinely** *adv.*, **genuineness** *n.*

genus *n.* (*pl.* **genera**) group of animals or plants, usu. containing several species; kind.

geocentric *a.* having the earth as a centre; as viewed from the earth's centre.

geode *n.* cavity lined with crystals; rock containing this.

geography *n.* study of earth's physical features, climate, etc.; features and arrangement of a place. **geographical** *a.*, **geographically** *adv.*, **geographer** *n.*

geology *n.* study of earth's crust; features of earth's crust. **geological** *a.*, **geologically** *adv.*, **geologist** *n.*

geometry *n.* branch of mathematics dealing with lines, angles, surfaces, and solids. **geometric** *a.*, **geometrical** *a.*, **geometrically** *adv.*, **geometrician** *n.*

Georgian *a.* of the time of the Georges, kings of England, esp. 1714–1830.

geranium *n.* garden plant with red, pink, or white flowers.

gerbil *n.* rodent with long hind legs.

geriatrics *n.* branch of medicine dealing with the diseases and care of old people. **geriatric** *a.*

germ *n.* micro-organism, esp. one capable of causing disease; portion (of an organism) capable of developing into a new organism; basis from which a thing may develop.

German *a.* & *n.* (native, language) of Germany. **German measles** disease like mild measles.

germane *a.* relevant.

germinate *v.* begin or cause to grow. **germination** *n.*

gerontology *n.* study of ageing. **gerontologist** *n.*

gerrymander *v.* arrange boundaries of (a constituency etc.) so as to gain unfair electoral advantage.

gerund *n.* English verbal noun ending in *-ing*.

Gestapo *n.* German secret police of the Nazi regime.

gestation *n.* carrying in the womb between conception and birth; period of this.

gesticulate *v.* make expressive movements with the hands and arms. **gesticulation** *n.*

gesture *n.* expressive movement or action. — *v.* make a gesture.

get *v.* (**got, getting**) come into possession of; earn; win; fetch; capture, catch; prepare (a meal); bring or come into a certain state; persuade; (*colloq.*) understand; (*colloq.*) annoy. **get at** reach; (*colloq.*) imply; (*sl.*) tamper with, bribe. **get by** pass; manage to survive. **get off** be acquitted. **get on** manage; make progress; be on harmonious terms; advance in age. **get out of** evade. **get-out** *n.* means of evading something. **get over** recover from. **get round** influence in one's favour; evade (a law or rule). **get-together** *n.* (*colloq.*) social gathering. **get up** stand up; get out of bed; prepare, organize; dress. **get-up** *n.* outfit.

getaway *n.* escape after a crime.

gewgaw *n.* gaudy ornament etc.

geyser /geézər/ *n.* spring that spouts hot water or steam; a kind of water heater.

ghastly *a.* (**-ier, -iest**) causing horror; (*colloq.*) very bad; pale and ill-looking. **ghastliness** *n.*

gherkin *n.* small cucumber used for pickling.

ghetto *n.* (*pl.* **-os**) slum area occupied by a particular group. **ghetto-blaster** *n.* (*sl.*) large portable cassette player.

ghost *n.* person's spirit appearing after their death. — *v.* write as a ghost writer. **ghost writer** person who writes a book etc. for another to pass off as their own. **ghostly** *a.*, **ghostliness** *n.*

ghoul /gōōl/ *n.* person who enjoys gruesome things; (in Muslim stories) spirit that robs and devours corpses. **ghoulish** *a.*, **ghoulishly** *adv.*, **ghoulishness** *n.*

giant *n.* (in fairy tales) a being of superhuman size; abnormally large person, animal, or thing; person of outstanding ability. — *a.* very large. **giantess** *n.fem.*

gibber *v.* make meaningless sounds, esp. in shock or terror.

gibberish *n.* unintelligible talk, nonsense.

gibbet *n.* gallows.

gibbon *n.* long-armed ape.

gibe /jīb/ *n.* & *v.* jeer.

giblets *n.pl.* edible organs from a bird.

giddy *a.* (**-ier, -iest**) having or causing the feeling that everything is spinning round; excitable, flighty. **giddily** *adv.*, **giddiness** *n.*

gift *n.* thing given or received without payment; natural ability; easy task. — *v.* bestow.

gifted *a.* having great natural ability.

gig ¹ *n.* light two-wheeled horse-drawn carriage.

gig ² *n.* (*colloq.*) engagement to play jazz etc. — *v.* (**gigged**) (*colloq.*) perform a gig.

giga- *pref.* multiplied by 10^9, as in *gigametre*.

gigantic *a.* very large.

giggle *v.* give small bursts of half-suppressed laughter. — *n.* this laughter.

gigolo /zhíggəlō/ *n.* (*pl.* **-os**) man paid by a woman to be her escort or lover.

gild *v.* (**gilded**) cover with a thin layer of gold or gold paint.

gilet /jiláy/ *n.* waistcoat as a woman's garment.

gill ¹ /gil/ *n.* (usu. *pl.*) respiratory opening on the body of a fish etc.; each of the vertical plates on the under side of a mushroom cap.

gill ² /jil/ *n.* one-quarter of a pint.

gilt *a.* gilded, gold-coloured. — *n.* substance used in gilding; gilt-edged investment. **gilt-edged** *a.* (of an investment etc.) very safe.
gimbals *n.pl.* contrivance of rings to keep instruments horizontal in a moving ship etc.
gimcrack /jimkrak/ *a.* cheap and flimsy.
gimlet *n.* small tool with a screw-like tip for boring holes.
gimmick *n.* trick or device to attract attention or publicity. **gimmicky** *a.*
gin *n.* alcoholic spirit flavoured with juniper berries.
ginger *n.* hot-tasting root of a tropical plant; liveliness; reddish yellow. — *a.* ginger-coloured. **ginger ale**, **ginger beer** ginger-flavoured fizzy drinks. **ginger group** group urging a more active policy. **gingery** *a.*
gingerbread *n.* ginger-flavoured cake or biscuit.
gingerly *a.* & *adv.* cautious(ly).
gingham *n.* cotton fabric, often with a checked or striped pattern.
ginseng *n.* plant with a fragrant root used in medicine.
gipsy *n.* = gypsy.
giraffe *n.* long-necked African animal.
girder *n.* metal beam supporting part of a building or bridge.
girdle *n.* cord worn round the waist; elastic corset; ring of bones in the body. — *v.* surround.
girl *n.* female child; young woman; female assistant or employee; man's girlfriend. **girlfriend** *n.* female friend, esp. man's usual companion. **girlhood** *n.*, **girlish** *a.*
giro /jīrō/ *n.* (*pl.* **-os**) banking system by which payment can be made by transferring credit from one account to another; cheque or payment made by this.
girth *n.* distance round something; band under a horse's belly, holding a saddle in place.
gist /jist/ *n.* essential points or general sense of a speech etc.
give *v.* **(gave, given)** cause to receive or have, supply; provide; utter; pledge; present (a play etc.) in public; yield as a product or result; be flexible. — *n.* springiness, elasticity. **give and take** willingness to make reciprocal concessions. **give away** give as a gift; reveal (a secret etc.) unintentionally. **give-away** *n.* (*colloq.*) unintentional disclosure. **give in** acknowledge that one is defeated. **give off** emit. **give out** announce; become exhausted or used up. **give over** devote; (*colloq.*) cease. **give up** cease; part with, hand over; abandon hope or an attempt. **give way** yield; allow other traffic to go first; collapse. **giver** *n.*
given *see* **give**. — *a.* specified; having a tendency. **given name** first name (given in addition to the family name).
gizzard *n.* bird's second stomach, in which food is ground.
glacé /glássay/ *a.* iced with sugar; preserved in sugar.
glacial *a.* icy; of or from glaciers. **glacially** *adv.*
glaciated *a.* covered with or affected by a glacier. **glaciation** *n.*
glacier *n.* mass or river of ice moving very slowly.
glad *a.* pleased, joyful. **gladly** *adv.*, **gladness** *n.*
gladden *v.* make glad.
glade *n.* open space in a forest.
gladiator *n.* man trained to fight at public shows in ancient Rome. **gladiatorial** *a.*
gladiolus *n.* (*pl.* **-li**) garden plant with spikes of flowers.
glamour *n.* alluring beauty; attractive exciting qualities. **glamorize** *v.*, **glamorous** *a.*, **glamorously** *adv.*
glance *v.* look briefly; strike and glide off. — *n.* brief look.
gland *n.* organ that secretes substances to be used or expelled by the body. **glandular** *a.*
glare *v.* shine with a harsh dazzling light; stare angrily or fiercely. — *n.* glaring light or stare.
glaring *a.* conspicuous.
glass *n.* hard brittle usu. transparent substance; things made of this; mirror; glass drinking vessel; barometer; (*pl.*) spectacles, binoculars. — *v.* fit or cover with glass. **glassy** *a.*, **glassily** *adv.*, **glassiness** *n.*
glasshouse *n.* greenhouse; (*sl.*) military prison.
glaze *v.* fit or cover with glass; coat with a glossy surface; become glassy. — *n.* shiny surface or coating.
glazier *n.* person whose trade is to fit glass in windows etc.
gleam *n.* beam or ray of soft light; brief show of a quality. — *v.* send out gleams.
glean *v.* pick up (grain left by harvesters); gather scraps of. **gleaner** *n.*, **gleanings** *n.pl.*
glee *n.* lively or triumphant joy. **gleeful** *a.*, **gleefully** *adv.*
glen *n.* narrow valley.
glib *a.* ready with words but insincere or superficial.
glide *v.* move smoothly; fly in a glider or aircraft without engine power. — *n.* gliding movement.

glider *n.* aeroplane with no engine.

glimmer *n.* faint gleam. — *v.* gleam faintly.

glimpse *n.* brief view. — *v.* catch a glimpse of.

glint *n.* very brief flash of light. — *v.* send out a glint.

glisten *v.* shine like something wet.

glitter *v.* & *n.* sparkle.

gloaming *n.* evening twilight.

gloat *v.* be full of greedy or malicious delight.

global *a.* worldwide; of a whole group of items. **global warming** worldwide rise in temperature. **globally** *adv.*

globe *n.* ball-shaped object, esp. with a map of the earth on it; the world; hollow round glass object. **globe-trotting** *n.* travelling widely as a tourist.

globular *a.* shaped like a globe.

globule *n.* small rounded drop.

globulin *n.* a kind of protein found in animal and plant tissue.

glockenspiel *n.* musical instrument of tuned steel bars or tubes struck by hammers.

gloom *n.* semi-darkness; feeling of sadness and depression. **gloomy** *a.*, **gloomily** *adv.*

glorify *v.* praise highly; worship; make seem grander than it is. **glorification** *n.*

glorious *a.* having or bringing glory; splendid. **gloriously** *adv.*

glory *n.* fame, honour, and praise; thing deserving this; magnificence. — *v.* rejoice, pride oneself. **glory-hole** *n.* (*colloq.*) untidy room or cupboard etc.

gloss *n.* shine on a smooth surface. — *v.* make glossy. **gloss over** cover up (a mistake etc.).

glossary *n.* list of technical or special words, with definitions.

glossy *a.* (**-ier, -iest**) shiny. **glossily** *adv.*, **glossiness** *n.*

glottis *n.* opening at the upper end of the windpipe between the vocal cords. **glottal** *a.*

glove *n.* covering for the hand, usu. with separate divisions for fingers and thumb.

glow *v.* send out light and heat without flame; have a warm or flushed look, colour, or feeling. — *n.* glowing state, look, or feeling. **glow-worm** *n.* beetle that can give out a greenish light.

glower /glowr/ *v.* scowl.

glucose *n.* form of sugar found in fruit juice.

glue *n.* sticky substance used for joining things together. — *v.* (**gluing**) fasten with glue; attach closely. **gluey** *a.*

glum *a.* (**glummer, glummest**) sad and gloomy. **glumly** *adv.*, **glumness** *n.*

glut *v.* (**glutted**) supply with more than is needed; satisfy fully with food. — *n.* excessive supply.

gluten *n.* sticky protein substance found in cereals.

glutinous *a.* glue-like, sticky. **glutinously** *adv.*

glutton *n.* a greedy person; one who is eager for something. **gluttonous** *a.*, **gluttony** *n.*

glycerine *n.* thick sweet liquid used in medicines etc.

gnarled /naarld/ *a.* knobbly; twisted and misshapen.

gnash /nash/ *v.* (of teeth) strike together; grind (one's teeth).

gnat /nat/ *n.* small biting fly.

gnaw /naw/ *v.* bite persistently (at something hard).

gnome /nōm/ *n.* dwarf in fairy tales, living underground.

gnomic /nōmik/ *a.* sententious.

gnu /noo/ *n.* ox-like antelope.

go *v.* (**went, gone**) move; depart; extend; be functioning; make (a specified movement or sound); (of time) pass; belong in a specified place; become; proceed; be sold; be spent or used up; collapse, fail, die. — *n.* (*pl.* **goes**) energy; turn, try; attack of illness. **go-ahead** *n.* signal to proceed; (*a.*) enterprising. **go back on** fail to keep (a promise). **go-between** *n.* one who acts as messenger or negotiator. **go for** (*sl.*) attack. **go-getter** *n.* pushily enterprising person. **go-kart** *n.* miniature racing car. **go off** explode. **go out** be extinguished. **go round** be enough for everyone. **go slow** work at a deliberately slow pace as a form of industrial protest. **go-slow** *n.* this procedure. **go under** succumb; fail. **go up** rise in price; explode; burn rapidly. **go with** match, harmonize with. **on the go** in constant motion, active.

goad *n.* pointed stick for driving cattle; stimulus to activity. — *v.* stimulate by annoying.

goal *n.* structure or area into which players try to send the ball in certain games; point scored thus; objective. **goalpost** *n.* either of the posts marking the limit of a goal.

goalie *n.* (*colloq.*) goalkeeper.

goalkeeper *n.* player whose task is to keep the ball out of the goal.

goat *n.* small horned animal.

gobble *v.* eat quickly and greedily; make a throaty sound like a turkeycock. **gobbler** *n.*

gobbledegook *n.* (*colloq.*) pompous language used by officials.
goblet *n.* drinking glass with a stem and foot; container for the liquid in a liquidizer.
goblin *n.* mischievous ugly elf.
God *n.* creator and ruler of the universe in Christian, Jewish, and Muslim teaching. **god** *n.* superhuman being worshipped as having power over nature and human affairs; person or thing that is greatly admired or adored. **God-fearing** *a.* sincerely religious. **God-forsaken** *a.* wretched, dismal.
godchild *n.* (*pl.* **-children**) child in relation to its godparent(s).
god-daughter *n.* female godchild.
goddess *n.* female god.
godetia *n.* hardy annual plant with showy flowers.
godfather *n.* male godparent.
godhead *n.* divine nature; deity.
godmother *n.* female godparent.
godparent *n.* person who promises at a child's baptism to see that it is brought up as a Christian.
godsend *n.* piece of unexpected good fortune.
godson *n.* male godchild.
goggle *v.* stare with wide-open eyes.
goggles *n.pl.* spectacles for protecting the eyes from wind, water, etc.
goitre /góytər/ *n.* enlarged thyroid gland.
gold *n.* yellow metal of high value; coins or articles made of this; its colour. — *a.* made of or coloured like gold. **goldfield** *n.* area where gold is found. **gold rush** rush to a newly discovered goldfield.
golden *a.* gold; precious, excellent. **golden handshake** generous cash payment to a person dismissed or forced to retire. **golden jubilee**, **golden wedding** 50th anniversary.
goldfinch *n.* songbird with a band of yellow across each wing.
goldfish *n.* (*pl.* **goldfish**) reddish carp kept in a bowl or pond.
goldsmith *n.* person whose trade is making articles in gold.
golf *n.* game in which a ball is struck with clubs into a series of holes. — *v.* play golf. **golf course, golf links** land on which golf is played. **golfer** *n.*
golliwog *n.* black-faced soft doll with fuzzy hair.
gonad *n.* animal organ producing gametes.
gondola *n.* boat with high pointed ends, used on canals in Venice.
gondolier *n.* man who propels a gondola by means of a pole.
gone *see* **go**.
gong *n.* metal plate that resounds when struck; (*sl.*) medal.
gonorrhoea *n.* venereal disease with a discharge from the genitals.
goo *n.* (*colloq.*) sticky wet substance.
good *a.* (**better, best**) having the right or desirable qualities; proper, expedient; morally correct, kindly; well-behaved; enjoyable, beneficial; efficient; thorough; considerable, full; valid. — *n.* morally right thing; profit, benefit; (*pl.*) movable property, articles of trade, things to be carried by road or rail. **as good as** practically, almost. **good-for-nothing** *a.* & *n.* worthless (person). **Good Friday** Friday before Easter, commemorating the Crucifixion. **good name** good reputation. **good will** intention that good shall result.
goodbye *int.* & *n.* expression used when parting.
goodness *n.* quality of being good; good element.
goodwill *n.* friendly feeling; established popularity of a business, treated as a saleable asset.
goody *n.* (*colloq.*) something good or attractive, esp. to eat. **goody-goody** *a.* & *n.* smugly virtuous (person).
gooey *a.* (*colloq.*) wet and sticky.
goose *n.* (*pl.* **geese**) web-footed bird larger than a duck; female of this. **goose-flesh, goose pimples** bristling skin caused by cold or fear. **goose-step** *n.* way of marching without bending the knees.
gooseberry *n.* thorny shrub; its edible (usu. green) berry.
gore [1] *n.* clotted blood from a wound.
gore [2] *v.* pierce with a horn or tusk.
gore [3] *n.* triangular or tapering section of a skirt or sail. **gored** *a.*
gorge *n.* narrow steep-sided valley. — *v.* eat greedily; fill full, choke up.
gorgeous *a.* richly coloured, magnificent; (*colloq.*) very pleasant, beautiful. **gorgeously** *adv.*
gorgon *n.* terrifying woman.
gorilla *n.* large powerful ape.
gorse *n.* wild evergreen thorny shrub with yellow flowers.
gory *a.* (**-ier, -iest**) covered with blood; involving bloodshed.
gosling *n.* young goose.
Gospel *n.* book(s) of the New Testament recording Christ's life and teachings. **gospel** *n.* undeniable truth; set of principles believed in.
gossamer *n.* fine filmy piece of cobweb; flimsy delicate material.
gossip *n.* casual talk, esp. about other

people's affairs; person fond of gossiping. — *v.* (**gossiped**) engage in gossip.
got *see* **get**. **have got** possess. **have got to do it** must do it.
Gothic *a.* of an architectural style of the 12th–16th centuries, with pointed arches; (of a novel etc.) in a horrific style popular in the 18th–19th centuries.
gouge *n.* chisel with a concave blade. — *v.* cut out with a gouge; scoop or force out.
goulash *n.* stew of meat and vegetables, seasoned with paprika.
gourd *n.* fleshy fruit of a climbing plant; container made from its dried rind.
gourmand *n.* glutton.
gourmet /goórmay/ *n.* connoisseur of good food and drink.
gout *n.* disease causing inflammation of the joints. **gouty** *a.*
govern *v.* rule with authority; keep under control; influence, direct. **governor** *n.*
governable *a.* able to be governed.
governance *n.* governing, control.
government *n.* governing; group or organization governing a country; State as an agent. **governmental** *a.*
gown *n.* loose flowing garment; woman's long dress; official robe.
GP *abbr.* general practitioner.
grab *v.* (**grabbed**) grasp suddenly; take greedily. — *n.* sudden clutch or attempt to seize; mechanical device for gripping things.
grace *n.* attractiveness and elegance, esp. of manner or movement; favour; mercy; short prayer of thanks for a meal. — *v.* confer honour or dignity on, be an ornament to.
graceful *a.* having or showing grace. **gracefully** *adv.*, **gracefulness** *n.*
graceless *a.* inelegant; ungracious. **gracelessly** *adv.*
gracious *a.* kind and pleasant towards inferiors; elegant. **graciously** *adv.*, **graciousness** *n.*
gradation *n.* stage in a process of gradual change; this process.
grade *n.* level of rank, quality, or value; mark given to a student for his or her standard of work; slope. — *v.* arrange in grades; assign a grade to; adjust the slope of (a road). **make the grade** be successful.
gradient *n.* slope, amount of this.
gradual *a.* taking place by degrees. **gradually** *adv.*
graduate *n.* /grádyooət/ person who holds a university degree. — *v.* /grádyoo-ayt/ take a university degree; divide into graded sections; mark into regular divisions. **graduation** *n.*
graffiti *n.pl.* words or drawings scribbled or scratched on a wall etc.
graft *n.* shoot fixed into a cut in a tree to form a new growth; living tissue transplanted surgically; (*sl.*) hard work. — *v.* put a graft in or on; join inseparably; (*sl.*) work hard.
grain *n.* small hard seed(s) of a food plant such as wheat or rice; these plants; small hard particle; unit of weight (about 65 mg); texture or pattern made by fibres or particles. **grainy** *a.*
gram *n.* one-thousandth of a kilogram.
grammar *n.* use of words in their correct forms and relationships.
grammatical *a.* according to the rules of grammar. **grammatically** *adv.*
grampus *n.* dolphin-like sea animal.
gran *n.* (*colloq.*) grandmother.
granary *n.* storehouse for grain.
grand *a.* great; splendid; imposing; (*colloq.*) very good. — *n.* grand piano. **grand piano** large full-toned piano with horizontal strings. **grandly** *adv.*, **grandness** *n.*
grandad *n.* (*colloq.*) grandfather.
grandchild *n.* (*pl.* **-children**) child of one's son or daughter.
granddaughter *n.* female grandchild.
grandeur *n.* splendour, grandness.
grandfather *n.* male grandparent. **grandfather clock** one in a tall wooden case.
grandiloquent *a.* using pompous language. **grandiloquently** *adv.*, **grandiloquence** *n.*
grandiose *a.* imposing; planned on a large scale. **grandiosely** *adv.*, **grandiosity** *n.*
grandma *n.* (*colloq.*) grandmother.
grandmother *n.* female grandparent.
grandpa *n.* (*colloq.*) grandfather.
grandparent *n.* parent of one's father or mother.
grandson *n.* male grandchild.
grandstand *n.* principal stand for spectators at races and sports.
grange *n.* country house with farm buildings that belong to it.
granite *n.* hard grey stone.
granny *n.* (*colloq.*) grandmother. **granny flat** self-contained accommodation in one's house for a relative.
grant *v.* give or allow as a privilege; admit to be true. — *n.* thing granted; student's allowance from public funds; granting. **take for granted** assume to be true or sure to happen or continue.
granular *a.* like grains.
granulate *v.* form into grains; roughen the surface of. **granulation** *n.*
granule *n.* small grain.
grape *n.* green or purple berry used for

making wine. **grapevine** *n.* vine bearing grapes; way news spreads unofficially.
grapefruit *n.* large round yellow citrus fruit.
graph *n.* diagram showing the relationship between quantities.
graphic *a.* of drawing, painting, or engraving; giving a vivid description. **graphics** *n.pl.* diagrams etc. used in calculation and design. **graphically** *adv.*
graphical *a.* using diagrams or graphs. **graphically** *adv.*
graphite *n.* a form of carbon.
graphology *n.* study of handwriting. **graphologist** *n.*
grapnel *n.* small anchor with several hooks; hooked device for dragging a river bed.
grapple *v.* seize, hold firmly; struggle. **grappling-iron** *n.* grapnel.
grasp *v.* seize and hold; understand. — *n.* firm hold or grip; understanding.
grasping *a.* greedy, avaricious.
grass *n.* wild plant with green blades eaten by animals; species of this (e.g. a cereal plant); ground covered with grass. — *v.* cover with grass. **grass roots** fundamental level or source; rank-and-file members. **grass widow** wife whose husband is absent for some time. **grassy** *a.*
grasshopper *n.* jumping insect that makes a chirping noise.
grassland *n.* wide grass-covered area with few trees.
grate [1] *n.* metal framework keeping fuel in a fireplace; hearth.
grate [2] *v.* shred finely by rubbing against a jagged surface; make a harsh noise by rubbing; sound harshly; have an irritating effect.
grateful *a.* feeling that one values a kindness or benefit received. **gratefully** *adv.*
grater *n.* device for grating food.
gratify *v.* give pleasure to; satisfy (wishes). **gratification** *n.*
grating *n.* screen of spaced bars placed across an opening.
gratis *a.* & *adv.* free of charge.
gratitude *n.* being grateful.
gratuitous *a.* given or done free; uncalled for. **gratuitously** *adv.*
gratuity *n.* money given as a present for services rendered.
grave [1] *n.* hole dug to bury a corpse.
grave [2] *a.* serious, causing great anxiety; solemn. **grave accent** /graav/ the accent `. **gravely** *adv.*
gravel *n.* coarse sand with small stones. **gravelly** *a.*
gravestone *n.* stone placed over a grave.
graveyard *n.* burial ground.
gravitate *v.* move or be attracted towards something.
gravitation *n.* gravitating; force of gravity. **gravitational** *a.*
gravity *n.* seriousness; solemnity; force that attracts bodies towards the centre of the earth.
gravy *n.* juice from cooked meat; sauce made from this.
gray *a.* & *n.* = grey.
graze [1] *v.* feed on growing grass; pasture animals in (a field).
graze [2] *v.* injure by scraping the skin; touch or scrape lightly in passing. — *n.* grazed place on the skin.
grease *n.* fatty or oily matter, esp. as a lubricant. — *v.* put grease on. **greasepaint** *n.* make-up used by actors. **greaser** *n.*, **greasy** *a.*
great *a.* much above average in size, amount, or intensity; of remarkable ability or character, important; (*colloq.*) very good. **greatness** *n.*
great- *pref.* (of a family relationship) one generation removed in ancestry or descent.
greatly *adv.* very much.
grebe *n.* a diving bird.
Grecian *a.* Greek.
greed *n.* excessive desire, esp. for food or wealth. **greedy** *a.*, **greedily** *adv.*, **greediness** *n.*
Greek *a.* & *n.* (native, language) of Greece.
green *a.* of the colour between blue and yellow, coloured like grass; unripe; concerned with protecting the environment; inexperienced, easily deceived. — *n.* green colour or thing; piece of grassy public land; (*pl.*) green vegetables. **green belt** area of open land round a town. **green fingers** skill in making plants grow. **green light** signal or (*colloq.*) permission to proceed. **Green Paper** government report of proposals being considered. **green pound** agreed value of the £ used for reckoning payments to EEC agricultural producers. **green-room** *n.* room in a theatre for the use of actors when off stage. **greenness** *n.*
greenery *n.* green foliage or plants.
greenfinch *n.* finch with green and yellow feathers.
greenfly *n.* (*pl.* **-fly**) small green insect that sucks juices from plants.
greengage *n.* round plum with a greenish skin.
greengrocer *n.* shopkeeper selling vegetables and fruit.
greenhorn *n.* inexperienced person.
greenhouse *n.* building with glass sides and roof, for rearing plants. **greenhouse**

effect trapping of the sun's radiation by the atmosphere. **greenhouse gas** gas causing this.
greenish *a.* rather green.
greenstone *n.* a kind of jade.
greet *v.* address politely on meeting or arrival; react to; present itself to (sight or hearing).
gregarious *a.* living in flocks or communities; fond of company. **gregariousness** *n.*
gremlin *n.* (*colloq.*) mischievous spirit said to cause mishaps to machinery.
grenade *n.* small bomb thrown by hand or fired from a rifle.
grenadine *n.* flavouring syrup made from pomegranates etc.
grew *see* **grow**.
grey *a.* of the colour between black and white, coloured like ashes. — *n.* grey colour or thing. — *v.* make or become grey. **greyness** *n.*
greyhound *n.* slender smooth-haired dog noted for its swiftness.
greyish *a.* rather grey.
grid *n.* grating; system of numbered squares for map references; network of lines, power cables, etc.; gridiron. **gridded** *a.*
gridiron *n.* framework of metal bars for cooking on; field for American football, marked with parallel lines.
grief *n.* deep sorrow. **come to grief** meet with disaster; fail; fall.
grievance *n.* ground of complaint.
grieve *v.* cause grief to; feel grief.
grievous *a.* causing grief; serious. **grievously** *adv.*
griffin *n.* mythological creature with an eagle's head and wings on a lion's body.
griffon *n.* small terrier-like dog; a kind of vulture; griffin.
grill *n.* metal grid, grating; device on a cooker for radiating heat downwards; grilled food. — *v.* cook under a grill or on a gridiron; question closely and severely.
grille *n.* grating, esp. in a door or window.
grim *a.* (**grimmer**, **grimmest**) stern, severe; without cheerfulness, unattractive. **grimly** *adv.*, **grimness** *n.*
grimace *n.* contortion of the face in pain or disgust, or done to cause amusement. — *v.* make a grimace.
grime *n.* ingrained dirt. — *v.* blacken with grime. **grimily** *adv.*, **griminess** *n.*, **grimy** *a.*
grin *v.* (**grinned**) smile broadly, showing the teeth. — *n.* broad smile.
grind *v.* (**ground**) crush into grains or powder; crush or oppress by cruelty; sharpen or smooth by friction; rub harshly together. — *n.* grinding process; hard monotonous work. **grinder** *n.*
grindstone *n.* thick revolving disc for sharpening or grinding things.
grip *v.* (**gripped**) take or keep firm hold of; hold the attention of. — *n.* firm grasp or hold; way of or thing for gripping; understanding; (*US*) travelling bag.
gripe *v.* (*colloq.*) grumble. — *n.* colic pain; (*colloq.*) grievance.
grisly *a.* (**-ier**, **-iest**) causing fear, horror, or disgust. **grisliness** *n.*
gristle *n.* tough tissue of animal bodies, esp. in meat. **gristly** *a.*
grit *n.* particles of stone or sand; (*colloq.*) courage and endurance. — *v.* (**gritted**) make a grating sound; clench; spread grit on. **gritty** *a.*, **grittiness** *n.*
grizzle *v.* & *n.* whimper, whine.
grizzled *a.* grey; grey-haired.
grizzly bear large brown bear of North America.
groan *v.* make a long deep sound in pain, grief, or disapproval; make a deep creaking sound. — *n.* sound made by groaning.
grocer *n.* shopkeeper selling foods and household stores.
grocery *n.* grocer's shop or goods.
grog *n.* drink of spirits mixed with water.
groggy *a.* (**-ier**, **-iest**) weak and unsteady, esp. after illness. **groggily** *adv.*, **grogginess** *n.*
groin *n.* groove where each thigh joins the trunk; curved edge where two vaults meet. **groined** *a.*
grommet *n.* insulating washer; tube placed through the eardrum.
groom *n.* person employed to look after horses; bridegroom. — *v.* clean and brush (an animal); make neat and trim; prepare (a person) for a career or position.
groove *n.* long narrow channel. — *v.* make groove(s) in.
grope *v.* feel about as one does in the dark.
gross *a.* thick, large-bodied; vulgar; outrageous; total, without deductions. — *n.* (*pl.* **gross**) twelve dozen. — *v.* produce or earn as total profit. **grossly** *adv.*
grotesque *a.* very odd or ugly. — *n.* comically distorted figure; design using fantastic forms. **grotesquely** *adv.*, **grotesqueness** *n.*
grotto *n.* (*pl.* **-oes**) picturesque cave.
grouch *v.* & *n.* (*colloq.*) grumble.
ground [1] *n.* solid surface of earth; area, position, or distance on this, (*pl.*) enclosed land of a large house; foundation for a theory, reason for action; (*pl.*)

coffee dregs. — *v.* prevent (an aircraft or airman) from flying; base; give basic training to. **ground-rent** *n.* rent paid for land leased for building. **ground swell** slow heavy waves.
ground [2] *see* **grind**. — *a.* **ground glass** glass made opaque by grinding.
grounding *n.* basic training.
groundless *a.* without foundation.
groundnut *n.* peanut.
groundsheet *n.* waterproof sheet for spreading on the ground.
groundsman *n.* (*pl.* **-men**) person employed to look after a sports ground.
groundwork *n.* preliminary or basic work.
group *n.* number of persons or things near, belonging, classed, or working together. — *v.* form or gather into group(s).
grouse [1] *n.* a kind of game bird.
grouse [2] *v.* & *n.* (*colloq.*) grumble.
grout *n.* thin fluid mortar. — *v.* fill with grout.
grove *n.* group of trees.
grovel *v.* (**grovelled**) crawl face downwards; humble oneself.
grow *v.* (**grew, grown**) increase in size or amount; develop or exist as a living plant; become; allow to grow; produce by cultivation. **grow up** become adult or mature. **grower** *n.*
growl *v.* make a low threatening sound as a dog does. — *n.* this sound.
grown *see* **grow**. — *a.* adult. **grown-up** *a.* & *n.* adult.
growth *n.* process of growing; thing that grows or has grown; tumour. **growth industry** one developing faster than others.
groyne *n.* solid structure projecting towards the sea to prevent erosion.
grub *n.* worm-like larva of certain insects; (*sl.*) food. — *v.* (**grubbed**) dig the surface of soil; dig up by the roots; rummage.
grubby *a.* (**-ier, -iest**) dirty; infested with grubs. **grubbiness** *n.*
grudge *n.* feeling of resentment or ill will. — *v.* begrudge.
gruel *n.* thin oatmeal porridge.
gruelling *a.* very tiring.
gruesome *a.* filling one with horror or disgust.
gruff *a.* (of the voice) low and hoarse; surly. **gruffly** *adv.*, **gruffness** *n.*
grumble *v.* complain in a bad-tempered way; rumble. — *n.* complaint; rumble. **grumbler** *n.*
grumpy *a.* (**-ier, -iest**) bad-tempered. **grumpily** *adv.*, **grumpiness** *n.*
grunt *n.* gruff snorting sound made by a pig. — *v.* make this or a similar sound.
gryphon *n.* = griffin.
G-string *n.* narrow strip of cloth etc. covering the genitals, attached to a string round the waist.
guano /gwaánō/ *n.* dung of seabirds, used as manure.
guarantee *n.* formal promise to do something or that a thing is of specified quality and durability; thing offered as security; guarantor. — *v.* give or be a guarantee of or to.
guarantor *n.* giver of a guarantee.
guard *v.* watch over and protect or supervise; restrain; take precautions. — *n.* state of watchfulness for danger; defensive attitude in boxing, cricket, etc.; person(s) guarding something; railway official in charge of a train; protecting part or device.
guarded *a.* cautious, discreet.
guardian *n.* one who guards or protects; person undertaking legal responsibility for an orphan. **guardianship** *n.*
guardsman *n.* (*pl.* **-men**) soldier acting as guard.
guava /gwaávə/ *n.* orange-coloured fruit of a tropical American tree.
gudgeon [1] *n.* small freshwater fish.
gudgeon [2] *n.* a kind of pivot; socket for a rudder; metal pin.
guerrilla *n.* person who takes part in **guerrilla warfare**, fighting or harassment by small groups acting independently.
guess *v.* form an opinion or state without definite knowledge; think likely. — *n.* opinion formed by guessing. **guesser** *n.*
guesswork *n.* guessing.
guest *n.* person entertained at another's house or table etc., or lodging at a hotel; visiting performer. **guest house** superior boarding house.
guffaw *n.* coarse noisy laugh. — *v.* utter a guffaw.
guidance *n.* guiding; advising or advice on problems.
guide *n.* person who shows others the way; one employed to point out interesting sights to travellers; book of information; thing directing actions or movements. — *v.* act as guide to.
guidebook *n.* book of information about a place, for visitors.
guild *n.* society for mutual aid or with a common purpose; association of craftsmen or merchants.
guilder *n.* unit of money of the Netherlands.
guile *n.* treacherous cunning, craftiness. **guileful** *a.*, **guileless** *a.*
guillotine *n.* machine for beheading criminals; machine for cutting paper or metal; fixing of times for voting in Parliament,

to prevent a lengthy debate. — *v.* use a guillotine on.

guilt *n.* fact of having committed an offence; feeling that one is to blame. **guiltless** *a.*

guilty *a.* (**-ier, -iest**) having done wrong; feeling or showing guilt. **guiltily** *adv.*, **guiltiness** *n.*

guinea *n.* former British coin worth 21 shillings (£1.05); this amount. **guinea pig** rodent kept as a pet or for biological experiments; person or thing used as a subject for an experiment.

guise *n.* false outward manner or appearance; pretence.

guitar *n.* a kind of stringed musical instrument. **guitarist** *n.*

gulf *n.* large area of sea partly surrounded by land; deep hollow; wide difference in opinion.

gull *n.* seabird with long wings.

gullet *n.* passage by which food goes from mouth to stomach.

gullible *a.* easily deceived. **gullibility** *n.*

gully *n.* narrow channel cut by water or carrying rainwater from a building.

gulp *v.* swallow (food etc.) hastily or greedily; make a gulping movement. — *n.* act of gulping; large mouthful of liquid gulped.

gum [1] *n.* firm flesh in which teeth are rooted.

gum [2] *n.* sticky substance exuded by certain trees; adhesive; chewing gum; gumdrop. — *v.* (**gummed**) smear or stick together with gum. **gum tree** tree that exudes gum; eucalyptus. **gummy** *a.*

gumboil *n.* abscess on the gum.

gumboot *n.* rubber boot.

gumdrop *n.* hard gelatine sweet.

gumption *n.* (*colloq.*) common sense.

gun *n.* weapon that sends shells or bullets from a metal tube; device operating similarly. — *v.* (**gunned**) shoot with a gun.

gunfire *n.* firing of guns.

gunman *n.* (*pl.* **-men**) man armed with a gun.

gunner *n.* artillery soldier; naval officer in charge of a battery of guns.

gunnery *n.* construction and operating of large guns.

gunny *n.* coarse material for making sacks; sack made of this.

gunpowder *n.* explosive of saltpetre, sulphur, and charcoal.

gunroom *n.* room where sporting guns are kept; room for junior officers in a warship.

gunrunning *n.* smuggling of firearms. **gunrunner** *n.*

gunshot *n.* shot fired from a gun.

gunsmith *n.* maker and repairer of small firearms.

gunwale /gúnn'l/ *n.* upper edge of a small ship's or boat's side.

guppy *n.* very small brightly coloured tropical fish.

gurgle *n.* low bubbling sound. — *v.* make or utter with this sound.

guru *n.* (*pl.* **-us**) Hindu spiritual teacher; revered teacher.

gush *v.* flow or pour suddenly or in great quantities; talk effusively. — *n.* sudden or great outflow; effusiveness. **gushy** *a.*

gusset *n.* piece of cloth inserted to strengthen or enlarge a garment etc. **gusseted** *a.*

gust *n.* sudden rush of wind, rain, smoke, or sound. — *v.* blow in gusts. **gusty** *a.*, **gustily** *adv.*

gustatory *a.* of the sense of taste.

gusto *n.* zest.

gut *n.* intestine; thread made from animal intestines; (*pl.*) abdominal organs; (*pl.*, *colloq.*) courage and determination. — *v.* (**gutted**) remove guts from (fish); remove or destroy internal fittings or parts of.

gutsy *a.* (*colloq.*) courageous, greedy. **gutsily** *adv.*, **gutsiness** *n.*

gutta-percha *n.* rubbery substance made from the juice of certain Malaysian trees.

gutter *n.* trough round a roof, or channel at a roadside, for carrying away rainwater; slum environment. — *v.* (of a candle) burn unsteadily.

guttural *a.* throaty, harsh-sounding. **gutturally** *adv.*

guy [1] *n.* effigy of Guy Fawkes burnt on 5 Nov.; (*colloq.*) man. — *v.* ridicule.

guy [2] *n.* rope or chain used to keep a thing steady or secured.

guzzle *v.* eat or drink greedily.

gybe *v.* (of a sail or boom) swing across; (of a boat) change course thus. — *n.* this change.

gym *n.* (*colloq.*) gymnasium, gymnastics.

gymkhana *n.* horse-riding competition; mounted games.

gymnasium *n.* room equipped for physical training and gymnastics.

gymnast *n.* expert in gymnastics.

gymnastics *n.* & *n.pl.* exercises to develop the muscles or demonstrate agility. **gymnastic** *a.*

gynaecology /gīnikólləji/ *n.* study of the physiological functions and diseases of women. **gynaecological** *a.*, **gynaecologist** *n.*

gypsophila *n.* garden plant with many small white flowers.

gypsum *n.* chalk-like substance.

gypsy *n.* member of a wandering people of Europe.

gyrate *v.* move in circles or spirals, revolve. **gyration** *n.*

gyratory *a.* gyrating, following a circular or spiral path.

gyro *n.* (*pl.* **-os**) (*colloq.*) gyroscope.

gyrocompass *n.* navigation compass using a gyroscope.

gyroscope *n.* rotating device used to keep navigation instruments steady. **gyroscopic** *a.*

H

ha *int.* exclamation of triumph.

habeas corpus order requiring a person to be brought into court.

habit *n.* settled way of behaving; monk's or nun's long dress; a woman's riding-dress.

habitable *a.* suitable for living in.

habitat *n.* animal's or plant's natural environment.

habitation *n.* place to live in.

habitual *a.* done or doing something constantly, esp. as a habit; usual. **habitually** *adv.*

habituate *v.* accustom. **habituation** *n.*

hacienda *n.* ranch or large estate in South America.

hack [1] *n.* horse for ordinary riding; person doing routine work, esp. as a writer. — *v.* ride on horseback at an ordinary pace.

hack [2] *v.* cut, chop, or hit roughly. — *n.* blow given thus.

hacker *n.* (*colloq.*) computer enthusiast, esp. one gaining unauthorized access to files.

hacking *a.* (of a cough) dry and frequent.

hackles *n.pl.* feathers or hairs on some birds or animals, raised in anger.

hackneyed *a.* (of sayings) over-used and therefore lacking impact.

hacksaw *n.* saw for metal.

haddock *n.* (*pl.* **haddock**) sea fish like a cod, used as food.

haematology /hée-/ *n.* study of blood. **haematologist** *n.*

haemoglobin /hée-/ *n.* red oxygen-carrying substance in blood.

haemophilia /hée-/ *n.* tendency to bleed excessively. **haemophiliac** *n.*

haemorrhage /hém-/ *n.* profuse bleeding. — *v.* bleed profusely.

haemorrhoids /hém-/ *n.pl.* varicose veins at or near the anus.

haft *n.* handle of a knife or dagger.

hag *n.* ugly old woman.

haggard *a.* looking ugly from exhaustion. **haggardness** *n.*

haggis *n.* Scottish dish made from sheep's heart, lungs, and liver.

haggle *v.* argue about price or terms when settling a bargain.

ha-ha *n.* sunk fence.

hail [1] *v.* greet; call to; signal to and summon.

hail [2] *n.* pellets of frozen rain falling in a shower; shower of blows, questions, etc. — *v.* pour down as or like hail. **hailstone** *n.*

hair *n.* fine thread-like strand growing from the skin; mass of these, esp. on the head. **hair-raising** *a.* terrifying. **hair-trigger** *n.* trigger operated by the slightest pressure.

haircut *n.* shortening of hair by cutting it; style of this.

hairdo *n.* (*pl.* **-dos**) arrangement of the hair.

hairdresser *n.* person whose job is to cut and arrange hair. **hairdressing** *n.*

hairgrip *n.* springy hairpin.

hairline *n.* edge of the hair on the forehead etc.; very narrow crack or line.

hairpin *n.* U-shaped pin for keeping hair in place. **hairpin bend** sharp U-shaped bend in a road.

hairy *a.* (**-ier, -iest**) covered with hair; (*sl.*) hair-raising, unpleasant, difficult. **hairiness** *n.*

Haitian *a.* & *n.* (native) of Haiti.

hajji *n.* Muslim who has been to Mecca on pilgrimage.

hake *n.* (*pl.* **hake**) sea fish of the cod family, used as food.

halal *v.* kill (animals for meat) according to Muslim law. — *n.* meat prepared thus.

halcyon *a.* calm and peaceful; (of a period) happy and prosperous.

hale *a.* strong and healthy.

half *n.* (*pl.* **halves**) each of two equal parts; this amount; (*colloq.*) half-back, half-pint, etc. — *a.* amounting to a half. — *adv.* to the extent of a half, partly. **half a dozen** six. **half and half** half one thing and half another. **half-back** *n.* player between forwards and full back(s). **half-brother** *n.* brother with only one parent in common with another. **half-caste** *n.* person of mixed race. **half-hearted** *a.* not very enthusiastic. **half-life** *n.* time after which radioactivity etc. is half its original level. **at half-mast** (of a flag) lowered in mourning. **half nelson** a kind of wrestling hold. **half-term** *n.* short holiday halfway through a school term. **half-timbered** *a.* built with a timber frame with brick or plaster filling. **half-time** *n.* interval between two halves of a game. **halfway** *a.* & *adv.* at a point equidistant between two others. **halfwit** *n.* halfwitted person. **halfwitted** *a.* stupid.

halfpenny /háypni/ *n.* (*pl.* **-pennies** for

single coins, **-pence** for a sum of money) coin worth half a penny.

halibut *n.* (*pl.* **halibut**) large flatfish used as food.

halitosis *n.* breath that smells unpleasant.

hall *n.* large room or building for meetings, concerts, etc.; large country house; space inside the front entrance of a house.

hallmark *n.* official mark on precious metals to indicate their standard; distinguishing characteristic. **hallmarked** *a.*

hallo *int.* & *n.* = hello.

Hallowe'en *n.* 31 Oct., eve of All Saints' Day.

hallucinate *v.* experience hallucinations.

hallucination *n.* illusion of seeing or hearing something not actually present. **hallucinatory** *a.*

hallucinogenic *a.* causing hallucinations.

halo *n.* (*pl.* **-oes**) circle of light esp. round the head of a sacred figure.

halogen *n.* any of a group of certain non-metallic elements.

halt *n.* & *v.* stop.

halter *n.* strap round the head of a horse for leading or fastening it.

halting *a.* slow and hesitant.

halve *v.* divide or share equally between two; reduce by half.

halyard *n.* rope for raising or lowering a sail or flag.

ham *n.* (meat from) a pig's thigh, salted or smoked; (*sl.*) poor actor or performer; (*colloq.*) amateur radio operator. — *v.* (**hammed**) (*sl.*) overact. **ham-fisted, ham-handed** *adjs.* (*sl.*) clumsy.

hamburger *n.* flat round cake of minced beef.

hamlet *n.* small village.

hammer *n.* tool with a head for hitting things or driving nails in; metal ball attached to a wire for throwing as an athletic contest. — *v.* hit or beat with a hammer; strike loudly.

hammock *n.* hanging bed of canvas or netting.

hamper[1] *n.* basketwork packing-case; selection of food packed as a gift.

hamper[2] *v.* prevent free movement or activity of, hinder.

hamster *n.* small rodent with cheek-pouches.

hamstring *n.* tendon at the back of a knee or hock. — *v.* (**hamstrung**) cripple by cutting hamstring(s); cripple the activity of.

hand *n.* end part of the arm, below the wrist; control, influence, or help in doing something; manual worker; style of handwriting; pointer on a dial etc.; (right or left) side; round of a card game, player's cards. — *v.* give or pass. **at hand** close by. **handout** *n.* thing distributed free of charge. **hands down** easily. **on hand** available. **out of hand** out of control. **to hand** within reach.

handbag *n.* bag to hold a purse and small personal articles; travelling bag.

handbill *n.* printed notice circulated by hand.

handbook *n.* small book giving useful facts.

handcuff *n.* metal ring linked to another, for securing a prisoner's wrists. — *v.* put handcuffs on.

handful *n.* quantity that fills the hand; a few; (*colloq.*) person difficult to control, difficult task.

handicap *n.* disadvantage imposed on a superior competitor to equalize chances; race etc. in which handicaps are imposed; thing that makes progress difficult; physical or mental disability. — *v.* (**handicapped**) impose or be a handicap on.

handkerchief *n.* (*pl.* **-fs**) small square of cloth for wiping the nose etc.

handle *n.* part by which a thing is to be held, carried, or controlled. — *v.* touch or move with the hands; deal with; manage; deal in.

handlebar *n.* steering bar of a bicycle etc.

handler *n.* person in charge of a trained dog etc.

handrail *n.* rail beside stairs etc.

handshake *n.* act of shaking hands as a greeting etc.

handsome *a.* good-looking; generous; (of a price etc.) very large.

handstand *n.* balancing on one's hands with feet in the air.

handwriting *n.* writing by hand with pen or pencil; style of this.

handy *a.* (**-ier, -iest**) convenient; clever with one's hands. **handily** *adv.*, **handiness** *n.*

handyman *n.* (*pl.* **-men**) person who does odd jobs.

hang *v.* (**hung**) support or be supported from above with the lower end free; kill or be killed by suspension from a rope round the neck (**hanged**); droop; remain. — *n.* way a thing hangs. **get the hang of** (*colloq.*) get the knack of, understand. **hang about** loiter. **hang back** hesitate. **hang-glider** *n.* frame used in **hang-gliding**, sport of being suspended in an airborne frame controlled by one's own movements. **hang on** hold tightly; depend on; (*sl.*) wait.

hangar *n.* shed for aircraft.

hangdog *a.* shamefaced.

hanger *n.* loop or hook by which a thing is hung; shaped piece of wood etc. to hang a garment on.

hangings *n.pl.* draperies hung on walls.

hangman *n.* (*pl.* **-men**) person whose job is to hang persons condemned to death.

hangnail *n.* torn skin at the root of a fingernail.

hangover *n.* unpleasant after-effects from drinking much alcohol.

hank *n.* coil or length of thread.

hanker *v.* crave, feel a longing.

hanky *n.* (*colloq.*) handkerchief.

Hanukkah *n.* Jewish festival of lights, beginning in December.

haphazard *a.* done or chosen at random. **haphazardly** *adv.*

hapless *a.* unlucky.

happen *v.* occur; chance. **happen to** be the fate or experience of.

happy *a.* (**-ier, -iest**) contented, pleased; fortunate. **happy-go-lucky** *a.* taking events cheerfully. **happily** *adv.*, **happiness** *n.*

harangue *n.* lengthy earnest speech. — *v.* make a harangue to.

harass *v.* worry or annoy continually; make repeated attacks on. **harassment** *n.*

harbour *n.* place of shelter for ships. — *v.* shelter; keep in one's mind.

hard *a.* firm, not easily cut; difficult; not easy to bear; harsh; strenuous; (of drugs) strong and addictive; (of currency) not likely to drop suddenly in value; (of drinks) strongly alcoholic; (of water) containing mineral salts that prevent soap from lathering freely. — *adv.* intensively; with difficulty; so as to be hard. **hard-boiled** *a.* (of eggs) boiled until yolk and white are set; callous. **hard copy** material produced in printed form by a computer. **hard-headed** *a.* shrewd and practical. **hard-hearted** *a.* unfeeling. **hard of hearing** slightly deaf. **hard sell** aggressive salesmanship. **hard shoulder** extra strip of road beside a motorway, for use in an emergency. **hard up** short of money. **hardness** *n.*

hardbitten *a.* tough and tenacious.

hardboard *n.* stiff board made of compressed wood pulp.

harden *v.* make or become hard or hardy.

hardly *adv.* only with difficulty; scarcely.

hardship *n.* harsh circumstance.

hardware *n.* tools and household implements sold by a shop; weapons; machinery used in a computer system.

hardwood *n.* hard heavy wood of deciduous trees.

hardy *a.* (**-ier, -iest**) capable of enduring cold or harsh conditions. **hardiness** *n.*

hare *n.* field animal like a large rabbit. — *v.* run rapidly. **hare-brained** *a.* wild and foolish, rash.

harebell *n.* wild plant with blue bell-shaped flowers.

harem /haáreem/ *n.* women of a Muslim household; their apartments.

haricot bean /hárrikō/ white dried seed of a kind of bean.

hark *v.* listen. **hark back** return to an earlier subject.

harlequin *a.* in varied colours.

harm *n.* damage, injury. — *v.* cause harm to. **harmful** *a.*, **harmless** *a.*

harmonic *a.* full of harmony.

harmonica *n.* mouth-organ.

harmonious *a.* forming a pleasing or consistent whole; free from ill feeling; sweet-sounding. **harmoniously** *adv.*

harmonium *n.* musical instrument like a small organ.

harmonize *v.* make or be harmonious; add notes to form chords. **harmonization** *n.*

harmony *n.* being harmonious; combination of musical notes to form chords; melodious sound.

harness *n.* straps and fittings by which a horse is controlled; similar fastenings. — *v.* put harness on, attach by this; control and use.

harp *n.* musical instrument with strings in a triangular frame. — *v.* **harp on** talk repeatedly about. **harpist** *n.*

harpoon *n.* spear-like missile with a rope attached. — *v.* spear with a harpoon. **harpooner** *n.*

harpsichord *n.* piano-like instrument.

harpy *n.* grasping unscrupulous woman.

harridan *n.* bad-tempered old woman.

harrow *n.* heavy frame with metal spikes or discs for breaking up clods. — *v.* draw a harrow over (soil); distress greatly.

harry *v.* harass.

harsh *a.* rough and disagreeable; severe, cruel. **harshly** *adv.*, **harshness** *n.*

hart *n.* adult male deer.

hartebeest *n.* large African antelope.

harum-scarum *a.* & *n.* wild and reckless (person).

harvest *n.* gathering of crop(s); season for this; season's yield of a natural product. — *v.* gather a crop; reap. **harvester** *n.*

hash *n.* dish of chopped re-cooked meat; jumble. — *v.* make into hash. **make a hash of** (*colloq.*) make a mess of, bungle.

hashish *n.* hemp dried for chewing or smoking as a narcotic.

hasp *n.* clasp fitting over a staple, secured by a pin or padlock.

hassle *n.* & *v.* (*colloq.*) quarrel, struggle; trouble, inconvenience.

hassock *n.* thick firm cushion for kneeling on in church.

haste *n.* hurry. **make haste** hurry.

hasten *v.* hurry.

hasty *a.* **(-ier, -iest)** hurried; acting or done too quickly. **hastily** *adv.*, **hastiness** *n.*

hat *n.* covering for the head, worn out of doors. **hat trick** three successes in a row, esp. in sports.

hatch [1] *n.* opening in a door, floor, ship's deck, etc.; its cover.

hatch [2] *v.* emerge or produce (young) from an egg; devise (a plot). — *n.* brood hatched.

hatch [3] *v.* mark with close parallel lines. **hatching** *n.* these marks.

hatchback *n.* a car with a back door that opens upwards.

hatchery *n.* place for hatching eggs.

hatchet *n.* small axe. **bury the hatchet** cease quarrelling and become friendly.

hatchway *n.* = hatch [1].

hate *n.* hatred. — *v.* feel hatred towards; dislike greatly. **hater** *n.*

hateful *a.* arousing hatred.

hatred *n.* violent dislike or enmity.

haughty *a.* **(-ier, -iest)** proud of oneself and looking down on others. **haughtily** *adv.*, **haughtiness** *n.*

haul *v.* pull or drag forcibly; transport by truck etc. — *n.* process of hauling; amount gained by effort, booty.

haulage *n.* transport of goods.

haulier *n.* person or firm that transports goods by road.

haunch *n.* fleshy part of the buttock and thigh; leg and loin of meat.

haunt *v.* linger in the mind of; (esp. of a ghost) repeatedly visit (a person or place). — *n.* place often visited by person(s) named. **haunted** *a.*

haute couture /ōt kootyoor/ high fashion.

have *v.* possess; contain; experience, undergo; give birth to; cause to be or do or be done; allow; be compelled (to do); (*colloq.*) cheat, deceive. — *v.aux.* (used with past participle to form past tenses). **have it out** settle a problem by frank discussion. **have up** bring (a person) to trial. **haves and have-nots** people with and without wealth or privilege.

haven *n.* refuge; harbour.

haversack *n.* strong bag carried on the back or shoulder.

havoc *n.* great destruction or disorder.

haw *n.* hawthorn berry.

hawk [1] *n.* bird of prey; person who favours an aggressive policy. **hawk-eyed** *a.* having very keen sight.

hawk [2] *v.* clear one's throat of phlegm noisily.

hawser *n.* heavy rope or cable for mooring or towing a ship.

hawthorn *n.* thorny tree or shrub with small red berries.

hay *n.* grass mown and dried for fodder. **hay fever** catarrh caused by pollen or dust.

haymaking *n.* mowing grass and spreading it to dry.

haystack *n.* regular pile of hay firmly packed for storing.

haywire *a.* badly disorganized.

hazard *n.* risk, danger; source of this; obstacle. — *v.* risk. **hazardous** *a.*

haze *n.* thin mist.

hazel *n.* bush with small edible nuts; light brown. **hazelnut** *n.*

hazy *a.* **(-ier, -iest)** misty; indistinct; vague. **hazily** *adv.*, **haziness** *n.*

H-bomb *n.* hydrogen bomb.

he *pron.* male previously mentioned. — *n.* male animal.

head *n.* part of the body containing the eyes, nose, mouth, and brain; intellect; individual person or animal; (*colloq.*) headache; thing like the head in form or position, top or leading part or position; foam on beer etc.; chief person; headmaster, headmistress; body of water or steam confined for exerting pressure; **heads** side of a coin showing a head, turned upwards after being tossed. — *v.* be at the head or top of; strike (a ball) with one's head; direct one's course. **head-hunt** *v.* seek to recruit (senior staff) from another firm. **head off** force to turn by getting in front. **head-on** *a.* & *adv.* with head or front foremost. **head wind** wind blowing from directly in front.

headache *n.* continuous pain in the head; worrying problem.

headdress *n.* ornamental covering worn on the head.

header *n.* dive with the head first; heading of the ball in football.

headgear *n.* hat or headdress.

heading *n.* word(s) at the top of written matter as a title.

headlamp *n.* headlight.

headland *n.* promontory.

headlight *n.* powerful light on the front of a vehicle etc.; its beam.

headline *n.* heading in a newspaper; (*pl.*) summary of broadcast news.

headlong *a.* & *adv.* falling or plunging with the head first; in a hasty and rash way.

headmaster, headmistress *ns.* principal

teacher in a school, responsible for organizing it.

headphone *n.* receiver held over the ear(s) by a band over the head.

headquarters *n.pl.* place from which an organization is controlled.

headstone *n.* stone set up at the head of a grave.

headstrong *a.* self-willed and obstinate.

headway *n.* progress.

heady *a.* (**-ier**, **-iest**) likely to cause intoxication. **headiness** *n.*

heal *v.* make or become healthy after injury; cure. **healer** *n.*

health *n.* state of being well and free from illness; condition of the body.

healthful *a.* health-giving.

healthy *a.* (**-ier**, **-iest**) having or showing or producing good health; functioning well. **healthily** *adv.*, **healthiness** *n.*

heap *n.* a number of things or particles lying one on top of another; (usu. *pl.*, *colloq.*) plenty. — *v.* pile or become piled in a heap; load with large quantities.

hear *v.* (**heard**) perceive (sounds) with the ear; pay attention to; receive information. **hear! hear!** I agree. **hearer** *n.*

hearing *n.* ability to hear; opportunity of being heard, trial of a lawsuit. **hearing aid** small sound-amplifier worn by a deaf person to improve the hearing.

hearsay *n.* things heard in rumour.

hearse *n.* vehicle for carrying the coffin at a funeral.

heart *n.* muscular organ that keeps blood circulating; centre of a person's emotions or inmost thoughts; courage; enthusiasm; central part; figure representing a heart; playing card of the suit marked with these. **break the heart of** cause overwhelming grief to. **by heart** memorized thoroughly. **heart attack** sudden failure of the heart to function normally. **heart-searching** *n.* examination of one's own feelings and motives. **heart-to-heart** *a.* frank and personal. **heart-warming** *a.* emotionally moving and encouraging.

heartache *n.* mental pain, sorrow.

heartbeat *n.* pulsation of the heart.

heartbreak *n.* overwhelming grief.

heartbroken *a.* broken-hearted.

heartburn *n.* burning sensation in the lower part of the chest.

hearten *v.* encourage.

heartfelt *a.* felt deeply, sincere.

hearth *n.* floor of a fireplace; fireside.

heartless *a.* not feeling pity or sympathy. **heartlessly** *adv.*

heart-throb *n.* (*colloq.*) object of romantic affection.

hearty *a.* (**-ier**, **-iest**) vigorous; enthusiastic; (of meals) large. **heartily** *adv.*, **heartiness** *n.*

heat *n.* form of energy produced by movement of molecules; hotness; passion, anger; preliminary contest. — *v.* make or become hot. **heatstroke** *n.* illness caused by overexposure to sun.

heated *a.* (of a person or discussion) angry. **heatedly** *adv.*

heater *n.* device supplying heat.

heath *n.* flat uncultivated land with low shrubs.

heathen *n.* person who does not believe in an established religion. **heathenish** *a.*

heather *n.* evergreen plant with purple, pink, or white flowers.

heave *v.* lift or haul with great effort; utter (a sigh); (*colloq.*) throw; rise and fall like waves; pant, retch. — *n.* act of heaving.

heaven *n.* abode of God; place or state of bliss; **the heavens** the sky as seen from the earth.

heavenly *a.* of heaven, divine; of or in the heavens; (*colloq.*) very pleasing. **heavenly bodies** sun, moon, stars, etc.

heavy *a.* (**-ier**, **-iest**) having great weight, force, or intensity; dense; stodgy; serious. **heavy-hearted** *a.* sad. **heavy industry** that producing metal or heavy machines etc. **heavily** *adv.*, **heaviness** *n.*

heavyweight *a.* having great weight or influence. — *n.* heavyweight person.

Hebrew *n.* & *a.* (member) of a Semitic people in ancient Palestine; (of) their language or a modern form of this. **Hebraic** *a.*

heckle *v.* interrupt (a public speaker) with aggressive questions and abuse. **heckler** *n.*

hectare *n.* unit of area, 10,000 sq. metres (about 2½ acres).

hectic *a.* with feverish activity. **hectically** *adv.*

hectogram *n.* 100 grams.

hector *v.* intimidate by bullying.

hedge *n.* fence of bushes or shrubs; barrier. — *v.* surround with a hedge; make or trim hedges; avoid giving a direct answer or commitment.

hedgehog *n.* small animal with a back covered in stiff spines.

hedgerow *n.* bushes etc. forming a hedge.

hedonist *n.* person who believes pleasure is the chief good. **hedonism** *n.*, **hedonistic** *a.*

heed *v.* pay attention to. — *n.* careful attention. **heedful** *a.*, **heedless** *a.*, **heedlessly** *adv.*

heel[1] *n.* back part of the human foot; part of a stocking or shoe covering or supporting this; (*sl.*) dishonourable man.

— *v.* make or repair the heel(s) of. **down at heel** shabby. **take to one's heels** run away.

heel [2] *v.* tilt (a ship) or become tilted to one side. — *n.* this tilt.

hefty *a.* (**-ier, -iest**) large and heavy. **heftily** *adv.*, **heftiness** *n.*

hegemony /hijémmәni/ *n.* leadership, esp. by one country.

Hegira /héjirә/ *n.* Muhammad's flight from Mecca (AD 622), from which the Muslim era is reckoned.

heifer /héffәr/ *n.* young cow.

height *n.* measurement from base to top or head to foot; distance above ground or sea level; highest degree of something.

heighten *v.* make or become higher or more intense.

heinous /háynәss/ *a.* very wicked.

heir /air/ *n.* person entitled to inherit property or a rank etc.

heiress /áiriss/ *n.* female heir, esp. to great wealth.

heirloom /áirlōōm/ *n.* possession handed down in a family for several generations.

held *see* **hold** [1].

helical *a.* like a helix.

helicopter *n.* aircraft with blades that revolve horizontally.

heliport *n.* helicopter station.

helium *n.* light colourless gas that does not burn.

helix *n.* (*pl.* **-ices**) spiral.

hell *n.* place of punishment for the wicked after death; place or state of supreme misery. **hell-bent** *a.* recklessly determined. **hell for leather** at great speed.

Hellenistic *a.* of Greece in the 4th–1st centuries BC.

hello *int.* & *n.* exclamation used in greeting or to call attention.

helm *n.* tiller or wheel by which a ship's rudder is controlled.

helmet *n.* protective head-covering.

helmsman *n.* (*pl.* **-men**) person controlling a ship's helm.

help *v.* do part of another's work; be useful (to); make easier; serve with food. — *n.* act of helping; person or thing that helps. **helper** *n.*

helpful *a.* giving help, useful. **helpfully** *adv.*, **helpfulness** *n.*

helping *n.* portion of food served.

helpless *a.* unable to manage without help; powerless. **helplessly** *adv.*, **helplessness** *n.*

helpline *n.* telephone service providing help with problems.

helter-skelter *adv.* in disorderly haste. — *n.* spiral slide at a funfair.

hem *n.* edge (of cloth) turned under and sewn or fixed down. — *v.* (**hemmed**) sew thus. **hem in** *or* **round** surround and restrict.

hemisphere *n.* half a sphere; half the earth. **hemispherical** *a.*

hemlock *n.* poisonous plant.

hemp *n.* plant with coarse fibres used in making rope and cloth; narcotic drug made from it.

hempen *a.* made of hemp.

hen *n.* female bird, esp. of the domestic fowl. **hen-party** *n.* (*colloq.*) party of women only.

hence *adv.* from this time; for this reason; (*old use*) from here.

henceforth, henceforward *advs.* from this time on, in future.

henchman *n.* (*pl.* **-men**) trusty supporter.

henna *n.* reddish dye used esp. on the hair; tropical plant from which it is obtained. **hennaed** *a.*

henpecked *a.* (of a man) nagged by his wife.

henry *n.* unit of inductance.

hepatic *a.* of the liver.

hepatitis *n.* inflammation of the liver.

heptagon *n.* geometric figure with seven sides. **heptagonal** *a.*

heptathlon *n.* athletic contest involving seven events.

her *pron.* objective case of *she.* — *a.* belonging to her.

herald *n.* person or thing heralding something. — *v.* proclaim the approach of.

heraldic *a.* of heraldry.

heraldry *n.* study of armorial bearings.

herb *n.* plant used in making medicines or flavourings.

herbaceous *a.* soft-stemmed. **herbaceous border** border containing esp. perennial plants.

herbal *a.* of herbs. — *n.* book about herbs.

herbalist *n.* dealer in medicinal herbs.

herbicide *n.* substance used to destroy plants. **herbicidal** *a.*

herbivore *n.* herbivorous animal.

herbivorous *a.* feeding on plants.

herculean *a.* needing or showing great strength or effort.

herd *n.* group of animals feeding or staying together; mob. — *v.* gather, stay, or drive as a group; tend (a herd). **herdsman** *n.*

here *adv.* in, at, or to this place; at this point. — *n.* this place.

hereabouts *adv.* near here.

hereafter *adv.* from now on. — *n.* the future; the next world.

hereby *adv.* by this act.

hereditary *a.* inherited; holding a position by inheritance.

heredity *n.* inheritance of characteristics from parents.
herein *adv.* in this place or book etc.
heresy *n.* opinion contrary to accepted beliefs; holding of this.
heretic *n.* person who holds a heresy. **heretical** *a.*, **heretically** *adv.*
hereto *adv.* to this
herewith *adv.* with this.
heritage *n.* thing(s) inherited.
hermaphrodite *n.* creature with male and female sexual organs.
hermetic *a.* with airtight closure. **hermetically** *adv.*
hermit *n.* person living in solitude.
hermitage *n.* hermit's dwelling.
hernia *n.* protrusion of part of an organ through the wall of the cavity (esp. the abdomen) containing it.
hero *n.* (*pl.* **-oes**) man admired for his brave deeds; chief male character in a story etc.
heroic *a.* very brave. **heroics** *n.pl.* over-dramatic behaviour. **heroically** *adv.*
heroin *n.* powerful drug prepared from morphine.
heroine *n.* female hero.
heroism *n.* heroic conduct.
heron *n.* long-legged wading bird.
herpes /hérpeez/ *n.* virus disease causing blisters.
herring *n.* North Atlantic fish much used for food. **herringbone** *n.* zigzag pattern or arrangement.
hers *poss.pron.* belonging to her.
herself *pron.* emphatic and reflexive form of *she* and *her*.
hertz *n.* (*pl.* **hertz**) unit of frequency of electromagnetic waves.
hesitant *a.* hesitating. **hesitantly** *adv.*, **hesitancy** *n.*
hesitate *v.* pause doubtfully; be reluctant, scruple. **hesitation** *n.*
hessian *n.* strong coarse cloth of hemp or jute.
heterodox *a.* not orthodox.
heterogeneous *a.* made up of people or things of various sorts. **heterogeneity** *n.*
heterosexual *a.* & *n.* (person) sexually attracted to people of the opposite sex. **heterosexuality** *n.*
hew *v.* (**hewn**) chop or cut with an axe etc.; cut into shape.
hexagon *n.* geometric figure with six sides. **hexagonal** *a.*
hey *int.* exclamation of surprise or inquiry, or calling attention.
heyday *n.* time of greatest success.
hi *int.* exclamation calling attention or greeting.
hiatus *n.* (*pl.* **-tuses**) break or gap in a sequence or series.
hibernate *v.* spend the winter in sleep-like state. **hibernation** *n.*
Hibernian *a.* & *n.* (native) of Ireland.
hibiscus *n.* shrub or tree with trumpet-shaped flowers.
hiccup *n.* cough-like stopping of breath. — *v.* (**hiccuped**) make this sound.
hide ¹ *v.* (**hid, hidden**) put or keep out of sight; keep secret; conceal oneself. **hideout** *n.* (*colloq.*) hiding place.
hide ² *n.* animal's skin.
hidebound *a.* rigidly conventional.
hideous *a.* very ugly. **hideously** *adv.*, **hideousness** *n.*
hiding *n.* (*colloq.*) thrashing.
hierarchy *n.* system with grades of status. **hierarchical** *a.*
hieroglyph *n.* pictorial symbol used in ancient Egyptian and other writing. **hieroglyphic** *a.*, **hieroglyphics** *n.pl.*
hi-fi *a.* & *n.* (*colloq.*) high fidelity, (equipment) reproducing sound with little or no distortion.
higgledy-piggledy *a.* & *adv.* in complete confusion.
high *a.* extending far or a specified distance upwards; far above ground or sea level; ranking above others; greater than normal; (of sound or a voice) not deep or low; (of meat) slightly decomposed; (*sl.*) intoxicated, under the influence of a drug. — *n.* high level; area of high pressure. — *adv.* in, at, or to a high level. **higher education** education above the level given in schools. **high-handed** *a.* using authority arrogantly. **high-rise** *a.* with many storeys. **high road** main road. **high sea(s)** sea outside a country's territorial waters. **high season** busiest season. **high-spirited** *a.* lively. **high spot** (*sl.*) important place or feature. **high street** principal shopping street. **high tea** early evening meal with tea and cooked food. **high tech, high technology** advanced technology, esp. in electronics. **high-water mark** level reached by the tide at its highest level.
highbrow *a.* very intellectual, cultured. — *n.* highbrow person.
highlands *n.pl.* mountainous region. **highland** *a.*, **highlander** *n.*
highlight *n.* bright area in a picture; best feature. — *v.* emphasize.
highly *adv.* in a high degree, extremely; very favourably. **highly-strung** *a.* (of a person) easily upset.
highway *n.* public road; main route.
highwayman *n.* (*pl.* **-men**) person (usu.

on horseback) who robbed travellers in former times.

hijack *v.* seize control illegally of (a vehicle or aircraft in transit). — *n.* hijacking. **hijacker** *n.*

hike *n.* long walk. — *v.* go for a hike. **hiker** *n.*

hilarious *a.* noisily merry; extremely funny. **hilariously** *adv.*, **hilarity** *n.*

hill *n.* raised part of earth's surface, less high than a mountain; slope in a road etc.; mound. **hill-billy** *n.* (*US*) rustic person.

hillock *n.* small hill, mound.

hilt *n.* handle of a sword or dagger. **to the hilt** completely.

him *pron.* objective case of *he*.

Himalayan *a.* of the Himalaya Mountains.

himself *pron.* emphatic and reflexive form of *he* and *him*.

hind [1] *n.* female deer.

hind [2] *a.* situated at the back.

hinder *v.* delay progress of.

Hindi *n.* group of languages of northern India.

hindmost *a.* furthest behind.

hindrance *n.* thing that hinders; hindering, being hindered.

hindsight *n.* wisdom about an event after it has occurred.

Hindu *n.* person whose religion is Hinduism. — *a.* of Hindus.

Hinduism *n.* principal religion and philosophy of India.

Hindustani *n.* language of much of northern India and Pakistan.

hinge *n.* movable joint such as that on which a door or lid turns. — *v.* attach or be attached by hinge(s). **hinge on** depend on.

hint *n.* slight indication; indirect suggestion; piece of practical information. — *v.* make a hint.

hinterland *n.* district behind a coast etc. or served by a port or other centre.

hip [1] *n.* projection of the pelvis on each side of body. **hipped** *a.*

hip [2] *n.* fruit of wild rose.

hippopotamus *n.* (*pl.* **-muses**) large African river animal with a thick skin.

hire *v.* engage or grant temporary use of, for payment. — *n.* hiring. **hire purchase** system by which a thing becomes the hirer's after a number of payments. **hirer** *n.*

hireling *n.* (*derog.*) hired helper.

hirsute /hûrsyo͞ot/ *a.* hairy, shaggy.

his *a.* & *poss.pron.* belonging to him.

Hispanic *a.* & *n.* (native) of Spain or a Spanish-speaking country.

hiss *n.* sound like 's'. — *v.* make this sound; utter with a hiss; express disapproval in this way.

histamine *n.* substance present in the body and causing some allergic reactions.

histology *n.* study of organic tissues. **histological** *a.*

historian *n.* expert in or writer of history.

historic *a.* famous in history.

historical *a.* of or concerned with history. **historically** *adv.*

history *n.* past events; methodical record of these; study of past events; story. **make history** do something memorable.

histrionic *a.* of acting; theatrical in manner. **histrionics** *n.pl.* theatricals; theatrical behaviour.

hit *v.* (**hit, hitting**) strike with a blow or missile, come forcefully against; affect badly; reach; find. — *n.* blow, stroke; shot that hits its target; success. **hit it off** get on well together. **hit list** (*sl.*) list of prospective victims. **hit-or-miss** *a.* aimed or done carelessly. **hitter** *n.*

hitch *v.* move (a thing) with a slight jerk; fasten with a loop or hook; hitchhike, obtain (a lift) in this way. — *n.* slight jerk; noose or knot of various kinds; snag.

hitchhike *v.* travel by seeking free lifts in passing vehicles. **hitchhiker** *n.*

hi-tech *n.* high tech(nology).

hither *adv.* to or towards this place. **hither and thither** to and fro.

hitherto *adv.* until this time.

HIV *abbr.* human immunodeficiency virus (causing Aids).

hive *n.* structure in which bees live. — *v.* **hive off** separate from a larger group.

hives *n.pl.* skin eruption, esp. nettle-rash.

hoard *v.* save and store away. — *n.* things hoarded. **hoarder** *n.*

hoarding *n.* fence of boards, often bearing advertisements.

hoar-frost *n.* white frost.

hoarse *a.* (of a voice) sounding rough as if from a dry throat; having such a voice. **hoarsely** *adv.*, **hoarseness** *n.*

hoary *a.* (**-ier, -iest**) grey with age; (of a joke etc.) old.

hoax *v.* deceive jokingly. — *n.* joking deception. **hoaxer** *n.*

hob *n.* top of a cooker, with hotplates.

hobble *v.* walk lamely; fasten the legs of (a horse) to limit its movement. — *n.* hobbling walk; rope etc. used to hobble a horse.

hobby *n.* thing done often and for pleasure in one's spare time.

hobby horse stick with a horse's head, as a toy; favourite topic.

hobgoblin *n.* mischievous imp.

hobnail *n.* heavy-headed nail for boot-soles. **hobnailed** *a.*
hobnob *v.* (**-nobbed**) spend time together in a friendly way.
hock [1] *n.* middle joint of an animal's hind leg.
hock [2] *n.* German white wine.
hockey *n.* field game played with curved sticks and a small hard ball; ice hockey.
hocus-pocus *n.* trickery.
hod *n.* trough on a pole for carrying mortar or bricks; container for shovelling and holding coal.
hoe *n.* tool for loosening soil or scraping up weeds. — *v.* (**hoeing**) dig or scrape with a hoe.
hog *n.* castrated male pig reared for meat; (*colloq.*) greedy person. — *v.* (**hogged**) (*colloq.*) take greedily; hoard selfishly.
hoick *v.* (*colloq.*) lift or bring out, esp. with a jerk.
hoi polloi ordinary people.
hoist *v.* raise or haul up. — *n.* apparatus for hoisting things.
hoity-toity *a.* haughty.
hokum *n.* (*sl.*) bunkum.
hold [1] *v.* (**held**) keep in one's arms or hands etc. or in one's possession or control; keep in a position or condition; contain; bear the weight of; remain unbroken under strain; continue; occupy; cause to take place; believe. — *n.* act, manner, or means of holding; means of exerting influence. **hold out** offer; last; continue to make a demand. **hold up** hinder; stop and rob by use of threats or force. **hold-up** *n.* delay; robbery. **hold with** (*colloq.*) approve of. **holder** *n.*
hold [2] *n.* storage cavity below a ship's deck.
holdall *n.* large soft travel bag.
holding *n.* something held or owned; land held by an owner or tenant.
hole *n.* hollow place; burrow; aperture; wretched place; (*colloq.*) awkward situation. — *v.* make hole(s) in.
holey *a.* full of holes.
holiday *n.* day(s) of recreation. — *v.* spend a holiday.
holiness *n.* being holy.
holistic *a.* (of treatment) involving the mind, body, social factors, etc.
hollow *a.* empty within, not solid; sunken; echoing as if in something hollow; worthless. — *n.* cavity; sunken place; valley. — *v.* make hollow. **hollowly** *adv.*, **hollowness** *n.*
holly *n.* evergreen shrub with prickly leaves and red berries.
hollyhock *n.* plant with large flowers on a tall stem.
holocaust *n.* large-scale destruction, esp. by fire.
hologram *n.* three-dimensional photographic image.
holograph [1] *v.* record as a hologram. **holography** *n.*
holograph [2] *a.* & *n.* (document) written wholly in the handwriting of the author.
holster *n.* leather case holding a pistol or revolver.
holy *a.* (**-ier, -iest**) belonging or devoted to God and reverenced; consecrated. **holy of holies** most sacred place.
homage *n.* things said or done as a mark of respect or loyalty.
home *n.* place where one lives; dwelling house; institution where those needing care may live. — *a.* of one's home or country; played on one's own ground. — *adv.* at or to one's home; to the point aimed at. — *v.* make its way home or to a target. **home truth** unpleasant truth about oneself.
homeland *n.* native land.
homeless *a.* lacking a home. **homelessness** *n.*
homely *a.* (**-ier, -iest**) simple and informal; (*US*) plain, not beautiful. **homeliness** *n.*
homesick *a.* longing for home.
homeward *a.* & *adv.* going towards home. **homewards** *adv.*
homework *n.* work set for a pupil to do away from school.
homicide *n.* killing of one person by another. **homicidal** *a.*
homily *n.* moralizing lecture. **homiletic** *a.*, **homiletics** *n.pl.*
hominid *a.* & *n.* (member) of the family of existing and fossil man.
homoeopathy /hōmióppəthi/ *n.* treatment of a disease by very small doses of a substance that would produce the same symptoms in a healthy person. **homoeopathic** *a.*
homogeneous *a.* of the same kind, uniform. **homogeneously** *adv.*, **homogeneity** *n.*
homogenize *v.* treat (milk) so that cream does not separate and rise to the top.
homonym *n.* word with the same spelling as another.
homophobia *n.* fear of homosexuals.
homophone *n.* word with the same sound as another.
homosexual *a.* & *n.* (person) sexually attracted to people of the same sex. **homosexuality** *n.*
hone *v.* sharpen on a whetstone.
honest *a.* truthful, trustworthy; fairly earned. **honestly** *adv.*, **honesty** *n.*

honey *n.* (*pl.* **-eys**) sweet substance made by bees from nectar; darling. **honey bee** common bee living in a hive. **honeyed** *a.*

honeycomb *n.* bees' wax structure for holding their honey and eggs; pattern of six-sided sections.

honeydew melon melon with pale skin and sweet green flesh.

honeymoon *n.* holiday spent together by a newly married couple; initial period of goodwill. — *v.* spend a honeymoon.

honeysuckle *n.* climbing shrub with fragrant pink and yellow flowers.

honk *n.* noise like the cry of a wild goose or the sound of a car horn. — *v.* make this noise.

honorary *a.* given as an honour; unpaid.

honour *n.* great respect or public regard; mark of this, privilege; good personal character or reputation. — *v.* feel honour for; confer honour on; pay (a cheque) or fulfil (a promise etc.).

honourable *a.* deserving, possessing, or showing honour. **honourably** *adv.*

hood [1] *n.* covering for the head and neck, esp. forming part of a garment; hood-like thing or cover, folding roof over a car. **hooded** *a.*

hood [2] *n.* (*US*) gangster, gunman.

hoodlum *n.* hooligan, young thug.

hoodoo *n.* (*US*) bad luck; thing causing this.

hoodwink *v.* deceive.

hoof *n.* (*pl.* **hoofs** *or* **hooves**) horny part of a horse's foot.

hook *n.* bent or curved device for catching hold or hanging things on; short blow made with the elbow bent. — *v.* grasp, catch, or fasten with hook(s); scoop or propel with a curving movement. **hook-up** *n.* interconnection. **off the hook** freed from a difficulty.

hookah *n.* oriental tobacco pipe with a long tube passing through water.

hooked *a.* hook-shaped. **hooked on** (*sl.*) addicted to.

hookworm *n.* parasitic worm with hook-like mouthparts.

hooligan *n.* young ruffian. **hooliganism** *n.*

hoop *n.* circular band of metal or wood; metal arch used in croquet. **hooped** *a.*

hoopla *n.* game in which rings are thrown to encircle a prize.

hoopoe *n.* bird with a crest and striped plumage.

hooray *int.* & *n.* = hurrah.

hoot *n.* owl's cry; sound of a hooter; cry of laughter or disapproval; cause of laughter. — *v.* (cause to) make a hoot.

hooter *n.* siren or steam whistle used as a signal; car horn.

Hoover *n.* [P.] a kind of vacuum cleaner. **hoover** *v.* clean with a vacuum cleaner.

hop [1] *v.* (**hopped**) jump on one foot or (of an animal) from both or all feet; (*colloq.*) make a quick short trip. — *n.* hopping movement; informal dance; short flight.

hop [2] *n.* plant cultivated for its cones (**hops**) which are used to give a bitter flavour to beer.

hope *n.* feeling of expectation and desire; person or thing giving cause for this; what one hopes for. — *v.* feel hope. **hopeful** *a.*, **hopefully** *adv.*

hopeless *a.* without hope; inadequate, incompetent. **hopelessly** *adv.*, **hopelessness** *n.*

hopper *n.* one who hops; container with an opening at its base through which its contents can be discharged.

hopscotch *n.* game involving hopping over marked squares.

horde *n.* large group or crowd.

horizon *n.* line at which earth and sky appear to meet; limit of knowledge or interests.

horizontal *a.* parallel to the horizon, going straight across. **horizontally** *adv.*

hormone *n.* secretion (or synthetic substance) that stimulates an organ or growth. **hormonal** *a.*

horn *n.* hard pointed growth on the heads of certain animals; substance of this; similar projection; wind instrument with a trumpet-shaped end; device for sounding a warning signal. **horn-rimmed** *a.* with frames of material like horn or tortoiseshell.

hornblende *n.* dark mineral constituent of granite etc.

hornet *n.* a kind of large wasp.

hornpipe *n.* lively solo dance performed by sailors.

horny *a.* (**-ier**, **-iest**) of or like horn; hardened and calloused. **horniness** *n.*

horology *n.* art of making clocks etc. **horologist** *n.*

horoscope *n.* forecast of events based on the relative positions of stars.

horrendous *a.* horrifying. **horrendously** *adv.*

horrible *a.* causing horror; (*colloq.*) unpleasant. **horribly** *adv.*

horrid *a.* horrible.

horrific *a.* horrifying. **horrifically** *adv.*

horrify *v.* arouse horror in.

horror *n.* loathing and fear; intense dislike or dismay; person or thing causing horror.

hors d'oeuvre /or dúrvrə/ food served as an appetizer.
horse *n.* quadruped with a mane and tail; padded structure for vaulting over in a gymnasium. — *v.* (*colloq.*) fool, play. **horse chestnut** brown shiny nut; tree bearing this. **horse sense** (*colloq.*) common sense.
horseback *n.* **on horseback** riding on a horse.
horsebox *n.* closed vehicle for transporting a horse.
horseman *n.* (*pl.* **-men**) rider on horseback. **horsewoman** *n.fem.* (*pl.* **-women**), **horsemanship** *n.*
horseplay *n.* boisterous play.
horsepower *n.* unit for measuring the power of an engine.
horseradish *n.* plant with a hot-tasting root used to make sauce.
horseshoe *n.* U-shaped strip of metal nailed to a horse's hoof; thing shaped like this.
horsy *a.* of or like a horse; interested in horses and horse racing.
horticulture *n.* art of garden cultivation. **horticultural** *a.*, **horticulturist** *n.*
hose *n.* hose-pipe; stockings and socks. — *v.* water or spray with a hose-pipe. **hose-pipe** *n.* flexible tube for conveying water.
hosiery *n.* stockings, socks, etc.
hospice *n.* hospital or home for the terminally ill.
hospitable *a.* giving hospitality. **hospitably** *adv.*
hospital *n.* institution for treatment of sick or injured people.
hospitality *n.* friendly and generous entertainment of guests.
hospitalize *v.* send or admit to a hospital. **hospitalization** *n.*
host [1] *n.* large number of people or things.
host [2] *n.* person who entertains guest(s); organism on which another lives as a parasite. — *v.* act as host to.
hostage *n.* person held as security that the holder's demands will be satisfied.
hostel *n.* lodging house for students, nurses, etc.
hostess *n.* woman host.
hostile *a.* of an enemy; unfriendly.
hostility *n.* being hostile, enmity; (*pl.*) acts of warfare.
hot *a.* (**hotter, hottest**) at or having a high temperature; producing a burning sensation to the taste; eager, angry; excited, excitable. — *v.* (**hotted**) (*colloq.*) make or become hot or exciting. **hot air** (*sl.*) excited or boastful talk. **hot dog** hot sausage in a bread roll. **hot line** direct line for speedy communication. **in hot water** in trouble or disgrace.
hotbed *n.* place favourable to the growth of something evil.
hotchpotch *n.* jumble.
hotel *n.* building where meals and rooms are provided for travellers.
hotelier *n.* hotel-keeper.
hotfoot *adv.* in eager haste.
hothead *n.* impetuous person.
hotheaded *a.* impetuous.
hothouse *n.* heated greenhouse.
hotplate *n.* heated surface on a cooker.
hound *n.* dog used in hunting. — *v.* pursue, harass; urge, incite.
hour *n.* one twenty-fourth part of a day and night; point of time; occasion; (*pl.*) period for daily work.
hourglass *n.* glass containing sand that takes one hour to trickle from upper to lower section through a narrow opening.
houri /hoóri/ *n.* (*pl.* **-is**) nymph of the Muslim paradise.
hourly *a.* done or occurring once an hour; continual. — *adv.* every hour.
house [1] /howss/ *n.* building for people (usu. one family) to live in, or for a specific purpose; household; legislative assembly; business firm; theatre audience or performance; family, dynasty. **house arrest** detention in one's own home. **house-proud** *a.* giving great attention to the appearance of one's home. **house-trained** *a.* trained to be clean in the house. **house-warming** *n.* party to celebrate occupation of a new home.
house [2] /howz/ *v.* provide accommodation or storage space for; encase.
houseboat *n.* barge-like boat fitted up as a dwelling.
housebound *a.* unable to leave one's house, esp. through infirmity.
housebreaker *n.* burglar. **housebreaking** *n.*
housecoat *n.* woman's long dress-like garment for informal wear.
household *n.* occupants of a house living as a family. **household word** familiar saying or name.
householder *n.* person owning or renting a house or flat.
housekeeper *n.* person employed to look after a household.
housekeeping *n.* management of household affairs; (*colloq.*) money to be used for this.
housemaid *n.* woman servant in a house, esp. one who cleans rooms.
housemaster, **housemistress** *ns.* teacher in charge of a school boarding house.

housewife *n.* woman managing a household. **housewifely** *adv.*

housework *n.* cleaning and cooking etc. done in housekeeping.

housing *n.* accommodation; rigid case enclosing machinery.

hovel *n.* small miserable dwelling.

hover *v.* (of a bird etc.) remain in one place in the air; linger, wait close at hand. **hover fly** wasp-like insect that hovers.

hovercraft *n.* (*pl.* **-craft**) vehicle supported by air thrust downwards from its engines.

how *adv.* by what means, in what way; to what extent or amount etc.; in what condition.

howdah *n.* seat, usu. with a canopy, on an elephant's back.

however *adv.* in whatever way, to whatever extent; nevertheless.

howitzer *n.* short gun firing shells at high elevation.

howl *n.* long loud wailing cry or sound. — *v.* make or utter with a howl; weep loudly.

howler *n.* one that howls; (*colloq.*) stupid mistake.

hoyden *n.* girl who behaves boisterously. **hoydenish** *a.*

h.p. *abbr.* hire purchase; horsepower.

hub *n.* central part of a wheel; centre of activity. **hubcap** *n.* cover for the hub of a car wheel.

hubbub *n.* confused noise of voices.

hubris /hyo͞obriss/ *n.* arrogant pride.

huckleberry *n.* low shrub common in North America; its fruit.

huddle *v.* crowd into a small place. — *n.* close mass.

hue¹ *n.* colour.

hue² *n.* **hue and cry** outcry.

huff *n.* fit of annoyance. — *v.* blow. **huffy** *a.* **huffily** *adv.*

hug *v.* (**hugged**) squeeze tightly in one's arms; keep close to. — *n.* hugging movement.

huge *a.* extremely large. **hugely** *adv.*, **hugeness** *n.*

hula *n.* Hawaiian women's dance. **hula hoop** large hoop for spinning round the body.

hulk *n.* body of an old ship; large clumsy-looking person or thing.

hulking *a.* (*colloq.*) large and clumsy.

hull¹ *n.* framework of a ship.

hull² *n.* pod of a pea or bean; cluster of leaves on a strawberry. — *v.* remove the hull of.

hullabaloo *n.* uproar.

hullo *int.* = hello.

hum *v.* (**hummed**) sing with closed lips; make a similar sound; (*colloq.*) be in state of activity. — *n.* humming sound.

human *a.* of mankind; of persons. — *n.* human being. **humanly** *adv.*

humane *a.* kind-hearted, merciful. **humanely** *adv.*

humanism *n.* system of thought concerned with human affairs and ethics (not theology); promotion of human welfare. **humanist** *n.*, **humanistic** *a.*

humanitarian *a.* promoting human welfare and reduction of suffering. **humanitarianism** *n.*

humanity *n.* human nature or qualities; kindness; human race; (*pl.*) arts subjects.

humanize *v.* make human; make humane. **humanization** *n.*

humble *a.* having or showing a modest estimate of one's own importance; of low rank; not large or expensive. — *v.* lower the rank or self-importance of. **humbly** *adv.*

humbug *n.* misleading behaviour or talk to win support or sympathy; person behaving thus; hard usu. peppermint-flavoured boiled sweet. — *v.* (**humbugged**) delude.

humdrum *a.* dull, commonplace.

humerus *n.* (*pl.* **-ri**) bone of the upper arm. **humeral** *a.*

humid *a.* (of air) damp. **humidity** *n.*

humidify *v.* keep (air) moist in a room etc. **humidifier** *n.*

humiliate *v.* cause to feel disgraced. **humiliation** *n.*

humility *n.* humble condition or attitude of mind.

hummock *n.* hump in the ground.

humour *n.* quality of being amusing; ability to perceive and enjoy this; state of mind. — *v.* keep (a person) contented by doing as he or she wishes. **humorous** *a.*, **humorously** *adv.*

hump *n.* rounded projecting part; curved deformity of the spine. — *v.* form into a hump; hoist and carry. **humped** *a.*

humpback *n.* hunchback. **humpback bridge** small steeply arched bridge.

humus *n.* soil-fertilizing substance formed by decay of dead leaves and plants etc.

hunch *v.* bend into a hump. — *n.* hump; hunk; intuitive feeling.

hunchback *n.* person with a humped back.

hundred *n.* ten times ten (100, C). **hundredth** *a.* & *n.*

hundredfold *a.* & *adv.* 100 times as much or as many.

hundredweight *n.* measure of weight, 112 lb or (**metric hundredweight**) 50 kg (110.25 lb).

hung *see* **hang**. — *a.* **hung-over** *a.* (*colloq.*) having a hangover.

Hungarian *a.* & *n.* (native, language) of Hungary.

hunger *n.* pain or discomfort felt when one has not eaten for some time; strong desire. — *v.* feel hunger. **hunger strike** refusal of food as a form of protest.

hungry *a.* (**-ier, -iest**) feeling hunger. **hungrily** *adv.*

hunk *n.* large or clumsy piece.

hunt *v.* pursue (wild animals) for food or sport; pursue with hostility; seek; search. — *n.* process of hunting; hunting group.

hunter *n.* one who hunts; horse used for hunting.

hurdle *n.* portable frame with bars, used as a temporary fence; frame to be jumped over in a race; obstacle, difficulty. **hurdler** *n.*

hurl *v.* throw violently. — *n.* violent throw.

hurly-burly *n.* rough bustle.

hurrah, hurray *int.* & *n.* exclamation of joy or approval.

hurricane *n.* violent storm-wind. **hurricane lamp** lamp with the flame protected from the wind.

hurried *a.* done with great haste. **hurriedly** *adv.*

hurry *v.* act or move with eagerness or too quickly; cause to do this. — *n.* hurrying.

hurt *v.* (**hurt**) cause pain, harm, or injury (to); feel pain. — *n.* injury, harm. **hurtful** *a.*

hurtle *v.* move or hurl rapidly.

husband *n.* married man in relation to his wife. — *v.* use economically, try to save.

husbandry *n.* farming; management of resources.

hush *v.* make or become silent. — *n.* silence. **hush-hush** *a.* secret.

husk *n.* dry outer covering of certain seeds and fruits. — *v.* remove the husk from.

husky [1] *a.* (**-ier, -iest**) dry; hoarse; burly. **huskily** *adv.*, **huskiness** *n.*

husky [2] *n.* Arctic sledge-dog.

hustle *v.* push roughly; hurry. — *n.* hustling.

hut *n.* small simple or roughly made house or shelter.

hutch *n.* box-like pen for rabbits.

hyacinth *n.* plant with fragrant bell-shaped flowers.

hybrid *n.* offspring of two different species or varieties; thing made by combining different elements. — *a.* produced in this way. **hybridism** *n.*

hybridize *v.* cross-breed; produce hybrids; interbreed. **hybridization** *n.*

hydrangea *n.* shrub with pink, blue, or white flowers in clusters.

hydrant *n.* pipe from a water main (esp. in a street) to which a hose can be attached.

hydrate *n.* chemical compound of water with another substance.

hydraulic *a.* operated by pressure of fluid conveyed in pipes; hardening under water. **hydraulics** *n.* science of hydraulic operations. **hydraulically** *adv.*

hydrocarbon *n.* compound of hydrogen and carbon.

hydrochloric acid corrosive acid containing hydrogen and chlorine.

hydrodynamic *a.* of the forces exerted by liquids in motion. **hydrodynamics** *n.*

hydroelectric *a.* using water-power to produce electricity.

hydrofoil *n.* boat with a structure that raises its hull out of the water when the boat is in motion; this structure.

hydrogen *n.* odourless gas, the lightest element. **hydrogen bomb** powerful bomb releasing energy by fusion of hydrogen nuclei.

hydrolysis *n.* decomposition by chemical reaction with water. **hydrolytic** *a.*

hydrometer *n.* device measuring the density of liquids.

hydrophobia *n.* abnormal fear of water; rabies.

hydroponics *n.* art of growing plants in water impregnated with chemicals.

hydrostatic *a.* of the pressure and other characteristics of liquid at rest. **hydrostatics** *n.*

hydrotherapy *n.* use of water to treat diseases etc.

hydrous *a.* containing water.

hyena *n.* wolf-like animal with a howl that sounds like laughter.

hygiene *n.* cleanliness as a means of preventing disease. **hygienic** *a.*, **hygienically** *adv.*, **hygienist** *n.*

hymen *n.* membrane partly closing the opening of the vagina of a virgin girl or woman.

hymn *n.* song of praise to God or a sacred being.

hyper- *pref.* excessively.

hyperactive *a.* abnormally active. **hyperactivity** *n.*

hypermarket *n.* very large self-service store selling a wide variety of goods and services.

hypersonic *a.* of speeds more than five times that of sound.

hypertension *n.* abnormally high blood pressure; extreme tension.

hyphen *n.* the sign - used to join words together or divide a word into parts. — *v.* hyphenate.

hyphenate *v.* join or divide with a hyphen. **hyphenation** *n.*

hypnosis *n.* sleep-like condition produced in a person who then obeys suggestions; production of this.

hypnotic *a.* of or producing hypnosis. **hypnotically** *adv.*

hypnotism *n.* hypnosis.

hypnotize *v.* produce hypnosis in; fascinate, dominate the mind or will of. **hypnotist** *n.*

hypochondria *n.* state of constantly imagining that one is ill. **hypochondriac** *n.* person suffering from this.

hypocrisy *n.* falsely pretending to be virtuous; insincerity.

hypocrite *n.* person guilty of hypocrisy. **hypocritical** *a.*, **hypocritically** *adv.*

hypodermic *a.* injected beneath the skin; used for such injections. — *n.* hypodermic syringe.

hypotenuse *n.* longest side of a right-angled triangle.

hypothermia *n.* condition of having an abnormally low body temperature.

hypothesis *n.* (*pl.* **-theses**) supposition put forward as a basis for reasoning or investigation.

hypothetical *a.* supposed but not necessarily true. **hypothetically** *adv.*

hysterectomy *n.* surgical removal of the womb.

hysteria *n.* wild uncontrollable emotion. **hysterical** *a.*, **hysterically** *adv.*

hysterics *n.pl.* hysterical outburst.

Hz *abbr.* hertz.

I

I *pron.* person speaking or writing and referring to himself or herself.

iambic *a.* & *n.* (verse) using iambuses, metrical feet of one long and one short syllable.

iatrogenic *a.* (of disease) caused unintentionally by medical treatment.

Iberian *a.* of the peninsula comprising Spain and Portugal.

ibex *n.* (*pl.* **ibex** or **ibexes**) mountain goat with curving horns.

ibis *n.* wading bird found in warm climates.

ice *n.* frozen water; portion of ice cream. — *v.* become frozen; make very cold; decorate with icing. **ice cream** sweet creamy frozen food. **ice hockey** game like hockey played on ice by skaters. **ice lolly** water-ice or ice cream on a stick.

iceberg *n.* mass of ice floating in the sea.

Icelandic *a.* & *n.* (language) of Iceland.

ichthyology /ikthiólləji/ *n.* study of fishes. **ichthyologist** *n.*

icicle *n.* hanging ice formed when dripping water freezes.

icing *n.* mixture of powdered sugar etc. used to decorate food.

icon *n.* (in the Eastern Church) sacred painting or mosaic; (in computing) graphic symbol on a computer screen.

iconoclast *n.* person who attacks cherished beliefs. **iconoclasm** *n.*, **iconoclastic** *a.*

icy *a.* (**-ier**, **-iest**) very cold; covered with ice; very unfriendly. **icily** *adv.*, **iciness** *n.*

idea *n.* plan etc. formed in the mind by thinking; opinion; mental impression; vague belief.

ideal *a.* satisfying one's idea of what is perfect. — *n.* person or thing regarded as perfect or as a standard to aim at. **ideally** *adv.*

idealist *n.* person with high ideals. **idealism** *n.*, **idealistic** *a.*

idealize *v.* regard or represent as perfect. **idealization** *n.*

identical *a.* the same; exactly alike. **identically** *adv.*

identify *v.* recognize as being a specified person or thing; associate (oneself) closely in feeling or interest. **identifiable** *a.*, **identification** *n.*

identikit *n.* set of pictures of features that can be put together to form a likeness.

identity *n.* who or what a person or thing is; sameness.

ideology *n.* ideas that form the basis of a political or economic theory. **ideological** *a.*

idiocy *n.* state of being an idiot; extreme foolishness.

idiom *n.* phrase or usage peculiar to a language.

idiomatic *a.* full of idioms. **idiomatically** *adv.*

idiosyncrasy *n.* person's own characteristic way of behaving. **idiosyncratic** *a.*

idiot *n.* very stupid person. **idiotic** *a.*, **idiotically** *adv.*

idle *a.* not employed or in use; lazy; aimless. — *v.* be idle, pass (time) aimlessly; (of an engine) run slowly in neutral gear. **idly** *adv.*, **idleness** *n.*, **idler** *n.*

idol *n.* image worshipped as a god; idolized person or thing.

idolatry *n.* worship of idols. **idolater** *n.*, **idolatrous** *a.*

idolize *v.* love or admire excessively. **idolization** *n.*

idyll /íddil/ *n.* peaceful or romantic scene or incident; description of this, usu. in verse. **idyllic** *a.*, **idyllically** *adv.*

i.e. *abbr.* (Latin *id est*) that is.

if *conj.* on condition that; supposing that; whether. — *n.* condition, supposition.

igloo *n.* Eskimo's snow hut.

igneous *a.* (of rock) formed by volcanic action.

ignite *v.* set fire to; catch fire.

ignition *n.* igniting; mechanism producing a spark to ignite the fuel in an engine.

ignoble *a.* not noble in character, aims, or purpose. **ignobly** *adv.*

ignominy *n.* disgrace, humiliation. **ignominious** *a.*, **ignominiously** *adv.*

ignoramus *n.* (*pl.* **-muses**) ignorant person.

ignorant *a.* lacking knowledge; behaving rudely through not knowing good manners. **ignorantly** *adv.*, **ignorance** *n.*

ignore *v.* take no notice of.

iguana *n.* tropical tree-climbing lizard.

il- *pref. see* **in-**.

ileum *n.* part of the small intestine.

ill *a.* unwell; bad; harmful; hostile, unkind. — *adv.* badly. — *n.* evil, harm, injury. **ill-advised** *a.* unwise. **ill at ease** uncomfortable, embarrassed. **ill-gotten** *a.* gained by evil or unlawful means.

ill-mannered *a.* having bad manners. **ill-treat** *v.* treat badly or cruelly. **ill will** hostility, unkind feeling.

illegal *a.* against the law. **illegally** *adv.*, **illegality** *n.*

illegible *a.* not legible. **illegibly** *adv.*, **illegibility** *n.*

illegitimate *a.* born of parents not married to each other; contrary to a law or rule. **illegitimately** *adv.*, **illegitimacy** *n.*

illicit *a.* unlawful, not allowed. **illicitly** *adv.*

illiterate *a.* unable to read and write; uneducated. **illiteracy** *n.*

illness *n.* state of being ill; particular form of ill health.

illogical *a.* not logical. **illogically** *adv.*, **illogicality** *n.*

illuminate *v.* light up; throw light on (a subject); decorate with lights. **illumination** *n.*, **illuminator** *n.*

illumine *v.* light up; enlighten.

illusion *n.* false belief; thing wrongly supposed to exist. **illusive** *a.*

illusionist *n.* conjuror.

illusory *a.* based on illusion.

illustrate *v.* supply (a book etc.) with drawings or pictures; make clear by example(s) or picture(s) etc.; serve as an example of. **illustration** *n.*, **illustrative** *a.*, **illustrator** *n.*

illustrious *a.* distinguished.

im- *pref. see* **in-**.

image *n.* optical appearance of a thing produced in a mirror or through a lens; likeness; mental picture; reputation. — *v.* picture.

imaginable *a.* able to be imagined.

imaginary *a.* existing only in the imagination, not real.

imagination *n.* imagining; ability to imagine or to plan creatively. **imaginative** *a.*, **imaginatively** *adv.*

imagine *v.* form a mental image of; think, suppose; guess.

imago /imáygō/ *n.* (*pl.* **-gines**) insect in its fully developed adult stage.

imam *n.* Muslim spiritual leader.

imbalance *n.* lack of balance.

imbecile *n.* extremely stupid person. — *a.* idiotic. **imbecilic** *a.*, **imbecility** *n.*

imbibe *v.* drink; absorb (ideas).

imbroglio /imbrṓliō/ *n.* (*pl.* **-os**) confused situation.

imbue *v.* fill with feelings, qualities, or emotions.

imitable *a.* able to be imitated.

imitate *v.* try to act or be like; copy. **imitation** *n.*, **imitator** *n.*

imitative *a.* imitating.

immaculate *a.* free from stain, blemish, or fault. **immaculately** *adv.*, **immaculacy** *n.*

immanent *a.* inherent. **immanence** *n.*

immaterial *a.* having no physical substance; of no importance.

immature *a.* not mature. **immaturity** *n.*

immeasurable *a.* not measurable, immense. **immeasurably** *adv.*, **immeasurability** *n.*

immediate *a.* with no delay; nearest, with nothing between. **immediately** *adv.* & *conj.*, **immediacy** *n.*

immemorial *a.* existing from before what can be remembered.

immense *a.* extremely great. **immensely** *adv.*, **immensity** *n.*

immerse *v.* put completely into liquid; involve deeply.

immersion *n.* immersing. **immersion heater** electric heater placed in the liquid to be heated.

immigrate *v.* come into a foreign country as a permanent resident. **immigrant** *a.* & *n.*, **immigration** *n.*

imminent *a.* about to occur. **imminently** *adv.*, **imminence** *n.*

immobile *a.* immovable; not moving. **immobility** *n.*

immobilize *v.* make or keep immobile. **immobilization** *n.*

immoderate *a.* excessive. **immoderately** *adv.*, **immoderation** *n.*

immolate *v.* kill as a sacrifice. **immolation** *n.*

immoral *a.* morally wrong. **immorally** *adv.*, **immorality** *n.*

immortal *a.* living for ever, not mortal; famous for all time. — *n.* immortal being. **immortality** *n.*

immortalize *v.* make immortal.

immovable *a.* unable to be moved; unyielding. **immovably** *adv.*, **immovability** *n.*

immune *a.* having immunity.

immunity *n.* ability to resist infection; special exemption.

immunize *v.* make immune to infection. **immunization** *n.*

immunodeficiency *n.* reduction in normal resistance to infection.

immunology *n.* study of immunity. **immunological** *a.*, **immunologist** *n.*

immure *v.* imprison, shut in.

immutable *a.* unchangeable. **immutably** *adv.*, **immutability** *n.*

imp *n.* small devil; mischievous child.

impact *n.* /impakt/ collision, force of this; strong effect. — *v.* /impákt/ press or wedge firmly. **impaction** *n.*

impair *v.* damage, weaken. **impairment** *n.*

impala *n.* (*pl.* **impala**) small antelope.

impale *v.* fix or pierce with a pointed object. **impalement** *n.*
impalpable *a.* intangible. **impalpably** *adv.*
impart *v.* give; make (information etc.) known.
impartial *a.* not favouring one more than another. **impartially** *adv.*, **impartiality** *n.*
impassable *a.* impossible to travel on or over.
impasse /ámpass/ *n.* deadlock.
impassioned *a.* passionate.
impassive *a.* not feeling or showing emotion. **impassively** *adv.*
impatient *a.* feeling or showing lack of patience; intolerant. **impatiently** *adv.*, **impatience** *n.*
impeach *v.* accuse of a serious crime against the State and bring for trial. **impeachment** *n.*
impeccable *a.* faultless. **impeccably** *adv.*, **impeccability** *n.*
impecunious *a.* having little or no money. **impecuniosity** *n.*
impedance *n.* resistance of an electric circuit to the flow of current.
impede *v.* hinder.
impediment *n.* hindrance, obstruction; lisp or stammer.
impel *v.* (**impelled**) urge; drive forward.
impending *a.* imminent.
impenetrable *a.* unable to be penetrated. **impenetrably** *adv.*, **impenetrability** *n.*
imperative *a.* expressing a command; essential. — *n.* command; essential thing.
imperceptible *a.* too slight to be noticed. **imperceptibly** *adv.*
imperfect *a.* not perfect; (of a tense) implying action going on but not completed. **imperfectly** *adv.*, **imperfection** *n.*
imperial *a.* of an empire; majestic; (of measures) belonging to the British official non-metric system. **imperially** *adv.*
imperialism *n.* policy of having or extending an empire. **imperialist** *n.*, **imperialistic** *a.*
imperil *v.* (**imperilled**) endanger.
imperious *a.* commanding, bossy. **imperiously** *adv.*, **imperiousness** *n.*
impersonal *a.* not showing or influenced by personal feeling. **impersonally** *adv.*, **impersonality** *n.*
impersonate *v.* pretend to be (another person). **impersonation** *n.*, **impersonator** *n.*
impertinent *a.* not showing proper respect. **impertinently** *adv.*, **impertinence** *n.*
imperturbable *a.* not excitable, calm. **imperturbably** *adv.*, **imperturbability** *n.*
impervious *a.* **impervious to** not able to be penetrated or influenced by. **imperviousness** *n.*
impetigo /impitígō/ *n.* contagious skin disease.
impetuous *a.* acting or done on impulse. **impetuously** *adv.*, **impetuosity** *n.*
impetus *n.* moving force.
impinge *v.* make an impact; encroach. **impingement** *n.*
impious *a.* not reverent, wicked. **impiously** *adv.*
implacable *a.* inexorable; relentless. **implacably** *adv.*, **implacability** *n.*
implant *v.* /implaánt/ plant, insert; insert (tissue) in a living thing. — *n.* /implaant/ implanted tissue. **implantation** *n.*
implement *n.* tool. — *v.* put into effect. **implementation** *n.*
implicate *v.* show or cause to be concerned in a crime etc.
implication *n.* implicating; implying; thing implied.
implicit *a.* implied, not explicit; absolute. **implicitly** *adv.*
implode *v.* (cause to) burst inwards. **implosion** *n.*, **implosive** *a.*
implore *v.* request earnestly.
imply *v.* suggest without stating directly; mean.
impolitic *a.* unwise; inexpedient.
imponderable *a.* not able to be estimated. — *n.* imponderable thing. **imponderably** *adv.*, **imponderability** *n.*
import *v.* /impórt/ bring in from abroad or from an outside source; imply. — *n.* /import/ importing; thing imported; meaning; importance. **importation** *n.*, **importer** *n.*
important *a.* having a great effect; having great authority or influence. **importance** *n.*
importunate *a.* making persistent requests. **importunity** *n.*
importune *v.* solicit.
impose *v.* levy (a tax); inflict; force acceptance of. **impose on** take unfair advantage of.
imposing *a.* impressive.
imposition *n.* act of imposing something; thing imposed; burden imposed unfairly.
impossible *a.* not possible; unendurable. **impossibly** *adv.*, **impossibility** *n.*
impostor *n.* person who fraudulently pretends to be someone else.
imposture *n.* fraudulent deception.
impotent *a.* powerless; (of a male) unable to copulate successfully. **impotently** *adv.*, **impotence** *n.*
impound *v.* take (property) into legal custody; confiscate.

impoverish *v.* cause to become poor; exhaust the strength or fertility of. **impoverishment** *n.*

imprecation *n.* spoken curse.

impregnable *a.* safe against attack. **impregnability** *n.*

impregnate *v.* introduce sperm or pollen into and fertilize; penetrate all parts of. **impregnation** *n.*

impresario *n.* (*pl.* **-os**) manager of an operatic or concert company.

impress *v.* cause to form a strong (usu. favourable) opinion; fix in the mind; press a mark into.

impression *n.* effect produced on the mind; uncertain idea; imitation done for entertainment; impressed mark; reprint.

impressionable *a.* easily influenced. **impressionability** *n.*

impressionism *n.* style of painting etc. giving a general impression without detail. **impressionist** *n.*, **impressionistic** *a.*

impressive *a.* making a strong favourable impression. **impressively** *adv.*, **impressiveness** *n.*

imprint *n.* /ímprint/ mark made by pressing on a surface; publisher's name etc. on a title-page. — *v.* /imprínt/ impress or stamp a mark etc. on.

imprison *v.* put into prison; keep in confinement. **imprisonment** *n.*

improbable *a.* not likely to be true or to happen. **improbably** *adv.*, **improbability** *n.*

impromptu *a.* & *adv.* without preparation or rehearsal.

improper *a.* unsuitable; not conforming to social conventions. **improperly** *adv.*, **impropriety** *n.*

improve *v.* make or become better. **improvement** *n.*

improvident *a.* not providing for future needs. **improvidently** *adv.*, **improvidence** *n.*

improvise *v.* compose impromptu; provide from whatever materials are at hand. **improvisation** *n.*

imprudent *a.* unwise, rash. **imprudently** *adv.*, **imprudence** *n.*

impudent *a.* cheeky, impertinent. **impudently** *adv.*, **impudence** *n.*

impugn /impyo͞on/ *v.* express doubts about the truth or honesty of.

impulse *n.* impetus; stimulating force in a nerve; sudden urge to do something.

impulsion *n.* impelling; impulse; impetus.

impulsive *a.* acting or done on impulse. **impulsively** *adv.*, **impulsiveness** *n.*

impunity *n.* freedom from punishment or injury.

impure *a.* not pure.

impurity *n.* being impure; substance that makes another impure.

impute *v.* attribute (a fault etc.). **imputation** *n.*

in *prep.* having as a position or state within (limits of space, time, surroundings, etc.); having as a state or manner; into, towards. — *adv.* in a position bounded by limits, or to a point enclosed by these; inside; in fashion, season, or office. — *a.* internal; living etc. inside; fashionable. **in for** about to experience; competing in. **ins and outs** details of activity or procedure. **in so far** to such an extent.

in- *pref.* (**il-** before *l*; **im-** before *b*, *m*, *p*; **ir-** before *r*) not; without, lacking.

in. *abbr.* inch(es).

inability *n.* being unable.

inaction *n.* lack of action.

inactive *a.* not active. **inactivity** *n.*

inadequate *a.* not adequate; not sufficiently able. **inadequately** *adv.*, **inadequacy** *n.*

inadmissible *a.* not allowable.

inadvertent *a.* unintentional.

inalienable *a.* not able to be given or taken away. **inalienably** *adv.*, **inalienability** *n.*

inane *a.* silly, lacking sense. **inanely** *adv.*, **inanity** *n.*

inanimate *a.* lacking animal life; showing no sign of being alive.

inanition *n.* loss or lack of vitality.

inappropriate *a.* unsuitable.

inarticulate *a.* not expressed in words; unable to speak distinctly; unable to express ideas clearly.

inasmuch *adv.* **inasmuch as** seeing that, because.

inattentive *a.* not paying attention. **inattentiveness** *n.*

inaugural *a.* of an inauguration.

inaugurate *v.* admit to office ceremonially; begin (an undertaking), open (a building etc.) formally; be the beginning of. **inauguration** *n.*, **inaugurator** *n.*

inborn *a.* existing in a person or animal from birth, natural.

inbred *a.* produced by inbreeding; inborn.

inbreeding *n.* breeding from closely related individuals.

Inc. *abbr.* (*US*) Incorporated.

incalculable *a.* unable to be calculated. **incalculably** *adv.*

incandescent *a.* glowing with heat. **incandescence** *n.*

incantation *n.* words or sounds uttered as a magic spell.

incapable *a.* not capable; helpless. **incapability** *n.*

incapacitate *v.* disable; make ineligible. **incapacitation** *n.*
incapacity *n.* inability, lack of sufficient strength or power.
incarcerate *v.* imprison. **incarceration** *n.*
incarnate *a.* embodied, esp. in human form.
incarnation *n.* embodiment, esp. in human form; **the Incarnation** that of God as Christ.
incautious *a.* rash. **incautiously** *adv.*
incendiary *a.* designed to cause fire. — *n.* incendiary bomb; arsonist. **incendiarism** *n.*
incense [1] /insenss/ *n.* substance burnt to produce fragrant smoke, esp. in religious ceremonies; this smoke.
incense [2] /insénss/ *v.* make angry.
incentive *n.* thing that encourages an action or effort.
inception *n.* beginning.
incessant *a.* not ceasing. **incessantly** *adv.*
incest *n.* sexual intercourse between very closely related people. **incestuous** *a.*
inch *n.* measure of length (= 2.54 cm). — *v.* move gradually.
incidence *n.* rate at which a thing occurs; falling.
incident *n.* event, esp. one causing trouble.
incidental *a.* occurring in connection with something; casual.
incidentally *adv.* in an incidental way; by the way.
incinerate *v.* burn to ashes. **incineration** *n.*, **incinerator** *n.*
incipient *a.* beginning to exist.
incise *v.* make a cut in; engrave. **incision** *n.*
incisive *a.* clear and decisive. **incisively** *adv.*, **incisiveness** *n.*
incisor *n.* any of the front teeth.
incite *v.* urge on to action; stir up. **incitement** *n.*
incivility *n.* rudeness.
inclination *n.* slope; bending; tendency; liking, preference.
incline *v.* /inklīn/ slope; bend; (cause to) have a certain tendency, influence. — *n.* /inklīn/ slope.
include *v.* have or treat as part of a whole; put into a specified category. **inclusion** *n.*
inclusive *a.* & *adv.* including what is mentioned; including everything. **inclusively** *adv.*, **inclusiveness** *n.*
incognito *a.* & *adv.* with one's identity kept secret. — *n.* (*pl.* **-os**) pretended identity.
incoherent *a.* rambling in speech or reasoning. **incoherently** *adv.*, **incoherence** *n.*
incombustible *a.* not able to be burnt. **incombustibility** *n.*
income *n.* money received during a period as wages, interest, etc.
incoming *a.* coming in.
incommunicado *a.* not allowed or not wishing to communicate with others.
incomparable *a.* beyond comparison, without an equal.
incomprehensible *a.* not able to be understood. **incomprehension** *n.*
inconceivable *a.* unable to be imagined; (*colloq.*) most unlikely.
inconclusive *a.* not fully convincing. **inconclusively** *adv.*
incongruous *a.* unsuitable, not harmonious. **incongruously** *adv.*, **incongruity** *n.*
inconsequential *a.* unimportant; not following logically. **inconsequentially** *adv.*
inconsiderable *a.* negligible.
inconsolable *a.* not able to be consoled. **inconsolably** *adv.*
inconstant *a.* fickle; variable; irregular. **inconstantly** *adv.*, **inconstancy** *n.*
incontestable *a.* indisputable. **incontestably** *adv.*, **incontestability** *n.*
incontinent *a.* unable to control one's excretion of urine and faeces; lacking self-restraint. **incontinence** *n.*
incontrovertible *a.* indisputable. **incontrovertibly** *adv.*, **incontrovertibility** *n.*
inconvenience *n.* lack of convenience; thing causing this. — *v.* cause inconvenience to.
inconvenient *a.* not convenient, slightly troublesome. **inconveniently** *adv.*
incorporate *v.* include as a part; form into a corporation. **incorporation** *n.*
incorrigible *a.* not able to be reformed. **incorrigibly** *adv.*
incorruptible *a.* not liable to decay; not corruptible morally. **incorruptibility** *n.*
increase *v.* /inkreéss/ make or become greater. — *n.* /inkreess/ increasing; amount by which a thing increases.
increasingly *adv.* more and more.
incredible *a.* unbelievable. **incredibly** *adv.*, **incredibility** *n.*
incredulous *a.* unbelieving, showing disbelief. **incredulously** *adv.*, **incredulity** *n.*
increment *n.* increase, added amount. **incremental** *a.*
incriminate *v.* indicate as involved in wrongdoing. **incrimination** *n.*, **incriminatory** *a.*
incrustation *n.* encrusting; crust or deposit formed on a surface.
incubate *v.* hatch (eggs) by warmth; cause (bacteria etc.) to develop. **incubation** *n.*
incubator *n.* apparatus for incubating eggs

or bacteria; enclosed heated compartment in which a premature baby can be kept.

inculcate *v.* implant (a habit etc.) by constant urging. **inculcation** *n.*

incumbent *a.* forming an obligation or duty. — *n.* holder of an office; rector, vicar.

incur *v.* (**incurred**) bring upon oneself.

incursion *n.* brief invasion, raid.

indebted /indéttid/ *a.* owing a debt.

indecent *a.* offending against standards of decency; unseemly. **indecently** *adv.*, **indecency** *n.*

indecipherable *a.* unable to be read or deciphered.

indecision *n.* inability to decide something, hesitation.

indecorous *a.* unseemly.

indeed *adv.* in truth, really.

indefatigable *a.* untiring. **indefatigably** *adv.*

indefensible *a.* unable to be defended; not justifiable.

indefinable *a.* unable to be defined or described clearly. **indefinably** *adv.*

indefinite *a.* not clearly stated or fixed, vague. **indefinite article** the word 'a' or 'an'.

indefinitely *adv.* in an indefinite way; for an unlimited period.

indelible *a.* (of a mark) unable to be removed or washed away; making such a mark. **indelibly** *adv.*, **indelibility** *n.*

indelicate *a.* slightly indecent; tactless. **indelicately** *adv.*, **indelicacy** *n.*

indemnify *v.* provide indemnity to. **indemnification** *n.*

indemnity *n.* protection against penalties incurred by one's actions; compensation for injury.

indent *v.* start inwards from a margin; place an official order (for goods etc.). **indentation** *n.*

indenture *n.* written contract, esp. of apprenticeship. — *v.* bind by this.

independent *a.* not dependent on or not controlled by another person or thing. **independently** *adv.*, **independence** *n.*

indescribable *a.* unable to be described. **indescribably** *adv.*

indestructible *a.* unable to be destroyed. **indestructibly** *adv.*

indeterminable *a.* impossible to discover or decide.

indeterminate *a.* not fixed in extent or character.

index *n.* (*pl.* **indexes** *or* **indices**) list (usu. alphabetical) of names, subjects, etc., with references; figure showing the current level of prices etc. compared with a previous level. — *v.* make an index to; enter in an index; adjust (wages etc.) according to a price index. **index finger** forefinger. **indexation** *n.*

Indian *a.* of India or Indians. — *n.* native of India; any of the original inhabitants of the American continent or their descendants. **Indian ink** a black pigment. **Indian summer** dry sunny weather in autumn.

indiarubber *n.* rubber for rubbing out pencil or ink marks.

indicate *v.* point out; be a sign of; state briefly. **indication** *n.*, **indicative** *a.*

indicator *n.* thing that indicates; pointer; device on a vehicle showing when the direction of travel is about to be altered.

indict /indít/ *v.* make a formal accusation against. **indictment** *n.*

indifferent *a.* showing no interest or sympathy; neither good nor bad; not very good. **indifferently** *adv.*, **indifference** *n.*

indigenous *a.* native.

indigent *a.* needy. **indigence** *n.*

indigestible *a.* difficult or impossible to digest.

indigestion *n.* pain caused by difficulty in digesting food.

indignant *a.* feeling or showing indignation. **indignantly** *adv.*

indignation *n.* anger aroused by something unjust or wicked.

indignity *n.* unworthy treatment, humiliation.

indigo *n.* deep blue dye or colour.

indiscernible *a.* unable to be discerned. **indiscernibly** *adv.*

indiscreet *a.* revealing secrets; not cautious. **indiscreetly** *adv.*, **indiscretion** *n.*

indiscriminate *a.* not discriminating, not making a careful choice. **indiscriminately** *adv.*

indispensable *a.* essential.

indisposed *a.* slightly ill; unwilling. **indisposition** *n.*

indisputable *a.* undeniable. **indisputably** *adv.*

indissoluble *a.* firm and lasting, not able to be destroyed.

individual *a.* single, separate; characteristic of one particular person or thing. — *n.* one person or animal or plant considered separately; (*colloq.*) person. **individually** *adv.*, **individuality** *n.*

individualist *n.* person who is very independent in thought or action. **individualism** *n.*

indoctrinate *v.* fill (a person's mind) with particular ideas or doctrines. **indoctrination** *n.*

indolent *a.* lazy. **indolently** *adv.*, **indolence** *n.*

indomitable *a.* unyielding, untiringly persistent. **indomitably** *adv.*
indoor *a.* situated, used, or done inside a building. **indoors** *adv.* inside a building.
indubitable *a.* that cannot reasonably be doubted. **indubitably** *adv.*
induce *v.* persuade; cause; bring on (labour) artificially.
inducement *n.* inducing; incentive.
induct *v.* install (a clergyman) ceremonially into a benefice.
inductance *n.* amount of induction of electric current.
induction *n.* inducting; inducing; reasoning (from observed examples) that a general law exists; production of an electric or magnetic state by proximity of an electrified or magnetic object; drawing of a fuel mixture into the cylinder(s) of an engine. **inductive** *a.*
indulge *v.* allow (a person) to have what he or she wishes; gratify. **indulgence** *n.*
indulgent *a.* indulging a person's wishes too freely; kind, lenient. **indulgently** *adv.*
industrial *a.* of, for, or full of industries. **industrially** *adv.*
industrialist *n.* owner or manager of an industrial business. **industrialism** *n.*
industrialized *a.* full of highly developed industries.
industrious *a.* hard-working. **industriously** *adv.*
industry *n.* manufacture or production of goods; business activity; being industrious.
inebriated *a.* drunken. **inebriation** *n.*
inedible *a.* not edible.
ineducable *a.* incapable of being educated.
ineffable *a.* too great to be described. **ineffably** *adv.*
ineluctable *a.* against which it is useless to struggle.
inept *a.* unsuitable, absurd; unskilful. **ineptly** *adv.*, **ineptitude** *n.*, **ineptness** *n.*
inequality *n.* lack of equality.
inequitable *a.* unfair, unjust. **inequitably** *adv.*
ineradicable *a.* not able to be eradicated. **ineradicably** *adv.*
inert *a.* without the power of moving; without active properties; not moving or taking action. **inertly** *adv.*, **inertness** *n.*
inertia *n.* being inert; property by which matter continues in its state of rest or line of motion.
inescapable *a.* unavoidable. **inescapably** *adv.*
inessential *a.* not essential. — *n.* inessential thing.
inestimable *a.* too great or intense to be estimated. **inestimably** *adv.*
inevitable *a.* not able to be prevented, sure to happen or appear. **inevitably** *adv.*, **inevitability** *n.*
inexact *a.* not exact. **inexactly** *adv.*, **inexactitude** *n.*
inexhaustible *a.* available in unlimited quantity.
inexorable *a.* relentless. **inexorably** *adv.*, **inexorability** *n.*
inexperience *n.* lack of experience. **inexperienced** *a.*
inexpert *a.* not expert, unskilful. **inexpertly** *adv.*
inexplicable *a.* unable to be explained. **inexplicably** *adv.*, **inexplicability** *n.*
inextricable *a.* unable to be extricated or disentangled. **inextricably** *adv.*
infallible *a.* incapable of being wrong; never failing. **infallibly** *adv.*, **infallibility** *n.*
infamous /infəməss/ *a.* having a bad reputation. **infamously** *adv.*, **infamy** *n.*
infancy *n.* early childhood, babyhood; early stage of development.
infant *n.* child during the earliest stage of its life.
infanticide *n.* killing or killer of an infant soon after its birth. **infanticidal** *a.*
infantile *a.* of infants or infancy; very childish.
infantry *n.* troops who fight on foot.
infatuated *a.* filled with intense unreasoning love. **infatuation** *n.*
infect *v.* affect or contaminate with a disease or its germs; affect with one's feeling.
infection *n.* infecting, being infected; disease or condition so caused.
infectious *a.* (of disease) able to spread by air or water; infecting others. **infectiousness** *n.*
infer *v.* (**inferred**) reach (an opinion) from facts or reasoning. **inference** *n.*
inferior *a.* low or lower in rank, importance, quality, or ability. — *n.* person inferior to another, esp. in rank. **inferiority** *n.*
infernal *a.* of hell; (*colloq.*) detestable, tiresome. **infernally** *adv.*
inferno *n.* (*pl.* **-os**) hell; intensely hot place; raging fire.
infest *v.* be numerous or troublesome in (a place). **infestation** *n.*
infidel *n.* person with no religious faith; opponent of a religion, esp. Christianity.
infidelity *n.* unfaithfulness.
infighting *n.* hidden conflict within an organization.
infiltrate *v.* enter gradually and unperceived. **infiltration** *n.*, **infiltrator** *n.*
infinite /infinit/ *a.* having no limit; too

great or too many to be measured. **infinitely** *adv.*

infinitesimal *a.* extremely small. **infinitesimally** *adv.*

infinitive *n.* form of a verb not indicating tense, number, or person (e.g. *to go*).

infinity *n.* infinite number, extent, or time.

infirm *a.* weak from age or illness. **infirmity** *n.*

infirmary *n.* hospital.

inflame *v.* arouse strong feeling in; cause inflammation in.

inflammable *a.* able to be set on fire. **inflammability** *n.*

inflammation *n.* redness and heat in a part of the body.

inflammatory *a.* arousing strong feeling or anger.

inflatable *a.* able to be inflated.

inflate *v.* fill with air or gas so as to swell; increase artificially.

inflation *n.* inflating; general increase in prices and fall in the purchasing power of money.

inflationary *a.* causing inflation.

inflect *v.* change the pitch of (a voice) in speaking; change the ending or form of (a word) grammatically. **inflection** *n.*

inflexible *a.* not flexible; unyielding. **inflexibly** *adv.*, **inflexibility** *n.*

inflict *v.* cause (a blow, penalty, etc.) to be suffered. **infliction** *n.*

influence *n.* ability to produce an effect or to affect character, beliefs, or actions; person or thing with this. — *v.* exert influence on.

influential *a.* having great influence. **influentially** *adv.*

influenza *n.* virus disease causing fever, muscular pain, and catarrh.

influx *n.* inward flow.

inform *v.* give information to; reveal secret or criminal activities to police etc. **informer** *n.*

informal *a.* not formal, without formality or ceremony. **informally** *adv.*, **informality** *n.*

informant *n.* giver of information.

information *n.* facts told or heard or discovered.

informative *a.* giving information. **informatively** *adv.*

infra-red *a.* of or using radiation with a wavelength longer than that of visible light rays.

infrastructure *n.* subordinate parts forming the basis of an enterprise.

infringe *v.* break (a rule or agreement); encroach. **infringement** *n.*

infuriate *v.* make very angry.

infuse *v.* imbue, instil; soak to bring out flavour.

infusion *n.* infusing; liquid made by this; thing added to a stock.

ingenious *a.* clever at inventing things; cleverly contrived. **ingeniously** *adv.*, **ingenuity** *n.*

ingenuous *a.* without artfulness, unsophisticated. **ingenuously** *adv.*, **ingenuousness** *n.*

ingest *v.* take in as food.

ingot *n.* oblong lump of cast metal.

ingrained *a.* deeply fixed in a surface or character.

ingratiate *v.* bring (oneself) into a person's favour, esp. to gain advantage. **ingratiation** *n.*

ingratitude *n.* lack of gratitude.

ingredient *n.* one element in a mixture or combination.

ingress *n.* going in; right of entry.

ingrowing *a.* growing abnormally into the flesh.

inhabit *v.* live in as one's home. **inhabitable** *a.*, **inhabitant** *n.*

inhalant *n.* medicinal substance to be inhaled.

inhale *v.* breathe in; draw tobacco smoke into the lungs.

inhaler *n.* device producing a medicinal vapour to be inhaled.

inherent *a.* existing in a thing as a permanent quality. **inherently** *adv.*

inherit *v.* receive from a predecessor, esp. someone who has died; derive from parents etc. **inheritance** *n.*

inhibit *v.* restrain, prevent; cause inhibitions in. **inhibitor** *n.*, **inhibitive** *a.*

inhibition *n.* inhibiting; resistance to an impulse or feeling.

inhuman *a.* brutal, extremely cruel. **inhumanly** *adv.*, **inhumanity** *n.*

inhumane *a.* not humane. **inhumanely** *adv.*, **inhumanity** *n.*

inimical *a.* hostile. **inimically** *adv.*

inimitable *a.* impossible to imitate. **inimitably** *adv.*

iniquity *n.* great injustice; wickedness.

initial *n.* first letter of a word or name. — *v.* (**initialled**) mark or sign with initials. — *a.* of the beginning. **initially** *adv.*

initiate *v.* /inishiayt/ cause to begin; admit into membership; give instruction to. — *n.* /inishiət/ initiated person. **initiation** *n.*, **initiator** *n.*, **initiatory** *a.*

initiative *n.* first step in a process; readiness to initiate things.

inject *v.* force (liquid) into the body with a syringe. **injection** *n.*

injudicious *a.* unwise. **injudiciously** *adv.*, **injudiciousness** *n.*

injunction *n.* court order.
injure *v.* cause injury to.
injurious *a.* causing injury.
injury *n.* damage, harm; form of this; wrong or unjust act.
injustice *n.* lack of justice; unjust action or treatment.
ink *n.* coloured liquid used in writing, printing, etc. — *v.* apply ink to. **inky** *a.*
inkling *n.* slight suspicion.
inlaid *see* **inlay**.
inland *a.* & *adv.* in or towards the interior of a country.
in-laws *n.pl.* (*colloq.*) one's relatives by marriage.
inlay *v.* /ínláy/ (**inlaid**) set (one thing in another) so that the surfaces are flush. — *n.* /ínlay/ inlaid material or design.
inlet *n.* strip of water extending inland; way in (e.g. for water into a tank).
inmate *n.* inhabitant, esp. of an institution.
inmost *a.* furthest inward.
inn *n.* hotel, esp. in the country; public house.
innards *n.pl.* (*colloq.*) entrails; inner parts.
innate *a.* inborn. **innately** *adv.*
inner *a.* nearer to the centre or inside; interior, internal. **inner city** central densely populated urban area.
innermost *a.* furthest inward.
innocent *a.* not guilty, free of evil; foolishly trustful. **innocently** *adv.*, **innocence** *n.*
innocuous *a.* harmless. **innocuously** *adv.*, **innocuousness** *n.*
innovate *v.* introduce something new. **innovation** *n.*, **innovative** *a.*, **innovator** *n.*
innuendo *n.* (*pl.* **-oes**) insinuation.
innumerable *a.* too many to be counted.
innumerate *a.* without knowledge of basic mathematics and science. **innumeracy** *n.*
inoculate *v.* protect (against disease) with vaccines or serums. **inoculation** *n.*
inoperable *a.* unable to be cured by surgical operation.
inoperative *a.* not functioning.
inopportune *a.* happening at an unsuitable time. **inopportunely** *adv.*
inordinate *a.* excessive. **inordinately** *adv.*
inorganic *a.* of mineral origin, not organic. **inorganically** *adv.*
in-patient *n.* patient residing in a hospital during treatment.
input *n.* what is put in. — *v.* (**input** *or* **inputted**) put in; supply (data etc.) to a computer.
inquest *n.* judicial investigation, esp. of a sudden death.
inquire *v.* make an inquiry. **inquirer** *n.*
inquiry *n.* investigation.
inquisition *n.* detailed or relentless questioning. **inquisitor** *n.*, **inquisitorial** *a.*
inquisitive *a.* eagerly seeking knowledge; prying. **inquisitively** *adv.*, **inquisitiveness** *n.*
inroad *n.* incursion.
insalubrious *a.* unhealthy.
insane *a.* mad; extremely foolish. **insanely** *adv.*, **insanity** *n.*
insanitary *a.* not clean, not hygienic.
insatiable *a.* unable to be satisfied. **insatiably** *adv.*, **insatiability** *n.*
inscribe *v.* write or engrave.
inscription *n.* words inscribed.
inscrutable *a.* baffling, impossible to interpret. **inscrutably** *adv.*, **inscrutability** *n.*
insect *n.* small creature with six legs, no backbone, and a segmented body.
insecticide *n.* substance for killing insects.
insectivorous *a.* insect-eating.
inseminate *v.* insert semen into. **insemination** *n.*
insensible *a.* unconscious; unaware; callous; imperceptible. **insensibly** *adv.*
insensitive *a.* not sensitive.
inseparable *a.* unable to be separated or kept apart. **inseparably** *adv.*, **inseparability** *n.*
insert *v.* /insért/ put into or between or among. — *n.* /ínsert/ thing inserted. **insertion** *n.*
inset *v.* /ínsét/ (**inset, insetting**) place in; decorate with an inset. — *n.* /ínset/ thing set into a larger thing.
inshore *a.* & *adv.* near or nearer to the shore.
inside *n.* inner side, surface, or part. — *a.* of or from the inside. — *adv.* on, in, or to the inside. — *prep.* on or to the inside of; within. **inside out** with the inner side outwards; thoroughly.
insidious *a.* proceeding inconspicuously but harmfully. **insidiously** *adv.*, **insidiousness** *n.*
insight *n.* perception and understanding of a thing's nature.
insignia *n.pl.* symbols of authority or office; identifying badge.
insignificant *a.* unimportant. **insignificantly** *adv.*, **insignificance** *n.*
insinuate *v.* insert gradually or craftily; hint artfully. **insinuation** *n.*, **insinuator** *n.*
insipid *a.* lacking flavour, interest, or liveliness. **insipidity** *n.*
insist *v.* declare or demand emphatically.
insistent *a.* insisting; forcing itself on one's attention. **insistently** *adv.*, **insistence** *n.*

in situ /in sityo͞o/ in its original place.

insolent *a.* disrespectful, arrogant. **insolently** *adv.*, **insolence** *n.*

insoluble *a.* unable to be dissolved; unable to be solved.

insolvent *a.* unable to pay one's debts. **insolvency** *n.*

insomnia *n.* inability to sleep.

insomniac *n.* sufferer from insomnia.

insouciant *a.* carefree, unconcerned. **insouciantly** *adv.*, **insouciance** *n.*

inspect *v.* examine critically or officially. **inspection** *n.*

inspector *n.* person who inspects; police officer above sergeant.

inspiration *n.* inspiring; inspiring influence; sudden brilliant idea. **inspirational** *a.*

inspire *v.* stimulate to activity; instil (a feeling or idea) into; animate.

install *v.* place (a person) into office ceremonially; set in position and ready for use; establish.

installation *n.* process of installing; apparatus etc. installed.

instalment *n.* one of the parts in which a thing is presented or a debt paid over a period of time.

instance *n.* example; particular case. — *v.* mention as an instance.

instant *a.* immediate; (of food) quickly and easily prepared. — *n.* exact moment. **instantly** *adv.*

instantaneous *a.* occurring or done instantly. **instantaneously** *adv.*, **instantaneousness** *n.*

instead *adv.* as an alternative.

instep *n.* middle part of the foot; part of a shoe etc. covering this.

instigate *v.* incite; initiate. **instigation** *n.*, **instigator** *n.*

instil *v.* (**instilled**) implant (ideas etc.) gradually. **instillation** *n.*

instinct *n.* inborn impulse; natural tendency or ability. **instinctive** *a.*, **instinctively** *adv.*

institute *n.* organization for promotion of a specified activity; its premises. — *v.* set up; establish. **institutor** *n.*

institution *n.* process of instituting; institute; home for people with special needs; established rule or custom. **institutional** *a.*

institutionalize *v.* accustom to living in an institution. **institutionalization** *n.*

instruct *v.* teach (a person) a subject or skill; give instructions to. **instructor** *n.*, **instructress** *n.fem.*

instruction *n.* process of teaching; knowledge or teaching imparted; (*pl.*) statements telling a person what to do.

instructive *a.* giving instruction, enlightening. **instructively** *adv.*

instrument *n.* implement for delicate work; measuring device of an engine or vehicle; device for producing musical sounds.

instrumental *a.* serving as a means; performed on musical instruments. **instrumentally** *adv.*, **instrumentality** *n.*

instrumentalist *n.* player of a musical instrument.

insubordinate *a.* disobedient, rebellious. **insubordination** *n.*

insubstantial *a.* lacking reality or solidity. **insubstantiality** *n.*

insufferable *a.* unbearable. **insufferably** *adv.*

insular *a.* of an island; of islanders, narrow-minded. **insularity** *n.*

insulate *v.* cover with a substance that prevents the passage of electricity, sound, or heat; isolate from influences. **insulation** *n.*, **insulator** *n.*

insulin *n.* hormone controlling the body's absorption of sugar.

insult *v.* /insúlt/ speak or act so as to offend someone. — *n.* /ínsult/ insulting remark or action. **insulting** *a.*

insuperable *a.* unable to be overcome. **insuperably** *adv.*, **insuperability** *n.*

insupportable *a.* unbearable.

insurance *n.* contract to provide compensation for loss, damage, or death; sum payable as a premium or in compensation; safeguard against loss or failure.

insure *v.* protect by insurance; (*US*) ensure. **insurer** *n.*

insurgent *a.* rebellious, rising in revolt. — *n.* rebel. **insurgency** *n.*

insurmountable *a.* insuperable.

insurrection *n.* rebellion. **insurrectionist** *n.*

intact *a.* undamaged, complete.

intake *n.* taking thing(s) in; place or amount of this.

integral *a.* forming or necessary to form a whole.

integrate *v.* combine (parts) into a whole; bring or come into full membership of a community. **integration** *n.*

integrity *n.* honesty.

intellect *n.* mind's power of reasoning and acquiring knowledge.

intellectual *a.* of or using the intellect; having a strong intellect. — *n.* intellectual person. **intellectually** *adv.*

intelligence *n.* mental ability to learn and understand things; information, esp. that of military value; people collecting this.

intelligent *a.* having mental ability. **intelligently** *adv.*

intelligible *a.* able to be understood. **intelligibly** *adv.*, **intelligibility** *n.*

intend *v.* have in mind as what one wishes to do or achieve.

intense *a.* strong in quality or degree; feeling strong emotion. **intensely** *adv.*, **intensity** *n.*

intensify *v.* make or become more intense. **intensification** *n.*

intensive *a.* employing much effort; concentrated. **intensively** *adv.*, **intensiveness** *n.*

intent *n.* intention. — *a.* with concentrated attention. **intent on** determined to. **intently** *adv.*, **intentness** *n.*

intention *n.* what one intends to do.

intentional *a.* done on purpose. **intentionally** *adv.*

inter *v.* (**interred**) bury.

inter- *prep.* between, among.

interact *v.* have an effect upon each other. **interaction** *n.*, **interactive** *a.*

interbreed *v.* (**interbred**) breed with each other, cross-breed.

intercede *v.* intervene on someone's behalf.

intercept *v.* stop or catch between starting point and destination. **interception** *n.*, **interceptor** *n.*

intercession *n.* interceding.

interchange *v.* /intərcháynj/ cause to change places; alternate. — *n.* /íntərchaynj/ process of interchanging; road junction designed so that streams of traffic do not intersect on the same level.

interchangeable *a.* able to be interchanged.

intercom *n.* (*colloq.*) communication system operating like a telephone.

interconnect *v.* connect with each other. **interconnection** *n.*

intercontinental *a.* between continents.

intercourse *n.* dealings between people or countries; copulation.

interdict *n.* formal prohibition.

interest *n.* feeling of curiosity or concern; object of it; advantage; legal share; money paid for use of money borrowed. — *v.* arouse the interest of.

interested *a.* feeling interest; having an interest, not impartial.

interesting *a.* arousing interest.

interface *n.* place where interaction occurs.

interfere *v.* take part in dealing with others' affairs without right or invitation; be an obstruction.

interference *n.* interfering; disturbance of radio signals.

interferon *n.* protein preventing the development of a virus.

interim *n.* intervening period. — *a.* of or in such a period, temporary.

interior *a.* inner. — *n.* interior part.

interject *v.* put in (a remark) when someone is speaking.

interjection *n.* process of interjecting; remark interjected; exclamation.

interlace *v.* weave or lace together.

interlink *v.* link together.

interlock *v.* fit into each other. — *n.* fine machine-knitted fabric.

interloper *n.* intruder.

interlude *n.* interval; thing happening or performed in this.

intermarry *v.* marry members of the same or another group. **intermarriage** *n.*

intermediary *n.* mediator, messenger. — *a.* acting as intermediary; intermediate.

intermediate *a.* coming between two things in time, place, or order.

interment *n.* burial.

intermezzo /intərmétsō/ *n.* (*pl.* **-os**) short piece of music.

interminable *a.* very long and boring. **interminably** *adv.*

intermission *n.* interval, pause.

intermittent *a.* occurring at intervals. **intermittently** *adv.*

intern *v.* compel (esp. an enemy alien) to live in a special area.

internal *a.* of or in the inside; of a country's domestic affairs. **internal-combustion engine** engine producing motive power from fuel exploded within a cylinder. **internally** *adv.*

international *a.* between countries. — *n.* sports contest between players representing different countries; one of these players. **internationally** *adv.*

internecine /intərnéessīn/ *a.* mutually destructive.

internee *n.* interned person.

internment *n.* interning.

interplay *n.* interaction.

interpolate *v.* interject; insert. **interpolation** *n.*

interpose *v.* insert; intervene. **interposition** *n.*

interpret *v.* explain the meaning of; act as interpreter. **interpretation** *n.*

interpreter *n.* person who orally translates speech between persons speaking different languages.

interregnum *n.* period between the rule of two successive rulers.

interrogate *v.* question closely. **interrogation** *n.*, **interrogator** *n.*

interrogative *a.* forming or having the form of a question. **interrogatively** *adv.*

interrupt *v.* break the continuity of; break

the flow of (speech etc.) by a remark. **interruption** *n.*

intersect *v.* divide or cross by passing or lying across. **intersection** *n.*

intersperse *v.* insert here and there.

interval *n.* time or pause between two events or parts of an action; space between two things; difference in musical pitch.

intervene *v.* occur between events; enter a situation to change its course or resolve it. **intervention** *n.*

interview *n.* formal meeting with a person to assess his or her merits or obtain information. — *v.* hold an interview with. **interviewer** *n.*, **interviewee** *n.*

interweave *v.* (**interwove, interwoven**) weave together.

intestate *a.* not having made a valid will. **intestacy** *n.*

intestine *n.* long tubular section of the alimentary canal between stomach and anus. **intestinal** *a.*

intimate [1] /íntimət/ *a.* closely acquainted or familiar; having a sexual relationship (esp. outside marriage); private and personal. — *n.* intimate friend. **intimately** *adv.*, **intimacy** *n.*

intimate [2] /íntimayt/ *v.* make known, esp. by hinting. **intimation** *n.*

intimidate *v.* influence by frightening. **intimidation** *n.*

into *prep.* to the inside of, to a point within; to a particular state or occupation; dividing (a number) mathematically; (*colloq.*) interested and involved in.

intolerable *a.* unbearable. **intolerably** *adv.*, **intolerability** *n.*

intonation *n.* intoning; pitch of the voice in speaking.

intone *v.* chant, esp. on one note.

intoxicate *v.* make drunk; excite excessively. **intoxication** *n.*

intra- *pref.* within.

intractable *a.* hard to deal with or control. **intractability** *n.*

intransigent *a.* stubborn. **intransigently** *adv.*, **intransigence** *n.*

intra-uterine *a.* within the uterus.

intravenous *a.* into a vein. **intravenously** *adv.*

intrepid *a.* fearless, brave. **intrepidly** *adv.*, **intrepidity** *n.*

intricate *a.* very complicated. **intricately** *adv.*, **intricacy** *n.*

intrigue *v.* plot secretly; rouse the interest of. — *n.* underhand plot or plotting; secret love affair.

intrinsic *a.* belonging to the basic nature of. **intrinsically** *adv.*

introduce *v.* make (a person) known to another; present to an audience; bring into use; insert.

introduction *n.* introducing; introductory section or treatise.

introductory *a.* preliminary.

introspection *n.* examination of one's own thoughts and feelings. **introspective** *a.*

introvert *n.* introspective and shy person. **introverted** *a.*

intrude *v.* come or join in without being invited or wanted; thrust in. **intruder** *n.*, **intrusion** *n.*, **intrusive** *a.*

intuition *n.* power of knowing without learning or reasoning. **intuitive** *a.*, **intuitively** *adv.*

Inuit /ínyoo-it/ *n.* (*pl.* same or **-s**) North American Eskimo.

inundate *v.* flood. **inundation** *n.*

inure *v.* accustom, esp. to something unpleasant.

invade *v.* enter (territory) with hostile intent; crowd into; penetrate harmfully. **invader** *n.*

invalid [1] /ínvəleed/ *n.* person suffering from ill health.

invalid [2] /inválid/ *a.* not valid.

invalidate *v.* make no longer valid. **invalidation** *n.*

invaluable *a.* having value too great to be measured.

invariable *a.* not variable, always the same. **invariably** *adv.*

invasion *n.* hostile or harmful intrusion.

invective *n.* abusive language.

invent *v.* make or design (something new); make up (a lie, a story). **inventor** *n.*

inventive *a.* able to invent things. **inventiveness** *n.*

inventory *n.* detailed list of goods or furniture.

inverse *a.* inverted. **inversely** *adv.*

invert *v.* turn upside down; reverse the position, order, or relationship of. **inverted commas** quotation marks. **inversion** *n.*

invertebrate *a.* & *n.* (animal) having no backbone.

invest *v.* use (money, time, etc.) to earn interest or bring profit; confer rank or power upon; endow with a quality. **investment** *n.*, **investor** *n.*

investigate *v.* study carefully; inquire into. **investigation** *n.*, **investigator** *n.*, **investigative** *a.*

inveterate *a.* habitual; firmly established. **inveterately** *adv.*

invidious *a.* liable to cause resentment. **invidiously** *adv.*

invigilate *v.* supervise examination candidates. **invigilator** *n.*

invigorate *v.* fill with vigour, give strength or courage to.

invincible *a.* unconquerable. **invincibly** *adv.*, **invincibility** *n.*

invisible *a.* not able to be seen. **invisibly** *adv.*, **invisibility** *n.*

invite *v.* ask (a person) politely to come or to do something; ask for; attract. **invitation** *n.*

inviting *a.* pleasant and tempting. **invitingly** *adv.*

in vitro in a test-tube or other laboratory environment.

invoice *n.* bill for goods or services. — *v.* send an invoice to.

invoke *v.* call for the help or protection of; summon (a spirit).

involuntary *a.* done without intention. **involuntarily** *adv.*

involve *v.* have as a consequence; include or affect; implicate. **involvement** *n.*

involved *a.* complicated; concerned.

invulnerable *a.* not vulnerable. **invulnerability** *n.*

inward *a.* situated on or going towards the inside; in the mind or spirit. — *adv.* inwards. **inwardly** *adv.*, **inwards** *adv.*

iodine *n.* chemical used in solution as an antiseptic.

ion *n.* electrically charged particle. **ionic** *a.*

ionize *v.* convert or be converted into ions. **ionization** *n.*

ionosphere *n.* ionized region of the atmosphere. **ionospheric** *a.*

iota *n.* Greek letter i; very small amount.

IOU *n.* signed paper given as a receipt for money borrowed.

ir- *see* **in-**.

irascible *a.* hot-tempered. **irascibly** *adv.*, **irascibility** *n.*

irate *a.* angry. **irately** *adv.*

ire *n.* anger.

iridescent *a.* coloured like a rainbow; shimmering. **iridescence** *n.*

iris *n.* coloured part of the eyeball, round the pupil; lily-like flower.

Irish *a.* & *n.* (language) of Ireland. **Irishman** *n.* (*pl.* **-men**), **Irishwoman** *n.* (*pl.* **-women**).

irk *v.* annoy, be tiresome to.

irksome *a.* tiresome.

iron *n.* hard grey metal; tool etc. made of this; implement with a flat base heated for smoothing cloth or clothes; (*pl.*) fetters. — *a.* made of iron; strong as iron. — *v.* smooth (clothes etc.) with an iron. **ironing board** narrow folding table for ironing clothes on.

ironic, ironical *adjs.* using irony. **ironically** *adv.*

ironmonger *n.* shopkeeper selling tools and household implements.

ironstone *n.* hard iron ore; a kind of hard white pottery.

irony *n.* expression of meaning by use of words normally conveying the opposite; apparent perversity of fate or circumstances.

irradiate *v.* throw light or other radiation on; treat (food) by radiation. **irradiation** *n.*

irrecoverable *a.* unable to be recovered. **irrecoverably** *adv.*

irrefutable *a.* unable to be refuted. **irrefutably** *adv.*

irregular *a.* not regular; contrary to rules or custom. **irregularly** *adv.*, **irregularity** *n.*

irrelevant *a.* not relevant. **irrelevantly** *adv.*, **irrelevance** *n.*

irreparable *a.* unable to be repaired. **irreparably** *adv.*

irreplaceable *a.* unable to be replaced.

irrepressible *a.* unable to be repressed. **irrepressibly** *adv.*

irreproachable *a.* blameless, faultless. **irreproachably** *adv.*

irresistible *a.* too strong or delightful to be resisted. **irresistibly** *adv.*, **irresistibility** *n.*

irresolute *a.* unable to make up one's mind. **irresolutely** *adv.*, **irresolution** *n.*

irrespective *a.* **irrespective of** not taking (a thing) into account.

irresponsible *a.* not showing a proper sense of responsibility. **irresponsibly** *adv.*, **irresponsibility** *n.*

irreverent *a.* not reverent; not respectful. **irreverently** *adv.*, **irreverence** *n.*

irreversible *a.* not reversible, unable to be altered or revoked. **irreversibly** *adv.*, **irreversibility** *n.*

irrevocable *a.* unalterable. **irrevocably** *adv.*

irrigate *v.* supply (land) with water by streams, pipes, etc. **irrigation** *n.*

irritable *a.* easily annoyed, bad-tempered. **irritably** *adv.*, **irritability** *n.*

irritant *a.* & *n.* (thing) causing irritation.

irritate *v.* annoy; cause itching in. **irritation** *n.*

irrupt *v.* make a violent entry. **irruption** *n.*

Islam *n.* Muslim religion; Muslim world. **Islamic** *a.*

island *n.* piece of land surrounded by water.

islander *n.* inhabitant of an island.

isle *n.* island.

islet *n.* small island.

isobar *n.* line on a map, connecting places with the same atmospheric pressure. **isobaric** *a.*

isolate *v.* place apart or alone; separate from others or from a compound. **isolation** *n.*

isolationism *n.* policy of holding aloof from other countries or groups. **isolationist** *n.*

isosceles /īsóssileez/ *a.* (of a triangle) having two sides equal.

isotherm *n.* line on a map, connecting places with the same temperature.

isotope *n.* one of two or more forms of a chemical element differing in their atomic weight. **isotopic** *a.*

issue *n.* outflow; issuing, quantity issued; one edition (e.g. of a magazine); important topic; offspring. — *v.* flow out; supply for use; publish; send out.

isthmus /ísməss/ *n.* (*pl.* **-muses**) narrow strip of land connecting two larger masses of land.

it *pron.* thing mentioned or being discussed; impersonal subject of a verb.

Italian *a.* & *n.* (native, language) of Italy.

italic *a.* (of type) sloping like *this.* **italics** *n.pl.* italic type.

italicize *v.* print in italics.

itch *n.* tickling sensation in the skin, causing a desire to scratch; restless desire. — *v.* have or feel an itch. **itchy** *a.*

item *n.* single thing in a list or collection; single piece of news.

itemize *v.* list, state the individual items of. **itemization** *n.*

itinerant *a.* travelling.

itinerary *n.* route, list of places to be visited on a journey.

its *poss.pron.* of it.

it's = it is, it has.

itself *pron.* emphatic and reflexive form of *it.*

ivory *n.* hard creamy-white substance forming tusks of elephant etc.; object made of this; its colour. — *a.* creamy-white. **ivory tower** seclusion from the harsh realities of life.

ivy *n.* climbing evergreen shrub.

J

jab *v.* (**jabbed**) poke roughly. — *n.* rough poke; (*colloq.*) injection.

jabber *v.* talk rapidly, often unintelligibly. — *n.* jabbering talk.

jack *n.* portable device for raising heavy weights off the ground; playing card next below queen; ship's small flag showing nationality; electrical connection with a single plug; small ball aimed at in bowls; male donkey. — *v.* **jack up** raise with a jack.

jackal *n.* dog-like wild animal.

jackass *n.* male ass; stupid person. **laughing jackass** kookaburra.

jackboot *n.* large high boot.

jackdaw *n.* bird of the crow family.

jacket *n.* short coat usu. reaching to the hips; outer covering.

jackknife *n.* large folding knife. — *v.* fold accidentally.

jackpot *n.* large prize of money that has accumulated until won. **hit the jackpot** (*colloq.*) have a sudden success.

Jacobean *a.* of the reign of James I of England (1603–25).

Jacuzzi *n.* [P.] large bath with underwater jets of water.

jade *n.* hard green, blue, or white stone; its green colour.

jaded *a.* tired and bored.

jagged *a.* having sharp projections.

jaguar *n.* large flesh-eating animal of the cat family.

jail *n.* prison. — *v.* put into jail.

jailer *n.* person in charge of a jail or its prisoners.

jam [1] *n.* thick sweet substance made by boiling fruit with sugar. — *v.* (**jammed**) spread with jam; make into jam.

jam [2] *v.* (**jammed**) squeeze or wedge into a space; become wedged; crowd (an area); make (a broadcast) unintelligible by causing interference. — *n.* squeeze, crush; stoppage caused by jamming; crowded mass; (*colloq.*) difficult situation. **jam-packed** *a.* (*colloq.*) very full.

jamb *n.* side post of a door or window.

jamboree *n.* large party; rally.

jangle *n.* harsh metallic sound. — *v.* make or cause to make this sound; upset by discord.

janitor *n.* caretaker of a building.

japan *n.* hard usu. black varnish. — *v.* (**japanned**) coat with this.

Japanese *a.* & *n.* (native, language) of Japan.

jar [1] *n.* cylindrical glass or earthenware container.

jar [2] *v.* (**jarred**) jolt; have a harsh or disagreeable effect (upon). — *n.* jolt.

jargon *n.* words or expressions developed for use within a particular group of people.

jasmine *n.* shrub with white or yellow flowers.

jasper *n.* a kind of quartz.

jaundice *n.* condition in which the skin becomes abnormally yellow.

jaundiced *a.* affected by jaundice; filled with resentment.

jaunt *n.* short pleasure trip. — *v.* make a jaunt.

jaunty *a.* (**-ier**, **-iest**) cheerful, self-confident. **jauntily** *adv.*, **jauntiness** *n.*

javelin *n.* light spear.

jaw *n.* bone(s) forming the framework of the mouth; (*pl.*) gripping-parts; (*colloq.*) lengthy talk. — *v.* (*colloq.*) talk lengthily (to).

jay *n.* bird of the crow family.

jaywalking *n.* crossing a road carelessly. **jaywalker** *n.*

jazz *n.* type of music with strong rhythm and much syncopation.

jealous *a.* resentful towards a rival; taking watchful care. **jealously** *adv.*, **jealousy** *n.*

jeans *n.pl.* denim trousers.

Jeep *n.* [P.] small sturdy motor vehicle with four-wheel drive.

jeer *v.* laugh or shout rudely or scornfully (at). — *n.* jeering.

Jehovah *n.* name of God in the Old Testament.

jell *v.* (*colloq.*) set as a jelly; take definite form.

jelly *n.* soft solid food made of liquid set with gelatine; substance of similar consistency; jam made of strained fruit juice.

jellyfish *n.* sea animal with a jelly-like body.

jemmy *n.* burglar's short crowbar. — *v.* open with this.

jenny *n.* female donkey.

jeopardize /jéppərdīz/ *v.* endanger.

jeopardy /jéppərdi/ *n.* danger.

jerboa *n.* rat-like desert animal with long hind legs.

jerk *n.* sudden sharp movement or pull. — *v.* move, pull, or stop with jerk(s). **jerky** *a.*, **jerkily** *adv.*, **jerkiness** *n.*

jerkin *n.* sleeveless jacket.

jerrycan *n.* five-gallon can for petrol or water.

jersey *n.* (*pl.* **-eys**) knitted woollen pullover with sleeves; machine-knitted fabric.

jest *n.* & *v.* joke.

jester *n.* person who makes jokes; entertainer at a medieval court.

jet [1] *n.* hard black mineral; glossy black. **jet-black** *a.*

jet [2] *n.* stream of water, gas, or flame from a small opening; burner on a gas cooker; engine or aircraft using jet propulsion. — *v.* (**jetted**) travel by jet. **jet lag** delayed tiredness etc. after a long flight. **jet-propelled** *a.* using **jet propulsion**, propulsion by engines that send out a high-speed jet of gases at the back.

jetsam *n.* goods jettisoned by a ship and washed ashore.

jettison *v.* throw overboard, eject; discard.

jetty *n.* breakwater; landing-stage.

Jew *n.* person of Hebrew descent or whose religion is Judaism. **Jewish** *a.*

jewel *n.* precious stone cut or set as an ornament; person or thing that is highly valued. **jewelled** *a.*

jeweller *n.* person who makes or deals in jewels or jewellery.

jewellery *n.* jewels or similar ornaments to be worn.

Jewry *n.* the Jewish people.

jib *n.* triangular sail stretching forward from a mast; projecting arm of a crane. — *v.* (**jibbed**) refuse to proceed. **jib at** object to.

jig *n.* lively dance; device that holds work and guides tools working on it; template. — *v.* (**jigged**) move quickly up and down.

jiggery-pokery *n.* (*colloq.*) trickery.

jiggle *v.* rock or jerk lightly.

jigsaw *n.* machine fretsaw. **jigsaw puzzle** picture cut into pieces which are then shuffled and reassembled for amusement.

jilt *v.* abandon (a person) after having courted him or her.

jingle *v.* (cause to) make a ringing or clinking sound. — *n.* this sound; simple rhyme.

jingoism *n.* excessive patriotism and contempt for other countries. **jingoist** *n.*, **jingoistic** *a.*

jink *v.* dodge by a sudden turn. **high jinks** boisterous fun.

jinx *n.* (*colloq.*) influence causing bad luck.

jitters *n.pl.* (*colloq.*) nervousness. **jittery** *a.*

jive *n.* fast lively jazz; dance to this. — *v.* dance to this music.

job *n.* piece of work; paid position of employment; (*colloq.*) difficult task. **good** *or* **bad job** fortunate or unfortunate state of affairs. **job lot** miscellaneous articles sold together.

jobbing *a.* doing single pieces of work for payment.

jobless *a.* out of work.

jockey *n.* (*pl.* **-eys**) person who rides in horse races. — *v.* manoeuvre to gain advantage.

jocose *a.* joking. **jocosely** *adv.*, **jocosity** *n.*

jocular *a.* joking. **jocularly** *adv.*, **jocularity** *n.*

jocund *a.* merry, cheerful. **jocundity** *n.*

jodhpurs *n.pl.* riding-breeches fitting closely from knee to ankle.

jog *v.* (**jogged**) nudge; stimulate; run at a slow regular pace. — *n.* slow run; nudge. **jogger** *n.*

joggle *v.* shake slightly. — *n.* slight shake.

jogtrot *n.* slow regular trot.

joie de vivre /zhwaá də veévrə/ exuberant enjoyment of life.

join *v.* unite; connect; come into the company of; take one's place in; become a member of. — *n.* place where things join. **join up** enlist in the forces.

joiner *n.* maker of wooden doors, windows, etc. **joinery** *n.* this work.

joint *a.* shared by two or more people. — *n.* join; structure where parts or bones fit together; large piece of meat. — *v.* connect by joint(s); divide into joints. **out of joint** dislocated; in disorder. **jointly** *adv.*

jointure *n.* estate settled on a widow for her lifetime.

joist *n.* one of the beams supporting a floor or ceiling.

jojoba /hōhṓbə/ *n.* plant producing seeds containing oil used in cosmetics.

joke *n.* thing said or done to cause laughter; ridiculous person or thing. — *v.* make jokes.

joker *n.* person who jokes; extra playing card with no fixed value.

jollification *n.* merrymaking.

jollity *n.* being jolly; merrymaking.

jolly *a.* (**-ier, -iest**) cheerful, merry; very pleasant. — *adv.* (*colloq.*) very. — *v.* keep in good humour.

jolt *v.* shake or dislodge with a jerk; move jerkily; shock. — *n.* jolting movement; shock.

jonquil *n.* a kind of narcissus.

joss-stick *n.* thin stick that burns with a smell of incense.
jostle *v.* push roughly.
jot *n.* very small amount. — *v.* **(jotted)** write down briefly.
jotter *n.* notepad, notebook.
joule *n.* unit of energy.
journal *n.* daily record of events; newspaper or periodical.
journalese *n.* style of language used in inferior journalism.
journalist *n.* person employed in writing for a newspaper or magazine. **journalism** *n.* this work.
journey *n.* (*pl.* **-eys**) continued course of going or travelling. — *v.* make a journey.
joust *v.* & *n.* fight on horseback with lances.
jovial *a.* full of cheerful good humour. **jovially** *adv.*, **joviality** *n.*
jowl *n.* jaw, cheek; dewlap, loose skin on the throat.
joy *n.* deep emotion of pleasure; thing causing delight.
joyful *a.* full of joy. **joyfully** *adv.*, **joyfulness** *n.*
joyous *a.* joyful. **joyously** *adv.*
joyride *n.* (*colloq.*) car ride taken for pleasure, usu. without the owner's permission. **joyriding** *n.*
joystick *n.* aircraft's control lever; device for moving a cursor on a VDU screen.
jubilant *a.* rejoicing. **jubilantly** *adv.*, **jubilation** *n.*
jubilee *n.* special anniversary.
Judaic *a.* Jewish.
Judaism *n.* religion of the Jewish people, based on the teachings of the Old Testament and Talmud.
judder *v.* shake noisily or violently. — *n.* this movement.
judge *n.* public officer appointed to hear and try cases in law courts; person appointed to decide who has won a contest; person able to give an authoritative opinion. — *v.* try (a case) in a law court; act as judge of.
judgement *n.* (in law contexts **judgment**) judging; judge's decision. **judgemental** *a.*
judicial *a.* of the administration of justice; of a judge or judgement. **judicially** *adv.*
judiciary *n.* the whole body of judges in a country.
judicious *a.* judging wisely, showing good sense. **judiciously** *adv.*, **judiciousness** *n.*
judo *n.* Japanese system of unarmed combat. **judoist** *n.*
jug *n.* vessel with a handle and a shaped lip, for holding and pouring liquids. **jugful** *n.*
juggernaut *n.* very large transport vehicle; overwhelmingly powerful object or institution.
juggle *v.* toss and catch objects skilfully for entertainment; manipulate skilfully. **juggler** *n.*
jugular vein either of the two large veins in the neck.
juice *n.* fluid content of fruits, vegetables, or meat; fluid secreted by an organ of the body. **juicy** *a.*
ju-jitsu *n.* Japanese system of unarmed combat.
jukebox *n.* coin-operated record player.
julep *n.* drink of spirits and water flavoured esp. with mint.
jumble *v.* mix in a confused way. — *n.* jumbled articles; items for a jumble sale. **jumble sale** sale of miscellaneous second-hand articles to raise money for charity.
jumbo *n.* (*pl.* **-os**) very large thing. **jumbo jet** very large jet aircraft.
jump *v.* move up off the ground etc. by muscular movement of the legs; make a sudden upward movement; pass over by jumping; leave (rails or track) accidentally; pounce on. — *n.* jumping movement; sudden rise or change; gap in a series; obstacle to be jumped. **jump-lead** *n.* cable for conveying electric current from one battery through another. **jump suit** one-piece garment for the whole body. **jump the gun** act before the permitted time. **jump the queue** obtain something without waiting one's turn.
jumper [1] *n.* one who jumps.
jumper [2] *n.* knitted garment for the upper part of the body.
jumpy *a.* **(-ier, -iest)** nervous.
junction *n.* join; place where roads or railway lines unite.
juncture *n.* point of time, convergence of events.
jungle *n.* tropical forest with tangled vegetation; scene of ruthless struggle.
junior *a.* younger in age; lower in rank or authority; for younger children. — *n.* junior person.
juniper *n.* evergreen shrub with dark berries.
junk [1] *n.* useless or discarded articles, rubbish. **junk food** food with low nutritional value.
junk [2] *n.* flat-bottomed ship with sails, used in China seas.
junket *n.* sweet custard-like food made of milk and rennet.
junkie *n.* (*sl.*) drug addict.

junta *n.* group who combine to rule a country, esp. after a revolution.
jurisdiction *n.* authority to administer justice or exercise power.
jurist *n.* person skilled in law.
juror *n.* member of a jury.
jury *n.* group of people sworn to give a verdict on a case in a court of law.
jury-rigged *a.* with makeshift rigging.
just *a.* fair to all concerned; right in amount etc., deserved. — *adv.* exactly; by only a short amount etc.; only a moment ago; merely; positively. **just now** a very short time ago. **justly** *adv.*
justice *n.* just treatment, fairness; legal proceedings; judge.
justifiable *a.* able to be justified. **justifiably** *adv.*, **justifiability** *n.*
justify *v.* show to be right or reasonable; be sufficient reason for; adjust (a line of type) to fill a space neatly. **justification** *n.*
jut *v.* (**jutted**) project.
jute *n.* fibre from the bark of certain tropical plants.
juvenile *a.* youthful, childish; for young people. — *n.* young person. **juvenility** *n.*
juxtapose *v.* put (things) side by side. **juxtaposition** *n.*

K

kale *n.* cabbage with curly leaves.

kaleidoscope *n.* toy tube containing mirrors and coloured fragments reflected to produce changing patterns. **kaleidoscopic** *a.*

kamikaze /kámmikaázi/ *n.* (in the Second World War) Japanese explosive-laden aircraft deliberately crashed on its target.

kangaroo *n.* Australian marsupial that jumps along on its strong hind legs. **kangaroo court** court formed illegally by a group to settle disputes among themselves.

kaolin *n.* fine white clay used in porcelain and medicine.

kapok *n.* fluffy fibre used for padding things.

karate /kəraáti/ *n.* Japanese system of unarmed combat.

karma *n.* (in Buddhism & Hinduism) person's actions as affecting his or her next reincarnation.

kayak /kíak/ *n.* small covered canoe, esp. of Eskimos.

kc/s *abbr.* kilocycle(s) per second.

kebabs *n.pl.* small pieces of meat cooked on a skewer.

kedge *n.* small anchor. — *v.* move by hauling on a kedge.

kedgeree *n.* cooked dish of rice and fish or eggs.

keel *n.* timber or steel structure along the base of a ship. — *v.* overturn; become tilted.

keen *a.* sharp; penetrating; piercingly cold; intense; very eager. **keen on** (*colloq.*) liking greatly. **keenly** *adv.*, **keenness** *n.*

keep *v.* (**kept**) retain possession of, have charge of; remain or cause to remain in a specified state or position; detain; put aside for a future time; provide with food and other necessities; own and look after (animals); manage (a shop etc.); continue doing something; remain in good condition. — *n.* person's food and other necessities; strongly fortified structure in a castle. **keep house** look after a house or household. **keep up** progress at the same pace as others; continue; maintain.

keeper *n.* person who keeps or looks after something, custodian.

keeping *n.* custody, charge. **in keeping with** suited to.

keepsake *n.* thing kept in memory of the giver.

keg *n.* small barrel. **keg beer** beer from a pressurized metal container.

kelp *n.* large brown seaweed.

kelvin *n.* degree of the **Kelvin scale** of temperature which has zero at absolute zero (–273.15°C).

kendo *n.* Japanese sport of fencing with bamboo swords.

kennel *n.* shelter for a dog; (*pl.*) boarding place for dogs.

kept *see* **keep**.

kerb *n.* stone edging to a pavement.

kerchief *n.* square scarf worn on the head.

kerfuffle *n.* (*colloq.*) fuss, commotion.

kermes *n.* insect used in making a red dye.

kernel *n.* seed within a husk, nut, or fruit stone; central or important part.

kerosene *n.* paraffin oil.

kestrel *n.* a kind of small falcon.

ketch *n.* two-masted sailing boat.

ketchup *n.* thick sauce made from tomatoes and vinegar.

kettle *n.* container with a spout and handle, for boiling water in.

kettledrum *n.* drum with parchment stretched over a large metal bowl.

Kevlar *n.* [P.] strong synthetic fibre used to reinforce rubber etc.

key *n.* piece of metal shaped for moving the bolt of a lock, tightening a spring, etc.; thing giving access or control or insight; system of related notes in music; lever for a finger to press on a piano, typewriter, etc. **key up** stimulate, make nervously tense.

keyboard *n.* set of keys on a piano, typewriter, or computer. — *v.* enter (data) by using a keyboard. **keyboarder** *n.*

keyhole *n.* hole by which a key is put into a lock.

keynote *n.* note on which a key in music is based; prevailing tone.

keypad *n.* small keyboard or set of buttons for operating an electronic device, telephone, etc.

keyring *n.* ring on which keys are threaded.

keystone *n.* central stone of an arch, locking others into position.

keyword *n.* key to a cipher etc.

kg *abbr.* kilogram(s).

khaki *a.* & *n.* dull brownish-yellow, colour of military uniforms.

kHz *abbr.* kilohertz.
kibbutz *n.* (*pl.* **-im**) communal settlement in Israel.
kick *v.* strike or propel with the foot; (of a gun) recoil when fired. — *n.* act of kicking; blow with the foot; (*colloq.*) thrill, interest. **kick-off** *n.* start of a football game. **kick out** (*colloq.*) expel forcibly; dismiss. **kick-start** *n.* lever pressed with the foot to start a motor cycle. **kick up** (*colloq.*) create (a fuss or noise).
kid *n.* young goat; (*sl.*) child. — *v.* (**kidded**) (*colloq.*) hoax, tease.
kiddy *n.* (*sl.*) child.
kidnap *v.* (**kidnapped**) carry off (a person) illegally in order to obtain a ransom. **kidnapper** *n.*
kidney *n.* (*pl.* **-eys**) either of a pair of organs that remove waste products from the blood and secrete urine. **kidney bean** kidney-shaped bean.
kill *v.* cause the death of; put an end to; spend (time) unprofitably by waiting. — *n.* killing; animal(s) killed by a hunter. **killer** *n.*
killjoy *n.* person who spoils the enjoyment of others.
kiln *n.* oven for hardening or drying things (e.g. pottery, hops).
kilo *n.* (*pl.* **-os**) kilogram.
kilo- *pref.* one thousand.
kilocycle *n.* 1000 cycles as a unit of wave frequency; kilohertz.
kilogram *n.* unit of weight or mass in the metric system (2.205 lb).
kilohertz *n.* unit of frequency of electromagnetic waves, = 1000 cycles per second.
kilometre *n.* 1000 metres (0.62 mile).
kilovolt *n.* 1000 volts.
kilowatt *n.* 1000 watts.
kilt *n.* knee-length pleated skirt of tartan wool, esp. as part of Highland man's dress.
kimono *n.* (*pl.* **-os**) loose Japanese robe worn with a sash; dressing gown resembling this.
kin *n.* person's relatives.
kind ¹ *n.* class of similar things. **in kind** (of payment) in goods etc. not money.
kind ² *a.* gentle and considerate towards others. **kind-hearted** *a.*, **kindness** *n.*
kindergarten *n.* school for very young children.
kindle *v.* set on fire; arouse, stimulate; become kindled.
kindling *n.* small pieces of wood for lighting fires.
kindly *a.* (**-ier**, **-iest**) kind. — *adv.* in a kind way; please. **kindliness** *n.*
kindred *n.* kin. — *a.* related; of similar kind.
kinetic *a.* of movement.
king *n.* male ruler of a country by right of birth; man or thing regarded as supreme; chess piece to be protected; playing card next above queen. **king-size, king-sized** *adjs.* extra large. **kingly** *a.*, **kingship** *n.*
kingdom *n.* country ruled by a king or queen; division of the natural world.
kingfisher *n.* small bird that dives to catch fish.
kingpin *n.* indispensable person or thing.
kink *n.* short twist in thread or wire etc.; mental peculiarity. — *v.* form or cause to form kink(s). **kinky** *a.*
kinsfolk *n.pl.* kin. **kinsman** *n.* (*pl.* **-men**), **kinswoman** *n.fem.* (*pl.* **-women**).
kiosk *n.* booth where newspapers or refreshments are sold, or containing a public telephone.
kipper *n.* smoked herring.
kirk *n.* (*Sc.*) church.
kirsch /keersh/ *n.* colourless liqueur made from wild cherries.
kismet *n.* destiny, fate.
kiss *n.* & *v.* touch or caress with the lips.
kissogram *n.* novelty greetings message delivered with a kiss.
kit *n.* outfit of clothing, tools, etc.; set of parts to be assembled. — *v.* (**kitted**) equip with kit.
kitbag *n.* bag for holding kit.
kitchen *n.* room where meals are prepared. **kitchen garden** vegetable garden.
kitchenette *n.* small kitchen.
kite *n.* large bird of the hawk family; light framework on a string, for flying in the wind as a toy.
kith *n.* **kith and kin** relatives.
kitsch /kich/ *n.* worthless pretentiousness in art; art showing this.
kitten *n.* young of cat, rabbit, or ferret. **kittenish** *a.*
kitty *n.* communal fund.
kiwi *n.* (*pl.* **-is**) New Zealand bird that does not fly.
kleptomania *n.* compulsive desire to steal. **kleptomaniac** *n.*
km *abbr.* kilometre(s).
knack *n.* ability to do something skilfully.
knacker *n.* person who buys and slaughters useless horses. — *v.* (*sl.*) kill; exhaust.
knapsack *n.* bag worn strapped on the back.
knave *n.* (*old use*) rogue; jack in playing cards.
knead *v.* press and stretch (dough) with the hands; massage with similar movements.

knee *n.* joint between the thigh and the lower part of the leg; part of a garment covering this. — *v.* (**kneed**) touch or strike with the knee. **knee-jerk** *a.* (of a reaction) automatic and predictable. **knees-up** *n.* (*colloq.*) lively party.

kneecap *n.* small bone over the front of the knee. — *v.* (**kneecapped**) shoot in the knee as a punishment.

kneel *v.* (**knelt**) lower one's body to rest on the knees.

knell *n.* sound of a bell tolled after a death or at a funeral.

knelt *see* **kneel**.

knew *see* **know**.

knickerbockers *n.pl.* loose breeches gathered in at the knee.

knickers *n.pl.* woman's or girl's undergarment for the lower body, with separate legs or leg-holes.

knick-knack *n.* small ornament.

knife *n.* (*pl.* **knives**) cutting instrument with a sharp blade and a handle. — *v.* cut or stab with a knife.

knight *n.* man given a rank below baronet, with the title 'Sir'; chess piece shaped like horse's head. — *v.* confer a knighthood on.

knighthood *n.* rank of knight.

knit *v.* (**knitted** *or* **knit**) form (yarn) into fabric of interlocking loops; make in this way; grow together so as to unite. **knitter** *n.*, **knitting** *n.*

knob *n.* rounded projecting part, esp. as a handle; small lump. **knobby** *a.*, **knobbly** *a.*

knock *v.* strike with an audible sharp blow; strike a door to gain admittance; drive or make by knocking; (*sl.*) criticize insultingly. — *n.* act or sound of knocking; sharp blow. **knock about** treat roughly; wander casually. **knock-down** *a.* (of price) very low. **knock-kneed** *a.* having an abnormal inward curvature of the legs at the knees (**knock knees**). **knock off** (*colloq.*) cease work; complete quickly; (*sl.*) steal. **knock-on effect** secondary or cumulative effect. **knockout** *n.* knocking a person out; (*colloq.*) outstanding or irresistible person or thing. **knock out** make unconscious; eliminate; disable. **knock up** rouse by knocking at a door; make or arrange hastily. **knock-up** *n.* practice or casual game at tennis etc.

knocker *n.* one who knocks; hinged flap for rapping on a door.

knoll *n.* hillock, mound.

knot *n.* intertwining of one or more pieces of thread or rope etc. as a fastening; tangle; hard mass esp. where a branch joins a tree trunk; round spot in timber; cluster; unit of speed used by ships and aircraft, = one nautical mile per hour. — *v.* (**knotted**) tie or fasten with a knot; entangle.

knotty *a.* (**-ier, -iest**) full of knots; puzzling, difficult.

know *v.* (**knew, known**) have in one's mind or memory; feel certain; recognize, be familiar with; understand. **in the know** (*colloq.*) having inside information. **know-all** *n.* person who behaves as if he knows everything. **know-how** *n.* practical knowledge or skill.

knowing *a.* aware; cunning. **knowingly** *adv.*

knowledge *n.* knowing about things; all a person knows; all that is known, information.

knowledgeable *a.* intelligent; well-informed.

knuckle *n.* finger-joint; animal's leg-joint as meat. — *v.* **knuckle under** yield, submit.

knuckleduster *n.* metal device worn over the knuckles to increase the effect of a blow.

koala *n.* **koala bear** Australian tree-climbing animal with thick grey fur.

kohl *n.* powder used to darken the eyelids.

kohlrabi *n.* cabbage with a turnip-like edible stem.

kookaburra *n.* Australian giant kingfisher with a harsh cry.

kopeck *n.* Russian coin, one-hundredth of a rouble.

Koran *n.* sacred book of Muslims, containing the revelations of Muhammad.

kosher *a.* conforming to Jewish dietary laws.

kowtow *v.* behave with exaggerated respect.

k.p.h. *abbr.* kilometres per hour.

krill *n.* tiny plankton crustaceans that are food for whales etc.

kudos *n.* (*colloq.*) honour and glory.

kudu *n.* African antelope.

kummel /koŏ mm'l/ *n.* liqueur flavoured with caraway seeds.

kumquat *n.* tiny variety of orange.

kung fu Chinese form of unarmed combat similar to karate.

Kurd *n.* member of a people of SW Asia. **Kurdish** *a.*

kV *abbr.* kilovolt(s).

kW *abbr.* kilowatt(s).

L

l *abbr.* litre(s).

lab *n.* (*colloq.*) laboratory.

label *n.* note fixed on or beside an object to show its nature, destination, etc. — *v.* (**labelled**) fix a label to; describe as. **labeller** *n.*

labial *a.* of the lips.

laboratory *n.* room or building equipped for scientific work.

laborious *a.* needing or showing much effort. **laboriously** *adv.*

labour *n.* work, exertion; contractions of the womb at childbirth; workers. — *v.* work hard; emphasize lengthily.

laboured *a.* showing signs of great effort, not spontaneous.

labourer *n.* person employed to do unskilled work.

Labrador *n.* dog of the retriever breed with a black or golden coat.

laburnum *n.* tree with hanging clusters of yellow flowers.

labyrinth *n.* maze. **labyrinthine** *a.*

lace *n.* ornamental openwork fabric or trimming; cord etc. threaded through holes or hooks to pull opposite edges together. — *v.* fasten with lace(s); intertwine; add a dash of spirits to (drink).

lacerate *v.* tear (flesh); wound (feelings). **laceration** *n.*

lachrymose *a.* tearful.

lack *n.* state or fact of not having something. — *v.* be without.

lackadaisical *a.* lacking vigour or determination, unenthusiastic.

lackey *n.* (*pl.* **-eys**) footman, servant; servile follower.

lacking *a.* undesirably absent; without.

lacklustre *a.* lacking brightness or enthusiasm.

laconic *a.* terse. **laconically** *adv.*

lacquer *n.* hard glossy varnish. — *v.* coat with lacquer.

lactation *n.* suckling; secretion of milk.

lacy *a.* (**-ier, -iest**) of or like lace.

lad *n.* boy, young fellow.

ladder *n.* set of crossbars between uprights, used as a means of climbing; vertical ladder-like flaw where stitches become undone in a stocking etc. — *v.* cause or develop a ladder (in).

laden *a.* loaded.

ladle *n.* deep long-handled spoon for transferring liquids. — *v.* transfer with a ladle.

lady *n.* woman, esp. of good social position; well-mannered woman; **Lady** title of wives, widows, or daughters of certain noblemen. **lady-in-waiting** *n.* lady attending a queen or princess.

ladybird *n.* small flying beetle, usu. red with black spots.

ladylike *a.* polite and appropriate to a lady.

ladyship *n.* title used of or to a woman with rank of *Lady.*

lag [1] *v.* (**lagged**) go too slow, not keep up. — *n.* lagging, delay.

lag [2] *v.* (**lagged**) encase in material that prevents loss of heat.

lager *n.* light beer. **lager lout** (*colloq.*) youth behaving badly after drinking.

laggard *n.* person who lags behind.

lagging *n.* material used to lag a boiler etc.

lagoon *n.* salt-water lake beside a sea; freshwater lake beside a river or larger lake.

laid *see* **lay** [2].

lain *see* **lie** [2].

lair *n.* place where a wild animal rests.

laird *n.* (*Sc.*) landowner.

laissez-faire /léssayfáir/ *n.* policy of non-interference.

laity *n.* laymen.

lake [1] *n.* large body of water surrounded by land.

lake [2] *n.* reddish pigment.

lam *v.* (**lammed**) (*sl.*) hit hard.

lama *n.* Buddhist priest in Tibet and Mongolia.

lamb *n.* young sheep; its flesh as food; gentle or endearing person. — *v.* give birth to a lamb.

lambaste *v.* (*colloq.*) thrash; reprimand severely.

lame *a.* unable to walk normally; weak, unconvincing. — *v.* make lame. **lame duck** person etc. unable to manage without help. **lamely** *adv.*, **lameness** *n.*

lamé /laámay/ *n.* fabric with gold or silver thread interwoven.

lament *n.* passionate expression of grief; song or poem expressing grief. — *v.* feel or express grief or regret. **lamentation** *n.*

lamentable *a.* regrettable, deplorable. **lamentably** *adv.*

laminate *n.* laminated material.

laminated *a.* made of layers joined one upon another.

lamp *n.* device for giving light.

lamplight *n.* light from a lamp.

lampoon *n.* piece of writing that attacks a person by ridiculing him. — *v.* ridicule in a lampoon.

lamppost *n.* tall post of a street lamp.

lamprey *n.* (*pl.* **-eys**) small eel-like water animal.

lampshade *n.* shade placed over a lamp to screen its light.

lance *n.* long spear. — *v.* prick or cut open with a lancet. **lance-corporal** *n.* army rank below corporal.

lanceolate *a.* tapering to each end like a spearhead.

lancet *n.* surgeon's pointed two-edged knife; tall narrow pointed arch or window.

land *n.* part of earth's surface not covered by water; expanse of this; ground, soil; country, State; (*pl.*) estates. — *v.* set or go ashore; come or bring to the ground; bring to or reach a place or situation; deal (a person) a blow; bring (a fish) to land; obtain (a prize, appointment, etc.). **landlocked** *a.* surrounded by land.

landau /lándaw/ *n.* a kind of horse-drawn carriage.

landed *a.* owning land; consisting of land.

landfall *n.* approach to land after a journey by sea or air.

landfill *n.* waste material etc. used in landscaping or reclaiming ground; use of this.

landing *n.* coming or bringing ashore or to ground; place for this; level area at the top of a flight of stairs. **landing-stage** *n.* platform for landing from a boat.

landlord *n.* man who lets land or a house or room to a tenant; one who keeps an inn or boarding house. **landlady** *n.fem.*

landlubber *n.* person not accustomed to the sea and seamanship.

landmark *n.* conspicuous feature of a landscape; event marking a stage in a thing's history.

landscape *n.* scenery of a land area; picture of this. — *v.* lay out (an area) attractively with natural-looking features.

landslide *n.* landslip; overwhelming majority of votes.

landslip *n.* sliding down of a mass of land on a slope.

landward *a.* & *adv.* towards the land. **landwards** *adv.*

lane *n.* narrow road, track, or passage; strip of road for a single line of traffic; track to which ships or aircraft etc. must keep.

language *n.* words and their use; system of this used by a nation or group.

languid *a.* lacking vigour or vitality. **languidly** *adv.*

languish *v.* lose or lack vitality; live under miserable conditions.

languor *n.* state of being languid; tender mood or effect. **languorous** *a.*, **languorously** *adv.*

lank *a.* tall and lean; straight and limp. **lanky** *a.*, **lankiness** *n.*

lanolin *n.* fat extracted from sheep's wool, used in ointments.

lantern *n.* transparent case for holding and shielding a light.

lanyard *n.* short rope for securing things on a ship; cord for hanging a whistle etc. round the neck or shoulder.

lap [1] *n.* flat area over the thighs of a seated person; single circuit; section of a journey. — *v.* (**lapped**) wrap round; be lap(s) ahead of (a competitor). **lap-dog** *n.* small pampered dog.

lap [2] *v.* (**lapped**) take up (liquid) by movements of tongue; flow (against) with ripples.

lapel *n.* flap folded back at the front of a coat etc.

lapidary *a.* of stones.

lapis lazuli blue semiprecious stone.

Lapp *n.* native or language of Lapland.

lapse *v.* fail to maintain one's position or standard; become void or no longer valid. — *n.* slight error; lapsing; passage of time.

laptop *n.* portable microcomputer.

lapwing *n.* kind of plover.

larch *n.* deciduous tree of the pine family.

lard *n.* white greasy substance prepared from pig-fat. — *v.* put strips of fat bacon in or on (meat) before cooking.

larder *n.* storeroom for food.

large *a.* of great size or extent. **at large** free to roam about; in general. **largeness** *n.*

largely *adv.* to a great extent.

largess *n.* (also **largesse**) money or gifts generously given.

lariat *n.* lasso.

lark [1] *n.* small brown bird, skylark.

lark [2] *n.* light-hearted adventurous action; amusing incident; activity. — *v.* play light-heartedly.

larkspur *n.* plant with spur-shaped blue or pink flowers.

larva *n.* (*pl.* **-vae**) insect in the first stage after coming out of the egg. **larval** *a.*

laryngitis *n.* inflammation of the larynx.

larynx *n.* part of the throat containing the vocal cords. **laryngeal** *a.*

lasagne /ləsányə/ *n.pl.* pasta in wide ribbon-like strips.

lascivious *a.* lustful. **lasciviously** *adv.*, **lasciviousness** *n.*

laser *n.* device emitting an intense narrow beam of light.

lash *v.* move in a whip-like movement; beat with a whip; strike violently; fasten with a cord etc. — *n.* flexible part of a whip; stroke with this; eyelash. **lash out** attack with blows or words; spend lavishly.

lashings *n.pl.* (*colloq.*) a lot.

lass, lassie *ns.* (*Sc.* & *N. Engl.*) girl, young woman.

lassitude *n.* tiredness, listlessness.

lasso *n.* (*pl.* **-oes**) rope with a noose for catching cattle. — *v.* (**lassoed, lassoing**) catch with a lasso.

last [1] *n.* foot-shaped block used in making and repairing shoes.

last [2] *a.* & *adv.* coming after all others; most recent(ly). — *n.* last person or thing. **at last, at long last** after much delay. **last post** military bugle-call sounded at sunset or military funerals. **last straw** slight addition to difficulties, making them unbearable. **last word** final statement in a dispute; latest fashion.

last [3] *v.* continue, endure; suffice for a period of time. **lasting** *a.*

lastly *adv.* finally.

latch *n.* bar lifted from its catch by a lever, used to fasten a gate etc.; spring-lock that catches when a door is closed. — *v.* fasten with a latch.

latchkey *n.* key of an outer door.

late *a.* & *adv.* after the proper or usual time; far on in a day or night or period; recent; no longer living or holding a position. **of late** lately. **lateness** *n.*

lately *adv.* recently.

latent *a.* existing but not active or developed or visible. **latency** *n.*

lateral *a.* of, at, to, or from the side(s). **laterally** *adv.*

latex *n.* milky fluid from certain plants, esp. the rubber tree; similar synthetic substance.

lath *n.* (*pl.* **laths**) narrow thin strip of wood, e.g. in trellis.

lathe *n.* machine for holding and turning pieces of wood or metal etc. while they are worked.

lather *n.* froth from soap and water; frothy sweat. — *v.* cover with or form lather.

Latin *n.* language of the ancient Romans. — *a.* of or in Latin; speaking a language based on Latin. **Latin America** parts of Central and South America where Spanish or Portuguese is the main language.

latitude *n.* distance of a place from the equator, measured in degrees; region; freedom from restrictions. **latitudinal** *a.*

latrine *n.* lavatory in a camp or barracks.

latter *a.* mentioned after another; nearer to the end; recent. **latter-day** *a.* modern, recent.

latterly *adv.* recently; nowadays.

lattice *n.* framework of crossed strips.

laudable *a.* praiseworthy.

laudanum *n.* opium prepared for use as a sedative.

laudatory *a.* praising.

laugh *v.* make sounds and movements of the face that express amusement or scorn; treat with a laugh. — *n.* act or manner of laughing; (*colloq.*) amusing incident. **laughing-stock** *n.* person or thing that is ridiculed.

laughable *a.* ridiculous.

laughter *n.* act or sound of laughing.

launch [1] *v.* put or go into action; cause (a ship) to slide into the water. — *n.* process of launching something. **launcher** *n.*

launch [2] *n.* large motor boat.

launder *v.* wash and iron (clothes etc.); (*colloq.*) transfer (funds) to conceal their origin.

launderette *n.* establishment fitted with washing machines to be used for a fee.

laundry *n.* place where clothes etc. are laundered; batch of clothes etc. sent to or from this.

laurel *n.* evergreen shrub with smooth glossy leaves; (*pl.*) victories or honours gained.

lava *n.* flowing or hardened molten rock from a volcano.

lavatory *n.* fixture into which urine and faeces are discharged for disposal; room equipped with this.

lavender *n.* shrub with fragrant purple flowers; light purple. **lavender-water** *n.* delicate perfume made from lavender.

laver *n.* edible seaweed.

lavish *a.* giving or producing something in large quantities; plentiful. — *v.* bestow lavishly. **lavishly** *adv.*, **lavishness** *n.*

law *n.* rule(s) established by authority or custom; their influence or operation; statement of what always happens in certain circumstances. **law-abiding** *a.* obeying the law. **lawgiver** *n.*

lawful *a.* permitted or recognized by law. **lawfully** *adv.*, **lawfulness** *n.*

lawless *a.* disregarding the law, uncontrolled. **lawlessness** *n.*

lawn [1] *n.* fine woven cotton fabric.

lawn [2] *n.* area of closely cut grass. **lawnmower** *n.* machine for cutting the grass of lawns. **lawn tennis** (*see* **tennis**).

lawsuit *n.* process of bringing a problem or claim etc. before a court of law for settlement.

lawyer *n.* person trained and qualified in legal matters.

lax *a.* slack, not strict or severe. **laxity** *n.*

laxative *a.* & *n.* (medicine) stimulating the bowels to empty.

lay [1] *a.* not ordained into the clergy; non-professional.

lay [2] *v.* **(laid)** place on a surface; arrange ready for use; cause to be in a certain condition; (of a hen) produce (an egg or eggs). — *n.* way a thing lies. **lay about one** hit out on all sides. **lay bare** expose, reveal. **lay into** (*sl.*) thrash; scold harshly. **lay off** discharge (workers) temporarily; (*colloq.*) cease. **lay-off** *n.* temporary discharge. **lay on** provide. **lay out** arrange; prepare (a body) for burial; spend (money) for a purpose; knock unconscious. **lay up** store; cause (a person) to be ill. **lay waste** devastate (an area).

lay [3] *see* **lie** [2].

layabout *n.* loafer, one who lazily avoids working for a living.

lay-by *n.* strip of road beside a carriageway, where vehicles may stop.

layer *n.* one thickness of material laid over a surface; attached shoot fastened down to take root; one who lays something. — *v.* arrange in layers; propagate (a plant) by layers.

layette *n.* outfit for a newborn baby.

lay figure artist's jointed model of the human body.

layman *n.* (*pl.* **-men**) non-professional person.

layout *n.* arrangement of parts etc. according to a plan.

laze *v.* spend time idly. — *n.* act or period of lazing.

lazy *a.* **(-ier, -iest)** unwilling to work, doing little work; showing lack of energy. **lazybones** *n.* (*colloq.*) lazy person. **lazily** *adv.*, **laziness** *n.*

lb *abbr.* pound(s) weight.

lea *n.* (*poetic*) piece of meadow etc.

leach *v.* percolate (liquid) through soil etc.; remove (soluble matter) or be removed in this way.

lead [1] /leed/ *v.* **(led)** guide; influence into an action, opinion, or state; be a route or means of access; pass (one's life); be or go first; be ahead. — *n.* guidance; clue; leading place, amount by which one competitor is in front; wire conveying electric current; strap or cord for leading an animal; chief role in a play etc. **lead up to** serve as introduction to or preparation for; direct conversation towards. **leading question** one worded to prompt the desired answer.

lead [2] /led/ *n.* heavy grey metal; graphite in a pencil; lump of lead used for sounding depths; (*pl.*) strips of lead.

leaden *a.* made of lead; heavy, slow-moving; dark grey.

leader *n.* one that leads; newspaper article giving editorial opinions. **leadership** *n.*

leaf *n.* flat (usu. green) organ growing from the stem, branch, or root of a plant; single thickness of paper as a page of a book; very thin sheet of metal; hinged flap or extra section of a table. — *v.* **leaf through** turn over the leaves of (a book). **leaf-mould** *n.* soil or compost consisting of decayed leaves.

leaflet *n.* small leaf of a plant; printed sheet of paper giving information. — *v.* **(leafleted)** distribute leaflets to.

leafy *a.* **(-ier, -iest)** with many leaves.

league *n.* union of people or countries; association of sports clubs which compete against each other; class of contestants. **in league with** conspiring with.

leak *n.* hole through which liquid or gas makes its way wrongly; liquid etc. passing through this; process of leaking; similar escape of an electric charge; disclosure of secret information. — *v.* escape or let out from a container; disclose. **leak out** become known. **leakage** *n.*, **leaky** *a.*

lean [1] *a.* without much flesh; (of meat) with little or no fat; scanty. — *n.* lean part of meat. **leanness** *n.*

lean [2] *v.* **(leaned, leant)** put or be in a sloping position; rest against; have leanings. **lean on** depend on for help; (*colloq.*) influence by intimidating. **lean-to** *n.* shed etc. against the side of a building.

leaning *n.* inclination, preference.

leap *v.* **(leaped, leapt)** jump vigorously. — *n.* vigorous jump. **leap year** year with an extra day (29 Feb.).

leap-frog *n.* game in which each player vaults over another who is bending down. — *v.* **(-frogged)** perform this vault (over); overtake alternately.

learn *v.* **(learned** *or* **learnt)** gain knowledge of or skill in; become aware of. **learner** *n.*

learned /lérnid/ *a.* having or showing great learning.

learning *n.* knowledge obtained by study.

lease *n.* contract allowing the use of land or a building for a specified time. — *v.* allow, obtain, or hold by lease. **leasehold** *n.*, **leaseholder** *n.*

leash *n.* dog's lead.

least *a.* smallest in amount or degree; lowest in importance. — *n.* least amount etc. — *adv.* in the least degree.

leather *n.* material made by treating animal

skins; piece of soft leather for polishing with. — *v.* thrash. **leather-jacket** *n.* crane-fly grub with tough skin.

leathery *a.* leather-like; tough.

leave *v.* (**left**) go away (from); go away finally or permanently; let remain; deposit; entrust with; abandon. — *n.* permission; official permission to be absent from duty, period for which this lasts. **on leave** absent in this way. **leave out** not insert or include.

leaven *n.* raising agent; enlivening influence. — *v.* add leaven to; enliven.

lecher *n.* lecherous man.

lechery *n.* unrestrained indulgence in sexual lust. **lecherous** *a.*

lectern *n.* stand with a sloping top from which a bible etc. is read.

lecture *n.* speech giving information about a subject; lengthy reproof or warning. — *v.* give lecture(s); reprove at length. **lecturer** *n.*

led *see* **lead** [1].

ledge *n.* narrow horizontal projection; narrow shelf.

ledger *n.* book used as an account book.

lee *n.* sheltered side, shelter in this.

leech *n.* small blood-sucking worm.

leek *n.* plant related to the onion, with a cylindrical white bulb.

leer *v.* look slyly or maliciously or lustfully. — *n.* leering look.

lees *n.pl.* sediment in wine.

leeward *a.* & *n.* (on) the side away from the wind.

leeway *n.* degree of freedom of action.

left [1] *see* **leave**.

left [2] *a.* & *adv.* of, on, or to the side or region opposite right. — *n.* left side or region; left hand or foot; people supporting a more extreme form of socialism than others in their group. **left-handed** *a.* using the left hand.

leftovers *n.pl.* things remaining when the rest is finished.

leg *n.* each of the limbs on which a person, animal, etc., stands or moves; part of a garment covering a person's leg; projecting support of piece of furniture; one section of a journey or contest.

legacy *n.* thing left to someone in a will, or handed down by a predecessor.

legal *a.* of or based on law; authorized or required by law. **legalistic** *a.*, **legally** *adv.*, **legality** *n.*

legalize *v.* make legal. **legalization** *n.*

legate *n.* envoy.

legatee *n.* recipient of a legacy.

legation *n.* diplomatic minister and staff; their headquarters.

legend *n.* story handed down from the past; such stories collectively; inscription on a coin or medal.

legendary *a.* of or described in legend; (*colloq.*) famous.

legerdemain /léjərdəmáyn/ *n.* sleight of hand.

legible *a.* clear enough to be deciphered, readable. **legibly** *adv.*, **legibility** *n.*

legion *n.* division of the ancient Roman army; organized group; multitude.

legionnaire *n.* member of a legion. **legionnaires' disease** form of bacterial pneumonia.

legislate *v.* make laws. **legislator** *n.*

legislation *n.* legislating; law(s) made.

legislative *a.* making laws.

legislature *n.* country's legislative assembly.

legitimate *a.* in accordance with a law or rule; justifiable; born of parents married to each other. **legitimately** *adv.*, **legitimacy** *n.*

legitimize *v.* make legitimate. **legitimization** *n.*

legless *a.* without legs; (*sl.*) drunk.

legume *n.* leguminous plant; pod of this.

leguminous *a.* of the family of plants bearing seeds in pods.

leisure *n.* time free from work. **at one's leisure** when one has time.

leisured *a.* having plenty of leisure.

leisurely *a.* & *adv.* without hurry.

lemming *n.* mouse-like Arctic rodent (said to rush headlong into the sea and drown in its migration).

lemon *n.* oval fruit with acid juice; tree bearing it; pale yellow colour; (*colloq.*) unsatisfactory person or thing. **lemony** *a.*

lemonade *n.* lemon-flavoured soft drink.

lemon sole a kind of plaice.

lemur *n.* nocturnal monkey-like animal of Madagascar.

lend *v.* (**lent**) give or allow to use temporarily; provide (money) temporarily in return for payment of interest; contribute as a help or effect. **lend itself to** be suitable for. **lender** *n.*

length *n.* measurement or extent from end to end; great extent; piece (of cloth etc.). **at length** after or taking a long time.

lengthen *v.* make or become longer.

lengthways *adv.* in the direction of a thing's length. **lengthwise** *adv.* & *a.*

lengthy *a.* (**-ier, -iest**) very long; long and boring. **lengthily** *adv.*

lenient *a.* merciful, not severe. **leniently** *adv.*, **lenience** *n.*

lens *n.* piece of glass or similar substance shaped for use in an optical instrument; transparent part of the eye, behind the pupil.

Lent *n.* Christian period of fasting and repentance before Easter.

lent *see* **lend**.

lentil *n.* a kind of bean.

leonine *a.* of or like a lion.

leopard /léppərd/ *n.* large flesh-eating animal of the cat family, with a dark-spotted yellowish or a black coat. **leopardess** *n.fem.*

leotard *n.* close-fitting garment worn by acrobats etc.

leper *n.* person with leprosy.

leprechaun *n.* (in Irish folklore) elf resembling a little old man.

leprosy *n.* infectious disease affecting the skin and nerves and causing deformities. **leprous** *a.*

lesbian *a.* & *n.* homosexual (woman). **lesbianism** *n.*

lesion *n.* harmful change in the tissue of an organ of the body.

less *a.* not so much of; smaller in amount or degree. — *adv.* to a smaller extent. — *n.* smaller amount. — *prep.* minus.

lessee *n.* person holding property by lease.

lessen *v.* make or become less.

lesser *a.* not so great as the other.

lesson *n.* amount of teaching given at one time; thing to be learnt by a pupil; experience by which one can learn; passage from the Bible read aloud in church.

lessor *n.* person who lets property on lease.

lest *conj.* for fear that.

let *v.* (**let, letting**) allow or cause to; allow the use of (rooms or land) in return for payment. — *v.aux.* (used in requests, commands, assumptions, or challenges). — *n.* letting of property etc. **let alone** refrain from interfering with or doing; not to mention. **let down** let out air from (a tyre etc.); fail to support, disappoint. **let-down** *n.* disappointment. **let in** allow to enter; insert. **let off** fire or explode (a weapon etc.); excuse from. **let on** (*sl.*) reveal a secret. **let out** allow to go out; make looser. **let up** (*colloq.*) relax.

lethal *a.* causing death.

lethargy *n.* extreme lack of energy or vitality. **lethargic** *a.*, **lethargically** *adv.*

letter *n.* symbol representing a speech sound; written message, usu. sent by post; (*pl.*) literature. — *v.* inscribe letters (on). **letter box** slit in a door, with a movable flap, through which letters are delivered; postbox.

letterhead *n.* printed heading on stationery; stationery with this.

lettuce *n.* plant with broad crisp leaves used as salad.

leucocyte *n.* white blood cell.

leukaemia /lookeémiə/ *n.* disease in which leucocytes multiply uncontrollably.

levee *n.* (*US*) embankment against floods; quay.

level *a.* horizontal; without projections or hollows; on a level with; steady, uniform. — *n.* horizontal line or plane; device for testing this; measured height or value etc.; relative position; level surface or area. — *v.* (**levelled**) make or become level; knock down (a building); aim (a gun etc.). **level crossing** place where a road and railway cross at the same level. **level-headed** *a.* sensible. **level pegging** equality in score. **on the level** honest(ly).

lever *n.* bar pivoted on a fixed point to lift something; pivoted handle used to operate machinery; means of power or influence. — *v.* use a lever; lift by this.

leverage *n.* action or power of a lever; power, influence.

leveret /lévvərit/ *n.* young hare.

leviathan *n.* thing of enormous size and power.

levitate *v.* rise or cause to rise and float in the air. **levitation** *n.*

levity *n.* humorous attitude.

levy *v.* impose (payment) or collect (an army etc.) by authority or force. — *n.* levying; payment or (*pl.*) troops levied.

lewd *a.* treating sexual matters vulgarly; lascivious. **lewdly** *adv.*, **lewdness** *n.*

lexical *a.* of words. **lexically** *adv.*

lexicography *n.* process of compiling a dictionary. **lexicographer** *n.*

lexicon *n.* dictionary.

liability *n.* being liable; (*colloq.*) disadvantage; (*pl.*) debts.

liable *a.* held responsible by law, legally obliged to pay a tax or penalty etc.; likely to do or suffer something.

liaise *v.* (*colloq.*) act as liaison.

liaison *n.* communication and cooperation; illicit sexual relationship.

liana *n.* climbing plant of tropical forests.

liar *n.* person who tells lies.

libation *n.* drink-offering to a god.

libel *n.* published false statement that damages a person's reputation; act of publishing it. — *v.* (**libelled**) publish a libel against. **libellous** *a.*

liberal *a.* generous; tolerant. **liberally** *adv.*, **liberality** *n.*

liberalize *v.* make less strict. **liberalization** *n.*, **liberalizer** *n.*

liberate *v.* set free. **liberation** *n.*, **liberator** *n.*

libertine *n.* man who lives an irresponsible immoral life.

liberty *n.* freedom. **take liberties** behave with undue freedom or familiarity.

librarian *n.* person in charge of or assisting in a library.

library *n.* collection of books (or records, films, etc.) for consulting or borrowing; room or building containing these.

lice *see* **louse**.

licence *n.* official permit to own or do something; permission; disregard of rules etc.

license *v.* grant a licence to or for.

licensee *n.* holder of a licence.

licentiate *n.* holder of a certificate of competence in a profession.

licentious *a.* sexually immoral. **licentiousness** *n.*

lichen /líkən/ *n.* dry-looking plant that grows on rocks etc.

lick *v.* pass the tongue over; (of waves or flame) touch lightly; (*colloq.*) defeat. — *n.* act of licking; slight application (of paint etc.); (*colloq.*) fast pace.

lid *n.* hinged or removable cover for a box, pot, etc.; eyelid.

lie [1] *n.* statement the speaker knows to be untrue. — *v.* (**lied, lying**) tell lie(s).

lie [2] *v.* (**lay, lain, lying**) have or put one's body in a flat or resting position; be at rest on something; be in a specified state; be situated. — *n.* way a thing lies. **lie in** lie idly in bed late in the morning. **lie-in** *n.* such lying. **lie low** conceal oneself or one's intentions.

lieu /lyo͞o/ *n.* **in lieu** instead.

lieutenant /lefténnənt/ *n.* army officer next below captain; naval officer next below lieutenant commander; rank just below a specified officer; chief assistant.

life *n.* (*pl.* **lives**) animals' and plants' ability to function and grow; being alive; period of this; living things; liveliness; activities or manner of living; biography. **life cycle** series of forms into which a living thing changes. **life-jacket** *n.* jacket of buoyant material to keep a person afloat. **life-size, life-sized** *adjs.* of the same size as a real person. **life-support** *a.*(of equipment etc.) enabling the body to function in a hostile environment or in cases of physical failure.

lifebelt *n.* belt of buoyant material to keep a person afloat.

lifeboat *n.* boat for rescuing people in danger on the sea; ship's boat for emergency use.

lifebuoy *n.* buoyant device to keep a person afloat.

lifeguard *n.* expert swimmer employed to rescue bathers who are in danger.

lifeless *a.* without life; dead; unconscious; lacking liveliness.

lifelike *n.* exactly like a real person or thing.

lifeline *n.* rope used in rescue; vital means of communication.

lifelong *a.* for all one's life.

lifetime *n.* duration of a person's life.

lift *v.* raise; take up; rise; remove (restrictions); steal, plagiarize. — *n.* lifting; apparatus for transporting people or goods from one level to another; free ride in a motor vehicle; feeling of elation. **lift-off** *n.* vertical take-off of a spacecraft etc.

ligament *n.* tough flexible tissue holding bones together.

ligature *n.* thing that ties something, esp. in surgical operations. — *v.* tie with a ligature.

light [1] *n.* a kind of radiation that stimulates sight; brightness, light part of a picture etc.; source of light, electric lamp; flame or spark; enlightenment; aspect, way a thing appears to the mind. — *a.* full of light, not in darkness; pale. — *v.* (**lit** *or* **lighted**) set burning, begin to burn; provide with light; brighten. **bring to light** reveal. **come to light** be revealed. **light-pen** *n.* light-emitting device for reading bar codes; (also **light-gun**) device for passing information to a computer screen. **light up** put lights on at dusk; brighten; make or become animated; begin to smoke a cigarette etc. **light year** distance light travels in one year, about 6 million million miles.

light [2] *a.* having little weight; not heavy, easy to lift or carry or do; of less than average weight or force or intensity; cheerful; not profound or serious; (of food) easy to digest. — *adv.* lightly, with little load. **light-fingered** *a.* apt to steal. **light-headed** *a.* feeling slightly faint; delirious. **light-hearted** *a.* cheerful. **light industry** that producing small or light articles. **make light of** treat as unimportant. **lightly** *adv.*, **lightness** *n.*

light [3] *v.* (**lit** *or* **lighted**) **light on** find accidentally. **light out** (*sl.*) depart.

lighten [1] *v.* shed light on; make or become brighter.

lighten [2] *v.* make or become less heavy.

lighter [1] *n.* device for lighting cigarettes and cigars.

lighter [2] *n.* flat-bottomed boat for unloading ships. **lighterman** *n.*

lighthouse *n.* tower with a beacon light to warn or guide ships.

lighting *n.* means of providing light; the light itself.

lightning *n.* flash of bright light produced from cloud by natural electricity. — *a.* very quick.

lights *n.pl.* lungs of certain animals, used as animal food.

lightship *n.* moored ship with a light, serving as a lighthouse.

lightweight *a.* not having great weight or influence. — *n.* lightweight person.

lignite *n.* brown coal of woody texture.

like [1] *a.* having the qualities or appearance of; characteristic of. — *prep.* in the manner of, to the same degree as. — *conj.* (*colloq.*) as; (*US*) as if. — *adv.* (*colloq.*) likely. — *n.* person or thing like another. **like-minded** *a.* with similar tastes or opinions.

like [2] *v.* find pleasant or satisfactory; wish for. **likes** *n.pl.* things one likes or prefers.

likeable *a.* pleasant, easy to like.

likelihood *n.* probability.

likely *a.* (**-ier, -iest**) such as may reasonably be expected to occur or be true; seeming to be suitable or have a chance of success. — *adv.* probably. **likeliness** *n.*

liken *v.* point out the likeness of (one thing to another).

likeness *n.* being like; copy, portrait.

likewise *adv.* also; in the same way.

liking *n.* what one likes; one's taste for something.

lilac *n.* shrub with fragrant purple or white flowers; pale purple. — *a.* pale purple.

lilt *n.* light pleasant rhythm; song with this. **lilting** *a.*

lily *n.* plant growing from a bulb, with large flowers.

limb *n.* projecting part of a person's or animal's body, used in movement or in grasping things; large branch of a tree.

limber *v.* **limber up** exercise in preparation for athletic activity.

limbo [1] *n.* intermediate inactive or neglected state.

limbo [2] *n.* (*pl.* **-os**) West Indian dance in which the dancer bends back to pass under a bar.

lime [1] *n.* white substance used in making cement etc.

lime [2] *n.* round yellowish-green fruit like a lemon; its colour.

lime [3] *n.* tree with heart-shaped leaves.

limelight *n.* great publicity.

limerick *n.* a type of humorous poem with five lines.

limestone *n.* a kind of rock from which lime is obtained.

limit *n.* point beyond which something does not continue; greatest amount allowed. — *v.* set or serve as a limit, keep within limits. **limitation** *n.*

limousine *n.* large luxurious car.

limp [1] *v.* walk or proceed lamely. — *n.* limping walk.

limp [2] *a.* not stiff or firm; wilting. **limply** *adv.*, **limpness** *n.*

limpet *n.* small shellfish that sticks tightly to rocks.

limpid *a.* (of liquids) clear. **limpidly** *adv.*, **limpidity** *n.*

linchpin *n.* pin passed through the end of an axle to secure a wheel; person or thing vital to something.

linctus *n.* soothing cough mixture.

linden *n.* lime tree.

line [1] *n.* long narrow mark; outline; boundary; row of people or things; row of words; (*pl.*) words of an actor's part; brief letter; service of ships, buses, or aircraft; series, several generations of a family; direction, course; railway track; type of activity, business, or goods; piece of cord for a particular purpose; electrical or telephone cable, connection by this; each of a set of military fieldworks; **the Line** the equator. — *v.* mark with lines; arrange in line(s).

line [2] *v.* cover the inside surface of. **line one's pockets** make money, esp. in underhand ways.

lineage *n.* line of ancestors or descendants.

lineal *a.* of or in a line.

linear *a.* of a line, of length; arranged in a line.

linen *n.* cloth made of flax; household articles (e.g. sheets, tablecloths) formerly made of this.

liner [1] *n.* passenger ship or aircraft of a regular line.

liner [2] *n.* removable lining.

linesman *n.* (*pl.* **-men**) umpire's assistant at the boundary line; workman who maintains railway, electrical, or telephone lines.

ling [1] *n.* a kind of heather.

ling [2] *n.* sea fish of north Europe.

linger *v.* delay departure; dawdle.

lingerie /lánzhəri/ *n.* women's underwear.

lingua franca language used between people of an area where several languages are spoken.

lingual *a.* of the tongue; of speech or languages.

linguist *n.* person who knows foreign languages well; expert in linguistics.

linguistic *a.* of language. **linguistics** *n.* study of language. **linguistically** *adv.*

liniment *n.* embrocation.

lining *n.* layer of material or substance covering an inner surface.

link *n.* each ring of a chain; person or thing connecting others. — *v.* connect; intertwine. **linkage** *n.*

linnet *n.* a kind of finch.

lino *n.* linoleum.
linocut *n.* design cut in relief on a block of linoleum; print made from this.
linoleum *n.* a kind of smooth covering for floors.
linseed *n.* seed of flax.
lint *n.* soft fabric for dressing wounds; fluff.
lintel *n.* horizontal timber or stone over a doorway etc.
lion *n.* large flesh-eating animal of the cat family. **lion's share** largest part. **lioness** *n.fem.*
lionize *v.* treat as a celebrity.
lip *n.* either of the fleshy edges of the mouth-opening; edge of a container or opening; slight projection shaped for pouring from. **lip-read** *v.* understand (what is said) from movements of a speaker's lips.
lipsalve *n.* ointment for the lips.
lipstick *n.* cosmetic for colouring the lips; stick of this.
liquefy *v.* make or become liquid. **liquefaction** *n.*
liqueur /likyoór/ *n.* strong alcoholic spirit with fragrant flavouring.
liquid *n.* flowing substance like water or oil. — *a.* in the form of liquid; (of assets) easy to convert into cash. **liquidity** *n.*
liquidate *v.* pay (a debt); close down (a business) and divide its assets between creditors; get rid of, esp. by killing. **liquidation** *n.*, **liquidator** *n.*
liquidize *v.* reduce to liquid.
liquidizer *n.* machine for making purées etc.
liquor *n.* alcoholic drink; juice from cooked food.
liquorice *n.* black substance used in medicine and as a sweet; plant from whose root it is made.
lira *n.* (*pl.* **lire**) unit of money in Italy and Turkey.
lisp *n.* speech defect in which *s* and *z* are pronounced like *th.* — *v.* speak or utter with a lisp.
lissom *a.* lithe.
list [1] *n.* written or printed series of names, items, figures, etc. — *v.* make a list of; enter in a list.
list [2] *v.* (of a ship) lean over to one side. — *n.* listing position.
listen *v.* make an effort to hear; pay attention; be persuaded by advice or a request. **listen in** overhear a conversation; listen to a broadcast. **listener** *n.*
listless *a.* without energy or enthusiasm. **listlessly** *adv.*, **listlessness** *n.*
lit *see* **light** [1], **light** [3].
litany *n.* a set form of prayer.
literacy *n.* being literate.
literal *a.* taking the primary meaning of a word or words, not a metaphorical or exaggerated one. **literally** *adv.*, **literalness** *n.*
literary *a.* of literature.
literate *a.* able to read and write.
literature *n.* writings, esp. great novels, poetry, and plays.
lithe *a.* supple, agile.
litho *a.* & *n.* lithographic (process).
lithograph *n.* picture printed by lithography.
lithography *n.* printing from a design on a smooth surface. **lithographic** *a.*
litigant *a.* & *n.* (person) involved in or initiating a lawsuit.
litigate *v.* carry on a lawsuit; contest in law.
litigious *a.* fond of litigation.
litmus *n.* substance turned red by acids and blue by alkalis. **litmus paper** paper stained with this.
litre *n.* metric unit of capacity (about 1¾ pints) for measuring liquids.
litter *n.* rubbish left lying about; young animals born at one birth; material used as bedding for animals or to absorb their excrement. — *v.* scatter as litter; make untidy by litter; give birth to (a litter).
little *a.* small in size, amount, or intensity etc. — *n.* small amount, time, or distance. — *adv.* to a small extent; not at all.
littoral *a.* & *n.* (region) of or by the shore.
liturgy *n.* set form of public worship. **liturgical** *a.*
live [1] /līv/ *a.* alive; burning; unexploded; charged with electricity; (of broadcasts) transmitted while actually happening. **live wire** energetic forceful person.
live [2] /liv/ *v.* have life, remain alive; have one's dwelling place; conduct (one's life) in a certain way; enjoy life fully. **live down** live until (scandal etc.) is forgotten. **live on** keep oneself alive on.
livelihood *n.* means of earning or providing enough food etc. to sustain life.
lively *a.* (**-ier, -iest**) full of energy or action. **liveliness** *n.*
liven *v.* make or become lively.
liver *n.* large organ in the abdomen, secreting bile; animal's liver as food.
liveried *a.* wearing livery.
livery *n.* distinctive uniform worn by male servants.
livestock *n.* farm animals.
livid *a.* bluish-grey; (*colloq.*) furiously angry.
living *a.* having life, not dead; currently in use. — *n.* being alive; manner of life;

livelihood. **living room** room for general daytime use.

lizard *n.* reptile with four legs and a long tail.

llama *n.* South American animal related to the camel.

load *n.* thing or quantity carried; amount of electric current supplied; burden of responsibility or worry; (*pl., colloq.*) plenty. — *v.* put a load in or on; receive a load; fill heavily; weight; put ammunition into (a gun) or film into (a camera); put (data etc.) into (a computer).

loaf [1] *n.* (*pl.* **loaves**) mass of bread shaped in one piece; (*sl.*) head.

loaf [2] *v.* spend time idly, stand or saunter about. **loafer** *n.*

loam *n.* rich soil. **loamy** *a.*

loan *n.* lending; thing lent, esp. money. — *v.* grant a loan of.

loath *a.* unwilling.

loathe *v.* feel hatred and disgust for. **loathing** *n.*, **loathsome** *a.*

lob *v.* (**lobbed**) send or strike (a ball) slowly in a high arc. — *n.* lobbed ball.

lobar *a.* of a lobe, esp. of the lung.

lobby *n.* porch, entrance hall, ante-room; body of people seeking to influence legislation. — *v.* seek to persuade (an MP etc.) to support one's cause.

lobbyist *n.* person who lobbies an MP etc.

lobe *n.* rounded part or projection; lower soft part of the ear.

lobelia *n.* low-growing garden plant used esp. for edging.

lobster *n.* shellfish with large claws; its flesh as food.

local *a.* of or affecting a particular place or small area. — *n.* inhabitant of a particular district; (*colloq.*) public house of a neighbourhood. **local government** administration of a district by representatives elected locally. **locally** *adv.*

locality *n.* thing's position; site, neighbourhood.

localize *v.* confine within an area; decentralize. **localization** *n.*

locate *v.* discover the position of; situate in a particular location.

location *n.* locating; place where a thing is situated. **on location** (of filming) in a suitable environment, not in a film studio.

loch *n.* (*Sc.*) lake, arm of the sea.

lock [1] *n.* portion of hair that hangs together; (*pl.*) hair.

lock [2] *n.* device (opened by a key) for fastening a door or lid etc.; gated section of a canal where the water level can be changed; secure hold; interlocking. — *v.* fasten with a lock; shut into a locked place; make or become rigidly fixed. **lock out** shut out by locking a door. **lock-up** *n.* lockable premises; place where prisoners can be kept temporarily.

lockable *a.* able to be locked.

locker *n.* cupboard where things can be stowed securely.

locket *n.* small ornamental case worn on a chain round the neck.

lockjaw *n.* tetanus.

lockout *n.* employer's procedure of locking out employees during a dispute.

locksmith *n.* maker and mender of locks.

locomotion *n.* ability to move from place to place.

locomotive *n.* self-propelled engine for moving railway trains. — *a.* of or effecting locomotion.

locum *n.* temporary stand-in for a doctor, clergyman, etc.

locus *n.* (*pl.* **-ci**) thing's exact place; line or curve etc. formed by certain points or by the movement of a point or line.

locust *n.* a kind of grasshopper that devours vegetation.

lode *n.* vein of metal ore.

lodestar *n.* star (esp. pole star) used as a guide in navigation.

lodestone *n.* oxide of iron used as a magnet.

lodge *n.* cabin for use by hunters, skiers, etc.; gatekeeper's house; porter's room at the entrance to a building; members or meeting place of a branch of certain societies; beaver's or otter's lair. — *v.* provide with sleeping quarters or temporary accommodation; live as a lodger; deposit; be or become embedded.

lodger *n.* person paying for accommodation in another's house.

lodging *n.* place where one lodges; (*pl.*) room(s) rented for living in.

loft *n.* space under a roof; gallery in a church. — *v.* hit, throw, or kick (a ball) in a high arc.

lofty *a.* (**-ier, -iest**) very tall; noble; haughty. **loftily** *adv.*, **loftiness** *n.*

log [1] *n.* piece cut from a trunk or branch of a tree; device for gauging a ship's speed; logbook, entry in this. — *v.* (**logged**) enter (facts) in a logbook. **logbook** *n.* book in which details of a voyage or journey are recorded. **log on** *or* **off** begin or finish operations at a computer terminal.

log [2] *n.* logarithm.

loganberry *n.* large dark red fruit resembling a blackberry.

logarithm *n.* one of a series of numbers set out in tables, used to simplify calculations.

logic *n.* science or method of reasoning; correct reasoning.
logical *a.* of or according to logic; reasonable; reasoning correctly. **logically** *adv.*, **logicality** *n.*
logician *n.* person skilled in logic.
logistics *n.* organization of supplies and services. **logistical** *a.*
logo *n.* (*pl.* **-os**) design used as an emblem.
loin *n.* side and back of the body between ribs and hip bone.
loincloth *n.* cloth worn round the loins.
loiter *v.* linger, stand about idly. **loiterer** *n.*
loll *v.* stand, sit, or rest lazily; hang loosely.
lollipop *n.* large usu. flat boiled sweet on a small stick. **lollipop lady** *or* **man** official using a circular sign on a stick to halt traffic for children to cross a road.
lollop *v.* (**lolloped**) (*colloq.*) move in clumsy bounds; flop.
lolly *n.* (*colloq.*) lollipop, ice lolly; (*sl.*) money.
lone *a.* solitary.
lonely *a.* solitary; sad because lacking companions; not much frequented. **loneliness** *n.*
loner *n.* person who prefers not to associate with others.
lonesome *a.* lonely.
long [1] *a.* of great or specified length. — *adv.* for a long time; throughout a specified time. **as** *or* **so long as** provided that. **long-distance** *a.* travelling or operated between distant places. **long face** dismal expression. **long johns** (*colloq.*) underpants with long legs. **long-life** *a.* (of milk etc.) treated to prolong its shelf-life. **long-lived** *a.* living or lasting for a long time. **long-range** *a.* having a relatively long range; relating to a long period of future time. **long shot** wild guess or venture. **long-sighted** *a.* able to see clearly only what is at a distance. **long-standing** *a.* having existed for a long time. **long-suffering** *a.* bearing provocation patiently. **long-term** *a.* of or for a long period. **long ton** (*see* **ton**); **long wave** radio wave of frequency less than 300 kHz. **long-winded** *a.* talking or writing at tedious length.
long [2] *v.* feel a longing.
longevity /lonjévviti/ *n.* long life.
longhand *n.* ordinary writing, not shorthand or typing etc.
longhorn *n.* one of a breed of cattle with long horns.
longing *n.* intense wish.
longitude *n.* distance east or west (measured in degrees on a map) from the Greenwich meridian.
longitudinal *a.* of longitude; of length, lengthwise. **longitudinally** *adv.*
loo *n.* (*colloq.*) lavatory.
loofah *n.* dried pod of a gourd, used as a rough sponge.
look *v.* use or direct one's eyes in order to see, search, or examine; face; seem. — *n.* act of looking; inspection, search; appearance. **look after** take care of; attend to. **look down on** despise. **look forward to** await eagerly. **look into** investigate. **lookout** *n.* watch; watcher(s); observation post; prospect; person's own concern. **look out** be vigilant. **look up** search for information about; improve in prospects; go to visit. **look up to** admire and respect.
looker-on *n.* (*pl.* **lookers-on**) mere spectator.
loom [1] *n.* apparatus for weaving cloth.
loom [2] *v.* appear, esp. close at hand or threateningly.
loop *n.* curve that is U-shaped or crosses itself; thing shaped like this, esp. length of cord or wire etc. fastened at the crossing. — *v.* form into loop(s); fasten or join with loop(s); enclose in a loop. **loop the loop** fly in a vertical circle.
loophole *n.* means of evading a rule or contract.
loose *a.* not tight; not fastened, held, or fixed; not packed together. — *adv.* loosely. — *v.* release; untie, loosen. **at a loose end** without a definite occupation. **loose-leaf** *a.* with each page removable. **loosely** *adv.*, **looseness** *n.*
loosen *v.* make or become loose or looser.
loot *n.* goods taken from an enemy or by theft. — *v.* take loot (from); take as loot. **looter** *n.*
lop *v.* (**lopped**) cut branches or twigs of; cut off.
lope *v.* run with a long bounding stride. — *n.* this stride.
lop-eared *a.* with drooping ears.
lopsided *a.* with one side lower, smaller, or heavier.
loquacious *a.* talkative. **loquaciously** *adv.*, **loquacity** *n.*
lord *n.* master, ruler; nobleman; title of certain peers or high officials. **the Lord** God; **Our Lord** Christ.
lordship *n.* title used of or to a man with the rank of *Lord*.
lore *n.* body of traditions and knowledge.
lorgnette /lornyét/ *n.* eyeglasses or opera-glasses held to the eyes on a long handle.
lorry *n.* large motor vehicle for transporting heavy loads.
lose *v.* (**lost**) cease to have or maintain; become unable to find; fail to

get; get rid of; be defeated in a contest etc.; suffer loss (of); cause the loss of. **loser** *n.*

loss *n.* losing; person or thing or amount lost; disadvantage caused by losing something. **be at a loss** not know what to do or say. **loss-leader** *n.* article sold at a loss to attract customers.

lost *see* **lose**. — *a.* strayed or separated from its owner.

lot [1] *n.* each of a set of objects drawn at random to decide something; person's share or destiny; piece of land; item being sold at auction.

lot [2] *n.* number of people or things of the same kind; large number or amount; much; **the lot** the total quantity. **bad lot** person of bad character.

lotion *n.* medicinal or cosmetic liquid applied to the skin.

lottery *n.* system of raising money by selling numbered tickets and giving prizes to holders of numbers drawn at random; thing where the outcome is governed by luck.

lotus *n.* (*pl.* **-uses**) tropical water lily; mythical fruit.

loud *a.* producing much noise, easily heard; gaudy. — *adv.* loudly. **loud hailer** electronically operated megaphone. **loudly** *adv.*, **loudness** *n.*

loudspeaker *n.* apparatus that converts electrical impulses into audible sound.

lough /lok/ *n.* (*Ir.*) = loch.

lounge *v.* loll; sit or stand about idly. — *n.* sitting room; waiting-room at an airport etc. **lounge suit** man's ordinary suit for day wear. **lounger** *n.*

louse *n.* (*pl.* **lice**) small parasitic insect; (*pl.* **louses**) contemptible person.

lousy *a.* (**-ier**, **-iest**) infested with lice; (*sl.*) very bad.

lout *n.* clumsy ill-mannered young man. **loutish** *a.*

louvre *n.* each of a set of overlapping slats arranged to admit air but exclude light or rain. **louvred** *a.*

lovable *a.* easy to love.

lovage *n.* herb used for flavouring.

love *n.* warm liking or affection; sexual passion; loved person; (in games) no score, nil. — *v.* feel love for; like greatly. **in love** feeling (esp. sexual) love for another person. **love affair** romantic or sexual relationship between people who are in love. **lovebird** *n.* small parakeet that shows great affection for its mate. **make love** have sexual intercourse.

lovelorn *a.* pining with love.

lovely *a.* (**-ier**, **-iest**) beautiful, attractive; (*colloq.*) delightful. **loveliness** *n.*

lover *n.* person in love with another or having an illicit love affair; one who likes or enjoys something.

loving *a.* feeling or showing love. **lovingly** *adv.*

low [1] *n.* deep sound made by cattle. — *v.* make this sound.

low [2] *a.* not high, not extending or lying far up; ranking below others; ignoble, vulgar; less than normal in amount or intensity; not loud or shrill; lacking vigour, depressed. — *n.* low level; area of low pressure. — *adv.* in, at, or to a low level. **low-class** *a.* of low quality or social class. **low-down** *a.* dishonourable; (*n.*, *sl.*) relevant information. **low-key** *a.* restrained, not intense or emotional. **low season** season that is least busy.

lowbrow *a.* not intellectual or cultured. — *n.* lowbrow person.

lower *v.* let or haul down; make or become lower. **lower case** letters (for printing or typing) that are not capitals.

lowlands *n.pl.* low-lying land. **lowland** *a.*, **lowlander** *n.*

lowly *a.* (**-ier**, **-iest**) of humble rank or condition. **lowliness** *n.*

loyal *a.* firm in one's allegiance. **loyally** *adv.*, **loyalty** *n.*

loyalist *n.* person who is loyal, esp. while others revolt.

lozenge *n.* four-sided diamond-shaped figure; small tablet to be dissolved in the mouth.

Ltd. *abbr.* Limited.

lubricant *n.* lubricating substance.

lubricate *v.* oil or grease (machinery etc.). **lubrication** *n.*

lubricious *a.* slippery; lewd.

lucid *a.* clearly expressed; sane. **lucidly** *adv.*, **lucidity** *n.*

luck *n.* good or bad fortune; chance thought of as a force bringing this.

luckless *a.* unlucky.

lucky *a.* (**-ier**, **-iest**) having, bringing, or resulting from good luck. **lucky dip** tub containing articles from which one takes at random. **luckily** *adv.*

lucrative *a.* producing much money.

lucre /lo͞okər/ *n.* (*derog.*) money.

ludicrous *a.* ridiculous. **ludicrously** *adv.*, **ludicrousness** *n.*

ludo *n.* simple game played with counters on a special board.

lug [1] *v.* (**lugged**) drag or carry with great effort.

lug [2] *n.* ear-like projection; (*colloq.*) ear.

luggage *n.* suitcases and bags etc. holding a traveller's possessions.

lugubrious *a.* dismal, mournful. **lugubriously** *adv.*

lukewarm *a.* only slightly warm; not enthusiastic.

lull *v.* soothe or send to sleep; calm; become quiet. — *n.* period of quiet or inactivity.

lullaby *n.* soothing song sung to send a child to sleep.

lumbago *n.* rheumatic pain in muscles of the lower back.

lumbar *a.* of or in the lower back.

lumber *n.* useless or unwanted articles, esp. furniture; (*US*) timber sawn into planks. — *v.* encumber; move heavily and clumsily.

lumberjack *n.* (*US*) workman cutting or conveying lumber.

lumen *n.* unit of luminous flux.

luminary *n.* natural light-giving body, esp. the sun or moon; eminent person.

luminescent *a.* emitting light without heat. **luminescence** *n.*

luminous *a.* emitting light, glowing in the dark. **luminously** *adv.*, **luminosity** *n.*

lump *n.* hard or compact mass; swelling. — *v.* put or consider together. **lump sum** money paid as a single amount.

lumpectomy *n.* surgical removal of a lump from the breast.

lumpy *a.* (**-ier, -iest**) full of lumps; covered in lumps. **lumpiness** *n.*

lunacy *n.* insanity; great folly.

lunar *a.* of the moon. **lunar month** period between new moons (29½ days), four weeks.

lunatic *n.* person who is insane or very foolish or reckless.

lunation *n.* lunar month

lunch *n.* midday meal. — *v.* eat lunch.

luncheon *n.* lunch. **luncheon meat** tinned cured meat ready for serving. **luncheon voucher** voucher given to an employee, exchangeable for food.

lung *n.* either of the pair of breathing-organs in the chest of man and most vertebrates.

lunge *n.* sudden forward movement of the body; thrust. — *v.* make this movement.

lupin *n.* garden plant with tall spikes of flowers.

lurch [1] *n.* **leave in the lurch** leave (a person) in difficulties.

lurch [2] *v.* & *n.* (make) an unsteady swaying movement, stagger.

lure *v.* entice. — *n.* enticement; bait or decoy to attract wild animals.

lurid *a.* in glaring colours; vivid and sensational or shocking. **luridly** *adv.*, **luridness** *n.*

lurk *v.* wait furtively or keeping out of sight; be latent.

luscious *a.* delicious; voluptuously attractive. **lusciously** *adv.*, **lusciousness** *n.*

lush *a.* (of grass etc.) growing thickly and strongly; luxurious. **lushly** *adv.*, **lushness** *n.*

lust *n.* intense sexual desire; any intense desire. — *v.* feel lust. **lustful** *a.*, **lustfully** *adv.*

lustre *n.* soft brightness of a surface; glory; metallic glaze on pottery. **lustrous** *a.*

lusty *a.* (**-ier, -iest**) strong and vigorous. **lustily** *adv.*

lute *n.* guitar-like instrument. **lutenist** *n.*

luxuriant *a.* growing profusely. **luxuriantly** *adv.*, **luxuriance** *n.*

luxuriate *v.* feel great enjoyment in something.

luxurious *a.* supplied with luxuries, very comfortable. **luxuriously** *adv.*, **luxuriousness** *n.*

luxury *n.* choice and costly surroundings, food, etc.; self-indulgence; thing that is enjoyable but not essential.

lying *see* **lie** [1], **lie** [2].

lymph *n.* colourless fluid from body tissue or organs. **lymphatic** *a.*

lynch *v.* execute or punish violently by a mob, without trial.

lynx *n.* wild animal of the cat family with keen sight.

lyre *n.* ancient musical instrument with strings in a U-shaped frame. **lyre-bird** *n.* Australian bird with a lyre-shaped tail.

lyric *a.* of poetry that expresses the poet's thoughts and feelings. — *n.* lyric poem; words of a song.

lyrical *a.* resembling or using language suitable for lyric poetry; (*colloq.*) expressing oneself enthusiastically. **lyrically** *adv.*

lyricist *n.* person who writes lyrics.

M

m *abbr.* metre(s); mile(s); million(s).
ma'am *n.* madam.
mac *n.* (*colloq.*) mackintosh.
macabre *a.* gruesome.
macadam *n.* layers of broken stone used in road-making.
macadamize *v.* pave with macadam.
macaroni *n.* tube-shaped pasta.
macaroon *n.* biscuit or small cake made with ground almonds.
macaw *n.* American parrot.
mace [1] *n.* ceremonial staff carried or placed before an official.
mace [2] *n.* spice made from the dried outer covering of nutmeg.
Mach /maak/ *n.* **Mach number** ratio of the speed of a moving body to the speed of sound.
machete /məchétti/ *n.* broad heavy knife used in Central America and the West Indies.
machiavellian *a.* elaborately cunning or deceitful.
machinations *n.pl.* clever scheming.
machine *n.* apparatus for applying mechanical power; thing operated by this; controlling system of an organization etc. — *v.* produce or work on with a machine. **machine-gun** *n.* gun that can fire continuously; (*v.*) shoot at with this. **machine-readable** *a.* in a form that a computer can process.
machinery *n.* machines; mechanism.
machinist *n.* person who works machinery.
machismo *n.* manly courage; show of this.
macho *a.* ostentatiously manly.
mackerel *n.* (*pl.* **mackerel**) edible sea fish.
mackintosh *n.* cloth waterproofed with rubber; raincoat.
macramé /məkraámi/ *n.* art of knotting cord in patterns; work done thus.
macrocosm *n.* the universe; any great whole.
mad *a.* (**madder, maddest**) having a disordered mind, not sane; extremely foolish; wildly enthusiastic; frenzied; (*colloq.*) very annoyed. **like mad** with great haste or energy or enthusiasm. **madly** *adv.*, **madness** *n.*
madam *n.* polite form of address to a woman.
madcap *a.* & *n.* wildly impulsive (person).
madden *v.* make mad or angry.
made *see* **make**.
Madeira *n.* fortified wine from Madeira. **Madeira cake** rich plain cake.
madonna *n.* picture or statue of the Virgin Mary.
madrigal *n.* part-song for voices.
maelstrom /máylstrəm/ *n.* great whirlpool.
maestro /mīstrō/ *n.* (*pl.* **-i**) great conductor or composer of music; master of any art.
magazine *n.* illustrated periodical; store for arms or explosives; chamber holding cartridges in a gun, slides in a projector, etc.
magenta *a.* & *n.* purplish-red.
maggot *n.* larva, esp. of the bluebottle. **maggoty** *a.*
magic *n.* supposed art of controlling things by supernatural power. — *a.* using or used in magic. **magical** *a.*, **magically** *adv.*
magician *n.* person skilled in magic; conjuror.
magisterial *a.* of a magistrate; imperious.
magistrate *n.* official or citizen with authority to hold preliminary hearings and judge minor cases. **magistracy** *n.*
magnanimous *a.* noble and generous in conduct, not petty. **magnanimously** *adv.*, **magnanimity** *n.*
magnate *n.* wealthy influential person, esp. in business.
magnesia *n.* compound of magnesium used in medicine.
magnesium *n.* white metal that burns with an intensely bright flame.
magnet *n.* piece of iron or steel that can attract iron and point north when suspended; thing exerting powerful attraction.
magnetic *a.* having the properties of a magnet; produced or acting by magnetism. **magnetic disk** computer storage device formed from magnetically coated plates. **magnetic tape** strip of plastic with magnetic particles, used in recording, computers, etc. **magnetically** *adv.*
magnetism *n.* properties and effects of magnetic substances; great charm and attraction.
magnetize *v.* make magnetic; attract. **magnetization** *n.*
magneto /magneétō/ *n.* (*pl.* **-os**) small electric generator using magnets.
magnification *n.* magnifying.

magnificent *a.* splendid in appearance etc.; excellent in quality. **magnificently** *adv.*, **magnificence** *n.*

magnify *v.* make (an object) appear larger by use of a lens; exaggerate. **magnifier** *n.*

magnitude *n.* largeness, size; importance.

magnolia *n.* tree with large wax-like white or pink flowers.

magnum *n.* bottle holding two quarts (2.27 litres) of wine or spirits.

magpie *n.* bird of the crow family with black and white plumage.

Magyar *a.* & *n.* (member, language) of a people now predominant in Hungary.

maharajah *n.* former title of certain Indian princes. **maharanee** *n.fem.*

maharishi *n.* Hindu man of great wisdom.

mahatma *n.* (in India etc.) title of a man regarded with reverence.

mah-jong *n.* Chinese game played with 136 or 144 pieces (tiles).

mahogany *n.* very hard reddish-brown wood; its colour.

maid *n.* woman servant.

maiden *n.* (*old use*) young unmarried woman, virgin. —*a.* unmarried; first. **maiden name** woman's family name before she married. **maidenly** *a.*, **maidenhood** *n.*

maidenhair *n.* fern with very thin stalks and delicate foliage.

maidservant *n.* female servant.

mail [1] *n.* = post [3]. —*v.* send by post. **mail order** purchase of goods by post. **mailshot** *n.* material sent to potential customers in an advertising campaign.

mail [2] *n.* body-armour made of metal rings or chains. **mailed** *a.*

maim *v.* wound or injure so that a part of the body is useless.

main *a.* principal, most important, greatest in size or extent. —*n.* main pipe or channel conveying water, gas, or (*pl.*) electricity. **mainly** *adv.*

mainframe *n.* large computer.

mainland *n.* country or continent without its adjacent islands.

mainmast *n.* principal mast.

mainsail *n.* lowest sail or sail set on the after part of the mainmast.

mainspring *n.* chief spring of a watch or clock; chief motivating force.

mainstay *n.* cable securing the mainmast; chief support.

mainstream *n.* dominant trend of opinion or style etc.

maintain *v.* cause to continue, keep in existence; keep in repair; bear the expenses of; assert.

maintenance *n.* process of maintaining something; provision of means to support life, allowance of money for this.

maisonette *n.* part of a house (usu. not all on one floor) used as a separate dwelling.

maize *n.* tall cereal plant bearing grain on large cobs; its grain.

majestic *a.* stately and dignified, imposing. **majestically** *adv.*

majesty *n.* impressive stateliness; sovereign power; title of a king or queen.

major *a.* greater; very important. —*n.* army officer next below lieutenant colonel. —*v.* (*US*) specialize (in a subject) at college. **major-general** *n.* army officer next below lieutenant general.

majority *n.* greatest part of a group or class; number by which votes for one party etc. exceed those for the next or for all combined; age when a person legally becomes adult.

make *v.* (**made**) form, prepare, produce; cause to exist or be or become; succeed in arriving at or achieving; gain, acquire; reckon to be; compel; perform (an action etc.). —*n.* brand of goods. **make believe** pretend. **make-believe** *n.* pretence. **make do** manage with something not fully satisfactory. **make for** try to reach; tend to bring about. **make good** become successful; repair or pay compensation for. **make much of** treat as important; give flattering attention to. **make off** go away hastily. **make off with** carry away, steal. **make out** write out (a list etc.); manage to see or understand; assert to be. **make over** transfer the ownership of; refashion (a garment etc.). **make up** form, constitute; invent (a story); compensate (for a loss etc.); become reconciled after (a quarrel); complete (an amount); apply cosmetics (to). **make-up** *n.* cosmetics applied to the skin; way a thing is made; person's character. **make up one's mind** decide.

maker *n.* one who makes something; manufacturer.

makeshift *a.* & *n.* (thing) used as an improvised substitute.

makeweight *n.* something added to make up for a deficiency.

maladjusted *a.* not happily adapted to one's circumstances. **maladjustment** *n.*

maladminister *v.* manage (business or public affairs) badly or improperly.

maladroit *a.* bungling, clumsy.

malady *n.* illness, disease.

malaise *n.* feeling of illness or uneasiness.

malapropism *n.* comical confusion of words.

malaria *n.* disease causing a recurring fever. **malarial** *a.*

Malay *a.* & *n.* (member, language) of a people of Malaysia and Indonesia.
malcontent *n.* discontented person.
male *a.* of the sex that can fertilize egg cells produced by a female; (of a plant) producing pollen, not seeds; (of a screw etc.) for insertion into a corresponding hollow part. — *n.* male person, animal, or plant.
malefactor /mállifaktər/ *n.* wrongdoer.
malevolent *a.* wishing harm to others. **malevolently** *adv.*, **malevolence** *n.*
malformation *n.* faulty formation. **malformed** *a.*
malfunction *n.* faulty functioning. — *v.* function faultily.
malice *n.* desire to harm others. **malicious** *a.*, **maliciously** *adv.*
malign /məlīn/ *a.* harmful; showing malice. — *v.* say unpleasant and untrue things about.
malignant *a.* showing great ill-will; (of a tumour) growing harmfully and uncontrollably. **malignantly** *adv.*, **malignancy** *n.*
malinger *v.* pretend illness to avoid work. **malingerer** *n.*
mall *n.* sheltered walk or promenade; shopping precinct.
mallard *n.* wild duck, male of which has a glossy green head.
malleable *a.* able to be hammered or pressed into shape; easy to influence. **malleability** *n.*
mallet *n.* hammer, usu. of wood; instrument for striking the ball in croquet or polo.
malmsey /maámzi/ *n.* a kind of strong sweet wine.
malnutrition *n.* insufficient nutrition.
malodorous *a.* stinking.
malpractice *n.* wrongdoing; improper professional behaviour.
malt *n.* barley or other grain prepared for brewing or distilling; (*colloq.*) beer or whisky made with this. **malted milk** drink made from dried milk and malt.
maltreat *v.* ill-treat. **maltreatment** *n.*
mamba *n.* poisonous South African tree-snake.
mammal *n.* member of the class of animals that suckle their young. **mammalian** *a.*
mammary *a.* of the breasts.
mammoth *n.* large extinct elephant with curved tusks. — *a.* huge.
man *n.* (*pl.* **men**) adult male person; human being; mankind; individual person; male servant or employee; ordinary soldier etc., not an officer; one of the small objects used in board games. — *v.* (**manned**) supply with people to guard or operate something. **man-hour** *n.* one hour's work by one person. **manhunt** *n.* organized search for a person, esp. a criminal. **man-made** *a.* synthetic. **man-sized** *a.* adequate for a man; large. **man to man** with frankness.
manacle *n.* & *v.* handcuff.
manage *v.* have control of; be manager of; operate (a tool etc.) effectively; contrive; deal with (a person) tactfully. **manageable** *a.*
management *n.* managing; people engaged in managing a business.
manager *n.* person in charge of a business etc. **manageress** *n.fem.*, **managerial** *a.*
manatee *n.* large tropical aquatic mammal.
Mandarin *n.* northern variety of the Chinese language.
mandarin *n.* senior influential official; a kind of small orange.
mandate *n.* & *v.* (give) authority to perform certain tasks.
mandatory *a.* compulsory.
mandible *n.* jaw or jaw-like part.
mandolin *n.* guitar-like musical instrument.
mandrake *n.* poisonous plant with a large yellow fruit.
mandrel *n.* shaft holding work in a lathe.
mandrill *n.* a kind of large baboon.
mane *n.* long hair on a horse's or lion's neck.
manful *a.* brave, resolute. **manfully** *adv.*
manganese *n.* hard brittle grey metal or its black oxide.
mange *n.* skin disease affecting hairy animals.
mangel-wurzel *n.* large beet used as cattle food.
manger *n.* open trough for horses or cattle to feed from.
mangle *v.* damage by cutting or crushing roughly, mutilate.
mango *n.* (*pl.* **-oes**) tropical fruit with juicy flesh; tree bearing it.
mangrove *n.* tropical tree or shrub growing in shore-mud and swamps.
mangy *a.* having mange; squalid.
manhandle *v.* move by human effort alone; treat roughly.
manhole *n.* opening through which a person can enter a drain etc. to inspect it.
manhood *n.* state of being a man; manly qualities.
mania *n.* violent madness; extreme enthusiasm for something.
maniac *n.* person with a mania.
maniacal *a.* of or like a mania or maniac.
manic *a.* of or affected by mania.

manicure *n.* cosmetic treatment of fingernails. — *v.* apply such treatment to. **manicurist** *n.*

manifest *a.* clear and unmistakable. — *v.* show clearly, give signs of. — *n.* list of cargo or passengers carried by a ship or aircraft. **manifestation** *n.*

manifesto *n.* (*pl.* **-os**) public declaration of principles and policy.

manifold *a.* of many kinds. — *n.* (in a machine) pipe or chamber with several openings.

manikin *n.* little man, dwarf.

manila *n.* brown paper used for wrapping and for envelopes.

manipulate *v.* handle or manage in a skilful or cunning way. **manipulation** *n.*, **manipulator** *n.*

mankind *n.* human beings in general.

manly *a.* brave, strong; considered suitable for a man. **manliness** *n.*

mannequin /mánnikin/ *n.* woman who models clothes.

manner *n.* way a thing is done or happens; person's way of behaving towards others; kind, sort; (*pl.*) polite social behaviour.

mannered *a.* having manners of a certain kind; stilted.

mannerism *n.* distinctive personal habit or way of doing something.

manoeuvrable *a.* able to be manoeuvred. **manoevrability** *a.*

manoeuvre *n.* planned movement of a vehicle, troops, etc.; skilful or crafty proceeding. — *v.* perform manoeuvre(s); move or guide skilfully or craftily.

manor *n.* large country house, usu. with lands. **manorial** *a.*

manpower *n.* number of people available for work or service.

manservant *n.* (*pl.* **menservants**) male servant.

mansion *n.* large stately house.

manslaughter *n.* act of killing a person unlawfully but not intentionally, or by negligence.

mantelpiece *n.* shelf above a fireplace.

mantilla *n.* Spanish lace veil worn over a woman's hair and shoulders.

mantis *n.* grasshopper-like insect.

mantle *n.* loose cloak; covering.

manual *a.* of the hands; done or operated by the hand(s). — *n.* handbook. **manually** *adv.*

manufacture *v.* make or produce (goods) on a large scale by machinery; invent. — *n.* process of manufacturing. **manufacturer** *n.*

manure *n.* substance, esp. dung, used as a fertilizer. — *v.* apply manure to.

manuscript *n.* book or document written by hand or typed, not printed.

Manx *a.* & *n.* (language) of the Isle of Man.

many *a.* numerous. — *n.* many people or things.

Maori /mówrī/ *n.* & *a.* (*pl.* **Maori** or **-is**) (member, language) of the indigenous race of New Zealand.

map *n.* representation of earth's surface or a part of it. — *v.* (**mapped**) make a map of. **map out** plan in detail.

maple *n.* a kind of tree with broad leaves.

mar *v.* (**marred**) damage, spoil.

maraca *n.* club-like gourd containing beads etc., shaken as a musical instrument.

marathon *n.* long-distance foot race; long test of endurance.

marauding *a.* & *n.* going about in search of plunder. **marauder** *n.*

marble *n.* a kind of limestone that can be polished; piece of sculpture in this; small ball of glass or clay used in children's games. — *v.* give a veined or mottled appearance to.

marcasite *n.* crystals of iron pyrites, used in jewellery.

march *v.* walk in a regular rhythm or an organized column; walk purposefully; cause to march or walk; progress steadily. — *n.* act of marching; distance covered by marching; music suitable for marching to; progress. **marcher** *n.*

marchioness *n.* wife or widow of a marquess; woman with the rank of marquess.

mare *n.* female of the horse or a related animal.

margarine *n.* substance made from animal or vegetable fat and used like butter.

marge *n.* (*colloq.*) margarine.

margin *n.* edge or border of a surface; blank space round the edges of a page; amount over the essential minimum.

marginal *a.* of or in a margin; near a limit; only very slight. **marginally** *adv.*

marginalize *v.* make or treat as insignificant. **marginalization** *n.*

marguerite *n.* large daisy.

marigold *n.* garden plant with golden daisy-like flowers.

marijuana /márrihwaánə/ *n.* dried hemp, smoked as a hallucinogenic drug.

marimba *n.* a kind of xylophone.

marina *n.* harbour for yachts and pleasure boats.

marinade *n.* flavoured liquid in which meat or fish is steeped before cooking. — *v.* steep in a marinade.

marine *a.* of the sea; of shipping. — *n.*

soldier trained to serve on land or sea; a country's shipping.

mariner *n.* sailor, seaman.

marionette *n.* puppet worked by strings.

marital *a.* of marriage, of husband and wife.

maritime *a.* living or found near the sea; of seafaring.

marjoram *n.* fragrant herb.

mark [1] *n.* thing that visibly breaks the uniformity of a surface; distinguishing feature; thing indicating the presence of a quality or feeling etc.; symbol; point given for merit; target; line or object serving to indicate a position; numbered design of a piece of equipment etc. — *v.* make a mark on; characterize; assign marks of merit to; notice, watch carefully; keep close to and ready to hamper (an opponent in football etc.). **mark down** reduce the price of. **mark time** move the feet as if marching but without advancing.

mark [2] *n.* unit of money in Germany.

marked *a.* clearly noticeable. **markedly** *adv.*

marker *n.* person or object that marks something.

market *n.* gathering or place for the sale of provisions, livestock, etc.; demand (for a commodity). — *v.* sell in a market; offer for sale. **market garden** one in which vegetables are grown for market. **on the market** offered for sale.

marking *n.* mark(s); colouring of an animal's skin, feathers, or fur.

marksman *n.* (*pl.* **-men**) person who is a skilled shot. **marksmanship** *n.*

marl *n.* soil composed of clay and lime, used as a fertilizer.

marmalade *n.* a kind of jam made from citrus fruit, esp. oranges.

marmoset *n.* small bushy-tailed monkey of tropical America.

marmot *n.* small burrowing animal of the squirrel family.

maroon [1] *n.* brownish-red colour; explosive device used as a warning signal. — *a.* brownish-red.

maroon [2] *v.* put and leave (a person) ashore in a desolate place; leave stranded.

marquee *n.* large tent used for a party or exhibition etc.

marquess *n.* nobleman ranking between duke and earl.

marquetry *n.* inlaid work of wood.

marquis *n.* rank in some European nobilities; marquess.

marram *n.* shore grass that binds sand.

marriage *n.* formal union of a man and woman to live together; act or ceremony of marrying.

marriageable *a.* suitable or old enough for marriage.

marrow *n.* soft fatty substance in the cavities of bones; a type of gourd used as a vegetable.

marry *v.* unite or give or take in marriage; unite (things).

marsh *n.* low-lying watery ground. **marsh marigold** a kind of large buttercup. **marshy** *a.*

marshal *n.* high-ranking officer; official controlling an event or ceremony. — *v.* (**marshalled**) arrange in proper order; assemble; usher.

marshmallow *n.* soft sweet made from sugar, egg white, and gelatine.

marsupial *n.* mammal that usu. carries its young in a pouch.

mart *n.* market.

marten *n.* weasel-like animal with thick soft fur.

martial *a.* of war, warlike. **martial law** military government suspending ordinary law.

martin *n.* bird of the swallow family.

martinet *n.* person who demands strict obedience.

martyr *n.* person who undergoes death or suffering for his or her beliefs. — *v.* kill or torment as a martyr. **martyrdom** *n.*

marvel *n.* wonderful thing. — *v.* (**marvelled**) feel wonder.

marvellous *a.* wonderful. **marvellously** *adv.*

Marxism *n.* socialist theories of Karl Marx. **Marxist** *a.* & *n.*

marzipan *n.* edible paste made from ground almonds.

mascara *n.* cosmetic for darkening the eyelashes.

mascot *n.* thing believed to bring good luck to its owner.

masculine *a.* of, like, or traditionally considered suitable for men; of the grammatical form suitable for the names of males. — *n.* masculine word. **masculinity** *n.*

mash *n.* soft mixture of grain or bran; mashed potatoes. — *v.* beat into a soft mass.

mask *n.* covering worn over the face as a disguise or protection. — *v.* cover with a mask; disguise, screen, conceal.

masochism *n.* pleasure in suffering pain. **masochist** *n.*, **masochistic** *a.*

mason *n.* person who builds or works with stone.

masonry *n.* stonework.

masquerade *n.* false show or pretence. — *v.* pretend to be what one is not.

mass [1] *n.* celebration (esp. in the RC Church) of the Eucharist; form of liturgy used in this.

mass [2] *n.* coherent unit of matter; large quantity or heap or expanse; quantity of matter a body contains; **the masses** ordinary people. — *v.* gather or assemble into a mass. **mass-produce** *v.* manufacture in large quantities by a standardized process.

massacre *n.* great slaughter. — *v.* slaughter in large numbers.

massage *n.* rubbing and kneading the body to reduce pain or stiffness. — *v.* treat in this way.

masseur *n.* man who practises massage professionally. **masseuse** *n.fem.*

massive *a.* large and heavy or solid; huge. **massively** *adv.*

mast [1] *n.* tall pole, esp. supporting a ship's sails.

mast [2] *n.* fruit of beech, oak, chestnut, etc., used as food for pigs.

mastectomy *n.* surgical removal of a breast.

master *n.* man who has control of people or things; male teacher; person with very great skill, great artist; thing from which a series of copies is made; **Master** title of a boy not old enough to be called *Mr.* — *a.* superior; principal; controlling others. — *v.* bring under control; acquire knowledge or skill in. **master-key** *n.* key that opens a number of different locks. **Master of Arts** etc., person with a high university degree. **master-stroke** *n.* very skilful act of policy.

masterful *a.* domineering. **masterfully** *adv.*

masterly *a.* very skilful.

mastermind *n.* person of outstanding mental ability; one directing an enterprise. — *v.* plan and direct.

masterpiece *n.* outstanding piece of work.

mastery *n.* control, supremacy; thorough knowledge or skill.

mastic *n.* gum or resin from certain trees; a kind of cement.

masticate *v.* chew. **mastication** *n.*

mastiff *n.* large strong dog.

mastodon *n.* extinct animal resembling an elephant.

mastoid *n.* part of a bone behind the ear.

masturbate *v.* stimulate the genitals (of) manually. **masturbation** *n.*

mat *n.* piece of material placed on a floor or other surface as an ornament or to protect it. — *v.* (**matted**) make or become tangled into a thick mass.

matador *n.* bullfighter.

match [1] *n.* short stick tipped with material that catches fire when rubbed on a rough surface.

match [2] *n.* contest in a game or sport; person or thing exactly like or corresponding or equal to another; matrimonial alliance. — *v.* set against each other in a contest; equal in ability or achievement; be alike; find a match for.

matchmaking *n.* scheming to arrange marriages. **matchmaker** *n.*

matchstick *n.* stick of a match.

matchwood *n.* wood that splinters easily; wood broken into splinters.

mate [1] *n.* companion or fellow worker; male or female of mated animals; merchant ship's officer. — *v.* put or come together as a pair; come or bring (animals) together to breed.

mate [2] *n.* checkmate.

material *n.* that from which something is or can be made; cloth, fabric. — *a.* of matter; of the physical (not spiritual) world; significant. **materially** *adv.*

materialism *n.* belief that only the material world exists; excessive concern with material possessions. **materialist** *n.*, **materialistic** *a.*

materialize *v.* appear, become visible; become a fact, happen. **materialization** *n.*

maternal *a.* of a mother; motherly; related through one's mother. **maternally** *adv.*

maternity *n.* motherhood; (*attrib.*) of or for women in pregnancy and childbirth.

mathematician *n.* person skilled in mathematics.

mathematics *n.* science of numbers, quantities, and measurements; (as *pl.*) use of this. **mathematical** *a.*, **mathematically** *adv.*

maths *n.* & *n.pl.* (*colloq.*) mathematics.

matinée *n.* afternoon performance. **matinée coat** baby's jacket.

matriarch *n.* female head of a family or tribe. **matriarchal** *a.*

matriarchy *n.* social organization in which a female is head of the family.

matricide *n.* killing or killer of own mother. **matricidal** *a.*

matriculate *v.* admit or be admitted to a university. **matriculation** *n.*

matrimony *n.* marriage. **matrimonial** *a.*

matrix *n.* (*pl.* **matrices**) mould in which a thing is cast or shaped; rectangular array of mathematical quantities.

matron *n.* married woman; woman in charge of domestic affairs or nursing in a school etc.

matronly *a.* like or suitable for a dignified married woman.

matt *a.* dull, not shiny.

matter *n.* that which occupies space in

the visible world; specified substance, material, or things; business etc. being discussed; pus. — *v.* be of importance. **what is the matter?** what is amiss?

mattress *n.* fabric case filled with padding or springy material, used on or as a bed.

maturation *n.* maturing.

mature *a.* fully grown or developed; (of a bill of exchange etc.) due for payment. — *v.* make or become mature. **maturity** *n.*

maudlin *a.* sentimental in a silly or tearful way.

maul *v.* treat roughly, injure by rough handling.

maunder *v.* talk in a dreamy or rambling way; move idly.

mausoleum *n.* magnificent tomb.

mauve /mōv/ *a.* & *n.* pale purple.

maverick *n.* unorthodox or undisciplined person.

mawkish *a.* sentimental in a sickly way. **mawkishly** *adv.*, **mawkishness** *n.*

maxim *n.* sentence giving a general truth or rule of conduct.

maximize *v.* increase to a maximum. **maximization** *n.*

maximum *a.* & *n.* (*pl.* **-ima**) greatest (amount) possible. **maximal** *a.*, **maximally** *adv.*

may [1] *v.aux.* (**might**) used to express a wish, possibility, or permission.

may [2] *n.* hawthorn blossom.

maybe *adv.* perhaps.

mayday *n.* international radio signal of distress.

May Day 1 May, esp. as a festival.

mayfly *n.* insect with long hair-like tails, living in spring.

mayhem *n.* violent action.

mayonnaise *n.* creamy sauce made with eggs and oil.

mayor *n.* head of the municipal corporation of a city or borough. **mayoral** *a.*, **mayoralty** *n.*

mayoress *n.* female mayor; mayor's wife, or other woman with her ceremonial duties.

maypole *n.* tall pole for dancing round on May Day.

maze *n.* complex and baffling network of paths, lines, etc.

ME *abbr.* myalgic encephalomyelitis (disease characterized by prolonged tiredness).

me *pron.* objective case of *I*.

mead *n.* alcoholic drink made from fermented honey and water.

meadow *n.* field of grass.

meagre *a.* scant in amount.

meal [1] *n.* occasion when food is eaten; the food itself.

meal [2] *n.* coarsely ground grain.

mealy *a.* of or like meal. **mealy-mouthed** *a.* trying excessively to avoid offending people.

mean [1] *a.* miserly; selfish; unkind; poor in quality or appearance; low in rank; (*US*) vicious. **meanly** *adv.*, **meanness** *n.*

mean [2] *a.* & *n.* (thing) midway between two extremes; average.

mean [3] *v.* (**meant**) intend; convey or express; be likely to result in; be of specified importance.

meander *v.* follow a winding course; wander in a leisurely way. — *n.* winding course.

meaning *n.* what is meant. — *a.* expressive. **meaningful** *a.*, **meaningless** *a.*

means *n.* that by which a result is brought about; (*pl.*) resources. **by all means** certainly. **by no means** not nearly. **means test** official inquiry to establish neediness before giving help from public funds.

meant *see* **mean** [3].

meantime *adv.* meanwhile.

meanwhile *adv.* in the intervening period; at the same time.

measles *n.* infectious disease producing red spots on the body.

measly *a.* (*sl.*) meagre.

measurable *a.* able to be measured. **measurably** *adv.*

measure *n.* size or quantity found by measuring; unit, standard, device, or system used in measuring; rhythm; action taken for a purpose, (proposed) law. — *v.* find the size etc. of by comparison with a known standard; be of a certain size; mark or deal (a measured amount). **measure up to** reach the standard required by.

measured *a.* rhythmical; carefully considered.

measurement *n.* measuring; size etc. found by measuring.

meat *n.* animal flesh as food.

meaty *a.* (**-ier, -iest**) like meat; full of meat; full of subject-matter. **meatiness** *n.*

mechanic *n.* skilled workman who uses or repairs machines.

mechanical *a.* of or worked by machinery; done without conscious thought. **mechanically** *adv.*

mechanics *n.* study of motion and force; science of machinery; (as *pl.*) way a thing works.

mechanism *n.* way a machine works; its parts.

mechanize *v.* equip with machinery. **mechanization** *n.*

medal *n.* coin-like piece of metal commemorating an event or awarded for an achievement.

medallion *n.* large medal; circular ornamental design.

medallist *n.* winner of a medal.

meddle *v.* interfere in people's affairs; tinker. **meddler** *n.*

meddlesome *a.* often meddling.

media *see* **medium**. — *n.pl.* **the media** newspapers and broadcasting as conveying information to the public.

mediaeval *a.* = medieval.

medial *a.* situated in the middle. **medially** *adv.*

median *a.* in or passing through the middle. — *n.* median point or line.

mediate *v.* act as peacemaker between disputants; bring about (a settlement) thus. **mediation** *n.*, **mediator** *n.*

medical *a.* of the science of medicine. — *n.* (*colloq.*) medical examination. **medically** *adv.*

medicament *n.* any medicine, ointment, etc.

medicate *v.* treat with a medicinal substance. **medication** *n.*

medicinal *a.* having healing properties. **medicinally** *adv.*

medicine *n.* science of the prevention and cure of disease; substance used to treat disease. **medicine man** witch-doctor.

medieval *a.* of the Middle Ages.

mediocre *a.* of medium quality; second-rate. **mediocrity** *n.*

meditate *v.* think deeply. **meditation** *n.*, **meditative** *a.*, **meditatively** *adv.*

medium *n.* (*pl.* **media**) middle size, quality, etc.; substance or surroundings in which a thing exists; agency, means. — *a.* intermediate; average; moderate.

medley *n.* (*pl.* **-eys**) assortment; excerpts of music from various sources.

medulla *n.* spinal or bone marrow; hindmost segment of the brain. **medullary** *a.*

meek *a.* quiet and obedient, not protesting. **meekly** *adv.*, **meekness** *n.*

meerschaum /meérshəm/ *n.* tobacco pipe with a white clay bowl; this clay.

meet *v.* (**met**) come into contact (with); be present at the arrival of; make the acquaintance of; experience; satisfy (needs etc.). — *n.* assembly for a hunt etc.

meeting *n.* coming together; an assembly for discussion.

mega- *pref.* large; one million (as in *megavolts*, *megawatts*).

megabyte *n.* one million bytes.

megahertz *n.* one million cycles per second, as a unit of frequency of electromagnetic waves.

megalith *n.* large stone, esp. as a prehistoric monument. **megalithic** *a.*

megalomania *n.* excessive self-esteem, esp. as a form of insanity. **megalomaniac** *a.* & *n.*

megaphone *n.* funnel-shaped device for amplifying the voice.

megaton *n.* unit of explosive power equal to one million tons of TNT.

melancholy *n.* mental depression, sadness; gloom. — *a.* sad, gloomy.

mêlée /méllay/ *n.* confused fight; muddle.

melanin *n.* dark pigment in the skin, hair, etc.

mellifluous *a.* sweet-sounding.

mellow *a.* (of fruit) ripe and sweet; (of sound or colour) soft and rich; (of persons) having become kindly, e.g. with age. — *v.* make or become mellow.

melodic *a.* of melody. **melodically** *adv.*

melodious *a.* full of melody. **melodiously** *adv.*

melodrama *n.* sensational drama. **melodramatic** *a.*, **melodramatically** *adv.*

melody *n.* sweet music; main part in a piece of harmonized music.

melon *n.* large sweet fruit.

melt *v.* make into or become liquid, esp. by heat; soften through pity or love; fade away.

meltdown *n.* melting of an overheated reactor core.

member *n.* person or thing belonging to a particular group or society. **membership** *n.*

membrane *n.* thin flexible skin-like tissue. **membranous** *a.*

memento *n.* (*pl.* **-oes**) souvenir.

memo *n.* (*pl.* **-os**) (*colloq.*) memorandum.

memoir /mémwaar/ *n.* written account of events etc. that one remembers.

memorable *a.* worth remembering, easy to remember. **memorably** *adv.*, **memorability** *n.*

memorandum *n.* (*pl.* **-da**) note written as a reminder; (*pl.* **-dums**) written message from one colleague to another.

memorial *n.* object or custom etc. established in memory of an event or person(s). — *a.* serving as a memorial.

memorize *v.* learn (a thing) so as to know it from memory.

memory *n.* ability to remember things; thing(s) remembered; computer store for data etc.

men *see* **man**.

menace *n.* threat; annoying or troublesome person or thing. — *v.* threaten. **menacingly** *adv.*
menagerie *n.* collection of wild or strange animals for exhibition.
mend *v.* repair; make or become better. — *n.* repaired place. **on the mend** recovering after illness.
mendacious *a.* untruthful. **mendaciously** *adv.*, **mendacity** *n.*
mendicant *a.* & *n.* (person) living by begging.
menfolk *n.* men in general; men of one's family.
menhir /ménheer/ *n.* tall stone set up in prehistoric times.
menial *a.* lowly, degrading. — *n.* person who does menial tasks. **menially** *adv.*
meningitis *n.* inflammation of the membranes covering the brain and spinal cord.
meniscus *n.* curved surface of a liquid; lens convex on one side and concave on the other.
menopause *n.* time of life when a woman finally ceases to menstruate. **menopausal** *a.*
menorah *n.* seven-armed candelabrum used in Jewish worship.
menstrual *a.* of or in menstruation.
menstruate *v.* experience a monthly discharge of blood from the womb. **menstruation** *n.*
mensuration *n.* measuring; mathematical rules for this.
mental *a.* of, in, or performed by the mind; (*colloq.*) mad. **mental handicap** lack of normal intelligence through imperfect mental development. **mental hospital** (*colloq.*) psychiatric hospital. **mentally** *adv.*
mentality *n.* characteristic attitude of mind.
menthol *n.* camphor-like substance.
mentholated *a.* impregnated with menthol.
mention *v.* speak or write about briefly; refer to by name. — *n.* act of mentioning, being mentioned.
mentor *n.* trusted adviser.
menu *n.* (*pl.* **-us**) list of dishes to be served; list of options displayed on a computer screen.
mercantile *a.* trading, of trade or merchants.
mercenary *a.* working merely for money or reward; grasping. — *n.* professional soldier hired by a foreign country.
merchandise *n.* goods bought and sold or for sale. — *v.* trade; promote sales of (goods). **merchandiser** *n.*
merchant *n.* wholesale trader; (*US* & *Sc.*) retail trader. **merchant bank** one dealing in commercial loans and the financing of businesses. **merchant navy** shipping employed in commerce. **merchant ship** ship carrying merchandise.
merchantable *a.* saleable.
merchantman *n.* (*pl.* **-men**) merchant ship.
merciful *a.* showing mercy; giving relief from pain and suffering. **mercifulness** *n.*
mercifully *adv.* in a merciful way; (*colloq.*) thank goodness.
merciless *a.* showing no mercy. **mercilessly** *adv.*
mercurial *a.* of or caused by mercury; lively in temperament; liable to sudden changes of mood.
mercury *n.* heavy silvery usu. liquid metal. **mercuric** *a.*
mercy *n.* kindness shown to an offender or enemy etc. who is in one's power; merciful act. **at the mercy of** wholly in the power of or subject to.
mere [1] *a.* no more or no better than what is specified. **merest** *a.* very small or insignificant. **merely** *adv.*
mere [2] *n.* (*poetic*) lake.
merge *v.* combine into a whole; blend gradually.
merger *n.* combining of commercial companies etc. into one.
meridian *n.* great semicircle on the globe, passing through the North and South Poles.
meringue /məráng/ *n.* baked mixture of sugar and egg white; small cake of this.
merino *n.* (*pl.* **-os**) a kind of sheep with fine soft wool; soft woollen fabric.
merit *n.* feature or quality that deserves praise; worthiness. — *v.* **(merited)** deserve.
meritocracy *n.* government by persons selected for merit.
meritorious *a.* deserving praise.
merlin *n.* a kind of falcon.
mermaid *n.*, **merman** *n.* (*pl.* **-men**) imaginary half-human sea creature with a fish's tail instead of legs.
merry *a.* **(-ier, -iest)** cheerful and lively, joyous. **merry-go-round** *n.* roundabout at a funfair. **merrymaking** *n.* revelry. **merrily** *adv.*, **merriment** *n.*
mesh *n.* space between threads in net, sieve, etc.; network fabric. — *v.* (of a toothed wheel) engage with another.
mesmerize *v.* hypnotize, dominate the attention or will of.
mesolithic *a.* of the period between palaeolithic and neolithic.

mess *n.* dirty or untidy condition; unpleasant or untidy thing(s); difficult or confused situation, trouble; (in the armed forces) group who eat together, their dining room. — *v.* make untidy or dirty; muddle, bungle; (in the armed forces) eat with a group. **make a mess of** bungle. **mess about** potter; fool about.

message *n.* spoken or written communication; moral or social teaching.

messenger *n.* bearer of a message.

Messiah *n.* deliverer expected by Jews; Christ as this. **Messianic** *a.*

Messrs *see* **Mr**.

messy *a.* (**-ier**, **-iest**) untidy or dirty, slovenly. **messily** *adv.*, **messiness** *n.*

met *see* **meet**.

metabolism *n.* process by which nutrition takes place. **metabolic** *a.*, **metabolically** *adv.*

metabolize *v.* process (food) in metabolism.

metal *n.* any of a class of mineral substances such as gold, silver, iron, etc., or an alloy of these; road-metal. — *v.* make or mend (a road) with road-metal.

metallic *a.* of or like metal.

metallurgy *n.* science of extracting and working metals.

metamorphose *v.* change by metamorphosis.

metamorphosis *n.* (*pl.* **-phoses**) change of form or character. **metamorphic** *a.*

metaphor *n.* transferred use of a word or phrase (e.g. the *evening* of one's life, *food* for thought). **metaphorical** *a.*, **metaphorically** *adv.*

metaphysics *n.* branch of philosophy dealing with the nature of existence and of knowledge. **metaphysical** *a.*

mete *v.* **mete out** deal out.

meteor *n.* small mass of matter from outer space.

meteoric *a.* of meteors; swift and brilliant. **meteorically** *adv.*

meteorite *n.* meteor fallen to earth.

meteorology *n.* study of atmospheric conditions esp. in order to forecast weather. **meteorological** *a.*, **meteorologist** *n.*

meter [1] *n.* device measuring and indicating the quantity supplied, distance travelled, time elapsed, etc. — *v.* measure by a meter.

meter [2] *n.* (*US*) = metre.

methane *n.* colourless inflammable gas.

method *n.* procedure or way of doing something; orderliness.

methodical *a.* orderly, systematic. **methodically** *adv.*

meths *n.* (*colloq.*) methylated spirit.

methylated spirit form of alcohol used as a solvent and for heating.

meticulous *a.* very careful and exact. **meticulously** *adv.*, **meticulousness** *n.*

metre *n.* metric unit of length (about 39.4 inches); rhythm in poetry.

metric *a.* of or using the metric system; of poetic metre. **metric system** decimal system of weights and measures, using the metre, litre, and gram as units.

metrical *a.* of or composed in rhythmic metre, not prose.

metricate *v.* convert to a metric system. **metrication** *n.*

metronome *n.* device used to indicate tempo while practising music.

metropolis *n.* chief city of country or region.

metropolitan *a.* of a metropolis.

mettle *n.* courage, strength of character.

mettlesome *a.* spirited, brave.

mew *n.* cat's characteristic cry. — *v.* make this sound.

mews *n.* set of stables converted into dwellings etc.

mezzanine *n.* extra storey set between two others.

mezzotint *n.* a kind of engraving.

mg *abbr.* milligram(s).

MHz *abbr.* megahertz.

miaow *n.* & *v.* = mew.

miasma *n.* unpleasant or unwholesome air.

mica /mī́kə/ *n.* mineral substance used as an electrical insulator.

mice *see* **mouse**.

micro- *pref.* extremely small; one-millionth part of (as in *microgram*).

microbe *n.* micro-organism.

microbiology *n.* study of micro-organisms.

microchip *n.* tiny piece of a semiconductor holding a complex electronic circuit.

microcomputer *n.* computer in which the central processor is contained on microchip(s).

microcosm *n.* community or complex resembling something else but on a very small scale.

microfiche /mī́krōfeesh/ *n.* (*pl.* **-fiche**) small sheet of microfilm.

microfilm *n.* length of film bearing miniature photographs of document(s). — *v.* photograph on this.

microlight *n.* a kind of motorized hang-glider.

micrometer *n.* instrument for measuring small lengths or angles.

micron *n.* one-millionth of a metre.

micro-organism *n.* organism invisible to the naked eye.

microphone *n.* instrument for amplifying or broadcasting sound.

microprocessor *n.* data processor contained on microchip(s).

microscope *n.* instrument with lenses that magnify very small things and make them visible.

microscopic *a.* of a microscope; very small; too small to be seen without a microscope. **microscopically** *adv.*, **microscopy** *n.*

microsurgery *n.* surgery using a microscope.

microwave *n.* electromagnetic wave of length between about 50 cm and 1 mm; microwave oven. **microwave oven** oven using such waves to heat food quickly.

mid *a.* middle.

midday *n.* noon.

middle *a.* occurring at an equal distance from extremes or outer limits. — *n.* middle point, position, area, etc. **middle age** part of life between youth and old age. **middle-aged** *a.* **Middle Ages** 5th c.–1453, or *c.* 1000–1453. **middle class** class of society between upper and working classes. **Middle East** area from Egypt to Iran inclusive.

middleman *n.* (*pl.* **-men**) trader handling a commodity between producer and consumer.

middling *a.* moderately good.

midge *n.* small biting insect.

midget *n.* extremely small person or thing. — *a.* extremely small.

Midlands *n.pl.* inland counties of central England. **midland** *a.*

midnight *n.* 12 o'clock at night.

midriff *n.* front part of the body just above the waist.

midshipman *n.* (*pl.* **-men**) naval rank just below sub-lieutenant.

midst *n.* **in the midst of** in the middle of; surrounded by.

midway *adv.* halfway.

midwife *n.* (*pl.* **-wives**) person trained to assist at childbirth.

mien /meen/ *n.* person's manner or bearing.

might [1] *n.* great strength or power. **with might and main** with all one's power and energy.

might [2] *see* **may** [1]. — *v.aux.* (used to request permission or (like *may*) to express possibility).

mighty *a.* (**-ier**, **-iest**) very strong or powerful; very great. **mightily** *adv.*

migraine /meegrayn/ *n.* severe form of headache.

migrant *a.* & *n.* migrating (person or animal).

migrate *v.* leave one place and settle in another; (of animals) go from one place to another at each season. **migration** *n.*, **migratory** *a.*

mihrab *n.* niche or slab in a mosque, showing the direction of Mecca.

mild *a.* moderate in intensity, not harsh or drastic; gentle; not strongly flavoured. **mildly** *adv.*, **mildness** *n.*

mildew *n.* tiny fungi forming a coating on things exposed to damp. **mildewed** *a.*

mile *n.* measure of length, 1760 yds (about 1.609 km); (*colloq.*) great distance. **nautical mile** unit used in navigation, 2025 yds (1.852 km).

mileage *n.* distance in miles.

milestone *n.* stone showing the distance to a certain place; significant event or stage reached.

milieu /milyű/ *n.* (*pl.* **-eus**) environment, surroundings.

militant *a.* & *n.* (person) prepared to take aggressive action. **militancy** *n.*

militarism *n.* reliance on military attitudes. **militaristic** *n.*

military *a.* of soldiers or the army or all armed forces.

militate *v.* serve as a strong influence.

militia /milishə/ *n.* a military force, esp. of trained civilians available in an emergency.

milk *n.* white fluid secreted by female mammals as food for their young; cow's milk as food for human beings; milk-like liquid. — *v.* draw milk from; exploit. **milk teeth** first (temporary) teeth in young mammals. **milker** *n.*

milkman *n.* (*pl.* **-men**) person who delivers milk to customers.

milky *a.* of or like milk; containing much milk. **Milky Way** broad luminous band of stars.

mill *n.* machinery for grinding or processing specified material; building containing this. — *v.* process in a mill; produce grooves in (metal); move in a confused mass. **miller** *n.*

millennium *n.* (*pl.* **-ums**) period of 1000 years; future period of great happiness for everyone.

millepede *n.* small crawling creature with many legs.

millet *n.* cereal plant; its seeds.

milli- *pref.* one-thousandth part of (as in *milligram*, *millilitre*, *millimetre*).

milliner *n.* person who makes or sells women's hats. **millinery** *n.*

million *n.* one thousand thousand (1,000,000). **millionth** *a.* & *n.*

millionaire *n.* person who possesses a million pounds.

millstone *n.* heavy circular stone for grinding corn; great burden.
milometer *n.* instrument measuring the distance in miles travelled by a vehicle.
milt *n.* sperm discharged by a male fish over eggs laid by the female.
mime *n.* acting with gestures without words. — *v.* act with mime.
mimic *v.* (**mimicked**) imitate, esp. playfully or for entertainment. — *n.* person who is clever at mimicking others. **mimicry** *n.*
mimosa *n.* tropical shrub with small ball-shaped flowers.
minaret *n.* tall slender tower on or beside a mosque.
mince *v.* cut into small pieces in a mincer; walk or speak with affected refinement. — *n.* minced meat. **mince pie** pie containing mincemeat.
mincemeat *n.* mixture of dried fruit, sugar, etc., used in pies.
mincer *n.* machine with revolving blades for cutting food into very small pieces.
mind *n.* ability to be aware of things and to think and reason; a person's attention, remembrance, intention, or opinion; sanity. — *v.* have charge of; object to; remember and be careful (about).
minded *a.* having inclinations or interests of a certain kind.
minder *n.* person whose job is to have charge of a person or thing; (*sl.*) bodyguard.
mindful *a.* taking thought or care (of something). **mindfulness** *n.*
mindless *a.* without intelligence. **mindlessness** *n.*
mine [1] *a.* & *poss.pron.* belonging to me.
mine [2] *n.* excavation for extracting metal or coal etc.; abundant source; explosive device laid in or on the ground or in water. — *v.* dig for minerals, extract in this way; lay explosive mines under or in.
minefield *n.* area where explosive mines have been laid.
miner *n.* person who works in a mine.
mineral *n.* inorganic natural substance; fizzy soft drink. — *a.* of or containing minerals. **mineral water** water naturally containing dissolved mineral salts or gases.
mineralogy *n.* study of minerals. **mineralogist** *n.*
minesweeper *n.* ship for clearing away mines laid in the sea.
mingle *v.* blend together; mix socially.
mini- *pref.* miniature.
miniature *a.* very small, on a small scale. — *n.* small-scale portrait, copy, or model.
miniaturize *v.* make miniature, produce in a very small version. **miniaturization** *n.*
minibus *n.* small bus-like vehicle with seats for only a few people.
minim *n.* note in music, lasting half as long as a semibreve; one-sixtieth of a fluid drachm.
minimal *a.* very small, least possible. **minimally** *adv.*
minimize *v.* reduce to a minimum; represent as small or unimportant. **minimization** *n.*
minimum *a.* & *n.* (*pl.* **-ima**) smallest (amount) possible.
minion *n.* (*derog.*) assistant.
minister *n.* head of a government department; clergyman; senior diplomatic representative. — *v.* **minister to** attend to the needs of. **ministerial** *a.*
ministry *n.* government department headed by a minister; period of government under one leader; work of a clergyman.
mink *n.* small stoat-like animal; its valuable fur; coat made of this.
minnow *n.* small fish of the carp family.
minor *a.* lesser; not very important. — *n.* person not yet legally of adult age.
minority *n.* smallest part of a group or class; small group differing from others; age when a person is not yet legally adult.
minstrel *n.* medieval singer and musician.
mint [1] *n.* place authorized to make a country's coins. — *v.* make (coins). **in mint condition** new-looking.
mint [2] *n.* fragrant herb; peppermint, sweet flavoured with this. **minty** *a.*
minuet /minyoo-ét/ *n.* slow stately dance.
minus *prep.* reduced by subtraction of; below zero; (*colloq.*) without. — *a.* less than zero; less than the amount indicated.
minuscule *a.* extremely small.
minute [1] /minnit/ *n.* one-sixtieth of an hour or degree; moment of time; (*pl.*) official summary of an assembly's proceedings. — *v.* record in the minutes.
minute [2] /mīnyo͞ot/ *a.* extremely small; very precise. **minutely** *adv.*, **minuteness** *n.*
minutiae /mīnyo͞oshi-ee/ *n.pl.* very small details.
miracle *n.* wonderful event attributed to a supernatural agency; remarkable event or thing. **miraculous** *a.*, **miraculously** *adv.*
mirage *n.* optical illusion caused by atmospheric conditions.
mire *n.* swampy ground, bog; mud or sticky dirt. **miry** *a.*
mirror *n.* glass coated so that reflections can be seen in it. — *v.* reflect in a mirror.

mirth *n.* merriment, laughter.
mis- *pref.* badly, wrongly.
misadventure *n.* piece of bad luck.
misanthrope, misanthropist *ns.* person who dislikes people in general. **misanthropy** *n.*, **misanthropic** *a.*
misapprehend *v.* misunderstand. **misapprehension** *n.*
misappropriate *v.* take dishonestly. **misappropriation** *n.*
misbehave *v.* behave badly.
miscalculate *v.* calculate incorrectly. **miscalculation** *n.*
miscarriage *n.* abortion occurring naturally.
miscarry *v.* have a miscarriage; go wrong, be unsuccessful.
miscellaneous *a.* assorted.
miscellany *n.* collection of assorted items.
mischance *n.* misfortune.
mischief *n.* children's annoying but not malicious conduct; playful malice; harm, damage.
mischievous *a.* full of mischief. **mischievously** *adv.*, **mischievousness** *n.*
misconception *n.* wrong interpretation.
misconduct *n.* bad behaviour; mismanagement.
misconstrue *v.* misinterpret. **misconstruction** *n.*
miscreant *n.* wrongdoer.
misdeed *n.* wrongful act.
misdemeanour *n.* misdeed.
miser *n.* person who hoards money and spends as little as possible. **miserly** *a.*, **miserliness** *n.*
miserable *a.* full of misery; wretchedly poor in quality or surroundings. **miserably** *adv.*
misery *n.* great unhappiness or discomfort; (*colloq.*) discontented or disagreeable person.
misfire *v.* (of a gun or engine) fail to fire correctly; go wrong.
misfit *n.* person not well suited to his work or environment.
misfortune *n.* bad luck, unfortunate event.
misgiving *n.* feeling of doubt or slight fear or mistrust.
misguided *a.* mistaken in one's opinions or actions.
mishap *n.* unlucky accident.
misinform *v.* give wrong information to. **misinformation** *n.*
misinterpret *v.* interpret incorrectly. **misinterpretation** *n.*
misjudge *v.* form a wrong opinion or estimate of.
mislay *v.* (**mislaid**) lose temporarily.
mislead *v.* (**misled**) cause to form a wrong impression.
mismanage *v.* manage badly or wrongly. **mismanagement** *n.*
misnomer *n.* wrongly applied name or description.
misogynist *n.* person who hates women. **misogyny** *n.*
misplace *v.* put in a wrong place; place (confidence etc.) unwisely; mislay.
misprint *n.* error in printing.
misquote *v.* quote incorrectly. **misquotation** *n.*
misread *v.* (**-read**) read or interpret incorrectly.
misrepresent *v.* represent in a false way. **misrepresentation** *n.*
misrule *n.* bad government.
Miss *n.* (*pl.* **Misses**) title of a girl or unmarried woman.
miss *v.* fail to hit, catch, see, hear, understand, etc.; notice or regret the absence or loss of. — *n.* failure to hit or attain what is aimed at.
missel thrush = mistle thrush.
misshapen *a.* badly shaped.
missile *n.* object or weapon suitable for projecting at a target.
missing *a.* not present; not in its place, lost.
mission *n.* task that a person or group is sent to perform; this group; missionaries' headquarters.
missionary *n.* person sent to spread religious faith.
misspell *v.* (**misspelt**) spell incorrectly. **misspelling** *n.*
mist *n.* water vapour near the ground or clouding a window etc.; thing resembling this. — *v.* cover or become covered with mist.
mistake *n.* incorrect idea or opinion; thing done incorrectly. — *v.* (**mistook, mistaken**) misunderstand; choose or identify wrongly.
mistle thrush large thrush.
mistletoe *n.* plant with white berries, growing on trees.
mistral *n.* cold north or north-west wind in southern France.
mistress *n.* woman who has control of people or things; female teacher; man's illicit female lover.
mistrust *v.* feel no trust in. — *n.* lack of trust. **mistrustful** *a.*
misty *a.* (**-ier, -iest**) full of mist; indistinct. **mistily** *adv.*, **mistiness** *n.*
misunderstand *v.* (**-stood**) fail to understand correctly. **misunderstanding** *n.*
misuse *v.* /missyōōz/ use wrongly; treat badly. — *n.* /missyōōss/ wrong use.
mite *n.* very small spider-like animal; small creature, esp. a child; small amount.

mitigate *v.* make seem less serious or severe. **mitigation** *n.*
mitre *n.* pointed headdress of bishops and abbots; join with tapered ends that form a right angle. — *v.* join in this way.
mitt *n.* mitten.
mitten *n.* glove with no partitions between the fingers, or leaving the fingertips bare.
mix *v.* combine (different things); blend; prepare by doing this; be compatible; be sociable. — *n.* mixture. **mix up** mix thoroughly; confuse. **mixer** *n.*
mixed *a.* composed of various elements; of or for both sexes. **mixed-up** *a.* (*colloq.*) muddled; not well adjusted emotionally.
mixture *n.* thing made by mixing; process of mixing things.
ml *abbr.* millilitre(s).
mm *abbr.* millimetre(s).
mnemonic /nimónnik/ *a.* & *n.* (verse etc.) aiding the memory.
moan *n.* low mournful sound; grumble. — *v.* make or utter with a moan. **moaner** *n.*
moat *n.* deep wide usu. water-filled ditch round a castle etc.
mob *n.* large disorderly crowd; (*sl.*) gang. — *v.* (**mobbed**) crowd round in great numbers.
mobile *a.* able to move or be moved easily. — *n.* artistic hanging structure whose parts move in currents of air. **mobility** *n.*
mobilize *v.* assemble (troops etc.) for active service. **mobilization** *n.*, **mobilizer** *n.*
moccasin *n.* soft flat-soled leather shoe.
mock *v.* make fun of by imitating; jeer. — *a.* imitation. **mock-up** *n.* model for testing or study.
mockery *n.* mocking, ridicule; absurd or unsatisfactory imitation.
mode *n.* way a thing is done; current fashion; specific state of operation in a computer. **modal** *a.*
model *n.* three-dimensional reproduction, usu. on a smaller scale; pattern; exemplary person or thing; person employed to pose for an artist or display clothes in a shop etc. by wearing them. — *a.* exemplary. — *v.* (**modelled**) make a model of; shape; work as artist's or fashion model, display (clothes) thus.
modem *n.* device for sending and receiving computer data through a telephone line.
moderate *a.* /móddərət/ medium; not extreme or excessive. — *n.* /móddərət/ holder of moderate views. — *v.* /móddərayt/ make or become moderate. **moderately** *adv.*
moderation *n.* moderating. **in moderation** in moderate amounts.
modern *a.* of present or recent times; in current style. **modernity** *n.*
modernist *n.* person who favours modern ideas or methods. **modernism** *n.*
modernize *v.* make modern, adapt to modern ways. **modernization** *n.*, **modernizer** *n.*
modest *a.* not vain or boastful; moderate in size etc., not showy; showing regard for conventional decencies. **modestly** *adv.*, **modesty** *n.*
modicum *n.* small amount.
modify *v.* make less severe; make partial changes in. **modification** *n.*
modish /módish/ *a.* fashionable.
modulate *v.* regulate, moderate; vary in tone or pitch. **modulation** *n.*
module *n.* standardized part or independent unit; unit of training or education. **modular** *a.*
mogul *n.* (*colloq.*) important or influential person.
mohair *n.* fine silky hair of the angora goat; yarn or fabric made from this.
moiety /móyəti/ *n.* half.
moist *a.* slightly wet.
moisten *v.* make or become moist.
moisture *n.* water or other liquid diffused through a substance or as vapour or condensed on a surface.
moisturize *v.* make (skin) less dry. **moisturizer** *n.*
molar *n.* back tooth with a broad top, used in chewing.
molasses *n.* syrup from raw sugar; (*US*) treacle.
mole [1] *n.* small dark spot on human skin.
mole [2] *n.* small burrowing animal with dark fur; spy established within an organization.
molecule *n.* very small unit (usu. a group of atoms) of a substance. **molecular** *a.*
molehill *n.* mound of earth thrown up by a mole.
molest *v.* attack or interfere with, esp. sexually. **molestation** *n.*
mollify *v.* soothe the anger of. **mollification** *n.*
mollusc *n.* animal with a soft body and often a hard shell.
mollycoddle *v.* pamper.
molten *a.* liquefied by heat.
molybdenum *n.* hard metal used in steel.
moment *n.* point or brief portion of time; importance.
momentary *a.* lasting only a moment. **momentarily** *adv.*
momentous *a.* of great importance. **momentously** *adv.*

momentum *n.* impetus gained by a moving body.
monarch *n.* ruler with the title of king, queen, emperor, or empress. **monarchic** *a.*, **monarchical** *a.*
monarchist *n.* supporter of monarchy. **monarchism** *n.*
monarchy *n.* form of government with a monarch as the supreme ruler; country governed thus.
monastery *n.* residence of a community of monks.
monastic *a.* of monks or monasteries. **monasticism** *n.*
monetarist *n.* person who advocates control of the money supply in order to curb inflation. **monetarism** *n.*
monetary *a.* of money or currency.
money *n.* current coins; coins and banknotes; (*pl.* **-eys**) any form of currency; wealth. **money-spinner** *n.* profitable thing.
moneyed *a.* wealthy.
Mongol *n.* & *a.* (native) of Mongolia.
mongoose *n.* (*pl.* **-gooses**) stoat-like tropical animal that can attack and kill snakes.
mongrel *n.* animal (esp. a dog) of mixed breed. — *a.* of mixed origin or character.
monitor *n.* device used to observe or test the operation of something; pupil with special duties in a school. — *v.* keep watch over; record and test or control.
monk *n.* member of a male religious community. **monkish** *a.*
monkey *n.* (*pl.* **-eys**) animal of a group closely related to man; mischievous person. — *v.* (**monkeyed**) tamper mischievously. **monkey-nut** *n.* peanut. **monkey-puzzle** *n.* evergreen tree with sharp stiff leaves. **monkey wrench** wrench with an adjustable jaw.
mono *a.* & *n.* (*pl.* **-os**) monophonic (sound or recording).
mono- *pref.* one, alone, single.
monochrome *a.* done in only one colour, black and white.
monocle *n.* eyeglass for one eye only.
monocular *a.* with or for one eye.
monogamy *n.* system of being married to only one person at a time. **monogamous** *a.*
monogram *n.* letters (esp. a person's initials) combined in a design. **monogrammed** *a.*
monolith *n.* large single upright block of stone; massive organization etc. **monolithic** *a.*
monologue *n.* long speech.
monomania *n.* obsession with one idea or interest. **monomaniac** *n.*
monophonic *a.* using only one transmission channel for reproduction of sound.
monoplane *n.* aeroplane with only one set of wings.
monopolize *v.* have a monopoly of; not allow others to share in. **monopolization** *n.*
monopoly *n.* sole possession or control of something, esp. of trade in a specified commodity. **monopolist** *n.*
monorail *n.* railway in which the track is a single rail.
monosodium glutamate substance added to food to enhance its flavour.
monosyllable *n.* word of one syllable. **monosyllabic** *a.*
monotheism *n.* doctrine that there is only one God. **monotheist** *n.*, **monotheistic** *a.*
monotone *n.* level unchanging tone of voice.
monotonous *a.* dull because lacking in variety or variation. **monotonously** *adv.*, **monotony** *n.*
monsoon *n.* seasonal wind in South Asia; rainy season accompanying this.
monster *n.* thing that is huge or very abnormal in form; huge ugly or frightening creature; very cruel or wicked person.
monstrosity *n.* monstrous thing.
monstrous *a.* like a monster, huge; outrageous, absurd.
montage *n.* making of a composite picture from pieces of others; this picture; joining of disconnected shots in a cinema film.
month *n.* each of the twelve portions into which the year is divided; period of 28 days.
monthly *a.* & *adv.* (produced or occurring) once a month. — *n.* monthly periodical.
monument *n.* thing commemorating a person or event etc.; structure of historical importance.
monumental *a.* of or serving as a monument; massive; extremely great.
moo *n.* cow's low deep cry. — *v.* make this sound.
mooch *v.* (*colloq.*) walk slowly and aimlessly.
mood *n.* temporary state of mind or spirits; fit of bad temper or depression.
moody *a.* (**-ier**, **-iest**) gloomy, sullen; liable to become like this. **moodily** *adv.*, **moodiness** *n.*
moon *n.* earth's satellite, made visible by light it reflects from the sun; natural satellite of any planet. — *v.* behave dreamily.
moonlight *n.* light from the moon. — *v.*

(*colloq.*) have two paid jobs, one by day and the other in the evening.

moonlit *a.* lit by the moon.

moonstone *n.* pearly semiprecious stone.

Moor *n.* member of a Muslim people of north-west Africa. **Moorish** *a.*

moor [1] *n.* stretch of open uncultivated land with low shrubs.

moor [2] *v.* secure (a boat etc.) to a fixed object by means of cable(s).

moorhen *n.* small waterbird.

moorings *n.pl.* cables or place for mooring a boat.

moose *n.* (*pl.* **moose**) elk of North America.

mop *n.* pad or bundle of yarn on a stick, used for cleaning things; thick mass of hair. — *v.* (**mopped**) clean with a mop. **mop up** wipe up with a mop or cloth etc.

mope *v.* be unhappy and listless.

moped *n.* motorized bicycle.

moraine *n.* mass of stones etc. deposited by a glacier.

moral *a.* concerned with right and wrong conduct; virtuous. — *n.* moral lesson or principle; (*pl.*) person's moral habits, esp. sexual conduct. **moral support** encouragement. **moral victory** a triumph though without concrete gain. **morally** *adv.*

morale /mərraál/ *n.* state of a person's or group's spirits and confidence.

moralist *n.* person who expresses or teaches moral principles.

morality *n.* moral principles or rules; goodness or rightness.

moralize *v.* talk or write about the morality of something.

morass *n.* marsh, bog; complex entanglement.

moratorium *n.* (*pl.* **-ums**) temporary agreed ban on an activity.

morbid *a.* preoccupied with gloomy or unpleasant things; unhealthy. **morbidly** *adv.*, **morbidness** *n.*, **morbidity** *n.*

mordant *a.* (of wit etc.) caustic.

more *a.* greater in quantity or intensity etc. — *n.* greater amount or number. — *adv.* to a greater extent; again. **more or less** approximately.

moreover *adv.* besides.

morgue /morg/ *n.* mortuary.

moribund *a.* in a dying state.

Mormon *n.* member of a Christian sect founded in the USA.

morning *n.* part of the day before noon or the midday meal.

morocco *n.* goatskin leather.

moron *n.* (*colloq.*) mentally handicapped person; fool. **moronic** *a.*

morose *a.* gloomy and unsociable, sullen. **morosely** *adv.*, **moroseness** *n.*

morphia *n.* morphine.

morphine *n.* drug made from opium, used to relieve pain.

morphology *n.* study of forms of animals and plants or of words. **morphological** *a.*

morris dance English folk dance by men in costume.

Morse *n.* **Morse code** code of signals using short and long sounds or flashes of light.

morsel *n.* small amount; small piece of food.

mortal *a.* subject to death; fatal; deadly. — *n.* mortal being. **mortally** *adv.*

mortality *n.* being mortal; loss of life on a large scale; death rate.

mortar *n.* mixture of lime or cement with sand and water for joining bricks or stones; bowl in which substances are pounded with a pestle; short cannon.

mortarboard *n.* stiff square cap worn as part of academic dress.

mortgage /mórgij/ *n.* loan for purchase of property, in which the property itself is pledged as security; agreement effecting this. — *v.* pledge (property) as security thus.

mortgagee /mórgijeé/ *n.* borrower in a mortgage.

mortgager /mórgijər/ *n.* (in law **mortgagor**) lender in a mortgage.

mortify *v.* humiliate greatly; (of flesh) become gangrenous. **mortification** *n.*

mortise *n.* hole in one part of a framework shaped to receive the end of another part. **mortise lock** lock set in (not on) a door.

mortuary *n.* place where dead bodies may be kept temporarily.

mosaic *n.* pattern or picture made with small pieces of glass or stone of different colours.

Moslem *a.* & *n.* = Muslim.

mosque *n.* Muslim place of worship.

mosquito *n.* (*pl.* **-oes**) a kind of gnat.

moss *n.* small flowerless plant forming a dense growth in moist places. **mossy** *a.*

most *a.* greatest in quantity or intensity etc. — *n.* greatest amount or number. — *adv.* to the greatest extent; very. **at most** not more than. **for the most part** in most cases; in most of its extent.

mostly *adv.* for the most part.

motel *n.* roadside hotel for motorists.

moth *n.* insect like a butterfly but usu. flying at night; similar insect whose larvae feed on cloth or fur. **moth-eaten** *a.* damaged by the larvae of moths.

mothball *n.* small ball of pungent substance for keeping moths away from clothes.

mother *n.* female parent; title of the female head of a religious community. — *v.* look after in a motherly way. **mother-in-law** *n.* (*pl.* **mothers-in-law**) mother of one's wife or husband. **mother-of-pearl** *n.* pearly substance lining shells of oysters and mussels etc. **mother tongue** one's native language. **motherhood** *n.*

motherland *n.* one's native country.

motherless *a.* without a living mother.

motherly *a.* showing a mother's kindness. **motherliness** *n.*

motif *n.* recurring design, feature, or melody.

motion *n.* moving; movement; formal proposal put to a meeting for discussion; emptying of the bowels, faeces. — *v.* make a gesture directing (a person) to do something. **motion picture** cinema film.

motionless *a.* not moving.

motivate *v.* supply a motive to; cause to feel active interest. **motivation** *n.*

motive *n.* that which induces a person to act in a certain way. — *a.* producing movement or action.

motley *a.* multicoloured; assorted. — *n.* (*old use*) jester's particoloured costume.

motor *n.* machine supplying motive power; car. — *a.* producing motion; driven by a motor. **motor bike** (*colloq.*) motor cycle. **motor cycle** motor-driven two-wheeled vehicle. **motor cyclist** rider of a motor cycle. **motor vehicle** vehicle with a motor engine, for use on ordinary roads.

motorcade *n.* procession or parade of motor vehicles.

motorist *n.* driver of a car.

motorize *v.* equip with motor(s) or motor vehicles.

motorway *n.* road designed for fast long-distance traffic.

mottled *a.* patterned with irregular patches of colour.

motto *n.* (*pl.* **-oes**) short sentence or phrase expressing an ideal or rule of conduct; maxim, riddle, etc., inside a paper cracker.

mould [1] *n.* hollow container into which a liquid is poured to set in a desired shape; pudding etc. made in this. — *v.* shape; guide or control the development of.

mould [2] *n.* furry growth of tiny fungi on a damp substance. **mouldy** *a.*

mould [3] *n.* soft fine earth rich in organic matter.

moulder *v.* decay and rot away.

moult *v.* shed feathers, hair, or skin before new growth. — *n.* process of moulting.

mound *n.* mass of piled-up earth or small stones; small hill.

mount [1] *n.* mountain, hill.

mount [2] *v.* go up; get on a horse etc.; increase; fix on or in support(s) or setting; organize, arrange. — *n.* horse for riding; thing on which something is fixed.

mountain *n.* mass of land rising to a great height; large heap or pile. **mountain ash** rowan tree. **mountain bike** strong bicycle suitable for riding on rough hilly ground.

mountaineer *n.* person who climbs mountains. — *v.* climb mountains as a recreation.

mountainous *a.* full of mountains; huge.

mourn *v.* feel or express sorrow or regret about (a dead person or lost thing). **mourner** *n.*

mournful *a.* sorrowful. **mournfully** *adv.*, **mournfulness** *n.*

mourning *n.* dark clothes worn as a symbol of bereavement.

mouse *n.* (*pl.* **mice**) small rodent with a long tail; quiet timid person; small rolling device for moving the cursor on a VDU screen.

moussaka *n.* Greek dish of minced meat and aubergine.

mousse *n.* frothy creamy dish; substance of similar texture.

moustache /məstaásh/ *n.* hair on the upper lip.

mousy *a.* dull greyish-brown; quiet and timid. **mousiness** *n.*

mouth *n.* /mowth/ opening in the head through which food is taken in and sounds uttered; opening of a bag, cave, cannon, etc.; place where a river enters the sea. — *v.* /mowth/ form (words) soundlessly with the lips. **mouth-organ** *n.* small instrument played by blowing and sucking.

mouthpiece *n.* part of an instrument placed between or near the lips; spokesperson.

mouthwash *n.* liquid for cleansing the mouth.

movable *a.* able to be moved.

move *v.* (cause to) change in place, position, or attitude; change one's residence; provoke an emotion in; take action; put to a meeting for discussion. — *n.* act of moving; moving of a piece in chess etc.; calculated action. **mover** *n.*

movement *n.* moving; move; moving parts; group with a common cause; section of a long piece of music.

movie *n.* (*US colloq.*) cinema film.

moving *a.* arousing pity or sympathy. **movingly** *adv.*

mow *v.* (**mown**) cut down (grass or grain etc.); cut grass etc. from. **mow down** kill or destroy by a moving force. **mower** *n.*

m.p.h. *abbr.* miles per hour.

Mr *n.* (*pl.* **Messrs**) title prefixed to a man's name.

Mrs *n.* (*pl.* **Mrs**) title prefixed to a married woman's name.

Ms *n.* title prefixed to a married or unmarried woman's name.

much *a.* & *n.* (existing in) great quantity. — *adv.* in a great degree; to a great extent.

mucilage *n.* sticky substance got from plants; adhesive gum.

muck *n.* farmyard manure; (*colloq.*) dirt, a mess. **mucky** *a.*

muckraking *n.* seeking and exposing scandal.

mucous *a.* like or covered with mucus.

mucus *n.* slimy substance coating the inner surface of hollow organs of the body.

mud *n.* wet soft earth. **muddy** *a.*

muddle *v.* confuse, mix up; progress in a haphazard way. — *n.* muddled condition or things.

mudguard *n.* curved cover above a wheel as a protection against spray thrown up by it.

muesli *n.* food of mixed crushed cereals, dried fruit, nuts, etc.

muezzin /moo-ézzin/ *n.* man who proclaims the hours of prayer for Muslims.

muff [1] *n.* tube-shaped usu. furry covering for the hands.

muff [2] *v.* (*colloq.*) bungle.

muffin *n.* light round yeast cake eaten toasted and buttered.

muffle *v.* wrap for warmth or protection, or to deaden sound; make less loud or less distinct.

muffler *n.* scarf worn for warmth.

mufti *n.* plain clothes worn by one who usually wears a uniform.

mug *n.* large drinking vessel with a handle, for use without a saucer; (*sl.*) face; (*sl.*) person who is easily outwitted. — *v.* (**mugged**) rob (a person) with violence, esp. in a public place. **mugger** *n.*

muggy *a.* (**-ier, -iest**) (of weather) oppressively damp and warm. **mugginess** *n.*

mulberry *n.* purple or white fruit resembling a blackberry; tree bearing this; dull purplish-red.

mulch *n.* mixture of wet straw, leaves, etc., spread on ground to protect plants or retain moisture. — *v.* cover with mulch.

mulct *v.* take money from (a person) by a fine, taxation, etc.

mule [1] *n.* animal that is the offspring of a horse and a donkey.

mule [2] *n.* backless slipper.

mull [1] *v.* heat (wine etc.) with sugar and spices, as a drink.

mull [2] *v.* **mull over** think over.

mullah *n.* Muslim learned in Islamic law.

mullet *n.* small edible sea fish.

mulligatawny *n.* curry-flavoured soup.

mullion *n.* upright bar between the sections of a tall window.

multi- *pref.* many.

multicultural *a.* of or involving several cultural or ethnic groups. **multiculturalism** *n.*

multifarious *a.* very varied. **multifariously** *adv.*

multinational *a.* & *n.* (business company) operating in several countries.

multiple *a.* having or affecting many parts. — *n.* quantity containing another a number of times without remainder.

multiplex *a.* having many elements.

multiplication *n.* multiplying.

multiplicity *n.* great variety.

multiply *v.* add a quantity to itself a specified number of times; increase in number. **multiplier** *n.*

multiracial *a.* of or involving people of several races.

multitude *n.* great number of things or people.

multitudinous *a.* very numerous.

mum [1] *a.* (*colloq.*) silent.

mum [2] *n.* (*colloq.*) mother.

mumble *v.* speak or utter indistinctly. — *n.* indistinct speech.

mumbo-jumbo *n.* meaningless ritual; deliberately obscure language.

mummify *v.* preserve (a corpse) by embalming as in ancient Egypt. **mummification** *n.*

mummy [1] *n.* corpse embalmed and wrapped for burial, esp. in ancient Egypt.

mummy [2] *n.* (*colloq.*) mother.

mumps *n.* virus disease with painful swellings in the neck.

munch *v.* chew vigorously.

mundane *a.* dull, routine; worldly.

municipal *a.* of a town or city.

municipality *n.* self-governing town or district.

munificent *a.* splendidly generous. **munificently** *adv.*, **munificence** *n.*

munitions *n.pl.* weapons, ammunition, etc., used in war.

mural *a.* of or on a wall. — *n.* a painting made on a wall.

murder *n.* intentional unlawful killing. — *v.* kill intentionally and unlawfully. **murderer** *n.*, **murderess** *n.fem.*
murderous *a.* involving or capable of murder.
murk *n.* darkness, gloom. **murky** *a.*
murmur *n.* low continuous sound; softly spoken words. — *v.* make a murmur; speak or utter softly.
murrain *n.* infectious disease of cattle.
muscle /múss'l/ *n.* strip of fibrous tissue able to contract and so move a part of the body; muscular power; strength. — *v.* **muscle in** (*colloq.*) force one's way.
muscular *a.* of muscles; having well-developed muscles. **muscularity** *n.*
muse *v.* ponder.
museum *n.* place where objects of historical interest are collected and displayed.
mush *n.* soft pulp.
mushroom *n.* edible fungus with a stem and a domed cap. — *v.* spring up in large numbers; rise and spread in a mushroom shape.
mushy *a.* as or like mush; feebly sentimental. **mushiness** *n.*
music *n.* arrangement of sounds of one or more voices or instruments; written form of this.
musical *a.* of or involving music; fond of or skilled in music; sweet-sounding. — *n.* play with songs and dancing. **musically** *adv.*
musician *n.* person skilled in music.
musicology *n.* study of the history and forms of music. **musicologist** *n.*
musk *n.* substance secreted by certain animals or produced synthetically, used in perfumes. **musky** *a.*
musket *n.* long-barrelled gun formerly used by infantry.
Muslim *a.* of or believing in Muhammad's teaching. — *n.* believer in this faith.
muslin *n.* a kind of thin cotton cloth.
musquash *n.* rat-like North American water animal; its fur.
mussel *n.* a kind of bivalve mollusc.
must *v.aux.* (used to express necessity or obligation, certainty, or insistence). — *n.* (*colloq.*) thing that must be done or visited etc.
mustang *n.* wild horse of Mexico and California.
mustard *n.* sharp-tasting yellow condiment made from the seeds of a plant; this plant.
musty *a.* (**-ier**, **-iest**) smelling mouldy, stale. **mustiness** *n.*
mutable *a.* liable to change, fickle. **mutability** *n.*
mutant *a.* & *n.* (living thing) differing from its parents as a result of genetic change.
mutate *v.* change in form.
mutation *n.* change in form; mutant.
mute *a.* silent; dumb. — *n.* dumb person; device muffling the sound of a musical instrument. — *v.* deaden or muffle the sound of. **mutely** *adv.*, **muteness** *n.*
mutilate *v.* injure or disfigure by cutting off a part. **mutilation** *n.*
mutineer *n.* person who mutinies.
mutinous *a.* rebellious, ready to mutiny. **mutinously** *adv.*
mutiny *n.* rebellion against authority, esp. by members of the armed forces. — *v.* engage in mutiny.
mutter *v.* speak or utter in a low unclear tone; utter subdued grumbles. — *n.* muttering.
mutton *n.* flesh of sheep as food.
mutual *a.* felt or done by each to the other; (*colloq.*) common to two or more. **mutually** *adv.*, **mutuality** *n.*
muzzle *n.* projecting nose and jaws of certain animals; open end of a firearm; strap etc. over an animal's head to prevent it from biting or feeding. — *v.* put a muzzle on; prevent from expressing opinions freely.
muzzy *a.* dazed, feeling stupefied. **muzziness** *n.*
my *a.* belonging to me.
mycology *n.* study of fungi.
myna *n.* bird of the starling family that can mimic sounds.
myopia /mīópiə/ *n.* short sight. **myopic** /mīóppik/ *a.*
myriad *n.* vast number.
myrrh /mur/ *n.* gum resin used in perfumes, medicines, and incense.
myrtle *n.* evergreen shrub.
myself *pron.* emphatic and reflexive form of *I* and *me*.
mysterious *a.* full of mystery, puzzling. **mysteriously** *adv.*
mystery *n.* a matter that remains unexplained; quality of being unexplained or obscure; story dealing with a puzzling crime.
mystic *a.* having a hidden or symbolic meaning, esp. in religion; inspiring a sense of mystery and awe. — *n.* person who seeks to obtain union with God by spiritual contemplation. **mystical** *a.*, **mystically** *adv.*, **mysticism** *n.*
mystify *v.* cause to feel puzzled. **mystification** *n.*
mystique *n.* aura of mystery or mystical power.

myth *n.* traditional tale(s) containing beliefs about ancient times or natural events; imaginary person or thing. **mythical** *a.*

mythology *n.* myths; study of myths. **mythological** *a.*

myxomatosis *n.* fatal virus disease of rabbits.

N

N. *abbr.* north; northern.

nab *v.* (**nabbed**) (*sl.*) catch in wrongdoing, arrest; seize.

nadir *n.* lowest point.

naevus /neévəss/ *n.* (*pl.* **-vi**) red birthmark.

nag [1] *n.* (*colloq.*) horse.

nag [2] *v.* (**nagged**) scold continually; (of pain) be felt persistently.

naiad /nīad/ *n.* water nymph.

nail *n.* layer of horny substance over the outer tip of a finger or toe; claw; small metal spike. — *v.* fasten with nail(s); catch, arrest.

naive /naa-éev/ *a.* showing lack of experience or of informed judgement. **naively** *adv.*, **naivety** *n.*

naked *a.* without clothes on; without coverings. **naked eye** the eye unassisted by a telescope or microscope etc. **nakedness** *n.*

namby-pamby *a.* & *n.* feeble or unmanly (person).

name *n.* word(s) by which a person, place, or thing is known or indicated; reputation. — *v.* give as a name; nominate, specify.

namely *adv.* that is to say.

namesake *n.* person or thing with the same name as another.

nanny *n.* child's nurse. **nanny goat** female goat.

nano- *pref.* one thousand millionth.

nap [1] *n.* short sleep, esp. during the day. — *v.* (**napped**) have a nap. **catch a person napping** catch him or her unawares.

nap [2] *n.* short raised fibres on the surface of cloth or leather.

napalm /náypaam/ *n.* jelly-like petrol substance used in incendiary bombs.

nape *n.* back part of neck.

naphtha /náfthə/ *n.* inflammable oil.

naphthalene *n.* pungent white substance obtained from coal tar.

napkin *n.* piece of cloth or paper used to protect clothes or for wiping one's lips at meals; nappy.

nappy *n.* piece of absorbent material worn by a baby to absorb or retain its excreta.

narcissism *n.* abnormal self-admiration. **narcissistic** *a.*

narcissus *n.* (*pl.* **-cissi**) flower of the group including the daffodil.

narcotic *a.* & *n.* (drug) causing sleep or drowsiness.

narrate *v.* tell (a story), give an account of. **narration** *n.*, **narrator** *n.*

narrative *n.* spoken or written account of something. — *a.* in this form.

narrow *a.* small across, not wide; with little margin or scope. — *v.* make or become narrower. **narrow-minded** *a.* intolerant. **narrowly** *adv.*, **narrowness** *n.*

narwhal *n.* Arctic whale with a spirally grooved tusk.

nasal *a.* of the nose; sounding as if breath came out through the nose. **nasally** *adv.*

nascent *a.* just coming into existence. **nascence** *n.*

nasty *a.* (**-ier**, **-iest**) unpleasant; unkind; difficult. **nastily** *adv.*, **nastiness** *n.*

natal *a.* of or from one's birth.

nation *n.* people of mainly common descent and history usu. inhabiting a particular country under one government.

national *a.* of a nation; common to a whole nation. — *n.* citizen of a particular country. **nationally** *adv.*

nationalism *n.* patriotic feeling; policy of national independence. **nationalist** *n.*, **nationalistic** *a.*

nationality *n.* condition of belonging to a particular nation.

nationalize *v.* convert from private to State ownership. **nationalization** *n.*

native *a.* natural, inborn; belonging to a place by birth. — *n.* person born in a specified place; local inhabitant.

nativity *n.* birth; **the Nativity** that of Christ.

natter *v.* & *n.* (*colloq.*) chat.

natural *a.* of or produced by nature; normal; not seeming artificial or affected. — *n.* person or thing that seems naturally suited for something. **natural history** study of animal and plant life. **naturalness** *n.*

naturalism *n.* realism in art and literature. **naturalistic** *a.*

naturalist *n.* expert in natural history.

naturalize *v.* admit (a person of foreign birth) to full citizenship of a country; introduce and acclimatize (an animal or plant) into a country; make look natural. **naturalization** *n.*

naturally *adv.* in a natural manner; as might be expected, of course.

nature *n.* the world with all its features and living things; physical power producing these; kind, sort; innate characteristics; all that makes a thing what it is.

naturist *n.* nudist. **naturism** *n.*

naughty *a.* **(-ier, -iest)** behaving badly, disobedient; slightly indecent. **naughtily** *adv.*, **naughtiness** *n.*

nausea *n.* feeling of sickness.

nauseate *v.* affect with nausea.

nauseous *a.* causing nausea.

nautical *a.* of sailors or seamanship.

nautilus *n.* (*pl.* **-luses**) mollusc with a spiral shell.

naval *a.* of a navy.

nave *n.* main part of a church.

navel *n.* small hollow in the centre of the abdomen.

navigable *a.* suitable for ships to sail in; able to be steered and sailed. **navigability** *n.*

navigate *v.* sail in or through (a sea or river etc.); direct the course of (a ship or vehicle etc.). **navigation** *n.*, **navigator** *n.*

navvy *n.* labourer making roads etc. where digging is necessary.

navy *n.* a country's warships; officers and men of these; navy blue. **navy blue** very dark blue.

NB *abbr.* (Latin *nota bene*) note well.

NE *abbr.* north-east; north-eastern.

neap tide tide when there is least rise and fall of water.

near *adv.* at, to, or within a short distance or interval; nearly. — *prep.* near to. — *a.* with only a short distance or interval between; closely related; with little margin; of the left side of a horse, vehicle, or road; stingy. — *v.* draw near. **nearness** *n.*

nearby *a.* & *adv.* near in position.

nearly *adv.* closely; almost.

neat *a.* clean and orderly in appearance or workmanship; undiluted. **neatly** *adv.*, **neatness** *n.*

neaten *v.* make neat.

nebula *n.* (*pl.* **-ae**) a cloud of gas or dust in space. **nebular** *a.*

nebulous *a.* indistinct. **nebulously** *adv.*, **nebulosity** *n.*

necessarily *adv.* as a necessary result, inevitably.

necessary *a.* essential in order to achieve something; happening or existing by necessity.

necessitate *v.* make necessary; involve as a condition or result.

necessitous *a.* needy.

necessity *n.* compelling power of circumstances; state or fact of being necessary; necessary thing; state of need or hardship.

neck *n.* narrow part connecting the head to the body; part of a garment round this; narrow part of a bottle, cavity, etc. **neck and neck** running level in a race.

necklace *n.* piece of jewellery etc. worn round the neck.

neckline *n.* outline formed by the edge of a garment at the neck.

necromancy *n.* art of predicting things by communicating with the dead. **necromancer** *n.*

necrosis *n.* death of bone or tissue. **necrotic** *a.*

nectar *n.* sweet fluid from plants, collected by bees; any delicious drink.

nectarine *n.* a kind of peach with no down on the skin.

née /nay/ *a.* born (used in stating a married woman's maiden name).

need *n.* requirement; state of great difficulty or misfortune; poverty. — *v.* be in need of, require; be obliged.

needful *a.* necessary.

needle *n.* small thin pointed piece of steel used in sewing; thing shaped like this; pointer of a compass or gauge. — *v.* annoy, provoke.

needless *a.* unnecessary. **needlessly** *adv.*

needlework *n.* sewing or embroidery.

needy *a.* **(-ier, -iest)** very poor.

nefarious *a.* wicked. **nefariously** *adv.*

negate *v.* nullify, disprove. **negation** *n.*

negative *a.* expressing denial, refusal, or prohibition; not positive; (of a quantity) less than zero; (of a battery terminal) through which electric current leaves. — *n.* negative statement or word; negative quality or quantity; photograph with lights and shades or colours reversed, from which positive pictures can be obtained. **negatively** *adv.*

neglect *v.* pay insufficient attention to; fail to take proper care of or to do something. — *n.* neglecting, being neglected. **neglectful** *a.*

negligee /néglizhay/ *n.* woman's light dressing gown.

negligence *n.* lack of proper care or attention. **negligent** *a.*, **negligently** *adv.*

negligible *a.* too small to be worth taking into account.

negotiate *v.* hold a discussion so as to reach agreement; arrange by such discussion; get past (an obstacle) successfully. **negotiation** *n.*, **negotiator** *n.*

Negro *n.* (*pl.* **-oes**) member of the black-skinned race that originated in Africa. **Negress** *n.fem.*, **Negroid** *a.*

neigh *n.* horse's long high-pitched cry. — *v.* make this cry.

neighbour *n.* person or thing living or situated near or next to another.

neighbourhood *n.* district. **neighbourhood watch** systematic vigilance by residents to deter crime in their area.
neighbouring *a.* living or situated nearby.
neighbourly *a.* kind and friendly towards neighbours. **neighbourliness** *n.*
neither *a.* & *pron.* not either. — *adv.* & *conj.* not either; also not.
nemesis /némmisiss/ *n.* inevitable retribution.
neo- *pref.* new.
neolithic *a.* of the later part of the Stone Age.
neologism *n.* new word.
neon *n.* a kind of gas much used in illuminated signs.
nephew *n.* one's brother's or sister's son.
nephritis *n.* inflammation of the kidneys.
nepotism *n.* favouritism shown to relatives in appointing them to jobs. **nepotistic** *a.*
nerve *n.* fibre carrying impulses of sensation or movement between the brain and a part of the body; courage; (*colloq.*) impudence; (*pl.*) nervousness, effect of mental stress. — *v.* give courage to.
nervous *a.* of the nerves; easily alarmed; slightly afraid. **nervously** *adv.*, **nervousness** *n.*
nervy *a.* nervous. **nerviness** *n.*
nest *n.* structure or place in which a bird lays eggs and shelters its young; breeding place, lair; snug place, shelter; set of articles (esp. tables) designed to fit inside each other. — *v.* make or have a nest. **nest egg** sum of money saved for future use.
nestle *v.* settle oneself comfortably; lie sheltered.
nestling *n.* bird too young to leave the nest.
net [1] *n.* open-work material of thread, cord, or wire etc.; piece of this used for a particular purpose. — *v.* (**netted**) place nets in or on; catch in a net.
net [2] *a.* remaining after all deductions; (of weight) not including wrappings etc. — *v.* (**netted**) obtain or yield as net profit.
netball *n.* team game in which a ball has to be thrown into a high net.
nether *a.* lower.
netting *n.* netted fabric.
nettle *n.* wild plant with leaves that sting when touched. — *v.* irritate, provoke.
network *n.* arrangement with intersecting lines; complex system; group of interconnected people or things.
neural *a.* of nerves.
neuralgia *n.* sharp pain along a nerve. **neuralgic** *a.*
neuritis *n.* inflammation of nerve(s).
neurology *n.* study of nerve systems. **neurological** *a.*, **neurologist** *n.*
neurosis *n.* (*pl.* **-oses**) mental disorder sometimes with physical symptoms but with no evidence of disease.
neurotic *a.* of or caused by a neurosis; subject to abnormal anxieties or obsessive behaviour. — *n.* neurotic person. **neurotically** *adv.*
neuter *a.* neither masculine nor feminine; without male or female parts. — *n.* neuter word or being; castrated animal. — *v.* castrate.
neutral *a.* not supporting either side in a conflict; without distinctive or positive characteristics. — *n.* neutral person, country, or colour; neutral gear. **neutral gear** position of gear mechanism in which the engine is disconnected from driven parts. **neutrally** *adv.*, **neutrality** *n.*
neutralize *v.* make ineffective. **neutralization** *n.*
neutrino *n.* (*pl.* **-os**) particle with zero electric charge and (probably) zero mass.
neutron *n.* nuclear particle with no electric charge. **neutron bomb** nuclear bomb that kills people but does little damage to buildings etc.
never *adv.* at no time, on no occasion; not; (*colloq.*) surely not. **never mind** do not be troubled.
nevermore *adv.* at no future time.
nevertheless *adv.* & *conj.* in spite of this.
new *a.* not existing before, recently made or discovered or experienced etc.; unfamiliar, unaccustomed. — *adv.* newly, recently. **new moon** moon seen as a crescent. **New Testament** (*see* **testament**). **new year** first days of January. **New Year's Day** 1 Jan.
newcomer *n.* one who has arrived recently.
newel *n.* top or bottom post of the handrail of a stair; central pillar of a winding stair.
newfangled *a.* objectionably new in method or style.
newly *adv.* recently, freshly. **newly-wed** *a.* & *n.* recently married (person).
news *n.* new or interesting information about recent events; broadcast report of this. **newsy** *a.*
newsagent *n.* shopkeeper who sells newspapers.
newscaster *n.* newsreader.
newsletter *n.* informal printed report containing news of interest to members of a club etc.
newspaper *n.* printed daily or weekly publication containing news reports; paper forming this.

newsprint *n.* type of paper on which newspapers are printed.

newsreader *n.* person who reads broadcast news reports.

newsworthy *a.* worth reporting as news. **newsworthiness** *n.*

newt *n.* small lizard-like amphibious creature.

next *a.* nearest in position or time etc.; soonest come to. — *adv.* in the next place or degree; on the next occasion. — *n.* next person or thing. **next door** in the next house or room. **next of kin** one's closest relative.

nexus *n.* (*pl.* **-uses**) connected group or series.

nib *n.* metal point of a pen.

nibble *v.* take small quick or gentle bites (at). — *n.* small quick bite; snack. **nibbler** *n.*

nice *a.* pleasant, satisfactory; precise; fastidious. **nicely** *adv.*, **niceness** *n.*

nicety *n.* precision; detail. **to a nicety** exactly.

niche *n.* shallow recess esp. in a wall; suitable position in life or employment.

nick *n.* small cut or notch. — *v.* make a nick in; (*sl.*) steal; (*sl.*) arrest. **in good nick** (*colloq.*) in good condition. **in the nick of time** only just in time.

nickel *n.* hard silvery-white metal; (*US*) 5-cent piece.

nickname *n.* name given humorously to a person or thing. — *v.* give as a nickname.

nicotine *n.* poisonous substance found in tobacco.

niece *n.* one's brother's or sister's daughter.

niggardly *a.* stingy. **niggard** *n.*

niggle *v.* fuss over details.

nigh *adv.* & *prep.* near.

night *n.* dark hours between sunset and sunrise; nightfall. **night-life** *n.* entertainments available in public places at night. **night school** instruction provided in the evening.

nightcap *n.* (alcoholic) drink taken just before going to bed.

nightclub *n.* club open at night, providing meals and entertainment.

nightdress *n.* woman's or child's loose garment for sleeping in.

nightfall *n.* onset of night.

nightgown *n.* nightdress.

nightie *n.* (*colloq.*) nightdress.

nightingale *n.* small thrush, male of which sings melodiously.

nightjar *n.* night-flying bird with a harsh cry.

nightly *a.* & *adv.* (happening) at night or every night.

nightmare *n.* unpleasant dream or (*colloq.*) experience. **nightmarish** *a.*

nightshade *n.* plant with poisonous berries.

nightshirt *n.* man's or boy's long shirt for sleeping in.

nihilism *n.* rejection of all religious and moral principles. **nihilist** *n.*, **nihilistic** *a.*

nil *n.* nothing.

nimble *a.* able to move quickly. **nimbly** *adv.*

nincompoop *n.* foolish person.

nine *a.* & *n.* one more than eight (9, IX). **ninth** *a.* & *n.*

ninepins *n.* game of skittles played with nine objects.

nineteen *a.* & *n.* one more than eighteen (19, XIX). **nineteenth** *a.* & *n.*

ninety *a.* & *n.* nine times ten (90, XC). **ninetieth** *a.* & *n.*

ninny *n.* foolish person.

nip [1] *v.* (**nipped**) pinch or squeeze sharply; bite quickly with the front teeth; (*sl.*) go quickly. — *n.* sharp pinch, squeeze, or bite; biting coldness.

nip [2] *n.* small drink of spirits.

nipple *n.* small projection at the centre of a breast; similar protuberance; teat of a feeding bottle.

nippy *a.* (**-ier, -iest**) (*colloq.*) nimble, quick; bitingly cold.

nirvana *n.* (in Buddhism and Hinduism) state of perfect bliss achieved by the soul.

nit *n.* egg of a louse or similar parasite. **nit-picking** *n.* & *a.* (*colloq.*) petty fault-finding.

nitrate *n.* substance formed from nitric acid, esp. used as a fertilizer.

nitric *a.* **nitric acid** corrosive acid containing nitrogen.

nitrogen *n.* gas forming about four-fifths of the atmosphere.

nitroglycerine *n.* a kind of powerful explosive.

nitrous oxide gas used as an anaesthetic.

nitty-gritty *n.* (*sl.*) basic facts or realities of a matter.

nitwit *n.* (*colloq.*) stupid or foolish person.

no *a.* not any; not a. — *adv.* (used as a denial or refusal of something); not at all. — *n.* (*pl.* **noes**) negative reply, vote against a proposal. **no-go area** area to which entry is forbidden or restricted. **no man's land** area not controlled by anyone, esp. between opposing armies. **no one** no person, nobody.

No., no. *abbrs.* number.

nobble *v.* (*sl.*) get hold of, tamper with or influence dishonestly.

nobility *n.* nobleness of character or of rank; titled people.

noble *a.* aristocratic; possessing excellent qualities, esp. of character, not mean or petty; imposing. — *n.* member of the nobility. **nobly** *adv.*, **nobleness** *n.*

nobleman, **noblewoman** *ns.* (*pl.* **-men**, **-women**) member of the nobility.

nobody *pron.* no person. — *n.* person of no importance.

nocturnal *a.* of or happening in or active in the night. **nocturnally** *adv.*

nod *v.* (**nodded**) move the head down and up quickly, indicate (agreement or casual greeting) thus; let the head droop, be drowsy; bend and sway. — *n.* nodding movement esp. in agreement or greeting.

node *n.* knob-like swelling; point on a stem where a leaf or bud grows out. **nodal** *a.*

nodule *n.* small rounded lump, small node. **nodular** *a.*

noise *n.* sound, esp. loud or harsh or undesired. **noiseless** *a.*

noisome *a.* noxious, disgusting.

noisy *a.* (**-ier**, **-iest**) making much noise. **noisily** *adv.*, **noisiness** *n.*

nomad *n.* member of a tribe that roams seeking pasture for its animals; wanderer. **nomadic** *a.*

nom de plume writer's pseudonym.

nomenclature *n.* system of names, e.g. in a science.

nominal *a.* in name only; (of a fee) very small. **nominal value** face value of a coin etc. **nominally** *adv.*

nominate *v.* name as candidate for or future holder of an office; appoint as a place or date. **nomination** *n.*, **nominator** *n.*

nominee *n.* person nominated.

non- *pref.* not.

nonagenarian *n.* person in his or her nineties.

nonchalant *a.* calm and casual. **nonchalantly** *adv.*, **nonchalance** *n.*

noncommittal *a.* not revealing one's opinion.

nonconformist *n.* person not conforming to established practices; **Nonconformist**, member of a Protestant sect not conforming to Anglican practices.

nondescript *a.* lacking distinctive characteristics.

none *pron.* not any; no person(s). — *adv.* not at all.

nonentity *n.* person of no importance.

non-event *n.* event that was expected to be important but proves disappointing.

non-existent *a.* not existing. **non-existence** *n.*

nonplussed *a.* completely perplexed.

nonsense *n.* words put together in a way that does not make sense; foolish talk or behaviour. **nonsensical** *a.*

non sequitur conclusion that does not follow from the evidence given.

non-starter *n.* horse entered for a race but not running in it; person or idea etc. not worth considering for a purpose.

non-stop *a.* & *adv.* not ceasing; (of a train etc.) not stopping at intermediate places.

noodles *n.pl.* pasta in narrow strips, used in soups etc.

nook *n.* secluded place; recess.

noon *n.* twelve o'clock in the day.

noose *n.* loop of rope etc. with a knot that tightens when pulled.

nor *conj.* & *adv.* and not.

norm *n.* standard.

normal *a.* conforming to what is standard or usual; free from mental or emotional disorders. **normally** *adv.*, **normality** *n.*

north *n.* point or direction to the left of person facing east; northern part. — *a.* in the north; (of wind) from the north. — *adv.* towards the north. **north-east** *n.* point or direction midway between north and east. **north-easterly** *a.* & *n.*, **north-eastern** *a.* **north-west** *n.* point or direction midway between north and west. **north-westerly** *a.* & *n.*, **north-western** *a.*

northerly *a.* towards or blowing from the north.

northern *a.* of or in the north.

northerner *n.* native of the north.

northernmost *a.* furthest north.

northward *a.* towards the north. **northwards** *adv.*

Norwegian *a.* & *n.* (native, language) of Norway.

Nos., **nos.** *abbrs.* numbers.

nose *n.* organ at the front of the head, used in breathing and smelling; sense of smell; open end of a tube; front end or projecting part. — *v.* detect or search by use of the sense of smell; push one's nose against or into; push one's way cautiously ahead.

nosebag *n.* bag of fodder for hanging on a horse's head.

nosedive *n.* steep downward plunge, esp. of an aeroplane. — *v.* make this plunge.

nostalgia *n.* sentimental memory of or longing for things of the past. **nostalgic** *a.*, **nostalgically** *adv.*

nostril *n.* either of the two external openings in the nose.

nosy *a.* (**-ier**, **-iest**) (*colloq.*) inquisitive. **nosily** *adv.*, **nosiness** *n.*

not *adv.* expressing a negative or denial or refusal.

notable *a.* worthy of notice, remarkable, eminent. — *n.* eminent person. **notably** *adv.*

notation *n.* system of signs or symbols representing numbers, quantities, musical notes, etc.

notch *n.* V-shaped cut or indentation. — *v.* make notch(es) in. **notch up** score, achieve.

note *n.* brief record written down to aid memory; short or informal letter; short written comment; banknote; musical tone of definite pitch; symbol representing the pitch and duration of a musical sound; each of the keys on a piano etc.; eminence; notice, attention. — *v.* notice, pay attention to; write down.

notebook *n.* book with blank pages on which to write notes.

notecase *n.* wallet for banknotes.

noted *a.* famous, well known.

notelet *n.* small folded card etc. for a short informal letter.

notepaper *n.* paper for writing letters on.

noteworthy *a.* worthy of notice, remarkable.

nothing *n.* no thing, not anything; no amount, nought; non-existence; person or thing of no importance. — *adv.* not at all.

notice *n.* attention, observation; intimation, warning; formal announcement of the termination of an agreement or employment; written or printed information displayed; review in a newspaper. — *v.* perceive; take notice of; remark upon. **take notice** show interest. **take no notice (of)** pay no attention (to).

noticeable *a.* easily seen or noticed. **noticeably** *adv.*

notifiable *a.* that must be notified.

notify *v.* inform; report, make known. **notification** *n.*

notion *n.* concept; idea; whim.

notional *a.* hypothetical. **notionally** *adv.*

notorious *a.* well known, esp. unfavourably. **notoriously** *adv.*, **notoriety** *n.*

notwithstanding *prep.* in spite of. — *adv.* nevertheless.

nougat /nōōgaa/ *n.* chewy sweet.

nought *n.* the figure 0; nothing.

noun *n.* word used as the name of a person, place, or thing.

nourish *v.* keep alive and well by food; encourage (a feeling).

nourishment *n.* nourishing; food.

nous /nowss/ *n.* (*colloq.*) common sense.

nova *n.* (*pl.* **-ae**) star that suddenly becomes much brighter for a short time.

novel *n.* book-length story. — *a.* of a new kind.

novelette *n.* short (esp. romantic) novel.

novelist *n.* writer of novels.

novelty *n.* novel thing or quality; small unusual object.

novice *n.* inexperienced person; probationary member of a religious order. **noviciate** *n.*

now *adv.* at the present time; immediately; (without temporal sense) I wonder or am telling you. — *conj.* as a consequence of or simultaneously with the fact that. — *n.* the present time. **now and again, now and then** occasionally.

nowadays *adv.* in present times.

nowhere *adv.* not anywhere.

noxious *a.* unpleasant and harmful.

nozzle *n.* vent or spout of a hosepipe etc.

nuance /nyōō-onss/ *n.* shade of meaning.

nub *n.* small lump; central point or core of a matter or problem.

nubile *a.* (of a woman) marriageable. **nubility** *n.*

nuclear *a.* of a nucleus; of the nuclei of atoms; using energy released or absorbed during reactions in these.

nucleus *n.* (*pl.* **-lei**) central part or thing round which others are collected; central portion of an atom, seed, or cell.

nude *a.* naked. — *n.* nude figure in a picture etc. **nudity** *n.*

nudge *v.* poke gently with the elbow to attract attention quietly; push slightly or gradually. — *n.* this movement.

nudist *n.* person who believes that going unclothed is good for the health. **nudism** *n.*

nugget *n.* rough lump of gold or platinum found in the earth.

nuisance *n.* annoying person or thing.

null *a.* having no legal force. **nullity** *n.*

nullify *v.* make null; neutralize the effect of. **nullification** *n.*

numb *a.* deprived of power to feel. — *v.* make numb. **numbness** *n.*

number *n.* symbol or word indicating how many; total; numeral assigned to a person or thing; single issue of a magazine; item. — *v.* count; amount to; mark or distinguish with a number. **number one** (*colloq.*) oneself. **number plate** plate on a motor vehicle, bearing its registration number.

numberless *a.* innumerable.

numeral *n.* written symbol of a number.

numerate *a.* having a good basic understanding of mathematics and science. **numeracy** *n.*

numerator *n.* number above the line in a vulgar fraction.

numerical *a.* of number(s). **numerically** *adv.*

numerous *a.* great in number.

nun *n.* member of a female religious community.

nunnery *n.* residence of a community of nuns.

nuptial *a.* of marriage or a wedding. **nuptials** *n.pl.* wedding ceremony.

nurse *n.* person trained to look after sick or injured people; woman employed to take charge of young children. — *v.* work as a nurse, act as nurse (to); feed at the breast or udder; hold carefully; give special care to. **nursing home** privately run hospital or home for invalids.

nursery *n.* room(s) for young children; place where plants are reared, esp. for sale. **nursery rhyme** traditional verse for children. **nursery school** school for children below normal school age. **nursery slopes** slopes suitable for beginners at skiing.

nurseryman *n.* (*pl.* **-men**) person growing plants etc. at a nursery.

nurture *v.* nourish, rear; bring up. — *n.* nurturing.

nut *n.* fruit with a hard shell round an edible kernel; this kernel; small threaded metal ring for use with a bolt; (*sl.*) head.

nutcase *n.* (*sl.*) crazy person.

nuthatch *n.* small climbing bird.

nutmeg *n.* hard fragrant tropical seed ground or grated as spice.

nutria *n.* fur of the coypu.

nutrient *a.* & *n.* nourishing (substance).

nutriment *n.* nourishing substance.

nutrition *n.* nourishment; study of nourishment. **nutritional** *a.*, **nutritionally** *adv.*

nutritious *a.* nourishing.

nuts *a.* (*sl.*) crazy.

nutshell *n.* hard shell of a nut. **in a nutshell** expressed very briefly.

nutty *a.* (**-ier**, **-iest**) full of nuts; tasting like nuts; (*sl.*) crazy.

nuzzle *v.* press or rub gently with the nose.

NW *abbr.* north-west; north-western.

nylon *n.* very light strong synthetic fibre; fabric made of this.

nymph *n.* mythological semi-divine maiden; young insect.

nymphomania *n.* excessive sexual desire in a woman. **nymphomaniac** *n.*

NZ *abbr.* New Zealand.

O

oaf *n.* (*pl.* **oafs**) awkward lout.

oak *n.* deciduous forest tree bearing acorns; its hard wood. **oak-apple** *n.* = gall[3]. **oaken** *a.*

oar *n.* pole with a flat blade used to propel a boat by its leverage against water; rower.

oasis *n.* (*pl.* **oases**) fertile spot in a desert, with a spring or well.

oath *n.* solemn promise; swear word.

oatmeal *n.* ground oats; greyish-fawn colour.

oats *n.* hardy cereal plant; its grain.

obdurate *a.* stubborn. **obdurately** *adv.*, **obduracy** *n.*

obedient *a.* doing what one is told to do. **obediently** *adv.*, **obedience** *n.*

obeisance *n.* bow or curtsy.

obelisk *n.* tall pillar set up as a monument.

obese *a.* very fat. **obesity** *n.*

obey *v.* do what is commanded (by).

obfuscate *v.* darken; confuse, bewilder. **obfuscation** *n.*

obituary *n.* printed statement of person's death (esp. in a newspaper).

object[1] /óbjikt/ *n.* something solid that can be seen or touched; person or thing to which an action or feeling is directed; purpose, intention; noun etc. acted upon by a verb or preposition. **no object** not a limiting factor. **object lesson** practical illustration of a principle.

object[2] /əbjékt/ *v.* state that one is opposed to, protest. **objector** *n.*

objection *n.* disapproval, opposition; statement of this; reason for objecting.

objectionable *a.* unpleasant. **objectionably** *adv.*

objective *a.* not influenced by personal feelings or opinions; of the form of a word used when it is the object of a verb or preposition. — *n.* thing one is trying to achieve, reach, or capture. **objectively** *adv.*, **objectiveness** *n.*, **objectivity** *n.*

objet d'art /óbzhay daar/ (*pl.* ***objets d'art***) small artistic object.

oblation *n.* offering made to God.

obligate *v.* oblige.

obligation *n.* being obliged to do something; what one must do to comply with an agreement or law.

obligatory *a.* compulsory.

oblige *v.* compel; help or gratify by a small service.

obliged *a.* indebted.

obliging *a.* polite and helpful. **obligingly** *adv.*

oblique *a.* slanting; indirect. **obliquely** *adv.*, **obliqueness** *n.*

obliterate *v.* blot out, destroy. **obliteration** *n.*

oblivion *n.* state of being forgotten; state of being oblivious.

oblivious *a.* unaware. **obliviously** *adv.*, **obliviousness** *n.*

oblong *a.* & *n.* (having) rectangular shape with length greater than breadth.

obloquy *n.* verbal abuse; disgrace.

obnoxious *a.* very unpleasant. **obnoxiously** *adv.*, **obnoxiousness** *n.*

oboe *n.* woodwind instrument of treble pitch. **oboist** *n.*

obscene *a.* indecent in a repulsive or offensive way. **obscenely** *adv.*, **obscenity** *n.*

obscure *a.* indistinct; not famous; not easily understood. — *v.* make obscure, conceal. **obscurely** *adv.*, **obscurity** *n.*

obsequies *n.pl.* funeral rites.

obsequious *a.* excessively respectful. **obsequiously** *adv.*, **obsequiousness** *n.*

observance *n.* keeping of a law, custom, or festival.

observant *a.* quick at noticing. **observantly** *adv.*

observation *n.* observing; remark. **observational** *a.*

observatory *n.* building equipped for observation of stars or weather.

observe *v.* perceive, watch carefully; pay attention to; keep or celebrate (a festival); remark. **observer** *n.*

obsess *v.* occupy the thoughts of continually.

obsession *n.* state of being obsessed; persistent idea. **obsessional** *a.*

obsessive *a.* of, causing, or showing obsession. **obsessively** *adv.*

obsolescent *a.* becoming obsolete. **obsolescence** *n.*

obsolete *a.* no longer used.

obstacle *n.* thing that obstructs progress.

obstetrics *n.* branch of medicine and surgery dealing with childbirth. **obstetric, obstetrical** *adjs.*, **obstetrician** *n.*

obstinate *a.* not easily persuaded or influenced or overcome. **obstinately** *adv.*, **obstinacy** *n.*

obstreperous *a.* noisy, unruly.

obstruct *v.* block; hinder movement or progress. **obstruction** *n.*, **obstructive** *a.*
obtain *v.* get, come into possession of; be customary.
obtrude *v.* force (ideas or oneself) upon others. **obtrusion** *n.*
obtrusive *a.* obtruding oneself, unpleasantly noticeable. **obtrusively** *adv.*, **obtrusiveness** *n.*
obtuse *a.* of blunt shape, (of an angle) more than 90° but less than 180°; slow at understanding. **obtusely** *adv.*, **obtuseness** *n.*
obverse *n.* side of a coin bearing a head or the principal design.
obviate *v.* make unnecessary.
obvious *a.* easy to perceive or understand. **obviously** *adv.*, **obviousness** *n.*
ocarina *n.* egg-shaped wind instrument.
occasion *n.* time at which a particular event takes place; special event; opportunity; need or cause. — *v.* cause.
occasional *a.* happening sometimes but not frequently; for a special occasion. **occasionally** *adv.*
Occident /óksid'nt/ *n.* the West, the western world. **occidental** *a.*
Occidental /óksidént'l/ *n.* native of the Occident.
occlude *v.* stop up, obstruct.
occlusion *n.* upward movement of a mass of warm air caused by a cold front overtaking it.
occult *a.* secret; supernatural.
occupant *n.* person occupying a place or dwelling. **occupancy** *n.*
occupation *n.* occupying; activity that keeps a person busy; employment.
occupational *a.* of or caused by one's employment. **occupational therapy** creative activities designed to assist recovery from certain illnesses.
occupy *v.* dwell in; take possession of (a place) by force; fill (a space or position); keep busy; fill up (time). **occupier** *n.*
occur *v.* (**occurred**) come into being as an event or process; exist.
occurrence *n.* occurring; incident, event.
ocean *n.* sea surrounding the continents of the earth. **oceanic** *a.*
oceanography *n.* study of the ocean.
ocelot *n.* leopard-like animal of Central and South America; its fur.
ochre *n.* type of clay used as pigment; pale brownish-yellow.
o'clock *adv.* by the clock.
octagon *n.* geometric figure with eight sides. **octagonal** *a.*
octahedron *n.* solid with eight sides. **octahedral** *a.*
octane *n.* hydrocarbon occurring in petrol.
octave *n.* note six whole tones above or below a given note; interval or notes between these.
octet *n.* group of eight voices or instruments; music for these.
octogenarian *n.* person in his or her eighties.
octopus *n.* (*pl.* **-puses**) sea animal with eight tentacles.
ocular *a.* of, for, or by the eyes.
oculist *n.* specialist in the treatment of eye disorders and defects.
odd *a.* unusual; occasional; (of a number) not exactly divisible by 2; not part of a set; exceeding a round number or amount. **oddly** *adv.*, **oddness** *n.*
oddity *n.* strangeness; unusual person or thing.
oddment *n.* thing left over, isolated article.
odds *n.pl.* probability; ratio between amounts staked by parties to a bet. **at odds with** in conflict with. **odds and ends** oddments. **odds-on** *a.* with success more likely than failure.
ode *n.* type of poem addressed to a person or celebrating an event.
odious *a.* hateful. **odiously** *adv.*, **odiousness** *n.*
odium *n.* widespread hatred or disgust.
odoriferous *a.* diffusing (usu. pleasant) odours.
odour *n.* smell. **odorous** *a.*
odyssey *n.* (*pl.* **-eys**) long adventurous journey.
oedema /ideémə/ *n.* excess fluid in tissues, causing swelling.
oesophagus /eesóffəgəss/ *n.* gullet.
of *prep.* belonging to; from; composed or made from; concerning; for, involving.
off *adv.* away; out of position, disconnected; not operating, cancelled; (of food) beginning to decay. — *prep.* away from; below the normal standard of. — *a.* of the right-hand side of a horse, vehicle, or road. **off chance** remote possibility. **off colour** not in the best of health. **off-licence** *n.* licence to sell alcohol for consumption away from the premises; shop with this. **off-putting** *a.* (*colloq.*) repellent. **off-white** *a.* not quite pure white.
offal *n.* edible organs from an animal carcass.
offbeat *a.* unusual, unconventional.
offence *n.* illegal act; feeling of annoyance or resentment.
offend *v.* cause offence to; do wrong. **offender** *n.*
offensive *a.* causing offence, insulting; disgusting; used in attacking. — *n.*

aggressive action. **offensively** *adv.*, **offensiveness** *n.*

offer *v.* (**offered**) present for acceptance or refusal, or for consideration or use; state what one is willing to do or pay or give; show an intention. — *n.* expression of willingness to do, give, or pay something; amount offered.

offering *n.* gift, contribution.

offhand *a.* unceremonious, casual. — *adv.* in an offhand way. **offhanded** *a.*

office *n.* room or building used for clerical and similar work; position of authority or trust.

officer *n.* official; person holding authority on a ship or in the armed services; policeman.

official *a.* of office or officials; authorized. — *n.* person holding office. **officially** *adv.*

officiate *v.* act in an official capacity, be in charge.

officious *a.* asserting one's authority, bossy. **officiously** *adv.*

offload *v.* unload.

offset *v.* (**-set, -setting**) counterbalance, compensate for.

offshoot *n.* side shoot; subsidiary product.

offside *a.* & *adv.* in a position where one may not legally play the ball (in football etc.).

offspring *n.* (*pl.* **-spring**) person's child or children; animal's young.

often *adv.* many times, at short intervals; in many instances.

ogle *v.* eye flirtatiously.

ogre *n.* man-eating giant in fairy tales; terrifying person.

oh *int.* exclamation of delight or pain, or used for emphasis.

ohm *n.* unit of electrical resistance.

oil *n.* thick slippery liquid that will not dissolve in water; petroleum, a form of this; oil colour. — *v.* lubricate or treat with oil. **oil colour, oil paint** paint made by mixing pigment in oil. **oil painting** picture painted in this. **oily** *a.*

oilfield *n.* area where oil is found in the ground.

oilskin *n.* cloth waterproofed by treatment with oil etc.; (*pl.*) waterproof clothing made of this.

ointment *n.* paste for rubbing on skin to heal it.

OK, okay *a.* & *adv.* (*colloq.*) all right.

okapi *n.* (*pl.* **-is**) giraffe-like animal of Central Africa.

okra *n.* African plant with seed pods used as food.

old *a.* having lived or existed or been known etc. for a long time; of specified age; shabby from age or wear; former, not recent or modern. **old age** later part of life. **old-fashioned** *a.* no longer fashionable. **Old Testament** (*see* **testament**). **old wives' tale** traditional but foolish belief.

oleaginous *a.* producing oil; oily.

oleander *n.* flowering shrub of Mediterranean regions.

olfactory *a.* concerned with smelling.

oligarch *n.* member of an oligarchy.

oligarchy *n.* government by a small group; country governed thus. **oligarchic** *a.*

olive *n.* small oval fruit from which an oil (**olive oil**) is obtained; tree bearing this; greenish colour. — *a.* of this colour; (of the complexion) yellowish-brown. **olive branch** thing done or offered to show one's desire to make peace.

ombudsman *n.* (*pl.* **-men**) official appointed to investigate people's complaints about maladministration by public authorities etc.

omega *n.* last letter of the Greek alphabet, = o.

omelette *n.* dish of beaten eggs cooked in a frying pan.

omen *n.* event regarded as a prophetic sign.

ominous *a.* seeming as if trouble is imminent. **ominously** *adv.*, **ominousness** *n.*

omit *v.* (**omitted**) leave out, not include; neglect (to do something). **omission** *n.*

omnibus *n.* bus; comprehensive publication containing several items.

omnipotent *a.* having unlimited or very great power. **omnipotence** *n.*

omnipresent *a.* present everywhere. **omnipresence** *n.*

omniscient *a.* knowing everything. **omniscience** *n.*

omnivorous *a.* feeding on all kinds of food.

on *prep.* supported by, attached to, covering; close to; towards; (of time) exactly at, during; in the state or process of; concerning; added to. — *adv.* so as to be on or covering something; further forward, towards something; with continued movement or action; operating, taking place. **be** *or* **keep on at** (*colloq.*) nag. **on and off** from time to time.

onager /ónnəgər/ *n.* wild ass.

once *adv., conj.,* & *n.* on one occasion, one time or occurrence; as soon as; formerly. **once-over** *n.* (*colloq.*) rapid inspection. **once upon a time** at some vague time in the past.

oncology *n.* study of tumours.

oncoming *a.* approaching.

one *a.* single, individual, forming a unity. — *n.* smallest whole number (1, I);

single thing or person. — *pron.* person; any person (esp. used by a speaker or writer of himself as representing people in general). **one another** each other. **one day** at some unspecified date. **one-sided** *a.* unfair, prejudiced. **one-way street** street where traffic is permitted to move in one direction only.

onerous *a.* burdensome.

oneself *pron.* emphatic and reflexive form of *one*.

ongoing *a.* continuing, in progress.

onion *n.* vegetable with a bulb that has a strong taste and smell.

onlooker *n.* spectator.

only *a.* being the one specimen or all the specimens of a class, sole. — *adv.* without anything or anyone else; and that is all; no longer ago than. — *conj.* but then. **only too** extremely.

onomatopoeia /ónnəmattəpeéə/ *n.* formation of words that imitate the sound of what they stand for. **onomatopoeic** *a.*

onset *n.* beginning; attack.

onslaught *n.* fierce attack.

onus *n.* duty or responsibility.

onward *adv.* & *a.* with an advancing motion; further on. **onwards** *adv.*

onyx *n.* stone like marble.

oodles *n.pl.* (*colloq.*) very great amount.

oolite /ṓəlīt/ *n.* type of limestone.

ooze *v.* trickle or flow out slowly; exude. — *n.* wet mud.

opacity *n.* being opaque.

opal *n.* iridescent quartz-like stone. **opaline** *a.*

opalescent *a.* iridescent like an opal. **opalescence** *n.*

opaque *a.* not clear, not transparent. **opaqueness** *n.*

open *a.* able to be entered, not closed or sealed or locked; not covered or concealed or restricted; unfolded; frank; not yet decided; willing to receive. — *v.* make or become open or more open; begin, establish. **in the open air** not in a house or building etc. **open-ended** *a.* with no fixed limit. **open-handed** *a.* giving generously. **open house** hospitality to all comers. **open letter** one addressed to a person by name but printed in a newspaper. **open-plan** *a.* without partition walls or fences. **open secret** one known to so many people that it is no longer secret. **openness** *n.*

opencast *a.* (of mining) on the surface of the ground.

opener *n.* device for opening tins or bottles etc.

opening *n.* gap, place where a thing opens; beginning; opportunity.

openly *adv.* publicly, frankly.

opera *n.* play(s) in which words are sung to music. **opera-glasses** *n.pl.* small binoculars.

operable *a.* able to be operated; suitable for treatment by surgery.

operate *v.* be in action; produce an effect; control the functioning of; perform an operation on.

operatic *a.* of or like opera.

operation *n.* operating; way a thing works; planned action; a surgical treatment.

operational *a.* of or used in operations; able to function.

operative *a.* working, functioning; of surgical operations. — *n.* worker, esp. in a factory.

operator *n.* person who operates a machine; one who connects lines at a telephone exchange.

operetta *n.* short or light opera.

ophidian *a.* & *n.* (member) of the snake family.

ophthalmic *a.* of or for the eyes.

ophthalmology *n.* study of the eye and its diseases. **ophthalmologist** *n.*

ophthalmoscope *n.* instrument for examining the eye.

opiate *n.* sedative containing opium.

opine *v.* express or hold as an opinion.

opinion *n.* belief or judgement held without actual proof; what one thinks on a particular point.

opinionated *a.* holding strong opinions obstinately.

opium *n.* narcotic drug made from the juice of certain poppies.

opossum *n.* small furry marsupial.

opponent *n.* one who opposes another.

opportune *a.* (of time) favourable; well-timed. **opportunely** *adv.*, **opportuneness** *n.*

opportunist *n.* person who grasps opportunities. **opportunism** *n.*, **opportunistic** *a.*

opportunity *n.* circumstances suitable for a particular purpose.

oppose *v.* argue or fight against; place opposite; place or be in opposition to; contrast.

opposite *a.* facing, on the further side; as different as possible from. — *n.* opposite thing or person. — *adv.* & *prep.* in an opposite position or direction (to).

opposition *n.* antagonism, resistance; placing or being placed opposite; people opposing something.

oppress *v.* govern or treat harshly; weigh down with cares. **oppression** *n.*, **oppressor** *n.*

oppressive *a.* oppressing; hard to endure; sultry and tiring. **oppressively** *adv.*, **oppressiveness** *n.*

opprobrious *a.* abusive.

opprobrium *n.* great disgrace from shameful conduct.

opt *v.* make a choice. **opt out** choose not to participate.

optic *a.* of the eye or sight.

optical *a.* of or aiding sight; visual. **optically** *adv.*

optician *n.* maker or seller of spectacles.

optics *n.* study of sight and of light as its medium.

optimism *n.* tendency to take a hopeful view of things. **optimist** *n.*, **optimistic** *a.*, **optimistically** *adv.*

optimum *a.* & *n.* best or most favourable (conditions, amount, etc.).

option *n.* freedom to choose; thing that is or may be chosen; right to buy or sell a thing within a limited time.

optional *a.* not compulsory. **optionally** *adv.*

opulent *a.* wealthy; abundant. **opulently** *adv.*, **opulence** *n.*

or *conj.* as an alternative; because if not; also known as.

oracle *n.* person or thing giving wise guidance. **oracular** *a.*

oral *a.* spoken not written; of the mouth, taken by mouth. — *n.* spoken examination. **orally** *adv.*

orange *n.* round juicy citrus fruit with reddish-yellow peel; this colour. — *a.* reddish-yellow.

orangeade *n.* orange-flavoured soft drink.

orang-utan *n.* large ape of Borneo and Sumatra.

oration *n.* long speech, esp. of a ceremonial kind.

orator *n.* person who makes public speeches, skilful speaker.

oratorio *n.* (*pl.* **-os**) musical composition for voices and orchestra, usu. with a biblical theme.

oratory *n.* art of public speaking; eloquent speech. **oratorical** *a.*

orb *n.* sphere, globe.

orbit *n.* curved path of a planet, satellite, or spacecraft round another; sphere of influence. — *v.* (**orbited**) move in an orbit (round).

orbital *a.* of orbits; (of a road) round the outside of a city.

orchard *n.* piece of land planted with fruit trees; these trees.

orchestra *n.* large body of people playing various musical instruments. **orchestral** *a.*

orchestrate *v.* compose or arrange (music) for an orchestra; coordinate. **orchestration** *n.*

orchid *n.* a kind of showy often irregularly shaped flower.

ordain *v.* appoint ceremonially to the Christian ministry; destine; decree authoritatively.

ordeal *n.* difficult experience.

order *n.* way things are placed in relation to each other; proper or usual sequence; efficient state; law-abiding state; command; request to supply goods etc., things supplied; written instruction or permission; rank; kind, quality; group of plants or animals classified as similar; monastic organization. — *v.* arrange in order; command; give an order for (goods etc.). **in order to** *or* **that** with the purpose of or intention that.

orderly *a.* in due order; not unruly. — *n.* soldier assisting an officer; hospital attendant. **orderliness** *n.*

ordinal *a.* **ordinal numbers** those defining position in a series (*first*, *second*, etc.).

ordinance *n.* decree.

ordinary *a.* usual, not exceptional. **ordinarily** *adv.*

ordination *n.* ordaining.

ordnance *n.* military materials. **Ordnance Survey** official survey of the British Isles, preparing maps.

ordure *n.* dung.

ore *n.* solid rock or mineral from which metal is obtained.

organ *n.* musical instrument with pipes supplied with wind by bellows and sounded by keys; distinct part with a specific function in an animal or plant body; medium of communication, esp. a newspaper.

organic *a.* of bodily organ(s); of or formed from living things; organized as a system; using no artificial fertilizers or pesticides. **organically** *adv.*

organism *n.* a living being, individual animal or plant.

organist *n.* person who plays the organ.

organization *n.* organizing; organized system or body of people. **organizational** *a.*

organize *v.* arrange systematically; make arrangements for; form (people) into an association for a common purpose. **organizer** *n.*

orgasm *n.* climax of sexual excitement.

orgy *n.* wild revelry; unrestrained activity. **orgiastic** *a.*

Orient *n.* the East, the eastern world.

orient *v.* place or determine the position of (a thing) with regard to points of the compass. **orient oneself** get one's bearings; become accustomed to a new situation. **orientation** *n.*

Oriental *n.* native of the Orient.

oriental *a.* of the Orient.

orientate *v.* orient.

orienteering *n.* sport of finding one's way across country by map and compass.

orifice *n.* opening of a cavity etc.

origin *n.* point, source, or cause from which a thing begins its existence; ancestry, parentage.

original *a.* existing from the first, earliest; being the first form of something; new in character or design; inventive, creative. — *n.* first form, thing from which another is copied. **originally** *adv.*, **originality** *n.*

originate *v.* bring or come into being. **origination** *n.*, **originator** *n.*

oriole *n.* bird with black and yellow plumage.

ormolu *n.* gold-coloured alloy of copper; things made of this.

ornament *n.* decorative object or detail; decoration. — *v.* decorate with ornament(s). **ornamentation** *n.*

ornamental *a.* serving as an ornament. **ornamentally** *adv.*

ornate *a.* elaborately ornamented. **ornately** *adv.*, **ornateness** *n.*

ornithology *n.* study of birds. **ornithological** *a.*, **ornithologist** *n.*

orphan *n.* child whose parents are dead. — *v.* make (a child) an orphan.

orphanage *n.* institution where orphans are cared for.

orrisroot *n.* violet-scented iris root.

orthodontics *n.* correction of irregularities in teeth. **orthodontic** *a.*, **orthodontist** *n.*

orthodox *a.* of or holding conventional or currently accepted beliefs, esp. in religion. **Orthodox Church** Eastern or Greek Church. **orthodoxy** *n.*

orthopaedics /orthəpeédiks/ *n.* surgical correction of deformities in bones or muscles. **orthopaedic** *a.*, **orthopaedist** *n.*

oryx *n.* large African antelope.

oscillate *v.* move to and fro; vary. **oscillation** *n.*

oscilloscope *n.* device for recording oscillations.

osier *n.* willow with flexible twigs; twig of this.

osmium *n.* heavy hard metallic element.

osmosis *n.* diffusion of fluid through a porous partition into another fluid. **osmotic** *a.*

osprey *n.* (*pl.* **-eys**) large bird preying on fish in inland waters.

osseous *a.* like bone, bony.

ossify *v.* turn into bone, harden; make or become rigid and unprogressive. **ossification** *n.*

ostensible *a.* pretended, used as a pretext. **ostensibly** *adv.*

ostentation *n.* showy display intended to impress people. **ostentatious** *a.*, **ostentatiously** *adv.*

osteopath *n.* practitioner who treats certain diseases and abnormalities by manipulating bones and muscles. **osteopathic** *a.*, **osteopathy** *n.*

ostracize *v.* refuse to associate with. **ostracism** *n.*

ostrich *n.* large swift-running African bird, unable to fly.

other *a.* alternative, additional, being the remaining one of a set of two or more; not the same. — *n.* & *pron.* the other person or thing. — *adv.* otherwise. **the other day** *or* **week** a few days or weeks ago.

otherwise *adv.* in a different way; in other respects; if circumstances are or were different.

otter *n.* fish-eating water animal with thick brown fur.

ottoman *n.* storage box with a padded top.

ought *v.aux.* expressing duty, rightness, advisability, or strong probability.

ounce *n.* unit of weight, one-sixteenth of a pound (about 28 grams). **fluid ounce** one-twentieth (in USA, one-sixteenth) of a pint (about 28 ml, in USA 35 ml).

our *a.*, **ours** *poss.pron.* belonging to us.

ourselves *pron.* emphatic and reflexive form of *we* and *us*.

oust *v.* drive out, eject.

out *adv.* away from or not in a place; not at home; not in effective action; in error; not possible; unconscious; into the open, so as to be heard or seen. — *prep.* out of. — *n.* way of escape. **be out to** be intending to. **out and out** thorough, extreme. **out of** from within or among; without a supply of; (of an animal) having as its dam. **out of date** no longer fashionable or current or valid. **out of doors** in the open air. **out of the way** no longer an obstacle; remote; unusual.

out- *pref.* more than, so as to exceed.

outboard *a.* (of a motor) attached to the outside of a boat.

outbreak *n.* breaking out of anger or war or disease etc.

outbuilding *n.* outhouse.

outburst *n.* explosion of feeling.

outcast *n.* person driven out of a group or by society.

outclass *v.* surpass in quality.

outcome *n.* result of an event.

outcrop *n.* part of an underlying layer of

rock that projects on the surface of the ground.
outcry *n.* loud cry; strong protest.
outdistance *v.* get far ahead of.
outdo *v.* (**-did**, **-done**) be or do better than.
outdoor *a.* of or for use in the open air. **outdoors** *adv.*
outer *a.* further from the centre or inside; exterior, external.
outermost *adv.* furthest outward.
outface *v.* disconcert by staring or by a confident manner.
outfit *n.* set of clothes or equipment.
outfitter *n.* supplier of equipment or men's clothing.
outflank *v.* get round the flank of (an enemy).
outgoing *a.* going out; sociable.
outgoings *n.pl.* expenditure.
outgrow *v.* (**-grew**, **-grown**) grow faster than; grow too large for; leave aside as one develops.
outhouse *n.* shed, barn, etc.
outing *n.* pleasure trip.
outlandish *a.* looking or sounding strange or foreign.
outlast *v.* last longer than.
outlaw *n.* (*old use*) person punished by being deprived of the law's protection; bandit. — *v.* make (a person) an outlaw; declare illegal.
outlay *n.* money etc. spent.
outlet *n.* way out; means for giving vent to energies or feelings; market for goods.
outline *n.* line(s) showing a thing's shape or boundary; summary. — *v.* draw or describe in outline; mark the outline of.
outlook *n.* view, prospect; mental attitude; future prospects.
outlying *a.* remote.
outmoded *a.* no longer fashionable or accepted.
outnumber *v.* exceed in number.
outpace *v.* go faster than.
out-patient *n.* person visiting a hospital for treatment but not remaining resident there.
outpost *n.* outlying settlement or detachment of troops.
output *n.* amount of electrical power etc. produced. — *v.* (**-put** *or* **-putted**) (of a computer) supply (results etc.).
outrage *n.* act that shocks public opinion; violation of rights. — *v.* shock and anger greatly.
outrageous *a.* greatly exceeding what is moderate or reasonable, shocking. **outrageously** *adv.*
outrider *n.* mounted attendant or motor cyclist riding as guard.
outrigger *n.* stabilizing strip of wood fixed outside and parallel to a canoe; canoe with this.
outright *adv.* completely, not gradually; frankly. — *a.* thorough, complete.
outrun *v.* (**-ran, -run, -running**) run faster or further than.
outset *n.* beginning.
outside *n.* outer side, surface, or part. — *a.* of or from the outside. — *adv.* on, at, or to the outside. — *prep.* on, at, or to the outside of; other than.
outsider *n.* non-member of a group; horse etc. thought to have no chance in a contest.
outsize *a.* much larger than average.
outskirts *n.pl.* outer districts.
outspoken *a.* very frank.
outstanding *a.* conspicuous; exceptionally good; not yet paid or settled. **outstandingly** *adv.*
outstrip *v.* (**-stripped**) run faster or further than; surpass.
outvote *v.* defeat by a majority of votes.
outward *a.* on or to the outside. — *adv.* outwards. **outwardly** *adv.*, **outwards** *adv.*
outweigh *v.* be of greater weight or importance than.
outwit *v.* (**-witted**) defeat by one's craftiness.
ouzel /o͞oz'l/ *n.* small bird of the thrush family; diving bird.
ouzo /o͞ozō/ *n.* Greek aniseed-flavoured spirits.
ova *see* **ovum**.
oval *n.* & *a.* (of) rounded symmetrical shape longer than it is broad.
ovary *n.* organ producing egg cells; that part of a pistil from which fruit is formed. **ovarian** *a.*
ovation *n.* enthusiastic applause.
oven *n.* enclosed chamber in which things are cooked or heated.
over *prep.* in or to a position higher than; above and across; throughout, during; more than. — *adv.* outwards and downwards from the brink or an upright position etc.; from one side or end etc. to the other; across a space or distance; besides; with repetition; at an end.
over- *pref.* above; excessively.
overall *n.* garment worn to protect other clothing, which it covers; (*pl.*) one-piece garment of this kind covering the body and legs. — *a.* total; taking all aspects into account. — *adv.* taken as a whole.
overarm *a.* & *adv.* with the arm brought forward and down from above shoulder level.

overawe *v.* overcome with awe.

overbalance *v.* lose balance and fall; cause to do this.

overbearing *a.* domineering.

overboard *adv.* from a ship into the water. **go overboard** (*colloq.*) show extreme enthusiasm.

overcast *a.* covered with cloud.

overcharge *v.* charge too much.

overcoat *n.* warm outdoor coat.

overcome *v.* win a victory over; succeed in subduing or dealing with; be victorious; make helpless.

overdo *v.* (**-did, -done**) do too much; cook too long.

overdose *n.* too large a dose. — *v.* give an overdose to; take an overdose.

overdraft *n.* overdrawing of a bank account; amount of this.

overdraw *v.* (**-drew, -drawn**) draw more from (a bank account) than the amount credited.

overdrive *n.* mechanism providing an extra gear above top gear.

overdue *a.* not paid or arrived etc. by the due time.

overestimate *v.* form too high an estimate of.

overflow *v.* flow over the edge or limits (of). — *n.* what overflows; outlet for excess liquid.

overgrown *a.* grown too large; covered with weeds etc.

overhaul *v.* examine and repair; overtake. — *n.* examination and repair.

overhead *a.* & *adv.* above the level of one's head; in the sky.

overheads *n.pl.* expenses involved in running a business etc.

overhear *v.* (**-heard**) hear accidentally or without the speaker's knowledge.

overjoyed *a.* filled with great joy.

overland *a.* & *adv.* (travelling) by land. **overlander** *n.*

overlap *v.* (**-lapped**) extend beyond the edge of; coincide partially. — *n.* overlapping; part or amount that overlaps.

overleaf *adv.* on the other side of a leaf of a book etc.

overload *v.* put too great a load on or in. — *n.* load that is too great.

overlook *v.* have a view over; oversee; fail to observe or consider; ignore, not punish.

overman *v.* (**-manned**) provide with too many people as workmen or crew.

overnight *adv.* & *a.* during a night.

overpass *n.* road crossing another by means of a bridge.

overpower *v.* overcome by greater strength or numbers.

overpowering *a.* (of heat or feelings) extremely intense.

overrate *v.* have too high an opinion of.

overreach *v.* **overreach oneself** fail through being too ambitious.

override *v.* (**-rode, -ridden**) overrule; prevail over; intervene and cancel the operation of.

overrule *v.* set aside (a decision etc.) by using one's authority.

overrun *v.* (**-ran, -run, -running**) spread over and occupy or injure; exceed (a limit).

overseas *a.* & *adv.* across or beyond the sea, abroad.

oversee *v.* (**-saw, -seen**) superintend. **overseer** *n.*

oversew *v.* (**-sewn**) sew (edges) together so that each stitch lies over the edges.

overshadow *v.* cast a shadow over; cause to seem unimportant in comparison.

overshoot *v.* (**-shot**) pass beyond (a target or limit etc.).

oversight *n.* supervision; unintentional omission or mistake.

overspill *n.* what spills over; district's surplus population seeking accommodation elsewhere.

overstay *v.* **overstay one's welcome**, stay so long that one is no longer welcome.

oversteer *v.* (of a car) tend to turn more sharply than was intended. — *n.* this tendency.

overstep *v.* (**-stepped**) go beyond (a limit).

overt *a.* done or shown openly. **overtly** *adv.*

overtake *v.* (**-took, -taken**) come abreast or level with; pass (a moving person or thing).

overthrow *v.* (**-threw, -thrown**) cause the downfall of. — *n.* downfall, defeat.

overtime *adv.* in addition to regular working hours. — *n.* time worked thus; payment for this.

overtone *n.* additional quality or implication.

overture *n.* orchestral composition forming a prelude to a performance; (*pl.*) initial approach or proposal.

overturn *v.* turn over; fall down or over, cause to fall.

overview *n.* general survey.

overwhelm *v.* bury beneath a huge mass; overcome completely; make helpless with emotion. **overwhelming** *a.*

overwrought *a.* in a state of nervous agitation.

oviduct *n.* tube through which ova pass from the ovary.

oviparous *a.* egg-laying.

ovoid *a.* egg-shaped, oval.

ovulate *v.* produce or discharge an egg cell from an ovary. **ovulation** *n.*

ovule *n.* germ cell of a plant.

ovum *n.* (*pl.* **ova**) egg cell, reproductive cell produced by a female.

owe *v.* be under an obligation to pay or repay or render; have (a thing) as the result of the action of another person or cause.

owing *a.* owed and not yet paid. **owing to** caused by; because of.

owl *n.* bird of prey with large eyes, usu. flying at night. **owlish** *a.*

own *a.* belonging to oneself or itself. — *v.* have as one's own; acknowledge ownership of. **of one's own** belonging to oneself. **on one's own** alone; independently. **own up** (*colloq.*) confess. **owner** *n.*, **ownership** *n.*

ox *n.* (*pl.* **oxen**) animal of or related to the kind kept as domestic cattle; fully grown bullock.

oxidation *n.* process of combining with oxygen.

oxide *n.* compound of oxygen and one other element.

oxidize *v.* combine with oxygen; coat with an oxide; make or become rusty. **oxidization** *n.*

oxyacetylene *a.* using a mixture of oxygen and acetylene, esp. in metal-cutting and welding.

oxygen *n.* colourless gas existing in air.

oyster *n.* shellfish used as food.

oz. *abbr.* ounce(s).

ozone *n.* form of oxygen; protective layer of this in the stratosphere.

P

pa *n.* (*colloq.*) father.

pace *n.* single step in walking or running; rate of progress. — *v.* walk steadily or to and fro; measure by pacing; set the pace for.

pacemaker *n.* runner etc. who sets the pace for another; device regulating heart contractions.

pachyderm /pákkiderm/ *n.* large thick-skinned mammal such as the elephant. **pachydermatous** *a.*

pacific *a.* making or loving peace. **pacifically** *adv.*

pacifist *n.* person totally opposed to war. **pacifism** *n.*

pacify *v.* calm and soothe; establish peace in. **pacification** *n.*

pack *n.* collection of things wrapped or tied for carrying or selling; set of playing cards; group of hounds or wolves. — *v.* put into or fill a container; press or crowd together, fill (a space) thus; cover or protect with something pressed tightly. **pack off** send away. **send packing** dismiss abruptly. **packer** *n.*

package *n.* parcel; box etc. in which goods are packed; package deal. — *v.* put together in a package. **package deal** set of proposals offered or accepted as a whole. **package holiday** one with set arrangements at an inclusive price. **packager** *n.*

packet *n.* small package; (*colloq.*) large sum of money; mail-boat.

pact *n.* agreement, treaty.

pad *n.* piece of padding; set of sheets of paper fastened together at one edge; soft fleshy part under an animal's paw; flat surface for use by helicopters or for launching rockets. — *v.* (**padded**) put padding on or into; fill out; walk softly or steadily.

padding *n.* soft material used to protect against jarring, add bulk, absorb fluid, etc.

paddle [1] *n.* short oar with broad blade(s). — *v.* propel by use of paddle(s); row gently.

paddle [2] *v.* walk with bare feet in shallow water for pleasure.

paddock *n.* small field where horses are kept; enclosure for horses at a racecourse.

padlock *n.* detachable lock with a U-shaped bar secured through the object fastened. — *v.* fasten with a padlock.

padre /paádri/ *n.* (*colloq.*) chaplain in the army etc.

paean /peéən/ *n.* song of triumph.

paediatrics /peédiátriks/ *n.* study of children's diseases. **paediatric** *a.*, **paediatrician** *n.*

paella /pī-éllə/ *n.* Spanish dish of rice, saffron, seafood, etc.

pagan *a.* & *n.* heathen.

page [1] *n.* sheet of paper in a book etc.; one side of this.

page [2] *n.* boy attendant of a bride. — *v.* summon by an announcement, messenger, or pager.

pageant *n.* public show or procession, esp. with people in costume. **pageantry** *n.*

pager *n.* radio device with a bleeper for summoning the wearer.

pagoda *n.* Hindu temple or Buddhist tower in India, China, etc.

paid *see* **pay**. — *a.* **put paid to** end (hopes or prospects etc.).

pail *n.* bucket.

pain *n.* unpleasant feeling caused by injury or disease of the body; mental suffering; (*pl.*) careful effort. — *v.* cause pain to.

painful *a.* causing or suffering pain; laborious. **painfully** *adv.*

painless *a.* not causing pain. **painlessly** *adv.*

painstaking *a.* very careful.

paint *n.* colouring matter for applying in liquid form to a surface; (*pl.*) tubes or cakes of paint. — *v.* coat with paint; portray by using paint(s) or in words; apply (liquid) to.

painter [1] *n.* person who paints as artist or decorator.

painter [2] *n.* rope attached to a boat's bow for tying it up.

painting *n.* painted picture.

pair *n.* set of two things or people, couple; article consisting of two parts; other member of a pair. — *v.* arrange or be arranged in pair(s).

pal *n.* (*colloq.*) friend.

palace *n.* official residence of a sovereign, archbishop, or bishop; splendid mansion.

palaeography /pálliógrəfi/ *n.* study of ancient writing and inscriptions. **palaeographer** *n.*

palaeolithic /pálliō-/ *a.* of the early part of the Stone Age.

palaeontology /pálli-/ *n.* study of life in the geological past. **palaeontologist** *n.*

palatable *a.* pleasant to the taste or mind.

palate *n.* roof of the mouth; sense of taste.

palatial /pəláysh'l/ *a.* of or like a palace.

palaver *n.* (*colloq.*) fuss.

pale [1] *a.* (of face) having less colour than normal; (of colour or light) faint. — *v.* turn pale. **palely** *adv.*, **paleness** *n.*

pale [2] *n.* **beyond the pale** outside the bounds of acceptable behaviour.

Palestinian *a.* & *n.* (native) of Palestine.

palette *n.* board on which an artist mixes colours. **palette-knife** *n.* blade with a handle, used for spreading paint or for smoothing soft substances in cookery.

paling *n.* railing(s).

pall /pawl/ *n.* cloth spread over a coffin; heavy dark covering. — *v.* become uninteresting.

pallbearer *n.* person helping to carry or walking beside the coffin at a funeral.

pallet [1] *n.* straw-stuffed mattress; hard narrow or makeshift bed.

pallet [2] *n.* tray or platform for goods being lifted or stored.

palliasse *n.* straw-stuffed mattress.

palliate *v.* alleviate; partially excuse. **palliation** *n.*, **palliative** *a.*

pallid *a.* pale, esp. from illness. **pallidness** *n.*, **pallor** *n.*

pally *a.* (*colloq.*) friendly.

palm *n.* inner surface of the hand; part of a glove covering this; tree of warm and tropical climates, with large leaves and no branches. — *v.* conceal in one's hand. **palm off** get (a thing) accepted fraudulently. **palm tree**.

palmist *n.* person who tells people's fortunes or characters from lines in their palms. **palmistry** *n.*

palomino *n.* (*pl.* **-os**) golden or cream-coloured horse.

palpable *a.* able to be touched or felt; obvious. **palpably** *adv.*, **palpability** *n.*

palpate *v.* examine medically by touch. **palpation** *n.*

palpitate *v.* throb rapidly; quiver with fear or excitement. **palpitation** *n.*

palsy *n.* paralysis, esp. with involuntary tremors. **palsied** *a.*

paltry *a.* (**-ier, -iest**) worthless. **paltriness** *n.*

pampas *n.* vast grassy plains in South America. **pampas-grass** *n.* large ornamental grass.

pamper *v.* treat very indulgently.

pamphlet *n.* leaflet or paper-covered booklet. **pamphleteer** *n.*

pan [1] *n.* metal or earthenware vessel with a flat base, used in cooking; similar vessel. — *v.* (**panned**) wash (gravel) in a pan in searching for gold; (*colloq.*) criticize severely. **pan out** turn out (well). **panful** *n.*

pan [2] *v.* (**panned**) turn horizontally in filming.

pan- *pref.* all-, whole.

panacea /pánnəséeə/ *n.* remedy for all kinds of diseases or troubles.

panache *n.* confident stylish manner.

panama *n.* straw hat.

panatella *n.* thin cigar.

pancake *n.* thin round cake of fried batter.

panchromatic *a.* sensitive to all colours of the visible spectrum.

pancreas *n.* gland near the stomach, discharging insulin into the blood. **pancreatic** *a.*

panda *n.* bear-like black and white animal of south-west China; racoon-like animal of India.

pandemic *a.* (of a disease) occurring country-wide or world-wide.

pandemonium *n.* uproar.

pander *v.* **pander to** gratify by satisfying a weakness or vulgar taste.

pane *n.* sheet of glass in a window or door.

panegyric *n.* piece of written or spoken praise.

panel *n.* distinct usu. rectangular section; strip of board etc. forming this; group assembled to discuss or decide something; list of jurors, jury. — *v.* (**panelled**) cover or decorate with panels.

panelling *n.* series of wooden panels in a wall; wood used for making panels.

panellist *n.* member of a panel.

pang *n.* sudden sharp pain.

pangolin *n.* scaly anteater.

panic *n.* sudden strong fear. — *v.* (**panicked**) affect or be affected with panic. **panic-stricken**, **panic-struck** *adjs.*, **panicky** *a.*

pannier *n.* large basket carried by a donkey etc.; bag fitted on a motor cycle or bicycle.

panoply *n.* splendid array.

panorama *n.* view of a wide area or set of events. **panoramic** *a.*

pansy *n.* garden flower of violet family with broad petals; (*derog.*) effeminate or homosexual man.

pant *v.* breathe with short quick breaths; utter breathlessly.

pantechnicon *n.* large van for transporting furniture.

pantheism *n.* doctrine that God is in everything. **pantheist** *n.*, **pantheistic** *a.*

panther *n.* leopard.

panties *n.pl.* (*colloq.*) short knickers.

pantile *n.* curved roof tile.

pantograph *n.* device for copying a plan etc. on any scale.

pantomime *n.* Christmas play based on a fairy tale.

pantry *n.* room for storing china, glass, etc.; larder.

pants *n.pl.* (*colloq.*) trousers; underpants; knickers.

pap *n.* soft food suitable for infants or invalids; pulp.

papacy *n.* position or authority of the pope.

papal *a.* of the pope or papacy.

paper *n.* substance manufactured in thin sheets from wood fibre, rags, etc., used for writing on, wrapping things, etc.; newspaper; set of examination questions; document; dissertation. — *v.* cover (walls etc.) with wallpaper.

paperback *a.* & *n.* (book) bound in flexible paper binding.

paperweight *n.* small heavy object to hold loose papers down.

papier mâché /pápyay máshay/ moulded paper pulp used for making small objects.

papoose *n.* young North American Indian child.

paprika *n.* red pepper.

papyrus *n.* reed-like water plant from which the ancient Egyptians made a kind of paper; this paper; (*pl.* **-ri**) manuscript written on this.

par *n.* average or normal amount or condition etc.; equal footing.

parable *n.* story told to illustrate a moral or spiritual truth.

paracetamol *n.* drug that relieves pain and reduces fever.

parachute *n.* device used to slow the descent of a person or object dropping from a great height. — *v.* descend or drop by parachute. **parachutist** *n.*

parade *n.* formal assembly of troops; procession; ostentatious display; public square or promenade. — *v.* assemble for parade; march or walk with display; make a display of.

paradigm /párrədīm/ *n.* example, model.

paradise *n.* heaven; Eden.

paradox *n.* statement that seems self-contradictory but contains a truth. **paradoxical** *a.*, **paradoxically** *adv.*

paraffin *n.* oil from petroleum or shale, used as fuel.

paragon *n.* apparently perfect person or thing.

paragraph *n.* one or more sentences on a single theme, beginning on a new line. — *v.* arrange in paragraphs.

parakeet *n.* a kind of small parrot.

parallax *n.* apparent difference in an object's position when viewed from different points. **parallactic** *a.*

parallel *a.* (of lines or planes) going continuously at the same distance from each other; similar, corresponding. — *n.* parallel line or thing; line of latitude; analogy. — *v.* (**paralleled**) be parallel to; compare. **parallelism** *n.*

parallelogram *n.* four-sided geometric figure with its opposite sides parallel to each other.

paralyse *v.* affect with paralysis; bring to a standstill.

paralysis *n.* loss of power of movement. **paralytic** *a.* & *n.*

paramedic *n.* skilled person working in support of medical staff.

parameter *n.* variable quantity or quality that restricts what it characterizes.

paramilitary *a.* organized like a military force.

paramount *a.* chief in importance.

paranoia *n.* mental disorder in which a person has delusions of grandeur or persecution; abnormal tendency to mistrust others. **paranoiac** *a.*, **paranoid** *a.*

parapet *n.* low wall along the edge of a balcony or bridge.

paraphernalia *n.* numerous belongings or pieces of equipment.

paraphrase *v.* express in other words. — *n.* rewording in this way.

paraplegia *n.* paralysis of the legs and part or all of the trunk. **paraplegic** *a.* & *n.*

parapsychology *n.* study of mental perceptions that seem outside normal abilities.

paraquat *n.* extremely poisonous weed-killer.

parasite *n.* animal or plant living on or in another; person living off another or others and giving no useful return. **parasitic** *a.*

parasol *n.* light umbrella used to give shade from the sun.

parboil *v.* cook partially by boiling.

parcel *n.* thing(s) wrapped for carrying or post; piece of land. — *v.* (**parcelled**) wrap as a parcel; divide into portions.

parch *v.* make hot and dry; make thirsty.

parchment *n.* writing material made from animal skins; paper resembling this.

pardon *n.* forgiveness. — *v.* (**pardoned**) forgive. **pardonable** *a.*, **pardonably** *adv.*

pare *v.* trim the edges of; peel; reduce little by little.

parent *n.* father or mother; ancestor; source from which other things are derived. **parental** *a.*, **parenthood** *n.*

parentage *n.* ancestry.

parenthesis *n.* (*pl.* **-theses**) word, phrase, or sentence inserted into a passage; brackets (like these) placed round this.

parenthetic *a.*, **parenthetical** *a.*, **parenthetically** *adv.*
parenting *n.* being a parent.
pariah /pərīə/ *n.* outcast.
parietal bone each of a pair of bones forming part of the skull.
paring *n.* piece pared off.
parish *n.* area with its own church and clergyman; local government area within a county.
parishioner *n.* inhabitant of a parish.
Parisian *a.* & *n.* (native) of Paris.
parity *n.* equality.
park *n.* public garden or recreation ground; enclosed land of a country house; parking area. — *v.* place and leave (a vehicle) temporarily.
parka *n.* a type of thick jacket with a hood attached.
parlance *n.* phraseology.
parley *n.* (*pl.* **-eys**) discussion, esp. between enemies, to settle a dispute. — *v.* (**parleyed**) hold a parley.
parliament *n.* assembly that makes a country's laws. **parliamentary** *a.*, **parliamentarian** *n.*
Parmesan *n.* a kind of hard cheese.
parochial *a.* of a church parish; interested in a limited area only. **parochially** *adv.*, **parochialism** *n.*
parody *n.* comic or grotesque imitation. — *v.* make a parody of.
parole *n.* person's word of honour; release of a prisoner before the end of his or her sentence on condition of good behaviour. — *v.* release in this way.
paroxysm *n.* spasm; outburst of laughter, rage, etc.
parquet /paárki/ *n.* flooring of wooden blocks arranged in a pattern.
parricide *n.* killing or killer of own parent. **parricidal** *a.*
parrot *n.* tropical bird with a short hooked bill; unintelligent imitator. — *v.* (**parroted**) repeat mechanically.
parry *v.* ward off (a blow); evade (a question) skilfully.
parsec *n.* unit of distance used in astronomy, about 3.25 light years.
parsimonious *a.* stingy, very sparing. **parsimoniously** *adv.*, **parsimony** *n.*
parsley *n.* herb with crinkled green leaves.
parsnip *n.* vegetable with a large yellowish tapering root.
parson *n.* (*colloq.*) clergyman. **parson's nose** fatty lump on the rump of a cooked fowl.
parsonage *n.* rectory, vicarage.
part *n.* some but not all; distinct portion; component; portion allotted; character assigned to an actor in a play etc. *adv.* partly. — *v.* separate, divide. **in good part** without taking offence. **part of speech** word's grammatical class (noun, verb, adjective, etc.). **part-time** *a.* for or during only part of the working week. **part with** give up possession of.
partake *v.* (**-took, -taken**) participate; take a portion, esp. of food. **partaker** *n.*
partial *a.* favouring one side or person, biased; not complete or total. **be partial to** have a strong liking for. **partially** *adv.*
partiality *n.* bias, favouritism; strong liking.
participate *v.* have a share, take part in something. **participation** *n.*, **participator** *n.*
participle *n.* word formed from a verb, as a **past participle** (e.g. *burnt*, *frightened*), **present participle** (e.g. *burning*, *frightening*). **participial** *a.*
particle *n.* very small portion of matter; minor part of speech.
particoloured *a.* coloured partly in one colour, partly in another.
particular *a.* relating to one person or thing and not others; carefully insisting on certain standards. — *n.* detail; piece of information. **in particular** specifically. **particularly** *adv.*
parting *n.* leave-taking; line from which hair is combed in different directions.
partisan *n.* strong supporter; guerrilla. **partisanship** *n.*
partition *n.* division into parts; structure dividing a room or space, thin wall. — *v.* divide into parts or by a partition.
partly *adv.* partially.
partner *n.* person sharing with another or others in an activity; each of a pair; husband or wife or member of an unmarried couple. — *v.* be the partner of; put together as partners. **partnership** *n.*
partridge *n.* plump brown game bird.
parturition *n.* process of giving birth to young; childbirth.
party *n.* social gathering; group travelling or working as a unit; group with common aims, esp. in politics; one side in an agreement or dispute. **party line** set policy of a political party. **party wall** wall common to two buildings or rooms.
paschal /pásk'l/ *a.* of the Passover; of Easter.
pass *v.* (**passed**) move onward or past; go or send to another person or place; discharge from the body as excreta; change from one state into another; happen; occupy (time); be accepted; examine and declare satisfactory; achieve the required standard in a test; go beyond; (in a game)

refuse one's turn. — *n.* passing, movement made with the hands or thing held; permit to enter or leave; gap in mountains, allowing passage to the other side. **make a pass at** (*colloq.*) make sexual advances to. **pass away** cease; die. **pass out** (*colloq.*) become unconscious. **pass over** disregard. **pass up** (*colloq.*) refuse to accept.

passable *a.* able to be traversed; just satisfactory. **passably** *adv.*

passage *n.* passing; right to pass or be a passenger; way through, esp. with a wall on each side; tube-like structure; journey by sea; section of a literary or musical work. **passageway** *n.*

passbook *n.* book recording a customer's deposits and withdrawals from a bank etc.

passenger *n.* person (other than the driver, pilot, or crew) travelling in a vehicle, train, ship, or aircraft; ineffective member of a team.

passer-by *n.* (*pl.* **passers-by**) person who happens to be going past.

passion *n.* strong emotion; sexual love; great enthusiasm; **the Passion** sufferings of Christ on the Cross.

passionate *a.* full of passion, intense. **passionately** *adv.*

passive *a.* acted upon and not active; not resisting; lacking initiative or forceful qualities. **passively** *adv.*, **passiveness** *n.*, **passivity** *n.*

Passover *n.* Jewish festival commemorating the escape of Jews from slavery in Egypt.

passport *n.* official document for use by a person travelling abroad.

password *n.* secret word(s), knowledge of which distinguishes friend from enemy.

past *a.* belonging to the time before the present, gone by. — *n.* past time or events; person's past life. — *prep.* & *adv.* beyond. **past master** thorough master, expert.

pasta *n.* dried dough produced in various shapes; cooked dish made with this.

paste *n.* moist mixture; adhesive; edible doughy substance; glass-like substance used in imitation gems. — *v.* fasten or coat with paste; (*sl.*) thrash.

pasteboard *n.* cardboard.

pastel *n.* chalk-like crayon; drawing made with this; light delicate shade of colour.

pasteurize *v.* sterilize by heating. **pasteurization** *n.*

pastille *n.* small flavoured sweet for sucking; lozenge.

pastime *n.* something done to pass time pleasantly.

pastor *n.* clergyman in charge of a church or congregation.

pastoral *a.* of country life; of a pastor, of spiritual guidance.

pastry *n.* dough made of flour, fat, and water, used for making pies etc.; article(s) made with this.

pasturage *n.* pasture land.

pasture *n.* grassy land suitable for grazing cattle. — *v.* put (animals) to graze.

pasty [1] /pásti/ *n.* pastry with sweet or savoury filling, baked without a dish.

pasty [2] /páysti/ *a.* (**-ier**, **-iest**) of or like paste; unhealthily pale.

pat *v.* (**patted**) tap gently with an open hand. — *n.* patting movement; small mass of a soft substance. — *adv.* & *a.* known and ready.

patch *n.* piece put on, esp. in mending; distinct area or period; piece of ground. — *v.* put patch(es) on; piece (things) together. **not a patch on** (*colloq.*) not nearly as good as. **patch up** repair; settle (a quarrel etc.).

patchwork *n.* needlework in which small pieces of cloth are joined decoratively; thing made of assorted pieces.

patchy *a.* (**-ier**, **-iest**) existing in patches; uneven in quality. **patchily** *adv.*, **patchiness** *n.*

pâté /páttay/ *n.* paste of meat etc.

patella *n.* (*pl.* **-ae**) kneecap.

patent *a.* obvious; patented. — *v.* obtain or hold a patent for. — *n.* official right to be the sole maker or user of an invention or process; invention etc. protected by this. **patent leather** leather with glossy varnished surface. **patently** *adv.*

patentee *n.* holder of a patent.

paternal *a.* of a father; fatherly; related through one's father. **paternally** *adv.*

paternalism *n.* policy of making kindly provision for people's needs but giving them no responsibility. **paternalistic** *a.*

paternity *n.* fatherhood.

path *n.* way by which people pass on foot; line along which a person or thing moves; course of action.

pathetic *a.* arousing pity or sadness; miserably inadequate. **pathetically** *adv.*

pathogenic *a.* causing disease.

pathology *n.* study of disease. **pathological** *a.*, **pathologist** *n.*

pathos *n.* pathetic quality.

patience *n.* calm endurance; card game for one player.

patient *a.* showing patience. — *n.* person treated by a doctor or dentist etc. **patiently** *adv.*

patina *n.* sheen on a surface produced by age or use.

patio *n.* (*pl.* **-os**) paved courtyard.

patois /pátwaa/ *n.* dialect.

patriarch *n.* male head of a family or tribe; bishop of high rank in certain Churches. **patriarchal** *a.*, **patriarchate** *n.*

patriarchy *n.* social organization in which a male is head of the family.

patricide *n.* killing or killer of own father. **patricidal** *a.*

patrimony *n.* heritage.

patriot *n.* patriotic person.

patriotic *a.* loyally supporting one's country. **patriotically** *adv.*, **patriotism** *n.*

patrol *v.* (**patrolled**) walk or travel regularly through (an area or building) to see that all is well. — *n.* patrolling; person(s) patrolling.

patron /páytrən/ *n.* person giving influential or financial support to a cause; regular customer. **patron saint** saint regarded as a protector.

patronage *n.* patron's support; patronizing behaviour.

patronize *v.* act as patron to; treat in a condescending way.

patronymic *n.* name derived from that of a father or ancestor.

patter[1] *v.* make a series of quick tapping sounds; run with short quick steps. — *n.* pattering sound.

patter[2] *n.* rapid glib speech.

pattern *n.* decorative design; model, design, or instructions showing how a thing is to be made; sample of cloth etc.; excellent example; regular manner in which things occur. **patterned** *a.*

patty *n.* small pie or pasty.

paucity *n.* smallness of quantity.

paunch *n.* protruding stomach.

pauper *n.* very poor person.

pause *n.* temporary stop. — *v.* make a pause.

pave *v.* cover (a path etc.) with stones etc. to make a hard surface.

pavement *n.* paved surface; paved path at the side of a road.

pavilion *n.* building on a sports ground for use by players and spectators; ornamental building.

pavlova *n.* meringue cake containing cream and fruit.

paw *n.* foot of an animal that has claws. — *v.* strike with a paw; scrape (the ground) with a hoof; (*colloq.*) touch with the hands.

pawl *n.* lever with a catch that engages with the notches of a ratchet.

pawn[1] *n.* chessman of the smallest size and value; person whose actions are controlled by others.

pawn[2] *v.* deposit with a pawnbroker as security for money borrowed.

pawnbroker *n.* person licensed to lend money on the security of personal property deposited.

pawnshop *n.* pawnbroker's premises.

pawpaw *n.* edible fruit of a palm-like tropical tree; this tree.

pay *v.* (**paid**) give (money) in return for goods or services; give what is owed; be profitable or worth while; suffer (a penalty). — *n.* payment; wages. **pay off** pay (a debt) in full; discharge (an employee); yield good results. **pay-off** *n.* (*sl.*) payment; reward, retribution, climax. **payer** *n.*

payable *a.* which must or may be paid.

payee *n.* person to whom money is paid or is to be paid.

payload *n.* aircraft's or rocket's total load.

payment *n.* paying; money etc. paid.

payola *n.* bribery offered for dishonest use of influence to promote a commercial product.

payroll *n.* list of a firm's employees receiving regular pay.

pea *n.* plant bearing seeds in pods; its round seed used as a vegetable. **pea-green** *a.* & *n.* bright green.

peace *n.* state of freedom from war or disturbance.

peaceable *a.* fond of peace, not quarrelsome; peaceful. **peaceably** *adv.*

peaceful *a.* characterized by peace. **peacefully** *adv.*, **peacefulness** *n.*

peacemaker *n.* person who brings about peace.

peach *n.* round juicy fruit with a rough stone; tree bearing this; its yellowish-pink colour.

peacock *n.* male bird with splendid plumage and a long fan-like tail. **peahen** *n.fem.*, **peafowl** *n.*

peak *n.* pointed top, esp. of a mountain; projecting part of the edge of a cap; point of highest value or intensity etc. **peaked** *a.*

peaky *a.* (**-ier, -iest**) looking drawn and sickly.

peal *n.* sound of ringing bell(s); set of bells with different notes; loud burst of thunder or laughter. — *v.* sound in a peal.

peanut *n.* plant bearing underground pods with two edible seeds; this seed; (*pl.*) very trivial sum of money.

pear *n.* rounded fruit tapering towards the stalk; tree bearing this.

pearl *n.* round usu. white gem formed inside the shell of certain oysters. **pearly** *a.*

peasant *n.* person working on the land, esp. in the Middle Ages.

peasantry *n.* peasants collectively.
peat *n.* decomposed vegetable matter from bogs etc., used in horticulture or as fuel. **peaty** *a.*
pebble *n.* small smooth round stone. **pebbly** *a.*
pecan *n.* smooth pinkish-brown nut; tree bearing this.
peccary *n.* small wild pig of Central and South America.
peck *v.* strike, nip, or pick up with the beak; kiss hastily. — *n.* pecking movement.
peckish *a.* (*colloq.*) hungry.
pectin *n.* substance found in fruits that makes jam set.
pectoral *a.* of, in, or on the chest or breast. — *n.* pectoral fin or muscle.
peculiar *a.* strange, eccentric; belonging exclusively to one person or place or thing; special. **peculiarly** *adv.*, **peculiarity** *n.*
pecuniary *a.* of or in money.
pedagogue *n.* (*derog.*) person who teaches pedantically.
pedal *n.* lever operated by the foot. — *v.* (**pedalled**) work the pedal(s) of; operate by pedals.
pedant *n.* pedantic person. **pedantry** *n.*
pedantic *a.* insisting on strict observance of rules and details in presenting knowledge; parading one's learning. **pedantically** *adv.*
peddle *v.* sell (goods) as a pedlar.
pedestal *n.* base supporting a column or statue etc.
pedestrian *n.* person walking, esp. in a street. — *a.* of or for pedestrians; unimaginative, dull.
pedicure *n.* care or treatment of the feet and toenails.
pedigree *n.* line or list of (esp. distinguished) ancestors. — *a.* (of an animal) of recorded and pure breeding.
pediment *n.* triangular part crowning the front of a building.
pedlar *n.* person who sells small articles from door to door.
pedometer *n.* device for estimating the distance travelled on foot.
peduncle *n.* stalk of a flower etc.
pee *v.* (*colloq.*) urinate. — *n.* (*colloq.*) urine.
peek *v.* & *n.* peep, glance.
peel *n.* skin of certain fruits and vegetables etc. — *v.* remove the peel of; strip off; come off in strips or layers, lose skin or bark etc. thus. **peeler** *n.*, **peelings** *n.pl.*
peep *v.* look through a narrow opening; look quickly or surreptitiously; show slightly. — *n.* brief or surreptitious look.
peep-hole *n.* small hole to peep through.
peeping Tom furtive voyeur.
peer [1] *v.* look searchingly or with difficulty or effort.
peer [2] *n.* duke, marquess, earl, viscount, or baron; one who is the equal of another in rank or merit etc. **peeress** *n.fem.*
peerage *n.* peers as a group; rank of peer or peeress.
peerless *a.* without equal, superb.
peeved *a.* (*colloq.*) annoyed.
peevish *a.* irritable. **peevishly** *adv.*, **peevishness** *n.*
peewit *n.* lapwing.
peg *n.* wooden or metal pin or stake; clip for holding clothes on a washing-line. — *v.* (**pegged**) fix or mark by means of peg(s); keep (wages or prices) at a fixed level. **off the peg** (of clothes) ready-made.
pejorative *a.* derogatory.
peke *n.* Pekingese dog.
Pekingese *n.* dog of a breed with short legs, flat face, and silky hair.
pelargonium *n.* plant with showy flowers.
pelican *n.* waterbird with a pouch in its long bill for storing fish. **pelican crossing** pedestrian crossing with lights operated by pedestrians.
pellagra *n.* deficiency disease causing cracking of the skin.
pellet *n.* small round mass of a substance; small shot. **pelleted** *a.*
pell-mell *a.* & *adv.* in a hurrying disorderly manner, headlong.
pellucid *a.* very clear.
pelmet *n.* ornamental strip above a window etc.
pelt [1] *n.* an animal skin.
pelt [2] *v.* throw missiles at; run fast. **at full pelt** as fast as possible.
pelvis *n.* framework of bones round the body below the waist. **pelvic** *a.*
pen [1] *n.* small fenced enclosure, esp. for animals. — *v.* (**penned**) shut in or as if in a pen.
pen [2] *n.* device with a metal point for writing with ink. — *v.* (**penned**) write (a letter etc.). **penfriend** *n.* friend with whom a person corresponds without meeting. **pen-name** *n.* author's pseudonym.
penal *a.* of or involving punishment.
penalize *v.* inflict a penalty on; put at a disadvantage. **penalization** *n.*
penalty *n.* punishment for breaking a law or rule or contract.
penance *n.* act performed as an expression of penitence.
pence *see* **penny**.
penchant /pónshon/ *n.* liking.

pencil *n.* instrument containing graphite, used for drawing or writing. — *v.* (**pencilled**) write, draw, or mark with a pencil.
pendant *n.* ornament hung from a chain round the neck.
pendent *a.* hanging.
pending *a.* waiting to be decided or settled. — *prep.* during; until.
pendulous *a.* hanging loosely.
pendulum *n.* weight hung from a cord and swinging freely; rod with a weighted end that regulates a clock's movement.
penetrable *a.* able to be penetrated. **penetrability** *n.*
penetrate *v.* make a way into or through, pierce; see into or through. **penetration** *n.*
penetrating *a.* showing great insight; (of sound) piercing.
penguin *n.* flightless seabird of Antarctic regions.
penicillin *n.* antibiotic obtained from mould fungi.
peninsula *n.* piece of land almost surrounded by water. **peninsular** *a.*
penis *n.* organ by which a male mammal copulates and urinates.
penitent *a.* feeling or showing regret that one has done wrong. — *n.* penitent person. **penitently** *adv.*, **penitence** *n.*
penitential *a.* of penitence or penance.
pennant *n.* long tapering flag.
penniless *a.* having no money, destitute.
pennon *n.* flag, esp. a long triangular or forked one.
penny *n.* (*pl.* **pennies** for separate coins, **pence** for a sum of money) British bronze coin worth one-hundredth of £1; former coin worth one-twelfth of a shilling. **penny-pinching** *a.* niggardly.
pension *n.* income consisting of a periodic payment made in consideration of past service or on retirement or widowhood etc. — *v.* pay a pension to. **pension off** dismiss with a pension.
pensionable *a.* entitled or (of a job) entitling one to a pension.
pensioner *n.* person who receives a pension.
pensive *a.* deep in thought. **pensively** *adv.*, **pensiveness** *n.*
pentagon *n.* geometric figure with five sides. **pentagonal** *a.*
pentagram *n.* five-pointed star.
pentathlon *n.* athletic contest involving five events.
Pentecost *n.* Jewish harvest festival, 50 days after second day of Passover; Whit Sunday.
penthouse *n.* dwelling (usu. with a terrace) on the roof of a tall building.
penultimate *a.* last but one.
penumbra *n.* (*pl.* **-ae**) area of partial shadow, esp. in an eclipse.
penury *n.* poverty. **penurious** *a.*
peony *n.* garden plant with large round red, pink, or white flowers.
people *n.pl.* human beings; persons; subjects of a State; parents or other relatives. — *n.* persons composing a race or nation. — *v.* fill with people, populate.
pep *n.* vigour. — *v.* (**pepped**) **pep up** fill with vigour, enliven. **pep talk** talk urging great effort.
pepper *n.* hot-tasting seasoning powder made from the dried berries of certain plants; capsicum. — *v.* sprinkle with pepper; pelt; sprinkle. **peppery** *a.*
peppercorn *n.* dried black berry from which pepper is made. **peppercorn rent** very low rent.
peppermint *n.* a kind of mint with strong fragrant oil; this oil; sweet flavoured with this.
pepsin *n.* enzyme in gastric juice.
peptic *a.* of digestion.
per *prep.* for each; in accordance with; by means of. **per annum** for each year. **per capita** for each person. **per cent** in or for every hundred.
perambulate *v.* walk through or round (an area). **perambulation** *n.*
perceive *v.* become aware of, see or notice.
percentage *n.* rate or proportion per hundred; proportion, part.
perceptible *a.* able to be perceived. **perceptibly** *adv.*, **perceptibility** *n.*
perception *n.* perceiving, ability to perceive.
perceptive *a.* showing insight and understanding. **perceptively** *adv.*, **perceptiveness** *n.*
perch [1] *n.* bird's resting place, rod etc. for this; high seat. — *v.* rest or place on or as if on a perch.
perch [2] *n.* (*pl.* **perch**) edible freshwater fish with spiny fins.
percipient *a.* perceptive. **percipience** *n.*
percolate *v.* filter, esp. through small holes; prepare in a percolator. **percolation** *n.*
percolator *n.* coffee pot in which boiling water is circulated repeatedly through ground coffee held in a perforated drum.
percussion *n.* striking of one object against another. **percussion instrument** musical instrument (e.g. drum, cymbals) played by striking. **percussive** *a.*
perdition *n.* eternal damnation.
peregrine *n.* a kind of falcon.

peremptory *a.* imperious. **peremptorily** *adv.*
perennial *a.* lasting a long time; constantly recurring; (of plants) living for several years. — *n.* perennial plant. **perennially** *adv.*
perfect *a.* /pérfikt/ complete, entire; faultless, excellent; exact. — *v.* /pərfékt/ make perfect. **perfectly** *adv.*, **perfection** *n.*
perfectionist *n.* person who seeks perfection. **perfectionism** *n.*
perfidious *a.* treacherous, disloyal. **perfidy** *n.*
perforate *v.* make hole(s) through. **perforation** *n.*
perform *v.* carry into effect; go through (a piece of music, ceremony, etc.); function; act in a play, sing, do tricks etc. before an audience. **performer** *n.*, **performance** *n.*
perfume *n.* sweet smell; fragrant liquid for applying to the body. — *v.* give a sweet smell to.
perfumery *n.* perfumes.
perfunctory *a.* done or doing things without much care or interest. **perfunctorily** *adv.*
pergola *n.* arch of trellis-work with climbing plants trained over it.
perhaps *adv.* it may be, possibly.
pericardium *n.* membranous sac enclosing the heart.
perigee *n.* point nearest to the earth in the moon's orbit.
peril *n.* serious danger.
perilous *a.* full of risk, dangerous. **perilously** *adv.*
perimeter *n.* outer edge of an area; length of this.
period *n.* length or portion of time; occurrence of menstruation; sentence; full stop in punctuation. — *a.* (of dress or furniture) belonging to a past age.
periodic *a.* happening at intervals. **periodicity** *n.*
periodical *a.* periodic. — *n.* magazine etc. published at regular intervals. **periodically** *adv.*
peripatetic *a.* going from place to place.
peripheral *a.* of or on the periphery; of minor but not central importance to something.
periphery *n.* boundary, edge; fringes of a subject etc.
periscope *n.* tube with mirror(s) by which a person in a submarine etc. can see things above.
perish *v.* suffer destruction, die; rot; distress or wither by cold or exposure. **perishing** *a.*
perishable *a.* liable to decay or go bad in a short time.
peritoneum *n.* membrane lining the abdominal cavity.
peritonitis *n.* inflammation of the peritoneum.
periwinkle [1] *n.* trailing plant with blue or white flowers.
periwinkle [2] *n.* winkle.
perjure *v.* **perjure oneself** lie under oath.
perjury *n.* deliberate giving of false evidence while under oath; this evidence.
perk [1] *v.* **perk up** (*colloq.*) cheer or brighten or smarten up.
perk [2] *n.* (*colloq.*) perquisite.
perky *a.* (**-ier, -iest**) (*colloq.*) lively and cheerful. **perkily** *adv.*, **perkiness** *n.*
perm [1] *n.* permanent artificial wave in the hair. — *v.* give a perm to.
perm [2] *n.* permutation. — *v.* make a permutation of.
permafrost *n.* permanently frozen subsoil in arctic regions.
permanent *a.* lasting indefinitely. **permanently** *adv.*, **permanence** *n.*, **permanency** *n.*
permeable *a.* able to be permeated by fluids etc. **permeability** *n.*
permeate *v.* pass or flow into every part of. **permeation** *n.*
permissible *a.* allowable.
permission *n.* consent or authorization to do something.
permissive *a.* tolerant, esp. in social and sexual matters. **permissiveness** *n.*
permit *v.* /pərmít/ (**permitted**) give permission to or for; make possible. — *n.* /pérmit/ written permission, esp. for entry to a place.
permutation *n.* variation of the order of or choice from a set of things.
pernicious *a.* harmful.
pernickety *a.* (*colloq.*) fastidious, scrupulous.
peroration *n.* lengthy speech; last part of this.
peroxide *n.* compound of hydrogen used to bleach hair. — *v.* bleach with this.
perpendicular *a.* at an angle of 90° to a line or surface; upright, vertical. — *n.* perpendicular line or direction. **perpendicularly** *adv.*
perpetrate *v.* commit (a crime), be guilty of (a blunder). **perpetration** *n.*, **perpetrator** *n.*
perpetual *a.* lasting, not ceasing. **perpetually** *adv.*
perpetuate *v.* preserve from being forgotten or from going out of use. **perpetuation** *n.*
perpetuity *n.* **in perpetuity** for ever.

perplex *v.* bewilder, puzzle.
perplexity *n.* bewilderment.
perquisite *n.* profit or privilege given in addition to wages.
perry *n.* drink resembling cider, made from fermented pears.
persecute *v.* treat with hostility because of race or religion; harass. **persecution** *n.*, **persecutor** *n.*
persevere *v.* continue in spite of difficulties. **perseverance** *n.*
persimmon *n.* edible orange plum-like fruit; tree bearing this.
persist *v.* continue firmly or obstinately; continue to exist. **persistent** *a.*, **persistently** *adv.*, **persistence** *n.*, **persistency** *n.*
person *n.* individual human being; one's body; (in grammar) one of the three classes of personal pronouns and verb forms, referring to the person(s) speaking, spoken to, or spoken of. **in person** physically present.
persona *n.* (*pl.* **-ae**) personality as perceived by others.
personable *a.* attractive in appearance or manner.
personage *n.* person, esp. an important one.
personal *a.* of one's own; of or involving a person's private life; referring to a person; done in person. **personally** *adv.*
personality *n.* person's distinctive character; person with distinctive qualities; celebrity.
personalize *v.* identify as belonging to a particular person. **personalization** *n.*
personify *v.* represent in human form or as having human characteristics; embody in one's behaviour. **personification** *n.*
personnel *n.* employees, staff.
perspective *n.* art of drawing so as to give an effect of solidity and relative position; point of view. **in perspective** according to the rules of perspective; not distorting a thing's relative importance.
perspicacious *a.* showing great insight. **perspicaciously** *adv.*, **perspicacity** *n.*
perspire *v.* sweat. **perspiration** *n.*
persuade *v.* cause (a person) to believe or do something by reasoning. **persuader** *n.*
persuasion *n.* persuading; persuasiveness; belief.
persuasive *a.* able or trying to persuade people. **persuasively** *adv.*, **persuasiveness** *n.*
pert *a.* cheeky; (*US*) lively. **pertly** *adv.*, **pertness** *n.*
pertain *v.* be relevant; belong as a part.
pertinacious *a.* persistent and determined. **pertinaciously** *adv.*, **pertinacity** *n.*
pertinent *a.* pertaining, relevant. **pertinently** *adv.*, **pertinence** *n.*
perturb *v.* disturb greatly, make uneasy. **perturbation** *n.*
peruse /pərōōz/ *v.* read carefully. **perusal** *n.*
pervade *v.* spread throughout (a thing). **pervasive** *a.*
perverse *a.* obstinately doing something different from what is reasonable or required. **perversely** *adv.*, **perversity** *n.*
pervert *v.* /pərvért/ misapply, lead astray, corrupt. — *n.* /pérvert/ perverted person. **perversion** *n.*
pervious *a.* permeable; penetrable.
peseta *n.* unit of money in Spain.
peso *n.* (*pl.* **-os**) unit of money in several South American countries.
pessimism *n.* tendency to take a gloomy view of things. **pessimist** *n.*, **pessimistic** *a.*, **pessimistically** *adv.*
pest *n.* troublesome person or thing; insect or animal harmful to plants, stored food, etc.
pester *v.* annoy continually, esp. with requests or questions.
pesticide *n.* substance used to destroy harmful insects etc.
pestilence *n.* deadly epidemic disease. **pestilential** *a.*
pestle /péss'l/ *n.* club-shaped instrument for pounding things to powder.
pet *n.* tame animal treated with affection; darling, favourite. — *a.* kept as a pet; favourite. — *v.* (**petted**) treat with affection; fondle. **pet name** name used affectionately.
petal *n.* one of the coloured outer parts of a flower head.
petite *a.* of small dainty build.
petition *n.* formal written request, esp. one signed by many people. — *v.* make a petition to.
petrel *n.* a kind of seabird.
petrify *v.* change into a stony mass; paralyse with astonishment or fear. **petrifaction** *n.*
petrochemical *n.* chemical substance obtained from petroleum or gas.
petrol *n.* inflammable liquid made from petroleum for use as fuel in internal-combustion engines.
petroleum *n.* mineral oil found underground, refined for use as fuel or in dry-cleaning etc.
petticoat *n.* dress-length undergarment worn hanging from the shoulders or waist beneath a dress or skirt.

pettifogging *a.* trivial; quibbling about unimportant details.

pettish *a.* peevish, irritable. **pettishly** *adv.*, **pettishness** *n.*

petty *a.* (**-ier, -iest**) unimportant; minor, on a small scale; small-minded. **petty cash** money kept by an office etc. for or from small payments. **pettily** *adv.*, **pettiness** *n.*

petulant *a.* peevish. **petulantly** *adv.*, **petulance** *n.*

petunia *n.* garden plant with funnel-shaped flowers.

pew *n.* long bench-like seat in a church; (*colloq.*) seat.

pewter *n.* grey alloy of tin with lead or other metal.

phalanx *n.* compact mass esp. of people.

phallus *n.* (image of) the penis. **phallic** *a.*

phantom *n.* ghost.

Pharaoh /fáirō/ *n.* title of the king of ancient Egypt.

pharmaceutical *a.* of or engaged in pharmacy.

pharmacist *n.* person skilled in pharmacy.

pharmacology *n.* study of the action of drugs. **pharmacological** *a.*, **pharmacologist** *n.*

pharmacopoeia /faáməkəpeéə/ *n.* list or stock of drugs.

pharmacy *n.* preparation and dispensing of medicinal drugs; pharmacist's shop, dispensary.

pharynx *n.* cavity at the back of the nose and throat. **pharyngeal** *a.*

phase *n.* stage of change or development. — *v.* carry out (a programme etc.) in stages. **phase in** *or* **out** bring gradually into or out of use.

pheasant *n.* game bird with bright feathers.

phenomenal *a.* extraordinary, remarkable. **phenomenally** *adv.*

phenomenon *n.* (*pl.* **-ena**) fact, occurrence, or change perceived by the senses or the mind; remarkable person or thing.

phial *n.* small bottle.

philander *v.* (of a man) flirt. **philanderer** *n.*

philanthropy *n.* love of mankind, esp. shown in benevolent acts. **philanthropist** *n.*, **philanthropic** *a.*, **philanthropically** *adv.*

philately *n.* stamp-collecting. **philatelic** *a.*, **philatelist** *n.*

philistine *a.* & *n.* uncultured (person).

philology *n.* study of languages. **philologist** *n.*, **philological** *a.*

philosopher *n.* person skilled in philosophy; philosophical person.

philosophical *a.* of philosophy; bearing misfortune calmly. **philosophically** *adv.*

philosophize *v.* theorize; moralize.

philosophy *n.* system or study of the basic truths and principles of the universe, life, and morals, and of human understanding of these; person's principles.

philtre *n.* magic potion.

phlegm /flem/ *n.* thick mucus in the bronchial passages, ejected by coughing.

phlegmatic *a.* not easily excited or agitated; sluggish, apathetic. **phlegmatically** *adv.*

phlox *n.* plant bearing a cluster of red, purple, or white flowers.

phobia *n.* lasting abnormal fear or great dislike. **phobic** *a.* & *n.*

phoenix /feéniks/ *n.* mythical Arabian bird said to burn itself and rise young again from its ashes.

phone *n.* & *v.* (*colloq.*) telephone. **phone book** telephone directory. **phone-in** *n.* broadcast programme in which listeners participate by telephoning the studio.

phonetic *a.* of or representing speech sounds; (of spelling) corresponding to pronunciation. **phonetically** *adv.*

phonetics *n.* study or (as *pl.*) representation of speech sounds. **phonetician** *n.*

phoney *a.* (**-ier, -iest**) (*colloq.*) sham. — *n.* (*colloq.*) phoney person or thing.

phosphate *n.* fertilizer containing phosphorus.

phosphorescent *a.* luminous. **phosphorescence** *n.*

phosphorus *n.* non-metallic chemical element; wax-like form of this appearing luminous in the dark.

photo *n.* (*pl.* **-os**) (*colloq.*) photograph. **photo finish** close finish where the winner is decided by a photograph.

photocopy *n.* photographed copy of a document. — *v.* make a photocopy of. **photocopier** *n.*

photoelectric cell electronic device emitting an electric current when light falls on it.

photogenic *a.* coming out attractively in photographs.

photograph *n.* picture formed by the chemical action of light or other radiation on sensitive material. — *v.* take a photograph of; come out (well or badly) when photographed. **photographer** *n.*, **photography** *n.*, **photographic** *a.*, **photographically** *adv.*

photosynthesis *n.* process by which green plants use sunlight to convert carbon dioxide and water into complex substances.

phrase *n.* group of words forming a unit; unit in a melody. — *v.* express in words; divide (music) into phrases. **phrasal** *a.*

phraseology *n.* the way something is worded.

phylum *n.* (*pl.* **phyla**) major division of the plant or animal kingdom.

physical *a.* of the body; of matter or the laws of nature; of physics. **physical geography** study of earth's natural features. **physically** *adv.*

physician *n.* doctor, esp. one specializing in medicine as distinct from surgery.

physicist *n.* expert in physics.

physics *n.* study of the properties and interactions of matter and energy.

physiognomy /fizziónnəmi/ *n.* features of a person's face.

physiology *n.* study of the bodily functions of living organisms. **physiological** *a.*, **physiologist** *n.*

physiotherapy *n.* treatment of an injury etc. by massage and exercises. **physiotherapist** *n.*

physique *n.* person's physical build and muscular development.

pi *n.* Greek letter used as a symbol for the ratio of a circle's circumference to its diameter (about 3.14).

pianist *n.* person who plays the piano.

piano *n.* (*pl.* **-os**) musical instrument with strings struck by hammers operated by a keyboard.

pianoforte *n.* piano.

piazza /piátsə/ *n.* public square or market place.

picador *n.* mounted bullfighter with a lance.

picaresque *a.* (of fiction) dealing with the adventures of rogues.

piccalilli *n.* pickle of chopped vegetables and hot spices.

piccolo *n.* (*pl.* **-os**) small flute.

pick [1] *n.* pickaxe; plectrum.

pick [2] *v.* select; use a pointed instrument or the fingers or beak etc. to make (a hole) in or remove bits from (a thing); detach (flower or fruit) from the plant bearing it. — *n.* picking; selection; best part. **pick a lock** open it with a tool other than a key. **pick a pocket** steal its contents. **pick a quarrel** provoke one deliberately. **pick holes in** find fault with. **pick off** pluck off; shoot or destroy one by one. **pick on** nag, find fault with; select. **pick out** select; discern. **pick up** lift or take up; call for and take away; acquire or become acquainted with casually; succeed in seeing or hearing by use of apparatus; recover health, improve; gather (speed). **pick-up** *n.* small open motor truck; stylus-holder in a record player. **picker** *n.*

pickaxe *n.* heavy tool with a pointed iron bar mounted at right angles to its handle, used for breaking ground etc.

picket *n.* person(s) stationed at a workplace to dissuade others from entering during a strike; party of sentries; pointed stake set in the ground. — *v.* (**picketed**) form a picket on (a workplace); enclose with stakes.

pickings *n.pl.* odd gains or perquisites.

pickle *n.* vegetables preserved in vinegar or brine; this liquid; (*colloq.*) plight, mess. — *v.* preserve in pickle.

pickpocket *n.* thief who picks people's pockets.

picnic *n.* informal outdoor meal. — *v.* (**picnicked**) take part in a picnic. **picnicker** *n.*

pictograph *n.* pictorial symbol used as a form of writing.

pictorial *a.* of or in or like a picture or pictures; illustrated. — *n.* newspaper etc. with many pictures. **pictorially** *adv.*

picture *n.* representation of person(s) or object(s) etc. made by painting, drawing, or photography etc.; thing that looks beautiful; scene; description; cinema film. — *v.* depict; imagine.

picturesque *a.* forming a pleasant scene; (of words or description) very expressive.

pidgin *n.* **pidgin English** simplified form of English with elements of a local language.

pie *n.* baked dish of meat, fish, or fruit covered with pastry or other crust. **pie chart** diagram representing quantities as sectors of a circle.

piebald *a.* (of a horse) with irregular patches of white and black.

piece *n.* part, portion; thing regarded as a unit; musical, literary, or artistic composition; small object used in board games. — *v.* make by putting pieces together. **of a piece** of the same kind; consistent. **piece-work** *n.* work paid according to the quantity done.

piecemeal *a.* & *adv.* done piece by piece, part at a time.

pied *a.* particoloured.

pied-à-terre /pyáydaatáir/ *n.* (*pl.* **pieds-à-terre**) small dwelling for occasional use.

pier *n.* structure built out into the sea; pillar supporting an arch or bridge.

pierce *v.* go into or through like a sharp-pointed instrument; make (a hole) in; force one's way into or through.

piercing *a.* (of cold or wind) penetrating sharply; (of sound) shrilly audible. **piercingly** *adv.*

piety *n.* piousness.

piffle *n.* (*colloq.*) nonsense.

pig *n.* animal with short legs, cloven hooves, and a blunt snout; (*colloq.*) greedy or unpleasant person. **pig-iron** *n.* crude iron from a smelting-furnace.

pigeon *n.* bird of the dove family; (*colloq.*) person's business or responsibility.

pigeon-hole *n.* small compartment in a desk or cabinet. — *v.* put away for future consideration or indefinitely; classify.

piggery *n.* pig-breeding establishment; pigsty.

piggy *a.* like a pig. **piggyback** *adv.* & *n.* (ride) on a person's back or on top of a larger object. **piggy bank** money box shaped like a pig.

pigheaded *a.* obstinate.

piglet *n.* young pig.

pigment *n.* colouring matter.

pigsty *n.* partly covered pen for pigs.

pigtail *n.* long hair worn in a plait at the back of the head.

pike *n.* spear with long wooden shaft; (*pl.* **pike**) large voracious freshwater fish.

pilaff *n.* = pilau.

pilaster *n.* rectangular usu. ornamental column.

pilau *n.* oriental dish of rice with meat, spices, etc.

pilchard *n.* small sea fish related to the herring.

pile [1] *n.* a number of things lying one upon another; (*colloq.*) large amount; lofty building. — *v.* heap, stack, load. **pile up** accumulate. **pile-up** *n.* collision of several vehicles.

pile [2] *n.* heavy beam driven vertically into ground as a support for a building or bridge.

pile [3] *n.* cut or uncut loops on the surface of fabric.

pile [4] *n.* haemorrhoid.

pilfer *v.* steal (small items or in small quantities). **pilferer** *n.*

pilgrim *n.* person who travels to a sacred place as an act of religious devotion. **pilgrimage** *n.*

pill *n.* small ball or piece of medicinal substance for swallowing whole; **the pill** contraceptive pill.

pillage *n.* & *v.* plunder.

pillar *n.* vertical structure used as a support or ornament.

pillion *n.* saddle for a passenger behind the driver of a motor cycle. **ride pillion** ride on this.

pillory *n.* wooden frame in which offenders were locked and exposed to public abuse. — *v.* ridicule publicly.

pillow *n.* cushion used (esp. in bed) for supporting the head. — *v.* rest on or as if on a pillow.

pilot *n.* person who operates an aircraft's flying-controls; person qualified to steer ships into or out of a harbour; guide. — *v.* (**piloted**) act as pilot of; guide. **pilot-light** *n.* small burning jet of gas which lights a larger burner; electric indicator light.

pimento *n.* (*pl.* **-os**) allspice; sweet pepper.

pimp *n.* man who solicits clients for a prostitute or brothel.

pimple *n.* small inflamed spot on the skin. **pimply** *a.*

pin *n.* short pointed piece of metal usu. with a round broadened head, used for fastening things together; peg or stake of wood or metal. — *v.* (**pinned**) fasten with pin(s); transfix; hold down and make unable to move; attach, fix. **pin down** establish clearly; bind by a promise. **pins and needles** tingling sensation. **pin-up** *n.* (*colloq.*) picture of an attractive or famous person.

pinafore *n.* apron. **pinafore dress** sleeveless dress worn over a blouse or jumper.

pincers *n.* tool with pivoted jaws for gripping and pulling things; claw-like part of a lobster etc.

pinch *v.* squeeze between two surfaces, esp. between finger and thumb; (*sl.*) steal. — *n.* pinching; stress of circumstances; small amount. **at a pinch** if really necessary.

pine [1] *n.* evergreen tree with needle-shaped leaves; its wood.

pine [2] *v.* lose strength through grief or yearning; feel an intense longing.

pineapple *n.* large juicy tropical fruit; plant bearing this.

ping *n.* short sharp ringing sound. — *v.* make this sound. **pinger** *n.*

ping-pong *n.* table tennis.

pinion [1] *n.* bird's wing. — *v.* restrain by holding or binding the arms or legs.

pinion [2] *n.* small cogwheel.

pink [1] *a.* pale red. — *n.* pink colour; garden plant with fragrant flowers. **in the pink** (*colloq.*) in very good health.

pink [2] *v.* pierce slightly; cut a zigzag edge on (fabric).

pink [3] *v.* (of an engine) make slight explosive sounds when running imperfectly.

pinnacle *n.* pointed ornament on a roof; peak; highest point.

pinpoint *v.* locate precisely.

pinstripe *n.* very narrow stripe in cloth fabric. **pinstriped** *a.*

pint *n.* measure for liquids, one-eighth of a gallon (0.568 litre).

pioneer *n.* person who is one of the first to explore a new region or subject. — *v.* be a pioneer (in).

pious *a.* devout in religion; ostentatiously virtuous. **piously** *adv.*, **piousness** *n.*

pip [1] *n.* small seed in fruit.

pip [2] *n.* star showing rank on an army officer's uniform.

pip [3] *v.* (**pipped**) (*colloq.*) defeat by a small margin.

pip [4] *n.* short high-pitched sound.

pipe *n.* tube through which something can flow; wind instrument, (*pl.*) bagpipes; narrow tube with a bowl at one end for smoking tobacco. — *v.* convey through pipe(s); play (music) on pipe(s); utter in a shrill voice. **pipe down** (*colloq.*) be quiet. **pipedream** *n.* impractical hope or scheme.

pipeline *n.* long pipe for conveying petroleum etc. to a distance; channel of supply or information. **in the pipeline** on the way, in preparation.

piper *n.* player of pipe(s).

pipette *n.* slender tube for transferring or measuring small amounts of liquid.

pipit *n.* small bird resembling a lark.

pippin *n.* a kind of apple.

piquant *a.* pleasantly sharp in taste or smell. **piquancy** *n.*

pique /peek/ *v.* hurt the pride of. — *n.* feeling of hurt pride.

piquet /peékay/ *n.* card game for two players.

piranha /piraánə/ *n.* fierce tropical American freshwater fish.

pirate *n.* person on a ship who robs another ship at sea or raids a coast; one who infringes copyright or business rights, or broadcasts without due authorization. — *v.* reproduce (a book etc.) without due authorization. **piratical** *a.*, **piracy** *n.*

pirouette *n.* & *v.* spin on the toe in dancing.

pistachio /pistaáshiō/ *n.* (*pl.* **-os**) a kind of nut.

piste *n.* ski run.

pistil *n.* seed-producing part of a flower.

pistol *n.* small gun.

piston *n.* sliding disc or cylinder inside a tube, esp. as part of an engine or pump.

pit *n.* hole in the ground; coal mine; sunken area; place where racing cars are refuelled etc. during a race. — *v.* (**pitted**) make pits or depressions in; match or set in competition.

pitch [1] *n.* dark tarry substance. **pitch-black, pitch-dark** *adjs.*

pitch [2] *v.* throw; erect (a tent or camp); set at a particular slope or level; fall heavily; (of a ship) plunge forward and back alternately. — *n.* process of pitching; steepness; intensity; degree of highness or lowness of a music note or voice; place where a street trader or performer is stationed; playing field. **pitched battle** one fought from prepared positions. **pitch in** (*colloq.*) set to work vigorously.

pitchblende *n.* mineral ore (uranium oxide) yielding radium.

pitcher [1] *n.* baseball player who delivers the ball to the batter.

pitcher [2] *n.* large usu. earthenware jug.

pitchfork *n.* long-handled fork for lifting and tossing hay.

piteous *a.* deserving or arousing pity. **piteously** *adv.*

pitfall *n.* unsuspected danger or difficulty.

pith *n.* spongy tissue in stems or fruits; essential part.

pithy *a.* (**-ier**, **-iest**) like pith, containing much pith; brief and full of meaning. **pithily** *adv.*

pitiful *a.* deserving or arousing pity or contempt. **pitifully** *adv.*

pitta *n.* a kind of flat bread.

pittance *n.* very small allowance of money.

pituitary gland gland at the base of the brain, with important influence on bodily growth and functions.

pity *n.* feeling of sorrow for another's suffering; cause for regret. — *v.* feel pity for. **take pity on** pity and try to help.

pivot *n.* central point or shaft on which a thing turns or swings. — *v.* (**pivoted**) turn on a pivot. **pivotal** *a.*

pixel *n.* each minute area of uniform illumination in an image on a VDU screen.

pixie *n.* a kind of fairy.

pizza *n.* layer of dough baked with a savoury topping.

pizzicato *adv.* by plucking the strings of a violin etc. instead of using the bow.

placard *n.* poster or similar notice. — *v.* put up placards on.

placate *v.* conciliate. **placation** *n.*, **placatory** *a.*

place *n.* particular part of space or of an area etc.; particular town, district, building, etc.; position; duty appropriate to one's rank. — *v.* put into a place, find a place for; locate, identify; put or give (an order for goods etc.). **be placed** (in a race) be among the first three.

placebo /pləseébō/ *n.* (*pl.* **-os**) harmless substance given as medicine, esp. to humour a patient.

placement *n.* placing.

placenta *n.* (*pl.* **-ae**) organ in the womb that nourishes the foetus. **placental** *a.*

placid *a.* calm, not easily upset. **placidly** *adv.*, **placidity** *n.*

plagiarize /pláyjərīz/ *v.* take and use (another's writings etc.) as one's own. **plagiarism** *n.*, **plagiarist** *n.*

plague *n.* deadly contagious disease; infestation. — *v.* (*colloq.*) annoy, pester.

plaice *n.* (*pl.* **plaice**) a kind of flatfish used as food.

plaid /plad/ *n.* long piece of woollen cloth worn as part of Highland costume; tartan pattern.

plain *a.* unmistakable, easy to see or hear or understand; not elaborate; in exact terms, candid; ordinary, without affectation; not good-looking. — *adv.* plainly. — *n.* large area of level country. **plain clothes** civilian clothes, not a uniform. **plain sailing** easy course of action. **plainly** *adv.*, **plainness** *n.*

plaintiff *n.* person that brings an action in a court of law.

plaintive *a.* sounding sad. **plaintively** *adv.*

plait /plat/ *v.* weave (three or more strands) into one rope-like length. — *n.* something plaited.

plan *n.* diagram showing the relative position of parts of a building or town etc.; method thought out in advance. — *v.* (**planned**) make a plan (of). **planner** *n.*

plane ¹ *n.* tall spreading tree with broad leaves.

plane ² *n.* level surface; level of thought or development; aeroplane. — *a.* level.

plane ³ *n.* tool for smoothing wood or metal by paring shavings from it. — *v.* smooth or pare with this.

planet *n.* large body in space that revolves round the sun. **planetary** *a.*

planetarium *n.* room with a domed ceiling on which lights are projected to show the positions of the stars and planets.

plangent *a.* resonant, loud and mournful. **plangently** *adv.*, **plangency** *n.*

plank *n.* long flat piece of timber.

plankton *n.* minute life-forms floating in the sea, rivers, etc.

plant *n.* living organism with neither the power of movement nor special organs of digestion; factory; its machinery. — *v.* place in soil for growing; place in position. **planter** *n.*

plantain ¹ *n.* herb whose seed is used as birdseed.

plantain ² *n.* tropical banana-like fruit; tree bearing this.

plantation *n.* area planted with trees or cultivated plants; estate on which cotton, tobacco, or tea etc. is cultivated.

plaque *n.* commemorative plate fixed on a wall; film forming on teeth and gums.

plasma *n.* colourless fluid part of blood; a kind of gas. **plasmic** *a.*

plaster *n.* mixture of lime, sand, and water etc. used for coating walls; sticking plaster. — *v.* cover with plaster; coat, daub.

plaster of Paris white paste made from gypsum. **plasterer** *n.*

plastic *a.* able to be moulded; made of plastic. — *n.* synthetic substance moulded to a permanent shape. **plastic surgery** operation(s) to replace injured or defective external tissue. **plasticity** *n.*

Plasticine *n.* [P.] plastic substance used for modelling.

plate *n.* almost flat usu. circular utensil for holding food; articles of gold, silver, or other metal; flat thin sheet of metal, glass, or other material; illustration on special paper in a book; (*colloq.*) denture. — *v.* cover or coat with metal. **plate glass** thick glass for windows etc. **plateful** *n.* (*pl.* **-fuls**).

plateau *n.* (*pl.* **-eaux**) area of level high ground; steady state following an increase.

platform *n.* raised level surface or area, esp. from which a speaker addresses an audience.

platinum *n.* silver-white metal that does not tarnish. **platinum blonde** woman with very light blonde hair.

platitude *n.* commonplace remark. **platitudinous** *a.*

platonic *a.* involving affection but not sexual love.

platoon *n.* subdivision of a military company.

platter *n.* large plate for food.

platypus *n.* (*pl.* **-puses**) Australian animal with a duck-like beak that lays eggs but suckles its young.

plaudits *n.pl.* applause, expression of approval.

plausible *a.* seeming probable; persuasive but deceptive. **plausibly** *adv.*, **plausibility** *n.*

play *v.* occupy oneself in (a game) or in other recreational activity; compete against in a game; move (a piece, a ball, etc.) in a game; act the part of; perform on (a musical instrument); cause (a radio, recording, etc.) to produce sound; move lightly, allow (light or water) to fall on something. — *n.* playing; activity, operation; literary work for stage or broadcast performance; free movement. **play at** perform in a half-hearted way. **play down** minimize the importance of. **play-pen** *n.* portable enclosure for a young child to play in. **play safe** not take risks. **play the game** behave honourably. **play up** play vigorously; (*colloq.*) be unruly, annoy by doing this. **player** *n.*

playboy *n.* pleasure-loving usu. rich man.

playful *a.* full of fun; in a mood for

play, not serious. **playfully** *adv.*, **playfulness** *n.*

playgroup *n.* group of preschool children who play regularly together under supervision.

playhouse *n.* theatre.

playing card one of a pack or set of (usu. 52) pieces of pasteboard used in card games.

playing field field used for outdoor games.

playmate *n.* child's companion in play.

playwright *n.* writer of plays.

plea *n.* defendant's answer to a charge in a law court; appeal, entreaty; excuse.

plead *v.* give as one's plea; put forward (a case) in a law court; make an appeal or entreaty; put forward as an excuse.

pleasant *a.* pleasing; having an agreeable manner. **pleasantly** *adv.*, **pleasantness** *n.*

pleasantry *n.* friendly or humorous remark.

please *v.* give pleasure to; think fit. — *adv.* polite word of request. **please oneself** do as one chooses.

pleased *a.* feeling or showing pleasure or satisfaction.

pleasurable *a.* causing pleasure. **pleasurably** *adv.*

pleasure *n.* feeling of satisfaction or joy; source of this.

pleat *n.* flat fold of cloth. — *v.* make a pleat or pleats in.

plebiscite /plébbisit/ *n.* referendum.

plectrum *n.* small piece of metal, bone, or ivory for plucking the strings of a musical instrument.

pledge *n.* thing deposited as a guarantee (e.g. that a debt will be paid); token of something; solemn promise. — *v.* deposit as a pledge; promise solemnly.

plenary /pleénəri/ *a.* entire; attended by all members.

plenipotentiary *a.* & *n.* (envoy) with full powers to take action.

plenitude *n.* abundance, completeness.

plentiful *a.* existing in large amounts. **plentifully** *adv.*

plenty *n.* enough and more. — *adv.* (*colloq.*) quite, fully. **plenteous** *a.*

plethora *n.* over-abundance.

pleurisy *n.* inflammation of the membrane round the lungs.

pliable *a.* flexible. **pliability** *n.*

pliant *a.* pliable. **pliancy** *n.*

pliers *n.pl.* pincers with flat surfaces for gripping things.

plight *n.* predicament.

plimsoll *n.* canvas sports shoe.

Plimsoll line *or* **mark** mark on a ship's side showing the legal water level when loaded.

plinth *n.* slab forming the base of a column or statue etc.

plod *v.* (**plodded**) walk doggedly, trudge; work slowly but steadily. **plodder** *n.*

plonk *n.* (*colloq.*) cheap or inferior wine.

plop *n.* & *v.* (**plopped**) sound like something small dropping into water with no splash.

plot *n.* small piece of land; story in a play or novel or film; conspiracy, secret plan. — *v.* (**plotted**) make a map or chart of, mark on this; plan secretly. **plotter** *n.*

plough /plow/ *n.* implement for cutting furrows in soil and turning it up. — *v.* cut or turn up (soil etc.) with a plough; make one's way laboriously. **ploughman** *n.*

plover *n.* a wading bird.

ploy *n.* cunning manoeuvre.

pluck *v.* pull at or out or off; pick (a flower etc.); strip (a bird) of its feathers. — *n.* plucking movement; courage.

plucky *a.* (**-ier**, **-iest**) showing pluck, brave. **pluckily** *adv.*

plug *n.* thing fitting into and stopping or filling a hole or cavity; device of this kind for making an electrical connection. — *v.* (**plugged**) put a plug into; (*colloq.*) work diligently; (*colloq.*) seek to popularize by constant commendation. **plug in** connect electrically by putting a plug into a socket.

plum *n.* fruit with sweet pulp round a pointed stone; tree bearing this; reddish-purple; something desirable, the best.

plumage *n.* bird's feathers.

plumb /plum/ *n.* lead weight hung on a cord (**plumb line**), used for testing depths or verticality. — *adv.* exactly; (*US*) completely. — *v.* measure or test with a plumb line; reach (depths); get to the bottom of; work or fit (things) as a plumber.

plumber /plúmmər/ *n.* person who fits and repairs plumbing.

plumbing /plúmming/ *n.* system of water pipes and drainage pipes etc. in a building.

plume *n.* feather, esp. as an ornament; thing(s) resembling this. **plumed** *a.*

plummet *v.* (**plummeted**) fall steeply.

plump[1] *a.* having a full rounded shape. — *v.* make or become plump. **plumpness** *n.*

plump[2] *v.* plunge abruptly. **plump for** choose, decide on.

plunder *v.* rob. — *n.* plundering; goods etc. acquired by this.

plunge *v.* thrust or go forcefully into

something; go down suddenly. — *n.* plunging, dive.

plunger *n.* thing that works with a plunging movement.

plural *n.* form of a noun or verb used in referring to more than one person or thing. — *a.* of this form; of more than one. **plurality** *n.*

plus *prep.* with the addition of; above zero. — *a.* more than zero; more than the amount indicated. — *n.* the sign +; advantage.

plush *n.* cloth with a long soft nap. — *a.* made of plush; plushy.

plushy *a.* (**-ier**, **-iest**) luxurious.

plutocrat *n.* wealthy and influential person. **plutocracy** *n.*, **plutocratic** *a.*

plutonium *n.* radioactive substance used in nuclear weapons and reactors.

pluvial *a.* of or caused by rain.

ply [1] *n.* thickness or layer of wood or cloth etc.; plywood.

ply [2] *v.* use or wield (a tool etc.); work (at a trade); keep offering or supplying; go to and fro regularly or looking for custom.

plywood *n.* board made by gluing layers with the grain crosswise.

p.m. *abbr.* (Latin *post meridiem*) after noon.

pneumatic /nyoomáttik/ *a.* filled with or operated by compressed air. **pneumatically** *adv.*

pneumonia /nyoomṓniə/ *n.* inflammation of one or both lungs.

poach *v.* cook (an egg without its shell) in or over boiling water; simmer in a small amount of liquid; take (game or fish) illegally; trespass, encroach. **poacher** *n.*

pocket *n.* small bag-like part in or on a garment; one's resources of money; pouch-like compartment; isolated group or area. — *a.* suitable for carrying in one's pocket. — *v.* put into one's pocket; appropriate. **in** *or* **out of pocket** having made a profit or loss. **pocket money** money for small personal expenses; money allowed to children. **pocketful** *n.* (*pl.* **-fuls**).

pock-marked *a.* marked by scars or pits.

pod *n.* long narrow seed case.

podgy *a.* (**-ier**, **-iest**) short and fat. **podginess** *n.*

podium *n.* (*pl.* **-ia**) projecting base; rostrum.

poem *n.* literary composition in verse.

poet *n.* writer of poems.

poetic, poetical *adjs.* of or like poetry. **poetically** *adv.*

poetry *n.* poems; poet's work; quality that pleases the mind similarly.

pogo stick stilt-like toy with a spring, for jumping about on.

pogrom *n.* organized massacre.

poignant *a.* arousing sympathy, moving; keenly felt. **poignantly** *adv.*, **poignancy** *n.*

poinsettia *n.* plant with large scarlet bracts.

point *n.* tapered or sharp end, tip; promontory; particular place, moment, or stage; unit of measurement or scoring; item, detail; characteristic; chief or important feature; effectiveness; electrical socket; movable rail for directing a train from one line to another. — *v.* aim, direct (a finger or weapon etc.); have a certain direction; indicate; fill in (joints of brickwork) with mortar or cement. **on the point of** on the verge of (an action). **point-blank** *a.* aimed or fired at very close range; (of a remark) direct; (*adv.*) in a point-blank manner. **point-duty** *n.* that of a policeman stationed to regulate traffic. **point of view** way of looking at a matter. **point out** draw attention to. **point up** emphasize. **to the point** relevant(ly).

pointed *a.* tapering to a point; (of a remark or manner) emphasized, clearly aimed at a person or thing. **pointedly** *adv.*

pointer *n.* thing that points to something; dog that points towards game which it scents.

pointless *a.* having no purpose or meaning. **pointlessly** *adv.*

poise *n.* balance; dignified self-assured manner.

poison *n.* substance that can destroy life or harm health. — *v.* give poison to; put poison on or in; corrupt, fill with prejudice. **poison-pen letter** malicious unsigned letter. **poisoner** *n.*, **poisonous** *a.*

poke *v.* thrust with the end of a finger or stick etc.; thrust forward; search, pry. — *n.* poking movement. **poke fun at** ridicule.

poker [1] *n.* stiff metal rod for stirring up a fire.

poker [2] *n.* gambling card game. **poker-face** *n.* one that does not reveal thoughts or feelings.

poky *a.* (**-ier**, **-iest**) small and cramped. **pokiness** *n.*

polar *a.* of or near the North or South Pole; of a pole of a magnet. **polar bear** white bear of Arctic regions.

polarize *v.* confine similar vibrations of (light waves) to one direction or plane; give magnetic poles to; set at opposite extremes of opinion. **polarization** *n.*

Pole *n.* Polish person.

pole [1] *n.* long rod or post. — *v.* push along

by using a pole. **pole position** most favourable starting position in a motor race.

pole [2] *n.* north (**North Pole**) or south (**South Pole**) end of earth's axis; one of the opposite ends of a magnet or terminals of an electric cell or battery. **pole star** star near the North Pole in the sky.

polecat *n.* small animal of the weasel family; (*US*) skunk.

polemic *n.* verbal attack on a belief or opinion. **polemical** *a.*

police *n.* civil force responsible for keeping public order. — *v.* keep order in by means of police. **police state** country where political police supervise and control citizens' activities. **policeman** *n.* (*pl.* **-men**), **policewoman** (*pl.* **-women**).

policy [1] *n.* course or general plan of action.

policy [2] *n.* insurance contract.

polio *n.* (*colloq.*) poliomyelitis.

poliomyelitis *n.* infectious disease causing temporary or permanent paralysis.

Polish *a.* & *n.* (language) of Poland.

polish *v.* make smooth and glossy by rubbing; refine, perfect. — *n.* glossiness; polishing, substance used for this; elegance. **polish off** finish off. **polisher** *n.*

polished *a.* (of manner or performance) elegant, perfected.

polite *a.* having good manners, socially correct; refined. **politely** *adv.*, **politeness** *n.*

political *a.* of or involving politics; of the way a country is governed. **politically** *adv.*

politician *n.* person engaged in politics.

politics *n.* science and art of government; political affairs or life; (*pl.*) political principles.

polka *n.* lively dance for couples. **polka dots** round evenly spaced dots on fabric.

poll *n.* votes at an election; place for this; estimate of public opinion made by questioning people. — *v.* receive as votes; cut off the horns of (cattle) or the top of (a tree etc.). **poll tax** tax on each member of the population.

pollard *v.* poll (a tree) to produce a close head of young branches. — *n.* pollarded tree; hornless animal.

pollen *n.* fertilizing powder from the anthers of flowers.

pollinate *v.* fertilize with pollen. **pollination** *n.*

pollute *v.* make dirty or impure. **pollution** *n.*, **pollutant** *n.*

polo *n.* game like hockey played by teams on horseback. **polo-neck** *n.* high turned-over collar.

polonaise *n.* slow processional dance.

poltergeist *n.* spirit that throws things about noisily.

polyandry *n.* system of having more than one husband at a time.

polyanthus *n.* (*pl.* **-thuses** *or* **-thus**) cultivated primrose.

polychrome *a.* multicoloured. **polychromatic** *a.*

polyester *n.* synthetic resin or fibre.

polygamy *n.* system of having more than one wife at a time. **polygamist** *n.*, **polygamous** *a.*

polyglot *a.* & *n.* (person) knowing or using several languages.

polygon *n.* geometric figure with many sides. **polygonal** *a.*

polyhedron *n.* (*pl.* **-dra**) solid with many sides. **polyhedral** *a.*

polymath *n.* person with knowledge of many subjects.

polymer *n.* compound whose molecule is formed from a large number of simple molecules.

polymerize *v.* combine into a polymer. **polymerization** *n.*

polyp *n.* simple organism with a tube-shaped body; abnormal growth projecting from mucous membrane.

polyphony *n.* combination of melodies. **polyphonal** *a.*

polystyrene *n.* a kind of plastic.

polytheism *n.* belief in or worship of more than one god. **polytheist** *n.*, **polytheistic** *a.*

polythene *n.* a kind of tough light plastic.

polyunsaturated *a.* (of fat) not associated with the formation of cholesterol in the blood.

polyurethane *n.* synthetic resin or plastic.

pomander *n.* ball of mixed sweet-smelling substances.

pomegranate *n.* tropical fruit with many seeds; tree bearing this.

Pomeranian *n.* dog of a small silky-haired breed.

pommel /púmm'l/ *n.* knob on the hilt of a sword; upward projection on a saddle.

pomp *n.* stately and splendid ceremonial.

pom-pom *n.* decorative tuft or ball.

pompous *a.* full of ostentatious dignity and self-importance. **pompously** *adv.*, **pomposity** *n.*

poncho *n.* (*pl.* **-os**) type of cloak made like a blanket with a hole for the head.

pond *n.* small area of still water.

ponder *v.* be deep in thought; think over.

ponderous *a.* heavy, unwieldy; laborious. **ponderously** *adv.*

pong *n.* & *v.* (*sl.*) stink.

pontiff *n.* bishop; pope.

pontificate *v.* speak in a pompously dogmatic way.
pontoon [1] *n.* flat-bottomed boat; floating platform. **pontoon bridge** temporary bridge supported on pontoons.
pontoon [2] *n.* a kind of card game.
pony *n.* horse of any small breed. **ponytail** *n.* long hair drawn back and tied to hang down.
poodle *n.* dog with thick curly hair.
pooh *int.* exclamation of contempt. **pooh-pooh** *v.* express contempt for.
pool [1] *n.* small area of still water; puddle; swimming pool.
pool [2] *n.* shared fund or supply; game resembling snooker; (*pl.*) football pools. — *v.* put into a common fund or supply.
poop *n.* ship's stern; raised deck at the stern.
poor *a.* having little money or means; not abundant; not very good; pitiable. **poorness** *n.*
poorly *adv.* in a poor way, badly. — *a.* unwell.
pop [1] *n.* small explosive sound; fizzy drink. — *v.* (**popped**) make or cause to make a pop; put or come or go quickly.
pop [2] *a.* in a popular modern style. — *n.* pop record or music.
popcorn *n.* maize heated to burst and form puffy balls.
pope *n.* bishop of Rome, head of the Roman Catholic Church.
poplar *n.* tall slender tree.
poplin *n.* plain woven usu. cotton fabric.
poppadam *n.* large thin crisp savoury Indian biscuit.
poppy *n.* plant with showy flowers and milky juice.
poppycock *n.* (*sl.*) nonsense.
populace *n.* the general public.
popular *a.* liked or enjoyed or used etc. by many people; of or for the general public. **popularly** *adv.*, **popularity** *n.*
popularize *v.* make generally liked; present in a popular non-technical form.
populate *v.* fill with a population.
population *n.* inhabitants of an area.
populous *a.* thickly populated.
porcelain *n.* fine china.
porch *n.* roofed shelter over the entrance of a building.
porcine *a.* of or like a pig.
porcupine *n.* animal covered with protective spines.
pore [1] *n.* tiny opening on skin or on a leaf, for emitting or taking in moisture.
pore [2] *v.* **pore over** study closely.
pork *n.* unsalted pig-meat.
porn *n.* (*colloq.*) pornography.
pornography *n.* writings or pictures intended to stimulate erotic feelings by portraying sexual activity. **pornographer** *n.*, **pornographic** *a.*
porous *a.* permeable by fluid or air. **porosity** *n.*
porphyry *n.* rock containing mineral crystals.
porpoise *n.* small whale with a blunt rounded snout.
porridge *n.* food made by boiling oatmeal etc. to a thick paste.
port [1] *n.* harbour; town with this.
port [2] *n.* opening in a ship's side; porthole.
port [3] *n.* left-hand side of a ship or aircraft.
port [4] *n.* strong sweet wine.
portable *a.* able to be carried. **portability** *n.*
portal *n.* door or entrance, esp. an imposing one.
portcullis *n.* vertical grating that slides down in grooves to block the gateway to a castle.
portend *v.* foreshadow.
portent *n.* omen, significant sign. **portentous** *a.*
porter [1] *n.* doorkeeper of a large building.
porter [2] *n.* person employed to carry luggage or goods.
portfolio *n.* (*pl.* **-os**) case for loose sheets of paper; set of investments.
porthole *n.* window in the side of a ship or aircraft.
portico *n.* (*pl.* **-oes**) columns supporting a roof to form a porch or similar structure.
portion *n.* part, share; amount of food for one person. — *v.* divide into portions.
portly *a.* (**-ier, -iest**) stout and dignified. **portliness** *n.*
portrait *n.* picture of a person or animal; description.
portray *v.* make a picture of; describe; represent in a play etc. **portrayal** *n.*
Portuguese *a.* & *n.* (native, language) of Portugal. **Portuguese man-of-war** a kind of jellyfish.
pose *v.* put into or take a particular attitude; pretend to be; put forward, present (a problem etc.). — *n.* attitude in which someone is posed; pretence.
poser *n.* puzzling problem; poseur.
poseur *n.* person who behaves affectedly.
posh *a.* (*colloq.*) very smart, luxurious.
position *n.* place occupied by or intended for a person or thing; posture; situation; status; job. — *v.* place. **positional** *a.*
positive *a.* definite; explicit; constructive; (of a quantity) greater than zero; (of a battery terminal) through which electric current enters; (of a photograph) with

lights, shades, or colours as in the subject, not reversed. — *n.* positive quality or quantity or photograph. **positively** *adv.*, **positiveness** *n.*

positron *n.* particle with a positive electric charge.

posse /pόssi/ *n.* body of constables, strong force or company.

possess *v.* own; hold as belonging to oneself; dominate the mind of. **possessor** *n.*

possession *n.* possessing; thing possessed. **take possession of** become the possessor of.

possessive *a.* of or indicating possession; desiring to possess things. **possessively** *adv.*, **possessiveness** *n.*

possible *a.* capable of existing or happening or being done etc. **possibly** *adv.*, **possibility** *n.*

possum *n.* (*colloq.*) opossum. **play possum** pretend to be unaware.

post [1] *n.* piece of timber, metal, etc. set upright to support or mark something. — *v.* display (a notice etc.), announce thus.

post [2] *n.* place of duty; outpost of soldiers; trading station; job. — *v.* place, station.

post [3] *n.* official conveyance of letters etc.; the letters etc. conveyed. — *v.* send by post. **keep me posted** keep me informed. **postbox** *n.* box into which letters are inserted for transmission. **post-haste** *adv.* with great haste. **post office** building or room where postal business is carried on.

post- *pref.* after.

postage *n.* charge for sending something by post.

postal *a.* of the post; by post.

postcard *n.* card for sending messages by post without an envelope.

postcode *n.* group of letters and figures in a postal address to assist sorting.

poster *n.* large picture or notice announcing or advertising something.

poste restante /pōst restόnt/ post office department where letters are kept until called for.

posterior *a.* situated behind or at the back. — *n.* buttocks.

posterity *n.* future generations.

postern *n.* small back or side entrance to a fortress etc.

posthumous *a.* (of a child) born after its father's death; published or awarded after a person's death. **posthumously** *adv.*

postman *n.* (*pl.* **-men**) person who delivers or collects letters etc.

postmark *n.* official mark stamped on something sent by post, giving place and date of marking. — *v.* mark with this.

postmaster, postmistress *ns.* person in charge of certain post offices.

post-mortem *a.* & *n.* (examination) made after death.

postnatal *a.* after childbirth.

postpone *v.* keep (an event etc.) from occurring until a later time. **postponement** *n.*

postprandial *a.* after lunch or dinner.

postscript *n.* additional paragraph at the end of a letter etc.

postulate *v.* assume to be true, esp. as a basis for reasoning. **postulation** *n.*

posture *n.* attitude of the body. — *v.* assume a posture, esp. for effect. **postural** *a.*

posy *n.* small bunch of flowers.

pot *n.* vessel for holding liquids or solids, or for cooking in. — *v.* (**potted**) put into a pot; send (a ball in billiards etc.) into a pocket. **go to pot** (*sl.*) deteriorate. **pot-belly** *n.* protuberant belly. **pot-boiler** *n.* literary or artistic work produced merely to make a living. **potluck** *n.* whatever is available for a meal. **pot-roast** *n.* piece of meat cooked slowly in a covered dish; (*v.*) cook thus. **pot-shot** *n.* shot aimed casually.

potable *a.* drinkable.

potash *n.* potassium carbonate.

potassium *n.* soft silvery-white metallic element.

potation *n.* drinking; a drink.

potato *n.* (*pl.* **-oes**) plant with starchy tubers that are used as food; one of these tubers.

potent *a.* having great natural power; having a strong effect. **potently** *adv.*, **potency** *n.*

potentate *n.* monarch, ruler.

potential *a.* & *n.* (ability etc.) capable of being developed or used. **potentially** *adv.*, **potentiality** *n.*

pothole *n.* hole formed underground by the action of water; hole in a road surface.

potholing *n.* caving. **potholer** *n.*

potion *n.* liquid for drinking as a medicine or drug.

pot-pourri /pōpoόri/ *n.* scented mixture of dried petals and spices; medley.

potsherd *n.* broken piece of earthenware, esp. in archaeology.

potted *see* **pot**. — *a.* preserved in a pot; abridged.

potter [1] *n.* maker of pottery.

potter [2] *v.* work on trivial tasks in a leisurely way.

pottery *n.* vessels and other objects made of baked clay; potter's work or workshop.

potty [1] *a.* (**-ier, -iest**) (*sl.*) trivial; crazy.

potty [2] *n.* (*colloq.*) child's chamber pot.

pouch *n.* small bag or bag-like formation.
pouffe *n.* padded stool.
poulterer *n.* dealer in poultry.
poultice *n.* moist usu. hot dressing applied to inflammation. — *v.* put a poultice on.
poultry *n.* domestic fowls.
pounce *v.* swoop down and grasp or attack. — *n.* pouncing movement.
pound [1] *n.* measure of weight, 16 oz. avoirdupois (0.454 kg) or 12 oz. troy (0.373 kg); unit of money in Britain and certain other countries.
pound [2] *n.* enclosure where stray animals, or vehicles officially removed, are kept until claimed.
pound [3] *v.* beat or crush with heavy strokes; run heavily; (of the heart) beat heavily.
poundage *n.* charge or commission per £ or per pound weight.
pour *v.* flow, cause to flow; rain heavily; send out freely.
pout *v.* push out one's lips, (of lips) be pushed out. — *n.* pouting expression.
poverty *n.* state of being poor; scarcity, lack; inferiority.
powder *n.* mass of fine dry particles; medicine or cosmetic in this form; gunpowder. — *v.* cover with powder. **powdery** *a.*
power *n.* ability to do something; vigour, strength; control, influence, authority; influential person or country etc.; product of a number multiplied by itself a given number of times; mechanical or electrical energy; electricity supply. — *v.* supply with (esp. motive) power. **power station** building where electricity is generated for distribution.
powerful *a.* having great power or influence. **powerfully** *adv.*
powerless *a.* without power to take action, wholly unable.
practicable *a.* able to be done. **practicability** *n.*
practical *a.* involving activity as distinct from study or theory; suitable for use; clever at doing and making things; virtual. **practical joke** humorous trick played on a person. **practicality** *n.*
practically *adv.* in a practical way; virtually, almost.
practice *n.* action as opposed to theory; custom; repeated exercise to improve skill; doctor's or lawyer's business.
practise *v.* do something repeatedly or habitually; (of a doctor or lawyer) perform professional work.
practised *a.* experienced.
practitioner *n.* professional worker, esp. in medicine.
pragmatic *a.* treating things from a practical point of view. **pragmatically** *adv.*, **pragmatism** *n.*, **pragmatist** *n.*
prairie *n.* large treeless area of grassland, esp. in North America.
praise *v.* express approval or admiration of; honour (God) in words. — *n.* praising; approval expressed in words.
praiseworthy *a.* deserving praise. **praiseworthiness** *n.*
pram *n.* four-wheeled carriage for a baby.
prance *v.* move springily.
prank *n.* piece of mischief.
prankster *n.* person playing pranks.
prattle *v.* chatter in a childish way. — *n.* childish chatter.
prawn *n.* edible shellfish like a large shrimp.
pray *v.* say prayers; entreat.
prayer *n.* solemn request or thanksgiving to God; set form of words used in this; act of praying; entreaty.
pre- *pref.* before; beforehand.
preach *v.* deliver a sermon; expound (the Gospel etc.); advocate. **preacher** *n.*
preamble *n.* preliminary statement, introductory section.
prearrange *v.* arrange beforehand. **prearrangement** *n.*
precarious *a.* unsafe, not secure. **precariously** *adv.*, **precariousness** *n.*
precaution *n.* something done in advance to avoid a risk. **precautionary** *a.*
precede *v.* come or go or place before in time or order etc.
precedence *n.* priority.
precedent *n.* previous case serving as an example to be followed.
precept *n.* command, rule of conduct.
precession *n.* change by which equinoxes occur earlier in each sidereal year.
precinct *n.* enclosed area, esp. round a cathedral; area closed to traffic in a town; (*pl.*) environs.
precious *a.* of great value; beloved; affectedly refined. **precious stone** small valuable piece of mineral.
precipice *n.* very steep or vertical face of a cliff or rock.
precipitate *v.* /prisíppitayt/ throw headlong; cause to happen suddenly or soon; cause (a substance) to be deposited; condense (vapour). — *n.* /prisíppitət/ substance deposited from a solution; moisture condensed from vapour. — *a.* /prisíppitət/ hasty, rash. **precipitately** *adv.*, **precipitation** *n.*
precipitous *a.* very steep.

précis /práysee/ *n.* (*pl.* **précis**) summary. — *v.* make a précis of.
precise *a.* exact; correct and clearly stated. **precisely** *adv.*, **precision** *n.*
preclude *v.* exclude the possibility of, prevent.
precocious *a.* having developed earlier than is usual. **precociously** *adv.*
precognition *n.* foreknowledge, esp. supernatural.
preconceived *a.* (of an idea) formed beforehand. **preconception** *n.*
precondition *n.* condition to be fulfilled beforehand.
precursor *n.* forerunner.
predatory /préddətəri/ *a.* preying on others. **predator** *n.* predatory animal.
predecease *v.* die earlier than (another person).
predecessor *n.* former holder of an office or position; ancestor.
predicament *n.* difficult situation.
predicate *n.* the part of a sentence that says something about the subject (e.g. 'is short' in *life is short*). **predicative** *a.*
predict *v.* foretell. **prediction** *n.*, **predictive** *a.*, **predictor** *n.*
predictable *a.* able to be predicted. **predictably** *adv.*
predilection *n.* special liking.
predispose *v.* influence in advance; render liable or inclined. **predisposition** *n.*
predominate *v.* be most numerous or powerful; exert control. **predominant** *a.*, **predominantly** *adv.*, **predominance** *n.*
pre-eminent *a.* excelling others, outstanding. **pre-eminently** *adv.*, **pre-eminence** *n.*
pre-empt *v.* take (a thing) before anyone else can do so. **pre-emption** *n.*, **pre-emptive** *a.*
preen *v.* smooth (feathers) with the beak. **preen oneself** groom oneself; show self-satisfaction.
prefabricate *v.* manufacture in sections for assembly on a site. **prefabrication** *n.*
preface *n.* introductory statement. — *v.* introduce with a preface; lead up to (an event).
prefect *n.* senior pupil authorized to maintain discipline in a school; administrative official in certain countries. **prefecture** *n.*
prefer *v.* (**preferred**) choose as more desirable, like better; put forward (an accusation).
preferable *a.* more desirable. **preferably** *adv.*
preference *n.* preferring; thing preferred; prior right; favouring.
preferential *a.* giving preference. **preferentially** *adv.*
preferment *n.* promotion.
prefigure *v.* foreshadow.
prefix *n.* (*pl.* **-ixes**) word or syllable placed in front of a word to change its meaning. — *v.* add as a prefix or introduction.
pregnant *a.* having a child or young developing in the womb; full of meaning. **pregnancy** *n.*
prehensile *a.* able to grasp things. **prehensility** *n.*
prehistoric *a.* of the ancient period before written records were made. **prehistorically** *adv.*
prejudge *v.* form a judgement on before knowing all the facts. **prejudgement** *n.*
prejudice *n.* unreasoning opinion or dislike; harm to rights. — *v.* cause to have a prejudice; harm the rights of. **prejudiced** *a.*
prejudicial *a.* harmful to rights or interests. **prejudicially** *adv.*
prelate *n.* clergyman of high rank. **prelacy** *n.*
preliminary *a.* & *n.* (action or event etc.) preceding and preparing for a main action or event.
prelude *n.* action or event leading up to another; introductory part or piece of music.
premarital *a.* before marriage.
premature *a.* coming or done before the usual or proper time. **prematurely** *adv.*
premedication *n.* medication in preparation for an operation.
premeditated *a.* planned beforehand. **premeditation** *n.*
premenstrual *a.* before each menstruation.
premier *a.* first in importance or order or time. — *n.* prime minister. **premiership** *n.*
première /prémmiair/ *n.* first public performance.
premises *n.pl.* house or other building and its grounds.
premiss *n.* statement on which reasoning is based.
premium *n.* amount or instalment paid for an insurance policy; extra sum added to a wage or charge; fee for instruction. **at a premium** above the nominal or usual price; highly esteemed.
premonition *n.* presentiment. **premonitory** *a.*
prenatal *a.* before birth; before childbirth. **prenatally** *adv.*
preoccupation *n.* being preoccupied; thing that fills one's thoughts.
preoccupied *a.* mentally engrossed and inattentive to other things; already occupied.

preparation *n.* preparing; thing done to make ready; substance prepared for use.
preparatory *a.* preparing for something. — *adv.* in a preparatory way.
prepare *v.* make or get ready. **prepared to** ready and willing to.
preponderate *v.* be greater in number or intensity etc. **preponderant** *a.*, **preponderantly** *adv.*, **preponderance** *n.*
preposition *n.* word used with a noun or pronoun to show position, time, or means (e.g. *at* home, *by* train). **prepositional** *a.*
prepossessing *a.* attractive.
preposterous *a.* utterly absurd, outrageous. **preposterously** *adv.*, **preposterousness** *n.*
prepuce *n.* foreskin.
prerequisite *a.* & *n.* (thing) required before something can happen.
prerogative *n.* right or privilege belonging to a person or group.
presage *n.* omen; presentiment. — *v.* portend; foresee.
Presbyterian *a.* & *n.* (member) of a Church governed by elders of equal rank. **Presbyterianism** *n.*
prescribe *v.* advise the use of (a medicine etc.); lay down as a course or rule to be followed.
prescription *n.* prescribing; doctor's written instructions for the preparation and use of a medicine.
prescriptive *a.* prescribing.
presence *n.* being present; person's bearing; person or thing that is or seems present. **presence of mind** ability to act sensibly in a crisis.
present [1] /prézz'nt/ *a.* being in the place in question; existing or being dealt with now. — *n.* present time, time now passing. **at present** now. **for the present** for now, temporarily.
present [2] *n.* /prézz'nt/ gift. — *v.* /prizént/ give as a gift or award; introduce; bring to the public. **presenter** *n.*
presentable *a.* fit to be presented, of good appearance. **presentably** *adv.*
presentation *n.* presenting; thing presented.
presentiment *n.* feeling of something about to happen, foreboding.
presently *adv.* soon; (*Sc.* & *US*) now.
preservation *n.* preserving.
preservative *a.* preserving. — *n.* substance that preserves perishable food.
preserve *v.* keep safe, unchanged, or in existence; treat (food) to prevent decay. *n.* interests etc. regarded as one person's domain; (also *pl.*) jam. **preserver** *n.*
preside *v.* be president or chairman; have the position of control.
president *n.* head of an institution or club; head of a republic. **presidency** *n.*, **presidential** *a.*
press [1] *v.* apply weight or force against; squeeze; flatten, smooth; iron (clothes etc.); urge; throng closely. — *n.* process of pressing; instrument for pressing something; newspapers and periodicals, people involved in producing these. **be pressed for** have barely enough of. **press conference** interview before a number of reporters. **press cutting** report etc. cut from a newspaper. **press-stud** *n.* small fastener with two parts that engage when pressed together. **press-up** *n.* exercise of pressing on the hands to raise the trunk while prone.
press [2] *v.* bring into use as a makeshift. **press-gang** *v.* force into service.
pressing *a.* urgent.
pressure *n.* exertion of force against a thing; this force; compelling or oppressive influence. — *v.* pressurize (a person). **pressure cooker** pan for cooking things quickly by steam under pressure. **pressure group** organized group seeking to exert influence by concerted action.
pressurize *v.* try to compel into an action; maintain a constant atmospheric pressure in (a compartment). **pressurization** *n.*
prestige *n.* respect resulting from good reputation or achievements.
prestigious *a.* having or giving prestige.
presumably *adv.* it may be presumed.
presume *v.* suppose to be true; be presumptuous. **presumption** *n.*
presumptuous *a.* behaving with impudent boldness; acting beyond one's authority. **presumptuously** *adv.*
presuppose *v.* assume beforehand; assume the prior existence of. **presupposition** *n.*
pretence *n.* pretending, make-believe; claim (e.g. to merit or knowledge).
pretend *v.* create a false impression of (in play or deception); claim falsely that one has or is something. **pretender** *n.*
pretension *n.* asserting of a claim; pretentiousness.
pretentious *a.* claiming great merit or importance. **pretentiously** *adv.*, **pretentiousness** *n.*
preternatural *a.* beyond what is natural. **preternaturally** *adv.*
pretext *n.* reason put forward to conceal one's true reason.
pretty *a.* **(-ier, -iest)** attractive in a delicate way. — *adv.* fairly, moderately. **prettily** *adv.*, **prettiness** *n.*
pretzel *n.* salted biscuit.

prevail *v.* be victorious, gain the mastery; be the most usual. **prevail on** persuade.

prevalent *a.* existing generally, widespread. **prevalence** *n.*

prevaricate *v.* speak evasively. **prevarication** *n.*

prevent *v.* keep from happening; keep from doing something. **prevention** *n.*, **preventable** *a.*

preventative *a.* & *n.* preventive.

preventive *a.* & *n.* (thing) preventing something.

previous *a.* coming before in time or order. **previously** *adv.*

prey *n.* animal hunted or killed by another for food; victim. — *v.* **prey on** seek or take as prey; cause worry to. **bird of prey** one that kills and eats animals.

price *n.* amount of money for which a thing is bought or sold; what must be given or done etc. to achieve something. — *v.* fix, find, or estimate the price of.

priceless *a.* invaluable; (*sl.*) very amusing or absurd.

prick *v.* pierce slightly; feel a pricking sensation; erect (the ears). — *n.* act of pricking; sensation of being pricked. **prick up one's ears** listen alertly.

prickle *n.* small thorn or spine; pricking sensation. — *v.* feel or cause a pricking sensation.

prickly *a.* (**-ier**, **-iest**) having prickles; irritable, touchy.

pride *n.* feeling of pleasure or satisfaction about one's actions, qualities, or possessions; source of this; sense of dignity; group (of lions). — *v.* **pride oneself on** be proud of. **pride of place** most prominent position.

priest *n.* member of the clergy; official of a non-Christian religion. **priestess** *n.fem.*, **priesthood** *n.*, **priestly** *a.*

prig *n.* self-righteous person. **priggish** *a.*, **priggishness** *n.*

prim *a.* (**primmer**, **primmest**) formal and precise; prudish. **primly** *adv.*, **primness** *n.*

prima *a.* **prima ballerina** chief ballerina. **prima donna** chief female singer in opera.

primal *a.* primitive, primeval; fundamental.

primary *a.* first in time, order, or importance. — *n.* primary thing. **primary colours** those not made by mixing others, i.e. red, green, violet, or (for pigments) red, blue, yellow. **primary education**, **primary school** that in which the rudiments of knowledge are taught. **primarily** *adv.*

primate *n.* archbishop; member of the highly developed order of animals that includes man, apes, and monkeys.

prime [1] *a.* chief; first-rate; fundamental. — *n.* state of greatest perfection. **prime minister** leader of a government. **prime number** number that can be divided exactly only by itself and one.

prime [2] *v.* prepare for use or action; provide with information in preparation for something.

primer *n.* substance used to prime a surface for painting; elementary textbook.

primeval *a.* of the earliest times of the world.

primitive *a.* of or at an early stage of civilization; simple, crude.

primogeniture *n.* system by which an eldest son inherits all his parents' property.

primordial *a.* primeval.

primrose *n.* pale yellow spring flower; its colour.

primula *n.* perennial plant of a kind that includes the primrose.

prince *n.* male member of a royal family; sovereign's son or grandson; the greatest or best.

princely *a.* like a prince; splendid, generous.

princess *n.* female member of a royal family; sovereign's daughter or granddaughter; prince's wife.

principal *a.* first in rank or importance. — *n.* head of certain schools or colleges; person with highest authority or playing the leading part; capital sum as distinct from interest or income.

principality *n.* country ruled by a prince.

principally *adv.* mainly.

principle *n.* general truth used as a basis of reasoning or action; scientific law shown or used in the working of something. **in principle** as regards the main elements. **on principle** because of one's moral beliefs.

print *v.* press (a mark) on a surface, impress (a surface etc.) in this way; produce by applying inked type to paper; write with unjoined letters; produce a positive picture from (a photographic negative). — *n.* mark left by pressing; printed lettering or words; printed design or picture or fabric. **printed circuit** electric circuit with lines of conducting material printed on a flat sheet.

printer *n.* person who prints books or newspapers etc.

printout *n.* computer output in printed form.

prior [1] *a.* coming before in time or order or importance.

prior [2] *n.* monk who is head of a religious

community, or one ranking next below an abbot. **prioress** *n.fem.*

prioritize *v.* treat as a priority. **prioritization** *n.*

priority *n.* right to be first; thing that should be treated as most important.

priory *n.* monastery or nunnery governed by a prior or prioress.

prise *v.* force out or open by leverage.

prism *n.* solid geometric shape with ends that are equal and parallel; transparent object of this shape with refracting surfaces.

prismatic *a.* of or like a prism; (of colours) rainbow-like.

prison *n.* building used to confine people convicted of crimes; place of custody or confinement.

prisoner *n.* person kept in prison; captive; person in confinement.

prissy *a.* (**-ier**, **-iest**) prim. **prissily** *adv.*, **prissiness** *n.*

pristine *a.* in its original and unspoilt condition.

privacy *n.* being private.

private *a.* belonging to a person or group, not public; confidential; secluded; not provided by the State. — *n.* soldier of the lowest rank. **in private** privately. **privately** *adv.*

privation *n.* loss, lack; hardship. **privative** *a.*

privatize *v.* transfer from State to private ownership. **privatization** *n.*

privet *n.* bushy evergreen shrub much used for hedges.

privilege *n.* special right granted to a person or group. **privileged** *a.*

prize [1] *n.* award for victory or superiority; thing that can be won. — *a.* winning a prize; excellent. — *v.* value highly.

prize [2] *v.* = prise.

pro [1] *n.* (*pl.* **-os**) (*colloq.*) professional.

pro [2] *n.* **pros and cons** arguments for and against something.

pro- *pref.* in favour of.

probable *a.* likely to happen or be true. **probably** *adv.*, **probability** *n.*

probate *n.* official process of proving that a will is valid; certified copy of a will.

probation *n.* testing of behaviour or abilities; system whereby certain offenders are supervised by an official (**probation officer**) instead of being imprisoned. **probationary** *a.*

probationer *n.* person undergoing a probationary period.

probe *n.* blunt surgical instrument for exploring a wound; unmanned exploratory spacecraft; investigation. — *v.* explore with a probe; investigate.

probity *n.* honesty.

problem *n.* something difficult to deal with or understand; thing to be solved or dealt with. **problematic**, **problematical** *adjs.*

proboscis *n.* long flexible snout; insect's elongated mouthpart used for sucking things.

procedure *n.* series of actions done to accomplish something. **procedural** *a.*

proceed *v.* go forward or onward; continue; start a lawsuit; come forth, originate.

proceedings *n.pl.* what takes place; published report of a conference; lawsuit.

proceeds *n.pl.* profit from a sale or performance etc.

process *n.* series of operations used in making something; procedure; series of changes or events. — *v.* subject to a process; deal with.

procession *n.* number of people or vehicles or boats etc. going along in an orderly line.

processor *n.* machine that processes things.

proclaim *v.* announce publicly. **proclamation** *n.*

proclivity *n.* tendency.

procrastinate *v.* postpone action. **procrastination** *n.*

procreate *v.* beget or generate (offspring). **procreation** *n.*

procure *v.* obtain by care or effort, acquire; act as procurer. **procurement** *n.*

procurer *n.* person who obtains women for prostitution. **procuress** *n.fem.*

prod *v.* (**prodded**) poke; stimulate to action. — *n.* prodding action; stimulus; instrument for prodding things.

prodigal *a.* wasteful, extravagant. **prodigally** *adv.*, **prodigality** *n.*

prodigious *a.* amazing; enormous. **prodigiously** *adv.*

prodigy *n.* person with exceptional qualities or abilities; wonderful thing.

produce *v.* /prədyōōss/ bring forward for inspection; bring (a performance etc.) before the public; bring into existence, cause; manufacture. — *n.* /pródyooss/ amount or thing(s) produced. **producer** *n.*, **production** *n.*

product *n.* thing produced; number obtained by multiplying.

productive *a.* producing things, esp. in large quantities.

productivity *n.* efficiency in industrial production.

profane *a.* secular; irreverent, blasphemous. — *v.* treat irreverently. **profanely** *adv.*, **profanity** *n.*, **profanation** *n.*

profess *v.* claim (a quality etc.), pretend; affirm faith in (a religion).

professed *a.* self-acknowledged; alleged. **professedly** *adv.*

profession *n.* occupation requiring advanced learning; people engaged in this; declaration.

professional *a.* belonging to a profession; skilful and conscientious; doing something for payment, not as a pastime. — *n.* professional worker or player. **professionalism** *n.*, **professionally** *adv.*

professor *n.* university teacher of the highest rank. **professorial** *a.*

proffer *v.* & *n.* offer.

proficient *a.* competent, skilled. **proficiently** *adv.*, **proficiency** *n.*

profile *n.* side view, esp. of the face; short account of a person's character or career.

profit *n.* advantage, benefit; money gained. — *v.* (**profited**) obtain a profit; benefit.

profitable *a.* bringing profit. **profitably** *adv.*, **profitability** *n.*

profiteer *n.* person who makes excessive profits. **profiteering** *n.*

profiterole *n.* small hollow cake of choux pastry with filling.

profligate *a.* wasteful, extravagant; dissolute. — *n.* profligate person. **profligacy** *n.*

profound *a.* intense; showing or needing great insight. **profoundly** *adv.*, **profundity** *n.*

profuse *a.* lavish; plentiful. **profusely** *adv.*, **profusion** *n.*

progenitor *n.* ancestor.

progeny *n.* offspring.

progesterone *n.* sex hormone that maintains pregnancy.

prognosis *n.* (*pl.* **-oses**) forecast, esp. of the course of a disease. **prognostic** *a.*

prognosticate *v.* forecast. **prognostication** *n.*

program *n.* (*US*) = programme; series of coded instructions for a computer. — *v.* (**programmed**) instruct (a computer) by means of this. **programmer** *n.*

programme *n.* plan of procedure; list of items in an entertainment; these items; broadcast performance.

progress *n.* /prógress/ forward or onward movement; development. — *v.* /prəgréss/ make progress; develop. **in progress** taking place. **progression** *n.*

progressive *a.* favouring progress or reform; (of a disease) gradually increasing in its effect. **progressively** *adv.*

prohibit *v.* forbid. **prohibition** *n.*

prohibitive *a.* prohibiting; intended to prevent the use or purchase of something.

project [1] /prəjékt/ *v.* extend outwards; cast, throw; estimate; plan.

project [2] /prójekt/ *n.* plan, undertaking; task involving research.

projectile *n.* missile.

projection *n.* process of projecting something; thing projecting from a surface; estimate of future situations based on a study of present ones.

projectionist *n.* person who operates a projector.

projector *n.* apparatus for projecting images on to a screen.

proletariat *n.* working-class people. **proletarian** *a.* & *n.*

proliferate *v.* reproduce rapidly, multiply. **proliferation** *n.*

prolific *a.* producing things abundantly. **prolifically** *adv.*

prologue *n.* introduction to a poem or play etc.

prolong *v.* lengthen in extent or duration. **prolongation** *n.*

prolonged *a.* continuing for a long time.

prom *n.* (*colloq.*) promenade; promenade concert.

promenade *n.* paved public walk (esp. along a sea front). **promenade concert** one where part of the audience is not seated and can move about.

prominent *a.* projecting; conspicuous; well-known. **prominently** *adv.*, **prominence** *n.*

promiscuous *a.* indiscriminate; having sexual relations with many people. **promiscuously** *adv.*, **promiscuity** *n.*

promise *n.* declaration that one will give or do or not do a certain thing; indication of future results. — *v.* make a promise (to); say that one will do or give (a thing); seem likely, produce expectation of.

promising *a.* likely to turn out well or produce good results.

promontory *n.* high land jutting out into the sea or a lake.

promote *v.* raise to a higher rank or office; help the progress of; publicize in order to sell. **promotion** *n.*, **promotional** *a.*, **promoter** *n.*

prompt *a.* done without delay; punctual. — *adv.* punctually. — *v.* incite; assist (an actor) by supplying words. **promptly** *adv.*, **promptness** *n.*

prompter *n.* person stationed off stage to prompt actors.

promulgate *v.* make known to the public. **promulgation** *n.*, **promulgator** *n.*

prone *a.* lying face downwards; likely to do or suffer something.

prong *n.* each of the pointed parts of a fork. **pronged** *a.*

pronoun *n.* word used as a substitute for a noun (e.g. *I*, *me*, *who*, *which*). **pronominal** *a.*

pronounce *v.* utter (a sound or word) distinctly or in a certain way; declare. **pronunciation** *n.*

pronounced *a.* noticeable.

pronouncement *n.* declaration.

proof *n.* evidence that something is true or exists; copy of printed matter for correction. — *a.* able to resist penetration or damage. — *v.* make (fabric) proof against something (e.g. water).

proofread *v.* read and correct (printed proofs). **proofreader** *n.*

prop ¹ *n.* & *v.* (**propped**) support to prevent something from falling or sagging or failing.

prop ² *n.* (*colloq.*) a stage property.

prop ³ *n.* (*colloq.*) propeller.

propaganda *n.* publicity intended to persuade or convince people.

propagate *v.* breed or reproduce from parent stock; spread (news etc.); transmit. **propagation** *n.*

propane *n.* hydrocarbon fuel gas.

propel *v.* (**propelled**) push forwards or onwards.

propellant *n.* thing that propels something. **propellent** *a.*

propeller *n.* revolving device with blades, for propelling a ship or aircraft.

propensity *n.* tendency; inclination.

proper *a.* suitable; correct; conforming to social conventions; (*colloq.*) thorough. **proper name** *or* **noun** name of an individual person or thing.

property *n.* thing(s) owned; real estate, land; movable object used in a play etc.; quality, characteristic.

prophecy *n.* power of prophesying; statement prophesying something.

prophesy *v.* foretell (what will happen).

prophet *n.* person who foretells the future; religious teacher inspired by God. **prophetess** *n.fem.*

prophetic, prophetical *adjs.* prophesying. **prophetically** *adv.*

prophylactic *a.* & *n.* (medicine or action etc.) preventing disease or misfortune. **prophylaxis** *n.*

propinquity *n.* nearness.

propitiate /prəpishiayt/ *v.* win the favour of. **propitiation** *n.*, **propitiatory** *a.*

propitious /prəpĭshəss/ *a.* auspicious, favourable. **propitiously** *adv.*, **propitiousness** *n.*

proponent *n.* person putting forward a proposal.

proportion *n.* fraction or share of a whole; ratio; correct relation in size or amount or degree; (*pl.*) dimensions. **proportional** *a.*, **proportionally** *adv.*

proportionate *a.* in due proportion. **proportionately** *adv.*

proposal *n.* proposing of something; thing proposed; request to marry the person asking.

propose *v.* put forward for consideration; declare as one's plan; nominate; make a proposal of marriage. **proposer** *n.*

proposition *n.* statement; proposal, scheme proposed; (*colloq.*) undertaking. — *v.* (*colloq.*) put a proposal to.

propound *v.* put forward for consideration.

proprietary *a.* made and sold by a particular firm, usu. under a patent; of an owner or ownership.

proprietor *n.* owner of a business. **proprietorial** *a.*

propriety *n.* correctness of behaviour.

propulsion *n.* process of propelling or being propelled.

pro rata proportional(ly).

prosaic *a.* plain and ordinary, unimaginative. **prosaically** *adv.*

proscribe *v.* forbid by law.

prose *n.* written or spoken language not in verse form.

prosecute *v.* take legal proceedings against (a person) for a crime; carry on, conduct. **prosecution** *n.*, **prosecutor** *n.*

proselyte *n.* recent convert to a religion.

proselytize *v.* seek to convert.

prospect *n.* /próspekt/ what one is to expect; chance of advancement. — *v.* /prəspékt/ explore in search of something. **prospector** *n.*

prospective *a.* expected to be or to occur; future, possible.

prospectus *n.* document giving details of a school, business, etc.

prosper *v.* be successful, thrive.

prosperous *a.* financially successful. **prosperity** *n.*

prostate gland gland round the neck of the bladder in males.

prosthesis *n.* (*pl.* **-theses**) artificial limb or similar appliance. **prosthetic** *a.*

prostitute *n.* woman who engages in sexual intercourse for payment. — *v.* make a prostitute of; put (talent etc.) to an unworthy use. **prostitution** *n.*

prostrate *a.* /próstrayt/ face downwards; lying horizontally; overcome, exhausted. — *v.* /prostráyt/ cause to be prostrate. **prostration** *n.*

protagonist *n.* one of the chief contenders; supporter.

protean *a.* variable; versatile.

protect *v.* keep from harm or injury. **protection** *n.*, **protector** *n.*
protectionism *n.* policy of protecting home industries by tariffs etc. **protectionist** *n.*
protective *a.* protecting, giving protection. **protectively** *adv.*
protectorate *n.* country that is under the official protection and partial control of a stronger one.
protégé /próttizhay/ *n.* (*fem.* **protégée**) person under the protection or patronage of another.
protein *n.* organic compound forming an essential part of humans' and animals' food.
protest *n.* /prṓtest/ statement or action indicating disapproval. — *v.* /prətést/ express disapproval; declare firmly.
Protestant *n.* member of one of the western Churches that are separated from the Roman Catholic Church. **Protestantism** *n.*
protestation *n.* firm declaration.
protocol *n.* etiquette applying to rank or status; draft of a treaty.
proton *n.* particle of matter with a positive electric charge.
protoplasm *n.* contents of a living cell.
prototype *n.* original example from which others are developed.
protozoon /prṓtəzṓ-on/ *n.* (*pl.* **-zoa**) one-celled microscopic animal. **protozoan** *a.* & *n.*
protract *v.* prolong in duration. **protraction** *n.*
protractor *n.* instrument for measuring angles.
protrude *v.* project, stick out. **protrusion** *n.*, **protrusive** *a.*
protuberance *n.* bulging part.
protuberant *a.* bulging.
proud *a.* full of pride; imposing; slightly projecting. **proudly** *adv.*
prove *v.* give or be proof of; be found to be.
proven *a.* proved.
provenance *n.* place of origin.
proverb *n.* short well-known saying.
proverbial *a.* of or mentioned in a proverb; well-known.
provide *v.* cause to have possession or use of; supply the necessities of life; make preparations. **provider** *n.*
provided *conj.* on condition (that).
providence *n.* being provident; God's or nature's protection.
provident *a.* showing wise forethought for future needs, thrifty.
providential *a.* happening very luckily. **providentially** *adv.*
providing *conj.* = provided.
province *n.* administrative division of a country; range of learning or responsibility; (*pl.*) all parts of a country outside its capital city.
provincial *a.* of a province or provinces; having limited interests and narrow-minded views. — *n.* inhabitant of province(s).
provision *n.* process of providing things; stipulation in a treaty or contract etc.; (*pl.*) supply of food and drink.
provisional *a.* arranged temporarily. **provisionally** *adv.*
proviso /prəvī́sō/ *n.* (*pl.* **-os**) stipulation. **provisory** *a.*
provoke *v.* make angry; rouse to action; produce as a reaction. **provocation** *n.*, **provocative** *a.*, **provocatively** *adv.*
prow *n.* projecting front part of a ship or boat.
prowess *n.* great ability or daring.
prowl *v.* go about stealthily. — *n.* prowling. **prowler** *n.*
proximate *a.* nearest.
proximity *n.* nearness.
proxy *n.* person authorized to represent or act for another; use of such a person.
prude *n.* person of exaggerated propriety, one who is easily shocked. **prudery** *n.*
prudent *a.* showing carefulness and foresight. **prudently** *adv.*, **prudence** *n.*
prudish *a.* showing prudery. **prudishly** *adv.*, **prudishness** *n.*
prune [1] *n.* dried plum.
prune [2] *v.* trim by cutting away dead or unwanted parts; reduce.
prurient *a.* having or arising from lewd thoughts. **pruriently** *adv.*, **prurience** *n.*
pry *v.* inquire or peer impertinently (often furtively).
psalm /saam/ *n.* sacred song.
psalmist /saám-/ *n.* writer of psalms.
psalter /sáwl-/ *n.* copy of the Book of Psalms in the Old Testament.
psephology /sef-/ *n.* study of trends in election. **psephological** *a.*, **psephologist** *n.*
pseudo- /syṓ͞odō/ *pref.* false.
pseudonym /syṓ͞o-/ *n.* fictitious name, esp. used by an author. **pseudonymous** *a.*
psoriasis /sərī́əsiss/ *n.* skin disease causing scaly red patches.
psyche /sī́ki/ *n.* soul, self; mind.
psychiatric /sī-/ *a.* of psychiatry. **psychiatric hospital** one for the care of patients with mental illnesses.
psychiatry /sī-/ *n.* study and treatment of mental illness. **psychiatrist** *n.*
psychic /sī́kik/ *a.* of the soul or mind; of

or having apparently supernatural powers. — *n.* person with such powers.

psychoanalyse /sī-/ *v.* treat by psychoanalysis. **psychoanalyst** *n.*

psychoanalysis /sī-/ *n.* method of examining and treating mental conditions by investigating the interaction of conscious and unconscious elements.

psychology /sī-/ *n.* study of the mind and how it works; mental characteristics. **psychological** *a.*, **psychologically** *adv.*, **psychologist** *n.*

psychopath /sī-/ *n.* person suffering from a severe mental disorder sometimes resulting in antisocial or violent behaviour. **psychopathic** *a.*

psychosis /sī-/ *n.* (*pl.* **-oses**) severe mental disorder involving a person's whole personality. **psychotic** *a.* & *n.*

psychosomatic /sī-/ *a.* (of illness) caused or aggravated by mental stress.

psychotherapy /sī-/ *n.* treatment of mental disorders by the use of psychological methods. **psychotherapist** *n.*

ptarmigan /taármigən/ *n.* bird of the grouse family with plumage that turns white in winter.

pterodactyl /térrədáktil/ *n.* extinct reptile with wings.

ptomaine /tómayn/ *n.* (toxic) compound found in putrefying matter.

pub *n.* (*colloq.*) public house.

puberty *n.* stage in life at which a person's reproductive organs become able to function. **pubertal** *a.*

pubic *a.* of the abdomen at the lower front part of the pelvis.

public *a.* of, for, or known to people in general. — *n.* members of a community in general. **public house** building (other than a hotel) licensed to serve alcoholic drinks. **public school** secondary school for fee-paying pupils; (in Scotland, USA, etc.) school run by public authorities. **public-spirited** *a.* showing readiness to do things for the benefit of people in general. **publicly** *adv.*

publican *n.* keeper of a public house.

publication *n.* publishing; published book or newspaper etc.

publicity *n.* public attention directed upon a person or thing; process of attracting this.

publicize *v.* bring to the attention of the public. **publicist** *n.*

publish *v.* issue copies of (a book etc.) to the public; make generally known. **publisher** *n.*

puce *a.* & *n.* brownish purple.

puck *n.* hard rubber disc used in ice hockey.

pucker *v.* & *n.* wrinkle.

pudding *n.* baked, boiled, or steamed dish made of or enclosed in a mixture of flour and other ingredients; sweet course of a meal; a kind of sausage.

puddle *n.* small pool of rainwater or of liquid on a surface.

pudenda *n.pl.* genitals.

puerile *a.* childish. **puerility** *n.*

puerperal *a.* of or resulting from childbirth.

puff *n.* short light blowing of breath, wind, smoke, etc.; soft pad for applying powder to the skin; piece of advertising. — *v.* send (air etc.) or come out in puffs; breathe hard, pant; swell. **puffball** *n.* globular fungus. **puff pastry** very light flaky pastry.

puffin *n.* seabird with a short striped bill.

puffy *a.* (**-ier**, **-iest**) puffed out, swollen. **puffiness** *n.*

pug *n.* dog of a small breed with a flat nose and wrinkled face.

pugilist /pyoōjilist/ *n.* professional boxer. **pugilism** *n.*

pugnacious *a.* eager to fight, aggressive. **pugnaciously** *adv.*, **pugnacity** *n.*

puke *v.* & *n.* vomit.

pull *v.* exert force upon (a thing) so as to move it towards the source of the force; remove by pulling; exert a pulling or driving force; attract. — *n.* act or force of pulling; means of exerting influence; deep drink; draw at a pipe etc. **pull in** move towards the side of the road or into a stopping place. **pull off** succeed in doing or achieving. **pull out** withdraw; move away from the side of a road or a stopping place. **pull through** come or bring successfully through an illness or difficulty. **pull up** stop.

pullet *n.* young hen.

pulley *n.* (*pl.* **-eys**) wheel over which a rope etc. passes, used in lifting things.

pullover *n.* sweater (with or without sleeves) with no fastenings.

pulmonary *a.* of the lungs.

pulp *n.* soft moist part (esp. of fruit) or substance. — *v.* reduce to pulp. **pulpy** *a.*

pulpit *n.* raised enclosed platform from which a preacher speaks.

pulsar *n.* cosmic source of radio pulses.

pulsate *v.* expand and contract rhythmically. **pulsation** *n.*

pulse [1] *n.* rhythmical throbbing of arteries as blood is propelled along them, esp. as felt in the wrists or temples etc.; single beat, throb, or vibration. — *v.* pulsate.

pulse [2] *n.* edible seed of beans, peas, lentils, etc.

pulverize *v.* crush into powder; become

powder; defeat thoroughly. **pulverization** *n.*

puma *n.* large brown American animal of the cat family.

pumice *n.* solidified lava used for scouring or polishing. **pumice-stone** *n.* piece of this.

pummel *v.* (**pummelled**) strike repeatedly esp. with the fists.

pump *n.* machine for moving liquid, gas, or air. — *v.* use a pump; move or inflate or empty by using a pump; move vigorously up and down; pour forth; question persistently.

pumpkin *n.* large round orange-coloured fruit of a vine.

pun *n.* humorous use of a word to suggest another that sounds the same. **punning** *a.* & *n.*

punch[1] *v.* strike with the fist; cut (a hole etc.) with a device. — *n.* blow with the fist; device for cutting holes or impressing a design. **punch-drunk** *a.* stupefied by repeated blows. **punchline** *n.* words giving the climax of a joke.

punch[2] *n.* drink made of wine or spirits mixed with fruit juices etc. **punch-bowl** *n.*

punctilious *a.* very careful about details; conscientious. **punctiliously** *adv.*, **punctiliousness** *n.*

punctual *a.* arriving or doing things at the appointed time. **punctually** *adv.*, **punctuality** *n.*

punctuate *v.* insert the appropriate marks in written material to separate sentences etc.; interrupt at intervals. **punctuation** *n.*

puncture *n.* small hole made by something sharp, esp. in a tyre. — *v.* make a puncture in; suffer a puncture.

pundit *n.* learned expert.

pungent *a.* having a strong sharp taste or smell. **pungently** *adv.*, **pungency** *n.*

punish *v.* cause (an offender) to suffer for his offence; inflict a penalty for; treat roughly. **punishment** *n.*

punitive *a.* inflicting or intended to inflict punishment.

punk *n.* (*sl.*) worthless person; (devotee of) punk rock. — *a.* (*sl.*) of punk rock or its devotees. **punk rock** deliberately outrageous type of rock music.

punnet *n.* small basket or similar container for fruit etc.

punt[1] *n.* shallow flat-bottomed boat with broad square ends. — *v.* propel (a punt) by thrusting with a pole against the bottom of a river; travel in a punt.

punt[2] *v.* kick (a dropped football) before it touches the ground. — *n.* this kick.

punter *n.* person who gambles; (*colloq.*) customer.

puny *a.* (**-ier, -iest**) undersized; feeble. **puniness** *n.*

pup *n.* young dog; young wolf, rat, or seal. — *v.* (**pupped**) give birth to pup(s).

pupa *n.* (*pl.* **-ae**) chrysalis.

pupate *v.* become a pupa. **pupation** *n.*

pupil *n.* person who is taught by another; opening in the centre of the iris of the eye.

puppet *n.* a kind of doll made to move as an entertainment; person or State controlled by another. **puppetry** *n.*

puppy *n.* young dog.

purchase *v.* buy. — *n.* buying; thing bought; firm hold to pull or raise something, leverage. **purchaser** *n.*

purdah *n.* Muslim or Hindu system of secluding women.

pure *a.* not mixed with any other substances; mere; innocent; chaste; (of mathematics or sciences) dealing with theory, not with practical applications.

purée *n.* pulped fruit or vegetables etc. — *v.* make into purée.

purely *adv.* in a pure way; entirely; only.

purgative *a.* strongly laxative. — *n.* purgative substance.

purgatory *n.* place or condition of suffering, esp. (in RC belief) in which souls undergo purification. **purgatorial** *a.*

purge *v.* clear the bowels of by a purgative; rid of undesirable people or things. — *n.* process of purging.

purify *v.* make pure. **purification** *n.*, **purifier** *n.*

purist *n.* stickler for correctness. **purism** *n.*

puritan *n.* person who is strict in morals and regards certain pleasures as sinful. **puritanical** *a.*

purity *n.* pure state or condition.

purl *n.* a kind of knitting stitch. — *v.* produce this stitch (in).

purloin *v.* steal.

purple *a.* & *n.* (of) a colour made by mixing red and blue.

purport *n.* /púrport/ meaning. — *v.* /pərpórt/ have as its apparent meaning; be intended to seem. **purportedly** *adv.*

purpose *n.* intended result of effort; intention to act, determination. — *v.* intend. **on purpose** by intention. **purpose-built** *a.* built for a particular purpose.

purposeful *a.* having or showing a conscious purpose, with determination. **purposefully** *adv.*

purposely *adv.* on purpose.

purr *n.* low vibrant sound that a cat makes

when pleased; similar sound. — *v.* make this sound.

purse *n.* small pouch for carrying money; (*US*) handbag; money, funds. — *v.* pucker (one's lips).

purser *n.* ship's officer in charge of accounts.

pursuance *n.* performance (of duties etc.).

pursue *v.* chase in order to catch or kill; continue, proceed along; engage in. **pursuer** *n.*

pursuit *n.* pursuing; activity to which one gives time or effort.

purulent *a.* of or containing pus. **purulence** *n.*

purvey *v.* supply (articles of food) as a trader. **purveyance** *n.*, **purveyor** *n.*

pus *n.* thick yellowish matter produced from infected tissue.

push *v.* move away by exerting force; thrust forward; make demands on the abilities or tolerance of; urge; sell (drugs) illegally. — *n.* act or force of pushing; vigorous effort. **push off** (*sl.*) go away. **pusher** *n.*

pushchair *n.* folding chair on wheels, in which a child can be pushed along.

pushy *a.* (**-ier, -iest**) (*colloq.*) self-assertive, determined to get on. **pushiness** *n.*

pusillanimous *a.* cowardly. **pusillanimity** *n.*

puss *n.* cat.

pussy *n.* cat. **pussy willow** willow with furry catkins.

pussyfoot *v.* move stealthily; act cautiously.

pustule *n.* pimple, blister. **pustular** *a.*

put *v.* (**put, putting**) cause to be in a certain place, position, state, or relationship; express, phrase; throw (the shot or weight) as an athletic exercise. — *n.* throw of the shot or weight. **put by** save for future use. **put down** suppress; snub; have (an animal) killed; record in writing. **put off** postpone; dissuade, repel. **put out** disconcert; inconvenience; extinguish; dislocate. **put up** construct, build; raise the price of; provide (money etc.); give temporary accommodation. **put-up job** scheme concocted fraudulently. **put upon** (*colloq.*) unfairly burdened. **put up to** instigate (a person) in. **put up with** endure, tolerate.

putative *a.* reputed, supposed. **putatively** *adv.*

putrefy *v.* rot. **putrefaction** *n.*

putrescent *a.* rotting. **putrescence** *n.*

putrid *a.* rotten; stinking.

putt *v.* strike (a golf ball) gently to make it roll along the ground. — *n.* this stroke. **putter** *n.* club used for this.

putty *n.* soft paste that sets hard, used for fixing glass in frames, filling up holes, etc.

puzzle *n.* difficult question or problem; problem or toy designed to test knowledge or ingenuity. — *v.* (cause to) think hard. **puzzlement** *n.*

Pygmy *n.* member of a dwarf Black African people; **pygmy** *a.* unusually small; dwarf.

pyjamas *n.pl.* loose jacket and trousers esp. for sleeping in.

pylon *n.* lattice-work tower used for carrying electricity cables.

pyorrhoea /pīreéə/ *n.* discharge of pus, esp. from tooth-sockets.

pyramid *n.* structure with triangular sloping sides that meet at the top. **pyramidal** *a.*

pyre *n.* pile of wood etc. for burning a dead body.

pyrethrum *n.* a kind of chrysanthemum; insecticide made from its dried flowers.

pyrites /pīrīteez/ *n.* mineral sulphide of (copper and) iron.

pyromaniac *n.* person with an uncontrollable impulse to set things on fire.

pyrotechnics *n.pl.* firework display. **pyrotechnic** *a.*

Pyrrhic victory /pírrik/ one gained at too great a cost.

python *n.* large snake that crushes its prey.

Q

quack [1] *n.* duck's harsh cry. — *v.* make this sound.

quack [2] *n.* person who falsely claims to have medical skill.

quad *n.* (*colloq.*) quadrangle; quadruplet.

quadrangle *n.* four-sided courtyard bordered by large buildings.

quadrant *n.* one-quarter of a circle or of its circumference; graduated instrument for taking angular measurements.

quadraphonic *a.* & *n.* (sound reproduction) using four transmission channels.

quadratic *a.* & *n.* (equation) involving the second and no higher power of an unknown quantity or variable.

quadrilateral *n.* geometric figure with four sides.

quadrille *n.* a kind of square dance.

quadruped *n.* four-footed animal.

quadruple *a.* having four parts or members; four times as much as. — *v.* increase by four times its amount.

quadruplet *n.* one of four children born at one birth.

quaff *v.* drink in large draughts.

quagmire *n.* bog, marsh.

quail [1] *n.* bird related to the partridge.

quail [2] *v.* flinch, show fear.

quaint *a.* odd in a pleasing way. **quaintly** *adv.*, **quaintness** *n.*

quake *v.* shake or tremble, esp. with fear.

qualification *n.* qualifying; thing that qualifies.

qualify *v.* make or become competent, eligible, or legally entitled to do something; limit the meaning of. **qualifier** *n.*

qualitative *a.* of or concerned with quality.

quality *n.* degree of excellence; characteristic, something that is special in a person or thing.

qualm /kwaam/ *n.* misgiving, pang of conscience.

quandary *n.* state of perplexity, difficult situation.

quango *n.* (*pl.* **-os**) administrative body (outside the Civil Service) with senior members appointed by the government.

quantify *v.* express as a quantity. **quantifiable** *a.*

quantitative *a.* of or concerned with quantity.

quantity *n.* amount or number of things; ability to be measured; (*pl.*) large amounts. **quantity surveyor** person who measures and prices building work.

quantum *n.* **quantum theory** theory of physics based on the assumption that energy exists in indivisible units.

quarantine *n.* isolation imposed on those who have been exposed to an infection which they could spread. — *v.* put into quarantine.

quark *n.* component of elementary particles.

quarrel *n.* angry disagreement. — *v.* (**quarrelled**) engage in a quarrel.

quarrelsome *a.* liable to quarrel.

quarry [1] *n.* intended prey or victim; thing sought or pursued.

quarry [2] *n.* open excavation from which stone etc. is obtained. — *v.* obtain from a quarry.

quart *n.* quarter of a gallon, two pints (1.137 litres).

quarter *n.* one of four equal parts; this amount; (*US* & *Canada*) (coin worth) 25 cents; fourth part of a year; point of time 15 minutes before or after every hour; direction, district; mercy towards an opponent; (*pl.*) lodgings, accommodation. — *v.* divide into quarters; put into lodgings. **quarter-final** *n.* contest preceding a semifinal.

quarterdeck *n.* part of a ship's upper deck nearest the stern.

quarterly *a.* & *adv.* (produced or occurring) once in every quarter of a year. — *n.* quarterly periodical.

quartermaster *n.* regimental officer in charge of stores etc.; naval petty officer in charge of steering and signals.

quartet *n.* group of four instruments or voices; music for these.

quartz *n.* a kind of hard mineral. **quartz clock** one operated by electric vibrations of a quartz crystal.

quasar *n.* star-like object that is the source of intense electromagnetic radiation.

quash *v.* annul; suppress.

quasi- *pref.* seeming to be but not really so.

quatrain *n.* stanza of four lines.

quaver *v.* tremble, vibrate; speak or utter in a trembling voice. — *n.* trembling sound; note in music, half a crotchet.

quay /kee/ *n.* landing place built for ships to load or unload alongside. **quayside** *n.*

queasy *a.* feeling slightly sick; squeamish. **queasiness** *n.*

queen *n.* female ruler of a country by right of birth; king's wife; woman or thing regarded as supreme in some way; piece in chess; playing card bearing a picture of a queen; fertile female of bee or ant etc.; (*sl.*) male homosexual. **queen mother** dowager queen who is the reigning sovereign's mother. **queenly** *a.*

queer *a.* strange, odd, eccentric; slightly ill or faint; (*derog.*) homosexual. — *n.* (*derog.*) homosexual. — *v.* spoil. **queer a person's pitch** spoil a person's chances.

quell *v.* suppress.

quench *v.* extinguish (a fire or flame); satisfy (one's thirst) by drinking something; cool by water.

quern *n.* hand-mill for grinding corn or pepper.

querulous *a.* complaining peevishly. **querulously** *adv.*, **querulousness** *n.*

query *n.* question; question mark. — *v.* ask a question or express doubt about.

quest *n.* seeking, search.

question *n.* sentence requesting information; matter for discussion or solution; doubt. — *v.* ask or raise question(s) about. **in question** being discussed or disputed. **no question of** no possibility of. **out of the question** completely impracticable. **question mark** punctuation mark ? placed after a question.

questionable *a.* open to doubt.

questionnaire *n.* list of questions seeking information.

queue /kyoo/ *n.* line of people waiting for something. — *v.* (**queuing**) wait in a queue.

quibble *n.* petty objection. — *v.* make petty objections.

quiche /keesh/ *n.* open tart, usu. with a savoury filling.

quick *a.* taking only a short time; able to learn or think quickly; (of temper) easily roused. — *n.* sensitive flesh below the nails. **quickly** *adv.*, **quickness** *n.*

quicken *v.* make or become quicker or livelier.

quicklime *n.* = lime [1].

quicksand *n.* area of loose wet deep sand into which heavy objects will sink.

quicksilver *n.* mercury.

quid *n.* (*pl.* **quid**) (*sl.*) £1.

quid pro quo thing given in return.

quiescent *a.* inactive, quiet. **quiescence** *n.*

quiet *a.* with little or no sound; free from disturbance or vigorous activity; silent; subdued. — *n.* quietness. — *v.* quieten. **on the quiet** unobtrusively, secretly. **quietly** *adv.*, **quietness** *n.*

quieten *v.* make or become quiet.

quiff *n.* upright tuft of hair.

quill *n.* large wing or tail feather; pen made from this; each of a porcupine's spines.

quilt *n.* padded bed-covering. — *v.* line with padding and fix with lines of stitching.

quin *n.* (*colloq.*) quintuplet.

quince *n.* hard yellowish fruit; tree bearing this.

quinine *n.* bitter-tasting medicine.

quinsy *n.* abscess on a tonsil.

quintessence *n.* essence; perfect example of a quality. **quintessential** *a.*, **quintessentially** *adv.*

quintet *n.* group of five instruments or voices; music for these.

quintuple *a.* having five parts or members; five times as much as. — *v.* increase by five times its amount.

quintuplet *n.* one of five children born at one birth.

quip *n.* witty or sarcastic remark. — *v.* (**quipped**) utter as a quip.

quire *n.* twenty-five or twenty-four sheets of writing paper.

quirk *n.* a peculiarity of behaviour; trick of fate.

quisling *n.* traitor who collaborates with occupying forces.

quit *v.* (**quitted**) leave; abandon; (*colloq.*) cease.

quite *adv.* completely; somewhat; really, actually; (as an answer) I agree. **quite a few** a considerable number.

quits *a.* on even terms after retaliation or repayment.

quiver [1] *n.* case for holding arrows.

quiver [2] *v.* shake or vibrate with a slight rapid motion. — *n.* quivering movement or sound.

quixotic *a.* chivalrous; visionary. **quixotically** *adv.*

quiz *n.* (*pl.* **quizzes**) series of questions testing knowledge, esp. as an entertainment. — *v.* (**quizzed**) interrogate.

quizzical *a.* done in a questioning way, esp. humorously. **quizzically** *adv.*

quoit /koyt/ *n.* ring thrown to encircle a peg in the game of **quoits**.

quorate *a.* having a quorum present.

quorum *n.* minimum number of people that must be present to constitute a valid meeting.

quota *n.* fixed share; maximum number or amount that may be admitted, manufactured, etc.

quotable *a.* worth quoting.

quotation *n.* quoting; passage or price quoted. **quotation marks** punctuation marks (‘ ’ or “ ”) enclosing words quoted.

quote *v.* repeat words from a book or speech; mention in support of a statement; state the price of, estimate.

quotidian *a.* daily.

quotient /kwŏsh'nt/ *n.* result of a division sum.

R

rabbi *n.* (*pl.* **-is**) religious leader of a Jewish congregation.

rabbinical *a.* of rabbis or Jewish doctrines or law.

rabbit *n.* burrowing animal with long ears and a short furry tail.

rabble *n.* disorderly crowd, mob.

rabid *a.* furious, fanatical; affected with rabies. **rabidity** *n.*

rabies *n.* contagious fatal virus disease of dogs etc., that can be transmitted to man.

race [1] *n.* contest of speed; (*pl.*) series of races for horses or dogs. — *v.* compete in a race (with); move or operate at full or excessive speed. **racer** *n.*

race [2] *n.* large group of people with common ancestry and inherited physical characteristics; genus, species, breed, or variety of animals or plants.

racecourse *n.* ground where horse races are run.

racetrack *n.* racecourse; track for motor racing.

raceme *n.* flower cluster with flowers attached by short stalks along a central stem.

racial *a.* of or based on race. **racially** *adv.*

racialism *n.* racism. **racialist** *a.* & *n.*

racism *n.* belief in the superiority of a particular race; antagonism between races; theory that human abilities are determined by race. **racist** *a.* & *n.*

rack [1] *n.* framework for keeping or placing things on; bar with teeth that engage with those of a wheel; instrument of torture on which people were tied and stretched. — *v.* inflict great torment on. **rack one's brains** think hard about a problem.

rack [2] *n.* **rack and ruin** destruction.

racket [1] *n.* stringed bat used in tennis and similar games.

racket [2] *n.* din, noisy fuss; (*sl.*) fraudulent business or scheme.

racketeer *n.* person who operates a fraudulent business etc. **racketeering** *n.*

raconteur *n.* person who is good at telling anecdotes.

racoon *n.* small arboreal mammal of North America.

racy *a.* (**-ier, -iest**) spirited and vigorous in style. **racily** *adv.*

radar *n.* system for detecting objects by means of radio waves.

radial *a.* of rays or radii; having spokes or lines etc. that radiate from a central point; (of a tyre; also **radial-ply**) having the fabric layers parallel and the tread strengthened. — *n.* radial-ply tyre. **radially** *adv.*

radiant *a.* emitting rays of light or heat; emitted in rays; looking very bright and happy. **radiantly** *adv.*, **radiance** *n.*

radiate *v.* spread outwards from a central point; send or be sent out in rays.

radiation *n.* process of radiating; sending out of rays and atomic particles characteristic of radioactive substances; these rays and particles.

radiator *n.* apparatus that radiates heat, esp. a metal case through which steam or hot water circulates; engine-cooling apparatus.

radical *a.* fundamental; drastic, thorough; holding extremist views. — *n.* person desiring radical reforms or holding radical views. **radically** *adv.*

radicle *n.* embryo root.

radio *n.* (*pl.* **-os**) process of sending and receiving messages etc. by electromagnetic waves; transmitter or receiver for this; sound broadcasting, station for this. — *a.* of or involving radio. — *v.* transmit or communicate by radio.

radioactive *a.* emitting radiation caused by decay of atomic nuclei. **radioactivity** *n.*

radiography *n.* production of X-ray photographs. **radiographer** *n.*

radiology *n.* study of X-rays and similar radiation. **radiological** *a.*, **radiologist** *n.*

radiotherapy *n.* treatment of disease by X-rays or similar radiation. **radiotherapist** *n.*

radish *n.* plant with a crisp hot-tasting root that is eaten raw.

radium *n.* radioactive metal obtained from pitchblende.

radius *n.* (*pl.* **-dii**) straight line from the centre to the circumference of a circle or sphere; its length; distance from a centre; thicker long bone of the forearm.

raffia *n.* strips of fibre from the leaves of a kind of palm tree.

raffish *a.* looking vulgarly flashy or rakish. **raffishness** *n.*

raffle *n.* lottery with an object as the prize. — *v.* offer as the prize in a raffle.

raft *n.* flat floating structure of timber etc., used as a boat.

rafter *n.* one of the sloping beams forming the framework of a roof.

rag [1] *n.* torn or worn piece of cloth; (*derog.*) newspaper; (*pl.*) old and torn clothes.

rag [2] *v.* (**ragged**) (*sl.*) tease. — *n.* students' carnival in aid of charity.

ragamuffin *n.* person in ragged dirty clothes.

rage *n.* violent anger; craze, fashion. — *v.* show violent anger; (of a storm or battle) continue furiously.

ragged *a.* torn, frayed; wearing torn clothes; jagged.

raglan *n.* type of sleeve joined to a garment by sloping seams.

ragout /ragōō/ *n.* stew of meat and vegetables.

raid *n.* brief attack to destroy or seize something; surprise visit by police etc. to arrest suspected people or seize illicit goods. — *v.* make a raid on. **raider** *n.*

rail [1] *n.* horizontal bar; any of the lines of metal bars on which trains or trams run; railway(s). — *v.* fit or protect with a rail.

rail [2] *v.* utter angry reproaches.

railing *n.* fence of rails supported on upright metal bars.

railroad *n.* (*US*) railway. — *v.* force into hasty action.

railway *n.* set of rails on which trains run; system of transport using these.

rain *n.* atmospheric moisture falling as drops; a fall of this; shower of things. — *v.* send down or fall as or like rain.

rainbow *n.* arch of colours formed in rain or spray by the sun's rays.

raincoat *n.* rain-resistant coat.

raindrop *n.* single drop of rain.

rainfall *n.* total amount of rain falling in a given time.

rainforest *n.* dense wet tropical forest.

rainwater *n.* water that has fallen as rain.

rainy *a.* (**-ier**, **-iest**) in or on which much rain falls.

raise *v.* bring to or towards a higher level or an upright position; breed, grow; bring up (a child); procure. — *n.* (*US*) increase in salary etc. **raising agent** substance that makes bread etc. swell in cooking.

raisin *n.* dried grape.

raison d'être /ráysoN détrə/ reason for or purpose of a thing's existence.

rake [1] *n.* tool with prongs for gathering of leaves etc. or smoothing loose soil; implement used similarly. — *v.* gather or smooth with a rake; search; direct (gunfire etc.) along. **rake-off** *n.* (*colloq.*) share of profits. **rake up** revive the memory of (an unpleasant incident).

rake [2] *n.* backward slope of an object. — *v.* set at a sloping angle.

rake [3] *n.* man who lives an irresponsible and immoral life. **rakish** *a.* like a rake; jaunty.

rally *v.* bring or come (back) together for a united effort; revive; recover strength. — *n.* act of rallying, recovery; series of strokes in tennis etc.; mass meeting; driving competition over public roads.

ram *n.* uncastrated male sheep; striking or plunging device. — *v.* (**rammed**) strike or push heavily, crash against.

Ramadan *n.* ninth month of the Muslim year, when Muslims fast during daylight hours.

ramble *n.* walk taken for pleasure. — *v.* take a ramble; wander, straggle; talk or write disconnectedly. **rambler** *n.*

ramify *v.* form branches or subdivisions; become complex. **ramification** *n.*

ramp *n.* slope joining two levels.

rampage *v.* /rampáyj/ behave or race about violently. — *n.* /rámpayj/ violent behaviour. **on the rampage** rampaging.

rampant *a.* flourishing excessively, unrestrained.

rampart *n.* broad-topped defensive wall or bank of earth.

ramshackle *a.* tumbledown, rickety.

ran *see* **run**.

ranch *n.* cattle-breeding establishment in North America; farm where certain other animals are bred. — *v.* farm on a ranch. **rancher** *n.*

rancid *a.* smelling or tasting like stale fat. **rancidity** *n.*

rancour *n.* bitter feeling or ill will. **rancorous** *a.*

rand *n.* unit of money in South African countries.

random *a.* done or made etc. at random. — *n.* **at random** without a particular aim or purpose. **randomness** *n.*

randy *a.* (**-ier**, **-iest**) lustful.

rang *see* **ring** [2].

range *n.* line or series of things; limits between which something operates or varies; distance a thing can travel or be effective; distance to an objective; large open area for grazing or hunting; place with targets for shooting practice. — *v.* arrange in row(s) etc.; extend; vary between limits; go about a place. **rangefinder** *n.* device for calculating the distance to a target etc.

rangy *a.* (**-ier**, **-iest**) tall and thin.

rank [1] *n.* line of people or things; place in a scale of quality or value etc.; high social position; (*pl.*) ordinary soldiers, not officers. — *v.* arrange in a rank; assign

a rank to; have a certain rank. **the rank and file** the ordinary people of an organization.
rank [2] *a.* growing too thickly and coarsely; full of weeds; foul-smelling; unmistakably bad. **rankness** *n.*
rankle *v.* cause lasting resentment.
ransack *v.* search thoroughly or roughly; rob or pillage (a place).
ransom *n.* price demanded or paid for the release of a captive. — *v.* demand or pay ransom for.
rant *v.* make a violent speech.
rap *n.* quick sharp blow; knocking sound; monologue recited to music; rock music with recited words; (*sl.*) blame, punishment. — *v.* (**rapped**) knock; (*sl.*) reprimand.
rapacious *a.* grasping, violently greedy. **rapacity** *n.*
rape [1] *v.* have sexual intercourse with (esp. a woman) without consent. — *n.* this act or crime.
rape [2] *n.* plant grown as fodder and for its seeds, which yield oil.
rapid *a.* quick, swift. **rapidly** *adv.*, **rapidity** *n.*
rapids *n.pl.* swift current where a river bed slopes steeply.
rapier *n.* thin light sword.
rapist *n.* person who commits rape.
rapport /rapór/ *n.* harmonious understanding relationship.
rapt *a.* very intent and absorbed, enraptured. **raptly** *adv.*
rapture *n.* intense delight. **rapturous** *a.*, **rapturously** *adv.*
rare [1] *a.* very uncommon; exceptionally good; of low density. **rarely** *adv.*, **rareness** *n.*
rare [2] *a.* (of meat) cooked lightly not thoroughly.
rarebit *n. see* **Welsh rabbit**.
rarefied *a.* (of air) of low density, thin. **rarefaction** *n.*
rarity *n.* rareness; rare thing.
rascal *n.* dishonest or mischievous person. **rascally** *adv.*
rash [1] *n.* eruption of spots or patches on the skin.
rash [2] *a.* acting or done without due consideration of the risks. **rashly** *adv.*, **rashness** *n.*
rasher *n.* slice of bacon or ham.
rasp *n.* coarse file; grating sound. — *v.* scrape with a rasp; utter with or make a grating sound.
raspberry *n.* edible red berry; plant bearing this; (*sl.*) vulgar sound of disapproval.
rat *n.* rodent like a large mouse; scoundrel, treacherous deserter. — *v.* (**ratted**) **rat on** desert or betray. **rat race** fiercely competitive struggle for success.
ratafia *n.* liqueur or biscuit flavoured with fruit kernels.
ratchet *n.* bar or wheel with notches in which a pawl engages to prevent backward movement.
rate *n.* standard of reckoning, ratio of one quantity or amount etc. to another; rapidity. — *v.* estimate the worth or value of; consider, regard as; deserve. **at any rate** no matter what happens; at least.
rather *adv.* slightly; more exactly; by preference; emphatically yes.
ratify *v.* confirm (an agreement etc.) formally. **ratification** *n.*
rating *n.* level at which a thing is rated; non-commissioned sailor.
ratio *n.* (*pl.* **-os**) relationship between two amounts, reckoned as the number of times one contains the other.
ratiocinate *v.* reason logically. **ratiocination** *n.*
ration *n.* fixed allowance of food etc. — *v.* limit to a ration.
rational *a.* able to reason; sane; based on reasoning. **rationally** *adv.*, **rationality** *n.*
rationale /rashənaál/ *n.* fundamental reason; logical basis.
rationalism *n.* treating reason as the basis of belief and knowledge. **rationalist** *n.*, **rationalistic** *a.*
rationalize *v.* invent a rational explanation for; make more efficient by reorganizing. **rationalization** *n.*
rattan *n.* palm with jointed stems.
rattle *v.* (cause to) make a rapid series of short hard sounds; (*sl.*) make nervous. — *n.* rattling sound; device for making this. **rattle off** utter rapidly.
rattlesnake *n.* poisonous American snake with a rattling tail.
raucous *a.* loud and harsh. **raucously** *adv.*, **raucousness** *n.*
raunchy *a.* (**-ier, -iest**) coarsely outspoken; sexually provocative. **raunchily** *adv.*, **raunchiness** *n.*
ravage *v.* do great damage to.
ravages *n.pl.* damage.
rave *v.* talk wildly or furiously; speak with rapturous enthusiasm.
ravel *v.* (**ravelled**) tangle.
raven *n.* black bird with a hoarse cry. — *a.* (of hair) glossy black.
ravenous *a.* very hungry. **ravenously** *adv.*, **ravenousness** *n.*
ravine /rəveén/ *n.* deep narrow gorge.
raving *a.* completely (mad).
ravioli *n.* Italian dish of small pasta cases containing meat.
ravish *v.* rape; enrapture.

raw *a.* not cooked; not yet processed; stripped of skin, sensitive because of this; (of weather) damp and chilly. **raw deal** unfair treatment. **rawness** *n.*

rawhide *n.* untanned leather.

ray [1] *n.* single line or narrow beam of radiation; radiating line.

ray [2] *n.* large marine flatfish.

rayon *n.* synthetic fibre or fabric, made from cellulose.

raze *v.* tear down (a building).

razor *n.* sharp-edged instrument used esp. for shaving hair from the skin.

razzmatazz *n.* excitement; extravagant publicity etc.

RC *abbr.* Roman Catholic.

re *prep.* concerning.

re- *pref.* again; back again.

reach *v.* extend, go as far as; arrive at; stretch out a hand in order to touch or take; establish communication with; achieve, attain. — *n.* distance over which a person or thing can reach; section of a river.

react *v.* cause or undergo a reaction. **reactive** *a.*

reaction *n.* response to a stimulus or act or situation etc.; chemical change produced by substances acting upon each other; occurrence of one condition after a period of the opposite.

reactionary *a.* & *n.* (person) opposed to progress and reform.

reactor *n.* apparatus for the production of nuclear energy.

read *v.* (**read**) understand the meaning of (written or printed words or symbols); speak (such words etc.) aloud; study or discover by reading; interpret mentally; have as wording; (of an instrument) indicate as a measurement. — *n.* (*colloq.*) session of reading.

readable *a.* pleasant to read; legible. **readably** *adv.*

reader *n.* person who reads; senior lecturer at a university; device producing a readable image from a microfilm etc.

readership *n.* readers of a newspaper etc.

readily *adv.* willingly; easily.

readiness *n.* being ready.

readjust *v.* adjust again; adapt oneself again. **readjustment** *n.*

ready *a.* (**-ier, -iest**) fit or available for action or use; willing; about or inclined (to do something); quick. — *adv.* beforehand.

reagent *n.* substance used to produce a chemical reaction.

real *a.* existing as a thing or occurring as a fact; genuine, natural. **real estate** immovable assets, i.e. buildings, land.

realism *n.* representing or viewing things as they are in reality. **realist** *n.*

realistic *a.* showing realism; practical. **realistically** *adv.*

reality *n.* quality of being real; something real and not imaginary.

realize *v.* be or become aware of; accept as a fact; fulfil (a hope or plan). **realization** *n.*

really *adv.* in fact; thoroughly; indeed, I assure you, I protest.

realm *n.* kingdom; field of activity or interest.

ream *n.* quantity of paper (usu. 500 sheets); (*pl.*) great quantity of written matter.

reap *v.* cut (grain etc.) as harvest; receive as the consequence of actions. **reaper** *n.*

reappear *v.* appear again.

rear [1] *n.* back part. — *a.* situated at the rear. **bring up the rear** be last. **rear admiral** naval officer next below vice admiral.

rear [2] *v.* bring up (children); breed and look after (animals); cultivate (crops); set up; (of a horse etc.) raise itself on its hind legs; extend to a great height.

rearguard *n.* troops protecting an army's rear.

rearm *v.* arm again. **rearmament** *n.*

rearrange *v.* arrange in a different way. **rearrangement** *n.*

rearward *a.*, *adv.*, & *n.* (towards or at) the rear. **rearwards** *adv.*

reason *n.* motive, cause, justification; ability to think and draw conclusions; sanity; good sense or judgement. — *v.* use one's ability to think and draw conclusions. **reason with** try to persuade by argument.

reasonable *a.* ready to use or listen to reason; in accordance with reason, logical; moderate, not expensive. **reasonably** *adv.*

reassemble *v.* assemble again.

reassure *v.* restore confidence to. **reassurance** *n.*

rebate *n.* partial refund.

rebel *n.* /rébb'l/ person who rebels. — *v.* /ribél/ (**rebelled**) fight against or refuse allegiance to established government or conventions; resist control. **rebellion** *n.*, **rebellious** *a.*

rebound *v.* /ribównd/ spring back after impact. — *n.* /réebownd/ act of rebounding. **on the rebound** while still reacting to a disappointment etc.

rebuff *v.* & *n.* snub.

rebuild *v.* (**rebuilt**) build again after destruction.

rebuke *v.* reprove. — *n.* reproof.

rebus *n.* representation of a word by pictures etc. suggesting its parts.

rebut *v.* (**rebutted**) disprove. **rebuttal** *n.*

recalcitrant *a.* obstinately disobedient. **recalcitrance** *n.*

recall *v.* summon to return; remember. — *n.* recalling, being recalled.

recant *v.* withdraw and reject (one's former statement or belief). **recantation** *n.*

recap *v.* (**recapped**) (*colloq.*) recapitulate. — *n.* (*colloq.*) recapitulation.

recapitulate *v.* state again briefly. **recapitulation** *n.*

recapture *v.* capture again; experience again. — *n.* recapturing.

recede *v.* go or shrink back; become more distant.

receipt /riseét/ *n.* act of receiving; written acknowledgement that something has been received or money paid.

receive *v.* acquire, accept, or take in; experience, be treated with; greet on arrival.

receiver *n.* person or thing that receives something; one who deals in stolen goods; official who handles the affairs of a bankrupt person or firm; apparatus that receives electrical signals and converts them into sound or a picture; earpiece of a telephone.

recent *a.* happening in a time shortly before the present. **recently** *adv.*

receptacle *n.* thing for holding what is put into it.

reception *n.* act, process, or way of receiving; assembly held to receive guests; place where clients etc. are received on arrival.

receptionist *n.* person employed to receive and direct clients etc.

receptive *a.* quick to receive ideas. **receptiveness** *n.*, **receptivity** *n.*

recess *n.* part or space set back from the line of a wall or room etc.; temporary cessation from business. — *v.* make a recess in or of.

recession *n.* receding from a point or level; temporary decline in economic activity.

recessive *a.* tending to recede.

recidivist *n.* person who persistently relapses into crime. **recidivism** *n.*

recipe /réssipi/ *n.* directions for preparing a dish; way of achieving something.

recipient *n.* person who receives something.

reciprocal *a.* both given and received. **reciprocally** *adv.*, **reciprocity** *n.*

reciprocate *v.* give and receive; make a return for something; move backward and forward alternately. **reciprocation** *n.*

recital *n.* reciting; long account of events; musical entertainment.

recitation *n.* reciting; thing recited.

recite *v.* repeat aloud from memory; state (facts) in order.

reckless *a.* wildly impulsive. **recklessly** *adv.*, **recklessness** *n.*

reckon *v.* count up; have as one's opinion; rely. **reckon with** take into account.

reclaim *v.* take action to recover possession of; make (waste land) usable. **reclamation** *n.*

recline *v.* lean (one's body), lie down.

recluse *n.* person who avoids social life.

recognition *n.* recognizing.

recognizance *n.* pledge made to a law court or magistrate; surety for this.

recognize *v.* know again from one's previous experience; acknowledge as genuine or valid or worthy. **recognizable** *a.*

recoil *v.* spring back; shrink in fear or disgust; have an adverse effect (on the originator). — *n.* act of recoiling.

recollect *v.* remember, call to mind. **recollection** *n.*

recommend *v.* advise; praise as worthy of employment or use etc.; (of qualities etc.) make desirable. **recommendation** *n.*

recompense *v.* repay, compensate. — *n.* repayment.

reconcile *v.* make friendly after an estrangement; induce to tolerate something unwelcome; make compatible. **reconciliation** *n.*

recondite *a.* obscure, dealing with an obscure subject.

recondition *v.* overhaul, repair.

reconnaissance *n.* preliminary survey, esp. exploration of an area for military purposes.

reconnoitre *v.* (**reconnoitring**) make a reconnaissance (of).

reconsider *v.* consider again; consider changing. **reconsideration** *n.*

reconstitute *v.* reconstruct; restore to its original form. **reconstitution** *n.*

reconstruct *v.* construct or enact again. **reconstruction** *n.*

record *v.* /rikórd/ set down in writing or other permanent form; preserve (sound) on a disc or magnetic tape for later reproduction; (of a measuring instrument) indicate, register. — *n.* /rékkord/ information set down in writing etc.; document bearing this; disc bearing recorded sound; facts known about a person's past; best performance or most remarkable event etc. of its kind. — *a.* /rékkord/ best or most extreme hitherto recorded. **off the record** unofficially or not for publication.

recorder *n.* person or thing that records; a kind of flute.

recount *v.* narrate, tell in detail.
re-count *v.* count again. — *n.* second or subsequent counting.
recoup *v.* reimburse or compensate (for); make up (a loss).
recourse *n.* source of help to which one may turn. **have recourse to** turn to for help.
recover *v.* regain possession or control of; return to health. **recovery** *n.*
recreation *n.* pastime; relaxation. **recreational** *a.*
recriminate *v.* make angry accusations in retaliation. **recrimination** *n.*, **recriminatory** *a.*
recruit *n.* new member, esp. of the armed forces. — *v.* form by enlisting recruits; enlist as a recruit. **recruitment** *n.*
rectal *a.* of the rectum.
rectangle *n.* geometric figure with four sides and four right angles, esp. with adjacent sides unequal in length. **rectangular** *a.*
rectify *v.* put right; purify, refine; convert to direct current. **rectification** *n.*, **rectifier** *n.*
rectilinear *a.* bounded by straight lines.
rectitude *n.* correctness of behaviour or procedure.
rector *n.* clergyman in charge of a parish; head of certain schools, colleges, and universities.
rectory *n.* house of a rector.
rectum *n.* last section of the intestine, between colon and anus.
recumbent *a.* lying down.
recuperate *v.* recover (health, strength, or losses). **recuperation** *n.*, **recuperative** *a.*
recur *v.* **(recurred)** happen again or repeatedly.
recurrent *a.* recurring. **recurrence** *n.*
recusant *n.* person who refuses to submit or comply.
recycle *v.* convert (waste material) for reuse.
red *a.* **(redder, reddest)** of or like the colour of blood; (of hair) reddish-brown; Communist, favouring Communism. — *n.* red colour or thing; Communist. **in the red** having a debit balance, in debt. **red carpet** privileged treatment for an important visitor. **red-handed** *a.* in the act of crime. **red herring** misleading clue or diversion. **red-hot** *a.* glowing red from heat; (of news) completely new. **red-letter day** day of a very joyful occurrence. **red light** signal to stop; danger signal. **red tape** excessive formalities in official transactions. **redness** *n.*
redbrick *a.* (of universities) founded in the 19th century or later.
redcurrant *n.* small edible red berry; bush bearing this.
redden *v.* make or become red.
reddish *a.* rather red.
redeem *v.* buy back; convert (tokens etc.) into goods or cash; reclaim; free from sin; make up for (faults). **redemption** *n.*, **redemptive** *a.*
redeploy *v.* send to a new place or task. **redeployment** *n.*
redhead *n.* person with red hair.
redirect *v.* direct or send to another place. **redirection** *n.*
redolent *a.* smelling strongly; reminiscent. **redolence** *n.*
redouble *v.* increase or intensify.
redoubtable *a.* formidable.
redress *v.* set right. — *n.* reparation, amends.
reduce *v.* make or become smaller or less; make lower in rank; slim; subdue; bring into a specified state; convert into a simpler or more general form. **reduction** *n.*, **reducible** *a.*
redundant *a.* superfluous; no longer needed. **redundancy** *n.*
redwood *n.* very tall evergreen Californian tree; its wood.
re-echo *v.* echo; echo repeatedly; resound.
reed *n.* water or marsh plant with tall hollow stems; its stem; vibrating part producing sound in certain wind instruments.
reedy *a.* (of the voice) having a thin high tone. **reediness** *n.*
reef *n.* ridge of rock or sand etc. reaching to or near the surface of water; part of a sail that can be drawn in when there is a high wind. — *v.* shorten (a sail). **reef-knot** *n.* symmetrical double knot.
reefer *n.* thick double-breasted jacket.
reek *n.* strong usu. unpleasant smell. — *v.* smell strongly.
reel *n.* cylinder on which something is wound; lively Scottish or folk dance. — *v.* wind on or off a reel; stagger. **reel off** rattle off without effort.
refectory *n.* dining room of a monastery or college etc.
refer *v.* **(referred) refer to** mention; direct to an authority or specialist; turn to for information.
referee *n.* umpire, esp. in football and boxing; person to whom disputes are referred for decision; person willing to testify to the character or ability of one applying for a job. — *v.* **(refereed)** act as referee in (a match etc.).
reference *n.* act of referring; mention; source of information; testimonial; person willing to testify to another's

character, ability, etc. **in** *or* **with reference to** in connection with, about. **reference book** book providing information. **reference library** one containing books that can be consulted but not taken away.

referendum *n.* (*pl.* **-ums**) referring of a question to the people for decision by a general vote.

referral *n.* referring.

refill *v.* /reéfil/ fill again. — *n.* /reéfil/ second or later filling; material used for this.

refine *v.* remove impurities or defects from; make elegant or cultured. **refined** *a.*

refinement *n.* refining; elegance of behaviour; improvement added; fine distinction.

refinery *n.* establishment where crude substances are refined.

reflate *v.* restore (a financial system) after deflation. **reflation** *n.*, **reflationary** *a.*

reflect *v.* throw back (light, heat, or sound); show an image of; bring (credit or discredit); think deeply. **reflection** *n.*

reflective *a.* reflecting; thoughtful.

reflector *n.* thing that reflects light or heat.

reflex *n.* reflex action. **reflex action** involuntary or instinctive movement in response to a stimulus. **reflex angle** angle of more than 180°.

reflexive *a.* & *n.* (word or form) showing that the action of the verb is performed on its subject (e.g. *he washed himself*).

reflux *n.* flowing back.

reform *v.* improve by removing faults; (cause to) give up bad behaviour. — *n.* reforming. **reformation** *n.*, **reformer** *n.*, **reformist** *n.*

reformatory *a.* reforming. — *n.* institution to which offenders are sent to be reformed.

refract *v.* bend (a ray of light) where it enters water or glass etc. obliquely. **refraction** *n.*, **refractor** *n.*, **refractive** *a.*

refractory *a.* resisting control or discipline; resistant to treatment or heat.

refrain [1] *n.* recurring lines of a song; music for these.

refrain [2] *v.* keep oneself from doing something.

refresh *v.* restore the vigour of by food, drink, or rest; stimulate (a person's memory).

refreshing *a.* restoring vigour, cooling; interesting because of its novelty. **refreshingly** *adv.*

refreshment *n.* process of refreshing; thing that refreshes, (usu. *pl.*) food and drink.

refrigerate *v.* make extremely cold, esp. in order to preserve. **refrigerant** *n.*, **refrigeration** *n.*

refrigerator *n.* cabinet or room in which food is stored at a very low temperature.

refuge *n.* shelter from pursuit or danger or trouble.

refugee *n.* person who has left home and seeks refuge (e.g. from war or persecution) elsewhere.

refund *v.* /rifúnd/ pay back. — *n.* /reéfund/ repayment, money refunded.

refurbish *v.* make clean or bright again, redecorate. **refurbishment** *n.*

refuse [1] /rifyōōz/ *v.* say or show that one is unwilling to accept or give or do (what is asked or required). **refusal** *n.*

refuse [2] /réfyōōss/ *n.* waste material.

refute *v.* prove (a statement or person) to be wrong. **refutation** *n.*

regain *v.* obtain again after loss; reach again.

regal *a.* like or fit for a king. **regally** *adv.*, **regality** *n.*

regale *v.* feed or entertain well.

regalia *n.pl.* emblems of royalty or rank.

regard *v.* look steadily at; consider to be. — *n.* steady gaze; heed; respect; (*pl.*) kindly greetings conveyed in a message. **as regards** regarding.

regarding *prep.* with reference to.

regardless *a.* & *adv.* heedless(ly).

regatta *n.* boat or yacht races organized as a sporting event.

regency *n.* rule by a regent; period of this.

regenerate *v.* give new life or vigour to. **regeneration** *n.*, **regenerative** *a.*

regent *n.* person appointed to rule while the monarch is a minor or ill or absent.

reggae *n.* West Indian style of music, with a strong beat.

regicide *n.* killing or killer of a king. **regicidal** *a.*

regime /rayzheém/ *n.* method or system of government.

regimen *n.* prescribed course of treatment etc.; way of life.

regiment *n.* permanent unit of an army; large array or number of things. — *v.* organize rigidly. **regimentation** *n.*

regimental *a.* of an army regiment.

region *n.* part of a surface, space, or body; administrative division of a country. **in the region of** approximately. **regional** *a.*

register *n.* official list; range of a voice or musical instrument. — *v.* enter in a register; record in writing; notice and remember; indicate, record; make an impression. **register office** place where records of births, marriages, and deaths are kept and civil marriages are performed. **registration** *n.*

registrar *n.* official responsible for keeping written records; hospital doctor ranking just below specialist.

registry *n.* registration; place where written records are kept. **registry office** register office.

regress *v.* relapse to an earlier or more primitive state. **regression** *n.*, **regressive** *a.*

regret *n.* feeling of sorrow about a loss, or of annoyance or repentance. — *v.* (**regretted**) feel regret about. **regretful** *a.*, **regretfully** *adv.*

regrettable *a.* that is to be regretted. **regrettably** *adv.*

regular *a.* acting or occurring or done in a uniform manner or at a fixed time or interval; conforming to a rule or habit; even, symmetrical; forming a country's permanent armed forces. — *n.* regular soldier etc.; (*colloq.*) regular customer etc. **regularly** *adv.*, **regularity** *n.*

regularize *v.* make regular; make lawful or correct. **regularization** *n.*

regulate *v.* control by rules; adjust to work correctly or according to one's requirements. **regulator** *n.*

regulation *n.* process of regulating; rule.

regurgitate *v.* bring (swallowed food) up again to the mouth; cast out again. **regurgitation** *n.*

rehabilitate *v.* restore to a normal life or good condition. **rehabilitation** *n.*

rehash *v.* /reéhásh/ put (old material) into a new form. — *n.* /reéhash/ rehashing; thing made of rehashed material.

rehearse *v.* practise beforehand; enumerate. **rehearsal** *n.*

rehouse *v.* provide with new accommodation.

reign *n.* sovereignty, rule. — *v.* rule as king or queen; be supreme.

reimburse *v.* repay (a person), refund. **reimbursement** *n.*

rein *n.* (also *pl.*) long strap fastened to a bridle, used to guide or check a horse; means of control. — *v.* check or control with reins.

reincarnation *n.* rebirth of the soul in another body after death of the first. **reincarnate** *v.*

reindeer *n.* (*pl.* **reindeer**) deer of Arctic regions, with large antlers.

reinforce *v.* strengthen with additional men, material, or quantity. **reinforcement** *n.*

reinstate *v.* restore to a previous position. **reinstatement** *n.*

reiterate *v.* say or do again or repeatedly. **reiteration** *n.*

reject *v.* /rijékt/ refuse to accept. — *n.* /reéjekt/ person or thing rejected. **rejection** *n.*

rejig *v.* (**rejigged**) re-equip for new work; rearrange.

rejoice *v.* feel or show great joy; gladden.

rejoin *v.* join again; retort.

rejoinder *n.* answer, retort.

rejuvenate *v.* restore youthful appearance or vigour to. **rejuvenation** *n.*, **rejuvenator** *n.*

relapse *v.* fall back into a previous state; become worse after improvement. — *n.* relapsing.

relate *v.* narrate; establish a relation between; have a connection with; establish a successful relationship.

related *a.* having a common descent or origin.

relation *n.* similarity connecting persons or things; relative; narrating; (*pl.*) dealings with others; (*pl.*) sexual intercourse. **relationship** *n.*

relative *a.* considered in relation to something else; having a connection. — *n.* person related to another by descent or marriage. **relatively** *adv.*

relativity *n.* being relative; Einstein's theory of the universe, showing that all motion is relative and treating time as a fourth dimension related to space.

relax *v.* make or become less tight or less tense or less strict; rest from work, indulge in recreation. **relaxation** *n.*

relay *n.* /reélay/ fresh set of workers relieving others; relay race; relayed message or transmission; device relaying things or activating an electrical circuit. — *v.* /riláy/ (**relayed**) receive and pass on or retransmit. **relay race** race between teams in which each person in turn covers a part of the total distance.

release *v.* set free; remove from a fixed position; make (information, a film or recording) available to the public. — *n.* releasing; handle or catch etc. that unfastens something; information or a film etc. released.

relegate *v.* consign to a less important place or state or group. **relegation** *n.*

relent *v.* become less severe or more lenient. **relentless** *a.*, **relentlessly** *adv.*

relevant *a.* related to the matter in hand. **relevance** *n.*

reliable *a.* able to be relied on; consistently good. **reliably** *adv.*, **reliability** *n.*

reliance *n.* relying; trust, confidence. **reliant** *a.*

relic *n.* thing that survives from earlier times; (*pl.*) remains.

relief *n.* ease given by reduction or removal of pain or anxiety etc.; thing that breaks up monotony; assistance to those in need; person replacing one who is on duty; carving etc. in which the design projects from a surface; similar effect given by colour or shading. **relief road** road by which traffic can avoid a congested area.

relieve *v.* give or bring relief to; release from a task or duty; raise the siege of. **relieve oneself** urinate or defecate.

religion *n.* belief in and worship of a superhuman controlling power; system of this; influence compared to religious faith.

religious *a.* of religion; devout, pious; very conscientious. **religiously** *adv.*

relinquish *v.* give up, cease from. **relinquishment** *n.*

reliquary *n.* receptacle for relic(s) of a holy person.

relish *n.* great enjoyment of something; appetizing flavour, thing giving this. — *v.* enjoy greatly.

relocate *v.* move to a different place. **relocation** *n.*

reluctant *a.* unwilling, grudging one's consent. **reluctantly** *adv.*, **reluctance** *n.*

rely *v.* **rely on** trust confidently, depend on for help etc.

remain *v.* stay; be left or left behind; continue in the same condition.

remainder *n.* remaining people or things or part; quantity left after subtraction or division. — *v.* dispose of unsold copies of (a book) at a reduced price.

remains *n.pl.* what remains, surviving parts; dead body.

remand *v.* send back (a prisoner) into custody while further evidence is sought. — *n.* **on remand** remanded.

remark *n.* spoken or written comment, thing said. — *v.* make a remark, say; notice.

remarkable *a.* worth noticing, unusual. **remarkably** *adv.*

remedy *n.* thing that cures or relieves a disease or puts right a matter. — *v.* be a remedy for, put right. **remedial** *a.*

remember *v.* keep in one's mind and recall at will. **remembrance** *n.*

remind *v.* cause to remember.

reminder *n.* thing that reminds someone, letter sent as this.

reminisce *v.* think or talk about past events.

reminiscence *n.* reminiscing; (usu. *pl.*) account of what one remembers.

reminiscent *a.* having characteristics that remind one (of something).

remiss *a.* negligent.

remission *n.* remitting of a debt or penalty; reduction of force or intensity.

remit *v.* /rimít/ (**remitted**) cancel (a debt or punishment); make or become less intense; send (money etc.); refer (a matter for decision) to an authority. — *n.* /reémit/ terms of reference.

remittance *n.* sending of money; money sent.

remnant *n.* small remaining quantity; surviving trace.

remonstrate *v.* make a protest. **remonstrance** *n.*

remorse *n.* deep regret for one's wrongdoing. **remorseful** *a.*, **remorsefully** *adv.*

remorseless *a.* relentless. **remorselessly** *adv.*

remote *a.* far away in place or time; not close; slight. **remotely** *adv.*, **remoteness** *n.*

removable *a.* able to be removed.

remove *v.* take off or away; dismiss from office; get rid of. — *n.* degree of remoteness or difference. **remover** *n.*, **removal** *n.*

remunerate *v.* pay or reward for services. **remuneration** *n.*

remunerative *a.* giving good remuneration, profitable.

Renaissance *n.* revival of art and learning in Europe in the 14th–16th centuries; **renaissance** any similar revival.

renal *a.* of the kidneys.

rend *v.* (**rent**) tear.

render *v.* give, esp. in return; submit (a bill etc.); cause to become; give a performance of; translate; melt down (fat).

rendezvous /róndivoo/ *n.* (*pl.* **-vous**) prearranged meeting or meeting place. — *v.* meet at a rendezvous.

rendition *n.* way something is rendered or performed.

renegade *n.* person who deserts from a group or cause etc.

renege /rináyg/ *v.* fail to keep a promise or agreement.

renew *v.* restore to its original state; replace with a fresh thing or supply; get or make or give again. **renewal** *n.*

rennet *n.* substance used to curdle milk in making cheese.

renounce *v.* give up formally; reject. **renouncement** *n.*

renovate *v.* repair, restore to good condition. **renovation** *n.*, **renovator** *n.*

renown *n.* fame.

renowned *a.* famous.

rent [1] *see* **rend**. — *n.* torn place.

rent [2] *n.* periodical payment for use of land, rooms, machinery, etc. — *v.* pay or receive rent for.
rental *n.* rent; renting.
renunciation *n.* renouncing.
reorganize *v.* organize in a new way. **reorganization** *n.*
rep [1] *n.* (*colloq.*) business firm's travelling representative.
rep [2] *n.* (*colloq.*) repertory.
repair *v.* put into good condition after damage or wear; make amends for. — *n.* process of repairing; repaired place; condition as regards being repaired. **repairer** *n.*
repartee *n.* witty reply; exchange of witty remarks.
repast *n.* (*formal*) a meal.
repatriate *v.* send or bring back (a person) to his or her own country. **repatriation** *n.*
repay *v.* (**repaid**) pay back. **repayment** *n.*, **repayable** *a.*
repeal *v.* withdraw (a law) officially. — *n.* repealing of a law.
repeat *v.* say or do or produce or occur again; tell (a thing told to oneself) to another person. — *n.* repeating; thing repeated.
repeatedly *adv.* again and again.
repel *v.* (**repelled**) drive away; be impossible for (a substance) to penetrate; be repulsive or distasteful to. **repellent** *a.* & *n.*
repent *v.* feel regret about (what one has done or failed to do). **repentance** *n.*, **repentant** *a.*
repercussion *n.* recoil; echo; indirect effect or reaction.
repertoire /réppərtwaar/ *n.* stock of songs, plays, etc., that a person or company is prepared to perform.
repertory *n.* repertoire; theatrical performances of various plays for short periods by one company (**repertory company**).
repetition *n.* repeating; instance of this.
repetitious *a.* repetitive.
repetitive *a.* characterized by repetition. **repetitively** *adv.*
repine *v.* fret, be discontented.
replace *v.* put back in its place; substitute for. **replacement** *n.*
replay *v.* /reepláy/ play again. — *n.* /reeplay/ replaying.
replenish *v.* refill; renew (a supply etc.). **replenishment** *n.*
replica *n.* exact copy.
replicate *v.* make a replica of. **replication** *n.*
reply *v.* & *n.* answer.
report *v.* give an account of; tell as news; make a formal complaint about; present oneself on arrival. — *n.* spoken or written account; written statement about a pupil's work etc.; rumour; explosive sound.
reporter *n.* person employed to report news etc. for publication or broadcasting.
repose *n.* rest, sleep; tranquillity. — *v.* rest, lie.
repository *n.* storage place.
repossess *v.* take back something for which payments have not been made. **repossession** *n.*
reprehend *v.* rebuke.
reprehensible *a.* deserving rebuke. **reprehensibly** *adv.*
represent *v.* show in a picture or play etc.; describe or declare (to be); be an example or embodiment of; act on behalf of. **representation** *n.*
representative *a.* typical of a group or class. — *n.* person's or firm's agent; person chosen to represent others.
repress *v.* suppress, keep (emotions) from finding an outlet. **repression** *n.*, **repressive** *a.*
reprieve *n.* postponement or cancellation of punishment (esp. death sentence); temporary relief from trouble. — *v.* give a reprieve to.
reprimand *v.* & *n.* rebuke.
reprint *v.* /reeprínt/ print again. — *n.* /reeprint/ book reprinted.
reprisal *n.* act of retaliation.
reproach *v.* express disapproval to (a person) for a fault or offence. — *n.* act or instance of reproaching; (cause of) discredit. **reproachful** *a.*, **reproachfully** *adv.*
reprobate *n.* immoral or unprincipled person.
reproduce *v.* produce again; produce a copy of; produce further members of the same species. **reproduction** *n.*
reproductive *a.* of reproduction.
reproof *n.* expression of condemnation for a fault or offence.
reprove *v.* give a reproof to.
reptile *n.* member of the class of cold-blooded animals with a backbone and rough or scaly skin. **reptilian** *a.* & *n.*
republic *n.* country in which the supreme power is held by the people or their representatives.
republican *a.* of or advocating a republic. — *n.* person advocating republican government.
repudiate *v.* reject or disown utterly, deny. **repudiation** *n.*
repugnant *a.* distasteful, objectionable. **repugnance** *n.*

repulse *v.* drive back (an attacking force); reject, rebuff. — *n.* driving back; rejection, rebuff.

repulsion *n.* repelling; strong feeling of distaste, revulsion.

repulsive *a.* arousing disgust; able to repel. **repulsively** *adv.*, **repulsiveness** *n.*

reputable *a.* having a good reputation, respected.

reputation *n.* what is generally believed about a person or thing.

repute *n.* reputation.

reputed *a.* said or thought to be.

reputedly *adv.* by repute.

request *n.* asking for something; thing asked for. — *v.* make a request (for or of).

requiem /rékwi-em/ *n.* special Mass for the repose of the soul(s) of the dead; music for this.

require *v.* need, depend on for success or fulfilment; order, oblige.

requirement *n.* need.

requisite *a.* required, necessary. — *n.* thing needed.

requisition *n.* formal written demand, order laying claim to use of property or materials. — *v.* demand or order by this.

requite *v.* make a return for.

resale *n.* sale to another person of something one has bought.

rescind *v.* repeal or cancel (a law or rule etc.).

rescue *v.* save from danger or capture etc. — *n.* rescuing. **rescuer** *n.*

research *n.* study and investigation, esp. to discover new facts. — *v.* perform research (into). **researcher** *n.*

resemble *v.* be like. **resemblance** *n.*

resent *v.* feel displeased and indignant about. **resentment** *n.*, **resentful** *a.*, **resentfully** *adv.*

reservation *n.* reserving; reserved accommodation etc.; doubt; land set aside, esp. for occupation by American Indians.

reserve *v.* put aside for future or special use; order or set aside for a particular person; retain. — *n.* thing(s) reserved, extra stock available; (also *pl.*) forces outside the regular armed services; land set aside for special use; substitute player in team games; lowest acceptable price for an item to be auctioned; tendency to avoid showing feelings or friendliness. **in reserve** unused and available.

reserved *a.* (of a person) showing reserve of manner.

reservist *n.* member of a reserve force.

reservoir /rézzərvwaar/ *n.* natural or artificial lake that is a source or store of water to a town etc.; container for a supply of fluid.

reshuffle *v.* interchange; reorganize. — *n.* reshuffling.

reside *v.* dwell permanently.

residence *n.* residing; one's dwelling. **in residence** living in a specified place to perform one's work.

resident *a.* residing, in residence. — *n.* permanent inhabitant; (at a hotel) person staying overnight.

residential *a.* containing dwellings; of or based on residence.

residual *a.* left over as a residue. **residually** *adv.*

residue *n.* what is left over.

resign *v.* give up (one's job or property or claim etc.). **resign oneself to** be ready to accept and endure. **resignation** *n.*

resigned *a.* having resigned oneself. **resignedly** *adv.*

resilient *a.* springy; readily recovering from shock etc. **resiliently** *adv.*, **resilience** *n.*

resin *n.* sticky substance from plants and certain trees; similar substance made synthetically, used in plastics. **resinous** *a.*

resist *v.* oppose strongly or forcibly; withstand; refrain from accepting or yielding to. **resistance** *n.*, **resistant** *a.*

resistible *a.* able to be resisted.

resistivity *n.* resistance to the passage of electric current.

resistor *n.* device having resistance to the passage of electric current.

resolute *a.* showing great determination. **resolutely** *adv.*, **resoluteness** *n.*

resolution *n.* resolving; great determination; formal statement of a committee's opinion.

resolve *v.* decide firmly; solve or settle (a problem or doubts); separate into constituent parts. — *n.* great determination.

resonant *a.* resounding, echoing; reinforcing sound, esp. by vibration. **resonance** *n.*

resonate *v.* produce or show resonance. **resonator** *n.*

resort *v.* turn for help, adopt as an expedient. — *n.* expedient; popular holiday place.

resound *v.* fill a place or be filled with sound; echo.

resource *n.* something to which one can turn for help; ingenuity; (*pl.*) available assets.

resourceful *a.* clever at finding ways of doing things. **resourcefully** *adv.*, **resourcefulness** *n.*

respect *n.* admiration or esteem; politeness arising from this; consideration; relation, reference; particular aspect. — *v.* feel or show respect for.

respectable *a.* worthy of respect; considerable. **respectably** *adv.*, **respectability** *n.*

respective *a.* belonging to each as an individual. **respectively** *adv.*

respiration *n.* breathing.

respirator *n.* device worn over the nose and mouth to purify air before it is inhaled; device for giving artificial respiration.

respiratory *a.* of respiration.

respire *v.* breathe.

respite *n.* interval of rest or relief; permitted delay.

resplendent *a.* brilliant with colour or decorations. **resplendently** *adv.*

respond *v.* answer; react.

respondent *n.* defendant in a lawsuit, esp. in a divorce case.

response *n.* answer; act, feeling, or movement produced by a stimulus or another's action.

responsibility *n.* being responsible; thing for which one is responsible.

responsible *a.* liable to be blamed for loss or failure etc.; having to account for one's actions; sensible; trustworthy; involving important duties; being the cause of something. **responsibly** *adv.*

responsive *a.* responding well to an influence. **responsiveness** *n.*

rest [1] *v.* be still; (cause or allow to) cease from tiring activity; (of a matter) be left without further discussion; place or be placed for support; rely. — *n.* (period of) inactivity or sleep; prop or support for an object.

rest [2] *v.* remain in a specified state. — *n.* **the rest** the remaining part; the others.

restaurant *n.* place where meals can be bought and eaten.

restaurateur *n.* restaurant-keeper.

restful *a.* giving rest; relaxing. **restfully** *adv.*, **restfulness** *n.*

restitution *n.* restoring of a thing to its proper owner or original state; compensation.

restive *a.* restless; impatient. **restively** *adv.*, **restiveness** *n.*

restless *a.* unable to rest or be still. **restlessly** *adv.*, **restlessness** *n.*

restoration *n.* restoring; restored thing.

restorative *a.* restoring health or strength. — *n.* restorative food, medicine, or treatment.

restore *v.* bring back to its original state (e.g. by repairing), or to good health or vigour; put back in a former position. **restorer** *n.*

restrain *v.* hold back from movement or action, keep under control. **restraint** *n.*

restrict *v.* put a limit on, subject to limitations. **restriction** *n.*, **restrictive** *a.*

result *n.* product of an activity or operation or calculation; score, marks, or name of the winner in a sports event or competition. — *v.* occur or have as a result.

resultant *a.* occurring as a result.

resume *v.* get or take again; begin again after stopping. **resumption** *n.*, **resumptive** *a.*

résumé /rézyoomay/ *n.* summary.

resurface *v.* put a new surface on; return to the surface.

resurgence *n.* revival after destruction or disappearance.

resurrect *v.* bring back into use.

resurrection *n.* rising from the dead; revival after disuse.

resuscitate *v.* revive. **resuscitation** *n.*

retail *n.* selling of goods to the public. — *a.* & *adv.* in the retail trade. — *v.* sell or be sold in the retail trade; relate details of. **retailer** *n.*

retain *v.* keep, esp. in one's possession or in use; hold in place.

retainer *n.* fee paid to retain services.

retaliate *v.* repay an injury or insult etc. by inflicting one in return. **retaliation** *n.*, **retaliatory** *a.*

retard *v.* cause delay to. **retardation** *n.*

retarded *a.* backward in mental or physical development.

retch *v.* strain one's throat as if vomiting.

retention *n.* retaining.

retentive *a.* able to retain things.

rethink *v.* (**rethought**) reconsider; plan again and differently.

reticent *a.* not revealing one's thoughts. **reticence** *n.*

retina *n.* (*pl.* **-as**) membrane at the back of the eyeball, sensitive to light.

retinue *n.* attendants accompanying an important person.

retire *v.* give up one's regular work because of age; cause (an employee) to do this; withdraw, retreat; go to bed. **retirement** *n.*

retiring *a.* shy, avoiding society.

retort [1] *v.* make (as) a witty or angry reply. — *n.* retorting; reply of this kind.

retort [2] *n.* vessel with a bent neck, used in distilling; vessel used in making gas or steel.

retouch *v.* touch up (a picture or photograph).

retrace *v.* go back over or repeat (a route).

retract *v.* withdraw. **retraction** *n.*, **retractor** *n.*, **retractable** *a.*

retractile *a.* able to be retracted.

retreat *v.* withdraw, esp. after defeat or when faced with difficulty. — *n.*

retreating, withdrawal; military signal for this; place of shelter or seclusion.

retrench *v.* reduce (expenditure or operations). **retrenchment** *n.*

retrial *n.* trial of a lawsuit or defendant again.

retribution *n.* deserved punishment.

retrieve *v.* regain possession of; extract; bring back; set right (an error etc.). **retrieval** *n.*

retriever *n.* dog of a breed used to retrieve game.

retroactive *a.* operating retrospectively. **retroactively** *adv.*

retrograde *a.* going backwards; reverting to an inferior state.

retrogress *v.* move backwards, deteriorate. **retrogression** *n.*, **retrogressive** *a.*

retrospect *n.* **in retrospect** when one looks back on a past event.

retrospective *a.* looking back on the past; (of a law etc.) made to apply to the past as well as the future. **retrospectively** *adv.*

retroverted *a.* turned backwards. **retroversion** *n.*

retry *v.* (**-tried**) try (a lawsuit or defendant) again.

return *v.* come or go back; bring, give, put, or send back. — *n.* returning; profit; return ticket; return match; formal report submitted by order. **return match** second match between the same opponents. **return ticket** ticket for a journey to a place and back again.

reunion *n.* gathering of people who were formerly associated.

reunite *v.* bring or come together again.

reusable *a.* able to be used again.

rev *n.* (*colloq.*) revolution of an engine. — *v.* (**revved**) (*colloq.*) cause (an engine) to run quickly; (of an engine) revolve.

Rev. *abbr.* Reverend.

revalue *v.* put a new (esp. higher) value on. **revaluation** *n.*

revamp *v.* renovate, give a new appearance to.

reveal *v.* make visible by uncovering; make known.

reveille /riválli/ *n.* military waking-signal.

revel *v.* (**revelled**) take great delight; hold revels. **revels** *n.pl.* lively festivities, merrymaking. **reveller** *n.*, **revelry** *n.*

revelation *n.* revealing; (surprising) thing revealed.

revenge *n.* injury inflicted in return for what one has suffered; opportunity to defeat a victorious opponent. — *v.* avenge.

revenue *n.* country's income from taxes etc.; department collecting this.

reverberate *v.* echo, resound. **reverberation** *n.*

revere *v.* feel deep respect or religious veneration for.

reverence *n.* feeling of awe and respect or veneration.

reverend *a.* deserving to be treated with respect; **Reverend** title of a member of the clergy.

reverent *a.* feeling or showing reverence. **reverently** *adv.*

reverie *n.* daydream.

revers /riveér/ *n.* (*pl.* **revers**) turned-back front edge at the neck of a jacket or bodice.

reversal *n.* reversing.

reverse *a.* opposite in character or order; upside down. — *v.* turn the other way round or upside down or inside out; convert to the opposite; annul (a decree etc.); move backwards or in the opposite direction. — *n.* reverse side or effect; piece of misfortune. **reversely** *adv.*, **reversible** *a.*

revert *v.* return to a former condition or habit; return to a subject in talk etc.; (of property etc.) pass to another holder when its present holder relinquishes it. **reversion** *n.*, **reversionary** *a.*

review *n.* general survey of events or a subject; reconsideration; ceremonial inspection of troops etc.; critical report of a book or play etc. — *v.* make or write a review of. **reviewer** *n.*

revile *v.* criticize angrily in abusive language.

revise *v.* re-examine and alter or correct; study again (work already learnt) in preparation for an examination. **reviser** *n.*, **revision** *n.*, **revisory** *a.*

revivalist *n.* person who seeks to promote religious fervour. **revivalism** *n.*, **revivalistic** *a.*

revive *v.* come or bring back to life or consciousness or vigour, or into use. **revival** *n.*

revocable *a.* able to be revoked.

revoke *v.* withdraw (a decree or licence etc.). **revocation** *n.*

revolt *v.* take part in a rebellion; be in a mood of protest or defiance; cause strong disgust in. — *n.* act or state of rebelling; sense of disgust.

revolting *a.* in revolt; causing disgust.

revolution *n.* revolving, single complete orbit or rotation; complete change of method or conditions; substitution of a new system of government, esp. by force.

revolutionary *a.* involving a great change; of political revolution. — *n.* person who begins or supports a political revolution.

revolutionize *v.* alter completely.

revolve *v.* turn round; move in an orbit.

revolver *n.* a kind of pistol.

revue *n.* entertainment consisting of a series of items.

revulsion *n.* strong disgust; sudden violent change of feeling.

reward *n.* something given or received in return for a service or merit etc. — *v.* give a reward to.

rewire *v.* renew the electrical wiring of.

rewrite *v.* (**rewrote, rewritten**) write again in a different form or style.

rhapsodize *v.* talk or write about something ecstatically.

rhapsody *n.* ecstatic statement; romantic musical composition. **rhapsodic** *a.*

rheostat *n.* device for varying the resistance to electric current. **rheostatic** *a.*

rhesus *n.* small Indian monkey used in biological experiments. **rhesus factor** substance usu. present in human blood (**rhesus-positive** having this; **rhesus-negative** not having it).

rhetoric *n.* art of using words impressively; impressive language.

rhetorical *a.* expressed so as to sound impressive. **rhetorical question** one used for dramatic effect, not seeking an answer. **rhetorically** *adv.*

rheumatic *a.* of or affected with rheumatism. **rheumaticky** *a.*

rheumatism *n.* disease causing pain in the joints, muscles, or fibrous tissue.

rheumatoid *a.* having the character of rheumatism.

rhinestone *n.* imitation diamond.

rhino *n.* (*pl.* **rhino** *or* **-os**) (*colloq.*) rhinoceros.

rhinoceros *n.* (*pl.* **-oses**) large thick-skinned animal with one horn or two horns on its nose.

rhizome *n.* root-like stem producing roots and shoots.

rhodium *n.* metal resembling platinum.

rhododendron *n.* evergreen shrub with clusters of flowers.

rhomboid *a.* like a rhombus. — *n.* rhomboid figure.

rhombus *n.* quadrilateral with opposite sides and angles equal (and not right angles).

rhubarb *n.* garden plant with red leaf-stalks that are used like fruit.

rhyme *n.* identity of sound between words or syllables; word providing a rhyme to another; poem with line-endings that rhyme. — *v.* form a rhyme.

rhythm *n.* pattern produced by emphasis and duration of notes in music or of syllables in words, or by regular movements or events. **rhythmic, rhythmical** *adjs.*, **rhythmically** *adv.*

rib *n.* one of the curved bones round the chest; structural part resembling this; pattern of raised lines in knitting. — *v.* (**ribbed**) support with ribs; knit as rib; (*colloq.*) tease.

ribald *a.* humorous in a cheerful but vulgar or disrespectful way. **ribaldry** *n.*

riband *n.* ribbon.

ribbon *n.* narrow band of silky material; strip resembling this.

ribonucleic acid substance controlling protein synthesis in cells.

rice *n.* cereal plant grown in marshes in hot countries, with seeds used as food; these seeds.

rich *a.* having much wealth; abundant; containing a large proportion of something (e.g. fat, fuel); (of soil) fertile; (of colour or sound or smell) pleasantly deep and strong. **riches** *n.pl.* wealth. **richness** *n.*

richly *adv.* in a rich way; fully, thoroughly.

rick [1] *n.* built stack of hay etc.

rick [2] *n.* slight sprain or strain. — *v.* sprain or strain slightly.

rickety *a.* shaky, insecure.

rickshaw *n.* two-wheeled hooded vehicle used in the Far East, drawn by one or more people.

ricochet /ríkkəshay/ *n.* & *v.* (**ricocheted**) rebound from a surface after striking it with a glancing blow.

rid *v.* (**rid, ridding**) free from something unpleasant or unwanted. **get rid of** cause to go away; free oneself of.

ridden *see* **ride**. — *a.* full of.

riddle [1] *n.* question etc. designed to test ingenuity esp. for amusement; something puzzling or mysterious.

riddle [2] *n.* coarse sieve. — *v.* pass through a riddle; permeate thoroughly.

ride *v.* (**rode, ridden**) sit on and be carried by (a horse or bicycle etc.); travel in a vehicle; float (on). — *n.* spell of riding; journey in a vehicle; track for riding on.

rider *n.* one who rides a horse etc.; additional statement.

ridge *n.* narrow raised strip; line where two upward slopes meet; elongated region of high barometric pressure. **ridged** *a.*

ridicule *n.* making or being made to seem ridiculous. — *v.* subject to ridicule, make fun of.

ridiculous *a.* deserving to be laughed at; not worth serious consideration. **ridiculously** *adv.*

rife *a.* occurring frequently, widespread. **rife with** full of.

riff *n.* short repeated phrase in jazz etc.

riffle *v.* flick through (pages etc.).

riff-raff *n.* rabble; disreputable people.

rifle *n.* a kind of gun with a long barrel.

— *v.* search and rob; cut spiral grooves in (a gun barrel).

rift *n.* cleft in earth or rock; crack, split; breach in friendly relations. **rift-valley** *n.* steep-sided valley formed by subsidence.

rig [1] *v.* (**rigged**) provide with clothes or equipment; fit (a ship) with spars, ropes, etc.; set up, esp. in a makeshift way. — *n.* way a ship's masts and sails etc. are arranged; apparatus for drilling an oil well etc. **rig-out** *n.* (*colloq.*) outfit.

rig [2] *v.* (**rigged**) manage or control fraudulently.

rigging *n.* ropes etc. used to support a ship's masts and sails.

right *a.* morally good; in accordance with justice; proper; correct, true; in a good condition; of or on the side of the body which in most people has the more-used hand. — *n.* what is just; something one is entitled to; right hand or foot; people supporting more conservative policies than others in their group. — *v.* restore to a correct or upright position; set right. — *adv.* on or towards the right-hand side; directly. **in the right** having truth or justice on one's side. **right angle** angle of 90°. **right away** immediately. **right-hand man** indispensable assistant. **right-handed** *a.* using the right hand. **right of way** right to pass over another's land; path subject to this; right to proceed while another vehicle must wait. **rightly** *adv.*, **rightness** *n.*

righteous /ríchəss/ *a.* doing what is morally right, making a show of this; morally justifiable. **righteously** *adv.*, **righteousness** *n.*

rightful *a.* just, proper, legal. **rightfully** *adv.*, **rightfulness** *n.*

rigid *a.* stiff; strict, inflexible. **rigidly** *adv.*, **rigidity** *n.*

rigmarole *n.* long rambling statement; complicated formal procedure.

rigor *n.* **rigor mortis** stiffening of the body after death.

rigour *n.* strictness, severity; harshness of weather or conditions. **rigorous** *a.*, **rigorously** *adv.*, **rigorousness** *n.*

rile *v.* (*colloq.*) annoy.

rim *n.* edge or border of something more or less circular. **rimmed** *a.*

rind *n.* tough outer layer on fruit, cheese, bacon, etc.

ring [1] *n.* outline of a circle; circular metal band usu. worn on a finger; enclosure where a performance or activity takes place; group of people acting together dishonestly. — *v.* put a ring on or round; surround.

ring [2] *v.* (**rang, rung**) give out a loud clear resonant sound; cause (a bell) to do this; signal by ringing; be filled with sound; telephone. — *n.* act or sound of ringing; specified tone or feeling of a statement etc.; (*colloq.*) telephone call. **ring off** end a telephone call. **ring the changes** vary things. **ring up** make a telephone call.

ringleader *n.* person who leads others in wrongdoing or riot etc.

ringlet *n.* long tubular curl.

ringside *n.* area beside a boxing ring. **ringside seat** position from which one has a clear view of the scene of action.

ringworm *n.* skin disease producing round scaly patches on the skin.

rink *n.* skating-rink.

rinse *v.* wash lightly; wash out soap etc. from. — *n.* process of rinsing; solution washed through hair to tint or condition it.

riot *n.* wild disturbance by a crowd of people; profuse display; (*colloq.*) very amusing person or thing. — *v.* take part in a riot. **run riot** behave in an unruly way; grow in an uncontrolled way.

riotous *a.* disorderly, unruly; boisterous. **riotously** *adv.*

rip *v.* (**ripped**) tear apart; remove by pulling roughly; become torn; rush along. — *n.* act of ripping; torn place. **rip-cord** *n.* cord for pulling to release a parachute. **rip off** (*colloq.*) defraud; steal. **rip-off** *n.* **ripper** *n.*

ripe *a.* ready to be gathered and used; matured; (of age) advanced; ready. **ripeness** *n.*

ripen *v.* make or become ripe.

riposte /ripóst/ *n.* quick counterstroke or retort. — *v.* deliver a riposte.

ripple *n.* small wave(s); gentle sound that rises and falls. — *v.* form ripples (in).

rise *v.* (**rose, risen**) come or go or extend upwards; get up from lying or sitting or kneeling, get out of bed; rebel; become higher; increase; have its origin or source. — *n.* act or amount of rising, increase; upward slope; increase in wages. **give rise to** cause.

risible *a.* ridiculous; inclined to laugh. **risibly** *adv.*, **risibility** *n.*

risk *n.* possibility of meeting danger or suffering harm; person or thing representing a source of risk. — *v.* expose to the chance of injury or loss; accept the risk of.

risky *a.* (**-ier, -iest**) full of risk. **riskily** *adv.*, **riskiness** *n.*

risotto *n.* (*pl.* **-os**) dish of rice containing chopped meat or fish etc.

risqué /riskáy/ *a.* slightly indecent.

rissole *n.* fried cake of minced meat.

rite *n.* ritual.
ritual *n.* series of actions used in a religious or other ceremony. — *a.* of or done as a ritual. **ritually** *adv.*, **ritualistic** *a.*, **ritualism** *n.*
rival *n.* person or thing that competes with or can equal another. — *a.* being a rival or rivals. — *v.* (**rivalled**) be a rival of; seem as good as. **rivalry** *n.*
river *n.* large natural stream of water; great flow.
rivet *n.* bolt for holding pieces of metal together, with its end pressed down to form a head when in place. — *v.* (**riveted**) fasten with a rivet; attract and hold (the attention of). **riveter** *n.*
rivulet *n.* small stream.
RNA *abbr.* ribonucleic acid.
roach *n.* (*pl.* **roach**) small freshwater fish of the carp family.
road *n.* prepared track along which people and vehicles may travel; way of reaching something. **on the road** travelling. **road-hog** *n.* reckless or inconsiderate driver. **road-metal** *n.* broken stone for making the foundation of a road or railway.
roadway *n.* road, esp. as distinct from a footpath beside it.
roadworks *n.pl.* construction or repair of roads.
roadworthy *a.* (of a vehicle) fit to be used on a road. **roadworthiness** *n.*
roam *v.* & *n.* wander.
roan *n.* horse with a dark coat sprinkled with white hairs.
roar *n.* long deep sound like that made by a lion; loud laughter. — *v.* give a roar; express in this way. **roarer** *n.*
roaring *a.* noisy; briskly active.
roast *v.* cook (meat) in an oven or by exposure to heat; expose to great heat; undergo roasting. — *n.* roast joint of meat.
rob *v.* (**robbed**) steal from; deprive. **robber** *n.*, **robbery** *n.*
robe *n.* long loose esp. ceremonial garment. — *v.* dress in a robe.
robin *n.* brown red-breasted bird.
robot *n.* machine resembling and acting like a person; piece of apparatus operated by remote control. **robotic** *a.*
robotics *n.* study of robots and their design, operation, etc.
robust *a.* strong, vigorous. **robustly** *adv.*, **robustness** *n.*
rock [1] *n.* hard part of earth's crust, below the soil; mass of this, large stone; hard sugar sweet made in sticks. **on the rocks** (of a drink) served with ice cubes. **rock-bottom** *a.* (*colloq.*) very low. **rock-cake** *n.* small fruit cake with a rough surface.
rock [2] *v.* move to and fro while supported; disturb greatly by shock. — *n.* rocking movement; a kind of modern music with a strong beat. **rock and roll** rock music with elements of blues.
rocker *n.* thing that rocks; pivoting switch.
rockery *n.* collection of rough stones with soil between them on which small plants are grown.
rocket *n.* firework that shoots into the air when ignited and then explodes; structure that flies by expelling burning gases. — *v.* (**rocketed**) move rapidly upwards or away.
rocketry *n.* science or practice of rocket propulsion.
rocky [1] *a.* (**-ier, -iest**) of or like rock; full of rock. **rockiness** *n.*
rocky [2] *a.* (**-ier, -iest**) (*colloq.*) unsteady. **rockily** *adv.*, **rockiness** *n.*
rococo *a.* & *n.* (of or in) an ornate style of decoration in Europe in the 18th century.
rod *n.* slender straight round stick or metal bar; fishing rod.
rode *see* **ride**.
rodent *n.* animal with strong front teeth for gnawing things.
rodeo *n.* (*pl.* **-os**) competition or exhibition of cowboys' skill.
roe [1] *n.* mass of eggs in a female fish's ovary (**hard roe**); male fish's milt (**soft roe**).
roe [2] *n.* (*pl.* **roe** *or* **roes**) a kind of small deer. **roebuck** *n.* male roe.
roentgen /rúntgən/ *n.* unit of ionizing radiation.
roger *int.* (in signalling) message received and understood.
rogue *n.* dishonest or unprincipled or mischievous person; wild animal living apart from the herd. **roguery** *n.*
roguish *a.* mischievous; playful. **roguishly** *adv.*, **roguishness** *n.*
role *n.* actor's part; person's or thing's function.
roll *v.* move (on a surface) on wheels or by turning over and over; turn on an axis or over and over; form into a cylindrical or spherical shape; flatten with a roller; rock from side to side; undulate; move or pass steadily. — *n.* cylinder of flexible material turned over and over upon itself; undulation; small individual loaf of bread; official list or register; long deep sound. **be rolling (in money)** (*colloq.*) be wealthy. **roll-call** *n.* calling of a list of names to check that all are present. **rolled gold** thin coating of gold on another metal. **rolling-pin** *n.* roller for flattening dough. **rolling-stock** *n.* railway engines and carriages, wagons, etc. **rolling stone** person who does not settle in one place.

roller *n.* cylinder rolled over things to flatten or spread them, or on which something is wound; long swelling wave. **roller coaster** switchback at a fair etc. **roller skate** (*see* **skate** [2]). **roller skating** skating on roller skates.

rollicking *a.* full of boisterous high spirits.

roly-poly *n.* pudding of suet pastry spread with jam, rolled up, and boiled. — *a.* plump, podgy.

Roman *a.* & *n.* (native, inhabitant) of Rome or of the ancient Roman republic or empire; Roman Catholic. **Roman Catholic** (member) of the Church that acknowledges the Pope as its head. **Roman numerals** letters representing numbers (I = 1, V = 5, etc.).

roman *n.* plain upright type.

romance *n.* imaginative story or literature; romantic situation, event, or atmosphere; love story, love affair resembling this; picturesque exaggeration. — *v.* distort the truth or invent imaginatively. **Romance languages** those descended from Latin.

Romanesque *a.* & *n.* (of or in) a style of art and architecture in Europe about 1050–1200.

romantic *a.* appealing to the emotions by its imaginative or heroic or picturesque quality; involving a love affair; enjoying romantic situations etc. — *n.* romantic person. **romantically** *adv.*

romanticism *n.* romantic style.

romanticize *v.* make romantic; indulge in romance. **romanticization** *n.*

Romany *a.* & *n.* gypsy; (of) the gypsy language.

romp *v.* play about in a lively way; (*colloq.*) go along easily. — *n.* spell of romping.

rondeau *n.* short poem with the opening words used as a refrain.

rondo *n.* (*pl.* **-os**) piece of music with a recurring theme.

roof *n.* (*pl.* **roofs**) upper covering of a building, car, cavity, etc. — *v.* cover with a roof; be the roof of. **roofer** *n.*

rook [1] *n.* bird of the crow family.

rook [2] *n.* chess piece with a top shaped like battlements.

rookery *n.* colony of rooks.

room *n.* space that is or could be occupied; enclosed part of a building; scope to allow something.

roomy *a.* (**-ier**, **-iest**) having plenty of space.

roost *n.* place where birds perch or rest. *v.* perch, esp. for sleep.

root [1] *n.* part of a plant that grows into the earth and absorbs water and nourishment from the soil; embedded part of hair, tooth, etc.; source, basis; number in relation to another which it produces when multiplied by itself a specified number of times; (*pl.*) emotional attachment to a place. — *v.* (cause to) take root; cause to stand fixed and unmoving. **root out** *or* **up** drag or dig up by the roots; get rid of. **take root** send down roots; become established.

root [2] *v.* (of an animal) turn up ground with the snout or beak in search of food; rummage, extract.

rootless *a.* without roots. **rootlessness** *n.*

rope *n.* strong thick cord. — *v.* fasten or secure with rope; fence off with rope(s). **know** *or* **show the ropes** know or show the procedure. **rope in** persuade to take part in.

rosary *n.* set series of prayers; string of beads for keeping count in this; rose-garden.

rose [1] *n.* ornamental usu. fragrant flower; bush or shrub bearing this; deep pink colour.

rose [2] *see* **rise**.

rosé /rōzay/ *n.* light pink wine.

rosemary *n.* shrub with fragrant leaves used to flavour food.

rosette *n.* round badge or ornament made of ribbons.

rosewood *n.* dark fragrant wood used for making furniture.

rosin *n.* a kind of resin.

roster *n.* & *v.* list showing people's turns of duty etc.

rostrum *n.* (*pl.* **-tra**) platform for one person.

rosy *a.* (**-ier**, **-iest**) deep pink; promising, hopeful.

rot *v.* (**rotted**) lose its original form by chemical action caused by bacteria or fungi etc.; cause to do this; perish through lack of use. — *n.* rotting, rottenness; (*sl.*) nonsense.

rota *n.* list of duties to be done or people to do them in rotation.

rotary *a.* acting by rotating.

rotate *v.* revolve; arrange or occur or deal with in a recurrent series. **rotation** *n.*, **rotatory** *a.*

rote *n.* **by rote** by memory without thought of the meaning; by a fixed procedure.

rotor *n.* rotating part.

rotten *a.* rotted, breaking easily from age or use; worthless, unpleasant. **rottenness** *n.*

Rottweiler *n.* dog of a large black and tan breed.

rotund *a.* rounded, plump. **rotundity** *n.*

rotunda *n.* circular domed building or hall.

rouble *n.* unit of money in Russia.

rouge *n.* reddish cosmetic colouring for the cheeks. — *v.* colour with rouge.

rough *a.* having an uneven or irregular surface; not gentle or careful, violent, (of weather) stormy; not perfected or detailed; approximate. — *adv.* roughly; in rough conditions. — *n.* rough thing or state; rough ground. — *v.* make rough. **rough-and-ready** *a.* rough but effective. **rough-and-tumble** *n.* haphazard struggle. **rough diamond** person of good nature but lacking polished manners. **rough it** do without ordinary comforts. **rough out** plan or sketch roughly. **roughly** *adv.*, **roughness** *n.*

roughage *n.* dietary fibre.

roughen *v.* make or become rough.

roughshod *a.* **ride roughshod over** treat inconsiderately or arrogantly.

roulette *n.* gambling game played with a small ball on a revolving disc.

round *a.* curved, circular, spherical, or cylindrical; complete. — *n.* round object; circular or recurring course or series; song for two or more voices that start at different times; shot from a firearm, ammunition for this; one section of a competition. — *prep.* so as to circle or enclose; visiting in a series; to all points of interest in. — *adv.* in a circle or curve; by a circuitous route; so as to face in a different direction; round a place or group; to a person's house etc. — *v.* make or become round; make into a round figure; travel round. **in the round** with all sides visible. **round about** nearby; approximately. **round figure** *or* **number** approximation without odd units. **round off** complete. **round robin** statement signed by a number of people. **round the clock** continuously through day and night. **round trip** circular tour; outward and return journey. **round up** gather into one place. **round-up** *n.* **roundness** *n.*

roundabout *n.* revolving platform at a funfair, with model horses etc. to ride on; road junction with a circular island round which traffic has to pass in one direction. — *a.* indirect.

roundel *n.* small disc; rondeau.

rounders *n.* team game played with bat and ball, in which players have to run round a circuit. **rounder** *n.* unit of scoring in this.

roundly *adv.* thoroughly, severely; in a rounded shape.

roundworm *n.* parasitic worm with a rounded body.

rouse *v.* wake; cause to become active or excited.

rousing *a.* vigorous, stirring.

rout [1] *n.* utter defeat; disorderly retreat. — *v.* defeat completely; put to flight.

rout [2] *v.* fetch (out); rummage.

route *n.* course or way from starting point to finishing point. **route march** training-march for troops.

routine *n.* standard procedure; set sequence of movements. — *a.* in accordance with routine. **routinely** *adv.*

roux /roo/ *n.* mixture of heated fat and flour as a basis for a sauce.

rove *v.* wander. **rover** *n.*

row [1] /rō/ *n.* people or things in a line.

row [2] /rō/ *v.* propel (a boat) by using oars; carry in a boat that one rows. — *n.* spell of rowing. **rowboat, rowing boat** *ns.*

row [3] /row/ *n.* (*colloq.*) loud noise; quarrel, angry argument. — *v.* (*colloq.*) quarrel, argue angrily.

rowan *n.* tree bearing hanging clusters of red berries.

rowdy *a.* (**-ier, -iest**) noisy and disorderly. — *n.* rowdy person. **rowdily** *adv.*, **rowdiness** *n.*

rowlock /róllək/ *n.* device on the side of a boat securing and forming a fulcrum for an oar.

royal *a.* of or suited to a king or queen; of the family or in the service or under the patronage of royalty; splendid, of exceptional size. — *n.* (*colloq.*) member of a royal family. **royal blue** bright blue. **royally** *adv.*

royalist *n.* person supporting or advocating monarchy.

royalty *n.* being royal; royal person(s); payment to an author etc. for each copy or performance of his or her work, or to a patentee for use of his or her patent.

RSVP *abbr.* (French *répondez s'il vous plaît*) please reply.

rub *v.* (**rubbed**) press against a surface and slide to and fro; polish, clean, dry, or make sore etc. by rubbing. — *n.* act or process of rubbing; difficulty. **rub it in** emphasize or remind a person constantly of an unpleasant fact. **rub out** remove (marks etc.) by using a rubber.

rubber *n.* tough elastic substance made from the juice of certain plants or synthetically; piece of this for rubbing out pencil or ink marks; device for rubbing things. **rubber-stamp** *v.* approve automatically without consideration. **rubbery** *a.*

rubberize *v.* treat or coat with rubber.

rubbish *n.* waste or worthless material; nonsense.

rubble *n.* waste or rough fragments of stone or brick etc.

rubella *n.* German measles.
rubric *n.* words put as a heading or note of explanation.
ruby *n.* red gem; deep red colour. — *a.* deep red.
ruche /ro͞osh/ *n.* fabric gathered as trimming. — *v.* gather thus.
ruck *v.* & *n.* crease, wrinkle.
rucksack *n.* capacious bag carried on the back in hiking etc.
ructions *n.pl.* (*colloq.*) protests and noisy arguments, a row.
rudder *n.* vertical piece of metal or wood hinged to the stern of a boat or aircraft, used for steering.
ruddy *a.* (**-ier**, **-iest**) reddish. **ruddily** *adv.*, **ruddiness** *n.*
rude *a.* impolite, showing no respect; primitive, roughly made. **rudely** *adv.*, **rudeness** *n.*
rudiment *n.* rudimentary part; (*pl.*) elementary principles.
rudimentary *a.* incompletely developed; basic, elementary.
rue [1] *n.* shrub with bitter leaves formerly used in medicine.
rue [2] *v.* repent, regret.
rueful *a.* showing or feeling good-humoured regret. **ruefully** *adv.*
ruff *n.* pleated frill worn round the neck; projecting or coloured ring of feathers or fur round a bird's or animal's neck; bird of the sandpiper family.
ruffian *n.* violent lawless person.
ruffle *v.* disturb the calmness or smoothness (of); annoy. — *n.* gathered frill.
rufous *a.* reddish-brown.
rug *n.* thick floor-mat; piece of thick warm fabric used as a covering.
Rugby *n.* **Rugby football** a kind of football played with an oval ball which may be kicked or carried; this ball.
rugged *a.* uneven, irregular, craggy; rough but kindly. **ruggedly** *adv.*, **ruggedness** *n.*
rugger *n.* (*colloq.*) Rugby football.
ruin *n.* destruction; complete loss of one's fortune or prospects; broken remains; cause of ruin. — *v.* cause ruin to; reduce to ruins. **ruination** *n.*
ruinous *a.* bringing ruin; in ruins, ruined. **ruinously** *adv.*
rule *n.* statement of what can or should be done in certain circumstances or in a game; dominant custom; governing, control; ruler used by carpenters etc. — *v.* govern; keep under control; give an authoritative decision; draw (a line) using a ruler. **as a rule** usually. **rule of thumb** rough practical method of procedure. **rule out** exclude.
ruler *n.* person who rules; straight strip used in measuring or for drawing straight lines.
ruling *n.* authoritative decision.
rum [1] *n.* alcoholic spirit distilled from sugar cane or molasses.
rum [2] *a.* (*colloq.*) strange, odd.
rumba *n.* ballroom dance of Cuban origin.
rumble [1] *v.* make a low continuous sound. — *n.* rumbling sound.
rumble [2] *v.* (*sl.*) detect the true character of.
rumbustious *a.* (*colloq.*) boisterous, uproarious.
ruminant *n.* animal that chews the cud. — *a.* ruminating.
ruminate *v.* chew the cud; meditate, ponder. **rumination** *n.*, **ruminative** *a.*
rummage *v.* & *n.* search by disarranging things. **rummage sale** jumble sale.
rummy *n.* card game in which players try to form sets or sequences of cards.
rumour *n.* information spread by talking but not certainly true. **be rumoured** be spread as a rumour.
rump *n.* buttocks; bird's back near the tail.
rumple *v.* make or become crumpled; make untidy.
rumpus *n.* (*colloq.*) uproar, angry dispute.
run *v.* (**ran**, **run**, **running**) move with quick steps and with always at least one foot off the ground; go smoothly or swiftly; compete in a race; spread; flow, exude liquid; function; travel or convey from one point to another; extend; be current or valid; manage, organize; own and use (a vehicle etc.). — *n.* spell of running; point scored in cricket or baseball; ladder in fabric; continuous stretch or sequence; enclosure where domestic animals can range; permission to make unrestricted use of something. **in** *or* **out of the running** with a good *or* with no chance of winning. **in the long run** in the end, over a long period. **on the run** fleeing. **run across** happen to meet or find. **run a risk** take a risk. **run a temperature** be feverish. **run away** flee; leave secretly. **run down** reduce the numbers of; knock down with a vehicle; discover after searching; speak of in a slighting way. **be run down** be weak or exhausted. **run-down** *n.* detailed analysis. **run into** collide with; happen to meet. **run-of-the-mill** *a.* ordinary. **run out** become used up. **run out of** have used up (one's stock). **run over** knock down or crush with a vehicle. **run up** allow (a bill) to mount. **run-up** *n.* period leading up to an event.

rune *n.* any of the letters in an early Germanic alphabet. **runic** *a.*

rung [1] *n.* crosspiece of a ladder etc.

rung [2] *see* **ring** [2].

runner *n.* person or animal that runs; messenger; creeping stem that roots; groove, strip, or roller etc. for a thing to move on; long narrow strip of carpet or ornamental cloth. **runner-up** *n.* one who finishes second in a competition.

runny *a.* semi-liquid; tending to flow or exude fluid.

runt *n.* undersized person or animal.

runway *n.* prepared surface on which aircraft may take off and land.

rupee *n.* unit of money in India, Pakistan, etc.

rupture *n.* breaking, breach; abdominal hernia. — *v.* burst, break; cause hernia in.

rural *a.* of or in or like the countryside.

ruse *n.* deception, trick.

rush [1] *n.* marsh plant with a slender pithy stem.

rush [2] *v.* go or come or convey with great speed; act hastily; force into hasty action; attack with a sudden assault. — *n.* rushing, instance of this; period of great activity. **rush hour** one of the times of day when traffic is busiest.

rusk *n.* a kind of biscuit.

russet *a.* soft reddish-brown. — *n.* russet colour; a kind of apple with a rough skin.

rust *n.* brownish corrosive coating formed on iron exposed to moisture. — *a.* reddish-brown. — *v.* make or become rusty. **rustproof** *a.* & *v.*, **rustless** *a.*

rustic *a.* of or like country life or people; made of rough timber or untrimmed branches. **rusticity** *n.*

rustle *v.* (cause to) make a sound like paper being crumpled; (*US*) steal (horses or cattle). — *n.* rustling sound. **rustler** *n.*

rusty *a.* **(-ier, -iest)** affected with rust; rust-coloured; having lost quality by lack of use. **rustiness** *n.*

rut [1] *n.* deep track made by wheels; habitual usu. dull course of life.

rut [2] *n.* periodic sexual excitement of a male deer, goat, etc. — *v.* **(rutted)** be affected with this.

ruthless *a.* having no pity. **ruthlessly** *adv.*, **ruthlessness** *n.*

rye *n.* a kind of cereal; whisky made from rye.

S

S. *abbr.* south; southern.
sabbath *n.* day of worship and rest from work (Saturday for Jews, Sunday for Christians).
sabbatical *n.* leave granted at intervals to a university professor etc. for study and travel.
sable *n.* small Arctic mammal with dark fur; its fur. — *a.* black.
sabotage *n.* wilful damage to machinery or materials, or disruption of work. — *v.* commit sabotage on. **saboteur** *n.*
sabre *n.* curved sword.
sac *n.* bag-like part in an animal or plant.
saccharin *n.* very sweet substance used instead of sugar.
saccharine *a.* intensely and unpleasantly sweet.
sachet /sáshay/ *n.* small bag or sealed pack.
sack [1] *n.* large bag of strong coarse fabric; **the sack** (*colloq.*) dismissal from one's employment. — *v.* (*colloq.*) dismiss. **sackful** *n.* (*pl.* **-fuls**).
sack [2] *v.* plunder (a captured town). — *n.* this act or process.
sackcloth, sacking *ns.* coarse fabric for making sacks.
sacral /sáykrəl/ *a.* of the sacrum.
sacrament *n.* any of the symbolic Christian religious ceremonies. **sacramental** *a.*
sacred *a.* holy; dedicated (to a person or purpose); connected with religion; sacrosanct. **sacred cow** idea etc. which its supporters will not allow to be criticized.
sacrifice *n.* slaughter of a victim or presenting of a gift to win a god's favour; this victim or gift; giving up of a valued thing for the sake of something else; thing given up, loss entailed. — *v.* offer or kill or give up as a sacrifice. **sacrificial** *a.*
sacrilege *n.* disrespect to a sacred thing. **sacrilegious** *a.*
sacrosanct *a.* reverenced or respected and not to be harmed.
sacrum /sáykrəm/ *n.* bone at the base of the spine.
sad *a.* (**sadder**, **saddest**) showing or causing sorrow; regrettable. **sadly** *adv.*, **sadness** *n.*
sadden *v.* make or become sad.
saddle *n.* seat for a rider; joint of meat consisting of the two loins. — *v.* put a saddle on (an animal); burden with a task.
saddler *n.* person who makes or deals in saddles and harness.
sadism *n.* (sexual) pleasure from inflicting or watching cruelty. **sadist** *n.*, **sadistic** *a.*, **sadistically** *adv.*
safari *n.* expedition to hunt or observe wild animals. **safari park** park where exotic wild animals are kept in the open for visitors to see.
safe *a.* free from risk or danger; providing security. — *adv.* safely. — *n.* strong lockable cupboard for valuables. **safe conduct** immunity from arrest or harm. **safe deposit** building containing safes and strongrooms for hire. **safely** *adv.*
safeguard *n.* means of protection. — *v.* protect.
safety *n.* being safe, freedom from risk or danger. **safety pin** brooch-like pin with a guard protecting and securing the point. **safety-valve** *n.* valve that opens automatically to relieve excessive pressure in a steam boiler; harmless outlet for emotion.
saffron *n.* orange-coloured stigmas of a crocus, used to colour and flavour food; colour of these.
sag *v.* (**sagged**) droop or curve down in the middle under weight or pressure. — *n.* sagging.
saga *n.* long story.
sagacious *a.* wise. **sagaciously** *adv.*, **sagacity** *n.*
sage [1] *n.* herb with fragrant grey-green leaves used to flavour food.
sage [2] *a.* wise. — *n.* old and wise man. **sagely** *adv.*
sago *n.* starchy pith of the sago palm, used in puddings.
said *see* **say**.
sail *n.* piece of fabric spread to catch the wind and drive a boat along; journey by boat; arm of a windmill. — *v.* travel by water; start on a voyage; control (a boat); move smoothly. **sailboat, sailing ship** *ns.*
sailboard *n.* board with a mast and sail, used in windsurfing. **sailboarder** *n.*, **sailboarding** *n.*
sailcloth *n.* canvas for sails; canvas-like dress material.
sailor *n.* member of a ship's crew; traveller

considered as liable (**bad sailor**) or not liable (**good sailor**) to seasickness.

saint *n.* holy person, esp. one venerated by the RC or Orthodox Church; very good or patient or unselfish person. **sainthood** *n.*, **saintly** *a.*, **saintliness** *n.*

sake [1] *n.* **for the sake of** in order to please or honour (a person) or to get or keep (a thing).

sake [2] /saáki/ *n.* Japanese fermented liquor made from rice.

salacious *a.* lewd, erotic. **salaciously** *adv.*, **salaciousness** *n.*, **salacity** *n.*

salad *n.* cold dish of (usu. raw) vegetables etc.

salamander *n.* lizard-like animal.

salami *n.* strongly flavoured sausage, eaten cold.

salaried *a.* receiving a salary.

salary *n.* fixed regular (usu. monthly) payment to an employee.

sale *n.* selling, exchange of a commodity for money; event at which goods are sold; disposal of stock at reduced prices. **for** *or* **on sale** offered for purchase.

saleable *a.* fit to be sold, likely to find a purchaser.

salesman, saleswoman, salesperson *ns.* (*pl.* **-men, -women, -people**) one employed to sell goods.

salesmanship *n.* skill at selling.

salient *a.* projecting, most noticeable. — *n.* projecting part.

saline *a.* salty, containing salt(s). **salinity** *n.*

saliva *n.* colourless liquid that forms in the mouth.

salivary *a.* of or producing saliva.

salivate *v.* produce saliva. **salivation** *n.*

sallow [1] *a.* (of the complexion) yellowish.

sallow [2] *n.* low-growing willow.

sally *n.* sudden swift attack; lively or witty remark. — *v.* **sally forth** rush out in attack; set out on a journey.

salmon /sámmən/ *n.* (*pl.* **salmon**) large fish with pinkish flesh; salmon-pink. **salmon-pink** *a.* & *n.* yellowish-pink.

salmonella *n.* a kind of bacterium causing food poisoning.

salon *n.* elegant room for receiving guests; place where a hairdresser, couturier, etc. receives clients.

saloon *n.* public room, esp. on board ship; saloon car. **saloon car** car for a driver and passengers, with a closed body.

salsify *n.* plant with a long fleshy root used as a vegetable.

salt *n.* sodium chloride used to season and preserve food; chemical compound of a metal and an acid; (*pl.*) substance resembling salt in form, esp. a laxative. — *a.* tasting of salt; impregnated with salt. — *v.* season with salt; preserve in salt. **old salt** experienced sailor. **salt away** (*colloq.*) put aside for the future. **salt-cellar** *n.* small container for salt used at meals. **salt marsh** marsh flooded by the sea at high tide. **take with a grain** (*or* **pinch**) **of salt** regard sceptically. **worth one's salt** competent. **salty** *a.*, **saltiness** *n.*

salting *n.* salt marsh.

saltpetre *n.* salty white powder used in gunpowder, in medicine, and in preserving meat.

salubrious *a.* health-giving.

saluki *n.* (*pl.* **-is**) tall swift silky-coated dog.

salutary *a.* producing a beneficial or wholesome effect.

salutation *n.* word(s) or gesture of greeting; expression of respect.

salute *n.* gesture of respect or greeting. — *v.* make a salute to.

salvage *n.* rescue of a ship or its cargo from loss at sea, or of property from fire etc.; saving and use of waste material; items saved thus. — *v.* save from loss or for use as salvage.

salvation *n.* saving from disaster, esp. from the consequences of sin.

salve *n.* soothing ointment; thing that soothes. — *v.* soothe (conscience etc.).

salver *n.* a kind of small tray.

salvo *n.* (*pl.* **-oes**) firing of guns simultaneously; volley of applause.

sal volatile /sál voláttili/ solution of ammonium carbonate used as a remedy for faintness.

samba *n.* ballroom dance of Brazilian origin.

same *a.* being of one kind, not changed or different; previously mentioned. **sameness** *n.*

samphire *n.* plant with edible fleshy leaves, growing by the sea.

sample *n.* small part showing the quality of the whole; specimen. — *v.* test by taking a sample or getting an experience of.

sampler *n.* piece of embroidery worked in various stitches to show one's skill.

sanatorium *n.* (*pl.* **-ums**) establishment for treating chronic diseases or convalescents; room for sick persons in a school.

sanctify *v.* make holy or sacred. **sanctification** *n.*

sanctimonious *a.* making a show of righteousness or piety. **sanctimoniously** *adv.*, **sanctimoniousness** *n.*

sanction *n.* permission, approval; penalty imposed on a country or organization. — *v.* give sanction to, authorize.

sanctity *n.* sacredness, holiness.
sanctuary *n.* sacred place; place where birds or wild animals are protected; refuge.
sanctum *n.* holy place; person's private room.
sand *n.* very fine loose fragments of crushed rock; (*pl.*) expanse of sand, sandbank. — *v.* sprinkle with sand; smooth with sandpaper.
sandal *n.* light shoe with straps.
sandalwood *n.* a kind of scented wood.
sandbag *n.* bag filled with sand, used to protect a wall or building. — *v.* (**sandbagged**) protect with sandbags.
sandbank *n.* underwater deposit of sand.
sandblast *v.* treat with a jet of sand driven by compressed air or steam.
sandcastle *n.* structure of sand, usu. made by a child.
sandpaper *n.* paper with a coating of sand or other abrasive substance, used for smoothing surfaces. — *v.* smooth with this.
sandstone *n.* rock formed of compressed sand.
sandstorm *n.* desert storm of wind with blown sand.
sandwich *n.* two or more slices of bread with a layer of filling between; thing arranged like this. — *v.* put between two others.
sandy *a.* (**-ier**, **-iest**) like sand; covered with sand; yellowish-red.
sane *a.* having a sound mind; rational. **sanely** *adv.*
sang *see* **sing**.
sangria *n.* Spanish drink of red wine, lemonade, and fruit.
sanguinary *a.* full of bloodshed; bloodthirsty.
sanguine *a.* optimistic.
sanitary *a.* of hygiene; hygienic; of sanitation.
sanitation *n.* arrangements to protect public health, esp. drainage and disposal of sewage.
sanitize *v.* make sanitary.
sanity *n.* condition of being sane.
sank *see* **sink**.
sap *n.* vital liquid in plants; (*sl.*) foolish person. — *v.* (**sapped**) exhaust gradually. **sappy** *a.*
sapele /səpéeli/ *n.* mahogany-like wood; tree producing this.
sapling *n.* young tree.
sapphire *n.* blue precious stone; its colour. — *a.* bright blue.
saprophyte *n.* fungus or related plant living on decayed matter. **saprophytic** *a.*
sarcasm *n.* ironical remark; use of such remarks. **sarcastic** *a.*, **sarcastically** *adv.*
sarcophagus *n.* (*pl.* **-gi**) stone coffin.
sardine *n.* young pilchard or similar small fish.
sardonic *a.* humorous in a grim or sarcastic way. **sardonically** *adv.*
sargasso *n.* seaweed with berry-like air-vessels.
sari *n.* (*pl.* **-is**) length of cloth draped round the body, worn by Hindu women.
sarong *n.* strip of cloth worn round the body, esp. in Malaya.
sarsen *n.* sandstone boulder.
sartorial *a.* of tailoring; of men's clothing.
sash [1] *n.* strip of cloth worn round the waist or over one shoulder.
sash [2] *n.* frame holding a pane of a window and sliding up and down in grooves. **sash-window** *n.*
sat *see* **sit**.
Satanic *a.* of Satan. **satanic** *a.* devilish, hellish.
Satanism *n.* worship of Satan.
satchel *n.* bag for school books, hung over the shoulder(s).
sate *v.* satiate.
sateen *n.* closely woven cotton fabric resembling satin.
satellite *n.* heavenly or artificial body revolving round a planet; country that is subservient to another. **satellite dish** dish-shaped aerial for receiving broadcasts transmitted by satellite.
satiate /sáyshiayt/ *v.* satisfy fully, glut. **satiation** *n.*
satiety /sətī́-iti/ *n.* condition of being satiated.
satin *n.* silky material that is glossy on one side. — *a.* smooth as satin. **satiny** *a.*
satire *n.* use of ridicule, irony, or sarcasm; novel or play etc. that ridicules something. **satirical** *a.*, **satirically** *adv.*
satirize *v.* attack with satire; describe satirically. **satirist** *n.*
satisfactory *a.* satisfying; adequate. **satisfactorily** *adv.*
satisfy *v.* give (a person) what he or she wants or needs; make pleased or contented; end (a demand etc.) by giving what is required; convince. **satisfaction** *n.*
satsuma *n.* a kind of mandarin orange.
saturate *v.* make thoroughly wet; cause to absorb or accept as much as possible. **saturation** *n.*
saturnine *a.* having a gloomy temperament or appearance.
satyr /sáttər/ *n.* woodland god in classical mythology, with a goat's ears, tail, and legs.
sauce *n.* liquid preparation added to food

to give flavour or richness; (*sl.*) impudence.

saucepan *n.* metal cooking pot with a long handle.

saucer *n.* curved dish on which a cup stands; thing shaped like this.

saucy *a.* (**-ier**, **-iest**) impudent; jaunty. **saucily** *adv.*

sauerkraut /sówərkrowt/ *n.* chopped pickled cabbage.

sauna *n.* Finnish-style steam bath.

saunter *v.* & *n.* stroll.

saurian *a.* of or like a lizard. — *n.* animal of the lizard family.

sausage *n.* minced seasoned meat in a tubular case of thin skin.

savage *a.* uncivilized; wild and fierce; cruel and hostile. — *n.* uncivilized person. — *v.* maul savagely. **savagely** *adv.*, **savagery** *n.*

savannah *n.* grassy plain in hot regions.

save *v.* rescue; protect; avoid wasting; keep for future use, put aside money thus; prevent the scoring of (a goal etc.). — *n.* act of saving in football etc. **saver** *n.*

saveloy *n.* highly seasoned sausage.

savings *n.pl.* money put aside for future use.

saviour *n.* person who rescues people from harm or danger; **the** *or* **our Saviour** Christ.

savory *n.* spicy herb.

savour *n.* flavour; smell. — *v.* have a certain savour; taste or smell with enjoyment.

savoury *a.* having an appetizing taste or smell; salty or piquant, not sweet. — *n.* savoury dish, esp. at the end of a meal.

savoy *n.* a kind of cabbage.

saw [1] *see* **see** [1].

saw [2] *n.* cutting tool with a zigzag edge. — *v.* (**sawed**, **sawn**) cut with a saw; make a to-and-fro movement.

saw [3] *n.* old saying, maxim.

sawdust *n.* powdery fragments of wood, made in sawing timber.

sawfish *n.* large sea fish with a jagged blade-like snout.

sawmill *n.* mill where timber is cut into planks etc.

sawn *see* **saw** [2].

sax *n.* (*colloq.*) saxophone.

saxe blue *a.* & *n.* greyish-blue.

saxifrage *n.* a kind of rock plant.

saxophone *n.* brass wind instrument with finger-operated keys. **saxophonist** *n.*

say *v.* (**said**) utter, recite; express in words, state; give as an opinion; suppose as a possibility etc. — *n.* power to decide.

saying *n.* well-known phrase or proverb or other statement.

scab *n.* crust forming over a sore; skin disease or plant disease causing similar roughness; (*colloq.*, *derog.*) blackleg. **scabby** *a.*

scabbard *n.* sheath of a sword etc.

scabies *n.* contagious skin disease causing itching.

scabious *n.* herbaceous plant with clustered flowers.

scabrous *a.* rough-surfaced; indecent.

scaffold *n.* platform for the execution of criminals; scaffolding.

scaffolding *n.* poles and planks providing platforms for workmen building or repairing a house etc.

scald *v.* injure with hot liquid or steam; cleanse with boiling water. — *n.* injury by scalding.

scale [1] *n.* each of the overlapping plates of horny membrane protecting the skin of many fishes and reptiles; thing resembling this; incrustation caused by hard water or forming on teeth. — *v.* remove scale(s) from; come off in scales. **scaly** *a.*

scale [2] *n.* pan of a balance; (*pl.*) instrument for weighing things.

scale [3] *n.* ordered series of units or qualities etc. for measuring or classifying things; fixed series of notes in a system of music; relative size or extent. — *v.* climb; represent in proportion to the size of the original.

scallop *n.* shellfish with hinged fan-shaped shells; one shell of this; (*pl.*) semicircular curves as an ornamental edging. **scalloped** *a.*

scallywag *n.* rascal.

scalp *n.* skin of the head excluding the face. — *v.* cut the scalp from.

scalpel *n.* surgeon's or painter's small straight knife.

scamp *n.* rascal.

scamper *v.* run hastily or in play. — *n.* scampering run.

scampi *n.pl.* large prawns.

scan *v.* (**scanned**) look at all parts of, esp. quickly; pass a radar or electronic beam over; (of verse) have a regular rhythm. — *n.* scanning. **scanner** *n.*

scandal *n.* something disgraceful; gossip about wrongdoing. **scandalous** *a.*, **scandalously** *adv.*

scandalize *v.* shock; outrage.

scandalmonger *n.* person who invents or spreads scandal.

Scandinavian *a.* & *n.* (native) of Scandinavia.

scansion *n.* scanning of verse.

scant *a.* not or barely enough.
scanty *a.* (**-ier**, **-iest**) small in amount or extent; barely enough. **scantily** *adv.*, **scantiness** *n.*
scapegoat *n.* person made to bear blame that should fall on others.
scapula *n.* (*pl.* **-lae**) shoulder blade. **scapular** *a.*
scar *n.* mark where a wound has healed. — *v.* (**scarred**) mark with a scar; form scar(s).
scarab *n.* sacred beetle of ancient Egypt.
scarce *a.* not enough to supply a demand, rare.
scarcely *adv.* only just, almost not; not, surely not.
scarcity *n.* being scarce, shortage.
scare *v.* frighten; be frightened. — *n.* fright, alarm.
scarecrow *n.* figure dressed in old clothes and set up to scare birds away from crops.
scaremonger *n.* alarmist. **scaremongering** *n.*
scarf *n.* (*pl.* **scarves**) piece or strip of material worn round the neck or tied over a woman's head.
scarify *v.* make slight cuts in; criticize harshly.
scarlet *a.* & *n.* brilliant red. **scarlet fever** infectious fever producing a scarlet rash.
scarp *n.* steep slope on a hillside.
scary *a.* (**-ier**, **-iest**) (*colloq.*) frightening.
scathing *a.* (of criticism) very severe.
scatter *v.* throw or put here and there; go or send in different directions. — *n.* small scattered amount.
scatterbrain *n.* careless or forgetful person. **scatterbrained** *a.*
scatty *a.* (**-ier**, **-iest**) (*colloq.*) crazy.
scavenge *v.* search for (usable objects) among rubbish etc.; (of animals) search for decaying flesh as food. **scavenger** *n.*
scenario *n.* (*pl.* **-os**) script or summary of a film or play; imagined sequence of events.
scene *n.* place of an event; piece of continuous action in a play or film; display of temper or emotion; stage scenery; view of a place or incident; (*sl.*) area of activity. **behind the scenes** hidden from public view.
scenery *n.* general (esp. picturesque) appearance of a landscape; structures used on a theatre stage to represent the scene of action.
scenic *a.* picturesque.
scent *n.* pleasant smell; liquid perfume; animal's trail perceptible to a hound's sense of smell. — *v.* discover by smell; suspect the presence or existence of; apply scent to, make fragrant.
sceptic /sképtik/ *n.* sceptical person.
sceptical /sképtik'l/ *a.* unwilling to believe things. **sceptically** *adv.*, **scepticism** *n.*
sceptre *n.* ornamental rod carried as a symbol of sovereignty.
schedule *n.* programme or timetable of events. — *v.* appoint in a schedule.
schematic *a.* in the form of a diagram. **schematically** *adv.*
schematize *v.* put into schematic form. **schematization** *n.*
scheme *n.* plan of work or action. — *v.* make plans, plot. **schemer** *n.*
scherzo /skáirtsō/ *n.* (*pl.* **-os**) lively piece of music.
schism /síss'm/ *n.* division into opposing groups through difference in belief or opinion. **schismatic** *a.* & *n.*
schist /shist/ *n.* rock with components in layers.
schizoid *a.* like or suffering from schizophrenia. — *n.* schizoid person.
schizophrenia *n.* mental disorder in which a person is unable to act or reason rationally. **schizophrenic** *a.* & *n.*
scholar *n.* learned person; pupil; holder of a scholarship. **scholarly** *a.*, **scholarliness** *n.*
scholarship *n.* grant of money towards education; scholars' methods and achievements.
scholastic *a.* of schools or education; academic.
school [1] *n.* shoal of fish or whales.
school [2] *n.* institution for educating children or giving instruction; group of artists etc. following the same principles. — *v.* train, discipline. **schoolboy** *n.*, **schoolchild** *n.* (*pl.* **-children**), **schoolgirl** *n.fem.*
schoolteacher *n.* teacher in a school.
schooner *n.* a kind of sailing ship; measure for sherry etc.
science *n.* branch of knowledge requiring systematic study and method, esp. dealing with substances, life, and natural laws. **scientific** *a.*, **scientifically** *adv.*
scientist *n.* expert in science(s).
scimitar *n.* short curved oriental sword.
scintillating *a.* lively; witty.
scion /sī́ən/ *n.* shoot, esp. cut for grafting; descendant.
scissors *n.pl.* cutting instrument with two pivoted blades.
sclerosis *n.* abnormal hardening of tissue.
scoff [1] *v.* speak contemptuously, jeer. **scoffer** *n.*
scoff [2] *v.* (*colloq.*) eat quickly.

scold *v.* rebuke (esp. a child). **scolding** *n.*

sconce *n.* ornamental bracket on a wall, holding a light.

scone /skon, skōn/ *n.* a kind of soft flat cake eaten buttered.

scoop *n.* deep shovel-like tool; a kind of ladle; piece of news published by one newspaper before its rivals. — *v.* lift or hollow with (or as if with) a scoop; forestall with a news scoop.

scoot *v.* run, dart.

scooter *n.* child's toy vehicle with a footboard and long steering-handle; a kind of lightweight motor cycle. **scooterist** *n.*

scope *n.* range of a subject etc.; opportunity, outlet.

scorch *v.* burn or become burnt on the surface.

scorching *a.* extremely hot.

score *n.* number of points gained in a game or competition; set of twenty; line or mark cut into something; written or printed music; music for a film or play. — *v.* gain (points etc.) in a game or competition; keep a record of the score; achieve; cut a line or mark into; write or compose as a musical score. **score out** cross out. **scorer** *n.*

scorn *n.* strong contempt. — *v.* feel or show scorn for; reject with scorn. **scornful** *a.*, **scornfully** *adv.*, **scornfulness** *n.*

scorpion *n.* small animal of the spider group with lobster-like claws and a sting in its long tail.

Scot *n.* native of Scotland.

Scotch *a.* Scottish. — *n.* Scotch whisky.

scotch *v.* put an end to (a rumour).

scot-free *a.* unharmed, not punished; free of charge.

Scots *a.* Scottish. — *n.* Scottish form of the English language. **Scotsman** *n.* (*pl.* **-men**), **Scotswoman** *n.fem.* (*pl.* **-women**).

Scottish *a.* of Scotland or its people or their form of the English language.

scoundrel *n.* dishonest or unprincipled person.

scour [1] *v.* cleanse by rubbing; clear out (a channel etc.) by flowing water; purge drastically. — *n.* scouring; action of water on a channel etc. **scourer** *n.*

scour [2] *v.* search thoroughly.

scourge /skurj/ *n.* whip; great affliction. — *v.* flog; afflict greatly.

scout *n.* person sent to gather information, esp. about enemy movements etc. — *v.* act as scout, search.

scow *n.* a kind of flat-bottomed boat.

scowl *n.* sullen or angry frown. — *v.* make a scowl.

scrabble *v.* scratch with the hands or feet; grope busily.

scraggy *a.* (**-ier**, **-iest**) lean and bony. **scragginess** *n.*

scram *v.* (**scrammed**) (*colloq.*) go away.

scramble *v.* clamber; move hastily or awkwardly; mix indiscriminately; cook (eggs) by heating and stirring; make (a transmission) unintelligible except by means of a special receiver; (of aircraft or crew) hurry to take off quickly. — *n.* scrambling walk or movement; eager struggle; motor cycle race over rough ground. **scrambler** *n.*

scrap [1] *n.* fragment; waste material; discarded metal suitable for reprocessing. — *v.* (**scrapped**) discard as useless.

scrap [2] *n.* & *v.* (**scrapped**) (*colloq.*) fight, quarrel.

scrapbook *n.* book in which to mount newspaper cuttings or similar souvenirs.

scrape *v.* clean, smooth, or damage by passing a hard edge across a surface; pass (an edge) across in this way; make the sound of scraping; get along or through etc. with difficulty; be very economical. — *n.* scraping movement or sound; scraped place; awkward situation resulting from an escapade. **scraper** *n.*

scraping *n.* fragment produced by scraping.

scrappy *a.* (**-ier**, **-iest**) made up of scraps or disconnected elements. **scrappily** *adv.*, **scrappiness** *n.*

scratch *v.* scrape with the fingernails; make a thin scraping sound; obtain with difficulty; withdraw from a race or competition. — *n.* mark, wound, or sound made by scratching; spell of scratching. — *a.* collected from what is available. **from scratch** from the very beginning or with no preparation. **up to scratch** up to the required standard. **scratchy** *a.*

scratchings *n.pl.* crisp residue of pork fat left after rendering lard.

scrawl *n.* bad handwriting; something written in this. — *v.* write in a scrawl.

scrawny *a.* (**-ier**, **-iest**) scraggy.

scream *v.* make a long piercing cry or sound. — *n.* screaming cry or sound; (*sl.*) extremely amusing person or thing.

scree *n.* mass of loose stones on a mountain side.

screech *n.* harsh high-pitched scream or sound. — *v.* make or utter with a screech.

screed *n.* tiresomely long list or letter etc.; thin layer of cement.

screen *n.* structure used to conceal or protect or divide something; windscreen; blank surface on which pictures or cinema films or television transmissions etc.

are projected. — *v.* shelter, conceal; show (images etc.) on a screen; examine for the presence or absence of a disease or quality etc.

screw *n.* metal pin with a spiral ridge round its length, fastened by turning; thing twisted to tighten or press something; propeller; act of screwing. — *v.* fasten or tighten with screw(s); turn (a screw); twist, become twisted; oppress, extort. **screw up** summon up (one's courage etc.); (*sl.*) bungle.

screwdriver *n.* tool for turning screws.

scribble *v.* write hurriedly or carelessly; make meaningless marks. — *n.* something scribbled.

scribe *n.* person who (before the invention of printing) made copies of writings; (in New Testament times) professional religious scholar. **scribal** *a.*

scrimmage *n.* confused struggle. — *v.* engage in this.

scrimp *v.* skimp.

script *n.* handwriting; style of printed characters resembling this; text of a play or film or broadcast talk etc.

scripture *n.* sacred writings; **the Scriptures** those of the Christians or the Jews. **scriptural** *a.*

scroll *n.* roll of paper or parchment; ornamental design in this shape. — *v.* move (a display on a VDU screen) up or down as the screen is filled.

scrotum *n.* (*pl.* **-ta**) pouch of skin enclosing the testicles.

scrounge *v.* cadge; collect by foraging. **scrounger** *n.*

scrub [1] *n.* vegetation consisting of stunted trees and shrubs; land covered with this.

scrub [2] *v.* (**scrubbed**) rub hard esp. with something coarse or bristly. — *n.* process of scrubbing.

scruff *n.* back of the neck.

scruffy *a.* (**-ier, -iest**) (*colloq.*) shabby and untidy. **scruffily** *adv.*, **scruffiness** *n.*

scrum *n.* scrummage; confused struggle.

scrummage *n.* grouping of forwards in Rugby football to struggle for possession of the ball by pushing.

scrumptious *a.* (*colloq.*) delicious.

scrunch *v.* & *n.* crunch, crush.

scruple *n.* doubt about doing something, produced by one's conscience. — *v.* hesitate because of scruples.

scrupulous *a.* very conscientious or careful. **scrupulously** *adv.*, **scrupulousness** *n.*

scrutinize *v.* make a scrutiny of.

scrutiny *n.* careful look or examination.

scuba *n.* an aqualung (acronym from *s*elf-*c*ontained *u*nderwater *b*reathing *a*pparatus). **scuba-diving** *n.*

scud *v.* (**scudded**) move along fast and smoothly.

scuff *v.* scrape or drag (one's feet) in walking; mark or scrape by doing this.

scuffle *n.* confused struggle or fight. — *v.* take part in a scuffle.

scull *n.* one of a pair of small oars; oar that rests on a boat's stern, worked with a screw-like movement. — *v.* row with scull(s).

sculpt *v.* (*colloq.*) sculpture.

sculptor *n.* maker of sculptures.

sculpture *n.* art of carving or modelling; work made thus. — *v.* represent in or decorate with sculpture; be a sculptor. **sculptural** *a.*

scum *n.* layer of impurities or froth etc. on the surface of a liquid; worthless person(s).

scupper *n.* opening in a ship's side to drain water from the deck. — *v.* sink (a ship) deliberately; (*sl.*) ruin.

scurf *n.* flakes of dry skin, esp. from the scalp; similar scaly matter. **scurfy** *a.*

scurrilous *a.* abusive and insulting; coarsely humorous. **scurrilously** *adv.*, **scurrility** *n.*

scurry *v.* run hurriedly, scamper. — *n.* scurrying, rush.

scurvy *n.* disease caused by lack of vitamin C in the diet.

scuttle [1] *n.* box or bucket for holding coal in a room.

scuttle [2] *v.* sink (a ship) by letting in water.

scuttle [3] *v.* & *n.* scurry.

scythe /sīth/ *n.* implement with a curved blade on a long handle, for cutting long grass or grain.

SE *abbr.* south-east; south-eastern.

sea *n.* expanse of salt water surrounding the continents; section of this; large inland lake; waves of the sea; vast expanse. **at sea** in a ship on the sea; perplexed. **sea dog** old sailor. **sea-green** *a.* & *n.* bluish-green. **sea horse** small fish with a horse-like head. **sea level** level corresponding to the mean level of the sea's surface. **sea lion** a kind of large seal. **sea urchin** sea animal with a round spiky shell.

seaboard *n.* coast.

seafarer *n.* seafaring person.

seafaring *a.* & *n.* working or travelling on the sea.

seafood *n.* fish or shellfish from the sea eaten as food.

seagoing *a.* for sea voyages.

seagull *n.* gull.

seal [1] *n.* amphibious sea animal with thick fur or bristles.

seal [2] *n.* engraved piece of metal used to stamp a design; its impression; action etc. serving to confirm or guarantee something; paper sticker; thing used to close an opening very tightly. — *v.* affix a seal to; close or coat so as to prevent penetration; stick down; settle (e.g. a bargain). **seal off** prevent access to (an area).

sealant *n.* substance for coating a surface to seal it.

sealskin *n.* seal's skin or fur used as a clothing material.

seam *n.* line where two edges join; layer of coal etc. in the ground. — *v.* join by a seam. **seamless** *a.*

seaman *n.* (*pl.* **-men**) sailor; person skilled in seafaring. **seamanship** *n.*

seamstress *n.* woman who sews, esp. for a living.

seance /sáyoNss/ *n.* spiritualist meeting.

seaplane *n.* aeroplane designed to take off from and land on water.

sear *v.* scorch, burn.

search *v.* look, feel, or go over (a person or place etc.) in order to find something. — *n.* process of searching. **searcher** *n.*

searching *a.* thorough.

searchlight *n.* outdoor lamp with a powerful beam; its beam.

seascape *n.* picture or view of the sea.

seasick *a.* made sick by the motion of a ship. **seasickness** *n.*

seaside *n.* coast, esp. as a place for holidays.

season *n.* section of the year associated with a type of weather; time when something takes place or is plentiful. — *v.* give extra flavour to (food); dry or treat until ready for use. **season ticket** ticket valid for any number of journeys or performances in a specified period.

seasonable *a.* suitable for the season; timely. **seasonably** *adv.*

seasonal *a.* of a season or seasons; varying with the seasons. **seasonally** *adv.*, **seasonality** *n.*

seasoned *a.* experienced.

seasoning *n.* substance used to season food.

seat *n.* thing made or used for sitting on; place as member of a committee or parliament etc.; buttocks, part of a garment covering these; place where something is based; country mansion. — *v.* cause to sit; have seats for. **seat belt** strap securing a person to a seat in a vehicle or aircraft. **be seated** sit down.

seaward *a.* & *adv.* towards the sea. **seawards** *adv.*

seaweed *n.* any plant that grows in the sea.

seaworthy *a.* (of ships) fit for a sea voyage. **seaworthiness** *n.*

sebaceous *a.* secreting an oily or greasy substance.

secateurs *n.pl.* clippers for pruning plants.

secede *v.* withdraw from membership. **secession** *n.*

seclude *v.* keep (a person) apart from others. **secluded** *a.* screened from view. **seclusion** *n.*

second [1] /sékkənd/ *a.* next after the first; secondary; inferior. — *n.* second thing, class, etc.; attendant in a duel or boxing match; sixtieth part of a minute of time or (in measuring angles) degree. — *v.* state one's support of (a proposal) formally. **second-best** *a.* next to the best in quality; inferior. **second-class** *a.* & *adv.* next or inferior to first-class in quality etc. **second cousin** (*see* **cousin**). **second-hand** *a.* bought after use by a previous owner. **second nature** habit or characteristic that has become automatic. **second-rate** *a.* inferior in quality. **second sight** supposed power to foresee future events. **second thoughts** change of mind after reconsideration. **second wind** renewed capacity for effort.

second [2] /sikónd/ *v.* transfer temporarily to another job or department. **secondment** *n.*

secondary *a.* coming after or derived from what is primary. — *n.* secondary thing. **secondary colours** those obtained by mixing two primary colours. **secondary education**, **secondary school** that for children who have received primary education. **secondarily** *adv.*

secondly *adv.* second.

secret *a.* kept from the knowledge of most people. — *n.* something secret; mystery. **in secret** secretly. **secretly** *adv.*, **secrecy** *n.*

secretariat *n.* administrative office or department.

secretary *n.* person employed to deal with correspondence and routine office work; official in charge of an organization's correspondence; ambassador's or government minister's chief assistant. **Secretary-General** *n.* principal administrative officer. **secretarial** *a.*

secrete *v.* put into a place of concealment; produce by secretion. **secretor** *n.*

secretion *n.* process of secreting; production of a substance within the body; this substance.

secretive *a.* making a secret of things. **secretively** *adv.*, **secretiveness** *n.*

secretory *a.* of physiological secretion.

sect *n.* group with beliefs that differ from those generally accepted.

sectarian *a.* of a sect or sects; narrow-mindedly promoting the interests of one's sect.

section *n.* distinct part; cross-section; subdivision. — *v.* divide into sections.

sectional *a.* of a section or sections; made in sections.

sector *n.* part of an area; branch of an activity; section of a circular area between two lines drawn from centre to circumference.

secular *a.* of worldly (not religious or spiritual) matters.

secure *a.* safe; certain not to slip or fail. — *v.* make secure; fasten securely; obtain; guarantee by pledging something as security. **securely** *adv.*

security *n.* safety; safety or precaution against espionage, theft, or other danger; thing serving as a pledge; certificate showing ownership of financial stocks etc.

sedate[1] *a.* calm and dignified. **sedately** *adv.*, **sedateness** *n.*

sedate[2] *v.* treat with sedatives. **sedation** *n.*

sedative *a.* having a calming effect. — *n.* sedative drug.

sedentary *a.* seated; (of work) done while sitting.

sedge *n.* grass-like plant(s) growing in marshes or by water.

sediment *n.* particles of solid matter in a liquid or deposited by water or wind. **sedimentary** *a.*, **sedimentation** *n.*

sedition *n.* words or actions inciting rebellion. **seditious** *a.*, **seditiously** *adv.*

seduce *v.* tempt (esp. into wrongdoing); persuade into sexual intercourse. **seducer** *n.*, **seductress** *n.fem.*, **seduction** *n.*, **seductive** *a.*

sedulous *a.* diligent and persevering. **sedulously** *adv.*

see[1] *v.* (**saw, seen**) perceive with the eye(s) or mind; understand; consider; watch; meet; experience; interview; escort; make sure. **see about** attend to. **seeing that** in view of the fact that. **see to** attend to.

see[2] *n.* district of a bishop or archbishop.

seed *n.* (*pl.* **seeds** *or* **seed**) plant's fertilized ovule; semen, milt; origin. — *v.* produce seed; sprinkle with seeds; remove seeds from. **go** *or* **run to seed** cease flowering as seed develops; become shabby or less efficient. **seed-cake** *n.* cake flavoured with caraway seeds.

seedless *a.* not containing seeds.

seedling *n.* very young plant growing from a seed.

seedy *a.* (**-ier, -iest**) looking shabby and disreputable; (*colloq.*) feeling slightly ill.

seek *v.* (**sought**) try to find or obtain; try (to do something).

seem *v.* appear to be or exist or be true. **seemingly** *adv.*

seen *see* **see**[1].

seep *v.* ooze slowly out or through. **seepage** *n.*

seer *n.* prophet.

seersucker *n.* fabric woven with a puckered surface.

see-saw *n.* a long board balanced on a central support so that children sitting on each end can ride up and down alternately; constantly repeated up-and-down change. — *v.* make this movement or change; vacillate.

seethe *v.* bubble as if boiling; be very agitated or excited.

segment *n.* part cut off or marked off or separable from others; part of a circle or sphere cut off by a straight line or plane. **segmented** *a.*

segregate *v.* put apart from others. **segregation** *n.*

seine /sayn/ *n.* a kind of fishing net that hangs from floats.

seismic /sízmik/ *a.* of earthquake(s).

seismograph *n.* instrument for recording earthquakes.

seismology *n.* study of earthquakes. **seismological** *a.*, **seismologist** *n.*

seize *v.* take hold of forcibly or suddenly; take possession of by force or legal right; affect suddenly; seize up. **seize on** make use of eagerly. **seize up** become stuck through overheating.

seizure *n.* seizing; sudden violent attack of an illness.

seldom *adv.* rarely, not often.

select *v.* pick out as best or most suitable. — *a.* carefully chosen; exclusive. **selector** *n.*

selection *n.* selecting; things selected; things from which to choose.

selective *a.* chosen or choosing carefully. **selectively** *adv.*, **selectivity** *n.*

self *n.* (*pl.* **selves**) person as an individual; person's special nature; person or thing as the object of reflexive action; one's own advantage or interests.

self- *pref.* of or to or done by oneself or itself. **self-assured** *a.* being self-confident. **self-centred** *a.* thinking chiefly of oneself or one's own affairs.

self-confidence *n.*, **self-confident** *a.* being confident of one's own abilities. **self-conscious** *a.*, **self-consciousness** *n.* being embarrassed from knowing that one is observed. **self-contained** *a.* complete in itself, having all the necessary facilities. **self-control** *n.*, **self-controlled** *a.* being able to control one's behaviour and not act emotionally. **self-denial** *n.* deliberately going without things one would like to have. **self-determination** *n.* free will; nation's own choice of its form of government or allegiance etc. **self-evident** *a.* clear without proof; obvious. **self-interest** *n.* one's own advantage. **self-made** *a.* having risen from poverty or obscurity by one's own efforts. **self-possessed** *a.* calm and dignified. **self-respect** *n.* proper regard for oneself and one's own dignity and principles etc. **self-righteous** *a.* smugly sure of one's own righteousness. **self-satisfied** *a.* smugly pleased with oneself and one's achievements. **self-seeking** *a.* & *n.* seeking to promote one's own interests rather than those of others. **self-service** *a.* at which customers help themselves and pay a cashier for goods taken. **self-styled** *a.* using a name or description one has adopted without right. **self-sufficient** *a.* able to provide what one needs without outside help. **self-willed** *a.* obstinately doing what one wishes.

selfish *a.* acting or done according to one's own interests without regard to those of others; keeping good things for oneself. **selfishly** *adv.*, **selfishness** *n.*

selfless *a.* unselfish. **selflessly** *adv.*

selfsame *a.* the very same.

sell *v.* (**sold**) exchange (goods etc.) for money; keep (goods) for sale; promote sales of; (of goods) be sold; have a specified price; persuade into accepting (an idea etc.). — *n.* manner of selling. **sell off** dispose of by selling, esp. at a reduced price. **sell out** dispose of all one's stock etc. by selling; betray. **sell up** sell one's house or business. **seller** *n.*

Sellotape *n.* [P.] adhesive usu. transparent tape.

selvage *n.* edge of cloth woven so that it does not unravel.

selvedge *n.* = selvage.

semantic *a.* of meaning in language. **semantically** *adv.*

semantics *n.* study of meaning.

semaphore *n.* system of signalling with the arms; signalling device with mechanical arms.

semblance *n.* outward appearance, show; resemblance.

semen *n.* sperm-bearing fluid produced by male animals.

semi- *pref.* half; partly.

semibreve *n.* note in music, equal to two minims.

semicircle *n.* half of a circle. **semicircular** *a.*

semicolon *n.* punctuation mark ;.

semiconductor *n.* substance that conducts electricity in certain conditions.

semi-detached *a.* (of a house) joined to another on one side.

semifinal *n.* match or round preceding the final. **semifinalist** *n.*

seminal *a.* of seed or semen; giving rise to new developments. **seminally** *adv.*

seminar *n.* small class for discussion and research.

seminary *n.* training college for priests or rabbis.

semiprecious *a.* (of gems) less valuable than those called precious.

semiquaver *n.* note in music, equal to half a quaver.

Semite *n.* member of the group of races that includes Jews and Arabs. **Semitic** *a.*

semitone *n.* half a tone in music.

semolina *n.* hard particles left when wheat is ground and sifted, used to make puddings.

senate *n.* upper house of certain parliaments; governing body of certain universities.

senator *n.* member of a senate.

send *v.* (**sent**) order or cause to go to a certain destination; send a message; cause to move or go or become. **send for** order to come or be brought. **send-off** *n.* friendly demonstration of goodwill at a person's departure. **send up** make fun of by imitating.

senescent *a.* growing old. **senescence** *n.*

senile *a.* weak in body or mind because of old age. **senility** *n.*

senior *a.* older; higher in rank or authority; for older children. — *n.* senior person; member of a senior school. **senior citizen** elderly person. **seniority** *n.*

senna *n.* dried pods or leaves of a tropical tree, used as a laxative.

sensation *n.* feeling produced by stimulation of a sense organ or of the mind; excited interest, person or thing producing this.

sensational *a.* causing great excitement or admiration. **sensationally** *adv.*

sensationalism *n.* use of or interest in sensational matters. **sensationalist** *n.*

sense *n.* any of the special powers (sight, hearing, smell, taste, touch) by which a living thing becomes aware of the external world; ability to perceive or be conscious of a thing; practical wisdom; meaning; (*pl.*) consciousness, sanity. — *v.* perceive by sense(s) or by a mental impression. **make sense** have a meaning; be a sensible idea. **make sense of** find a meaning in. **sense organ** any of the organs by which the body becomes aware of the external world.

senseless *a.* foolish; unconscious.

sensibility *n.* sensitiveness.

sensible *a.* having or showing good sense; aware. **sensibly** *adv.*

sensitive *a.* receiving impressions or responding to stimuli easily; easily hurt or offended; requiring tact. **sensitively** *adv.*, **sensitivity** *n.*

sensitize *v.* make sensitive. **sensitization** *n.*, **sensitizer** *n.*

sensor *n.* device that responds to a certain stimulus.

sensory *a.* of the senses; receiving and transmitting sensations.

sensual *a.* gratifying to the body; indulging oneself with physical pleasures. **sensualism** *n.*, **sensually** *adv.*, **sensuality** *n.*

sensuous *a.* affecting the senses pleasantly. **sensuously** *adv.*, **sensuousness** *n.*

sent *see* **send**.

sentence *n.* series of words making a single complete statement; punishment awarded by a law court. — *v.* declare condemned (to punishment).

sententious *a.* dull and moralizing. **sententiously** *adv.*, **sententiousness** *n.*

sentient *a.* capable of perceiving and feeling things. **sentiently** *adv.*, **sentience** *n.*

sentiment *n.* mental feeling; opinion; sentimentality.

sentimental *a.* full of romantic or nostalgic feeling. **sentimentalism** *n.*, **sentimentally** *adv.*, **sentimentality** *n.*

sentinel *n.* sentry.

sentry *n.* soldier posted to keep watch and guard something.

sepal *n.* each of the leaf-like parts forming a calyx.

separable *a.* able to be separated. **separability** *n.*

separate *a.* /séppərət/ not joined or united with others. — *v.* /séppərayt/ divide; set, move, or keep apart; cease to live together as a married couple. **separately** *adv.*, **separation** *n.*, **separator** *n.*

separatist *n.* person who favours separation from a larger (esp. political) unit. **separatism** *n.*

sepia *n.* brown colouring matter; rich reddish-brown.

sepsis *n.* septic condition.

septet *n.* group of seven instruments or voices; music for these.

septic *a.* infected with harmful micro-organisms. **septic tank** tank in which sewage is liquefied by bacterial activity.

septicaemia /séptiseémiə/ *n.* blood poisoning.

septuagenarian *n.* person in his or her seventies.

sepulchre /séppəlkər/ *n.* tomb.

sequel *n.* what follows, esp. as a result; novel or film etc. continuing the story of an earlier one.

sequence *n.* following of one thing after another; set of things belonging next to each other in a particular order; section dealing with one topic in a film.

sequential *a.* forming a sequence; occurring as a result; serial. **sequentially** *adv.*

sequester *v.* seclude; confiscate.

sequestrate *v.* confiscate. **sequestration** *n.*

sequin *n.* circular spangle. **sequinned** *a.*

sequoia /sikwóyə/ *n.* Californian tree growing to a great height.

seraglio /seraáliō/ *n.* (*pl.* **-os**) harem of a Muslim palace.

seraph *n.* (*pl.* **-im**) member of the highest order of angels. **seraphic** *a.*

serenade *n.* music played by a lover to his lady, or suitable for this. — *v.* sing or play a serenade to.

serendipity *n.* making of pleasant discoveries by accident.

serene *a.* calm and cheerful. **serenely** *adv.*, **serenity** *n.*

serf *n.* medieval farm labourer forced to work for his landowner; oppressed labourer. **serfdom** *n.*

serge *n.* strong twilled fabric.

sergeant /saárjənt/ *n.* non-commissioned army officer ranking just above corporal; police officer ranking just below inspector. **sergeant major** warrant officer assisting an adjutant.

serial *n.* story presented in a series of instalments. — *a.* of or forming a series. **serially** *adv.*

serialize *v.* produce as a serial. **serialization** *n.*

series *n.* (*pl.* **series**) number of things of the same kind, or related to each other, occurring or arranged or produced in order.

serious *a.* solemn; sincere; important; not slight. **seriously** *adv.*, **seriousness** *n.*

sermon *n.* talk on a religious or moral subject, esp. during a religious service.

sermonize *v.* give a long moralizing talk. **sermonizer** *n.*

serpent *n.* snake, esp. a large one.

serpentine *a.* twisting like a snake.

serrated *a.* having a series of small projections. **serration** *n.*

serried /sérrid/ *a.* arranged in a close series.

serum *n.* (*pl.* **sera**) fluid left when blood has clotted; this used for inoculation; watery fluid from animal tissue. **serous** *a.*

servant *n.* person employed to do domestic work in a household or as an attendant; employee.

serve *v.* perform or provide services for; be employed (in the army etc.); be suitable (for); present (food etc.) for others to consume; attend to (customers); (of food) be enough for; set the ball in play at tennis etc.; deliver (a legal writ etc.) to (a person). — *n.* service in tennis etc. **server** *n.*

service *n.* act of serving; being a servant; working for an employer; department of people employed by a public organization; (*pl.*) armed forces; system that performs work for customers or supplies public needs; religious ceremony or meeting; set of dishes etc. for serving a meal; game in which one serves in tennis etc.; maintenance and repair of machinery. — *v.* maintain and repair (machinery); supply with service(s); pay the interest on (a loan). **service area** area beside a motorway where petrol and refreshments etc. are available. **service flat** flat where domestic service is provided. **service road** road giving access to houses etc. but not for use by through traffic. **service station** garage selling petrol etc.

serviceable *a.* usable; hard-wearing.

serviceman, servicewoman *ns.* (*pl.* **-men, -women**) member of the armed services.

serviette *n.* table napkin.

servile *a.* menial; excessively submissive. **servilely** *adv.*, **servility** *n.*

servitude *n.* condition of being forced to work for others.

servo- *pref.* power-assisted.

sesame /séssəmi/ *n.* tropical plant with seeds that yield oil or are used as food; its seeds.

session *n.* meeting(s) for discussing or deciding something; period spent in an activity; academic year in certain universities.

set [1] *v.* (**set, setting**) put, place, fix in position or readiness; make or become hard or firm or established; fix or appoint (a date etc.); establish; assign as something to be done; put into a specified state; have a certain movement; be brought towards or below the horizon by earth's movement. — *n.* way a thing sets or is set; process of setting hair; scenery or stage for a play or film; (also **sett**) badger's burrow. **be set on** be determined about. **set about** begin (a task); attack. **set back** halt or slow the progress of; (*sl.*) cost (a person) a specified amount. **set-back** *n.* setting back of progress. **set eyes on** catch sight of. **set fire to** cause to burn. **set forth** set out. **set in** become established. **set off** begin a journey; cause to begin; cause to explode; improve the appearance of by contrast. **set out** declare, make known; begin a journey. **set piece** formal or elaborate construction. **set sail** begin a voyage. **set square** right-angled triangular drawing instrument. **set-up** *n.* (*colloq.*) structure of an organization.

set [2] *n.* people or things grouped as similar or forming a unit; games forming part of a match in tennis etc.; radio or television receiver.

sett *n.* (*see* **set** [1] *n.*)

settee *n.* sofa.

setter *n.* person or thing that sets; dog of a long-haired breed.

setting *n.* way or place in which a thing is set; set of cutlery or crockery for one person.

settle [1] *n.* wooden seat with a high back and arms.

settle [2] *v.* place so as to stay in position; establish, become established; make one's home; occupy (a previously unoccupied area); sink, come to rest; arrange as desired or conclusively, deal with; make or become calm or orderly; pay (a bill etc.); bestow legally. **settle up** pay what is owing. **settler** *n.*

settlement *n.* settling; business or financial arrangement; amount or property settled legally on a person; place occupied by settlers.

seven *a.* & *n.* one more than six (7, VII). **seventh** *a.* & *n.*

seventeen *a.* & *n.* one more than sixteen (17, XVII). **seventeenth** *a.* & *n.*

seventy *a.* & *n.* seven times ten (70, LXX). **seventieth** *a.* & *n.*

sever *v.* cut or break off. **severance** *n.*

several *a.* a few, more than two but not many. — *pron.* several people or things.

severe *a.* strict; harsh; intense; (of style) plain, without decoration. **severely** *adv.*, **severity** *n.*

sew /sō/ *v.* (**sewed, sewn** *or* **sewed**) fasten by passing thread through material, using a threaded needle or an awl etc.; make or fasten (a thing) by sewing. **sewing** *n.*

sewage /so͞o-ij/ *n.* liquid waste drained from houses etc. for disposal.

sewer [1] /so͞oər/ *n.* one who sews.

sewer [2] /so͞o ər/ *n.* drain for carrying sewage.

sewerage *n.* system of sewers.

sewn *see* **sew**.

sex *n.* either of the two main groups (*male* and *female*) into which living things are placed according to their reproductive functions; fact of belonging to one of these; sexual feelings or impulses; sexual intercourse. — *v.* judge the sex of. **sexer** *n.*

sexagenarian *n.* person in his or her sixties.

sexist *a.* discriminating in favour of members of one sex; assuming a person's abilities and social functions are predetermined by his or her sex. — *n.* person who does this. **sexism** *n.*

sexless *a.* lacking sex, neuter; not involving sexual feelings.

sextant *n.* instrument for finding one's position by measuring the height of the sun etc.

sextet *n.* group of six instruments or voices; music for these.

sexton *n.* official in charge of a church and churchyard.

sextuplet *n.* one of six children born at one birth.

sexual *a.* of sex or the sexes; (of reproduction) occurring by fusion of male and female cells. **sexual intercourse** copulation, insertion of the penis into the vagina. **sexually** *adv.*, **sexuality** *n.*

sexy *a.* (**-ier, -iest**) sexually attractive or stimulating. **sexily** *adv.*, **sexiness** *n.*

shabby *a.* (**-ier, -iest**) worn; dilapidated; poorly dressed; unfair, dishonourable. **shabbily** *adv.*, **shabbiness** *n.*

shack *n.* roughly built hut.

shackle *n.* one of a pair of metal rings joined by a chain, for fastening a prisoner's wrists or ankles. — *v.* put shackles on; impede, restrict.

shade *n.* comparative darkness; place sheltered from the sun; degree or depth of colour; differing variety; small amount; screen or cover used to block or moderate light; (*pl.*) darkness of night or evening. — *v.* block the rays of; give shade to; darken (parts of a drawing etc.); pass gradually into another colour or variety.

shadow *n.* shade; patch of this where a body blocks light rays; person's inseparable companion; slight trace; gloom. — *v.* cast shadow over; follow and watch secretly. **shadow-boxing** *n.* boxing against an imaginary opponent as a form of training. **shadower** *n.*, **shadowy** *a.*

shady *a.* (**-ier, -iest**) giving shade; situated in shade; disreputable, not completely honest. **shadily** *adv.*, **shadiness** *n.*

shaft *n.* arrow, spear; long slender straight part of a thing; long bar; large axle; vertical or sloping passage or opening.

shag *n.* shaggy mass; strong coarse tobacco; cormorant.

shaggy *a.* (**-ier, -iest**) having long rough hair or fibre; (of hair etc.) rough and thick. **shaggy-dog story** lengthy anecdote with a twist of humour at the end. **shagginess** *n.*

shagreen *n.* untanned leather with a granulated surface; sharkskin.

shake *v.* (**shook, shaken**) move quickly up and down or to and fro; dislodge by doing this; shock; make less firm; (of the voice) become uneven; (*colloq.*) shake hands. — *n.* shaking, being shaken; shock. **shake hands** clasp right hands in greeting or parting or agreement. **shake up** mix by shaking; rouse from lethargy, shock. **shake-up** *n.* upheaval, reorganization. **shaker** *n.*

shaky *a.* (**-ier, -iest**) shaking, unsteady; unreliable. **shakily** *adv.*, **shakiness** *n.*

shale *n.* slate-like stone. **shaly** *a.*

shall *v.aux.* used with *I* and *we* to express future tense, and with other words in promises or statements of obligation.

shallot *n.* onion-like plant.

shallow *a.* of little depth; superficial. — *n.* shallow place. — *v.* make or become shallow. **shallowness** *n.*

sham *n.* pretence; thing that is not genuine. — *a.* pretended; not genuine. — *v.* (**shammed**) pretend; pretend to be.

shamble *v.* & *n.* walk or run in a shuffling or lazy way.

shambles *n.* scene or condition of great bloodshed or disorder.

shame *n.* painful mental feeling aroused by having done something dishonourable or ridiculous; ability to feel this; person or thing causing shame; something regrettable. — *v.* bring shame on; make ashamed; compel by arousing shame. **shameful** *a.*, **shamefully** *adv.*, **shameless** *a.*, **shamelessly** *adv.*

shamefaced *a.* looking ashamed.

shammy *n.* chamois leather.

shampoo *n.* liquid used to wash hair; preparation for cleaning upholstery etc.; process of shampooing. — *v.* wash or clean with shampoo.

shamrock *n.* clover-like plant.

shandy *n.* mixed drink of beer and ginger beer or lemonade.

shank *n.* leg, esp. from knee to ankle; thing's shaft or stem.
shantung *n.* soft Chinese silk.
shanty [1] *n.* shack. **shanty town** poor area of town, consisting of shanties.
shanty [2] *n.* sailors' traditional song.
shape *n.* area or form with a definite outline; form, condition; orderly arrangement. — *v.* give shape to; develop into a certain condition. **shapeless** *a.*
shapely *a.* (**-ier**, **-iest**) having a pleasant shape. **shapeliness** *n.*
shard *n.* broken piece of pottery.
share *n.* part of something that one is entitled to have or do; one of the equal parts forming a business company's capital and entitling the holder to a proportion of the profits. — *v.* give or have a share (of). **share-out** *n.* division into shares. **shareholder** *n.*, **sharer** *n.*
shark *n.* large voracious sea fish; (*colloq.*) person who ruthlessly extorts money, swindler.
sharkskin *n.* fabric with a slightly lustrous textured weave.
sharp *a.* having a fine edge or point capable of cutting; abrupt, not gradual; well-defined; (of tastes or smells) causing a smarting sensation; mentally alert; unscrupulous; above the correct pitch in music. — *adv.* punctually; suddenly; at a sharp angle. — *n.* (sign indicating) music note raised by a semitone. **sharp practice** barely honest dealing. **sharply** *adv.*, **sharpness** *n.*
sharpen *v.* make or become sharp or sharper. **sharpener** *n.*
sharpshooter *n.* marksman.
shatter *v.* break violently into small pieces; destroy utterly; upset the calmness of.
shave *v.* scrape (growing hair) off the skin; clear (the chin etc.) of hair thus; cut thin slices from; graze gently in passing. — *n.* shaving of hair from the face. **shaver** *n.*
shaven *a.* shaved.
shaving *n.* thin strip of wood etc. shaved off.
shawl *n.* large piece of soft fabric worn round the shoulders or wrapped round a baby.
she *pron.* female (or thing personified as female) previously mentioned. — *n.* female animal.
sheaf *n.* (*pl.* **sheaves**) bundle of papers; tied bundle of cornstalks.
shear *v.* (**shorn** *or* **sheared**) cut or trim with shears or other sharp device; break because of strain. **shearer** *n.*
shears *n.pl.* large cutting instrument shaped like scissors.
sheath /sheeth/ *n.* close-fitting cover, esp. for a blade or tool.
sheathe /sheeth/ *v.* put into a case; encase in a covering.
shed [1] *n.* building for storing things, or for use as a workshop.
shed [2] *v.* (**shed**, **shedding**) lose by a natural falling off; take off; allow to fall or flow.
sheen *n.* gloss, lustre. **sheeny** *a.*
sheep *n.* (*pl.* **sheep**) grass-eating animal with a thick fleecy coat.
sheepdog *n.* dog trained to guard and herd sheep.
sheepish *a.* bashful, embarrassed. **sheepishly** *adv.*, **sheepishness** *n.*
sheepskin *n.* sheep's skin with the fleece on.
sheer [1] *a.* pure, not mixed or qualified; very steep; (of fabric) very thin, transparent. — *adv.* directly, straight up or down. **sheerly** *adv.*, **sheerness** *n.*
sheer [2] *v.* swerve from a course.
sheet *n.* piece of cotton used in pairs as inner bedclothes; large thin piece of glass, metal, paper, etc.; expanse of water, flame, etc.; rope securing the lower corner of a sail. **sheet anchor** large anchor for emergency use; thing on which one relies.
sheikh /shayk/ *n.* Arab ruler. **sheikhdom** *n.* his territory.
shekel *n.* unit of money in Israel; (*pl.*, *colloq.*) money, riches.
shelf *n.* (*pl.* **shelves**) board or slab fastened horizontally for things to be placed on; thing resembling this, ledge. **shelf-life** *n.* time for which a stored thing remains usable.
shell *n.* hard outer covering of eggs, nut kernels, and of animals such as snails and tortoises; firm framework or covering; metal case filled with explosive, for firing from a large gun. — *v.* remove the shell(s) of; fire explosive shells at. **shell-shock** *n.* nervous breakdown from exposure to battle conditions.
shellac *n.* resinous substance used in varnish. — *v.* (**shellacked**) coat with this.
shellfish *n.* water animal that has a shell.
shelter *n.* structure that shields against danger, wind, rain, etc.; refuge, shielded condition. — *v.* provide with shelter; find or take shelter.
shelve *v.* put aside for later consideration or permanently; slope.
shelving *n.* shelves; material for these.
shepherd *n.* person who tends sheep. — *v.* guide (people). **shepherd's pie** pie of minced meat topped with mashed potato.

sherbet *n.* fizzy sweet drink, powder from which this is made.

sheriff *n.* Crown's chief executive officer in a county; chief judge of a district in Scotland; (*US*) chief law-enforcing officer of a county.

Sherpa *n.* member of a Himalayan people of Nepal and Tibet.

sherry *n.* strong wine orig. from southern Spain.

shibboleth *n.* old slogan or principle still considered essential by some members of a party.

shield *n.* piece of armour carried on the arm to protect the body; trophy in the form of this; protective structure. — *v.* protect, screen.

shift *v.* change or move from one position or form to another; transfer (blame etc.); (*sl.*) move quickly. — *n.* change of place or form etc.; set of workers who start work when another set finishes; time for which they work.

shiftless *a.* lazy and inefficient.

shifty *a.* **(-ier, -iest)** evasive; untrustworthy. **shiftily** *adv.*, **shiftiness** *n.*

Shiite /shée-īt/ *n.* & *a.* (member) of a Muslim sect opposed to the Sunni.

shilly-shally *v.* be unable to make up one's mind firmly.

shimmer *v.* & *n.* (shine with) a soft quivering light.

shin *n.* front of the leg below the knee; lower foreleg. — *v.* **(shinned) shin up** climb.

shindig *n.* (*colloq.*) din, brawl.

shine *v.* **(shone)** give out or reflect light, be bright; excel; cause to shine; **(shined)** polish. — *n.* brightness; high polish.

shingle [1] *n.* wooden roof tile.

shingle [2] *n.* small rounded pebbles; stretch of these, esp. on a shore. **shingly** *a.*

shingles *n.* disease with a rash of small blisters.

Shinto *n.* Japanese religion revering ancestors and nature-spirits. **Shintoism** *n.*, **Shintoist** *n.*

shiny *a.* **(-ier, -iest)** shining, glossy. **shininess** *n.*

ship *n.* large sea-going vessel. — *v.* **(shipped)** put or take on board a ship; transport. **shipper** *n.*

shipmate *n.* person travelling or working on the same ship as another.

shipment *n.* shipping of goods; consignment shipped.

shipping *n.* ships collectively.

shipshape *adv.* & *a.* in good order, tidy.

shipwreck *n.* destruction of a ship by storm or striking rock etc. **shipwrecked** *a.*

shipyard *n.* establishment where ships are built.

shire *n.* county. **shire-horse** *n.* horse of a heavy powerful breed.

shirk *v.* avoid (duty or work etc.) selfishly. **shirker** *n.*

shirt *n.* lightweight garment for the upper part of the body.

shirty *a.* (*colloq.*) annoyed, angry.

shiver [1] *v.* tremble slightly esp. with cold or fear. — *n.* shivering movement. **shivery** *a.*

shiver [2] *v.* shatter.

shoal [1] *n.* great number of fish swimming together. — *v.* form shoals.

shoal [2] *n.* shallow place; underwater sandbank.

shock [1] *n.* effect of a violent impact or shake; sudden violent effect on the mind or emotions; acute weakness caused by injury, pain, or mental shock; effect of a sudden discharge of electricity through the body. — *v.* cause to suffer shock or a shock; horrify, disgust, seem scandalous to.

shock [2] *n.* bushy mass of hair.

shocker *n.* (*colloq.*) shocking person or thing.

shocking *a.* causing great astonishment, indignation, or disgust; scandalous; (*colloq.*) very bad.

shod *see* **shoe**.

shoddy *a.* **(-ier, -iest)** of poor quality. **shoddily** *adv.*, **shoddiness** *n.*

shoe *n.* outer covering for a person's foot; horseshoe; part of a brake that presses against a wheel. — *v.* **(shod, shoeing)** fit with a shoe or shoes. **shoe-tree** *n.* shaped block for keeping a shoe in shape.

shoehorn *n.* curved implement for easing one's heel into a shoe.

shoelace *n.* a cord for lacing up shoes.

shoeshine *n.* (*US*) polishing of shoes.

shoestring *n.* shoelace; (*colloq.*) barely adequate amount of capital.

shone *see* **shine**.

shoo *int.* sound uttered to frighten animals away. — *v.* **(shooed)** drive away by this.

shook *see* **shake**.

shoot *v.* **(shot)** fire (a gun etc., or a missile); kill or wound with a missile from a gun etc.; hunt with a gun for sport; send out or move swiftly; (of a plant) put forth buds or shoots; take a shot at goal; photograph, film. — *n.* young branch or new growth of a plant. **shoot up** rise suddenly; grow rapidly. **shooting star** small meteor seen to move quickly. **shooting stick** walking stick with a small folding seat in the handle. **shooter** *n.*

shop *n.* building or room where goods

or services are sold to the public; workshop; one's own work as a subject of conversation. — *v.* (**shopped**) go into a shop or shops to buy things; (*sl.*) inform against. **shop around** look for the best bargain. **shop-floor** *n.* workers as distinct from management or senior union officials. **shop-soiled** *a.* soiled from being on display in a shop. **shop steward** trade union official elected by fellow workers as their spokesman.

shoplifter *n.* person who steals goods that are displayed in a shop. **shoplifting** *n.*

shopper *n.* person who shops; bag for holding shopping.

shopping *n.* buying goods in shops; goods bought.

shore [1] *n.* land along the edge of a sea or lake.

shore [2] *v.* prop or support with a length of timber.

shorn *see* **shear**.

short *a.* measuring little from end to end in space or time, or from head to foot; insufficient; having insufficient; concise, brief; curt; (of pastry) crisp and easily crumbled. — *adv.* abruptly. — *n.* (*colloq.*) drink of spirits; short circuit; (*pl.*) trousers that do not reach the knee. — *v.* (*colloq.*) short-circuit. **short-change** *v.* cheat, esp. by giving insufficient change. **short circuit** fault in an electrical circuit when current flows by a shorter route than the normal one. **short-circuit** *v.* cause a short circuit in; bypass. **short cut** quicker route or method. **short-handed** *a.* having insufficient workers. **short-list** *v.* put on a short list from which a final choice will be made. **short-sighted** *a.* able to see clearly only what is close; lacking foresight. **short ton** (*see* **ton**). **short wave** radio wave of frequency greater than 3 MHz.

shortage *n.* lack, insufficiency.

shortbread *n.* rich sweet biscuit.

shortcake *n.* shortbread.

shortcoming *n.* failure to reach a required standard; fault.

shorten *v.* make or become shorter.

shortfall *n.* deficit.

shorthand *n.* method of writing rapidly with quickly made symbols.

shortly *adv.* after a short time; in a few words; curtly.

shot *see* **shoot**. — *n.* firing of a gun etc.; sound of this; person of specified skill in shooting; missile(s) for a cannon or gun etc.; heavy ball thrown as a sport; attempt to hit something or reach a target; stroke in certain ball games; attempt; injection; photograph; (*colloq.*) dram of spirits. **like a shot** (*colloq.*) without hesitation.

shotgun *n.* gun for firing small shot at close range.

should *v.aux.* used to express duty or obligation, possible or expected future event, or (with *I* and *we*) a polite statement or a conditional or indefinite clause.

shoulder *n.* part of the body where the arm or foreleg is attached; animal's upper foreleg as a joint of meat. — *v.* push with one's shoulder; take (blame or responsibility) on oneself. **shoulder arms** hold a rifle with the barrel against one's shoulder. **shoulder blade** large flat bone of the shoulder.

shout *n.* loud cry or utterance. — *v.* utter a shout; call loudly. **shout down** silence by shouting.

shove *n.* rough push. — *v.* push roughly; (*colloq.*) put.

shovel *n.* spade-like tool for scooping earth etc.; mechanical scoop. — *v.* (**shovelled**) shift or clear with or as if with a shovel; scoop roughly.

shoveller *n.* duck with a broad shovel-like beak.

show *v.* (**showed, shown**) allow or cause to be seen, offer for inspection or viewing; demonstrate, point out, prove; cause to understand; conduct; present an image of; be able to be seen. — *n.* process of showing; display, public exhibition or performance; outward appearance. **show business** entertainment profession. **show off** display well or proudly or ostentatiously; try to impress people. **show of hands** raising of hands in voting. **show-piece** *n.* excellent specimen used for exhibition. **show up** make or be clearly visible; reveal (a fault etc.); (*colloq.*) arrive.

showdown *n.* confrontation that settles an argument.

shower *n.* brief fall of rain or of snow, stones, etc.; sudden influx of letters or gifts etc.; device or cabinet in which water is sprayed on a person's body; wash in this; (*US*) party for giving presents. — *v.* send or come in a shower; take a shower.

showerproof *a.* (of fabric) able to keep out slight rain. — *v.* make showerproof.

showery *a.* with showers of rain.

showjumping *n.* competitive sport of riding horses to jump over obstacles. **showjumper** *n.*

showman *n.* (*pl.* **-men**) organizer of circuses or theatrical entertainments.

showmanship *n.* skill in presenting entertainment or goods etc. well.

shown *see* **show**.

showroom *n.* room where goods are displayed for inspection.

showy *a.* (**-ier**, **-iest**) making a good display; brilliant, gaudy. **showily** *adv.*, **showiness** *n.*

shrank *see* **shrink**.

shrapnel *n.* pieces of metal scattered from an exploding bomb.

shred *n.* small strip torn or cut from something; small amount. — *v.* (**shredded**) tear or cut into shreds. **shredder** *n.*

shrew *n.* small mouse-like animal.

shrewd *a.* showing sound judgement, clever. **shrewdly** *adv.*, **shrewdness** *n.*

shriek *n.* shrill cry or scream. — *v.* utter (with) a shriek.

shrike *n.* bird with a strong hooked beak.

shrill *a.* piercing and high-pitched in sound. **shrilly** *adv.*, **shrillness** *n.*

shrimp *n.* small edible shellfish; (*colloq.*) very small person.

shrimping *n.* catching shrimps.

shrine *n.* sacred or revered place.

shrink *v.* (**shrank**, **shrunk**) make or become smaller; draw back to avoid something. — *n.* (*sl.*) psychiatrist.

shrinkage *n.* shrinking of textile fabric; loss by theft or wastage.

shrivel *v.* (**shrivelled**) shrink and wrinkle from great heat or cold or lack of moisture.

shroud *n.* cloth wrapping a dead body for burial; thing that conceals; one of the ropes supporting a ship's mast. — *v.* wrap in a shroud; conceal.

shrub *n.* woody plant smaller than a tree. **shrubby** *a.*

shrubbery *n.* area planted with shrubs.

shrug *v.* (**shrugged**) raise (one's shoulders) as a gesture of indifference or doubt or helplessness. — *n.* this movement.

shrunk *see* **shrink**.

shrunken *a.* having shrunk.

shudder *v.* shiver or shake violently. — *n.* this movement.

shuffle *v.* walk without lifting one's feet clear of the ground; rearrange, jumble. — *n.* shuffling movement or walk; rearrangement.

shun *v.* (**shunned**) avoid.

shunt *v.* move (a train) to a side track; divert.

shush *int.* & *v.* (*colloq.*) hush.

shut *v.* (**shut, shutting**) move (a door or window etc.) into position to block an opening; be moved thus; prevent access to (a place); bring or fold parts of (a thing) together; trap or exclude by shutting something. **shut down** stop or cease working or business. **shut-down** *n.* this process. **shut-eye** *n.* (*colloq.*) sleep. **shut up** shut securely; (*colloq.*) stop or cease talking or making a noise.

shutter *n.* screen that can be closed over a window; device that opens and closes the aperture of a camera. **shuttered** *a.*

shuttle *n.* device carrying the weft-thread in weaving; vehicle used in a shuttle service; spacecraft for repeated use. — *v.* move, travel, or send to and fro. **shuttle service** transport service making frequent journeys to and fro.

shuttlecock *n.* small cone-shaped feathered object struck to and fro in badminton.

shy [1] *a.* timid and lacking self-confidence. — *v.* jump or move suddenly in alarm. **shyly** *adv.*, **shyness** *n.*

shy [2] *v.* & *n.* (*colloq.*) throw.

SI *abbr.* (*Fr.*) Système International, the international metric system.

Siamese *a.* of Siam, former name of Thailand. **Siamese cat** cat with pale fur and darker face, paws, and tail. **Siamese twins** twins whose bodies are joined at birth.

sibling *n.* brother or sister.

sibyl *n.* pagan prophetess. **sibylline** *a.*

sic *adv.* used or spelt in the way quoted.

Sicilian *a.* & *n.* (native) of Sicily.

sick *a.* unwell; vomiting; likely to vomit; distressed, disgusted; finding amusement in misfortune or morbid subjects.

sicken *v.* become ill; distress; disgust. **be sickening for** be in the first stages of (a disease).

sickle *n.* curved blade used for cutting corn etc.

sickly *a.* (**-ier, -iest**) unhealthy; causing sickness or distaste; weak. **sickliness** *n.*

sickness *n.* illness; vomiting.

side *n.* surface of an object, esp. one that is not the top, bottom, front, back, or end; bounding line of a plane figure; either of the two halves into which something is divided; part near an edge; slope of a hill or ridge; region next to a person or thing; aspect of a problem etc.; one of two opposing groups or teams etc. — *a.* at or on the side. — *v.* join forces (with a person) in a dispute. **on the side** as a sideline; as a surreptitious activity. **side by side** close together. **side effect** secondary (usu. bad) effect. **side-saddle** *n.* saddle on which a woman rider sits with both legs on the same side of the horse; (*adv.*) sitting thus.

sideboard *n.* piece of dining-room furniture with drawers and cupboards for china etc.; (*pl.*, *colloq.*) sideburns.

sideburns *n.pl.* short whiskers on the cheek.

sidelight *n.* incidental information; either of two small lights on the front of a vehicle.

sideline *n.* thing done in addition to one's main activity; (*pl.*) lines bounding the sides of a football pitch etc., place for spectators; (*pl.*) position etc. apart from the main action.

sidelong *a.* & *adv.* sideways.

sidereal /sīdeeriəl/ *a.* of or measured by the stars.

sideshow *n.* small show forming part of a large one.

sideslip *n.* sideways movement, skid. — *v.* (**-slipped**) move thus.

sidestep *v.* (**-stepped**) avoid by stepping sideways; evade.

sidetrack *v.* divert.

sidewalk *n.* (*US*) pavement.

sideways *adv.* & *a.* to or from one side; with one side forward.

siding *n.* short track by the side of a railway, used in shunting.

sidle *v.* advance in a timid, furtive, or cringing way.

siege *n.* surrounding and blockading of a place by armed forces, in order to capture it.

sienna *n.* a kind of clay used as colouring matter. **burnt sienna** reddish-brown. **raw sienna** brownish-yellow.

sierra *n.* chain of mountains with jagged peaks in Spain or Spanish America.

siesta *n.* afternoon nap or rest, esp. in hot countries.

sieve /siv/ *n.* utensil with a mesh through which liquids or fine particles can pass. — *v.* put through a sieve.

sift *v.* sieve; examine carefully and select or analyse.

sigh *n.* long deep breath given out audibly in sadness, tiredness, relief, etc. — *v.* give or express with a sigh.

sight *n.* ability to see; seeing, being seen; thing seen or worth seeing; unsightly thing; device looked through to aim or observe with a gun or telescope etc. — *v.* get a sight of; aim or observe with a gunsight etc. **at** *or* **on sight** as soon as seen. **sight-read** *v.* play or sing (music) without preliminary study of the score.

sightless *a.* blind.

sightseeing *n.* visiting places of interest. **sightseer** *n.*

sign *n.* thing perceived that suggests the existence of something; board bearing the name of a shop etc.; notice displayed; action or gesture conveying information etc.; any of the twelve divisions of the zodiac. — *v.* make a sign; write (one's name) on a document, convey or engage or acknowledge by this.

signal *n.* sign or gesture giving information or a command; object placed to give notice or warning; sequence of electrical impulses or radio waves transmitted or received. — *v.* (**signalled**) make a signal or signals; communicate with or announce thus. — *a.* noteworthy. **signal-box** *n.* small railway building with signalling apparatus. **signaller** *n.*, **signally** *adv.*

signalman *n.* (*pl.* **-men**) person responsible for operating railway signals.

signatory *n.* one of the parties who sign an agreement.

signature *n.* person's name or initials written by himself in signing something; indication of key or tempo at the beginning of a musical score. **signature tune** tune used to announce a particular performer or programme.

signet ring finger ring with an engraved design.

significance *n.* meaning; importance. **significant** *a.*, **significantly** *adv.*

signification *n.* meaning.

signify *v.* be a sign or symbol of; have as a meaning; make known; matter.

signpost *n.* post with arms showing the direction of certain places.

Sikh /seek/ *n.* member of an Indian religion believing in one God. **Sikhism** *n.*

silage *n.* green fodder stored and fermented in a silo.

silence *n.* absence of sound or of speaking. — *v.* make silent.

silencer *n.* device for reducing sound.

silent *a.* without sound; not speaking. **silently** *adv.*

silhouette /siloo-ét/ *n.* dark shadow or outline seen against a light background. — *v.* show as a silhouette.

silica *n.* compound of silicon occurring as quartz and in sandstone etc. **siliceous** *a.*

silicate *n.* compound of silicon.

silicon *n.* chemical substance found in the earth's crust in its compound forms. **silicon chip** silicon microchip.

silicone *n.* organic compound of silicon, used in paint, varnish, and lubricants.

silicosis *n.* lung disease caused by inhaling dust that contains silica.

silk *n.* fine strong soft fibre produced by silkworms; thread or cloth made from it or resembling this. **silky** *a.*

silken *a.* like silk.

silkworm *n.* caterpillar which spins its cocoon of silk.

sill *n.* strip of stone, wood, or metal

at the base of a doorway or window opening.

silly *a.* (**-ier**, **-iest**) lacking good sense, foolish, unwise; feeble-minded. **silliness** *n.*

silo *n.* (*pl.* **-os**) pit or airtight structure for holding silage; pit or tower for storing grain or cement or radioactive waste; underground place where a missile is kept ready for firing.

silt *n.* sediment deposited by water in a channel or harbour etc. — *v.* block or become blocked with silt.

silver *n.* white precious metal; articles made of this; coins made of an alloy resembling it; household cutlery; colour of silver. — *a.* made of or coloured like silver. **silver jubilee, silver wedding** 25th anniversary.

silverfish *n.* small wingless insect with a fish-like body.

silverside *n.* joint of beef cut from the haunch, below topside.

silvery *a.* like silver; having a clear gentle ringing sound.

simian *a.* monkey-like, ape-like. — *n.* monkey, ape.

similar *a.* alike but not the same; of the same kind or amount. **similarly** *adv.*, **similarity** *n.*

simile /simmili/ *n.* figure of speech in which one thing is compared to another.

similitude *n.* similarity.

simmer *v.* boil very gently; be in a state of barely suppressed anger or excitement. **simmer down** become less excited.

simper *v.* smile in an affected way. — *n.* affected smile.

simple *a.* of one element or kind; not complicated or showy; guileless; feeble-minded. **simply** *adv.*, **simplicity** *n.*

simpleton *n.* foolish or feeble-minded person.

simplify *v.* make simple; make easy to do or understand. **simplification** *n.*

simplistic *a.* over-simplified. **simplistically** *adv.*

simulate *v.* pretend; imitate the form or condition of. **simulation** *n.*, **simulator** *n.*

simultaneous *a.* occurring at the same time. **simultaneously** *adv.*, **simultaneity** *n.*

sin *n.* breaking of a religious or moral law; act which does this. — *v.* (**sinned**) commit a sin.

since *prep.* after; from (a specified time) until now, within that period. — *conj.* from the time that; because. — *adv.* since that time or event.

sincere *a.* without pretence or deceit. **sincerely** *adv.*, **sincerity** *n.*

sine *n.* ratio of the length of one side of a right-angled triangle to the hypotenuse.

sinecure *n.* position of profit with no work attached.

sinew *n.* tough fibrous tissue joining muscle to bone; tendon; (*pl.*) muscles, strength. **sinewy** *a.*

sinful *a.* full of sin, wicked. **sinfully** *adv.*, **sinfulness** *n.*

sing *v.* (**sang, sung**) make musical sounds with the voice; perform (a song); make a humming sound. **singer** *n.*

singe /sinj/ *v.* (**singeing**) burn slightly; burn the ends or edges of. — *n.* slight burn.

single *a.* one only, not double or multiple; designed for one person or thing; unmarried; (of a ticket) valid for an outward journey only. — *n.* one person or thing; room etc. for one person; single ticket; pop record with one piece of music on each side; (usu. *pl.*) game with one player on each side. — *v.* choose or distinguish from others. **single figures** numbers from 1 to 9. **single-handed** *a.* without help. **single-minded** *a.* with one's mind set on a single purpose. **single parent** person bringing up a child or children without a partner. **singly** *adv.*

singlet *n.* sleeveless vest.

singleton *n.* thing that occurs singly.

singsong *a.* with a monotonous rise and fall of the voice. — *n.* singsong manner; informal singing by a group of people.

singular *n.* form of a noun or verb used in referring to one person or thing. — *a.* of this form; uncommon, extraordinary. **singularly** *adv.*, **singularity** *n.*

sinister *a.* suggestive of evil; involving wickedness.

sink *v.* (**sank, sunk**) fall or come gradually downwards; make or become submerged; lose value or strength; send (a ball) into a pocket or hole; invest (money). — *n.* fixed basin with a drainage pipe. **sink in** become understood. **sinking fund** money set aside regularly for repayment of a debt etc.

sinker *n.* weight used to sink a fishing line etc.

sinner *n.* person who sins.

sinuous *a.* curving, undulating.

sinus /sīnəss/ *n.* (*pl.* **-uses**) cavity in bone or tissue, esp. that connecting with the nostrils.

sip *n.* & *v.* (**sipped**) drink in small mouthfuls.

siphon *n.* bent pipe or tube used for transferring liquid by utilizing atmospheric pressure; bottle from which soda water etc. is forced out by pressure of gas. — *v.*

flow or draw out through a siphon; take from a source.

sir *n.* polite form of address to a man; **Sir** title of a knight or baronet.

sire *n.* animal's male parent. — *v.* beget.

siren *n.* device that makes a loud prolonged sound as a signal; dangerously fascinating woman.

sirloin *n.* upper (best) part of loin of beef.

sirocco *n.* (*pl.* **-os**) hot wind that reaches Italy from Africa.

sisal /sīs'l/ *n.* rope-fibre made from a tropical plant; this plant.

sissy *n.* weak or timid person. — *a.* characteristic of a sissy.

sister *n.* daughter of the same parents as another person; woman who is a fellow member of a group or Church etc.; nun; senior female nurse. **sister-in-law** *n.* (*pl.* **sisters-in-law**) sister of one's husband or wife; wife of one's brother. **sisterly** *a.*

sisterhood *n.* relationship of sisters; order of nuns; group of women with common aims.

sit *v.* (**sat, sitting**) take or be in a position with the body resting on the buttocks; cause to sit; pose for a portrait; perch; (of animals) rest with legs bent and body on the ground; (of birds) remain on the nest to hatch eggs; be situated; be a candidate (for); (of a committee etc.) hold a session.

sitar *n.* guitar-like Indian musical instrument.

sitcom *n.* (*colloq.*) situation comedy.

site *n.* place where something is or was or is to be located. — *v.* locate, provide with a site.

sitter *n.* person sitting; babysitter.

sitting *see* **sit**. — *n.* time during which a person or assembly etc. sits; clutch of eggs. **sitting room** room used for sitting in, not a bedroom. **sitting tenant** one already in occupation.

situate *v.* place or put in a certain position. **be situated** be in a certain position.

situation *n.* place (with its surroundings) occupied by something; set of circumstances; position of employment. **situation comedy** broadcast comedy involving the same characters in a series of episodes. **situational** *a.*

six *a.* & *n.* one more than five (6, VI). **sixth** *a.* & *n.*

sixteen *n.* one more than fifteen (16, XVI). **sixteenth** *a.* & *n.*

sixty *a.* & *n.* six times ten (60, LX). **sixtieth** *a.* & *n.*

size [1] *n.* relative bigness, extent; one of a series of standard measurements in which things are made and sold. — *v.* group according to size. **size up** estimate the size of; (*colloq.*) form a judgement of.

size [2] *n.* gluey solution used to glaze paper or stiffen textiles etc. — *v.* treat with size.

sizeable *a.* large; fairly large.

sizzle *v.* make a hissing sound like that of frying.

skate [1] *n.* (*pl.* **skate**) marine flatfish used as food.

skate [2] *n.* boot with a blade or (**roller skate**) wheels attached, for gliding over ice or a hard surface. — *v.* move on skates. **skate over** make only a passing reference to. **skater** *n.*

skateboard *n.* small board with wheels for riding on while standing. — *v.* ride on a skateboard.

skedaddle *v.* (*colloq.*) run away.

skein /skayn/ *n.* loosely coiled bundle of yarn; flock of wild geese etc. in flight.

skeletal *a.* of or like a skeleton.

skeleton *n.* hard supporting structure of an animal body; any supporting structure; framework. **skeleton service** *or* **staff** one reduced to a minimum. **skeleton key** key made so as to fit many locks.

sketch *n.* rough drawing or painting; brief account; short usu. comic play. — *v.* make a sketch or sketches (of).

sketchy *a.* (**-ier, -iest**) rough and not detailed or substantial. **sketchily** *adv.*, **sketchiness** *n.*

skew *a.* slanting, askew. — *v.* make skew; turn or twist round.

skewbald *a.* (of an animal) with irregular patches of white and another colour.

skewer *n.* pin to hold meat or pieces of food together while cooking. — *v.* pierce with a skewer.

ski *n.* (*pl.* **-is**) one of a pair of long narrow strips of wood etc. fixed under the feet for travelling over snow. — *v.* (**ski'd, skiing**) travel on skis. **skier** *n.*

skid *v.* (**skidded**) (of a vehicle) slide uncontrollably. — *n.* skidding movement. **skid-pan** *n.* surface used for practising control of skidding vehicles.

skiff *n.* small light rowing boat.

skilful *a.* having or showing great skill. **skilfully** *adv.*

skill *n.* ability to do something well. **skilled** *a.*

skim *v.* (**skimmed**) take (matter) from the surface of (liquid); glide; read quickly. **skim milk** milk from which the cream has been skimmed.

skimp *v.* supply or use rather less than what is necessary.

skimpy *a.* (**-ier**, **-iest**) scanty. **skimpily** *adv.*, **skimpiness** *n.*

skin *n.* outer covering of the human or other animal body; material made from animal skin; complexion; outer layer; skin-like film on liquid. — *v.* (**skinned**) strip skin from. **skin diving** sport of swimming under water with flippers and breathing apparatus. **skin diver**.

skinflint *n.* miserly person.

skinny *a.* (**-ier**, **-iest**) very thin.

skint *a.* (*sl.*) with no money left.

skip [1] *v.* (**skipped**) move lightly, esp. taking two steps with each foot in turn; jump with a skipping rope; (*colloq.*) omit; (*colloq.*) go away hastily or secretly. — *n.* skipping movement.

skip [2] *n.* large container for builders' rubbish etc.

skipper *n.* & *v.* captain.

skipping rope rope turned over the head and under the feet while jumping.

skirmish *n.* minor fight or conflict. — *v.* take part in a skirmish.

skirt *n.* woman's garment hanging from the waist; this part of a garment; similar part; cut of beef from the lower flank. — *v.* go or be along the edge of.

skirting (board) *n.* narrow board round the bottom of the wall of a room.

skit *n.* short parody.

skittish *a.* frisky.

skittle *n.* one of the wooden pins set up to be bowled down with a ball in the game of **skittles**.

skua *n.* large seagull.

skulduggery *n.* (*colloq.*) trickery.

skulk *v.* loiter stealthily.

skull *n.* bony framework of the head; representation of this.

skullcap *n.* small cap with no peak.

skunk *n.* black bushy-tailed American animal able to spray an evil-smelling liquid; (*sl.*) contemptible person.

sky *n.* region of the clouds or upper air. **sky-blue** *a.* & *n.* bright clear blue.

skydiving *n.* parachuting in which the parachute is not opened until the last moment.

skylark *n.* lark that soars while singing. — *v.* play mischievously.

skylight *n.* window set in the line of a roof or ceiling.

skyscraper *n.* very tall building.

slab *n.* broad flat piece of something solid.

slack *a.* not tight; not busy; negligent. — *n.* slack part. — *v.* slacken; be lazy about work. **slacker** *n.*, **slackly** *adv.*, **slackness** *n.*

slacken *v.* make or become slack.

slacks *n.pl.* trousers for casual wear.

slag *n.* solid waste left when metal has been smelted; (*sl.*) promiscuous woman. — *v.* (**slagged**) (*sl.*) criticize, insult. **slag-heap** *n.* mound of waste matter.

slain *see* **slay**.

slake *v.* satisfy (thirst); combine (lime) with water.

slalom *n.* ski race down a zigzag course; obstacle race in canoes etc.

slam *v.* (**slammed**) shut forcefully and noisily; put or hit forcefully; (*sl.*) criticize severely. — *n.* slamming noise.

slander *n.* false statement uttered maliciously that damages a person's reputation; crime of uttering this. — *v.* utter slander about. **slanderer** *n.*, **slanderous** *a.*

slang *n.* words or phrases or particular meanings of these used very informally for vividness or novelty. **slangy** *a.*

slant *v.* slope; present (news etc.) from a particular point of view. — *n.* slope; way news etc. is slanted, bias. **slantwise** *adv.*

slap *v.* (**slapped**) strike with the open hand or with something flat; place forcefully or carelessly. — *n.* slapping blow. — *adv.* with a slap, directly. **slap-happy** *a.* (*colloq.*) cheerfully casual. **slap-up** *a.* (*colloq.*) first-class.

slapdash *a.* hasty and careless.

slapstick *n.* boisterous comedy.

slash *v.* gash; make a sweeping stroke; strike thus; reduce drastically. — *n.* slashing stroke; cut.

slat *n.* narrow strip of wood, metal, etc.

slate *n.* rock that splits easily into flat blue-grey plates; piece of this used as roofing-material or (formerly) for writing on. — *v.* cover with slates; (*colloq.*) criticize severely.

slaughter *v.* kill (animals) for food; kill ruthlessly or in great numbers. — *n.* this process.

slaughterhouse *n.* place where animals are killed for food.

Slav *a.* & *n.* (member) of any of the peoples of Europe who speak a Slavonic language.

slave *n.* person who is owned by and must work for another; victim of or to a dominating influence; drudge. — *v.* work very hard. **slave-driver** *n.* person who makes others work very hard. **slave-driving** *n.*

slaver *v.* have saliva flowing from the mouth.

slavery *n.* existence or condition of slaves; very hard work.

slavish *a.* excessively submissive or imitative. **slavishly** *adv.*

Slavonic *a.* & *n.* (of) the group of languages including Russian and Polish.

slay *v.* (**slew, slain**) kill.

sleazy *a.* (**-ier, -iest**) dirty; disreputable. **sleaziness** *n.*

sledge *n.* cart with runners instead of wheels, used on snow. — *v.* travel or convey in a sledge.

sledgehammer *n.* large heavy hammer.

sleek *a.* smooth and glossy; looking well fed and thriving. **sleekness** *n.*

sleep *n.* natural condition of rest with unconsciousness and relaxation of muscles; spell of this. — *v.* (**slept**) be or spend (time) in a state of sleep; provide with sleeping accommodation.

sleeper *n.* one who sleeps; beam on which the rails of a railway rest; railway coach fitted for sleeping in; ring worn in a pierced ear to keep the hole from closing.

sleeping bag padded bag for sleeping in.

sleepwalk *v.* walk about while asleep. **sleepwalker** *n.*

sleepy *a.* (**-ier, -iest**) feeling a desire to sleep; without stir or bustle. **sleepily** *adv.*, **sleepiness** *n.*

sleet *n.* hail or snow and rain falling simultaneously. — *v.* fall as sleet. **sleety** *a.*

sleeve *n.* part of a garment covering the arm; tube-like cover; cover for a record. **up one's sleeve** concealed but available.

sleigh /slay/ *n.* sledge, esp. drawn by horses.

sleight of hand /slīt/ skill in using the hands to perform conjuring tricks etc.

slender *a.* slim and graceful; small in amount. **slenderness** *n.*

slept *see* **sleep**.

sleuth /sloōth/ *n.* detective.

slew [1] *v.* turn or swing round.

slew [2] *see* **slay**.

slice *n.* thin flat piece (or a wedge) cut from something; portion; implement for lifting or serving food; slicing stroke. — *v.* cut, esp. into slices; strike (a ball) so that it spins away from the direction intended. **slicer** *n.*

slick *a.* (*colloq.*) quick and cunning; smooth in manner. — *n.* slippery place; patch of oil on the sea. — *v.* (*colloq.*) make sleek.

slide *v.* (**slid**) (cause to) move along a smooth surface touching it always with the same part; move or pass smoothly. — *n.* act of sliding; smooth slope or surface for sliding; sliding part; piece of glass for holding an object under a microscope; picture for projecting onto a screen; hinged clip for holding hair in place. **sliding scale** scale of fees or taxes etc. that varies according to the variation of some standard.

slight *a.* not much, not great, not thorough; slender. — *v.* & *n.* insult by treating with lack of respect. **slightly** *adv.*, **slightness** *n.*

slim *a.* (**slimmer, slimmest**) of small girth or thickness; small, slight, insufficient. — *v.* (**slimmed**) make (oneself) slimmer by dieting, exercise, etc. **slimmer** *n.*, **slimness** *n.*

slime *n.* unpleasant thick slippery liquid substance. **slimy** *a.*, **slimily** *adv.*, **sliminess** *n.*

sling *n.* belt or chain or bandage etc. looped round an object to support or lift it; looped strap used to throw a stone etc. — *v.* (**slung**) suspend or lift or hurl with a sling; (*colloq.*) throw.

slink *v.* (**slunk**) move in a stealthy or shamefaced way.

slinky *a.* smooth and sinuous.

slip [1] *v.* (**slipped**) slide accidentally; lose one's balance thus; go or put smoothly; escape hold or capture; detach, release; become detached from. — *n.* act of slipping; casual mistake; petticoat; liquid containing clay for coating pottery. **give a person the slip** escape from or avoid him or her. **slipped disc** disc of cartilage between vertebrae that has become displaced and causes pain. **slip-road** *n.* road for entering or leaving a motorway. **slip up** (*colloq.*) make a mistake. **slip-up** *n.*

slip [2] *n.* small piece of paper.

slipper *n.* light loose shoe for indoor wear.

slippery *a.* smooth or wet and difficult to hold or causing slipping; (of a person) not trustworthy. **slipperiness** *n.*

slipshod *a.* done or doing things carelessly.

slipstream *n.* current of air driven backward as something is propelled forward.

slipway *n.* sloping structure on which boats are landed or ships built or repaired.

slit *n.* narrow straight cut or opening. — *v.* (**slit, slitting**) cut a slit in; cut into strips.

slither *v.* slide unsteadily.

sliver *n.* small thin strip.

slobber *v.* slaver, dribble.

sloe *n.* blackthorn; its small dark plum-like fruit.

slog *v.* (**slogged**) hit hard; work or walk hard and steadily. — *n.* hard hit; spell of hard steady work or walking. **slogger** *n.*

slogan *n.* word or phrase adopted as a motto or in advertising.

sloop *n.* small ship with one mast.

slop *v.* (**slopped**) spill; splash. — *n.* unappetizing liquid; slopped liquid; (*pl.*) liquid refuse.

slope *v.* lie or put at an angle from the horizontal or vertical. — *n.* sloping surface; amount by which a thing slopes.

sloppy *a.* (**-ier, -iest**) wet, slushy; slipshod; weakly sentimental. **sloppily** *adv.*, **sloppiness** *n.*

slosh *v.* (*colloq.*) splash, pour clumsily; (*sl.*) hit. — *n.* (*colloq.*) splashing sound; (*sl.*) blow.

sloshed *a.* (*sl.*) drunk.

slot *n.* narrow opening into or through which something is to be put; position in a series or scheme. — *v.* (**slotted**) make slot(s) in; put or fit into a slot. **slot machine** machine operated by inserting a coin into a slot.

sloth /slōth/ *n.* laziness; slow-moving animal of tropical America.

slothful *a.* lazy. **slothfully** *adv.*

slouch *v.* stand, sit, or move in a lazy awkward way. — *n.* slouching movement or posture.

slough [1] /slow/ *n.* swamp, marsh.

slough [2] /sluf/ *v.* shed (skin); be shed in this way.

slovenly *a.* careless and untidy. **slovenliness** *n.*

slow *a.* not quick or fast; showing an earlier time than the correct one; stupid. — *adv.* slowly. — *v.* reduce the speed (of). **slowly** *adv.*, **slowness** *n.*

slowcoach *n.* person who is slow in his actions or work.

slow-worm *n.* legless lizard.

sludge *n.* thick mud.

slug [1] *n.* small slimy animal like a snail without a shell; small lump of metal; bullet.

slug [2] *v.* (**slugged**) (*US*) hit hard.

sluggard *n.* slow or lazy person.

sluggish *a.* slow-moving, not lively. **sluggishly** *adv.*, **sluggishness** *n.*

sluice /sloos/ *n.* sliding gate controlling a flow of water; this water; channel carrying off water.

slum *n.* squalid house or district

slumber *v.* & *n.* sleep. **slumberer** *n.*

slump *n.* sudden great fall in prices or demand. — *v.* undergo a slump; sit or flop down slackly.

slung *see* **sling**.

slunk *see* **slink**.

slur *v.* (**slurred**) utter with each letter or sound running into the next; pass lightly over (a fact). — *n.* slurred sound; curved line marking notes to be slurred in music; discredit.

slurp *v.* & *n.* (make) a noisy sucking sound.

slurry *n.* thin mud; thin liquid cement; fluid manure.

slush *n.* partly melted snow on the ground; silly sentimental talk or writing. **slushy** *a.*

slut *n.* slovenly or immoral woman. **sluttish** *a.*

sly *a.* unpleasantly cunning and secret; mischievous and knowing. **on the sly** secretly. **slyly** *adv.*, **slyness** *n.*

smack [1] *n.* slap; loud kiss. — *v.* slap, hit hard; close and part (lips) noisily.

smack [2] *n.* & *v.* (have) a slight flavour or trace.

smack [3] *n.* single-masted boat.

small *a.* not large or great; unimportant; petty. — *n.* narrowest part (of the back); (*pl.*, *colloq.*) underwear. — *adv.* in a small way. **small hours** period soon after midnight. **small-minded** *a.* narrow or selfish in outlook. **small talk** social conversation on unimportant subjects. **small-time** *a.* of an unimportant level. **smallness** *n.*

smallholding *n.* small farm. **smallholder** *n.*

smallpox *n.* disease with pustules that often leave bad scars.

smarmy *a.* (**-ier, -iest**) (*colloq.*) ingratiating, fulsome. **smarmily** *adv.*, **smarminess** *n.*

smart *a.* neat and elegant; clever; forceful, brisk. — *v.* & *n.* (feel) a stinging pain. **smartly** *adv.*, **smartness** *n.*

smarten *v.* make or become smarter.

smash *v.* break noisily into pieces; strike forcefully; crash; ruin. — *n.* act or sound of smashing; collision; disaster; ruin.

smashing *a.* (*colloq.*) excellent.

smattering *n.* slight knowledge.

smear *v.* spread with a greasy or dirty substance; try to damage the reputation of. — *n.* mark made by smearing; slander. **smeary** *a.*

smell *n.* ability to perceive things with the sense organs of the nose; quality perceived thus; unpleasant quality of this kind; act of smelling. — *v.* (**smelt** *or* **smelled**) perceive the smell of; give off a smell. **smelly** *a.*

smelt [1] *see* **smell**.

smelt [2] *v.* heat and melt (ore) to extract metal; obtain (metal) thus.

smelt [3] *n.* small fish related to the salmon.

smile *n.* facial expression indicating pleasure or amusement, with lips stretched and their ends upturned. — *v.* give a smile; look favourable.

smirch *v.* & *n.* discredit.

smirk *n.* self-satisfied smile. — *v.* give a smirk.

smite *v.* (**smote, smitten**) hit hard; affect suddenly.

smith *n.* person who makes things in metal; blacksmith.

smithereens *n.pl.* small fragments.
smithy *n.* blacksmith's workshop.
smitten *see* **smite**.
smock *n.* loose overall.
smog *n.* dense smoky fog.
smoke *n.* visible vapour given off by a burning substance; spell of smoking tobacco; (*sl.*) cigarette, cigar. — *v.* give out smoke or steam; preserve with smoke; draw smoke from (a cigarette or cigar or pipe) into the mouth; do this as a habit. **smoky** *a.*
smokeless *a.* with little or no smoke.
smoker *n.* person who smokes tobacco as a habit.
smokescreen *n.* thing intended to disguise or conceal activities.
smooth *a.* having an even surface with no projections; not harsh in sound or taste; moving evenly without bumping; polite but perhaps insincere. — *v.* make smooth. **smoothly** *adv.*, **smoothness** *n.*
smote *see* **smite**.
smother *v.* suffocate, stifle; cover thickly; suppress.
smoulder *v.* burn slowly with smoke but no flame; burn inwardly with concealed anger etc.
smudge *n.* dirty or blurred mark. — *v.* make a smudge on or with; become smudged; blur. **smudgy** *a.*, **smudginess** *n.*
smug *a.* (**smugger**, **smuggest**) self-satisfied. **smugly** *adv.*, **smugness** *n.*
smuggle *v.* convey secretly; bring (goods) illegally into or out of a country, esp. without paying customs duties. **smuggler** *n.*
smut *n.* small flake of soot; small black mark; indecent talk or pictures or stories. **smutty** *a.*
snack *n.* small or casual meal. **snack bar** place where snacks are sold.
snaffle *n.* horse's bit without a curb. — *v.* (*colloq.*) take for oneself.
snag *n.* jagged projection; tear caused by this. — *v.* (**snagged**) catch or tear on a snag.
snail *n.* soft-bodied animal with a shell. **snail's pace** very slow pace.
snake *n.* reptile with a long narrow body and no legs. — *v.* move in a winding course. **snaky** *a.*
snakeskin *n.* leather made from snakes' skins.
snap *v.* (**snapped**) (cause to) make a sharp cracking sound; break suddenly; bite at suddenly; speak with sudden irritation; move smartly; take a snapshot of. — *n.* act or sound of snapping; small crisp biscuit; snapshot. — *a.* sudden, done or arranged at short notice. **snap up** take eagerly.
snapdragon *n.* garden plant with flowers that have a mouth-like opening.
snapper *n.* any of several sea fish used as food.
snappy *a.* (**-ier**, **-iest**) (*colloq.*) irritable; brisk; neat and elegant. **snappily** *adv.*, **snappiness** *n.*
snapshot *n.* photograph taken informally or casually.
snare *n.* trap, usu. with a noose. — *v.* trap in a snare.
snarl [1] *v.* growl angrily with teeth bared; speak or utter in a bad-tempered way. — *n.* act or sound of snarling.
snarl [2] *v.* & *n.* tangle. **snarl-up** *n.*
snatch *v.* seize quickly or eagerly. — *n.* act of snatching; short or brief part.
snazzy *a.* (**-ier**, **-iest**) (*sl.*) stylish.
sneak *v.* go or convey or (*sl.*) steal furtively; (*school sl.*) tell tales. — *n.* (*school sl.*) tell-tale.
sneaking *a.* persistent but not openly acknowledged.
sneer *n.* scornful expression or remark. — *v.* show contempt by a sneer.
sneeze *n.* sudden audible involuntary expulsion of air through the nose. — *v.* give a sneeze.
snicker *v.* & *n.* snigger.
snide *a.* (*colloq.*) sneering slyly.
sniff *v.* draw air audibly through the nose; draw in as one breathes; try the smell of. — *n.* act or sound of sniffing. **sniffer** *n.*
sniffle *v.* sniff slightly or repeatedly. — *n.* this act or sound.
snifter *n.* (*sl.*) small drink of alcoholic liquor.
snigger *v.* & *n.* (give) a sly giggle.
snip *v.* (**snipped**) cut with scissors or shears in small quick strokes. — *n.* act or sound of snipping; (*sl.*) bargain, certainty.
snipe *n.* (*pl.* **snipe**) wading bird with a long straight bill. — *v.* fire shots from a hiding place; make sly critical remarks. **sniper** *n.*
snippet *n.* small piece.
snivel *v.* (**snivelled**) cry in a miserable whining way.
snob *n.* person with an exaggerated respect for social position, wealth, or certain tastes and who despises those he or she considers inferior. **snobbery** *n.*, **snobbish** *a.*
snooker *n.* game played on a baize-covered table with 15 red and 6 other coloured balls.
snoop *v.* (*colloq.*) pry. **snooper** *n.*

snooty *a.* (*colloq.*) haughty and contemptuous. **snootily** *adv.*

snooze *n.* & *v.* nap.

snore *n.* snorting or grunting sound made during sleep. — *v.* make such sounds. **snorer** *n.*

snorkel *n.* tube by which an underwater swimmer can breathe. — *v.* (**snorkelled**) swim with a snorkel.

snort *n.* sound made by forcing breath through the nose, esp. in indignation. — *v.* make a snort; (*sl.*) inhale (a powdered drug).

snout *n.* animal's long projecting nose or nose and jaws.

snow *n.* frozen atmospheric vapour falling to earth in white flakes; fall or layer of snow. — *v.* fall as or like snow. **snowed under** covered with snow; overwhelmed with work etc. **snowstorm** *n.*, **snowy** *a.*

snowball *n.* snow pressed into a compact mass for throwing. — *v.* increase in size or intensity.

snowblower *n.* machine that clears snow by blowing it to the side of the road etc.

snowdrift *n.* mass of snow piled up by the wind.

snowdrop *n.* plant with white flowers blooming in spring.

snowman *n.* (*pl.* **-men**) figure made of snow.

snowplough *n.* device for clearing roads etc. by pushing snow aside.

snub [1] *v.* (**snubbed**) reject (a person) contemptuously. — *n.* treatment of this kind.

snub [2] *a.* (of the nose) short and stumpy. **snub-nosed** *a.*

snuff [1] *n.* powdered tobacco for sniffing up the nostrils.

snuff [2] *v.* put out (a candle). **snuff it** (*sl.*) die. **snuffer** *n.*

snuffle *v.* breathe with a noisy sniff. — *n.* snuffling sound.

snug *a.* (**snugger, snuggest**) cosy; close-fitting. **snugly** *adv.*

snuggle *v.* nestle, cuddle.

so *adv.* & *conj.* to the extent or in the manner or with the result indicated; very; for that reason; also. — *pron.* that, the same thing. **so-and-so** *n.* person or thing that need not be named; (*colloq.*) disliked person. **so-called** *a.* called (wrongly) by that name. **so that** in order that.

soak *v.* place or lie in liquid so as to become thoroughly wet; (of liquid) penetrate; absorb. — *n.* soaking; (*sl.*) heavy drinker.

soap *n.* substance used in washing things, made of fat or oil and an alkali; (*colloq.*) soap opera. — *v.* apply soap to. **soap opera** television or radio serial usu. dealing with domestic issues.

soapstone *n.* steatite.

soapsuds *n.pl.* froth of soapy water.

soapy *a.* of or like soap; containing or smeared with soap; unctuous. **soapiness** *n.*

soar *v.* rise high esp. in flight.

sob *n.* uneven drawing of breath when weeping or gasping. — *v.* (**sobbed**) weep, breathe, or utter with sobs.

sober *a.* not drunk; serious; (of colour) not bright. — *v.* make or become sober. **soberly** *adv.*, **sobriety** *n.*

soccer *n.* football played with a spherical ball not to be handled in play except by the goalkeeper.

sociable *a.* fond of company; characterized by friendly companionship. **sociably** *adv.*, **sociability** *n.*

social *a.* living in a community; of society or its organization; sociable. — *n.* social gathering. **social security** State assistance for those who lack economic security. **social services** welfare services provided by the State. **social worker** person trained to help people with social problems. **socially** *adv.*

socialism *n.* political and economic theory that resources, industries, and transport should be owned and managed by the State. **socialist** *n.*, **socialistic** *a.*

socialite *n.* person prominent in fashionable society.

socialize *v.* behave sociably. **socialization** *n.*

society *n.* organized community; system of living in this; people of the higher social classes; mixing with other people; group organized for a common purpose.

sociology *n.* study of human society or of social problems. **sociological** *a.*, **sociologist** *n.*

sock [1] *n.* knitted covering for the foot; loose insole.

sock [2] *v.* (*colloq.*) hit forcefully. — *n.* (*colloq.*) forceful blow.

socket *n.* hollow into which something fits. **socketed** *a.*

sod *n.* turf; a piece of this.

soda *n.* compound of sodium; soda water. **soda water** water made fizzy by being charged with carbon dioxide under pressure.

sodden *a.* made very wet.

sodium *n.* soft silver-white metallic element.

sofa *n.* long upholstered seat with a back and raised ends.

soft *a.* not hard or firm or rough; not loud;

gentle; flabby, feeble, tender-hearted; (of drinks) non-alcoholic; (of drugs) not likely to cause addiction; (of currency) likely to fall suddenly in value. **soft fruit** small stoneless fruit (e.g. raspberry). **soft option** easy alternative. **soft-pedal** *v.* refrain from emphasizing. **soft spot** feeling of affection. **softly** *adv.*, **softness** *n.*

soften *v.* make or become soft or softer. **softener** *n.*

software *n.* computer programs or tapes containing these.

softwood *n.* soft wood of coniferous trees.

soggy *a.* (**-ier**, **-iest**) sodden; moist and heavy. **sogginess** *n.*

soil [1] *n.* loose earth; ground as territory.

soil [2] *v.* make or become dirty.

sojourn *n.* temporary stay. — *v.* stay temporarily.

solace *v.* & *n.* comfort in distress.

solar *a.* of or from the sun; reckoned by the sun. **solar cell** etc., device converting solar radiation into electricity. **solar plexus** network of nerves at the pit of the stomach; this area. **solar system** sun with the planets etc. that revolve round it.

sold *see* **sell.**

solder *n.* soft alloy used to cement metal parts together. — *v.* join with solder. **soldering iron** tool for melting and applying solder.

soldier *n.* member of an army. — *v.* serve as a soldier. **soldier on** (*colloq.*) persevere doggedly.

sole [1] *n.* under-surface of a foot; part of a shoe etc. covering this. — *v.* put a sole on.

sole [2] *n.* flatfish used as food.

sole [3] *a.* one and only; belonging exclusively to one person or group. **solely** *adv.*

solemn *a.* not smiling or cheerful; formal and dignified. **solemnly** *adv.*, **solemnity** *n.*

solemnize *v.* celebrate (a festival etc.); perform with formal rites. **solemnization** *n.*

solenoid *n.* coil of wire magnetized by electric current.

sol-fa *n.* system of syllables (*doh*, *ray*, *me*, etc.) representing the notes of a musical scale.

solicit *v.* seek to obtain by asking (for). **solicitation** *n.*

solicitor *n.* lawyer who advises clients and instructs barristers.

solicitous *a.* anxious about a person's welfare or comfort. **solicitously** *adv.*, **solicitude** *n.*

solid *a.* keeping its shape, firm; not liquid or gas; not hollow; of the same substance throughout; continuous; of solids; three-dimensional; sound and reliable. — *n.* solid substance or body or food. **solidly** *adv.*, **solidity** *n.*

solidarity *n.* unity resulting from common aims or interests etc.

solidify *v.* make or become solid. **solidification** *n.*

soliloquize *v.* utter a soliloquy.

soliloquy *n.* speech made aloud to oneself.

solitaire *n.* gem set by itself; game for one person played on a board with pegs.

solitary *a.* alone; single; not frequented, lonely. — *n.* recluse.

solitude *n.* being solitary.

solo *n.* (*pl.* **-os**) music for a single performer; unaccompanied performance etc. — *a.* & *adv.* unaccompanied, alone.

soloist *n.* performer of a solo.

solstice *n.* either of the times (about 21 June and 22 Dec.) or points reached when the sun is furthest from the equator.

soluble *a.* able to be dissolved; able to be solved. **solubility** *n.*

solution *n.* liquid containing something dissolved; process of dissolving; process of solving a problem etc.; answer found.

solvable *a.* able to be solved.

solve *v.* find the answer to.

solvent *a.* having enough money to pay one's debts etc.; able to dissolve another substance. — *n.* liquid used for dissolving something. **solvency** *n.*

sombre *a.* dark, gloomy.

sombrero *n.* (*pl.* **-os**) man's hat with a very wide brim.

some *a.* unspecified quantity or number of; unknown, unnamed; considerable quantity; approximately; (*sl.*) remarkable. — *pron.* some persons or things.

somebody *n.* & *pron.* unspecified person; person of importance.

somehow *adv.* in an unspecified or unexplained manner.

someone *n.* & *pron.* somebody.

somersault *n.* & *v.* leap or roll turning one's body upside down and over.

something *n.* & *pron.* unspecified thing or extent; important or praiseworthy thing. **something like** rather like; approximately.

sometime *a.* former. — *adv.* at some unspecified time.

sometimes *adv.* at some times but not all the time.

somewhat *adv.* to some extent.

somewhere *adv.* at, in, or to an unspecified place.

somnambulist *n.* sleepwalker. **somnambulism** *n.*

somnolent *a.* sleepy; asleep. **somnolence** *n.*

son *n.* male in relation to his parents. **son-in-law** *n.* (*pl.* **sons-in-law**) daughter's husband.

sonar *n.* device for detecting objects under water by reflection of sound waves.

sonata *n.* musical composition for one instrument or two, usu. in several movements.

song *n.* singing; music for singing. **going for a song** (*colloq.*) being sold very cheaply.

songbird *n.* bird with a musical cry.

songster *n.* singer; songbird.

sonic *a.* of sound waves.

sonnet *n.* type of poem of 14 lines.

sonorous *a.* resonant. **sonorously** *adv.*, **sonority** *n.*

soon *adv.* in a short time; early; readily. **sooner or later** at some time, eventually.

soot *n.* black powdery substance in smoke. **sooty** *a.*

soothe *v.* calm, ease (pain etc.). **soothing** *a.*

soothsayer *n.* prophet.

sop *n.* concession to pacify a troublesome person. — *v.* (**sopped**) dip in liquid; soak up (liquid).

sophisticated *a.* characteristic of or experienced in fashionable life and its ways; complicated, elaborate. **sophistication** *n.*

sophistry, **sophism** *ns.* clever and subtle but perhaps misleading reasoning. **sophist** *n.*

soporific *a.* tending to cause sleep. — *n.* soporific drug etc.

sopping *a.* very wet, drenched.

soppy *a.* (**-ier**, **-iest**) (*colloq.*) sentimental in a sickly way. **soppiness** *n.*

soprano *n.* (*pl.* **-os**) highest female or boy's singing voice.

sorbet /sórbay/ *n.* flavoured water ice.

sorcerer *n.* magician. **sorceress** *n.fem.*, **sorcery** *n.*

sordid *a.* dirty, squalid; (of motives etc.) not honourable. **sordidly** *adv.*, **sordidness** *n.*

sore *a.* causing or suffering pain from injury or disease; distressed, vexed. — *n.* sore place; source of distress or annoyance. **soreness** *n.*

sorely *adv.* very much, severely.

sorghum *n.* tropical cereal plant.

sorrel [1] *n.* sharp-tasting herb.

sorrel [2] *a.* reddish-brown.

sorrow *n.* mental suffering caused by loss or disappointment etc.; thing causing this. — *v.* feel sorrow, grieve. **sorrowful** *a.*, **sorrowfully** *adv.*

sorry *a.* (**-ier**, **-iest**) feeling pity or regret or sympathy; wretched.

sort *n.* particular kind or variety. — *v.* arrange according to sort or size or destination etc.

sortie *n.* sally by troops from a besieged place; flight of an aircraft on a military operation.

SOS international code-signal of distress. — *n.* urgent appeal for help.

sot *n.* habitual drunkard.

soufflé *n.* light dish made with beaten egg white.

sough /sow, suf/ *n.* & *v.* (make) a moaning or whispering sound as of wind in trees.

sought *see* **seek**.

soul *n.* person's spiritual or immortal element; mental, moral, or emotional nature; personification, pattern (of honesty etc.); person; black American culture. **soul music** emotional style of jazz-playing.

soulful *a.* showing deep feeling, emotional. **soulfully** *adv.*

soulless *a.* lacking sensitivity or noble qualities; dull.

sound [1] *n.* vibrations of air detectable by the ear; sensation produced by these; what is or may be heard. — *v.* produce or cause to produce sound; utter, pronounce; seem when heard. **sound barrier** high resistance of air to objects moving at speeds near that of sound. **sound off** (*colloq.*) express one's opinions loudly. **sounder** *n.*

sound [2] *a.* healthy; not diseased or damaged; secure; correct, well-founded; thorough. **soundly** *adv.*, **soundness** *n.*

sound [3] *v.* test the depth of (a river or sea etc.); examine with a probe. **sounder** *n.*

sound [4] *n.* strait.

sounding board board to reflect sound or increase resonance.

soundproof *a.* impervious to sound. — *v.* make soundproof.

soup *n.* liquid food made from meat or vegetables etc. — *v.* **soup up** (*colloq.*) increase the power of (an engine etc.). **soup-kitchen** *n.* place where soup etc. is served free to the needy. **soupy** *a.*

sour *a.* tasting sharp; not fresh, tasting or smelling stale; bad-tempered. — *v.* make or become sour. **sourly** *adv.*, **sourness** *n.*

source *n.* place from which something comes or is obtained; river's starting point; person or book etc. supplying information.

sourpuss *n.* (*colloq.*) bad-tempered person.

souse *v.* steep in pickle; drench.
south *n.* point or direction to the right of a person facing east; southern part. — *a.* in the south; (of wind) from the south. — *adv.* towards the south. **south-east** *n.* point or direction midway between south and east. **south-easterly** *a.* & *n.*, **south-eastern** *a.* **south-west** *n.* point or direction midway between south and west. **south-westerly** *a.* & *n.*, **south-western** *a.*
southerly *a.* towards or blowing from the south.
southern *a.* of or in the south.
southerner *n.* native of the south.
southernmost *a.* furthest south.
southpaw *n.* (*colloq.*) left-handed person.
southward *a.* towards the south. **southwards** *adv.*
souvenir *n.* thing serving as a reminder of an incident or place visited.
sou'wester *n.* waterproof usu. oilskin hat with a broad flap at the back.
sovereign *n.* king or queen who is the supreme ruler of a country. — *a.* supreme; (of a State) independent. **sovereignty** *n.*
sow [1] /sō/ *v.* (**sowed, sown** or **sowed**) plant or scatter (seed) for growth; plant seed in; implant (ideas etc.). **sower** *n.*
sow [2] /sow/ *n.* adult female pig.
soy *n.* soya bean.
soya *n.* plant from whose seed (**soya bean**) an edible oil and flour are obtained.
sozzled *a.* (*sl.*) drunk.
spa *n.* place with a curative mineral spring.
space *n.* boundless expanse in which all objects exist and move; portion of this; empty area or extent; universe beyond earth's atmosphere; interval. — *v.* arrange with spaces between.
spacecraft *n.* (*pl.* **-craft**) vehicle for travelling in outer space.
spaceship *n.* spacecraft.
spacious *a.* providing much space, roomy. **spaciousness** *n.*
spade [1] *n.* tool for digging, with a broad metal blade on a handle.
spade [2] *n.* playing card of the suit marked with black figures shaped like an inverted heart with a small stem.
spadework *n.* hard preparatory work.
spaghetti *n.* pasta made in long strings.
span *n.* extent from end to end; distance or part between the uprights of an arch or bridge. — *v.* (**spanned**) extend across.
spangle *n.* small piece of glittering material ornamenting a dress etc. — *v.* cover with spangles or sparkling objects.
Spaniard *n.* native of Spain.
spaniel *n.* a kind of dog with drooping ears and a silky coat.
Spanish *a.* & *n.* (language) of Spain.
spank *v.* slap on the buttocks.
spanner *n.* tool for gripping and turning the nut on a screw etc.
spar [1] *n.* strong pole used as a ship's mast or yard or boom.
spar [2] *v.* (**sparred**) box, esp. for practice; quarrel, argue.
spare *v.* refrain from hurting or harming; use with restraint; afford to give. — *a.* additional to what is usually needed or used, kept in reserve; thin. — *n.* extra thing kept in reserve. **to spare** additional to what is needed.
sparing *a.* economical, not generous or wasteful.
spark *n.* fiery particle; flash of light produced by an electrical discharge; particle (of energy, genius, etc.). — *v.* give off spark(s). **spark(ing) plug** device for making a spark in an internal-combustion engine.
sparkle *v.* shine with flashes of light; be lively or witty. — *n.* sparkling light.
sparkler *n.* sparking firework.
sparkling *a.* (of wine or mineral water) effervescent.
sparrow *n.* small brownish-grey bird.
sparrowhawk *n.* small hawk.
sparse *a.* thinly scattered. **sparsely** *adv.*, **sparseness** *n.*
spartan *a.* (of conditions) simple and sometimes harsh.
spasm *n.* strong involuntary contraction of a muscle; sudden brief spell of activity or emotion etc.
spasmodic *a.* of or occurring in spasms. **spasmodically** *adv.*
spastic *a.* affected by cerebral palsy which causes jerky, involuntary movements. — *n.* person with this condition. **spasticity** *n.*
spat [1] *see* **spit** [1].
spat [2] *n.* short gaiter.
spate *n.* sudden flood.
spatial *a.* of or existing in space. **spatially** *adv.*
spatter *v.* scatter or fall in small drops (on). — *n.* splash(es); sound of spattering.
spatula *n.* knife-like tool with a blunt blade; medical instrument for pressing down the tongue.
spawn *n.* eggs of fish or frogs or shellfish. — *v.* deposit spawn; generate.
spay *v.* sterilize (a female animal) by removing the ovaries.
speak *v.* (**spoke, spoken**) utter (words)

in an ordinary voice; say something; converse; express by speaking.

speaker *n.* person who speaks, one who makes a speech; loudspeaker.

spear *n.* weapon for hurling, with a long shaft and pointed tip; pointed stem. — *v.* pierce with or as if with a spear.

spearhead *n.* foremost part of an advancing force. — *v.* be the spearhead of.

spearmint *n.* a kind of mint.

spec *n.* **on spec** (*colloq.*) as a speculation.

special *a.* of a particular kind; for a particular purpose; exceptional. **specially** *adv.*

specialist *n.* expert in a particular branch of a subject.

speciality *n.* special quality or product or activity.

specialize *v.* be or become a specialist; adapt for a particular purpose. **specialization** *n.*

species *n.* (*pl.* **species**) group of similar animals or plants which can interbreed.

specific *a.* particular; exact, not vague. — *n.* specific aspect; remedy for a specific disease. **specifically** *adv.*

specification *n.* specifying; details describing a thing to be made or done.

specify *v.* mention definitely; include in specifications.

specimen *n.* part or individual taken as an example or for examination or testing.

specious *a.* seeming good or sound but lacking real merit. **speciously** *adv.*, **speciousness** *n.*

speck *n.* small spot or particle.

speckle *n.* small spot, esp. as a natural marking. **speckled** *a.*

spectacle *n.* impressive sight; lavish public show; ridiculous sight; (*pl.*) pair of lenses set in a frame, worn to assist sight.

spectacular *a.* impressive. — *n.* spectacular performance or production. **spectacularly** *adv.*

spectator *n.* person who watches a show or game or incident.

spectral *a.* of or like a spectre; of the spectrum.

spectre *n.* ghost; haunting fear.

spectrum *n.* (*pl.* **-tra**) bands of colour or sound forming a series according to their wavelengths; entire range of ideas etc.

speculate *v.* form opinions by guessing; buy in the hope of making a profit. **speculation** *n.*, **speculator** *n.*, **speculative** *a.*

speculum *n.* medical instrument for looking into bodily cavities.

sped *see* **speed**.

speech *n.* act or power or manner of speaking; spoken communication, esp. to an audience; language, dialect.

speechless *a.* unable to speak because of great emotion.

speed *n.* rate of time at which something moves or operates; rapidity. — *v.* (**sped**) move, pass, or send quickly; (**speeded**) travel at an illegal speed. **speed up** accelerate. **speed-up** *n.*

speedboat *n.* fast motor boat.

speedometer *n.* device in a vehicle, showing its speed.

speedway *n.* arena for motor cycle racing; (*US*) road for fast traffic.

speedy *a.* (**-ier, -iest**) rapid. **speedily** *adv.*, **speediness** *n.*

spell [1] *n.* words supposed to have magic power; their influence; fascination, attraction.

spell [2] *v.* (**spelt**) give in correct order the letters that form (a word); produce as a result. **spell out** state explicitly. **speller** *n.*

spell [3] *n.* period of time or weather or activity.

spellbound *a.* entranced.

spelt *see* **spell** [2].

spend *v.* (**spent**) pay out (money) in buying something; use up; pass (time etc.). **spender** *n.*

spendthrift *n.* wasteful spender.

spent *see* **spend**.

sperm *n.* (*pl.* **sperms** *or* **sperm**) male reproductive cell; semen. **sperm whale** a kind of large whale.

spermatozoon /spérmətōzṓ-on/ *n.* (*pl.* **-zoa**) fertilizing cell of a male organism.

spermicidal *a.* killing sperm.

spew *v.* vomit; cast out in a stream.

sphagnum *n.* moss growing on bogs.

sphere *n.* perfectly round solid geometric figure or object; field of action or influence etc.

spherical *a.* shaped like a sphere.

sphincter *n.* ring of muscle controlling an opening in the body.

sphinx *n.* ancient Egyptian statue with a lion's body and human or ram's head; enigmatic person.

spice *n.* flavouring substance with a strong taste or smell; thing that adds zest. — *v.* flavour with spice. **spicy** *a.*

spider *n.* small animal with a segmented body and eight legs. **spidery** *a.*

spigot *n.* plug stopping the vent-hole of a cask or controlling the flow of a tap.

spike *n.* pointed thing; pointed piece of metal. — *v.* put spikes on; pierce or fasten with a spike; (*colloq.*) add alcohol to (drink). **spiky** *a.*

spill [1] *n.* thin strip of wood or paper for transferring flame.

spill [2] *v.* (**spilt**) cause or allow to run over the edge of a container; become spilt. — *n.* fall. **spillage** *n.*

spin *v.* (**spun, spinning**) turn rapidly on its axis; draw out and twist into threads; make (yarn etc.) thus. — *n.* spinning movement; short drive for pleasure. **spin-off** *n.* incidental benefit. **spin out** prolong. **spinner** *n.*

spinach *n.* vegetable with dark-green leaves.

spinal *a.* of the spine.

spindle *n.* rod on which thread is wound in spinning; revolving pin or axis.

spindly *a.* long or tall and thin.

spindrift *n.* sea spray.

spine *n.* backbone; needle-like projection; part of a book where the pages are hinged.

spineless *a.* having no backbone; lacking determination.

spinet *n.* a kind of small harpsichord.

spinnaker *n.* large extra sail on a racing yacht.

spinneret *n.* thread-producing organ in a spider, silkworm, etc.

spinney *n.* (*pl.* **-eys**) thicket.

spinster *n.* unmarried woman.

spiny *a.* full of spines, prickly.

spiral *a.* forming a continuous curve round a central point or axis. — *n.* spiral line or thing; continuous increase or decrease in two or more quantities alternately. — *v.* (**spiralled**) move in a spiral course. **spirally** *adv.*

spire *n.* tall pointed structure esp. on a church tower.

spirit *n.* mind or animating principle as distinct from body; soul; ghost; person's nature; characteristic quality; real meaning; liveliness, boldness; distilled extract; (*pl.*) person's feeling of cheerfulness or depression; (*pl.*) strong distilled alcoholic drink. — *v.* carry off swiftly and mysteriously. **spirit level** sealed glass tube containing a bubble in liquid, used to test levelness.

spirited *a.* lively, bold. **spiritedly** *adv.*

spiritual *a.* of the human spirit or soul; of the Church or religion. — *n.* religious folk song of black Americans. **spiritually** *adv.*, **spirituality** *n.*

spiritualism *n.* attempted communication with spirits of the dead. **spiritualist** *n.*, **spiritualistic** *a.*

spirituous *a.* strongly alcoholic.

spit [1] *v.* (**spat** *or* **spit, spitting**) eject from the mouth; eject saliva; (of rain) fall lightly. — *n.* spittle; act of spitting.

spit [2] *n.* metal spike holding meat while it is roasted; narrow strip of land projecting into the sea.

spite *n.* malicious desire to hurt or annoy someone. — *v.* hurt or annoy from spite. **in spite of** not being prevented by. **spiteful** *a.*, **spitefully** *adv.*, **spitefulness** *n.*

spitfire *n.* fiery-tempered person.

spittle *n.* saliva.

splash *v.* cause (liquid) to fly about in drops; move or fall or wet with such drops; decorate with irregular patches of colour etc.; display in large print; spend (money) freely. — *n.* act or mark or sound of splashing; patch of colour or light; striking display. **splashy** *a.*

splatter *v.* & *n.* splash, spatter.

splay *v.* spread apart; slant outwards or inwards. — *a.* splayed.

spleen *n.* abdominal organ, involved in maintaining the proper condition of the blood. **splenic** *a.*

splendid *a.* brilliant, very impressive; excellent. **splendidly** *adv.*

splendour *n.* splendid appearance.

splenetic *a.* bad-tempered.

splice *v.* join by interweaving or overlapping the ends.

splint *n.* rigid framework preventing a limb etc. from movement, e.g. while a broken bone heals. — *v.* secure with a splint.

splinter *n.* thin sharp piece of broken wood etc. — *v.* break into splinters. **splinter group** small group that has broken away from a larger one.

split *v.* (**split, splitting**) break or come apart, esp. lengthwise; divide, share. — *n.* splitting; split thing or place; (*pl.*) acrobatic position with legs stretched fully apart. **split second** very brief moment.

splodge *v.* & *n.* = splotch.

splotch *v.* & *n.* splash, blotch.

splurge *n.* ostentatious display, esp. of wealth. — *v.* make a splurge, spend money freely.

splutter *v.* make a rapid series of spitting sounds; speak or utter incoherently. — *n.* spluttering sound.

spoil *v.* (**spoilt** *or* **spoiled**) make useless or unsatisfactory; become unfit for use; harm the character of (a person) by being indulgent. — *n.* (also *pl.*) plunder. **be spoiling for** (*colloq.*) desire (a fight etc.) eagerly.

spoilsport *n.* person who spoils others' enjoyment.

spoke [1] *n.* any of the bars connecting the hub to the rim of a wheel.

spoke [2], **spoken** *see* **speak**.

spokesman *n.* (*pl.* **-men**) person who speaks on behalf of a group.

spoliation *n.* pillaging.

sponge *n.* water animal with a porous structure; its skeleton, or a similar substance, esp. used for washing or cleaning or padding; sponge cake. — *v.* wipe or wash with a sponge; live off the generosity of others. **sponge cake, sponge pudding** one with a light open texture. **spongeable** *a.*, **spongy** *a.*

sponger *n.* person who sponges on others.

sponsor *n.* person who gives to charity in return for another's activity; godparent; one who provides funds for a broadcast, sporting event, etc. — *v.* act as sponsor for. **sponsorship** *n.*

spontaneous *a.* resulting from natural impulse; not caused or suggested from outside. **spontaneously** *adv.*, **spontaneity** *n.*

spoof *n.* (*colloq.*) hoax, parody.

spook *n.* (*colloq.*) ghost. **spooky** *a.*

spool *n.* reel on which something is wound. — *v.* wind on a spool.

spoon *n.* utensil with a rounded bowl and a handle, used for eating, serving, or stirring food; amount it contains. — *v.* take or lift with a spoon. **spoonful** *n.* (*pl.* **-fuls**).

spoonfeed *v.* (**-fed**) feed from a spoon; give excessive help to.

spoor *n.* track or scent left by an animal.

sporadic *a.* occurring here and there or now and again. **sporadically** *adv.*

spore *n.* one of the tiny reproductive cells of fungi, ferns, etc.

sporran *n.* pouch worn hanging in front of a kilt.

sport *n.* athletic (esp. outdoor) activity; game(s), pastime(s); (*colloq.*) sportsmanlike person. — *v.* play, amuse oneself; wear. **sports car** open low-built fast car. **sports jacket** man's jacket for informal wear.

sporting *a.* of sport; like a sportsman. **sporting chance** reasonable chance of success.

sportive *a.* playful. **sportively** *adv.*, **sportiveness** *n.*

sportsman *n.* (*pl.* **-men**), **sportswoman** *n.fem.* (*pl.* **-women**) one who takes part in sports; one who plays fairly and generously. **sportsmanlike** *a.*, **sportsmanship** *n.*

spot *n.* round mark or stain; pimple; place; drop; (*colloq.*) small amount; spotlight. — *v.* (**spotted**) mark with a spot or spots; rain slightly; (*colloq.*) notice; watch for and take note of. **on the spot** without delay or change of place; alert; (*colloq.*) compelled to take action or justify oneself. **spot check** random check. **spotter** *n.*

spotless *a.* free from stain or blemish. **spotlessly** *adv.*, **spotlessness** *n.*

spotlight *n.* lamp or its beam directed on a small area. — *v.* (**-lit** *or* **-lighted**) direct a spotlight on; draw attention to.

spotty *a.* marked with spots.

spouse *n.* husband or wife.

spout *n.* projecting tube through which liquid is poured or conveyed; jet of liquid. — *v.* come or send out forcefully as a jet of liquid; utter or speak lengthily.

sprain *v.* injure by wrenching violently. — *n.* this injury

sprang *see* **spring**.

sprat *n.* small herring-like fish.

sprawl *v.* sit, lie, or fall with arms and legs spread loosely; spread out irregularly. — *n.* sprawling attitude or arrangement.

spray [1] *n.* branch with its leaves and flowers; bunch of cut flowers; ornament in similar form.

spray [2] *n.* liquid dispersed in very small drops; liquid for spraying; device for spraying liquid. — *v.* come or send out as spray; wet with liquid thus. **spray-gun** *n.* device for spraying paint etc. **sprayer** *n.*

spread *v.* (**spread**) open out; become longer or wider; apply as a layer; be able to be spread; make or become widely known or felt or suffered; distribute, become distributed. — *n.* spreading; (*colloq.*) lavish meal; thing's range; paste for spreading on bread. **spread-eagled** *a.* with arms and legs spread.

spreadsheet *n.* computer program for manipulating esp. tabulated numerical data.

spree *n.* (*colloq.*) lively outing, piece of fun.

sprig *n.* twig, shoot.

sprightly *a.* (**-ier, -iest**) lively, full of energy. **sprightliness** *n.*

spring *v.* (**sprang, sprung**) jump; move rapidly; issue, arise; produce or cause to operate suddenly. — *n.* act of springing, jump; device that reverts to its original position after being compressed, tightened, or stretched; elasticity; place where water or oil flows naturally from the ground; season between winter and summer. **spring-clean** *v.* clean (one's home etc.) thoroughly. **spring tide** tide when there is the largest rise and fall of water.

springboard *n.* flexible board giving impetus to a gymnast or diver.

springbok *n.* South African gazelle.

springtime *n.* season of spring.

springy *a.* (**-ier**, **-iest**) able to spring back easily after being squeezed or tightened or stretched. **springiness** *n.*

sprinkle *v.* scatter or fall in drops or particles on (a surface). — *n.* light shower. **sprinkler** *n.*

sprinkling *n.* something sprinkled; a few here and there.

sprint *v.* & *n.* run or swim etc. at full speed. **sprinter** *n.*

sprite *n.* elf, fairy, or goblin.

sprocket *n.* projection engaging with links on a chain etc.

sprout *v.* begin to grow or appear; put forth. — *n.* plant's shoot; Brussels sprout.

spruce [1] *a.* neat, smart. — *v.* smarten. **sprucely** *adv.*, **spruceness** *n.*

spruce [2] *n.* a kind of fir.

sprung *see* **spring**. — *a.* fitted with springs.

spry *a.* active, lively. **spryly** *adv.*, **spryness** n.

spud *n.* narrow spade; (*sl.*) potato.

spume *n.* froth.

spun *see* **spin**.

spur *n.* pricking-device worn on a horseman's heel; stimulus, incentive; projection. — *v.* (**spurred**) urge on (a horse) with one's spurs; urge on, incite; stimulate. **on the spur of the moment** on impulse. **win one's spurs** prove one's ability.

spurious *a.* not genuine or authentic. **spuriously** *adv.*, **spuriousness** *n.*

spurn *v.* reject contemptuously.

spurt *v.* gush; send out (liquid) suddenly; increase speed suddenly. — *n.* sudden gush; short burst of activity; sudden increase in speed.

sputter *v.* & *n.* splutter.

sputum *n.* expectorated matter; saliva.

spy *n.* person who secretly watches or gathers information. — *v.* catch sight of; be a spy, watch secretly.

sq. *abbr.* square.

squabble *v.* quarrel pettily or noisily. — *n.* quarrel of this kind.

squad *n.* small group working or being trained together.

squadron *n.* division of a cavalry unit or of an airforce; detachment of warships.

squalid *a.* dirty and unpleasant; morally degrading. **squalidly** *adv.*, **squalor** *n.*

squall *n.* sudden storm or wind. **squally** *a.*

squander *v.* spend wastefully.

square *n.* geometric figure with four equal sides and four right angles; area or object shaped like this; product of a number multiplied by itself. — *a.* of square shape; right-angled; of or using units expressing the measure of an area; properly arranged; equal, not owed or owing anything; straightforward; honest. — *adv.* squarely, directly. — *v.* make right-angled; mark with squares; place evenly; multiply by itself; settle (an account etc.); make or be consistent; (*colloq.*) bribe. **square dance** dance in which four couples face inwards from four sides. **square meal** substantial meal. **square root** number of which a given number is the square. **square up to** face in a fighting attitude; face resolutely. **squarely** *adv.*, **squareness** *n.*

squash *v.* crush, squeeze or become squeezed flat or into pulp; suppress; silence with a crushing reply. — *n.* crowd of people squashed together; fruit-flavoured soft drink; (also **squash rackets**) game played with rackets and a small ball in a closed court. **squashy** *a.*

squat *v.* (**squatted**) sit on one's heels; crouch; (*colloq.*) sit; be a squatter (in). — *n.* squatting posture; being a squatter, place occupied thus. — *a.* dumpy.

squatter *n.* person who takes unauthorized possession of unoccupied premises.

squawk *n.* loud harsh cry. — *v.* make or utter with a squawk.

squeak *n.* short high-pitched cry or sound. — *v.* make or utter with a squeak. **narrow squeak** narrow escape. **squeaky** *a.*

squeal *n.* long shrill cry or sound. — *v.* make or utter with a squeal; (*sl.*) become an informer.

squeamish *a.* easily disgusted; over-scrupulous. **squeamishly** *adv.*, **squeamishness** *n.*

squeeze *v.* exert pressure on; treat thus to extract moisture; force into or through, force one's way, crowd; produce by pressure or effort or compulsion; extort money etc. from. — *n.* squeezing; affectionate clasp or hug; drops produced by squeezing; crowd, crush; restrictions on borrowing. **squeezer** *n.*

squelch *v.* & *n.* sound like someone treading in thick mud.

squib *n.* small exploding firework.

squid *n.* sea creature with ten arms round its mouth.

squiggle *n.* short curly line. **squiggly** *a.*

squint *v.* have one eye turned abnormally from the line of gaze of the other; look sideways or through a small opening. — *n.* squinting condition of one eye; sideways glance.

squire *n.* country gentleman, esp. landowner.

squirm *v.* wriggle; feel embarrassment. — *n.* wriggle.

squirrel *n.* small tree-climbing animal with a bushy tail.

squirt *v.* send out (liquid) or be sent out in a jet; wet thus. — *n.* jet of liquid.

squish *v.* & *n.* (move with) a soft squelching sound. **squishy** *a.*

St *abbr.* Saint.

St. *abbr.* Street.

stab *v.* (**stabbed**) pierce, wound or kill with something pointed; poke. — *n.* act of stabbing; sensation of being stabbed; (*colloq.*) attempt.

stabilize *v.* make or become stable. **stabilization** *n.*, **stabilizer** *n.*

stable [1] *a.* firmly fixed or established, not easily shaken or decomposed or destroyed. **stably** *adv.*, **stability** *n.*

stable [2] *n.* building in which horses are kept; establishment for training racehorses; horses, people, or products etc. from the same establishment. — *v.* put or keep in a stable. **stable lad** person who works in a stable.

staccato *a.* & *adv.* in a sharp disconnected manner.

stack *n.* orderly pile or heap; (*colloq.*) large quantity; isolated chimney; storage section of a library. — *v.* arrange in a stack or stacks; arrange (cards) secretly for cheating; cause (aircraft) to fly at different levels while waiting to land.

stadium *n.* sports ground surrounded by tiers of seats for spectators.

staff *n.* stick used as a weapon, support, or symbol of authority; the people employed by an organization, esp. those doing administrative work; (*pl.* **staves**) set of five horizontal lines on which music is written. — *v.* provide with a staff of people.

stag *n.* fully grown male deer. **stag beetle** beetle with branched projecting mouthparts. **stag-night** *n.* all-male party for a man about to marry.

stage *n.* raised floor or platform; one on which plays etc. are performed; theatrical work or profession; division of or point reached in a process or journey. — *v.* present on the stage; arrange and carry out. **go on the stage** become an actor or actress. **stage fright** nervousness on facing an audience. **stage whisper** one meant to be overheard.

stagger *v.* move or go unsteadily; shock deeply; arrange so as not to coincide exactly. — *n.* staggering movement.

staggering *a.* astonishing.

stagnant *a.* not flowing, still and stale; not developing; without activity. **stagnancy** *n.*

stagnate *v.* be or become stagnant. **stagnation** *n.*

staid *a.* steady and serious.

stain *v.* be or become discoloured; blemish; colour with a penetrating pigment. — *n.* mark caused by staining; blemish; liquid for staining things.

stainless *a.* free from stains. **stainless steel** steel alloy not liable to rust or tarnish.

stair *n.* one of a flight of fixed indoor steps; (*pl.*) a flight of these.

staircase *n.* stairs and their supporting structure.

stairway *n.* staircase.

stake *n.* pointed stick or post for driving into the ground; money etc. wagered; share or interest in an enterprise etc. — *v.* fasten or support or mark with a stake or stakes; wager. **at stake** being risked. **stake a claim** claim a right to something. **stake out** place under surveillance. **stake-out** *n.*

stalactite *n.* deposit of calcium carbonate hanging like an icicle.

stalagmite *n.* deposit of calcium carbonate standing like a pillar.

stale *a.* not fresh; unpleasant or uninteresting from lack of freshness; spoilt by too much practice. — *v.* make or become stale. **staleness** *n.*

stalemate *n.* drawn position in chess; drawn contest; deadlock. — *v.* bring to such a state.

stalk [1] *n.* stem or similar supporting part.

stalk [2] *v.* walk in a stately or imposing manner; track or pursue stealthily. **stalker** *n.*

stall *n.* stable, cowhouse; compartment in this; ground floor seat in a theatre; booth or stand where goods are displayed for sale; stalling of an aircraft. — *v.* place or keep in a stall; (of an engine) stop suddenly through lack of power; (of an aircraft) begin to drop because the speed is too low; cause to stall; play for time when being questioned.

stallion *n.* uncastrated male horse.

stalwart *a.* sturdy; strong and faithful. — *n.* stalwart person.

stamen *n.* pollen-bearing part of a flower.

stamina *n.* ability to withstand long physical or mental strain.

stammer *v.* speak with involuntary pauses or repetitions of a syllable. — *n.* this act or tendency.

stamp *v.* bring (one's foot) down heavily on the ground; press so as to cut or leave a mark or pattern; fix a postage stamp to; give a specified character to. — *n.* act or sound of stamping; instrument for stamping a mark etc., this mark; small adhesive label for affixing to an envelope or document to show the amount paid as postage or a fee etc.; characteristic feature. **stamping ground** usual haunt. **stamp out** suppress by force.

stampede *n.* sudden rush of animals or people. — *v.* (cause to) take part in a stampede.

stance *n.* manner of standing.

stanch *v.* stop or slow down the flow of (blood) from a wound.

stanchion *n.* upright post or support.

stand *v.* (**stood**) have, take, or keep a stationary upright position; be situated; place, set upright; stay firm or valid; offer oneself for election; endure; provide at one's own expense. — *n.* stationary condition; position taken up; resistance to attack; rack, pedestal; raised structure with seats at a sports ground etc.; stall for goods. **stand a chance** have a chance of success. **stand by** look on without interfering; stand ready for action; support in a difficulty; keep to (a promise etc.). **stand-by** *a.* & *n.* (person or thing) available as a substitute. **stand down** withdraw. **stand for** represent; (*colloq.*) tolerate. **stand in** deputize. **stand-in** *n.* deputy, substitute. **stand one's ground** not yield. **stand to reason** be logical. **stand up** come to or place in a standing position; be valid; (*colloq.*) fail to keep an appointment with. **stand up for** speak in defence of. **stand up to** resist courageously; be strong enough to endure.

standard *n.* thing against which something may be compared for testing or measurement; average quality; required level of quality or proficiency; distinctive flag; moral principle. — *a.* serving as or conforming to a standard; of average or usual quality. **standard lamp** household lamp set on a tall support.

standardize *v.* cause to conform to a standard. **standardization** *n.*

standing *n.* status; duration.

standoffish *a.* aloof.

standpipe *n.* vertical pipe for fluid to rise in, esp. for attachment to a water main.

standpoint *n.* point of view.

standstill *n.* inability to proceed.

stank *see* **stink**.

stanza *n.* verse of poetry.

staphylococcus *n.* (*pl.* **-ci**) pus-producing bacterium. **staphylococcal** *a.*

staple [1] *n.* U-shaped spike for holding something in place; piece of wire driven into papers and clenched to fasten them. — *v.* secure with staple(s). **stapler** *n.*

staple [2] *a.* & *n.* principal or standard (food or product etc.).

star *n.* heavenly body appearing as a point of light; asterisk; star-shaped mark indicating a category of excellence; famous actor or performer etc. — *v.* (**starred**) put an asterisk beside (an item); present or perform as a star actor.

starboard *n.* right-hand side of a ship or aircraft.

starch *n.* white carbohydrate; preparation for stiffening fabrics; stiffness of manner. — *v.* stiffen with starch. **starchy** *a.*

stardom *n.* being a star actor etc.

stare *v.* gaze fixedly esp. in astonishment. — *n.* staring gaze.

starfish *n.* star-shaped sea creature.

stark *n.* desolate, bare; sharply evident; downright; naked. — *adv.* completely. **starkly** *adv.*, **starkness** *n.*

starling *n.* noisy bird with glossy black speckled feathers.

starry *a.* set with stars; shining like stars. **starry-eyed** *a.* (*colloq.*) romantically enthusiastic.

start *v.* begin, cause to begin; begin operating; begin a journey; make a sudden movement, esp. from pain or surprise. — *n.* beginning; place where a race etc. starts; advantage gained or allowed in starting; sudden movement of pain or surprise. **starter** *n.*

startle *v.* shock, surprise.

starve *v.* die or suffer acutely from lack of food; cause to do this; force by starvation; (*colloq.*) feel very hungry or cold. **starvation** *n.*

stash *v.* (*sl.*) stow.

state *n.* mode of being, with regard to characteristics or circumstances; (*colloq.*) excited or agitated condition of mind; grand imposing style; (often **State**) political community under one government or forming part of a federation; civil government. — *a.* of or involving the State; ceremonial. — *v.* express in words; specify.

stateless *a.* not a citizen or subject of any country.

stately *a.* (**-ier**, **-iest**) dignified, grand. **stateliness** *n.*

statement *n.* process of stating; thing stated; formal account of facts; written report of a financial account.

stateroom *n.* room used on ceremonial occasions; passenger's private compartment on a ship.

statesman *n.* (*pl.* **-men**) experienced and respected political leader. **stateswoman** *n.fem.* (*pl.* **-women**), **statesmanship** *n.*

static *a.* of force acting by weight without motion; stationary; not changing. — *n.* electrical disturbances in the air, causing interference in telecommunications; (also

static electricity) electricity present in a body, not flowing as current.
station *n.* place where a person or thing stands or is stationed; place where a public service or specialized activity is based; broadcasting channel; stopping place on a railway; status. — *v.* put at or in a certain place for a purpose. **station wagon** (*US*) estate car.
stationary *a.* not moving; not movable.
stationer *n.* dealer in stationery.
stationery *n.* writing paper, envelopes, labels, etc.
statistic *n.* item of information expressed in numbers. **statistics** *n.* science of collecting and interpreting numerical information. **statistical** *a.*, **statistically** *adv.*
statistician *n.* expert in statistics.
statue *n.* sculptured, cast, or moulded figure.
statuesque *a.* like a statue in size or dignity or stillness.
statuette *n.* small statue.
stature *n.* bodily height; greatness gained by ability or achievement.
status *n.* (*pl.* **-uses**) person's position or rank in relation to others; high rank or prestige. **status quo** existing previous state of affairs.
statute *n.* law passed by Parliament or a similar body.
statutory *a.* fixed or done or required by statute.
staunch *a.* firm in opinion or loyalty. **staunchly** *adv.*
stave *n.* one of the strips of wood forming the side of a cask or tub; staff in music. — *v.* (**stove** or **staved**) dent, break a hole in. **stave off** (**staved**) ward off.
stay *v.* continue in the same place or state; dwell temporarily; postpone; show endurance. — *n.* period of staying; postponement. **stay the course** be able to reach the end of it. **staying power** endurance.
stead *n.* **in a person's** *or* **thing's stead** instead of him or her or it. **stand in good stead** be of great service to.
steadfast *a.* firm and not changing or yielding. **steadfastly** *adv.*
steady *a.* (**-ier, -iest**) not shaking; regular, uniform; dependable, not excitable. — *adv.* steadily. — *v.* make or become steady. **steadily** *adv.*, **steadiness** *n.*
steak *n.* slice of meat (esp. beef) or fish, usu. grilled or fried.
steal *v.* (**stole, stolen**) take dishonestly; move stealthily. — *n.* (*colloq.*) stealing; bargain, easy task. **steal the show** outshine other performers.
stealth *n.* stealthiness.
stealthy *a.* (**-ier, -iest**) quiet so as to avoid notice. **stealthily** *adv.*, **stealthiness** *n.*
steam *n.* gas into which water is changed by boiling; this as motive power; energy, power. — *v.* give out steam; cook or treat by steam; move by the power of steam; cover or become covered by steam. **steam engine** engine or locomotive driven by steam. **steamy** *a.*
steamer *n.* steam-driven ship; container in which things are cooked or heated by steam.
steamroller *n.* heavy engine with a large roller, used in road-making.
steatite /steéətīt/ *n.* greyish talc that feels smooth and soapy.
steel *n.* very strong alloy of iron and carbon; tapered steel rod for sharpening knives. — *v.* make resolute. **steel wool** mass of fine shavings of steel used as an abrasive. **steely** *a.* **steeliness** *n.*
steep [1] *v.* soak in liquid; permeate thoroughly.
steep [2] *a.* sloping sharply not gradually; (*colloq.*, of price) unreasonably high. **steeply** *adv.*, **steepness** *n.*
steeple *n.* tall tower with a spire, rising above a church roof.
steeplechase *n.* race for horses or athletes with fences to jump. **steeplechaser** *n.*, **steeplechasing** *n.*
steeplejack *n.* person who climbs tall chimneys etc. to do repairs.
steer [1] *n.* bullock.
steer [2] *v.* direct the course of, guide by mechanism; be able to be steered. **steer clear of** avoid.
stellar *a.* of a star or stars.
stem [1] *n.* supporting usu. cylindrical part, esp. of a plant; main usu. unchanging part of a noun or verb. — *v.* (**stemmed**) **stem from** have as its source.
stem [2] *v.* (**stemmed**) restrain the flow of; dam.
stench *n.* foul smell.
stencil *n.* sheet of card etc. with a cut-out design, painted over to reproduce this on the surface below; design reproduced thus. — *v.* (**stencilled**) produce or ornament by this.
stenographer *n.* shorthand writer.
stenography *n.* shorthand.
stentorian *a.* (of a voice) extremely loud.
step *v.* (**stepped**) lift and set down a foot or alternate feet; move a short distance thus; progress. — *n.* movement of a foot and leg in stepping; distance covered thus; short distance; pattern of steps in dancing; one of a series of actions; level surface for placing the foot on in climbing; stage in a scale; (*pl.*) stepladder.

in step stepping in time with others; conforming. **mind** *or* **watch one's step** take care. **step in** intervene; enter. **step up** increase.

step- *pref.* related by re-marriage of a parent, as **stepfather, stepmother, stepson,** etc. — *ns.*

stepladder *n.* short ladder with a supporting framework.

steppe *n.* grassy plain, esp. in south-east Europe and Siberia.

stepping-stone *n.* raised stone for stepping on in crossing a stream etc.; means of progress.

stereo *n.* (*pl.* **-os**) stereophonic sound or record player etc.; stereoscopic effect.

stereophonic *a.* using two transmission channels so as to give the effect of naturally distributed sound. **stereophony** *n.*

stereoscopic *a.* giving a three-dimensional effect.

stereotype *n.* standardized conventional idea or character etc. — *v.* standardize; cause to conform to a preconceived type. **stereotyped** *a.* standardized and hackneyed.

sterile *a.* barren; free from micro-organisms. **sterility** *n.*

sterilize *v.* make sterile. **sterilization** *n.*, **sterilizer** *n.*

sterling *n.* British money. — *a.* of standard purity; excellent.

stern [1] *a.* strict, severe. **sternly** *adv.*, **sternness** *n.*

stern [2] *n.* rear of a ship or aircraft.

sternum *n.* breastbone.

steroid *n.* any of a group of organic compounds that includes certain hormones.

stertorous *a.* making a snoring or rasping sound. **stertorously** *adv.*

stethoscope *n.* instrument for listening to sounds within the body.

stetson *n.* hat with a wide brim and high crown.

stevedore *n.* docker.

stew *v.* cook by simmering in a closed vessel; (*colloq.*) swelter. — *n.* dish made by stewing; (*colloq.*) state of great anxiety.

steward *n.* person employed to manage an estate etc.; passengers' attendant on a ship, aircraft, or train; official at a race meeting or show etc. **stewardess** *n.* female steward on a ship etc.

stick [1] *n.* thin piece of wood; thing shaped like this; walking stick; implement used to propel the ball in hockey, polo, etc.; (*colloq.*) criticism.

stick [2] *v.* (**stuck**) thrust (a thing) into something; (*colloq.*) put; fix or be fixed by glue or suction etc.; jam; (*colloq.*) remain in a specified place, not progress; (*colloq.*) endure. **stick-in-the-mud** *n.* person who will not adopt new ideas etc. **stick out** stand above the surrounding surface; be conspicuous. **stick to** remain faithful to; keep to (a subject or position etc.). **stick together** (*colloq.*) remain united or loyal. **stick to one's guns** not yield. **stick up for** (*colloq.*) stand up for.

sticker *n.* adhesive label or sign.

sticking plaster adhesive fabric for covering small cuts.

stickleback *n.* small fish with sharp spines on its back.

stickler *n.* **stickler for** one who insists on something.

sticky *a.* (**-ier, -iest**) sticking to what is touched; humid; (*colloq.*) unpleasant, difficult. **stickily** *adv.*, **stickiness** *n.*

stiff *a.* not bending or moving easily; difficult; formal in manner; (of wind) blowing briskly; (of a drink etc.) strong; (of a price or penalty) severe. — *n.* (*sl.*) corpse. **stiff-necked** *a.* obstinate; haughty. **stiffly** *adv.*, **stiffness** *n.*

stiffen *v.* make or become stiff. **stiffener** *n.*

stifle *v.* feel or cause to feel unable to breathe; suppress.

stigma *n.* (*pl.* **-as**) mark of shame; part of a pistil.

stigmatize *v.* brand as something disgraceful. **stigmatization** *n.*

stile *n.* steps or bars for people to climb over a fence.

stiletto *n.* (*pl.* **-os**) dagger with a narrow blade. **stiletto heel** long tapering heel of a shoe.

still [1] *a.* with little or no motion or sound; (of drinks) not fizzy. — *n.* silence and calm; photograph taken from a cinema film. — *adv.* without moving; then or now as before; nevertheless; in a greater amount or degree. **still life** picture of inanimate objects. **stillness** *n.*

still [2] *n.* distilling apparatus.

stillborn *a.* born dead.

stilted *a.* stiffly formal.

stilts *n.pl.* pair of poles with footrests, enabling the user to walk with feet at a distance above the ground; piles or posts on which a building stands.

stimulant *a.* stimulating. — *n.* stimulating drug or drink.

stimulate *v.* make more active; apply a stimulus to. **stimulation** *n.*, **stimulator** *n.*, **stimulative** *a.*

stimulus *n.* (*pl.* **-li**) something that rouses a person or thing to activity or energy.

sting *n.* sharp wounding part or organ of an insect or plant etc.; wound made thus; its infliction; sharp bodily or mental pain. — *v.* (**stung**) wound or affect with a sting; feel or cause sharp pain; (*sl.*) overcharge, extort money from.

stingy *a.* (**-ier, -iest**) spending, giving, or given grudgingly or in small amounts. **stingily** *adv.*, **stinginess** *n.*

stink *n.* offensive smell; (*colloq.*) row or fuss. — *v.* (**stank** or **stunk**) give off a stink; (*colloq.*) seem very unpleasant or dishonest.

stinker *n.* (*sl.*) very objectionable person; very difficult task.

stinking *a.* that stinks; (*sl.*) very objectionable.

stint *v.* restrict to a small allowance. — *n.* allotted amount of work.

stipend /stī́pend/ *n.* salary.

stipendiary *a.* receiving a stipend.

stipple *v.* paint, draw, or engrave in small dots. — *n.* this process or effect.

stipulate *v.* demand or insist (on) as part of an agreement. **stipulation** *n.*

stir *v.* (**stirred**) move; mix (a substance) by moving a spoon etc. round in it; stimulate, excite. — *n.* act or process of stirring; commotion, excitement.

stirrup *n.* support for a rider's foot, hanging from the saddle.

stitch *n.* single movement of a thread in and out of fabric in sewing, or of a needle or hook in knitting or crochet; loop made thus; method of making a stitch; sudden pain in the side. — *v.* sew; join or close with stitches. **in stitches** (*colloq.*) laughing uncontrollably.

stoat *n.* animal of the weasel family.

stock *n.* amount of something available; livestock; lineage; business company's capital, portion of this held by an investor; standing or status; liquid made by stewing bones, meat, fish, or vegetables; plant with fragrant flowers; plant into which a graft is inserted; handle of a rifle; cravat; (*pl.*) framework on which a ship rests during construction; (*pl.*) wooden frame with holes for a seated person's legs, used like the pillory. — *a.* stocked and regularly available; commonly used. — *v.* keep in stock; provide with a supply. **stock-car** *n.* car used in racing where deliberate bumping is allowed. **stock exchange** stock market. **stock-in-trade** *n.* all the requisites for carrying on a trade or business. **stock market** institution for buying and selling stocks and shares; transactions of this. **stock-still** *a.* motionless. **stocktaking** *n.* making an inventory of stock.

stockade *n.* protective fence.

stockbroker *n.* person who buys and sells shares for clients.

stockinet *n.* fine machine-knitted fabric used for underwear etc.

stocking *n.* close-fitting covering for the foot and leg.

stockist *n.* firm that stocks certain goods.

stockpile *n.* accumulated stock of goods etc. kept in reserve. — *v.* accumulate a stockpile of.

stocky *a.* (**-ier, -iest**) short and solidly built. **stockily** *adv.*, **stockiness** *n.*

stodge *n.* (*colloq.*) stodgy food.

stodgy *a.* (**-ier, -iest**) (of food) heavy and filling; dull.

stoic /stṓ-ik/ *n.* stoical person.

stoical *a.* calm and uncomplaining. **stoically** *adv.*, **stoicism** *n.*

stoke *v.* tend and put fuel on (a fire etc.). **stoker** *n.*

stole[1] *n.* woman's wide scarf-like garment.

stole[2], **stolen** *see* **steal**.

stolid *a.* not excitable. **stolidly** *adv.*, **stolidity** *n.*

stomach *n.* integral organ in which the first part of digestion occurs; abdomen; appetite. — *v.* endure, tolerate. **stomach-ache** *n.* pain in the belly or bowels.

stomp *v.* tread heavily.

stone *n.* piece of rock; stones or rock as a substance or material; gem; hard substance formed in the bladder or kidney etc.; hard case round the kernel of certain fruits; (*pl.* **stone**) unit of weight, 14 lb. — *a.* made of stone. — *v.* pelt with stones; remove stones from (fruit). **Stone Age** prehistoric period when weapons and tools were made of stone.

stonemason *n.* person who shapes stone or builds in stone.

stonewall *v.* give noncommittal replies.

stoneware *n.* heavy kind of pottery.

stony *a.* (**-ier, -iest**) full of stones, hard, unfeeling; unresponsive. **stonily** *adv.*

stood *see* **stand**.

stooge *n.* comedian's assistant; person who is another's puppet.

stool *n.* movable seat without arms or raised back; footstool; (*pl.*) faeces. **stool-pigeon** *n.* decoy, esp. to trap a criminal.

stoop *v.* bend forwards and down; condescend; lower oneself morally. — *n.* stooping posture.

stop *v.* (**stopped**) put an end to movement, progress, or operation (of); refuse to give or allow; close by plugging or obstructing. — *n.* stopping; place where a train or bus etc. stops regularly; thing that stops or regulates motion; row of organ pipes providing tones of one quality, knob etc. controlling these. **stop press**

late news inserted in a newspaper after printing has begun.

stopcock *n.* valve regulating the flow in a pipe etc.

stopgap *n.* temporary substitute.

stoppage *n.* stopping; obstruction.

stopper *n.* plug for closing a bottle etc. — *v.* close with a stopper.

stopwatch *n.* watch with mechanism for starting and stopping it at will.

storage *n.* storing; space for this.

store *n.* supply of something available for use; large shop; storehouse. — *v.* collect and keep for future use; deposit in a warehouse. **in store** being stored; destined to happen, imminent. **set store by** value greatly.

storehouse *n.* place where things are stored.

storeroom *n.* room used for storing things.

storey *n.* (*pl.* **-eys**) each horizontal section of a building. **storeyed** *a.*

stork *n.* large wading bird.

storm *n.* disturbance of the atmosphere with strong winds and usu. rain or snow; violent shower (of missiles etc.); great outbreak (of anger or abuse etc.). — *v.* rage, be violent; attack or capture suddenly. **stormy** *a.*

story *n.* account of an incident or series of incidents (true or invented).

stout *a.* thick and strong; fat; brave and resolute. — *n.* a kind of strong dark beer. **stoutly** *adv.*, **stoutness** *n.*

stove [1] *n.* apparatus containing an oven; closed apparatus used for heating rooms etc.

stove [2] *see* **stave**.

stow *v.* place in a receptacle for storage. **stow away** conceal oneself as a stowaway.

stowaway *n.* person who hides on a ship etc. so as to travel without charge or unseen.

straddle *v.* sit or stand (across) with legs wide apart; stand or place (things) in a line across.

strafe *v.* attack with gunfire from the air.

straggle *v.* grow or spread untidily; wander separately; lag behind others. **straggler** *n.*, **straggly** *a.*

straight *a.* extending or moving in one direction, not curved or bent; correctly or tidily arranged; in unbroken succession; honest, frank; not modified or elaborate; without additions. — *adv.* in a straight line; direct; without delay; frankly. — *n.* straight part. **go straight** live honestly after being a criminal. **straight away** without delay. **straight face** not smiling. **straight fight** contest between only two candidates. **straight off** (*colloq.*) immediately, without hesitation. **straightness** *n.*

straighten *v.* make or become straight.

straightforward *a.* honest, frank; without complications. **straightforwardly** *adv.*

strain [1] *n.* lineage; variety or breed of animals etc.; slight or inherited tendency.

strain [2] *v.* make taut; injure by excessive stretching or over-exertion; make an intense effort (with); sieve to separate solids from liquid. — *n.* straining, force exerted thus; injury or exhaustion caused by straining; severe demand on strength or resources; passage from a tune. **strainer** *n.*

strained *a.* (of manner etc.) tense, not natural or relaxed.

strait *n.* (also *pl.*) narrow stretch of water connecting two seas; (*pl.*) difficult state of affairs. **strait-jacket** *n.* strong garment put round a violent person to restrain their arms; (*v.*) restrict severely. **strait-laced** *a.* very prim and proper.

straitened *a.* (of conditions) poverty-stricken.

strand [1] *n.* single thread; each of those twisted to form a cable or yarn etc.; lock of hair.

strand [2] *n.* shore. — *v.* run aground; leave in difficulties.

strange *a.* not familiar; alien; unusual, odd; unaccustomed. **strangely** *adv.*, **strangeness** *n.*

stranger *n.* one who is strange to a place or company or experience.

strangle *v.* kill or be killed by squeezing the throat; restrict the growth or utterance of. **strangler** *n.*

stranglehold *n.* strangling grip.

strangulation *n.* strangling.

strap *n.* strip of leather or other flexible material for holding things together or in place, or supporting something. — *v.* (**strapped**) secure with strap(s). **strapped for** (*colloq.*) short of.

strapping *a.* tall and robust. — *n.* straps; sticking plaster used for binding injuries.

strata *see* **stratum**.

stratagem *n.* cunning method of achieving something; trick.

strategic *a.* of strategy; (of weapons) very long-range. **strategically** *adv.*

strategist *n.* expert in strategy.

strategy *n.* planning and directing of the whole operation of a campaign or war; plan, policy.

stratify *v.* arrange in strata. **stratification** *n.*

stratosphere *n.* layer of the atmosphere about 10–60 km above the earth's surface.

stratum *n.* (*pl.* **strata**) one of a series of layers or levels.

straw *n.* dry cut stalks of corn etc.; single piece of this; narrow tube for sucking up liquid in drinking. **straw poll** unofficial poll as a test of general feeling.

strawberry *n.* soft juicy edible red fruit with yellow seeds on the surface. **strawberry mark** red birthmark.

stray *v.* leave one's group or proper place aimlessly; wander; deviate from a subject. — *a.* having strayed; isolated. — *n.* stray domestic animal.

streak *n.* thin line or band of a colour or substance different from its surroundings; element, trait; spell, series. — *v.* mark with streaks; move very rapidly; (*colloq.*) run naked in a public place. **streaker** *n.*, **streaky** *a.*

stream *n.* small river; flow of liquid or things or people; direction of this; section into which schoolchildren of the same level of ability are placed. — *v.* flow; run with liquid; float or wave at full length; arrange (schoolchildren) in streams. **on stream** in active operation or production.

streamer *n.* long narrow flag; strip of ribbon or paper etc. attached at one or both ends.

streamline *v.* give a smooth even shape that offers least resistance to movement through water or air; make more efficient by simplifying.

street *n.* public road in a town or village lined with buildings. **street credibility** familiarity with a fashionable urban subculture.

strength *n.* quality of being strong; its intensity; advantageous skill or quality; total number of people making up a group. **on the strength of** relying on as a basis or support.

strengthen *v.* make or become stronger.

strenuous *a.* making or requiring great effort. **strenuously** *adv.*, **strenuousness** *n.*

streptococcus *n.* (*pl.* **-ci**) bacterium causing serious infections.

stress *n.* emphasis; extra force used on a sound in speech or music; pressure, tension, strain. — *v.* lay stress on.

stretch *v.* pull out tightly or to a greater extent; be able or tend to become stretched; be continuous; thrust out one's limbs; strain; exaggerate. — *n.* stretching; ability to be stretched; continuous expanse or period. — *a.* able to be stretched. **stretch a point** agree to something not normally allowed. **stretchy** *a.*

stretcher *n.* framework for carrying a sick or injured person in a lying position.

strew *v.* (**strewed**, **strewn** *or* **strewed**) scatter over a surface; cover with scattered things.

striation *n.* each of a series of lines or grooves.

stricken *a.* afflicted by an illness, shock, or grief.

strict *a.* precisely limited or defined; without exception or deviation; requiring or giving complete obedience or exactitude. **strictly** *adv.*, **strictness** *n.*

stricture *n.* severe criticism; abnormal constriction.

stride *v.* (**strode**, **stridden**) walk with long steps. — *n.* single long step; manner of striding; progress.

strident *a.* loud and harsh. **stridently** *adv.*, **stridency** *n.*

strife *n.* quarrelling, conflict.

strike *v.* (**struck**) hit; knock; attack suddenly; afflict; ignite (a match) by friction; agree on (a bargain); indicate (the hour) or be indicated by a sound; find (gold or mineral oil etc.); occur to the mind of, produce a mental impression on; take down (a flag or tent etc.); stop work in protest; assume (an attitude) dramatically. — *n.* act or instance of striking; attack; workers' refusal to work as a protest. **strike home** deal an effective blow. **strike off** *or* **out** cross out. **strike up** begin playing or singing; start (a friendship etc.) casually.

strikebound *a.* immobilized by a workers' strike.

striker *n.* person or thing that strikes; worker who is on strike; football player whose main function is to try to score goals.

striking *a.* sure to be noticed; impressive. **strikingly** *adv.*

string *n.* narrow cord; stretched piece of catgut or wire etc. in a musical instrument, vibrated to produce tones; set of objects strung together; series; (*pl.*) conditions insisted upon; (*pl.*) stringed instruments, (*attrib.*) of or for these. — *v.* (**strung**) fit or fasten with string(s); thread on a string. **pull strings** use one's influence. **string along** (*colloq.*) deceive; go along (with). **string out** spread out on a line. **string up** hang up on strings; kill by hanging.

stringent *a.* strict, with firm restrictions. **stringently** *adv.*, **stringency** *n.*

stringy *a.* like string; fibrous.

strip [1] *v.* (**stripped**) remove (clothes, coverings, or parts etc.); pull or tear away (from); undress; deprive, e.g. of property or titles. **stripper** *n.*

strip [2] *n.* long narrow piece or area.

comic strip *or* **strip cartoon** sequence of cartoons. **strip light** tubular fluorescent lamp.
stripe *n.* long narrow band on a surface, differing in colour or texture from its surroundings; chevron on a sleeve, indicating rank. **striped** *a.*, **stripy** *a.*
stripling *n.* a youth.
striptease *n.* entertainment in which a performer gradually undresses.
strive *v.* (**strove**, **striven**) make great efforts; carry on a conflict.
strobe *n.* (*colloq.*) stroboscope.
stroboscope *n.* apparatus for producing a rapidly flashing bright light. **stroboscopic** *a.*
strode *see* **stride**.
stroke [1] *n.* act of striking something; single movement or action or effort; particular sequence of movements (e.g. in swimming); mark made by a movement of a pen or paintbrush etc.; sound made by a clock striking; attack of apoplexy or paralysis.
stroke [2] *v.* pass the hand gently along the surface of. — *n.* act of stroking.
stroll *v.* & *n.* walk in a leisurely way. **stroller** *n.*
strong *a.* capable of exerting or resisting great power; powerful through numbers, resources, or quality; concentrated; containing much alcohol; having a considerable effect; having a specified number of members. — *adv.* strongly. **strong language** forcible language; swearing. **strong-minded** *a.* determined. **strongly** *adv.*
stronghold *n.* fortified place; centre of support for a cause.
strongroom *n.* room designed for safe storage of valuables.
strontium *n.* silver-white metallic element. **strontium 90** its radioactive isotope.
strove *see* **strive**.
struck *see* **strike**. — *a.* **struck on** (*colloq.*) impressed with, liking.
structure *n.* way a thing is constructed or organized; thing's supporting framework or essential parts; constructed thing, complex whole. **structural** *a.*, **structurally** *adv.*
struggle *v.* move in a vigorous effort to get free; make one's way or a living etc. with difficulty; make a vigorous effort. — *n.* spell of struggling; vigorous effort; hard contest.
strum *v.* (**strummed**) play unskilfully or monotonously on (a musical instrument). — *n.* sound made by strumming.
strung *see* **string**. — *a.* **strung up** mentally tense or excited.
strut *n.* bar of wood or metal supporting something; strutting walk. — *v.* (**strutted**) walk in a pompous self-satisfied way.
strychnine /strikneen/ *n.* bitter highly poisonous substance.
stub *n.* short stump; counterfoil of a cheque or receipt etc. — *v.* (**stubbed**) strike (one's toe) against a hard object; extinguish (a cigarette) by pressure.
stubble *n.* lower ends of cornstalks left in the ground after harvest; short stiff growth of hair or beard, esp. growing after shaving. **stubbly** *a.*
stubborn *a.* obstinate. **stubbornly** *adv.*, **stubbornness** *n.*
stubby *a.* (**-ier**, **-iest**) short and thick. **stubbiness** *n.*
stucco *n.* plaster or cement used for coating walls or moulding into decorations. **stuccoed** *a.*
stuck *see* **stick** [2]. — *a.* unable to move. **stuck-up** *a.* (*colloq.*) conceited; snobbish.
stud [1] *n.* projecting nail-head or similar knob on a surface; device for fastening e.g. a detachable shirt-collar. — *v.* (**studded**) decorate with studs or precious stones; strengthen with studs.
stud [2] *n.* horses kept for breeding; establishment keeping these.
student *n.* person engaged in studying something, esp. at a college or university.
studied *a.* deliberate and artificial.
studio *n.* (*pl.* **-os**) workroom of a painter, photographer, etc.; premises where cinema films are made; room from which broadcasts are transmitted or where recordings are made. **studio flat** one-room flat with a kitchen and bathroom.
studious *a.* spending much time in study; deliberate and careful. **studiously** *adv.*, **studiousness** *n.*
study *n.* process of studying; its subject; work presenting the results of studying; musical composition designed to develop a player's skill; preliminary drawing; room used for studying. — *v.* give one's attention to acquiring knowledge of (a subject); examine attentively.
stuff *n.* material; unnamed things, belongings, subjects, etc. — *v.* pack tightly; fill with padding or stuffing; eat greedily.
stuffing *n.* padding used to fill something; savoury mixture put inside poultry, rolled meat, etc., before cooking.
stuffy *a.* (**-ier**, **-iest**) lacking fresh air or ventilation; dull; (*colloq.*) old-fashioned, prim, narrow-minded. **stuffily** *adv.*, **stuffiness** *n.*
stultify *v.* impair, make ineffective. **stultification** *n.*

stumble *v.* trip and lose one's balance; walk with frequent stumbles; make mistakes in speaking etc. — *n.* act of stumbling. **stumbling block** obstacle, difficulty.

stump *n.* base of a tree left in the ground when the rest has gone; similar remnant of something cut or broken or worn down; one of the uprights of a wicket in cricket. — *v.* walk stiffly or noisily; (*colloq.*) baffle. **stump up** (*colloq.*) pay over (money required).

stumpy *a.* (**-ier, -iest**) short and thick. **stumpiness** *n.*

stun *v.* (**stunned**) knock senseless; astound.

stung *see* **sting**.

stunk *see* **stink**.

stunner *n.* (*colloq.*) stunning person or thing.

stunning *a.* (*colloq.*) very attractive. **stunningly** *adv.*

stunt [1] *v.* hinder the growth or development of.

stunt [2] *n.* something unusual or difficult done as a performance.

stupefy *v.* dull the wits or senses of; stun. **stupefaction** *n.*

stupendous *a.* amazing; exceedingly great. **stupendously** *adv.*

stupid *a.* not clever; slow at learning or understanding; in a stupor. **stupidly** *adv.*, **stupidity** *n.*

stupor *n.* dazed almost unconscious condition.

sturdy *a.* (**-ier, -iest**) strongly built, hardy, vigorous. **sturdily** *adv.*, **sturdiness** *n.*

sturgeon *n.* (*pl.* **sturgeon**) large shark-like fish yielding caviare.

stutter *v.* & *n.* stammer, esp. repeating consonants.

sty [1] *n.* pigsty.

sty [2] *n.* inflamed swelling on the edge of the eyelid.

style *n.* manner of writing, speaking, or doing something; design; elegance. — *v.* design, shape, or arrange, esp. fashionably. **in style** elegantly, luxuriously.

stylish *a.* fashionable, elegant. **stylishly** *adv.*, **stylishness** *n.*

stylist *n.* person who has a good style; person who styles things.

stylistic *a.* of literary or artistic style. **stylistically** *adv.*

stylized *a.* made to conform to a conventional style. **stylization** *n.*

stylus *n.* (*pl.* **-uses** *or* **-li**) needle-like device for cutting or following a groove in a record.

stymie *v.* (**stymieing**) thwart.

styptic *a.* checking bleeding by causing blood vessels to contract.

suave /swaav/ *a.* smooth-mannered. **suavely** *adv.*, **suavity** *n.*

sub *n.* (*colloq.*) submarine; subscription; substitute.

sub- *pref.* under; subordinate.

subaltern *n.* army officer below the rank of captain.

subatomic *a.* smaller than an atom; occurring in an atom.

subcommittee *n.* committee formed from some members of a main committee.

subconscious *a.* & *n.* (of) our own mental activities of which we are not aware. **subconsciously** *adv.*

subcontinent *n.* large land mass forming part of a continent.

subcontract *v.* give or accept a contract to carry out all or part of another contract. **subcontractor** *n.*

subculture *n.* culture within a larger one.

subcutaneous *a.* under the skin.

subdivide *v.* divide (a part) into smaller parts. **subdivision** *n.*

subdue *v.* bring under control; make quieter or less intense.

subhuman *a.* less than human; not fully human.

subject *a.* /súbjikt/ not politically independent. — *n.* /súbjikt/ person subject to a particular political rule or ruler; person or thing being discussed or studied; word(s) in a sentence that name who or what does the action of the verb. — *v.* /səbjékt/ subjugate; cause to undergo. **subject-matter** *n.* matter treated in a book or speech etc. **subject to** depending upon as a condition. **subjection** *n.*

subjective *a.* dependent on personal taste or views etc. **subjectively** *adv.*

subjugate *v.* bring (a country) into subjection. **subjugation** *n.*

sublet *v.* (**sublet, subletting**) let (rooms etc. that one holds by lease) to a tenant.

sublimate *v.* divert the energy of (an emotion or impulse) into a culturally higher activity. **sublimation** *n.*

sublime *a.* most exalted. **sublimely** *adv.*, **sublimity** *n.*

subliminal *a.* below the level of conscious awareness.

sub-machine-gun *n.* lightweight machine-gun held in the hand.

submarine *a.* under the surface of the sea. — *n.* vessel that can operate under water.

submerge *v.* put or go below the surface of water or other liquid; flood. **submersion** *n.*

submersible *a.* able to submerge. — *n.* submersible craft.

submission *n.* submitting; statement etc. submitted; obedience.

submissive *a.* submitting to authority. **submissively** *adv.*, **submissiveness** *n.*

submit *v.* (**submitted**) yield to authority or control, surrender; subject to a process; present for consideration.

subordinate *a.* /səbórdinət/ of lesser importance or rank; working under another's authority. — *n.* /səbórdinət/ subordinate person. — *v.* /səbórdinayt/ make or treat as subordinate. **subordination** *n.*

suborn *v.* induce by bribery to commit perjury or other unlawful act. **subornation** *n.*

subpoena /səbpeénə/ *n.* writ commanding a person to appear in a law court. — *v.* (**subpoenaed**) summon with a subpoena.

subscribe *v.* pay (a subscription); sign. **subscribe to a theory** etc., express agreement. **subscriber** *n.*

subscription *n.* sum of money contributed; fee for membership etc.; process of subscribing.

subsequent *a.* occurring after. **subsequently** *adv.*

subservient *a.* subordinate; servile. **subserviently** *adv.*, **subservience** *n.*

subside *v.* sink to a lower or normal level; become less intense. **subsidence** *n.*

subsidiary *a.* of secondary importance; (of a business company) controlled by another. — *n.* subsidiary thing.

subsidize *v.* pay a subsidy to or for. **subsidization** *n.*

subsidy *n.* money given to support an industry etc. or to keep prices down.

subsist *v.* keep oneself alive, exist. **subsistence** *n.*

subsoil *n.* soil lying immediately below the surface layer.

subsonic *a.* of or flying at speeds less than that of sound.

substance *n.* matter with more or less uniform properties; particular kind of this; essence of something spoken or written; reality, solidity.

substantial *a.* of solid material or structure; of considerable amount or intensity or validity; wealthy; in essentials. **substantially** *adv.*

substantiate *v.* support with evidence. **substantiation** *n.*

substitute *n.* person or thing that acts or serves in place of another. — *v.* use or serve as a substitute. **substitution** *n.*

subsume *v.* bring or include under a particular classification.

subtenant *n.* person to whom a room etc. is sublet.

subterfuge *n.* trick used to avoid blame or defeat etc.

subterranean *a.* underground.

subtitle *n.* subordinate title; caption on a cinema film. — *v.* provide with subtitle(s).

subtle /sútt'l/ *a.* slight and difficult to detect or identify; making fine distinctions; ingenious. **subtly** *adv.*, **subtlety** *n.*

subtotal *n.* total of part of a group of figures.

subtract *v.* remove (a part or quantity or number) from a greater one. **subtraction** *n.*

subtropical *a.* of regions bordering on the tropics.

suburb *n.* residential area outside the central part of a town. **suburban** *a.*, **suburbanite** *n.*

suburbia *n.* suburbs and their inhabitants.

subvention *n.* subsidy.

subvert *v.* overthrow the authority of, esp. by weakening people's trust. **subversion** *n.*, **subversive** *a.*

subway *n.* underground passage; (*US*) underground railway.

succeed *v.* be successful; take the place previously filled by; come next in order.

success *n.* favourable outcome; attainment of one's aims, or of wealth, fame, or position; successful person or thing.

successful *a.* having success. **successfully** *adv.*

succession *n.* following in order; series of people or things following each other; succeeding to a throne or other position. **in succession** one after another.

successive *a.* following in succession. **successively** *adv.*

successor *n.* person who succeeds another.

succinct /səksíngkt/ *a.* concise and clear. **succinctly** *adv.*

succour *v.* & *n.* help.

succulent *a.* juicy; (of plants) having thick fleshy leaves. — *n.* succulent plant. **succulence** *n.*

succumb *v.* give way to something overpowering.

such *a.* of the same or that kind or degree; so great or intense. — *pron.* that. **such-and-such** *a.* particular but not now specified.

suchlike *a.* of the same kind.

suck *v.* draw (liquid or air etc.) into the mouth; draw liquid from; squeeze in the mouth by using the tongue; draw in. — *n.* act or process of sucking. **suck up to** (*colloq.*) treat sycophantically.

sucker *n.* organ or device that can adhere to a surface by suction; (*sl.*) person who is easily deceived.
suckle *v.* feed at the breast.
suckling *n.* unweaned child or animal.
sucrose *n.* sugar.
suction *n.* sucking; production of a partial vacuum so that external atmospheric pressure forces fluid etc. into the vacant space or causes adhesion.
sudden *a.* happening or done quickly or without warning. **all of a sudden** suddenly. **suddenly** *adv.*, **suddenness** *n.*
suds *n.pl.* soapsuds.
sue *v.* (**suing**) take legal proceedings against.
suede /swayd/ *n.* leather with a velvety nap on one side.
suet *n.* hard white fat from round an animal's kidneys, used in cooking. **suety** *a.*
suffer *v.* undergo or be subjected to (pain, loss, damage, etc.); tolerate. **suffering** *n.*
sufferance *n.* **on sufferance** tolerated but only grudgingly.
suffice *v.* be enough (for).
sufficient *a.* enough. **sufficiently** *adv.*, **sufficiency** *n.*
suffix *n.* (*pl.* **-ixes**) letter(s) added at the end of a word to make another word.
suffocate *v.* kill by stopping the breathing; cause discomfort to by making breathing difficult; be suffocated. **suffocation** *n.*
suffrage *n.* right to vote in political elections.
suffuse *v.* spread throughout or over. **suffusion** *n.*
sugar *n.* sweet crystalline substance obtained from the juices of various plants. **sugar beet** white beet from which sugar is obtained. **sugar cane** tall tropical plant from which sugar is obtained. **sugar soap** abrasive cleaning compound. **sugary** *a.*
suggest *v.* bring to mind; propose for acceptance or rejection.
suggestible *a.* easily influenced. **suggestibility** *n.*
suggestion *n.* suggesting; thing suggested; slight trace.
suggestive *a.* conveying a suggestion; suggesting something indecent. **suggestively** *adv.*
suicidal *a.* of or involving suicide; liable to commit suicide. **suicidally** *adv.*
suicide *n.* intentional killing of oneself; person who commits suicide; act destructive to one's own interests. **commit suicide** kill oneself intentionally.
suit /soot/ *n.* set of clothing, esp. jacket and trousers or skirt; any of the four sets into which a pack of cards is divided; lawsuit. — *v.* make or be suitable or convenient for; give a pleasing appearance upon.
suitable *a.* right for the purpose or occasion. **suitably** *adv.*, **suitability** *n.*
suitcase *n.* rectangular case for carrying clothes.
suite /sweet/ *n.* set of rooms or furniture; retinue; set of musical pieces.
sulk *v.* be sullen because of resentment or bad temper. **sulks** *n.pl.* fit of sulking. **sulky** *a.*, **sulkily** *adv.*, **sulkiness** *n.*
sullen *a.* gloomy and unresponsive; dark and dismal. **sullenly** *adv.*, **sullenness** *n.*
sully *v.* stain, blemish.
sulphate *n.* salt of sulphuric acid.
sulphide *n.* compound of sulphur and an element or radical.
sulphite *n.* salt of sulphurous acid.
sulphur *n.* pale yellow non-metallic element. **sulphurous** *a.*
sulphuric acid strong corrosive acid.
sultan *n.* ruler of certain Muslim countries.
sultana *n.* seedless raisin; sultan's wife, mother, or daughter.
sultanate *n.* sultan's territory.
sultry *a.* (**-ier**, **-iest**) hot and humid; (of a woman) passionate and sensual. **sultriness** *n.*
sum *n.* total; amount of money; problem in arithmetic. **sum total** total. **sum up** give the total of; summarize; form an opinion of.
summarize *v.* make or be a summary of. **summarization** *n.*
summary *n.* statement giving the main points of something. — *a.* giving the main points only; without attention to details or formalities. **summarily** *adv.*
summation *n.* adding up; summarizing.
summer *n.* warmest season of the year. **summertime** *n.* summer. **summer time** time shown by clocks put forward in summer to give longer light evenings. **summery** *a.*
summit *n.* highest point; top of a mountain; conference between heads of States.
summon *v.* send for (a person); order to appear in a law court; gather together (one's courage etc.); call upon to do something.
summons *n.* command summoning a person; written order to appear in a law court. — *v.* serve with a summons.
sump *n.* reservoir of oil in a petrol engine; hole or low area into which liquid drains.
sumptuous *a.* splendid and costly-

looking. **sumptuously** *adv.*, **sumptuousness** *n.*

sun *n.* star around which the earth travels; light or warmth from this; any fixed star. — *v.* (**sunned**) expose to the sun.

sunbathe *v.* expose one's body to the sun. **sunbather** *n.*

sunbeam *n.* ray of sun.

sunburn *n.* inflammation caused by exposure to sun. — *v.* suffer sunburn. **sunburnt** *a.*

sundae /súnday/ *n.* dish of ice cream and fruit, nuts, syrup, etc.

Sunday school school for religious instruction of Christian children, held on Sundays.

sunder *v.* break or tear apart.

sundew *n.* bog plant that traps insects.

sundial *n.* device that shows the time by means of a shadow on a scaled dial.

sundown *n.* sunset.

sundry *a.* various. **all and sundry** everyone. **sundries** *n.pl.* various small items.

sunflower *n.* tall garden plant bearing large yellow flowers.

sung *see* **sing**.

sunk *see* **sink**.

sunken *a.* lying below the level of the surrounding surface.

Sunni *n.* & *a.* (*pl.* same or **-is**) (person) belonging to a Muslim sect opposed to Shiites.

sunny *a.* (**-ier**, **-iest**) full of sunshine; cheerful. **sunnily** *adv.*

sunrise *n.* rising of the sun.

sunset *n.* setting of the sun; sky full of colour at sunset.

sunshade *n.* parasol; awning.

sunshine *n.* direct sunlight.

sunspot *n.* dark patch observed on the sun's surface; (*colloq.*) place with a sunny climate.

sunstroke *n.* illness caused by too much exposure to sun.

super *a.* (*colloq.*) excellent, superb.

superb *a.* of the most impressive or splendid kind. **superbly** *adv.*

supercharge *v.* increase the power of (an engine) by a device that forces extra air or fuel into it. **supercharger** *n.*

supercilious *a.* haughty and superior. **superciliously** *adv.*, **superciliousness** *n.*

superficial *a.* of or on the surface, not deep or penetrating. **superficially** *adv.*, **superficiality** *n.*

superfluous *a.* more than is required. **superfluously** *adv.*, **superfluity** *n.*

superhuman *a.* beyond ordinary human capacity or power; higher than humanity, divine.

superimpose *v.* place on top of something else. **superimposition** *n.*

superintend *v.* supervise. **superintendence** *n.*

superintendent *n.* supervisor; police officer next above inspector.

superior *a.* higher in position or rank; better, greater; showing that one feels wiser or better etc. than others. — *n.* person or thing of higher rank or ability or quality. **superiority** *n.*

superlative *a.* of the highest quality; of the grammatical form expressing 'most'. — *n.* superlative form. **superlatively** *adv.*

superman *n.* (*pl.* **-men**) man of superhuman powers.

supermarket *n.* large self-service shop.

supernatural *a.* of or involving a power above the forces of nature. **supernaturally** *adv.*

supernumerary *a.* & *n.* extra.

superpower *n.* extremely powerful nation.

superscript *a.* written just above and to the right of a word etc.

supersede *v.* take the place of; put or use in place of.

supersonic *a.* of or flying at speeds greater than that of sound. **supersonically** *adv.*

superstition *n.* belief in magical and similar influences; idea or practice based on this; widely held but wrong idea. **superstitious** *a.*, **superstitiously** *adv.*

superstore *n.* supermarket.

superstructure *n.* structure that rests on something else.

supervene *v.* occur as an interruption or a change. **supervention** *n.*

supervise *v.* direct and inspect. **supervision** *n.*, **supervisor** *n.*, **supervisory** *a.*

supine /sōōpīn/ *a.* lying face upwards; indolent. **supinely** *adv.*

supper *n.* evening meal, last meal of the day.

supplant *v.* oust and take the place of. **supplanter** *n.*

supple *a.* bending easily. **supply** *adv.*, **suppleness** *n.*

supplement *n.* thing added as an extra part or to make up for a deficiency. — *v.* provide or be a supplement to.

supplementary *a.* serving as a supplement.

suppliant /súpliənt/ *n.* & *a.* (person) asking humbly for something.

supplicate *v.* ask humbly for; beseech. **supplication** *n.*

supply *v.* give or provide with, make available; satisfy (a need). — *n.* supplying; stock, amount provided or available.

support *v.* bear the weight of; strengthen; supply with necessaries; help, encourage. — *n.* act of supporting; person or thing that supports. **supporter** *n.*, **supportive** *a.*

suppose *v.* be inclined to think; assume to be true; consider as a proposal. **be supposed to** be expected to; have as a duty.

supposedly *adv.* according to supposition.

supposition *n.* process of supposing; what is supposed.

suppository *n.* solid medicinal substance placed in the rectum or vagina and left to melt.

suppress *v.* put an end to the activity or existence of; keep from being known. **suppression** *n.*, **suppressor** *n.*

suppurate *v.* form pus, fester. **suppuration** *n.*

supra- *pref.* above, over.

supreme *a.* highest in authority, rank, or quality. **supremely** *adv.*, **supremacy** *n.*

supremo *n.* (*pl.* **-os**) supreme leader.

surcharge *n.* additional charge. — *v.* make a surcharge on or to.

sure *a.* without doubt or uncertainty; reliable, unfailing. — *adv.* (*colloq.*) certainly. **make sure** act so as to be certain. **sure-footed** *a.* never slipping or stumbling. **sureness** *n.*

surely *adv.* in a sure manner; (used for emphasis) that must be right; (as an answer) certainly.

surety *n.* guarantee; guarantor of a person's promise.

surf *n.* white foam of breaking waves. **surfing** *n.* sport of riding on a surfboard.

surface *n.* outside or outward appearance of something; any side of an object; uppermost area, top. — *a.* of or on the surface. — *v.* put a specified surface on; come or bring to the surface.

surfboard *n.* narrow board for riding over surf.

surfeit /súrfit/ *n.* too much, esp. of food or drink. — *v.* cause to take too much of something; satiate.

surge *v.* move forward in or like waves; increase in volume or intensity. — *n.* wave(s); surging movement or increase.

surgeon *n.* doctor qualified to perform surgical operations.

surgery *n.* treatment by cutting or manipulation of affected parts of the body; place where or times when a doctor or dentist or an MP etc. is available for consultation. **surgical** *a.*, **surgically** *adv.*

surly *a.* (**-ier, -iest**) bad-tempered and unfriendly. **surliness** *n.*

surmise *v.* & *n.* conjecture.

surmount *v.* overcome (a difficulty); get over (an obstacle); be on the top of. **surmountable** *a.*

surname *n.* family name.

surpass *v.* outdo; excel.

surplus *n.* amount left over after what is needed has been used.

surprise *n.* emotion aroused by something sudden or unexpected; thing causing this. — *v.* cause to feel surprise; come upon or attack unexpectedly.

surrealism *n.* style of art and literature seeking to express what is in the subconscious mind. **surrealist** *n.*, **surrealistic** *a.*

surrender *v.* hand over, give into another's power or control, esp. under compulsion; give oneself up. — *n.* surrendering.

surreptitious *a.* acting or done stealthily. **surreptitiously** *adv.*

surrogate *n.* deputy. **surrogate mother** woman who bears a child on behalf of another. **surrogacy** *n.*

surround *v.* come, place, or be all round, encircle. — *n.* border.

surroundings *n.pl.* things or conditions around a person or place.

surveillance *n.* supervision; close watch.

survey *v.* /sərváy/ look at and take a general view of; examine the condition of (a building); measure and map out. — *n.* /súrvay/ general look at or examination of something; report or map produced by surveying.

surveyor *n.* person whose job is to survey land or buildings.

survival *n.* surviving; thing that has survived from an earlier time.

survive *v.* continue to live or exist; remain alive or in existence after. **survivable** *a.*, **survivability** *n.*, **survivor** *n.*

susceptible *a.* easily affected or influenced. **susceptibility** *n.*

sushi *n.* Japanese dish of flavoured balls of cold rice usu. garnished with fish.

suspect *v.* /səspékt/ feel that something may exist or be true; mistrust; feel to be guilty but have no proof. — *n.* /súspekt/ person suspected of a crime etc. — *a.* /súspekt/ suspected, open to suspicion.

suspend *v.* hang up; keep from falling or sinking in air or liquid; stop temporarily; deprive temporarily of a position or right.

suspender *n.* attachment to hold up a sock or stocking by its top.

suspense *n.* anxious uncertainty while awaiting an event etc.

suspension *n.* suspending; means by which a vehicle is supported on its axles. **suspension bridge** bridge suspended from cables that pass over supports at each end.

suspicion *n.* suspecting; unconfirmed belief; slight trace.
suspicious *a.* feeling or causing suspicion. **suspiciously** *adv.*
sustain *v.* support; keep alive; keep (a sound or effort) going continuously; undergo; endure; uphold the validity of.
sustenance *n.* food, nourishment.
suture /sōōchər/ *n.* surgical stitching of a wound; stitch or thread used in this. — *v.* stitch (a wound).
suzerain *n.* country or ruler with some authority over a self-governing country; overlord. **suzerainty** *n.*
svelte *a.* slender and graceful.
SW *abbr.* south-west; south-western.
swab *n.* mop or pad for cleansing, drying, or absorbing things; specimen of a secretion taken with this. — *v.* **(swabbed)** cleanse with a swab.
swaddle *v.* swathe in wraps or warm garments.
swag *n.* loot; carved festoon.
swagger *v.* walk or behave with aggressive pride. — *n.* this gait or manner.
Swahili *n.* Bantu language widely used in East Africa.
swallow [1] *v.* cause or allow to go down one's throat; work throat muscles in doing this; take in and engulf or absorb; accept. — *n.* act of swallowing; amount swallowed.
swallow [2] *n.* small migratory bird with a forked tail.
swam *see* **swim**.
swamp *n.* marsh. — *v.* flood, drench or submerge in water; overwhelm with a mass or number of things. **swampy** *a.*
swan *n.* large usu. white waterbird with a long slender neck.
swank *n.* (*colloq.*) boastful person or behaviour; ostentation. — *v.* (*colloq.*) behave with swank.
swansong *n.* person's last performance or achievement etc.
swap *v.* **(swapped)** & *n.* exchange.
swarm [1] *n.* large cluster of people, insects etc. — *v.* move in a swarm; be crowded.
swarm [2] *v.* **swarm up** climb by gripping with arms and legs.
swarthy *a.* **(-ier, -iest)** having a dark complexion. **swarthiness** *n.*
swashbuckling *a.* & *n.* swaggering boldly. **swashbuckler** *n.*
swastika *n.* symbol formed by a cross with ends bent at right angles.
swat *v.* **(swatted)** hit hard with something flat. **swatter** *n.*
swatch *n.* sample(s) of cloth etc.
swath /swawth/ *n.* (*pl.* **swaths**) strip cut in one sweep or passage by a scythe or mowing-machine.
swathe *v.* wrap with layers of coverings.
sway *v.* swing gently, lean to and fro; influence the opinions of; waver in one's opinion. — *n.* swaying movement; influence.
swear *v.* **(swore, sworn)** state or promise on oath; state emphatically; use a swear word. **swear by** have great confidence in. **swear word** profane or indecent word used in anger etc.
sweat *n.* moisture given off by the body through the pores; state of sweating; moisture forming in drops on a surface. — *v.* exude sweat or as sweat; be in a state of great anxiety; work long and hard. **sweat-band** *n.* band of material worn to absorb or wipe away sweat. **sweated labour** labour of workers with poor pay and conditions. **sweaty** *a.*
sweater *n.* jumper, pullover.
sweatshirt *n.* cotton sweater with sleeves.
sweatshop *n.* place employing sweated labour.
Swede *n.* native of Sweden.
swede *n.* large variety of turnip.
Swedish *a.* & *n.* (language) of Sweden.
sweep *v.* **(swept)** clear away with a broom or brush; clean or clear (a surface) thus; go smoothly and swiftly or majestically; extend in a continuous line. — *n.* sweeping movement or line; act of sweeping; chimney sweep; sweepstake. **sweep the board** win all the prizes. **sweeper** *n.*
sweeping *a.* comprehensive; making no exceptions.
sweepstake *n.* form of gambling in which the money staked is divided among those who have drawn numbered tickets for the winners.
sweet *a.* tasting as if containing sugar; fragrant; melodious; pleasant; (*colloq.*) charming. — *n.* small shaped piece of sweet substance; sweet dish forming one course of a meal; beloved person. **sweet pea** climbing plant with fragrant flowers. **sweet tooth** liking for sweet things. **sweetly** *adv.*, **sweetness** *n.*
sweetbread *n.* animal's thymus gland or pancreas used as food.
sweeten *v.* make or become sweet or sweeter. **sweetener** *n.*
sweetheart *n.* either of a pair of people in love with each other.
sweetmeal *a.* of sweetened wholemeal.
swell *v.* **(swelled, swollen** *or* **swelled)** make or become larger from pressure within; curve outwards; make or become greater in amount or intensity. — *n.* act or state of swelling; heaving of the sea;

gradual increase in loudness; (*colloq.*) person of high social position. **swelled head** (*sl.*) conceit.

swelling *n.* swollen place on the body.

swelter *v.* be uncomfortably hot.

swept *see* **sweep**.

swerve *v.* turn aside from a straight course. — *n.* swerving movement or direction.

swift *a.* quick, rapid. — *n.* swiftly flying bird with narrow wings. **swiftly** *adv.*, **swiftness** *n.*

swill *v.* wash, rinse; (of water) pour; drink greedily. — *n.* rinse; sloppy food fed to pigs.

swim *v.* (**swam, swum**) travel through water by movements of the body; be covered with liquid; seem to be whirling or waving; be dizzy. — *n.* act or period of swimming. **swimming bath, swimming pool** artificial pool for swimming in. **swimmer** *n.*

swimmingly *adv.* with easy unobstructed progress.

swindle *v.* cheat in a business transaction. — *n.* piece of swindling. **swindler** *n.*

swine *n.pl.* pigs. — *n.* (*pl.* **swine**) (*colloq.*) hated person or thing.

swing *v.* (**swung**) move to and fro while supported; turn in a curve; change from one mood or opinion to another; influence decisively. — *n.* act, movement, or extent of swinging; hanging seat for swinging in; jazz with the time of the melody varied. **in full swing** with activity at its greatest. **swing-bridge** *n.* bridge that can be swung aside for ships to pass. **swing-wing** *n.* aircraft wing that can be moved to slant backwards. **swinger** *n.*

swingeing *a.* forcible; huge in amount or scope.

swipe *v.* (*colloq.*) hit with a swinging blow; snatch, steal. — *n.* (*colloq.*) swinging blow.

swirl *v.* & *n.* whirl, flow with a whirling movement.

swish *v.* move with a hissing sound. — *n.* swishing sound. — *a.* (*colloq.*) smart, fashionable.

Swiss *a.* & *n.* (native) of Switzerland. **Swiss roll** thin flat sponge cake spread with jam etc. and rolled up.

switch *n.* device operated to turn electric current on or off; flexible stick or rod, whip; tress of hair tied at one end; shift in opinion or method etc. — *v.* turn (on or off) by means of a switch; transfer, divert; change; swing round quickly.

switchback *n.* railway used for amusement at a fair etc., with alternate steep ascents and descents; road with similar slopes.

switchboard *n.* panel of switches for making telephone connections or operating electric circuits.

swivel *n.* link or pivot enabling one part to revolve without turning another. — *v.* (**swivelled**) turn on or as if on a swivel.

swollen *see* **swell**.

swoop *v.* make a sudden downward rush, attack suddenly. — *n.* swooping movement or attack.

swop *v.* & *n.* = swap.

sword /sord/ *n.* weapon with a long blade and a hilt. **swordsman** *n.* (*pl.* **-men**).

swordfish *n.* sea fish with a long sword-like upper jaw.

swore *see* **swear**.

sworn *see* **swear**. — *a.* open and determined, esp. in enmity.

swot *v.* (**swotted**) (*school sl.*) study hard. — *n.* (*school sl.*) person who studies hard.

swum *see* **swim**.

swung *see* **swing**.

sybarite *n.* person who is excessively fond of comfort and luxury. **sybaritic** *a.*

sycamore *n.* large tree of the maple family.

sycophant *n.* person who tries to win favour by flattery. **sycophantic** *a.*, **sycophantically** *adv.*

syllable *n.* unit of sound in a word. **syllabic** *a.*

syllabub *n.* dish of whipped cream flavoured with wine.

syllabus *n.* (*pl.* **-buses**) statement of the subjects to be covered by a course of study.

sylph *n.* slender girl or woman.

symbiosis *n.* (*pl.* **-oses**) relationship of different organisms living in close association. **symbiotic** *a.*

symbol *n.* thing regarded as suggesting something; mark or sign with a special meaning.

symbolic, **symbolical** *adjs.* of, using, or used as a symbol. **symbolically** *adv.*

symbolism *n.* use of symbols to express things. **symbolist** *n.*

symbolize *v.* be a symbol of; represent by means of a symbol.

symmetry *n.* state of having parts that correspond in size, shape, and position on either side of a dividing line or round a centre. **symmetrical** *a.*, **symmetrically** *adv.*

sympathetic *a.* feeling or showing or resulting from sympathy; likeable. **sympathetically** *adv.*

sympathize *v.* feel or express sympathy. **sympathizer** *n.*

sympathy *n.* ability to share another's emotions or sensations; pity or tenderness towards a sufferer; liking for each other.

symphony *n.* long elaborate musical composition for a full orchestra. **symphonic** *a.*

symposium *n.* (*pl.* **-ia**) meeting for discussing a particular subject.

symptom *n.* sign of the existence of a condition.

symptomatic *a.* serving as a symptom.

synagogue *n.* building for public Jewish worship.

synchromesh *n.* device that makes gear wheels revolve at the same speed.

synchronize *v.* (cause to) occur or operate at the same time; cause (clocks etc.) to show the same time. **synchronization** *n.*

synchronous *a.* occurring or existing at the same time.

syncopate *v.* change the beats or accents in (music). **syncopation** *n.*

syndicate *n.* /sindikət/ association of people or firms to carry out a business undertaking. — *v.* /sindikayt/ combine into a syndicate; arrange publication in many newspapers etc. simultaneously. **syndication** *n.*

syndrome *n.* combination of signs, symptoms, etc. characteristic of a specified condition.

synonym *n.* word or phrase meaning the same as another in the same language. **synonymous** *a.*

synopsis *n.* (*pl.* **-opses**) summary, brief general survey.

syntax *n.* way words are arranged to form phrases and sentences. **syntactic** *a.*, **syntactically** *adv.*

synthesis *n.* (*pl.* **-theses**) combining; artificial production of a substance that occurs naturally.

synthesize *v.* make by synthesis.

synthesizer *n.* electronic musical instrument able to produce a great variety of sounds.

synthetic *a.* made by synthesis. — *n.* synthetic substance or fabric. **synthetically** *adv.*

syphilis *n.* a venereal disease. **syphilitic** *a.*

syringe *n.* device for drawing and injecting liquid. — *v.* wash out or spray with a syringe.

syrup *n.* thick sweet liquid; water sweetened with sugar. **syrupy** *a.*

system *n.* set of connected things that form a whole or work together; animal body as a whole; set of rules or practices used together; method of classification or notation or measurement; orderliness.

systematic *a.* methodical. **systematically** *adv.*

systematize *v.* arrange according to a system.

systemic *a.* of or affecting the body as a whole.

T

tab *n.* small projecting flap or strip. **keep tabs on** (*colloq.*) keep under observation.
tabard *n.* short sleeveless tunic-like garment.
tabby *n.* cat with grey or brown fur and dark stripes.
table *n.* piece of furniture with a flat top supported on one or more legs; food provided at table; list of facts or figures arranged in columns. — *v.* submit (a motion or report) for discussion. **at table** while taking a meal at the table. **table tennis** game played with bats and a light hollow ball on a table.
tableau /táblō/ *n.* (*pl.* **-eaux**) silent motionless group arranged to represent a scene.
table d'hôte /taab'l dőt/ (meal) served at a fixed inclusive price.
tableland *n.* plateau of land.
tablespoon *n.* large spoon for serving food; amount held by this. **tablespoonful** *n.* (*pl.* **-fuls**).
tablet *n.* slab bearing an inscription etc.; measured amount of a drug compressed into a solid form.
tabloid *n.* small-sized newspaper, often sensational in style.
taboo *n.* ban or prohibition made by religion or social custom. — *a.* prohibited by a taboo.
tabular *a.* arranged in a table or list.
tabulate *v.* arrange in tabular form. **tabulation** *n.*
tachograph *n.* device in a motor vehicle to record speed and travel time.
tacit *a.* implied or understood without being put into words. **tacitly** *adv.*
taciturn *a.* saying very little. **taciturnity** *n.*
tack [1] *n.* small broad-headed nail; long temporary stitch; sailing ship's oblique course. — *v.* nail with tack(s); stitch with tacks; add as an extra thing; sail a zigzag course.
tack [2] *n.* harness, saddles, etc.
tackle *n.* set of ropes and pulleys for lifting etc.; equipment for a task or sport; act of tackling in football etc. — *v.* try to deal with or overcome (an opponent or problem etc.); intercept (an opponent who has the ball in football etc.).
tacky *a.* (of paint etc.) sticky, not quite dry. **tackiness** *n.*
tact *n.* skill in avoiding offence or in winning goodwill. **tactful** *a.*, **tactfully** *adv.*
tactic *n.* piece of tactics.
tactical *a.* of tactics; (of weapons) for use in a battle or at close quarters. **tactically** *adv.*
tactician *n.* expert in tactics.
tactics *n.* skilful use of available means to achieve an (esp. military) objective; (*pl.*) manoeuvring; procedure adopted.
tactile *a.* of or using the sense of touch. **tactility** *n.*
tactless *a.* lacking in tact. **tactlessly** *adv.*, **tactlessness** *n.*
tadpole *n.* larva of a frog or toad etc. at the stage when it has gills and a tail.
taffeta *n.* shiny silk-like fabric.
tag *n.* metal point on a shoelace etc.; label; much-used phrase or quotation. — *v.* (**tagged**) label; attach, add.
tail *n.* animal's hindmost part, esp. when extending beyond its body; rear or hanging or inferior part; (*colloq.*) person tailing another; **tails** reverse of a coin, turned upwards after being tossed. — *v.* (*colloq.*) follow closely, shadow. **tail-end** *n.* very last part. **tail-light** *n.* light at the back of a motor vehicle or train etc. **tail off** become fewer or smaller or slighter; end inconclusively.
tailback *n.* queue of traffic extending back from an obstruction.
tailboard *n.* hinged or removable back of a lorry etc. **tailcoat** *n.* man's coat with the skirt tapering and divided at the back.
tailgate *n.* rear door in a motor vehicle.
tailor *n.* maker of men's clothes, esp. to order. — *v.* make (clothes) as a tailor; make or adapt for a special purpose. **tailor-made** *a.*
tailplane *n.* horizontal part of an aeroplane's tail.
tailspin *n.* aircraft's spinning dive.
taint *n.* trace of decay or infection or other bad quality. — *v.* affect with a taint.
take *v.* (**took, taken**) get possession of, capture; be effective; make use of; cause to come or go with one; carry, remove; accept, endure; study or teach (a subject); make a photograph (of). — *n.* amount taken or caught; instance of photographing a scene for a cinema film. **be taken by** *or* **with** find attractive. **be taken ill** become ill. **take after** resemble (a parent etc.). **take-away** *n.* & *a.* (cooked meal) bought at a restaurant etc. for eating elsewhere; (place) selling this. **take**

back withdraw (a statement). **take in** include; make (a garment etc.) smaller; understand; deceive, cheat. **take off** take (clothing etc.) from the body; mimic humorously; become airborne. **take-off** *n.* humorous mimicry; process of becoming airborne. **take on** acquire; undertake; engage (an employee); accept as an opponent. **take oneself off** depart. **take one's time** not hurry. **take out** remove. **take over** take control of. (**takeover** *n.*). **take part** share in an activity. **take place** occur. **take sides** support one side or another. **take to** adopt as a habit or custom; go to as a refuge; develop a liking or ability for. **take up** take as a hobby or business or protégé; occupy (time or space); resume; interrupt or question (a speaker); accept (an offer). **take up with** begin to associate with. **taker** *n.*

taking *a.* attractive, captivating.

takings *n.pl.* money taken in business.

talc *n.* a kind of smooth mineral; talcum powder.

talcum *n.* talc. **talcum powder** talc powdered and usu. perfumed for use on the skin.

tale *n.* narrative, story; report spread by gossip.

talent *n.* special ability.

talented *a.* having talent.

talisman *n.* (*pl.* **-mans**) object supposed to bring good luck.

talk *v.* convey or exchange ideas by spoken words; use (a specified language) in talking. — *n.* talking, conversation; style of speech; informal lecture; rumour. **talk over** discuss. **talking-to** *n.* reproof. **talker** *n.*

talkative *a.* talking very much.

tall *a.* of great or specified height. **tall order** difficult task. **tall story** (*colloq.*) one that is hard to believe. **tallness** *n.*

tallboy *n.* tall chest of drawers.

tallow *n.* animal fat used to make candles, lubricants, etc.

tally *n.* total of a debt or score. — *v.* correspond.

Talmud *n.* body of Jewish law and tradition. **Talmudic** *a.*

talon *n.* bird's large claw.

tambourine *n.* percussion instrument with jingling metal discs.

tame *a.* (of animals) gentle and not afraid of human beings; docile; not exciting. — *v.* make tame or manageable. **tamely** *adv.*, **tameness** *n.*

Tamil *n.* member or language of a people of south India and Sri Lanka.

tamp *v.* pack down tightly.

tamper *v.* **tamper with** meddle or interfere with.

tampon *n.* plug of absorbent material inserted into the body.

tan *v.* (**tanned**) convert (hide) into leather; make or become brown by exposure to sun; (*sl.*) thrash. — *n.* yellowish-brown; brown colour in sun-tanned skin. — *a.* yellowish-brown.

tandem *n.* bicycle for two people one behind another. — *adv.* one behind another. **in tandem** arranged thus.

tandoor *n.* Indian etc. clay oven.

tandoori *n.* food cooked in a tandoor.

tang *n.* strong taste or flavour or smell. **tangy** *a.*

tangent *n.* straight line that touches the outside of a curve without intersecting it. **go off at a tangent** diverge suddenly from a line of thought etc. **tangential** *a.*

tangerine *n.* a kind of small orange; its colour.

tangible *a.* able to be perceived by touch; clear and definite, real. **tangibly** *adv.*, **tangibility** *n.*

tangle *v.* twist into a confused mass; entangle; become involved in conflict with. — *n.* tangled mass or condition.

tango *n.* (*pl.* **-os**) ballroom dance with gliding steps. — *v.* dance a tango.

tank *n.* large container for liquid or gas; armoured fighting vehicle moving on Caterpillar tracks.

tankard *n.* large one-handled usu. metal drinking vessel.

tanker *n.* ship or aircraft or vehicle for carrying liquid in bulk.

tanner *n.* person who tans hides.

tannery *n.* place where hides are tanned into leather.

tannic acid tannin.

tannin *n.* substance used in tanning and dyeing.

tantalize *v.* torment by the sight of something desired but kept out of reach or withheld. **tantalization** *n.*

tantamount *a.* equivalent.

tantra *n.* any of a class of Hindu or Buddhist mystical or magical writings.

tantrum *n.* outburst of bad temper.

tap [1] *n.* tubular plug with a device for allowing liquid to flow through; connection for tapping a telephone. — *v.* (**tapped**) fit a tap into; draw off through a tap or incision; obtain supplies etc. or information from; cut a screw-thread in (a cavity); fit a listening device in (a telephone circuit). **on tap** (*colloq.*) available for use. **tap root** plant's chief root.

tap [2] *v.* (**tapped**) knock gently. — *n.* light blow; sound of this. **tap-dance** *n.*

dance in which the feet tap an elaborate rhythm.

tape *n.* narrow strip of material for tying or fastening or labelling things; magnetic tape; tape-measure; tape recording. — *v.* tie or fasten with tape; record on magnetic tape. **have a thing taped** (*sl.*) understand and be able to deal with it. **tape-measure** *n.* strip of tape etc. marked for measuring length. **tape recorder** apparatus for recording and reproducing sounds on magnetic tape. **tape recording**.

taper *n.* thin candle; narrowing. — *v.* make or become gradually narrower. **taper off** diminish.

tapestry *n.* textile fabric woven or embroidered ornamentally.

tapeworm *n.* tape-like worm living as a parasite in intestines.

tapioca *n.* starchy grains obtained from cassava, used in making puddings.

tapir /táypeer/ *n.* small pig-like animal with a long snout.

tappet *n.* projection used in machinery to tap against something.

tar *n.* thick dark liquid distilled from coal etc.; similar substance formed by burning tobacco. — *v.* (**tarred**) coat with tar.

tarantella *n.* rapid whirling dance.

tarantula *n.* large black hairy spider.

tardy *a.* (**-ier**, **-iest**) slow; late. **tardily** *adv.*, **tardiness** *n.*

tare [1] *n.* a kind of vetch.

tare [2] *n.* allowance for the weight of the container or vehicle weighed with the goods it holds.

target *n.* object or mark to be hit in shooting etc.; object of criticism; objective. — *v.* (**targeted**) aim at (as) a target.

tariff *n.* list of fixed charges; duty to be paid.

Tarmac *n.* [P.] broken stone or slag mixed with tar. **tarmac** *n.* area surfaced with this. **tarmacked** *a.*

tarnish *v.* lose or cause (metal) to lose lustre; blemish (a reputation). — *n.* loss of lustre; blemish.

tarot /tárrō/ *n.* pack of 78 cards mainly used for fortune-telling.

tarpaulin *n.* waterproof canvas.

tarragon *n.* aromatic herb.

tarsier *n.* small monkey-like animal of the East Indies.

tarsus *n.* (*pl.* **-si**) set of small bones forming the ankle.

tart [1] *a.* acid in taste or manner. **tartly** *adv.*, **tartness** *n.*

tart [2] *n.* pie or pastry flan with sweet filling; (*sl.*) prostitute. — *v.* **tart up** (*colloq.*) dress gaudily, smarten up.

tartan *n.* pattern (orig. of a Scottish clan) with coloured stripes crossing at right angles; cloth with this.

Tartar *n.* member of a group of Central Asian peoples; bad-tempered or difficult person.

tartar *n.* hard deposit forming on teeth; deposit formed by fermentation in a wine cask.

tartare sauce sauce of mayonnaise, chopped gherkins, etc.

tartlet *n.* small tart.

task *n.* piece of work to be done. **take to task** rebuke. **task force** group organized for a special task.

taskmaster *n.* person who imposes a task, esp. regularly or severely.

tassel *n.* ornamental bunch of hanging threads. **tasselled** *a.*

taste *n.* sensation caused in the tongue by things placed upon it; ability to perceive this; small quantity (of food or drink); slight experience; liking; ability to perceive what is beautiful or fitting. — *v.* discover or test the flavour of; have a certain flavour; experience. **taster** *n.*

tasteful *a.* showing good taste. **tastefully** *adv.*, **tastefulness** *n.*

tasteless *a.* having no flavour; showing poor taste. **tastelessly** *adv.*, **tastelessness** *n.*

tasty *a.* (**-ier**, **-iest**) having a strong flavour, appetizing.

tat *n.* (*colloq.*) tatty thing(s).

tattered *a.* ragged.

tatters *n.pl.* torn pieces.

tattle *v.* chatter idly, reveal information thus. — *n.* idle chatter.

tattoo [1] *n.* military display or pageant; tapping sound.

tattoo [2] *v.* mark (skin) by puncturing it and inserting pigments; make (a pattern) thus. — *n.* tattooed pattern.

tatty *a.* (**-ier**, **-iest**) (*colloq.*) ragged, shabby and untidy; tawdry. **tattily** *adv.*, **tattiness** *n.*

taught *see* **teach**.

taunt *v.* jeer at provocatively. — *n.* taunting remark.

taut *a.* stretched firmly, not slack.

tauten *v.* make or become taut.

tautology *n.* pointless repetition, esp. using a word or phrase of the same grammatical function (e.g. *free, gratis, and for nothing*). **tautological** *a.*, **tautologous** *a.*

tavern *n.* (*old use*) inn, public house.

tawdry *a.* (**-ier**, **-iest**) showy but without real value. **tawdrily** *adv.*, **tawdriness** *n.*

tawny *a.* orange-brown.

tax *n.* money to be paid to a government; thing that makes a heavy demand. — *v.*

impose a tax on; make heavy demands on. **taxation** *n.*, **taxable** *a.*

taxi *n.* (*pl.* **-is**) car with driver which may be hired. — *v.* (**taxied, taxiing**) (of an aircraft) move along ground under its own power. **taxi-cab** *n.* taxi.

taxidermy *n.* process of preparing, stuffing, and mounting the skins of animals in lifelike form. **taxidermist** *n.*

taxonomy *n.* scientific classification of organisms. **taxonomical** *a.*, **taxonomist** *n.*

taxpayer *n.* person who pays tax (esp. income tax).

tea *n.* dried leaves of a tropical evergreen shrub; hot drink made by infusing these (or other substances) in boiling water; afternoon or evening meal at which tea is drunk. **tea bag** small porous bag holding tea for infusion. **tea chest** wooden box in which tea is exported. **tea cloth** tea towel. **tea leaf** leaf of tea, esp. after infusion. **tea rose** rose with scent like tea. **tea towel** towel for drying washed crockery etc.

teacake *n.* bun for serving toasted and buttered.

teach *v.* (**taught**) impart information or skill to (a person) or about (a subject). **teachable** *a.*, **teacher** *n.*

teak *n.* strong heavy wood of an Asian evergreen tree; this tree.

teal *n.* (*pl.* **teal**) a kind of duck.

team *n.* set of players; set of people or animals working together. — *v.* combine into a team or set.

teamwork *n.* organized cooperation.

teapot *n.* vessel with a spout, in which tea is made.

tear [1] /tair/ *v.* (**tore, torn**) pull forcibly apart or away or to pieces; make (a hole etc.) thus; become torn: move or travel hurriedly. — *n.* hole etc. torn.

tear [2] /teer/ *n.* drop of liquid forming in and falling from the eye. **in tears** with tears flowing. **tear gas** gas causing severe irritation of the eyes.

tearaway *n.* impetuous hooligan.

tearful *a.* shedding or ready to shed tears. **tearfully** *adv.*

tease *v.* try to provoke in a playful or unkind way; pick into separate strands. — *n.* person fond of teasing others.

teasel *n.* plant with bristly heads.

teaset *n.* set of cups and plates etc. for serving tea.

teashop *n.* shop where tea is served to the public.

teaspoon *n.* small spoon for stirring tea etc.; amount held by this. **teaspoonful** *n.* (*pl.* **-fuls**).

teat *n.* nipple on a milk-secreting organ; device of rubber etc. on a feeding bottle, through which the contents are sucked.

technical *a.* of the mechanical arts and applied sciences; of a particular subject or craft etc.; using technical terms; in a strict legal sense. **technically** *adv.*, **technicality** *n.*

technician *n.* expert in the techniques of a subject or craft; skilled mechanic.

technique *n.* method of doing or performing something.

technocracy *n.* government by technical experts. **technocrat** *n.*

technology *n.* study of mechanical arts and applied sciences; these subjects; their application in industry etc. **technological** *a.*, **technologically** *adv.*, **technologist** *n.*

teddy bear toy bear.

tedious *a.* tiresome because of length, slowness, or dullness. **tediously** *adv.*, **tediousness** *n.*, **tedium** *n.*

tee *n.* cleared space from which a golf ball is driven at the start of play; small heap of sand or piece of wood for supporting this ball. — *v.* (**teed**) **tee off** make the first stroke in golf.

teem [1] *v.* be full of; be present in large numbers.

teem [2] *v.* (of water or rain) pour.

teenager *n.* person in his or her teens.

teens *n.pl.* years of age from 13 to 19. **teenage** *a.*, **teenaged** *a.*

teeny *a.* (**-ier, -iest**) (*colloq.*) tiny.

tee shirt = T-shirt.

teeter *v.* stand or move unsteadily.

teeth *see* **tooth**.

teethe *v.* (of a baby) have its first teeth appear through the gums. **teething troubles** problems in the early stages of an enterprise.

teetotal *a.* abstaining completely from alcohol. **teetotaller** *n.*

telecommunication *n.* communication by telephone, radio, etc.; (*pl.*) technology for this.

telegram *n.* message sent by telegraph.

telegraph *n.* system or apparatus for sending messages, esp. by electrical impulses along wires. — *v.* communicate thus.

telegraphist *n.* person employed in telegraphy.

telegraphy *n.* communication by telegraph. **telegraphic** *a.*, **telegraphically** *adv.*

telemeter *n.* apparatus for recording and transmitting the readings of an instrument at a distance. **telemetry** *n.*

telepathy *n.* communication between minds other than by the senses. **telepathic** *a.*, **telepath, telepathist** *ns.*

telephone *n.* device for transmitting speech by wire or radio. — *v.* send (a message) to (a person) by telephone. **telephonic** *a.*, **telephonically** *adv.*, **telephony** *n.*

telephonist *n.* operator of a telephone switchboard.

telephoto lens lens producing a large image of a distant object for photography.

teleprinter *n.* telegraph instrument for sending and receiving typewritten messages.

telerecording *n.* recorded television broadcast.

telesales *n.pl.* selling by telephone.

telescope *n.* optical instrument for making distant objects appear larger. — *v.* make or become shorter by sliding each section inside the next; compress or become compressed forcibly. **telescopic** *a.*, **telescopically** *adv.*

teletext *n.* service transmitting written information to subscribers' television screens.

televise *v.* transmit by television.

television *n.* system for reproducing on a screen a view of scenes etc. by radio transmission; televised programmes; (also **television set**) apparatus for receiving these. **televisual** *a.*

telex *n.* system of telegraphy using teleprinters and public transmission lines. — *v.* send (a message) to (a person) by telex.

tell *v.* **(told)** make known in words; give information to; reveal a secret; decide; distinguish; produce an effect; direct, order. **tell off** (*colloq.*) reprimand. **tell-tale** *n.* person who tells tales. **tell tales** reveal secrets.

teller *n.* narrator; person appointed to count votes; bank cashier.

telling *a.* having a noticeable effect.

telly *n.* (*colloq.*) television.

temerity *n.* audacity.

temp *n.* (*colloq.*) temporary employee.

temper *n.* state of mind as regards calmness or anger; fit of anger; calmness under provocation. — *v.* bring (metal or clay) to the required hardness or consistency; moderate the effects of.

tempera *n.* method of painting using colours mixed with egg.

temperament *n.* person's nature as it controls his or her behaviour.

temperamental *a.* of or relating to temperament; excitable or moody. **temperamentally** *adv.*

temperance *n.* self-restraint; total abstinence from alcohol.

temperate *a.* self-restrained, moderate; (of climate) without extremes. **temperately** *adv.*

temperature *n.* degree of heat or cold; body temperature above normal.

tempest *n.* violent storm.

tempestuous *a.* stormy.

template *n.* pattern or gauge, esp. for cutting shapes.

temple [1] *n.* building dedicated to the presence or service of god(s).

temple [2] *n.* flat part between forehead and ear.

tempo *n.* (*pl.* **-os** *or* **-i**) time, speed, or rhythm of a piece of music; rate of motion or activity.

temporal *a.* secular; of or denoting time; of the temple(s) of the head.

temporary *a.* lasting for a limited time. **temporarily** *adv.*

temporize *v.* avoid committing oneself in order to gain time. **temporization** *n.*

tempt *v.* persuade or try to persuade by the prospect of pleasure or advantage; arouse a desire in. **temptation** *n.*, **tempter** *n.*, **temptress** *n.fem.*

ten *a.* & *n.* one more than nine (10, X).

tenable *a.* able to be defended or held. **tenability** *n.*

tenacious *a.* holding or sticking firmly. **tenaciously** *adv.*, **tenacity** *n.*

tenancy *n.* use of land or a building etc. as a tenant.

tenant *n.* person who rents land or a building etc. from a landlord.

tench *n.* (*pl.* **tench**) fish of the carp family.

tend [1] *v.* take care of.

tend [2] *v.* have a specified tendency.

tendency *n.* way a person or thing is likely to be or behave or become; thing's direction.

tendentious *a.* biased, not impartial. **tendentiously** *adv.*

tender [1] *a.* not tough or hard; delicate; painful when touched; sensitive; loving, gentle. **tenderly** *adv.*, **tenderness** *n.*

tender [2] *v.* offer formally; make a tender for. — *n.* formal offer to supply goods or carry out work at a stated price. **legal tender** currency that must, by law, be accepted in payment.

tender [3] *n.* vessel or vehicle conveying goods or passengers to and from a larger one; truck attached to a steam locomotive and carrying fuel and water etc.

tendon *n.* strip of strong tissue connecting a muscle to a bone etc.

tendril *n.* thread-like part by which a climbing plant clings; slender curl of hair etc.

tenement *n.* large house let in portions to tenants.

tenet *n.* firm belief or principle.

tenfold *a.* & *adv.* ten times as much or as many.

tennis *n.* ball game played with rackets over a net, with a soft ball on an open court (**lawn tennis**) or with a hard ball in a walled court (**real tennis**).

tenon *n.* projection shaped to fit into a mortise.

tenor *n.* general meaning; highest ordinary male singing voice. — *a.* of tenor pitch.

tense [1] *n.* any of the forms of a verb that indicate the time of the action.

tense [2] *a.* stretched tightly; nervous, anxious. — *v.* make or become tense. **tensely** *adv.*, **tenseness** *n.*

tensile *a.* of tension; capable of being stretched.

tension *n.* stretching; tenseness, esp. of feelings; effect produced by forces pulling against each other; electromotive force.

tent *n.* portable shelter or dwelling made of canvas etc.

tentacle *n.* slender flexible part of certain animals, used for feeling or grasping things.

tentative *a.* hesitant; done as a trial. **tentatively** *adv.*

tenterhooks *n.pl.* **on tenterhooks** in suspense because of uncertainty.

tenth *a.* & *n.* next after ninth. **tenthly** *adv.*

tenuous *a.* very thin; very slight. **tenuousness** *n.*

tenure *n.* holding of office or of land or accommodation etc.

tepee /teepee/ *n.* conical tent used by North American Indians.

tepid *a.* slightly warm, lukewarm.

tequila *n.* Mexican liquor made from the sap of an agave plant.

tercentenary *n.* 300th anniversary.

term *n.* fixed or limited period; period of weeks during which a school etc. is open or in which a law court holds sessions; each quantity or expression in a mathematical series or ratio etc.; word or phrase; (*pl.*) conditions offered or accepted; (*pl.*) relation between people. **come to terms with** reconcile oneself to (a difficulty etc.).

termagant *n.* bullying woman.

terminal *a.* of or forming an end; of or undergoing the last stage of a fatal disease. — *n.* terminus; building where air passengers arrive and depart; point of connection in an electric circuit, or of input or output to a computer etc. **terminally** *adv.*

terminate *v.* end. **termination** *n.*

terminology *n.* technical terms of a subject. **terminological** *a.*

terminus *n.* (*pl.* **-i**) end; last stopping place on a rail or bus route.

termite *n.* small insect that is very destructive to timber.

tern *n.* seabird with long wings.

terrace *n.* raised level place; paved area beside a house; row of houses joined by party walls.

terracotta *n.* brownish-red unglazed pottery; its colour.

terra firma dry land, the ground.

terrain *n.* land with regard to its natural features.

terrapin *n.* freshwater tortoise.

terrestrial *a.* of the earth; of or living on land.

terrible *a.* appalling, distressing; (*colloq.*) very bad. **terribly** *adv.*

terrier *n.* small active dog.

terrific *a.* (*colloq.*) of great size; excellent. **terrifically** *adv.*

terrify *v.* fill with terror.

terrine *n.* pâté or similar food; earthenware dish for this.

territorial *a.* of territory. **Territorial Army** a volunteer reserve force.

territory *n.* land under the control of a person or State or city etc.; sphere of action or thought.

terror *n.* extreme fear; terrifying person or thing; (*colloq.*) troublesome person or thing.

terrorism *n.* use of violence and intimidation. **terrorist** *n.*

terrorize *v.* fill with terror; coerce by terrorism.

terry *n.* looped cotton fabric used for towels etc.

terse *a.* concise, curt. **tersely** *adv.*, **terseness** *n.*

tertiary /térshəri/ *a.* next after secondary.

tessellated *a.* resembling mosaic.

test *n.* something done to discover a person's or thing's qualities or abilities etc.; examination (esp. in a school) on a limited subject; test match. — *v.* subject to a test. **test match** one of a series of international cricket or Rugby football matches. **test-tube** *n.* tube of thin glass with one end closed, used in laboratories. **tester** *n.*

testament *n.* a will; written statement of beliefs. **Old Testament** books of the Bible telling the history and beliefs of the Jews. **New Testament** those telling the life and teachings of Christ.

testate *a.* having left a valid will at death. **testacy** *n.*

testator *n.* person who has made a will. **testatrix** *n.fem.*
testes *see* **testis**.
testicle *n.* male organ that secretes sperm-bearing fluid.
testify *v.* bear witness to; give evidence; be evidence of.
testimonial *n.* formal statement testifying to character, abilities, etc.; gift showing appreciation.
testimony *n.* declaration (esp. under oath); supporting evidence.
testis *n.* (*pl.* **testes**) testicle.
testosterone *n.* male sex hormone.
testy *a.* irritable. **testily** *adv.*
tetanus *n.* bacterial disease causing painful muscular spasms.
tête-à-tête /táytaatáyt/ *n.* private conversation, esp. between two people. — *a.* & *adv.* together in private.
tether *n.* rope etc. fastening an animal so that it can graze. — *v.* fasten with a tether. **at the end of one's tether** having reached the limit of one's endurance.
tetrahedron *n.* (*pl.* **-dra**) solid with four sides.
Teutonic *a.* of Germanic peoples or their languages.
text *n.* main body of a book as distinct from illustrations etc.; sentence from Scripture used as the subject of a sermon. **textual** *a.*
textbook *n.* book of information for use in studying a subject.
textile *n.* woven or machine-knitted fabric. — *a.* of textiles.
texture *n.* way a fabric etc. feels to the touch. **textured** *a.* having a noticeable texture. **textural** *a.*
than *conj.* used to introduce the second element in a comparison.
thank *v.* express gratitude to. **thank you** polite expression of thanks. **thanks** *n.pl.* expressions of gratitude; (*colloq.*) thank you.
thankful *a.* feeling or expressing gratitude. **thankfully** *adv.*
thankless *a.* not likely to win thanks. **thanklessness** *n.*
thanksgiving *n.* expression of gratitude, esp. to God.
that *a.* & *pron.* (*pl.* **those**) the (person or thing) referred to; further or less obvious (one) of two. — *adv.* to such an extent. — *rel.pron.* used to introduce a defining clause. — *conj.* introducing a dependent clause.
thatch *n.* roof made of straw or reeds etc. — *v.* roof with thatch. **thatcher** *n.*
thaw *v.* make or become unfrozen; become less cool or less formal in manner. — *n.* thawing, weather that thaws ice etc.
the *a.* applied to a noun standing for a specific person or thing, or one or all of a kind, or used to emphasize excellence or importance; (of prices) per.
theatre *n.* place for the performance of plays etc.; lecture hall with seats in tiers; room where surgical operations are performed; plays and acting.
theatrical *a.* of or for the theatre; exaggerated for effect. **theatricals** *n.pl.* theatrical (esp. amateur) performances. **theatrically** *adv.*, **theatricality** *n.*
thee *pron.* (*old use*) objective case of *thou.*
theft *n.* stealing.
their *a.*, **theirs** *poss.pron.* belonging to them.
theism /theé-iz'm/ *n.* belief that the universe was created by a god. **theist** *n.*, **theistic** *a.*
them *pron.* objective case of *they.*
theme *n.* subject being discussed; melody which is repeated. **theme park** park with amusements organized round one theme. **thematic** *a.*
themselves *pron.* emphatic and reflexive form of *they* and *them.*
then *adv.* at that time; next, and also; in that case. — *a.* & *n.* (of) that time.
thence *adv.* from that place or source.
thenceforth *adv.* from then on.
theocracy *n.* form of government by a divine being or by priests. **theocratic** *a.*, **theocratically** *adv.*
theodolite *n.* surveying instrument for measuring angles.
theology *n.* study or system of religion. **theological** *a.*, **theologian** *n.*
theorem *n.* mathematical statement to be proved by reasoning.
theoretical *a.* based on theory only. **theoretically** *adv.*
theorist *n.* person who theorizes.
theorize *v.* form theories.
theory *n.* set of ideas formulated to explain something; opinion, supposition; statement of the principles of a subject.
theosophy *n.* system of philosophy that aims at direct intuitive knowledge of God. **theosophical** *a.*
therapeutic /thérrəpyoōtik/ *a.* curative. **therapeutically** *adv.*
therapist *n.* specialist in therapy.
therapy *n.* curative treatment.
there *adv.* in, at, or to that place; at that point; in that matter. — *n.* that place. — *int.* exclamation of satisfaction or consolation.
thereabouts *adv.* near there.
thereafter *adv.* after that.

thereby *adv.* by that means.
therefore *adv.* for that reason.
therein *adv.* in that place.
thereof *adv.* of that.
thereto *adv.* to that.
thereupon *adv.* in consequence of that, because of that.
thermal *a.* of or using heat; warm, hot. — *n.* rising current of hot air.
thermodynamics *n.* science of the relationship between heat and other forms of energy.
thermometer *n.* instrument for measuring heat.
thermonuclear *a.* of or using nuclear reactions that occur only at very high temperatures.
thermoplastic *a.* & *n.* (substance) becoming soft when heated and hardening when cooled.
Thermos *n.* [P.] vacuum flask.
thermosetting *a.* setting permanently when heated.
thermostat *n.* device that regulates temperature automatically. **thermostatic** *a.*, **thermostatically** *adv.*
thesaurus *n.* (*pl.* **-ri**) dictionary of synonyms.
these *see* **this**.
thesis *n.* (*pl.* **theses**) theory put forward and supported by reasoning; lengthy written essay submitted for a university degree.
they *pron.* people or things mentioned or unspecified.
thick *a.* of great or specified distance between opposite surfaces; dense; fairly stiff in consistency; (*colloq.*) friendly. — *adv.* thickly. — *n.* busiest part. **thick-skinned** *a.* not sensitive to criticism or snubs. **thickly** *adv.*, **thickness** *n.*
thicken *v.* make or become thicker.
thicket *n.* close group of shrubs and small trees etc.
thickset *a.* set or growing close together; stocky, burly.
thief *n.* (*pl.* **thieves**) one who steals. **thievish** *a.*, **thievery** *n.*
thieve *v.* be a thief; steal.
thigh *n.* upper part of the leg, between hip and knee.
thimble *n.* hard cap worn to protect the end of the finger in sewing.
thin *a.* (**thinner**, **thinnest**) not thick; lean, not plump; lacking substance, weak. — *adv.* thinly. — *v.* (**thinned**) make or become thinner. **thin-skinned** *a.* oversensitive to criticism or snubs. **thinly** *adv.*, **thinness** *n.*, **thinner** *n.*
thine *a.* & *poss.pron.* (*old use*) belonging to thee.
thing *n.* whatever is or may be perceived, known, or thought about; act, fact, idea, task, etc.; item; inanimate object; (*pl.*) belongings, utensils, circumstances.
think *v.* (**thought**) exercise the mind, form ideas; form or have as an idea or opinion or plan. — *n.* (*colloq.*) act of thinking. **think better of it** change one's mind after thought. **think-tank** *n.* group providing ideas and advice on national or commercial problems. **thinker** *n.*
third *a.* next after second. — *n.* third thing, class, etc.; one of three equal parts. **third party** another person etc. besides the two principals. **third-rate** *a.* very inferior in quality. **Third World** developing countries of Asia, Africa, and Latin America. **thirdly** *adv.*
thirst *n.* feeling caused by a desire to drink; strong desire. — *v.* feel a thirst. **thirsty** *a.*, **thirstily** *adv.*
thirteen *a.* & *n.* one more than twelve (13, XIII). **thirteenth** *a.* & *n.*
thirty *a.* three times ten (30, XXX). **thirtieth** *a.* & *n.*
this *a.* & *pron.* (*pl.* **these**) the (person or thing) near or present or mentioned.
thistle *n.* prickly plant. **thistly** *a.*
thistledown *n.* very light fluff on thistle seeds.
thong *n.* strip of leather used as a fastening or lash etc.
thorax *n.* part of the body between head or neck and abdomen. **thoracic** *a.*
thorn *n.* small sharp pointed projection on a plant; thorn-bearing tree or shrub. **thorny** *a.*
thorough *a.* complete in every way; detailed; methodical. **thoroughly** *adv.*, **thoroughness** *n.*
thoroughbred *n.* & *a.* (horse etc.) bred of pure or pedigree stock.
thoroughfare *n.* public way open at both ends.
those *see* **that**.
thou *pron.* (*old use*) you.
though *conj.* in spite of the fact that, even supposing. — *adv.* (*colloq.*) however.
thought *see* **think**. — *n.* process or power or way of thinking; idea etc. produced by thinking; intention; consideration.
thoughtful *a.* thinking deeply; thought out carefully; considerate. **thoughtfully** *adv.*, **thoughtfulness** *n.*
thoughtless *a.* careless; inconsiderate. **thoughtlessly** *adv.*, **thoughtlessness** *n.*
thousand *a.* & *n.* ten hundred (1000, M). **thousandth** *a.* & *n.*
thrash *v.* beat, esp. with a stick or whip; defeat thoroughly; thresh; make

flailing movements. **thrash out** discuss thoroughly.

thread *n.* thin length of spun cotton or wool etc.; thing compared to this; spiral ridge of a screw. — *v.* pass a thread through; pass (a strip or thread etc.) through or round something; make (one's way) through a crowd etc. **threader** *n.*

threadbare *a.* with nap worn and threads visible; shabbily dressed.

threadworm *n.* small thread-like parasitic worm.

threat *n.* expression of intention to punish, hurt, or harm; person or thing thought likely to bring harm or danger.

threaten *v.* make or be a threat (to)..

three *a.* & *n.* one more than two (3, III). **three-dimensional** *a.* having or appearing to have length, breadth, and depth.

threefold *a.* & *adv.* three times as much or as many.

threesome *n.* three together, trio.

thresh *v.* beat out (grain) from husks of corn; make flailing movements.

threshold *n.* piece of wood or stone forming the bottom of a doorway; point of entry; lowest limit at which a stimulus is perceptible.

threw *see* **throw**.

thrice *adv.* (*old use*) three times.

thrift *n.* economical management of resources; plant with pink flowers. **thrifty** *a.*, **thriftily** *adv.*, **thriftiness** *n.*

thrill *n.* wave of feeling or excitement. — *v.* feel or cause to feel a thrill.

thriller *n.* exciting story or play etc., esp. involving crime.

thrive *v.* (**throve** or **thrived, thrived** or **thriven**) grow or develop well; prosper.

throat *n.* front of the neck; passage from mouth to oesophagus or lungs; narrow passage.

throaty *a.* uttered deep in the throat; hoarse. **throatily** *adv.*

throb *v.* (**throbbed**) (of the heart or pulse) beat with more than usual force; vibrate or sound with a persistent rhythm. — *n.* throbbing beat or sound.

throes *n.pl.* severe pangs of pain. **in the throes of** struggling with the task of.

thrombosis *n.* formation of a clot of blood in a blood vessel or organ of the body.

throne *n.* ceremonial seat for a monarch, bishop, etc.; sovereign power.

throng *n.* crowded mass of people. — *v.* move or press in a throng; fill with a throng.

throttle *n.* valve controlling the flow of fuel or steam etc. to an engine; lever controlling this. — *v.* strangle. **throttle back** *or* **down** reduce an engine's speed by means of the throttle.

through *prep.* & *adv.* from end to end or side to side (of), entering at one point and coming out at another; from beginning to end (of); so as to have finished, so as to have passed (an examination); so as to be connected by telephone (to); by the agency, means, or fault of. — *a.* going through; passing without stopping.

throughout *prep.* & *adv.* right through, from beginning to end (of).

throughput *n.* amount of material processed.

throve *see* **thrive**.

throw *v.* (**threw, thrown**) send with some force through the air; cause to fall; put (clothes etc.) on or off hastily; shape (pottery) on a wheel; cause to be in a certain state; (*colloq.*) disconcert; operate (a switch or lever); have (a fit or tantrum); (*colloq.*) give (a party). — *n.* act of throwing; distance something is thrown. **throw away** part with as useless or unwanted; fail to make use of. **throw-away** *a.* to be thrown away after use. **throw in the towel** admit defeat or failure. **throw out** discard; reject. **throw up** raise, erect; bring to notice; resign from; vomit. **thrower** *n.*

thrush [1] *n.* songbird, esp. one with a speckled breast.

thrush [2] *n.* fungoid infection of the mouth, throat, or vagina.

thrust *v.* (**thrust**) push forcibly; make a forward stroke with a sword etc. — *n.* thrusting movement or force.

thud *n.* dull low sound like that of a blow. — *v.* (**thudded**) make or fall with a thud.

thug *n.* vicious ruffian. **thuggish** *a.*, **thuggery** *n.*

thumb *n.* short thick finger set apart from the other four. — *v.* touch or turn (pages etc.) with the thumbs; request (a lift) by signalling with one's thumb. **under the thumb of** completely under the influence of.

thump *v.* strike or knock heavily (esp. with the fist), thud. — *n.* heavy blow; sound of thumping.

thunder *n.* loud noise that accompanies lightning; similar sound. — *v.* sound with or like thunder; utter loudly; make a forceful attack in words. **steal a person's thunder** forestall him or her. **thundery** *a.*

thunderbolt *n.* imaginary missile thought of as sent to earth with a lightning flash; startling formidable event or statement.

thunderclap *n.* clap of thunder.

thunderous *a.* like thunder.

thunderstorm *n.* storm accompanied by thunder.

thunderstruck *a.* amazed.

thus *adv.* in this way; as a result of this; to this extent.

thwack *v.* strike with a heavy blow. — *n.* this blow or sound.

thwart *v.* prevent from doing what is intended or from being accomplished. — *n.* oarsman's bench across a boat.

thy *a.* (*old use*) belonging to thee.

thyme /tīm/ *n.* herb with fragrant leaves.

thymus *n.* ductless gland near the base of the neck.

thyroid *a.* & *n.* **thyroid gland** large ductless gland in the neck.

thyself *pron.* emphatic and reflexive form of *thou* and *thee*.

tiara *n.* woman's jewelled semi-circular headdress.

tibia *n.* (*pl.* **-ae**) shin-bone.

tic *n.* involuntary muscular twitch.

tick [1] *n.* regular clicking sound, esp. made by a clock or watch; (*colloq.*) moment; small mark placed against an item in a list etc., esp. to show that it is correct. — *v.* (of a clock etc.) make a series of ticks; mark with a tick. **tick off** (*colloq.*) reprimand. **tick over** (of an engine) idle. **tick-tack** *n.* semaphore signalling by racecourse bookmakers.

tick [2] *n.* blood-sucking mite or parasitic insect.

tick [3] *n.* (*colloq.*) financial credit.

ticket *n.* marked piece of card or paper entitling the holder to a certain right (e.g. to travel by train etc.); certificate of qualification as a ship's master or pilot etc.; label; notification of a traffic offence; list of candidates for office; **the ticket** (*colloq.*) the correct or desirable thing. — *v.* (**ticketed**) put a ticket on.

tickle *v.* touch or stroke lightly so as to cause a slight tingling sensation; feel this sensation; amuse, please. — *n.* act or sensation of tickling.

ticklish *a.* sensitive to tickling; (of a problem) requiring careful handling.

tidal *a.* of or affected by tides.

tiddler *n.* (*colloq.*) small fish, esp. stickleback or minnow.

tiddly *a.* (*colloq.*) slightly drunk.

tiddly-winks *n.pl.* game of flicking small counters (**tiddly-winks**) into a receptacle.

tide *n.* sea's regular rise and fall; trend of feeling or events etc. **tide over** help temporarily.

tidings *n.pl.* news.

tidy *a.* (**-ier, -iest**) neat and orderly. — *v.* make tidy. **tidily** *adv.*, **tidiness** *n.*

tie *v.* (**tying**) attach or fasten with cord etc.; form into a knot or bow; unite; make the same score as another competitor; restrict, limit. — *n.* cord etc. used for tying something; strip of material worn below the collar and knotted at the front of the neck; thing that unites or restricts; equality of score between competitors; sports match between two of a set of teams or players. **tie-break** *n.* means of deciding the winner when competitors have tied. **tie-clip** *n.*, **tie-pin** *n.* ornamental clip or pin for holding a necktie in place. **tie in** link or (of information etc.) be connected with something else. **tie up** fasten with cord etc.; make (money etc.) not readily available for use; occupy fully. **tie-up** *n.* connection, link.

tied *a.* (of a public house) bound to supply only one brewer's beer; (of a house) for occupation only by a person working for its owner.

tier /teer/ *n.* any of a series of rows or ranks or units of a structure placed one above the other.

tiff *n.* petty quarrel.

tiger *n.* large striped animal of the cat family. **tiger lily** orange lily with dark spots.

tight *a.* held or fastened firmly, fitting closely; tense, not slack; (of money etc.) severely restricted; (*colloq.*) stingy; (*colloq.*) drunk. — *adv.* tightly. **tight corner** difficult situation. **tight-fisted** *a.* stingy. **tightly** *adv.*, **tightness** *n.*

tighten *v.* make or become tighter.

tightrope *n.* tightly stretched rope on which acrobats perform.

tights *n.pl.* garment covering the legs and lower part of the body.

tigress *n.* female tiger.

tile *n.* thin slab of baked clay etc. used in rows for covering roofs, walls, or floors. — *v.* cover with tiles.

till [1] *v.* prepare and use (land) for growing crops. **tillage** *n.*

till [2] *prep.* & *conj.* up to (a specified time).

till [3] *n.* receptacle for money in a shop etc.

tiller *n.* bar by which a rudder is turned.

tilt *v.* move into a sloping position. — *n.* sloping position. **at full tilt** at full speed or force.

tilth *n.* tillage; tilled soil.

timber *n.* wood prepared for use in building or carpentry; trees suitable for this; wooden beam used in constructing a house or ship.

timbered *a.* constructed of timber or with a timber framework; (of land) wooded.

timbre /támbər/ *n.* characteristic quality of the sound of a voice or instrument.

time *n.* all the years of the past, present, and future; point or portion of this; occasion, instance; rhythm in music; (*pl.*) contemporary circumstances; (*pl.*, in multiplication or comparison) taken a number of times. — *v.* choose the time for; measure the time taken by. **behind the times** out of date. **for the time being** until another arrangement is made. **from time to time** at intervals. **in time** not late; eventually. **time-and-motion** *a.* concerned with measuring the efficiency of effort. **time bomb** bomb that can be set to explode after an interval. **time-honoured** *a.* respected because of antiquity, traditional. **time-lag** *n.* interval between two connected events. **time-share** *n.* share in a property that allows use by several joint owners at agreed different times. **time switch** one operating automatically at a set time. **time zone** region (between parallels of longitude) where a common standard time is used.

timeless *a.* not affected by the passage of time. **timelessness** *n.*

timely *a.* occurring at just the right time. **timeliness** *n.*

timepiece *n.* clock or watch.

timetable *n.* list showing the times at which certain events take place.

timid *a.* easily alarmed, not bold, shy. **timidly** *adv.*, **timidity** *n.*

timorous *a.* timid. **timorously** *adv.*, **timorousness** *n.*

timpani *n.pl.* kettledrums. **timpanist** *n.*

tin *n.* silvery-white metal; metal box or other container, one in which food is sealed for preservation. — *v.* (**tinned**) coat with tin; seal (food) into a tin.

tincture *n.* solution of a medicinal substance in alcohol; slight tinge.

tinder *n.* any dry substance that catches fire easily.

tine *n.* prong or point of a fork, harrow, or antler.

tinge *v.* (**tingeing**) colour slightly; give a slight trace of an element or quality to. — *n.* slight colouring or trace.

tingle *v.* have a slight pricking or stinging sensation. — *n.* this sensation.

tinker *n.* travelling mender of pots and pans; (*colloq.*) mischievous person or animal. — *v.* work at something casually trying to repair or improve it.

tinkle *n.* series of short light ringing sounds. — *v.* make or cause to make a tinkle.

tinsel *n.* glittering decorative metallic strips or threads.

tint *n.* variety or slight trace of a colour. — *v.* colour slightly.

tiny *a.* (**-ier, -iest**) very small.

tip [1] *n.* end, esp. of something small or tapering. — *v.* (**tipped**) provide with a tip.

tip [2] *v.* (**tipped**) tilt, topple; discharge (a thing's contents) by tilting; name as a likely winner; make a small present of money to, esp. in acknowledgement of services. — *n.* small money present; useful piece of advice; place where rubbish etc. is tipped. **tip off** give a warning or hint to. **tip-off** *n.* such a warning etc. **tipper** *n.*

tipple *v.* drink (wine or spirits etc.) repeatedly. — *n.* (*colloq.*) alcoholic or other drink.

tipster *n.* person who gives tips about race-horses etc.

tipsy *a.* slightly drunk.

tiptoe *v.* (**tiptoeing**) walk very quietly or carefully.

tiptop *a.* (*colloq.*) first-rate.

tirade *n.* long angry piece of criticism or denunciation.

tire *v.* make or become tired.

tired *a.* feeling a desire to sleep or rest. **tired of** having had enough of and feeling impatient or bored.

tireless *a.* not tiring easily. **tirelessly** *adv.*, **tirelessness** *n.*

tiresome *a.* annoying; tedious.

tissue *n.* substance forming an animal or plant body; tissue-paper; piece of soft absorbent paper used as a handkerchief etc. **tissue-paper** *n.* thin soft paper used for packing things.

tit [1] *n.* any of several small birds.

tit [2] *n.* (*sl.*) breast, nipple.

titanic *a.* gigantic.

titanium *n.* dark-grey metal.

titbit *n.* choice bit of food or item of information.

tithe *n.* one-tenth of income or produce formerly paid to the Church.

titillate *v.* excite or stimulate pleasantly. **titillation** *n.*

titivate *v.* (*colloq.*) smarten up, put finishing touches to. **titivation** *n.*

title *n.* name of a book, poem, or picture etc.; word denoting rank or office, or used in speaking of or to the holder; championship in sport; legal right to ownership of property. **title-deed** *n.* legal document proving a person's title to a property. **title role** part in a play etc. from which the title is taken.

titled *a.* having a title of nobility.

titmouse *n.* (*pl.* **-mice**) = tit [1].

titter *n.* high-pitched giggle. — *v.* give a titter.

tittle-tattle *v.* & *n.* gossip.

titular *a.* of a title; having the title of ruler etc. but no real authority.

tizzy *n.* (*colloq.*) state of nervous agitation or confusion.

TNT *abbr.* trinitrotoluene, a powerful explosive.

to *prep.* towards; as far as; as compared with, in respect of; for (a person or thing) to hold or possess or be affected by. — (with a verb) forming an infinitive, or expressing purpose or consequence etc.; used alone when the infinitive is understood. — *adv.* to a closed position; into a state of consciousness or activity. **to and fro** backwards and forwards. **-to-be** soon to become. **to-do** *n.* fuss.

toad *n.* frog-like animal living chiefly on land. **toad-in-the-hole** *n.* sausages baked in batter.

toadflax *n.* wild plant with yellow or purple flowers.

toadstool *n.* fungus (usu. poisonous) with a round top on a stalk.

toady *n.* sycophant. — *v.* behave sycophantically.

toast *n.* toasted bread; person or thing in whose honour a company is requested to drink; this request or instance of drinking. — *v.* brown by heating; express good wishes to by drinking.

toaster *n.* electrical device for toasting bread.

tobacco *n.* plant with leaves that are used for smoking or snuff; its prepared leaves.

tobacconist *n.* shopkeeper who sells cigarettes etc.

toboggan *n.* small sledge used for sliding downhill. **tobogganing** *n.*

toby jug mug or jug in the form of a seated old man.

tocsin *n.* bell rung as an alarm signal; signal of disaster.

today *adv.* & *n.* (on) this present day; (at) the present time.

toddle *v.* (of a young child) walk with short unsteady steps.

toddler *n.* child who has only recently learnt to walk.

toddy *n.* sweetened drink of spirits and hot water.

toe *n.* any of the divisions (five in humans) of the front part of the foot; part of a shoe or stocking covering the toes. — *v.* touch with the toe(s). **be on one's toes** be alert or eager. **toe-hold** *n.* slight foothold. **toe the line** conform; obey orders.

toff *n.* (*sl.*) distinguished or well-dressed person.

toffee *n.* sweet made with heated butter and sugar. **toffee-apple** *n.* toffee-coated apple on a stick.

tog *n.* unit for measuring the warmth of duvets; (*pl.*, *colloq.*) clothes. — *v.* (**togged**) **tog out** *or* **up** (*colloq.*) dress.

toga *n.* loose outer garment worn by men in ancient Rome.

together *adv.* in or into company or conjunction, towards each other; simultaneously.

toggle *n.* short piece of wood etc. passed through a loop as a fastening device; switch that turns a function on and off alternately.

toil *v.* work or move laboriously. — *n.* laborious work; (*pl.*) net, snare. **toilsome** *a.*

toilet *n.* process of dressing and grooming oneself; lavatory. **toilet water** light perfume.

toiletries *n.pl.* articles used in washing and grooming oneself.

token *n.* sign, symbol; keepsake; voucher that can be exchanged for goods; disc used as money in a slot machine etc. — *a.* nominal; symbolic.

tokenism *n.* granting of minimal concessions.

told *see* **tell**. — *a.* **all told** counting everything or everyone.

tolerable *a.* endurable; passable. **tolerably** *adv.*

tolerance *n.* willingness to tolerate; permitted variation. **tolerant** *a.*, **tolerantly** *adv.*

tolerate *v.* permit without protest or interference; endure. **toleration** *n.*

toll [1] *n.* tax paid for the use of a public road etc.; loss or damage caused by a disaster etc. **toll-gate** *n.* barrier preventing passage until a toll is paid.

toll [2] *v.* ring with slow strokes, esp. to mark a death. — *n.* stroke of a tolling bell.

tom, tom-cat *ns.* male cat.

tomahawk *n.* light axe used by North American Indians.

tomato *n.* (*pl.* **-oes**) red fruit used as a vegetable.

tomb *n.* grave or other place of burial.

tombola *n.* lottery resembling bingo.

tomboy *n.* girl who enjoys rough and noisy activities.

tombstone *n.* memorial stone set up over a grave.

tome *n.* large book.

tommy-rot *n.* (*sl.*) nonsense.

tomorrow *adv.* & *n.* (on) the day after today; (in) the near future.

tom-tom *n.* drum beaten with the hands.

ton *n.* measure of weight, either 2240 lb (**long ton**) or 2000 lb (**short ton**) or 1000 kg (**metric ton**); unit of volume in shipping.

tone *n.* musical or vocal sound, esp. with

reference to its pitch and quality and strength; full interval between one note and the next in an octave; proper firmness of muscles etc.; shade of colour; general character. — *v.* give tone to; harmonize in colour. **tone-deaf** *a.* unable to perceive differences of musical pitch. **tone down** make less intense. **tonal** *a.*, **tonally** *adv.*, **tonality** *n.*

toneless *a.* without positive tone, not expressive. **tonelessly** *adv.*

tongs *n.pl.* instrument with two arms used for grasping things.

tongue *n.* muscular organ in the mouth, used in tasting and speaking; tongue of an ox etc. as food; language; projecting strip; tapering jet of flame. **tongue-tied** *a.* silent from shyness etc. **tongue-twister** *n.* sequence of words difficult to pronounce quickly and correctly. **tongue-in-cheek** *a.* with sly sarcasm.

tonic *n.* medicine etc. with an invigorating effect; keynote in music; tonic water. — *a.* invigorating. **tonic sol-fa** = sol-fa. **tonic water** mineral water, esp. flavoured with quinine.

tonight *adv.* & *n.* (on) the present evening or night, or that of today.

tonnage *n.* ship's carrying capacity expressed in tons; charge per ton for carrying cargo.

tonne *n.* metric ton, 1000 kg.

tonsil *n.* either of two small organs near the root of the tongue.

tonsillitis *n.* inflammation of the tonsils.

tonsure *n.* shaving the top or all of the head as a religious symbol; this shaven area. **tonsured** *a.*

too *adv.* to a greater extent than is desirable; (*colloq.*) very; also.

took *see* **take**.

tool *n.* thing used for working on something; person used by another for his or her own purposes. — *v.* shape or ornament with a tool; equip with tools.

toot *n.* short sound produced by a horn or whistle etc. — *v.* make or cause to make a toot.

tooth *n.* (*pl.* **teeth**) each of the white bony structures in the jaws, used in biting and chewing; tooth-like part or projection. **toothed** *a.*

toothpaste *n.* paste for cleaning the teeth.

toothpick *n.* small pointed instrument for removing bits of food from between the teeth.

toothy *a.* having many or large teeth.

top [1] *n.* highest point or part or position; upper surface; utmost degree or intensity; thing forming the upper part or covering; garment for the upper part of the body. — *a.* highest in position or rank etc. — *v.* (**topped**) provide or be a top for; reach the top of; be higher than; add as a final thing. **on top of** in addition to. **top dog** (*colloq.*) master, victor. **top dress** apply fertilizer on the top of (soil). **top hat** man's tall hat worn with formal dress. **top-heavy** *a.* heavy at the top and liable to fall over. **top-notch** *a.* (*colloq.*) first-rate. **top secret** of the highest category of secrecy. **top up** fill up (something half empty).

top [2] *n.* toy that spins on its point when set in motion.

topaz *n.* semiprecious stone of various colours, esp. yellow.

topcoat *n.* overcoat; final coat of paint etc.

topiary *a.* & *n.* (of) the art of clipping shrubs etc. into ornamental shapes.

topic *n.* subject of a discussion or written work.

topical *a.* having reference to current events. **topically** *adv.*, **topicality** *n.*

topknot *n.* tuft, crest, or bow etc. on top of the head.

topless *a.* leaving or having the breasts bare.

topmost *a.* highest.

topography *n.* local geography, position of the rivers, roads, buildings, etc., of a place or district. **topographical** *a.*

topper *n.* (*colloq.*) top hat.

topple *v.* be unsteady and fall; cause to do this.

topside *n.* beef from the upper part of the haunch.

topsoil *n.* top layer of the soil.

topsy-turvy *adv.* & *a.* upside down; in or into great disorder.

tor *n.* hill or rocky peak.

torch *n.* small hand-held electric lamp; burning piece of wood etc. carried as a light. **torchlight** *n.*

tore *see* **tear** [1].

toreador *n.* fighter (esp. on horseback) in a bullfight.

torment *n.* /tórment/ severe suffering; cause of this. — *v.* /tormént/ subject to torment; tease, annoy. **tormentor** *n.*

torn *see* **tear** [1].

tornado *n.* (*pl.* **-oes**) violent destructive whirlwind.

torpedo *n.* (*pl.* **-oes**) explosive underwater missile. — *v.* attack or destroy with a torpedo.

torpid *a.* sluggish and inactive. **torpidly** *adv.*, **torpidity** *n.*

torpor *n.* sluggish condition.

torque *n.* force that produces rotation.

torrent *n.* rushing stream or flow; downpour. **torrential** *a.*

torrid *a.* intensely hot.

torsion *n.* twisting, spiral twist.

torso *n.* (*pl.* **-os**) trunk of the human body.

tort *n.* any private or civil wrong (other than breach of contract) for which damages may be claimed.

tortoise *n.* slow-moving reptile with a hard shell.

tortoiseshell *n.* mottled yellowish-brown shell of certain turtles, used for making combs etc. **tortoiseshell cat** one with mottled colouring.

tortuous *a.* full of twists and turns. **tortuously** *adv.*

torture *n.* severe pain; infliction of this as a punishment or means of coercion. — *v.* inflict torture upon. **torturer** *n.*

toss *v.* throw lightly; throw up (a coin) to settle a question by the way it falls; roll about from side to side; coat (food) by gently shaking it in dressing etc. — *n.* tossing. **toss off** drink rapidly; compose rapidly. **toss-up** *n.* tossing of a coin; even chance.

tot [1] *n.* small child; small quantity of spirits.

tot [2] *v.* (**totted**) **tot up** (*colloq.*) add up.

total *a.* including everything or everyone; complete. — *n.* total amount. — *v.* (**totalled**) reckon the total of; amount to. **totally** *adv.*, **totality** *n.*

totalitarian *a.* of a regime in which no rival parties or loyalties are permitted. **totalitarianism** *n.*

totalizator *n.* device that automatically registers bets, so that the total amount can be divided among the winners.

tote [1] *n.* (*sl.*) totalizator.

tote [2] *v.* (*US*) carry. **tote bag** large capacious bag.

totem *n.* tribal emblem among North American Indians. **totem-pole** *n.* pole carved or painted with totems.

totter *v.* walk or rock unsteadily. — *n.* tottering walk or movement. **tottery** *a.*

toucan *n.* tropical American bird with an immense beak.

touch *v.* be, come, or bring into contact; feel or stroke; press or strike lightly; reach; affect; rouse sympathy in; (*sl.*) persuade to give or lend money. — *n.* act, fact, or manner of touching; ability to perceive things through touching them; style of workmanship; detail; slight trace. **touch-and-go** *a.* uncertain as regards result. **touch down** touch the ball on the ground behind the goal line in Rugby football; (of an aircraft) land. (**touchdown** *n.*). **touchline** *n.* side limit of a football field. **touch off** cause to explode; start (a process). **touch on** mention briefly. **touch up** improve by making small additions.

touché /tōōsháy/ *int.* acknowledgement of a hit in fencing, or of a valid criticism.

touching *a.* rousing kindly feelings or pity. — *prep.* concerning.

touchstone *n.* standard or criterion.

touchy *a.* (**-ier, -iest**) easily offended. **touchiness** *n.*

tough *a.* hard to break or cut or chew; hardy; unyielding, resolute; difficult; (*colloq.*, of luck) hard. — *n.* rough violent person. **toughness** *n.*

toughen *v.* make or become tough or tougher.

toupee /tōōpay/ *n.* small wig.

tour *n.* journey through a place, visiting things of interest or giving performances. — *v.* make a tour (of). **on tour** touring.

tour de force feat of strength or skill.

tourism *n.* organized touring or other services for tourists.

tourist *n.* person travelling or visiting a place for recreation.

tournament *n.* contest of skill involving a series of matches.

tousle *v.* make (hair etc.) untidy by ruffling.

tout *v.* pester people to buy. — *n.* person who touts; person who sells tickets for popular events at high prices.

tow [1] *n.* coarse fibres of flax or hemp.

tow [2] *v.* pull along behind one. — *n.* act of towing. **tow-path** *n.* path beside a canal or river, orig. for horses towing barges.

toward *prep.* towards.

towards *prep.* in the direction of; in relation to; as a contribution to; near, approaching.

towel *n.* piece of absorbent material for drying oneself or wiping things dry. — *v.* (**towelled**) rub with a towel.

towelling *n.* fabric for towels.

tower *n.* tall structure, esp. as part of a church or castle etc. — *v.* be very tall. **tower block** tall building with many storeys. **tower of strength** source of strong reliable support.

town *n.* collection of buildings (larger than a village); its inhabitants; central business and shopping area. **go to town** (*colloq.*) do something lavishly or with enthusiasm. **town hall** building containing local government offices etc. **townsman** *n.* (*pl.* **-men**), **townswoman** *n.fem.* (*pl.* **-women**).

township *n.* small town; (*S. Afr.*) urban area set aside for black people.

toxaemia /tokseémiə/ *n.* blood poisoning; abnormally high blood pressure in pregnancy.

toxic *a.* of or caused by poison; poisonous. **toxicity** *n.*

toxicology *n.* study of poisons. **toxicologist** *n.*

toxin *n.* poisonous substance, esp. formed in the body.

toy *n.* thing to play with; (*attrib.*, of a dog) of a diminutive variety. — *v.* **toy with** handle idly; deal with (a thing) without seriousness. **toy boy** (*colloq.*) woman's much younger male lover.

trace [1] *n.* track or mark left behind; sign of what has existed or occurred; very small quantity. — *v.* follow or discover by observing marks or other evidence; mark out; copy by using tracing-paper or carbon paper. **trace element** one required only in minute amounts. **tracer** *n.*

trace [2] *n.* each of the two side-straps by which a horse draws a vehicle. **kick over the traces** become insubordinate or reckless.

traceable *a.* able to be traced.

tracery *n.* openwork pattern in stone; similar decorative pattern of lines.

trachea /trəkeéə/ *n.* windpipe.

tracheotomy *n.* surgical opening into the trachea.

tracing *n.* copy of a map or drawing etc. made by tracing it. **tracing-paper** *n.* transparent paper used in this.

track *n.* mark(s) left by a moving person or thing; course; path, rough road; particular section on a record or recording tape; railway line; continuous band round the wheels of a tractor etc. — *v.* follow the track of, find or observe thus. **keep** *or* **lose track of** keep or fail to keep oneself informed about. **track suit** loose warm suit worn by an athlete during practice. **tracker** *n.*

tract [1] *n.* stretch of land; system of connected parts of the body, along which something passes.

tract [2] *n.* pamphlet with a short essay, esp. on a religious subject.

tractable *a.* easy to deal with or control, docile. **tractability** *n.*

traction *n.* pulling; grip of wheels on the ground; use of weights etc. to exert a steady pull on an injured limb etc.

tractor *n.* powerful motor vehicle for pulling heavy equipment.

trade *n.* exchange of goods for money or other goods; business of a particular kind, people engaged in this; trading. — *v.* engage in trade, buy and sell; exchange (goods) in trading. **trade in** give (a used article) as partial payment for a new one. (**trade-in** *n.*). **trade mark** company's registered emblem or name etc. used to identify its goods. **trade off** exchange as a compromise. **trade union** (*pl.* **trade unions**) organized association of employees formed to protect and promote their common interests. **trade-unionist** *n.* member of a trade union. **trade wind** constant wind blowing towards the equator. **trader** *n.*

tradesman *n.* (*pl.* **-men**) craftsman; shopkeeper; person who delivers goods to private houses.

tradition *n.* belief or custom handed down from one generation to another; long-established procedure. **traditional** *a.*, **traditionally** *adv.*

traditionalist *n.* person who upholds traditional beliefs etc. **traditionalism** *n.*

traduce *v.* slander. **traducement** *n.*

traffic *n.* vehicles, ships, or aircraft moving along a route; trading. — *v.* (**trafficked**) trade. **traffic warden** official who controls the movement and parking of road vehicles. **trafficker** *n.*

tragedian *n.* writer of tragedies; actor in tragedy.

tragedienne *n.* actress in tragedy.

tragedy *n.* serious drama with unhappy events or a sad ending; event causing great sadness.

tragic *a.* of or in tragedy; causing great sadness. **tragically** *adv.*

tragicomedy *n.* drama of mixed tragic and comic events.

trail *v.* drag behind, esp. on the ground; hang loosely; move wearily; lag, straggle; track. — *n.* thing that trails; line of people or things following something; track, trace; beaten path.

trailer *n.* truck etc. designed to be hauled by a vehicle; short extract from a film etc., shown in advance to advertise it.

train *n.* railway engine with linked carriages or trucks; retinue; sequence of things; part of a long robe that trails behind the wearer. — *v.* bring or come to a desired standard of efficiency or condition or behaviour etc. by instruction and practice; aim (a gun etc.); cause (a plant) to grow in the required direction. **in train** in preparation.

trainee *n.* person being trained.

trainer *n.* person who trains horses or athletes etc.; (*pl.*) soft sports or running shoes.

traipse *v.* (*colloq.*) trudge.

trait *n.* characteristic.

traitor *n.* person who behaves disloyally, esp. to his country. **traitorous** *a.*

trajectory *n.* path of a projectile.

tram *n.* public passenger vehicle running on rails laid in the road.

tramcar *n.* tram.

tramlines *n.pl.* rails on which a tram runs; (*colloq.*) pair of parallel sidelines in tennis etc.

trammel *v.* (**trammelled**) hamper, restrain.

tramp *v.* walk with heavy footsteps; go on foot across (an area); trample. — *n.* sound of heavy footsteps; long walk; vagrant; cargo boat that does not travel a regular route; (*sl.*) immoral woman.

trample *v.* tread repeatedly, crush or harm by treading.

trampoline *n.* sheet attached by springs to a frame, used for jumping on in acrobatic leaps. — *v.* use a trampoline.

trance *n.* sleep-like or dreamy state.

tranquil *a.* calm and undisturbed. **tranquilly** *adv.*, **tranquillity** *n.*

tranquillize *v.* make calm.

tranquillizer *n.* drug used to relieve anxiety and tension.

transact *v.* perform or carry out (business etc.). **transaction** *n.*

transatlantic *a.* on or from the other side of the Atlantic; crossing the Atlantic.

transcend *v.* go beyond the range of (experience, belief, etc.); surpass. **transcendent** *a.*, **transcendence** *n.*

transcendental *a.* transcendent; abstract, obscure, visionary.

transcontinental *a.* crossing or extending across a continent.

transcribe *v.* copy in writing; produce in written form; arrange (music) for a different instrument etc. **transcription** *n.*

transcript *n.* written copy.

transducer *n.* device that receives waves or other variations from one system and conveys related ones to another.

transept *n.* part lying at right angles to the nave in a church.

transfer *v.* /transfér/ (**transferred**) convey from one place or person or application to another. — *n.* /tránsfer/ transferring; document transferring property or a right; design for transferring from one surface to another. **transference** *n.*, **transferable** *a.*

transfigure *v.* change in appearance to something nobler or more beautiful. **transfiguration** *n.*

transfix *v.* pierce through, impale; make motionless with fear or astonishment.

transform *v.* change greatly in appearance or character; change the voltage of (electric current). **transformation** *n.*, **transformer** *n.*

transfuse *v.* give a transfusion of or to; permeate; imbue.

transfusion *n.* injection of blood or other fluid into a blood vessel.

transgress *v.* break (a rule or law). **transgression** *n.*, **transgressor** *n.*

transient *a.* passing away quickly. **transience** *n.*

transistor *n.* very small semiconductor device which controls the flow of an electric current; portable radio set using transistors. **transistorized** *a.*

transit *n.* process of going or conveying across, over, or through.

transition *n.* process of changing from one state or style etc. to another. **transitional** *a.*

transitory *a.* lasting only briefly.

translate *v.* express in another language or other words; be able to be translated; transfer. **translation** *n.*, **translator** *n.*

transliterate *v.* convert to the letters of another alphabet. **transliteration** *n.*

translucent *a.* allowing light to pass through but not transparent. **translucence** *n.*

transmigrate *v.* (of the soul) pass into another body after a person's death. **transmigration** *n.*

transmission *n.* transmitting; broadcast; gear transmitting power from engine to axle.

transmit *v.* (**transmitted**) pass on from one person, place, or thing to another; send out (a signal or programme etc.) by cable or radio waves. **transmitter** *n.*

transmute *v.* change in form or substance. **transmutation** *n.*

transom *n.* horizontal bar across the top of a door or window; fanlight.

transparency *n.* being transparent; photographic slide.

transparent *a.* able to be seen through; easily understood, obvious. **transparently** *adv.*

transpire *v.* become known; (of plants) give off (vapour) from leaves etc. **transpiration** *n.*

transplant *v.* /tranzplaánt/ remove and replant or establish elsewhere; transfer (living tissue). — *n.* /tránzplaant/ transplanting of tissue; thing transplanted. **transplantation** *n.*

transport *v.* /tranzpórt/ convey from one place to another. — *n.* /tránzport/ process of transporting; means of conveyance; (*pl.*) condition of strong emotion. **transportation** *n.*, **transporter** *n.*

transpose *v.* cause (two or more things) to change places; change the position of;

put (music) into a different key. **transposition** *n.*

transsexual *n.* & *a.* (person) having the physical characteristics of one sex and psychological characteristics of the other. **transsexualism** *n.*

transuranic *a.* having atoms heavier than those of uranium.

transverse *a.* crosswise.

transvestism *n.* dressing in clothing of the opposite sex. **transvestite** *n.*

trap *n.* device for capturing an animal; scheme for tricking or catching a person; trapdoor; compartment from which a dog is released in racing; curved section of a pipe holding liquid to prevent gases from coming upwards; two-wheeled horse-drawn carriage; (*sl.*) mouth. — *v.* (**trapped**) catch or hold in a trap.

trapdoor *n.* door in a floor, ceiling, or roof.

trapeze *n.* a kind of swing on which acrobatics are performed.

trapezium *n.* quadrilateral with only two opposite sides parallel; (*US*) trapezoid.

trapezoid *n.* quadrilateral with no sides parallel; (*US*) trapezium.

trapper *n.* person who traps animals, esp. for furs.

trappings *n.pl.* accessories; adjuncts.

trash *n.* worthless stuff. **trashy** *a.*

trauma *n.* wound, injury; emotional shock producing a lasting effect. **traumatic** *a.*

travail *n.* & *v.* labour.

travel *v.* (**travelled**) go from one place to another; journey along or through. — *n.* travelling, esp. abroad. **traveller** *n.*

traverse *v.* travel or lie or extend across. — *n.* thing that lies across another; lateral movement. **traversal** *n.*

travesty *n.* absurd or inferior imitation. — *v.* make or be a travesty of.

trawl *n.* large wide-mouthed fishing net. — *v.* fish with a trawl.

trawler *n.* boat used in trawling.

tray *n.* board with a rim for carrying small articles; open receptacle for office correspondence.

treacherous *a.* showing treachery; not to be relied on, deceptive. **treacherously** *adv.*

treachery *n.* betrayal of a person or cause; act of disloyalty.

treacle *n.* thick sticky liquid produced when sugar is refined. **treacly** *a.*

tread *v.* (**trod, trodden**) walk, step; walk on, press or crush with the feet. — *n.* manner or sound of walking; horizontal surface of a stair; part of a tyre that touches the ground. **tread water** keep upright in water by making treading movements.

treadle *n.* lever worked by the foot to drive a wheel.

treadmill *n.* mill-wheel formerly turned by people treading on steps round its edge; tiring monotonous routine work.

treason *n.* treachery towards one's country. **treasonous** *a.*

treasonable *a.* involving treason.

treasure *n.* collection of precious metals or gems; highly valued object or person. — *v.* value highly; store as precious. **treasure trove** treasure of unknown ownership, found hidden.

treasurer *n.* person in charge of the funds of an institution.

treasury *n.* place where treasure is kept; department managing a country's revenue.

treat *v.* act or behave towards or deal with in a specified way; give medical treatment to; subject to a chemical or other process; buy something for (a person) in order to give pleasure. — *n.* something special that gives pleasure; providing this.

treatise *n.* written work dealing with one subject.

treatment *n.* manner of dealing with a person or thing; something done to relieve illness etc.

treaty *n.* formal agreement made, esp. between countries.

treble *a.* three times as much or as many; (of a voice) high-pitched, soprano. — *n.* treble quantity or thing; treble voice, person with this. **trebly** *adv.*

tree *n.* perennial plant with a single thick woody stem.

trefoil *n.* plant with three leaflets (e.g. clover); thing shaped like this.

trek *n.* long arduous journey. — *v.* (**trekked**) make a trek.

trellis *n.* light framework of crossing strips of wood etc.

tremble *v.* shake, quiver; feel very anxious. — *n.* trembling movement. **trembly** *a.*

tremendous *a.* immense; (*colloq.*) excellent. **tremendously** *adv.*

tremor *n.* slight trembling movement; thrill of fear etc.

tremulous *a.* trembling, quivering. **tremulously** *adv.*

trench *n.* deep ditch. **trench coat** belted double-breasted raincoat.

trenchant *a.* (of comments, policies, etc.) strong and effective.

trend *n.* general tendency. **trend-setter** *n.* person who leads the way in fashion etc.

trendy *a.* (**-ier, -iest**) (*colloq.*) following the latest fashion. **trendily** *adv.*, **trendiness** *n.*

trepidation *n.* nervousness.

trespass *v.* enter land or property unlawfully; intrude. — *n.* act of trespassing. **trespasser** *n.*

tress *n.* lock of hair.

trestle *n.* one of a set of supports on which a board is rested to form a table. **trestle-table** *n.*

trews *n.pl.* close-fitting usu. tartan trousers.

tri- *pref.* three times, triple.

triad *n.* group of three; Chinese usu. criminal secret society.

trial *n.* examination in a law court by a judge; process of testing qualities or performance; person or thing that tries one's patience. **on trial** undergoing a trial.

triangle *n.* geometric figure with three sides and three angles; triangular steel rod used as a percussion instrument.

triangular *a.* shaped like a triangle; involving three people.

triangulation *n.* measurement or mapping of an area by means of a network of triangles.

tribe *n.* related group of families living as a community. **tribal** *a.*, **tribesman** *n.* (*pl.* **-men**).

tribulation *n.* great affliction.

tribunal *n.* board of officials appointed to adjudicate on a particular problem.

tributary *n.* & *a.* (stream) flowing into a larger stream or a lake.

tribute *n.* something said or done as a mark of respect; payment that one country or ruler was formerly obliged to pay to another.

trice *n.* **in a trice** in an instant.

trichology *n.* study of hair and its diseases. **trichologist** *n.*

trick *n.* something done to deceive or outwit someone; technique, knack; mannerism; mischievous act. — *v.* deceive or persuade by a trick; decorate. **do the trick** (*colloq.*) achieve what is required.

trickery *n.* use of tricks, deception.

trickle *v.* (cause to) flow in a thin stream; come or go gradually. — *n.* trickling flow.

tricky *a.* (**-ier, -iest**) crafty, deceitful; requiring careful handling. **trickiness** *n.*

tricolour *n.* flag with three colours in stripes.

tricycle *n.* three-wheeled pedal-driven vehicle. **tricyclist** *n.*

trident *n.* three-pronged spear.

triennial *a.* happening every third year; lasting three years.

trier *n.* person who tries hard.

trifle *n.* thing of only slight value or importance; very small amount; sweet dish of sponge cake and jelly etc. topped with custard and cream. — *v.* **trifle with** toy with. **trifler** *n.*

trifling *a.* trivial.

trigger *n.* lever for releasing a spring, esp. to fire a gun. — *v.* (also **trigger off**) set in action, cause. **trigger-happy** *a.* apt to shoot on slight provocation.

trigonometry *n.* branch of mathematics dealing with the relationship of sides and angles of triangles etc.

trike *n.* (*colloq.*) tricycle.

trilateral *a.* having three sides or three participants.

trilby *n.* man's soft felt hat.

trill *n.* vibrating sound, esp. in music or singing. — *v.* sound or sing with a trill.

trillion *n.* a million million million; (*US* etc.) a million million.

trilobite *n.* a kind of fossil crustacean.

trilogy *n.* group of three related books, plays, etc.

trim *a.* (**trimmer, trimmest**) neat and orderly. — *v.* (**trimmed**) reduce or neaten by cutting; ornament; make (a boat or aircraft) evenly balanced by distributing its load. — *n.* ornamentation; colour or type of upholstery etc. in a car; trimming of hair etc. **trimly** *adv.*, **trimness** *n.*

trimaran *n.* vessel like a catamaran, with three hulls.

trimming *n.* thing added as a decoration; (*pl.*) pieces cut off when something is trimmed.

trinity *n.* group of three; **the Trinity** the three persons of the Christian deity (Father, Son, Holy Spirit) as constituting one God.

trinket *n.* small fancy article or piece of jewellery.

trio *n.* (*pl.* **-os**) group or set of three; music for three instruments or voices.

trip *v.* (**tripped**) go lightly and quickly; (cause to) catch one's foot and lose balance; (cause to) make a blunder; release (a switch etc.) so as to operate a mechanism. — *n.* journey or excursion, esp. for pleasure; (*colloq.*) visionary experience caused by a drug; stumble; device for tripping a mechanism.

tripartite *a.* consisting of three parts.

tripe *n.* stomach of an ox etc. as food; (*sl.*) nonsense.

triple *a.* having three parts or members; three times as much or as many. — *v.* increase by three times its amount.

triplet *n.* one of three children born at one birth; set of three.

triplex *a.* triple, threefold.

triplicate *a.* & *n.* existing in three examples. **in triplicate** as three identical copies.

tripod *n.* three-legged stand.
tripper *n.* person who goes on a pleasure trip.
triptych /triptik/ *n.* picture or carving with three panels fixed or hinged side by side.
trite *a.* hackneyed.
triumph *n.* fact of being successful or victorious; joy at this; great success. — *v.* be successful or victorious, rejoice at this. **triumphant** *a.*, **triumphantly** *adv.*
triumphal *a.* celebrating or commemorating a triumph.
triumvirate *n.* government or control by a board of three.
trivet *n.* metal stand for a kettle or hot dish etc.
trivia *n.pl.* trivial things.
trivial *a.* of only small value or importance. **trivially** *adv.*, **triviality** *n.*
trod, trodden *see* **tread**.
troglodyte *n.* cave dweller. **troglodytic** *a.*
troll *n.* giant or dwarf in Scandinavian mythology.
trolley *n.* (*pl.* **-eys**) platform on wheels for transporting goods; small cart; small table on wheels.
trollop *n.* promiscuous or slovenly woman.
trombone *n.* large brass wind instrument with a sliding tube.
troop *n.* company of people or animals; cavalry or artillery unit. — *v.* go as a troop or in great numbers.
trooper *n.* soldier in a cavalry or armoured unit; (*US*) member of a State police force.
trophy *n.* thing taken in war or hunting etc. as a souvenir of success; object awarded as a prize.
tropic *n.* line of latitude 23° 27′ north or south of the equator; (*pl.*) region between these, with a hot climate. **tropical** *a.*
troposphere *n.* layer of the atmosphere between the earth's surface and the stratosphere.
trot *n.* running action of a horse etc.; moderate running pace. — *v.* (**trotted**) go or cause to go at a trot. **on the trot** (*colloq.*) continually busy; in succession. **trot out** (*colloq.*) produce.
troth *n.* promise, fidelity.
trotter *n.* animal's foot as food.
troubadour *n.* medieval romantic poet.
trouble *n.* difficulty, distress, misfortune; cause of this; conflict; inconvenience, exertion. — *v.* cause trouble to; make or be worried; exert oneself.
troubleshooter *n.* person employed to deal with faults or problems.
troublesome *a.* causing trouble.
trough *n.* long open receptacle, esp. for animals' food or water; depression between two waves or ridges; region of low atmospheric pressure.
trounce *v.* defeat heavily.
troupe /tro͞op/ *n.* company of actors or other performers.
trouper *n.* member of a troupe; staunch colleague.
trousers *n.pl.* two-legged outer garment reaching from the waist usu. to the ankles.
trousseau /tro͞ossō/ *n.* (*pl.* **-eaux**) bride's collection of clothing etc. for her marriage.
trout *n.* (*pl.* **trout**) freshwater fish valued as food and game.
trowel *n.* small garden tool for digging; similar tool for spreading mortar etc.
troy weight system of weights used for precious metals.
truant *n.* pupil who stays away from school without leave. **play truant** stay away as a truant. **truancy** *n.*
truce *n.* agreement to cease hostilities temporarily.
truck *n.* open container on wheels for transporting loads; open railway wagon; lorry.
trucker *n.* lorry driver.
truculent *a.* defiant and aggressive. **truculently** *adv.*, **truculence** *n.*
trudge *v.* walk laboriously. — *n.* laborious walk.
true *a.* in accordance with fact, genuine; exact, accurate; loyal, faithful. — *adv.* truly, accurately.
truffle *n.* rich-flavoured underground fungus valued as a delicacy; soft chocolate sweet.
truism *n.* statement that is obviously true, esp. a hackneyed one.
truly *adv.* truthfully; genuinely; faithfully.
trump *n.* playing card of a suit temporarily ranking above others; (*colloq.*) person who behaves in a helpful or useful way. — *v.* **trump up** invent fraudulently. **turn up trumps** (*colloq.*) be successful or helpful.
trumpet *n.* metal wind instrument with a flared tube; thing shaped like this. — *v.* (**trumpeted**) proclaim loudly; (of an elephant) make a loud sound with its trunk. **trumpeter** *n.*
truncate *v.* shorten by cutting off the end. **truncation** *n.*
truncheon *n.* short thick stick carried as a weapon.
trundle *v.* roll along, move along heavily on wheels.
trunk *n.* tree's main stem; body apart from head and limbs; large box with a hinged lid, for transporting or storing clothes

etc.; elephant's long flexible nose; (*US*) boot of a car; (*pl.*) shorts for swimming etc. **trunk road** important main road.

truss *n.* cluster of flowers or fruit; framework supporting a roof etc; device worn to support a hernia. — *v.* tie up securely.

trust *n.* firm belief in the reliability or truth or strength etc. of a person or thing; confident expectation; responsibility, care; property legally entrusted to someone; association of business firms, formed to defeat competition. — *v.* have or place trust in; entrust; hope earnestly. **in trust** held as a trust. **on trust** accepted without investigation. **trustful** *a.*, **trustfully** *adv.*

trustee *n.* person who administers property held as a trust; one of a group managing the business affairs of an institution.

trustworthy *a.* worthy of trust. **trustworthiness** *n.*

trusty *a.* trustworthy.

truth *n.* quality of being true; something that is true.

truthful *a.* habitually telling the truth; true. **truthfully** *adv.*, **truthfulness** *n.*

try *v.* attempt; test, esp. by use; be a strain on; hold a trial of. — *n.* attempt; touchdown in Rugby football, entitling the player's side to a kick at goal. **try on** put (a garment) on to see if it fits. **try out** test by use. **try-out** *n.*

trying *a.* annoying.

tsetse *n.* African fly that transmits disease by its bite.

T-shirt *n.* short-sleeved casual cotton top.

T-square *n.* large T-shaped ruler used in technical drawing.

tub *n.* open usu. round container.

tuba *n.* large low-pitched brass wind instrument.

tubby *a.* (**-ier, -iest**) short and fat. **tubbiness** *n.*

tube *n.* long hollow cylinder; thing shaped like this; cathode-ray tube.

tuber *n.* short thick rounded root or underground stem from which shoots will grow.

tubercle *n.* small rounded swelling.

tubercular *a.* of or affected with tuberculosis.

tuberculosis *n.* infectious wasting disease, esp. affecting lungs.

tuberous *a.* of or like a tuber; bearing tubers.

tubing *n.* tubes; a length of tube.

tubular *a.* tube-shaped.

tuck *n.* flat fold stitched in a garment etc. — *v.* put into or under something so as to be concealed or held in place; cover or put away compactly. **tuck in** *or* **into** (*colloq.*) eat heartily. **tuck shop** shop selling cakes and sweets etc. to schoolchildren.

tuft *n.* bunch of threads or grass or hair etc. held or growing together at the base. **tufted** *a.*

tug *v.* (**tugged**) pull vigorously; tow. — *n.* vigorous pull; small powerful boat for towing others. **tug of war** contest of strength in which two teams pull opposite ways on a rope.

tuition *n.* teaching or instruction, esp. of an individual or small group.

tulip *n.* garden plant with a cup-shaped flower. **tulip-tree** *n.* tree with tulip-like flowers.

tulle /tyo͞ol/ *n.* fine silky net fabric.

tumble *v.* (cause to) fall; roll, push, or move in a disorderly way; perform somersaults etc.; rumple. — *n.* fall; untidy state. **tumble-drier** *n.* machine for drying washing in a heated rotating drum. **tumble to** (*colloq.*) grasp the meaning of.

tumbledown *a.* dilapidated.

tumbler *n.* drinking glass with no handle or foot; pivoted piece in a lock etc.; acrobat.

tumescent *a.* swelling. **tumescence** *n.*

tummy *n.* (*colloq.*) stomach.

tumour *n.* abnormal mass of new tissue growing in or on the body.

tumult *n.* uproar; conflict of emotions.

tumultuous *a.* making an uproar.

tun *n.* large cask; fermenting-vat.

tuna *n.* (*pl.* **tuna**) tunny; its flesh as food.

tundra *n.* vast level Arctic regions where the subsoil is frozen.

tune *n.* melody. — *v.* put (a musical instrument) in tune; set (a radio) to the desired wavelength; adjust (an engine) to run smoothly. **in tune** playing or singing at the correct musical pitch; harmonious. **out of tune** not in tune. **tune up** bring musical instruments to the correct or uniform pitch. **tuner** *n.*

tuneful *a.* melodious.

tungsten *n.* heavy grey metal.

tunic *n.* close-fitting jacket worn as part of a uniform; loose garment reaching to the knees.

tunnel *n.* underground passage. — *v.* (**tunnelled**) make a tunnel (through), make (one's way) thus.

tunny *n.* large edible sea fish.

turban *n.* Muslim or Sikh man's headdress of cloth wound round the head; woman's hat resembling this.

turbid *a.* (of liquids) muddy, not clear; disordered. **turbidity** *n.*

turbine *n.* machine or motor driven by a wheel that is turned by a flow of water or gas.

turbo- *pref.* using a turbine; driven by such engines.

turbot *n.* large flat edible sea fish.

turbulent *a.* in a state of commotion or unrest; moving unevenly. **turbulently** *adv.*, **turbulence** *n.*

tureen *n.* deep covered dish from which soup is served.

turf *n.* (*pl.* **turfs** *or* **turves**) short grass and the soil just below it; piece of this; **the turf** horse racing. — *v.* lay (ground) with turf. **turf accountant** bookmaker. **turf out** (*colloq.*) throw out.

turgid *a.* swollen and not flexible; (of language) pompous. **turgidly** *adv.*, **turgidity** *n.*

Turk *n.* native of Turkey.

turkey *n.* (*pl.* **-eys**) large bird reared for its flesh; this as food.

Turkish *a.* & *n.* (language) of Turkey. **Turkish bath** hot air or steam bath followed by massage etc. **Turkish delight** sweet consisting of flavoured gelatine coated in powdered sugar.

turmeric *n.* bright yellow spice from the root of an Asian plant.

turmoil *n.* state of great disturbance or confusion.

turn *v.* move round a point or axis; take or give a new direction (to), aim; pass round (a point); pass (a certain hour or age); change in form or appearance etc.; make or become sour; shape in a lathe; give an elegant form to. — *n.* process of turning; change of direction or condition etc.; bend in a road; service of a specified kind; opportunity or obligation coming in succession; short performance in an entertainment; (*colloq.*) attack of illness, momentary nervous shock. **in turn** in succession. **out of turn** before or after one's proper turn; indiscreetly, presumptuously. **to a turn** so as to be cooked perfectly. **turn against** make or become hostile to. **turn down** fold down; reduce the volume or flow of; reject. **turn in** hand in; (*colloq.*) go to bed; (*colloq.*) abandon (work etc.). **turn off** (*or* **on**) stop (*or* start) the flow or operation of; (*colloq.*) cause to lose (*or* to feel) interest. **turn out** expel; turn off (a light etc.); equip, dress; produce by work; empty and search or clean; (*colloq.*) come out; prove to be the case eventually. **turn-out** *n.* process of turning out a room etc.; number of people attending a gathering; outfit. **turn the tables** reverse a situation and put oneself in a superior position. **turn up** discover; be found; make one's appearance; increase the volume or flow of. **turn-up** *n.* turned-up part, esp. at the lower end of a trouser leg.

turncoat *n.* person who changes his or her principles.

turner *n.* person who works with a lathe.

turning *n.* place where one road meets another, forming a corner. **turning point** point at which a decisive change takes place.

turnip *n.* (plant with) a round white root used as a vegetable.

turnover *n.* pasty; amount of money taken in a business; rate of replacement.

turnstile *n.* revolving barrier for admitting people one at a time.

turntable *n.* circular revolving platform.

turpentine *n.* oil used for thinning paint and as a solvent.

turpitude *n.* wickedness.

turps *n.* (*colloq.*) turpentine.

turquoise *n.* blue-green precious stone; its colour.

turret *n.* small tower-like structure. **turreted** *a.*

turtle *n.* sea creature like a tortoise. **turn turtle** capsize. **turtle-dove** *n.* wild dove noted for its soft cooing. **turtle-neck** *n.* high round close-fitting neckline.

tusk *n.* long pointed tooth outside the mouth of certain animals.

tussle *v.* & *n.* struggle, conflict.

tussock *n.* tuft or clump of grass.

tutelage *n.* guardianship; tuition.

tutor *n.* private or university teacher. — *v.* act as tutor (to).

tutorial *a.* of a tutor. — *n.* student's session with a tutor.

tut-tut *int.* exclamation of annoyance, impatience, or rebuke.

tutu *n.* dancer's short skirt made of layers of frills.

tuxedo /tukséedō/ *n.* (*pl.* **-os**) (*US*) dinner jacket.

twaddle *n.* nonsense.

twang *n.* sharp ringing sound like that made by a tense wire when plucked; nasal intonation. — *v.* make or cause to make a twang.

tweak *v.* & *n.* (pinch, twist, or pull with) a sharp jerk.

twee *a.* affectedly dainty or quaint.

tweed *n.* thick woollen fabric; (*pl.*) clothes made of tweed. **tweedy** *a.*

tweet *n.* & *v.* chirp.

tweeter *n.* loudspeaker for reproducing high-frequency signals.

tweezers *n.pl.* small pincers for handling very small things.

twelve *a.* & *n.* one more than eleven (12, XII). **twelfth** *a.* & *n.*

twenty *a.* & *n.* twice ten. **twentieth** *a.* & *n.*

twerp *n.* (*sl.*) stupid or insignificant person.

twice *adv.* two times; in double amount or degree.

twiddle *v.* twist idly about. — *n.* act of twiddling. **twiddle one's thumbs** have nothing to do.

twig [1] *n.* small shoot issuing from a branch or stem.

twig [2] *v.* **(twigged)** (*colloq.*) realize, grasp the meaning of.

twilight *n.* light from the sky after sunset; period of this.

twill *n.* fabric woven so that parallel diagonal lines are produced. **twilled** *a.*

twin *n.* one of two children or animals born at one birth; one of a pair that are exactly alike. — *a.* being a twin or twins. — *v.* **(twinned)** combine as a pair. **twin towns** two towns that establish special social and cultural links.

twine *n.* strong thread or string. — *v.* twist; wind or coil.

twinge *n.* slight or brief pang.

twinkle *v.* shine with a light that flickers rapidly. — *n.* twinkling light.

twirl *v.* twist lightly or rapidly. — *n.* twirling movement; twirled mark. **twirly** *a.*

twist *v.* wind (strands etc.) round each other, esp. to form a single cord; make by doing this; bend round; rotate; distort; (*sl.*) swindle. — *n.* process of twisting; thing formed by twisting; unexpected development etc.; (*sl.*) swindle. **twister** *n.*

twit *n.* (*sl.*) foolish or insignificant person.

twitch *v.* pull with a light jerk; quiver or contract spasmodically. — *n.* twitching movement.

twitter *v.* make light chirping sounds; talk rapidly in an anxious or nervous way. — *n.* twittering.

two *a.* & *n.* one more than one (2, II). **be in two minds** be undecided. **two-dimensional** *a.* having or appearing to have length and breadth but no depth. **two-faced** *a.* insincere, deceitful.

twofold *a.* & *adv.* twice as much or as many.

twosome *n.* two together, pair.

tycoon *n.* magnate.

tying *see* **tie**.

tympanum *n.* (*pl.* **-na**) eardrum; space between the lintel and the arch above a door.

type *n.* kind, class; typical example or instance; (*colloq.*) person of specified character; set of characters used in printing. — *v.* classify according to type; write with a typewriter.

typecast *v.* cast (an actor) in a role appropriate to his or her nature or previous successful roles.

typescript *n.* typewritten document.

typewriter *n.* machine for producing print-like characters on paper, by pressing keys. **typewritten** *a.*

typhoid *n.* **typhoid fever** serious infectious feverish disease.

typhoon *n.* violent hurricane.

typhus *n.* infectious feverish disease transmitted by parasites.

typical *a.* having the distinctive qualities of a particular type of person or thing. **typically** *adv.*

typify *v.* be a representative specimen of.

typist *n.* person who types.

typography *n.* art or style of printing. **typographical** *a.*

tyrannize *v.* rule as or like a tyrant.

tyranny *n.* government by a tyrant; tyrannical use of power. **tyrannical** *a.*, **tyrannically** *adv.*, **tyrannous** *a.*

tyrant *n.* ruler or other person who uses power in a harsh or oppressive way.

tyre *n.* covering round the rim of a wheel to absorb shocks.

U

ubiquitous *a.* found everywhere. **ubiquity** *n.*

udder *n.* bag-like milk-secreting organ of a cow, goat, etc.

ugly *a.* (**-ier**, **-iest**) unpleasant to look at or hear; threatening, hostile. **ugliness** *n.*

UHF *abbr.* ultra-high frequency.

UK *abbr.* United Kingdom.

ukulele /yōōkəláyli/ *n.* small four-stringed guitar.

ulcer *n.* open sore. **ulcerous** *a.*

ulcerated *a.* affected with ulcer(s). **ulceration** *n.*

ulna *n.* (*pl.* **-ae**) thinner long bone of the forearm. **ulnar** *a.*

ulterior *a.* beyond what is obvious or admitted.

ultimate *a.* last, final; fundamental. **ultimately** *adv.*

ultimatum *n.* (*pl.* **-ums**) final demand, with a threat of hostile action if this is rejected.

ultra- *pref.* beyond; extremely.

ultra-high *a.* (of frequency) between 300 and 3000 MHz.

ultramarine *a.* & *n.* deep bright blue.

ultrasonic *a.* above the range of normal human hearing.

ultrasound *n.* ultrasonic waves.

ultraviolet *a.* of or using radiation with a wavelength shorter than that of visible light rays.

ululate *v.* howl, wail. **ululation** *n.*

umber *n.* natural brownish colouring matter.

umbilical *a.* of the navel. **umbilical cord** flexible tube connecting the placenta to the navel of a foetus.

umbra *n.* (*pl.* **-ae**) area of total shadow cast by the moon or earth in an eclipse.

umbrage *n.* feeling of being offended. **take umbrage** take offence.

umbrella *n.* portable protection against rain, circle of fabric on a folding framework of spokes attached to a central stick.

umpire *n.* person appointed to supervise a game or contest etc. and see that rules are observed. — *v.* act as umpire in.

umpteen *a.* (*sl.*) very many. **umpteenth** *a.*

UN *abbr.* United Nations.

un- *pref.* not; reversing the action indicated by a verb, e.g. *unlock. The number of words with this prefix is almost unlimited and many of those whose meaning is obvious are not listed below.*

unaccountable *a.* unable to be accounted for; not having to account for one's actions etc. **unaccountably** *adv.*

unadopted *a.* (of a road) not maintained by a local authority.

unadulterated *a.* pure, complete.

unalloyed *a.* pure.

unanimous *a.* all agreeing; agreed by all. **unanimously** *adv.*, **unanimity** *n.*

unarmed *a.* without weapons.

unassuming *a.* not arrogant, unpretentious.

unattended *a.* (of a vehicle etc.) having no person in charge of it.

unavoidable *a.* unable to be avoided. **unavoidably** *adv.*

unawares *adv.* unexpectedly; without noticing.

unbalanced *a.* not balanced; biased; mentally unsound.

unbeknown *a.* (*colloq.*) unknown.

unbend *v.* (**unbent**) change from a bent position; become relaxed or affable.

unbending *a.* inflexible, refusing to alter one's demands.

unbidden *a.* not commanded or invited.

unblock *v.* remove an obstruction from.

unbolt *v.* release (a door) by drawing back the bolt(s).

unborn *a.* not yet born.

unbounded *a.* without limits.

unbridled *a.* unrestrained.

unburden *v.* **unburden oneself** reveal one's thoughts and feelings.

uncalled-for *a.* given or done impertinently or unjustifiably.

uncanny *a.* (**-ier**, **-iest**) strange and rather frightening; extraordinary. **uncannily** *adv.*

unceasing *a.* not ceasing.

unceremonious *a.* without proper formality or dignity.

uncertain *a.* not known or not knowing certainly; not to be depended on. **uncertainly** *adv.*, **uncertainty** *n.*

uncle *n.* brother or brother-in-law of one's father or mother.

unclean *a.* not clean; ritually impure.

uncoil *v.* unwind.

uncommon *a.* not common, unusual.

uncompromising *a.* not allowing or not seeking compromise, inflexible.

unconcern *n.* lack of concern.

unconditional *a.* not subject to conditions. **unconditionally** *adv.*

unconscionable *a.* unscrupulous; contrary to what one's conscience feels is right.

unconscious *a.* not conscious; not aware; done without conscious intention. **unconsciously** *adv.*, **unconsciousness** *n.*

unconsidered *a.* disregarded.

uncork *v.* pull the cork from.

uncouple *v.* disconnect (things joined by a coupling).

uncouth *a.* awkward in manner, boorish.

uncover *v.* remove a covering from; reveal, expose.

unction *n.* anointing with oil, esp. as a religious rite; excessive politeness.

unctuous *a.* having an oily manner; smugly virtuous. **unctuously** *adv.*, **unctuousness** *n.*

undeceive *v.* disillusion.

undecided *a.* not yet certain; not yet having made up one's mind.

undeniable *a.* undoubtedly true. **undeniably** *adv.*

under *prep.* in or to a position or rank etc. lower than; less than; governed or controlled by; subjected to; in accordance with; designated by. — *adv.* in or to a lower position or subordinate condition; in or into a state of unconsciousness; below a certain quantity, rank, or age etc. **under age** not old enough, esp. for some legal right; not yet of adult status. **under way** making progress.

under- *pref.* below; lower, subordinate; insufficiently.

underarm *a.* & *adv.* in the armpit; with the hand brought forwards and upwards.

undercarriage *n.* aircraft's landing wheels and their supports; supporting framework of a vehicle.

underclass *n.* social class below mainstream society.

undercliff *n.* terrace or lower cliff formed by a landslip.

underclothes *n.pl.* (also **underclothing**) underwear.

undercoat *n.* layer of paint used under a finishing coat.

undercover *a.* done or doing things secretly.

undercurrent *n.* current flowing below a surface; underlying feeling or influence or trend.

undercut *v.* (**undercut**) cut away the part below; sell or work for a lower price than.

underdog *n.* person etc. in an inferior or subordinate position.

underdone *a.* not thoroughly cooked.

underestimate *v.* & *n.* (make) too low an estimate (of).

underfelt *n.* felt for laying under a carpet.

underfoot *adv.* on the ground; under one's feet.

undergo *v.* (**-went, -gone**) experience; be subjected to.

undergraduate *n.* university student who has not yet taken a degree.

underground *a.* under the surface of the ground; secret. — *n.* underground railway.

undergrowth *n.* thick growth of shrubs and bushes under trees.

underhand *a.* done or doing things slyly or secretly; underarm.

underlay *n.* material laid under another as a support.

underlie *v.* (**-lay, -lain, -lying**) be the cause or basis of. **underlying** *a.*

underline *v.* draw a line under; emphasize.

underling *n.* subordinate.

undermanned *a.* having too few staff or crew etc.

undermine *v.* weaken gradually; weaken the foundations of.

underneath *prep.* & *adv.* below or on the inside of (a thing).

underpants *n.pl.* man's undergarment covering the lower part of the body and part of the legs.

underpass *n.* road passing under another.

underpin *v.* (**-pinned**) support, strengthen from beneath.

underprivileged *a.* not having the normal standard of living or rights in a community.

underrate *v.* underestimate.

underseal *v.* coat the lower surface of (a vehicle) with a protective layer. — *n.* this coating.

undersell *v.* (**-sold**) sell at a lower price than.

undershoot *v.* (**-shot**) land short of (a runway etc.).

undersigned *a.* who has or have signed this document.

underskirt *n.* skirt for wearing beneath another; petticoat.

underslung *a.* supported from above.

understand *v.* (**-stood**) see the meaning or importance of; know the ways or workings of: know the explanation; infer; take for granted. **understandable** *a.*

understanding *a.* showing insight or sympathy. — *n.* ability to understand; sympathetic insight; agreement; thing agreed.

understate *v.* express in restrained terms; represent as less than it really is. **understatement** *n.*

understeer *v.* (of a car) tend to turn less

sharply than was intended. — *n.* this tendency.

understudy *n.* actor who studies another's part in order to be able to take his or her place if necessary. — *v.* be an understudy for.

undertake *v.* (**-took, -taken**) agree or promise (to do something).

undertaker *n.* one whose business is to organize funerals.

undertaking *n.* work etc. undertaken; promise, guarantee.

undertone *n.* underlying quality or feeling.

undertow *n.* undercurrent moving in the opposite direction to the surface current.

underwear *n.* garments worn under indoor clothing.

underwent *see* **undergo**.

underworld *n.* (in mythology) abode of spirits of the dead, under the earth; part of society habitually involved in crime.

underwrite *v.* (**-wrote, -written**) accept liability under (an insurance policy); undertake to finance. **underwriter** *n.*

undesirable *a.* not desirable, objectionable. **undesirably** *adv.*

undies *n.pl.* (*colloq.*) women's underwear.

undo *v.* (**-did, -done**) unfasten, unwrap; cancel the effect of, ruin.

undone *a.* unfastened; not done.

undoubted *a.* not disputed. **undoubtedly** *adv.*

undress *v.* take clothes off.

undue *a.* excessive.

undulate *v.* have or cause to have a wavy movement or appearance. **undulation** *n.*

unduly *adv.* excessively.

undying *a.* everlasting.

unearth *v.* uncover or bring out from the ground; find by searching.

unearthly *a.* not of this earth; mysterious and frightening; (*colloq.*) absurdly early or inconvenient.

uneasy *a.* not comfortable; not confident; worrying. **uneasily** *adv.*, **uneasiness** *n.*

uneatable *a.* not fit to be eaten.

uneconomic *a.* not profitable.

unemployable *a.* not fit for paid employment.

unemployed *a.* without a paid job; not in use. **unemployment** *n.*

unending *a.* endless.

unequivocal *a.* clear and not ambiguous. **unequivocally** *adv.*

unerring *a.* making no mistake.

uneven *a.* not level, not smooth; not uniform. **unevenly** *adv.*, **unevenness** *n.*

unexampled *a.* without precedent.

unexceptionable *a.* with which no fault can be found.

unexceptional *a.* not exceptional.

unexpected *a.* not expected. **unexpectedly** *adv.*

unfailing *a.* constant, reliable.

unfair *a.* not impartial, not in accordance with justice. **unfairly** *adv.*, **unfairness** *n.*

unfaithful *a.* not loyal; having committed adultery. **unfaithfully** *adv.*, **unfaithfulness** *n.*

unfeeling *a.* lacking sensitivity; callous. **unfeelingly** *adv.*

unfit *a.* unsuitable; not in perfect physical condition. — *v.* (**unfitted**) make unsuitable.

unflappable *a.* (*colloq.*) remaining calm in a crisis.

unfold *v.* open, spread out; become known.

unforgettable *a.* impossible to forget. **unforgettably** *adv.*

unfortunate *a.* having bad luck; regrettable. **unfortunately** *adv.*

unfounded *a.* with no basis.

unfrock *v.* dismiss (a priest) from the priesthood.

unfurl *v.* unroll; spread out.

ungainly *adv.* awkward-looking, not graceful. **ungainliness** *n.*

ungodly *a.* irreligious; wicked; (*colloq.*) outrageous.

ungovernable *a.* uncontrollable.

ungracious *a.* not courteous or kindly. **ungraciously** *adv.*

unguarded *a.* not guarded; incautious.

unguent /únggwənt/ *n.* ointment, lubricant.

ungulate *a.* & *n.* hoofed (animal).

unhappy *a.* (**-ier, -iest**) not happy, sad; unfortunate; unsuitable. **unhappily** *adv.*, **unhappiness** *n.*

unhealthy *a.* (**-ier, -iest**) not healthy; harmful to health. **unhealthily** *adv.*

unheard-of *a.* unprecedented.

unhinge *v.* cause to become mentally unbalanced.

unholy *a.* (**-ier, -iest**) wicked, irreverent; (*colloq.*) very great.

unicorn *n.* mythical horse-like animal with one straight horn on its forehead.

uniform *n.* distinctive clothing identifying the wearer as a member of an organization or group. — *a.* always the same. **uniformly** *adv.*, **uniformity** *n.*

unify *v.* unite. **unification** *n.*

unilateral *a.* done by or affecting one person or group etc. and not another. **unilaterally** *adv.*

unimpeachable *a.* completely trustworthy.

uninviting *a.* unattractive, repellent.

union *n.* uniting, being united; a whole

formed by uniting parts; association; trade union (*see* **trade**). **Union Jack** national flag of the UK.
unionist *n.* member of a trade union; supporter of trade unions; one who favours union.
unionize *v.* organize into or cause to join a union. **unionization** *n.*
unique *a.* being the only one of its kind; unequalled. **uniquely** *adv.*
unisex *a.* designed in a style suitable for people of either sex.
unison *n.* **in unison** all together; sounding or singing together.
unit *n.* individual thing, person, or group, esp. as part of a complex whole; fixed quantity used as a standard of measurement. **unit trust** investment company paying dividends based on the average return from the various securities which they hold.
unitary *a.* of a unit or units.
unite *v.* join together, make or become one; act together, cooperate.
unity *n.* state of being one or a unit; complex whole; agreement.
universal *a.* of, for, or done by all. **universally** *adv.*
universe *n.* all existing things, including the earth and its creatures and all the heavenly bodies.
university *n.* educational institution for advanced learning.
unkempt *a.* looking untidy or neglected.
unkind *a.* harsh, hurtful; thoughtless. **unkindly** *adv.*, **unkindness** *n.*
unknown *a.* not known. —*n.* unknown person, thing, or place.
unleaded *a.* (of petrol etc.) without added lead.
unleash *v.* release, let loose.
unless *conj.* except when; except on condition that.
unlettered *a.* illiterate.
unlike *a.* not like. —*prep.* differently from.
unlikely *a.* not likely to happen or be true or be successful.
unlisted *a.* not included in a (published) list.
unload *v.* remove a load or cargo (from); get rid of; remove the ammunition from (a gun).
unlock *v.* release the lock of (a door etc.); release by unlocking.
unlooked-for *a.* unexpected.
unmanned *a.* operated without a crew.
unmask *v.* remove a mask (from); expose the true character of.
unmentionable *a.* not fit to be spoken of.
unmistakable *a.* clear, not able to be doubted or mistaken for another. **unmistakably** *adv.*
unmitigated *a.* not modified, absolute.
unmoved *a.* not moved, not persuaded, not affected by emotion.
unnatural *a.* not natural; not normal. **unnaturally** *adv.*
unnecessary *a.* not necessary; more than is necessary. **unnecessarily** *adv.*
unnerve *v.* cause to lose courage or determination.
unnumbered *a.* not marked with a number; countless.
unobtrusive *a.* not making oneself or itself noticed. **unobtrusively** *adv.*
unpack *v.* open and remove the contents of (a suitcase etc.); take out from its packaging.
unparalleled *a.* never yet equalled.
unpick *v.* undo the stitching of.
unplaced *a.* not placed as one of the first three in a race etc.
unpleasant *a.* not pleasant. **unpleasantly** *adv.*, **unpleasantness** *n.*
unpopular *a.* not popular; disliked. **unpopularity** *n.*
unprecedented *a.* for which there is no precedent; unparalleled.
unprepared *a.* not prepared beforehand; not ready or not equipped to do something.
unpretentious *a.* not pretentious, not showy or pompous.
unprincipled *a.* without good moral principles, unscrupulous.
unprintable *a.* too indecent or libellous etc. to be printed.
unprofessional *a.* contrary to the standards of behaviour for members of a profession. **unprofessionally** *adv.*
unprofitable *a.* not profitable; useless. **unprofitably** *adv.*
unqualified *a.* not qualified; not restricted or modified.
unquestionable *a.* too clear to be doubted. **unquestionably** *adv.*
unravel *v.* (**unravelled**) disentangle; undo (knitted fabric); become unravelled.
unreasonable *a.* not reasonable; excessive, unjust. **unreasonably** *adv.*
unrelieved *a.* not relieved; without anything to give variation.
unremitting *a.* not ceasing.
unrequited *a.* (of love) not returned or rewarded.
unreservedly *adv.* without reservation, completely.
unrest *n.* restlessness, agitation.
unrivalled *a.* having no equal, incomparable.
unroll *v.* open after being rolled.

unruly *a.* not easy to control, disorderly. **unruliness** *n.*
unsaid *a.* not spoken or expressed.
unsavoury *a.* disagreeable to the taste or smell; morally disgusting.
unscathed *a.* without suffering any injury.
unscramble *v.* sort out; make (a scrambled transmission) intelligible.
unscrew *v.* loosen (a screw etc.); unfasten by removing screw(s).
unscripted *a.* without a prepared script.
unscrupulous *a.* not prevented by scruples of conscience.
unseat *v.* dislodge (a rider); remove from a parliamentary seat.
unselfish *a.* not selfish; considering others' needs before one's own. **unselfishly** *adv.*, **unselfishness** *n.*
unsettle *v.* make uneasy, disturb.
unsettled *a.* (of weather) changeable.
unshakeable *a.* firm.
unsightly *a.* not pleasant to look at, ugly. **unsightliness** *n.*
unskilled *a.* not having or needing skill or special training.
unsocial *a.* not sociable; not conforming to normal social practices.
unsolicited *a.* not requested.
unsophisticated *a.* simple and natural or naive.
unsound *a.* not sound or strong, not free from defects. **of unsound mind** insane.
unsparing *a.* giving lavishly.
unspeakable *a.* too bad to be described in words.
unstable *a.* not stable; mentally or emotionally unbalanced.
unstick *v.* (**-stuck**) detach (what is stuck).
unstuck *a.* detached after being stuck on or together. **come unstuck** (*colloq.*) suffer disaster, fail.
unstudied *a.* natural in manner.
unsullied *a.* not sullied, pure.
unsuspecting *a.* feeling no suspicion.
unswerving *a.* not turning aside; unchanging.
unthinkable *a.* too bad or too unlikely to be thought about.
unthinking *a.* thoughtless.
untidy *a.* (**-ier, -iest**) not tidy. **untidily** *adv.*, **untidiness** *n.*
untie *v.* unfasten; release from being tied up.
until *prep.* & *conj.* = till ².
untimely *a.* inopportune; premature.
untold *a.* not told; too much or too many to be counted.
untouchable *a.* not able or not allowed to be touched. — *n.* member of the lowest Hindu social group.
untoward *a.* unexpected and inconvenient.
untraceable *a.* unable to be traced.
untruth *n.* untrue statement, lie; lack of truth. **untruthful** *a.*, **untruthfully** *adv.*
unusual *a.* not usual; remarkable, rare. **unusually** *adv.*
unutterable *a.* too great to be expressed in words. **unutterably** *adv.*
unvarnished *a.* not varnished; plain and straightforward.
unveil *v.* remove a veil (from); remove concealing drapery from; disclose, make publicly known.
unversed *a.* **unversed in** not experienced in.
unwarrantable *a.* unjustifiable.
unwarranted *a.* unjustified, unauthorized.
unwary *a.* not cautious.
unwell *a.* not in good health.
unwieldy *a.* awkward to move or control because of its size, shape, or weight. **unwieldiness** *n.*
unwind *v.* (**unwound**) draw out or become drawn out from being wound; (*colloq.*) relax from work or tension.
unwise *a.* not wise, foolish. **unwisely** *adv.*
unwitting *a.* unaware; unintentional. **unwittingly** *adv.*
unwonted *a.* not customary, not usual. **unwontedly** *adv.*
unworldly *a.* not materialistic; naïve. **unworldliness** *n.*
unworthy *a.* worthless; not deserving; unsuitable to the character (of a person or thing).
unwritten *a.* not written down; based on custom not statute.
unzip *v.* (**unzipped**) open by the undoing of a zip-fastener.
up *adv.* to, in, or at a higher place or state etc.; to a vertical position; to a larger size; as far as a stated place, time, or amount; out of bed; (*colloq.*) amiss, happening. — *prep.* upwards along or through or into; at a higher part of. — *a.* directed upwards; travelling towards a central place. — *v.* (**upped**) (*colloq.*) raise; get up (and do something). **time is up** is finished. **up in** (*colloq.*) knowledgeable about. **ups and downs** alternate good and bad fortune. **up to** occupied with, doing; required as a duty or obligation from; capable of. **up to date** in accordance with current fashion or information. **up-to-date** *a.*
upbeat *n.* unaccented beat. — *a.* (*colloq.*) optimistic, cheerful.
upbraid *v.* reproach.
upbringing *n.* training and education during childhood.
update *v.* bring up to date.
up-end *v.* set or rise up on end.

upgrade *v.* raise to higher grade.

upheaval *n.* sudden heaving upwards; violent disturbance.

uphill *a.* & *adv.* going or sloping upwards.

uphold *v.* (**upheld**) support.

upholster *v.* put fabric covering, padding, etc. on (furniture).

upholstery *n.* upholstering; material used in this.

upkeep *n.* keeping (a thing) in good condition and repair; cost of this.

upland *n.* & *a.* (of) higher or inland parts of a country.

uplift *v.* raise. — *n.* being raised; mentally elevating influence.

upon *prep.* on.

upper *a.* higher in place or position or rank. — *n.* part of a shoe above the sole. **upper case** capital letters in printing or typing. **upper class** highest social class. **upper crust** (*colloq.*) aristocracy. **upper hand** dominance.

uppermost *a.* & *adv.* in, on, or to the top or most prominent position.

uppish, uppity *adjs.* (*colloq.*) self-assertive; presumptuous.

upright *a.* in a vertical position; strictly honest or honourable. — *n.* vertical part or support.

uprising *n.* rebellion.

uproar *n.* outburst of noise and excitement or anger.

uproarious *a.* noisy, with loud laughter. **uproariously** *adv.*

uproot *v.* pull out of the ground together with its roots; force to leave an established place.

upset *v.* /úpsét/ (**upset, upsetting**) overturn; disrupt; distress; disturb the temper or digestion of. — *n.* /úpset/ upsetting.

upshot *n.* outcome.

upside down with the upper part underneath; in great disorder.

upstage *adv.* & *a.* nearer the back of a theatre stage. — *v.* divert attention from, outshine.

upstairs *adv.* & *a.* to or on a higher floor.

upstanding *a.* strong and healthy, well set up; standing up.

upstart *n.* person newly risen to a high position, esp. one who behaves arrogantly.

upstream *a.* & *adv.* in the direction from which a stream flows.

upsurge *n.* upward surge, rise.

upswing *n.* upward movement or trend.

uptake *n.* **quick on the uptake** (*colloq.*) quick to understand what is meant.

uptight *a.* (*colloq.*) nervously tense; annoyed.

upturn *v.* /úptúrn/ turn up or upwards or upside down. — *n.* /úpturn/ upheaval; upward trend, improvement.

upward *a.* moving or leading up.

upwards *adv.* towards a higher place etc.

uranium *n.* heavy grey metal used as a source of nuclear energy.

urban *a.* of a city or town.

urbane *a.* having smooth manners. **urbanely** *adv.*, **urbanity** *n.*

urbanize *v.* change (a place) into an urban area. **urbanization** *n.*

urchin *n.* mischievous child.

Urdu *n.* language related to Hindi.

ureter /yooréetər/ *n.* duct from the kidney to the bladder.

urethra /yooréethrə/ *n.* duct which carries urine from the body.

urge *v.* press, encourage to proceed; recommend strongly or earnestly. — *n.* feeling or desire urging a person to do something.

urgent *a.* needing or calling for immediate attention or action. **urgently** *adv.*, **urgency** *n.*

urinal *n.* receptacle or structure for receiving urine.

urinate *v.* discharge urine from the body. **urination** *n.*

urine *n.* waste liquid which collects in the bladder and is discharged from the body. **urinary** *a.*

urn *n.* a kind of vase, esp. for holding a cremated person's ashes; large metal container with a tap, for keeping water etc. hot.

ursine *a.* of or like a bear.

us *pron.* objective case of *we*.

US, USA *abbr.* United States (of America).

usable *a.* able or fit to be used.

usage *n.* manner of using or treating something; customary practice.

use *v.* /yo͞oz/ cause to act or to serve for a purpose; treat; exploit selfishly. — *n.* /yo͞oss/ using, being used; power of using; purpose for which a thing is used.

used /yo͞ozd/ *a.* second-hand.

used to /yo͞osst/ *v.* was accustomed to (do). — *a.* familiar with by practice or habit.

useful *a.* fit for a practical purpose; able to produce good results. **usefully** *adv.*, **usefulness** *n.*

useless *a.* not usable, not useful. **uselessly** *adv.*, **uselessness** *n.*

user *n.* one who uses something. **user-friendly** *a.* easy for a user to understand and operate.

usher *n.* person who shows people to their seats in a public hall etc. — *v.* lead, escort.

usherette *n.* woman who ushers people to seats in a cinema etc.

usual *a.* such as happens or is done or used etc. in many or most instances. **usually** *adv.*

usurer *n.* person who lends money at excessively high rates.

usurp *v.* take (power, position, or right) wrongfully or by force. **usurpation** *n.*, **usurper** *n.*

usury *n.* lending of money at excessively high rates of interest.

utensil *n.* instrument or container, esp. for domestic use.

uterus *n.* womb. **uterine** *a.*

utilitarian *a.* useful rather than decorative or luxurious.

utilitarianism *n.* theory that actions are justified if they benefit the majority.

utility *n.* usefulness; useful thing. — *a.* severely practical.

utilize *v.* use, find a use for. **utilization** *n.*

utmost *a.* & *n.* furthest, greatest, or extreme (point or degree etc.).

Utopia *n.* imaginary place or state where all is perfect. **Utopian** *a.*

utter [1] *a.* complete, absolute. **utterly** *adv.*

utter [2] *v.* make (a sound or words) with the mouth or voice; speak. **utterance** *n.*

uttermost *a.* & *n.* = utmost.

U-turn *n.* driving of a vehicle in a U-shaped course to reverse its direction; reversal of policy or opinion.

uvula /yo͞ovyoolər/ *n.* small fleshy projection hanging at the back of the throat. **uvular** *a.*

uxorious *a.* excessively fond of one's wife.

V

V *abbr.* volt(s).
vac *n.* (*colloq.*) vacation.
vacancy *n.* state of being vacant; vacant place or position etc.
vacant *a.* unoccupied; showing no interest. **vacantly** *adv.*
vacate *v.* cease to occupy.
vacation *n.* interval between terms in universities and law courts; (*US*) holiday; vacating of a place etc.
vaccinate *n.* inoculate with a vaccine. **vaccination** *n.*
vaccine /vákseen/ *n.* preparation that gives immunity from an infection.
vacillate *v.* keep changing one's mind. **vacillation** *n.*
vacuous *a.* inane; expressionless. **vacuously** *adv.*, **vacuity** *n.*
vacuum *n.* (*pl.* **-cua** *or* **-cuums**) space from which air has been removed. — *v.* (*colloq.*) clean with a vacuum cleaner. **vacuum cleaner** electrical apparatus that takes up dust by suction. **vacuum flask** container for keeping liquids hot or cold. **vacuum-packed** *a.* sealed after removal of air.
vagabond *n.* wanderer; vagrant.
vagary *n.* capricious act or idea or fluctuation.
vagina *n.* passage leading from the vulva to the womb. **vaginal** *a.*
vagrant *n.* person without a settled home. **vagrancy** *n.*
vague *a.* not clearly explained or perceived; not expressing oneself clearly. **vaguely** *adv.*, **vagueness** *n.*
vain *a.* conceited; useless, futile. **in vain** uselessly. **vainly** *adv.*
vainglory *n.* great vanity. **vainglorious** *a.*
valance *n.* short curtain or hanging frill.
vale *n.* valley.
valediction *n.* farewell. **valedictory** *a.*
valence, valency *ns.* combining power of an atom as compared with that of the hydrogen atom.
valentine *n.* person to whom one sends a romantic greetings card on St Valentine's Day (14 Feb.); this card.
valet *n.* man's personal attendant. — *v.* (**valeted**) act as valet to.
valetudinarian *n.* person who pays excessive attention to preserving his or her health.
valiant *a.* brave. **valiantly** *adv.*
valid *a.* having legal force, usable; logical. **validity** *n.*
validate *v.* make valid, confirm. **validation** *n.*
valley *n.* (*pl.* **-eys**) low area between hills.
valour *n.* bravery.
valuable *a.* of great value or worth.
valuables *n.pl.* valuable things.
valuation *n.* estimation or estimate of a thing's worth.
value *n.* amount of money or other commodity etc. considered equivalent to something else; usefulness, importance; (*pl.*) moral principles. — *v.* estimate the value of; consider to be of great worth. **value added tax** tax on the amount by which a thing's value has been increased at each stage of its production. **value judgement** subjective estimate of quality etc.
valuer *n.* person who estimates values professionally.
valve *n.* device controlling flow through a pipe; structure allowing blood to flow in one direction only; each half of the hinged shell of an oyster etc. **valvular** *a.*
vamoose *v.* (*US sl.*) depart hurriedly.
vamp *n.* upper front part of a boot or shoe. — *v.* improvise (esp. a musical accompaniment).
vampire *n.* ghost or reanimated body supposed to suck blood.
van [1] *n.* covered vehicle for transporting goods etc.; railway carriage for luggage or goods.
van [2] *n.* vanguard, forefront.
vandal *n.* person who damages things wilfully. **vandalism** *n.*
vandalize *v.* damage wilfully.
vanguard *n.* foremost part of an advancing army etc.
vanilla *n.* a kind of flavouring, esp. obtained from the pods of a tropical orchid.
vanish *v.* disappear completely.
vanity *n.* conceit; futility. **vanity case** woman's small case for carrying cosmetics etc.
vanquish *v.* conquer.
vantage *n.* advantage (esp. as a score in tennis). **vantage point** position giving a good view.
vapid *a.* insipid, uninteresting. **vapidly** *adv.*, **vapidity** *n.*
vaporize *v.* convert or be converted into vapour. **vaporization** *n.*

vapour *n.* moisture suspended in air, into which certain liquids or solids are converted by heating. **vaporous** *a.*

variable *a.* varying. — *n.* thing that varies. **variability** *n.*

variance *n.* **at variance** disagreeing.

variant *a.* differing. — *n.* variant form or spelling etc.

variation *n.* varying, extent of this; variant; repetition of a melody in a different form.

varicose *a.* (of veins) permanently swollen. **varicosity** *n.*

varied *a.* of different sorts.

variegated *a.* having irregular patches of colours. **variegation** *n.*

variety *n.* quality of not being the same; quantity of different things; sort or kind; entertainment with a series of short performances.

various *a.* of several kinds; several. **variously** *adv.*

varnish *n.* liquid that dries to form a shiny transparent coating. — *v.* coat with varnish.

vary *v.* make or be or become different.

vascular *a.* of vessels or ducts for conveying blood or sap.

vase *n.* decorative jar, esp. for holding cut flowers.

vasectomy *n.* surgical removal of part of the ducts that carry semen from the testicles, esp. as a method of birth control.

vassal *n.* humble subordinate.

vast *a.* very great in area or size. **vastly** *adv.*, **vastness** *n.*

VAT *abbr.* value added tax.

vat *n.* large tank for liquids.

vault [1] *n.* arched roof; cellar used as a storage place; burial chamber. **vaulted** *a.*

vault [2] *v.* & *n.* jump, esp. with the help of the hands or a pole.

vaunt *v.* & *n.* boast.

VDU *abbr.* visual display unit.

veal *n.* calf's flesh as food.

vector *n.* thing (e.g. velocity) that has both magnitude and direction; carrier of an infection.

veer *v.* change direction.

vegan /veégən/ *n.* person who eats no meat or animal products.

vegetable *n.* plant grown for food. — *a.* of or from plants.

vegetarian *n.* person who eats no meat. **vegetarianism** *n.*

vegetate *v.* live an uneventful life.

vegetation *n.* plants collectively.

vehement *a.* showing strong feeling. **vehemently** *adv.*, **vehemence** *n.*

vehicle *n.* conveyance for transporting passengers or goods on land or in space; means by which something is expressed or displayed. **vehicular** *a.*

veil *n.* piece of fine net or other fabric worn to protect or conceal the face. — *v.* cover with or as if with a veil.

vein *n.* any of the blood vessels conveying blood towards the heart; thread-like structure; narrow layer in rock etc.; mood, manner. **veined** *a.*

vellum *n.* fine parchment; smooth writing paper.

velocity *n.* speed.

velour /vəloór/ *n.* heavy plush-like fabric.

velvet *n.* woven fabric with thick short pile on one side. **velvet glove** outward gentleness concealing inflexibility. **velvety** *a.*

velveteen *n.* cotton velvet.

venal *a.* able to be bribed; influenced by bribery. **venality** *n.*

vend *v.* sell, offer for sale.

vendetta *n.* feud.

vending machine slot machine where small articles are obtained.

vendor *n.* seller.

veneer *n.* thin covering layer of fine wood; superficial show of a quality. — *v.* cover with a veneer.

venerate *v.* respect deeply. **veneration** *n.*, **venerable** *a.*

venereal *a.* (of infections) contracted by sexual intercourse with an infected person.

Venetian *a.* & *n.* (native) of Venice. **Venetian blind** window blind of adjustable horizontal slats.

vengeance *n.* retaliation. **with a vengeance** in an extreme degree.

vengeful *a.* seeking vengeance.

venial *a.* (of a sin) pardonable, not serious. **veniality** *n.*

venison *n.* deer's flesh as food.

venom *n.* poisonous fluid secreted by snakes etc.; bitter feeling or language. **venomous** *a.*

vent [1] *n.* slit at the lower edge of the back or side of a coat.

vent [2] *n.* opening allowing gas or liquid to pass through. — *v.* give vent to. **give vent to** give an outlet to (feelings).

ventilate *v.* cause air to enter or circulate freely in; express publicly. **ventilation** *n.*

ventilator *n.* device for ventilating a room etc.

ventral *a.* of or on the abdomen.

ventricle *n.* cavity, esp. in the heart or brain. **ventricular** *a.*

ventriloquist *n.* entertainer who can produce voice sounds so that they seem to come from a puppet etc. **ventriloquism** *n.*

venture *n.* undertaking that involves risk. — *v.* dare; dare to go or utter. **venturesome** *a.*

venue *n.* appointed place for a meeting etc.

veracious *a.* truthful; true. **veraciously** *adv.*, **veracity** *n.*

veranda *n.* roofed terrace.

verb *n.* word indicating action or occurrence or being.

verbal *a.* of or in words; spoken; of a verb. **verbally** *adv.*

verbalize *v.* express in words; be verbose. **verbalization** *n.*

verbatim /verbáytim/ *adv.* & *a.* in exactly the same words.

verbiage *n.* excessive number of words.

verbose *a.* using more words than are needed. **verbosely** *adv.*, **verbosity** *n.*

verdant *a.* (of grass etc.) green.

verdict *n.* decision reached by a jury; decision or opinion reached after testing something.

verdigris *n.* green deposit forming on copper or brass.

verdure *n.* green vegetation.

verge [1] *n.* extreme edge, brink; grass edging of a road etc.

verge [2] *v.* **verge on** border on.

verger *n.* church caretaker.

verify *v.* check the truth or correctness of. **verification** *n.*

verisimilitude *n.* appearance of being true.

veritable *a.* real, rightly named.

vermicelli *n.* pasta made in slender threads.

vermiform *a.* worm-like in shape.

vermilion *a.* & *n.* bright red.

vermin *n.* (*pl.* **vermin**) animal or insect regarded as a pest.

verminous *a.* infested with vermin.

vermouth *n.* wine flavoured with herbs.

vernacular *n.* ordinary language of a country or district.

vernal *a.* of or occurring in spring.

veronica *n.* a kind of flowering herb or shrub.

verruca /vəro͞okə/ *n.* (*pl.* **-ae**) wart, esp. on the foot.

versatile *a.* able to do or be used for many different things. **versatility** *n.*

verse *n.* metrical (not prose) composition; group of lines forming a unit in a poem or hymn; numbered division of a Bible chapter.

versed *a.* **versed in** experienced in.

versify *v.* express in verse; compose verse. **versification** *n.*

version *n.* particular account of a matter; translation; special or variant form.

versus *prep.* against.

vertebra *n.* (*pl.* **-brae**) segment of the backbone. **vertebral** *a.*

vertebrate *n.* & *a.* (animal) having a backbone.

vertex *n.* (*pl.* **vertices**) highest point of a hill etc.; apex.

vertical *a.* perpendicular to the horizontal, upright. — *n.* vertical line or position. **vertically** *adv.*

vertigo *n.* dizziness.

verve *n.* enthusiasm, vigour.

very *adv.* in a high degree, extremely; exactly. — *a.* actual, truly such; extreme. **very high frequency** frequency in the range 30–300 MHz. **very well** expression of consent.

vesicle *n.* sac, esp. containing liquid; blister.

vessel *n.* structure designed to travel on water and carry people or goods; receptacle, esp. for liquid; tube-like structure conveying blood or other fluid in the body of an animal or plant.

vest *n.* undergarment covering the trunk; (*US*) waistcoat. — *v.* confer or furnish with (power) as a firm or legal right. **vested interest** advantageous right held by a person or group.

vestibule *n.* entrance hall; porch.

vestige *n.* small remaining bit; very small amount. **vestigial** *a.*, **vestigially** *adv.*

vestment *n.* ceremonial garment, esp. of clergy or a church choir.

vet *n.* (*colloq.*) veterinary surgeon. — *v.* (**vetted**) (*colloq.*) examine critically for faults or errors etc.

vetch *n.* plant of the pea family used as fodder for cattle.

veteran *n.* person with long experience, esp. in the armed forces.

veterinarian *n.* veterinary surgeon.

veterinary *a.* of or for the treatment of diseases and disorders of animals. **veterinary surgeon** person skilled in such treatment.

veto *n.* (*pl.* **-oes**) authoritative rejection of something proposed; right to make this. — *v.* reject by a veto.

vex *v.* annoy. **vexed question** problem that is much discussed. **vexation** *n.*, **vexatious** *a.*

VHF *abbr.* very high frequency.

via *prep.* by way of, through.

viable *a.* capable of living or surviving; practicable. **viability** *n.*

viaduct *n.* long bridge over a valley.

vial *n.* small bottle.

viands *n.pl.* articles of food.

vibrant *a.* vibrating, resonant, thrilling with energy.

vibraphone *n.* percussion instrument like

a xylophone but with a vibrating effect.
vibrate *v.* move rapidly and continuously to and fro; sound with rapid slight variation of pitch. **vibrator** *n.*, **vibratory** *a.*
vibration *n.* vibrating; (*pl.*) emanations felt intuitively.
vicar *n.* member of the clergy in charge of a parish.
vicarage *n.* house of a vicar.
vicarious *a.* felt through sharing imaginatively in the feelings or activities etc. of another person; acting or done etc. for another. **vicariously** *adv.*
vice ¹ *n.* great wickedness; criminal and immoral practices.
vice ² *n.* instrument with two jaws for holding things firmly.
vice- *pref.* substitute or deputy for; next in rank to.
vice-chancellor *n.* chief administrator of a university.
viceroy *n.* person governing a colony etc. as the sovereign's representative. **viceregal** *a.*
vice versa with terms the other way round.
vicinity *n.* surrounding district. **in the vicinity (of)** near.
vicious *a.* brutal, strongly spiteful; savage and dangerous. **vicious circle** bad situation producing effects that intensify its original cause. **viciously** *adv.*
vicissitude *n.* change of circumstances or luck.
victim *n.* person injured or killed or made to suffer; living creature killed as a religious sacrifice.
victimize *v.* single out to suffer ill treatment. **victimization** *n.*
victor *n.* winner.
Victorian *n.* & *a.* (person) of the reign of Queen Victoria (1837–1901).
victorious *a.* having gained victory.
victory *n.* success achieved by gaining mastery over opponent(s) or having the highest score.
vicuña /vikyo͞onə/ *n.* South American animal related to the llama; soft cloth made from its wool.
video *n.* (*pl.* **-os**) recording or broadcasting of pictures; apparatus for this; videotape. — *v.* make a video of.
videotape *n.* magnetic tape suitable for recording television pictures and sound. — *v.* record on this.
videotex *n.* (also **videotext**) electronic information system, esp. teletext or viewdata.
vie *v.* **(vying)** carry on a rivalry, compete.
view *n.* range of vision; things within this; fine scenery; mental attitude, opinion. — *v.* regard, consider; watch television. **in view of** having regard to. **on view** displayed for inspection. **with a view to** with the hope or intention of. **viewer** *n.*
viewdata *n.* news and information service from a computer source to which a television screen is connected by a telephone link.
viewfinder *n.* device on a camera showing the extent of the area being photographed.
viewpoint *n.* point of view.
vigil *n.* period of staying awake to keep watch or pray.
vigilant *a.* watchful. **vigilantly** *adv.*, **vigilance** *n.*
vigilante /vijilánti/ *n.* member of a self-appointed group trying to prevent crime etc.
vignette /veenyét/ *n.* short written description.
vigour *n.* active physical or mental strength; forcefulness. **vigorous** *a.*, **vigorously** *adv.*, **vigorousness** *n.*
Viking *n.* ancient Scandinavian trader and pirate.
vile *a.* extremely disgusting or wicked. **vilely** *adv.*, **vileness** *n.*
vilify *v.* say evil things about. **vilification** *n.*, **vilifier** *n.*
villa *n.* house in a suburban district; house in Italy or France etc. used for holidays.
village *n.* collection of houses etc. in a country district. **villager** *n.*
villain *n.* wicked person. **villainous** *a.*, **villainy** *n.*
vim *n.* (*colloq.*) vigour.
vinaigrette *n.* salad dressing of oil and vinegar.
vindicate *v.* clear of blame; justify. **vindication** *n.*
vindictive *a.* showing a desire for vengeance. **vindictively** *adv.*, **vindictiveness** *n.*
vine *n.* climbing plant whose fruit is the grape.
vinegar *n.* sour liquid made from wine, malt, etc., by fermentation. **vinegary** *a.*
vineyard *n.* plantation of vines for wine-making.
vintage *n.* wine from a season's grapes, esp. when of high quality; date of origin or existence. — *a.* of high quality, esp. from a past period.
vintner *n.* wine-merchant.
vinyl /vīnil/ *n.* a kind of plastic.
viola ¹ /viṓlə/ *n.* instrument like a violin but of lower pitch.
viola ² /vīələ/ *n.* plant of the genus to which violets belong.
violate *v.* break (an oath or treaty etc.);

treat (a sacred place) irreverently; disturb; rape. **violation** *n.*, **violator** *n.*

violent *a.* involving great force or intensity; using excessive physical force. **violently** *adv.*, **violence** *n.*

violet *n.* small plant, often with purple flowers; bluish-purple colour. — *a.* bluish-purple.

violin *n.* musical instrument with four strings of treble pitch, played with a bow. **violinist** *n.*

violoncello /vīələnchéllō/ *n.* (*pl.* **-os**) cello.

viper *n.* small poisonous snake.

virago *n.* (*pl.* **-os**) aggressive woman.

viral /vīrəl/ *a.* of a virus.

virgin *n.* person (esp. a woman) who has never had sexual intercourse; **the Virgin** Mary, mother of Christ. — *a.* virginal; untouched, not yet used. **virginal** *a.*, **virginity** *n.*

virile *a.* having masculine strength or procreative power. **virility** *n.*

virology *n.* study of viruses. **virologist** *n.*

virtual *a.* being so in effect though not in name. **virtually** *adv.*

virtue *n.* moral excellence, goodness; chastity; good characteristic. **by** *or* **in virtue of** because of.

virtuoso *n.* (*pl.* **-si**) expert performer. **virtuosity** *n.*

virtuous *a.* morally good. **virtuously** *adv.*, **virtuousness** *n.*

virulent *a.* (of poison or disease) extremely strong or violent; bitterly hostile. **virulently** *adv.*, **virulence** *n.*

virus *n.* (*pl.* **-uses**) minute organism capable of causing disease; destructive code hidden in a computer program.

visa *n.* official mark on a passport, permitting the holder to enter a specified country.

visage *n.* person's face.

vis-à-vis /veezaavee/ *adv.* & *prep.* with regard to; as compared with.

viscera /vissərə/ *n.pl.* internal organs of the body. **visceral** *a.*

viscid /vissid/ *a.* thick and gluey. **viscidity** *n.*

viscose *n.* viscous cellulose; fabric made from this.

viscount /vīkownt/ *n.* nobleman ranking between earl and baron. **viscountess** *n.fem.*

viscous *a.* thick and gluey. **viscosity** *n.*

visibility *n.* state of being visible; range of vision or clarity.

visible *a.* able to be seen or noticed. **visibly** *adv.*

vision *n.* ability to see, sight; thing seen in the imagination or a dream; foresight; person of unusual beauty.

visionary *a.* fanciful; not practical. — *n.* person with visionary ideas.

visit *v.* go or come to see; stay temporarily with or at. — *n.* act of visiting. **visitor** *n.*

visitation *n.* official visit; trouble regarded as divine punishment.

visor /vīzər/ *n.* movable front part of a helmet, covering the face; shading device at the top of a vehicle's windscreen.

vista *n.* extensive view, esp. seen through a long opening.

visual *a.* of or used in seeing. **visual display unit** device displaying a computer output or input on a screen. **visually** *adv.*

visualize *v.* form a mental picture of. **visualization** *n.*

vital *a.* essential to life; essential to a thing's existence or success; full of vitality. **vitals** *n.pl.* vital organs of the body. **vital statistics** those relating to population figures; (*colloq.*) measurements of a woman's bust, waist, and hips. **vitally** *adv.*

vitality *n.* liveliness, persistent energy.

vitamin *n.* any of the organic substances present in food and essential to nutrition.

vitaminize *v.* add vitamins to.

vitiate /víshiayt/ *v.* make imperfect or ineffective. **vitiation** *n.*

viticulture *n.* vine-growing.

vitreous *a.* having a glass-like texture or finish.

vitrify *v.* change into a glassy substance. **vitrifaction** *n.*

vitriol *n.* sulphuric acid; savagely hostile remarks. **vitriolic** *a.*

vituperate *v.* use abusive language. **vituperation** *n.*, **vituperative** *a.*

vivacious *a.* lively, high-spirited. **vivaciously** *adv.*, **vivacity** *n.*

vivarium *n.* (*pl.* **-ia**) place for keeping living animals etc. in natural conditions.

vivid *a.* bright and strong; clear; (of imagination) lively. **vividly** *adv.*, **vividness** *n.*

vivify *v.* put life into.

viviparous *a.* bringing forth young alive, not egg-laying.

vivisection *n.* performance of experiments on living animals.

vixen *n.* female fox.

viz. *adv.* namely.

vocabulary *n.* list of words with their meanings; words known or used by a person or group.

vocal *a.* of, for, or uttered by the voice. — *n.* piece of sung music. **vocally** *adv.*

vocalist *n.* singer.

vocalize *v.* utter. **vocalization** *n.*

vocation *n.* strong desire or feeling of

fitness for a certain career; trade, profession. **vocational** *a.*

vociferate *v.* say loudly, shout. **vociferation** *n.*

vociferous *a.* making a great outcry. **vociferously** *adv.*

vodka *n.* alcoholic spirit distilled chiefly from rye.

vogue *n.* current fashion; popularity. **in vogue** in fashion.

voice *n.* sounds formed in the larynx and uttered by the mouth; expressed opinion, right to express an opinion. — *v.* express; utter. **voice-over** *n.* narration in a film etc. without a picture of the speaker.

void *a.* empty; not valid. — *n.* empty space, emptiness. — *v.* make void; excrete.

voile *n.* very thin dress fabric.

volatile *a.* evaporating rapidly; lively, changing quickly in mood. **volatility** *n.*

vol-au-vent /vóllōvoN/ *n.* puff pastry case filled with a savoury mixture.

volcano *n.* (*pl.* **-oes**) mountain with a vent through which lava is expelled. **volcanic** *a.*

vole *n.* small rodent.

volition *n.* use of one's own will in making a decision etc.

volley *n.* (*pl.* **-eys**) simultaneous discharge of missiles etc.; outburst of questions or other words; return of the ball in tennis etc. before it touches the ground. — *v.* send in a volley.

volleyball *n.* game for two teams of six persons sending a large ball by hand over a net.

volt *n.* unit of electromotive force.

voltage *n.* electromotive force expressed in volts.

volte-face /voltfaáss/ *n.* complete change of attitude to something.

voluble *a.* speaking or spoken with a great flow of words. **volubly** *adv.*, **volubility** *n.*

volume *n.* book; amount of space occupied or contained; amount; strength of sound.

voluminous *a.* having great volume, bulky; copious.

voluntary *a.* done, given, or acting by choice; working or done without payment; maintained by voluntary contributions. **voluntarily** *adv.*

volunteer *n.* person who offers to do something; one who enrols voluntarily for military service. — *v.* undertake or offer voluntarily; be a volunteer.

voluptuary *n.* person fond of luxury etc.

voluptuous *a.* full of or fond of sensual pleasures; having a full attractive figure. **voluptuously** *adv.*, **voluptuousness** *n.*

vomit *v.* (**vomited**) eject (matter) from the stomach through the mouth. — *n.* vomited matter.

voodoo *n.* form of religion based on witchcraft. **voodooism** *n.*

voracious *a.* greedy; ravenous; insatiable. **voraciously** *adv.*, **voracity** *n.*

vortex *n.* (*pl.* **-exes** *or* **-ices**) whirlpool; whirlwind.

vote *n.* formal expression of one's opinion or choice on a matter under discussion; choice etc. expressed thus; right to vote. — *v.* express, decide, or support etc. by a vote. **voter** *n.*

votive *a.* given to fulfil a vow.

vouch *v.* **vouch for** guarantee the accuracy or reliability etc. of.

voucher *n.* document exchangeable for certain goods or services; a kind of receipt.

vow *n.* solemn promise, esp. to a deity or saint. — *v.* make a vow.

vowel *n.* speech sound made without audible stopping of the breath; letter(s) representing this.

voyage *n.* journey made by water or in space. — *v.* make a voyage. **voyager** *n.*

voyeur /vwaayŭr/ *n.* person who gets sexual pleasure from watching others having sex or undressing.

vulcanite *n.* hard black vulcanized rubber.

vulcanize *v.* strengthen (rubber) by treating with sulphur. **vulcanization** *n.*

vulgar *a.* lacking refinement or good taste. **vulgar fraction** one represented by numbers above and below a line. **vulgarly** *adv.*, **vulgarity** *n.*

vulgarian *n.* vulgar (esp. rich) person.

vulgarism *n.* vulgar word(s) etc.

vulnerable *a.* able to be hurt or injured; exposed to danger or criticism. **vulnerability** *n.*

vulture *n.* large bird of prey that lives on the flesh of dead animals.

vulva *n.* external parts of the female genital organs.

vying *see* **vie**.

W

W. *abbr.* west; western.

wad *n.* pad of soft material; bunch of papers or banknotes. — *v.* (**wadded**) pad.

wadding *n.* padding.

waddle *v.* & *n.* walk with short steps and a swaying movement.

wade *v.* walk through water or mud; proceed slowly and laboriously (through work etc.).

wader *n.* long-legged waterbird; (*pl.*) high waterproof boots worn in fishing etc.

wafer *n.* thin light biscuit; small thin slice. **wafery** *a.*

waffle [1] *n.* (*colloq.*) vague wordy talk or writing. — *v.* (*colloq.*) talk or write waffle.

waffle [2] *n.* small cake of batter eaten hot, cooked in a **waffle-iron**.

waft *v.* carry or travel lightly through air or over water. — *n.* wafted odour.

wag *v.* (**wagged**) shake briskly to and fro. — *n.* wagging movement; humorous person.

wage [1] *v.* engage in (war).

wage [2] *n.*, **wages** *n.pl.* regular payment to an employee for his or her work.

wager *n.* & *v.* bet.

waggle *v.* & *n.* wag.

waggon *n.* = wagon.

wagon *n.* four-wheeled goods vehicle pulled by horses or oxen; open railway truck.

wagtail *n.* small bird with a long tail that wags up and down.

waif *n.* homeless child.

wail *v.* & *n.* (utter) a long sad cry; lament.

wainscot *n.* wooden panelling in a room. **wainscoting** *n.*

waist *n.* part of the human body between ribs and hips; narrow middle part.

waistcoat *n.* close-fitting waist-length sleeveless jacket.

waistline *n.* outline or size of the waist.

wait *v.* postpone an action until a specified time or event occurs; be postponed; wait on people at a meal; pause. — *n.* act or period of waiting. **wait on** hand food and drink to (persons) at a meal; fetch and carry things for.

waiter *n.* man employed to wait on customers in a restaurant etc. **waitress** *n.fem.*

waive *v.* refrain from using (a right etc.). **waiver** *n.*

wake [1] *v.* (**woke** or **waked**, **woken** or **waked**) cease to sleep; cause to cease sleeping; evoke. — *n.* (*Ir.*) watch by a corpse before burial; attendant lamentations and merrymaking. **wake up** wake; make or become alert.

wake [2] *n.* track left on water's surface by a ship etc. **in the wake of** behind; following.

wakeful *a.* unable to sleep; sleepless. **wakefulness** *n.*

waken *v.* wake.

walk *v.* progress by setting down one foot and then lifting the other(s) in turn; travel (over) in this way; accompany in walking. — *n.* journey on foot; manner or style of walking; place or route for walking. **walk of life** social rank; occupation. **walk out** depart suddenly and angrily; go on strike suddenly. (**walk-out** *n.*). **walk out on** desert. **walkover** *n.* easy victory. **walker** *n.*

walkabout *n.* informal stroll among a crowd by royalty etc.

walkie-talkie *n.* small portable radio transmitter and receiver.

walking stick stick carried or used as a support when walking.

wall *n.* continuous upright structure forming one side of a building or room or area; thing like this in form or function. — *v.* surround or enclose with a wall.

wallaby *n.* small species of kangaroo.

wallet *n.* small folding case for banknotes or documents.

wallflower *n.* garden plant with fragrant flowers.

wallop *v.* (**walloped**) (*sl.*) thrash, hit hard. — *n.* (*sl.*) heavy blow; beer or other drink.

wallow *v.* roll in mud or water etc. — *n.* act of wallowing. **wallow in** take unrestrained pleasure in.

wallpaper *n.* paper for covering the interior walls of rooms.

wally *n.* (*sl.*) stupid person.

walnut *n.* nut containing a wrinkled edible kernel; tree bearing this; its wood.

walrus *n.* large seal-like Arctic animal with long tusks.

waltz *n.* ballroom dance; music for this. — *v.* dance a waltz; (*colloq.*) move gaily or casually.

wan *a.* pallid. **wanly** *adv.*, **wanness** *n.*

wand *n.* slender rod, esp. associated with the working of magic.

wander *v.* go from place to place with no settled route or purpose; stray; digress. —*n.* act of wandering. **wanderer** *n.*
wanderlust *n.* strong desire to travel.
wane *v.* decrease in vigour or importance; (of the moon) show a decreasing bright area after being full. **on the wane** waning.
wangle *v.* (*sl.*) obtain or arrange by using trickery or scheming.
want *v.* desire; need; lack; fall short of. —*n.* desire; need; lack.
wanted *a.* (of a suspected criminal) sought by the police.
wanting *a.* lacking, deficient.
wanton *a.* irresponsible, lacking proper restraint.
wapiti /wóppiti/ *n.* large North American deer.
war *n.* (a period of) fighting (esp. between countries); open hostility; conflict. —*v.* (**warred**) make war. **at war** engaged in a war.
warble *v.* sing, esp. with a gentle trilling note. —*n.* warbling sound.
ward *n.* room with beds for patients in a hospital; division of a city or town, electing a councillor to represent it; person (esp. a child) under the care of a guardian or law court. —*v.* **ward off** keep at a distance; repel.
warden *n.* official with supervisory duties; churchwarden.
warder *n.* prison officer.
wardrobe *n.* large cupboard for storing hanging clothes; stock of clothes or costumes.
ware *n.* manufactured goods of the kind specified; (*pl.*) articles offered for sale.
warehouse *n.* building for storing goods or furniture.
warfare *n.* making war, fighting.
warhead *n.* explosive head of a missile.
warlike *a.* fond of making war, aggressive; of or for war.
warm *a.* moderately hot; providing warmth; enthusiastic, hearty; kindly and affectionate. —*v.* make or become warm. **warm-blooded** *a.* having blood that remains warm permanently. **warm to** become cordial towards (a person) or more animated about (a task). **warm up** warm; reheat; prepare for exercise etc. by practice beforehand; make or become more lively. **warmly** *adv.*, **warmness** *n.*
warmonger *n.* person who seeks to bring about war.
warmth *n.* warmness.
warn *v.* inform about a present or future danger or difficulty etc., advise about action in this. **warn off** tell (a person) to keep away or to avoid (a thing).
warning *n.* thing that serves to warn a person.
warp *v.* make or become bent by uneven shrinkage or expansion; distort, pervert. —*n.* warped condition; lengthwise threads in a loom.
warrant *n.* written authorization; voucher; proof, guarantee. —*v.* justify; prove, guarantee.
warranty *n.* guarantee.
warren *n.* series of burrows where rabbits live; building or district with many winding passages.
warrior *n.* person who fights in a battle.
wart *n.* small hard abnormal growth. **warthog** *n.* African wild pig with wart-like growths on its face. **warty** *a.*
wary *a.* (**-ier, -iest**) cautious, looking out for possible danger or difficulty. **warily** *adv.*, **wariness** *n.*
wash *v.* cleanse with water or other liquid; wash oneself or clothes etc.; be washable; flow past or against or over; carry by flowing; coat thinly with paint; (*colloq.*, of reasoning) be valid. —*n.* process of washing or being washed; clothes etc. to be washed; disturbed water or air behind a moving ship or aircraft etc.; thin coating of paint. **washed out** faded; pallid. **washed up** (*sl.*) defeated, having failed. **wash one's hands of** refuse to take responsibility for. **wash out** make (a sport) impossible by heavy rainfall; (*colloq.*) cancel. **wash-out** *n.* (*sl.*) complete failure. **wash up** wash (dishes etc.) after use; cast up on the shore.
washable *a.* able to be washed without suffering damage.
washbasin *n.* bowl (usu. fixed to a wall) for washing one's hands and face.
washer *n.* ring of rubber or metal etc. placed between two surfaces to give tightness.
washing *n.* clothes etc. to be washed. **washing-up** *n.* dishes etc. for washing after use; process of washing these.
washroom *n.* (*US*) room with a lavatory.
washy *a.* too watery or weak; lacking vigour.
wasp *n.* stinging insect with a black and yellow striped body.
waspish *a.* making sharp or irritable comments. **waspishly** *adv.*
wastage *n.* loss or diminution by waste; loss of employees by retirement or resignation.
waste *v.* use or be used extravagantly or without adequate result; fail to use; make or become gradually weaker. —*a.*

left or thrown away because not wanted; (of land) unfit for use. — *n.* process of wasting; waste material or food etc.; waste land; waste pipe. **waste pipe** pipe carrying off used or superfluous water or steam.

wasteful *a.* extravagant. **wastefully** *adv.*, **wastefulness** *n.*

waster *n.* wasteful person; good-for-nothing person.

watch *v.* keep under observation; wait alertly, take heed; exercise protective care. — *n.* act of watching, constant observation or attention; sailor's period of duty, persons on duty in this; small portable device indicating the time. **on the watch** waiting alertly. **watch out** be on one's guard. **watch-tower** *n.* tower from which observation can be kept. **watcher** *n.*

watchdog *n.* dog kept to guard property; guardian of people's rights etc.

watchful *a.* watching closely. **watchfully** *adv.*, **watchfulness** *n.*

watchmaker *n.* person who makes or repairs watches.

watchman *n.* (*pl.* **-men**) man employed to guard a building etc.

watchword *n.* word or phrase expressing a group's principles.

water *n.* colourless odourless tasteless liquid that is a compound of hydrogen and oxygen; this as supplied for domestic use; lake, sea; watery secretion, urine; level of the tide. — *v.* sprinkle, supply, or dilute with water; secrete tears or saliva. **by water** in a boat etc. **water-bed** *n.* mattress of rubber etc. filled with water. **water-biscuit** *n.* thin unsweetened biscuit. **water-butt** *n.* barrel used to catch rainwater. **water-cannon** *n.* device giving a powerful jet of water to dispel a crowd etc. **water-closet** *n.* lavatory flushed by water. **water colour** artists' paint mixed with water (not oil); painting done with this. **water down** dilute; make less forceful. **water ice** frozen flavoured water. **water lily** plant with broad floating leaves. **water main** main pipe in a water supply system. **water-meadow** *n.* meadow that is flooded periodically by a stream. **water melon** melon with red pulp and watery juice. **water-mill** *n.* mill worked by a waterwheel. **water-pistol** *n.* toy pistol that shoots a jet of water. **water polo** ball game played by teams of swimmers. **water-power** *n.* power obtained from flowing or falling water. **water-rat** *n.* small rodent living beside a lake or stream. **water-skiing** *n.* sport of skimming over water on flat boards while towed by a motor boat. **water-table** *n.* level below which the ground is saturated with water. **water-wings** *n.pl.* floats worn on the shoulders by a person learning to swim.

waterbrash *n.* watery fluid brought up from the stomach.

watercourse *n.* stream, brook, or artificial waterway; its channel.

watercress *n.* a kind of cress that grows in streams and ponds.

waterfall *n.* stream that falls from a height.

waterfront *n.* part of a town that borders on a river, lake, or sea.

watering-can *n.* container with a spout for watering plants.

watering place pool where animals drink; spa, seaside resort.

waterline *n.* line along which the surface of water touches a ship's side.

waterlogged *a.* saturated with water.

watermark *n.* manufacturer's design in paper, visible when the paper is held against light.

waterproof *a.* unable to be penetrated by water. — *n.* waterproof garment. — *v.* make waterproof.

watershed *n.* line of high land separating two river systems; turning point in the course of events.

waterspout *n.* column of water between sea and cloud, formed by a whirlwind.

watertight *a.* made or fastened so that water cannot get in or out; impossible to disprove.

waterway *n.* navigable channel.

waterwheel *n.* wheel turned by a flow of water to work machinery.

waterworks *n.* establishment with machinery etc. for supplying water to a district.

watery *a.* of or like water; containing too much water; (of colour) pale. **wateriness** *n.*

watt *n.* unit of electric power.

wattage *n.* amount of electric power, expressed in watts.

wattle [1] *n.* interwoven sticks used as material for fences, walls, etc.

wattle [2] *n.* fold of skin hanging from the neck of a turkey etc.

wave *n.* moving ridge of water; wave-like curve(s), e.g. in hair; advancing group; temporary increase of an influence or condition; act of waving; wave-like motion by which heat, light, sound, or electricity etc. is spread; single curve in this. — *v.* move loosely to and fro or up and down; move (one's arm etc.) thus as a signal; give or have a wavy course or appearance.

waveband *n.* range of wavelengths.

wavelength *n.* distance between corresponding points in a sound wave or electromagnetic wave.
wavelet *n.* small wave.
waver *v.* be or become unsteady; show hesitation or uncertainty. **waverer** *n.*
wavy *a.* (**-ier, -iest**) full of wave-like curves.
wax [1] *n.* beeswax; any of various similar soft substances; polish containing this. — *v.* coat, polish, or treat with wax. **waxy** *a.*
wax [2] *v.* increase in vigour or importance; (of the moon) show an increasing bright area until becoming full.
waxwing *n.* small bird with red tips on some of its wing-feathers.
waxwork *n.* wax model, esp. of a person.
way *n.* line of communication between two places; route; space free of obstacles so that people etc. can pass; progress; specified direction or aspect; method, style, manner; chosen or desired course of action; (*pl.*) habits. — *adv.* (*colloq.*) far. **by the way** incidentally, as an irrelevant comment. **by way of** by going through; serving as. **in a way** to a limited extent; in some respects. **in the way** forming an obstacle or hindrance. **on one's way** in the process of travelling or approaching. **on the way** on one's way; (of a baby) conceived but not yet born.
waybill *n.* list of the passengers or goods being carried by a vehicle.
wayfarer *n.* traveller.
waylay *v.* (**-laid**) lie in wait for.
wayside *n.* side of a road or path.
wayward *a.* childishly self-willed, hard to control. **waywardness** *n.*
we *pron.* used by a person referring to himself or herself and another or others; used instead of 'I' in newspaper editorials and by a royal person in formal proclamations.
weak *a.* lacking strength or power; not convincing; much diluted. **weak-kneed** *a.*, **weak-minded** *a.* lacking determination. **weakly** *adv.*
weaken *v.* make or become weaker.
weakling *n.* feeble person or animal.
weakness *n.* state of being weak; weak point, fault; self-indulgent liking.
weal *n.* ridge raised on flesh esp. by the stroke of a rod or whip.
wealth *n.* money and valuable possessions; possession of these; great quantity.
wealthy *a.* (**-ier, -iest**) having wealth, rich. **wealthiness** *n.*
wean *v.* accustom (a baby) to take food other than milk; cause to give up something gradually.
weapon *n.* thing designed or used for inflicting harm or damage; means of coercing someone.
wear *v.* (**wore, worn**) have on the body as clothing or ornament; damage or become damaged by prolonged use; endure continued use. — *n.* wearing, being worn; clothing; capacity to endure being used. **wear down** overcome (opposition etc.) by persistence. **wear off** pass off gradually. **wear out** use or be used until no longer usable; tire or become tired out. **wearer** *n.*, **wearable** *a.*
wearisome *a.* causing weariness.
weary *a.* (**-ier, -iest**) very tired; tiring, tedious. — *v.* make or become weary. **wearily** *adv.*, **weariness** *n.*
weasel *n.* small wild animal with a slender body and reddish-brown fur.
weather *n.* state of the atmosphere with reference to sunshine, rain, wind, etc. — *v.* (cause to) be changed by exposure to the weather; come safely through (a storm). **under the weather** feeling unwell or depressed. **weather-beaten** *a.* bronzed or worn by exposure to weather. **weather vane** weathercock.
weatherboard *n.* sloping board for keeping out rain.
weathercock *n.* revolving pointer to show the direction of the wind.
weave [1] *v.* (**wove, woven**) make (fabric etc.) by passing crosswise threads or strips under and over lengthwise ones; form (thread etc.) into fabric thus; compose (a story etc.). — *n.* style or pattern of weaving.
weave [2] *v.* move in an intricate course.
weaver *n.* person who weaves; tropical bird that builds an intricately woven nest.
web *n.* network of fine strands made by a spider etc.; skin filling the spaces between the toes of ducks, frogs, etc. **web-footed** *a.* having toes joined by web.
webbing *n.* strong band(s) of woven fabric used in upholstery.
wed *v.* (**wedded**) marry; unite.
wedding *n.* marriage ceremony and festivities.
wedge *n.* piece of solid substance thick at one end and tapering to a thin edge at the other. — *v.* force apart or fix firmly with a wedge; crowd tightly.
wedlock *n.* married state.
wee *a.* (*Sc.*) little; (*colloq.*) tiny.
weed *n.* wild plant growing where it is not wanted; thin weak-looking person. — *v.* uproot and remove weeds (from). **weed out** remove as inferior or undesirable. **weedy** *a.*
week *n.* period of seven successive days,

esp. from Monday to Sunday or Sunday to Saturday; the weekdays of this; working period during a week.

weekday *n.* day other than Sunday and usu. Saturday.

weekend *n.* Saturday and Sunday.

weekly *a.* & *adv.* (produced or occurring) once a week. — *n.* weekly periodical.

weeny *a.* (**-ier**, **-iest**) (*colloq.*) tiny.

weep *v.* (**wept**) shed (tears); shed or ooze (moisture) in drops. — *n.* spell of weeping. **weeper** *n.*, **weepy** *a.*

weeping *a.* (of a tree) having drooping branches.

weevil *n.* small beetle that feeds on grain, nuts, tree-bark, etc.

weft *n.* crosswise threads in weaving.

weigh *v.* measure the weight of; have a specified weight; consider the relative importance of; have influence; be burdensome. **weigh anchor** raise the anchor and start a voyage. **weigh down** bring or keep down by its weight; depress, oppress. **weigh up** form an estimate of.

weighbridge *n.* weighing machine with a plate set in a road etc. for weighing vehicles.

weight *n.* object's mass numerically expressed using a recognized scale of units; unit or system of units used thus; piece of metal of known weight used in weighing; heavy object; heaviness; load; influence. — *v.* attach a weight to; hold down with a weight; burden; bias. **weightless** *a.*, **weightlessness** *n.*

weighting *n.* extra pay given in special cases.

weighty *a.* (**-ier**, **-iest**) heavy; showing or deserving earnest thought; influential.

weir *n.* small dam built so that some of a stream's water flows over it; waterfall formed thus.

weird *a.* uncanny, bizarre. **weirdly** *adv.*, **weirdness** *n.*

welcome *a.* received with pleasure; freely permitted. — *int.* greeting expressing pleasure. — *n.* kindly greeting or reception. — *v.* give a welcome to; receive gladly.

weld *v.* unite or fuse (pieces of metal) by heating or pressure; unite into a whole. — *n.* welded joint. **welder** *n.*

welfare *n.* well-being; organized efforts to ensure people's well-being. **Welfare State** country with highly developed social services.

well [1] *n.* shaft sunk to obtain water or oil etc.; enclosed shaft-like space. — *v.* rise or spring.

well [2] *adv.* (**better**, **best**) in a good manner or style, rightly; thoroughly; favourably, kindly; with good reason; easily; probably. — *a.* in good health; satisfactory. — *int.* expressing surprise, relief, or resignation etc., or said when one is hesitating. **as well** in addition; desirable; desirably. **as well as** in addition to. **well-appointed** *a.* well-equipped. **well-being** *n.* good health, happiness, and prosperity. **well-disposed** *a.* having kindly or favourable feelings. **well-heeled** *a.* (*colloq.*) wealthy. **well-meaning** *a.*, **well-meant** *a.* acting or done with good intentions. **well off** in a satisfactory or good situation; fairly rich. **well-read** *a.* having read much literature. **well-spoken** *a.* speaking in a polite and correct way. **well-to-do** *a.* fairly rich.

wellington *n.* boot of rubber or other waterproof material.

well-nigh *adv.* almost.

Welsh *a.* & *n.* (language) of Wales. **Welsh rabbit** *or* **rarebit** melted or toasted cheese on toast. **Welshman** *n.* (*pl.* **-men**), **Welshwoman** *n.* (*pl.* **-women**).

welsh *v.* avoid paying one's debts; break an agreement. **welsher** *n.*

welt *n.* leather rim attaching the top of a boot or shoe to the sole; ribbed or strengthened border of a knitted garment; weal. — *v.* provide with a welt; raise weals on, thrash.

welter *n.* turmoil; disorderly mixture.

wen *n.* benign tumour on the skin.

wend *v.* **wend one's way** go.

went *see* **go**.

wept *see* **weep**.

werewolf /wéerwoolf/ *n.* (*pl.* **-wolves**) (in myths) person who at times turns into a wolf.

west *n.* point on the horizon where the sun sets; direction in which this lies; western part. — *a.* in the west; (of wind) from the west. — *adv.* towards the west. **go west** (*sl.*) be destroyed or lost or killed.

westerly *a.* towards or blowing from the west.

western *a.* of or in the west. — *n.* film or novel about cowboys in western North America.

westerner *n.* native or inhabitant of the west.

westernize *v.* make (an oriental country etc.) more like a western one in ideas and institutions. **westernization** *n.*

westernmost *a.* further west.

westward *a.* towards the west. **westwards** *adv.*

wet *a.* (**wetter**, **wettest**) soaked or covered with water or other liquid; rainy; not dry;

(*colloq.*) lacking vitality. — *v.* (**wetted**) make wet. — *n.* moisture, water; wet weather. **wet blanket** gloomy person. **wet-nurse** *n.* woman employed to suckle another's child; (*v.*) act as wet-nurse to, coddle as if helpless. **wetsuit** porous garment worn by a skin diver etc. **wetly** *adv.*, **wetness** *n.*

wether *n.* castrated ram.

whack *v.* & *n.* (*colloq.*) hit. **do one's whack** (*sl.*) do one's share.

whacked *a.* (*colloq.*) tired out.

whale *n.* very large sea mammal. **a whale of a** (*colloq.*) an exceedingly great or good (thing).

whalebone *n.* horny substance from the upper jaw of whales, formerly used as stiffening.

whaler *n.* whaling ship; seaman hunting whales.

whaling *n.* hunting whales.

wham *int.* & *n.* sound of a forcible impact.

wharf *n.* (*pl.* **wharfs**) landing stage where ships load and unload.

what *a.* asking for a statement of amount or number or kind; how great or remarkable; the or any that. — *pron.* what thing(s); what did you say? *adv.* to what extent or degree. — *int.* exclamation of surprise. **what about** what is the news or your opinion about (a subject)? **what's what** what things are important.

whatever *a.* of any kind or number. — *pron.* anything or everything; no matter what.

whatnot *n.* something trivial or indefinite.

whatsoever *a.* & *pron.* whatever.

wheat *n.* grain from which flour is made; plant producing this.

wheatear *n.* a kind of small bird.

wheaten *a.* made from wheat.

wheedle *v.* coax.

wheel *n.* disc or circular frame that revolves on a shaft passing through its centre; wheel-like motion. — *v.* push or pull (a cart or bicycle etc.) along; turn; move in circles or curves. **at the wheel** driving a vehicle, directing a ship; in control of affairs. **wheel and deal** engage in scheming to exert influence. **wheel-clamp** *v.* fix a clamp on (an illegally parked car etc.).

wheelbarrow *n.* open container for moving small loads, with a wheel at one end.

wheelbase *n.* distance between a vehicle's front and rear axles.

wheelchair *n.* chair on wheels for a person who cannot walk.

wheeze *v.* breathe with a hoarse whistling sound. — *n.* this sound. **wheezy** *a.*

whelk *n.* shellfish with a spiral shell.

whelp *n.* young dog, pup. — *v.* give birth to (a whelp or whelps).

when *adv.* at what time, on what occasion; at which time. — *conj.* at the time that; whenever; as soon as; although. — *pron.* what or which time.

whence *adv.* & *conj.* from where; from which.

whenever *conj.* & *adv.* at whatever time; every time that.

where *adv.* & *conj.* at or in which place or circumstances; in what respect; from what place or source; to what place. — *pron.* what place.

whereabouts *adv.* in or near what place. — *n.* a person's or thing's approximate location.

whereas *adv.* since it is the fact that; but in contrast.

whereby *adv.* by which.

whereupon *adv.* after which, and then.

wherever *adv.* at or to whatever place.

wherewith *adv.* with what, with which.

wherewithal *n.* things (esp. money) needed for a purpose.

wherry *n.* light rowing boat; large light barge.

whet *v.* (**whetted**) sharpen by rubbing against a stone etc.; stimulate (appetite or interest).

whether *conj.* introducing an alternative possibility.

whetstone *n.* shaped hard stone used for sharpening tools.

whey *n.* watery liquid left when milk forms curds.

which *a.* & *pron.* what particular one(s) of a set; and that. — *rel.pron.* thing or animal referred to.

whichever *a.* & *pron.* any which, that or those which.

whiff *n.* puff of air or odour etc.

while *n.* period of time; time spent in doing something. — *conj.* during the time that, as long as; although; on the other hand. — *v.* **while away** pass (time) in a leisurely or interesting way.

whilst *conj.* while.

whim *n.* sudden fancy.

whimper *v.* make feeble crying sounds. — *n.* whimpering sound.

whimsical *a.* impulsive and playful; fanciful, quaint. **whimsically** *adv.*, **whimsicality** *n.*

whine *v.* make a long high complaining cry or a similar shrill sound; complain or utter with a whine. — *n.* whining sound or complaint. **whiner** *n.*

whinge *v.* (*colloq.*) whine, complain.

whinny *n.* gentle or joyful neigh. — *v.* utter a whinny.

whip *n.* cord or strip of leather on a handle, used for striking a person or animal; food made with whipped cream etc. — *v.* (**whipped**) strike or urge on with a whip; beat into a froth; move or take suddenly; (*sl.*) steal. **have the whip hand** have control. **whip-round** *n.* appeal for contributions from a group. **whip up** incite.

whipcord *n.* cord of tightly twisted strands; twilled fabric with prominent ridges.

whiplash *n.* lash of a whip; jerk.

whippet *n.* small dog resembling a greyhound, used for racing.

whipping-boy *n.* scapegoat.

whippy *a.* flexible, springy.

whirl *v.* swing or spin round and round; convey or go rapidly in a vehicle. — *n.* whirling movement; confused state; bustling activity.

whirlpool *n.* current of water whirling in a circle.

whirlwind *n.* mass of air whirling rapidly about a central point.

whirr *n.* continuous buzzing or vibrating sound. — *v.* make this sound.

whisk *v.* convey or go rapidly; brush away lightly; beat into a froth. — *n.* whisking movement; instrument for beating eggs etc.; bunch of bristles etc. for brushing or flicking things.

whisker *n.* long hair-like bristle near the mouth of a cat etc.; (*pl.*) hair growing on a man's cheek. **whiskered** *a.*, **whiskery** *a.*

whiskey *n.* Irish whisky.

whisky *n.* spirit distilled from malted grain (esp. barley).

whisper *v.* speak or utter softly, not using the vocal cords; rustle. — *n.* whispering sound or speech or remark; rumour.

whist *n.* card game usu. for two pairs of players.

whistle *n.* shrill sound made by blowing through a narrow opening between the lips; similar sound; instrument for producing this. — *v.* make this sound; signal or produce (a tune) in this way. **whistler** *n.*

Whit *a.* of or close to **Whit Sunday**, seventh Sunday after Easter.

white *a.* of the colour of snow or common salt; having a light-coloured skin; pale from illness or fear etc. — *n.* white colour or thing; transparent substance round egg yolk; **White** member of the race with light-coloured skin. **white ant** termite. **white coffee** coffee with milk or cream. **white-collar worker** one not engaged in manual labour. **white elephant** useless possession. **white hope** person expected to achieve much. **white horses** white-crested waves on sea. **white-hot** *a.* (of metal) glowing white after heating. **white lie** harmless lie. **white sale** sale of household linen. **white spirit** light petroleum used as a solvent. **white wine** wine of yellow colour. **whitely** *adv.*, **whiteness** *n.*

whitebait *n.* (*pl.* **whitebait**) small silvery-white fish.

whiten *v.* make or become white or whiter.

whitewash *n.* liquid containing quicklime or powdered chalk, used for painting walls or ceilings etc.; means of glossing over mistakes. — *v.* paint with whitewash; gloss over mistakes in.

whither *adv.* (*old use*) to what place.

whiting *n.* (*pl.* **whiting**) small sea fish used as food.

whitlow *n.* small abscess under or affecting a nail.

Whitsun *n.* Whit Sunday and the days close to it. **Whitsuntide** *n.*

whittle *v.* trim (wood) by cutting thin slices from the surface; reduce by removing various amounts.

whiz *v.* (**whizzed**) make a sound like something moving at great speed through air; move very quickly. — *n.* whizzing sound. **whiz-kid** *n.* (*colloq.*) brilliant or successful young person.

who *pron.* what or which person(s)?; the particular person(s).

whodunit *n.* (*colloq.*) detective or mystery story or play etc.

whoever *pron.* any or every person who, no matter who.

whole *a.* with no part removed or left out; not injured or broken. — *n.* full amount, all parts or members; complete system made up of parts. **on the whole** considering everything; in respect of the whole though some details form exceptions. **wholehearted** *a.* without doubts or reservations. **whole number** number consisting of one or more units with no fractions.

wholemeal *a.* made from the whole grain of wheat etc.

wholesale *n.* selling of goods in large quantities to be retailed by others. — *a.* & *adv.* in the wholesale trade; on a large scale. **wholesaler** *n.*

wholesome *a.* good for health or well-being. **wholesomeness** *n.*

wholly *adv.* entirely.

whom *pron.* objective case of *who*.

whoop *v.* utter a loud cry of excitement. — *n.* this cry.

whooping cough infectious disease esp. of children, with a violent convulsive cough.

whopper *n.* (*sl.*) something very large; great lie.

whore *n.* prostitute.
whorl *n.* coiled form, one turn of a spiral; circle of ridges in a fingerprint; ring of leaves or petals.
whose *pron.* of whom; of which.
whosoever *pron.* whoever.
why *adv.* for what reason or purpose?; on account of which. — *int.* exclamation of surprised discovery or recognition.
wick *n.* length of thread in a candle or lamp etc., by which the flame is kept supplied with melted grease or fuel.
wicked *a.* morally bad, offending against what is right; formidable, severe; mischievous. **wickedly** *adv.*, **wickedness** *n.*
wicker *n.* osiers or thin canes interwoven to make furniture or baskets etc. **wickerwork** *n.*
wicket *n.* set of three stumps and two bails used in cricket; part of a cricket ground between or near the two wickets.
wide *a.* measuring much from side to side; having a specified width; extending far; fully opened; far from the target. — *adv.* widely. **wide awake** fully awake or (*colloq.*) alert. **widely** *adv.*, **wideness** *n.*
widen *v.* make or become wider.
widespread *a.* found or distributed over a wide area.
widgeon *n.* wild duck.
widow *n.* woman whose husband has died and who has not remarried. **widowhood** *n.*
widowed *a.* made a widow or widower.
widower *n.* man whose wife has died and who has not remarried.
width *n.* wideness; distance from side to side; piece of material of full width as woven.
wield *v.* hold and use (a tool etc.); have and use (power).
wife *n.* (*pl.* **wives**) married woman in relation to her husband. **wifely** *a.*
wig *n.* covering of hair worn on the head.
wiggle *v.* & *n.* move repeatedly from side to side, wriggle.
wigwam *n.* conical tent as formerly used by North American Indians.
wild *a.* not domesticated or tame or cultivated; not civilized; disorderly; stormy; full of strong unrestrained feeling; extremely foolish; random. — *adv.* in a wild manner. — *n.* (usu. *pl.*) desolate uninhabited place. **wild-goose chase** useless quest. **wildly** *adv.*, **wildness** *n.*
wildcat *a.* reckless; (of strikes) unofficial and irresponsible.
wildebeest *n.* gnu.
wilderness *n.* wild uncultivated area.
wildfire *n.* **spread like wildfire** spread very fast.
wildfowl *n.* birds hunted as game.
wildlife *n.* wild animals and plants.
wile *n.* piece of trickery.
wilful *a.* intentional, not accidental; self-willed. **wilfully** *adv.*, **wilfulness** *n.*
will [1] *v.aux.* used with *I* and *we* to express promises or obligations, and with other words to express a future tense.
will [2] *n.* mental faculty by which a person decides upon and controls his or her actions; determination; person's attitude in wishing good or bad to others; written directions made by a person for disposal of their property after their death. — *v.* exercise one's will-power, influence by doing this; bequeath by a will. **at will** whenever one pleases. **have one's will** get what one desires. **will-power** *n.* control exercised by one's will.
willing *a.* desiring to do what is required, not objecting; given or done readily. — *n.* willingness. **willingly** *adv.*, **willingness** *n.*
will-o'-the-wisp *n.* phosphorescent light seen on marshy ground; hope or aim that can never be fulfilled.
willow *n.* tree or shrub with flexible branches; its wood.
willowy *a.* full of willows; slender and supple.
willy *n.* (*sl.*) penis.
willy-nilly *adv.* whether one desires it or not.
wilt *v.* lose or cause to lose freshness and droop; become limp from exhaustion.
wily /wīli/ *a.* (**-ier, -iest**) full of wiles, cunning. **wiliness** *n.*
wimp *n.* (*sl.*) feeble or ineffective person.
win *v.* (**won, winning**) be victorious (in); obtain as the result of a contest etc., or by effort; gain the favour or support of. — *n.* victory, esp. in a game.
wince *v.* make a slight movement from pain or embarrassment etc. — *n.* this movement.
winceyette *n.* cotton fabric with a soft downy surface.
winch *n.* machine for hoisting or pulling things by a cable that winds round a revolving drum. — *v.* hoist or pull with a winch.
wind [1] /wind/ *n.* current of air; gas in the stomach or intestines; breath as needed in exertion or speech etc.; orchestra's wind instruments; useless or boastful talk. — *v.* detect by a smell; cause to be out of breath. **get wind of** hear a hint or rumour of. **in the wind** happening or about to happen. **put the wind up** (*colloq.*) frighten. **take the wind out of a person's sails** take away an

advantage, frustrate by anticipating him or her. **wind-break** *n.* screen shielding something from the wind. **wind-chill** *n.* cooling effect of the wind. **wind instrument** musical instrument sounded by a current of air, esp. by the player's breath. **wind-sock** *n.* canvas cylinder flown at an airfield to show the direction of the wind. **wind-tunnel** *n.* enclosed tunnel in which winds can be created for testing things.

wind² /wīnd/ *v.* (**wound**) move or go in a curving or spiral course; wrap closely around something or round upon itself; move by turning a windlass or handle etc.; wind up (a clock etc.). **wind up** set or keep (a clock etc.) going by tightening its spring; bring or come to an end; settle the affairs of and close (a business company). **winder** *n.*

windbag *n.* (*colloq.*) person who talks lengthily.

windfall *n.* fruit blown off a tree by the wind; unexpected gain, esp. a sum of money.

windlass *n.* winch-like device using a rope or chain that winds round a horizontal roller.

windmill *n.* mill worked by the action of wind on projecting parts that radiate from a shaft.

window *n.* opening in a wall etc. to admit light and often air, usu. filled with glass; this glass; space for display of goods behind the window of a shop. **window-box** *n.* trough fixed outside a window, for growing flowers etc. **window-dressing** *n.* arranging a display of goods in a shop window; presentation of facts so as to give a favourable impression. **window-shopping** *n.* looking at displayed goods without buying.

windpipe *n.* air passage from the throat to the bronchial tubes.

windscreen *n.* glass in the window at the front of a vehicle.

windsurfing *n.* sport of surfing on a board to which a sail is fixed.

windswept *a.* exposed to strong winds.

windward *a.* situated in the direction from which the wind blows. — *n.* this side or region.

wine *n.* fermented grape-juice as an alcoholic drink; fermented drink made from other fruits or plants; dark red. — *v.* drink wine; entertain with wine. **wine bar** bar or small restaurant serving wine as the main drink.

wing *n.* each of a pair of projecting parts by which a bird or insect etc. is able to fly; wing-like part of an aircraft; projecting part; bodywork above the wheel of a car; either end of a battle array; player at either end of the forward line in football or hockey etc., side part of playing area in these games; extreme section of a political party; (*pl.*) sides of a theatre stage. — *v.* fly, travel by wings; wound slightly in the wing or arm. **on the wing** flying. **take wing** fly away. **under one's wing** under one's protection. **wing-collar** *n.* high stiff collar with turned-down corners.

winged *a.* having wings.

winger *n.* wing player in football etc.

wink *v.* blink one eye as a signal; shine with a light that flashes or twinkles. — *n.* act of winking. **not a wink** no sleep at all.

winker *n.* flashing indicator.

winkle *n.* edible sea snail. — *v.* **winkle out** extract, prise out.

winner *n.* person or thing that wins; something successful.

winning *see* **win**. — *a.* charming, persuasive. **winning post** post marking the end of a race. **winnings** *n.pl.* money won in betting etc.

winnow *v.* fan or toss (grain) to free it of chaff.

winsome *a.* charming.

winter *n.* coldest season of the year. — *v.* spend the winter. **wintry** *a.*

winy *a.* wine-flavoured.

wipe *v.* clean or dry or remove by rubbing; spread thinly on a surface. — *n.* act of wiping. **wipe out** cancel; destroy completely.

wiper *n.* device that automatically wipes rain etc. from a windscreen.

wire *n.* strand of metal; length of this used for fencing, conducting electric current, etc. — *v.* provide or fasten or strengthen with wire(s). **wire-haired** *a.* having stiff wiry hair.

wireworm *n.* destructive larva of a beetle.

wiring *n.* system of electric wires in a building, vehicle, etc.

wiry *a.* (**-ier**, **-iest**) like wire; lean but strong. **wiriness** *n.*

wisdom *n.* being wise, soundness of judgement; wise sayings. **wisdom tooth** hindmost molar tooth, not usu. cut before the age of 20.

wise *a.* showing soundness of judgement; having knowledge. **wisely** *adv.*

wiseacre *n.* person who pretends to have great wisdom.

wisecrack *n.* (*colloq.*) witty remark. — *v.* (*colloq.*) make a wisecrack.

wish *n.* desire, mental aim; expression of desire. — *v.* have or express as a wish; hope or express hope about another person's welfare; (*colloq.*) foist.

wishbone *n.* forked bone between a bird's neck and breast.
wishful *a.* desiring. **wishful thinking** belief founded on wishes not facts.
wishy-washy *a.* weak in colour, character, etc.
wisp *n.* small separate bunch; small streak of smoke etc. **wispy** *a.*, **wispiness** *n.*
wisteria *n.* climbing shrub with hanging clusters of flowers.
wistful *a.* full of sad or vague longing. **wistfully** *adv.*, **wistfulness** *n.*
wit *n.* amusing ingenuity in expressing words or ideas; person who has this; intelligence. **at one's wits' end** worried and not knowing what to do.
witch *n.* person (esp. a woman) who practises witchcraft; bewitching woman. **witch-doctor** *n.* tribal magician. **witch hazel** North American shrub; astringent lotion made from its leaves and bark. **witch-hunt** *n.* persecution of persons thought to be witches or holders of unpopular views.
witchcraft *n.* practice of magic.
with *prep.* in the company of, among; having, characterized by; by means of; of the same opinion as; at the same time as; because of; under the conditions of; by addition or possession of; in regard to, towards.
withdraw *v.* (**withdrew, withdrawn**) take back; remove (deposited money) from a bank etc.; cancel (a statement); go away from a place or from company. **withdrawal** *n.*
withdrawn *a.* (of a person) unsociable.
wither *v.* shrivel, lose freshness or vitality; subdue by scorn.
withhold *v.* (**withheld**) refuse to give; restrain.
within *prep.* inside; not beyond the limit or scope of; in a time no longer than. — *adv.* inside.
without *prep.* not having; in the absence of; with no action of. — *adv.* outside.
withstand *v.* (**withstood**) endure successfully.
withy *n.* tough flexible willow branch or osier etc., used for tying things.
witless *a.* foolish.
witness *n.* person who sees or hears something; one who gives evidence in a law court; one who confirms another's signature; thing that serves as evidence. — *v.* be a witness of.
witticism *n.* witty remark.
witty *a.* (**-ier, -iest**) full of wit. **wittily** *adv.*, **wittiness** *n.*
wives *see* **wife**.
wizard *n.* male witch, magician; person with amazing abilities. **wizardry** *n.*
wizened /wizz'nd/ *a.* full of wrinkles, shrivelled with age.
woad *n.* blue dye obtained from a plant; this plant.
wobble *v.* stand or move unsteadily; quiver. — *n.* wobbling movement; quiver. **wobbly** *a.*
wodge *n.* (*colloq.*) chunk, wedge.
woe *n.* sorrow, distress; trouble causing this, misfortune. **woeful** *a.*, **woefully** *adv.*, **woefulness** *n.*
woebegone *a.* looking unhappy.
wok *n.* bowl-shaped frying pan used esp. in Chinese cookery.
woke, woken *see* **wake** [1].
wold *n.* (esp. in *pl.*) area of open upland country.
wolf *n.* (*pl.* **wolves**) wild animal of the dog family; (*sl.*) aggressive male flirt. — *v.* eat quickly and greedily. **cry wolf** raise false alarms. **wolf-whistle** *n.* man's admiring whistle at an attractive woman. **wolfish** *a.*
wolfram *n.* tungsten (ore).
wolverine *n.* North American animal of the weasel family.
woman *n.* (*pl.* **women**) adult female person; women in general.
womanhood *n.* state of being a woman.
womanize *v.* (of a man) seek women's company for sexual purposes. **womanizer** *n.*
womankind *n.* women in general.
womanly *a.* having qualities considered characteristic of a woman. **womanliness** *n.*
womb *n.* hollow organ in female mammals in which the young develop before birth.
wombat *n.* small bear-like Australian animal.
women *see* **woman**.
womenfolk *n.* women in general; women of one's family.
won *see* **win**.
wonder *n.* feeling of surprise and admiration or curiosity or bewilderment; remarkable thing. — *v.* feel wonder or surprise; desire to know; try to decide.
wonderful *a.* arousing admiration. **wonderfully** *adv.*
wonderland *n.* place full of wonderful things.
wonderment *n.* feeling of wonder.
woo *v.* (*old use*) court; try to achieve or obtain or coax.
wood *n.* tough fibrous substance of a tree; this cut for use; (also *pl.*) trees growing fairly densely over an area of ground. **out of the wood** clear of danger or difficulty.

woodbine *n.* wild honeysuckle.

woodcock *n.* a kind of game bird.

woodcut *n.* engraving made on wood; picture made from this.

wooded *a.* covered with trees.

wooden *a.* made of wood; showing no expression. **woodenly** *adv.*

woodland *n.* wooded country.

woodlouse *n.* (*pl.* **-lice**) small wingless creature with many legs, living in decaying wood etc.

woodpecker *n.* bird that taps tree trunks with its beak to discover insects.

woodpigeon *n.* a kind of large pigeon.

woodwind *n.* wind instruments made (or formerly made) of wood.

woodwork *n.* art or practice of making things from wood; wooden things or fittings.

woodworm *n.* larva of a kind of beetle that bores in wood.

woody *a.* like or consisting of wood; full of woods.

woof *n.* dog's gruff bark. — *v.* make this sound.

woofer *n.* loudspeaker for reproducing low-frequency signals.

wool *n.* soft hair from sheep or goats etc.; yarn or fabric made from this. **pull the wool over someone's eyes** deceive him or her.

woollen *a.* made of wool. **woollens** *n.pl.* woollen cloth or clothing.

woolly *a.* (**-ier**, **-iest**) covered with wool; like wool, woollen; vague. — *n.* (*colloq.*) woollen garment. **woolliness** *n.*

word *n.* sound(s) expressing a meaning independently and forming a basic element of speech; this represented by letters or symbols; thing said; message, news; promise; command. — *v.* express in words. **word of mouth** spoken (not written) words. **word-perfect** *a.* having memorized every word perfectly. **word processor** computer programmed for storing, correcting, and printing out text entered from a keyboard.

wording *n.* way a thing is worded.

wordy *a.* using too many words.

wore *see* **wear**.

work *n.* use of bodily or mental power in order to do or make something; thing to be undertaken; thing done or produced by work; literary or musical composition; employment; ornamentation of a certain kind, articles with this; things made of certain materials or with certain tools; (*pl.*) operations of building etc., operative parts of a machine; (*pl.*, usu. treated as *sing.*) factory; (usu. *pl.*) defensive structure; (*pl.*, *sl.*) all that is available. — *v.* perform work; make efforts; be employed; operate, do this effectively; bring about, accomplish; shape or knead or hammer etc. into a desired form or consistency; make (a way) or pass or cause to pass gradually by effort; become (loose etc.) through repeated stress or pressure; be in motion; ferment. **work off** get rid of by activity. **work out** find or solve by calculation; plan the details of; have a specified result; take exercise. **work to rule** cause delay by over-strict observance of rules, as a form of protest. **work up** bring gradually to a more developed state; excite progressively; advance (to a climax).

workable *a.* able to be done or used successfully.

workaday *a.* ordinary, everyday; practical.

worker *n.* person who works; member of the working class; neuter bee or ant etc. that does the work of the hive or colony.

workhouse *n.* former public institution where people unable to support themselves were housed.

working *a.* engaged in work, esp. manual labour, working-class. — *n.* excavation(s) made in mining, tunnelling, etc. **working class** class of people who are employed for wages, esp. in manual or industrial work. **working-class** *a.* of this class. **working knowledge** knowledge adequate to work with.

workman *n.* (*pl.* **-men**) man employed to do manual labour.

workmanlike *a.* characteristic of a good workman, practical.

workmanship *n.* skill in working or in a thing produced.

workout *n.* practice or test; exercising.

workshop *n.* room or building in which manual work or manufacture etc. is carried on.

workstation *n.* computer terminal and keyboard; desk with this; location of an individual worker or stage in manufacturing etc.

world *n.* the earth; people or things belonging to a certain class or sphere of activity; everything, all people; material things and occupations; very great amount.

worldly *a.* of or concerned with earthly life or material gains, not spiritual. **worldliness** *n.*

worldwide *a.* extending through the whole world.

worm *n.* animal with a long soft body and no backbone or limbs; (*pl.*) internal parasites; insignificant or contemptible person; spiral part of a screw. — *v.* make one's way with twisting movements; insinuate oneself; obtain by crafty persistence; rid of parasitic worms. **worm-cast** *n.* pile of earth cast up by an earthworm. **wormy** *a.*

wormeaten *a.* full of holes made by insect larvae.

wormwood *n.* woody plant with a bitter flavour.

worn *see* **wear**. — *a.* damaged or altered by use or wear; looking exhausted. **worn-out** *a.*

worried *a.* feeling or showing worry.

worry *v.* be troublesome to; give way to anxiety; seize with the teeth and shake or pull about. — *n.* worried state, mental uneasiness; thing causing this. **worrier** *n.*

worse *a.* & *adv.* more bad, more badly, more evil or ill; less good. — *n.* something worse.

worsen *v.* make or become worse.

worship *n.* reverence and respect paid to a deity; adoration of or devotion to a person or thing. — *v.* (**worshipped**) honour as a deity; take part in an act of worship; idolize, treat with adoration. **worshipper** *n.*

worst *a.* & *adv.* most bad, most badly, least good. — *n.* worst part or feature or event etc. — *v.* defeat, outdo. **get the worst of** be defeated in.

worsted /wŏŏstid/ *n.* a kind of smooth woollen yarn or fabric.

worth *a.* having a specified value; deserving; possessing as wealth. — *n.* value, merit, usefulness; amount that a specified sum will buy. **for all one is worth** (*colloq.*) with all one's energy. **worth while** *or* **worth one's while** worth the time or effort needed.

worthless *a.* having no value or usefulness. **worthlessness** *n.*

worthwhile *a.* worth while.

worthy *a.* (**-ier, -iest**) having great merit; deserving. — *n.* worthy person. **worthily** *adv.*, **worthiness** *n.*

would *v.aux.* used in senses corresponding to *will*[1] in the past tense, conditional statements, questions, polite requests and statements, and to express probability or something that happens from time to time. **would-be** *a.* desiring or pretending to be.

wound[1] /wōōnd/ *n.* injury done to tissue by violence; injury to feelings. — *v.* inflict a wound upon.

wound[2] /wownd/ *see* **wind**[2].

wove, woven *see* **weave**[1].

wow *int.* exclamation of astonishment. — *n.* (*sl.*) sensational success.

wrack *n.* a type of seaweed.

wraith *n.* ghost, spectral apparition of a living person.

wrangle *v.* argue or quarrel noisily. — *n.* noisy argument.

wrap *v.* (**wrapped**) arrange (a soft or flexible covering) round (a person or thing). — *n.* shawl. **be wrapped up in** have one's attention deeply occupied by.

wrapper *n.* cover of paper etc. wrapped round something.

wrapping *n.* material for wrapping things.

wrasse /rass/ *n.* brightly coloured sea fish.

wrath *n.* anger, indignation. **wrathful** *a.*, **wrathfully** *adv.*

wreak *v.* inflict (vengeance etc.).

wreath /reeth/ *n.* (*pl.* **-ths**) flowers or leaves etc. fastened into a ring, used as a decoration or placed on a grave etc.

wreathe /reeth/ *v.* encircle; twist into a wreath; wind, curve.

wreck *n.* destruction, esp. of a ship by storms or accident; ship that has suffered this; something ruined or dilapidated; person whose health or spirits have been destroyed. — *v.* cause the wreck of; involve in shipwreck. **wrecker** *n.*

wreckage *n.* remains of something wrecked.

wren *n.* very small bird.

wrench *v.* twist or pull violently round; damage or pull by twisting. — *n.* violent twisting pull; pain caused by parting; adjustable spanner-like tool.

wrest *v.* wrench away; obtain by force or effort; twist, distort.

wrestle *v.* fight (esp. as a sport) by grappling with and trying to throw an opponent to the ground; struggle to deal with.

wretch *n.* wretched or despicable person; rascal.

wretched *a.* miserable, unhappy; worthless; contemptible. **wretchedly** *adv.*, **wretchedness** *n.*

wriggle *v.* move with short twisting movements; escape (out of a difficulty etc.) cunningly. — *n.* wriggling movement.

wring *v.* (**wrung**) twist and squeeze, esp. to remove liquid; squeeze firmly or forcibly; obtain with effort or difficulty.

wrinkle *n.* small crease; small ridge or furrow in skin; (*colloq.*) useful hint. — *v.* form wrinkles (in). **wrinkly** *a.*

wrist *n.* joint connecting hand and forearm; part of a garment covering this. **wrist-watch** *n.* watch worn on the wrist.

wristlet *n.* band or bracelet etc. worn round the wrist.

writ *n.* formal written authoritative command.

write *v.* (**wrote**, **written**, **writing**) make letters or other symbols on a surface, esp. with a pen or pencil; compose in written form, esp. for publication; be an author; write and send a letter. **write off** recognize as lost. **write-off** *n.* something written off as lost, vehicle too damaged to be worth repairing. **write up** write an account of; write entries in. **write-up** *n.* (*colloq.*) published account of something, review.

writer *n.* person who writes; author. **writer's cramp** cramp in the muscles of the hand.

writhe *v.* twist one's body about, as in pain; wriggle; suffer because of embarrassment.

writing *n.* handwriting; literary work. **in writing** in written form. **writing paper** paper for writing (esp. letters) on.

written *see* **write**.

wrong *a.* incorrect, not true; morally bad; contrary to justice; not what is required or desirable; not in a satisfactory condition. — *adv.* in a wrong manner or direction, mistakenly. — *n.* what is wrong, wrong action etc.; injustice. — *v.* treat unjustly. **in the wrong** not having truth or justice on one's side. **wrongly** *adv.*, **wrongness** *n.*

wrongdoer *n.* person who acts illegally or immorally. **wrongdoing** *n.*

wrongful *a.* contrary to what is right or legal. **wrongfully** *adv.*

wrote *see* **write**.

wrought /rawt/ *a.* (of metals) shaped by hammering. **wrought iron** pure form of iron used for decorative work.

wrung *see* **wring**.

wry *a.* (of the face) contorted in disgust or disappointment; (of humour) dry, mocking. **wryly** *adv.*, **wryness** *n.*

wych elm elm with broad leaves and spreading branches.

wych hazel = witch hazel.

X Y Z

xenophobia /zénnəfṓbiə/ *n.* strong dislike or distrust of foreigners.
Xmas *n.* (*colloq.*) Christmas.
X-ray *n.* photograph or examination made by a kind of electromagnetic radiation (**X-rays**) that can penetrate solids. — *v.* photograph, examine, or treat by X-rays.
xylophone *n.* musical instrument with flat wooden bars struck with small hammers.
yacht /yot/ *n.* light sailing vessel for racing; vessel used for private pleasure excursions. **yachting** *n.*, **yachtsman** *n.* (*pl.* **-men**), **yachtswoman** *n.fem.* (*pl.* **-women**).
yak *n.* long-haired Asian ox.
yam *n.* tropical climbing plant; its edible tuber; sweet potato.
yank *v.* (*colloq.*) pull sharply. — *n.* (*colloq.*) sharp pull.
yap *n.* shrill bark. — *v.* (**yapped**) bark shrilly.
yard [1] *n.* measure of length, = 3 feet (0.9144 metre); pole slung from a mast to support a sail.
yard [2] *n.* piece of enclosed ground, esp. attached to a building.
yardage *n.* length measured in yards.
yardstick *n.* standard of comparison.
yarmulke /yaármәlkә/ *n.* skullcap worn by Jewish men.
yarn *n.* any spun thread; (*colloq.*) tale. — *v.* tell yarns.
yarrow *n.* plant with feathery leaves and strong-smelling flowers.
yashmak *n.* veil worn by Muslim women in certain countries.
yaw *v.* (of a ship or aircraft) fail to hold a straight course. — *n.* yawing.
yawl *n.* a kind of fishing boat or sailing boat.
yawn *v.* open the mouth wide and draw in breath, as when sleepy or bored; have a wide opening. — *n.* act of yawning.
yaws *n.* tropical skin disease.
yd *abbr.* yard. **yds** *abbr.* yards.
year *n.* time taken by the earth to orbit the sun (about 365¼ days); period from 1 Jan. to 31 Dec. inclusive; consecutive period of twelve months; (*pl.*) age.
yearling *n.* animal between 1 and 2 years old.
yearly *a.* happening, published, or payable once a year. — *adv.* annually.
yearn *v.* feel great longing.
yeast *n.* fungus used to cause fermentation in making beer and wine and as a raising agent.
yell *v.* & *n.* shout.
yellow *a.* of the colour of buttercups and ripe lemons; (*colloq.*) cowardly. — *n.* yellow colour or thing. — *v.* turn yellow.
yellowhammer *n.* bird of the finch family with a yellow head, neck, and breast.
yellowish *a.* rather yellow.
yelp *n.* shrill yell or bark. — *v.* utter a yelp.
yen [1] *n.* (*pl.* **yen**) unit of money in Japan.
yen [2] *n.* (*colloq.*) longing, yearning.
yes *adv.* & *n.* expression of agreement or consent, or of reply to a summons etc. **yes-man** *n.* person who is always ready to agree with his or her superiors.
yesterday *adv.* & *n.* (on) the day before today; (in) the recent past.
yet *adv.* up to this or that time, still; besides; eventually; even; nevertheless. — *conj.* nevertheless, in spite of that.
yeti *n.* (*pl.* **-is**) large human-like or bear-like animal said to exist in the Himalayas.
yew *n.* evergreen tree with dark needle-like leaves; its wood.
Yiddish *n.* language used by Jews from eastern Europe.
yield *v.* give as fruit or gain or result; surrender; allow (victory, right of way, etc.) to another; be able to be forced out of the natural shape. — *n.* amount yielded or produced.
yippee *int.* exclamation of delight or excitement.
yodel *v.* (**yodelled**) sing with a quickly alternating change of pitch. — *n.* yodelling cry. **yodeller** *n.*
yoga *n.* Hindu system of meditation and self-control.
yoghurt *n.* food made of milk that has been thickened by the action of certain bacteria.
yoke *n.* wooden crosspiece fastened over the necks of two oxen pulling a plough etc.; piece of wood shaped to fit a person's shoulders and hold a load slung from each end; top part of a garment; oppression. — *v.* harness with a yoke; unite.
yokel *n.* country fellow; bumpkin.
yolk *n.* round yellow internal part of an egg.
yomp *v.* & *n.* (*sl.*) march with heavy equipment across country.
yonder *a.* & *adv.* over there.

yonks *adv.* (*sl.*) a long time.
yore *n.* **of yore** long ago.
Yorkshire pudding baked batter pudding eaten with meat.
you *pron.* person(s) addressed; one, anyone, everyone.
young *a.* having lived or existed for only a short time; youthful; having little experience. — *n.* offspring of animals.
youngster *n.* young person, child.
your *a.*, **yours** *poss.pron.* belonging to you.
yourself *pron.* (*pl.* **yourselves**) emphatic and reflexive form of *you*.
youth *n.* (*pl.* **youths**) state or period of being young; young man; young people. **youth club** club where leisure activities are provided for young people. **youth hostel** hostel providing cheap accommodation for young travellers.
youthful *a.* young; characteristic of young people. **youthfulness** *n.*
yowl *v.* & *n.* howl.
Yo-yo *n.* (*pl.* **-os**) [P.] round toy that can be made to rise and fall on a string that winds round it in a groove.
yucca *n.* tall plant with white bell-like flowers and spiky leaves.
yule, yule-tide *ns.* (*old use*) Christmas festival.
yummy *a.* (*colloq.*) delicious.
yuppie *n.* (*colloq.*) young urban professional person.
zany *a.* (**-ier, -iest**) crazily funny. — *n.* zany person.
zeal *n.* enthusiasm, hearty and persistent effort.
zealot /zéllət/ *n.* zealous person, fanatic.
zealous /zélləss/ *a.* full of zeal. **zealously** *adv.*
zebra *n.* African horse-like animal with black and white stripes. **zebra crossing** pedestrian crossing where the road is marked with broad white stripes.
zebu *n.* ox with a humped back.
Zen *n.* form of Buddhism.
zenith *n.* the part of the sky that is directly overhead; highest point.
zephyr *n.* soft gentle wind.
zero *n.* (*pl.* **-os**) nought, the figure 0; nil; point marked 0 on a graduated scale, temperature corresponding to this. **zero hour** hour at which something is timed to begin. **zero in on** take aim at; focus attention on.
zest *n.* keen enjoyment or interest; orange or lemon peel as flavouring. **zestful** *a.*, **zestfully** *adv.*
zigzag *n.* line or course turning right and left alternately at sharp angles. — *a.* & *adv.* as or in a zigzag. — *v.* (**zigzagged**) move in a zigzag.
zinc *n.* bluish-white metal.
zing *n.* (*colloq.*) vigour. — *v.* (*colloq.*) move swiftly or shrilly.
Zionism *n.* movement to found and support a Jewish homeland (Israel). **Zionist** *n.*
zip *n.* short sharp sound; vigour, liveliness; zip-fastener. — *v.* (**zipped**) fasten with a zip-fastener; move with the sound of 'zip' or at high speed. **zip-fastener** *n.* fastening device with teeth that interlock when brought together by a sliding tab.
zipper *n.* zip-fastener.
zircon *n.* bluish-white gem cut from a translucent mineral.
zirconium *n.* grey metallic element.
zither *n.* stringed instrument played with the fingers.
zodiac *n.* (in astrology) band of the sky divided into twelve equal parts (**signs of the zodiac**) each named from a constellation. **zodiacal** *a.*
zombie *n.* (in voodoo) corpse said to have been revived by witchcraft; (*colloq.*) person who seems to have no mind or will.
zone *n.* area with particular characteristics, purpose, or use. — *v.* divide into zones. **zonal** *a.*
zoo *n.* place where wild animals are kept for exhibition and study.
zoology *n.* study of animals. **zoological** *a.*, **zoologist** *n.*
zoom *v.* move quickly, esp. with a buzzing sound; rise quickly; (in photography) make a distant object appear gradually closer by means of a **zoom lens**.
zucchini /zookéeni/ *n.* (*pl.* **-i** *or* **-is**) courgette.
Zulu *n.* (*pl.* **-us**) member or language of a Bantu people of South Africa.
zygote *n.* cell formed by the union of two gametes.

THE OXFORD POPULAR THESAURUS

Using the Thesaurus

In this thesaurus you will find:

Headwords

The words you want to look up are printed in bold and arranged in a single alphabetical sequence. In addition, there may be subheads in bold at the end of main entries for derived forms and phrases.

Synonyms

Synonyms are listed alphabetically, except that distinct senses of a headword are numbered and treated separately.

Under some headwords, in addition to the lists of synonyms given there, a cross-reference printed in SMALL CAPITALS takes you to another entry to provide an extended range of synonyms. These cross-references are marked by the arrowhead symbol ▷ .

Antonyms

Cross-references printed in SMALL CAPITALS introduce you to lists of opposites. These cross-references are preceded by the abbreviation *Opp*.

Part-of-speech labels

Part-of-speech labels are given throughout. (See list of abbreviations.) Under each headword, synonyms for *adjective, adverb, noun,* and *verb* uses are separated by the symbol

Illustrative phrases

Meanings of less obvious senses are indicated by illustrative phrases printed in *italic*.

Usage warnings

Usage markers in *italic* precede words which are normally only used in certain contexts—for example, slang, poetic, or jocular use. (See list of abbreviations.)

A

abandon *v* 1 evacuate, leave, quit, vacate, withdraw from. 2 break with, desert, *inf* dump, forsake, jilt, leave behind, *inf* leave in the lurch, maroon, renounce, strand, *inf* throw over, *inf* wash your hands of. 3 *abandon a claim.* abdicate, cancel, cede, *inf* chuck in, discontinue, disown, *inf* ditch, drop, forfeit, forgo, give up, relinquish, resign, surrender, waive, yield.

abbey *n* cathedral, church, convent, friary, monastery, nunnery, priory.

abbreviate *v* abridge, compress, condense, cut, edit, précis, reduce, shorten, summarize, truncate. *Opp* LENGTHEN.

abdicate *v* renounce the throne, *inf* step down. ⊳ ABANDON, RESIGN.

abduct *v* carry off, kidnap, *inf* make away with, seize.

abhor *v* detest, execrate, loathe, shudder at. ⊳ HATE.

abhorrent *adj* abominable, detestable, execrable, loathsome, nauseating, obnoxious, repellent, revolting. ⊳ HATEFUL. *Opp* ATTRACTIVE.

abide *v* 1 accept, bear, endure, put up with, stand, stomach, suffer, tolerate. 2 ⊳ STAY. **abide by** ⊳ OBEY.

ability *n* aptitude, bent, brains, capability, capacity, cleverness, competence, expertise, flair, genius, gift, intelligence, knack, *inf* know-how, knowledge, means, power, proficiency, prowess, resources, scope, skill, strength, talent, training, wit.

ablaze *adj* afire, aflame, aglow, alight, blazing, burning, flaming, lit up, on fire, raging.

able *adj* 1 accomplished, adept, capable, clever, competent, effective, efficient, experienced, expert, handy, intelligent, masterly, practised, proficient, skilful, skilled, talented. *Opp* INCOMPETENT. 2 allowed, at liberty, authorized, available, eligible, fit, free, permitted, willing. *Opp* UNABLE.

abnormal *adj* aberrant, anomalous, atypical, *inf* bent, bizarre, curious, deformed, deviant, distorted, eccentric, exceptional, extraordinary, freak, funny, idiosyncratic, irregular, *inf* kinky, malformed, odd, peculiar, perverted, queer, singular, strange, uncharacteristic, unnatural, unorthodox, unrepresentative, untypical, unusual, wayward, weird. *Opp* NORMAL.

abolish *v* abrogate, annul, delete, destroy, dispense with, do away with, eliminate, end, eradicate, finish, get rid of, liquidate, nullify, overturn, put an end to, quash, remove, suppress, terminate, withdraw. *Opp* CREATE.

abominable *adj* abhorrent, appalling, atrocious, awful, base, beastly, brutal, cruel, despicable, detestable, disgusting, dreadful, execrable, foul, hateful, heinous, horrible, inhuman, inhumane, loathsome, nasty, obnoxious, odious, repellent, repugnant, repulsive, revolting, terrible, vile. *Opp* PLEASANT.

abort *v* 1 be born prematurely, die, miscarry. 2 *abort take-off.* call off, end, halt, nullify, stop, terminate.

abortion *n* miscarriage, premature birth, termination of pregnancy.

abortive *adj* fruitless, futile, ineffective, pointless, stillborn, unfruitful, unsuccessful, vain. *Opp* SUCCESSFUL.

abound *v* be plentiful, flourish, prevail, swarm, teem, thrive.

abrasive *adj* biting, caustic, galling, grating, harsh, hurtful, irritating, rough, sharp. ⊳ UNKIND. *Opp* KIND.

abridge *v* abbreviate, compress, condense, cut, edit, précis, reduce, shorten, summarize, truncate. *Opp* EXPAND.

abridged *adj* abbreviated, bowdlerized, censored, compact, concise, cut, edited, *inf* potted, shortened.

abrupt *adj* 1 hasty, headlong, hurried, precipitate, quick, rapid, sudden, unexpected, unforeseen. 2 *abrupt drop.* precipitous, sharp, sheer, steep. 3 *abrupt manner.* blunt, brisk, brusque, curt, discourteous, rude, snappy, terse, uncivil, ungracious. *Opp* GENTLE, GRADUAL.

absent *adj* 1 away, *sl* bunking off, gone, missing, off, out, playing truant, *sl* skiving. *Opp* PRESENT. 2 ⊳ ABSENT-MINDED.

absent-minded *adj* absent, absorbed, abstracted, careless, distracted, dreamy, forgetful, inattentive, oblivious, preoccupied, scatterbrained, unaware, unthinking, vague, withdrawn, woolgathering. *Opp* ALERT.

absolute *adj* 1 categorical, certain, complete, conclusive, decided, definite, downright, genuine, implicit, inalienable, indubitable, out and out, perfect, positive, pure, sheer, sure, thorough, total, unadulterated, unambiguous, unconditional, unequivocal, unmitigated, unqualified, unreserved, unrestricted, utter. 2 *absolute ruler*. autocratic, despotic, dictatorial, omnipotent, totalitarian, tyrannical. 3 *absolute opposites*. *inf* dead, diametrical, exact.

absorb *v* 1 assimilate, consume, digest, drink in, hold, imbibe, incorporate, ingest, mop up, soak up, suck up, take in. *Opp* EMIT. 2 *absorb a blow*. cushion, deaden, lessen, soften. 3 *absorb a person*. captivate, engage, engross, enthrall, fascinate, occupy, preoccupy. ▷ INTEREST.
absorbed ▷ INTERESTED.

absorbent *adj* absorptive, permeable, pervious, porous, spongy. *Opp* IMPERVIOUS.

absorbing *adj* engrossing, fascinating, gripping, spellbinding. ▷ INTERESTING.

abstain *v*

abstain from avoid, cease, deny yourself, desist from, eschew, forgo, give up, go without, refrain from, refuse, resist, shun, withhold from.

abstemious *adj* ascetic, frugal, moderate, restrained, self-denying, sparing, temperate. *Opp* SELF-INDULGENT.

abstract *adj* 1 academic, hypothetical, indefinite, intangible, intellectual, metaphysical, notional, philosophical, theoretical, unreal. *Opp* CONCRETE. 2 *abstract art*. non-pictorial, non-representational, symbolic.
• *n* outline, précis, résumé, summary, synopsis.

abstruse *adj* complex, cryptic, deep, devious, difficult, enigmatic, esoteric, hard, incomprehensible, mysterious, obscure, perplexing, problematic, profound, unfathomable. *Opp* OBVIOUS.

absurd *adj* crazy, *inf* daft, eccentric, farcical, foolish, grotesque, illogical, incongruous, irrational, laughable, ludicrous, nonsensical, outlandish, paradoxical, preposterous, ridiculous, senseless, silly, stupid, surreal, unreasonable, zany. ▷ FUNNY, MAD. *Opp* RATIONAL.

abundant *adj* ample, bountiful, copious, excessive, flourishing, generous, lavish, liberal, luxuriant, overflowing, plentiful, profuse, rampant, rank, rich, well-supplied. *Opp* SCARCE.

abuse *n* 1 assault, ill-treatment, maltreatment, misappropriation, misuse, perversion. 2 *verbal abuse*. curse, execration, imprecation, insult, invective, obscenity, slander, vilification, vituperation.
• *v* 1 damage, exploit, harm, hurt, ill-treat, injure, maltreat, misuse, molest, rape, spoil, treat roughly. 2 *abuse verbally*. affront, berate, be rude to, *inf* call names, castigate, curse, defame, denigrate, insult, inveigh against, libel, malign, revile, slander, smear, sneer at, swear at, vilify, vituperate, wrong.

abusive *adj* acrimonious, angry, censorious, critical, cruel, defamatory, denigrating, derogatory, disparaging, hurtful, impolite, injurious, insulting, libellous, offensive, opprobrious, pejorative, rude, scathing, scornful, scurrilous, slanderous, vituperative. *Opp* POLITE.

abysmal *adj* 1 bottomless, boundless, deep, immeasurable, incalculable, infinite, profound, vast. 2 ▷ BAD.

abyss *n inf* bottomless pit, chasm, crater, fissure, gap, gulf, hole, pit, rift, void.

academic *adj* 1 collegiate, educational, scholastic. 2 bookish, *inf* brainy, clever, erudite, highbrow, intelligent, learned, scholarly, studious. 3 *academic study*. abstract, conjectural, hypothetical, impractical, intellectual, speculative, theoretical.
• *n inf* egghead, highbrow, intellectual, scholar, thinker.

accelerate *v* 1 *inf* get a move on, go faster, hasten, pick up speed, quicken, speed up. 2 bring on, expedite, spur on, step up, stimulate.

accent *n* 1 brogue, cadence, dialect, enunciation, intonation, pronunciation, speech pattern, tone. 2 accentuation, beat, emphasis, pulse, rhythm, stress.

accept *v* 1 get, *inf* jump at, receive, take, welcome. 2 acknowledge, admit, bear, put up with, reconcile yourself to, resign yourself to, submit to, suffer, tolerate, undertake. 3 *accept an argument*. abide by, accede to, acquiesce in, agree to, believe in, be reconciled to, consent to, defer to, grant, recognize, stomach, *inf* swallow, take in. *Opp* REJECT.

acceptable *adj* 1 agreeable, gratifying, pleasant, pleasing, worthwhile. 2 adequate, admissible, moderate, passable, satisfactory, suitable, tolerable. *Opp* UNACCEPTABLE.

acceptance *n* acquiescence, agreement, approval, consent. *Opp* REFUSAL.

accepted *adj* acknowledged, agreed, axiomatic, common, indisputable, recognized, standard, undisputed, unquestioned. *Opp* CONTROVERSIAL.

accessible *adj* approachable, at hand, attainable, available, close, convenient, handy, within reach. *Opp* INACCESSIBLE.

accessory *n* 1 addition, appendage, attachment, component, extra. 2 ▷ ACCOMPLICE.

accident *n* 1 blunder, chance, coincidence, fate, fluke, fortune, luck, misadventure, mischance, mishap, mistake, *inf* pot luck, serendipity. 2 catastrophe, collision, crash, disaster, *inf* pile-up, wreck.

accidental *adj* arbitrary, casual, chance, coincidental, *inf* fluky, fortuitous, fortunate, haphazard, inadvertent, lucky, random, unexpected, unforeseen, unintended, unintentional, unlucky, unplanned, unpremeditated. *Opp* INTENTIONAL.

acclaim *v* applaud, celebrate, cheer, clap, commend, extol, hail, honour, praise, salute, welcome.

accommodate *v* 1 assist, equip, fit, furnish, help, provide, serve, supply. 2 *accommodate guests.* billet, board, cater for, harbour, house, lodge, provide for, *inf* put up, quarter, shelter, take in. 3 *accommodate yourself to new surroundings.* accustom, adapt, reconcile. **accommodating** ▷ CONSIDERATE.

accommodation *n* board, *inf* digs, home, housing, lodgings, pied-à-terre, premises, rooms, shelter.

accompany *v* 1 attend, chaperon, conduct, escort, follow, go with, guard, guide, look after, partner, *inf* tag along with. 2 be associated with, be linked with, belong with, complement, occur with, supplement.

accompanying *adj* associated, attached, attendant, complementary, related.

accomplice *n* abettor, accessory, associate, collaborator, colleague, confederate, conspirator, helper, partner.

accomplish *v* achieve, attain, *inf* bring off, carry out, carry through, complete, consummate, discharge, do successfully, effect, finish, fulfil, realize, succeed in.

accomplished *adj* adept, expert, gifted, polished, proficient, skilful, talented.

accomplishment *n* ability, attainment, expertise, gift, skill, talent.

accord *n* agreement, concord, harmony, rapport, understanding.

account *n* 1 bill, calculation, check, computation, invoice, receipt, reckoning, *inf* score, statement. 2 commentary, description, diary, explanation, history, log, memoir, narrative, record, report, statement, story, tale, *inf* write-up. 3 *of no account.* advantage, benefit, concern, consequence, importance, interest, significance, use, value, worth. **account for** ▷ EXPLAIN.

accumulate *v* accrue, aggregate, amass, assemble, bring together, build up, collect, come together, gather, grow, heap up, hoard, increase, multiply, pile up, stockpile, store up. *Opp* DISPERSE.

accumulation *n* *inf* build-up, collection, conglomeration, gathering, heap, hoard, mass, stockpile, store.

accurate *adj* authentic, careful, correct, exact, factual, faultless, meticulous, minute, nice, perfect, precise, reliable, scrupulous, sound, *inf* spot-on, true, truthful, unerring, veracious. *Opp* INACCURATE.

accusation *n* allegation, charge, citation, complaint, impeachment, indictment, summons.

accuse *v* attack, blame, bring charges against, censure, charge, condemn, denounce, impeach, impugn, indict, *inf* point the finger at, prosecute, summons, tax. *Opp* DEFEND.

accustomed *adj* common, customary, established, expected, familiar, habitual, normal, ordinary, prevailing, routine, traditional, usual. **get accustomed** ▷ ADAPT.

ache *n* anguish, discomfort, hurt, pain, pang, smart, soreness, throbbing, twinge. • *v* 1 be painful, be sore, hurt, smart, sting, throb. 2 ▷ DESIRE.

achieve *v* 1 accomplish, attain, bring off, carry out, complete, conclude, do successfully, effect, engineer, execute, finish, fulfil, manage, succeed in. 2 *achieve fame.* acquire, earn, gain, get, obtain, reach, win.

acid *adj* sharp, sour, stinging, tangy, tart, vinegary. *Opp* SWEET.

acknowledge *v* 1 accede, accept, acquiesce, admit, allow, concede, confess, confirm, endorse, grant, own up to, profess. *Opp* DENY. 2 *acknowledge a greeting.* answer, react to, reply to, respond to, return. 3 *acknowledge a friend.* greet, hail, recognize, *inf* say hello to. *Opp* IGNORE.

acme *n* apex, crown, height, highest point,

peak, pinnacle, summit, top, zenith. *Opp* NADIR.

acquaint *v* announce, apprise, brief, enlighten, inform, make aware, make familiar, notify, reveal, tell.

acquaintance *n* 1 awareness, familiarity, knowledge, understanding. 2 ▷ FRIEND.

acquire *v* buy, come by, earn, get, obtain, procure, purchase.

acquisition *n* addition, *inf* buy, gain, possession, purchase.

acquit *v* absolve, clear, declare innocent, discharge, excuse, exonerate, find innocent, free, let off, release, reprieve, set free, vindicate. *Opp* CONDEMN. **acquit yourself** ▷ BEHAVE.

acrid *adj* bitter, caustic, pungent, sharp, unpleasant.

acrimonious *adj* abusive, acerbic, angry, bad-tempered, bitter, caustic, hostile, hot-tempered, ill-tempered, irascible, quarrelsome, rancorous, sarcastic, sharp, spiteful, tart, testy, venomous, virulent, waspish. *Opp* PEACEABLE.

act *n* 1 deed, exploit, feat, operation, undertaking. ▷ ACTION. 2 *act of parliament.* bill [= *draft act*], decree, edict, law, regulation, statute. 3 *stage act.* performance, routine, sketch, turn.
• *v* 1 behave, carry on, conduct yourself. 2 function, operate, serve, take effect, work. 3 *Act now!* do something, get involved, take steps. ▷ BEGIN. 4 *act a role.* appear (as), *derog* camp it up, characterize, dramatize, enact, *derog* ham it up, impersonate, mime, mimic, *derog* overact, perform, personify, play, portray, pose as, represent. ▷ PRETEND.

acting *adj* deputy, interim, stand-by, stopgap, substitute, temporary, vice-.

action *n* 1 act, deed, enterprise, exploit, feat, measure, performance, proceeding, step, undertaking, work. 2 activity, drama, energy, enterprise, excitement, exertion, liveliness, movement, vigour, vitality. 3 *action of a play.* events, happenings, story. 4 *action of a watch.* mechanism, operation, working, works. 5 *military action.* ▷ BATTLE.

activate *v* actuate, energize, excite, fire, galvanize, initiate, mobilize, rouse, set in motion, set off, start, stimulate, trigger.

active *adj* 1 animated, brisk, bustling, busy, dynamic, energetic, enthusiastic, functioning, hyperactive, live, lively, militant, nimble, *inf* on the go, restless, sprightly, strenuous, vigorous, vivacious, working. 2 *active support.* committed, dedicated, devoted, diligent, hardworking, industrious, involved, occupied, sedulous, staunch, zealous. *Opp* INACTIVE.

activity *n* 1 action, animation, bustle, commotion, energy, hurly-burly, hustle, industry, life, movement, stir. 2 hobby, interest, job, occupation, pastime, pursuit, task, venture. ▷ WORK.

actor, actress *n* artist, artiste, lead, leading lady, performer, player, star, supporting actor. **actors** cast, company, troupe.

actual *adj* authentic, bona fide, confirmed, corporeal, definite, existing, factual, genuine, indisputable, in existence, legitimate, living, material, real, tangible, true, verifiable. *Opp* IMAGINARY.

acute *adj* 1 narrow, pointed, sharp. 2 *acute pain.* excruciating, exquisite, extreme, intense, keen, piercing, racking, severe, sharp, shooting, violent. 3 *acute mind.* alert, analytical, astute, *inf* cute, discerning, incisive, intelligent, keen, penetrating, perceptive, sharp, subtle. ▷ CLEVER. 4 *acute problem.* crucial, immediate, important, overwhelming, pressing, serious, urgent. 5 *acute illness.* critical, sudden. *Opp* CHRONIC, STUPID.

adapt *v* 1 acclimatize, accustom, adjust, attune, become conditioned, become hardened, fit, get accustomed (to), get used (to), habituate, reconcile, suit, tailor, turn. 2 *adapt to a new use.* alter, amend, change, convert, modify, process, rearrange, rebuild, reconstruct, refashion, remake, reorganize, transform. ▷ EDIT.

add *v* annex, append, attach, combine, integrate, join, *inf* tack on, unite. *Opp* DEDUCT. **add to** ▷ INCREASE. **add up (to)** ▷ TOTAL.

addict *n* 1 alcoholic, *sl* junkie, *inf* user. 2 ▷ ENTHUSIAST.

addiction *n* compulsion, craving, dependence, fixation, habit, obsession.

addition *n* 1 adding up, calculation, computation, reckoning, totalling, *inf* totting up. 2 accessory, addendum, additive, adjunct, admixture, annexe, appendage, appendix, attachment, continuation, development, expansion, extension, extra, increase, increment, postscript, supplement.

additional *adj* added, extra, further, increased, more, new, other, spare, supplementary.

address *n* 1 directions, location, whereabouts. 2 *deliver an address.* discourse,

harangue, homily, lecture, sermon, speech, talk.
• *v* 1 accost, approach, *inf* buttonhole, greet, hail, salute, speak to, talk to. 2 *address an audience*. give a speech to, harangue, lecture. **address yourself to** ▷ TACKLE.

adept *adj* clever, competent, gifted, practised, proficient. ▷ SKILFUL. *Opp* UNSKILFUL.

adequate *adj* acceptable, all right, average, competent, fair, fitting, middling, *inf* OK, passable, presentable, satisfactory, *inf* so-so, sufficient, tolerable. *Opp* INADEQUATE.

adhere *v* bind, bond, cement, cling, glue, gum, paste. ▷ STICK.

adherent *n* aficionado, devotee, fan, follower, *inf* hanger-on, supporter.

adhesive *adj* glued, gluey, gummed. ▷ STICKY.

adjoining *adj* abutting, adjacent, bordering, juxtaposed, neighbouring, next, touching. *Opp* DISTANT.

adjourn *v* break off, defer, discontinue, interrupt, postpone, put off, suspend.

adjournment *n* break, interruption, pause, postponement, recess, stay, suspension.

adjust *v* 1 adapt, alter, amend, balance, change, convert, correct, modify, put right, rectify, regulate, remake, remodel, reorganize, reshape, set, tailor, temper, tune. 2 acclimatize, accommodate, accustom, fit, habituate, reconcile yourself.

administer *v* 1 administrate, conduct affairs, control, direct, govern, lead, manage, organize, oversee, preside over, regulate, rule, run, supervise. 2 *administer justice*. carry out, execute, implement, prosecute. 3 *administer medicine*. dispense, distribute, give, hand out, measure out, mete out, provide, supply.

administrator *n* bureaucrat, civil servant, controller, director, executive, manager, *derog* mandarin, organizer. ▷ CHIEF.

admirable *adj* awe-inspiring, commendable, creditable, deserving, estimable, excellent, exemplary, great, honourable, laudable, marvellous, meritorious, pleasing, praiseworthy, wonderful, worthy. *Opp* CONTEMPTIBLE.

admiration *n* appreciation, awe, commendation, esteem, hero-worship, high regard, honour, praise, respect. *Opp* CONTEMPT.

admire *v* applaud, appreciate, approve of, be delighted by, commend, esteem, have a high opinion of, hero-worship, honour, idolize, laud, look up to, marvel at, praise, respect, revere, think highly of, value, venerate, wonder at. ▷ LOVE. **admiring** ▷ COMPLIMENTARY, RESPECTFUL.

admission *n* 1 access, admittance, entrance, entry. 2 acceptance, acknowledgement, affirmation, concession, confession, declaration, disclosure, revelation. *Opp* DENIAL.

admit *v* 1 accept, allow in, let in, provide a place (in), receive, take in. 2 *admit guilt*. accept, acknowledge, allow, concede, confess, declare, disclose, own up, recognize, reveal, say reluctantly. *Opp* DENY.

adolescence *n* boyhood, girlhood, growing up, puberty, *inf* teens, youth.

adolescent *adj* boyish, girlish, immature, juvenile, pubescent, teenage, youthful.
• *n* boy, girl, juvenile, minor, *inf* teenager, youngster, youth.

adopt *v* 1 appropriate, approve, back, choose, embrace, endorse, follow, *inf* go for, patronize, support, take on, take up. 2 befriend, foster, stand by, take in.

adore *v* dote on, glorify, honour, love, revere, venerate, worship. ▷ ADMIRE. *Opp* HATE.

adorn *v* beautify, decorate, embellish, garnish, ornament, trim.

adrift *adj* 1 afloat, anchorless, drifting, floating. 2 aimless, astray, directionless, lost, purposeless.

adult *adj* full-grown, full-size, grown-up, marriageable, mature, of age. *Opp* IMMATURE.

adulterate *v* alloy, contaminate, corrupt, debase, dilute, *inf* doctor, pollute, taint, weaken.

advance *n* development, evolution, forward movement, growth, headway, improvement, progress.
• *v* 1 approach, bear down, come near, forge ahead, gain ground, go forward, make headway, make progress, move forward, press on, progress, *inf* push on. *Opp* RETREAT. 2 *our knowledge will advance*. develop, evolve, improve, prosper, thrive. 3 *advance your career*. accelerate, assist, benefit, boost, further, help the progress of, promote. *Opp* HINDER. 4 *advance a theory*. adduce, give, present, propose, submit, suggest. 5 *advance money*. lend, offer, pay, provide, supply. *Opp* WITHHOLD.

advanced *adj* 1 latest, modern, sophisticated, up-to-date. 2 *advanced ideas.* avant-garde, contemporary, experimental, forward-looking, futuristic, imaginative, innovative, new, novel, original, pioneering, progressive, revolutionary, trend-setting, *inf* way-out. 3 *advanced maths.* complex, difficult, hard, higher. 4 *advanced for her age.* grown-up, mature, precocious, sophisticated. *Opp* BACKWARD, BASIC.

advantage *n* 1 aid, asset, assistance, benefit, boon, gain, help, profit, usefulness. 2 *have an advantage.* dominance, edge, *inf* head start, superiority. **take advantage of** ▷ EXPLOIT.

advantageous *adj* beneficial, favourable, helpful, positive, profitable, salutary, useful, valuable, worthwhile. ▷ GOOD. *Opp* USELESS.

adventure *n* 1 chance, escapade, exploit, feat, gamble, occurrence, risk, undertaking, venture. 2 danger, excitement, hazard.

adventurous *adj* 1 audacious, bold, brave, courageous, daredevil, daring, *derog* foolhardy, intrepid, *derog* reckless, venturesome. 2 *adventurous trip.* challenging, dangerous, difficult, exciting, hazardous, risky. *Opp* UNADVENTUROUS.

adversary *n* antagonist, attacker, enemy, foe, opponent.

adverse *adj* 1 attacking, censorious, critical, derogatory, hostile, hurtful, inimical, negative, uncomplimentary, unfavourable, unkind, unsympathetic. 2 *adverse conditions.* detrimental, disadvantageous, harmful, inappropriate, inauspicious, opposing, prejudicial, uncongenial, unpropitious. *Opp* FAVOURABLE.

advertise *v* announce, broadcast, display, flaunt, make known, market, merchandise, *inf* plug, proclaim, promote, publicize, *inf* push, show off, tout.

advertisement *n* *inf* advert, bill, *inf* blurb, circular, commercial, leaflet, notice, placard, *inf* plug, poster, promotion, publicity, sign, *inf* small ad.

advice *n* 1 admonition, counsel, guidance, help, opinion, recommendation, tip, view, warning. 2 ▷ NEWS.

advisable *adj* expedient, judicious, politic, prudent, recommended, sensible. ▷ WISE.

advise *v* 1 admonish, caution, counsel, enjoin, exhort, guide, instruct, recommend, suggest, urge, warn. 2 ▷ INFORM.

adviser *n* confidant(e), consultant, counsellor, guide, mentor.

advocate *n* 1 apologist, backer, champion, proponent, supporter. 2 ▷ LAWYER. ▪ *v* argue for, back, champion, favour, recommend, speak for, uphold.

aesthetic *adj* artistic, beautiful, cultivated, sensitive, tasteful. *Opp* UGLY.

affair *n* 1 activity, business, concern, issue, interest, matter, project, subject, topic, undertaking. 2 circumstance, episode, event, happening, incident, occurrence, thing. 3 *love affair.* amour, attachment, intrigue, involvement, liaison, relationship, romance.

affect *v* 1 act on, agitate, alter, attack, change, concern, disturb, have an effect on, have an impact on, impinge on, impress, influence, move, perturb, relate to, stir, touch, trouble, upset. 2 *affect an accent.* adopt, assume, feign, *inf* put on. ▷ PRETEND.

affectation *n* artificiality, insincerity, mannerism, posturing. ▷ PRETENCE.

affected *adj* 1 artificial, contrived, insincere, *inf* put on, studied, unnatural. ▷ PRETENTIOUS. 2 *affected by disease.* afflicted, damaged, infected, injured, poisoned, stricken, troubled.

affection *n* attachment, fondness, friendliness, friendship, liking, partiality, *inf* soft spot, tenderness, warmth. ▷ LOVE.

affectionate *adj* caring, doting, fond, kind, tender. ▷ LOVING. *Opp* ALOOF.

affinity *n* closeness, compatibility, kinship, like-mindedness, likeness, rapport, relationship, similarity, sympathy.

affirm *v* assert, avow, declare, maintain, state, swear, testify.

affirmation *n* assertion, avowal, declaration, oath, promise, statement, testimony.

affirmative *adj* agreeing, assenting, concurring, confirming, positive. *Opp* NEGATIVE.

afflict *v* affect, annoy, beset, bother, burden, cause suffering to, distress, harass, harm, hurt, oppress, pain, plague, torment, torture, trouble, try, worry, wound.

affluent *adj* 1 *inf* flush, *sl* loaded, moneyed, prosperous, rich, wealthy, *inf* well-heeled, well-off, well-to-do. 2 *affluent life-style.* expensive, gracious, lavish, opulent, self-indulgent, sumptuous. *Opp* POOR.

afford *v* 1 be rich enough, have the means, manage to give, sacrifice, *inf* stand. 2 ▷ PROVIDE.

afloat *adj* aboard, adrift, floating, on board ship, under sail.

afraid *adj* 1 aghast, agitated, alarmed, anxious, apprehensive, cowardly, cowed, daunted, diffident, faint-hearted, fearful, frightened, hesitant, horrified, intimidated, *inf* jittery, nervous, panicky, panic-stricken, reluctant, scared, terrified, timid, timorous, trembling, unheroic. *Opp* FEARLESS. 2 [*inf*] *I'm afraid I'm late.* apologetic, regretful, sorry. **be afraid** ▷ FEAR.

afterthought *n* addendum, addition, extra, postscript.

age *n* 1 advancing years, decrepitude, dotage, old age, senility. 2 *bygone age.* days, epoch, era, time. 3 [*inf*] *ages ago.* lifetime, long time.
• *v* degenerate, grow older, look older, mature, mellow, ripen. **aged** ▷ OLD.

agenda *n* list, plan, programme, schedule, timetable.

agent *n* broker, delegate, envoy, executor, functionary, go-between, intermediary, mediator, middleman, negotiator, proxy, representative, surrogate, trustee.

aggravate *v* 1 add to, augment, compound, exacerbate, exaggerate, increase, inflame, intensify, make worse, worsen. *Opp* ALLEVIATE. 2 ▷ ANNOY.

aggressive *adj* antagonistic, assertive, bellicose, belligerent, bullying, *inf* butch, hostile, *inf* macho, militant, offensive, pugnacious, *inf* pushy, quarrelsome, violent, warlike. *Opp* DEFENSIVE, PEACEABLE.

aggressor *n* assailant, attacker, instigator, invader.

agile *adj* acrobatic, adroit, deft, fleet, graceful, lissom, lithe, mobile, nimble, quick-moving, sprightly, spry, supple. *Opp* CLUMSY.

agitate *v* 1 beat, churn, froth up, ruffle, shake, stimulate, stir, toss, work up. 2 alarm, arouse, confuse, discomfit, disconcert, excite, fluster, incite, perturb, stir up, trouble, unsettle, upset, worry. *Opp* CALM. **agitated** ▷ EXCITED, NERVOUS.

agitator *n* firebrand, rabble-rouser, revolutionary, troublemaker.

agonize *v* hurt, labour, suffer, worry, wrestle.

agony *n* anguish, distress, suffering, torment, torture. ▷ PAIN.

agree *v* 1 accede, acquiesce, admit, allow, assent, be willing, concede, consent, grant, make a contract, pledge yourself, promise, undertake. 2 accord, be unanimous, be united, concur, correspond, fit, get on, harmonize, match, *inf* see eye to eye. *Opp* DISAGREE. **agree on** ▷ CHOOSE. **agree with** ▷ ENDORSE.

agreeable *adj* acceptable, delightful, enjoyable, nice. ▷ PLEASANT. *Opp* DISAGREEABLE.

agreement *n* 1 accord, compatibility, concord, conformity, consensus, consent, consistency, correspondence, harmony, similarity, sympathy, unanimity, unity. 2 alliance, armistice, arrangement, bargain, compact, contract, convention, covenant, deal, entente, pact, settlement, treaty, truce, understanding. *Opp* DISAGREEMENT.

agricultural *adj* 1 agrarian, bucolic, pastoral, rural. 2 *agricultural land.* cultivated, farmed, productive, tilled.

agriculture *n* agronomy, crofting, cultivation, farming, husbandry, tilling.

aground *adj* beached, grounded, helpless, marooned, shipwrecked, stranded.

aid *n* assistance, avail, backing, benefit, cooperation, donation, funding, grant, guidance, help, loan, patronage, relief, sponsorship, subsidy, succour, support.
• *v* abet, assist, back, benefit, collaborate with, cooperate with, encourage, facilitate, help, *inf* lend a hand, promote, prop up, *inf* rally round, relieve, subsidize, succour, support.

ailing *adj* feeble, infirm, poorly, sick, unwell, weak. ▷ ILL.

ailment *n* affliction, disorder, infirmity, sickness. ▷ ILLNESS.

aim *n* ambition, cause, design, destination, direction, dream, focus, goal, hope, intent, intention, mark, object, objective, plan, purpose, wish.
• *v* 1 address, beam, direct, fire at, line up, point, sight, take aim, train, turn, zero in on. 2 *aim to win.* aspire, design, endeavour, essay, intend, plan, propose, resolve, strive, try, want, wish.

aimless *adj* chance, directionless, purposeless, rambling, random, undisciplined, unfocused. *Opp* PURPOSEFUL.

air *n* 1 airspace, atmosphere, ether, heavens, sky. 2 *fresh air.* breath, breeze, draught, wind. 3 *air of authority.* ambience, appearance, aspect, aura, bearing, character, demeanour, feeling, impression, look, manner, mood, style.
• *v* 1 aerate, dry off, freshen, ventilate. 2 *air opinions.* articulate, display, exhibit,

express, give vent to, make known, make public, vent, voice.

aircraft *n* aeroplane, *old use* flying-machine, plane.

airman *n old use* aviator, flier, pilot.

airport *n* aerodrome, airfield, airstrip, heliport, landing strip.

airy *adj* breezy, draughty, fresh, open, ventilated. *Opp* STUFFY.

aisle *n* corridor, gangway, passage, passageway.

akin *adj* allied, related, similar.

alarm *n* 1 alert, signal, warning. 2 anxiety, consternation, dismay, fright, nervousness, panic, uneasiness. ▷ FEAR.
• *v* agitate, dismay, distress, panic, *inf* put the wind up, shock, startle, unnerve, worry. ▷ FRIGHTEN. *Opp* REASSURE.

alcohol *n inf* booze, drink, hard stuff, liquor, spirits.

alcoholic *adj* brewed, distilled, fermented, intoxicating, *inf* strong.
• *n* addict, dipsomaniac, drunkard, inebriate. *Opp* TEETOTALLER.

alert *adj* active, alive (to), attentive, awake, careful, eagle-eyed, heedful, lively, observant, on the lookout, on the watch, on your guard, on your toes, perceptive, ready, sensitive, sharp-eyed, vigilant, watchful, wide awake. *Opp* ABSENT-MINDED, INATTENTIVE.
• *v* advise, alarm, forewarn, make aware, notify, signal, tip off, warn.

alibi *n* excuse, explanation.

alien *adj* extra-terrestrial, foreign, outlandish, strange, unfamiliar.
• *n* foreigner, newcomer, outsider, stranger.

alight *adj* ablaze, aflame, blazing, burning, fiery, ignited, illuminated, lit up, live, on fire.
• *v* come down, come to rest, disembark, dismount, get down, get off, land, touch down.

align *v* 1 arrange in line, line up, straighten up. 2 *align with the opposition*. affiliate, ally, associate, join, side, sympathize.

alike *adj* analogous, cognate, comparable, equivalent, identical, indistinguishable, like, matching, parallel, resembling, similar, twin, uniform. *Opp* DISSIMILAR.

alive *adj* 1 animate, breathing, existing, extant, flourishing, in existence, live, living, *old use* quick. 2 *alive to new ideas*. ▷ ALERT. *Opp* DEAD.

allay *v* calm, check, diminish, ease, mollify, pacify, quell, quench, quieten, reduce, slake (*thirst*), subdue. ▷ ALLEVIATE. *Opp* STIMULATE.

allegation *n* accusation, assertion, charge, claim, declaration, statement, testimony.

allege *v* assert, attest, avow, claim, contend, declare, maintain, make a charge, plead, state.

allegiance *n* devotion, duty, faithfulness, fidelity, loyalty.

allergic *adj* antipathetic, averse, hostile, incompatible (with), opposed.

alleviate *v* abate, allay, ameliorate, assuage, diminish, ease, lessen, lighten, mitigate, moderate, quell, quench, reduce, relieve, slake (*thirst*), soften, subdue, temper. *Opp* AGGRAVATE.

alliance *n* affiliation, agreement, bloc, cartel, coalition, compact, concordat, confederation, connection, consortium, covenant, entente, federation, guild, marriage, pact, partnership, relationship, treaty, union.

allot *v* allocate, allow, assign, deal out, *inf* dish out, *inf* dole out, dispense, distribute, give out, grant, provide, ration, share out.

allow *v* 1 approve, authorize, consent to, enable, grant permission for, let, license, permit, sanction, stand, tolerate. *Opp* FORBID. 2 acknowledge, admit, concede, grant, own. 3 ▷ ALLOT. *Opp* DENY.

allowance *n* 1 allocation, measure, portion, quota, ration, share. 2 alimony, annuity, grant, payment, pension, pocket money. 3 *allowance on the full price*. deduction, discount, rebate, reduction. **make allowances for** ▷ TOLERATE.

alloy *n* admixture, aggregate, amalgam, blend, compound, fusion, mixture.

allude *v* **allude to** make an allusion to, mention, refer to, speak of, touch on.

allure *v* attract, beguile, cajole, charm, draw, entice, fascinate, lead on, lure, seduce, tempt.

allusion *n* mention, reference, suggestion.

ally *n* abettor, accessory, accomplice, associate, backer, collaborator, colleague, companion, comrade, friend, helper, *inf* mate, partner, supporter. *Opp* ENEMY.
• *v* affiliate, amalgamate, associate, collaborate, combine, cooperate, form an alliance, fraternize, join, join forces, league, *inf* link up, side, *inf* team up, unite.

almighty *adj* 1 all-powerful, omnipotent, supreme. 2 ▷ BIG.

almost *adv* about, all but, approximately, around, as good as, just about, nearly, not quite, practically, virtually.

alone *adj* apart, deserted, desolate, forlorn, friendless, isolated, lonely, on your own, separate, single, solitary, unaccompanied, unassisted.

aloof *adj* chilly, cold, cool, detached, disinterested, dispassionate, distant, formal, haughty, inaccessible, indifferent, remote, reserved, reticent, self-contained, standoffish, supercilious, unapproachable, unconcerned, undemonstrative, unforthcoming, unfriendly, unresponsive, unsociable, unsympathetic. *Opp* FRIENDLY, SOCIABLE.

aloud *adv* audibly, clearly, distinctly, out loud.

also *adv* additionally, besides, furthermore, in addition, moreover, *joc* to boot, too.

alter *v* adapt, adjust, amend, change, convert, edit, modify, reconstruct, reform, remodel, reorganize, reshape, revise, transform, vary.

alteration *n* adjustment, amendment, change, difference, modification, reorganization, revision, transformation.

alternate *v* follow in turn, interchange, oscillate, rotate, *inf* see-saw, take turns.

alternative *n* 1 choice, option. 2 replacement, substitute.

altitude *n* elevation, height.

altogether *adv* absolutely, completely, entirely, fully, perfectly, quite, thoroughly, totally, utterly, wholly.

always *adv* consistently, constantly, continually, endlessly, eternally, evermore, forever, invariably, perpetually, persistently, regularly, repeatedly, unceasingly, unfailingly.

amalgamate *v* affiliate, ally, associate, band together, blend, coalesce, combine, come together, compound, form an alliance, fuse, integrate, join, join forces, *inf* link up, marry, merge, mix, synthesize, *inf* team up, unite. *Opp* SPLIT.

amateur *adj* inexperienced, lay, unpaid, unqualified. ▷ AMATEURISH.
• *n* dabbler, dilettante, layman, non-professional. *Opp* PROFESSIONAL.

amateurish *adj* clumsy, crude, *inf* do-it-yourself, incompetent, inept, *inf* rough-and-ready, second-rate, shoddy, unprofessional, unskilful, untrained. *Opp* SKILLED.

amaze *v* astonish, astound, awe, bewilder, daze, dumbfound, flabbergast, perplex, shock, stagger, startle, stun, stupefy, surprise. **amazed** ▷ SURPRISED.

amazing *adj* astonishing, astounding, breathtaking, exceptional, exciting, extraordinary, *inf* fantastic, incredible, miraculous, phenomenal, prodigious, remarkable, *inf* sensational, shocking, staggering, startling, stunning, stupendous, wonderful. *Opp* ORDINARY.

ambassador *n* agent, attaché, consul, delegate, diplomat, emissary, envoy, representative.

ambiguous *adj* ambivalent, confusing, enigmatic, indefinite, indeterminate, puzzling, unclear, vague, woolly. ▷ UNCERTAIN. *Opp* DEFINITE.

ambition *n* 1 commitment, drive, energy, enterprise, enthusiasm, *inf* go, initiative, *inf* push, thrust, zeal. 2 aim, aspiration, desire, dream, goal, hope, ideal, intention, object, objective, target, wish.

ambitious *adj* 1 committed, eager, enterprising, enthusiastic, go-ahead, *inf* go-getting, keen, *inf* pushy, zealous. 2 *ambitious ideas.* *inf* big, far-reaching, grand, grandiose, unrealistic. *Opp* APATHETIC.

ambivalent *adj* ambiguous, contradictory, equivocal, hesitant, indecisive, unclear, unresolved. ▷ UNCERTAIN.

ambush *n* attack, snare, surprise attack, trap.
• *v* attack, ensnare, intercept, lie in wait for, pounce on, surprise, trap, waylay.

amenable *adj* accommodating, acquiescent, adaptable, agreeable, complaisant, compliant, cooperative, docile, open-minded, persuadable, responsive, tractable, willing. *Opp* OBSTINATE.

amend *v* adapt, adjust, alter, ameliorate, change, correct, edit, improve, mend, modify, put right, rectify, reform, remedy, revise, transform, vary.

amiable *adj* affable, agreeable, amicable, friendly, genial, good-natured, kind-hearted, kindly, likeable, well-disposed. *Opp* UNFRIENDLY.

ammunition *n* bullets, cartridges, grenades, missiles, rounds, shells, shrapnel.

amoral *adj* unethical, unprincipled, without standards.

amorous *adj* affectionate, ardent, doting, enamoured, fond, impassioned, loving, lustful, passionate, *sl* randy, sexy. *Opp* COLD.

amount *n* aggregate, bulk, entirety, extent, lot, mass, measure, quantity, reckoning, size, sum, supply, total, value, volume, whole.
• *v* **amount to** add up to, come to, equal, make, mean, total.

ample *adj* abundant, bountiful, broad, capacious, commodious, considerable, copious, extensive, generous, great, large, lavish, liberal, munificent, plentiful, profuse, roomy, spacious, substantial, unstinting, voluminous. *Opp* INSUFFICIENT.

amplify *v* 1 add to, augment, broaden, develop, elaborate, enlarge, expand, expatiate on, extend, fill out, lengthen, make fuller, supplement. 2 *amplify sound.* boost, heighten, increase, intensify, magnify, make louder. *Opp* DECREASE.

amputate *v* chop off, cut off, dock, lop off, remove, sever, truncate. ▷ CUT.

amuse *v* absorb, cheer (up), delight, divert, engross, entertain, interest, involve, make laugh, occupy, please, *inf* tickle. *Opp* BORE. **amusing** ▷ ENJOYABLE, FUNNY.

amusement *n* 1 delight, enjoyment, fun, hilarity, laughter, mirth. ▷ MERRIMENT. 2 distraction, diversion, entertainment, game, hobby, interest, leisure activity, pastime, play, pleasure, recreation, sport.

anaemic *adj* bloodless, colourless, pale, pallid, pasty, sallow, sickly, unhealthy, wan, weak.

analogy *n* comparison, likeness, metaphor, parallel, resemblance, similarity, simile.

analyse *v* break down, dissect, evaluate, examine, interpret, investigate, scrutinize, separate out, test.

analysis *n* breakdown, critique, dissection, enquiry, evaluation, examination, interpretation, investigation, *inf* post-mortem, scrutiny, study, test.

analytical *adj* analytic, critical, *inf* in-depth, inquiring, investigative, logical, methodical, penetrating, questioning, rational, searching, systematic.

anarchy *n* bedlam, chaos, confusion, disorder, insurrection, lawlessness, misrule, mutiny, pandemonium, riot. *Opp* ORDER.

ancestor *n* antecedent, forebear, forefather, forerunner, precursor, predecessor.

ancestry *n* blood, derivation, descent, extraction, family, genealogy, heredity, line, lineage, origin, parentage, pedigree, roots, stock, strain.

anchor *v* berth, make fast, moor, secure, tie up. ▷ FASTEN.

anchorage *n* harbour, haven, moorings, port, shelter.

ancient *adj* 1 aged, antediluvian, antiquated, antique, archaic, fossilized, obsolete, old, old-fashioned, out-of-date, passé, superannuated, time-worn, venerable. 2 *ancient times.* bygone, earlier, early, former, olden (*days*), past, prehistoric, primitive, primordial, remote, *old use* of yore. *Opp* MODERN.

angel *n* archangel, cherub, divine messenger, seraph.

angelic *adj* 1 blessed, celestial, cherubic, divine, ethereal, heavenly, holy, seraphic, spiritual. 2 *angelic behaviour.* exemplary, saintly, virtuous. ▷ GOOD. *Opp* DEVILISH.

anger *n* annoyance, antagonism, bitterness, displeasure, exasperation, fury, hostility, indignation, ire, irritation, outrage, passion, rage, resentment, spleen, vexation, wrath.
• *v inf* aggravate, antagonize, displease, *inf* drive mad, enrage, exasperate, incense, inflame, infuriate, irritate, madden, *inf* make someone's blood boil, outrage, provoke, vex. ▷ ANNOY. *Opp* PACIFY.

angle *n* 1 bend, corner, crook, nook. 2 *new angle.* approach, outlook, perspective, point of view, position, slant, standpoint, viewpoint.
• *v* bend, slant, turn, twist.

angry *adj* apoplectic, bad-tempered, bitter, *inf* bristling, choleric, crabby, cross, disgruntled, enraged, exasperated, fiery, fuming, furious, heated, hostile, *inf* hot under the collar, incensed, indignant, infuriated, *inf* in high dudgeon, irascible, irate, irritated, livid, mad, outraged, raging, *inf* ratty, raving, resentful, seething, smouldering, *inf* sore, *inf* steamed up, vexed, *inf* up in arms, wild, wrathful. ▷ ANNOYED. *Opp* CALM. **be angry, become angry** *inf* blow up, boil, bridle, bristle, flare up, *inf* fly off the handle, fulminate, fume, *inf* get steamed up, lose your temper, rage, rant, rave, *inf* see red, seethe, snap, storm. **make angry** ▷ ANGER.

anguish *n* agony, anxiety, distress, grief, heartache, misery, pain, sorrow, suffering, torment, torture, woe.

angular *adj* bent, crooked, jagged, sharp-cornered, zigzag. *Opp* STRAIGHT.

animal *adj* beastly, bestial, brutish, carnal, fleshly, inhuman, instinctive, physical, savage, sensual, subhuman, wild.

• *n* 1 beast, being, brute, creature, *pl* fauna, organism, *pl* wildlife. 2 amphibian, bird, fish, insect, invertebrate, mammal, reptile, vertebrate.

animate *adj* alive, breathing, conscious, feeling, live, living, sentient. ▷ ANIMATED. *Opp* INANIMATE.
•*v* activate, arouse, brighten up, cheer up, encourage, energize, enliven, excite, fire, galvanize, incite, inspire, invigorate, kindle, move, *inf* pep up, quicken, revitalize, revive, rouse, spark, spur, stimulate, stir, urge.

animated *adj* active, alive, bright, brisk, bubbling, busy, eager, ebullient, energetic, enthusiastic, excited, exuberant, gay, impassioned, lively, passionate, quick, spirited, sprightly, vibrant, vigorous, vivacious. *Opp* LETHARGIC.

animation *n* activity, eagerness, ebullience, energy, enthusiasm, excitement, gaiety, high spirits, life, liveliness, *inf* pep, sparkle, spirit, verve, vigour, vitality, vivacity, zest. *Opp* LETHARGY.

animosity *n* acrimony, antagonism, antipathy, aversion, bad blood, bitterness, dislike, enmity, grudge, hate, hatred, hostility, ill will, loathing, malevolence, malice, odium, rancour, resentment, sourness, spite, unfriendliness, venom, vindictiveness, virulence. *Opp* FRIENDLINESS.

annex *v* acquire, appropriate, conquer, occupy, purloin, seize, take over, usurp.

annihilate *v* destroy, eliminate, eradicate, erase, exterminate, extinguish, extirpate, *inf* kill off, liquidate, obliterate, raze, slaughter, wipe out.

annotation *n* comment, commentary, elucidation, explanation, footnote, gloss, interpretation, note.

announce *v* 1 advertise, broadcast, declare, disclose, divulge, give notice of, make public, notify, proclaim, publicize, publish, put out, report, reveal, state. 2 *announce a speaker.* introduce, present.

announcement *n* advertisement, bulletin, communiqué, declaration, disclosure, notification, proclamation, publication, report, revelation, statement.

announcer *n* anchorman, broadcaster, commentator, compère, disc jockey, DJ, herald, master of ceremonies, *inf* MC, messenger, newscaster, newsreader, reporter.

annoy *v inf* aggravate, antagonize, badger, bother, *sl* bug, displease, drive mad, exasperate, fret, gall, *inf* get on your nerves, grate, harass, harry, infuriate, irk, irritate, jar, madden, make cross, molest, *inf* needle, *inf* nettle, offend, pester, pique, *inf* plague, provoke, put out, rankle, rile, *inf* rub up the wrong way, ruffle, tease, trouble, try (someone's patience), upset, vex, worry. ▷ ANGER. *Opp* PLEASE.

annoyance *n* 1 chagrin, displeasure, exasperation, irritation, pique, vexation. ▷ ANGER. 2 *Noise is an annoyance. inf* aggravation, bother, irritant, nuisance, *inf* pain in the neck, pest, provocation, worry.

annoyed *adj* chagrined, cross, displeased, exasperated, *inf* huffy, irritated, *inf* miffed, *inf* nettled, offended, *inf* peeved, piqued, put out, *inf* shirty, *inf* sore, upset, vexed. ▷ ANGRY. *Opp* PLEASED. **be annoyed** take offence, *inf* take umbrage.

annoying *adj inf* aggravating, displeasing, exasperating, galling, grating, inconvenient, infuriating, irksome, irritating, maddening, offensive, provocative, tiresome, troublesome, trying, upsetting, vexatious, vexing, worrying.

anoint *v* 1 lubricate, oil, smear. 2 baptize, consecrate, sanctify.

anonymous *adj* 1 incognito, nameless, unidentified, unknown, unnamed, unspecified, unsung. 2 *anonymous letters.* unsigned. 3 *anonymous style.* characterless, impersonal, nondescript, unidentifiable, unrecognizable.

answer *n* 1 acknowledgement, *inf* comeback, reaction, rejoinder, reply, response, retort, riposte. 2 explanation, solution. 3 *answer to a charge.* countercharge, defence, plea, refutation, vindication.
• *v* 1 acknowledge, give an answer, react, reply, respond, retort, return. 2 explain, resolve, solve. 3 *answer a charge.* counter, defend yourself against, refute. 4 *answer a need.* correspond to, fit, meet, satisfy, serve, suffice, suit. **answer back** ▷ ARGUE.

antagonism *n* antipathy, enmity, friction, opposition, rivalry, strife. ▷ HOSTILITY.

antagonize *v* alienate, anger, annoy, irritate, make an enemy of, offend, provoke, upset.

anthem *n* canticle, chant, hymn, psalm.

anthology *n* collection, compendium, compilation, digest, miscellany, selection, treasury.

anticipate *v* 1 forestall, pre-empt, prevent. 2 ▷ FORESEE.

anticlimax *n* bathos, *inf* come-down,

inf damp squib, disappointment, *inf* let-down.

antics *pl n* capers, clowning, escapades, *inf* larking-about, pranks, *inf* skylarking, tomfoolery, tricks.

antidote *n* antitoxin, corrective, countermeasure, cure, neutralizing agent, remedy.

antiquated *adj* anachronistic, ancient, antediluvian, archaic, dated, obsolete, old, old-fashioned, outmoded, out-of-date, passé, *inf* past it, *inf* prehistoric, primitive, quaint, superannuated, unfashionable. ▷ ANTIQUE. *Opp* NEW.

antique *adj* collectible, historic, traditional, veteran, vintage. ▷ ANTIQUATED.
▪ *n* collectible, collector's item, curio, curiosity, *Fr* objet d'art, rarity.

antiquity *n* classical times, days gone by, former times, olden days, the past.

antiseptic *adj* aseptic, clean, disinfectant, disinfected, germ free, germicidal, hygienic, medicated, sterile, sterilized, sterilizing.

antisocial *adj* alienated, disagreeable, disruptive, misanthropic, obnoxious, offensive, rebellious, rude, troublesome, uncooperative, unruly, unsociable. ▷ UNFRIENDLY. *Opp* SOCIABLE.

anxiety *n* 1 angst, apprehension, concern, disquiet, distress, doubt, dread, fear, foreboding, misgiving, nervousness, stress, tension, uncertainty, unease, worry. 2 *anxiety to succeed.* desire, eagerness, impatience, longing.

anxious *adj* 1 afraid, agitated, apprehensive, concerned, desperate, distraught, distressed, disturbed, edgy, fearful, *inf* fraught, fretful, *inf* jittery, nervous, *inf* on edge, perturbed, restless, solicitous, tense, troubled, uneasy, upset, worried. 2 *anxious to succeed.* *inf* desperate, *inf* dying, eager, impatient, itching, keen, longing, yearning. **be anxious** ▷ WORRY.

apathetic *adj* casual, cool, dispassionate, half-hearted, impassive, indifferent, languid, lethargic, listless, passive, phlegmatic, sluggish, tepid, torpid, unambitious, uncommitted, unconcerned, unenthusiastic, uninterested, uninvolved, unresponsive. *Opp* ENTHUSIASTIC.

apathy *n* coolness, indifference, lassitude, lethargy, listlessness, passivity, torpor. *Opp* ENTHUSIASM.

apex *n* 1 crest, crown, head, peak, pinnacle, point, summit, tip, top. 2 *apex of your career.* acme, climax, crowning moment, culmination, height, high point, zenith. *Opp* NADIR.

aphrodisiac *adj* arousing, erotic, sexy, stimulating.

apologetic *adj* ashamed, conscience-stricken, contrite, penitent, regretful, remorseful, repentant, rueful, sorry. *Opp* UNREPENTANT.

apologize *v* be apologetic, express regret, make an apology, repent, say sorry.

apology *n* defence, excuse, explanation, justification, plea.

apostle *n* crusader, disciple, evangelist, follower, missionary, preacher, teacher.

appal *v* disgust, dismay, distress, horrify, nauseate, outrage, revolt, shock, sicken. ▷ FRIGHTEN. **appalling** ▷ ATROCIOUS, BAD, FRIGHTENING.

apparatus *n* appliance, contraption, device, equipment, gadget, *inf* gear, implement, instrument, machine, machinery, mechanism, system, tackle, tool, utensil.

apparent *adj* blatant, clear, conspicuous, discernible, evident, manifest, noticeable, obvious, ostensible, overt, patent, perceptible, recognizable, self-explanatory, unconcealed, unmistakable, visible. *Opp* HIDDEN.

apparition *n* chimera, ghost, hallucination, illusion, manifestation, phantasm, phantom, presence, shade, spectre, spirit, *inf* spook, vision, wraith.

appeal *n* 1 application, call, cry, entreaty, petition, plea, prayer, request, supplication. 2 allure, charisma, charm, *inf* pull, seductiveness.
▪ *v* ask earnestly, beg, beseech, call, canvass, entreat, implore, invoke, petition, plead, pray, request, solicit, supplicate. **appeal to** ▷ ATTRACT.

appear *v* 1 arise, arrive, be published, be seen, *inf* bob up, come into view, come out, *inf* crop up, develop, emerge, *inf* heave into sight, loom, materialize, occur, show, spring up, surface, turn up. 2 *I appear to be wrong.* look, seem, transpire, turn out. 3 *appear in a play.* ▷ PERFORM.

appearance *n* 1 arrival, advent, presence. 2 *smart appearance.* air, aspect, bearing, demeanour, exterior, impression, likeness, look, mien, semblance.

appease *v* assuage, calm, conciliate, humour, mollify, pacify, placate, quiet, reconcile, satisfy, soothe, *inf* sweeten, win over. *Opp* ANGER.

appendix *n* addendum, addition, codicil, epilogue, postscript, rider, supplement.

appetite *n* craving, demand, desire, eagerness, greed, hankering, hunger, keenness, longing, lust, passion, predilection, relish, stomach, taste, thirst, urge, willingness, wish, yearning, *inf* yen, zest.

appetizing *adj* delicious, *inf* moreish, mouthwatering, tasty, tempting.

applaud *v* acclaim, approve, *inf* bring the house down, cheer, clap, commend, compliment, congratulate, eulogize, extol, give an ovation, laud, praise, salute. *Opp* CRITICIZE.

applause *n* acclaim, approval, cheering, clapping, ovation, plaudits. ▷ PRAISE.

appliance *n* apparatus, contraption, device, gadget, implement, instrument, machine, mechanism, tool, utensil.

applicant *n* candidate, competitor, entrant, interviewee.

apply *v* 1 administer, affix, put on, rub on, spread, stick. ▷ FASTEN. 2 *rules apply to all.* be relevant, have a bearing (on), pertain, refer, relate. 3 *apply common sense.* employ, exercise, implement, practise, use, utilize, wield. **apply for** ▷ REQUEST. **apply yourself** ▷ CONCENTRATE.

appoint *v* 1 arrange, decide on, determine, establish, fix, ordain, settle. 2 *appoint you to do a job.* assign, choose, delegate, depute, designate, detail, elect, name, nominate, *inf* plump for, select, settle on, vote for.

appointment *n* 1 arrangement, assignation, consultation, date, engagement, fixture, interview, meeting, rendezvous, session. 2 choice, choosing, election, naming, nomination, selection. 3 job, office, place, position, post, situation.

appreciate *v* 1 admire, approve of, be grateful for, cherish, commend, enjoy, esteem, find worthwhile, like, praise, prize, rate highly, respect, sympathize with, treasure, value, welcome. 2 *appreciate the facts.* acknowledge, comprehend, know, realize, recognize, see, understand. 3 *property value appreciates.* build up, escalate, go up, grow, improve, increase, inflate, mount, rise, soar. *Opp* DEPRECIATE, DESPISE, DISREGARD.

apprehensive *adj* afraid, concerned, disturbed, edgy, fearful, *inf* jittery, nervous, uneasy, worried. ▷ ANXIOUS. *Opp* FEARLESS.

apprentice *n* beginner, learner, novice, probationer, pupil, starter, trainee.

approach *n* 1 advance, advent, arrival, coming. 2 access, doorway, entrance, entry, road, way in. 3 attitude, method, mode, procedure, style, system, technique, way. 4 appeal, application, invitation, offer, overture, proposal, proposition.
• *v* 1 advance, bear down, catch up, draw near, gain (on), loom, move towards, near. *Opp* RETREAT. 2 *approach a task.* ▷ BEGIN. 3 *approach someone for help.* ▷ CONTACT.

approachable *adj* accessible, affable, informal, kind, open, relaxed, sympathetic, well-disposed. ▷ FRIENDLY. *Opp* ALOOF.

appropriate *adj* applicable, apposite, apt, befitting, compatible, correct, deserved, due, felicitous, fit, fitting, happy, just, opportune, pertinent, proper, relevant, right, seasonable, seemly, suitable, tactful, tasteful, timely, well-judged, well-timed. *Opp* INAPPROPRIATE.
• *v* annex, commandeer, confiscate, *inf* hijack, requisition, seize, take, take over, usurp. ▷ STEAL.

approval *n* 1 acclaim, acclamation, admiration, applause, appreciation, approbation, commendation, esteem, favour, liking, plaudits, praise, regard, respect, support. *Opp* DISAPPROVAL. 2 acceptance, acquiescence, agreement, assent, authorization, *inf* blessing, consent, endorsement, *inf* go-ahead, *inf* green light, *inf* OK, permission, ratification, sanction, seal, stamp, *inf* thumbs up. *Opp* REFUSAL.

approve *v* accede to, accept, agree to, allow, authorize, *inf* back, confirm, consent to, countenance, endorse, *inf* give your blessing to, pass, permit, ratify, *inf* rubber-stamp, sanction, sign, support, uphold. *Opp* REFUSE, VETO. **approve of** ▷ ADMIRE.

approximate *adj* estimated, imprecise, loose, rough. *Opp* EXACT.
• *v* **approximate to** approach, be similar to, come near to, equal roughly, resemble.

approximately *adv* about, approaching, around, close to, just about, more or less, nearly, *inf* nigh on, *inf* pushing, roughly, round about.

aptitude *n* ability, bent, capability, facility, fitness, flair, gift, suitability, talent. ▷ SKILL.

arbitrary *adj* 1 capricious, casual, chance, erratic, irrational, random, subjective, unpredictable, unreasonable, whimsical. *Opp* METHODICAL. 2 *arbitrary rule.* absolute, autocratic, despotic, dictatorial, high-handed, imperious, summary, tyrannical, uncompromising.

arbitrate *v* adjudicate, decide the outcome,

intercede, judge, make peace, mediate, negotiate, referee, settle, umpire.

arbitration *n* adjudication, intercession, judgement, mediation, negotiation, settlement.

arbitrator *n* adjudicator, arbiter, go-between, intermediary, judge, mediator, middleman, negotiator, ombudsman, peacemaker, referee, umpire.

arch *n* arc, archway, bridge.
• *v* bend, bow. ▷ CURVE.

archetype *n* classic, example, ideal, model, original, paradigm, pattern, precursor, prototype, standard.

archives *n* annals, chronicles, documents, papers, records, registers.

ardent *adj* eager, enthusiastic, fervent, hot, impassioned, intense, keen, passionate, warm, zealous. *Opp* APATHETIC.

arduous *adj* demanding, exhausting, gruelling, herculean, laborious, onerous, punishing, rigorous, severe, strenuous, taxing, tiring, uphill. ▷ DIFFICULT. *Opp* EASY.

area *n* 1 acreage, breadth, expanse, extent, patch, sheet, space, stretch, surface, tract, width. 2 district, environment, environs, locality, neighbourhood, part, precinct, province, quarter, region, sector, terrain, territory, vicinity, zone. 3 *area of study*. field, sphere, subject.

argue *v* 1 answer back, *inf* bandy words, bicker, debate, demur, differ, disagree, discuss, dispute, dissent, fall out, fight, haggle, *inf* have words, quarrel, *inf* row, spar, squabble, wrangle. 2 *argue a case*. assert, claim, contend, demonstrate, hold, maintain, plead, prove, reason, show, suggest.

argument *n* 1 altercation, bickering, clash, conflict, controversy, difference (of opinion), disagreement, dispute, fight, quarrel, *inf* row, *inf* set-to, squabble, *inf* tiff, wrangle. 2 debate, deliberation, discussion. 3 *argument of a lecture*. case, contention, gist, hypothesis, idea, outline, reasoning, theme, thesis, view.

arid *adj* 1 barren, desert, dry, fruitless, infertile, lifeless, parched, sterile, unproductive, waste, waterless. *Opp* FRUITFUL. 2 ▷ BORING.

arise *v* come up, *inf* crop up, get up, rise. ▷ APPEAR.

aristocrat *n* grandee, lady, lord, nobleman, noblewoman, peer.

aristocratic *adj inf* blue-blooded, courtly, élite, lordly, noble, patrician, princely, royal, thoroughbred, titled, upper class.

arm *n* appendage, bough, branch, extension, limb, offshoot, projection.
• *v* equip, fortify, furnish, provide, supply. **arms** ▷ WEAPON(S).

armed services *pl n* air force, army, forces, militia, navy, troops.

armistice *n* agreement, ceasefire, peace, treaty, truce.

armoury *n* ammunition-dump, arsenal, magazine, stockpile.

aroma *n* bouquet, fragrance, odour, perfume, redolence, savour, scent, smell, whiff.

arouse *v* awaken, call forth, encourage, foment, foster, kindle, provoke, quicken, stimulate, stir up, *inf* whip up. ▷ CAUSE. *Opp* ALLAY.

arrange *v* 1 adjust, align, array, categorize, classify, collate, display, dispose, distribute, grade, group, lay out, marshal, order, organize, position, put in order, range, set out, sort (out), systematize, tabulate, tidy up. 2 *arrange a meeting*. bring about, contrive, coordinate, devise, organize, plan, prepare, see to, set up. 3 *arrange music*. adapt, orchestrate.

arrangement *n* 1 adjustment, alignment, design, distribution, grouping, layout, organization, planning, positioning, spacing, tabulation. ▷ ARRAY. 2 agreement, bargain, contract, deal, pact, scheme, settlement, terms, understanding. 3 *musical arrangement*. adaptation, orchestration, setting, version.

array *n* arrangement, assemblage, collection, display, exhibition, formation, *inf* line-up, panoply, parade, show.
• *v* 1 adorn, attire, clothe, deck, decorate, dress, equip, fit out, garb, robe, wrap. 2 ▷ ARRANGE.

arrest *n* capture, detention, seizure.
• *v* 1 bar, block, check, delay, end, halt, hinder, impede, inhibit, interrupt, obstruct, prevent, restrain, retard, slow, stem, stop. 2 *arrest a suspect*. apprehend, capture, catch, *inf* collar, detain, have up, hold, *inf* nab, *inf* nick, seize, take into custody.

arrival *n* 1 advent, appearance, approach, entrance, homecoming, landing, return, touchdown. 2 *new arrival*. caller, newcomer, visitor.

arrive *v* 1 appear, come, disembark, enter, get in, land, make an entrance, *inf* roll up, show up, touch down, turn up. 2 ▷ SUCCEED. **arrive at** ▷ REACH.

arrogant *adj* boastful, brash, brazen, bumptious, cavalier, *inf* cocky, conceited, condescending, disdainful, egotistical, haughty, *inf* high and mighty, high-handed, imperious, lofty, overbearing, patronizing, pompous, presumptuous, proud, scornful, self-important, *inf* snooty, *inf* stuck-up, supercilious, superior, vain. *Opp* MODEST.

arsonist *n* fire-raiser, incendiary, pyromaniac.

art *n* 1 aptitude, artistry, cleverness, craft, craftsmanship, dexterity, expertise, facility, knack, proficiency, skilfulness, skill, talent, technique, touch, trick. 2 artwork, craft, fine art.

artful *adj* astute, canny, clever, crafty, cunning, designing, devious, *inf* foxy, ingenious, scheming, shrewd, skilful, sly, smart, subtle, tricky, wily. *Opp* NAÏVE.

article *n* 1 item, object, thing. 2 *magazine article.* feature, item, piece, story.

articulate *adj* clear, coherent, comprehensible, distinct, eloquent, expressive, fluent, *derog* glib, intelligible, lucid, understandable, vocal. *Opp* INARTICULATE.
• *v* ▷ SPEAK.

articulated *adj* bending, flexible, hinged, jointed.

artificial *adj* 1 fabricated, man-made, manufactured, synthetic, unnatural. 2 *artificial style.* affected, assumed, bogus, contrived, counterfeit, fake, false, feigned, forced, imitation, insincere, mock, *inf* phoney, pretended, *inf* pseudo, *inf* put on, sham, simulated, spurious, unreal. *Opp* NATURAL.

artist *n* craftsman, craftswoman, illustrator, painter, photographer, potter, sculptor, silversmith, weaver. ▷ ENTERTAINER, MUSICIAN, PERFORMER.

artistic *adj* aesthetic, attractive, beautiful, creative, cultured, decorative, imaginative, ornamental, tasteful.

ascend *v* climb, come up, fly, go up, lift off, make an ascent, mount, move up, rise, scale, soar, take off. *Opp* DESCEND.

ascent *n* climb, gradient, hill, incline, ramp, rise, slope. *Opp* DESCENT.

ascertain *v* confirm, determine, discover, establish, find out, identify, learn, make certain, make sure, verify.

ascetic *adj* abstemious, austere, celibate, chaste, frugal, harsh, hermit-like, plain, puritanical, restrained, rigorous, self-denying, severe, spartan, strict. *Opp* SELF-INDULGENT.

ash *n* burnt remains, cinders, embers.

ashamed *adj* 1 abashed, apologetic, chagrined, chastened, conscience-stricken, contrite, guilty, humiliated, mortified, penitent, remorseful, repentant, rueful, shamefaced, sorry. 2 bashful, blushing, demure, diffident, embarrassed, modest, prudish, self-conscious, sheepish, shy. *Opp* SHAMELESS.

ask *v* appeal, apply, badger, beg, beseech, crave, demand, enquire, entreat, implore, importune, inquire, interrogate, invite, petition, plead, pray, press, query, question, quiz, request, require, seek, solicit, supplicate. **ask for** ▷ ATTRACT.

asleep *adj* comatose, *inf* dead to the world, dormant, dozing, hibernating, inactive, *inf* in the land of nod, napping, *inf* out like a light, resting, sleeping, slumbering, snoozing, unconscious. ▷ NUMB. *Opp* AWAKE.

aspect *n* 1 angle, characteristic, circumstance, detail, element, facet, feature, quality, side, standpoint, viewpoint. 2 air, appearance, attitude, bearing, countenance, demeanour, expression, face, look, manner, mien, visage. 3 *southern aspect.* direction, outlook, position, prospect, situation, view.

asperity *n* abrasiveness, acidity, astringency, bitterness, harshness, hostility, rancour, roughness, severity, sharpness, sourness, virulence. *Opp* MILDNESS.

aspiration *n* aim, ambition, craving, desire, dream, goal, hope, longing, objective, purpose, wish, yearning.

aspire *v* **aspire to** aim for, crave, desire, dream of, hope for, pursue, seek, set your sights on, want, wish for. **aspiring** ▷ POTENTIAL.

assail *v* assault, bombard, pelt, set on. ▷ ATTACK.

assault *n* battery, *inf* GBH, mugging, rape. ▷ ATTACK.
• *v inf* beat up, molest, pounce on, rape, set about, set on, violate. ▷ ATTACK.

assemble *v* 1 come together, congregate, convene, converge, crowd, flock, gather, group, herd, join up, meet, rally round, swarm. 2 accumulate, amass, bring together, collect, get together, marshal, mobilize, muster, rally, round up. 3 build, construct, erect, fabricate, make, manufacture, piece together, produce, put together. *Opp* DISMANTLE, DISPERSE.

assembly *n* conference, congregation, congress, convention, convocation, council, gathering, meeting, parliament, rally, synod. ▷ CROWD.

assent *n* acceptance, accord, acquiescence, agreement, approbation, approval, consent, *inf* go-ahead, permission, sanction, willingness. *Opp* REFUSAL.
• *v* accede, accept, acquiesce, agree, approve, comply, concede, consent, submit, yield. *Opp* REFUSE.

assert *v* affirm, allege, argue, attest, claim, contend, declare, insist, maintain, proclaim, profess, protest, state, stress, swear, testify. **assert yourself** ▷ INSIST.

assertive *adj* aggressive, authoritative, *inf* bossy, certain, confident, decided, definite, dogmatic, emphatic, firm, forceful, insistent, *derog* opinionated, peremptory, positive, *derog* pushy, self-assured, strong, strong-willed. *Opp* SUBMISSIVE.

assess *v* appraise, calculate, compute, consider, determine, estimate, evaluate, fix, gauge, judge, price, reckon, review, *inf* size up, value, weigh up.

asset *n* advantage, aid, benefit, blessing, boon, *inf* godsend, good, help, profit, resource, strength, support. **assets** capital, effects, estate, funds, goods, holdings, means, money, possessions, property, resources, savings, securities, valuables, wealth, *inf* worldly goods.

assign *v* 1 allocate, allot, apportion, consign, dispense, distribute, give, hand over, share out. 2 appoint, authorize, delegate, designate, nominate, prescribe, select, specify. 3 *assign my success to luck.* ascribe, attribute, credit.

assignment *n* chore, duty, errand, job, mission, obligation, post, project, task. ▷ WORK.

assist *v* abet, advance, aid, benefit, collaborate, cooperate, facilitate, further, help, *inf* lend a hand, promote, reinforce, relieve, second, serve, succour, support, work with. *Opp* HINDER.

assistance *n* aid, backing, collaboration, contribution, cooperation, encouragement, help, patronage, relief, succour, support. *Opp* HINDRANCE.

assistant *n* accessory, accomplice, aide, ally, associate, backer, collaborator, colleague, companion, comrade, deputy, helper, *inf* henchman, mainstay, *derog* minion, partner, *inf* right-hand man, second, second-in-command, stand-by, subordinate, supporter.

associate *n* ▷ ASSISTANT, FRIEND.
• *v* 1 ally yourself, be friends, combine, consort, fraternize, *inf* gang up, *inf* hob nob (with), keep company, link up, mingle, mix, side, socialize. *Opp* DISSOCIATE. 2 *associate snow with winter.* connect, put together, relate, *inf* tie up.

association *n* affiliation, alliance, body, brotherhood, cartel, clique, club, coalition, combination, company, confederation, consortium, corporation, federation, fellowship, group, league, merger, organization, partnership, party, society, syndicate, union. ▷ FRIENDSHIP.

assorted *adj* different, diverse, mixed, various. ▷ MISCELLANEOUS.

assortment *n* array, choice, collection, diversity, jumble, medley, miscellany, *inf* mishmash, *inf* mixed bag, mixture, potpourri, range, selection, variety.

assume *v* 1 believe, deduce, expect, guess, imagine, infer, presume, suppose, surmise, suspect, take for granted, think. 2 *assume duties.* accept, take on, undertake. 3 *assume a disguise, an attitude.* acquire, adopt, affect, don, fake, feign, pretend, put on, simulate, try on.

assumption *n* belief, conjecture, expectation, guess, hypothesis, premise, premiss, supposition, surmise, theory.

assurance *n* guarantee, oath, pledge, promise, vow, undertaking, word (of honour).

assure *v* convince, guarantee, persuade, pledge, promise, reassure, swear, vow. **assured** ▷ CONFIDENT.

astonish *v* amaze, astound, baffle, bewilder, confound, daze, *inf* dazzle, dumbfound, flabbergast, leave speechless, nonplus, shock, stagger, startle, stun, stupefy, surprise, take by surprise. **astonishing** ▷ AMAZING.

astound *v* ▷ ASTONISH.

astray *adv* adrift, lost, off course, wide of the mark, wrong.

astute *adj* acute, artful, canny, clever, crafty, cunning, discerning, ingenious, intelligent, knowing, observant, perceptive, perspicacious, sharp, shrewd, sly, subtle, wily. *Opp* STUPID.

asylum *n* haven, refuge, retreat, safety, sanctuary, shelter.

asymmetrical *adj* awry, crooked, distorted, irregular, lop-sided, unbalanced, uneven, *inf* wonky. *Opp* SYMMETRICAL.

atheist *n* heathen, pagan, sceptic, unbeliever.

athletic *adj* acrobatic, active, energetic, fit,

muscular, powerful, robust, sinewy, *inf* sporty, strong, vigorous, well-built, wiry.

athletics *pl n* field events, sports, track events.

atmosphere *n* 1 air, ether, heavens, sky, stratosphere. 2 ambience, aura, character, climate, environment, feeling, mood, spirit, tone.

atom *n inf* bit, crumb, grain, iota, jot, molecule, morsel, particle, scrap, speck, spot.

atone *v* compensate, do penance, expiate, make amends, make reparation, pay the penalty, pay the price, redeem yourself, redress.

atrocious *adj* abominable, appalling, barbaric, brutal, callous, cruel, diabolical, dreadful, evil, fiendish, frightful, grim, gruesome, heartless, heinous, hideous, horrendous, horrible, horrific, horrifying, inhuman, monstrous, nauseating, revolting, sadistic, savage, shocking, sickening, terrible, vicious, vile, villainous, wicked.

atrocity *n* crime, cruelty, enormity, offence, outrage. ▷ EVIL.

attach *v* 1 add, append, bind, combine, connect, fix, join, link, secure, stick, tie, unite. ▷ FASTEN. *Opp* DETACH. 2 ascribe, assign, associate, attribute, impute. **attached** ▷ LOVING.

attack *n* 1 ambush, assault, battery, blitz, bombardment, charge, foray, incursion, invasion, offensive, onset, onslaught, raid, rush, sortie, strike. 2 *verbal attack*. abuse, censure, criticism, diatribe, invective, outburst, tirade. 3 *attack of coughing*. bout, convulsion, fit, outbreak, paroxysm, seizure, spasm, *inf* turn.
• *v* 1 ambush, assail, assault, *inf* beat up, bombard, charge, counterattack, *inf* do over, fall on, fight, fly at, invade, jump on, lash out at, *inf* lay into, mob, mug, *inf* pitch into, pounce on, raid, set about, set on, storm, strike at, *inf* wade into. 2 *attack verbally*. abuse, censure, criticize, denounce, impugn, inveigh against, libel, malign, round on, slander, snipe at, vilify. *Opp* DEFEND. 3 *attack a task*. ▷ BEGIN.

attacker *n* aggressor, assailant, critic, detractor, enemy, fighter, intruder, invader, mugger, opponent, persecutor, raider, slanderer.

attain *v* accomplish, achieve, acquire, arrive at, complete, fulfil, gain, get, grasp, *inf* make, obtain, reach, realize, secure, touch, win.

attempt *n* bid, effort, endeavour, *inf* go, start, try.
• *v* aim, aspire, do your best, endeavour, *inf* have a go, make a bid, make an effort, put yourself out, seek, strive, tackle, try, undertake, venture.

attend *v* 1 be present, go (to), frequent, present yourself, *inf* put in an appearance, visit. 2 accompany, chaperon, conduct, escort, follow, guard, usher. 3 *attend carefully*. concentrate, hear, heed, listen, mark, mind, note, notice, observe, pay attention, watch. **attend to** assist, care for, help, look after, mind, nurse, see to, take care of, tend.

attendant *n* assistant, escort, helper, usher. ▷ SERVANT.

attention *n* 1 care, concentration, concern, diligence, heed, notice, thought, vigilance. 2 consideration, courtesy, good manners, kindness, politeness, regard, respect, thoughtfulness.

attentive *adj* 1 alert, awake, concentrating, intent, observant, watchful. *Opp* INATTENTIVE. 2 ▷ POLITE. *Opp* RUDE.

attire *n* apparel, array, clothes, clothing, costume, dress, finery, garb, garments, *inf* gear, outfit, wear.
• *v* ▷ DRESS.

attitude *n* 1 air, approach, bearing, behaviour, demeanour, disposition, frame of mind, manner, mien, mood, posture, stance. 2 *attitude towards politics*. belief, feeling, opinion, outlook, position, standpoint, thought, view, viewpoint.

attract *v* 1 allure, appeal to, beguile, bewitch, captivate, charm, enchant, entice, fascinate, interest, lure, seduce, tempt, *sl* turn someone on. 2 *a magnet attracts iron*. draw, pull. 3 *attract attention*. ask for, cause, court, generate, induce, invite, provoke, seek out, *inf* stir up. *Opp* REPEL.

attractive *adj* adorable, alluring, appealing, appetizing, becoming, bewitching, captivating, charming, *inf* cute, delightful, desirable, enchanting, endearing, engaging, enticing, fascinating, fetching, glamorous, good-looking, gorgeous, handsome, hypnotic, interesting, inviting, irresistible, lovable, lovely, magnetic, personable, pleasing, pretty, seductive, stunning, *inf* taking, tasteful, tempting, winning. ▷ BEAUTIFUL. *Opp* REPULSIVE.

attribute *n* characteristic, feature, property, quality, trait.
• *v* ascribe, assign, charge, credit, impute, put down, refer.

audacious *adj* adventurous, courageous, daring, fearless, *derog* foolhardy, intrepid, *derog* rash, *derog* reckless. ▷ BOLD. *Opp* TIMID.

audacity *n* boldness, cheek, effrontery, impertinence, impudence, presumptuousness, rashness, temerity. ▷ COURAGE.

audible *adj* clear, detectable, distinct, high, perceptible. *Opp* INAUDIBLE.

audience *n* assembly, congregation, crowd, gathering, listeners, meeting, onlookers, spectators, *inf* turn-out, viewers.

auditorium *n* assembly room, concert hall, hall, theatre.

augment *v* add to, amplify, boost, enlarge, expand, fill out, grow, increase, magnify, make larger, multiply, raise, reinforce, strengthen, supplement, swell. *Opp* DECREASE.

augur *v* bode, forebode, foreshadow, forewarn, give an omen, herald, portend, predict, promise, prophesy, signal.

augury *n* forecast, omen, portent, prophecy, sign, warning.

auspicious *adj* favourable, *inf* hopeful, lucky, promising, propitious. *Opp* OMINOUS.

austere *adj* 1 abstemious, ascetic, chaste, cold, forbidding, formal, frugal, grave, hard, harsh, hermit-like, parsimonious, puritanical, restrained, rigorous, self-denying, serious, severe, sober, spartan, stern, strict, thrifty. 2 *austere dress.* modest, plain, simple, unadorned. *Opp* LUXURIOUS, ORNATE.

authentic *adj* accurate, actual, bona fide, certain, factual, genuine, honest, legitimate, original, real, reliable, true, truthful, undisputed, valid. ▷ AUTHORITATIVE. *Opp* FALSE.

authenticate *v* certify, confirm, corroborate, endorse, substantiate, validate, verify.

author *n* 1 composer, dramatist, novelist, playwright, poet, scriptwriter, writer. 2 creator, designer, father, founder, initiator, inventor, maker, originator, prime mover.

authoritarian *adj* autocratic, *inf* bossy, despotic, dictatorial, dogmatic, domineering, strict, tyrannical.

authoritative *adj* definitive, dependable, official, recognized, sanctioned. ▷ AUTHENTIC.

authority *n* 1 approval, authorization, consent, permission, permit, sanction, warrant. 2 command, control, force, influence, jurisdiction, might, power, prerogative, right, sovereignty, supremacy, sway, weight. 3 *authority on wine. inf* buff, connoisseur, expert, specialist. **the authorities** government, management, officialdom, *inf* powers that be.

authorize *v* accede to, agree to, allow, approve, *inf* back, commission, consent to, empower, endorse, entitle, legalize, license, make official, *inf* OK, pass, permit, ratify, *inf* rubber-stamp, sanction, validate. **authorized** ▷ OFFICIAL.

automatic *adj* 1 conditioned, habitual, impulsive, instinctive, involuntary, reflex, spontaneous, unconscious, unthinking. 2 automated, computerized, mechanical, programmed, self-regulating, unmanned.

autonomous *adj* free, independent, self-determining, self-governing, sovereign.

auxiliary *adj* additional, backup, emergency, extra, reserve, secondary, spare, subordinate, subsidiary, substitute, supplementary, supporting.

available *adj* accessible, at hand, convenient, disposable, free, handy, obtainable, ready, to hand, uncommitted, usable. *Opp* INACCESSIBLE.

avaricious *adj* ▷ GREEDY.

avenge *v inf* get your own back, repay, take revenge.

average *adj* commonplace, everyday, mediocre, medium, middling, moderate, normal, regular, *inf* run-of-the-mill, typical, unexceptional, usual. ▷ ORDINARY. *Opp* EXCEPTIONAL.
▪ *n* mean, mid-point, norm, standard.
▪ *v* even out, standardize.

averse *adj* antipathetic, disinclined, hostile, opposed, reluctant, resistant, unwilling.

aversion *n* antagonism, antipathy, dislike, distaste, hostility, reluctance, unwillingness. ▷ HATRED.

avert *v* change the course of, deflect, fend off, parry, prevent, stave off, turn aside, ward off.

avoid *v* abstain from, *inf* beg the question, *inf* bypass, circumvent, dodge, *inf* duck, elude, escape, evade, fend off, find a way round, *inf* get round, *inf* give a wide berth to, ignore, keep away from, refrain from, shirk, shun, side-step, skirt round, steer clear of. *Opp* SEEK.

await *v* be ready for, expect, hope for, lie in wait for, look out for, wait for.

awake *adj* 1 aware, conscious, sleepless, *inf* tossing and turning, wakeful, wide awake. 2 ▷ ALERT. *Opp* ASLEEP.

awaken *v* alert, arouse, call, excite,

kindle, revive, rouse, stimulate, stir up, wake.

award *n* cup, decoration, gift, grant, medal, prize, reward, trophy.
• *v* allot, assign, bestow, confer, endow, give, grant, hand over, present.

aware *adj* acquainted, alive (to), appreciative, attentive, conscious, familiar, heedful, informed, knowledgeable, mindful, observant, responsive, sensitive. *Opp* IGNORANT, INSENSITIVE.

awe *n* admiration, amazement, apprehension, dread, fear, respect, reverence, terror, veneration, wonder.

awe-inspiring *adj* awesome, breathtaking, dramatic, grand, imposing, impressive, magnificent, marvellous, overwhelming, solemn, *inf* stunning, stupendous, sublime. ▷ FRIGHTENING, WONDERFUL. *Opp* INSIGNIFICANT.

awful *adj* ▷ BAD.

awkward *adj* 1 blundering, bungling, clumsy, gauche, gawky, *inf* ham-fisted, inelegant, inept, maladroit, uncoordinated, ungainly, ungraceful, unskilful. 2 *awkward load.* bulky, cumbersome, unmanageable, unwieldy. 3 *awkward problem.* annoying, difficult, inconvenient, perplexing, *inf* thorny, ticklish, troublesome, trying, vexing. 4 *awkward silence.* embarrassing, touchy, tricky, uncomfortable, uneasy. 5 *awkward children. inf* bloody-minded, defiant, disobedient, exasperating, intractable, naughty, obstinate, perverse, rebellious, rude, stubborn, uncooperative, undisciplined, unruly, wayward. *Opp* COOPERATIVE, EASY, NEAT.

awning *n* canopy, screen, shade, shelter, tarpaulin.

axe *n* chopper, cleaver, hatchet.
• *v* cancel, cut, discontinue, dismiss, eliminate, get rid of, *inf* give the chop to, remove, sack, withdraw.

axle *n* rod, shaft, spindle.

B

baby *n* babe, child, infant, newborn, toddler.

babyish *adj* childish, immature, infantile, juvenile, puerile, simple. *Opp* MATURE.

back *adj* dorsal, end, hind, hindmost, last, rear, rearmost.
• *n* 1 end, hindquarters, posterior, rear, stern, tail, tail-end. 2 reverse, verso. *Opp* FRONT.
• *v* 1 back away, backtrack, *inf* beat a retreat, give way, move back, recede, recoil, retire, retreat, reverse. *Opp* ADVANCE. 2 ▷ SUPPORT. **back down** ▷ RETREAT. **back out** ▷ WITHDRAW.

backer *n* ▷ SPONSOR.

background *n* 1 circumstances, context, history, *inf* lead-up, setting, surroundings. 2 education, experience, tradition, training, upbringing.

backing *n* 1 aid, approval, assistance, encouragement, endorsement, funding, grant, help, investment, loan, patronage, sponsorship, subsidy, support. 2 *musical backing*. accompaniment, orchestration.

backward *adj* 1 retreating, retrograde, reverse. 2 bashful, coy, diffident, hesitant, inhibited, modest, reluctant, reserved, reticent, self-effacing, shy, timid, unassertive, unforthcoming. 3 *backward pupil*. disadvantaged, immature, late-starting, slow, undeveloped. *Opp* FORWARD.

bad *adj* 1 *bad men, deeds*. abhorrent, base, corrupt, criminal, cruel, dangerous, delinquent, deplorable, depraved, evil, guilty, immoral, infamous, malevolent, malicious, mean, mischievous, nasty, naughty, offensive, reprehensible, shameful, sinful, vicious, vile, villainous, wicked, wrong. 2 *bad accident*. appalling, awful, calamitous, dire, disastrous, dreadful, frightful, ghastly, grave, hair-raising, hideous, horrible, serious, severe, shocking, terrible, unfortunate, unpleasant, violent. 3 *bad driving, work*. abominable, abysmal, appalling, atrocious, awful, *inf* chronic, defective, diabolical, disgraceful, dreadful, faulty, feeble, hopeless, inadequate, incompetent, incorrect, inferior, *inf* lousy, pitiful, poor, shoddy, *inf* sorry, substandard, unsatisfactory, useless, weak, worthless. 4 *bad conditions*. adverse, detrimental, discouraging, *inf* frightful, harmful, harsh, hostile, inauspicious, prejudicial, uncongenial, unfavourable, unfortunate. 5 *bad smell*. decayed, decomposing, foul, loathsome, mildewed, mouldy, nauseating, noxious, obnoxious, odious, offensive, polluted, putrid, rancid, repulsive, revolting, sickening, rotten, sour. 6 *I feel bad*. ▷ ILL. *Opp* GOOD.

badge *n* chevron, crest, device, emblem, insignia, logo, mark, medal, sign, symbol, token.

bad-tempered *adj* angry, cantankerous, crabby, cross, crotchety, disgruntled, dyspeptic, gruff, grumpy, hostile, ill-humoured, irascible, irritable, moody, morose, peevish, petulant, quarrelsome, querulous, rude, short-tempered, shrewish, snappy, *inf* stroppy, sulky, sullen, truculent. *Opp* GOOD-TEMPERED.

baffle *v* 1 *inf* bamboozle, bemuse, bewilder, confound, confuse, *inf* floor, *inf* flummox, frustrate, mystify, perplex, puzzle, *inf* stump. **baffling** ▷ INEXPLICABLE.

bag *n* carrier, carrier bag, case, handbag, haversack, holdall, rucksack, sack, satchel, shopping bag. ▷ BAGGAGE.
• *v* capture, catch, ensnare, snare.

baggage *n* accoutrements, bags, belongings, *inf* gear, paraphernalia. ▷ LUGGAGE.

bait *n* attraction, bribe, *inf* carrot, decoy, inducement, lure, temptation.
• *v* annoy, goad, harass, hound, persecute, pester, provoke, tease, torment.

balance *n* 1 scales, weighing machine. 2 equilibrium, poise, stability, steadiness. 3 correspondence, equality, evenness, parity, symmetry. 4 *spend a bit & save the balance*. remainder, surplus.
• *v* 1 compensate for, counterbalance, equalize, even up, level, make steady, match, offset, stabilize. 2 keep balanced, poise, steady, support. **balanced** ▷ EVEN, IMPARTIAL, STABLE.

bald *adj* 1 bare, hairless, smooth, thin on top. 2 *bald truth*. direct, forthright, plain, simple, stark, unadorned, uncompromising.

bale *n* bunch, bundle, pack, package.
• *v* **bale out** eject, escape, jump out.

ball *n* 1 drop, globe, globule, orb, sphere. 2 dance, disco, party.

balloon *n* airship, dirigible, hot-air balloon.
• *v* ▷ BILLOW.

ballot *n* election, plebiscite, poll, referendum, vote.

ban *n* boycott, embargo, moratorium, prohibition, veto.
• *v* banish, bar, debar, disallow, exclude, forbid, make illegal, ostracize, outlaw, prevent, prohibit, proscribe, restrict, stop, suppress, veto. *Opp* PERMIT.

banal *adj* boring, clichéd, commonplace, *inf* corny, dull, hackneyed, humdrum, obvious, *inf* old hat, ordinary, over-used, pedestrian, platitudinous, stereotyped, trite, unimaginative, unoriginal.

band *n* 1 belt, border, hoop, line, loop, ribbon, ring, strip, stripe, swathe. 2 body, clique, club, company, crew, gang, horde, party, troop. ▷ GROUP. 3 [*music*] ensemble, group, orchestra.

bandage *n* dressing, gauze, lint, plaster.

bandit *n* brigand, buccaneer, desperado, gangster, gunman, highwayman, hijacker, marauder, outlaw, pirate, robber, thief.

bandy *adj* bandy-legged, bowed, bow-legged.
• *v* *bandy words.* exchange, swap. ▷ ARGUE.

bang *n* 1 blow, bump, collision, knock, punch, smack, thump, *sl* wallop, *inf* whack. 2 blast, boom, clap, crash, explosion, shot.

banish *v* 1 deport, drive out, eject, evict, exile, expatriate, expel, ostracize, oust, outlaw, send away. 2 ban, bar, debar, eliminate, exclude, make illegal, prohibit, proscribe, put an embargo on, remove, suppress, veto.

bank *n* 1 declivity, dyke, earthwork, embankment, gradient, incline, mound, ramp, ridge, rise, slope. 2 *river bank.* brink, edge, margin, shore, side. 3 *bank of controls.* array, collection, display, group, panel, row, series.
• *v* 1 incline, lean, list, pitch, slope, tilt, tip. 2 *bank money.* deposit, save.

bankrupt *adj inf* broke, failed, *sl* gone bust, gone into liquidation, insolvent, ruined, wound up. ▷ POOR. *Opp* SOLVENT.

banner *n* colours, ensign, flag, pennant, pennon, standard, streamer.

banquet *n inf* binge, *sl* blow-out, dinner, feast, repast, *inf* spread.

banter *n* chaffing, joking, raillery, repartee, teasing, wordplay.

bar *n* 1 beam, girder, pole, rail, railing, rod, shaft, stake, stick, strut. 2 barrier, deterrent, impediment, obstacle, obstruction. 3 *bar of colour.* band, line, streak, strip, stripe. 4 *bar of soap.* block, cake, chunk, hunk, ingot, lump, nugget, piece, slab, wedge. 5 café, counter, wine bar. ▷ PUB.
• *v* 1 ban, banish, debar, exclude, keep out, ostracize, outlaw, prohibit. 2 block, deter, halt, hinder, impede, obstruct, prevent, stop, thwart.

barbarian *adj* ▷ BARBARIC.
• *n* heathen, ignoramus, lout, pagan, philistine, savage, vandal, *sl* yob.

barbaric *adj* barbarous, brutal, brutish, crude, inhuman, primitive, rough, savage, uncivilized, wild. ▷ CRUEL. *Opp* CIVILIZED.

bare *adj* 1 bald, exposed, naked, nude, stark-naked, unclothed, uncovered, undressed. 2 *bare hills.* barren, bleak, desolate, open, treeless, unwooded, windswept. 3 *bare trees.* denuded, leafless, shorn, stripped. 4 *bare rooms.* austere, empty, plain, simple, unadorned, undecorated, unfurnished, vacant. 5 *bare walls.* blank, clean, unmarked. 6 *bare facts.* hard, literal, open, plain, straightforward, unconcealed, undisguised. 7 *the bare minimum.* basic, essential, just adequate, just sufficient, minimal.
• *v* expose, lay bare, make known, reveal, show, uncover, undress, unmask, unveil.

bargain *n* 1 agreement, arrangement, contract, deal, negotiation, pact, promise, settlement, transaction, understanding. 2 *bargain in the sales. inf* giveaway, good buy, *inf* snip, special offer.
• *v* argue, barter, discuss terms, do a deal, haggle, negotiate. **bargain for** ▷ EXPECT.

bark *v* 1 growl, yap. 2 *bark your shin.* chafe, graze, rub, scrape, scratch.

barmaid, barman *ns* server, steward, stewardess, waiter, waitress.

barracks *n* billet, camp, garrison, lodging, quarters.

barrage *n* 1 ▷ BARRIER. 2 *barrage of gunfire.* assault, attack, battery, bombardment, cannonade, fusillade, onslaught, salvo, storm, volley.

barrel *n* butt, cask, churn, drum, keg, tank, tub, water-butt.

barren *adj* 1 arid, bare, desert, desolate, dried-up, dry, lifeless, treeless, uncultivated, unproductive, useless, waste. 2 infertile, sterile, unfruitful. *Opp* FERTILE.

barricade *n* ▷ BARRIER.

• *v* bar, block off, defend, obstruct.

barrier *n* 1 bar, barrage, barricade, boom, bulwark, dam, embankment, fence, hurdle, obstacle, obstruction, palisade, railing, rampart, stockade, wall. 2 *barrier to progress.* handicap, hindrance, impediment, limitation, restriction, stumbling block.

barter *v* bargain, exchange, negotiate, trade.

base *adj* contemptible, cowardly, degrading, despicable, dishonourable, evil, ignoble, immoral, inferior, low, mean, selfish, shabby, shameful, sordid, undignified, unworthy, vulgar, vile. ▷ WICKED.
• *n* 1 basis, bed, bedrock, bottom, core, essentials, foot, footing, foundation, fundamentals, groundwork, infrastructure, pedestal, rest, root, stand, substructure, support, underpinning. 2 camp, centre, headquarters, starting point, station.
• *v* build, construct, establish, found, ground, locate, position, set up, station.

basement *n* cellar, crypt, vault.

bashful *adj* abashed, backward, blushing, coy, demure, diffident, embarrassed, inhibited, meek, modest, reserved, reticent, retiring, self-conscious, self-effacing, shamefaced, sheepish, shy, timid, unforthcoming. *Opp* ASSERTIVE.

basic *adj* central, chief, crucial, elementary, essential, fundamental, important, intrinsic, key, main, necessary, primary, principal, underlying, vital. *Opp* UNIMPORTANT.

basin *n* bath, bowl, container, dish, pool, sink.

basis *n* base, core, footing, foundation, ground, premise, principle, starting point, support.

bask *v* enjoy, glory, lie, lounge, luxuriate, relax, sunbathe, wallow.

basket *n* bag, hamper, pannier, punnet.

bastard *n* illegitimate child, *old use* love-child, natural child.

bat *n* club, racket, racquet.

bath *n* jacuzzi, pool, shower, *inf* soak, *inf* tub, wash.

bathe *v* 1 clean, cleanse, immerse, rinse, soak, steep, swill, wash. 2 go swimming, paddle, plunge, splash about, swim, *inf* take a dip.

bathos *n* anticlimax, *inf* come-down, disappointment, *inf* let-down. *Opp* CLIMAX.

baton *n* cane, club, cudgel, rod, staff, stick, truncheon.

batter *v* beat, bludgeon, cudgel, keep hitting, pound. ▷ HIT.

battery *n* 1 artillery unit, emplacement. 2 *electric battery.* accumulator, cell. 3 *assault and battery.* assault, attack, thrashing, violence.

battle *n* action, attack, blitz, campaign, clash, combat, conflict, contest, confrontation, crusade, encounter, engagement, fight, fray, hostilities, offensive, quarrel, *inf* shoot-out, siege, skirmish, strife, struggle, war, warfare.
• *v* ▷ FIGHT.

battlefield *n* arena, battleground, theatre of war.

bawdy *adj* earthy, erotic, lusty, *inf* naughty, racy, *inf* raunchy, ribald, sexy, *inf* spicy. [*derog*] blue, coarse, dirty, indecent, indelicate, lascivious, lewd, licentious, obscene, prurient, risqué, rude, smutty, suggestive, titillating, vulgar. *Opp* PROPER.

bawl *v* cry, roar, shout, thunder, wail, yell, yelp.

bay *n* 1 cove, creek, estuary, fjord, gulf, harbour, inlet, sound. 2 alcove, booth, compartment, opening, recess.

bazaar *n* auction, boot-sale, bring-and-buy, fair, fête, jumble sale, market, sale.

be *v* 1 be alive, breathe, endure, exist, live. 2 *be here all day.* continue, last, persist, remain, stay, survive. 3 *the next event will be at noon.* arise, happen, occur, take place. 4 *want to be a writer.* become.

beach *n* bank, coast, coastline, sand, sands, seashore, seaside, shore.

beacon *n* bonfire, fire, flare, light, lighthouse, signal.

bead *n* blob, drip, drop, droplet, globule, jewel, pearl.

beaker *n* cup, glass, goblet, jar, mug, tankard, tumbler.

beam *n* 1 bar, girder, joist, plank, post, rafter, spar, support, timber. 2 *beam of light.* gleam, ray, shaft, stream.
• *v* 1 aim, direct, emit, radiate, send out, shine, transmit. 2 *beam happily.* grin, laugh, look radiant, radiate happiness, smile.

bear *v* 1 carry, hold, shoulder, support, sustain, take. 2 *bear an inscription.* display, have, possess, show. 3 *bear gifts.* bring, carry, convey, deliver, take, transfer, transport. 4 *bear pain.* abide, accept, brook, cope with, endure, live with, put up with, stand, stomach, suffer, tolerate.

5 *bear young, fruit.* breed, develop, give birth to, produce, spawn, yield. **bear out** ▷ CONFIRM. **bear up** ▷ SURVIVE. **bear witness** ▷ TESTIFY.

bearable *adj* acceptable, endurable, supportable, tolerable.

bearing *n* 1 air, appearance, aspect, attitude, carriage, demeanour, deportment, look, manner, mien, posture, presence, stance, style. 2 *evidence had no bearing.* application, connection, pertinence, relationship, relevance, significance. **bearings** course, direction, orientation, position, sense of direction.

beast *n* brute, creature, monster, savage. ▷ ANIMAL.

beastly *adj* bestial, brutal, cruel, savage. ▷ VILE.

beat *n* 1 accent, pulse, rhythm, stress, tempo. 2 *policeman's beat.* course, itinerary, journey, path, rounds, route, way.
• *v* 1 batter, bludgeon, buffet, cane, clout, flog, hammer, knock about, lash, *inf* lay into, pound, punch, strike, *sl* tan, thrash, thump, *sl* wallop, *inf* whack, whip. ▷ HIT. 2 *beat eggs.* blend, mix, stir, whip, whisk. 3 *His heart beat faster.* palpitate, pound, pulsate, race, throb, thump. 5 *beat an opponent.* best, conquer, crush, defeat, get the better of, *inf* lick, outclass, outdistance, outdo, outwit, overcome, overpower, overthrow, overwhelm, rout, subdue, surpass, *inf* thrash, trounce, vanquish, worst. **beat up** ▷ ATTACK.

beautiful *adj* admirable, alluring, appealing, artistic, attractive, becoming, bewitching, brilliant, captivating, charming, *old use* comely, decorative, delightful, elegant, exquisite, *old use* fair, fascinating, fetching, fine, good-looking, glamorous, glorious, gorgeous, graceful, handsome, lovely, magnificent, picturesque, pleasing, pretty, radiant, ravishing, scenic, seductive, spectacular, splendid, stunning, superb, tasteful, tempting. *Opp* UGLY.

beautify *v* adorn, deck, decorate, embellish, ornament, prettify. *Opp* DISFIGURE.

beauty *n* allure, appeal, attractiveness, bloom, charm, elegance, glamour, glory, grace, loveliness, magnificence, prettiness, radiance, splendour.

becalmed *adj* helpless, idle, motionless, still, unmoving.

beckon *v* gesture, motion, signal, summon, wave.

become *v* 1 change into, develop into, grow into, mature into, turn into. 2 *Red becomes you.* be becoming to, enhance, flatter, suit. **becoming** ▷ ATTRACTIVE, SUITABLE.

bed *n* 1 berth, bunk, cot, couch, divan, resting place. 2 *bed of concrete.* base, foundation, layer, substratum. 3 *river bed.* bottom, channel, course. 4 *flower bed.* border, garden, patch, plot.

bedclothes *pl n* bedding, bed linen, blankets, duvets, pillows, pillowcases, quilts, sheets.

bedraggled *adj* dishevelled, drenched, messy, *inf* scruffy, sodden, unkempt, untidy, wet. *Opp* SMART.

beer *n* ale, bitter, lager, mild, stout.

befall *v* ▷ HAPPEN.

before *adv* already, earlier, in advance, previously.

befriend *v* get to know, make friends with, make the acquaintance of, *inf* pal up with.

beg *v* 1 *inf* cadge, scrounge, sponge. 2 *beg a favour.* ask, beseech, crave, entreat, implore, importune, petition, plead, pray, request, supplicate.

beget *v* ▷ CREATE.

beggar *n* destitute person, down-and-out, homeless person, mendicant, pauper, scrounger, sponger, tramp, vagrant.

begin *v* 1 activate, approach, attack, commence, conceive, create, embark on, enter into, found, *inf* get going, inaugurate, initiate, instigate, introduce, launch, lay the foundations, lead off, move off, open, originate, pioneer, precipitate, provoke, set about, set in motion, set out, set up, *inf* spark off, start, *inf* take steps, take the initiative, take up, touch off, trigger off, undertake. 2 *Spring will begin soon.* appear, arise, come into existence, emerge, happen, materialize, originate. *Opp* END.

beginner *n* 1 creator, founder, initiator, instigator, originator, pioneer. 2 *only a beginner.* apprentice, inexperienced person, initiate, learner, novice, recruit, starter, trainee.

beginning *n* 1 birth, commencement, conception, creation, dawn, embryo, emergence, establishment, foundation, genesis, germ, inauguration, inception, initiation, instigation, introduction, launch, onset, opening, origin, outset, point of departure, rise, source, start, starting point, threshold. 2 *beginning of a book.* preface, prelude, prologue. *Opp* END.

begrudge *v* be bitter about, covet, envy, grudge, mind, object to, resent.

behave *v* 1 acquit yourself, act, conduct yourself, function, operate, perform, react, respond, work. 2 *told to behave.* act properly, be good, be on best behaviour.

behaviour *n* actions, attitude, bearing, conduct, demeanour, deportment, manners, performance.

behead *v* decapitate, guillotine.

behold *v* descry, discern, espy, look at, note, notice, see, set eyes on, view.

being *n* 1 actuality, essence, existence, life, reality, substance. 2 animal, creature, individual, person, spirit, soul.

belated *adj* behindhand, delayed, last-minute, late, overdue, tardy, unpunctual.

belch *v* 1 *inf* burp. 2 *belch smoke.* discharge, emit, gush, send out, spew out.

belief *n* 1 acceptance, assent, assurance, certainty, confidence, credence, reliance, security, sureness, trust. 2 *religious belief.* conviction, creed, doctrine, dogma, ethos, faith, feeling, ideology, morality, notion, opinion, persuasion, principles, standards, tenets, theories, views. *Opp* SCEPTICISM.

believe *v* 1 accept, be certain of, credit, depend on, endorse, have faith in, rely on, subscribe to, *inf* swallow, swear by, trust. *Opp* DISBELIEVE. 2 assume, consider, *inf* dare say, feel, gather, guess, imagine, judge, maintain, presume, speculate, suppose, take it for granted, think. **make believe** ▷ IMAGINE.

believer *n* adherent, devotee, disciple, follower, supporter, upholder. *Opp* ATHEIST.

belittle *v* criticize, decry, denigrate, deprecate, detract from, disparage, minimize, *inf* play down, slight, speak slightingly of, undervalue. *Opp* EXAGGERATE, FLATTER, PRAISE.

bell *n* alarm, chime, knell, peal, signal. ▷ RING.

belligerent *adj* aggressive, antagonistic, argumentative, bellicose, bullying, combative, contentious, defiant, disputatious, fierce, hawkish, hostile, jingoistic, martial, militant, militaristic, provocative, pugnacious, quarrelsome, violent, warlike, warmongering, warring. ▷ UNFRIENDLY. *Opp* PEACEABLE.

belong *v* 1 be owned (by), be the property of. 2 be at home, feel welcome, have a place. 3 *belong to a club.* be a member of, be connected with, *inf* be in with.

belongings *n* chattels, effects, *inf* gear, goods, possessions, property, things.

belt *n* 1 band, circle, loop. 2 *belt round the waist.* cummerbund, girdle, girth, sash, strap, waistband. 3 *green belt.* area, district, stretch, strip, swathe, tract, zone.

bemuse *v* befuddle, bewilder, confuse, muddle, perplex, puzzle.

bench *n* 1 form, pew, seat, settle. 2 counter, table, workbench, work table. 3 *He was up before the bench.* court, courtroom, judge, magistrate, tribunal.

bend *n* angle, arc, corner, crook, curve, loop, turn, turning, twist, zigzag.
• *v* 1 arch, be flexible, bow, buckle, coil, contort, curl, curve, distort, flex, fold, *inf* give, loop, turn, twist, warp, wind, yield. 2 *bend down before the queen.* bow, crouch, curtsy, genuflect, kneel, stoop.

benefactor *n* *inf* angel, backer, donor, *inf* fairy godmother, patron, philanthropist, promoter, sponsor, supporter, well-wisher.

beneficial *adj* advantageous, benign, constructive, favourable, good, health-giving, healthy, helpful, improving, nourishing, nutritious, profitable, salubrious, salutary, supportive, useful, valuable, wholesome. *Opp* HARMFUL.

beneficiary *n* heir, heiress, inheritor, legatee, recipient, successor (*to title*).

benefit *n* 1 advantage, asset, blessing, convenience, gain, good thing, help, privilege, profit, service, use. *Opp* DISADVANTAGE. 2 *unemployment benefit.* aid, allowance, assistance, *inf* dole, grant, handout, income support, payment, social security, welfare.
• *v* aid, assist, better, boost, do good to, enhance, further, help, improve, profit, promote, serve.

benevolent *adj* altruistic, benign, caring, charitable, compassionate, considerate, friendly, generous, helpful, humane, kind-hearted, kindly, merciful, philanthropic, sympathetic, unselfish, warm-hearted. ▷ KIND. *Opp* UNKIND.

benign *adj* gentle, harmless, kind. ▷ BENEFICIAL, BENEVOLENT.

bent *adj* 1 arched, bowed, buckled, coiled, contorted, crooked, curved, distorted, hunched, twisted, warped. 2 [*inf*] *The dealer was bent.* corrupt, dishonest, immoral, untrustworthy, wicked. *Opp* HONEST, STRAIGHT.
• *n* ▷ APTITUDE, BIAS.

bequeath *v* endow, hand down, leave, make over, pass on, settle, will.

bequest *n* endowment, gift, inheritance, legacy, settlement.

bereavement *n* death, loss.

bereft *adj* deprived, devoid, lacking, wanting.

berserk *adj inf* beside yourself, crazy, demented, deranged, frantic, frenzied, furious, insane, mad, violent, wild. *Opp* CALM. **go berserk** ▷ RAGE, RAMPAGE.

berth *n* 1 bed, bunk. 2 *berth for ships.* anchorage, dock, harbour, haven, landing stage, moorings, pier, port, quay, wharf.
• *v* anchor, dock, drop anchor, land, moor, tie up. **give a wide berth to** ▷ AVOID.

beseech *v* ask, entreat, implore, plead. ▷ BEG.

besiege *v* beset, blockade, cut off, encircle, hem in, isolate, pester, plague, siege, surround.

best *adj* choicest, finest, first-class, foremost, incomparable, leading, matchless, optimum, outstanding, pre-eminent, superlative, supreme, top, unequalled, unrivalled, unsurpassed.

bestial *adj* animal, beastly, brutal, brutish, inhuman. ▷ SAVAGE.

bestow *v* award, confer, donate, give, grant, present.

bet *n inf* flutter, gamble, speculation, stake, wager.
•*v* bid, gamble, *inf* have a flutter, lay bets, speculate, stake, venture, wager.

betray *v* 1 be disloyal to, cheat, conspire against, deceive, double-cross, give away, inform against, inform on, let down, *inf* sell down the river, sell out, *inf* shop. 2 *betray secrets.* disclose, divulge, expose, give away, let out, let slip, reveal, show, tell.

better *adj* 1 preferable, recommended, superior. 2 convalescent, cured, fitter, healed, healthier, improved, *inf* on the mend, progressing, recovered, recovering, well.
• *v* ▷ IMPROVE, SURPASS.

beware *v* be careful, be on your guard, guard (against), heed, keep clear (of), look out, mind, steer clear (of), take care, take heed, watch out, *inf* watch your step.

bewilder *v* baffle, *inf* bamboozle, bemuse, confound, confuse, daze, disconcert, disorientate, *inf* floor, *inf* flummox, muddle, mystify, perplex, puzzle, *inf* stump.

bewitch *v* ▷ ENCHANT.

bias *n* 1 aptitude, bent, inclination, leaning, liking, partiality, penchant, predilection, predisposition, preference, proclivity, propensity, tendency. 2 [*derog*] bigotry, chauvinism, favouritism, injustice, nepotism, one-sidedness, partiality, partisanship, prejudice, racism, sexism, unfairness.
• *v* ▷ INFLUENCE.

biased *adj* bigoted, blinkered, chauvinistic, distorted, influenced, interested (*party*), loaded, one-sided, partial, partisan, prejudiced, racist, sexist, slanted, unfair, unjust. *Opp* UNBIASED.

bicycle *n inf* bike, cycle, *inf* push-bike, racer, tandem, *inf* two-wheeler.

bid *n* 1 offer, price, proposal, tender. 2 *winning bid.* attempt, effort, endeavour, *inf* go, try, venture.
•*v* 1 make an offer, offer, propose, tender. 2 ▷ COMMAND.

big *adj* 1 above average, *inf* almighty, ample, astronomical, broad, bulky, burly, capacious, colossal, commodious, considerable, elephantine, enormous, extensive, fat, formidable, gargantuan, generous, giant, gigantic, grand, great, heavy, hefty, huge, *inf* hulking, immeasurable, immense, impressive, infinite, *inf* jumbo, *inf* king-sized, large, lofty, long, mammoth, massive, mighty, monstrous, monumental, mountainous, oversized, prodigious, roomy, sizeable, spacious, substantial, swingeing (*increase*), tall, *inf* terrific, *inf* thumping, tidy (*sum*), titanic, towering, *inf* tremendous, vast, voluminous, weighty, *inf* whacking, *inf* whopping, wide. 2 *big decision.* grave, important, major, momentous, serious, significant. 3 *big in politics.* inflential, leading, principal, prominent, powerful. 4 *big name.* ▷ FAMOUS. 5 *big noise.* ▷ LOUD. *Opp* SMALL.

bigot *n* chauvinist, fanatic, prejudiced person, racist, sexist, zealot.

bigoted *adj* intolerant, one-sided, prejudiced. ▷ BIASED.

bill *n* 1 account, invoice, receipt, statement. 2 advertisement, broadsheet, circular, handbill, leaflet, notice, placard, poster. 3 *Parliamentary bill.* draft law. 4 *bird's bill.* beak.

billow *v* balloon, bulge, fill out, heave, puff out, rise, roll, surge, swell, undulate.

bind *v* 1 attach, combine, hitch, hold together, join, lash, link, rope, secure, strap, tie, unite. ▷ FASTEN. 2 *bind a wound.* bandage, cover, dress, swathe, wrap. 3 compel, constrain, force, oblige, require. **binding** ▷ COMPULSORY, FORMAL.

biography *n* autobiography, life, life-story, memoirs.

bird *n* chick, cock, *joc* feathered friend, fledgling, fowl, hen, nestling.

birth *n* 1 childbirth, confinement, delivery, labour. 2 ancestry, background, blood, breeding, derivation, descent, extraction, family, genealogy, line, lineage, parentage, pedigree, race, stock, strain. 3 ▷ BEGINNING. **give birth** bear, calve, farrow, foal. ▷ BEGIN.

bisect *v* cross, cut in half, divide, halve, intersect.

bit *n* 1 atom, chip, chunk, crumb, dollop, fraction, fragment, gobbet, grain, helping, hunk, iota, lump, morsel, mouthful, part, particle, piece, portion, sample, scrap, section, segment, share, slab, slice, snippet, speck, spot, taste, titbit, trace. 2 *Wait a bit.* instant, *inf* jiffy, minute, moment, second, *inf* tick, while.

bite *n* 1 nip, pinch, sting. 2 *bite to eat.* morsel, mouthful, nibble, snack, taste. ▷ BIT.
• *v* 1 champ, chew, crunch, cut into, gnaw, munch, nibble, nip, sting, tear at, wound. 2 *The screw won't bite.* grip, hold.

bitter *adj* 1 acid, acrid, harsh, sharp, sour, unpleasant. 2 *bitter experience.* distressing, galling, heartbreaking, painful, sorrowful, unhappy, unwelcome, upsetting. 3 *bitter remarks.* acrimonious, acerbic, angry, cruel, cynical, embittered, envious, hostile, jaundiced, jealous, malicious, rancorous, resentful, savage, sharp, spiteful, stinging, vicious, waspish. 4 *bitter wind.* biting, cold, freezing, perishing, piercing, raw. *Opp* KIND, MILD, PLEASANT.

bizarre *adj* curious, eccentric, fantastic, freakish, odd, outlandish, surreal, weird. ▷ STRANGE. *Opp* ORDINARY.

black *adj* coal-black, dark, dusky, ebony, funereal, gloomy, inky, jet, jet-black, moonless, murky, pitch-black, pitch-dark, raven, sable, sooty, starless.
• *v* 1 blacken, polish. 2 ▷ BLACKLIST.

blackleg *n inf* scab, strike-breaker, traitor.

blacklist *v* ban, boycott, exclude, ostracize, put an embargo on, repudiate, veto.

blade *n* dagger, edge, knife, razor, scalpel. ▷ SWORD.

blame *n* accusation, castigation, censure, criticism, culpability, fault, guilt, liability, *inf* rap, recrimination, reprimand, reproach, reproof, responsibility, *inf* stick, stricture.
• *v* accuse, admonish, censure, condemn, criticize, denounce, hold responsible, incriminate, reprehend, reprimand, reproach, reprove, scold, tax, upbraid. *Opp* EXCUSE.

blameless *adj* faultless, guiltless, innocent, irreproachable, moral, unimpeachable, upright. *Opp* GUILTY.

bland *adj* banal, boring, characterless, dull, flat, gentle, insipid, mild, nondescript, smooth, soft, soothing, tasteless, trite, unappetizing, unexciting, uninspiring, uninteresting, vapid, weak, *inf* wishy-washy. *Opp* INTERESTING.

blank *adj* 1 bare, clean, clear, empty, plain, spotless, unadorned, unmarked, unused. 2 *blank look.* apathetic, baffled, dead, *inf* deadpan, emotionless, expressionless, glazed, immobile, impassive, inscrutable, lifeless, poker-faced, uncomprehending, unresponsive, vacant, vacuous.
• *n* 1 emptiness, nothingness, vacuum, void. 2 *Fill in the blanks.* box, break, gap, line, space.

blaspheme *v* curse, utter profanities, swear.

blasphemous *adj* disrespectful, impious, irreverent, profane, sacrilegious, sinful, ungodly, wicked. *Opp* REVERENT.

blast *n* 1 gale, gust, wind. 2 blare, din, noise, racket, roar. 3 ▷ EXPLOSION.
• *v* ▷ ATTACK, EXPLODE. **blast off** ▷ LAUNCH.

blatant *adj* apparent, bare-faced, bold, brazen, conspicuous, evident, flagrant, glaring, obtrusive, obvious, open, overt, shameless, stark, unconcealed, undisguised, unmistakable, visible. *Opp* HIDDEN.

blaze *n* conflagration, fire, flame, flare-up, inferno, outburst.
• *v* burn, flame, flare.

bleach *v* blanch, discolour, fade, lighten, whiten.

bleak *adj* bare, barren, cheerless, chilly, cold, comfortless, depressing, desolate, dismal, dreary, exposed, grim, hopeless, joyless, sombre, unpromising, windswept, wintry.

bleary *adj* blurred, blurry, cloudy, dim, filmy, foggy, fuzzy, hazy, indistinct, misty, murky, obscured, smeary, unclear. *Opp* CLEAR.

blemish *n* blotch, blot, chip, crack, defect, deformity, disfigurement, eyesore, fault, flaw, imperfection, mark, mess, pimple, scar, smudge, speck, spot, stain.
• *v* deface, disfigure, flaw, mar, mark, scar, spoil, stain, tarnish.

blend *n* alloy, amalgam, amalgamation, combination, composite, compound, concoction, fusion, mix, mixture, synthesis, union.

▪ *v* 1 amalgamate, coalesce, combine, compound, fuse, harmonize, integrate, intermingle, merge, mingle, synthesize, unite. 2 *blend the ingredients.* beat, mix, stir together, whip, whisk.

bless *v* 1 anoint, consecrate, dedicate, grace, hallow, make sacred, ordain, sanctify. 2 *bless the Lord.* exalt, extol, glorify, praise. *Opp* CURSE.

blessed *adj* 1 divine, hallowed, holy, revered, sacred, sanctified. 2 ▷ HAPPY.

blessing *n.* 1 benediction, consecration, grace, prayer. 2 approbation, approval, backing, consent, leave, permission, sanction, support. 3 *The good weather was a blessing.* advantage, asset, benefit, *inf* godsend, help. *Opp* CURSE, MISFORTUNE.

blight *n* affliction, ailment, curse, decay, disease, evil, illness, infestation, misfortune, plague, rot, scourge, sickness, trouble.
▪ *v* ▷ SPOIL.

blind *adj* 1 blinded, eyeless, sightless, unseeing. 2 blinkered, heedless, ignorant, inattentive, indifferent, insensitive, irrational, mindless, oblivious, prejudiced, unaware, unobservant, unreasoning.
▪ *n* awning, cover, screen, shade, shutters.
▪ *v* 1 dazzle, make blind. 2 ▷ DECEIVE.

blink *v* flash, flicker, gleam, glimmer, shimmer, sparkle, twinkle, wink.

bliss *n* delight, ecstasy, euphoria, felicity, glee, happiness, heaven, joy, paradise, rapture. ▷ PLEASURE. *Opp* MISERY.

bloated *adj* distended, enlarged, inflated, puffy, swollen.

block *n* 1 bar, brick, cake, chunk, hunk, ingot, lump, mass, piece, slab. 2 ▷ BLOCKAGE.
▪ *v* 1 *block a drain. inf* bung up, choke, clog, close, congest, constrict, dam, fill, jam, plug, stop up. 2 *block a driveway.* bar, barricade, impede, obstruct. 3 *block a plan.* deter, halt, hamper, hinder, hold back, prevent, prohibit, resist, *inf* scotch, stop, thwart.

blockage *n* barrier, block, bottleneck, congestion, constriction, impediment, jam, obstacle, obstruction, stoppage.

blond, blonde *adj* bleached, fair, flaxen, golden, light, platinum, silvery, yellow.

bloodshed *n* butchery, carnage, killing, massacre, murder, slaughter, violence.

bloodthirsty *adj* barbaric, brutal, ferocious, fierce, homicidal, inhuman, murderous, pitiless, ruthless, sadistic, savage, vicious, violent, warlike. ▷ CRUEL. *Opp* HUMANE.

bloody *adj* 1 bleeding, bloodstained, raw. 2 *a bloody battle.* cruel, fierce, gory. ▷ BLOODTHIRSTY.

bloom *n* 1 blossom, bud, floret, flower. 2 *bloom of youth.* beauty, flush, glow, prime.
▪ *v* be healthy, blossom, bud, burgeon, *inf* come out, develop, flourish, flower, grow, open, prosper, sprout, thrive. *Opp* FADE.

blot *n* 1 blob, blotch, mark, smear, smudge, *inf* splodge, spot, stain. 2 *blot on the landscape.* blemish, defect, eyesore, fault, flaw.
▪ *v* bespatter, blemish, blur, disfigure, mar, mark, smudge, spoil, spot, stain. **blot out** ▷ OBLITERATE. **blot your copybook** ▷ MISBEHAVE.

blotchy *adj* blemished, discoloured, marked, patchy, smudged, spotty, streaked, uneven.

blow *n* 1 bang, bash, *sl* biff, buffet, bump, clip, clout, hit, jolt, knock, punch, rap, slap, *inf* slosh, smack, stroke, swat, swipe, thump, *sl* wallop, *inf* whack. 2 *inf* bombshell, calamity, disappointment, disaster, misfortune, shock, surprise, upset.
▪ *v* blast, breathe, exhale, fan, puff, waft, whirl, whistle. **blow up** 1 dilate, enlarge, expand, fill, inflate, pump up. 2 exaggerate, magnify, make worse, overstate. 3 blast, bomb, burst, detonate, dynamite, erupt, explode, go off, set off, shatter. 4 [*inf*] erupt, get angry, lose your temper, rage.

blue *adj* 1 aquamarine, azure, cobalt, indigo, navy, sapphire, sky-blue, turquoise, ultramarine. 2 ▷ BAWDY. 3 ▷ SAD.
▪ *v* ▷ SQUANDER.

blueprint *n* basis, design, draft, model, outline, pattern, plan, proposal, prototype, scheme.

bluff *v* deceive, delude, dupe, fool, mislead.

blunder *n sl* boob, error, fault, *Fr* faux pas, gaffe, howler, indiscretion, miscalculation, misjudgement, mistake, slip, slip-up.
▪ *v* be clumsy, *inf* botch up, bumble, bungle, *inf* drop a clanger, flounder, go wrong, *inf* make a hash of something, make a mistake, mess up, miscalculate, misjudge, *inf* put your foot in it, slip up, stumble.

blunt *adj* 1 dull, rounded, thick, unsharpened, worn. *Opp* SHARP. 2 *blunt*

criticism. abrupt, brusque, candid, curt, direct, downright, forthright, frank, honest, insensitive, outspoken, plain-spoken, rude, straightforward, tactless, undiplomatic. *Opp* TACTFUL.
• *v* abate, allay, anaesthetize, dampen, deaden, desensitize, dull, lessen, numb, soften, take the edge off, weaken. *Opp* SHARPEN.

blur *v* 1 cloud, darken, dim, fog, obscure, smear. 2 confuse, muddle.

blurred *adj* bleary, blurry, clouded, cloudy, confused, dim, faint, foggy, fuzzy, hazy, ill-defined, indistinct, misty, nebulous, out of focus, smoky, unclear, unfocused, vague. *Opp* CLEAR.

blurt *v* **blurt out** *inf* blab, burst out with, cry out, disclose, divulge, exclaim, *inf* give the game away, let out, let slip, reveal, *inf* spill the beans, tell.

blush *v* be embarrassed, colour, flush, go red, redden.

blustering *adj* angry, bullying, defiant, domineering, hectoring, noisy, ranting, self-assertive, storming, swaggering, threatening, violent. *Opp* MODEST.

blustery *adj* gusty, squally, unsettled, windy.

board *n* 1 chipboard, clapboard, panel, plank, plywood, slat, timber. 2 *board of directors.* cabinet, committee, council, directorate, jury, panel.
• *v* 1 accommodate, billet, feed, house, lodge, put up, quarter, stay. 2 *board a plane.* catch, enter, get on, go on board.

boast *v inf* blow your own trumpet, brag, crow, exaggerate, gloat, show off, *inf* sing your own praises, swagger, *inf* talk big.

boaster *n inf* big-head, braggart, *inf* loudmouth, *inf* poser, show-off, swaggerer.

boastful *adj inf* big-headed, bragging, *inf* cocky, conceited, egotistical, ostentatious, proud, puffed up, swaggering, swollen-headed, vain. *Opp* MODEST.

boat *n* craft, cruiser, motor boat, rowing boat, ship, speedboat, vessel, yacht.

boatman *n* ferryman, gondolier, oarsman, rower, sailor, yachtsman. ▷ SAILOR.

bob *v* bounce, dance, hop, jerk, jig about, jump, leap, nod, toss about, twitch. **bob up** ▷ APPEAR.

body *n* 1 anatomy, being, build, figure, form, frame, physique, shape, substance, torso, trunk. 2 cadaver, carcass, corpse, mortal remains, mummy, relics, remains, *sl* stiff. 3 association, band, committee, company, corporation, society. ▷ GROUP. 4 *body of material.* accumulation, collection, corpus, mass.

bodyguard *n* defender, guard, *sl* minder, protector.

bog *n* fen, marsh, marshland, mire, morass, mudflats, peat bog, quagmire, quicksands, swamp, wetlands. **get bogged down** get into difficulties, get stuck, grind to a halt, sink.

bogus *adj* counterfeit, fake, false, fraudulent, imitation, *inf* phoney, sham, spurious. *Opp* GENUINE.

Bohemian *adj inf* arty, eccentric, nonconformist, off-beat, unconventional, unorthodox, *inf* way-out, weird.

boil *n* abscess, blister, carbuncle, chilblain, eruption, inflammation, pimple, pustule, sore, spot, ulcer, *sl* zit.
• *v* 1 cook, heat, simmer, stew. 2 bubble, effervesce, foam, seethe, steam. 3 ▷ RAGE.

boisterous *adj* animated, disorderly, exuberant, irrepressible, lively, noisy, obstreperous, riotous, rough, rowdy, stormy, tempestuous, tumultuous, undisciplined, unruly, uproarious, wild. *Opp* CALM.

bold *adj* 1 adventurous, brave, confident, courageous, daredevil, daring, dauntless, enterprising, fearless, *derog* foolhardy, forceful, gallant, heroic, intrepid, plucky, *derog* rash, *derog* reckless, self-confident, valiant, valorous. 2 [*derog*] brash, brazen, cheeky, forward, impertinent, impudent, insolent, pert, presumptuous, rude, saucy, shameless. 3 *bold colours, writing.* big, bright, clear, conspicuous, eye-catching, large, prominent, pronounced, showy, striking, strong, vivid. *Opp* FAINT, TIMID.

bolster *n* cushion, pillow.
• *v* ▷ SUPPORT.

bolt *n* 1 arrow, dart, missile, projectile. 2 peg, pin, rivet, rod, screw. 3 *bolt on a door.* catch, fastening, latch, lock.
• *v* 1 close, fasten, latch, lock, secure. 2 dart away, dash away, escape, flee, fly, run off, rush off. 3 *bolt food.* ▷ EAT. **bolt from the blue** ▷ SURPRISE.

bomb *n* bombshell, explosive.
• *v* ▷ BOMBARD.

bombard *v* 1 attack, batter, blast, blitz, bomb, fire at, pelt, pound, shell, shoot at, strafe. 2 *bombard with questions.* assail, besiege, set upon, pester, plague.

bombardment *n* attack, barrage, blast,

blitz, broadside, burst, cannonade, discharge, fusillade, salvo, volley.

bombastic *adj* extravagant, grandiloquent, grandiose, high-flown, inflated, pompous, turgid.

bond *n* 1 chain, cord, fastening, fetter, manacle, restraint, rope, shackle. 2 *bond of friendship.* affinity, attachment, connection, link, relationship, tie, unity. 3 *legal bond.* agreement, compact, covenant, guarantee, pledge, promise, word.
• *v* ▷ STICK.

bondage *n* ▷ SLAVERY.

bonus *n* 1 commission, dividend, gift, gratuity, handout, payment, *inf* perk, reward, supplement, tip. 2 addition, advantage, benefit, extra, *inf* plus.

bony *adj* angular, emaciated, gangling, gawky, lanky, lean, scraggy, scrawny, skinny, thin. *Opp* PLUMP.

book *n* album, booklet, copy, edition, guidebook, handbook, hardback, paperback, publication, textbook, tome, volume, work.
• *v* 1 *book for speeding.* take your name, write down details. 2 *book in advance.* arrange, order, organize, reserve, sign up.

booklet *n* brochure, leaflet, pamphlet.

boom *n* 1 bang, blast, crash, explosion, reverberation, roar, rumble. 2 *boom in trade.* boost, expansion, growth, improvement, increase, spurt, upsurge, upturn. ▷ PROSPERITY. 3 *boom across a river.* ▷ BARRIER.
• *v* 1 crash, explode, reverberate, roar, rumble. 2 ▷ PROSPER.

boorish *adj* ignorant, ill-mannered, loutish, oafish, philistine, uncultured, vulgar. *Opp* CULTURED.

boost *n* aid, encouragement, fillip, help, impetus, lift, push, stimulus.
• *v* advance, aid, assist, augment, bolster, build up, buoy up, encourage, enhance, expand, foster, further, give an impetus to, heighten, help, improve, increase, lift, promote, push up, raise, support. *Opp* DEPRESS.

booth *n* box, compartment, cubicle, hut, kiosk, stall, stand.

booty *n* contraband, gains, haul, loot, pickings, plunder, spoils, *inf* swag, takings, winnings.

border *n* 1 brim, brink, edge, edging, frame, frieze, fringe, hem, margin, perimeter, periphery, rim, surround, verge. 2 borderline, boundary, frontier, limit. 3 *flower border.* bed.
• *v* be adjacent to, be alongside, join, share a border with, touch.

bore *v* 1 burrow, drill, mine, penetrate, sink, tunnel. ▷ PIERCE. 2 be tedious, fatigue, pall on, tire, *inf* turn off, weary. *Opp* INTEREST.

boring *adj* arid, commonplace, dreary, dry, dull, flat, humdrum, long-winded, monotonous, repetitive, soporific, stale, tedious, tiresome, trite, uneventful, unexciting, uninspiring, uninteresting, vapid, wearisome, wordy. *Opp* INTERESTING.

born *adj* congenital, instinctive, natural, untaught.

borrow *v* adopt, appropriate, *inf* cadge, copy, crib, make use of, obtain, pirate, plagiarize, scrounge, take, use. *Opp* LEND.

boss *n* employer, head. ▷ CHIEF.

bossy *adj* assertive, authoritarian, bullying, dictatorial, domineering, high-handed, imperious, officious, overbearing, peremptory, *inf* pushy, self-assertive, tyrannical. *Opp* SERVILE.

bother *n* 1 ado, difficulty, disorder, disturbance, fuss, *inf* hassle, problem, *inf* to-do. 2 annoyance, inconvenience, irritation, nuisance, pest, trouble, worry.
• *v* 1 annoy, concern, dismay, disturb, exasperate, harass, *inf* hassle, inconvenience, irk, irritate, molest, nag, perturb, pester, plague, trouble, upset, vex, worry. 2 be concerned, be worried, care, mind, take trouble. ▷ TROUBLE.

bottle *n* carafe, decanter, flagon, flask.
bottle up ▷ SUPPRESS.

bottom *adj* deepest, least, lowest, minimum.
• *n* 1 base, bed depth, floor, foot, foundation, lowest point, nadir, pedestal, substructure, underside. *Opp* TOP. 2 basis, essence, grounds, heart, origin, root, source. 3 *sl* arse, backside, behind, *inf* bum, buttocks, *joc* posterior, rear, rump, seat.

bottomless *adj* deep, immeasurable, unfathomable.

bounce *v* bob, bound, bump, jump, leap, rebound, recoil, ricochet, spring.

bound *adj* 1 *bound to obey.* compelled, committed, constrained, duty-bound, forced, obliged, required. 2 *bound to help.* certain, sure. 3 *bound to lose her job.* destined, doomed, fated. 4 *bound with rope.* fastened, joined, lashed together, roped, secured, tied.
• *v* bob, bounce, caper, gambol, hop,

hurdle, jump, leap, pounce, romp, skip, spring, vault. **bound for** directed towards, going to, heading for, making for, travelling towards.

boundary *n* border, borderline, bounds, brink, circumference, confines, demarcation, edge, end, extremity, fringe, frontier, limit, margin, perimeter, threshold, verge.

boundless *adj* endless, everlasting, immeasurable, incalculable, inexhaustible, infinite, limitless, unflagging, unlimited, unrestricted, untold. ▷ VAST. *Opp* FINITE.

bounty *n* alms, beneficence, charity, generosity, gift, goodness, largesse, liberality, munificence, philanthropy, unselfishness.

bouquet *n* 1 arrangement, bunch, buttonhole, corsage, garland, nosegay, posy, spray. 2 aroma, fragrance, scent, smell.

bout *n* 1 attack, fit, period, run, spell, time. 2 battle, combat, competition, contest, encounter, engagement, fight, match, round, *inf* set-to, struggle.

bow *v* 1 bend, bob, curtsy, genuflect, incline, kowtow, nod, stoop. 2 ▷ SUBMIT.

bowels *n* 1 entrails, guts, *inf* innards, insides, intestines, viscera, vitals. 2 core, depths, heart, inside.

bower *n* arbour, gazebo, hideaway, recess, retreat, shelter, summer house.

bowl *n* basin, casserole, container, dish, pan, tureen.
• *v* fling, hurl, lob, pitch, throw, toss.

box *n* caddy, canister, carton, case, casket, chest, coffer, container, crate, pack, trunk.
• *v inf* engage in fisticuffs, fight, punch, scrap, spar. ▷ HIT.

boy *n derog* brat, *inf* kid, lad, schoolboy, son, *derog* urchin, youngster, youth.

boycott *n* ban, blacklist, embargo, prohibition.
• *v* avoid, blacklist, exclude, *inf* give the cold-shoulder to, ignore, ostracize, outlaw, prohibit, spurn, stay away from.

bracing *adj* crisp, exhilarating, health-giving, invigorating, refreshing, restorative, stimulating, tonic.

brag *v* crow, gloat, show off. ▷ BOAST.

brain *n inf* grey matter, intellect, intelligence, mind, *inf* nous, reason, sense, understanding, wisdom, wit.

brainwash *v* condition, indoctrinate, re-educate.

branch *n* 1 arm, bough, limb, stem, twig. 2 department, division, office, offshoot, part, section, subdivision, wing.
• *v* diverge, divide, fork, split, subdivide. **branch out** ▷ DIVERSIFY.

brand *n* kind, label, line, make, sort, type, variety.
• *v* 1 burn, identify, label, mark, scar, stamp, tag. 2 characterize, denounce, discredit, expose, stigmatize.

brash *adj* brazen, insolent, rude, self-assertive. ▷ ARROGANT.

bravado *n* arrogance, bluster, swagger.

brave *adj* adventurous, audacious, bold, courageous, daring, dauntless, determined, fearless, gallant, game, *inf* gutsy, heroic, indomitable, intrepid, *derog* macho, plucky, resolute, spirited, stalwart, stoical, stout-hearted, tough, unafraid, undaunted, valiant, valorous, venturesome. *Opp* COWARDLY.

bravery *n* audacity, boldness, *sl* bottle, courage, daring, determination, fearlessness, fibre, firmness, fortitude, gallantry, *inf* grit, *inf* guts, heroism, mettle, *inf* nerve, pluck, prowess, resolution, spirit, stoicism, tenacity, valour. *Opp* COWARDICE.

brawl *n* affray, altercation, *inf* bust-up, clash, *inf* dust-up, fracas, fray, *inf* free-for-all, mêlée, *inf* punch-up, quarrel, *inf* row, scrap, scuffle, *inf* set-to, tussle.
• *v* ▷ FIGHT.

brazen *adj* barefaced, blatant, cheeky, defiant, flagrant, impertinent, impudent, insolent, rude, shameless, unabashed, unashamed. *Opp* SHAMEFACED.

breach *n* 1 aperture, break, chasm, crack, fissure, gap, hole, opening, rent, space, split. 2 difference, disagreement, drifting apart, estrangement, quarrel, rift, rupture, separation, split. 3 *breach of law.* contravention, infringement, offence, transgression, violation.

bread *n* 1 provisions, sustenance. ▷ FOOD. 2 [*inf*] ▷ MONEY.

break *n* 1 breach, breakage, burst, chink, cleft, crack, crevice, fissure, fracture, gap, hole, leak, opening, rift, rupture, split, tear. 2 *break from work. inf* breather, breathing-space, interlude, intermission, interval, *inf* let-up, lull, pause, respite, rest. 3 *break in service.* disruption, halt, interruption, lapse, suspension.
• *v* 1 breach, burst, *inf* bust, chip, crack, crumble, crush, damage, demolish, fracture, fragment, knock down, ruin, shatter, smash, snap, splinter, split, wreck. ▷ DESTROY. 2 *break the law.* contravene, defy, disobey, disregard, fail to observe, flout, transgress, violate.

3 break a record. beat, better, exceed, excel, go beyond, outdo, outstrip, pass, surpass. **break down** ▷ ANALYSE, DEMOLISH. **break in** ▷ INTERRUPT, INTRUDE. **break off** ▷ FINISH. **break out** ▷ ESCAPE. **break through** ▷ PENETRATE. **break up** ▷ DISINTEGRATE.

breakdown *n* 1 collapse, disintegration, downfall, failure, malfunction, stoppage. 2 analysis, classification, dissection, itemization.

breakthrough *n* advance, development, discovery, find, improvement, innovation, invention, leap forward, progress, revolution, success.

breakwater *n* jetty, pier.

breath *n* gust, murmur, puff, sigh, waft, whiff, whisper.

breathe *v* 1 exhale, inhale, pant, respire. 2 tell, whisper.

breathless *adj* exhausted, gasping, out of breath, panting, *inf* puffed, wheezy, winded.

breed *n* clan, family, kind, line, lineage, pedigree, race, sort, species, stock, strain, type, variety.
• *v* 1 bear, cultivate, increase, multiply, nourish, nurture, procreate, produce young, propagate (*plants*), raise, reproduce. 2 *breed contempt.* arouse, cause, create, develop, engender, generate, foster, induce, occasion.

breeze *n* air current, breath, draught, waft, wind.

breezy *adj* airy, blowy, draughty, fresh, gusty, windy.

brevity *n* compactness, compression, concision, curtness, economy, pithiness, succinctness, terseness.

brew *n* blend, concoction, drink, infusion, liquor, mixture, potion, punch.
•*v* 1 cook, ferment, infuse, make, simmer, steep. 2 *brew mischief.* concoct, contrive, *inf* cook up, devise, foment, hatch, plan, plot, scheme, stir up.

bribe *n sl* backhander, *inf* carrot, enticement, *sl* graft, incentive, inducement, *inf* payola, *inf* sweetener.
• *v* buy off, corrupt, entice, *inf* grease your palm, influence, offer a bribe, pervert, suborn, tempt.

brick *n* block, breeze-block, cube, stone.

bridge *n* arch, connection, crossing, link, span, way over.
• *v* connect, cross, fill, join, link, pass over, span, straddle, tie together, traverse, unite.

bridle *v* 1 check, control, curb, restrain. 2 ▷ BRISTLE.

brief *adj* 1 cursory, ephemeral, fleeting, hasty, limited, momentary, passing, quick, sharp, short, short-lived, temporary, transient. 2 *brief comment.* abbreviated, abridged, compressed, concise, condensed, crisp, curt, curtailed, laconic, pithy, shortened, succinct, terse, thumbnail, to the point. *Opp* LONG.
•*n* 1 advice, briefing, directions, information, instructions, orders, outline, plan. 2 *barrister's brief.* argument, case, defence, dossier.
•*v* advise, direct, enlighten, *inf* fill someone in, guide, inform, instruct, prepare, prime, *inf* put someone in the picture.

brigand *n* pirate, robber, ruffian, thief. ▷ BANDIT.

bright *adj* 1 alight, beaming, blazing, burnished, colourful, dazzling, *derog* flashy, fresh, *derog* gaudy, glaring, gleaming, glistening, glittering, glossy, glowing, incandescent, lambent, light, luminous, lustrous, pellucid, polished, radiant, resplendent, scintillating, shimmering, shining, shiny, showy, sparkling, twinkling, vivid. 2 *bright sky.* clear, cloudless, fair, sunny. 3 *bright prospects.* auspicious, favourable, optimistic, rosy. 4 *bright smile.* ▷ CHEERFUL. 5 *bright ideas.* ▷ CLEVER. *Opp* DULL.

brighten *v* 1 cheer (up), enliven, gladden, illuminate, light up, liven up, *inf* perk up. 2 become sunny, clear up, lighten.

brilliant *adj* 1 dazzling, glorious, intense, shining, sparkling, vivid. ▷ BRIGHT. *Opp* DULL. 2 [*inf*] *brilliant game.* ▷ EXCELLENT.

brim *n* edge, rim, top. ▷ BRINK.

bring *v* 1 carry, convey, deliver, fetch, take, transport. 2 *bring a friend.* accompany, escort, guide, lead, usher. 3 *The book will bring her fame.* attract, cause, draw, earn, engender, give rise to, lead to, occasion, produce, prompt, provoke, result in. **bring about** ▷ CREATE. **bring in** ▷ EARN, INTRODUCE. **bring off** ▷ ACHIEVE. **bring on** ▷ ACCELERATE, CAUSE. **bring out** ▷ EMPHASIZE, PRODUCE. **bring up** ▷ EDUCATE, RAISE.

brink *n* bank, border, boundary, brim, edge, fringe, limit, lip, margin, perimeter, periphery, rim, threshold, verge.

brisk *adj* 1 active, animated, bright, businesslike, bustling, busy, crisp, decisive, energetic, lively, nimble, quick, rapid, *inf* snappy, *inf* spanking (*pace*), speedy, spirited, sprightly, vigorous. *Opp*

LEISURELY. 2 *brisk wind.* bracing, fresh, invigorating, refreshing, stimulating.

bristle *n* barb, hair, prickle, quill, spine, stubble, thorn, whisker.
• *v* become angry, become defensive, become indignant, bridle, flare up.

brittle *adj* breakable, crisp, crumbling, delicate, easily broken, fragile, frail. *Opp* FLEXIBLE, RESILIENT.

broad *adj* 1 ample, capacious, expansive, extensive, large, open, spacious, sweeping, vast, wide. 2 *broad daylight.* clear, full, open, plain. 3 *broad outline.* general, imprecise, non-specific, sweeping, undetailed. 4 *broad tastes.* comprehensive, encyclopaedic, universal, wide-ranging. ▷ BROAD-MINDED. 5 *broad humour.* bawdy, blue, coarse, earthy, indecent, racy, ribald, suggestive, vulgar. *Opp* NARROW.

broadcast *n* programme, relay, show, transmission.
• *v* 1 advertise, announce, circulate, disseminate, make known, make public, proclaim, publish, relay, report, spread about, televise, transmit. 2 *broadcast seed.* scatter, sow at random.

broadcaster *n* anchorman, announcer, commentator, compère, disc jockey, DJ, newsreader, presenter.

broaden *v* branch out, develop, diversify, expand, extend, increase, open up, spread, widen. *Opp* LIMIT.

broad-minded *adj* all-embracing, broad, catholic, comprehensive, cosmopolitan, eclectic, enlightened, liberal, open-minded, tolerant, unbiased, unprejudiced, unshockable. *Opp* NARROW-MINDED.

brochure *n* booklet, catalogue, circular, handbill, leaflet, pamphlet, prospectus.

brooch *n* badge, clasp, clip.

brood *n* children, clutch (*of eggs*), family. ▷ YOUNG.
• *v* 1 hatch, incubate, sit on. 2 *brood over mistakes.* agonize, dwell (on), *inf* eat your heart out, fret, mope, worry. ▷ THINK.

brook *n* beck, burn, rivulet, stream, watercourse.
• *v* ▷ TOLERATE.

browbeat *v* badger, bully, coerce, cow, intimidate. ▷ FRIGHTEN.

brown *adj* beige, bronze, buff, chestnut, chocolate, fawn, khaki, russet, sepia, tan, tawny, terracotta, umber.
• *v* bronze, grill, tan, toast.

browse *v* 1 crop, feed, graze, pasture. 2 *browse in a book.* dip in, flick through, leaf through, look through, peruse, scan, skim.

bruise *n* bump, contusion, discoloration, *inf* shiner.
• *v* blacken, crush, damage, discolour, mark. ▷ WOUND.

brush *n* 1 besom, broom. 2 *brush with police.* ▷ CONFLICT.
• *v* 1 groom, scrub, sweep, tidy. 2 *brush the goalpost.* graze, touch. **brush aside** ▷ DISMISS. **brush-off** ▷ REBUFF. **brush up** ▷ REVISE.

brutal *adj* barbaric, bestial, bloodthirsty, brutish, callous, cold-blooded, cruel, dehumanized, ferocious, hard-hearted, heartless, inhuman, inhumane, merciless, murderous, pitiless, ruthless, sadistic, savage, vicious, violent, wild. ▷ UNKIND. *Opp* HUMANE.

brutalize *v* dehumanize, harden, inure.

brute *adj* irrational, mindless, physical, rough, unfeeling. ▷ BRUTISH.
• *n* 1 beast, creature. ▷ ANIMAL. 2 [*inf*] *cruel brute.* barbarian, bully, monster, ruffian, sadist, savage.

brutish *adj* animal, barbaric, bestial, boorish, brutal, coarse, cold-blooded, crude, cruel, *inf* gross, inhuman, insensitive, mindless, savage, senseless, stupid, unthinking. *Opp* HUMANE.

bubble *n* air pocket, blister, vesicle.
• *v* boil, effervesce, fizz, foam, froth, gurgle, sparkle. **bubbles** effervescence, fizz, foam, froth, head, suds.

bubbly *adj* effervescent, fizzy, foaming, sparkling. ▷ LIVELY.

buccaneer *n* adventurer, bandit, brigand, marauder, pirate, robber.

bucket *n* can, pail, scuttle, tub.

buckle *n* catch, clasp, clip, fastener.
• *v* 1 clasp, clip, do up, fasten, hook up, secure. 2 bend, bulge, cave in, collapse, crumple, distort, twist, warp.

bud *n* shoot, sprout.
• *v* begin to grow, burgeon, develop, shoot, sprout. **budding** ▷ POTENTIAL, PROMISING.

budge *v* 1 give way, move, stir, yield. 2 *can't budge him.* change, dislodge, move, persuade, propel, push, shift, sway.

budget *n* accounts, allocation of funds, allowance, estimate, financial planning, means, resources.
• *v* allocate money, allot resources, allow (for), estimate expenditure, ration your spending.

buff *n* ▷ ENTHUSIAST.
• *v* polish, rub, shine, smooth.

buffer *n* bumper, cushion, fender, safeguard, shield, shock-absorber.

buffet *n* 1 café, counter, snack bar. 2 *stand-up buffet.* ▷ MEAL.
• *v* ▷ HIT.

bug *n* 1 ▷ INSECT, MICROBE. 2 *bug in a computer program.* defect, error, failing, fault, flaw, *inf* gremlin, malfunction, mistake, virus.
• *v* 1 intercept, listen in to, spy on, tap. 2 [*sl*] *Don't let it bug you.* ▷ ANNOY.

build *v* assemble, construct, develop, erect, fabricate, form, found, *inf* knock together, make, put up, raise, rear, set up. **build up** ▷ INTENSIFY.

builder *n* bricklayer, construction worker, labourer.

building *n* construction, edifice, piece of architecture, *inf* pile, premises, structure.

bulb *n* 1 corm, tuber. 2 *electric bulb.* lamp, light.

bulbous *adj* bloated, bulging, convex, distended, pot-bellied, rotund, spherical, swollen.

bulge *n* bump, distension, knob, lump, protrusion, protuberance, swelling.
• *v* billow, dilate, distend, expand, project, protrude, stick out, swell.

bulk *n* 1 amplitude, body, dimensions, extent, immensity, magnitude, mass, size, substance, volume, weight. 2 *bulk of the work. inf* best part, greater part, majority, preponderance.

bulky *adj* awkward, chunky, cumbersome, unwieldy. ▷ BIG.

bulletin *n* announcement, communication, communiqué, dispatch, message, newsflash, notice, report, statement.

bull's-eye *n* centre, mark, target.

bully *v* browbeat, coerce, cow, harass, hector, intimidate, persecute, *inf* pick on, *inf* push around, terrorize, threaten, torment, tyrannize.

bulwark *n* defence, earthwork, fortification, protection, rampart, wall. ▷ BARRIER.

bump *n* 1 bang, blow, collision, crash, knock, thud, thump. 2 bulge, distension, hump, knob, lump, protrusion, protuberance, swelling, welt.
• *v* 1 bang, collide with, jar, knock, ram, smash into, thump, *sl* wallop. ▷ HIT. 2 bounce, jerk, jolt. **bump into** ▷ MEET. **bump off** ▷ KILL.

bumptious *adj* arrogant, *inf* big-headed, boastful, brash, *inf* cocky, conceited, egotistical, forward, officious, overbearing, pompous, presumptuous, *inf* pushy, self-assertive, self-important, smug, *inf* stuck-up, *inf* snooty, vain. *Opp* MODEST.

bumpy *adj* 1 bouncy, jarring, jerky, jolting. 2 *bumpy road.* broken, jagged, knobbly, pitted, rocky, rough, rutted, stony, uneven. *Opp* SMOOTH.

bunch *n* 1 batch, bundle, clump, cluster, heap, lot, quantity, set, sheaf, tuft. 2 *bunch of flowers.* bouquet, posy, spray. 3 [*inf*] *bunch of friends.* crowd, gang, gathering, party. ▷ GROUP.
• *v* cluster, congregate, crowd, flock, gather, herd, huddle, mass, pack. *Opp* DISPERSE.

bundle *n* bale, bunch, collection, package, packet, parcel, sheaf, truss.
• *v* bale, bind, fasten, pack, tie, truss, wrap. **bundle out** ▷ EJECT.

bung *n* cork, plug, stopper.
• *v* ▷ THROW.

bungle *v* blunder, botch, *sl* cock up, fluff, *inf* make a hash of, *inf* make a mess of, *inf* mess up, mismanage, *inf* muff, ruin, *inf* screw up, spoil.

buoy *n* beacon, float, marker, signal.
• *v* **buoy up** ▷ RAISE.

buoyant *adj* 1 floating, light. 2 *buoyant mood.* ▷ CHEERFUL.

burden *n* 1 cargo, encumbrance, load, weight. 2 *burden of guilt.* affliction, anxiety, care, cross, millstone, obligation, onus, problem, responsibility, trial, trouble, worry.
• *v* afflict, encumber, hamper, handicap, impose on, *inf* lumber (with), oppress, overload (with), *inf* saddle (with), tax, trouble, weigh down, worry.

burdensome *adj* difficult, exacting, heavy, onerous, oppressive, taxing, tiring, troublesome, wearisome, weighty, worrying. *Opp* EASY.

bureau *n* 1 desk, writing desk. 2 *travel bureau.* agency, department, office, service.

bureaucracy *n* administration, government, officialdom, paperwork, *inf* red tape, regulations.

burglar *n* housebreaker, intruder, robber. ▷ THIEF.

burglary *n* break-in, forcible entry, housebreaking, pilfering, robbery, stealing, theft.

burgle *v* break in, rob. ▷ STEAL.

burial *n* ▷ FUNERAL.

burlesque *n* caricature, imitation, mockery, parody, satire, *inf* send-up, *inf* spoof, *inf* take-off.

burly *adj* brawny, heavy, hefty, *inf* hulking, muscular, powerful, stocky, *inf* strapping, strong, sturdy, thickset, tough, well-built. *Opp* THIN.

burn *n* blister, charring.
• *v* 1 be alight, blaze, flame, flicker, glow, smoke, smoulder, spark. 2 consume, cremate, destroy by fire, ignite, incinerate, kindle, reduce to ashes, set on fire. 3 *burn your skin.* blister, char, scald, scorch, sear, shrivel, singe, sting. ▷ FIRE, HEAT.

burning *adj* 1 alight, blazing, flaming, glowing, incandescent, on fire, raging, smouldering. 2 *burning pain.* biting, blistering, fiery, scalding, scorching, searing, smarting, stinging. 3 *burning chemicals.* acid, caustic, corrosive. 4 *burning smell.* acrid, pungent, reeking, smoky. 5 *burning desire.* acute, ardent, consuming, eager, fervent, heated, impassioned, intense, passionate, red-hot, vehement. 6 *burning issue.* crucial, important, pressing, urgent, vital.

burrow *n* hole, retreat, set, shelter, tunnel, warren.
• *v* delve, dig, excavate, tunnel.

burst *v* 1 break, crack, erupt, explode, force open, give way, open suddenly, puncture, rupture, shatter, split. 2 ▷ RUSH.

bury *v* cover, embed, engulf, entomb, immerse, implant, inter, lay to rest, plant, secrete, submerge. ▷ HIDE.

bus *n* coach, double-decker, minibus.

bushy *adj* bristly, dense, fluffy, fuzzy, luxuriant, rough, shaggy, spreading, tangled, thick, unruly, untidy.

business *n* 1 affair, concern, duty, function, matter, problem, question, responsibility, subject, task. 2 calling, career, employment, job, line of work, occupation, profession, pursuit, trade, vocation. 3 buying and selling, commerce, dealings, industry, merchandising, trade, trading, transactions. 4 company, concern, corporation, enterprise, firm, organization, *inf* outfit, partnership, *inf* set-up, venture.

businesslike *adj* efficient, hard-headed, logical, methodical, orderly, practical, professional, systematic, well-organized. *Opp* DISORGANIZED.

businessman, businesswoman *ns* entrepreneur, executive, financier, industrialist, magnate, manager, tycoon.

bustle *n* activity, agitation, commotion, excitement, flurry, fuss, haste, hurly-burly, hustle, stir, *inf* to-do, *inf* toing and froing.
• *v* dash, fuss, hasten, hurry, hustle, rush, scamper, scramble, scurry, scuttle, *inf* tear, whirl.

busy *adj* 1 active, bustling about, diligent, employed, engaged, engrossed, *inf* hard at it, immersed, industrious, involved, occupied, *inf* on the go, slaving, *inf* tied up, *inf* up to your eyes, working. *Opp* IDLE. 2 *busy shops.* bustling, frantic, full, hectic, lively.

busybody *n* gossip, meddler, *inf* Nosey Parker, *inf* snooper. **be a busybody** ▷ INTERFERE.

butt *n* 1 handle, shaft. 2 *water-butt.* barrel, cask. 3 *cigar butt.* remains, remnant, stub. 4 *butt of ridicule.* object, subject, target, victim.
• *v* buffet, bump, jab, poke, prod, push, shove, thump. ▷ HIT. **butt in** ▷ INTERRUPT.

buttocks *n sl* arse, backside, behind, bottom, *inf* bum, *Amer* butt, haunches, *joc* posterior, rear, rump, seat.

buttress *n* prop, support.
• *v* brace, prop up, reinforce, strengthen, support.

buxom *adj* ample, bosomy, full-figured, plump, robust, voluptuous. *Opp* THIN.

buy *v* acquire, come by, get, *inf* invest in, obtain, pay for, procure, purchase. *Opp* SELL.

buyer *n* client, consumer, customer, purchaser, shopper.

bypass *v* avoid, circumvent, dodge, evade, go round, ignore, omit, sidestep, skirt.

by-product *n* consequence, corollary, repercussion, side-effect.

bystander *n* eye-witness, observer, onlooker, passer-by, spectator, witness.

C

cabin *n* 1 chalet, hut, lodge, shack, shanty, shed, shelter. 2 *cabin on a ship.* berth, compartment, quarters.

cable *n* 1 chain, cord, flex, guy, hawser, lead, rope, wire. 2 *news by cable.* message, telegram, wire.

cacophonous *adj* discordant, dissonant, harsh, noisy. *Opp* HARMONIOUS.

cacophony *n* caterwauling, din, discord, dissonance, harshness, jangle, racket, *inf* row, *inf* rumpus, tumult. *Opp* HARMONY.

cadence *n* accent, beat, intonation, lilt, metre, rhythm, rise and fall, stress, tune.

cadet *n* learner, recruit, trainee.

cadge *v* ask, beg, scrounge, sponge.

café *n* bar, bistro, brasserie, buffet, cafeteria, canteen, coffee bar, restaurant, snack bar, take-away, teashop.

cage *n* coop, enclosure, hutch, pen.
• *v* ▷ CONFINE.

cajole *v inf* butter up, coax, flatter, inveigle, persuade, seduce.

cake *n* 1 bun, gateau. 2 *cake of soap.* bar, block, chunk, lump, piece, slab.
• *v* 1 coat, clog, encrust, make muddy. 2 coagulate, congeal, dry, solidify, thicken.

calamitous *adj* cataclysmic, catastrophic, devastating, dire, disastrous, dreadful, fatal, ruinous, serious, terrible, tragic, unlucky.

calamity *n* accident, cataclysm, catastrophe, disaster, misadventure, misfortune, mishap, tragedy, tribulation.

calculate *v* add up, ascertain, assess, compute, count, determine, estimate, evaluate, figure out, gauge, judge, reckon, total, weigh, work out. **calculated** ▷ DELIBERATE. **calculating** ▷ CRAFTY.

calibre *n* 1 bore, diameter, gauge. 2 ability, capacity, character, distinction, excellence, genius, merit, proficiency, quality, skill, stature, talent, worth.

call *n* 1 bellow, cry, exclamation, shout, yell. 2 bidding, invitation, signal, summons. 3 *social call.* stay, visit. 4 *no call for it.* demand, excuse, justification, need, occasion, request.
• *v* 1 bellow, clamour, cry out, exclaim, hail, shout, yell. 2 *call on friends.* drop in, visit. 3 baptize, christen, entitle, name, title. 4 *call me at 7.* awaken, get someone up, rouse, wake. 5 *call a meeting.* convene, invite, order, summon. 6 *call by phone.* contact, ring, telephone. **call for** ▷ FETCH, REQUEST. **call off** ▷ CANCEL. **call someone names** ▷ INSULT.

calligraphy *n* copperplate, handwriting, lettering, script.

calling *n* career, employment, line of work, métier, occupation, profession, pursuit, trade, vocation.

callous *adj* cold, hard-bitten, *inf* hard-boiled, hardened, hard-hearted, heartless, inhuman, insensitive, merciless, ruthless, *inf* thick-skinned, uncaring, unemotional, unfeeling, unsympathetic. ▷ CRUEL. *Opp* SENSITIVE.

callow *adj* adolescent, immature, juvenile. ▷ INEXPERIENCED. *Opp* MATURE.

calm *adj* 1 even, flat, halcyon (*days*), like a millpond, motionless, placid, quiet, slow-moving, smooth, still, unclouded, windless. 2 collected, *derog* complacent, composed, controlled, cool, dispassionate, equable, impassive, imperturbable, *inf* laid-back, level-headed, patient, peaceful, poised, quiet, relaxed, restrained, sedate, self-possessed, sensible, serene, tranquil, unemotional, *inf* unflappable, unhurried, unperturbed, unruffled, untroubled. *Opp* EXCITABLE, STORMY.
• *n* flat sea, peace, quietness, stillness, tranquillity. ▷ CALMNESS.
• *v* appease, compose, control, cool, lull, mollify, pacify, placate, quieten, settle down, soothe. *Opp* DISTURB.

calmness *n* composure, equability, equanimity, imperturbability, level-headedness, peace of mind, sang-froid, self-possession, serenity, *inf* unflappability. *Opp* ANXIETY, EXCITEMENT.

camouflage *n* cloak, cover, disguise, façade, front, guise, mask, pretence, protective colouring, screen, veil.
• *v* cloak, conceal, cover up, disguise, hide, mask, screen, veil.

camp *n* bivouac, campsite, encampment, settlement.

campaign *n* battle, crusade, drive, effort, fight, movement, offensive, operation, struggle, war.

campus *n* grounds, setting, site.

canal *n* channel, waterway.

cancel *v* abandon, abolish, abort, annul, call off, countermand, cross out, delete, drop, eliminate, erase, expunge, invalidate, overrule, postpone, quash, repeal, rescind, revoke, scrap, *inf* scrub, wipe out, write off. **cancel out** ▷ NEUTRALIZE.

cancer *n* carcinoma, growth, malignancy, tumour.

candid *adj* blunt, direct, fair, forthright, frank, honest, ingenuous, *inf* no-nonsense, objective, open, outspoken, plain, sincere, straightforward, transparent, truthful, unbiased, undisguised, unprejudiced. *Opp* INSINCERE.

candidate *n* applicant, competitor, contender, contestant, entrant, nominee, *inf* possibility, runner.

cane *n* bamboo, rod, stick.
• *v* ▷ THRASH.

canoe *n* dug-out, kayak.

canopy *n* awning, covering, shade, shelter, umbrella.

canvass *n* census, examination, investigation, market research, opinion poll, poll, scrutiny, survey.
• *v* ask for, campaign, *inf* drum up support, electioneer, seek, solicit.

canyon *n* gap, gorge, pass, ravine, valley.

cap *n* covering, lid, top. ▷ HAT.
• *v* ▷ COVER.

capable *adj* able, accomplished, adept, clever, competent, efficient, experienced, expert, gifted, handy, intelligent, masterly, practised, proficient, qualified, skilful, talented. *Opp* INCAPABLE. **capable of** apt to, disposed to, equal to, liable to.

capacity *n* 1 content, dimensions, magnitude, room, size, volume. 2 ability, capability, competence, intelligence, potential, power, skill, talent, wit. 3 *in an official capacity.* duty, function, job, office, place, position, post, responsibility, role.

cape *n* 1 cloak, coat, mantle, shawl, wrap. 2 head, headland, point, promontory.

caper *v* bound, cavort, dance, frisk, frolic, gambol, hop, leap, play, prance, skip, spring.

capital *adj* 1 chief, first, foremost, important, leading, main, paramount, pre-eminent, primary, principal. 2 *capital letters.* block, large, upper-case. 3 ▷ EXCELLENT.
• *n* 1 chief city, centre of government. 2 assets, cash, finance, funds, investments, money, property, resources, savings, stock, wealth, *inf* the wherewithal.

capitulate *v* acquiesce, concede, give in, relent, submit, succumb, surrender, *inf* throw in the towel, yield.

capricious *adj* changeable, erratic, fanciful, fickle, flighty, impulsive, mercurial, moody, quirky, unpredictable, unreliable, unstable, variable, wayward. *Opp* STEADY.

capsize *v* flip over, keel over, overturn, tip over, *inf* turn turtle, turn upside down.

capsule *n* lozenge, medicine, pill, tablet.

captain *n* 1 boss, chief, head, leader. 2 commander, master, officer in charge, pilot, skipper.

caption *n* description, explanation, heading, title.

captivate *v* attract, beguile, bewitch, charm, delight, enchant, enslave, enthral, entrance, fascinate, hypnotize, infatuate, mesmerize, seduce, *inf* steal your heart. *Opp* DISGUST.

captive *adj* caged, captured, chained, confined, detained, enslaved, ensnared, imprisoned, incarcerated, jailed, secure, taken prisoner, *inf* under lock and key. *Opp* FREE.
• *n* convict, detainee, hostage, prisoner, slave.

captivity *n* bondage, confinement, custody, detention, imprisonment, incarceration, internment, restraint, slavery. ▷ PRISON. *Opp* FREEDOM.

capture *n* apprehension, arrest, seizure.
• *v* apprehend, arrest, *inf* bag, catch, *inf* collar, corner, ensnare, *inf* get, *inf* nab, net, *inf* nick, secure, seize, snare, take prisoner, trap. ▷ CONQUER. *Opp* LIBERATE.

car *n* automobile, *inf* banger, *joc* jalopy, motor, motor car, vehicle, *sl* wheels.

carcass *n* 1 body, corpse, meat, remains. 2 *carcass of a car.* framework, hulk, shell, skeleton.

card *n* 1 cardboard. 2 birthday card, business card, credit card, greetings card, playing card, postcard.

care *n* 1 attention, carefulness, caution, circumspection, concern, diligence, forethought, heed, meticulousness, pains, prudence, solicitude, thoroughness, thought, vigilance, watchfulness. 2 anxiety, concern, problem, responsibility, sorrow, stress, woe, worry. ▷ TROUBLE. 3 *left in my care.* charge, control,

custody, guardianship, protection, safekeeping, ward.
•*v* bother, concern yourself, mind, worry. **care for** ▷ LOVE, TEND.

career *n* calling, employment, job, livelihood, living, métier, occupation, profession, trade, vocation, work.
•*v* ▷ RUSH.

carefree *adj* 1 blasé, casual, debonair, easygoing, happy-go-lucky, insouciant, *inf* laid-back, light-hearted, nonchalant, relaxed, unconcerned, unworried. ▷ HAPPY. 2 *carefree holiday.* leisurely, peaceful, quiet, relaxing, restful, trouble-free. *Opp* ANXIOUS.

careful *adj* 1 alert, attentive, cautious, chary, circumspect, mindful, observant, prudent, solicitous, thoughtful, vigilant, wary. 2 *careful work.* accurate, conscientious, diligent, fastidious, *derog* fussy, judicious, methodical, meticulous, neat, orderly, organized, painstaking, particular, precise, punctilious, rigorous, scrupulous, systematic, thorough, well-organized. *Opp* CARELESS. **be careful** ▷ BEWARE.

careless *adj* 1 absent-minded, heedless, imprudent, inattentive, incautious, inconsiderate, irresponsible, negligent, rash, reckless, thoughtless, unguarded, unthinking. 2 *careless work.* casual, cursory, disorganized, hasty, inaccurate, jumbled, messy, perfunctory, scatter-brained, shoddy, slapdash, slipshod, *inf* sloppy, slovenly, untidy. *Opp* CAREFUL.

carelessness *n* inattention, irresponsibility, negligence, recklessness, *inf* sloppiness, slovenliness, thoughtlessness, untidiness. *Opp* CARE.

caress *v* cuddle, embrace, fondle, hug, kiss, make love to, nuzzle, pat, pet, rub against, stroke, touch.

caretaker *n* custodian, janitor, keeper, porter, warden, watchman.

careworn *adj* gaunt, grim, haggard. ▷ WEARY.

cargo *n* consignment, freight, goods, load, merchandise, payload, shipment.

caricature *n* burlesque, cartoon, parody, satire, *inf* send-up, *inf* spoof, *inf* take-off, travesty.
• *v* burlesque, distort, exaggerate, make fun of, mimic, overact, parody, ridicule, satirize, *inf* send up, *inf* take off.

caring *n* concern, kindness, nursing, solicitude.

carnage *n* bloodbath, bloodshed, butchery, holocaust, killing, massacre, pogrom, slaughter.

carnal *adj* animal, bodily, erotic, fleshly, physical, sexual. ▷ LUSTFUL. *Opp* SPIRITUAL.

carnival *n* celebration, fair, festival, fête, fun and games, gala, jamboree, merry-making, pageant, parade, revelry, show.

carp *v* cavil, find fault, *inf* go on, grumble, object, pick holes, quibble, *inf* split hairs, *inf* whinge. ▷ COMPLAIN.

carpentry *n* joinery, woodwork.

carriage *n* 1 coach. 2 bearing, demeanour, gait, manner, mien, posture, stance.

carrier *n* 1 bearer, conveyor, courier, delivery-man, delivery-woman, dispatch rider, haulier, messenger, postman, runner. 2 *carrier of a disease.* contact, host, transmitter.

carry *v* 1 bring, *inf* cart, ferry, fetch, haul, lead, lift, lug, manhandle, move, relay, ship, shoulder, take, transfer, transmit, transport. ▷ CONVEY. 2 *carry weight.* bear, maintain, support. 3 *carry a penalty.* demand, entail, involve, lead to, result in. **carry on** ▷ CONTINUE. **carry out** ▷ DO.

cart *n* truck, wagon, wheelbarrow.
•*v* ▷ CARRY.

carton *n* box, cartridge, case, container, pack, packet.

cartoon *n* animation, caricature, comic strip, drawing, sketch.

cartridge *n* 1 canister, capsule, case, cassette, container. 2 *cartridge for a gun.* magazine, round, shell.

carve *v* 1 slice. ▷ CUT. 2 *carve stone. inf* chip away at, chisel, engrave, hew, sculpture, shape.

cascade *n* cataract, flood, torrent, waterfall.
•*v* ▷ POUR.

case *n* 1 box, cabinet, carton, casket, chest, container, crate, pack, suitcase, trunk. 2 *case of mistaken identity.* example, illustration, instance, occurrence, specimen. 3 *rules don't apply in his case.* circumstances, condition, context, plight, predicament, situation. 4 *legal case.* action, argument, cause, dispute, inquiry, investigation, lawsuit.

cash *n* change, coins, currency, *inf* dough, funds, legal tender, money, notes, *inf* (the) ready, *inf* the wherewithal.
• *v* exchange for cash, realize, sell. **cash in on** ▷ PROFIT.

cashier *n* check-out person, clerk, teller.

cask *n* barrel, butt, tub, vat.

cast *n* 1 ▷ SCULPTURE. 2 *cast of a play.* characters, company, performers, players, troupe.
• *v* 1 *inf* chuck, drop, fling, hurl, launch, lob, pelt, pitch, project, scatter, shy, sling, throw, toss. 2 form, mould, shape. ▷ SCULPTURE. **cast off** ▷ SHED, UNTIE.

castaway *adj* abandoned, deserted, exiled, marooned, rejected, shipwrecked, stranded.

caste *n* class, degree, estate, grade, level, position, rank, standing, station, status.

castigate *v* chastise, correct, discipline, punish, rebuke, scold, *inf* tell off. ▷ CRITICIZE.

castle *n* chateau, citadel, fort, mansion, palace, stately home, stronghold, tower.

castrate *v* emasculate, geld, neuter, sterilize.

casual *adj* 1 accidental, chance, fortuitous, incidental, irregular, random, unexpected, unforeseen, unintentional, unplanned, unpremeditated, unstructured, unsystematic. *Opp* DELIBERATE. 2 *casual attitude.* blasé, careless, *inf* couldn't-care-less, easygoing, *inf* free-and-easy, lackadaisical, *inf* laid-back, lax, nonchalant, offhand, relaxed, *inf* slap-happy, *inf* throwaway, unconcerned, unenthusiastic, unprofessional. *Opp* ENTHUSIASTIC. 3 *casual clothes.* comfortable, informal. *Opp* FORMAL.

casualty *n* dead person, fatality, injured person, loss, victim.

cat *n* kitten, *inf* moggy, *inf* pussy, tabby, tom, tomcat.

catacombs *n* crypt, sepulchre, tomb, vault.

catalogue *n* brochure, directory, index, inventory, list, record, register, roll.
• *v* classify, file, index, list, make an inventory of, record, register.

catapult *v* fire, fling, hurl, launch. ▷ THROW.

cataract *n* cascade, falls, rapids, torrent, waterfall.

catastrophe *n* calamity, cataclysm, crushing blow, debacle, devastation, ruin, tragedy. ▷ MISFORTUNE.

catch *n* 1 bag, booty, haul, net, prize, take. 2 difficulty, disadvantage, drawback, obstacle, problem, snag, trap, trick. 3 bolt, clasp, clip, fastener, fastening, hook, latch, lock.
• *v* 1 clutch, ensnare, grab, grasp, grip, hang on to, hold, hook, net, seize, snatch, take, tangle, trap. 2 *catch a thief.* apprehend, arrest, capture, *inf* cop, corner, discover, expose, intercept, *inf* nab, *inf* nobble, stop, take by surprise. 3 *catch unawares.* come upon, discover, surprise. 4 *catch a bus.* be in time for, get on. 5 *catch a cold.* contract, get. **catch on** ▷ SUCCEED, UNDERSTAND. **catchphrase** ▷ SAYING. **catch-22** ▷ DILEMMA. **catch up** ▷ OVERTAKE.

catching *adj* ▷ CONTAGIOUS.

catchy *adj* attractive, haunting, memorable, popular, tuneful.

categorical *adj* absolute, certain, complete, decided, definite, direct, dogmatic, downright, emphatic, explicit, express, firm, forceful, out and out, positive, total, unambiguous, unconditional, unequivocal, unmitigated, unqualified, utter, vigorous. *Opp* TENTATIVE.

category *n* class, classification, division, grade, group, heading, kind, order, rank, section, set, sort, type, variety.

cater *v* cook, make arrangements, minister, provide, serve, supply.

catholic *adj* all-embracing, broad, broad-minded, comprehensive, cosmopolitan, eclectic, general, liberal, universal, varied, wide, wide-ranging.

cattle *pl n* bullocks, bulls, calves, cows, heifers, livestock.

catty *adj inf* bitchy, malicious, mean, nasty, sly, spiteful. ▷ UNKIND. *Opp* KIND.

cause *n* 1 basis, beginning, genesis, grounds, motive, occasion, origin, reason, root, source, stimulus. 2 agent, author, creator, initiator, inspiration, inventor, originator, producer. 3 excuse, explanation, pretext, reason. 4 *good cause.* aim, belief, concern, end, ideal, object, purpose, undertaking.
• *v* 1 arouse, awaken, begin, bring about, bring on, create, effect, engender, generate, give rise to, incite, kindle, lead to, occasion, precipitate, produce, provoke, result in, set off, stimulate, trigger off, *inf* whip up. 2 compel, force, induce, motivate.

caustic *adj* 1 acid, astringent, burning, corrosive. 2 *caustic criticism.* acrimonious, biting, bitter, cutting, mordant, sarcastic, scathing, severe, sharp, stinging, trenchant, waspish. *Opp* MILD.

caution *n* 1 alertness, care, carefulness, circumspection, discretion, forethought, heed, prudence, vigilance, wariness, watchfulness. 2 *let off with a caution.*

admonition, *inf* dressing-down, reprimand, *inf* talking-to, *inf* ticking-off, warning.
• *v* 1 advise, alert, counsel, inform, tip off, warn. 2 *the police will caution him.* admonish, give a warning, reprehend, reprimand, *inf* tell off, *inf* tick off.

cautious *adj* 1 alert, attentive, careful, heedful, prudent, vigilant, watchful. 2 *cautious comments. inf* cagey, calculating, chary, circumspect, discreet, grudging, guarded, hesitant, judicious, noncommittal, suspicious, tactful, tentative, wary, watchful. *Opp* RECKLESS.

cavalcade *n* march-past, parade, procession, spectacle, troop.

cave *n* cavern, cavity, den, grotto, hole, pothole, underground chamber.
• *v* **cave in** ▷ COLLAPSE, SURRENDER.

cavity *n* cave, crater, hole, pit.

cease *v* break off, call a halt, conclude, desist, discontinue, finish, halt, *inf* kick (*a habit*), *inf* knock off, *inf* lay off, leave off, *inf* pack in, refrain, stop, terminate. *Opp* BEGIN.

ceaseless *adj* chronic, constant, continuous, everlasting, incessant, interminable, never-ending, non-stop, perpetual, persistent, relentless, unending, unremitting, untiring. *Opp* INTERMITTENT, TEMPORARY.

celebrate *v* 1 have a celebration, let yourself go, *inf* live it up, make merry, *inf* paint the town red, rejoice, revel. 2 commemorate, hold, honour, keep, observe, officiate at, remember, solemnize. **celebrated** ▷ FAMOUS.

celebration *n* banquet, binge, carnival, commemoration, feast, festivity, *inf* jamboree, *inf* jollification, merrymaking, observance, *inf* orgy, party, *inf* rave-up, revelry, *inf* shindig, solemnization.

celebrity *n* 1 ▷ FAME. 2 big name, *inf* bigwig, famous person, idol, personality, public figure, star, *inf* superstar, VIP.

celestial *adj* 1 cosmic, galactic, interplanetary, starry, stellar. 2 *celestial beings.* angelic, divine, ethereal, godlike, heavenly, seraphic, spiritual, sublime, transcendental.

celibacy *n* bachelorhood, chastity, purity, self-restraint, spinsterhood, virginity.

celibate *adj* abstinent, chaste, single, unmarried, virgin.
• *n* bachelor, spinster, virgin.

cell *n* cavity, chamber, compartment, cubicle, den, enclosure, prison, room, space, unit.

cellar *n* basement, crypt, vault, wine cellar.

cemetery *n* burial ground, churchyard, graveyard.

censor *v* ban, bowdlerize, *inf* clean up, cut, edit, expurgate, prohibit, remove.

censorious *adj* fault-finding, judgemental, moralistic, self-righteous. ▷ CRITICAL.

censure *n* blame, castigation, condemnation, criticism, denunciation, diatribe, disapproval, *inf* dressing-down, harangue, rebuke, reprimand, reproach, reproof, *inf* slating, stricture, *inf* talking-to, *inf* telling-off, tirade, verbal attack.
• *v* admonish, berate, blame, *inf* carpet, castigate, caution, *old use* chide, condemn, criticize, denounce, rebuke, reproach, scold, take to task, *inf* tear (someone) off a strip, *inf* tell off, *inf* tick off, upbraid.

census *n* count, survey, tally.

central *adj* 1 focal, inner, innermost, middle. 2 *central facts.* chief, crucial, essential, fundamental, important, key, major, pivotal, primary, principal, vital. *Opp* PERIPHERAL.

centralize *v* amalgamate, concentrate, rationalize, streamline, unify. *Opp* DISPERSE.

centre *n* bull's-eye, core, focal point, focus, heart, hub, interior, kernel, midpoint, nucleus, pivot. *Opp* PERIMETER.
• *v* concentrate, converge, focus.

centrifugal *adj* dispersing, diverging, moving outwards, scattering, spreading. *Opp* CENTRIPETAL.

centripetal *adj* converging. *Opp* CENTRIFUGAL.

cereal *n* barley, corn, grain, maize, oats, rice, rye, wheat.

ceremonial *adj* celebratory, liturgical, majestic, official, ritual, stately. ▷ FORMAL. *Opp* INFORMAL.

ceremonious *adj* courtly, dignified, formal, grand, *derog* pompous, punctilious, *derog* starchy. ▷ POLITE. *Opp* CASUAL.

ceremony *n* 1 celebration, commemoration, *inf* do, function, occasion, parade, reception, rite, ritual, service, solemnity. 2 decorum, etiquette, formality, grandeur, pageantry, pomp and circumstance, protocol, ritual, spectacle.

certain *adj* 1 adamant, assured, confident, convinced, decided, determined, firm, invariable, positive, resolved, satisfied, settled, steady, sure, unshakable, unwavering. 2 *certain proof.* absolute, categorical, certified, clear, clear-cut, conclusive, convincing, definite, established, genuine, guaranteed, incontestable, incontrovertible, infallible, irrefutable, official, plain, reliable, settled, sure, true, trustworthy, unarguable, undeniable, undisputed, undoubted, unmistakable, unquestionable, valid, verifiable. 3 *certain disaster.* fated, guaranteed, imminent, inescapable, inevitable, inexorable, predestined, unavoidable. 4 *certain to pay up.* bound, compelled, required, sure. 5 *certain people.* individual, particular, some, specific, unnamed. *Opp* UNCERTAIN. **be certain** ▷ KNOW. **for certain** ▷ DEFINITELY. **make certain** ▷ ENSURE.

certainty *n* 1 actuality, certain fact, *inf* foregone conclusion, inevitability, *inf* sure thing. 2 assertiveness, assurance, authority, confidence, conviction, knowledge, proof, sureness, truth, validity. *Opp* DOUBT.

certificate *n* authorization, degree, diploma, document, guarantee, licence, pass, permit, qualification, warrant.

certify *v* 1 affirm, attest, authenticate, avow, bear witness, confirm, declare, endorse, guarantee, notify, sign, swear, testify, verify, vouch, witness. 2 *certify as competent.* authorize, charter, franchise, license, recognize, validate.

chain *n* 1 bond, coupling, fetter, link, manacle, shackle. 2 *chain of events.* combination, concatenation, line, progression, row, sequence, series, set, string, succession, train.
• *v* bind, fetter, handcuff, link, manacle, shackle, tether, tie. ▷ FASTEN.

chair *n* armchair, deckchair, easy chair, recliner, seat.
• *v* ▷ PRESIDE.

chairperson *n* chair, chairman, chairwoman, convenor, leader, moderator, president, speaker.

challenge *v* 1 accost, confront, dare, defy, *inf* have a go at, provoke, summon, take on, tax. 2 *challenge a decision.* argue against, call in doubt, contest, dispute, impugn, object to, oppose, protest against, query, question, take exception to.

challenging *adj* inspiring, stimulating, testing, thought-provoking. ▷ DIFFICULT. *Opp* EASY.

chamber *n* cavity, cell, compartment, niche, room, space.

champion *adj* great, leading, record-breaking, supreme, top, unrivalled, victorious, winning, world-beating.
• *n* 1 conqueror, hero, medallist, prizewinner, record-breaker, superman, superwoman, title-holder, victor, winner. 2 *champion of the poor.* backer, defender, guardian, patron, protector, supporter, upholder, vindicator.
• *v* ▷ SUPPORT.

championship *n* competition, contest, series, tournament.

chance *adj* accidental, casual, coincidental, *inf* fluky, fortuitous, fortunate, inadvertent, incidental, lucky, random, unexpected, unforeseen, unfortunate, unplanned, unpremeditated. *Opp* DELIBERATE.
• *n* 1 accident, coincidence, fate, fluke, fortune, gamble, luck, misfortune, serendipity. 2 *chance of rain.* danger, likelihood, possibility, probability, prospect, risk. 3 occasion, opportunity, time, turn.
• *v* 1 ▷ RISK. 2 ▷ HAPPEN.

chancy *adj* dangerous, *inf* dicey, *inf* dodgy, hazardous, *inf* iffy, insecure, precarious, risky, tricky, uncertain, unpredictable, unsafe. *Opp* SAFE.

change *n* 1 adaptation, adjustment, alteration, break, conversion, deterioration, development, difference, improvement, innovation, metamorphosis, modification, mutation, new look, rearrangement, reformation, reorganization, revolution, shift, substitution, swing, transfiguration, transformation, transition, translation, transposition, *inf* turn-about, U-turn, variation, variety, vicissitude. 2 *small change.* ▷ CASH.
• *v* 1 acclimatize, accommodate, adapt, adjust, affect, alter, amend, convert, diversify, influence, modify, rearrange, reconstruct, reform, remodel, reorganize, reshape, restyle, tailor, transfigure, transform, translate, transmute. 2 *opinions change.* alter, be transformed, *inf* chop and change, develop, fluctuate, move on, mutate, shift, vary. 3 *change one thing for another.* displace, exchange, replace, substitute, switch, swap, transpose. 4 *change money.* barter, convert, trade in. **change into** ▷ BECOME. **change someone's mind** ▷ CONVERT. **change your mind** ▷ RECONSIDER.

changeable *adj* capricious, chequered (*career*), erratic, fickle, fitful, fluctuating, fluid, inconsistent, irregular, mercurial, mutable, protean, shifting, temperamental, uncertain, unpredictable, unreliable, unsettled, unstable, *inf* up and down, vacillating, variable, volatile, wavering. *Opp* CONSTANT.

channel *n* 1 aqueduct, canal, conduit,

ditch, duct, groove, gully, gutter, moat, overflow, pipe, sluice, sound, strait, trench, trough, waterway. ▷ STREAM. 2 avenue, means, medium, path, route, way. 3 *TV channel.* *inf* side, station, wavelength.
• *v* conduct, convey, direct, guide, lead, route, transmit.

chant *n* hymn, plainsong, psalm. ▷ SONG.
• *v* intone. ▷ SING.

chaos *n* anarchy, bedlam, confusion, disorder, *inf* mayhem, muddle, pandemonium, *inf* shambles, tumult, turmoil. *Opp* ORDER.

chaotic *adj* anarchic, confused, disordered, disorganized, haphazard, *inf* haywire, *inf* higgledy-piggledy, jumbled, lawless, muddled, riotous, *inf* shambolic, *inf* topsy-turvy, tumultuous, uncontrolled, unruly, untidy, *inf* upside-down. *Opp* ORDERLY.

char *v* blacken, brown, burn, scorch, sear, singe.

character *n* 1 distinctiveness, flavour, individuality, integrity, stamp, uniqueness. ▷ CHARACTERISTIC. 2 *forceful character.* constitution, disposition, *inf* make-up, manner, nature, personality, reputation, temper, temperament. 3 *famous character.* figure, individual, person, personality, *inf* type. 4 *She's a character!* *inf* case, comedian, eccentric, *inf* nut-case, *derog* weirdo. 5 *character in a play.* part, persona, role. 6 *written character.* cipher, figure, hieroglyphic, letter, mark, sign, symbol.

characteristic *adj* 1 [*of an individual*] distinctive, distinguishing, essential, idiosyncratic, individual, particular, peculiar, singular, special, specific, symptomatic, unique. 2 [*of a kind*] representative, typical.
• *n* attribute, distinguishing feature, hallmark, idiosyncrasy, peculiarity, property, quality, symptom, trait.

characterize *v* brand, delineate, depict, describe, distinguish, draw, identify, mark, portray, present, typify.

charade *n* deception, fabrication, farce, make-believe, masquerade, mockery, *inf* play-acting, pose, pretence, *inf* put-up job, sham.

charge *n* 1 cost, expenditure, expense, fare, fee, payment, price, rate, terms, toll, value. 2 *in my charge.* care, control, custody, guardianship, jurisdiction, protection, responsibility, safe-keeping, supervision, trust. 3 *criminal charge.* accusation, allegation, imputation, indictment. 4 *cavalry charge.* assault, attack, drive, incursion, invasion, offensive, onslaught, raid, sally, sortie.
• *v* 1 debit, exact, levy, make you pay, require. 2 accuse, blame, impeach, indict, prosecute, tax. 3 *charge with a duty.* burden, entrust, give, impose on. 4 command, direct, exhort, instruct. 5 *charge an enemy.* assault, attack, *inf* fall on, rush, set on, storm, *inf* wade into.

charitable *adj* bountiful, liberal, munificent, open-handed, philanthropic. ▷ KIND. *Opp* MEAN.

charity *n* 1 altruism, benevolence, bounty, caring, compassion, consideration, generosity, helpfulness, humanity, kindness, love, mercy, philanthropy, self-sacrifice, sympathy, unselfishness, warm-heartedness. 2 alms-giving, bounty, donation, financial support, gift, handout, largesse, offering, patronage, relief.

charm *n* 1 allure, appeal, attractiveness, charisma, fascination, magic, magnetism, power, pull, seductiveness. ▷ BEAUTY. 2 *magic charm.* curse, enchantment, incantation, magic, mumbo-jumbo, sorcery, spell, witchcraft. 3 *lucky charm.* amulet, mascot, ornament, talisman, trinket.
• *v* allure, attract, beguile, bewitch, captivate, cast a spell on, delight, disarm, enchant, enthral, entrance, fascinate, hold spellbound, hypnotize, intrigue, mesmerize, please, seduce, win over. **charming** ▷ ATTRACTIVE.

chart *n* diagram, graph, map, plan, sketch-map, table.

charter *v* 1 employ, engage, hire, lease, rent. 2 ▷ CERTIFY.

chase *v* drive, follow, hound, hunt, pursue, run after, track.

chasm *n* abyss, canyon, cleft, crater, crevasse, fissure, gap, gulf, hole, opening, pit, ravine, rift, split, void.

chaste *adj* 1 abstinent, celibate, *inf* clean, inexperienced, innocent, moral, pure, sinless, undefiled, unmarried, virgin, virginal, virtuous. *Opp* IMMORAL. 2 *chaste dress.* austere, decent, decorous, modest, plain, restrained, severe, simple, unadorned. *Opp* INDECENT.

chasten *v* 1 restrain, subdue. ▷ HUMILIATE. 2 ▷ CHASTISE.

chastise *v* castigate, correct, discipline, rebuke, scold. ▷ PUNISH, REPRIMAND.

chastity *n* abstinence, celibacy, innocence, integrity, morality, purity, restraint, virginity, virtue. *Opp* LUST.

chat *n* chatter, *inf* chin-wag, *inf* chit-chat, conversation, gossip, *inf* heart-to-heart.
• *v* chatter, gossip, *inf* natter, prattle. ▷ TALK. **chat up** ▷ WOO.

chauvinist *n* bigot, *inf* MCP (= *male chauvinist pig*), patriot, sexist, xenophobe.

cheap *adj* 1 bargain, budget, cut-price, *inf* dirt-cheap, discount, economical, economy, inexpensive, *inf* knock-down, low-priced, reasonable, reduced, *inf* rock-bottom, sale. 2 *cheap quality*. base, inferior, poor, second-rate, shoddy, tawdry, *inf* tinny, worthless. 3 *cheap insult*. contemptible, despicable, facile, glib, ill-mannered, mean, silly, tasteless, unworthy, vulgar. *Opp* EXPENSIVE, WORTHY.

cheapen *v* belittle, debase, degrade, demean, devalue, discredit, downgrade, lower the tone (of), vulgarize.

cheat *n* 1 charlatan, *inf* con-man, counterfeiter, deceiver, double-crosser, forger, fraud, hoaxer, impersonator, impostor, *inf* phoney, quack, rogue, *inf* shark, swindler, trickster. 2 artifice, chicanery, *inf* con, confidence trick, deception, *inf* fiddle, fraud, hoax, lie, misrepresentation, pretence, *inf* put-up job, *inf* racket, *inf* rip-off, ruse, sham, swindle, *inf* swizz, trick.
• *v* 1 *inf* bamboozle, beguile, *inf* con, deceive, defraud, *inf* diddle, *inf* do, double-cross, dupe, *inf* fiddle, fleece, fool, hoax, hoodwink, outwit, *inf* rip off, *inf* short-change, swindle, take in, trick. 2 *cheat in an exam*. copy, crib.

check *adj* ▷ CHEQUERED.
• *n* 1 delay, hesitation, hindrance, interruption, pause, restraint, stoppage. 2 *medical check*. check-up, examination, *inf* going-over, inspection, investigation, *inf* once-over, scrutiny, test.
• *v* 1 arrest, bar, bridle, control, curb, delay, halt, hamper, hinder, hold back, impede, inhibit, keep in check, obstruct, regulate, rein, repress, restrain, slow down, stem, stop, stunt (*growth*), thwart. 2 *check answers*. compare, cross-check, examine, inspect, investigate, monitor, scrutinize, test, verify.

cheek *n* audacity, boldness, effrontery, impertinence, impudence, insolence, presumptuousness, rudeness, temerity.

cheeky *adj* audacious, bold, brazen, disrespectful, flippant, forward, impertinent, impolite, impudent, insolent, irreverent, pert, presumptuous, rude, saucy, shameless, *inf* tongue-in-cheek. *Opp* RESPECTFUL.

cheer *n* 1 cry of approval, hurrah, shout of applause. 2 ▷ HAPPINESS.
• *v* 1 acclaim, applaud, clap, encourage, shout, yell. *Opp* JEER. 2 comfort, console, encourage, exhilarate, gladden, please, solace, uplift. *Opp* SADDEN. **cheer someone up** ▷ COMFORT, ENTERTAIN. **cheer up** ▷ BRIGHTEN. **Cheer up!** *inf* buck up, smile, *sl* snap out of it, take heart.

cheerful *adj* animated, bouncy, bright, *inf* chirpy, contented, convivial, festive, genial, good-humoured, hearty, hopeful, jaunty, jolly, jovial, joyful, light-hearted, merry, optimistic, *inf* perky, pleased, positive, sparkling, spirited, sprightly, sunny, warm-hearted. ▷ HAPPY. *Opp* BAD-TEMPERED, CHEERLESS.

cheerless *adj* bleak, comfortless, dark, depressing, desolate, dingy, drab, dreary, dull, forbidding, gloomy, lacklustre, melancholy, miserable, sombre, sullen, sunless, uncongenial, uninviting, unpleasant, unpromising, woeful. ▷ SAD. *Opp* CHEERFUL.

chemical *n* compound, element, substance.

chemist *n Amer* drugstore, pharmacist, pharmacy.

chequered *adj* 1 check, criss-cross, in squares, patchwork, tartan, tessellated. 2 *chequered career*. ▷ CHANGEABLE.

cherish *v* be fond of, care for, cosset, foster, hold dear, keep safe, love, nurse, nurture, prize, protect, treasure, value.

chest *n* 1 box, caddy, case, casket, coffer, crate, strongbox, trunk. 2 breast, ribcage, thorax.

chew *v* bite, champ, crunch, gnaw, masticate, munch, nibble. **chew over** ▷ CONSIDER.

chick *n* fledgling, nestling.

chicken *n* bantam, cockerel, fowl, hen, pullet, rooster.

chief *adj* 1 arch, first, greatest, head, highest, leading, major, most experienced, most important, oldest, outstanding, premier, principal, senior, supreme, top, unequalled, unrivalled. 2 *chief facts*. basic, cardinal, central, especial, essential, foremost, fundamental, high-priority, indispensable, key, main, necessary, overriding, paramount, predominant, primary, prime, salient, significant, uppermost, vital. *Opp* UNIMPORTANT.
• *n inf* bigwig, *inf* boss, captain, commander, commanding officer, commissioner, controller, director, employer,

executive, foreman, forewoman, *inf* gaffer, *inf* godfather, governor, head, king, leader, manager, managing director, master, *inf* number one, organizer, overseer, owner, president, principal, proprietor, ringleader, ruler, superintendent, supervisor, *inf* supremo.

chiefly *adv* especially, essentially, generally, mainly, mostly, particularly, predominantly, primarily, principally.

child *n* 1 *inf* babe, baby, *inf* bambino, boy, *derog* brat, girl, infant, juvenile, *inf* kid, lad, lass, minor, newborn, *inf* nipper, *inf* stripling, toddler, *inf* tot, *derog* urchin, youngster, youth. 2 daughter, descendant, heir, issue, offspring, progeny, son.

childhood *n* babyhood, boyhood, girlhood, infancy, minority, schooldays, *inf* teens, youth.

childish *adj* babyish, credulous, immature, juvenile, puerile. ▷ SILLY. *Opp* MATURE.

childlike *adj* artless, guileless, ingenuous, innocent, naive, simple, trustful, unaffected, unsophisticated. *Opp* ARTFUL.

chill *n* ▷ COLD.
• *v* cool, freeze, keep cold, make cold, refrigerate. *Opp* WARM.

chilly *adj* 1 cold, cool, crisp, frosty, icy, *inf* nippy, *inf* parky, raw, sharp, wintry. 2 *chilly greeting.* aloof, cool, frigid, hostile, remote, reserved, standoffish, unforthcoming, unfriendly, unresponsive, unsympathetic, unwelcoming. *Opp* WARM.

chime *n* peal, striking, tintinnabulation, tolling.
• *v* ▷ RING.

chimney *n* flue, funnel, smokestack.

china *n* porcelain. ▷ CROCKERY.

chink *n* 1 cleft, crack, cranny, crevice, fissure, gap, opening, rift, slit, slot, space. 2 clink, chime, jingle, ring, tinkle.

chip *n* 1 bit, flake, fleck, fragment, piece, scrap, shard, shaving, sliver, splinter, wedge. 2 *chip in a cup.* crack, damage, flaw, nick, notch, scratch.
• *v* break, crack, damage, nick, notch, scratch, splinter. **chip away** ▷ CHISEL. **chip in** ▷ CONTRIBUTE, INTERRUPT.

chisel *v* carve, *inf* chip away, cut, engrave, fashion, model, sculpture, shape.

chivalrous *adj* bold, brave, courageous, courteous, courtly, gallant, generous, gentlemanly, heroic, honourable, noble, polite, respectable, true, trustworthy, valiant, worthy. *Opp* COWARDLY, RUDE.

choice *adj* ▷ EXCELLENT.
• *n* 1 alternative, dilemma, option. 2 *make your choice.* choosing, decision, election, nomination, pick, preference, say, vote. 3 *choice of food.* array, assortment, miscellany, mixture, range, selection, variety.

choke *v* 1 asphyxiate, garrotte, smother, stifle, strangle, suffocate, throttle. 2 *choke in smoke.* cough, gag, gasp, retch. 3 *cars choke the roads.* block, *inf* bung up, clog, congest, constrict, dam, fill, jam, obstruct, stop up. **choke back** ▷ SUPPRESS.

choose *v* adopt, agree on, appoint, decide on, determine on, distinguish, draw lots for, elect, fix on, identify, name, nominate, opt for, pick out, *inf* plump for, prefer, select, settle on, single out, vote for.

choosy *adj* dainty, discerning, discriminating, fastidious, finicky, fussy, hard to please, particular, *inf* pernickety, *inf* picky, selective. *Opp* INDIFFERENT.

chop *v* hack, lop, split. ▷ CUT. **chop and change** ▷ CHANGE.

chopper *n* axe, cleaver.

choppy *adj* rough, ruffled, turbulent, uneven. *Opp* SMOOTH.

chore *n* burden, drudgery, duty, errand, job, task, work.

chorus *n* 1 choir, ensemble, singers. 2 *join in the chorus.* refrain, response.

christen *v* anoint, baptize, call, dub, name.

chronic *adj* 1 ceaseless, constant, deep-rooted, habitual, incessant, incurable, ineradicable, ingrained, lasting, lifelong, lingering, long-standing, never-ending, non-stop, permanent, persistent, unending. *Opp* ACUTE, TEMPORARY. 2 [*inf*] *chronic driving.* ▷ BAD.

chronicle *n* account, annals, archive, description, diary, history, journal, narrative, record, register, saga, story.

chronological *adj* consecutive, in order, sequential.

chronology *n* 1 calendar, diary, journal, log, timetable. 2 *establish the chronology.* dating, order, sequence, timing.

chubby *adj* buxom, plump, stout, tubby. ▷ FAT. *Opp* THIN.

chunk *n* bar, block, brick, hunk, lump, mass, piece, portion, slab, wedge, *inf* wodge.

church *n* abbey, basilica, cathedral, chapel, convent, monastery, nunnery, priory.

churchyard *n* burial ground, cemetery, graveyard.

chute *n* channel, incline, ramp, rapid, slide, slope.

cinema *n* films, *inf* flicks, *inf* movies, *inf* pictures.

circle *n* 1 band, circlet, circuit, cycle, disc, hoop, loop, orbit, ring, rotation, sphere. 2 *circle of friends*. association, band, body, clique, club, company, fellowship, gang, party, set, society. ▷ GROUP.
• *v* 1 circulate, circumnavigate, coil, curl, curve, go round, gyrate, loop, orbit, reel, revolve, rotate, spin, spiral, swirl, swivel, tour, turn, wheel, whirl, wind. 2 *trees circle the lawn*. encircle, enclose, encompass, girdle, hem in, ring, skirt, surround.

circuit *n* journey round, lap, orbit, revolution, tour.

circuitous *adj* devious, indirect, labyrinthine, meandering, rambling, roundabout, serpentine, tortuous, twisting, winding, zigzag. *Opp* DIRECT.

circular *adj* 1 ringlike, round. 2 *circular conversation*. circumlocutory, cyclic, repetitive, roundabout, tautologous.
• *n* advertisement, leaflet, letter, notice, pamphlet.

circulate *v* 1 go round, move about, move round, orbit. ▷ CIRCLE. 2 *circulate gossip*. advertise, disseminate, distribute, issue, make known, promulgate, publicize, *inf* put about, send round, spread about.

circulation *n* 1 flow, movement, pumping, recycling. 2 broadcasting, diffusion, dissemination, distribution, publication, spreading, transmission. 3 *newspaper circulation*. distribution, sales-figures.

circumference *n* border, boundary, circuit, edge, fringe, limit, margin, outline, perimeter, periphery, rim, verge.

circumstance *n* affair, event, happening, incident, occasion, occurrence. **circumstances** 1 background, conditions, considerations, context, contingencies, details, factors, facts, particulars, position, situation, state of affairs, surroundings. 2 finances, income, resources.

circumstantial *adj* conjectural, deduced, inferred, unprovable. *Opp* PROVABLE.

cistern *n* bath, reservoir, tank.

citadel *n* acropolis, bastion, castle, fort, fortress, garrison, stronghold, tower.

cite *v* adduce, advance, *inf* bring up, mention, name, quote, *inf* reel off, refer to.

citizen *n* denizen, dweller, freeman, householder, inhabitant, national, native, passport-holder, resident, subject, taxpayer, voter.

city *n* capital, conurbation, metropolis, town.

civil *adj* 1 affable, civilized, courteous, respectful, urbane. ▷ POLITE. *Opp* IMPOLITE. 2 *civil administration*. civilian, domestic, internal, national. 3 *civil liberties*. communal, public, social, state. **civil rights** human rights, legal rights, liberty, political rights. **civil servant** administrator, bureaucrat, *derog* mandarin.

civilization *n* achievements, attainments, culture, customs, mores, refinement, sophistication, urbanity, urbanization.

civilize *v* cultivate, domesticate, educate, enlighten, humanize, improve, refine, socialize, urbanize.

civilized *adj* cultivated, cultured, democratic, developed, domesticated, educated, enlightened, humane, orderly, polite, refined, sociable, sophisticated, urbane, urbanized, well-behaved, well-run. *Opp* UNCIVILIZED.

claim *v* 1 ask for, collect, demand, exact, insist on, request, require, take. 2 affirm, allege, argue, assert, contend, declare, insist, maintain, pretend, profess, state.

clairvoyant *adj* extra-sensory, prophetic, psychic, telepathic.
• *n* fortune-teller, oracle, prophet, seer, soothsayer.

clamber *v* climb, crawl, move awkwardly, scramble.

clammy *adj* close, damp, dank, humid, moist, muggy, slimy, sticky, sweaty, wet.

clamour *n* babel, commotion, din, hubbub, hullabaloo, noise, outcry, racket, *inf* row, shouting, storm, uproar.
• *v* cry out, exclaim, shout, yell.

clan *n* family, house, tribe.

clannish *adj* cliquish, close-knit, insular, united.

clap *n* bang, crack, crash, report, smack.
• *v* 1 applaud, *sl* put your hands together. 2 *clap on the back*. ▷ HIT.

clarify *v* 1 clear up, define, elucidate, explain, gloss, illuminate, make clear, simplify, spell out, throw light on. *Opp* CONFUSE. 2 *clarify wine*. cleanse, filter, purify, refine.

clash *v* 1 bang, clang, clank, crash, ring. 2 ▷ CONFLICT. 3 *The events clash*. ▷ COINCIDE.

clasp *n* 1 brooch, buckle, catch, clip, fastener, fastening, hasp, hook, pin. 2 cuddle, embrace, grip, hold, hug.
• *v* 1 ▷ FASTEN. 2 cling to, clutch,

embrace, grasp, grip, hold, hug, squeeze. 3 *clasp your hands.* hold together, wring.

class *n* 1 category, classification, division, genre, genus, grade, group, kind, league, order, quality, rank, set, sort, species, sphere, type. 2 *social class.* caste, degree, grouping, lineage, pedigree, standing, station, status. 3 *class in school.* band, form, *Amer* grade, group, set, stream, year.
• *v* ▷ CLASSIFY.

classic *adj* 1 abiding, ageless, deathless, enduring, flawless, ideal, immortal, lasting, legendary, memorable, outstanding, perfect, time-honoured, undying, unforgettable, *inf* vintage. ▷ EXCELLENT. *Opp* COMMONPLACE, EPHEMERAL. 2 *classic case.* archetypal, characteristic, copybook, definitive, exemplary, model, standard, typical, usual. *Opp* UNUSUAL.
• *n* masterpiece, masterwork, model.

classical *adj* 1 ancient, Attic, Greek, Hellenic, Latin, Roman. 2 *classical style.* austere, dignified, elegant, pure, restrained, symmetrical, well-proportioned. 3 *classical music.* harmonious, highbrow, serious.

classification *n* categorization, codification, organization, tabulation, taxonomy. ▷ CLASS.

classify *v* arrange, catalogue, categorize, class, grade, group, order, organize, pigeon-hole, sort, systematize, tabulate. **classified** ▷ SECRET.

clause *n* article, condition, item, paragraph, part, passage, proviso, section, subsection.

claw *n* nail, talon.
• *v* injure, lacerate, maul, rip, scrape, scratch, slash, tear.

clean *adj* 1 decontaminated, disinfected, hygienic, immaculate, laundered, perfect, polished, sanitary, scrubbed, spotless, sterile, sterilized, unsoiled, unstained, unsullied, washed, wholesome. 2 *clean water.* clarified, clear, distilled, fresh, pure, purified, unpolluted. 3 *clean paper.* blank, new, plain, uncreased, unmarked, untouched, unused. 4 *clean edge.* neat, regular, smooth, straight, tidy. 5 *clean fight.* chivalrous, fair, honest, honourable, sporting, sportsmanlike. 6 *clean fun.* chaste, decent, good, innocent, moral, respectable, upright, virtuous. *Opp* DIRTY.
• *v* cleanse, clear up, purify, sterilize, tidy up, wash. *Opp* CONTAMINATE. **make a clean breast of** ▷ CONFESS.

clean-shaven *adj* beardless, shaved, shorn, smooth.

clear *adj* 1 clean, colourless, crystalline, glassy, limpid, pellucid, pure, transparent. 2 *clear sky.* cloudless, fair, fine, sunny, starlit, unclouded. *Opp* CLOUDY. 3 *clear colours.* bright, lustrous, shining, strong, vivid. 4 *clear conscience.* blameless, easy, guiltless, innocent, quiet, satisfied, undisturbed, untarnished, untroubled, unworried. 5 *clear handwriting.* bold, definite, distinct, focused, legible, recognizable, sharp, simple, visible, well-defined. 6 *clear sound.* audible, distinct, penetrating, sharp. 7 *clear instructions.* coherent, comprehensible, explicit, intelligible, lucid, precise, specific, straightforward, unambiguous, understandable, well-presented. 8 *clear case of cheating.* apparent, blatant, clear-cut, conspicuous, evident, indisputable, manifest, obvious, palpable, perceptible, plain, pronounced, straightforward, undisguised, unmistakable. *Opp* UNCERTAIN. 9 *clear space.* empty, free, open, passable, uncluttered, uncrowded, unhindered, unimpeded, unobstructed.
• *v* 1 disappear, evaporate, fade, melt away, vanish. 2 brighten, lighten. 3 clean, make clean, polish, wipe. 4 *clear weeds.* disentangle, get rid of, remove, strip. 5 *clear a drain.* clean out, free, open up, unblock, unclog. 6 *clear of blame.* absolve, acquit, exculpate, excuse, exonerate, free, let off, release, vindicate. 7 *clear a building.* empty, evacuate. 8 *clear a fence.* bound over, jump, leap over, pass over, vault. **clear away** ▷ REMOVE. **clear off** ▷ DEPART. **clear up** ▷ CLEAN, EXPLAIN.

clearing *n* gap, glade, opening, space.

cleave *v* divide, halve, rive, slit, split. ▷ CUT.

clench *v* 1 clamp, close tightly, double up, grit (*your teeth*), squeeze tightly. 2 clasp, grasp, grip, hold.

clergyman *n* archbishop, bishop, canon, cardinal, chaplain, churchman, cleric, curate, deacon, deaconess, dean, divine, ecclesiastic, friar, guru, imam, *inf* man of the cloth, minister, missionary, monk, padre, parson, pastor, preacher, prebend, prelate, priest, rabbi, rector, vicar. *Opp* LAYMAN.

clerical *adj* 1 *clerical work.* office, secretarial, *inf* white-collar. 2 *clerical collar.* canonical, ecclesiastical, episcopal, ministerial, monastic, pastoral, priestly, rabbinical, spiritual.

clerk *n* assistant, bookkeeper, computer operator, filing clerk, office worker, *inf* pen-pusher, receptionist, scribe, secretary, shorthand-typist, stenographer, typist, word-processor operator.

clever *adj* able, academic, accomplished, acute, adroit, artful, astute, *inf* brainy, bright, brilliant, canny, capable, *derog* crafty, creative, *derog* cunning, *inf* cute, *inf* deep, deft, dexterous, discerning, expert, gifted, handy, ingenious, intellectual, intelligent, inventive, judicious, keen, knowing, knowledgeable, observant, penetrating, perceptive, perspicacious, precocious, quick, quick-witted, resourceful, sagacious, sensible, sharp, shrewd, skilful, skilled, *derog* sly, smart, subtle, talented, *derog* wily, wise, witty. *Opp* STUPID, UNSKILFUL. **clever person** *inf* egghead, expert, genius, *derog* know-all, mastermind, prodigy, sage, *derog* smart-arse, virtuoso, wizard.

cleverness *n* ability, acuteness, astuteness, brilliance, *derog* cunning, expertise, ingenuity, intellect, intelligence, mastery, sagacity, sharpness, shrewdness, skill, subtlety, talent, wisdom, wit. *Opp* STUPIDITY.

cliché *n* banality, *inf* chestnut, commonplace, hackneyed phrase, platitude, stereotype, truism, well-worn phrase.

client *n pl* clientele, consumer, customer, patient, patron, shopper, user.

cliff *n* bluff, crag, escarpment, precipice, rock face, scar.

climate *n* 1 ▷ WEATHER. 2 *climate of opinion.* ambience, atmosphere, environment, feeling, mood, spirit, temper, trend.

climax *n* 1 acme, crisis, culmination, head, highlight, high point, peak, summit, zenith. *Opp* BATHOS. 2 *sexual climax.* orgasm.

climb *n* ascent, gradient, hill, incline, rise, slope.
• *v* 1 ascend, clamber up, go up, mount, move up, scale, shin up, soar, take off. 2 incline, rise, slope up. 3 *climb a mountain.* conquer, reach the top of. **climb down** ▷ DESCEND.

clinch *v* close, complete, conclude, confirm, determine, finalize, make certain of, ratify, secure, settle, shake hands on, verify.

cling *v* adhere, attach, fasten, fix, hold fast, stick. **cling to** ▷ EMBRACE.

clinic *n* health centre, infirmary, medical centre, surgery.

clip *n* 1 ▷ FASTENER. 2 *clip from a film.* cutting, excerpt, extract, fragment, part, passage, quotation, section, snippet, trailer.
• *v* 1 pin, staple. ▷ FASTEN. 2 crop, shear, snip, trim. ▷ CUT.

cloak *n* 1 cape, cope, mantle, poncho, robe, wrap. 2 ▷ COVER.
• *v* cover, mask, shroud, veil, wrap. ▷ HIDE.

clock *n* chronometer, timepiece, watch.

clog *v* block, *inf* bung up, choke, congest, dam, impede, jam, obstruct, plug, stop up.

close *adj* 1 accessible, adjacent, at hand, convenient, handy, near, neighbouring, point-blank. 2 *close friends.* affectionate, attached, dear, devoted, familiar, fond, friendly, intimate, loving, *inf* thick. 3 *close comparison.* alike, analogous, comparable, corresponding, related, similar. 4 *close crowd.* compact, congested, cramped, crowded, dense, *inf* jam-packed, packed, thick. 5 *close scrutiny.* attentive, careful, detailed, minute, painstaking, precise, rigorous, searching, thorough. 6 *close with information.* private, reserved, reticent, secretive, taciturn. 7 *close with money.* mean, *inf* mingy, miserly, niggardly, parsimonious, penurious, stingy, tight, tight-fisted. 8 *close atmosphere.* airless, fuggy, humid, muggy, oppressive, stale, stifling, stuffy, suffocating, sweltering, unventilated. *Opp* DISTANT, OPEN.
• *n* 1 completion, conclusion, culmination, end, finish, termination. 2 cadence, coda, finale. 3 *close of a play.* denouement, last act.
• *v* 1 bolt, fasten, lock, make inaccessible, padlock, seal, secure, shut. 2 *close a road.* bar, barricade, block, make impassable, obstruct, seal off, stop up. 3 *close proceedings.* complete, conclude, culminate, discontinue, end, finish, stop, terminate, *inf* wind up. 4 *close a gap.* fill, join up, reduce, shorten. *Opp* OPEN.

closed *adj* 1 fastened, locked, sealed, shut. 2 concluded, done with, ended, finished, over, resolved, settled, tied up.

clot *n* embolism, lump, mass, thrombosis.
• *v* coagulate, coalesce, congeal, curdle, set, solidify, stiffen, thicken.

cloth *n* fabric, material, stuff, textile.

clothe *v* array, attire, cover, deck, drape, dress, fit out, garb, *inf* kit out, robe, swathe. *Opp* STRIP. **clothe yourself in** ▷ WEAR.

clothes *pl n* apparel, attire, *inf* clobber, clothing, costume, dress, ensemble, finery, footwear, garb, garments, *inf* gear, *inf* get-up, headgear, outfit, *inf* rig-out, *sl* togs, trousseau, underclothes, uniform, vestments, wardrobe, wear, weeds.

cloud *n* billow, haze, mist, storm cloud.
• *v* blur, conceal, cover, darken, eclipse, enshroud, hide, mantle, mist up, obscure, screen, shroud, veil.

cloudless *adj* bright, clear, starlit, sunny. *Opp* CLOUDY.

cloudy *adj* 1 dark, dull, gloomy, grey, leaden, lowering, overcast, sunless. *Opp* CLOUDLESS. 2 *cloudy windows.* blurred, blurry, dim, misty, opaque, steamy. 3 *cloudy liquid.* hazy, milky, muddy, murky. *Opp* CLEAR.

clown *n* buffoon, comedian, fool, jester, joker. ▷ IDIOT.

club *n* 1 bat, baton, cosh, cudgel, mace, staff, stick, truncheon. 2 association, circle, company, federation, fellowship, fraternity, group, guild, league, order, organization, party, set, society, sorority, union.
• *v* ▷ HIT. **club together** ▷ COMBINE.

clue *n* hint, idea, indication, inkling, key, lead, pointer, sign, suggestion, suspicion, tip, tip-off, trace.

clump *n* bunch, bundle, cluster, mass, shock (*of hair*), thicket, tuft. ▷ GROUP.

clumsy *adj* 1 awkward, blundering, bungling, fumbling, gangling, gawky, graceless, *inf* ham-fisted, heavy-handed, *inf* hulking, lumbering, maladroit, uncoordinated, ungainly, ungraceful. *Opp* SKILFUL. 2 amateurish, badly-made, bulky, cumbersome, heavy, inelegant, large, ponderous, rough, unmanageable, unwieldy. *Opp* NEAT. 3 *clumsy remark.* gauche, ill-judged, inappropriate, indelicate, indiscreet, inept, insensitive, tactless, uncouth, undiplomatic, unsubtle.

cluster *n* batch, bunch, clump, collection, knot. ▷ GROUP.
• *v* ▷ GATHER.

clutch *n* clasp, control, grasp, grip, hold, possession, power.
• *v* catch, clasp, cling to, grab, grasp, embrace, hang on to, seize, snatch, take hold of.

clutter *n* chaos, confusion, disorder, jumble, junk, litter, mess, muddle, odds and ends, rubbish, tangle, untidiness.
• *v* be scattered about, litter, make untidy, *inf* mess up, muddle, strew.

coach *n* 1 bus, carriage. 2 *games coach.* instructor, teacher, trainer, tutor.
• *v* direct, drill, guide, instruct, prepare, teach, train, tutor.

coagulate *v* clot, congeal, curdle, *inf* jell, set, solidify, thicken.

coarse *adj* 1 bristly, gritty, hairy, harsh, prickly, rough, scratchy, sharp, stony, uneven. *Opp* FINE, SOFT. 2 *coarse language.* bawdy, blasphemous, boorish, common, crude, earthy, foul, impolite, improper, indecent, indelicate, offensive, ribald, rude, smutty, uncouth, vulgar. *Opp* REFINED.

coast *n* beach, coastline, seaboard, seashore, seaside, shore.
• *v* cruise, drift, freewheel, glide, sail, skim, slide, slip.

coastal *adj* maritime, nautical, seaside.

coat *n* 1 jacket, *inf* mac, overcoat, raincoat. 2 *animal's coat.* fleece, fur, hair, hide, pelt, skin. 3 *coat of paint.* coating, finish, glaze, layer, overlay, patina, veneer, wash. ▷ COVERING.
• *v* ▷ COVER. **coat of arms** ▷ CREST.

coax *v* allure, cajole, charm, entice, induce, inveigle, manipulate, persuade, tempt, wheedle.

cobble *v* **cobble together** botch, knock up, make, mend, patch up, put together.

code *n* 1 etiquette, laws, regulations, rulebook, rules, system. 2 *message in code.* cipher, secret language, signals.

coerce *v* bludgeon, browbeat, bully, compel, constrain, dragoon, force, intimidate, press-gang, pressurize, terrorize.

coercion *n* browbeating, bullying, compulsion, conscription, constraint, duress, force, intimidation, pressure, *inf* strong-arm tactics, threats.

coffer *n* box, cabinet, case, casket, chest, crate, trunk.

cog *n* ratchet, sprocket, tooth.

cogent *adj* compelling, conclusive, convincing, effective, forceful, indisputable, irresistible, persuasive, potent, powerful, strong, unanswerable, well-argued. ▷ COHERENT. *Opp* IRRATIONAL.

cohere *v* bind, cake, coalesce, combine, fuse, hold together, join, stick together, unite.

coherent *adj* articulate, cohesive, connected, consistent, integrated, logical, lucid, orderly, organized, rational, reasoned, sound, systematic, unified, united, well-ordered, well-structured. *Opp* INCOHERENT.

coil *n* convolution, corkscrew, curl, helix, kink, loop, roll, spiral, twist, vortex, whirl, whorl.
• *v* curl, entwine, loop, roll, snake, spiral, twine, twirl, twist, wind, writhe.

coin *n* 1 bit, piece. 2 [*pl*] change, coppers, silver, small change. ▷ MONEY.
• *v* 1 make, mint, mould, stamp. 2 *coin a name.* conceive, concoct, create, devise, dream up, fabricate, introduce, invent, make up, originate, think up.

coincide *v* accord, agree, be congruent, be identical, be in unison, clash, coexist, concur, correspond, happen together, harmonize, match, square, synchronize, tally.

coincidence *n* 1 accord, agreement, coexistence, concurrence, congruence, correspondence, harmony, similarity. 2 *meet by coincidence.* accident, chance, fluke, luck.

cold *adj* 1 arctic, biting, bitter, bleak, chill, chilly, cool, crisp, cutting, draughty, freezing, fresh, frosty, glacial, ice-cold, icy, inclement, keen, *inf* nippy, numbing, *inf* parky, perishing, piercing, polar, raw, shivery, Siberian, snowy, unheated, wintry. 2 *cold hands.* blue with cold, chilled, frostbitten, frozen, numbed, shivering. 3 *cold heart.* aloof, callous, cold-blooded, hard-hearted, heartless, indifferent, inhuman, insensitive, passionless, stony, uncaring, unconcerned, undemonstrative, unemotional, unfeeling, unresponsive. ▷ UNFRIENDLY. *Opp* HOT, KIND.
• *n* 1 chill, coolness, frostiness, iciness, wintriness. *Opp* HEAT. 2 *cold in the head.* catarrh, *inf* flu, *inf* the sniffles. **feel the cold** freeze, quiver, shake, shiver, shudder, tremble.

cold-blooded *adj* brutal, callous, inhuman, ruthless, savage. ▷ CRUEL. *Opp* HUMANE.

cold-hearted *adj* callous, dispassionate, heartless, impassive, insensitive, *inf* thick-skinned, uncaring, unemotional, unfeeling. ▷ UNFRIENDLY.

collaborate *v* 1 cooperate, join forces, *inf* pull together, team up, work together. 2 [*derog*] collude, connive, conspire, join the opposition, *inf* rat, turn traitor.

collaboration *n* 1 association, concerted effort, cooperation, partnership, teamwork. 2 [*derog*] collusion, connivance, conspiracy, treachery.

collaborator *n* 1 accomplice, ally, assistant, associate, co-author, colleague, confederate, fellow-worker, helper, partner, *joc* partner-in-crime, team-mate. 2 [*derog*] blackleg, *inf* Judas, quisling, *inf* scab, traitor, turncoat.

collapse *n* breakdown, break-up, cave-in, disintegration, downfall, end, fall, ruin, subsidence.
• *v* 1 break down, break up, buckle, cave in, crumble, crumple, deflate, disintegrate, double up, fall apart, fall in, fold up, give in, sink, subside, tumble down. 2 *collapse in the heat.* become ill, *inf* bite the dust, black out, *inf* crack up, faint, *inf* keel over, pass out, swoon. 3 *sales will collapse.* crash, deteriorate, diminish, drop, fall, slump, worsen.

collapsible *adj* adjustable, folding, retractable, telescopic.

colleague *n* associate, business partner, fellow-worker. ▷ COLLABORATOR.

collect *v* 1 accumulate, amass, assemble, bring together, cluster, come together, concentrate, congregate, convene, converge, crowd, garner, gather, group, harvest, heap, hoard, lay up, muster, pile up, put by, rally, save, scrape together, stack up, stockpile, store. *Opp* DISPERSE. 2 *collect money for charity.* be given, raise, secure, take. 3 *collect goods from a shop.* bring, fetch, get, load up, obtain, pick up. **collected** ▷ CALM.

collection *n* 1 accumulation, array, assortment, cluster, heap, mass, pile, set, stack, store. ▷ GROUP. 2 flag-day, voluntary contributions, *inf* whip-round.

collective *adj* combined, common, co-operative, corporate, group, joint, shared, united. *Opp* INDIVIDUAL.

college *n* academy, conservatory, institute, polytechnic, school, university.

collide *v* **collide with** bump into, cannon into, crash into, knock, meet, run into, smash into, strike. ▷ HIT.

collision *n* accident, bump, clash, crash, head-on collision, impact, knock, pile-up, smash.

colloquial *adj* conversational, informal, slangy, vernacular. *Opp* FORMAL.

colonist *n* colonizer, explorer, pioneer, settler. *Opp* NATIVE.

colonize *v* occupy, people, populate, settle in, subjugate.

colony *n* 1 dependency, dominion, possession, province, settlement, territory. 2 ▷ GROUP.

colossal *adj* enormous, gargantuan, giant, gigantic, herculean, huge, immense, *inf* jumbo, mammoth, massive, monstrous, prodigious, vast. ▷ BIG. *Opp* SMALL.

colour *n* 1 coloration, colouring, hue, pigment, pigmentation, shade, tincture, tinge, tint, tone. 2 *colour in your cheeks.* bloom, blush, flush, glow, rosiness, ruddiness.

• *v* 1 crayon, dye, paint, pigment, shade, stain, tinge, tint. 2 blush, bronze, brown, burn, flush, redden, tan. *Opp* FADE. 3 *It will not colour his decision.* affect, bias, distort, influence, pervert, prejudice, slant, sway. **colours** ▷ FLAG.

colourful *adj* 1 bright, brilliant, chromatic, gaudy, iridescent, multicoloured, psychedelic, showy, vibrant. 2 *colourful personality.* dashing, distinctive, dynamic, eccentric, energetic, exciting, flamboyant, glamorous, unusual, vigorous. 3 *colourful description.* graphic, lively, picturesque, rich, stimulating, striking, telling, vivid. *Opp* COLOURLESS.

colouring *n* colourant, dye, pigment, stain. ▷ COLOUR.

colourless *adj* 1 ashen, blanched, grey, monochrome, neutral, pale, pallid, sickly, wan, *inf* washed out, waxen. ▷ WHITE. 2 bland, boring, characterless, dowdy, drab, dreary, dull, insipid, lacklustre, lifeless, tame, uninspiring, uninteresting, vacuous, vapid. *Opp* COLOURFUL.

column *n* 1 pilaster, pillar, pole, post, shaft, support, upright. 2 *newspaper column.* article, feature, leader, piece. 3 *column of soldiers.* cavalcade, file, line, procession, queue, rank, row, string, train.

comb *v* 1 arrange, groom, neaten, smarten up, tidy, untangle. 2 *comb the house.* ransack, rummage through, scour, search thoroughly.

combat *n* action, battle, conflict, contest, encounter, fight, skirmish, struggle, warfare.
• *v* battle against, contest, counter, defy, face up to, oppose, resist, stand up to, struggle against, tackle, withstand. ▷ FIGHT.

combination *n* aggregate, amalgam, blend, compound, conjunction, fusion, marriage, mix, mixture, synthesis, unification. 2 alliance, amalgamation, association, coalition, confederation, consortium, conspiracy, federation, grouping, link-up, merger, partnership, syndicate, union.

combine *v* 1 add together, amalgamate, bind, blend, compound, fuse, incorporate, integrate, interweave, join, link, *inf* lump together, marry, merge, mingle, mix, pool, put together, synthesize, unify, unite. *Opp* DIVIDE. 2 *combine as a team.* ally, associate, band together, club together, coalesce, connect, cooperate, form an alliance, *inf* gang up, join forces, team up. *Opp* DISPERSE.

combustible *adj* flammable, inflammable. *Opp* INCOMBUSTIBLE.

come *v* 1 advance, appear, approach, arrive, draw near, enter, get to, move (towards), near, reach, visit. 2 *whatever may come.* happen, materialize, occur, turn up. **come about** ▷ HAPPEN. **come across** ▷ FIND. **come apart** ▷ DISINTEGRATE. **come clean** ▷ CONFESS. **come out with** ▷ SAY. **come round** ▷ RECOVER. **come up** ▷ ARISE. **come upon** ▷ FIND.

comedian *n* buffoon, clown, comic, fool, humorist, jester, joker, wag.

comedy *n* clowning, facetiousness, farce, hilarity, humour, jesting, joking, slapstick, wit.

comfort *n* 1 aid, cheer, consolation, encouragement, help, moral support, reassurance, relief, solace, succour. 2 *living in comfort.* abundance, affluence, contentment, cosiness, ease, luxury, plenty, relaxation, well-being. *Opp* DISCOMFORT, POVERTY.
• *v* calm, cheer up, console, ease, encourage, gladden, hearten, help, reassure, relieve, solace, soothe, sympathize with.

comfortable *adj* 1 *inf* comfy, convenient, cosy, easy, padded, relaxing, roomy, snug, soft, upholstered. 2 *comfortable clothes.* informal, loose-fitting, well-fitting. 3 *comfortable life.* affluent, agreeable, contented, happy, homely, luxurious, pleasant, prosperous, relaxed, restful, serene, tranquil, untroubled, well-off. *Opp* UNCOMFORTABLE.

comic *adj* absurd, amusing, comical, diverting, droll, facetious, farcical, funny, hilarious, humorous, hysterical, joking, laughable, ludicrous, *inf* priceless, *inf* rich, ridiculous, satirical, *inf* side-splitting, silly, uproarious, waggish, witty. *Opp* SERIOUS.
• *n* 1 ▷ COMEDIAN. 2 ▷ MAGAZINE.

command *n* 1 behest, bidding, decree, directive, edict, injunction, instruction, mandate, order, requirement, ultimatum. 2 authority, charge, control, direction, government, jurisdiction, management, power, rule, sovereignty, supervision, sway. 3 *command of a language.* grasp, knowledge, mastery.
• *v* 1 bid, charge, compel, decree, demand, direct, enjoin, instruct, ordain, order, prescribe, request, require. 2 *command a ship.* administer, be in charge of, control, govern, have authority over, head, lead, manage, reign over, rule, supervise.

commandeer *v* appropriate, confiscate, hijack, requisition, seize, take over.

commander *n* captain, commandant, general, head, leader, officer-in-charge. ▷ CHIEF.

commemorate *v* be a memorial to, celebrate, honour, immortalize, keep alive the memory of, pay your respects to, pay tribute to, remember, salute, solemnize.

commence *v* embark on, enter on, initiate, launch, set off, set up, start. ▷ BEGIN. *Opp* FINISH.

commend *v* acclaim, applaud, approve of, compliment, congratulate, eulogize, extol, praise, recommend. *Opp* CRITICIZE.

commendable *adj* admirable, creditable, deserving, laudable, meritorious, praiseworthy. ▷ GOOD. *Opp* DEPLORABLE.

comment *n* annotation, commentary, criticism, elucidation, explanation, footnote, gloss, interjection, interpolation, mention, note, observation, opinion, reaction, reference, remark, statement.
• *v* criticize, elucidate, explain, interject, interpose, mention, note, observe, remark, say, state.

commentary *n* 1 account, broadcast, description, report. 2 *commentary on a poem.* analysis, criticism, critique, discourse, explanation, interpretation, notes, review.

commentator *n* broadcaster, journalist, reporter.

commerce *n* business, buying and selling, dealings, financial transactions, marketing, trade, trading, traffic.

commercial *adj* business, economic, financial, mercantile, monetary, money-making, profitable, profit-making, trading.
• *n inf* advert, advertisement, *inf* break, *inf* plug.

commiserate *v* be sorry (for), be sympathetic, comfort, condole, console, feel (for), grieve, mourn, sympathize. *Opp* CONGRATULATE.

commission *n* 1 appointment, warrant. 2 *commission to do a job.* order, request. 3 *commission on a sale.* allowance, *inf* cut, fee, percentage, *inf* rake-off, reward. 4 ▷ COMMITTEE.

commit *v* 1 carry out, do, enact, execute, perform, perpetrate. 2 *commit to safekeeping.* consign, deliver, entrust, give, hand over, transfer. **commit yourself** ▷ PROMISE.

commitment *n* 1 assurance, duty, guarantee, liability, pledge, promise, undertaking, vow, word. 2 *commitment to a cause.* adherence, dedication, determination, devotion, loyalty, zeal. 3 *social commitment.* appointment, arrangement, engagement.

committed *adj* active, ardent, *inf* card-carrying, dedicated, devoted, earnest, enthusiastic, fervent, firm, keen, passionate, resolute, staunch, unwavering, wholehearted, zealous. *Opp* APATHETIC.

committee *n* board, body, commission, council, panel, think-tank. ▷ GROUP.

common *adj* 1 average, *inf* common or garden, conventional, customary, daily, everyday, familiar, frequent, habitual, normal, ordinary, popular, prevalent, regular, *inf* run-of-the-mill, standard, stock, traditional, typical, undistinguished, unexceptional, usual, well-known, widespread, workaday. ▷ COMMONPLACE. 2 *common knowledge.* accepted, collective, communal, general, joint, mutual, open, popular, public, shared, universal. 3 boorish, churlish, coarse, crude, disreputable, loutish, low, plebeian, proletarian, rude, uncouth, unrefined, vulgar, *inf* yobbish. *Opp* ARISTOCRATIC, DISTINCTIVE, UNUSUAL.
• *n* heath, park, parkland.

commonplace *adj* banal, boring, forgettable, hackneyed, humdrum, mediocre, obvious, ordinary, pedestrian, plain, platitudinous, predictable, prosaic, routine, standard, trite, unexciting, unremarkable. ▷ COMMON. *Opp* MEMORABLE.
• *n* ▷ PLATITUDE.

commotion *n inf* ado, agitation, bedlam, bother, brawl, *inf* brouhaha, *inf* bust-up, chaos, clamour, confusion, contretemps, din, disorder, disturbance, excitement, ferment, fracas, fray, furore, fuss, hubbub, hullabaloo, *inf* kerfuffle, noise, *inf* palaver, pandemonium, racket, riot, *inf* row, *inf* rumpus, sensation, *inf* shemozzle, *inf* stir, *inf* to-do, tumult, turmoil, upheaval, uproar, upset.

communal *adj* collective, common, general, joint, mutual, open, public, shared. *Opp* PRIVATE.

communicate *v* 1 commune, confer, converse, correspond, discuss, get in touch, speak, talk, write (to). 2 *communicate information.* announce, broadcast, convey, declare, disclose, divulge, express, get across, impart, indicate, inform, intimate, make known, mention, network, notify, pass on, proclaim, promulgate, publish, put over, relay, report, reveal, show, speak, spread, state, transfer, transmit, write. 3 *communicate a disease.* give, infect someone with, pass on, spread, transmit.

4 *The rooms communicate with each other.* be connected, lead (to).

communication *n* 1 announcement, communion, contact, conversation, correspondence, dispatch, information, intelligence, interaction, message, report, statement. 2 *mass communication.* advertising, radio, television, the media, the press.

communicative *adj* chatty, frank, informative, outgoing, responsive, sociable. ▷ TALKATIVE. *Opp* SECRETIVE.

community *n* commonwealth, commune, kibbutz, nation, society, state. ▷ GROUP.

commute *v* 1 adjust, decrease, mitigate, reduce, shorten. 2 ▷ TRAVEL.

compact *adj* 1 compressed, consolidated, dense, firm, packed, solid, tight-packed. *Opp* LOOSE. 2 handy, neat, portable, small. 3 abridged, brief, concentrated, condensed, short, small, succinct, terse. ▷ CONCISE. *Opp* LARGE.
• *n* ▷ AGREEMENT.

companion *n* accomplice, chaperon, colleague, confederate, confidant(e), consort, *inf* crony, escort, fellow, follower, *inf* henchman, partner. ▷ FRIEND, HELPER.

company *n* 1 companionship, friendship, society. 2 [*inf*] *company for tea.* callers, guests, visitors. 3 *mixed company.* assemblage, band, body, circle, club, community, coterie, crew, crowd, entourage, gang, gathering, society, throng, troop, troupe (*of actors*). 4 *trading company.* business, cartel, concern, consortium, corporation, establishment, firm, house, organization, partnership, *inf* set-up, syndicate. ▷ GROUP.

comparable *adj* analogous, cognate, commensurate, compatible, corresponding, equal, equivalent, matching, parallel, proportionate, related, similar, twin. *Opp* DISSIMILAR.

compare *v* check, contrast, correlate, draw parallels (between), equate, juxtapose, liken, make comparisons, measure (against), relate (to), set side by side, weigh (against). **compare with** ▷ EQUAL.

comparison *n* analogy, contrast, correlation, difference, distinction, juxtaposition, likeness, parallel, relationship, resemblance, similarity.

compartment *n* alcove, bay, berth, booth, cell, chamber, *inf* cubbyhole, cubicle, division, kiosk, locker, niche, nook, pigeon-hole, section, slot, space.

compatible *adj* 1 harmonious, like-minded, similar, well-matched. ▷ FRIENDLY. 2 *compatible claims.* congruent, consistent, matching, reconcilable. *Opp* INCOMPATIBLE.

compel *v* coerce, constrain, dragoon, drive, force, impel, necessitate, oblige, order, press, press-gang, pressurize, require, *inf* shanghai, urge.

compendium *n* anthology, collection, digest, handbook, summary.

compensate *v* 1 atone, expiate, indemnify, make amends, make good, make restitution, make up for, pay back, recompense, redress, reimburse, remunerate, repay, requite. 2 counterbalance, even up, neutralize, offset.

compensation *n* amends, damages, indemnity, recompense, reimbursement, reparation, repayment, restitution.

compère *n* announcer, disc jockey, host, hostess, Master of Ceremonies, MC, presenter.

compete *v* 1 enter, participate, perform, take part. 2 be in competition, contend, emulate, oppose, rival, strive, undercut, vie. ▷ FIGHT. *Opp* COOPERATE. **compete with** ▷ RIVAL.

competent *adj* able, accomplished, adept, adequate, capable, clever, effective, efficient, experienced, expert, fit, handy, practical, proficient, qualified, satisfactory, skilful, skilled, trained, workmanlike. *Opp* INCOMPETENT.

competition *n* 1 competitiveness, conflict, contention, emulation, rivalry, struggle. 2 challenge, championship, contest, event, game, heat, match, quiz, race, rally, tournament, trial.

competitive *adj* 1 aggressive, antagonistic, combative, contentious, hard-fought, keen, lively, sporting. 2 *competitive prices.* fair, moderate, reasonable, similar to others.

competitor *n* adversary, antagonist, candidate, contender, contestant, entrant, finalist, opponent, participant, rival.

compile *v* accumulate, amass, arrange, assemble, collate, collect, compose, edit, gather, marshal, organize, put together.

complain *v inf* beef, *inf* bellyache, carp, cavil, find fault, fuss, *inf* gripe, *inf* grouch, *inf* grouse, grumble, lament, *inf* moan, object, protest, wail, whine, *inf* whinge. *Opp* PRAISE. **complain about** ▷ CRITICIZE.

complaint *n* 1 accusation, *inf* beef, charge, criticism, grievance, *inf* gripe, *inf* grouse, grumble, *inf* moan, objection, protest, whine, *inf* whinge. 2 *medical complaint.* disease, infection, sickness. ▷ ILLNESS.

complaisant *adj* accommodating, acquiescent, amenable, biddable, compliant, cooperative, docile, obedient, obliging, pliant, polite, tractable, willing. *Opp* OBSTINATE.

complement *n* 1 completion, *inf* finishing touch. 2 *full complement.* aggregate, capacity, quota, sum, total.
• *v* complete, make whole, perfect, round off.

complementary *adj* interdependent, matching, reciprocal, toning, twin.

complete *adj* 1 comprehensive, entire, exhaustive, full, intact, total, unabridged, uncut, unedited, unexpurgated, whole. 2 accomplished, achieved, concluded, done, finished, over. ▷ PERFECT. 3 *complete disaster.* absolute, downright, extreme, out and out, outright, pure, rank, sheer, thorough, total, unmitigated, unmixed, unqualified, utter, *inf* wholesale. *Opp* INCOMPLETE.
• *v* 1 accomplish, achieve, carry out, clinch, close, conclude, crown, do, end, finalize, finish, fulfil, perfect, perform, round off, terminate, *inf* wind up. 2 *complete forms.* answer, fill in.

complex *adj* complicated, composite, compound, convoluted, elaborate, *inf* fiddly, intricate, involved, *inf* knotty, labyrinthine, mixed, multifarious, multiple, ornate, problematic, sophisticated, tortuous, tricky. *Opp* SIMPLE.

complexion *n* appearance, colour, colouring, look, pigmentation, skin, texture.

complicate *v* compound, confound, confuse, elaborate, entangle, make complicated, mix up, muddle, *inf* snarl up, tangle, twist. *Opp* SIMPLIFY. **complicated** ▷ COMPLEX.

complication *n* complexity, confusion, convolution, difficulty, intricacy, *inf* mix-up, obstacle, problem, ramification, set-back, snag, tangle.

compliment *n* [often *pl*] accolade, admiration, appreciation, commendation, congratulations, eulogy, felicitations, flattery, honour, plaudits, praise, tribute.
• *v* applaud, commend, congratulate, eulogize, felicitate, flatter, give credit, laud, praise, salute, speak highly of. *Opp* INSULT.

complimentary *adj* admiring, appreciative, approving, commendatory, congratulatory, eulogistic, favourable, flattering, *derog* fulsome, generous, laudatory, rapturous, supportive. *Opp* ABUSIVE, CRITICAL.

comply *v* abide (by), accede, accord, acquiesce, adhere (to), agree, assent, be in accordance, concur, consent, defer, fall in (with), fit in, follow, fulfil, harmonize, keep (to), match, meet, obey, observe, perform, respect, satisfy, square (with), submit, yield. ▷ CONFORM. *Opp* DEFY.

component *n* bit, constituent, element, essential part, ingredient, item, part, piece, *inf* spare, spare part, unit.

compose *v* 1 build, constitute, construct, fashion, form, frame, make, put together. 2 *compose music.* arrange, create, devise, imagine, produce, write. 3 *compose yourself.* calm, control, pacify, quieten, soothe. **be composed of** ▷ COMPRISE. **composed** ▷ CALM.

composition *n* 1 assembly, constitution, creation, establishment, formation, *inf* make-up, setting up. 2 configuration, layout, organization, structure. 3 *literary composition.* article, essay, story. 4 *musical composition.* opus, piece, work.

compound *adj* complex, complicated, composite, intricate, involved, multiple. *Opp* SIMPLE.
• *n* 1 alloy, amalgam, blend, combination, composite, composition, fusion, mixture, synthesis. 2 *compound for cattle.* corral, enclosure, pen, run.
• *v* ▷ COMBINE, COMPLICATE.

comprehend *v* appreciate, conceive, fathom, grasp, realize. ▷ UNDERSTAND.

comprehensible *adj* clear, easy, intelligible, lucid, meaningful, plain, self-explanatory, simple, straightforward, understandable. *Opp* INCOMPREHENSIBLE.

comprehensive *adj* all-embracing, broad, catholic, compendious, complete, detailed, encyclopaedic, exhaustive, extensive, far-reaching, full, sweeping, thorough, total, universal, wholesale, wide-ranging. *Opp* SELECTIVE.

compress *v* abbreviate, abridge, concentrate, condense, constrict, contract, cram, crush, flatten, *inf* jam, précis, press, shorten, squash, squeeze, stuff, summarize, truncate. *Opp* EXPAND. **compressed** ▷ COMPACT, CONCISE.

comprise *v* be composed of, comprehend, consist of, contain, cover, embody, include, incorporate, involve.

compromise *n* bargain, concession, *inf* give-and-take, *inf* halfway house, middle way, settlement.

• *v* 1 concede a point, make concessions, meet halfway, negotiate a settlement, reach a formula, settle, *inf* split the difference, strike a balance. 2 *compromise your reputation.* damage, discredit, disgrace, dishonour, jeopardize, prejudice, risk, undermine, weaken. **compromising** ▷ SHAMEFUL.

compulsion *n* 1 coercion, duress, force, necessity. 2 *compulsion to smoke.* addiction, drive, habit, pressure, urge.

compulsive *adj* 1 besetting, compelling, driving, involuntary, irresistible, overpowering, overwhelming, uncontrollable, urgent. 2 *compulsive drinker.* addicted, habitual, incorrigible, obsessive, persistent.

compulsory *adj* binding, contractual, enforceable, essential, imperative, incumbent, indispensable, mandatory, necessary, obligatory, official, prescribed, required, requisite, set, statutory, stipulated, unavoidable. *Opp* OPTIONAL.

compunction *n* contrition, hesitation, pang of conscience, qualm, regret, remorse, scruple.

compute *v* add up, ascertain, assess, calculate, count, determine, estimate, evaluate, measure, reckon, total, work out.

computer *n* mainframe, micro, microcomputer, PC, personal computer, word-processor.

comrade *n* associate, colleague, companion. ▷ FRIEND.

conceal *v* blot out, bury, camouflage, cloak, cover up, disguise, gloss over, hide, hush up, keep secret, mask, obscure, screen, secrete, suppress, veil. *Opp* REVEAL. **concealed** ▷ HIDDEN.

concede *v* accept, acknowledge, admit, agree, allow, confess, grant, own, profess, recognize. **concede defeat** capitulate, *inf* cave in, cede, give in, resign, submit, surrender, yield.

conceit *n* self-love, vanity. ▷ PRIDE.

conceited *adj* arrogant, *inf* big-headed, boastful, bumptious, *inf* cocky, egocentric, egotistical, haughty, *inf* high and mighty, immodest, narcissistic, overweening, pleased with yourself, proud, self-centred, self-important, self-satisfied, smug, snobbish, *inf* snooty, *inf* stuck-up, supercilious, *inf* swollen-headed, *inf* toffee-nosed, vain. *Opp* MODEST.

conceive *v* 1 become pregnant. 2 *conceive a plan.* conjure up, contrive, create, design, devise, *inf* dream up, envisage, form, formulate, frame, hatch, imagine, invent, make up, originate, plan, plot, produce, realize, suggest, think up, visualize, work out. ▷ THINK.

concentrate *n* distillation, essence, extract.

• *v* 1 apply yourself, attend, be attentive, engross yourself, think, work hard. 2 centre, cluster, collect, congregate, converge, crowd, focus, gather, mass. *Opp* DISPERSE. 3 *concentrate a liquid.* condense, reduce, thicken. *Opp* DILUTE. **concentrated** 1 ▷ INTENSIVE. 2 condensed, evaporated, reduced, strong, thick, undiluted.

conception *n* 1 begetting, conceiving, fathering, fertilization, genesis, impregnation, origin. ▷ BEGINNING. 2 ▷ IDEA.

concern *n* 1 attention, care, consideration, heed, interest, regard. 2 *no concern of yours.* affair, business, involvement, matter, problem, responsibility, task. 3 *matter for concern.* anxiety, disquiet, distress, fear, solicitude, worry. 4 *business concern.* company, corporation, enterprise, establishment, firm, organization.

• *v* affect, be important to, interest, involve, matter to, pertain to, refer to, relate to.

concerned *adj* 1 *concerned parents.* bothered, caring, distressed, solicitous, troubled, unhappy, worried. ▷ ANXIOUS. 2 *the people concerned.* connected, implicated, interested, involved, referred to, relevant. ▷ RESPONSIBLE.

concerning *prep* about, apropos of, involving, re, regarding, relating to, relevant to, with reference to, with regard to.

concert *n* performance, programme, show.

concerted *adj* collaborative, collective, combined, cooperative, joint, mutual, united.

concession *n* adjustment, allowance, reduction.

concise *adj* brief, compact, compressed, concentrated, condensed, laconic, pithy, short, small, succinct, terse. ▷ ABRIDGED. *Opp* DIFFUSE.

conclude *v* 1 cease, close, complete, culminate, end, finish, round off, stop, terminate. 2 assume, decide, deduce, gather, infer, judge. ▷ THINK.

conclusion *n* 1 close, completion, culmination, end, epilogue, finale, finish, termination. 2 answer, belief, decision, deduction, inference, judgement, opinion, outcome, resolution, result, solution, upshot, verdict.

conclusive *adj* certain, convincing, decisive, definite, persuasive, unanswerable, unequivocal. *Opp* INCONCLUSIVE.

concoct *v* contrive, devise, fabricate, feign, formulate, hatch, invent, make up, plan, prepare, put together, think up.

concord *n* agreement, euphony, harmony, peace.

concrete *adj* actual, definite, existing, factual, firm, material, objective, palpable, physical, real, solid, substantial, tangible, visible. *Opp* ABSTRACT.

concur *v* accord, agree. ▷ COMPLY.

concurrent *adj* coexisting, coinciding, concomitant, contemporary, overlapping, parallel, simultaneous, synchronous.

condemn *v* 1 blame, castigate, censure, criticize, damn, decry, denounce, deplore, deprecate, disapprove of, disparage, execrate, rebuke, reprove, revile, *inf* slam, *inf* slate, upbraid. *Opp* COMMEND. 2 convict, find guilty, judge, punish, sentence. *Opp* ACQUIT.

condense *v* 1 abbreviate, abridge, compress, curtail, précis, reduce, shorten, summarize. *Opp* EXPAND. 2 *condense a liquid.* concentrate, distil, reduce, solidify, thicken. *Opp* DILUTE.

condensation *n* haze, mist, precipitation, steam.

condescend *v* deign, demean yourself, lower yourself, stoop. **condescending** ▷ HAUGHTY.

condition *n* 1 case, circumstance, *inf* fettle, fitness, form, health, *inf* nick, order, shape, situation, state, *inf* trim, working order. 2 limitation, prerequisite, proviso, qualification, requirement, requisite, restriction, stipulation, terms. 3 *medical condition.* ▷ ILLNESS.
• *v* acclimatize, accustom, brainwash, educate, mould, prepare, *inf* soften up, train.

conditional *adj* dependent, limited, provisional, qualified, restricted, *inf* with strings attached. *Opp* UNCONDITIONAL.

condone *v* connive at, disregard, endorse, excuse, forgive, overlook, pardon, tolerate.

conducive *adj* advantageous, beneficial, encouraging, favourable, helpful, supportive. **be conducive to** ▷ ENCOURAGE.

conduct *n* 1 actions, attitude, bearing, behaviour, demeanour, deportment, manners, ways. 2 *conduct of affairs.* administration, control, direction, discharge, government, guidance, handling, management, organization, regulation, running, supervision.
• *v* 1 administer, be in charge of, chair, command, control, direct, govern, handle, head, manage, organize, oversee, preside over, regulate, rule, run, steer, supervise. 2 accompany, escort, guide, lead, take, usher. 3 *conduct electricity.* carry, channel, convey, transmit. **conduct yourself** ▷ BEHAVE.

confer *v* 1 accord, award, bestow, give, grant, honour with, impart, invest, present. 2 compare notes, consult, debate, deliberate, discuss, exchange ideas, *inf* put your heads together. ▷ TALK.

conference *n* congress, consultation, convention, council, discussion, forum, meeting, seminar, symposium.

confess *v* acknowledge, admit, *inf* come clean, concede, disclose, divulge, *inf* make a clean breast (of), own up, unburden yourself.

confession *n* acknowledgement, admission, declaration, disclosure, expression, revelation.

confide *v* consult, speak confidentially, *inf* spill the beans, open your heart, *inf* tell all, tell secrets, trust.

confidence *n* 1 belief, certainty, faith, hope, optimism, reliance, trust. 2 aplomb, assurance, boldness, composure, conviction, firmness, *inf* nerve, panache, self-assurance, self-possession, spirit, verve. *Opp* DOUBT, HESITATION. **have confidence in** ▷ TRUST.

confident *adj* 1 certain, convinced, hopeful, optimistic, positive, sanguine, sure. 2 *confident person.* assertive, assured, bold, *derog* cocksure, composed, cool, definite, fearless, secure, self-assured, self-possessed, unafraid. *Opp* DOUBTFUL.

confidential *adj* 1 classified, *inf* hush-hush, *inf* off the record, restricted, secret, top secret. 2 *confidential secretary.* personal, private, trusted.

confine *v* box in, cage, circumscribe, constrain, *inf* coop up, cramp, enclose, hedge in, hem in, *inf* hold down, isolate, keep in, limit, localize, restrain, restrict, rope off, shut in, shut up, surround, wall up. ▷ IMPRISON. *Opp* FREE.

confirm *v* 1 authenticate, back up, bear out, corroborate, demonstrate, endorse, establish, give credence to, justify, lend force to, prove, reinforce, settle, strengthen, substantiate, support, underline, vindicate. 2 *confirm a deal.* clinch, formalize, guarantee, make official, ratify, sanction, validate, verify.

confiscate *v* appropriate, commandeer, expropriate, impound, remove, seize, sequestrate, take away, take possession of.

conflict *n* 1 antagonism, antipathy, contradiction, disagreement, dissension, friction, hostility, incompatibility, inconsistency, opposition, strife. 2 battle, *inf* brush, clash, combat, confrontation, dispute, encounter, engagement, feud, *inf* row, *inf* set-to, skirmish, struggle, war, wrangle.
• *v* 1 be at variance, be incompatible, clash, compete, contradict, contrast, *inf* cross swords, disagree. ▷ FIGHT, QUARREL.

conform *v* agree, behave conventionally, blend in, *inf* do what you are told, *inf* keep in step, obey, *inf* toe the line. ▷ COMPLY.

conformist *n* traditionalist, yes-man. *Opp* REBEL.

conformity *n* compliance, conventionality, orthodoxy, submission, uniformity.

confront *v* accost, challenge, defy, encounter, face up to, oppose, resist, stand up to, take on, withstand. *Opp* AVOID.

confuse *v* 1 disarrange, disorder, garble, jumble, *inf* mess up, mix up, muddle, tangle, *inf* throw into disarray, upset. 2 *rules confuse me.* baffle, befuddle, bemuse, bewilder, confound, disconcert, disorientate, distract, *inf* flummox, fluster, mislead, mystify, perplex, puzzle, *inf* rattle, *inf* throw. **confusing** ▷ PUZZLING.

confused *adj* 1 chaotic, disordered, disorganized, *inf* higgledy-piggledy, jumbled, messy, mixed up, muddled, *inf* shambolic, *inf* topsy-turvy, twisted. 2 *confused ideas.* aimless, contradictory, disjointed, garbled, incoherent, inconsistent, irrational, misleading, obscure, rambling, unclear, unstructured, woolly. 3 *confused mind.* addled, baffled, bewildered, dazed, disorientated, distracted, flustered, fuddled, *inf* in a tizzy, muddle-headed, mystified, nonplussed, perplexed, puzzled. ▷ MAD. *Opp* ORDERLY.

confusion *n* 1 *inf* ado, anarchy, bedlam, bother, chaos, clutter, commotion, disorder, disorganization, fuss, hubbub, hullabaloo, jumble, *inf* mayhem, mêlée, mess, *inf* mix-up, muddle, pandemonium, riot, *inf* rumpus, *inf* shambles, tumult, turmoil, upheaval, uproar, whirl. 2 *mental confusion.* bemusement, bewilderment, disorientation, distraction, mystification, perplexity, puzzlement. *Opp* ORDER.

congeal *v* clot, coagulate, curdle, harden, *inf* jell, set, solidify, stiffen, thicken.

congenial *adj* acceptable, agreeable, pleasant, suitable, understanding. ▷ FRIENDLY. *Opp* UNCONGENIAL.

congenital *adj* hereditary, inborn, inherent, inherited, innate, natural.

congested *adj* blocked, choked, clogged, crammed, crowded, full, jammed, obstructed, overcrowded, stuffed. *Opp* CLEAR.

congratulate *v* applaud, compliment, felicitate, praise.

congregate *v* assemble, collect, convene, converge, gather, mass, meet, muster, rally, rendezvous. ▷ GROUP.

conjure *v* invoke, raise, summon. **conjure up** ▷ PRODUCE.

conjuring *n* illusions, magic, sleight of hand, tricks.

connect *v* 1 attach, combine, couple, fix, interlock, join, link, switch on, tie, unite. ▷ FASTEN. 2 associate, bracket together, compare, put together, relate, tie up. *Opp* SEPARATE.

connection *n* affinity, association, bond, contact, correlation, correspondence, link, relationship, relevance, tie, *inf* tie-up, unity. *Opp* SEPARATION.

conquer *v* 1 annex, best, capture, crush, defeat, get the better of, humble, *inf* lick, master, occupy, outdo, overpower, overrun, overthrow, overwhelm, quell, rout, seize, subdue, subjugate, surmount, take, *inf* thrash, triumph over, vanquish, worst. ▷ WIN. 2 *conquer a mountain.* climb, reach the top of.

conquest *n* annexation, appropriation, capture, defeat, domination, invasion, occupation, overthrow, subjection, subjugation, *inf* takeover. ▷ VICTORY.

conscience *n* compunction, ethics, honour, morality, principles, qualms, reservations, scruples, standards.

conscientious *adj* attentive, careful, diligent, dutiful, hard-working, honest, meticulous, painstaking, particular, punctilious, responsible, rigorous, scrupulous, serious, thorough. *Opp* CARELESS.

conscious *adj* 1 alert, awake, aware, compos mentis, sensible. 2 *conscious act.* calculated, deliberate, intended, intentional, knowing, planned, premeditated, studied, voluntary, wilful. *Opp* UNCONSCIOUS.

consecrate *v* bless, dedicate, devote,

hallow, make sacred, sanctify. *Opp* DESECRATE.

consecutive *adj* continuous, following, one after the other, running (*3 days running*), sequential, successive.

consent *n* acquiescence, agreement, assent, concurrence, permission, seal of approval.
• *v* accede, acquiesce, agree, approve, comply, concede, concur, undertake, yield. *Opp* REFUSE. **consent to** ▷ ALLOW.

consequence *n* 1 aftermath, by-product, corollary, effect, end, *inf* follow-up, outcome, repercussion, result, side-effect, upshot. 2 *of no consequence*. concern, importance, moment, note, significance, value.

consequent *adj* consequential, ensuing, following, resultant, resulting, subsequent.

conservation *n* economy, maintenance, preservation, protection, safeguarding, saving, upkeep. *Opp* DESTRUCTION.

conservationist *n* ecologist, environmentalist, *inf* green.

conservative *adj* 1 conventional, die-hard, hidebound, moderate, narrow-minded, old-fashioned, reactionary, sober, traditional, unadventurous. 2 *conservative estimate*. cautious, reasonable, understated. 3 *conservative politics*. right-of-centre, right-wing, Tory. *Opp* PROGRESSIVE.
• *n* conformist, die-hard, right-winger, Tory, traditionalist.

conserve *v* hold in reserve, keep, look after, maintain, preserve, protect, safeguard, save, store up, use sparingly. *Opp* DESTROY, WASTE.

consider *v* 1 *inf* chew over, contemplate, discuss, examine, muse, puzzle over, reflect, study, *inf* turn over, weigh up. ▷ THINK. 2 believe, deem, judge, reckon.

considerable *adj* appreciable, big, comfortable, noteworthy, noticeable, perceptible, reasonable, respectable, significant, sizeable, substantial, *inf* tidy (amount), tolerable, worthwhile. *Opp* NEGLIGIBLE.

considerate *adj* accommodating, altruistic, caring, cooperative, friendly, generous, gracious, helpful, kind, kind-hearted, neighbourly, obliging, polite, sensitive, solicitous, sympathetic, tactful, thoughtful, unselfish. *Opp* SELFISH.

consign *v* commit, convey, deliver, devote, entrust, give, hand over, pass on, relegate, send, ship, transfer.

consignment *n* batch, cargo, delivery, goods, load, shipment.

consist *v* **consist of** add up to, amount to, be composed of, comprise, contain, embody, include, incorporate, involve.

consistent *adj* 1 constant, dependable, faithful, predictable, regular, reliable, stable, steady, unchanging, undeviating, unfailing, uniform. 2 *The stories are consistent*. compatible, consonant, in accordance, in agreement, of a piece. *Opp* INCONSISTENT.

console *v* calm, cheer, comfort, ease, hearten, relieve, solace, soothe, sympathize with.

consolidate *v* make secure, make strong, reinforce, stabilize, strengthen. *Opp* WEAKEN.

consort *v* **consort with** associate with, be seen with, fraternize with, *inf* gang up with, keep company with, mix with.

conspicuous *adj* apparent, blatant, clear, discernible, dominant, eminent, evident, flagrant, glaring, impressive, manifest, marked, notable, noticeable, obtrusive, obvious, ostentatious, outstanding, patent, perceptible, plain, prominent, pronounced, self-evident, shining (*example*), showy, striking, unmistakable, visible. *Opp* INCONSPICUOUS.

conspiracy *n* collusion, *inf* frame-up, insider dealing, intrigue, machinations, plot, *inf* racket, scheme, treason.

conspirator *n* plotter, schemer.

conspire *v* be in league, collude, combine, connive, cooperate, hatch a plot, have designs, intrigue, plot, scheme.

constant *adj* 1 ceaseless, chronic, consistent, continuous, endless, everlasting, fixed, immutable, incessant, invariable, non-stop, permanent, perpetual, persistent, regular, relentless, repeated, stable, steady, sustained, unbroken, unchanging, unending, unflagging, uniform, uninterrupted, unremitting. 2 *constant friend*. dedicated, dependable, devoted, faithful, firm, indefatigable, loyal, reliable, resolute, staunch, steadfast, tireless, true, trustworthy, trusty, unswerving. *Opp* CHANGEABLE.

constitute *v* appoint, bring together, compose, comprise, create, establish, form, found, inaugurate, make (up), set up.

construct *v* assemble, build, create, engineer, erect, fabricate, fashion, form, *inf* knock together, make, manufacture, produce, put together, put up, set up. *Opp* DEMOLISH.

construction *n* 1 assembly, building, creation, manufacture, production, putting-up, setting-up. 2 building, edifice, structure.

constructive *adj* advantageous, beneficial, cooperative, creative, helpful, positive, practical, productive, useful, valuable, worthwhile. *Opp* DESTRUCTIVE.

consult *v* confer, debate, discuss, exchange views, *inf* put your heads together, refer (to), seek advice, speak (to), *inf* talk things over. ▷ QUESTION.

consume *v* 1 devour, drink, *inf* gobble up, guzzle, *inf* put away. ▷ EAT. 2 *consume energy.* absorb, deplete, drain, exhaust, expend, swallow up, use up, utilize.

contact *n* connection, junction, touch, union. ▷ COMMUNICATION.
• *v* apply to, approach, call on, communicate with, *inf* drop a line to, *inf* get hold of, get in touch with, make overtures to, notify, ring, speak to, telephone.

contagious *adj* catching, communicable, infectious, spreading, transmissible, transmittable.

contain *v* 1 accommodate, enclose, hold. 2 comprise, consist of, embody, embrace, include, incorporate, involve. 3 *contain your anger.* check, control, curb, hold back, limit, repress, restrain, stifle.

container *n* holder, receptacle, vessel.

contaminate *v* adulterate, corrupt, debase, defile, foul, infect, poison, pollute, soil, spoil, stain, taint. *Opp* PURIFY.

contemplate *v* 1 eye, gaze at, observe, stare at, survey, watch. ▷ SEE. 2 consider, examine, mull over, muse, plan, reflect, ruminate, study. ▷ THINK. 3 envisage, expect, intend, propose.

contemporary *adj* 1 *contemporary events.* coexistent, concurrent, contemporaneous, simultaneous, synchronous. 2 *contemporary music.* current, fashionable, the latest, modern, novel, present-day, *inf* trendy, topical, up-to-date.

contempt *n* derision, disdain, disgust, disrespect, ridicule, scorn. ▷ HATRED. *Opp* ADMIRATION. **feel contempt for** ▷ DESPISE.

contemptible *adj* base, beneath contempt, discreditable, disgraceful, disreputable, ignominious, mean, pitiful, shabby, shameful, worthless, wretched. ▷ HATEFUL. *Opp* ADMIRABLE.

contemptuous *adj* arrogant, belittling, condescending, derisive, disdainful, dismissive, haughty, insolent, insulting, jeering, patronizing, sarcastic, scornful, sneering, *inf* snide, *inf* snooty, *sl* snotty, supercilious, superior, withering. *Opp* RESPECTFUL. **be contemptuous of** ▷ DESPISE.

contend *v* 1 compete, contest, cope, grapple, strive, struggle, vie. ▷ FIGHT, QUARREL. 2 *contend that you're innocent.* affirm, allege, argue, assert, claim, declare, maintain, plead.

content *adj* ▷ CONTENTED.
• *n* 1 constituent, element, ingredient, part. 2 ▷ CONTENTMENT.
• *v* ▷ SATISFY.

contented *adj* comfortable, fulfilled, peaceful, relaxed, satisfied, serene, smug, uncomplaining, untroubled, well-fed. ▷ HAPPY. *Opp* DISSATISFIED.

contentment *n* comfort, content, ease, fulfilment, relaxation, satisfaction, serenity, smugness, tranquillity, well-being. ▷ HAPPINESS. *Opp* DISSATISFACTION.

contest *n* ▷ COMPETITION, FIGHT.
• *v* 1 compete for, contend for, fight for, *inf* make a bid for, strive for, struggle for, vie for. 2 *contest a decision.* argue against, challenge, debate, dispute, doubt, oppose, query, question, refute, resist.

contestant *n* candidate, opponent, participant. ▷ ENTRANT.

context *n* background, environment, frame of reference, framework, milieu, setting, situation, surroundings.

continual *adj* eternal, everlasting, frequent, limitless, ongoing, perennial, perpetual, recurrent, regular, repeated. ▷ CONTINUOUS. *Opp* OCCASIONAL.

continuation *n* 1 extension, prolongation, protraction, resumption. 2 addition, appendix, postscript, sequel, supplement.

continue *v* 1 carry on, endure, go on, last, linger, persevere, persist, proceed, pursue, remain, stay, *inf* stick at, survive, sustain. 2 *continue after lunch. inf* pick up the threads, restart, resume. 3 *continue a series.* extend, keep going, lengthen, maintain, prolong.

continuous *adj* constant, continuing, endless, incessant, interminable, never-ending, non-stop, relentless, *inf* round-the-clock, solid, sustained, unbroken, unceasing, uninterrupted, unremitting. ▷ CHRONIC, CONTINUAL. *Opp* INTERMITTENT.

contour *n* form, outline, shape.

contract *n* agreement, bargain, bond, commitment, concordat, covenant, deal, lease, pact, settlement, treaty, understanding, undertaking.

• *v* 1 become smaller, close up, condense, decrease, diminish, draw together, dwindle, lessen, narrow, reduce, shrink, shrivel, slim down, wither. *Opp* EXPAND. 2 agree, arrange, close a deal, covenant, negotiate a deal, promise, sign an agreement, undertake. 3 *contract a disease.* become infected by, catch, develop, get.

contraction *n* 1 diminution, narrowing, shortening, shrinkage, shrivelling. 2 abbreviation, diminutive, shortened form.

contradict *v* argue with, challenge, confute, deny, disagree with, dispute, gainsay, impugn, oppose, speak against.

contradictory *adj* antithetical, conflicting, contrary, different, incompatible, inconsistent, irreconcilable, opposed, opposite. *Opp* COMPATIBLE.

contraption *n* apparatus, contrivance, device, gadget, invention, machine, mechanism.

contrary *adj* 1 conflicting, contradictory, different, opposed, opposite, reverse. 2 *contrary winds.* adverse, hostile, opposing, unfavourable. 3 *contrary child.* awkward, cantankerous, defiant, difficult, disobedient, disruptive, intractable, obstinate, perverse, rebellious, *inf* stroppy, stubborn, uncooperative, unhelpful, wayward, wilful. *Opp* HELPFUL.

contrast *n* antithesis, comparison, difference, disparity, dissimilarity, distinction, divergence, foil, opposition. *Opp* SIMILARITY.
•*v* 1 compare, differentiate, discriminate, distinguish, make a distinction, set one against the other. 2 be set off (by), clash, conflict, differ (from). **contrasting** ▷ DISSIMILAR.

contribute *v* add, bestow, *inf* chip in, donate, *inf* fork out, furnish, give, present, provide, put up, subscribe, supply. **contribute to** ▷ SUPPORT.

contribution *n* 1 donation, fee, gift, grant, handout, offering, payment, sponsorship, subscription. 2 addition, input, support. ▷ HELP.

contributor *n* 1 backer, benefactor, donor, giver, helper, patron, sponsor, subscriber, supporter. 2 ▷ WRITER.

control *n* 1 administration, authority, charge, command, direction, discipline, government, grip, guidance, influence, jurisdiction, leadership, management, mastery, organization, oversight, power, regulation, restraint, rule, supervision, supremacy, sway. 2 dial, key, lever, switch.
• *v* 1 administer, *inf* be at the helm, be in charge, command, conduct, cope with, deal with, direct, dominate, engineer, govern, guide, handle, lead, look after, manage, manipulate, order about, oversee, regulate, rule, run, superintend, supervise. 2 *control animals.* check, confine, contain, curb, hold back, keep in check, master, repress, restrain, subdue.

controversial *adj* 1 arguable, debatable, disputable, doubtful, problematic, questionable. *Opp* ACCEPTED. 2 argumentative, contentious, litigious, polemical, provocative.

controversy *n* argument, contention, debate, disagreement, dispute, dissension, polemic, quarrel, war of words, wrangle.

convalesce *v* get better, make progress, mend, recover, recuperate, regain strength.

convalescent *adj* getting better, healing, improving, making progress, *inf* on the mend, recovering, recuperating.

convene *v* bring together, call, convoke, summon. ▷ GATHER.

convenient *adj* accessible, appropriate, at hand, available, expedient, handy, helpful, labour-saving, nearby, opportune, suitable, timely, useful. *Opp* INCONVENIENT.

convention *n* 1 custom, etiquette, formality, practice, rule, tradition. 2 ▷ ASSEMBLY.

conventional *adj* 1 accepted, correct, customary, decorous, expected, formal, mainstream, orthodox, prevalent, received, standard, *inf* straight, traditional, unadventurous, unimaginative, unoriginal. ▷ ORDINARY. 2 [*derog*] bourgeois, conservative, hidebound, pedestrian, reactionary, rigid, stereotyped, *inf* stuffy. *Opp* UNCONVENTIONAL.

converge *v* coincide, combine, come together, join, link up, meet, merge, unite. *Opp* DIVERGE.

conversation *n* *inf* chat, communication, discourse, discussion, gossip, *inf* heart-to-heart, intercourse, *inf* natter, tête-à-tête. ▷ TALK.

convert *v* change someone's mind, convince, persuade, re-educate, reform, rehabilitate, save, win over. ▷ CHANGE.

convey *v* 1 bear, bring, carry, conduct, deliver, ferry, fetch, forward, move, send, shift, ship, take, transfer, transport. 2 *convey a message.* communicate, disclose, impart, imply, indicate, mean, relay, reveal, signify, tell, transmit.

convict *n* criminal, culprit, felon, malefactor, prisoner, wrongdoer.
•*v* condemn, declare guilty, prove guilty, sentence. *Opp* ACQUIT.

conviction *n* 1 assurance, certainty, confidence. 2 *religious conviction.* belief, creed, faith, opinion, persuasion, position, principle, tenet, view.

convince *v* assure, *inf* bring round, convert, persuade, reassure, satisfy, sway, win over. **convincing** ▷ PERSUASIVE.

convulsion *n* 1 eruption, tremor, turbulence, upheaval. 2 [*medical*] attack, fit, paroxysm, seizure, spasm.

convulsive *adj* jerky, shaking, spasmodic, *inf* twitchy, uncontrolled, violent, wrenching.

cook *v* bake, cater, concoct, make, prepare. **cook up** ▷ PLOT.

cooking *n* baking, catering, cookery, cuisine.

cool *adj* 1 chilled, chilly, iced, refreshing. ▷ COLD. *Opp* HOT. 2 calm, collected, composed, dignified, *inf* laid-back, level-headed, phlegmatic, quiet, relaxed, self-possessed, sensible, serene, unexcited, unflustered, unruffled, urbane. 3 [*derog*] aloof, apathetic, cold-blooded, dispassionate, distant, frigid, half-hearted, indifferent, lukewarm, offhand, reserved, standoffish, unemotional, unenthusiastic, unfriendly, unresponsive, unsociable, unwelcoming. *Opp* PASSIONATE. 4 [*inf*] *cool customer.* ▷ INSOLENT.
•*v* 1 chill, freeze, refrigerate. *Opp* HEAT. 2 *cool your enthusiasm.* abate, allay, assuage, calm, dampen, diminish, lessen, moderate, *inf* pour cold water on, quiet, temper. *Opp* INFLAME.

cooperate *v* collaborate, combine, conspire, help, *inf* join forces, *inf* pitch in, *inf* play along, *inf* play ball, *inf* pull together, unite, work as a team, work together. *Opp* COMPETE.

cooperation *n* assistance, collaboration, help, joint action, mutual support, teamwork. *Opp* COMPETITION.

cooperative *adj* 1 accommodating, hard-working, helpful, obliging, supportive, united, willing, working as a team. 2 *cooperative effort.* collective, combined, communal, concerted, coordinated, corporate, joint, shared.

cope *v* get by, make do, manage, survive, win through. **cope with** ▷ ENDURE, MANAGE.

copious *adj* abundant, ample, bountiful, extravagant, generous, great, inexhaustible, large, lavish, liberal, luxuriant, overflowing, plentiful, profuse, unstinting. *Opp* SCARCE.

copy *n* 1 carbon copy, clone, counterfeit, double, duplicate, facsimile, fake, forgery, imitation, likeness, model, pattern, photocopy, print, replica, representation, reproduction, tracing, transcript, twin, Xerox. 2 *copy of a book.* edition, volume.
•*v* 1 counterfeit, crib, duplicate, emulate, follow, forge, imitate, photocopy, plagiarize, reproduce, simulate, transcribe. 2 ape, imitate, impersonate, mimic.

cord *n* cable, lace, line, rope, strand, string, twine, wire.

cordon *n* barrier, chain, line. **cordon off** ▷ ISOLATE.

core *n* 1 centre, heart, nucleus. 2 *core of a problem.* central issue, crux, essence, gist, kernel, *sl* nitty-gritty, nub.

cork *n* bung, plug, stopper.

corner *n* 1 angle, crook, joint. 2 bend, crossroads, intersection, junction, turning. 3 *quiet corner.* hideaway, hiding-place, niche, nook, recess, retreat.
•*v* capture, catch, trap.

corporation *n* company, concern, council, enterprise, firm, organization.

corpse *n* body, cadaver, carcass, mortal remains, *sl* stiff.

correct *adj* 1 accurate, confirmed, exact, factual, faithful, faultless, flawless, genuine, literal, precise, reliable, right, strict, true, truthful, verified. 2 acceptable, appropriate, fitting, just, proper, regular, standard, suitable, tactful, well-mannered. *Opp* WRONG.
•*v* 1 adjust, alter, cure, put right, rectify, redress, remedy, repair. 2 *correct pupils' work.* assess, mark. 3 ▷ REPRIMAND.

correspond *v* accord, agree, be consistent, coincide, concur, conform, correlate, fit, harmonize, match, parallel, square, tally. **corresponding** ▷ EQUIVALENT. **correspond with** communicate with, write to.

correspondence *n* letters, memoranda, *inf* memos, messages, notes, writings.

correspondent *n* contributor, journalist, reporter, writer.

corridor *n* aisle, hallway, passage, passageway.

corrode *v* 1 consume, eat into, erode, oxidize, rot, rust, tarnish. 2 crumble, deteriorate.

corrugated *adj* creased, *inf* crinkly, furrowed, lined, puckered, ridged, wrinkled.

corrupt *adj inf* bent, criminal, *inf* crooked, debauched, decadent, degenerate, depraved, *inf* dirty, dishonest, dishonourable, dissolute, evil, false, fraudulent, illegal, immoral, iniquitous, low, perverted, rotten, sinful, unethical, unprincipled, unscrupulous, untrustworthy, venal, vicious, wicked. *Opp* HONEST.
• *v* 1 bribe, divert, *inf* fix, influence, pervert, suborn, subvert. 2 *corrupt the innocent.* debauch, deprave, lead astray, tempt, seduce.

cosmetics *n* make-up, toiletries.

cosmic *adj* boundless, endless, infinite, limitless, universal.

cosmopolitan *adj* international, multicultural, sophisticated, urbane. *Opp* PROVINCIAL.

cost *n* amount, charge, expenditure, expense, fare, figure, outlay, payment, price, rate, tariff, value.
• *v* be worth, fetch, go for, realize, sell for, *inf* set you back.

costume *n* clothing, dress, fancy-dress, livery, period dress, *old use* raiment, robes. ▷ CLOTHES.

cosy *adj* comfortable, *inf* comfy, homely, intimate, reassuring, restful, secure, snug, warm. *Opp* UNCOMFORTABLE.

council *n* committee, corporation, meeting. ▷ ASSEMBLY.

counsel *n* ▷ LAWYER.
• *v* advise, discuss (with), give help, guide, warn.

count *v* 1 add up, calculate, check, compute, enumerate, estimate, figure out, *inf* notch up, number, reckon, score, take stock of, tell, total, *inf* tot up, work out. 2 be important, matter, signify. **count on** ▷ EXPECT.

countenance *n* aspect, demeanour, expression, face, features, look.
• *v* ▷ APPROVE.

counter *n* 1 bar, service-point, table. 2 chip, disc, piece, token.
• *v* answer, *inf* come back at, contradict, defend yourself against, hit back at, parry, react to, refute, reply to, ward off.

counteract *v* act against, annul, be an antidote to, cancel out, counterbalance, foil, invalidate, negate, neutralize, offset, oppose, resist, thwart, withstand, work against.

counterbalance *v* balance, compensate for, counteract, counterpoise, equalize.

counterfeit *adj* artificial, bogus, copied, ersatz, fake, false, feigned, forged, fraudulent, imitation, *inf* phoney, *inf* pseudo, sham, simulated, spurious, synthetic. *Opp* GENUINE.
• *v* copy, fake, falsify, feign, forge, imitate, pretend, *inf* put on, simulate.

countless *adj* endless, immeasurable, incalculable, infinite, innumerable, limitless, many, myriad, numerous, unnumbered, untold. *Opp* FINITE.

country *n* 1 commonwealth, domain, empire, kingdom, land, nation, people, power, realm, state, territory. 2 *open country.* countryside, green belt, landscape, scenery.

couple *n* brace, duo, pair, twosome.
• *v* 1 connect, fasten, hitch, join, link, match, pair, unite, yoke. ▷ MATE.

coupon *n* tear-off slip, ticket, token, voucher.

courage *n* audacity, boldness, *sl* bottle, bravery, daring, determination, fearlessness, firmness, fortitude, gallantry, *inf* grit, *inf* guts, heroism, indomitability, mettle, *inf* nerve, patience, pluck, resolution, spirit, stoicism, tenacity, valour. *Opp* COWARDICE.

courageous *adj* audacious, bold, brave, daring, dauntless, determined, fearless, gallant, game, *inf* gutsy, heroic, indomitable, intrepid, noble, plucky, resolute, spirited, stalwart, stout-hearted, tough, unafraid, uncomplaining, undaunted, unshrinking, valiant, valorous. *Opp* COWARDLY.

course *n* 1 bearings, direction, orbit, path, route, track, way. 2 *course of events.* development, movement, passage, progress, progression, succession. 3 *course of lectures.* curriculum, programme, schedule, series, syllabus.

court *n* 1 assizes, bench, law court, tribunal. 2 entourage, followers, retinue. 3 ▷ COURTYARD.
• *v* 1 *inf* ask for, invite, provoke, seek, solicit. 2 date, *inf* go out with, pursue, try to win, woo.

courteous *adj* civil, considerate, gentlemanly, ladylike, urbane, well-mannered. ▷ POLITE.

courtier *n* attendant, follower, lady, lord, noble, page, steward.

courtyard *n* court, enclosure, patio, *inf* quad, quadrangle.

cover *n* 1 ▷ COVERING. 2 binding, case,

dust jacket, envelope, folder, wrapper. 3 camouflage, cloak, concealment, cover-up, deception, disguise, façade, front, hiding-place, mask, pretence, refuge, shelter, smokescreen. 3 *air cover.* defence, guard, protection.
• *v* 1 blot out, bury, camouflage, cap, cloak, clothe, coat, conceal, curtain, disguise, drape, dress, encase, enclose, envelop, hide, hood, mantle, mask, obscure, overlay, plaster, protect, screen, shade, sheathe, shield, shroud, spread over, surface, veil, veneer, wrap up. 2 *cover expenses.* be enough for, match, meet, pay for, suffice for. 3 *The talk will cover many subjects.* comprise, deal with, embrace, encompass, include, involve, treat.

covering *n* blanket, canopy, cap, carpet, casing, cloak, coat, cocoon, crust, facing, film, incrustation, layer, mantle, rind, roof, screen, sheath, sheet, shell, shield, shroud, skin, tarpaulin, veil, veneer, wrapping. ▷ BEDCLOTHES.

coward *n inf* chicken, deserter, *inf* wimp.

cowardice *n* cowardliness, desertion, faint-heartedness, *inf* funk, spinelessness, timidity. ▷ FEAR. *Opp* COURAGE.

cowardly *adj* abject, afraid, cowering, craven, faint-hearted, fearful, *inf* gutless, *inf* lily-livered, pusillanimous, spineless, submissive, timid, unchivalrous, unheroic, *inf* wimpish, *sl* yellow. ▷ FRIGHTENED. *Opp* COURAGEOUS.

cower *v* cringe, crouch, flinch, quail, shiver, shrink, tremble.

coy *adj* bashful, coquettish, demure, diffident, embarrassed, evasive, hesitant, modest, timid, unforthcoming. ▷ SHY. *Opp* BOLD.

crack *n* 1 break, chink, cranny, crevice, fissure, flaw, fracture, gap, opening, rift, rupture, slit, split. 2 bang, clap, explosion, shot, snap. 3 ▷ JOKE.
• *v* break, fracture, snap, splinter, split.
crack up ▷ DISINTEGRATE.

craft *n* 1 handicraft, job, trade. ▷ CRAFTSMANSHIP, CUNNING. 2 *sea-going craft.* boat, ship, vessel.
• *v* ▷ MAKE.

craftsmanship *n* art, artistry, expertise, handiwork, *inf* know-how, workmanship. ▷ SKILL.

crafty *adj* artful, astute, calculating, canny, clever, conniving, cunning, deceitful, devious, *inf* dodgy, furtive, ingenious, knowing, machiavellian, manipulative, scheming, shrewd, sly, sneaky, wily. *Opp* HONEST, NAÏVE.

craggy *adj* jagged, rocky, rough, rugged.

cram *v* 1 compress, crowd, crush, force, jam, overfill, pack, press, squeeze, stuff. 2 ▷ STUDY.

cramped *adj* crowded, restricted, tight, uncomfortable. *Opp* ROOMY.

crash *n* 1 bang, blast, boom, explosion, smash. 2 accident, collision, disaster, impact, pile-up, smash, wreck. 3 *crash on the stock market.* collapse, depression, fall.
• *v* 1 bump, collide, knock, smash. ▷ HIT. 2 collapse, crash-dive, dive, fall, plummet, plunge, topple.

crate *n* box, case, packing case.

crater *n* abyss, chasm, hole, hollow, pit.

crawl *v* 1 clamber, creep, edge, slither, wriggle. 2 [*inf*] be obsequious, fawn, flatter, grovel, *inf* suck up, toady. 3 ▷ TEEM.

craze *n* enthusiasm, fad, fashion, infatuation, mania, novelty, obsession, passion, rage, trend.

crazy *adj* 1 berserk, demented, deranged, frantic, hysterical, insane, *inf* potty, unbalanced, unhinged, wild. ▷ MAD. 2 *crazy ideas.* absurd, confused, foolish, idiotic, illogical, impractical, ridiculous, senseless, silly, unrealistic, unreasonable, unwise. ▷ STUPID. 3 ▷ ENTHUSIASTIC. *Opp* SENSIBLE.

creamy *adj* milky, oily, smooth, thick, velvety.

crease *n* corrugation, fold, furrow, groove, pleat, pucker, ridge, tuck, wrinkle.
• *v* crimp, crinkle, crumple, crush, fold, pleat, pucker, rumple, wrinkle.

create *v old use* beget, breed, bring into existence, build, cause, compose, conceive, constitute, construct, design, *inf* dream up, engender, engineer, establish, father, forge, found, generate, give rise to, imagine, institute, invent, make up, manufacture, originate, produce, shape, sire, think up. ▷ MAKE. *Opp* DESTROY.

creation *n* 1 beginning, birth, conception, constitution, construction, formation, foundation, genesis, inception, institution, making, origin, procreation, production. 2 achievement, brainchild, concept, handiwork, invention, product. *Opp* DESTRUCTION.

creative *adj* artistic, clever, fertile, imaginative, ingenious, inspired, inventive, original, productive, resourceful, talented. *Opp* DESTRUCTIVE.

creator *n* architect, author, begetter, composer, craftsman, designer, deviser, initiator, inventor, manufacturer, originator. ▷ ARTIST.

creature *n* beast, being, brute, organism. ▷ ANIMAL.

credentials *n* authorization, documents, licence, passport, proof of identity, warrant.

credible *adj* believable, conceivable, convincing, likely, persuasive, plausible, possible, tenable, trustworthy. *Opp* INCREDIBLE.

credit *n* approval, commendation, distinction, esteem, fame, honour, *inf* kudos, merit, praise, prestige, recognition, reputation.
• *v* 1 accept, believe, count on, depend on, have faith in, rely on, subscribe to, *inf* swallow, swear by, trust. *Opp* DOUBT. 2 *credit you with sense.* assign to, attribute to. 3 *credit £10 to my account.* add, enter. *Opp* DEBIT.

creditable *adj* admirable, commendable, estimable, honourable, laudable, meritorious, praiseworthy, worthy. *Opp* UNWORTHY.

credulous *adj* easily taken in, *inf* green, gullible, trusting, unsuspecting. ▷ NAÏVE. *Opp* SCEPTICAL.

creed *n* belief, conviction, doctrine, dogma, faith, principle, tenet.

creek *n* bay, cove, estuary, harbour, inlet.

creep *v* crawl, edge, move quietly, move slowly, slip, slither, sneak, steal, tiptoe, worm.

creepy *adj* disturbing, eerie, frightening, hair-raising, macabre, ominous, *inf* scary, sinister, spine-chilling, *inf* spooky, supernatural, threatening, weird.

crest *n* 1 comb, plume. 2 *crest of a hill.* apex, brow, crown, peak, pinnacle, summit. 3 badge, coat of arms, device, emblem, heraldic device, insignia, seal, shield, symbol.

crevice *n* break, chink, cleft, crack, cranny, fissure, groove, rift, slit.

crew *n* band, company, gang, team. ▷ GROUP.

crime *n* delinquency, dishonesty, felony, law-breaking, lawlessness, misconduct, misdemeanour, offence, *inf* racket, sin, wrongdoing.

criminal *adj inf* bent, corrupt, *inf* crooked, culpable, dishonest, felonious, illegal, indictable, nefarious, *inf* shady, unlawful. ▷ WICKED, WRONG. *Opp* LAWFUL.
• *n* convict, *inf* crook, culprit, delinquent, desperado, felon, lawbreaker, malefactor, miscreant, offender, outlaw, recidivist, transgressor, villain. ▷ GANGSTER.

cringe *v* cower, crouch, flinch, grovel, quail, quiver, shy away, wince.

cripple *v* 1 disable, hamper, hamstring, incapacitate, lame, maim, mutilate, paralyse, weaken. 2 damage, make useless, sabotage. **crippled** ▷ HANDICAPPED.

crisis *n* calamity, catastrophe, critical moment, danger, difficulty, disaster, emergency, turning point.

crisp *adj* 1 brittle, crackly, crunchy, friable, hard and dry. 2 ▷ BRACING, BRISK.

criterion *n* measure, principle, standard, yardstick.

critic *n* 1 authority, judge, pundit, reviewer. 2 attacker, detractor.

critical *adj* 1 carping, censorious, criticizing, deprecatory, derogatory, disapproving, disparaging, hypercritical, judgemental, *inf* nit-picking, scathing, uncomplimentary. *Opp* COMPLIMENTARY. 2 analytical, discerning, discriminating, intelligent, perceptive, probing, sharp. 3 *critical moment.* crucial, dangerous, decisive, important, key, momentous, pivotal, vital. *Opp* UNIMPORTANT.

criticism *n* 1 censure, condemnation, disapproval, disparagement, reprimand, verbal attack. 2 *literary criticism.* analysis, appraisal, appreciation, commentary, critique, evaluation, judgement.

criticize *v* 1 belittle, berate, blame, *inf* cast aspersions on, castigate, censure, *old use* chide, condemn, complain about, disapprove of, disparage, find fault with, *inf* get at, impugn, *inf* knock, *inf* pan, *inf* pick holes in, *inf* rap, rate, rebuke, reprimand, satirize, scold, *inf* slam, *inf* slate. *Opp* PRAISE. 2 analyse, appraise, assess, evaluate, judge, review.

crockery *n* china, crocks, dishes, earthenware, porcelain, pottery, tableware.

crook *n* 1 angle, corner, hook. 2 ▷ CRIMINAL.

crooked *adj* 1 angled, askew, bent, contorted, curved, deformed, gnarled, lopsided, misshapen, off-centre, tortuous, twisted, warped, winding. ▷ INDIRECT. 2 ▷ CRIMINAL.

crop *n* harvest, produce, yield.
• *v* browse, graze, nibble, shear, trim. ▷ CUT, HARVEST. **crop up** ▷ ARISE.

cross *adj* bad-tempered, cantankerous, grumpy, irascible, irate, irritable, peevish, short-tempered, testy, upset. ▷ ANGRY, ANNOYED. *Opp* GOOD-TEMPERED.

• *n* 1 intersection, X. 2 *cross to bear.* burden, grief, misfortune, problem, trial, tribulation, trouble. 3 *cross of breeds.* amalgam, combination, cross-breed, hybrid, mixture, mongrel.
• *v* 1 criss-cross, intersect, meet. 2 *cross a river.* bridge, ford, go across, traverse. 3 *cross someone.* annoy, block, frustrate, impede, oppose, thwart. **cross out** ▷ CANCEL. **cross swords** ▷ CONFLICT.

crossing *v* 1 bridge, causeway, flyover, ford, overpass, pedestrian crossing, underpass. 2 *sea crossing.* ▷ JOURNEY.

crossroads *n* interchange, intersection, junction.

crouch *v* bend, cower, cringe, duck, squat, stoop.

crowd *n* 1 assembly, bunch, cluster, collection, company, crush, flock, gathering, horde, mob, multitude, pack, swarm, throng. ▷ GROUP. 2 *football crowd.* audience, spectators.
• *v* assemble, cluster, collect, compress, congregate, cram, flock, gather, jostle, mass, muster, overcrowd, pack, *inf* pile, press, push, squeeze, swarm, throng.

crowded *adj* congested, cramped, full, jammed, jostling, overcrowded, overflowing, packed, teeming. *Opp* EMPTY.

crown *n* 1 circlet, coronet, tiara. 2 *crown of a hill.* apex, brow, peak, summit, top.
• *v* 1 anoint, appoint, enthrone, install. 2 complete, conclude, culminate, finish off, perfect, round off.

crucial *adj* central, critical, essential, important, momentous, pivotal. *Opp* UNIMPORTANT.

crude *adj* 1 natural, raw, unprocessed, unrefined. 2 *crude work.* amateurish, awkward, clumsy, inelegant, inept, makeshift, primitive, rough, rudimentary, unpolished, unskilful. *Opp* REFINED. 3 ▷ VULGAR.

cruel *adj* atrocious, barbaric, beastly, bestial, bloodthirsty, brutal, callous, cold-blooded, diabolical, ferocious, fiendish, fierce, grim, hard, hard-hearted, harsh, heartless, hellish, implacable, inhuman, malevolent, merciless, murderous, pitiless, relentless, ruthless, sadistic, savage, spiteful, tyrannical, unfeeling, unjust, unkind, unmerciful, unrelenting, vengeful, venomous, vicious, violent. *Opp* KIND.

cruelty *n* barbarity, brutality, callousness, cold-bloodedness, ferocity, heartlessness, inhumanity, malevolence, ruthlessness, sadism, savagery, unkindness, viciousness, violence.

cruise *v* coast, sail, travel, voyage.
• *n* boat-trip, journey, passage, voyage.

crumb *n* bit, fragment, grain, morsel, particle, scrap, speck.

crumble *v* break into pieces, crush, decompose, deteriorate, disintegrate, fall apart, fragment, perish, powder, pulverize.

crumbly *adj* friable, granular, powdery. *Opp* SOLID.

crumple *v* crease, crush, dent, mangle, rumple, wrinkle.

crunch *v* chew, crush, grind, masticate, munch, scrunch, smash.

crusade *n* campaign, holy war, jihad, struggle, war.

crush *n* congestion, jam. ▷ CROWD.
• *v* 1 break, bruise, compress, crunch, mangle, mash, pound, press, pulp, pulverize, smash, squeeze. 2 *crush opponents.* humiliate, mortify, overwhelm, rout, thrash, vanquish. ▷ CONQUER.

crust *n* incrustation, outer layer, rind, scab, shell, skin, surface. ▷ COVERING.

crux *n* centre, core, crucial issue, essence, nub.

cry *n* bellow, call, caterwaul, exclamation, howl, roar, scream, shout, shriek, whoop, yell.
• *v* bawl, blubber, shed tears, snivel, sob, weep, *inf* whinge. **cry off** ▷ WITHDRAW. **cry out** ▷ SHOUT.

crypt *n* catacomb, cellar, grave, sepulchre, tomb, vault.

cryptic *adj* arcane, coded, enigmatic, hidden, mysterious, mystical, obscure, perplexing, recondite, secret, unintelligible, veiled. *Opp* INTELLIGIBLE.

cuddle *v* caress, clasp lovingly, embrace, fondle, hold closely, hug, make love, nestle against, nurse, pet, snuggle up to.

cudgel *n* baton, bludgeon, club, cosh, truncheon.
• *v* batter, beat, bludgeon, *inf* clobber, cosh, pummel, thrash, thump. ▷ HIT.

cue *n* hint, prompt, sign, signal.

culminate *v* climax, conclude, reach a finale. ▷ END.

culpable *adj* criminal, guilty, liable, punishable, reprehensible, wrong. ▷ DELIBERATE. *Opp* INNOCENT.

culprit *n* miscreant, offender, troublemaker, wrongdoer. ▷ CRIMINAL.

cult *n* 1 craze, fan-club, fashion, party, trend, vogue. 2 *religious cult*. ▷ DENOMINATION.

cultivate *v* 1 dig, farm, manure, plough, prepare, till, turn, work. 2 grow, plant, produce, raise, take cuttings, tend. 3 *cultivate a friendship*. court, develop, encourage, foster, further, improve, promote, pursue.

cultivated *adj* 1 farmed, planted, prepared, tilled. 2 ▷ CULTURED.

cultivation *n* agriculture, agronomy, breeding, farming, gardening, horticulture, husbandry, nurturing.

cultural *adj* aesthetic, artistic, educational, enlightening, highbrow, intellectual.

culture *n* 1 art, civilization, customs, education, learning, traditions, way of life. 2 ▷ CULTIVATION.

cultured *adj* 1 civilized, discriminating, educated, elegant, erudite, refined, scholarly, sophisticated, well-bred, well-educated. *Opp* IGNORANT. 2 ▷ CULTIVATED.

cunning *adj* 1 devious, guileful, knowing, machiavellian, sly, subtle, tricky, wily. ▷ CRAFTY. 2 adroit, astute, ingenious, skilful. ▷ CLEVER.
• *n* 1 artfulness, chicanery, craft, deceit, deviousness, duplicity, guile, trickery. 2 cleverness, expertise, ingenuity, skill.

cup *n* 1 mug, tankard, teacup. 2 award, prize, trophy.

cupboard *n* cabinet, chiffonier, closet, larder, locker, wardrobe.

curable *adj* remediable, treatable. *Opp* INCURABLE.

curb *v* check, control, deter, hinder, hold back, impede, inhibit, moderate, restrain, restrict, suppress. *Opp* ENCOURAGE.

curdle *v* clot, coagulate, congeal, go sour.

cure *n* 1 antidote, medication, medicine, palliative, panacea, prescription, remedy, therapy. 2 healing, recovery, restoration, revival.
• *v* alleviate, correct, counteract, ease, *inf* fix, heal, mend, rectify, relieve, remedy, repair, treat. *Opp* AGGRAVATE.

curiosity *n* inquisitiveness, interest, interference, nosiness, *inf* snooping.

curious *adj* 1 inquiring, inquisitive, interested, puzzled, questioning, searching. 2 meddlesome, *inf* nosy, prying. 3 ▷ STRANGE. **be curious** ▷ PRY.

curl *n* coil, curve, kink, loop, ringlet, scroll, spiral, swirl, twist, whorl.
• *v* 1 coil, corkscrew, curve, entwine, loop, spiral, twist, wreathe, writhe. 2 *curl your hair*. crimp, frizz, perm.

curly *adj* crimped, curled, frizzy, permed, wavy. *Opp* STRAIGHT.

current *adj* 1 contemporary, existing, fashionable, living, modern, ongoing, present-day, prevailing, reigning, remaining, *inf* trendy, up-to-date. 2 *current passport*. valid. *Opp* OLD.
• *n* course, drift, flow, river, tide, trend, undertow.

curriculum *n* course, programme of study, syllabus.

curse *n* blasphemy, expletive, imprecation, malediction, oath, profanity, swear word. *Opp* BLESSING.
• *v* blaspheme, damn, swear. *Opp* BLESS.
cursed ▷ HATEFUL.

cursory *adj* brief, careless, casual, desultory, hasty, perfunctory, slapdash, superficial. *Opp* THOROUGH.

curt *adj* abrupt, blunt, brief, brusque, crusty, gruff, monosyllabic, offhand, rude, short, succinct, tart, terse, uncommunicative, ungracious. ▷ RUDE. *Opp* EXPANSIVE.

curtail *v* abbreviate, break off, cut short, decrease, *inf* dock, halt, lessen, restrict, shorten, truncate. ▷ SHORTEN. *Opp* EXTEND.

curtain *n* blind, drape, screen.
• *v* drape, mask, screen, veil. ▷ HIDE.

curtsy *v* bend the knee, bow, genuflect.

curve *n* arc, arch, bend, bow, bulge, circle, corkscrew, crescent, curl, loop, spiral, swirl, trajectory, turn, twist, undulation, whorl.
• *v* arc, arch, bend, bow, bulge, corkscrew, curl, loop, snake, spiral, swerve, twist. ▷ CIRCLE.

curved *adj* concave, convex, crescent, crooked, curvy, rounded, serpentine, sinuous, swelling, tortuous, turned, undulating.

cushion *n* bolster, hassock, pad, pillow.
• *v* absorb, deaden, insulate, mitigate, protect from, reduce the effect of, support.

custodian *n* caretaker, curator, guardian, keeper, warder, *inf* watchdog, watchman.

custody *n* 1 care, guardianship, observation, possession, preservation, protection, safe-keeping. 2 *in police custody*. confinement, detention, imprisonment, incarceration, remand.

custom *n* 1 convention, etiquette, fashion, formality, habit, institution, observance, policy, practice, procedure, routine, tradition, way. 2 business, customers, patronage, support, trade.

customary *adj* accepted, accustomed, common, commonplace, conventional, established, everyday, expected, fashionable, general, habitual, normal, ordinary, popular, prevailing, regular, routine, traditional, typical, usual, wonted. *Opp* UNUSUAL.

customer *n* buyer, client, consumer, patron, purchaser, shopper. *Opp* SELLER.

cut *n* 1 gash, graze, incision, laceration, nick, rent, rip, slash, slit, snick, snip, stab, tear. ▷ INJURY. 2 *cut in prices.* cutback, decrease, fall, lowering, reduction, saving.
• *v* 1 amputate, axe, carve, chisel, chop, cleave, crop, dice, dissect, divide, dock, engrave, gash, gouge, grate, graze, guillotine, hack, halve, hew, incise, knife, lacerate, lance, lop, mince, mow, nick, notch, pierce, prune, reap, saw, scalp, score, sever, shave, shear, shred, slash, slice, slit, snick, snip, split, stab, trim, wound. 2 abbreviate, abridge, censor, condense, edit, précis, shorten, summarize, truncate. ▷ REDUCE. **cut and dried** ▷ DEFINITE. **cut in** ▷ INTERRUPT. **cut off** ▷ REMOVE, STOP. **cut short** ▷ CURTAIL.

cutlery *n* knives, forks, and spoons, silver, tableware.

cutting *adj* acute, biting, caustic, incisive, keen, sarcastic, satirical, sharp. ▷ HURTFUL.

cycle *n* 1 circle, repetition, revolution, rotation, sequence, series. 2 bicycle, *inf* bike, moped, *inf* motor bike, scooter.
• *v* travel by cycle.

cyclic *adj* circular, recurring, repeating, repetitive, rotating.

cynical *adj* doubting, *inf* hard, incredulous, mocking, negative, pessimistic, questioning, sceptical. *Opp* OPTIMISTIC.

D

dabble *v* 1 dip, paddle, splash. 2 *dabble in a hobby.* potter about, tinker, work casually.

dabbler *n* ▷ AMATEUR.

dagger *n* bayonet, blade, knife, stiletto.

daily *adj* diurnal, everyday, regular.

dainty *adj* 1 charming, delicate, exquisite, fine, meticulous, neat, pretty, skilful. 2 discriminating, fastidious, finicky, fussy, genteel, sensitive, squeamish, well-mannered. 3 *dainty morsel.* appealing, appetizing, choice, delectable, delicious. *Opp* CLUMSY, GROSS.

dally *v* dawdle, delay, *inf* dilly-dally, hang about, idle, linger, loaf, loiter, play about, procrastinate, *old use* tarry.

dam *n* bank, barrage, barrier, dyke, embankment, wall, weir.
• *v* block, check, hold back, obstruct, stanch, stem, stop.

damage *n* destruction, devastation, harm, havoc, injury, mutilation, sabotage.
• *v* 1 break, buckle, burst, *inf* bust, chip, crack, cripple, deface, destroy, disable, disfigure, harm, hurt, immobilize, impair, incapacitate, injure, make inoperative, make useless, mar, mark, mutilate, ruin, rupture, sabotage, scar, scratch, spoil, vandalize, warp, weaken, wound, wreck. **damaged** ▷ FAULTY. **damages** ▷ COMPENSATION. **damaging** ▷ HARMFUL.

damn *v* attack, berate, castigate, condemn, criticize, curse, denounce, doom, execrate, swear at.

damnation *n* doom, everlasting fire, hell, perdition, ruin. *Opp* SALVATION.

damp *adj* clammy, dank, dripping, drizzly, foggy, humid, misty, moist, muggy, perspiring, rainy, soggy, steamy, sticky, sweaty, unaired, unventilated, wet. *Opp* DRY.
• *v* 1 dampen, moisten, sprinkle. 2 ▷ DISCOURAGE.

dance *n* disco, ball, party.
• *v* caper, cavort, frisk, frolic, gambol, hop about, jig, leap, prance, skip, whirl.

danger *n* 1 hazard, insecurity, jeopardy, menace, peril, pitfall, trouble. 2 chance, possibility, risk, threat.

dangerous *adj* 1 critical, destructive, explosive, grave, harmful, hazardous, insecure, menacing, *inf* nasty, noxious, perilous, precarious, reckless, risky, threatening, toxic, unsafe. 2 *dangerous men.* desperate, ruthless, treacherous, unmanageable, unpredictable, violent, volatile, wild. *Opp* HARMLESS.

dangle *v* be suspended, flap, hang, sway, swing, trail, wave about.

dank *adj* chilly, clammy, damp, moist, unaired.

dappled *adj* blotchy, brindled, dotted, flecked, freckled, marbled, mottled, patchy, pied, speckled, spotted, stippled, streaked, variegated.

dare *v* 1 gamble, have the courage, risk, take a chance, venture. 2 challenge, defy, provoke, taunt. **daring** ▷ BOLD.

dark *adj* 1 black, cheerless, cloudy, dim, dingy, dismal, drab, dreary, dull, dusky, funereal, gloomy, glowering, glum, grim, inky, moonless, murky, overcast, pitch-black, pitch-dark, shadowy, shady, sombre, starless, sullen, sunless, unlit. 2 *dark colours.* dense, heavy, strong. 3 *dark complexion.* black, brown, dark-skinned, dusky, swarthy, tanned. 4 ▷ HIDDEN, MYSTERIOUS. *Opp* LIGHT, PALE.

darken *v* 1 become overcast, cloud over. 2 blacken, dim, eclipse, obscure, overshadow, shade. *Opp* LIGHTEN.

darling *n* beloved, *inf* blue-eyed boy, dear, dearest, favourite, honey, love, loved one, pet, sweetheart, true love.

dart *n* arrow, bolt, missile, shaft.
• *v* bound, flit, fly, hurtle, leap, move suddenly, shoot, spring, streak, *inf* whiz, *inf* zip. ▷ DASH.

dash *n* race, run, rush, sprint, spurt.
• *v* 1 bolt, chase, dart, fly, hasten, hurry, move quickly, rush, speed, tear, zoom. 2 ▷ HIT.

dashing *adj* dapper, dynamic, elegant, lively, smart, spirited, stylish, vigorous.

data *pl n* details, facts, figures, information, statistics.

date *n* 1 day. ▷ TIME. 2 *date with a friend.* appointment, assignation, engagement, meeting, rendezvous. **out-of-date** ▷ OBSOLETE. **up-to-date** ▷ MODERN.

daunt *v* deter, discourage, dishearten, dismay, intimidate, overawe, put off, unnerve. ▷ FRIGHTEN. *Opp* ENCOURAGE.

dawdle *v* be slow, dally, delay, *inf* dilly-dally, hang about, idle, lag behind, linger, loaf about, loiter, *inf inf* take your time, trail behind. *Opp* HURRY.

dawn *n* daybreak, first light, sunrise. ▷ BEGINNING.

day *n* 1 daylight, daytime. 2 age, epoch, era, period, time.

daydream *n* fantasy, hope, illusion, meditation, reverie, vision, woolgathering.
• *v* dream, fantasize, imagine, meditate.

daze *v* paralyse, shock, stun, stupefy. ▷ AMAZE.

dazzle *v* blind, confuse, disorientate. **dazzling** ▷ BRILLIANT.

dead *adj* 1 deceased, *inf* done for, inanimate, inert, killed, late, lifeless, perished, rigid, stiff. *Opp* ALIVE. 2 *dead language.* died out, extinct, obsolete. 3 *dead with cold.* insensitive, numb, paralysed, without feeling. 4 *dead battery, engine.* burnt out, defunct, flat, inoperative, not working, out of order, unresponsive, used up, useless, worn out. 5 *dead party.* boring, dull, slow, uninteresting. *Opp* LIVELY. 6 *dead centre.* ▷ EXACT. **dead person** ▷ CORPSE. **dead to the world** ▷ ASLEEP.

deaden *v* 1 anaesthetize, desensitize, numb, paralyse. 2 blunt, cushion, damp, dampen, diminish, lessen, muffle, mute, quieten, reduce, smother, soften, stifle, suppress, weaken.

deadlock *n* impasse, stalemate, standstill, stop, stoppage, tie.

deadly *adj* dangerous, fatal, lethal, mortal, noxious, terminal. ▷ HARMFUL.

deafen *v* drown out, make deaf, overwhelm. **deafening** ▷ LOUD.

deal *n* 1 agreement, arrangement, bargain, contract, pact, understanding. 2 amount, quantity, volume.
• *v* 1 allot, dispense, distribute, divide, *inf* dole out, give out, share out. 2 *deal someone a blow.* administer, deliver, inflict, mete out. 3 *deal in stocks and shares.* buy and sell, do business, trade, traffic. **deal with** ▷ MANAGE, TREAT.

dealer *n* agent, broker, distributor, merchant, retailer, shopkeeper, trader, tradesman, vendor, wholesaler.

dear *adj* 1 adored, beloved, darling, intimate, loved, precious, treasured, valued. ▷ LOVABLE. *Opp* HATEFUL. 2 costly, exorbitant, expensive, high-priced, overpriced. *Opp* CHEAP.
• *n* ▷ DARLING.

death *n* 1 demise, dying, loss. ▷ END. 2 casualty, fatality. **put to death** ▷ EXECUTE.

debase *v* belittle, commercialize, degrade, demean, depreciate, devalue, diminish, reduce the value of, ruin, spoil, vulgarize.

debatable *adj* arguable, contentious, controversial, disputable, doubtful, dubious, open to question, problematic, questionable, uncertain, unsettled. *Opp* CERTAIN.

debate *n* argument, conference, consultation, controversy, deliberation, dialectic, discussion, disputation.
• *v* argue, consider, deliberate, discuss, dispute, mull over, question, reflect on, wrangle.

debit *v* subtract, take away. *Opp* CREDIT.

debris *n* bits, detritus, flotsam, fragments, litter, pieces, remains, rubbish, ruins, wreckage.

debt *n* account, arrears, bill, debit, dues, liability, obligation. **in debt** bankrupt, defaulting, insolvent. ▷ POOR.

decadent *adj* corrupt, debauched, declining, degenerate, immoral, self-indulgent. *Opp* MORAL.

decay *v* atrophy, break down, corrode, decompose, degenerate, deteriorate, disintegrate, dissolve, fester, go bad, mortify, moulder, oxidize, putrefy, rot, spoil, waste away, weaken, wither.

deceit *n* artifice, chicanery, craftiness, cunning, deceitfulness, dishonesty, dissimulation, duplicity, guile, hypocrisy, insincerity, lying, pretence, slyness, treachery, trickery, underhandedness, untruthfulness. ▷ DECEPTION. *Opp* HONESTY.

deceitful *adj* crafty, cunning, deceiving, deceptive, dishonest, double-dealing, duplicitous, false, fraudulent, furtive, insincere, lying, secretive, sneaky, treacherous, tricky, underhand, untrustworthy, wily. *Opp* HONEST.

deceive *v inf* bamboozle, beguile, betray, bluff, cheat, *inf* con, defraud, delude, *inf* double-cross, dupe, fool, *inf* fox, hoax, hoodwink, *inf* kid, *inf* lead on, lie, mislead, mystify, *inf* outsmart, outwit, swindle, *inf* take for a ride, take in, trick.

decelerate *v* brake, decrease speed, go slower, slow down. *Opp* ACCELERATE.

decent *adj* 1 appropriate, chaste, courteous, decorous, delicate, fitting, honourable, modest, polite, presentable, proper, respectable, seemly, sensitive, tasteful. *Opp* INDECENT. 2 agreeable, pleasant, satisfactory. ▷ GOOD. *Opp* BAD.

deception *n* charade, cheat, *inf* con, confidence trick, cover-up, *inf* fiddle, fraud, hoax, lie, pretence, ruse, sham, subterfuge, swindle, trick, wile. ▷ DECEIT.

deceptive *adj* ambiguous, deceiving, dishonest, equivocal, fallacious, false, fraudulent, illusory, insincere, lying, mendacious, misleading, specious, spurious, unreliable, wrong. *Opp* GENUINE.

decide *v* adjudicate, arbitrate, choose, conclude, determine, elect, judge, make up your mind, opt for, reach a decision, resolve, select, settle. **decided** ▷ DEFINITE.

decipher *v* disentangle, *inf* figure out, work out. ▷ DECODE.

decision *n* conclusion, decree, finding, judgement, outcome, ruling, verdict.

decisive *adj* 1 conclusive, convincing, crucial, final, positive, significant. 2 *decisive action.* certain, confident, definite, determined, firm, forceful, forthright, incisive, resolute, unhesitating. *Opp* TENTATIVE.

declaration *n* affirmation, announcement, assertion, avowal, confirmation, deposition, disclosure, edict, manifesto, proclamation, profession, pronouncement, protestation, statement, testimony.

declare *v* affirm, announce, assert, attest, avow, broadcast, certify, claim, confirm, contend, disclose, insist, maintain, make known, proclaim, profess, pronounce, protest, report, reveal, state, swear, testify.

decline *n* decrease, degeneration, deterioration, downturn, drop, fall, recession, reduction, slump.
• *v* 1 decrease, degenerate, deteriorate, die away, diminish, dwindle, ebb, fail, fall off, flag, lessen, peter out, reduce, slacken, subside, tail off, taper off, wane, weaken, wilt, worsen. *Opp* IMPROVE. 2 *decline an invitation.* abstain from, forgo, refuse, reject, *inf* turn down, veto. *Opp* ACCEPT.

decode *v* *inf* crack, decipher, explain, *inf* figure out, interpret, make out, read, solve, understand, unscramble.

decompose *v* break down, decay, disintegrate, *inf* go off, moulder, putrefy, rot.

decorate *v* 1 adorn, beautify, *old use* bedeck, colour, *inf* do up, embellish, embroider, festoon, garnish, ornament, paint, *derog* prettify, refurbish, renovate, smarten up, spruce up, trim, wallpaper. 2 give a medal to, honour, reward.

decoration *n* 1 adornment, elaboration, embellishment, finery, flourish, ornament, ornamentation, trimming. 2 award, badge, colours, medal, order, ribbon, star.

decorative *adj* elaborate, fancy, non-functional, ornamental, ornate. *Opp* FUNCTIONAL.

decorous *adj* appropriate, becoming, befitting, correct, dignified, genteel, polite, presentable, proper, refined, respectable, sedate, seemly, suitable, well-behaved. ▷ DECENT. *Opp* INDECOROUS.

decorum *n* decency, dignity, etiquette, good manners, gravity, modesty, politeness, propriety, protocol, respectability, seemliness.

decoy *n* bait, distraction, diversion, enticement, inducement, lure, red herring, trap.
• *v* bait, draw, entice, inveigle, lead, lure, seduce, tempt, trick.

decrease *n* abatement, contraction, curtailment, cut, decline, diminution, downturn, drop, dwindling, easing-off, ebb, fall, falling off, lessening, lowering, reduction, shrinkage, wane. *Opp* INCREASE.
• *v* 1 abate, cut, ease off, lower, reduce, turn down. 2 condense, contract, decline, die away, diminish, dwindle, lessen, peter out, shrink, slacken, subside, tail off, taper off, wane. *Opp* INCREASE.

decree *n* act, command, declaration, dictate, dictum, directive, edict, enactment, fiat, injunction, judgement, law, mandate, order, ordinance, proclamation, regulation, ruling, statute.
• *v* command, decide, declare, determine, dictate, direct, order, prescribe, proclaim, promulgate, pronounce, rule.

decrepit *adj* battered, broken down, derelict, dilapidated, feeble, frail, ramshackle, tumbledown, weak, worn out. ▷ OLD.

dedicate *v* 1 commit, consecrate, devote, give, pledge, sanctify. 2 *dedicate a book.* address, inscribe. **dedicated** ▷ KEEN, LOYAL.

dedication *n* 1 allegiance, commitment, devotion, enthusiasm, faithfulness, fidelity, loyalty, single-mindedness, zeal. 2 inscription, legend.

deduce *v* conclude, divine, draw the conclusion, extrapolate, glean, infer, *inf* reason, surmise, *sl* suss out, understand, work out.

deduct *v* subtract, take away. *Opp* ADD.

deduction *n* 1 allowance, decrease, diminution, discount, reduction, subtraction, withdrawal. 2 conclusion, finding, inference, reasoning.

deed *n* 1 accomplishment, achievement, act, adventure, effort, endeavour, enterprise, exploit, feat, stunt, undertaking. 2 ▷ DOCUMENT.

deep *adj* 1 profound, unfathomable, unplumbed, yawning. 2 *deep feelings.* earnest, extreme, genuine, heartfelt, intense, serious, sincere. 3 *deep in thought.* absorbed, concentrating, engrossed, immersed, preoccupied, rapt, thoughtful. 4 *deep matters.* esoteric, intellectual, learned, obscure, recondite. ▷ DIFFICULT. 5 *deep sleep.* heavy, sound. 6 *deep colour.* dark, rich, strong, vivid. 7 *deep sound.* bass, booming, growling, low-pitched, resonant, reverberating, sonorous. *Opp* SHALLOW, SUPERFICIAL.

deface *v* blemish, damage, disfigure, harm, impair, injure, mar, mutilate, ruin, spoil, vandalize.

defeat *n* beating, downfall, *inf* drubbing, failure, humiliation, *inf* licking, overthrow, rebuff, repulse, rout, set-back, subjugation, thrashing, trouncing. *Opp* VICTORY.
• *v* beat, be victorious over, check, *inf* clobber, confound, conquer, crush, destroy, *inf* flatten, foil, frustrate, get the better of, *sl* hammer, *inf* lick, master, outdo, outwit, overcome, overpower, overthrow, overwhelm, prevail over, put down, quell, repulse, rout, ruin, *inf* smash, stop, subdue, subjugate, suppress, *inf* thrash, thwart, triumph over, vanquish, whip. *Opp* LOSE. **be defeated** ▷ LOSE. **defeated** ▷ UNSUCCESSFUL.

defect *n* blemish, (*computing*) bug, deficiency, error, failing, fault, flaw, imperfection, irregularity, mark, mistake, shortcoming, shortfall, spot, stain, weakness, weak point.
• *v* change sides, desert, go over.

defective *adj* broken, deficient, faulty, flawed, imperfect, incomplete, *inf* on the blink, unsatisfactory. *Opp* PERFECT.

defence *n* 1 deterrence, guard, protection, safeguard, security, shelter, shield. ▷ BARRIER. 2 alibi, apology, case, excuse, explanation, justification, plea, testimony, vindication.

defenceless *adj* exposed, helpless, insecure, powerless, unguarded, unprotected, vulnerable, weak.

defend *v* 1 fight for, fortify, guard, keep safe, preserve, protect, safeguard, screen, shelter, shield, *inf* stick up for, watch over. 2 champion, justify, plead for, speak up for, stand up for, support, uphold, vindicate. *Opp* ATTACK.

defendant *n* accused, appellant, offender, prisoner.

defensive *adj* 1 protective, wary, watchful. 2 apologetic, faint-hearted. *Opp* AGGRESSIVE.

defer *v* 1 adjourn, delay, hold over, postpone, prorogue (*parliament*), put off, *inf* shelve, suspend. 2 ▷ YIELD.

deference *n* acquiescence, compliance, obedience, submission. ▷ RESPECT.

defiant *adj* antagonistic, belligerent, bold, brazen, challenging, daring, disobedient, headstrong, insolent, insubordinate, mutinous, obstinate, rebellious, recalcitrant, self-willed, stubborn, truculent, uncooperative, unruly, unyielding. *Opp* COOPERATIVE.

deficient *adj* defective, inadequate, insufficient, lacking, scanty, scarce, short, unsatisfactory, wanting, weak. *Opp* ADEQUATE, EXCESSIVE.

defile *v* contaminate, corrupt, degrade, desecrate, dirty, dishonour, foul, poison, pollute, soil, stain, sully, taint, tarnish.

define *v* 1 be the boundary of, bound, circumscribe, delineate, demarcate, describe, fix, limit, mark off, mark out, outline, specify. 2 *define a word.* explain, formulate, give the meaning of, interpret, spell out.

definite *adj* assured, categorical, certain, clear, clear-cut, confident, confirmed, cut and dried, decided, determined, distinct, emphatic, exact, explicit, fixed, incisive, marked, noticeable, obvious, particular, perceptible, positive, precise, pronounced, settled, specific, sure, unambiguous, unequivocal, unmistakable, well-defined. *Opp* VAGUE.

definitely *adv* beyond doubt, certainly, doubtless, for certain, indubitably, positively, surely, unquestionably, without doubt, without fail.

definition *n* 1 elucidation, explanation, interpretation. 2 clarity, clearness, focus, precision, sharpness.

definitive *adj* agreed, authoritative, complete, conclusive, correct, decisive, final, last (*word*), official, reliable, settled, standard, ultimate. *Opp* PROVISIONAL.

deflect *v* avert, deviate, divert, fend off, head off, intercept, parry, sidetrack, swerve, turn aside, veer, ward off.

deformed *adj* bent, buckled, contorted, crippled, crooked, disfigured, distorted, gnarled, grotesque, malformed, mangled, misshapen, mutilated, twisted, ugly, warped.

defraud *v inf* con, *inf* diddle, embezzle, fleece, rob, swindle. ▷ CHEAT.

deft *adj* adept, adroit, agile, clever, dexterous, expert, neat, *inf* nifty, nimble, proficient, quick, skilful. *Opp* CLUMSY.

defy *v* 1 challenge, confront, dare, disobey, rebel against, refuse to obey, resist, stand up to, withstand. 2 baffle, beat, elude, foil, frustrate, repel, repulse, resist, thwart, withstand.

degenerate *adj* ▷ CORRUPT.
• *v* become worse, decline, deteriorate, retrogress, sink, weaken, worsen. *Opp* IMPROVE.

degrade *v* 1 demote, depose, downgrade. 2 abase, brutalize, cheapen, corrupt, debase, dehumanize, deprave, desensitize, dishonour, humiliate. **degrading** ▷ SHAMEFUL.

degree *n* 1 calibre, class, grade, order, position, rank, standard, standing, station, status. 2 extent, intensity, level, measure.

deify *v* idolize, treat as a god, venerate, worship.

deign *v* concede, condescend, demean yourself, lower yourself, stoop.

deity *n* divinity, god, goddess, godhead, idol, immortal, spirit, supreme being.

dejected *adj* depressed, disconsolate, dispirited, downhearted, heavy-hearted, in low spirits. ▷ SAD.

delay *n* check, deferment, hiatus, hitch, hold-up, interruption, pause, postponement, set-back, stay (*of execution*), stoppage, wait.
• *v* 1 defer, detain, halt, hinder, hold up, impede, keep back, keep waiting, obstruct, postpone, put off, retard, set back, slow down, stay, stop, suspend. 2 be late, be slow, dally, dawdle, *inf* drag your feet, *inf* get bogged down, hang about, hang back, hang fire, hesitate, loiter, mark time, pause, *inf* play for time, procrastinate, stall, *old use* tarry, temporize, vacillate. *Opp* HURRY.

delegate *n* agent, ambassador, emissary, envoy, go-between, legate, messenger, representative, spokesperson.
• *v* appoint, assign, authorize, charge, commission, depute, entrust, mandate, nominate.

delegation *n* commission, deputation, mission.

delete *v* blot out, cancel, cross out, cut out, efface, eliminate, eradicate, erase, expunge, obliterate, remove, rub out, wipe out.

deliberate *adj* 1 arranged, calculated, cold-blooded, conscious, contrived, intentional, malicious, organized, planned, pre-arranged, preconceived, premeditated, prepared, purposeful, studied, thought out, wilful, worked out. 2 careful, cautious, circumspect, considered, diligent, measured, methodical, orderly, painstaking, regular, slow, thoughtful, unhurried. *Opp* HASTY, INSTINCTIVE.
• *v* ▷ THINK.

delicacy *n* accuracy, care, cleverness, daintiness, discrimination, exquisiteness, fineness, finesse, fragility, intricacy, precision, sensitivity, subtlety, tact.

delicate *adj* 1 dainty, easily broken, easily damaged, elegant, exquisite, fine, flimsy, fragile, frail, gauzy, gentle, feathery, intricate, light, sensitive, soft, tender. *Opp* TOUGH. 2 *delicate work*. accurate, careful, clever, deft, precise, skilled. *Opp* CLUMSY. 3 *delicate flavour*, *colour*. faint, muted, pale, slight, subtle. 4 *delicate health*. feeble, puny, sickly, squeamish, unhealthy, weak. 5 *delicate situation*. awkward, confidential, embarrassing, private, problematic, ticklish, touchy. 6 *delicate handling*. considerate, diplomatic, discreet, judicious, prudent, sensitive, tactful. *Opp* CRUDE.

delicious *adj* appetizing, choice, delectable, enjoyable, luscious, *inf* mouth-watering, savoury, *inf* scrumptious, succulent, tasty, tempting, *sl* yummy.

delight *n* bliss, delectation, ecstasy, enchantment, enjoyment, felicity, gratification, happiness, joy, pleasure, rapture, satisfaction.
• *v* amuse, bewitch, captivate, charm, cheer, enchant, entertain, enthral, entrance, fascinate, gladden, gratify, please, thrill, transport. *Opp* DISMAY. **delighted** ▷ HAPPY, PLEASED.

delightful *adj* agreeable, attractive, captivating, charming, congenial, delectable, enjoyable, *inf* nice, pleasant, pleasing, pleasurable, rewarding, satisfying. ▷ BEAUTIFUL.

delinquent *n* culprit, hooligan, lawbreaker, malefactor, miscreant, offender, roughneck, ruffian, *inf* tearaway, vandal, wrongdoer.

delirious *adj inf* beside yourself, crazy,

demented, distracted, ecstatic, excited, feverish, frantic, frenzied, hysterical, incoherent, light-headed, rambling, wild. ▷ DRUNK, MAD. *Opp* SANE, SOBER.

deliver *v* 1 bear, bring, carry, convey, distribute, give out, hand over, present, purvey, supply, surrender, take round, transfer, transport, turn over. 2 *deliver a lecture.* broadcast, express, give, make, read. ▷ SPEAK. 3 *deliver a blow.* administer, aim, deal, direct, fire, inflict, launch, strike, throw. ▷ HIT. 4 ▷ RESCUE.

delivery *n* 1 dispatch, distribution, shipment, transmission, transportation. 2 *delivery of goods.* batch, consignment. 3 *delivery of a speech.* execution, performance, presentation. 4 childbirth, confinement, parturition.

deluge *n* downpour, flood, inundation, rainfall, rainstorm, spate.
• *v* drown, engulf, flood, inundate, overwhelm, submerge, swamp.

delusion *n* dream, fantasy, hallucination, illusion, mirage, misconception, self-deception.

delve *v* burrow, dig, explore, investigate, probe, search.

demand *n old use* behest, claim, command, desire, expectation, importunity, need, order, request, requirement, requisition, want.
• *v* call for, claim, cry out for, exact, insist on, order, request, require, requisition. ▷ ASK. **demanding** ▷ DIFFICULT, IMPORTUNATE. **in demand** ▷ POPULAR.

demean *v* cheapen, debase, degrade, disgrace, humble, humiliate, lower, make (yourself) cheap, sacrifice (your) pride, undervalue. **demeaning** ▷ SHAMEFUL.

democratic *adj* 1 classless, egalitarian. 2 chosen, elected, popular, representative. *Opp* TOTALITARIAN.

demolish *v* bulldoze, dismantle, flatten, knock down, level, raze, tear down, wreck. ▷ DESTROY. *Opp* BUILD.

demon *n* devil, evil spirit, fiend, goblin, imp, spirit.

demonstrable *adj* conclusive, confirmable, evident, incontrovertible, indisputable, irrefutable, palpable, provable, undeniable, unquestionable, verifiable.

demonstrate *v* 1 display, embody, establish, evince, exemplify, exhibit, explain, express, illustrate, indicate, manifest, prove, represent, show, substantiate, teach, typify, verify. 2 lobby, march, parade, picket, protest, rally.

demonstration *n* 1 confirmation, display, exhibition, experiment, expression, illustration, indication, manifestation, presentation, proof, representation, substantiation, test, verification. 2 *inf* demo, march, parade, picket, protest, rally, sit-in, vigil.

demonstrative *adj* affectionate, effusive, emotional, fulsome, loving, open, uninhibited, unreserved. *Opp* RETICENT.

demote *v* downgrade, reduce, relegate. *Opp* PROMOTE.

demure *adj* bashful, coy, diffident, modest, prim, reserved, reticent, sedate, shy, sober, staid. *Opp* CONCEITED.

den *n* hideaway, *inf* hideout, hiding-place, lair, retreat, sanctuary, secret place, shelter.

denial *n* abnegation, disavowal, disclaimer, negation, refutation, rejection, renunciation, repudiation, veto. *Opp* ADMISSION.

denigrate *v* belittle, blacken the reputation of, criticize, decry, disparage, impugn, malign, *inf* put down, *inf* run down, sneer at, *inf* turn your nose up, vilify. ▷ DESPISE. *Opp* PRAISE.

denomination *n* 1 category, classification, designation, kind, size, sort, species, type, value. 2 church, communion, creed, cult, persuasion, schism, sect.

denote *v* be the sign for, designate, express, indicate, represent, signify, stand for, symbolize.

denouement *n* climax, *inf* pay-off, resolution, solution, *inf* sorting out, *inf* tidying up. ▷ END.

denounce *v* accuse, attack verbally, betray, blame, censure, complain about, condemn, criticize, declaim against, decry, *inf* hold forth against, impugn, incriminate, inform against, pillory, report, reveal, stigmatize, vilify, vituperate. *Opp* PRAISE.

dense *adj* 1 close, compact, concentrated, heavy, impassable, impenetrable, *inf* jam-packed, packed, solid, thick, tight. *Opp* THIN. 2 ▷ STUPID.

dent *n* concavity, depression, dimple, dint, hollow, indentation.
• *v* bend, crumple, knock in.

denude *v* defoliate, deforest, expose, remove, strip, unclothe, uncover. *Opp* CLOTHE.

deny *v* 1 contradict, disagree with, disclaim, disown, dispute, gainsay, negate, refute, reject, repudiate. *Opp* AGREE.

2 begrudge, deprive of, disallow, refuse, withhold. *Opp* GRANT. **deny yourself** ▷ ABSTAIN.

depart *v* 1 abscond, *inf* clear off, decamp, disappear, embark, exit, go away, *sl* hit the road, leave, make off, *inf* make tracks, *inf* make yourself scarce, migrate, move away, move off, *inf* push off, quit, retreat, run away, run off, *sl* scarper, *sl* scram, set off, set out, start, take your leave, vanish, withdraw. 2 ▷ DEVIATE. **departed** ▷ DEAD.

department *n* 1 branch, division, office, section, sector, subdivision, unit. 2 [*inf*] *not my department.* area, concern, field, function, job, line, province, responsibility, specialism, sphere.

departure *n* disappearance, embarkation, exit, exodus, going, retirement, withdrawal. *Opp* ARRIVAL.

depend *v* 1 **depend on** *inf* bank on, count on, hinge on, need, put your faith in, *inf* reckon on, rely on, trust. 2 hang, dangle.

dependable *adj* conscientious, consistent, faithful, honest, regular, reliable, safe, steady, true, trustworthy, unfailing. *Opp* UNRELIABLE.

dependence *n* 1 need, reliance, trust. 2 ▷ ADDICTION.

dependent *adj* **dependent on** 1 conditional on, determined by, subject to, vulnerable to. *Opp* INDEPENDENT. 2 *dependent on drugs.* addicted to, *inf* hooked on, reliant on.

depict *v* describe, draw, illustrate, narrate, outline, paint, picture, portray, represent, reproduce, show.

deplete *v* consume, cut, decrease, drain, reduce, use up. *Opp* INCREASE.

deplorable *adj* awful, discreditable, disgraceful, disreputable, dreadful, execrable, lamentable, regrettable, reprehensible, scandalous, shameful, shocking, unfortunate. ▷ BAD. *Opp* COMMENDABLE.

deplore *v* 1 lament, mourn, regret. 2 ▷ CONDEMN.

deploy *v* arrange, distribute, manage, position, use systematically, utilize.

deport *v* banish, exile, expatriate, expel, send abroad, transport.

depose *v* demote, dethrone, displace, get rid of, oust, remove, *inf* topple.

deposit *n* 1 advance payment, down-payment, initial payment, part-payment, retainer, security. 2 accumulation, dregs, layer, precipitate, sediment, silt, sludge.
• *v* 1 drop, *inf* dump, leave, *inf* place, put down, set down. 2 *deposit money.* bank, pay in, save.

depot *n* 1 arsenal, cache, depository, dump, store, storehouse. 2 *bus depot.* garage, headquarters, station, terminus.

deprave *v* brutalize, corrupt, debase, degrade. **depraved** ▷ CORRUPT.

depreciate *v* become less, decrease, deflate, drop, fall, lessen, reduce, slump, weaken. *Opp* APPRECIATE.

depress *v* 1 burden, discourage, dishearten, dismay, dispirit, enervate, lower the spirits of, oppress, sadden, tire, upset, weary. *Opp* CHEER. 2 *depress the market.* bring down, deflate, make less active, push down, weaken. *Opp* BOOST. **depressed, depressing** ▷ SAD.

depression *n* 1 *inf* blues, dejection, desolation, despair, despondency, gloom, glumness, hopelessness, low spirits, melancholy, misery, pessimism, sadness, weariness. *Opp* HAPPINESS. 2 cavity, concavity, dent, dimple, dip, excavation, hole, hollow, indentation, recess, sunken area. *Opp* BUMP. 3 *economic depression.* decline, hard times, recession, slump. *Opp* BOOM, HIGH.

deprive *v* **deprive of** deny, prevent from using, refuse, starve of, strip of, take away, withdraw, withhold. **deprived** ▷ POOR.

deputize *v* **deputize for** act as stand-in for, cover for, do the job of, replace, represent, stand in for, substitute for, take over from, understudy.

deputy *n* agent, assistant, delegate, emissary, *inf* locum, proxy, relief, replacement, representative, reserve, second-in-command, stand-in, substitute, supply, surrogate, understudy, vice-president.

derelict *adj* abandoned, broken down, decrepit, deserted, desolate, dilapidated, forsaken, neglected, overgrown, ruined, run-down, tumbledown, uncared-for, untended.

derivation *n* ancestry, descent, etymology, extraction, origin. ▷ BEGINNING.

derive *v* draw, extract, gain, gather, get, glean, *inf* lift, obtain, pick up, procure, receive, secure, take. **be derived** ▷ ORIGINATE.

descend *v* 1 climb down, come down, drop, fall, move down, plummet, plunge, sink. 2 dip, incline, slant, slope. 3 alight, dismount, get down, get off. *Opp* ASCEND. **be descended** ▷ ORIGINATE. **descend on** ▷ ATTACK.

descendant *n* child, heir, scion, successor. *Opp* ANCESTOR. **descendants** family, issue, line, lineage, offspring, progeny.

descent *n* 1 declivity, dip, drop, fall, incline, slant, slope, way down. *Opp* ASCENT. 2 *aristocratic descent.* ancestry, extraction, family, genealogy, heredity, lineage, parentage, pedigree, stock. ▷ ORIGIN.

describe *v* 1 characterize, define, delineate, depict, detail, explain, give an account of, narrate, outline, portray, present, recount, relate, report, represent, sketch, speak of. 2 *describe a circle.* draw, mark out, trace.

description *n* account, characterization, commentary, definition, delineation, depiction, explanation, narration, outline, portrait, report, representation, sketch, story.

descriptive *adj* detailed, explanatory, expressive, graphic, illustrative, vivid.

desecrate *v* contaminate, corrupt, debase, defile, degrade, dishonour, pervert, pollute, profane, treat disrespectfully, treat irreverently, vandalize, violate. *Opp* REVERE.

desert *adj* arid, barren, desolate, infertile, isolated, lonely, sterile, uncultivated, uninhabited, waterless. *Opp* FERTILE.
• *n* dust bowl, wasteland, wilderness.
• *v* 1 abandon, betray, forsake, jilt, *inf* leave in the lurch, maroon, renounce, strand, vacate, *inf* walk out on, *inf* wash your hands of. 2 abscond, defect, go absent, run away. **deserted** ▷ EMPTY, LONELY.

deserter *n* absconder, betrayer, defector, escapee, fugitive, outlaw, renegade, runaway, traitor, truant, turncoat.

deserve *v* be worthy of, earn, justify, merit, rate, warrant. **deserving** ▷ WORTHY.

design *n* 1 blueprint, conception, drawing, model, pattern, plan, proposal, prototype, sketch. 2 style, type, version. 3 arrangement, composition, configuration, form, pattern, shape. 4 aim, goal, intention, objective, purpose.
• *v* conceive, construct, create, devise, draft, draw, draw up, fashion, form, intend, invent, lay out, make, originate, plan, plot, project, propose, shape. **designing** ▷ CRAFTY. **have designs** ▷ PLOT.

designer *n* architect, artist, creator, inventor, originator.

desire *n* 1 ambition, appetite, craving, fancy, hankering, hunger, longing, urge, want, wish, yearning, *inf* yen. 2 covetousness, cupidity, greed. 3 *sexual desire.* ardour, libido, love, lust, passion.
• *v* ache for, ask for, covet, crave, dream of, fancy, *inf* have a yen for, hope for, hunger for, itch for, long for, lust after, need, pursue, *inf* set your heart on, want, wish for, yearn for.

desolate *adj* 1 abandoned, bare, barren, bleak, cheerless, deserted, dismal, dreary, empty, forsaken, gloomy, godforsaken, inhospitable, isolated, lonely, remote, uninhabited, wild. 2 bereft, dejected, depressed, despairing, disconsolate, forlorn, forsaken, inconsolable, lonely, melancholy, miserable, neglected, solitary, wretched. ▷ SAD. *Opp* CHEERFUL.

despair *n* anguish, depression, desperation, despondency, hopelessness, pessimism, resignation, wretchedness. ▷ MISERY.
• *v* give in, give up, lose heart, lose hope. *Opp* HOPE.

desperate *adj* 1 *inf* at your wits' end, beyond hope, despairing, wretched. 2 *desperate situation.* acute, critical, dangerous, grave, hopeless, irretrievable, pressing, serious, severe, urgent. 3 *desperate criminals.* dangerous, impetuous, rash, reckless, violent, wild. 4 ▷ ANXIOUS.

despise *v* be contemptuous of, condemn, deride, disapprove of, disdain, feel contempt for, hate, look down on, scorn, spurn, undervalue. ▷ DENIGRATE. *Opp* ADMIRE.

despondent *adj* dejected, depressed, disheartened, downcast, *inf* down in the mouth, melancholy, morose, pessimistic, sorrowful. ▷ MISERABLE.

despotic *adj* ▷ DICTATORIAL. *Opp* DEMOCRATIC.

destination *n* goal, objective, purpose, target.

destined *adj* 1 inescapable, inevitable, intended, ordained, predetermined, unavoidable. 2 *destined to fail.* bound, certain, doomed.

destiny *n* doom, fate, fortune, karma, kismet, luck, providence.

destitute *adj* deprived, down-and-out, homeless, impecunious, impoverished, penniless, poverty-stricken. ▷ POOR. *Opp* WEALTHY.

destroy *v* annihilate, blast, break down, burst, *inf* bust, crush, decimate, demolish, devastate, devour, dismantle, eliminate, eradicate, erase, exterminate, extinguish, flatten, get rid of, knock down, lay waste, level, liquidate, nullify, pull down, pulverize, raze, ruin, sabotage, scuttle, shatter, smash, stamp out, uproot, vaporize, wipe out, wreck, write off. ▷ DEFEAT, END, KILL. *Opp* CONSERVE, CREATE.

destruction *n* annihilation, decimation, demolition, depredation, devastation, elimination, eradication, extermination, extinction, liquidation, overthrow, ruin, ruination, shattering, smashing, undoing, uprooting, wiping out, wrecking. ▷ KILLING. *Opp* CONSERVATION, CREATION.

destructive *adj* adverse, antagonistic, baleful, catastrophic, damaging, dangerous, deadly, deleterious, detrimental, devastating, disastrous, fatal, harmful, injurious, lethal, malignant, negative, pernicious, pestilential, ruinous, violent. *Opp* CONSTRUCTIVE.

detach *v* cut loose, cut off, disconnect, disengage, disentangle, free, isolate, pull off, release, remove, separate, sever, take off, tear off, uncouple, undo, unfasten, unfix, unhitch. *Opp* ATTACH. **detached** ▷ ALOOF, IMPARTIAL, SEPARATE.

detail *n* aspect, complexity, complication, component, element, fact, factor, feature, intricacy, item, *pl* minutiae, nicety, particular, point, refinement, specific, technicality.

detailed *adj inf* blow-by-blow, complete, complex, comprehensive, descriptive, exact, exhaustive, full, *derog* fussy, *derog* hair-splitting, intricate, itemized, minute, specific. *Opp* GENERAL.

detain *v* 1 arrest, capture, confine, hold, imprison, intern. 2 delay, hinder, hold up, impede, keep, keep waiting, restrain, slow, waylay.

detect *v* ascertain, become aware of, diagnose, discern, discover, expose, feel, *inf* ferret out, find, identify, locate, note, observe, perceive, recognize, reveal, scent, see, sense, sniff out, spot, spy, taste, track down, uncover, unearth.

detective *n* investigator, police officer, *inf* private eye, sleuth.

detention *n* captivity, confinement, custody, imprisonment, incarceration, internment.

deter *v* check, daunt, discourage, dismay, dissuade, hinder, impede, intimidate, obstruct, prevent, put off, repel, *inf* turn off, warn off. *Opp* ENCOURAGE.

deteriorate *v* decay, decline, degenerate, depreciate, disintegrate, fall off, get worse, *inf* go downhill, slip, weaken, worsen. *Opp* IMPROVE.

determination *n* backbone, commitment, courage, dedication, doggedness, firmness, fortitude, *inf* grit, *inf* guts, perseverance, persistence, resoluteness, resolve, single-mindedness, spirit, steadfastness, *derog* stubbornness, tenacity, will-power.

determine *v* 1 conclude, decide, establish, find out, identify, judge, settle. 2 choose, decide on, resolve, select. 3 *What determined your choice?* affect, dictate, govern, influence, regulate.

determined *adj* adamant, assertive, certain, convinced, decided, decisive, definite, dogged, firm, insistent, intent, *derog* obstinate, persistent, purposeful, resolute, single-minded, steadfast, strong-minded, strong-willed, *derog* stubborn, sure, tenacious, tough, unwavering. *Opp* IRRESOLUTE.

deterrent *n* barrier, check, curb, discouragement, disincentive, hindrance, impediment, obstacle, restraint, threat, warning. *Opp* ENCOURAGEMENT.

detest *v* abhor, abominate, despise, execrate, loathe. ▷ HATE.

detour *n* deviation, diversion, indirect route. **make a detour** ▷ DEVIATE.

detract *v* **detract from** diminish, lessen, lower, reduce, take away from.

detrimental *adj* damaging, deleterious, disadvantageous, harmful, hurtful, injurious, prejudicial, unfavourable. *Opp* ADVANTAGEOUS.

devastate *v* 1 damage severely, demolish, destroy, flatten, lay waste, level, obliterate, ravage, raze, ruin, waste, wreck. 2 ▷ DISMAY.

develop *v* 1 advance, age, *inf* blow up, come into existence, evolve, grow, flourish, improve, mature, move on, progress, ripen. *Opp* REGRESS. 2 *develop habits.* acquire, contract, cultivate, evolve, foster, pick up. 3 *develop ideas.* amplify, augment, elaborate, enlarge on. 4 *develop a business.* branch out, build up, diversify, enlarge, expand, extend, increase.

development *n* 1 advancement, enlargement, evolution, expansion, extension, furtherance, growth, improvement, increase, progress, promotion, regeneration, reinforcement, spread. 2 incident, occurrence, outcome, result, upshot.

deviate *v* branch off, digress, diverge, divert, drift, go astray, go round, make a detour, stray, swerve, turn aside, turn off, veer, wander.

device *n* 1 apparatus, appliance, contraption, contrivance, gadget, implement, invention, machine, tool, utensil. 2 expedient, gambit, manoeuvre, plan, ploy, ruse, scheme, stratagem, tactic, trick. 3 *heraldic device.* badge, crest, design, logo, motif, symbol.

devil *n* demon, fiend, imp, spirit. **The Devil** Beelzebub, Lucifer, *inf* Old Nick, the Prince of Darkness, Satan.

devilish *adj* demoniac(al), demonic, diabolic(al), fiendish, impish, inhuman, satanic. ▷ EVIL. *Opp* ANGELIC.

devious *adj* 1 circuitous, crooked, indirect, periphrastic, round-about, sinuous, tortuous, winding. 2 [*derog*] calculating, cunning, deceitful, evasive, insincere, misleading, scheming, slippery, sly, sneaky, treacherous, underhand, wily. ▷ DISHONEST. *Opp* DIRECT.

devise *v* arrange, conceive, concoct, contrive, *inf* cook up, create, design, formulate, invent, make up, plan, plot, prepare, project, scheme, think up, work out.

devoted *adj* committed, dedicated, enthusiastic, faithful, loving, staunch, true, zealous. ▷ LOYAL. *Opp* DISLOYAL, HALF-HEARTED.

devotee *n inf* addict, aficionado, *inf* buff, enthusiast, fan, follower, supporter.

devotion *n* allegiance, attachment, commitment, dedication, *derog* fanaticism, fervour, loyalty, zeal. ▷ LOVE, PIETY.

devour *v* consume, demolish, eat up, engulf, swallow up, take in. ▷ DESTROY, EAT.

devout *adj* God-fearing, godly, holy, religious, sincere, spiritual. ▷ PIOUS. *Opp* IRRELIGIOUS.

dexterous *adj* adroit, agile, clever, deft, nimble, quick, skilful. *Opp* CLUMSY.

diabolical *adj* evil, fiendish, inhuman, satanic, wicked. ▷ DEVILISH. *Opp* SAINTLY.

diagnose *v* detect, determine, identify, isolate, name, recognize.

diagnosis *n* analysis, conclusion, explanation, identification, interpretation, verdict.

diagram *n* chart, drawing, figure, graph, illustration, outline, plan, representation, sketch, table.

dial *n* clock, digital display, face, instrument, speedometer.

dialect *n* accent, brogue, creole, idiom, language, patois, pronunciation, register, slang, tongue, vernacular.

dialogue *n inf* chat, *inf* chin-wag, communication, conversation, debate, discourse, discussion, exchange, interchange, intercourse, talk, *inf* tête-à-tête.

diary *n* appointment book, calendar, chronicle, engagement book, journal, log, record.

dictate *v* 1 read aloud, recite. 2 command, decree, enforce, give orders, impose, *inf* lay down the law, make the rules, order, prescribe.

dictator *n* autocrat, despot, tyrant. ▷ RULER.

dictatorial *adj* absolute, authoritarian, autocratic, *inf* bossy, despotic, dogmatic, dominant, domineering, imperious, intolerant, omnipotent, oppressive, overbearing, repressive, totalitarian, tyrannical, undemocratic. *Opp* DEMOCRATIC.

dictionary *n* glossary, lexicon, thesaurus, vocabulary.

didactic *adj* instructive, lecturing, pedagogic, pedantic.

die *v* 1 *inf* bite the dust, cease to exist, decease, depart, expire, *inf* give up the ghost, *sl* kick the bucket, pass away, *sl* peg out, perish, *sl* snuff it. 2 decline, decrease, die away, disappear, droop, dwindle, end, fade, fail, fizzle out, go out, languish, lessen, stop, subside, vanish, wane, weaken, wilt, wither.

diet *n* fare, food, intake, nourishment, nutriment, nutrition, sustenance.
• *v inf* cut down, fast, lose weight, ration yourself, reduce, slim.

differ *v* 1 be different, be distinct, contrast, deviate, diverge, vary. 2 argue, be at odds, be at variance, clash, conflict, contradict, disagree, dispute, dissent, fall out, quarrel. *Opp* AGREE.

difference *n* 1 alteration, change, comparison, contrast, deviation, dissimilarity, distinction, diversity, incompatibility, inconsistency, modification, variation, variety. *Opp* SIMILARITY. 2 argument, clash, conflict, controversy, debate, disagreement, dispute, dissent, quarrel, strife, tiff, wrangle. *Opp* AGREEMENT.

different *adj* 1 assorted, conflicting, contradictory, contrasting, discordant, disparate, dissimilar, divergent, diverse, heterogeneous, inconsistent, miscellaneous, mixed, multifarious, opposed, opposite, varied, various. *Opp* SIMILAR. 2 abnormal, anomalous, atypical, bizarre, distinct, distinctive, eccentric, extraordinary, fresh, individual, new, original, particular, peculiar, separate, singular, special, specific, strange, uncommon, unconventional, unique, unorthodox, unusual. *Opp* CONVENTIONAL.

differentiate *v* discriminate, distinguish.

difficult *adj* 1 baffling, complex, complicated, deep, enigmatic, hard, intractable, intricate, involved, *inf* knotty, obscure, perplexing, problematic, *inf* thorny, ticklish, tricky. 2 arduous, back-breaking, burdensome, challenging, daunting, demanding, exacting, formidable, gruelling, heavy, herculean, laborious, onerous, punishing, rigorous, severe, strenuous, taxing, tough. 3 *difficult children.* annoying, disruptive, fussy, headstrong, intractable, obstinate, obstreperous, tiresome, troublesome, trying, uncooperative, unfriendly, unhelpful, unresponsive, unruly. *Opp* COOPERATIVE, EASY.

difficulty *n* adversity, complication, dilemma, embarrassment, *inf* fix, hardship, hindrance, hurdle, impediment, *inf* jam, *inf* mess, obstacle, perplexity, *inf* pickle, plight, predicament, problem, puzzle, quandary, snag, *inf* spot, stumbling block, tribulation, trouble.

diffident *adj* backward, bashful, coy, distrustful, doubtful, fearful, hesitant, inhibited, insecure, introvert, meek, modest, nervous, private, reluctant, reserved, retiring, self-effacing, sheepish, shrinking, shy, tentative, timid, timorous, unadventurous, unassuming, unsure, withdrawn. *Opp* CONFIDENT.

diffuse *adj* discursive, long-winded, meandering, rambling, spread out, unstructured, vague, *inf* waffly, wandering. ▷ WORDY. *Opp* CONCISE.
• *v* ▷ SPREAD.

dig *v* 1 burrow, delve, excavate, gouge, hollow, mine, quarry, tunnel. 2 cultivate, fork over, till, trench, turn over. 3 jab, nudge, poke, prod, punch, shove. **dig out** ▷ FIND. **dig up** disinter, exhume.

digest *n* ▷ SUMMARY.
• *v* 1 absorb, assimilate, dissolve, process, utilize. ▷ EAT. 2 consider, ponder, study, take in, understand.

digit *n* 1 figure, integer, number, numeral. 2 finger, toe.

dignified *adj* august, calm, courtly, decorous, distinguished, elegant, exalted, formal, grave, imposing, impressive, lofty, lordly, majestic, noble, proper, refined, regal, sedate, serious, sober, solemn, stately. ▷ PROUD. *Opp* UNBECOMING.

dignitary *n* important person, luminary, official, *inf* VIP, worthy.

dignity *n* calmness, decorum, formality, grandeur, gravity, majesty, nobility, propriety, respectability, seriousness, sobriety, solemnity, stateliness.

digress *v* depart, deviate, diverge, drift, get off the subject, *inf* lose the thread, ramble, stray, veer, wander.

dilapidated *adj* broken down, crumbling, decayed, decrepit, derelict, falling down, in disrepair, in ruins, neglected, ramshackle, rickety, ruined, run-down, shaky, tumbledown, uncared-for.

dilemma *n inf* catch-22, deadlock, difficulty, *inf* fix, impasse, *inf* jam, *inf* pickle, plight, predicament, problem, quandary, stalemate.

diligent *adj* assiduous, busy, careful, conscientious, devoted, earnest, hardworking, indefatigable, industrious, meticulous, painstaking, persevering, persistent, punctilious, scrupulous, sedulous, studious, thorough, tireless. *Opp* LAZY.

dilute *v* adulterate, reduce the strength of, thin, water down, weaken. *Opp* CONCENTRATE.

dim *adj* 1 bleary, blurred, clouded, cloudy, dark, dull, faint, foggy, fuzzy, gloomy, grey, hazy, ill-defined, indistinct, misty, murky, nebulous, obscure, pale, shadowy, sombre, unclear, vague. 2 ▷ STUPID. *Opp* BRIGHT.
• *v* 1 blacken, cloud, darken, dull, obscure, shade, shroud. 2 become dim, fade, go out. *Opp* BRIGHTEN. **take a dim view** ▷ DISAPPROVE.

dimensions *pl n* capacity, extent, magnitude, measurements, proportions, scale, scope, size.

diminish *v* 1 abate, contract, decline, decrease, depreciate, die down, dwindle, ease off, ebb, fade, lessen, *inf* let up, peter out, recede, reduce, shrink, subside, wane, *inf* wind down. *Opp* INCREASE. 2 belittle, demean, deprecate, devalue, disparage, minimize, undervalue. *Opp* EXAGGERATE.

diminutive *adj* microscopic, miniature, minuscule, minute, tiny. ▷ SMALL.

din *n* clamour, clatter, commotion, crash, hubbub, hullabaloo, noise, outcry, pandemonium, racket, roar, *inf* row, *inf* rumpus, shouting, tumult, uproar.

dingy *adj* colourless, dark, depressing, dim, dirty, dismal, drab, dreary, dull, faded, gloomy, grimy, murky, old, seedy, shabby, soiled, worn. *Opp* BRIGHT.

dinner *n* banquet, feast. ▷ MEAL.

dip *n* 1 concavity, declivity, dent, depression, fall, hollow, incline, slope. 2 *dip in the sea.* bathe, dive, immersion, plunge, swim.
• *v* 1 decline, descend, dive, fall, go down, sag, sink, slope down, slump, subside. 2 douse, drop, duck, dunk, immerse, lower, plunge, submerge. **take a dip** ▷ BATHE.

diplomacy *n* delicacy, discretion, finesse, negotiation, skill, tact.

diplomat *n* ambassador, consul, negotiator, official, peacemaker, politician, statesman.

diplomatic *adj* careful, delicate, discreet, judicious, polite, politic, prudent, sensitive, subtle, tactful, understanding. *Opp* TACTLESS.

direct *adj* 1 non-stop, shortest, straight, undeviating, unswerving. 2 blunt, candid, clear, decided, explicit, forthright, frank, honest, open, outspoken, plain, sincere, straightforward, *derog* tactless, to the point, unambiguous, uncomplicated, *derog* undiplomatic, unequivocal, unreserved. 3 *direct experience.* empirical, first-hand, personal. 4 *direct opposites.* absolute, complete, diametrical, exact, out and out, utter. *Opp* INDIRECT.
• *v* 1 escort, guide, indicate the way, point, send, show the way, usher. 2 aim, focus, target. 3 administer, be in charge of, conduct, control, govern, handle, lead, manage, mastermind, oversee, regulate, rule, run, stage-manage, supervise, take charge of. 4 advise, bid, command, counsel, instruct, order, require, tell.

direction *n* aim, approach, (*compass*) bearing, course, orientation, path, road, route, tack, track, way. **directions** guidelines, instructions, orders, plans.

director *n* administrator, *inf* boss, governor, manager, organizer, president, principal. ▷ CHIEF.

directory *n* catalogue, index, list, register.

dirt *n* 1 dust, filth, grime, impurity, mess, mire, muck, ooze, pollution, smut, soot, stain. ▷ OBSCENITY, RUBBISH. 2 clay, earth, loam, mud, soil.

dirty *adj* 1 dingy, dusty, filthy, foul, grimy, grubby, marked, messy, mucky, muddy, smeary, smudged, soiled, sooty, sordid, squalid, stained, sullied, tarnished, travel-stained, unclean, unwashed. 2 *dirty water.* cloudy, contaminated, impure, muddy, murky, polluted, tainted, untreated. 3 *dirty tactics.* dishonest, dishonourable, illegal, *inf* low-down, mean, rough, treacherous, unfair, unscrupulous, unsporting. ▷ CORRUPT. 4 *dirty talk.* coarse, crude, improper, indecent, offensive, rude, smutty, vulgar. ▷ OBSCENE. *Opp* CLEAN.
• *v* foul, mark, *inf* mess up, smear, smudge, soil, spatter, spot, stain, streak, tarnish. ▷ DEFILE. *Opp* CLEAN.

disability *n* affliction, defect, disablement, handicap, impairment, incapacity, infirmity, weakness.

disable *v* cripple, damage, debilitate, enfeeble, *inf* hamstring, handicap, immobilize, impair, incapacitate, injure, lame, maim, paralyse, put out of action, weaken. **disabled** ▷ HANDICAPPED.

disadvantage *n* drawback, handicap, hardship, hindrance, impediment, inconvenience, liability, *inf* minus, nuisance, snag, trouble, weakness.

disagree *v* argue, bicker, conflict, contend, differ, dispute, dissent, fall out, fight, quarrel, squabble, wrangle. **disagree with** ▷ OPPOSE.

disagreeable *adj* distasteful, nasty, objectionable, offensive, sickening, unsavoury. ▷ UNPLEASANT. *Opp* PLEASANT.

disagreement *n* altercation, argument, clash, conflict, controversy, debate, difference, disharmony, dispute, dissension, dissent, divergence, incompatibility, inconsistency, misunderstanding, opposition, quarrel, squabble, strife, *inf* tiff, variance, wrangle. *Opp* AGREEMENT.

disappear *v* 1 become invisible, clear, disperse, dissolve, dwindle, ebb, evaporate, fade, melt away, recede, vanish, vaporize, wane. ▷ DIE. 2 escape, flee, fly, run away, walk away, withdraw. *Opp* APPEAR.

disappoint *v* disenchant, disillusion, dismay, displease, dissatisfy, fail to satisfy, *inf* let down, sadden, upset. ▷ FRUSTRATE. *Opp* SATISFY. **disappointed** disillusioned, frustrated, *inf* let down. ▷ SAD.

disapproval *n* censure, condemnation, criticism, disfavour, dislike, displeasure, dissatisfaction, hostility. *Opp* APPROVAL.

disapprove *v* **disapprove of** be displeased by, censure, condemn, criticize, denounce, deplore, deprecate, dislike, disparage, frown on, look askance at, make unwelcome, object to, reject, *inf* take a dim view of, take exception to. *Opp* APPROVE. **disapproving** ▷ CRITICAL.

disarm *v* 1 demilitarize, demobilize, make powerless, take weapons from. 2 charm, mollify, pacify, placate.

disaster *n* accident, blow, calamity,

cataclysm, catastrophe, crash, debacle, failure, fiasco, *inf* flop, misadventure, mischance, misfortune, mishap, reverse, tragedy, *inf* wash-out. *Opp* SUCCESS.

disastrous *adj* appalling, awful, calamitous, cataclysmic, catastrophic, devastating, dire, dreadful, fatal, ruinous, terrible, tragic. *Opp* SUCCESSFUL.

disbelieve *v* be sceptical of, discount, discredit, doubt, have no faith in, mistrust, reject, suspect. *Opp* BELIEVE. **disbelieving** ▷ INCREDULOUS.

disc *n* 1 circle, counter, token. 2 album, CD, LP, record, single. 3 [*computing*] CD-ROM, disk, diskette, floppy disk, hard disk.

discard *v* abandon, cast off, dispense with, dispose of, *inf* ditch, dump, get rid of, jettison, junk, reject, scrap, shed, throw away, toss out.

discern *v* be aware of, detect, discover, distinguish, make out, mark, notice, observe, perceive, recognize, spy. ▷ SEE. **discerning** ▷ PERCEPTIVE.

discernible *adj* detectable, distinguishable, measurable, perceptible. ▷ NOTICEABLE.

discharge *n* 1 release, dismissal. 2 emission, ooze, pus, secretion, suppuration. • *v* 1 belch, eject, emit, expel, exude, give off, pour out, produce, release, secrete, send out, spew, spit out. 2 *discharge guns.* detonate, explode, fire, let off, shoot. 3 *discharge employees.* dismiss, fire, make redundant, sack, throw out. 4 *discharge a prisoner.* absolve, acquit, clear, dismiss, excuse, exonerate, free, liberate, pardon, release. 5 *discharge duties.* accomplish, carry out, execute, fulfil, perform.

disciple *n* adherent, admirer, apostle, apprentice, devotee, follower, learner, pupil, scholar, student, supporter.

disciplinarian *n* authoritarian, autocrat, despot, dictator, *inf* hard taskmaster, *inf* slave-driver, tyrant.

discipline *n* 1 control, drill, indoctrination, instruction, management, training. 2 obedience, order, orderliness, routine, self-control, self-restraint. • *v* 1 coach, control, drill, educate, govern, indoctrinate, instruct, keep in check, manage, restrain, school, train. 2 castigate, chastise, correct, penalize, punish, rebuke, reprimand, reprove, scold. **disciplined** ▷ OBEDIENT.

disclaim *v* deny, disown, reject, renounce, repudiate. *Opp* ACKNOWLEDGE.

disclose *v* divulge, expose, let out, make known. ▷ REVEAL.

discolour *v* bleach, dirty, fade, mark, stain, tarnish, tinge.

discomfort *n* distress, inconvenience, irritation, soreness, uneasiness. ▷ PAIN. *Opp* COMFORT.

disconcert *v* agitate, bewilder, confuse, discomfit, distract, disturb, fluster, nonplus, perplex, puzzle, *inf* rattle, ruffle, throw off balance, trouble, unsettle, upset, worry. *Opp* REASSURE.

disconnect *v* break off, cut off, detach, disengage, divide, part, sever, switch off, turn off, undo, unhook, unplug. **disconnected** ▷ INCOHERENT.

discontented *adj* annoyed, disgruntled, displeased, dissatisfied, fed up, restless, sulky, unhappy, unsettled.

discord *n* 1 argument, conflict, difference of opinion, disagreement, disharmony, dispute, friction, strife. ▷ QUARREL. 2 [*music*] cacophony, jangle. ▷ NOISE. *Opp* HARMONY.

discordant *adj* 1 conflicting, contrary, differing, dissimilar, divergent, incompatible, inconsistent, opposed, opposite. 2 cacophonous, clashing, dissonant, grating, harsh, jangling, jarring, shrill, strident, tuneless, unmusical. *Opp* HARMONIOUS.

discount *n* concession, cut, deduction, *inf* mark-down, rebate, reduction. • *v* disbelieve, dismiss, disregard, ignore, overlook, reject.

discourage *v* 1 cow, damp, dampen, daunt, demoralize, depress, disenchant, dishearten, dismay, dispirit, frighten, inhibit, intimidate, overawe, *inf* put off, scare, *inf* throw cold water on, unnerve. 2 *discourage vandalism.* check, deter, dissuade, hinder, prevent, put an end to, repress, restrain, stop, suppress. *Opp* ENCOURAGE.

discouragement *n* constraint, *inf* damper, deterrent, disincentive, hindrance, impediment, obstacle, restraint. *Opp* ENCOURAGEMENT.

discourse *n* 1 ▷ CONVERSATION. 2 dissertation, essay, paper, thesis, treatise. • *v* ▷ SPEAK.

discover *v* ascertain, bring to light, come across, detect, dig up, disclose, expose, *inf* ferret out, find, hit on, identify, learn, locate, notice, observe, perceive, recognize, reveal, search out, spot, track down, turn up, uncover, unearth. ▷ INVENT. *Opp* HIDE.

discoverer *n* explorer, finder, initiator, inventor, originator, pioneer, traveller.

discovery *n* breakthrough, detection, disclosure, exploration, *inf* find, innovation, invention, revelation.

discredit *v* 1 defame, disgrace, dishonour, slander, slur, smear, vilify. 2 challenge, disbelieve, disprove, refuse to believe.

discreet *adj* careful, cautious, circumspect, considerate, delicate, diplomatic, guarded, judicious, low-key, muted, politic, prudent, restrained, sensitive, subdued, tactful, thoughtful, wary. *Opp* INDISCREET.

discrepancy *n* conflict, difference, disparity, dissimilarity, divergence, incompatibility, incongruity, inconsistency, variance. *Opp* SIMILARITY.

discretion *n* circumspection, diplomacy, good sense, judgement, maturity, prudence, responsibility, sensitivity, tact, wisdom. *Opp* TACTLESSNESS.

discriminate *v* 1 differentiate, distinguish, draw a distinction, separate, tell apart. 2 be biased, be prejudiced. **discriminating** ▷ PERCEPTIVE.

discrimination *n* 1 discernment, good taste, insight, judgement, perceptiveness, refinement, subtlety, taste. 2 [*derog*] bias, bigotry, chauvinism, favouritism, prejudice, racism, sexism, unfairness. *Opp* IMPARTIALITY.

discuss *v* confer about, consider, consult, debate, deliberate, examine, talk about, *inf* weigh up the pros and cons of.

discussion *n* argument, colloquy, conference, consideration, consultation, debate, deliberation, dialogue, discourse, examination, exchange of views, symposium. ▷ TALK.

disdainful *adj* contemptuous, mocking, scornful, supercilious, superior. ▷ PROUD.

disease *n* affliction, ailment, *inf* bug, complaint, contagion, disorder, infection, infirmity, malady, sickness. ▷ ILLNESS.

diseased *adj* ailing, infirm, sick, unwell. ▷ ILL.

disembark *v* alight, get off, go ashore, land. *Opp* EMBARK.

disfigure *v* blemish, damage, deface, deform, distort, impair, injure, make ugly, mar, mutilate, ruin, scar, spoil. *Opp* BEAUTIFY.

disgrace *n* 1 degradation, discredit, dishonour, disrepute, embarrassment, humiliation, ignominy, opprobrium, scandal, shame, slur, stain, stigma. 2 ▷ OUTRAGE.

disgraceful *adj* contemptible, degrading, dishonourable, embarrassing, humiliating, ignominious, shameful, shaming, wicked. ▷ BAD.

disgruntled *adj* annoyed, cross, disaffected, disappointed, discontented, dissatisfied, fed up, grumpy, moody, sulky, sullen. ▷ BAD-TEMPERED.

disguise *n* camouflage, costume, cover, front, *inf* get-up, impersonation, mask, pretence, smokescreen.
• *v* camouflage, conceal, cover up, dress up, falsify, gloss over, hide, make inconspicuous, mask, misrepresent, screen, shroud, veil. **disguise yourself as** ▷ IMPERSONATE.

disgust *n* abhorrence, aversion, contempt, detestation, dislike, distaste, hatred, loathing, nausea, outrage, repugnance, revulsion, sickness.
• *v* appal, be distasteful to, horrify, nauseate, offend, outrage, repel, revolt, sicken, shock, *inf* turn your stomach. *Opp* PLEASE. **disgusting** ▷ HATEFUL.

dish *n* 1 basin, bowl, casserole, container, plate, platter, tureen. 2 entrée, food, item on the menu, recipe. **dish out** ▷ DISTRIBUTE. **dish up** ▷ SERVE.

dishearten *v* depress, deter, discourage, dismay, put off, sadden. *Opp* ENCOURAGE. **disheartened** ▷ SAD.

dishevelled *adj* bedraggled, disordered, messy, ruffled, rumpled, *inf* scruffy, slovenly, tangled, tousled, uncombed, unkempt, untidy. *Opp* NEAT.

dishonest *adj inf* bent, cheating, corrupt, criminal, *inf* crooked, deceitful, deceptive, devious, dishonourable, disreputable, false, fraudulent, hypocritical, immoral, insincere, lying, mendacious, misleading, perfidious, *inf* shady, slippery, swindling, thieving, treacherous, *inf* two-faced, *inf* underhand, unprincipled, unscrupulous, untrustworthy, untruthful. *Opp* HONEST.

dishonour *n* blot, degradation, discredit, disgrace, humiliation, ignominy, indignity, loss of face, opprobrium, reproach, scandal, shame, slander, slur, stain, stigma. *Opp* HONOUR.
• *v* abuse, debase, defile, degrade, disgrace, profane, shame, slight.

dishonourable *adj* base, despicable, discreditable, disgraceful, dishonest, disloyal, disreputable, ignoble, ignominious, improper, infamous, mean, outrageous, perfidious, reprehensible, scandalous, shabby, shameful, shameless, treacherous, unchivalrous, unscrupulous, unworthy. ▷ CORRUPT. *Opp* HONOURABLE.

disillusion *v* disabuse, disappoint, disenchant, enlighten.

disinfect *v* chlorinate, clean, cleanse, decontaminate, fumigate, purify, sanitize, sterilize.

disinfectant *n* antiseptic, decontaminant, germicide.

disinherit *v* cut off, cut out of a will, deprive someone of their inheritance.

disintegrate *v* break up, come apart, crack up, crumble, decay, decompose, deteriorate, fall apart, rot, shatter, smash, splinter.

disinterested *adj* detached, dispassionate, impartial, impersonal, neutral, objective, unbiased, uninvolved, unprejudiced. *Opp* BIASED.

disjointed *adj* confused, disconnected, dislocated, disordered, incoherent, jumbled, mixed up, muddled, rambling, uncoordinated, wandering. *Opp* COHERENT.

dislike *n* antagonism, antipathy, aversion, detestation, disapproval, disgust, distaste, hatred, hostility, ill will, loathing, repugnance, revulsion.
• *v* despise, detest, disapprove of, scorn, *inf* take against. ▷ HATE. *Opp* LOVE.

dislocate *v* disengage, disjoint, displace, put out of joint.

disloyal *adj* faithless, false, insincere, perfidious, renegade, seditious, subversive, treacherous, *inf* two-faced, unfaithful, unreliable, untrustworthy. *Opp* LOYAL.

disloyalty *n* betrayal, double-dealing, duplicity, inconstancy, infidelity, perfidy, treachery, treason, unfaithfulness. *Opp* LOYALTY.

dismal *adj* bleak, cheerless, depressing, dreary, dull, funereal, gloomy, grey, grim, miserable, sombre, wretched. ▷ SAD.

dismantle *v* demolish, strip down, take apart, take down. *Opp* ASSEMBLE.

dismay *n* agitation, alarm, anxiety, apprehension, consternation, disappointment, distress, dread, gloom, horror, surprise. ▷ FEAR.
• *v* alarm, appal, daunt, depress, devastate, disappoint, discourage, dishearten, dispirit, distress, shock, take aback, unnerve. ▷ FRIGHTEN. *Opp* PLEASE.

dismiss *v* 1 disband, free, let go, *inf* pack off, release, send away. 2 belittle, brush aside, discount, disregard, drop, give up, reject, repudiate, set aside, shrug off, wave aside. 3 *dismiss a worker.* discharge, *inf* fire, get rid of, give notice to, *inf* give someone their cards, give the push to, lay off, make redundant, sack.

disobedient *adj* anarchic, contrary, defiant, disorderly, disruptive, headstrong, insubordinate, intractable, mutinous, obstinate, obstreperous, perverse, rebellious, recalcitrant, refractory, riotous, self-willed, uncontrollable, undisciplined, unmanageable, unruly, wayward, wild, wilful. ▷ NAUGHTY. *Opp* OBEDIENT.

disobey *v* 1 be disobedient, mutiny, protest, rebel, revolt, rise up. 2 break, contravene, defy, disregard, flout, ignore, infringe, oppose, transgress, violate. *Opp* OBEY.

disorder *n* 1 anarchy, chaos, confusion, disarray, disorganization, disturbance, fighting, fracas, fuss, jumble, lawlessness, mess, muddle, *inf* shambles, tangle, untidiness, uproar. ▷ COMMOTION. *Opp* ORDER. 2 ▷ ILLNESS.

disorderly *adj* ▷ DISOBEDIENT, DISORGANIZED.

disorganized *adj* aimless, careless, chaaoic, confused, disorderly, haphazard, jumbled, messy, muddled, rambling, scatterbrained, slapdash, slipshod, *inf* sloppy, slovenly, unplanned, unstructured, unsystematic, untidy. *Opp* SYSTEMATIC.

disown *v* disclaim knowledge of, renounce, repudiate.

disparage *v* belittle, demean, discredit, insult, *inf* put down, slight, undervalue. ▷ CRITICIZE. **disparaging** ▷ UNCOMPLIMENTARY.

dispassionate *adj* calm, composed, cool, equable, even-tempered, level-headed, sober. ▷ IMPARTIAL, UNEMOTIONAL. *Opp* EMOTIONAL.

dispatch *n* bulletin, communiqué, letter, message, report.
• *v* 1 consign, convey, forward, mail, post, send, ship. 2 ▷ KILL.

dispense *v* 1 allocate, allot, apportion, assign, distribute, *inf* dole out, give out, issue, measure out, provide, ration out, share. 2 *dispense medicine.* make up, prepare, supply. **dispense with** ▷ OMIT, REMOVE.

disperse *v* 1 break up, disband, dismiss, dispel, dissipate, drive away, send in different directions, separate, spread. *Opp* GATHER. 2 disappear, dissolve, melt away, scatter, spread out, vanish.

displace *v* 1 disarrange, dislocate, dislodge, disturb, move, put out of place, shift. 2 crowd out, depose, oust, replace, succeed, supersede, supplant, take the place of, unseat, usurp.

display *n* 1 array, demonstration, exhibition, manifestation, pageant, parade, presentation, show, spectacle. 2 ceremony, ostentation, pageantry, pomp.
• *v* advertise, air, demonstrate, disclose, exhibit, expose, flaunt, flourish, give evidence of, parade, present, produce, put on show, reveal, show, show off, unfold, unfurl, unveil, vaunt. *Opp* HIDE.

displease *v* anger, offend, put out, upset. ▷ ANNOY.

disposable *adj* 1 available, usable. 2 expendable, non-returnable, replaceable, *inf* throwaway.

dispose *v* distribute, place, position. ▷ ARRANGE. **disposed** ▷ LIABLE. **dispose of** ▷ DESTROY, DISCARD.

disproportionate *adj* excessive, incongruous, inordinate, out of proportion, unbalanced, uneven, unreasonable. *Opp* PROPORTIONAL.

disprove *v* confute, contradict, discredit, *inf* explode, invalidate, negate, rebut, refute, show to be wrong. *Opp* PROVE.

dispute *n* ▷ QUARREL.
• *v* argue against, challenge, contest, contradict, deny, disagree with, doubt, gainsay, impugn, object to, oppose, *inf* pick holes in, quarrel with, query, question, raise doubts about. ▷ DEBATE. *Opp* ACCEPT.

disqualify *v* debar, declare ineligible, exclude, preclude, prohibit, reject.

disregard *v* brush aside, discount, dismiss, disobey, *inf* fly in the face of, forget, ignore, leave out, *inf* make light of, miss out, neglect, omit, overlook, pass over, pay no attention to, reject, shrug off, skip, *inf* turn a blind eye to. *Opp* HEED.

disreputable *adj* dishonest, dishonourable, *inf* dodgy, dubious, infamous, questionable, *inf* shady, suspect, suspicious, untrustworthy. *Opp* REPUTABLE.

disrespectful *adj* bad-mannered, discourteous, disparaging, impolite, impudent, inconsiderate, insolent, insulting, irreverent, mocking, scornful, uncivil. ▷ RUDE. *Opp* RESPECTFUL.

disrupt *v* break up, dislocate, disorder, disturb, interfere with, interrupt, intrude on, spoil, throw into disorder, unsettle, upset.

dissatisfaction *n* annoyance, chagrin, disappointment, discontentment, dismay, displeasure, disquiet, exasperation, frustration, irritation, malaise, regret, unhappiness. *Opp* SATISFACTION.

dissatisfied *adj* disaffected, disappointed, discontented, disgruntled, displeased, fed up, frustrated, unfulfilled. ▷ UNHAPPY. *Opp* CONTENTED.

dissident *n derog* agitator, dissenter, independent thinker, protester, rebel, revolutionary. *Opp* CONFORMIST.

dissimilar *adj* antithetical, conflicting, contrasting, different, disparate, distinct, distinguishable, divergent, diverse, heterogeneous, incompatible, opposite, unrelated, various. *Opp* SIMILAR.

dissipate *v* 1 break up, diffuse, disappear, disperse, scatter. 2 ▷ SQUANDER. **dissipated** ▷ IMMORAL.

dissociate *v* cut off, detach, distance, divorce, isolate. ▷ SEPARATE. *Opp* ASSOCIATE.

dissolve *v* 1 become liquid, decompose, dematerialize, diffuse, disappear, disintegrate, disperse, liquefy, melt away, vanish. 2 *dissolve a meeting, partnership.* break up, cancel, dismiss, divorce, end, sever, split up, terminate, *inf* wind up.

dissuade *v* **dissuade from** advise against, argue out of, deter from, discourage from, persuade not to, put off, warn against. *Opp* PERSUADE.

distance *n* 1 breadth, extent, gap, interval, journey, length, measurement, mileage, range, reach, space, span, stretch, width. 2 aloofness, coolness, unfriendliness.
• *v* **distance yourself** be unfriendly, dissociate yourself, keep away, separate yourself, set yourself apart, stay away. *Opp* INVOLVE.

distant *adj* 1 far, far-away, far-flung, outlying, out-of-the-way, remote. *Opp* CLOSE. 2 aloof, cool, formal, haughty, reserved, reticent, stiff, unapproachable, unfriendly, withdrawn. *Opp* FRIENDLY.

distasteful *adj* disgusting, displeasing, nasty, objectionable, offensive, *inf* off-putting, revolting, unpalatable. ▷ UNPLEASANT. *Opp* PLEASANT.

distinct *adj* 1 apparent, clear, clear-cut, definite, evident, noticeable, obvious, patent, perceptible, plain, precise, recognizable, sharp, unambiguous, unequivocal, unmistakable, visible, well-defined. *Opp* INDISTINCT. 2 contrasting, detached, different, dissimilar, distinguishable, individual, separate, unconnected, unique.

distinction *n* 1 contrast, difference, differentiation, dissimilarity, distinctiveness, dividing line, division, individuality, particularity, peculiarity, separation. *Opp* SIMILARITY. 2 celebrity, credit, eminence, excellence, fame, glory, greatness, honour, importance, merit, prestige, renown, reputation, superiority.

distinctive *adj* characteristic, different, distinguishing, idiosyncratic, individual, original, peculiar, personal, singular, special, striking, typical, uncommon, unique. *Opp* COMMON.

distinguish *v* 1 choose, decide, differentiate, discriminate, judge, make a distinction, separate, tell apart. 2 ascertain, determine, discern, know, make out, perceive, pick out, recognize, see, single out, tell. **distinguished** ▷ FAMOUS.

distort *v* 1 bend, buckle, contort, deform, twist, warp, wrench. 2 exaggerate, falsify, garble, misrepresent, pervert, slant, twist. **distorted** ▷ GNARLED, FALSE.

distract *v* bewilder, bother, confuse, deflect, disconcert, divert, harass, mystify, perplex, puzzle, sidetrack, trouble, worry. **distracted** ▷ DISTRAUGHT, MAD.

distraction *n* 1 disturbance, interference, interruption. 2 agitation, bewilderment, confusion, delirium, frenzy, insanity, madness. 3 ▷ DIVERSION.

distraught *adj* agitated, *inf* beside yourself, distracted, distressed, disturbed, emotional, excited, frantic, hysterical, overwrought, troubled, upset, worked up. ▷ ANXIOUS. *Opp* CALM.

distress *n* adversity, affliction, angst, anguish, anxiety, danger, desolation, difficulty, dismay, fright, grief, heartache, misery, privation, sadness, sorrow, stress, suffering, torment, tribulation, trouble, unhappiness, woe, worry, wretchedness. ▷ PAIN.
• *v* afflict, alarm, bother, dismay, disturb, frighten, grieve, harass, hurt, make miserable, pain, perplex, perturb, plague, sadden, shake, shock, terrify, torment, torture, trouble, upset, worry, wound. *Opp* COMFORT.

distribute *v* allocate, allot, apportion, arrange, assign, circulate, deliver, *inf* dish out, dispense, disperse, disseminate, *inf* dole out, give out, hand round, issue, partition, scatter, share out, spread, strew, take round. *Opp* COLLECT.

district *n* area, community, division, locality, neighbourhood, parish, part, province, quarter, region, sector, territory, vicinity, ward, zone.

distrust *v* disbelieve, doubt, have misgivings about, have qualms about, mistrust, question, suspect. *Opp* TRUST.

distrustful *adj* cautious, dubious, uncertain. ▷ SUSPICIOUS. *Opp* TRUSTFUL.

disturb *v* 1 agitate, alarm, annoy, bother, disrupt, distract, distress, excite, fluster, frighten, interrupt, intrude on, perturb, pester, ruffle, scare, shake, startle, stir up, trouble, unsettle, upset, worry. 2 disorder, interfere with, jumble up, move, muddle, rearrange. **disturbed** ▷ DISTRAUGHT.

disturbance *n* disruption, interference, upheaval, upset. ▷ COMMOTION.

disunited *adj* divided, opposed, polarized, split. *Opp* UNITED.

disunity *n* difference, disagreement, discord, disharmony, disintegration, division, fragmentation, incoherence, opposition, polarization. *Opp* UNITY.

disused *adj* abandoned, closed, dead, discarded, discontinued, idle, neglected, obsolete, superannuated, withdrawn. ▷ OLD. *Opp* CURRENT.

ditch *n* channel, drain, dyke, gully, gutter, moat, trench.
• *v* ▷ ABANDON.

dive *v* crash-dive, dip, drop, fall, go under, jump, leap, nosedive, pitch, plummet, plunge, sink, submerge, subside, swoop.

diverge *v* branch, deviate, divide, fork, part, radiate, separate, split, spread, subdivide. ▷ DIFFER. *Opp* CONVERGE.

diverse *adj* ▷ VARIOUS.

diversify *v* branch out, develop, divide, enlarge, expand, extend, spread out, vary.

diversion *n* 1 detour, deviation. 2 amusement, distraction, entertainment, fun, game, hobby, interest, pastime, play, recreation, relaxation, sport.

divert *v* 1 avert, change direction, deflect, deviate, redirect, reroute, shunt, sidetrack, switch, turn aside. 2 amuse, beguile, cheer up, delight, distract, engage, entertain, keep happy, occupy, regale. **diverting** ▷ FUNNY.

divide *v* 1 branch, diverge, fork, move apart, part, separate, sunder. 2 allocate, allot, apportion, deal out, dispense, distribute, *inf* dole out, give out, halve, measure out, parcel out, pass round, share out. 3 disunite, polarize, split. 4 *divide into sets.* arrange, categorize, classify, grade, group, sort out, subdivide. *Opp* GATHER, UNITE.

divine *adj* angelic, celestial, godlike, hallowed, heavenly, holy, immortal, mystical, religious, sacred, saintly, seraphic, spiritual, transcendental. *Opp* MORTAL.
• *n* ▷ CLERGYMAN.
• *v* ▷ PROPHESY.

divinity *n* 1 ▷ GOD. 2 religion, religious studies, theology.

division *n* 1 allocation, allotment, cutting up, dividing, partition, segmentation, separation. 2 disagreement, discord, disunity, feud, quarrel, rupture, schism, split. 3 alcove, compartment, part, recess, section, segment. 4 border, borderline, boundary line, demarcation, dividing wall, fence, frontier, margin, partition, screen. 5 *division of a business.* branch, department, section, subdivision, unit.

divorce *n* annulment, *inf* break-up, dissolution, separation, *inf* split-up.
• *v* annul marriage, dissolve marriage, part, separate, *inf* split up.

dizziness *n* faintness, giddiness, light-headedness, vertigo.

dizzy *adj* confused, dazed, faint, giddy, light-headed, muddled, reeling, shaky, unsteady, *inf* woozy.

do *v* 1 accomplish, achieve, carry out, commit, complete, effect, execute, finish, fulfil, implement, initiate, instigate, organize, perform, produce, undertake. 2 *do the garden.* arrange, attend to, cope with, deal with, handle, look after, manage, work at. 3 *do sums.* give your mind to, solve, work out. 4 *Will this do?* be acceptable, be enough, be suitable, satisfy, serve, suffice. 5 *Do as you like.* act, behave, conduct yourself. **do away with** ▷ ABOLISH. **do up** ▷ DECORATE, FASTEN.

docile *adj* cooperative, domesticated, obedient. ▷ TAME.

dock *n* berth, dockyard, dry dock, harbour, jetty, landing stage, pier, quay, wharf.
• *v* 1 anchor, berth, drop anchor, land, moor, put in, tie up. 2 ▷ CUT.

doctor *n* general practitioner, *inf* GP, medical officer, medical practitioner, *inf* MO, physician, *derog* quack, surgeon.

doctrine *n* axiom, belief, conviction, creed, dogma, precept, principle, teaching, tenet.

document *n* certificate, charter, chronicle, deed, diploma, form, instrument, licence, manuscript, *inf* MS, paper, passport, policy, record, typescript, visa, warrant, will.
• *v* ▷ RECORD.

documentary *adj* 1 authenticated, recorded, substantiated, written. 2 factual, historical, non-fiction, real life.

dodge *n* contrivance, device, manoeuvre, ploy, ruse, scheme, stratagem, subterfuge, trick, *inf* wheeze.
• *v* 1 avoid, duck, elude, escape, evade, fend off, move out of the way, sidestep, swerve, turn away, veer. 2 *dodge work.* shirk, *sl* skive, *inf* wriggle out of. 3 *dodge a question.* equivocate, fudge, hedge, *inf* waffle.

dog *n* bitch, hound, mongrel, pedigree, pup, puppy.
• *v* ▷ FOLLOW.

dogma *n* article of faith, belief, conviction, creed, doctrine, precept, principle, teaching, tenet.

dogmatic *adj* assertive, arbitrary, authoritarian, categorical, certain, dictatorial, doctrinaire, *inf* hard-line, imperious, inflexible, intolerant, narrow-minded, obdurate, opinionated. ▷ STUBBORN. *Opp* AMENABLE.

dole *n* [*inf*] benefit, income support, social security, unemployment benefit. **dole out** ▷ DISTRIBUTE. **on the dole** ▷ UNEMPLOYED.

doll *n* marionette, puppet, rag doll.

domestic *adj* 1 family, household, private. 2 internal, national.

domesticated *adj* house-trained, tame, trained. *Opp* WILD.

dominant *adj* 1 biggest, chief, commanding, conspicuous, eye-catching, highest, largest, main, major, obvious, outstanding, pre-eminent, prevailing, primary, principal, uppermost. 2 ascendant, controlling, domineering, governing, influential, leading, powerful, predominant, presiding, reigning, ruling, supreme.

dominate *v* 1 be in the majority, control, direct, govern, influence, lead, manage, master, monopolize, outnumber, prevail, rule, subjugate, take control, tyrannize. 2 look down on, overshadow, tower over.

domineering *adj* authoritarian, autocratic, *inf* bossy, despotic, dictatorial, high-handed, oppressive, overbearing, *inf* pushy, strict, tyrannical. *Opp* SUBMISSIVE.

donate *v* contribute, give, grant, hand over, make a donation, present, supply.

donation *n* alms, contribution, offering. ▷ GIFT.

donor *n* backer, benefactor, contributor, giver, philanthropist, sponsor, supporter.

doom *n* destiny, end, fate, fortune, karma, kismet, lot.

doomed *adj* 1 condemned, destined, fated, ordained, predestined. 2 *doomed enterprise.* cursed, damned, hopeless, ill-fated, ill-starred, luckless, star-crossed, unlucky.

door *n* barrier, doorway, entrance, exit, gate, gateway, opening, portal, swing door, way out.

dormant *adj* 1 asleep, hibernating, inactive, inert, passive, quiescent, quiet, resting, sleeping. 2 *dormant talent.* hidden, latent, potential, untapped, unused. *Opp* ACTIVE.

dose *n* amount, dosage, measure, prescribed amount, quantity.
• *v* administer, dispense, prescribe.

dossier *n* file, folder, records, set of documents.

dot *n* decimal point, fleck, full stop, iota, jot, mark, point, speck, spot.
• *v* fleck, speckle, spot, stipple.

dote *v* **dote on** adore, idolize, worship. ▷ LOVE.

double *adj* doubled, dual, duplicated, paired, twin, twofold.
• *n* clone, copy, counterpart, duplicate, *inf* look-alike, *inf* spitting image, twin.
• *v* duplicate, multiply by two, repeat. **double back** ▷ RETURN. **double up** ▷ COLLAPSE.

double-cross *v* cheat, deceive, let down, trick. ▷ BETRAY.

doubt *n* 1 anxiety, apprehension, cynicism, diffidence, disbelief, disquiet, distrust, fear, hesitation, incredulity, indecision, misgiving, mistrust, perplexity, qualm, reservation, scepticism, suspicion, worry. 2 ambiguity, difficulty, dilemma, problem, query, question, uncertainty. *Opp* CERTAINTY.
• *v* be dubious, be sceptical about, disbelieve, distrust, fear, feel uncertain about, have misgivings about, hesitate, lack confidence, mistrust, query, question, suspect. *Opp* TRUST.

doubtful *adj* 1 cynical, diffident, distrustful, dubious, hesitant, incredulous, sceptical, suspicious, tentative, uncertain, unconvinced, undecided, unsure. 2 *doubtful decision.* ambiguous, debatable, dubious, equivocal, inconclusive, problematic, questionable, suspect, worrying. 3 *doubtful ally.* irresolute, uncommitted, unreliable, untrustworthy, vacillating, wavering. *Opp* CERTAIN, DEPENDABLE.

dowdy *adj* colourless, dingy, drab, dull, *inf* frumpish, shabby, unattractive, unstylish. *Opp* SMART.

downfall *n* collapse, defeat, overthrow, ruin, undoing.

downhearted *adj* dejected, depressed, discouraged, downcast, miserable. ▷ SAD.

downward *adj* declining, descending, downhill, falling, going down. *Opp* UPWARD.

downy *adj* feathery, fleecy, fluffy, furry, fuzzy, soft, woolly.

drab *adj* cheerless, colourless, dingy, dismal, dowdy, dreary, dull, flat, gloomy, grey, lacklustre, shabby, sombre, uninteresting. *Opp* BRIGHT.

draft *n* 1 notes, outline, plan, rough version, sketch. 2 *bank draft.* cheque, order.
• *v* compose, draw up, outline, plan, prepare, put together, sketch out, work out.

drag *v* 1 draw, haul, lug, pull, tow, trail, tug. 2 crawl, creep, go slowly, lose momentum, pass slowly.

drain *n* channel, conduit, ditch, dyke, drainpipe, duct, gutter, outlet, pipe, sewer, trench, watercourse.
• *v* 1 bleed, draw off, dry out, empty, extract, pump out, remove, tap. 2 drip, ebb, leak out, ooze, seep, strain, trickle. 3 *drain resources.* consume, deplete, exhaust, sap, spend, use up.

drama *n* 1 acting, dramatics, improvisation, stagecraft, theatre, theatricals. 2 comedy, dramatization, farce, melodrama, musical, opera, operetta, pantomime, performance, play, production, screenplay, script, show, tragedy. 3 *real-life drama.* action, crisis, excitement, suspense.

dramatic *adj* 1 ▷ THEATRICAL. 2 *dramatic gestures.* exaggerated, flamboyant, showy. 3 ▷ EXCITING.

dramatist *n* playwright, scriptwriter.

dramatize *v* 1 adapt, make into a play. 2 exaggerate, make too much of, overdo, overstate.

drape *n* curtain, hanging, screen.
• *v* cover, decorate, festoon, hang, swathe.

drastic *adj* desperate, dire, draconian, extreme, far-reaching, harsh, radical, rigorous, severe, strong.

draught *n* 1 breeze, current, movement, puff, wind. 2 dose, drink, gulp, measure, pull, swallow, *inf* swig.

draw *n* 1 attraction, enticement, lure, *inf* pull. 2 dead-heat, stalemate, tie. 3 competition, lottery, raffle.
• *v* 1 drag, haul, lug, pull, tow, tug.

2 *draw a crowd.* attract, bring in, entice, lure, persuade, pull in, win over. 3 *draw a sword.* extract, remove, take out, unsheathe. 4 *draw lots.* choose, pick, select. 5 *draw a conclusion.* arrive at, come to, deduce, infer, work out. 6 *draw 1-1.* be equal, finish equal, tie. 7 *draw pictures.* depict, map out, outline, paint, pen, portray, represent, sketch, trace. **draw off** ▷ DRAIN. **draw out** ▷ EXTEND. **draw up** ▷ DRAFT, HALT.

drawback *n* difficulty, disadvantage, hindrance, obstacle, problem, snag, stumbling block.

drawing *n* cartoon, design, illustration, outline, picture, sketch.

dread *n* anxiety, apprehension, awe, dismay, fear, nervousness, qualm, trepidation, uneasiness, worry.
• *v* be afraid of, shrink from, view with horror. ▷ FEAR.

dreadful *adj* alarming, appalling, awful, dire, distressing, frightful, ghastly, grisly, gruesome, harrowing, hideous, horrible, indescribable, monstrous, shocking, terrible, tragic, unspeakable, upsetting. ▷ BAD, FRIGHTENING.

dream *n* 1 daydream, delusion, fantasy, hallucination, illusion, mirage, nightmare, reverie, trance, vision. 2 ambition, aspiration, ideal, pipedream, wish.
• *v* conjure up, daydream, fancy, fantasize, hallucinate, imagine, think. **dream up** ▷ INVENT.

dreary *adj* bleak, boring, depressing, dismal, dull, gloomy, sombre, uninteresting. ▷ MISERABLE.

dregs *n* deposit, grounds (*of coffee*), lees, precipitate, remains, residue, sediment.

drench *v* douse, drown, flood, inundate, saturate, soak, souse, steep, wet thoroughly.

dress *n* 1 apparel, attire, clothing, costume, garb, garments, *inf* gear, *inf* get-up, outfit, *old use* raiment. ▷ CLOTHES. 2 frock, gown, robe, shift.
• *v* 1 array, attire, clothe, cover, fit out, provide clothes for, robe. 2 *dress a wound.* bandage, bind up, put a dressing on, tend, treat.

dressing *n* bandage, compress, plaster, poultice.

dribble *v* 1 drool, slaver, slobber. 2 drip, flow, leak, ooze, run, seep, trickle.

drift *n* 1 bank, dune, heap, mound, pile, ridge. 2 *drift of a speech.* ▷ GIST.
• *v* 1 be carried, coast, float, meander, move casually, ramble, roam, stray, waft, walk aimlessly, wander. 2 accumulate, gather, make drifts, pile up.

drill *n* discipline, exercises, instruction, practice, training.
• *v* 1 coach, discipline, exercise, indoctrinate, instruct, practise, rehearse, school, teach, train. 2 bore, penetrate, perforate, pierce.

drink *n* 1 beverage, *inf* dram, draught, glass, *inf* nightcap, *inf* nip, pint, sip, swallow, swig, *inf* tipple, tot. 2 alcohol, *inf* booze, *joc* liquid refreshment, liquor.
• *v* 1 gulp, guzzle, imbibe, *inf* knock back, lap, partake of, quaff, sip, swallow, swig, *inf* swill. 2 *inf* booze, carouse, *inf* indulge, tipple.

drip *n* bead, drop, splash, spot, tear, trickle.
• *v* dribble, drizzle, drop, leak, plop, splash, sprinkle, trickle, weep.

drive *n* 1 excursion, jaunt, journey, outing, ride, run, *inf* spin, trip. 2 ambition, determination, energy, enterprise, enthusiasm, *inf* get-up-and-go, impetus, initiative, keenness, motivation, persistence, *inf* push, vigour, zeal. 3 campaign, crusade, effort.
• *v* 1 bang, dig, hammer, hit, knock, push, ram, sink, stab, strike, thrust. 2 coerce, compel, constrain, force, oblige, press, urge. 3 control, direct, guide, handle, manage, pilot, propel, send, steer. ▷ TRAVEL. **drive out** ▷ EXPEL.

droop *v* be limp, fall, flop, hang, sag, slump, wilt, wither.

drop *n* 1 bead, blob, bubble, dab, drip, droplet, globule, pearl, spot, tear. 2 *drop of whisky.* dash, *inf* nip, *inf* tot. 3 *steep drop.* declivity, descent, dive, fall, incline, plunge, precipice. 4 *drop in price.* cut, decrease, reduction, slump. *Opp* RISE.
• *v* 1 collapse, descend, dip, dive, fall, jump down, lower, nosedive, plummet, plunge, sink, slump, subside, swoop, tumble. 2 *drop from a team.* eliminate, exclude, leave out, omit. 3 *drop a friend, a plan.* abandon, discard, *inf* dump, forsake, give up, jilt, leave, reject, scrap. **drop behind** ▷ LAG. **drop in on** ▷ VISIT. **drop off** ▷ SLEEP.

drown *v* 1 engulf, flood, immerse, submerge, swamp. 2 be louder than, overpower, overwhelm, silence.

drowsy *adj* dozing, heavy-eyed, *inf* nodding off, sleepy, sluggish, somnolent, tired. *Opp* LIVELY.

drudgery *n* chore, *inf* donkey work, *inf*

grind, labour, slavery, *inf* slog, toil. ▷ WORK.

drug *n* 1 cure, medicament, medication, medicine, remedy, treatment. 2 *inf* dope, narcotic, opiate.
• *v* anaesthetize, *inf* dope, dose, *inf* knock out, medicate, poison, sedate, stupefy, tranquillize.

drum *n* ▷ BARREL.

drunk *adj* delirious, fuddled, incapable, inebriate, inebriated, intoxicated, maudlin. [*sl*] blotto, legless, merry, paralytic, pie-eyed, pissed, plastered, sloshed, sozzled, tiddly, tight, tipsy. *Opp* SOBER.

drunkard *n* alcoholic, dipsomaniac, drunk, *inf* sot, tippler, *sl* wino. *Opp* TEETOTALLER.

dry *adj* 1 arid, baked, barren, dead, dehydrated, desiccated, parched, scorched, shrivelled, thirsty, waterless. *Opp* WET. 2 boring, dreary, dull, flat, prosaic, tedious, tiresome, uninspired, uninteresting. *Opp* LIVELY. 3 *dry humour. inf* dead-pan, droll, laconic.
• *v* become dry, dehumidify, dehydrate, desiccate, parch, shrivel, wilt, wither.

dual *adj* double, duplicate, linked, paired, twin.

dubious *adj* 1 ▷ DOUBTFUL. 2 *a dubious character. inf* fishy, *inf* shady, suspect, suspicious, unreliable, untrustworthy.

duck *v* 1 avoid, bob down, crouch, dodge, evade, sidestep, stoop, swerve. 2 immerse, plunge, push under, submerge.

due *adj* 1 outstanding, owed, owing, payable, unpaid. 2 *due consideration.* adequate, appropriate, deserved, fitting, just, merited, proper, requisite, right, rightful, sufficient, suitable, well-earned.
• *n* deserts, entitlement, merits, reward, rights. **dues** ▷ DUTY.

dull *adj* 1 dim, dingy, dowdy, drab, dreary, faded, flat, gloomy, lacklustre, lifeless, sombre, subdued. 2 *dull sky.* cloudy, dismal, grey, heavy, leaden, murky, overcast, sunless. 3 *dull sound.* deadened, indistinct, muffled, muted. 4 *dull student.* dense, dim, obtuse, *inf* thick, unimaginative, unintelligent, unresponsive. ▷ STUPID. 5 *dull edge.* blunt, blunted. 6 *dull book.* tedious, uninteresting. ▷ BORING. *Opp* BRIGHT, SHARP.

dumb *adj* mute, silent, speechless, tongue-tied, unable to speak.

dummy *n* 1 copy, counterfeit, duplicate, imitation, model, reproduction, sample, simulation, substitute, toy. 2 doll, figure, puppet.

dump *n* 1 rubbish-heap, tip. 2 *arms dump.* arsenal, cache, depot, hoard, store.
• *v* deposit, discard, dispose of, *inf* ditch, drop, get rid of, jettison, offload, put down, reject, scrap, throw away, tip, unload.

dune *n* drift, hillock, hummock, mound, sand dune.

dungeon *n* gaol, keep, lock-up, prison, vault.

duplicate *adj* copied, corresponding, identical, matching, second, twin.
• *n* carbon copy, clone, copy, double, facsimile, imitation, likeness, *inf* look-alike, match, photocopy, replica, reproduction, twin, Xerox.
• *v* copy, photocopy, print, repeat, reproduce, Xerox.

durable *adj* enduring, hard-wearing, indestructible, long-lasting, permanent, resilient, stout, strong, substantial, thick, tough. *Opp* IMPERMANENT, WEAK.

dusk *n* evening, sundown, sunset, twilight.

dust *n* dirt, grime, grit, particles, powder.

dusty *adj* 1 chalky, crumbly, dry, fine, friable, powdery, sandy, sooty. 2 dirty, grubby, uncleaned, unswept.

dutiful *adj* careful, compliant, conscientious, devoted, diligent, faithful, hard-working, loyal, obedient, obliging, reliable, responsible, scrupulous, thorough, trustworthy. *Opp* IRRESPONSIBLE.

duty *n* 1 allegiance, loyalty, obedience, obligation, onus, responsibility, service. 2 assignment, business, chore, function, job, office, role, stint, task, work. 3 charge, dues, fee, levy, tariff, tax, toll.

dwarf *adj* ▷ SMALL.
• *n* midget, pigmy.
• *v* dominate, overshadow, tower over.

dwell *v* **dwell in** ▷ INHABIT.

dwelling *n* abode, domicile, habitation, home, house, lodging, quarters, residence.

dying *adj* declining, expiring, fading, failing, moribund, obsolescent. *Opp* ALIVE.

dynamic *adj* active, driving, energetic, enterprising, enthusiastic, forceful, *inf* go-ahead, *inf* go-getting, high-powered, lively, motivated, powerful, *inf* pushy, spirited, vigorous, zealous. *Opp* APATHETIC.

E

eager *adj* agog, animated, anxious (*to please*), ardent, avid, desirous, earnest, enthusiastic, excited, fervent, hungry, impatient, intent, itching, keen, keyed up, motivated, passionate, *inf* raring (*to go*), voracious, yearning, zealous. *Opp* APATHETIC.

eagerness *n* alacrity, anxiety, appetite, ardour, desire, enthusiasm, excitement, fervour, hunger, impatience, interest, keenness, longing, motivation, passion, thirst, zeal. *Opp* APATHY.

early *adj* 1 advance, before time, first, forward, premature. *Opp* LATE. 2 ancient, initial, original. ▷ OLD. *Opp* RECENT.

earn *v* 1 be paid, *inf* bring in, *inf* clear, draw, gain, get, *inf* gross, make, net, obtain, pocket, realize, receive, *inf* take home, yield. 2 attain, be worthy of, deserve, merit, warrant, win.

earnest *adj* 1 assiduous, committed, conscientious, dedicated, determined, devoted, diligent, eager, hard-working, industrious, purposeful, resolved, zealous. *Opp* CASUAL. 2 grave, heartfelt, impassioned, serious, sincere, sober, solemn, thoughtful, well-meant.

earnings *n* income, salary, stipend, wages. ▷ PAY.

earth *n* clay, dirt, ground, land, loam, soil, topsoil.

earthenware *n* ceramics, china, crockery, porcelain, pottery.

earthly *adj* human, material, mortal, mundane, physical, secular, temporal, terrestrial, worldly. *Opp* SPIRITUAL.

earthquake *n* quake, shock, tremor, upheaval.

earthy *adj* bawdy, coarse, crude, down to earth, frank, lusty, ribald, uninhibited.

ease *n* 1 aplomb, calmness, comfort, composure, contentment, enjoyment, happiness, leisure, luxury, peace, quiet, relaxation, repose, rest, serenity, tranquillity. 2 dexterity, effortlessness, facility, skill, speed, straightforwardness. *Opp* DIFFICULTY.

• *v* 1 allay, alleviate, assuage, calm, comfort, decrease, lessen, lighten, mitigate, moderate, pacify, quell, quieten, reduce, relax, relieve, slacken, soothe. 2 edge, guide, inch, manœuvre, move gradually, slide.

easy *adj* 1 carefree, comfortable, contented, cosy, *inf* cushy, effortless, leisurely, light, painless, peaceful, pleasant, relaxed, relaxing, restful, serene, soft, tranquil, undemanding, unhurried, untroubled. 2 clear, elementary, foolproof, manageable, plain, simple, straightforward, uncomplicated, understandable, user-friendly. 3 ▷ EASYGOING. *Opp* DIFFICULT.

easygoing *adj* accommodating, affable, amenable, calm, carefree, casual, cheerful, even-tempered, flexible, *inf* free and easy, friendly, genial, *inf* happy-go-lucky, indulgent, informal, *inf* laid-back, *derog* lax, lenient, liberal, mellow, nonchalant, open, patient, permissive, placid, relaxed, tolerant, unruffled. *Opp* STRICT.

eat *v* 1 bolt, chew, consume, devour, digest, feed on, gnaw, gobble, gorge, graze, gulp, guzzle, live on, munch, nibble, *inf* scoff, swallow, *inf* tuck in. 2 breakfast, dine, feast, lunch. **eat away, eat into** ▷ ERODE.

eatable *adj* digestible, edible, fit to eat, palatable, wholesome. ▷ TASTY. *Opp* INEDIBLE.

ebb *v* fall, flow back, go down, recede, retreat, subside. ▷ DECLINE.

eccentric *adj* 1 aberrant, abnormal, anomalous, atypical, bizarre, curious, freakish, idiosyncratic, odd, outlandish, out of the ordinary, peculiar, quaint, queer, quirky, singular, strange, unconventional, unusual, *inf* way-out, *inf* weird, zany. ▷ ABSURD, MAD. 2 *eccentric circles.* irregular, off-centre.

• *n* ▷ CHARACTER.

echo *v* 1 resound, reverberate, ring, sound again. 2 copy, emulate, imitate, mimic, mirror, reiterate, repeat.

eclipse *v* 1 blot out, cloud, darken, dim, obscure, veil. ▷ COVER. 2 excel, outdo, outshine, overshadow, *inf* put in the shade, surpass, top.

economic *adj* business, commercial, financial, fiscal, monetary, trading.

economical *adj* 1 careful, frugal, provident, prudent, sparing, thrifty. ▷ MISERLY. *Opp* WASTEFUL. 2 cheap, cost-effective, inexpensive, low-priced, reasonable, *inf* value-for-money. *Opp* EXPENSIVE.

economize *v* cut back, save, *inf* scrimp, skimp, spend less, *inf* tighten your belt. *Opp* SQUANDER.

economy *n* 1 frugality, *derog* miserliness, parsimony, providence, prudence, saving, thrift. *Opp* WASTE. 2 *national economy.* budget, economic affairs, wealth. 3 ▷ BREVITY.

ecstasy *n* bliss, delight, elation, euphoria, exaltation, fervour, frenzy, happiness, joy, rapture, thrill, trance, transport.

ecstatic *adj* blissful, delighted, delirious, elated, enraptured, euphoric, exhilarated, exultant, frenzied, joyful, orgasmic, overjoyed, *inf* over the moon, rapturous, transported. ▷ HAPPY.

eddy *n* maelstrom, swirl, vortex, whirl, whirlpool, whirlwind.
• *v* move in circles, spin, swirl, turn, whirl.

edge *n* 1 border, boundary, brim, brink, circumference, frame, kerb, limit, lip, margin, outline, perimeter, periphery, rim, side, verge. 2 outskirts, suburbs. 3 incisiveness, keenness, sharpness. 4 *edge of a curtain.* edging, fringe, hem.
• *v* 1 bind, border, fringe, hem, trim. 2 *edge away.* crawl, creep, inch, move stealthily, sidle, slink, steal, worm.

edible *adj* digestible, eatable, fit to eat, palatable, wholesome. ▷ TASTY. *Opp* INEDIBLE.

edit *v* abridge, adapt, alter, amend, arrange, assemble, censor, compile, condense, correct, cut, emend, organize, polish, prepare, put together, rephrase, revise, rewrite, select.

edition *n* 1 copy, issue, number. 2 impression, printing, print-run, publication, version.

educate *v* bring up, civilize, coach, cultivate, discipline, drill, edify, enlighten, guide, improve, indoctrinate, inform, instruct, lecture, rear, school, teach, train, tutor.

educated *adj* cultured, enlightened, erudite, knowledgeable, learned, literate, numerate, trained, well-bred, well-read.

education *n* coaching, enlightenment, guidance, indoctrination, instruction, schooling, teaching, training, tuition.

eerie *adj inf* creepy, frightening, ghostly, mysterious, *inf* scary, *inf* spooky, strange, uncanny, unearthly, unnatural, weird.

effect *n* 1 aftermath, conclusion, consequence, impact, issue, outcome, repercussion, result, sequel, upshot. 2 feeling, illusion, impression, sensation, sense.
• *v* accomplish, achieve, bring about, carry out, cause, create, enforce, execute, implement, initiate, make, produce, put into effect, secure.

effective *adj* 1 capable, competent, functional, impressive, potent, powerful, productive, proficient, serviceable, strong, successful, useful, worthwhile. ▷ EFFICIENT. 2 *effective argument.* cogent, compelling, convincing, meaningful, persuasive, striking, telling. *Opp* INEFFECTIVE.

effeminate *adj* camp, effete, girlish, *inf* sissy, unmanly, weak. *Opp* MANLY.

effervesce *v* bubble, ferment, fizz, foam, froth, sparkle.

effervescent *adj* bubbling, bubbly, carbonated, fizzy, foaming, frothy, gassy, sparkling.

efficient *adj* businesslike, cost-effective, economic, streamlined. ▷ EFFECTIVE. *Opp* INEFFICIENT.

effort *n* 1 application, *inf* elbow grease, endeavour, exertion, industry, labour, pains, strain, stress, striving, struggle, toil, trouble, work. 2 *brave effort.* attempt, endeavour, go, try, venture. 3 *successful effort.* achievement, exploit, feat, outcome, product, production, result.

effusive *adj* demonstrative, ebullient, enthusiastic, exuberant, fulsome, gushing, lavish, *inf* over the top, profuse, voluble. *Opp* RETICENT.

egotism *n* egocentricity, egoism, narcissism, pride, self-importance, self-interest, selfishness, self-love, vanity.

egotistical *adj* self-centred, selfish. ▷ CONCEITED.

eject *v* 1 banish, *inf* bundle out, deport, discharge, dismiss, drive out, evict, exile, expel, *inf* kick out, oust, push out, put out, remove, sack, shoot out, throw out, turn out. 2 ▷ EMIT.

elaborate *adj* 1 complex, complicated, detailed, exhaustive, intricate, involved, painstaking, thorough. 2 *elaborate decor.* baroque, decorative, fancy, fantastic, fussy, intricate, ornamental, ornate, rococo, showy. *Opp* SIMPLE.
• *v* add to, adorn, amplify, complicate, decorate, develop, embellish, enlarge on, expand, fill out, give details of, improve on, ornament. *Opp* SIMPLIFY.

elapse *v* go by, pass, slip by.

elastic *adj inf* bendy, bouncy, flexible, plastic, pliable, pliant, resilient, rubbery, *inf* springy, *inf* stretchy, yielding. *Opp* RIGID.

elderly *adj* ageing, *inf* getting on. ▷ OLD.

elect *adj* chosen, elected, prospective, selected.
• *v* adopt, appoint, choose, name, nominate, opt for, pick, select, vote for.

election *n* ballot, choice, poll, referendum, selection, vote, voting.

electioneer *v* campaign, canvass.

electorate *n* constituents, electors, voters.

electric *adj* 1 battery-operated, electrical. 2 electrifying. ▷ EXCITING.

electricity *n* current, energy, power, power supply.

elegant *adj* beautiful, chic, courtly, cultivated, debonair, dignified, exquisite, fashionable, fine, genteel, graceful, gracious, handsome, luxurious, pleasing, *inf* plush, *inf* posh, refined, smart, sophisticated, splendid, stately, stylish, suave, tasteful, urbane, well-bred. *Opp* INELEGANT.

elegy *n* dirge, lament, requiem.

element *n* 1 component, constituent, detail, factor, feature, fragment, ingredient, part, piece, trace, unit. 2 *in your element*. domain, environment, habitat, medium, sphere, territory. **elements** ▷ RUDIMENTS, WEATHER.

elementary *adj* basic, early, first, fundamental, initial, introductory, primary, rudimentary, simple, straightforward. ▷ EASY. *Opp* ADVANCED.

elevate *v* exalt, lift, make higher, promote. ▷ RAISE. **elevated** ▷ HIGH, NOBLE.

elicit *v* bring out, derive, draw out, evoke, extract, get, obtain, wrest, wring.

eligible *adj* acceptable, allowed, appropriate, authorized, competent, equipped, fit, proper, qualified, suitable, worthy. *Opp* INELIGIBLE.

eliminate *v* 1 abolish, annihilate, delete, destroy, dispense with, do away with, eject, end, eradicate, exterminate, extinguish, get rid of, remove, stamp out. ▷ KILL. 2 drop, exclude, knock out, leave out, omit, reject.

elite *n* aristocracy, best, *inf* cream, flower, nobility, pick *inf* upper crust.

eloquent *adj* articulate, expressive, fluent, *derog* glib, persuasive, plausible, powerful. *Opp* INARTICULATE.

elude *v* avoid, circumvent, dodge, *inf* duck, escape, evade, foil, *inf* give (someone) the slip, shake off.

elusive *adj* 1 evasive, hard to find, slippery. 2 *elusive meaning*. ambiguous, baffling, deceptive, hard to pin down, indefinable, intangible, puzzling.

emaciated *adj* bony, cadaverous, gaunt, haggard, skeletal, skinny, starved, underfed, undernourished, wizened. ▷ THIN.

emancipate *v* deliver, discharge, enfranchise, free, let go, liberate, loose, release, set free. *Opp* ENSLAVE.

embankment *n* bank, dam, earthwork, mound.

embark *v* board, depart, go aboard, leave, set out. *Opp* DISEMBARK. **embark on** ▷ BEGIN.

embarrass *v* abash, confuse, discomfit, disconcert, disgrace, distress, fluster, humiliate, mortify, shame, *inf* show up, upset. **embarrassed** ▷ ASHAMED. **embarrassing** ▷ AWKWARD, SHAMEFUL.

embellish *v* adorn, beautify, deck, decorate, embroider, garnish, ornament. ▷ ELABORATE.

embezzle *v* appropriate, misappropriate, *inf* put your hand in the till. ▷ STEAL.

embezzlement *n* fraud, misappropriation, misuse of funds, stealing, theft.

embittered *adj* bitter, disillusioned, envious, rancorous, resentful, sour. ▷ ANGRY.

emblem *n* badge, crest, device, image, insignia, mark, regalia, seal, sign, symbol, token.

embody *v* 1 exemplify, express, incarnate, manifest, personify, represent, stand for, symbolize. 2 combine, comprise, embrace, enclose, include, incorporate, integrate, involve, unite.

embrace *v* 1 clasp, cling to, cuddle, enfold, grasp, hold, hug, kiss, snuggle up to. 2 *embrace new ideas*. accept, espouse, receive, take on, welcome. 3 ▷ EMBODY.

embryonic *adj* early, immature, just beginning, rudimentary, undeveloped, unformed. *Opp* MATURE.

emerge *v* appear, arise, be revealed, come out, come to light, emanate, leak out, *inf* pop up, proceed, surface, transpire, *inf* turn out.

emergency *n* crisis, danger, difficulty, predicament, serious situation.

emigrate *v* depart, go abroad, leave, relocate, resettle.

eminent *adj* august, celebrated, conspicuous, distinguished, elevated, esteemed, exalted, famous, great, honoured, illustrious, important, notable, noteworthy, outstanding, pre-eminent, prominent, renowned, well-known. *Opp* LOWLY.

emit *v* belch, discharge, eject, exhale, expel, exude, give off, give out, issue, radiate, send out, spew out, spout, transmit.

emotion *n* excitement, feeling, fervour, passion, sentiment, warmth.

emotional *adj* 1 ardent, demonstrative, enthusiastic, excited, fervent, fiery, heated, hot-headed, impassioned, intense, irrational, passionate, romantic, touched, warm-hearted, worked up. 2 *emotional language*. affecting, emotive, heart-rending, inflammatory, loaded, moving, pathetic, poignant, provocative, sentimental, stirring, subjective, *inf* tear-jerking, tender, touching. *Opp* UNEMOTIONAL.

emphasis *n* accent, attention, force, importance, intensity, priority, prominence, stress, urgency, weight.

emphasize *v* accent, accentuate, bring out, dwell on, focus on, highlight, impress, insist on, make obvious, *inf* play up, point up, *inf* press home, *inf* rub it in, spotlight, stress, underline, underscore.

emphatic *adj* assertive, categorical, dogmatic, definite, firm, forceful, insistent, positive, pronounced, resolute, strong, uncompromising, unequivocal. *Opp* TENTATIVE.

empirical *adj* experimental, observed, practical, pragmatic. *Opp* THEORETICAL.

employ *v* 1 commission, engage, enlist, hire, pay, sign up, take on, use the services of. 2 apply, use, utilize.

employed *adj* active, earning, hired, involved, in work, occupied, practising, working. ▷ BUSY. *Opp* UNEMPLOYED.

employee *n* worker. **employees** staff, workforce.

employer *n* boss, chief, *inf* gaffer, *inf* governor, head, manager, owner, proprietor.

employment *n* business, calling, craft, job, line, livelihood, living, métier, occupation, profession, pursuit, trade, vocation, work.

empty *adj* 1 bare, blank, clean, clear, deserted, desolate, forsaken, hollow, unfilled, unfurnished, uninhabited, unoccupied, unused, vacant, void. *Opp* FULL. 2 *empty threats*. futile, idle, impotent, ineffective, meaningless, pointless, purposeless, senseless, silly, worthless.
• *v* clear, discharge, drain, evacuate, exhaust, pour out, unload, vacate, void. *Opp* FILL.

enable *v* allow, assist, authorize, empower, entitle, equip, facilitate, help, license, make it possible, permit, provide the means, qualify. *Opp* PREVENT.

enchant *v* allure, beguile, bewitch, captivate, cast a spell on, charm, delight, enthral, entrance, fascinate, hypnotize, mesmerize. **enchanting** ▷ ATTRACTIVE.

enchantment *n* charm, magic, sorcery, spell, witchcraft, wizardry. ▷ DELIGHT.

enclose *v* box, cage, conceal, confine, contain, cover, encircle, encompass, enfold, envelop, fence in, hedge in, hem in, insert, limit, package, pen, restrict, ring, secure, sheathe, shut in, surround, wall in, wall up, wrap. ▷ IMPRISON.

enclosure *n* 1 cage, compound, coop, corral, courtyard, farmyard, field, fold, paddock, pen, pound, ring, run, stockade, sty, yard. 2 *enclosure in an envelope*. contents, insertion.

encounter *n* 1 confrontation, meeting. 2 [*military*] battle, clash, dispute, skirmish, struggle. ▷ FIGHT.
• *v inf* bump into, chance upon, clash with, come upon, confront, contend with, *inf* cross swords with, face, happen upon, meet, run into.

encourage *v* 1 applaud, cheer, egg on, give hope to, hearten, incite, inspire, persuade, prompt, rally, reassure, rouse, spur on, support, urge. 2 *encourage sales*. aid, be an incentive to, be conducive to, boost, foster, further, generate, help, increase, induce, promote, stimulate. *Opp* DISCOURAGE.

encouragement *n* approval, boost, cheer, exhortation, incentive, inspiration, reassurance, *inf* shot in the arm, stimulus, support. *Opp* DISCOURAGEMENT.

encouraging *adj* comforting, heartening, hopeful, inspiring, optimistic, positive, promising, reassuring. ▷ FAVOURABLE.

encroach *v* enter, impinge, infringe, intrude, invade, make inroads, trespass, violate.

end *n* 1 boundary, edge, extremity, limit, tip. 2 cessation, close, coda, completion, conclusion, culmination, curtain (*of play*), denouement (*of plot*), ending, expiry, finale, finish, *inf* pay-off, resolution. 3 *journey's end*. destination, home, termination. 4 *end of a queue*. back, rear,

tail. 5 *end of your life*. death, destruction, destiny, doom, extinction, fate, passing. 6 *end in view*. aim, aspiration, design, intention, objective, outcome, plan, purpose, result, upshot. *Opp* BEGINNING.
• *v* 1 abolish, break off, complete, conclude, cut off, destroy, discontinue, *inf* drop, eliminate, exterminate, finalize, *inf* get rid of, halt, phase out, *inf* round off, ruin, terminate, *inf* wind up. 2 break up, cease, close, culminate, die, disappear, expire, fade away, finish, *inf* pack up, stop. *Opp* BEGIN.

endanger *v* jeopardize, put at risk, threaten. *Opp* PROTECT.

endearing *adj* appealing, attractive, captivating, charming, disarming, enchanting, engaging, likable, lovable, sweet, winning. *Opp* REPULSIVE.

endeavour *v* ▷ TRY.

endless *adj* 1 boundless, immeasurable, inexhaustible, infinite, limitless, unbounded, unlimited. 2 abiding, ceaseless, constant, continual, continuous, enduring, eternal, everlasting, immortal, incessant, interminable, never-ending, nonstop, perpetual, persistent, unbroken, undying.

endorse *v* 1 advocate, agree with, approve, authorize, *inf* back, condone, confirm, *inf* OK, sanction, subscribe to, support. 2 *endorse a cheque*. countersign, sign.

endurance *n* determination, fortitude, patience, perseverance, persistence, resolution, stamina, staying-power, strength, tenacity.

endure *v* 1 carry on, continue, exist, last, live on, persevere, persist, prevail, remain, stay, survive. 2 bear, cope with, experience, go through, put up with, stand, stomach, submit to, suffer, tolerate, undergo, weather, withstand. **enduring** ▷ PERMANENT.

enemy *n* adversary, antagonist, competitor, foe, opponent, opposition, the other side, rival. *Opp* FRIEND.

energetic *adj* active, animated, brisk, dynamic, enthusiastic, forceful, indefatigable, lively, powerful, quick-moving, spirited, strenuous, tireless, unflagging, vigorous, zestful. *Opp* LETHARGIC.

energy *n* 1 animation, ardour, drive, dynamism, élan, enthusiasm, exertion, fire, force, *inf* get-up-and-go, *inf* go, life, liveliness, spirit, stamina, strength, verve, vigour, vitality, vivacity, zeal, zest. *Opp* LETHARGY. 2 fuel, power.

enforce *v* apply, carry out, compel, execute, implement, impose, inflict, insist on, prosecute, put into effect, require. *Opp* WAIVE.

engage *v* 1 employ, enlist, hire, recruit, sign up, take on. 2 *cogs engage*. bite, fit together, interlock. 3 *engage to do something*. ▷ PROMISE. 4 *engage in gossip*. ▷ OCCUPY. 5 *engage in sport*. ▷ PARTICIPATE.

engaged *adj* 1 affianced, betrothed, *old use* spoken for. 2 ▷ BUSY.

engagement *n* 1 betrothal, promise to marry. 2 *social engagement*. appointment, arrangement, commitment, date, fixture, meeting, obligation, rendezvous. 3 ▷ BATTLE.

engine *n* 1 machine, motor. 2 locomotive.

engineer *n* mechanic, technician.
• *v* ▷ CONSTRUCT, DEVISE.

engrave *v* carve, chisel, etch, inscribe. ▷ CUT.

enigma *n* conundrum, mystery, problem, puzzle, riddle.

enjoy *v* 1 appreciate, bask in, delight in, *inf* go in for, indulge in, *inf* lap up, luxuriate in, relish, revel in, savour, take pleasure in. ▷ LIKE. 2 benefit from, experience, take advantage of, use. **enjoy yourself** celebrate, have a good time, make merry.

enjoyable *adj* agreeable, amusing, delicious, delightful, entertaining, *inf* nice, pleasurable, rewarding, satisfying. ▷ PLEASANT. *Opp* UNPLEASANT.

enlarge *v* amplify, augment, blow up, broaden, build up, develop, dilate, distend, elongate, expand, extend, fill out, grow, increase, inflate, lengthen, magnify, multiply, spread, stretch, swell, widen. *Opp* DECREASE. **enlarge on** ▷ ELABORATE.

enlighten *v* edify, illuminate, inform, make aware. ▷ TEACH.

enlist *v* 1 conscript, muster, recruit, sign up. 2 *enlist in the army*. enrol, enter, join up, register, sign on, volunteer. 3 *enlist help*. ▷ OBTAIN.

enliven *v* animate, arouse, brighten, cheer up, energize, inspire, *inf* pep up, rouse, stimulate, wake up.

enormous *adj* colossal, elephantine, gargantuan, giant, gigantic, gross, huge, immense, *inf* jumbo, mammoth, massive, mighty, monstrous, mountainous, prodigious, stupendous, titanic, towering, vast. ▷ BIG. *Opp* SMALL.

enough *adj* adequate, ample, as much as necessary, sufficient.

enquire *v* ask, inquire, query, question. **enquire about** ▷ INVESTIGATE.

enrage *v* incense, infuriate, madden. ▷ ANGER.

enslave *v* dominate, subjugate, take away the rights of. *Opp* EMANCIPATE.

ensure *v* confirm, guarantee, make certain, secure.

entail *v* call for, demand, give rise to, involve, lead to, necessitate, require.

enter *v* 1 arrive, come in, get in, go in, infiltrate, invade, step in. *Opp* DEPART. 2 penetrate, pierce, puncture, push into. 3 *enter a contest.* engage in, enlist in, enrol in, *inf* go in for, join, participate in, sign up for, take part in, volunteer for. 4 *enter names on a list.* add, insert, note down, put down, record, register, sign, write. *Opp* REMOVE. **enter into** ▷ BEGIN.

enterprise *n* 1 adventure, effort, endeavour, operation, programme, project, undertaking, venture. 2 ambition, courage, daring, determination, drive, energy, *inf* get-up-and-go, initiative. 3 business, company, concern, firm, organization.

enterprising *adj* adventurous, ambitious, bold, courageous, daring, determined, eager, energetic, enthusiastic, *inf* go-ahead, *inf* go-getting, imaginative, indefatigable, industrious, intrepid, keen, purposeful, *inf* pushy, resourceful, spirited, vigorous, zealous. *Opp* UNADVENTUROUS.

entertain *v* 1 amuse, cheer up, delight, divert, occupy, please, regale, *inf* tickle. *Opp* BORE. 2 *entertain friends.* accommodate, be host to, cater for, *inf* put up, receive, treat, welcome. 3 *entertain an idea.* accept, agree to, approve, consent to, consider, contemplate, support, take seriously. *Opp* IGNORE. **entertaining** ▷ INTERESTING.

entertainer *n* actor, actress, artist, artiste, musician, performer, player, singer.

entertainment *n* 1 amusement, distraction, diversion, enjoyment, fun, nightlife, pastime, play, pleasure, recreation, sport. 2 drama, exhibition, extravaganza, performance, presentation, production, show, spectacle.

enthusiasm *n* 1 ambition, ardour, drive, eagerness, excitement, exuberance, *derog* fanaticism, fervour, gusto, keenness, passion, relish, spirit, verve, zeal, zest. *Opp* APATHY. 2 craze, fad, hobby, interest, passion, pastime.

enthusiast *n* addict, admirer, aficionado, *inf* buff, champion, devotee, fan, fanatic, *inf* fiend, lover, supporter.

enthusiastic *adj* ambitious, ardent, avid, committed, *inf* crazy, devoted, eager, earnest, ebullient, energetic, excited, exuberant, fervent, hearty, impassioned, interested, involved, irrepressible, keen, lively, *inf* mad (about), passionate, positive, rapturous, raring (*to go*), spirited, unstinting, vigorous, wholehearted, zealous. *Opp* APATHETIC. **be enthusiastic** enthuse, get excited, *inf* go into raptures, *inf* go overboard, rave.

entice *v* allure, attract, coax, decoy, inveigle, lead on, lure, persuade, seduce, tempt, trap.

entire *adj* complete, full, intact, sound, total, unbroken, undivided, uninterrupted, whole.

entitle *v* 1 call, christen, designate, dub, name, style, term, title. 2 allow, authorize, empower, enable, license, permit, qualify, warrant.

entitlement *n* claim, ownership, prerogative, right, title.

entity *n* article, being, object, organism, thing, whole.

entrails *n* bowels, guts, *inf* innards, inner organs, *inf* insides, intestines, viscera.

entrance *n* 1 access, admission, admittance. 2 appearance, arrival, entry. 3 door, doorway, gate, ingress, opening, turnstile, way in. 4 ante-room, foyer, lobby, passage, passageway, porch, vestibule. *Opp* EXIT.

entrant *n* applicant, candidate, competitor, contender, contestant, participant, player, rival.

entreat *v* beg, beseech, implore, sue. ▷ REQUEST.

entry *n* 1 insertion, item, listing, note, record. 2 ▷ ENTRANCE. 3 ▷ ENTRANT.

envelop *v* cloak, enfold, enshroud, swathe, wrap. ▷ HIDE.

envelope *n* cover, sheath, wrapper, wrapping.

enviable *adj* attractive, covetable, desirable, sought-after.

envious *adj* bitter, covetous, *inf* green with envy, grudging, jaundiced, jealous, resentful.

environment *n* conditions, context, ecosystem, environs, habitat, location, milieu, setting, situation, surroundings.

envisage *v* anticipate, contemplate, dream

of, envision, fancy, forecast, foresee, imagine, picture, predict, visualize.

envy *n* bitterness, covetousness, cupidity, desire, discontent, ill will, jealousy, longing, resentment.
• *v* begrudge, grudge, resent.

ephemeral *adj* brief, evanescent, fleeting, fugitive, impermanent, momentary, passing, short-lived, transient, transitory. *Opp* PERMANENT.

epidemic *adj* general, prevalent, rife, spreading, universal, widespread.
• *n* outbreak, pestilence, plague, rash, upsurge.

episode *n* 1 affair, event, happening, incident, matter, occurrence. 2 chapter, instalment, part, passage, scene.

epitome *n* 1 archetype, embodiment, essence, exemplar, incarnation, personification, quintessence, type. 2 ▷ SUMMARY.

equal *adj* balanced, commensurate, congruent, egalitarian, even, fair, identical, indistinguishable, interchangeable, level, like, matching, proportionate, regular, the same, symmetrical, uniform. ▷ EQUIVALENT. *Opp* UNEQUAL.
• *n* counterpart, equivalent, fellow, peer, twin.
• *v* 1 balance, correspond to, draw with, tie with. 2 *No one equals her.* be in the same class as, compare with, match, resemble, rival.

equality *n* 1 balance, correspondence, equivalence, identity, similarity, uniformity. 2 *social equality.* egalitarianism, even-handedness, fairness, parity. *Opp* BIAS, INEQUALITY.

equalize *v* balance, compensate, even up, level, match, regularize, square, standardize.

equate *v* assume to be equal, compare, juxtapose, liken, match, set side by side.

equilibrium *n* balance, equanimity, evenness, poise, stability, steadiness, symmetry.

equip *v* arm, array, attire, clothe, dress, fit out, fit up, furnish, *inf* kit out, provide, stock, supply.

equipment *n* accoutrements, apparatus, *inf* clobber, furnishings, *inf* gear, hardware, implements, instruments, kit, machinery, materials, outfit, paraphernalia, rig, stuff, supplies, tackle, things, tools, trappings.

equivalent *adj* alike, analogous, comparable, corresponding, parallel, similar, synonymous. ▷ EQUAL.

equivocal *adj* ambiguous, circumlocutory, doubtful, equivocating, evasive, noncommittal, questionable, roundabout.

equivocate *v inf* beat about the bush, dodge the issue, fence, *inf* have it both ways, hedge, prevaricate, quibble.

era *n* age, date, day, epoch, period, time.

eradicate *v* eliminate, get rid of, uproot. ▷ DESTROY.

erase *v* cancel, cross out, delete, eradicate, obliterate, rub out, wipe away. ▷ REMOVE.

erect *adj* perpendicular, rigid, standing, straight, upright, vertical.
• *v* build, construct, elevate, establish, lift up, pitch (*a tent*), put up, raise.

erode *v* corrode, eat away, eat into, gnaw away, grind down, wash away, wear away.

erotic *adj* aphrodisiac, arousing, seductive, sensual, voluptuous. ▷ SEXY.

err *v* be mistaken, *sl* boob, *inf* get it wrong, go astray, go wrong, misbehave, miscalculate, sin, *inf* slip up, transgress.

errand *n* assignment, commission, duty, job, journey, mission, task, trip.

erratic *adj* capricious, changeable, fickle, fitful, fluctuating, inconsistent, irregular, shifting, spasmodic, sporadic, uneven, unpredictable, unsteady, variable, wayward. *Opp* REGULAR. 2 aimless, haphazard, meandering, wandering.

error *n inf* bloomer, blunder, *sl* boob, fallacy, fault, flaw, gaffe, *inf* howler, inaccuracy, inconsistency, lapse, misapprehension, miscalculation, misconception, misprint, mistake, misunderstanding, omission, oversight, sin, *inf* slip-up, solecism, transgression, wrongdoing.

erupt *v* be discharged, belch, break out, burst out, explode, gush, issue, pour out, shoot out, spew, spout, spurt.

eruption *n* emission, explosion, outbreak, outburst, rash.

escapade *n* adventure, exploit, *inf* lark, mischief, practical joke, prank, scrape, stunt.

escape *n* 1 break-out, departure, flight, flit, getaway, retreat. 2 discharge, emission, leak, leakage, seepage. 3 avoidance, distraction, diversion, escapism, evasion, relaxation, relief.
• *v* 1 abscond, *sl* beat it, bolt, break free, break out, *inf* cut and run, decamp, disappear, *sl* do a bunk, elope, flee, fly, get away, *inf* give someone the slip, run away, *sl* scarper, *inf* slip the net, *inf* take to your heels, *inf* turn tail. 2 discharge,

drain, leak, ooze, pour out, seep. 3 *escape the nasty jobs.* avoid, dodge, duck, elude, evade, shirk, *sl* skive off.

escapism *n* daydreaming, fantasy, wishful thinking.

escort *n* 1 bodyguard, convoy, guard, guide, protection, protector, safe-conduct. 2 *royal escort.* attendant, entourage, retinue, train. 3 *escort at a dance.* chaperon, companion, *inf* date, partner. • *v* accompany, attend, chaperon, conduct, guard, look after, protect, shepherd, stay with, usher, watch.

essence *n* 1 centre, character, core, crux, essential quality, heart, kernel, life, meaning, nature, pith, quintessence, soul, spirit, substance. 2 concentrate, elixir, extract, flavouring, fragrance, perfume, scent, tincture.

essential *adj* basic, characteristic, chief, crucial, fundamental, important, indispensable, inherent, innate, intrinsic, irreplaceable, key, leading, main, necessary, primary, principal, quintessential, requisite, vital. *Opp* INESSENTIAL.

establish *v* 1 base, constitute, construct, create, decree, found, form, inaugurate, institute, introduce, organize, originate, set up, start. 2 *establish yourself in a job.* confirm, ensconce, entrench, install, lodge, secure, settle. 3 *establish facts.* accept, agree, authenticate, confirm, corroborate, decide, demonstrate, fix, prove, ratify, recognize, substantiate, verify.

established *adj* deep-rooted, deep-seated, ineradicable, ingrained, long-standing, permanent, proven, reliable, respected, secure, traditional, well-known, well-tried. *Opp* NEW.

establishment *n* 1 constitution, creation, formation, foundation, inauguration, institution, introduction, setting up. 2 *well-run establishment.* business, company, concern, enterprise, factory, household, institution, office, organization, shop.

estate *n* 1 area, development, domain, land. 2 assets, capital, chattels, effects, fortune, goods, inheritance, lands, possessions, property, wealth.

esteem *n* admiration, credit, estimation, favour, honour, regard, respect, reverence, veneration.
• *v* ▷ RESPECT.

estimate *n* appraisal, approximation, assessment, calculation, conjecture, estimation, evaluation, guess, judgement, opinion, price, quotation, reckoning, valuation. • *v* appraise, assess, calculate, compute, conjecture, consider, count up, evaluate, gauge, guess, judge, project, reckon, surmise, weigh up, work out.

estimation *n* appraisal, appreciation, assessment, calculation, consideration, estimate, evaluation, judgement, opinion, rating, view.

estuary *n* creek, firth, fjord, inlet, loch, river mouth.

eternal *adj* ceaseless, endless, everlasting, heavenly, immeasurable, immortal, infinite, lasting, measureless, never-ending, permanent, perpetual, timeless, unchanging, undying, unending, unlimited. ▷ CONTINUAL. *Opp* OCCASIONAL, TRANSIENT.

eternity *n* afterlife, immortality, infinity, perpetuity.

ethical *adj* decent, fair, good, honest, just, moral, noble, principled, righteous, upright, virtuous. *Opp* IMMORAL.

ethnic *adj* cultural, folk, national, racial, traditional.

etiquette *n* ceremony, civility, code, conventions, courtesy, decency, decorum, form, formalities, manners, politeness, propriety, protocol, rules, standards.

evacuate *v* 1 clear, move out, remove, send away. 2 abandon, desert, empty, leave, pull out of, quit, relinquish, vacate, withdraw from.

evade *v* 1 avoid, circumvent, dodge, duck, elude, escape from, fend off, get away from, shirk, shrink from, shun, sidestep, *sl* skive, steer clear of. 2 *evade a question.* fudge, hedge, parry. ▷ EQUIVOCATE. *Opp* CONFRONT.

evaluate *v* assess, estimate, judge, value, weigh up.

evaporate *v* disappear, disperse, dissipate, dissolve, dry up, melt away, vanish, vaporize.

evasive *adj* ambiguous, *inf* cagey, circumlocutory, deceptive, devious, equivocal, indirect, misleading, noncommittal, oblique, prevaricating, roundabout, *inf* shifty, uninformative. *Opp* DIRECT.

even *adj* 1 flat, flush, horizontal, level, plane, smooth, straight, true. 2 *even pulse.* consistent, constant, measured, regular, rhythmical, unbroken, uniform, unvarying. 3 *even scores.* balanced, equal, identical, level, matching, the same. 4 ▷ EVEN-TEMPERED. *Opp* IRREGULAR. **even out** ▷ FLATTEN. **even up** ▷ EQUALIZE. **get even** ▷ RETALIATE.

evening *n* dusk, nightfall, sundown, sunset, twilight.

event *n* 1 affair, business, chance, circumstance, contingency, episode, eventuality, experience, happening, incident, occurrence. 2 ceremony, entertainment, function, occasion. 3 *sporting event.* championship, competition, contest, engagement, fixture, game, match, meeting, tournament.

even-tempered *adj* balanced, calm, composed, cool, equable, impassive, imperturbable, peaceable, peaceful, placid, poised, reliable, self-possessed, serene, stable, steady, tranquil, unemotional, unexcitable, unruffled. *Opp* EXCITABLE.

eventual *adj* concluding, destined, ensuing, final, last, resultant, resulting, ultimate.

everlasting *adj* ceaseless, deathless, endless, eternal, immortal, incorruptible, infinite, limitless, measureless, never-ending, permanent, perpetual, timeless, unchanging, undying, unending. *Opp* TRANSIENT.

evermore *adv* always, eternally, for ever, unceasingly.

evict *v* dislodge, dispossess, eject, expel, *sl* give (someone) the boot, *inf* kick out, oust, remove, throw out, *inf* turf out.

evidence *n* attestation, confirmation, corroboration, data, demonstration, documentation, facts, grounds, information, proof, sign, statistics. **give evidence** ▷ TESTIFY.

evident *adj* apparent, clear, discernible, manifest, obvious, palpable, patent, perceptible, plain, self-explanatory, undeniable, unmistakable, visible. *Opp* UNCERTAIN.

evil *adj* 1 amoral, atrocious, base, black-hearted, blasphemous, corrupt, devilish, diabolical, dishonest, fiendish, foul, harmful, hateful, heinous, hellish, impious, iniquitous, irreligious, machiavellian, malevolent, nefarious, pernicious, perverted, reprobate, satanic, sinful, sinister, treacherous, ungodly, unprincipled, vicious, vile, wicked, wrong. ▷ BAD. *Opp* GOOD. 2 *evil smell.* foul, nasty, pestilential, poisonous, unpleasant, unspeakable, vile. *Opp* PLEASANT.
• *n* 1 amorality, blasphemy, corruption, criminality, cruelty, depravity, dishonesty, fiendishness, immorality, impiety, iniquity, malevolence, malice, mischief, sin, sinfulness, treachery, turpitude, ungodliness, unrighteousness, vice, viciousness, villainy, wickedness. 2 affliction, bane, calamity, catastrophe, curse, disaster, enormity, hardship, harm, ill, misfortune, wrong.

evocative *adj* atmospheric, emotive, graphic, imaginative, realistic, stimulating, suggestive, vivid.

evoke *v* arouse, awaken, call up, conjure up, elicit, excite, kindle, produce, provoke, raise, rouse, stimulate, stir up, suggest, summon up.

evolution *n* advance, development, emergence, formation, growth, improvement, maturation, progress, unfolding.

evolve *v* develop, emerge, grow, improve, mature, progress, unfold.

exact *adj* 1 accurate, correct, dead (*centre*), faithful, faultless, meticulous, painstaking, precise, punctilious, right, rigorous, scrupulous, specific, *inf* spot-on, strict, true, truthful. *Opp* IMPRECISE. 2 *exact copy.* identical, indistinguishable, literal, perfect.
• *v* claim, compel, demand, enforce, extort, extract, get, insist on, obtain, require. **exacting** ▷ DIFFICULT.

exaggerate *v* 1 amplify, embellish, embroider, enlarge, inflate, magnify, make too much of, maximize, overdo, overemphasize, overestimate, overstate, *inf* pile it on. *Opp* MINIMIZE. 2 ▷ CARICATURE. **exaggerated** ▷ EXCESSIVE.

exalt *v* boost, elevate, lift, promote, raise, uplift. ▷ PRAISE. **exalted** ▷ HIGH.

examination *n* 1 analysis, appraisal, assessment, audit, *inf* exam, inspection, investigation, paper, post-mortem, review, scrutiny, study, survey, test. 2 [*medical*] *inf* check-up, scan. 3 *police examination.* cross-examination, enquiry, inquiry, inquisition, interrogation, probe, questioning, trial.

examine *v* 1 analyse, appraise, audit (*accounts*), check, *inf* check out, explore, inquire into, inspect, investigate, peruse, probe, research, scan, scrutinize, sift, sort out, study, test, vet, weigh up. 2 *examine a witness.* catechize, cross-examine, cross-question, *inf* grill, interrogate, *inf* pump, question, sound out, try.

example *n* 1 case, illustration, instance, occurrence, sample, specimen. 2 *example to follow.* ideal, lesson, model, paragon, pattern, prototype. **make an example of** ▷ PUNISH.

exasperate *v* *inf* aggravate, gall, infuriate, irk, irritate, pique, vex. ▷ ANNOY.

excavate *v* burrow, dig, hollow out, mine, unearth.

exceed *v* do more than, go beyond, outnumber, outstrip, overstep, overtake, pass, transcend. ▷ EXCEL.

exceedingly *adv* amazingly, especially, exceptionally, excessively, extremely, outstandingly, unusually, very.

excel *v* beat, better, eclipse, exceed, outdo, outshine, shine, stand out, surpass, top.

excellent *adj inf* ace, admirable, *inf* brilliant, capital, champion, choice, consummate, distinguished, exceptional, exemplary, extraordinary, *inf* fabulous, *inf* fantastic, fine, first-class, first-rate, gorgeous, great, ideal, impressive, magnificent, marvellous, model, outstanding, perfect, *inf* phenomenal, remarkable, *inf* smashing, splendid, sterling, *inf* stunning, *inf* super, superb, superlative, supreme, surpassing, *inf* terrific, *inf* tip-top, *inf* top-notch, *inf* tremendous, unequalled, wonderful. *Opp* BAD.

except *v* exclude, leave out, omit.

exception *n* 1 exclusion, omission, rejection. 2 anomaly, departure, deviation, eccentricity, freak, irregularity, oddity, peculiarity, quirk, rarity. **take exception** ▷ OBJECT.

exceptional *adj* 1 abnormal, anomalous, atypical, curious, eccentric, extraordinary, isolated, memorable, notable, odd, out of the ordinary, peculiar, phenomenal, quirky, rare, remarkable, singular, special, strange, surprising, uncommon, unconventional, unexpected, unheard-of, unique, unparalleled, unprecedented, untypical, unusual. 2 ▷ EXCELLENT. *Opp* ORDINARY.

excerpt *n* citation, clip, extract, fragment, part, passage, quotation, section, selection.

excess *n* 1 abundance, glut, overabundance, overflow, profit, superfluity, surfeit, surplus. *Opp* SCARCITY. 2 debauchery, dissipation, extravagance, intemperance, overindulgence, profligacy, wastefulness. *Opp* MODERATION.

excessive *adj* 1 disproportionate, exaggerated, extravagant, extreme, immoderate, inordinate, intemperate, needless, overdone, prodigal, profligate, profuse, superfluous, undue, unnecessary, wasteful. ▷ HUGE. *Opp* INADEQUATE. 2 *excessive prices.* exorbitant, extortionate, unjustifiable, unrealistic, unreasonable. *Opp* MODERATE.

exchange *n* deal, interchange, replacement, substitution, swap, switch. • *v* bargain, barter, change, convert (*currency*), interchange, reciprocate, replace, substitute, swap, switch, trade, trade in. **exchange words** ▷ TALK.

excitable *adj* edgy, emotional, explosive, fidgety, fiery, highly-strung, hot-tempered, irrepressible, jumpy, lively, mercurial, nervous, passionate, quick-tempered, restive, temperamental, unstable, volatile. *Opp* CALM.

excite *v* 1 agitate, amaze, animate, arouse, awaken, disturb, elate, electrify, enthral, exhilarate, fluster, *inf* get going, incite, inflame, interest, intoxicate, move, perturb, provoke, rouse, stimulate, stir up, thrill, *inf* turn on, upset, urge, work up. 2 *excite interest.* activate, cause, elicit, encourage, engender, evoke, fire, generate, kindle, produce, whet. *Opp* CALM.

excited *adj* agitated, eager, enthusiastic, exuberant, feverish, frantic, frenzied, heated, *inf* het up, hysterical, impassioned, intoxicated, lively, nervous, overwrought, restless, spirited, vivacious, wild. *Opp* APATHETIC.

excitement *n* action, activity, adventure, agitation, animation, commotion, drama, eagerness, enthusiasm, furore, fuss, heat, intensity, *inf* kicks, passion, stimulation, suspense, tension, thrill, unrest.

exciting *adj* dramatic, electrifying, eventful, fast-moving, galvanizing, gripping, heady, hair-raising, intoxicating, *inf* nail-biting, provocative, riveting, rousing, sensational, spectacular, spine-tingling, stimulating, stirring, tense, thrilling. ▷ AMAZING. *Opp* BORING.

exclaim *v* bawl, bellow, blurt out, call, cry out, declare, proclaim, shout, utter, yell.

exclamation *n* bellow, call, cry, expletive, interjection, oath, shout, utterance, yell.

exclude *v* ban, bar, blacklist, debar, disallow, except, expel, forbid, keep out, leave out, omit, ostracize, outlaw, prohibit, proscribe, put an embargo on, refuse, reject, repudiate, rule out, shut out, veto. ▷ REMOVE. *Opp* INCLUDE.

exclusive *adj* 1 limiting, restricted, sole, unique, unshared. 2 *exclusive club. inf* classy, fashionable, *inf* posh, private, select, selective, snobbish, up-market.

excreta *pl n* droppings, dung, excrement, faeces, manure, sewage, waste matter.

excursion *n* expedition, jaunt, journey, outing, trip.

excuse *n* alibi, apology, defence, explanation, extenuation, justification, mitigation, plea, pretext, reason, vindication.

• *v* 1 apologize for, condone, disregard, explain away, forgive, ignore, justify, mitigate, overlook, pardon, pass over, sanction, tolerate, vindicate, warrant. 2 absolve, acquit, clear, discharge, exculpate, exempt, exonerate, free, let off, *inf* let off the hook, liberate, release. *Opp* BLAME.

execute *v* 1 accomplish, achieve, bring off, carry out, complete, discharge, do, effect, implement, perform, *inf* pull off. 2 kill, put to death.

executive *n* administrator, manager, officer. ▷ CHIEF.

exemplary *adj* admirable, commendable, faultless, flawless, ideal, model, perfect, praiseworthy.

exemplify *v* demonstrate, depict, embody, illustrate, personify, represent, show, symbolize, typify.

exempt *v* except, exclude, excuse, free, let off, liberate, release, spare.

exercise *n* 1 action, activity, aerobics, callisthenics, exertion, games, gymnastics, sport, *inf* work-out. 2 *military exercise.* discipline, drill, manoeuvre, operation, practice, training.
• *v* 1 apply, bring to bear, display, effect, employ, exert, expend, implement, put to use, show, use, utilize, wield. 2 *exercise your body.* discipline, drill, keep fit, practise, train, *inf* work out. 3 ▷ WORRY.

exertion *n* action, effort, endeavour, strain. ▷ WORK.

exhaust *n* emission, fumes, gases, smoke.
• *v* 1 consume, deplete, drain, dry up, empty, expend, finish off, *inf* run through, sap, spend, use up. 2 debilitate, enervate, fatigue, prostrate, tax, tire, wear out, weary. **exhausted** ▷ BREATHLESS, WEARY.

exhausting *adj* arduous, back-breaking, crippling, debilitating, demanding, enervating, gruelling, hard, laborious, punishing, severe, strenuous, taxing, tiring, wearying.

exhaustion *n* tiredness, weariness. ▷ FATIGUE.

exhaustive *adj* careful, comprehensive, full-scale, intensive, meticulous, thorough. *Opp* INCOMPLETE.

exhibit *v* 1 arrange, display, offer, present, put up, set up, show. 2 air, betray, demonstrate, disclose, express, *derog* flaunt, indicate, manifest, *derog* parade, reveal, *derog* show off. *Opp* HIDE.

exhibition *n* demonstration, display, *inf* expo, exposition, presentation, show.

exhilarating *adj* bracing, cheering, exciting, invigorating, refreshing, stimulating, tonic, uplifting. ▷ HAPPY.

exhort *v* advise, encourage, harangue, recommend, urge.

exile *n* 1 banishment, deportation, expatriation, expulsion. 2 displaced person, émigré, expatriate, outcast, refugee, wanderer.
• *v* ban, banish, bar, deport, drive out, eject, evict, expatriate, expel, oust, send away.

exist *v* 1 be, be found, be real, happen, occur. 2 continue, endure, hold out, keep going, last, live, remain alive, subsist, survive. **existing** ▷ ACTUAL, CURRENT, LIVING.

existence *n* actuality, being, continuance, life, living, persistence, reality, survival.

exit *n* 1 barrier, door, doorway, gate, gateway, opening, portal, way out. 2 *hurried exit.* departure, escape, exodus, flight, leave-taking, retreat, withdrawal.
• *v* ▷ DEPART.

exorbitant *adj* disproportionate, excessive, extortionate, extravagant, high, inordinate, outrageous, prohibitive, *inf* sky-high, *inf* steep, swingeing, unjustifiable, unrealistic, unreasonable, unwarranted. ▷ EXPENSIVE. *Opp* REASONABLE.

exotic *adj* 1 far-away, foreign, remote. 2 colourful, different, exciting, extraordinary, glamorous, novel, odd, outlandish, peculiar, rare, romantic, singular, strange, striking, unfamiliar, unusual, wonderful. *Opp* ORDINARY.

expand *v* 1 amplify, augment, broaden, build up, develop, diversify, elaborate, enlarge, extend, fill out, heighten, increase, prolong. 2 dilate, distend, grow, increase, lengthen, open out, stretch, swell, thicken, widen. *Opp* CONTRACT.

expanse *n* area, breadth, extent, range, space, spread, stretch, sweep, surface, tract.

expansive *adj* 1 affable, amiable, communicative, effusive, extrovert, friendly, genial, open, outgoing, sociable, well-disposed. ▷ TALKATIVE. *Opp* TACITURN. 2 ▷ BROAD.

expect *v* 1 anticipate, await, *inf* bank on, bargain for, be prepared for, contemplate, count on, envisage, forecast, foresee, hope for, imagine, look forward to, plan for, predict, prophesy, reckon on, wait for. 2 *expect obedience.* demand, insist on, look for, rely on, require, want. 3 *I expect he'll come.* assume, believe, conjecture, imagine, judge, presume, suppose, surmise, think. **expected** ▷ PREDICTABLE.

expectant *adj* 1 eager, hopeful, keyed up, *inf* on tenterhooks, optimistic, ready. 2 *expectant mother. inf* expecting, pregnant.

expedient *adj* advantageous, advisable, appropriate, beneficial, convenient, desirable, helpful, judicious, opportune, politic, practical, pragmatic, profitable, prudent, right, sensible, suitable, to your advantage, useful, worthwhile.
• *n* contrivance, device, means, measure, method, ploy, recourse, resort, ruse, scheme, stratagem, tactics.

expedition *n* crusade, excursion, exploration, journey, mission, pilgrimage, quest, raid, safari, tour, trek, trip, undertaking, voyage.

expel *v* 1 ban, banish, cast out, dismiss, drive out, eject, evict, exile, exorcise, *inf* kick out, oust, remove, send away, throw out, *inf* turf out, turn out. 2 *expel fumes.* belch, discharge, emit, exhale, give out, push out, send out, spew out.

expend *v* consume, employ, pay out, spend, use.

expendable *adj* disposable, inessential, replaceable, *inf* throw-away, unimportant.

expense *n* charge, cost, expenditure, fee, outgoings, outlay, overheads, payment, price, rate, spending.

expensive *adj* costly, dear, generous, high-priced, over-priced, *inf* pricey, *inf* steep, up-market, valuable. ▷ EXORBITANT. *Opp* CHEAP.

experience *n* 1 familiarity, involvement, observation, participation, practice, taking part. 2 background, expertise, *inf* know-how, knowledge, *Fr* savoir faire, skill, understanding, wisdom. 3 *nasty experience.* adventure, episode, event, happening, incident, occurrence, ordeal, trial.
• *v* encounter, endure, face, go through, have a taste of, know, meet, sample, suffer, test out, try, undergo. **experienced** ▷ EXPERT.

experiment *n* demonstration, investigation, *inf* practical, research, test, trial, try-out.
• *v* examine, investigate, probe, research, test, try out.

experimental *adj* 1 exploratory, pilot, provisional, tentative, trial. 2 *experimental evidence.* empirical, proved, tested.

expert *adj* able, *inf* ace, *inf* brilliant, capable, competent, *inf* crack, experienced, knowing, knowledgeable, master, masterly, practised, professional, proficient, qualified, skilful, skilled, specialized, trained, well-versed. ▷ CLEVER. *Opp* UNSKILFUL.
• *n inf* ace, authority, connoisseur, *inf* dab hand, genius, *derog* know-all, master, *inf* old hand, professional, pundit, specialist, virtuoso, *inf* wizard. *Opp* AMATEUR.

expertise *n* dexterity, judgement, *inf* know-how, knowledge, *Fr* savoir faire, skill.

expire *v* cease, come to an end, finish, lapse, *inf* run out, terminate. ▷ DIE.

explain *v* 1 clarify, clear up, decipher, define, demonstrate, describe, disentangle, elucidate, expound, *inf* get across, *inf* get over, gloss, illustrate, interpret, make clear, make plain, resolve, shed light on, simplify, solve, *inf* sort out, spell out, teach, translate, unravel. 2 *explain a mistake.* account for, excuse, give reasons for, justify, legitimize, make excuses for, rationalize, vindicate.

explanation *n* 1 account, analysis, clarification, definition, demonstration, description, elucidation, exegesis, exposition, gloss, illustration, interpretation, key, meaning, rubric, significance, solution. 2 cause, excuse, justification, motive, reason, vindication.

explanatory *adj* descriptive, expository, helpful, illuminating, illustrative.

explicit *adj* categorical, clear, definite, detailed, direct, exact, express, frank, manifest, open, outspoken, patent, plain, positive, precise, specific, *inf* spelt out, spoken, stated, straightforward, unambiguous, unconcealed, unequivocal, unreserved, well-defined. *Opp* IMPLICIT.

explode *v* 1 backfire, blast, blow up, burst, detonate, erupt, go off, set off, shatter. 2 *explode a theory.* debunk, destroy, discredit, disprove, put an end to, rebut, refute, reject.

exploit *n* achievement, adventure, attainment, deed, feat.
• *v* 1 build on, capitalize on, *inf* cash in on, develop, make use of, profit by, profit from, trade on, work on, use, utilize. 2 *exploit people. inf* bleed, ill-treat, impose on, keep down, manipulate, *inf* milk, misuse, oppress, *inf* rip off, *inf* squeeze dry, take advantage of, treat unfairly.

explore *v* 1 break new ground, prospect, reconnoitre, scout, search, survey, tour, travel through. 2 *explore a problem.* analyse, examine, inspect, investigate, look into, probe, research, scrutinize, study.

explosion *n* 1 bang, blast, burst, clap, crack, detonation, eruption, firing, report. 2 *explosion of anger.* fit, outbreak, outburst, paroxysm, spasm.

explosive *adj* dangerous, highly-charged, sensitive, unstable, volatile. *Opp* STABLE.
• *n* cordite, dynamite, gelignite, gunpowder, TNT.

exponent *n* 1 interpreter, performer, player. 2 advocate, champion, defender, expounder, presenter, proponent, supporter, upholder.

expose *v* bare, betray, dig up, disclose, display, show (up), uncover, unmask. ▷ REVEAL. *Opp* HIDE.

express *v* air, articulate, give vent to, phrase, put into words, release, vent, voice, word. ▷ COMMUNICATE.

expression *n* 1 cliché, formula, phrase, phraseology, remark, statement, term, turn of phrase, usage, utterance, wording. ▷ SAYING. 2 articulation, confession, declaration, disclosure, revelation, statement. 3 *expression in your voice.* depth, emotion, expressiveness, feeling, nuance, sensitivity, sympathy, tone. 4 *facial expression.* air, appearance, aspect, countenance, face, look, mien.

expressionless *adj* blank, *inf* dead-pan, emotionless, empty, glassy, impassive, inscrutable, poker-faced, uncommunicative, wooden. 2 boring, dull, flat, monotonous, uninspiring, unmodulated, unvarying. *Opp* EXPRESSIVE.

expressive *adj* 1 meaningful, revealing, significant, striking, suggestive, telling. 2 articulate, eloquent, lively, modulated, varied. *Opp* EXPRESSIONLESS.

exquisite *adj* delicate, elegant, fine, intricate, well-crafted. ▷ BEAUTIFUL. *Opp* CRUDE.

extend *v* 1 add to, broaden, build up, develop, draw out, enlarge, expand, increase, keep going, lengthen, open up, pad out, perpetuate, prolong, protract, *inf* spin out, spread, stretch, widen. 2 *extend a deadline.* defer, delay, postpone, put back, put off. 3 *extend your hand.* give, hold out, offer, outstretch, present, proffer, put out, raise, reach out, stretch out. 4 *The grounds extend to the lake.* continue, range, reach.

extensive *adj* broad, comprehensive, expansive, far-ranging, far-reaching, sweeping, vast, wide, widespread. ▷ LARGE.

extent *n* amount, area, bounds, breadth, compass, degree, dimensions, distance, expanse, length, limit, magnitude, measure, proportions, quantity, range, reach, scale, scope, size, spread, sweep, width.

exterior *adj* external, outer, outside, outward, superficial.
• *n* coating, covering, façade, front, outside, shell, skin, surface. *Opp* INTERIOR.

exterminate *v* annihilate, destroy, eliminate, eradicate, extirpate, get rid of, obliterate, root out, terminate. ▷ KILL.

external *adj* exterior, outer, outside, outward, superficial. *Opp* INTERNAL.

extinct *adj* dead, defunct, died out, extinguished, gone, inactive, vanished. ▷ OLD. *Opp* LIVING.

extinguish *v* blow out, damp down, douse, put out, quench, slake, smother, snuff out, switch off. ▷ DESTROY. *Opp* KINDLE.

extort *v* blackmail, bully, coerce, exact, extract, force, obtain by force.

extra *adj* accessory, added, additional, auxiliary, excess, further, left over, more, other, reserve, spare, superfluous, supplementary, surplus, temporary, unneeded, unused, unwanted.

extract *n* 1 concentrate, distillation, essence, quintessence. 2 abstract, citation, *inf* clip, clipping, cutting, excerpt, passage, quotation, selection.
• *v* 1 draw out, extricate, pull out, remove, take out, withdraw. 2 *extract a confession.* extort, force out, *inf* worm out, wrench, wrest, wring. 3 *extract what you need.* choose, derive, gather, glean, quote, select. ▷ OBTAIN.

extraordinary *adj* abnormal, amazing, astonishing, astounding, bizarre, breathtaking, curious, exceptional, extreme, fantastic, *inf* funny, incredible, marvellous, miraculous, mysterious, notable, noteworthy, odd, outstanding, peculiar, *inf* phenomenal, prodigious, queer, rare, remarkable, *inf* sensational, singular, special, staggering, strange, striking, stunning, stupendous, surprising, *inf* unbelievable, uncommon, unheard-of, unimaginable, unique, unprecedented, unusual, *inf* weird, wonderful. *Opp* ORDINARY.

extravagance *n* excess, improvidence, lavishness, overindulgence, prodigality, profligacy, self-indulgence, wastefulness. *Opp* ECONOMY.

extravagant *adj* exaggerated, excessive, flamboyant, grandiose, immoderate, improvident, lavish, outrageous, overdone, pretentious, prodigal, profligate, profuse, self-indulgent, *inf* showy, spendthrift, uneconomical, unreasonable, wasteful. ▷ EXPENSIVE. *Opp* ECONOMICAL.

extreme *adj* 1 acute, drastic, excessive, greatest, maximum, *inf* terrific, utmost. ▷ EXTRAORDINARY. 2 distant, furthermost, furthest, last, outermost, ultimate, uttermost. 3 *extreme opinions.* absolute, avant-garde, exaggerated, extravagant, extremist, fanatical, *inf* hardline, immoderate, intemperate, intransigent, left-wing, militant, outrageous, radical, right-wing, uncompromising, *inf* way-out.
• *n* bounds, edge, end, extremity, left wing, limit, maximum, minimum, pole, right wing, top, ultimate.

extroverted *adj* active, confident, exhibitionist, outgoing, positive. ▷ SOCIABLE. *Opp* INTROVERTED.

exuberant *adj* 1 animated, boisterous, *inf* bubbly, buoyant, eager, ebullient, effervescent, energetic, enthusiastic, excited, exhilarated, exultant, high-spirited, irrepressible, lively, spirited, sprightly, vivacious. ▷ CHEERFUL. 2 *exuberant decoration.* baroque, exaggerated, ornate, overdone, rich, rococo. 3 *exuberant growth.* abundant, copious, lush, luxuriant, overflowing, profuse, rank, teeming. *Opp* AUSTERE.

exultant *adj* delighted, ecstatic, elated, joyful, jubilant, *inf* on top of the world, overjoyed, rejoicing. ▷ EXUBERANT.

eye *n* 1 eyeball, *inf* peeper. 2 discernment, perception, sight, vision.
•*v* contemplate, examine, inspect, scrutinize, study, watch. ▷ SEE.

eye-witness *n* bystander, observer, onlooker, passer-by, spectator, watcher, witness.

F

fabric *n* 1 cloth, material, stuff, textile. 2 *fabric of a building.* construction, framework, make-up, structure, substance.

fabulous *adj* 1 fabled, fairy-tale, fanciful, fictitious, imaginary, legendary, mythical, story-book. 2 ⊳ EXCELLENT.

face *n* 1 appearance, countenance, expression, features, lineaments, look, *sl* mug, visage. 2 *face of building.* aspect, exterior, façade, front, outside, side, surface.
• *v* 1 be opposite, front onto, look towards, overlook. 2 *face danger.* brave, come to terms with, confront, cope with, defy, encounter, experience, face up to, meet, oppose, stand up to, tackle. 3 *face a wall with plaster.* ⊳ COVER.

facetious *adj* cheeky, flippant, impudent, irreverent. ⊳ FUNNY.

facile *adj* 1 cheap, easy, effortless, hasty, obvious, quick, simple, superficial, unconsidered. 2 *facile talker.* fluent, glib, insincere, plausible, ready, shallow, slick, *inf* smooth.

facility *n* 1 adroitness, ease, expertise, fluency, skill, smoothness. 2 *useful facility.* amenity, convenience, help, provision, resource, service.

fact *n* actuality, certainty, *Fr* fait accompli, reality, truth. *Opp* FICTION. **the facts** circumstances, data, details, evidence, information, *sl* the lowdown, particulars, statistics.

factor *n* aspect, cause, circumstance, component, consideration, constituent, contingency, detail, element, fact, influence, ingredient, item, part, particular.

factory *n* forge, foundry, manufacturing plant, mill, plant, refinery, works, workshop.

factual *adj* 1 accurate, bona fide, circumstantial, correct, demonstrable, empirical, faithful, genuine, matter-of-fact, objective, plain, prosaic, realistic, straightforward, true, unadorned, unbiased, unimaginative, unvarnished, valid, verifiable, well-documented. *Opp* FALSE. 2 *factual film.* biographical, documentary, historical, real-life. *Opp* FICTIONAL.

faculty *n* ability, aptitude, capability, capacity, flair, genius, gift, knack, power, talent.

fade *v* 1 blanch, bleach, dim, discolour, dull, grow pale, whiten. *Opp* BRIGHTEN. 2 become less, decline, diminish, disappear, dwindle, evanesce, fail, melt away, vanish, wane, weaken. 3 *flowers fade.* droop, flag, wilt, wither.

fail *v* 1 be unsuccessful, break down, close down, come to an end, *inf* come to grief, come to nothing, *sl* conk out, *inf* crash, cut out, fall through, *inf* fizzle out, *inf* flop, *inf* fold, founder, give up, go bankrupt, *inf* go bust, go out of business, miscarry, misfire, *inf* miss out, peter out, stop working. 2 *the light will fail soon.* decline, deteriorate, diminish, disappear, dwindle, ebb, fade, give out, melt away, vanish, wane, weaken. 3 *fail to do something.* forget, neglect, omit. 4 *fail someone.* disappoint, *inf* let down. *Opp* IMPROVE, SUCCEED.

failing *n* blemish, defect, fault, flaw, foible, imperfection, shortcoming, weakness, weak spot.

failure *n* 1 defeat, disappointment, disaster, downfall, fiasco, *inf* flop, loss, miscarriage, *inf* wash-out, wreck. 2 breakdown, collapse, crash, stoppage. 3 *failure to do your duty.* dereliction, neglect, omission. *Opp* SUCCESS.

faint *adj* 1 blurred, blurry, dim, faded, feeble, hazy, ill-defined, indistinct, misty, muzzy, pale, pastel (*colours*), shadowy, unclear, vague. 2 *faint smell.* delicate, slight. 3 *faint sounds.* distant, hushed, low, muffled, muted, soft, stifled, subdued, thin, weak. 4 *feel faint.* dizzy, exhausted, feeble, giddy, light-headed, unsteady, weak, *inf* woozy. *Opp* CLEAR, STRONG.
• *v* black out, collapse, *inf* flake out, *inf* keel over, pass out, swoon.

fair *adj* 1 blond, blonde, flaxen, golden, light, yellow. 2 *fair weather.* bright, clear, clement, cloudless, dry, favourable, fine, pleasant, sunny. *Opp* DARK. 3 *fair decision.* disinterested, even-handed, honest, honourable, impartial, just, lawful, legitimate, non-partisan, open-minded, proper, right, unbiased, unprejudiced, upright. *Opp* UNJUST. 4 *fair standard.* acceptable, adequate, average, mediocre,

middling, moderate, passable, reasonable, respectable, satisfactory, *inf* so-so, tolerable. *Opp* UNACCEPTABLE. 5 ▷ BEAUTIFUL.
• *n* 1 amusement park, funfair. 2 bazaar, carnival, exhibition, festival, fête, gala, market, sale, show.

fairly *adv* moderately, pretty, quite, rather, reasonably, somewhat, tolerably, up to a point.

faith *n* 1 assurance, belief, confidence, credence, reliance, trust. *Opp* DOUBT. 2 conviction, creed, doctrine, dogma, persuasion, religion.

faithful *adj* 1 constant, dependable, devoted, dutiful, loyal, reliable, staunch, steadfast, trusted, trustworthy, unswerving. 2 *faithful account.* accurate, exact, factual, literal, precise. ▷ TRUE. *Opp* FALSE.

fake *adj* artificial, bogus, counterfeit, ersatz, false, fictitious, forged, fraudulent, imitation, invented, made-up, mock, *inf* phoney, pretended, sham, simulated, spurious, synthetic, trumped-up, unreal. *Opp* GENUINE.
• *n* 1 copy, counterfeit, duplicate, forgery, hoax, imitation, replica, reproduction, sham, simulation. 2 charlatan, cheat, fraud, hoaxer, impostor, *inf* phoney, quack.
• *v* affect, copy, counterfeit, dissemble, falsify, feign, forge, fudge, imitate, pretend, put on, reproduce, sham, simulate.

fall *n* 1 collapse, crash, decline, decrease, depreciation, descent, dip, dive, downswing, downturn, drop, lowering, nosedive, plunge, reduction, slump, tumble. 2 *fall of a town.* capitulation, capture, defeat, overthrow, seizure, submission, surrender.
• *v* 1 collapse, *inf* come a cropper, crash down, dive, drop down, founder, keel over, overbalance, pitch, plummet, plunge, sink, slump, spiral, stumble, topple, trip over, tumble. 2 decline, decrease, diminish, dwindle, ebb, lessen, subside. 3 descend, drop, fall away, slope down. 4 *curtains fell in folds.* be suspended, cascade, dangle, hang. 5 *Christmas falls on a Friday this year.* come, happen, occur. 6 ▷ DIE. 7 ▷ SURRENDER. **fall apart** ▷ DISINTEGRATE. **fall back** ▷ RETREAT. **fall behind** ▷ LAG. **fall down, fall in** ▷ COLLAPSE. **fall off** ▷ DECLINE. **fall out** ▷ QUARREL. **fall through** ▷ FAIL.

fallacy *n* delusion, misconception. ▷ ERROR.

fallible *adj* erring, frail, human, imperfect, liable to make mistakes, uncertain, unpredictable, unreliable, weak. *Opp* INFALLIBLE.

fallow *adj* resting, uncultivated, unplanted, unused.

false *adj* 1 deceptive, distorted, erroneous, fabricated, fallacious, fictitious, flawed, imprecise, inaccurate, incorrect, invalid, misleading, mistaken, spurious, untrue, wrong. ▷ FAKE. 2 *false friends.* deceitful, dishonest, disloyal, double-dealing, faithless, lying, treacherous, *inf* two-faced, unfaithful, unreliable, untrustworthy. *Opp* TRUE. **false name** ▷ PSEUDONYM.

falsehood *n* fabrication, *inf* fib, *inf* story. ▷ LIE.

falsify *v* alter, *inf* cook (*the books*), counterfeit, distort, exaggerate, fake, forge, fudge, misrepresent, mock up, pervert, slant, tamper with, twist.

falter *v* 1 flag, flinch, hesitate, hold back, lose confidence, pause, quail, stagger, stumble, totter, waver. *Opp* PERSIST. 2 stammer, stutter. **faltering** ▷ HESITANT.

fame *n* acclaim, celebrity, distinction, eminence, glory, honour, importance, name, *derog* notoriety, pre-eminence, prestige, prominence, renown, reputation, repute, *inf* stardom.

familiar *adj* 1 accustomed, common, conventional, customary, everyday, frequent, habitual, mundane, normal, ordinary, predictable, regular, routine, stock, traditional, usual, well-known. *Opp* STRANGE. 2 chatty, close, confidential, *derog* forward, *inf* free-and-easy, *derog* impudent, informal, intimate, *derog* presumptuous, relaxed, sociable, unceremonious. ▷ FRIENDLY. *Opp* FORMAL. **familiar with** acquainted with, *inf* at home with, aware of, conscious of, knowledgeable about, trained in, versed in.

family *n* 1 brood, children, *inf* flesh and blood, issue, kindred, kith and kin, litter, *inf* nearest and dearest, offspring, progeny, relations, relatives, *inf* tribe. 2 ancestry, blood, clan, dynasty, extraction, forebears, genealogy, house, line, lineage, pedigree, race, strain, tribe.

famine *n* dearth, hunger, lack, malnutrition, scarcity, shortage, starvation, want. *Opp* PLENTY.

famished *adj* hungry, ravenous, starved, starving.

famous *adj* acclaimed, big, celebrated, distinguished, eminent, exalted, glorious, great, historic, illustrious, important, legendary, notable, noted, *derog* notorious, outstanding, popular, prominent, proverbial, renowned, revered, time-honoured, venerable, well-known, world-famous. *Opp* UNKNOWN.

fan *n* 1 extractor, ventilator. 2 *soccer fan.* addict, admirer, aficionado, *inf* buff, devotee, enthusiast, *inf* fiend, follower, lover, supporter. ▷ FANATIC.

fanatic *n* activist, adherent, bigot, extremist, fiend, freak, maniac, militant, zealot.

fanatical *adj* bigoted, extreme, fervent, immoderate, irrational, maniacal, militant, obsessive, over-enthusiastic, passionate, rabid, single-minded, zealous. *Opp* MODERATE.

fanciful *adj* capricious, fantastic, illusory, imaginary, make-believe, unrealistic, whimsical.

fancy *adj* decorative, elaborate, embellished, embroidered, intricate, ornate.
• *n* ▷ IMAGINATION, WHIM.
• *v* 1 envisage, imagine, picture, visualize. ▷ THINK. 2 be attracted to, crave, like, long for, prefer, want, wish for. ▷ DESIRE.

fantastic *adj* 1 absurd, amazing, elaborate, exaggerated, extraordinary, extravagant, fabulous, fanciful, far-fetched, grotesque, imaginative, implausible, incredible, odd, quaint, remarkable, strange, surreal, unbelievable, unlikely, weird. 2 ▷ EXCELLENT. *Opp* ORDINARY.

fantasy *n* chimera, daydream, delusion, dream, fancy, hallucination, illusion, make-believe, mirage, pipedream, reverie, vision. *Opp* REALITY.

far *adj* distant, far-away, far-off, outlying, remote. *Opp* NEAR.

farcical *adj* absurd, foolish, ludicrous, preposterous. ▷ FUNNY.

fare *n* 1 charge, cost, fee, payment, price. 2 ▷ FOOD.

farewell *adj* leaving, parting, valedictory.
• *n* departure, leave-taking, send-off, valediction. ▷ GOODBYE.

farm *n* farmhouse, farmstead, grange, smallholding.

farming *n* agriculture, crofting, cultivation, husbandry.

fascinate *v* allure, attract, beguile, bewitch, captivate, charm, delight, enchant, engross, enthral, entrance, interest, mesmerize, rivet. **fascinating** ▷ ATTRACTIVE.

fashion *n* 1 manner, method, mode, way. 2 convention, craze, fad, look, rage, style, taste, trend, vogue.

fashionable *adj* chic, contemporary, current, elegant, *inf* in, in vogue, the latest, modern, popular, smart, *inf* snazzy, sophisticated, stylish, tasteful, *inf* trendy, up-to-date. *Opp* UNFASHIONABLE.

fast *adv* at full tilt, briskly, post-haste, quickly, rapidly, swiftly.
• *adj* 1 breakneck, brisk, express, hasty, headlong, high-speed, hurried, lively, *inf* nippy, precipitate, quick, rapid, smart, *inf* spanking, speedy, swift. *Opp* SLOW. 2 attached, bound, fastened, firm, fixed, immobile, immovable, secure, tight. 3 *fast colours.* indelible, lasting, permanent, stable. 4 *fast living.* ▷ IMMORAL.
• *v* abstain, deny yourself, diet, go hungry, go without food, starve. *Opp* INDULGE.

fasten *v* affix, anchor, attach, bind, bolt, buckle, button, chain, clasp, cling, close, connect, couple, do up, fix, grip, hitch, hook, knot, join, lace, latch on, link, lock, make fast, moor, nail, padlock, paste, peg, pin, rope, screw down, seal, secure, staple, strap, tack, tape, tether, tie, unite, weld. ▷ STICK. *Opp* UNDO.

fastener *n* 1 bond, connection, connector, coupling, fastening, link, linkage. 2 buckle, button, catch, clasp, clip, hook, lace, latch, lock, peg, pin, zip.

fastidious *adj inf* choosy, dainty, discriminating, finicky, fussy, hard to please, nice, particular, *inf* pernickety, *inf* picky, selective, squeamish.

fat *adj* 1 bloated, *inf* broad in the beam, bulky, chubby, corpulent, dumpy, flabby, fleshy, gross, heavy, obese, overweight, paunchy, plump, podgy, portly, pot-bellied, pudgy, rotund, round, solid, squat, stocky, stout, thick, tubby, well-fed. ▷ BIG. 2 *fat meat.* fatty, greasy, oily. *Opp* LEAN.
• *n* blubber, grease, oil.

fatal *adj* 1 deadly, final, incurable, lethal, malignant, mortal, terminal. 2 ▷ DISASTROUS.

fatality *n* casualty, death, loss.

fate *n* 1 chance, destiny, doom, fortune, karma, kismet, lot, luck, nemesis, predestination, providence, the stars. 2 death, demise, destruction, downfall, end, ruin.

fated *adj* certain, cursed, damned, decreed, destined, doomed, inescapable, inevitable, intended, predestined, predetermined, preordained, sure.

father *n* begetter, *inf* dad, *inf* daddy,

inf pa, *inf* papa, parent, *inf* pop, sire.

fatigue *n* debility, exhaustion, languor, lassitude, lethargy, tiredness, weakness, weariness.
• *v* debilitate, drain, enervate, exhaust, tire, weaken, weary. **fatigued** ▷ WEARY.

fault *n* 1 blemish, defect, deficiency, failure, fallacy, flaw, foible, frailty, imperfection, inaccuracy, malfunction, snag, weakness. 2 blunder, *sl* boob, error, failing, *Fr* faux pas, gaffe, *inf* howler, indiscretion, lapse, miscalculation, misconduct, misdeed, mistake, negligence, offence, omission, oversight, peccadillo, shortcoming, sin, slip, transgression, vice, wrongdoing. 3 *It was my fault.* blame, culpability, guilt, liability, responsibility.
• *v* ▷ CRITICIZE.

faultless *adj* accurate, correct, exemplary, flawless, ideal, in mint condition, unimpeachable. ▷ PERFECT. *Opp* FAULTY.

faulty *adj* broken, damaged, defective, flawed, illogical, imperfect, inaccurate, incorrect, inoperative, invalid, not working, out of order, shop-soiled, unusable, useless. *Opp* FAULTLESS.

favour *n* 1 acceptance, approval, bias, favouritism, friendliness, goodwill, grace, liking, partiality, preference, support. 2 *Do me a favour.* courtesy, gift, good turn, indulgence, kindness, service.
• *v* 1 approve of, be in sympathy with, champion, choose, commend, esteem, *inf* fancy, *inf* go for, like, opt for, prefer, think well of, value. *Opp* DISLIKE. 2 abet, advance, back, be advantageous to, befriend, promote, support. ▷ HELP. *Opp* HINDER.

favourable *adj* 1 advantageous, appropriate, auspicious, beneficial, benign, convenient, following (*wind*), friendly, generous, helpful, kind, opportune, promising, propitious, reassuring, suitable, supportive, sympathetic, understanding, well-disposed. 2 *favourable review.* approving, commendatory, complimentary, encouraging, enthusiastic. 3 *favourable reputation.* desirable, enviable, good, pleasing, satisfactory. *Opp* UNFAVOURABLE.

favourite *adj* beloved, best, chosen, dearest, ideal, liked, loved, popular, preferred, well-liked.
• *n* 1 choice, pick, preference. 2 *inf* apple of your eye, darling, idol, pet.

fear *n* alarm, anxiety, apprehension, awe, concern, cowardice, dismay, doubt, dread, faint-heartedness, foreboding, fright, *inf* funk, horror, misgiving, nervousness, panic, qualm, suspicion, terror, timidity, trepidation, uneasiness, worry. ▷ PHOBIA. *Opp* COURAGE.
• *v* be afraid of, dread, quail at, shrink from, suspect, tremble at, worry about.

fearful *adj* 1 alarmed, apprehensive, frightened, nervous, scared, terrified, timid. ▷ AFRAID. *Opp* FEARLESS. 2 ▷ FEARSOME.

fearless *adj* bold, brave, dauntless, intrepid, resolute, stoical, unafraid, unconcerned, undaunted, valiant, valorous. ▷ COURAGEOUS. *Opp* FEARFUL.

fearsome *adj* appalling, awe-inspiring, awesome, dreadful, fearful, frightful, terrible, terrifying. ▷ FRIGHTENING.

feasible *adj* 1 attainable, easy, possible, practicable, practical, viable, workable. *Opp* IMPRACTICAL. 2 *feasible excuse.* credible, likely, plausible, reasonable. *Opp* IMPLAUSIBLE.

feast *n* banquet, *sl* blow-out, dinner, *inf* spread.
• *v* dine, gorge, *inf* wine and dine.

feat *n* accomplishment, achievement, act, action, attainment, deed, exploit, performance.

feather *n* plume, quill. **feathers** down, plumage.

feathery *adj* downy, fluffy, wispy.

feature *n* 1 aspect, attribute, characteristic, detail, facet, hallmark, idiosyncrasy, mark, peculiarity, point, property, quality, trait. 2 *newspaper feature.* article, column, item, piece, report, story.
• *v* 1 emphasize, focus on, highlight, *inf* play up, present, promote, show up, *inf* spotlight, stress. 2 *feature in a film.* act, appear, figure, participate, perform, play a role, star, take a part. **features** ▷ FACE.

fee *n* bill, charge, cost, dues, fare, payment, price, remuneration, subscription, sum, tariff, terms, toll, wage.

feeble *adj* 1 ailing, debilitated, decrepit, delicate, exhausted, faint, fragile, frail, helpless, ill, impotent, inadequate, ineffective, infirm, languid, listless, powerless, puny, sickly, slight, useless, weak. *Opp* STRONG. 2 hesitant, incompetent, indecisive, ineffectual, irresolute, *inf* namby-pamby, spineless, vacillating, weedy, *inf* wimpish, *inf* wishy-washy. 3 *feeble excuses.* flimsy, insubstantial, lame, poor, tame, thin, unconvincing.

feed *v* 1 cater for, nourish, nurture, provide for, provision, strengthen, suckle, support, sustain, *inf* wine and dine. 2 dine, eat, graze, pasture. **feed on** ▷ EAT.

feel *v* 1 caress, finger, handle, hold, manipulate, maul, *inf* paw, pet, stroke, touch. 2 *feel your way.* explore, fumble, grope. 3 *feel the cold.* be aware of, be conscious of, detect, experience, know, notice, perceive, sense, suffer, undergo. 4 *feel empty.* appear, seem. 5 *feel something's true.* believe, consider, deem, guess, *inf* have a feeling, *inf* have a hunch, judge, think.

feeling *n* 1 perception, sensation, sense of touch, sensitivity. 2 emotion, passion, sentiment. 3 *religious feelings.* attitude, belief, consciousness, guess, hunch, idea, impression, instinct, intuition, notion, opinion, thought, view. 4 *feeling for music.* sympathy, understanding. 5 [*inf*] *autumnal feeling.* atmosphere, mood, tone.

fell *v* cut down, flatten, floor, knock down, mow down, prostrate. ▷ KILL.

female *adj* ▷ FEMININE. *Opp* MALE.
• *n* girl, woman.

feminine *adj derog of men* effeminate, female, *derog* girlish, ladylike, womanly. *Opp* MASCULINE.

fen *n* bog, lowland, marsh, morass, quagmire, swamp.

fence *n* barricade, barrier, hedge, hurdle, paling, palisade, railing, rampart, stockade, wall, wire.
• *v* 1 bound, circumscribe, confine, coop up, encircle, enclose, hedge in, pen, surround, wall in. 2 ▷ FIGHT.

fend *v* **fend for yourself** *inf* get along, *inf* get by, look after yourself, manage, *inf* scrape along, support yourself, survive. **fend off** ▷ REPEL.

ferment *n* ▷ COMMOTION.
• *v* 1 boil, bubble, effervesce, *inf* fizz, foam, froth, seethe. 2 agitate, excite, foment, incite, instigate, provoke, rouse, stir up.

ferocious *adj* bestial, bloodthirsty, brutal, cruel, fiendish, fierce, harsh, inhuman, merciless, murderous, pitiless, sadistic, savage, vicious, wild. *Opp* GENTLE.

ferry *n* boat, craft, ship, vessel.
• *v* carry, export, import, ship, take across, transport. ▷ CONVEY.

fertile *adj* abundant, fecund, flourishing, fruitful, lush, luxuriant, productive, prolific, rich, teeming. *Opp* STERILE.

fertilize *v* 1 impregnate, inseminate, pollinate. 2 cultivate, enrich, feed, make fertile, manure, mulch, nourish.

fertilizer *n* compost, dressing, manure, mulch, nutrient.

fervent *adj* ardent, avid, burning, committed, devout, eager, emotional, enthusiastic, excited, fanatical, fervid, fiery, frenzied, heated, impassioned, intense, keen, passionate, spirited, vehement, vigorous, warm, wholehearted, zealous. *Opp* COOL.

fervour *n* ardour, eagerness, energy, enthusiasm, excitement, fire, heat, intensity, keenness, passion, sparkle, spirit, vehemence, vigour, warmth, zeal.

fester *v* become infected, decay, discharge, go bad, go septic, ooze, putrefy, rot, run, suppurate, ulcerate.

festival *n* anniversary, carnival, commemoration, fair, feast, fête, fiesta, gala, jamboree, jubilee. ▷ FESTIVITY.

festive *adj* celebratory, cheerful, cheery, convivial, gay, gleeful, jolly, jovial, joyful, joyous, light-hearted, merry. ▷ HAPPY.

festivity *n* celebration, conviviality, entertainment, feasting, *inf* jollification, jollity, jubilation, merrymaking, merriment, mirth, rejoicing, revelry, revels. ▷ PARTY.

fetch *v* 1 bear, bring, carry, collect, convey, get, obtain, pick up, retrieve, transfer, transport. 2 *fetch a good price.* bring in, earn, go for, make, produce, raise, realize, sell for. **fetching** ▷ ATTRACTIVE.

feud *n* animosity, antagonism, *inf* bad blood, dispute, enmity, grudge, hostility, rivalry, vendetta. ▷ QUARREL.

fever *n* delirium, feverishness, high temperature.

feverish *adj* 1 burning, febrile, fevered, flushed, hot, inflamed, trembling. *Opp* COOL. 2 *feverish activity.* agitated, excited, frantic, frenetic, frenzied, hectic, hurried, impatient, restless.

few *adj inf* few and far between, hardly any, inadequate, infrequent, rare, scarce, sparse, sporadic, *inf* thin on the ground, uncommon. *Opp* MANY.

fibre *n* 1 filament, hair, strand, thread. 2 *moral fibre.* backbone, character, determination, spirit, tenacity. ▷ COURAGE.

fickle *adj* capricious, changeable, changing, disloyal, erratic, faithless, flighty, inconsistent, inconstant, mercurial, mutable, treacherous, unfaithful, unpredictable, unreliable, unstable, unsteady, *inf* up and down, vacillating, volatile. *Opp* CONSTANT.

fiction *n* 1 concoction, fabrication, fantasy, figment of the imagination, flight of fancy, invention, lies, story-telling, *inf* tall story. 2 novel, romance, story, tale. *Opp* FACT.

fictional *adj* fabulous, fanciful, imaginary, invented, legendary, made-up, make-believe, mythical, story-book. *Opp* FACTUAL.

fictitious *adj* apocryphal, assumed, fabricated, fraudulent, imagined, invented, made-up, spurious, unreal, untrue. ▷ FALSE. *Opp* GENUINE.

fiddle *v* interfere, meddle, play about, tamper. ▷ FIDGET. **fiddling** ▷ TRIVIAL.

fidget *v* be restless, fiddle, fret, fuss, jiggle, *inf* mess about, *inf* play about, shuffle, squirm, twitch, worry, wriggle about.

fidgety *adj* agitated, impatient, *inf* jittery, jumpy, nervous, on edge, restless, *inf* twitchy, uneasy. *Opp* CALM.

field *n* 1 arable land, clearing, enclosure, grassland, green, meadow, paddock, pasture. 2 *games field*. arena, ground, pitch, playing field, stadium. 3 *field of activity*. area, *inf* department, domain, province, sphere, subject, territory.

fiend *n* 1 demon, devil, evil spirit, goblin, hobgoblin, imp, Satan, spirit. 2 ▷ FANATIC.

fierce *adj* 1 angry, barbaric, barbarous, bloodthirsty, bloody, brutal, cold-blooded, cruel, dangerous, fearsome, ferocious, fiendish, fiery, homicidal, inhuman, merciless, murderous, pitiless, ruthless, sadistic, savage, untamed, vicious, violent, wild. 2 *fierce opposition*. active, aggressive, competitive, eager, furious, heated, intense, keen, passionate, relentless, strong. *Opp* GENTLE.

fiery *adj* 1 aflame, blazing, burning, fierce, flaming, glowing, hot, incandescent, raging, red, red-hot. 2 *fiery temper*. angry, choleric, excitable, fervent, furious, hot-headed, intense, irascible, livid, mad, passionate, touchy, violent. *Opp* COOL.

fight *n* action, affray, attack, battle, bout, brawl, *inf* brush, *inf* bust-up, clash, combat, competition, conflict, confrontation, contest, dispute, dogfight, duel, *inf* dust-up, encounter, engagement, feud, fisticuffs, fracas, fray, *inf* free-for-all, hostilities, match, mêlée, *inf* punch-up, riot, rivalry, *inf* row, scramble, scrap, scrimmage, scuffle, *inf* set-to, skirmish, squabble, strife, struggle, tussle, war, wrangle. ▷ QUARREL.

• *v* 1 attack, battle, box, brawl, *inf* brush, clash, compete, conflict, contend, duel, engage, fence, feud, grapple, quarrel, *inf* row, scrap, scuffle, skirmish, spar, squabble, stand up (to), strive, struggle, tussle, wage war, wrestle. 2 *fight a decision*. campaign against, contest, defy, oppose, resist, take a stand against.

fighter *n* aggressor, antagonist, attacker, campaigner, combatant, contender, defender. ▷ SOLDIER.

figure *n* 1 amount, cipher, digit, integer, number, numeral, sum, symbol, value. 2 diagram, drawing, graph, illustration, outline, picture, plate, representation. 3 *plump figure*. body, build, form, outline, physique, shape, silhouette. 4 *bronze figure*. ▷ SCULPTURE. 5 *well-known figure*. ▷ PERSON.

• *v* ▷ FEATURE. **figure out** ▷ CALCULATE, UNDERSTAND. **figures** ▷ STATISTICS.

file *n* 1 binder, box-file, case, cover, dossier, folder, portfolio, ring-binder. 2 *single file*. column, line, procession, queue, rank, row, stream, string, train.

• *v* 1 arrange, categorize, classify, enter, organize, pigeon-hole, put away, record, register, store, systematize. 2 *file through a door*. march, parade, proceed in a line, stream, troop.

fill *v* 1 be full of, block, *inf* bung up, clog, close up, cram, crowd, flood, jam, load, pack, plug, refill, replenish, seal, stock up, stop up, stuff, *inf* top up. *Opp* EMPTY. 2 *fill a need*. answer, fulfil, meet, provide, satisfy, supply. 3 *fill a post*. hold, occupy, take over, take up. **fill out** ▷ SWELL.

filling *n* contents, insides, padding, stuffing, wadding.

film *n* 1 coat, coating, covering, haze, layer, membrane, mist, sheet, skin, slick, tissue, veil. 2 *inf* flick, *inf* movie, *inf* picture, video.

filter *n* colander, gauze, mesh, riddle, screen, sieve, strainer.

• *v* clarify, percolate, purify, refine, screen, sieve, sift, strain.

filth *n* decay, dirt, effluent, garbage, grime, *inf* gunge, muck, mud, ordure, pollution, refuse, rubbish, scum, sewage, slime, sludge. ▷ EXCRETA.

filthy *adj* 1 caked, defiled, dirty, disgusting, dusty, foul, grimy, grubby, messy, mucky, muddy, nasty, polluted, scummy, slimy, smelly, soiled, sooty, sordid, squalid, stinking, tainted, unkempt, unwashed, vile. 2 ▷ OBSCENE. *Opp* CLEAN.

final *adj* closing, concluding, conclusive, decisive, dying, end, eventual, finishing, last, settled, terminal, ultimate. *Opp* INITIAL.

finalize *v* clinch, complete, conclude, settle, *inf* sew up, *inf* wrap up.

finance *n* accounting, banking, business, commerce, economics, investment, stocks and shares.
• *v* back, fund, guarantee, invest in, pay for, provide money for, subsidize, support, underwrite. **finances** assets, capital, cash, funds, holdings, income, money, resources, wealth, *inf* the wherewithal.

financial *adj* economic, fiscal, monetary, pecuniary.

find *v* 1 acquire, become aware of, *inf* bump into, chance upon, come across, come upon, detect, diagnose, dig out, dig up, discover, encounter, expose, *inf* ferret out, happen on, hit on, identify, learn, light on, locate, meet, note, notice, observe, *inf* put your finger on, recognize, reveal, spot, stumble on, uncover, unearth. 2 get back, recover, rediscover, regain, repossess, retrieve, trace, track down. 3 *found me a job.* give, pass on, procure, provide, supply. *Opp* LOSE.

finding *n* conclusion, decision, decree, judgement, verdict.

fine *adj* 1 admirable, beautiful, choice, classic, excellent, first-class, handsome, noble, select, superior, worthy. ▷ GOOD. 2 *fine workmanship.* consummate, craftsmanlike, meticulous, skilful, skilled. 3 *fine sand.* minute, powdery, soft. 4 *fine fabric.* dainty, delicate, exquisite, flimsy, fragile, silky. 5 *fine distinction.* acute, discriminating, hair-splitting, nice, precise, subtle. 6 *fine weather.* bright, clear, cloudless, dry, fair, nice, pleasant, sunny. 7 *fine point.* ▷ SHARP.
• *n* charge, forfeit, penalty.

finish *n* 1 cessation, close, completion, conclusion, culmination, end, ending, finale, resolution, result, termination. 2 *finish on furniture.* appearance, gloss, lustre, patina, polish, shine, smoothness, surface, texture.
• *v* 1 accomplish, achieve, break off, bring to an end, cease, clinch, complete, conclude, discontinue, end, finalize, fulfil, halt, pack up, perfect, phase out, reach the end, round off, sign off, stop, terminate, *inf* wind up, *inf* wrap up. 2 consume, drink up, eat up, empty, exhaust, expend, get through, *inf* polish off, use up. **finish off** ▷ KILL.

finite *adj* bounded, definable, defined, fixed, known, limited, measurable, numbered, rationed, restricted. *Opp* INFINITE.

fire *n* 1 blaze, combustion, conflagration, flames, holocaust, inferno, pyre. 2 fireplace, furnace, grate, hearth. 3 *fire in your veins.* ▷ PASSION.
• *v* 1 bake, burn, heat, ignite, kindle, light, set alight, set fire to, spark off. 2 animate, awaken, enliven, excite, incite, inflame, inspire, motivate, rouse, stimulate, stir. 3 *fire a gun or missile.* catapult, detonate, discharge, explode, launch, let off, set off, shoot, trigger off. 4 *fire a worker.* dismiss, make redundant, sack, throw out. **fire at** ▷ BOMBARD. **hang fire** ▷ DELAY.

fireproof *adj* flameproof, incombustible, non-flammable. *Opp* INFLAMMABLE.

firm *adj* 1 compact, compressed, dense, hard, rigid, set, solid, stable, stiff, unyielding. 2 anchored, embedded, fast, fastened, fixed, immovable, secure, steady, tight. 3 *firm convictions.* adamant, decided, determined, dogged, inflexible, obstinate, persistent, resolute, unshakeable, unwavering. 4 *firm price.* agreed, settled, unchangeable. 5 *firm friends.* constant, dependable, devoted, faithful, loyal, reliable.
• *n* business, company, concern, corporation, establishment, organization, partnership.

first *adj* 1 cardinal, chief, dominant, foremost, head, key, leading, main, outstanding, paramount, predominant, primary, prime, principal, top, uppermost. 2 *first steps.* basic, elementary, initial, introductory, preliminary, rudimentary. 3 *first version.* archetypal, earliest, eldest, embryonic, oldest, original, primeval. **first-class, first-rate** ▷ EXCELLENT.

fish *v* angle, go fishing, trawl.

fisher *n* angler, fisherman, trawlerman.

fit *adj* 1 adapted, adequate, applicable, apposite, appropriate, apt, becoming, befitting, correct, decent, equipped, fitting, good enough, proper, right, satisfactory, seemly, sound, suitable, suited, timely. 2 able, capable, competent, in good form, on form, prepared, ready, strong, well enough. ▷ HEALTHY. *Opp* UNFIT.
• *n* attack, bout, convulsion, eruption, explosion, outbreak, outburst, paroxysm, seizure, spasm, spell.

• *v* 1 accord with, become, be fitting for, conform with, correspond to, go with, suit. 2 *fit things into place.* arrange, assemble, build, construct, dovetail, install, interlock, join, match, position, put in place, put together. **fit out, fit up** ▷ EQUIP.

fix *n inf* catch-22, corner, difficulty, dilemma, *inf* hole, *inf* jam, mess, *inf* pickle, plight, predicament, problem, quandary.
• *v* 1 attach, connect, implant, install, join, link, make firm, plant, position, secure, stabilize, stick. ▷ FASTEN. 2 *fix a price.* agree, appoint, arrange, arrive at, conclude, confirm, decide, define, establish, finalize, name, set, settle, sort out, specify. 3 *fix a broken window.* correct, make good, mend, put right, rectify, remedy, repair.

fixture *n* date, engagement, event, game, match, meeting.

fizz *v* bubble, effervesce, fizzle, foam, froth, hiss, sizzle, sparkle, sputter.

fizzy *adj* bubbly, effervescent, foaming, sparkling.

flag *n* banner, bunting, colours, ensign, pennant, pennon, standard, streamer.
• *v* 1 ▷ SIGNAL. 2 *enthusiasm began to flag.* ▷ DECLINE.

flake *n* chip, leaf, scale, shaving, sliver, splinter, wafer.

flame *n* blaze, light, tongue. ▷ FIRE.
• *v* ▷ FLARE.

flap *v* beat, flutter, sway, swing, thrash about, *inf* waggle, wave about.

flare *v* 1 blaze, brighten, burst out, erupt, flame, shine. ▷ BURN. 2 ▷ WIDEN.

flash *v* dazzle, flicker, glare, glint, glitter, light up, reflect, scintillate, shine, spark, sparkle, twinkle. ▷ BURN.

flat *adj* 1 calm, even, horizontal, level, smooth, unbroken, unruffled. 2 outstretched, prone, prostrate, recumbent, spread-eagled, spread out, supine. 3 *flat voice.* bland, boring, dead, dull, featureless, insipid, lacklustre, lifeless, monotonous, stale, tedious, tired, unexciting, uninteresting, unvarying. 4 *flat tyre.* blown out, burst, deflated, punctured.
• *n* apartment, bedsitter, penthouse, rooms.

flatten *v* 1 compress, even out, iron out, level out, press, roll, smooth. 2 crush, demolish, level, raze, run over, squash, trample. ▷ DESTROY. 3 *flatten an opponent.* fell, floor, knock down, prostrate. ▷ DEFEAT.

flatter *v inf* butter up, compliment, court, curry favour with, fawn on, humour, *inf* play up to, praise, *inf* suck up to. *Opp* INSULT. **flattering** ▷ COMPLIMENTARY, OBSEQUIOUS.

flatterer *n inf* crawler, *inf* creep, groveller, sycophant, toady, *inf* yes-man.

flattery *n* adulation, blandishments, *inf* blarney, cajolery, fawning, *inf* flannel, insincerity, obsequiousness, servility, *inf* soft soap, sycophancy.

flavour *n* 1 savour, taste. ▷ FLAVOURING. 2 air, ambience, atmosphere, aura, character, characteristic, feel, feeling, property, quality, style.
• *v* add flavour to, season, spice.

flavouring *n* additive, essence, extract, seasoning.

flaw *n* break, defect, error, fallacy, fault, imperfection, inaccuracy, loophole, mistake, slip, weakness. ▷ BLEMISH. **flawed** ▷ IMPERFECT.

flawless *adj* accurate, clean, faultless, immaculate, mint, pristine, sound, spotless, undamaged, unmarked. ▷ PERFECT. *Opp* IMPERFECT.

flee *v* abscond, *inf* beat a retreat, *sl* beat it, bolt, clear off, *inf* cut and run, decamp, disappear, escape, fly, get away, *inf* make a run for it, make off, retreat, run away, *sl* scarper, take flight, *inf* take to your heels, vanish, withdraw.

fleet *n* armada, convoy, flotilla, navy, squadron, task force.

fleeting *adj* brief, ephemeral, evanescent, fugitive, impermanent, momentary, passing, short, short-lived, temporary, transient, transitory. *Opp* PERMANENT.

flesh *n* carrion, fat, meat, muscle, tissue.

flex *n* cable, cord, extension, lead, wire.
• *v* ▷ BEND.

flexible *adj* 1 bendable, *inf* bendy, elastic, floppy, lithe, plastic, pliable, pliant, rubbery, soft, springy, stretchy, supple, whippy, yielding. 2 adjustable, fluid, open, provisional, variable. 3 *flexible person.* accommodating, adaptable, amenable, compliant, cooperative, docile, easygoing, malleable, open-minded, responsive, tractable, willing. *Opp* RIGID.

flicker *v* blink, flutter, glimmer, quiver, shimmer, sparkle, tremble, twinkle, waver.

flight *n* 1 journey, trajectory. 2 ▷ ESCAPE.

flimsy *adj* 1 breakable, brittle, delicate, fine, fragile, frail, insubstantial, light, slight, thin, weak. 2 *flimsy building.* decrepit, dilapidated, gimcrack, makeshift, rickety, shaky, tottering, wobbly. 3 *flimsy argument.* feeble, implausible, inadequate, superficial, trivial, unbelievable, unconvincing, unsatisfactory. *Opp* STRONG.

flinch *v* blench, cower, cringe, dodge, draw back, duck, falter, jump, quail, recoil, shrink back, shy away, start, swerve, wince. **flinch from** ▷ EVADE.

fling *v* *inf* bung, cast, *inf* chuck, heave, hurl, launch, lob, pitch, sling, throw, toss.

flippant *adj* cheeky, facetious, *inf* flip, frivolous, light-hearted, shallow, superficial, thoughtless. *Opp* SERIOUS.

flirt *n* *female* coquette, *male* philanderer, *inf* tease.
• *v* *sl* chat someone up, lead someone on, make love, philander.

flirtatious *adj* amorous, coquettish, flirty, playful, teasing.

float *v* 1 bob, drift, glide, hang, hover, sail, swim, waft. 2 *float a ship.* launch. *Opp* SINK.

flock *n* congregation, crowd, drove, gathering, herd, horde. ▷ GROUP.
• *v* ▷ GATHER.

flog *v* beat, birch, cane, flagellate, flay, lash, scourge, thrash, whip. ▷ HIT.

flood *n* 1 cataract, deluge, downpour, flash-flood, inundation, overflow, rush, spate, stream, tide, torrent. 2 abundance, excess, glut, plethora, superfluity, surfeit, surge.
• *v* cover, deluge, drown, engulf, fill up, immerse, inundate, overflow, overwhelm, saturate, sink, submerge, swamp.

floor *n* 1 floorboards, flooring. 2 deck, level, storey, tier.

flop *v* 1 collapse, dangle, droop, drop, fall, flag, sag, slump, topple, tumble, wilt. 2 ▷ FAIL.

floppy *adj* dangling, droopy, loose, limp, pliable, soft. ▷ FLEXIBLE. *Opp* RIGID.

flounder *v* 1 blunder, flail, fumble, grope, move clumsily, plunge about, stagger, struggle, tumble, wallow. 2 falter, get confused, make mistakes.

flourish *n* ▷ GESTURE.
• *v* 1 be successful, bloom, blossom, boom, burgeon, develop, do well, flower, grow, increase, prosper, strengthen, succeed, thrive. 2 *flourish an umbrella.* brandish, flaunt, gesture with, shake, swing, twirl, wag, wave, wield.

flow *n* cascade, course, current, drift, ebb, effusion, flood, gush, outpouring, spate, spurt, stream, tide, trickle.
• *v* cascade, course, dribble, drift, drip, flood, flush, glide, gush, issue, leak, ooze, overflow, pour, ripple, roll, run, seep, spill, spring, spurt, squirt, stream, swirl, trickle, well, well up.

flower *n* 1 bloom, blossom, bud, floret, petal.
• *v* bloom, blossom, bud, burgeon, come out, open out, unfold. ▷ FLOURISH. **bunch of flowers** arrangement, bouquet, corsage, garland, posy, spray, wreath.

fluctuate *v* alternate, be unsteady, change, go up and down, oscillate, seesaw, shift, swing, vacillate, vary, waver.

fluent *adj* articulate, effortless, eloquent, *derog* facile, flowing, *derog* glib, natural, polished, ready, smooth, voluble, unhesitating. *Opp* HESITANT.

fluff *n* down, dust, feathers, fuzz, thistledown.

fluffy *adj* downy, feathery, fleecy, furry, fuzzy, light, silky, soft, velvety, wispy, woolly.

fluid *adj* 1 aqueous, flowing, liquefied, liquid, melted, molten, running, *inf* runny, sloppy, watery. *Opp* SOLID. 2 *fluid situation.* changing, flexible, open, variable, undefined.
• *n* juice, liquid, plasma, sap.

fluke *n* accident, chance, stroke of good luck.

flush *v* 1 blush, colour, glow, go red, redden. 2 *flush a lavatory.* cleanse, rinse out. 3 *flush from a hiding-place.* chase out, drive out, expel.

fluster *v* agitate, bewilder, bother, distract, flurry, perplex, put off, put out, *inf* rattle, *inf* throw, upset. ▷ CONFUSE.

flutter *v* bat (*eyelid*), flap, flicker, flit, oscillate, palpitate, quiver, shake, tremble, twitch, vibrate, wave.

fly *v* 1 ascend, flit, glide, hover, rise, sail, soar, swoop, take flight, take wing. 2 *fly a plane.* control, pilot. 3 *fly a flag.* display, flutter, hang up, hoist, raise, show, wave. 4 *fly from danger.* flee, hurry, run. ▷ ESCAPE. **fly at** ▷ ATTACK. **fly in the face of** ▷ DISREGARD.

flying *n* aeronautics, air-travel, aviation, flight.

foam *n* 1 bubbles, effervescence, froth, head (*on beer*), lather, scum, spume, suds. 2 sponge.

• *v* boil, bubble, effervesce, fizz, froth, lather.

focus *n* centre, core, focal point, heart, hub, pivot, target.
• *v* aim, centre, concentrate, direct attention, home in, spotlight.

fog *n* cloud, haze, miasma, mist, smog, smoke, vapour.

foggy *adj* blurred, cloudy, dim, hazy, indistinct, misty, murky, obscure. *Opp* CLEAR.

foil *v* baffle, block, check, frustrate, halt, hamper, hinder, obstruct, outwit, prevent, stop, thwart. ▷ DEFEAT.

foist *v inf* fob off, get rid of, impose, offload, palm off.

fold *n* 1 bend, corrugation, crease, crinkle, furrow, pleat, pucker, wrinkle. 2 *fold for sheep.* ▷ ENCLOSURE.
• *v* 1 bend, crease, crinkle, double over, jack-knife, overlap, pleat, pucker, tuck in, turn over. 2 close, collapse, let down, put down, shut. 3 *fold in your arms.* clasp, embrace, enclose, enfold, envelop, hold, hug, wrap. 4 *business folded.* ▷ FAIL.

folk *n* clan, nation, people, the public, race, society, tribe.

follow *v* 1 accompany, chase, come after, dog, escort, go after, hound, hunt, keep pace with, pursue, replace, shadow, stalk, succeed, supersede, supplant, *inf* tag along with, *inf* tail, take the place of, track, trail. 2 *follow a path.* keep to, trace. 3 *follow rules.* abide by, adhere to, comply with, conform to, heed, honour, obey, observe, pay attention to, stick to, take notice of. 4 *follow my example.* adopt, copy, imitate, mirror. 5 *follow an argument.* appreciate, comprehend, grasp, keep up with, take in, understand. 6 *follow football.* be a fan of, keep abreast of, know about, take an interest in, support. 7 *It doesn't follow.* be inevitable, be logical, ensue, happen, mean, result. **following** ▷ SUBSEQUENT.

folly *n* foolishness, insanity, lunacy, madness. ▷ STUPIDITY.

foment *v* arouse, incite, instigate, kindle, provoke, rouse, stir up. ▷ STIMULATE.

fond *adj* 1 adoring, affectionate, caring, loving, tender, warm. 2 *a fond hope.* ▷ FOOLISH. **be fond of** ▷ LOVE.

fondle *v* caress, cuddle, handle, pat, pet, squeeze, touch.

food *n* comestibles, cooking, cuisine, delicacies, diet, eatables, *inf* eats, fare, feed, fodder, foodstuff, *inf* grub, meat, *sl* nosh, nourishment, nutriments, provisions, rations, recipe, refreshments, sustenance, *old use* victuals.

fool *n* 1 [*most synonyms inf*] ass, blockhead, buffoon, dimwit, dope, dunce, dunderhead, dupe, half-wit, ignoramus, mug, muggins, ninny, nit, nitwit, simpleton, sucker, twerp, wally. ▷ IDIOT. 2 clown, comedian, comic, entertainer, jester.
• *v inf* bamboozle, bluff, cheat, *inf* con, deceive, defraud, delude, dupe, fleece, gull, hoax, hoodwink, *inf* kid, mislead, swindle, take in, tease, trick. **fool about** ▷ MISBEHAVE.

foolish *adj* absurd, asinine, brainless, childish, crazy, *inf* daft, *inf* dopey, *inf* dotty, fatuous, feather-brained, frivolous, *inf* half-baked, hare-brained, idiotic, immature, inane, infantile, irrational, laughable, ludicrous, mad, meaningless, mindless, misguided, naive, nonsensical, pointless, preposterous, ridiculous, *inf* scatty, senseless, shallow, silly, simple, simple-minded, simplistic, *inf* soppy, stupid, thoughtless, unintelligent, unreasonable, unwise, witless. *Opp* WISE.

foot *n* 1 claw, hoof, paw, trotter. 2 ▷ BASE.

footprint *n* footmark, spoor, track.

forbid *v* ban, bar, debar, deny, disallow, exclude, outlaw, preclude, prevent, prohibit, proscribe, refuse, rule out, stop, veto. *Opp* ALLOW.

forbidden *adj* 1 against the law, taboo, unlawful, wrong. 2 *forbidden area.* closed, out of bounds, restricted, secret.

forbidding *adj* gloomy, grim, menacing, ominous, stern, threatening, uninviting. ▷ UNFRIENDLY. *Opp* FRIENDLY.

force *n* 1 aggression, *inf* arm-twisting, coercion, compulsion, constraint, duress, effort, might, power, pressure, strength, vehemence, vigour, violence. 2 energy, impact, intensity, momentum, shock. 3 *military force.* army, body, group, troops. 4 *force of an argument.* cogency, effectiveness, persuasiveness, thrust, validity, weight.
• *v* 1 *inf* bulldoze, coerce, compel, constrain, drive, impel, make, oblige, order, press-gang, pressurize. 2 *force a door.* break open, burst open, prise open, smash, wrench. 3 *force something on someone.* impose, inflict.

foreboding *n* anxiety, apprehension, dread, fear, intimation, intuition, misgiving, omen, portent, premonition, presentiment, suspicion, warning, worry.

forecast *n* augury, outlook, prediction, prognosis, projection, prophecy.
• *v* ▷ FORESEE.

forefront *n* avant-garde, front, lead, vanguard.

foreign *adj* 1 distant, exotic, far-away, outlandish, remote, strange, unfamiliar, unknown. 2 alien, external, imported, incoming, international, outside, overseas, visiting. 3 extraneous, odd, uncharacteristic, unnatural, untypical, unusual, unwanted. *Opp* NATIVE.

foreigner *n* alien, immigrant, newcomer, outsider, overseas visitor, stranger. *Opp* NATIVE.

foremost *adj* first, leading, main, primary. ▷ CHIEF.

forerunner *n* advance messenger, harbinger, herald, precursor, predecessor. ▷ ANCESTOR.

foresee *v* anticipate, envisage, expect, forecast, picture. ▷ FORETELL.

foresight *n* ▷ FORETHOUGHT.

forest *n* jungle, plantation, trees, woodland, woods.

foretaste *n* advance warning, augury, example, forewarning, indication, omen, premonition, preview, sample, specimen, tip-off, trailer.

foretell *v* augur, bode, forebode, foreshadow, forewarn, herald, portend, predict, presage, prophesy, signify. ▷ FORESEE.

forethought *n* anticipation, caution, far-sightedness, foresight, looking ahead, perspicacity, planning, preparation, prudence, readiness, vision.

forewarning *n* advance warning, augury, omen, premonition, tip-off. ▷ FORETASTE.

forfeit *n* damages, fee, fine, penalty.
• *v* abandon, give up, let go, lose, pay up, relinquish, renounce, surrender.

forge *n* furnace, smithy, workshop.
• *v* 1 beat into shape, cast, construct, hammer out, manufacture, mould, shape, work. 2 coin, copy, counterfeit, fake, falsify, imitate, reproduce. **forge ahead** ▷ ADVANCE.

forgery *n* copy, counterfeit, *inf* dud, fake, fraud, imitation, *inf* phoney, reproduction.

forget *v* 1 dismiss from your mind, disregard, fail to remember, ignore, leave out, lose track (of), miss out, neglect, omit, overlook, skip. 2 be without, leave behind. *Opp* REMEMBER.

forgetful *adj* absent-minded, careless, distracted, neglectful, negligent, oblivious, preoccupied, unmindful, unreliable, vague, *inf* woolly-minded.

forgivable *adj* allowable, excusable, justifiable, pardonable, petty, understandable, venial (*sin*). *Opp* UNFORGIVABLE.

forgive *v* 1 absolve, acquit, clear, excuse, exonerate, let off, pardon, spare. 2 *forgive a crime.* condone, ignore, make allowances for, overlook, pass over.

forgiveness *n* absolution, amnesty, clemency, compassion, exoneration, indulgence, leniency, mercy, pardon, reprieve. *Opp* RETRIBUTION.

forgiving *adj* compassionate, forbearing, generous, merciful, tolerant, understanding. ▷ KIND. *Opp* VENGEFUL.

forgo *v* abandon, abstain from, do without, forswear, give up, go without, pass up, relinquish, renounce, sacrifice, waive.

forked *adj* branched, cleft, divided, pronged, V-shaped.

forlorn *adj* abandoned, alone, bereft, deserted, forsaken, friendless, lonely, outcast, solitary, unloved. ▷ SAD.

form *n* 1 appearance, arrangement, cast, character, configuration, design, format, framework, genre, guise, kind, manifestation, model, mould, nature, pattern, semblance, sort, species, structure, style, system, type, variety. 2 *human form.* anatomy, body, build, figure, frame, outline, physique, shape, silhouette. 3 *school form.* class, grade, group, level, set, stream. 4 *good form.* behaviour, convention, custom, etiquette, fashion, manners, practice. 5 *application form.* document, paper. 6 *in good form.* condition, *inf* fettle, fitness, health, performance, spirits. 7 ▷ SEAT.
• *v* 1 cast, constitute, construct, create, design, establish, forge, found, give form to, make, model, mould, organize, produce, shape. 2 appear, arise, develop, grow, materialize, take shape. 3 *form a team.* act as, compose, comprise, make up. 4 *form a habit.* acquire, develop, get.

formal *adj* 1 aloof, ceremonial, conventional, cool, correct, customary, dignified, orthodox, *inf* posh, proper, punctilious, ritualistic, solemn, sophisticated, *inf* starchy, stately, stiff, unbending, unfriendly. 2 *formal language.* academic, impersonal, official, precise, specialist, stilted, technical. 3 *formal agreement.* binding, contractual, enforceable, legal, *inf* signed and sealed. 4 *formal design.*

geometrical, orderly, organized, regular, rigid, symmetrical. *Opp* INFORMAL.

format *n* appearance, design, layout, plan, shape, size, style.

former *adj* bygone, departed, ex-, last, late, old, one-time, past, previous, prior, recent. **the former** earlier, first, first-mentioned. *Opp* LATTER.

formidable *adj* awesome, challenging, daunting, difficult, dreadful, frightening, intimidating, *inf* mind-boggling, onerous, overwhelming, prodigious, taxing. *Opp* EASY.

formula *n* 1 ritual, rubric, spell, wording. 2 *formula for success.* blueprint, method, prescription, procedure, recipe, rule, technique, way.

formulate *v* 1 codify, define, express clearly, set out in detail, specify, systematize. 2 concoct, create, devise, evolve, form, invent, map out, originate, plan, work out.

forsake *v* abandon, desert, forgo, forswear, give up, jilt, leave, quit, renounce, repudiate, surrender, throw over, *inf* turn your back on.

fort *n* castle, citadel, fortress, garrison, stronghold, tower.

forthright *adj* blunt, candid, decisive, direct, outspoken, straightforward, unequivocal, unhesitating, uninhibited. ▷ FRANK. *Opp* EVASIVE.

fortify *v* 1 defend, garrison, protect, reinforce, secure against attack, shore up. 2 bolster, boost, brace, buoy up, cheer, encourage, hearten, invigorate, reassure, strengthen, support, sustain. *Opp* WEAKEN.

fortitude *n* backbone, bravery, determination, endurance, firmness, patience, resolution, stoicism, valour, will-power. ▷ COURAGE. *Opp* COWARDICE.

fortunate *adj* auspicious, blessed, favourable, lucky, opportune, propitious, prosperous, providential, timely. ▷ HAPPY.

fortune *n* 1 accident, chance, destiny, fate, karma, kismet, luck, providence. 2 affluence, assets, estate, holdings, inheritance, *inf* millions, money, *inf* pile, possessions, property, prosperity, riches, treasure, wealth.

fortune-teller *n* clairvoyant, crystal-gazer, oracle, palmist, prophet, seer, soothsayer.

forward *adj* 1 advancing, frontal, head-first, leading, onward, progressive. 2 *forward planning.* advance, early, future. 3 *forward child.* assertive, bold, brazen, cheeky, familiar, *inf* fresh, impertinent, impudent, insolent, over-confident, precocious, presumptuous, *inf* pushy, shameless, uninhibited. *Opp* BACKWARD.
• *v* 1 dispatch, freight, post on, re-address, send, send on, ship, transmit, transport. 2 *forward your career.* accelerate, advance, encourage, facilitate, foster, further, hasten, help along, promote, speed up, support. ▷ HELP. *Opp* HINDER.

foster *v* 1 advance, cultivate, encourage, further, promote, stimulate. ▷ HELP. 2 *foster a child.* adopt, bring up, care for, look after, raise, rear, take care of.

foul *adj* 1 bad, contaminated, disgusting, fetid, filthy, hateful, impure, loathsome, nasty, nauseating, noisome, obnoxious, offensive, polluted, putrid, repugnant, repulsive, revolting, rotten, sickening, squalid, stinking, vile. ▷ DIRTY, SMELLING. 2 *foul crimes.* abhorrent, abominable, atrocious, beastly, cruel, evil, monstrous, scandalous, shameful, vicious, villainous, violent, wicked. 3 *foul language.* abusive, blasphemous, coarse, common, crude, improper, indecent, insulting, offensive, rude, uncouth, vulgar. ▷ OBSCENE. 4 *foul weather.* foggy, rainy, rough, stormy, violent, windy. ▷ UNPLEASANT. 5 *foul play.* dishonest, illegal, invalid, unfair, unsportsmanlike. *Opp* CLEAN, FAIR.
• *n* infringement, violation.
• *v* ▷ DIRTY. **foul up** ▷ MUDDLE.

found *v* 1 begin, create, endow, establish, fund, *inf* get going, inaugurate, initiate, institute, organize, originate, raise, set up, start. 2 base, build, construct, erect, ground.

foundation *n* 1 beginning, endowment, establishment, inauguration, initiation, institution, setting up. 2 base, basis, bottom, cornerstone, foot, footing, substructure, underpinning. 3 *foundations of science.* basic principle, element, essential, fundamental, origin, *pl* rudiments.

founder *v* be wrecked, *inf* come to grief, fail, fall through, go down, miscarry, sink.

fountain *n* fount, jet, source, spout, spray, spring, well.

foyer *n* ante-room, entrance, entrance hall, hall, lobby.

fraction *n* division, part, portion, section, subdivision.

fracture *n* break, breakage, chip, cleft, crack, fissure, gap, opening, rent, rift, rupture, split.

• *v* breach, break, crack, rupture, separate, snap, split.

fragile *adj* ▷ FRAIL.

fragment *n* atom, bit, chip, crumb, *pl* debris, morsel, part, particle, piece, portion, remnant, scrap, shard, shred, sliver, *pl* smithereens, snippet, speck.
• *v* ▷ BREAK.

fragmentary *adj inf* bitty, broken, disconnected, disjointed, fragmented, imperfect, in bits, incoherent, incomplete, partial, scattered, scrappy, sketchy, uncoordinated. *Opp* COMPLETE.

fragrance *n* aroma, bouquet, nose (*of wine*), odour, perfume, redolence, scent, smell.

fragrant *adj* aromatic, odorous, perfumed, redolent, scented, sweet-smelling.

frail *adj* breakable, brittle, delicate, easily damaged, flimsy, fragile, insubstantial, light, *derog* puny, rickety, slight, thin, unsound, unsteady, vulnerable, *derog* weedy. ▷ ILL. *Opp* STRONG.

frame *n* 1 bodywork, chassis, construction, scaffolding, structure. ▷ FRAMEWORK. 2 *photo frame*. border, case, casing, edge, edging, mount, mounting.
• *v* 1 box in, enclose, mount, set off, surround. 2 ▷ COMPOSE. **frame of mind** ▷ ATTITUDE.

framework *n* bare bones, frame, outline, plan, shell, skeleton, support, trellis.

frank *adj* blunt, candid, direct, downright, explicit, forthright, genuine, *inf* heart-to-heart, honest, *inf* no-nonsense, open, outright, outspoken, plain, plain-spoken, revealing, sincere, straightforward, straight from the heart, to the point, trustworthy, truthful, unconcealed, undisguised, unreserved. *Opp* INSINCERE.

frantic *adj* agitated, anxious, berserk, *inf* beside yourself, crazy, delirious, demented, desperate, distraught, excitable, feverish, *inf* fraught, frenetic, frenzied, furious, hectic, hysterical, mad, overwrought, panicky, violent, wild, worked up. *Opp* CALM.

fraud *n* 1 cheating, chicanery, *inf* con-trick, counterfeit, deceit, deception, dishonesty, double-dealing, duplicity, fake, forgery, hoax, pretence, *inf* put-up job, ruse, sham, *inf* sharp practice, swindle, trick, trickery. 2 charlatan, cheat, *inf* con-man, hoaxer, impostor, *inf* phoney, quack, rogue, scoundrel, swindler.

fraudulent *adj inf* bent, bogus, cheating, corrupt, counterfeit, criminal, *inf* crooked, deceitful, devious, *inf* dirty, dishonest, duplicitous, fake, false, forged, illegal, lying, *inf* phoney, sham, specious, swindling, underhand. *Opp* HONEST.

fray *n* brawl, commotion, conflict, fracas, mêlée, quarrel, *inf* rumpus. ▷ FIGHT.

frayed *adj* tattered, threadbare, worn. ▷ RAGGED.

freak *adj* aberrant, abnormal, anomalous, atypical, bizarre, exceptional, extraordinary, odd, peculiar, queer, rare, unaccountable, unforeseeable, unpredictable, unusual, weird. *Opp* NORMAL.
• *n* 1 aberration, abnormality, anomaly, curiosity, irregularity, monster, monstrosity, mutant, oddity, *inf* one-off, quirk, rarity, variant. 2 ▷ FANATIC.

free *adj* 1 able, allowed, at leisure, at liberty, idle, independent, loose, not working, uncommitted, unconfined, unconstrained, unrestrained, untrammelled. 2 emancipated, liberated, released, unchained, unfettered, unshackled. 3 *free country*. autonomous, democratic, independent, self-governing, sovereign. 4 *free access*. clear, open, permitted, unhindered, unimpeded, unrestricted. 5 *free gifts*. complimentary, gratis, *sl* on the house, unasked-for, unsolicited. 6 *free space*. available, empty, uninhabited, unoccupied, vacant. 7 *free with money*. casual, generous, lavish, liberal, ready, unstinting, willing.
• *v* 1 absolve, acquit, clear, deliver, discharge, emancipate, exculpate, exonerate, let go, let off, let out, liberate, loose, pardon, parole, ransom, release, reprieve, rescue, save, set free, spare, turn loose, unchain, unfetter, unleash, unlock, unloose. *Opp* CONFINE. 2 *free tangled ropes*. clear, disengage, disentangle, extricate, loose, undo, untie. *Opp* TANGLE. **free and easy** ▷ INFORMAL.

freedom *n* 1 autonomy, independence, liberty, self-determination, self-government, sovereignty. *Opp* CAPTIVITY. 2 deliverance, emancipation, exemption, immunity, liberation, release. 3 *freedom to choose*. ability, discretion, free hand, latitude, leeway, leisure, licence, opportunity, permission, power, privilege, right, scope.

freeze *v* 1 congeal, harden, ice over, ice up, solidify, stiffen. 2 chill, cool, make cold, numb. 3 chill, deep-freeze, ice, preserve, refrigerate. 4 fix, hold, immobilize, peg, stand still, stick, stop. **freezing** ▷ COLD.

freight *n* ▷ CARGO.

frenzy *n* agitation, delirium, excitement, fever, fit, fury, hysteria, insanity, lunacy, madness, mania, outburst, paroxysm, passion, turmoil.

frequent *adj* common, constant, continual, customary, everyday, familiar, habitual, incessant, innumerable, many, normal, numerous, persistent, recurrent, regular, repeated, usual. *Opp* INFREQUENT.
• *v* ▷ HAUNT.

fresh *adj* 1 additional, alternative, different, extra, new, recent, supplementary, unfamiliar, up-to-date. 2 alert, energetic, healthy, invigorated, lively, *inf* perky, rested, revived, sprightly, tingling, vigorous, vital. 3 *fresh recruit.* ▷ INEXPERIENCED. 4 *fresh water.* clear, drinkable, pure, refreshing, sweet, uncontaminated. 5 *fresh air.* airy, breezy, circulating, clean, cool, unpolluted. 6 *fresh wind.* bracing, invigorating, sharp, stiff. 7 *fresh food.* healthy, natural, unprocessed, untreated, wholesome. 8 *fresh sheets.* clean, crisp, laundered, unused, washed-and-ironed. 9 *fresh colours.* bright, clean, glowing, renewed, restored, sparkling, vivid. *Opp* OLD, STALE.

fret *v* 1 agonize, be anxious, brood, worry. 2 ▷ ANNOY.

fretful *adj* anxious, distressed, disturbed, edgy, irritable, *inf* jittery, peevish, petulant, restless, touchy, worried. *Opp* CALM.

friction *n* 1 abrasion, chafing, grating, resistance, rubbing, scraping. 2 ▷ CONFLICT.

friend *n* acquaintance, associate, *inf* buddy, *inf* chum, companion, comrade, confidant(e), *inf* crony, intimate, *inf* mate, *inf* pal, partner, playmate, supporter, well-wisher. ▷ ALLY, LOVER. *Opp* ENEMY. **be friends** ▷ ASSOCIATE. **make friends with** ▷ BEFRIEND.

friendless *adj* alienated, alone, deserted, estranged, forlorn, isolated, lonely, ostracized, shunned, solitary, unattached, unloved, unpopular.

friendliness *n* benevolence, camaraderie, conviviality, devotion, esteem, familiarity, goodwill, helpfulness, hospitality, kindness, regard, sociability, warmth. *Opp* HOSTILITY.

friendly *adj* accessible, affable, affectionate, agreeable, amiable, amicable, approachable, benevolent, benign, *inf* chummy, civil, close, companionable, compatible, conciliatory, congenial, convivial, cordial, demonstrative, expansive, favourable, genial, good-natured, gracious, helpful, hospitable, intimate, kind, kind-hearted, kindly, likeable, *inf* matey, neighbourly, outgoing, *inf* pally, sympathetic, tender, *inf* thick, warm, welcoming, well-disposed. ▷ FAMILIAR, LOVING, SOCIABLE. *Opp* UNFRIENDLY.

friendship *n* affection, alliance, association, attachment, closeness, fellowship, fondness, harmony, intimacy, rapport, relationship. ▷ FRIENDLINESS, LOVE. *Opp* HOSTILITY.

fright *n* 1 jolt, scare, shock, surprise. 2 alarm, apprehension, consternation, dismay, dread, fear, horror, panic, terror, trepidation.

frighten *v* agitate, alarm, appal, browbeat, bully, cow, daunt, dismay, distress, horrify, intimidate, *inf* make your blood run cold, make your hair stand on end, menace, panic, petrify, *inf* put the wind up, scare, shake, shock, startle, terrify, terrorize, threaten, traumatize, tyrannize, unnerve, upset. ▷ DISCOURAGE. *Opp* REASSURE.

frightened *adj* afraid, aghast, alarmed, anxious, appalled, apprehensive, *inf* chicken, cowardly, daunted, fearful, horrified, horror-struck, panicky, panic-stricken, petrified, scared, shocked, terrified, trembling, unnerved, upset.

frightening *adj* alarming, appalling, blood-curdling, *inf* creepy, daunting, dire, dreadful, eerie, fearsome, formidable, ghostly, grim, hair-raising, horrifying, intimidating, *inf* scary, sinister, spine-chilling, *inf* spooky, terrifying, traumatic, uncanny, unnerving, upsetting, weird, worrying. ▷ FRIGHTFUL.

frightful *adj* 1 awful, ghastly, grisly, gruesome, harrowing, hideous, horrid, horrific, macabre, shocking, terrible. ▷ FRIGHTENING. 2 ▷ BAD.

fringe *n* 1 borders, boundary, edge, limits, marches, margin, outskirts, perimeter, periphery. 2 border, edging, flounce, frill, gathering, ruffle, trimming.

frisky *adj* active, animated, frolicsome, high-spirited, jaunty, lively, perky, playful, skittish, spirited, sportive, sprightly.

frivolity *n* facetiousness, flippancy, levity, light-heartedness, nonsense, silliness, triviality. ▷ FUN.

frivolous *adj* casual, facetious, flighty, *inf* flip, flippant, foolish, inconsequential, insignificant, jocular, joking, minor, paltry, petty, pointless, shallow, silly, superficial, trifling, trivial, unimportant, vacuous, worthless. *Opp* SERIOUS.

frock *n* dress, gown, robe.

frolic *v* caper, cavort, dance, frisk about, gambol, have fun, jump about, lark around, leap about, play about, prance, revel, romp, skip, skylark, sport.

front *adj* facing, first, foremost, leading, most advanced.
• *n* 1 bow (*of ship*), façade, face, facing, forefront, foreground, frontage, head, nose, van, vanguard. 2 battle area, danger zone, front line. 3 *brave front*. appearance, aspect, bearing, blind, *inf* cover-up, demeanour, disguise, expression, look, mask, pretence, show. *Opp* BACK.

frontal *adj* direct, facing, head-on, oncoming, straight.

frontier *n* border, borderline, boundary, bounds, limit.

froth *n* bubbles, effervescence, foam, head (*on beer*), lather, scum, spume, suds.

frown *v* glare, glower, grimace, knit your brows, look sullen, lour, scowl. **frown on** ▷ DISAPPROVE.

fruit *n* outcome, product, profit, result.

fruitful *adj* 1 abundant, bountiful, copious, fecund, fertile, flourishing, lush, luxurious, plenteous, productive, profuse, prolific, rich. 2 advantageous, beneficial, effective, gainful, profitable, rewarding, successful, useful, worthwhile. *Opp* FRUITLESS.

fruitless *adj* 1 barren, sterile, unfruitful, unproductive. 2 abortive, disappointing, futile, ineffective, pointless, profitless, unavailing, unprofitable, unrewarding, unsuccessful, useless, vain. *Opp* FRUITFUL.

frustrate *v* baffle, block, check, disappoint, foil, halt, hinder, impede, inhibit, nullify, prevent, *inf* scotch, stop, *inf* stymie, thwart. ▷ DEFEAT. *Opp* ENCOURAGE.

frustrated *adj* disappointed, loveless, lovesick, resentful, thwarted, unfulfilled, unsatisfied.

fuel *n* ammunition, energy, food, nourishment.
• *v* encourage, feed, inflame, keep going, nourish, stoke up, supply with fuel.

fugitive *adj* ▷ TRANSIENT.
• *n* deserter, escapee, escaper, refugee, renegade, runaway.

fulfil *v* 1 accomplish, achieve, bring about, bring off, carry out, complete, consummate, discharge, do, effect, execute, implement, perform, realize. 2 *fulfil a need*. answer, comply with, conform to, meet, obey, respond to, satisfy.

full *adj* 1 brimming, bursting, *inf* chock-a-block, *inf* chock-full, congested, crammed, crowded, filled, jammed, *inf* jam-packed, loaded, overflowing, packed, stuffed, topped-up, well-stocked. 2 *full stomach*. gorged, replete, sated, satiated, satisfied, well-fed. 3 *the full story*. complete, comprehensive, detailed, entire, exhaustive, thorough, total, unabridged, uncensored, uncut, unedited, unexpurgated, whole. 4 *full speed*. greatest, highest, maximum, top, utmost. 5 *full figure*. ample, broad, buxom, fat, large, plump, rounded, voluptuous, well-built. 6 *full skirt*. baggy, voluminous, wide. *Opp* EMPTY, INCOMPLETE, SMALL.

full-grown *adj* adult, grown-up, mature, ready, ripe.

fumble *v* grope at, feel your way, mishandle, stumble.

fume *v* emit fumes, smoke, smoulder. **fuming** ▷ ANGRY.

fumes *pl n* exhaust, fog, gases, pollution, smog, smoke, vapour.

fun *n* amusement, clowning, diversion, enjoyment, entertainment, festivity, fun and games, gaiety, games, *inf* high jinks, horseplay, jocularity, joking, *inf* jollification, jollity, laughter, merriment, merrymaking, mirth, pastimes, play, playfulness, pleasure, pranks, recreation, romp, *inf* skylarking, sport, teasing, tomfoolery. ▷ FRIVOLITY. **make fun of** ▷ MOCK.

function *n* 1 aim, purpose, use. ▷ JOB. 2 *official function*. affair, ceremony, *inf* do, event, occasion, party, reception.
• *v* act, behave, go, operate, perform, run, work.

functional *adj* functioning, practical, serviceable, useful, utilitarian, working. *Opp* DECORATIVE.

fund *n* cache, hoard, *inf* kitty, mine, pool, reserve, reservoir, stock, store, supply, treasure-house. **funds** capital, investments, resources, riches, savings, wealth. ▷ MONEY.

fundamental *adj* axiomatic, basic, cardinal, central, crucial, elementary, essential, important, key, main, necessary, primary, prime, principal, underlying. *Opp* INESSENTIAL.

funeral *n* burial, cremation, entombment, exequies, interment, obsequies, wake.

funereal *adj* dark, depressing, dismal,

gloomy, grave, mournful, sepulchral, solemn, sombre. ▷ SAD. *Opp* CHEERFUL.

funnel *n* chimney, flue.
• *v* channel, direct, filter, pour.

funny *adj* 1 absurd, amusing, comic, comical, crazy, *inf* daft, diverting, droll, eccentric, entertaining, facetious, farcical, hilarious, humorous, *inf* hysterical, ironic, jocular, laughable, ludicrous, mad, merry, nonsensical, *inf* priceless, *inf* rich, ridiculous, satirical, *inf* side-splitting, silly, slapstick, uproarious, waggish, witty, zany. *Opp* SERIOUS. 2 ▷ PECULIAR.

fur *n* bristles, coat, down, fleece, hair, hide, pelt, skin, wool.

furious *adj* 1 enraged, fuming, incensed, infuriated, irate, livid, mad, raging, savage, wrathful. ▷ ANGRY. 2 *furious activity.* agitated, frantic, frenzied, intense, tempestuous, tumultuous, turbulent, violent, wild. *Opp* CALM.

furnish *v* 1 equip, fit out, fit up, *inf* kit out. 2 *furnish information.* give, grant, provide, supply.

furniture *n* antiques, effects, equipment, fittings, fixtures, furnishings, household goods, *inf* movables, possessions.

furrow *n* channel, corrugation, crease, cut, ditch, fissure, fluting, gash, groove, hollow, line, rut, track, trench, wrinkle.

furrowed *adj* 1 creased, crinkled, corrugated, fluted, grooved, ploughed, ribbed, ridged, rutted, scored. 2 *furrowed brow.* frowning, lined, worried, wrinkled. *Opp* SMOOTH.

furry *adj* bristly, downy, feathery, fleecy, fuzzy, hairy, woolly.

further *adj* additional, another, auxiliary, extra, fresh, more, new, supplementary.

furthermore *adv* additionally, also, besides, moreover, too.

furtive *adj* clandestine, concealed, conspiratorial, covert, deceitful, disguised, hidden, mysterious, private, secret, secretive, *inf* shifty, sly, sneaky, stealthy, surreptitious, underhand. ▷ CRAFTY. *Opp* BLATANT.

fury *n* ferocity, fierceness, force, intensity, madness, power, rage, savagery, tempestuousness, turbulence, vehemence, violence, wrath. ▷ ANGER.

fuse *v* amalgamate, blend, coalesce, combine, compound, consolidate, join, melt, merge, mix, solder, unite, weld.

fusillade *n* barrage, burst, firing, outburst, salvo, volley.

fuss *n* ▷ COMMOTION.
• *v* agitate, bother, complain, *inf* create, fidget, *inf* flap, get worked up, grumble, worry.

fussy *adj* 1 *inf* choosy, difficult, discriminating, *inf* faddy, fastidious, finicky, hard to please, niggling, *inf* nit-picking, particular, *inf* pernickety, scrupulous, squeamish. 2 *fussy decorations.* complicated, detailed, elaborate, fancy, ornate, overdone.

futile *adj* abortive, barren, empty, foolish, forlorn, fruitless, hollow, ineffective, ineffectual, pointless, profitless, silly, sterile, unavailing, unproductive, unprofitable, unsuccessful, useless, vain, wasted, worthless. *Opp* FRUITFUL.

future *adj* approaching, awaited, coming, destined, expected, forthcoming, impending, intended, planned, prospective, subsequent, unborn.
• *n* expectations, outlook, prospects, time to come, tomorrow. *Opp* PAST.

fuzz *n* down, floss, fluff, hair.

fuzzy *adj* 1 downy, feathery, fleecy, fluffy, furry, woolly. 2 bleary, blurred, cloudy, dim, faint, hazy, ill-defined, indistinct, misty, obscure, out of focus, shadowy, unclear, unfocused, vague. *Opp* CLEAR.

G

gadget *n* apparatus, appliance, contraption, device, implement, instrument, invention, machine, tool, utensil.

gag *n* ▷ JOKE.
• *v* check, curb, keep quiet, muffle, muzzle, silence, stifle, still, suppress.

gaiety *n* brightness, cheerfulness, delight, exhilaration, felicity, glee, happiness, high spirits, hilarity, jollity, joyfulness, light-heartedness, liveliness, merriment, merrymaking, mirth.

gain *n* achievement, acquisition, advantage, asset, attainment, benefit, dividend, earnings, income, increase, proceeds, profit, return, revenue, winnings, yield. *Opp* LOSS.
• *v* 1 acquire, bring in, capture, earn, gather in, get, harvest, make, net, obtain, pick up, procure, profit, realize, reap, receive, win. *Opp* LOSE. 2 *gain your objective.* achieve, arrive at, attain, get to, reach, secure. *Opp* MISS. **gain on** approach, catch up with, close the gap, go faster than, overtake.

gainful *adj* ▷ PROFITABLE.

gala *n* carnival, celebration, fair, festival, festivity, fête, *inf* jamboree, party.

gale *n* ▷ WIND.

gallant *adj* attentive, chivalrous, courteous, courtly, dashing, gentlemanly, gracious, heroic, honourable, magnanimous, noble, polite, valiant, well-bred. ▷ BRAVE. *Opp* VILLAINOUS.

gallows *n* gibbet, scaffold.

gamble *v* back, bet, chance, draw lots, *inf* have a flutter, hazard, lay bets, risk money, speculate, *inf* take a chance, take risks, *inf* try your luck, venture, wager.

game *adj* ▷ BRAVE, WILLING.
• *n* 1 amusement, diversion, entertainment, frolic, fun, jest, joke, *inf* lark, pastime, play, playing, recreation, romp, sport. 2 competition, contest, match, round, *pl* sport, tournament. 3 animals, game birds, prey, quarry. **give the game away** ▷ REVEAL.

gang *n* band, crowd, pack, team. ▷ GROUP. **gang together**, **gang up** ▷ COMBINE.

gangster *n* bandit, brigand, criminal, *inf* crook, desperado, gunman, hoodlum, mafioso, racketeer, robber, thug.

gaol *n* cell, custody, dungeon, jail, *Amer* penitentiary. ▷ PRISON.
• *v* confine, detain, imprison, incarcerate, intern, *inf* send down, send to prison, *inf* shut away.

gaoler *n* guard, jailer, prison officer, *sl* screw, warder.

gap *n* 1 aperture, breach, break, cavity, chink, cleft, crack, cranny, crevice, gulf, hole, opening, rent, rift, rip, space, void. 2 breathing-space, discontinuity, hiatus, interlude, intermission, interruption, interval, lacuna, lapse, lull, pause, recess, respite, rest, suspension, wait. 3 *gap between political parties.* difference, disagreement, discrepancy, disparity, distance, divergence, division, incompatibility.

gape *v* 1 open, part, yawn. 2 *inf* gawp, gaze, goggle, stare.

garbage *n* debris, junk, litter, refuse, trash. ▷ RUBBISH.

garble *v* distort, falsify, misquote, misrepresent, mutilate, slant, twist, warp. ▷ CONFUSE.

garden *n* allotment, patch, plot, yard. **gardens** grounds, park.

garish *adj* ▷ GAUDY.

garment *n* ▷ CLOTHES.

garrison *n* 1 contingent, detachment, force, unit. 2 barracks, camp, citadel, fort, fortification, fortress, station, stronghold.

gas *n* exhalation, exhaust, fumes, miasma, vapour.

gash *v* chop, cleave, cut, lacerate, score, slash, slit, split, wound.

gasp *v* breathe with difficulty, choke, fight for breath, gulp, pant, puff, wheeze. **gasping** ▷ BREATHLESS, THIRSTY.

gate *n* access, barrier, door, entrance, entry, exit, gateway, opening, portal, portcullis, turnstile, way in, way out, wicket.

gather *v* 1 accumulate, amass, assemble, bring together, build up, cluster, collect, come together, concentrate, congregate, convene, crowd, flock, get together, group, grow, heap up, herd, hoard, huddle together, marshal, mass, meet, mobilize, muster, rally, round up, pick up, stockpile, store up, swarm, throng.

Opp DISPERSE. 2 *gather flowers.* garner, glean, harvest, pick, pluck, reap. 3 *I gather he's ill.* assume, be led to believe, conclude, deduce, guess, infer, learn, surmise, understand.

gathering *n* assembly, congress, convention, convocation, function, *inf* get-together, meeting, party, rally, social. ▷ GROUP.

gaudy *adj* bright, cheap, crude, flamboyant, *inf* flashy, garish, harsh, loud, lurid, ostentatious, raffish, showy, startling, tasteless, tawdry, vivid, vulgar. *Opp* DRAB, TASTEFUL.

gauge *n* 1 benchmark, criterion, guideline, measurement, norm, standard, test, yardstick. 2 capacity, dimensions, extent, measure, size, span, thickness, width. • *v* ▷ ESTIMATE, MEASURE.

gaunt *adj* 1 bony, cadaverous, emaciated, haggard, hollow-eyed, lean, pinched, scraggy, scrawny, skeletal, starving, underweight, wasted away. ▷ THIN. *Opp* PLUMP. 2 *gaunt ruin.* bare, bleak, desolate, dreary, forbidding, grim, stark, stern. *Opp* ATTRACTIVE.

gawky *adj* awkward, blundering, clumsy, gangling, gauche, gawky, inept, lumbering, maladroit, uncoordinated, ungainly. *Opp* GRACEFUL.

gay *adj* 1 animated, bright, carefree, cheerful, colourful, festive, fun-loving, jolly, jovial, joyful, light-hearted, lively, merry, sparkling, sunny, vivacious. ▷ HAPPY. 2 ▷ HOMOSEXUAL.

gaze *v* contemplate, gape, look, regard, stare, view, wonder (at).

gear *n* accessories, accoutrements, apparatus, appliances, baggage, belongings, equipment, *inf* get-up, harness, kit, luggage, materials, paraphernalia, rig, stuff, tackle, things, tools, trappings. ▷ CLOTHES.

gem *n* gemstone, jewel, precious stone, *sl* sparkler.

general *adj* 1 accepted, accustomed, collective, common, communal, conventional, customary, everyday, familiar, habitual, normal, ordinary, popular, prevailing, public, regular, *inf* run-of-the-mill, shared, typical, usual. 2 *general discussion.* across-the-board, all-embracing, broad-based, catholic, comprehensive, encyclopaedic, extensive, far-reaching, global, heterogeneous, hybrid, inclusive, sweeping, universal, wholesale, wide-ranging, widespread, worldwide. 3 *general idea.* approximate, broad, ill-defined, imprecise, indefinite, inexact, loose, simplified, superficial, unclear, unspecific, vague. *Opp* SPECIFIC.

generally *adv* as a rule, broadly, chiefly, in the main, mainly, mostly, normally, on the whole, predominantly, principally, usually.

generate *v* beget, breed, bring about, cause, create, engender, father, give rise to, make, originate, procreate, produce, propagate, sire, spawn, *inf* whip up.

generosity *n* bounty, largesse, liberality, munificence, philanthropy.

generous *adj* 1 benevolent, big-hearted, bounteous, bountiful, charitable, forgiving, *inf* free, impartial, kind, liberal, magnanimous, munificent, noble, open, open-handed, philanthropic, public-spirited, unselfish, unsparing, unstinting. 2 *generous gifts.* handsome, princely, valuable. ▷ EXPENSIVE. 3 *generous portions.* abundant, ample, copious, lavish, plentiful, sizeable, substantial. ▷ BIG. *Opp* MEAN, SELFISH.

genial *adj* affable, agreeable, amiable, cheerful, convivial, easygoing, happy, jolly, jovial, kindly, pleasant, relaxed, sociable, sunny, warm, warmhearted. ▷ FRIENDLY. *Opp* UNFRIENDLY.

genitals *n* genitalia, *inf* private parts, pudenda, sex organs.

genius *n* 1 ability, aptitude, bent, brains, brilliance, flair, gift, intellect, intelligence, knack, talent, wit. 2 academic, *inf* egghead, expert, intellectual, *derog* know-all, mastermind, thinker, virtuoso.

genteel *adj derog* affected, courtly, ladylike, mannered, overpolite, *inf* posh, refined, stylish, *inf* upper-crust. ▷ POLITE.

gentle *adj* 1 amiable, compassionate, docile, easygoing, good-tempered, harmless, humane, kind, kindly, lenient, loving, meek, merciful, mild, moderate, passive, peaceful, placid, pleasant, quiet, soft-hearted, sweet-tempered, sympathetic, tame, tender. 2 *gentle music.* low, muted, reassuring, relaxing, soft, soothing. 3 *gentle wind.* balmy, faint, light, soft, warm. 4 *gentle hint.* indirect, polite, subtle, tactful. 5 *gentle hill.* easy, gradual, imperceptible, moderate, slight. *Opp* HARSH, SEVERE.

genuine *adj* 1 actual, authentic, authenticated, bona fide, legitimate, original, real, sterling, veritable. 2 *genuine feelings.* earnest, frank, heartfelt, honest, sincere, true, unaffected, unfeigned. *Opp* FALSE.

germ *n* 1 beginning, cause, embryo, genesis, nucleus, origin, root, seed, source. 2 bacterium, *inf* bug, microbe, micro-organism, virus.

germinate *v* bud, develop, grow, root, shoot, spring up, sprout, start growing, take root.

gesture *n* action, flourish, gesticulation, indication, motion, movement, sign, signal.
•*v* gesticulate, indicate, motion, sign, signal.

get *v* 1 acquire, be given, bring, buy, come by, earn, fetch, gain, *inf* get hold of, inherit, *inf* land, *inf* lay hands on, obtain, pick up, procure, purchase, receive, retrieve, secure, take, win. 2 *get her by phone.* contact, reach, speak to. 3 *get a cold.* catch, come down with, contract, develop, fall ill with. 4 *get a criminal.* apprehend, arrest, capture, catch, *inf* collar, *inf* nab, *sl* pinch, seize. 5 *get him to help.* cajole, cause, induce, persuade, prevail on, *inf* twist someone's arm, wheedle. 6 *get tea.* cook, prepare. 7 *get what he means.* appreciate, comprehend, fathom, follow, grasp, know, take in, understand, work out. 8 *get what he says.* catch, distinguish, hear, make out. 9 *get somewhere.* arrive, come, go, reach, travel. 10 *get cold.* become, grow, turn. **get across** ▷ COMMUNICATE. **get ahead** ▷ PROSPER. **get at** ▷ CRITICIZE. **get away** ▷ ESCAPE. **get down** ▷ DESCEND. **get in** ▷ ENTER. **get off** ▷ DESCEND. **get on** ▷ PROSPER. **get out** ▷ LEAVE. **get together** ▷ GATHER.

getaway *n* escape, flight, retreat.

ghastly *adj* appalling, awful, dreadful, frightful, grim, grisly, gruesome, hideous, horrible, macabre, nasty, shocking, terrible, upsetting. ▷ UNPLEASANT.

ghost *n* apparition, banshee, ghoul, hallucination, illusion, phantasm, phantom, poltergeist, shade, shadow, spectre, spirit, *inf* spook, vision, visitant, wraith. **give up the ghost** ▷ DIE.

ghostly *adj* creepy, disembodied, eerie, frightening, *inf* scary, sinister, spectral, *inf* spooky, supernatural, uncanny, unearthly, weird, wraith-like.

giant *adj* ▷ GIGANTIC.
•*n* colossus, Goliath, leviathan, monster, ogre, superhuman, titan, *inf* whopper.

giddiness *n* dizziness, faintness, unsteadiness, vertigo.

giddy *adj* dizzy, faint, light-headed, reeling, silly, spinning, unbalanced, unsteady.

gift *n* 1 bequest, bounty, charity, contribution, donation, favour, *inf* give-away, grant, gratuity, handout, largesse, offering, present, tip. 2 ability, aptitude, bent, capability, capacity, facility, flair, genius, knack, talent.

gifted *adj* expert, skilful, skilled, talented. ▷ CLEVER.

gigantic *adj* colossal, elephantine, enormous, gargantuan, giant, huge, immense, *inf* jumbo, *inf* king-size, mammoth, massive, mighty, monstrous, prodigious, titanic, towering, vast. ▷ BIG. *Opp* SMALL.

giggle *v* laugh, snicker, snigger, titter.

gimcrack *adj* cheap, *inf* cheap and nasty, flimsy, *inf* rubbishy, shoddy, tawdry, *inf* trashy, useless, worthless.

gimmick *n* device, ploy, ruse, stratagem, stunt, trick.

girder *n* bar, beam, joist, rafter.

girdle *n* band, belt, corset, waistband.
•*v* ▷ SURROUND.

girl *n sl* bird, daughter, debutante, girlfriend, fiancée, lass, *old use* maiden, *inf* miss, schoolgirl, tomboy, wench. ▷ WOMAN.

girth *n* circumference, measurement round, perimeter.

gist *n* core, direction, drift, essence, general sense, main idea, meaning, nub, pith, point.

give *v* 1 allocate, allot, allow, apportion, assign, award, bestow, confer, contribute, deal out, *inf* dish out, distribute, *inf* dole out, donate, endow, entrust, *inf* fork out, furnish, give away, give out, grant, hand over, lend, offer, pay, present, provide, render, share out, supply. 2 *give information.* deliver, display, express, impart, issue, notify, publish, put across, put into words, reveal, set out, show, tell, transmit. 3 *give a shout.* emit, let out, utter, voice. 4 *give treatment.* administer, dispense, dose with, impose, inflict, mete out, prescribe. 5 *give a party.* arrange, organize, provide, put on. 6 *give trouble.* cause, create, engender, occasion. 7 *give under pressure.* bend, buckle, collapse, distort, fail, fall apart, give way, warp, yield. *Opp* RECEIVE, TAKE. **give away** ▷ BETRAY. **give in** ▷ SURRENDER. **give off, give out** ▷ EMIT. **give up** ▷ ABANDON, SURRENDER.

glad *adj* 1 content, delighted, overjoyed, pleased. ▷ HAPPY. *Opp* GLOOMY. 2 *glad to help.* disposed, eager, inclined, keen, ready, willing. *Opp* RELUCTANT.

glamorize *v* idealize, romanticize.

glamorous *adj* alluring, appealing, colourful, dazzling, enviable, exciting, exotic, fascinating, glittering, prestigious, romantic, smart, spectacular, wealthy. ▷ BEAUTIFUL.

glamour *n* allure, appeal, attraction, brilliance, charm, excitement, fascination, glitter, magic, romance. ▷ BEAUTY.

glance *v* glimpse, have a quick look, peep, scan. ▷ LOOK.

glare *v* 1 frown, *inf* give a nasty look, glower, *inf* look daggers, scowl, stare angrily. 2 blaze, dazzle, flare, reflect, shine. **glaring** ▷ BRIGHT.

glass *n* 1 crystal, glassware. 2 glazing, pane, plate glass, window. 3 looking-glass, mirror, reflector. 4 beaker, goblet, tumbler, wineglass. **glasses** *inf* specs, spectacles.

glasshouse *n* conservatory, greenhouse, hothouse, orangery.

glassy *adj* 1 glazed, gleaming, glossy, icy, polished, shining, shiny, smooth. 2 *glassy stare*. ▷ EXPRESSIONLESS.

glaze *v* burnish, enamel, gloss, lacquer, polish, shine, varnish.

gleam *v* flash, glimmer, glint, glisten, glow, reflect, shine. ▷ LIGHT. **gleaming** ▷ BRIGHT.

gleeful *adj* delighted, ecstatic, exuberant, gay, jovial, joyful, jubilant, pleased, rapturous, triumphant. ▷ HAPPY. *Opp* SAD.

glib *adj* articulate, facile, fast-talking, fluent, insincere, plausible, quick, ready, slick, smooth, smooth-tongued, superficial. ▷ TALKATIVE. *Opp* INARTICULATE, SINCERE.

glide *v* coast, drift, float, fly, freewheel, move smoothly, sail, skate, ski, skid, skim, slide, slip, soar, stream.

glimpse *n* glance, look, peep, sight, view. • *v* discern, distinguish, espy, get a glimpse of, make out, notice, observe, sight, spot, spy.

glisten *v* flash, gleam, glint, glitter, reflect, shine. ▷ LIGHT.

glitter *v* flash, scintillate, spark, sparkle, twinkle. ▷ LIGHT. **glittering** ▷ BRIGHT.

gloat *v* boast, brag, *inf* crow, exult, glory, rejoice, *inf* rub it in, show off, triumph.

global *adj* broad, international, total, universal, wide-ranging, worldwide. *Opp* LOCAL.

globe *n* 1 ball, globule, orb, sphere. 2 earth, planet, world.

gloom *n* cloudiness, darkness, dimness, dullness, dusk, murk, obscurity, semi-darkness, shade, shadow, twilight. ▷ DEPRESSION.

gloomy *adj* 1 cheerless, cloudy, dark, depressing, dim, dingy, dismal, dreary, glum, grim, murky, obscure, overcast, shadowy, shady, sombre. 2 *gloomy mood*. depressed, downhearted, lugubrious, mournful, pessimistic, saturnine. ▷ SAD. *Opp* CHEERFUL.

glorious *adj* 1 celebrated, distinguished, eminent, famous, heroic, illustrious, noble, noted, renowned, triumphant. 2 *glorious weather*. beautiful, bright, brilliant, dazzling, delightful, excellent, fine, gorgeous, grand, impressive, lovely, magnificent, marvellous, resplendent, spectacular, splendid, *inf* super, superb, wonderful. *Opp* ORDINARY.

glory *n* 1 credit, distinction, eminence, fame, honour, *inf* kudos, praise, prestige, renown, reputation, success, triumph. 2 *glory to God*. adoration, exaltation, glorification, homage, praise, thanksgiving, veneration, worship. 3 *glory of sunrise*. brightness, brilliance, grandeur, magnificence, majesty, radiance, splendour. ▷ BEAUTY.

gloss *n* 1 brightness, brilliance, burnish, finish, glaze, gleam, lustre, polish, sheen, shine, varnish. 2 annotation, comment, definition, elucidation, explanation, footnote, note, paraphrase. • *v* annotate, comment on, define, elucidate, explain, interpret, paraphrase. **gloss over** ▷ CONCEAL.

glossary *n* dictionary, phrasebook, vocabulary, word-list.

glossy *adj* bright, burnished, glazed, gleaming, glistening, lustrous, polished, reflective, shiny, silky, sleek, smooth, waxed. *Opp* DULL.

glove *n* gauntlet, mitt, mitten.

glow *n* 1 burning, fieriness, heat, incandescence, luminosity, lustre, phosphorescence, radiation, redness. 2 ardour, blush, enthusiasm, fervour, flush, passion, rosiness, warmth. • *v* blush, flush, gleam, light up, radiate heat, redden, smoulder. ▷ LIGHT.

glower *v* frown, glare, lour, scowl, stare angrily.

glowing *adj* 1 aglow, bright, hot, incandescent, lambent, luminous, phosphorescent, radiant, red, red-hot. 2 *glowing praise*. enthusiastic, fervent, passionate, warm.

glue *n* adhesive, cement, fixative, gum, paste, size.

• *v* affix, bond, cement, fasten, fix, gum, paste, seal, stick.

glum *adj* cheerless, gloomy, lugubrious, moody, mournful, *inf* out of sorts, saturnine, sullen. ▷ SAD. *Opp* CHEERFUL.

glut *n* abundance, excess, overabundance, overflow, plenty, superfluity, surfeit, surplus. *Opp* SCARCITY.

glutton *n joc* gourmand, *inf* greedy-guts, guzzler, *inf* pig.

gluttonous *adj* insatiable, voracious. ▷ GREEDY.

gnarled *adj* contorted, crooked, distorted, knobbly, knotted, lumpy, misshapen, rough, rugged, twisted.

gnaw *v* bite, chew, erode, wear away. ▷ EAT.

go *n* attempt, chance, *inf* crack, opportunity, *inf* shot, *inf* stab, try, turn.
• *v* 1 advance, begin, be off, depart, disappear, embark, escape, *inf* get going, get moving, get under way, leave, make off, move, pass along, pass on, proceed, retire, retreat, set off, set out, start, take off, take your leave, vanish, wend your way, withdraw. ▷ RUN, TRAVEL, WALK. 2 die, fade, fail, give way. 3 extend, lead, reach, stretch. 4 *The car won't go.* function, operate, perform, run, work. 5 *The days go slowly.* elapse, lapse, pass. 7 *The milk will go sour.* become, grow, turn. 8 *Do the eggs go in the fridge?* belong, live. **go away** ▷ DEPART. **go down** ▷ DESCEND, SINK. **go in for** ▷ LIKE. **go into** ▷ INVESTIGATE. **go off** ▷ EXPLODE. **go on** ▷ CONTINUE. **go through** ▷ SUFFER. **go to** ▷ VISIT. **go together** ▷ MATCH. **go with** ▷ ACCOMPANY. **go without** ▷ ABSTAIN.

goad *v* badger, chivvy, egg on, *inf* needle, prod, prompt, spur, urge. ▷ STIMULATE.

go-ahead *adj* ambitious, enterprising, forward-looking, progressive.
• *n* approval, *inf* green light, permission, sanction, *inf* thumbs-up.

goal *n* aim, ambition, aspiration, design, intention, object, objective, purpose, target.

gobble *v* bolt, devour, gulp, guzzle. ▷ EAT.

go-between *n* agent, broker, envoy, intermediary, mediator, messenger, middleman, negotiator. **act as go-between** ▷ MEDIATE.

god, goddess *ns* deity, divinity, godhead. **God** the Almighty, the Creator, the supreme being. **the gods** the immortals, the powers above.

godsend *n* blessing, boon, gift, miracle, stroke of good luck, windfall.

golden *adj* 1 gilded, gilt. 2 *golden hair.* blond(e), flaxen, yellow.

good *adj* 1 acceptable, admirable, agreeable, appropriate, commendable, delightful, enjoyable, esteemed, *inf* fabulous, fair, *inf* fantastic, fine, gratifying, happy, lovely, marvellous, nice, perfect, pleasant, pleasing, praiseworthy, proper, remarkable, right, satisfactory, *inf* sensational, sound, splendid, suitable, *inf* super, superb, useful, valid, valuable, wonderful, worthy. ▷ EXCELLENT. 2 *good person.* angelic, benevolent, caring, charitable, considerate, decent, dependable, dutiful, ethical, friendly, helpful, holy, honest, honourable, humane, incorruptible, innocent, just, law-abiding, loyal, merciful, moral, noble, obedient, pure, reliable, religious, righteous, saintly, sound, *inf* straight, thoughtful, true, trustworthy, upright, virtuous, well-behaved, well-mannered, worthy. ▷ KIND. 3 *good worker.* able, accomplished, capable, conscientious, efficient, gifted, proficient, skilful, skilled, talented. ▷ CLEVER. 4 *good work.* careful, competent, correct, creditable, efficient, neat, orderly, presentable, professional, thorough, well-done. 5 *good food.* delicious, healthy, nourishing, nutritious, tasty, well-cooked, wholesome. 6 *good book.* classic, exciting, great, interesting, readable, well-written. *Opp* BAD. **good-humoured** ▷ GOOD-TEMPERED. **good-looking** ▷ HANDSOME. **good-natured** ▷ GOOD-TEMPERED. **good person** *inf* angel, *inf* saint, Samaritan, worthy. **goods** 1 belongings, chattels, effects, possessions, property. 2 commodities, freight, load, mechandise, produce, stock, wares.

goodbye *n* departure, farewell, leave-taking, parting words, send-off, valediction.

good-tempered *adj* accommodating, amenable, amiable, benevolent, benign, cheerful, cheery, considerate, cooperative, cordial, friendly, genial, good-humoured, good-natured, helpful, obliging, patient, pleasant, relaxed, smiling, sympathetic, thoughtful, willing. ▷ KIND. *Opp* BAD-TEMPERED.

gorge *v* be greedy, fill up, guzzle, indulge yourself, *inf* make a pig of yourself, overeat, stuff yourself.

gorgeous *adj* dazzling, glorious, magnificent, resplendent, splendid, sumptuous. ▷ BEAUTIFUL.

gory *adj* bloodstained, bloody, grisly, gruesome, savage.

gospel *n* creed, doctrine, good news, good tidings, message, religion, revelation, teaching, testament.

gossip *n* 1 chatter, *inf* the grapevine, hearsay, prattle, rumour, scandal, small talk, *inf* tattle, *inf* tittle-tattle. 2 busybody, chatterbox, *inf* Nosey Parker, scandalmonger, tell-tale.
• *v* *inf* blab, *inf* chat, chatter, *inf* natter, prattle, *inf* tattle, tell tales, *inf* tittle-tattle. ▷ TALK.

gouge *v* chisel, dig, gash, hollow, scoop. ▷ CUT.

gourmet *n* connoisseur, epicure, *derog* gourmand.

govern *v* 1 administer, be in charge of, command, conduct affairs, control, direct, guide, head, lead, look after, manage, oversee, preside over, reign, rule, run, steer, superintend, supervise. 2 *govern your anger.* bridle, check, control, curb, discipline, keep under control, master, regulate, restrain, tame.

government *n* administration, authority, bureaucracy, conduct of state affairs, constitution, control, direction, dominion, management, oversight, regime, regulation, rule, sovereignty, supervision, sway.

gown *n* dress, frock. ▷ CLOTHES.

grab *v* appropriate, *inf* bag, capture, catch, clutch, *inf* collar, commandeer, expropriate, get hold of, grasp, hold, *inf* nab, pluck, seize, snap up, snatch, usurp.

grace *n* 1 attractiveness, beauty, charm, ease, elegance, fluidity, gracefulness, loveliness, poise, refinement, tastefulness. 2 *God's grace.* beneficence, benevolence, compassion, favour, forgiveness, goodness, graciousness, kindness, love, mercy. 3 *grace before meals.* blessing, prayer, thanksgiving.

graceful *adj* 1 agile, deft, dignified, easy, elegant, flowing, fluid, natural, nimble, pliant, smooth, supple, willowy. ▷ BEAUTIFUL. 2 *graceful compliments.* courteous, courtly, kind, polite, refined, suave, tactful, urbane. *Opp* GRACELESS.

graceless *adj* 1 awkward, clumsy, gawky, inelegant, ungainly. ▷ CLUMSY. *Opp* GRACEFUL. 2 *graceless manners.* boorish, gauche, inept, tactless, uncouth. ▷ RUDE.

gracious *adj* 1 affable, agreeable, civilized, cordial, courteous, dignified, elegant, friendly, good-natured, pleasant, polite. ▷ KIND. 2 clement, compassionate, forgiving, generous, indulgent, lenient, magnanimous, pitying, sympathetic. ▷ MERCIFUL. 3 *gracious living.* affluent, expensive, lavish, luxurious, opulent, sumptuous.

grade *n* category, class, condition, degree, echelon, estate, level, mark, notch, point, position, quality, rank, rung, situation, standard, standing, status, step.
• *v* 1 arrange, categorize, classify, differentiate, group, organize, range, size, sort. 2 *grade students' work.* assess, evaluate, mark, rank, rate.

gradient *n* ascent, bank, declivity, hill, incline, rise, slope.

gradual *adj* continuous, easy, even, gentle, leisurely, moderate, regular, slow, steady, unhurried. *Opp* SUDDEN.

graduate *v* 1 get a degree, pass, qualify. 2 *graduate a measuring rod.* calibrate, mark off, mark with a scale.

graft *v* implant, join, splice.

grain *n* 1 atom, bit, crumb, fleck, fragment, granule, iota, jot, mite, molecule, morsel, mote, particle, scrap, seed, speck, trace. 2 ▷ CEREAL.

grand *adj* 1 aristocratic, august, dignified, eminent, glorious, great, imposing, impressive, lordly, magnificent, majestic, noble, opulent, palatial, regal, royal, splendid, stately, sumptuous, superb. ▷ BIG. 2 [*derog*] haughty, *inf* high-and-mighty, lofty, patronizing, pompous, posh. ▷ GRANDIOSE. *Opp* MODEST.

grandiloquent *adj* bombastic, elaborate, florid, flowery, grandiose, high-flown, inflated, ornate, pompous, rhetorical, turgid. *Opp* SIMPLE.

grandiose *adj* affected, ambitious, exaggerated, extravagant, flamboyant, grand, ostentatious, *inf* over the top, pretentious, showy. ▷ GRANDILOQUENT. *Opp* MODEST.

grant *n* allocation, allowance, annuity, award, bequest, bursary, concession, contribution, donation, endowment, expenses, gift, investment, loan, pension, scholarship, sponsorship, subsidy.
• *v* 1 allocate, allot, allow, assign, award, bestow, confer, donate, give, pay, provide, supply. 2 *Grant that I'm right.* accept, acknowledge, admit, agree, concede, consent.

graph *n* chart, column-graph, diagram, grid, pie chart, tab.

graphic *adj* clear, descriptive, detailed, lifelike, lucid, photographic, plain, realistic, representational, vivid, well-drawn.

grapple *v* clutch (at), tackle, wrestle. ▷ GRASP, FIGHT. **grapple with** attend to, come to grips with, contend with, cope with, deal with, get involved with, handle, *inf* have a go at, manage, try to solve.

grasp *v* 1 catch, clasp, clutch, get hold of, grab, grapple with, grip, hang on to, hold, *inf* nab, seize, snatch, take hold of. 2 *grasp an idea*. appreciate, comprehend, *inf* cotton on to, follow, *inf* get the drift of, get the hang of, learn, master, realize, take in, understand. **grasping** ▷ GREEDY.

grass *n* field, grassland, green, lawn, meadow, pasture, prairie, savannah, steppe, turf, veld.
• *v* ▷ INFORM.

grate *n* fireplace, hearth.
• *v* cut, grind, rasp, scrape, shred. **grate on** ▷ ANNOY. **grating** ▷ ANNOYING, HARSH.

grateful *adj* appreciative, beholden, gratified, indebted, obliged, thankful. *Opp* UNGRATEFUL.

gratify *v* delight, fulfil, indulge, please, satisfy.

gratis *adj* complimentary, free, free of charge, gratuitous.

gratitude *n* appreciation, gratefulness, thankfulness, thanks.

gratuitous *adj* 1 ▷ GRATIS. 2 *gratuitous insults*. baseless, groundless, inappropriate, needless, uncalled-for, undeserved, unjustifiable, unnecessary, unprovoked, unsolicited, unwarranted. *Opp* JUSTIFIABLE.

gratuity *n* bonus, *inf* perk, present, reward, tip.

grave *adj* 1 acute, critical, crucial, dangerous, *inf* life and death, major, momentous, pressing, serious, severe, significant, terminal (*illness*), threatening, urgent, vital, weighty, worrying. 2 *grave offence*. criminal, indictable, punishable. 3 *grave look*. dignified, earnest, grim, long-faced, pensive, serious, severe, sober, solemn, sombre, subdued, thoughtful, unsmiling. ▷ SAD. *Opp* CHEERFUL, TRIVIAL.
• *n* barrow, burial place, crypt, *inf* last resting place, mausoleum, sepulchre, tomb, vault. ▷ GRAVESTONE.

gravel *n* grit, pebbles, shingle, stones.

gravestone *n* headstone, memorial, monument, tombstone.

graveyard *n* burial ground, cemetery, churchyard.

gravity *n* 1 acuteness, danger, importance, magnitude, momentousness, seriousness, severity, significance. 2 *behave with gravity*. ceremony, dignity, earnestness, pomp, reserve, sedateness, sobriety, solemnity. 3 *force of gravity*. attraction, gravitation, heaviness, pull, weight.

graze *n* abrasion, laceration, raw spot, scrape, scratch. ▷ WOUND.

grease *n* fat, lubrication, oil.

greasy *adj* 1 buttery, fatty, oily, slippery, smeary, waxy. 2 *greasy manner*. fawning, flattering, fulsome, ingratiating, slick, *inf* smarmy, sycophantic, toadying, unctuous.

great *adj* 1 colossal, enormous, extensive, giant, gigantic, grand, huge, immense, massive, prodigious, *inf* tremendous, vast. ▷ BIG. 2 *great pain*. acute, considerable, excessive, extreme, intense, marked, pronounced. ▷ SEVERE. 3 *great events*. grand, imposing, momentous, serious, significant, spectacular. ▷ IMPORTANT. 4 *great music*. brilliant, *inf* fabulous, *inf* fantastic, fine, first-rate, outstanding, wonderful. ▷ EXCELLENT. 5 *great athlete*. able, celebrated, distinguished, eminent, gifted, noted, prominent, renowned, talented, well-known. ▷ FAMOUS. 6 *great friend*. close, dedicated, devoted, faithful, fast, loyal, true, valued. 7 *great reader*. active, ardent, assiduous, eager, enthusiastic, habitual, keen, passionate, zealous. 8 ▷ GOOD. *Opp* SMALL, UNIMPORTANT.

greed *n* 1 appetite, craving, gluttony, hunger, insatiability, intemperance, ravenousness, self-indulgence, voracity. 2 *greed for wealth*. avarice, covetousness, cupidity, desire, rapacity, self-interest. ▷ SELFISHNESS.

greedy *adj* 1 famished, gluttonous, *inf* hoggish, hungry, insatiable, intemperate, *inf* piggish, ravenous, self-indulgent, starving, voracious. *Opp* ABSTEMIOUS. 2 *greedy for wealth*. acquisitive, avaricious, avid, covetous, desirous, eager, grasping, materialistic, mean, mercenary, rapacious, selfish. *Opp* UNSELFISH. **be greedy** ▷ GORGE. **greedy person** ▷ GLUTTON.

green *adj* 1 grassy, leafy, verdant. 2 emerald, jade, lime, olive.

greenery *n* foliage, leaves, plants, vegetation.

greet *v* accost, acknowledge, address, hail, receive, salute, *inf* say hello to, usher in, welcome.

greeting *n* salutation, reception, welcome. **greetings** compliments, congratulations, felicitations, good wishes, regards.

grey *adj* ashen, colourless, greying, grizzled, grizzly, hoary, leaden, livid, pearly, silvery, slate-grey, smoky, sooty. ▷ GLOOMY.

grid *n* framework, grating, grille, lattice, network.

grief *n* affliction, anguish, depression, desolation, distress, heartache, heartbreak, melancholy, misery, mourning, regret, remorse, sadness, sorrow, suffering, tragedy, unhappiness, woe, wretchedness. ▷ PAIN. *Opp* HAPPINESS. **come to grief** ▷ FAIL.

grievance *n* 1 calamity, damage, hardship, harm, indignity, injury, injustice. 2 allegation, *inf* bone to pick, charge, complaint, *inf* gripe, objection.

grieve *v* 1 afflict, depress, dismay, distress, hurt, pain, sadden, upset, wound. *Opp* PLEASE. 2 be in mourning, *inf* eat your heart out, lament, mourn, suffer, wail, weep. *Opp* REJOICE.

grim *adj* appalling, cruel, dreadful, fearsome, fierce, forbidding, formidable, frightful, frowning, ghastly, grisly, gruesome, harsh, hideous, horrible, horrid, inexorable, inflexible, menacing, merciless, ominous, relentless, ruthless, savage, severe, sinister, stark, stern, sullen, surly, terrible, threatening, unattractive, unfriendly, unpleasant, unrelenting, unsmiling, unyielding. ▷ GLOOMY. *Opp* CHEERFUL.

grime *n* dirt, dust, filth, grit, muck, scum, soot.

grind *v* 1 crumble, crush, erode, granulate, grate, mill, pound, powder, pulverize, rasp. 2 file, polish, sand, sandpaper, scrape, sharpen, smooth, wear away, whet. 3 *grind your teeth*. gnash, grate. **grind away** ▷ WORK. **grind down** ▷ OPPRESS.

grip *n* clasp, clutch, grasp, hold, purchase, stranglehold. ▷ CONTROL.
• *v* 1 clasp, clutch, grab, grasp, hold, seize, take hold of. 2 *grip the imagination*. absorb, compel, engage, engross, enthral, fascinate, hypnotize, mesmerize, rivet. **come to grips with** ▷ TACKLE.

grisly *adj* ▷ GRUESOME.

gristly *adj* leathery, stringy, tough, uneatable.

gritty *adj* abrasive, dusty, grainy, granular, gravelly, harsh, rasping, rough, sandy.

groan *v* 1 cry out, moan, sigh, wail. 2 ▷ COMPLAIN.

groom *n* 1 ostler, stable-lad, stableman. 2 bridegroom, husband.
• *v* 1 brush, clean, neaten, preen, smarten up, spruce up, tidy. 2 *groom someone for a job*. coach, drill, educate, get ready, prepare, prime, train up, tutor.

groove *n* channel, cut, fluting, furrow, gutter, hollow, indentation, rut, scratch, slot, track.

grope *v* feel about, fish, flounder, fumble, search blindly.

gross *adj* 1 bloated, massive, obese, repellent, repulsive, revolting. ▷ FAT. 2 churlish, coarse, crude, rude, unrefined, vulgar. 3 *gross injustice*. blatant, flagrant, glaring, manifest, monstrous, obvious, outrageous, shameful. 4 *gross income*. before tax, inclusive, overall, total, whole.

grotesque *adj* absurd, bizarre, deformed, distorted, fantastic, freakish, ludicrous, macabre, malformed, misshapen, monstrous, outlandish, preposterous, queer, ridiculous, strange, surreal, twisted, ugly, unnatural, weird.

ground *n* 1 clay, dirt, earth, loam, mud, soil. 2 area, land, property, terrain. 3 campus, estate, garden, park, surroundings. 4 *sports ground*. arena, court, field, pitch, playing field, stadium. 5 *grounds for complaint*. argument, base, basis, case, cause, evidence, foundation, justification, motive, reason.
• *v* 1 base, establish, found, set, settle. 2 coach, educate, instruct, prepare, teach, train, tutor. 3 beach, run ashore, shipwreck, strand, wreck.

groundless *adj* baseless, false, gratuitous, hypothetical, illusory, imaginary, irrational, needless, speculative, uncalled-for, unfounded, unjustifiable, unjustified, unreasonable, unsubstantiated, unsupported, unwarranted.

group *n* 1 [*people*] alliance, assemblage, assembly, association, band, body, brotherhood, *inf* bunch, cartel, caste, caucus, circle, clan, class, clique, club, colony, committee, community, company, congregation, consortium, contingent, corps, coterie, crew, crowd, delegation, faction, family, federation, fraternity, gang, gathering, horde, host, knot, league, meeting, *derog* mob, multitude, number, organization, party, platoon, posse, *derog* rabble, ring, sect, *derog* shower, sisterhood, society, squad, swarm, team, throng, troop, troupe, union, unit. 2 [*things, animals*] accumulation, assemblage, assortment, batch, battery (*guns*), brood (*chicks*), bunch, bundle, category, class, clump, cluster, clutch (*eggs*), collection, combination, conglomeration,

constellation, convoy, covey (*birds*), fleet, flock, gaggle (*geese*), galaxy, heap, herd, hoard, litter, mass, pack, pile, pride (*lions*), school, set, shoal (*fish*), species. 3 ▷ MUSICIAN.
• *v* 1 arrange, assemble, bring together, categorize, classify, collect, deploy, gather, herd, marshal, order, organize, put together, set out, sort. 2 associate, band, cluster, come together, congregate, crowd, flock, gather, get together, herd, swarm, team up, throng.

grovel *v* abase yourself, cower, *inf* crawl, *inf* creep, cringe, demean yourself, fawn, flatter, kowtow, *inf* lick someone's boots, prostrate yourself, snivel, *inf* suck up, toady. **grovelling** ▷ OBSEQUIOUS.

grow *v* 1 augment, broaden, build up, burgeon, develop, emerge, enlarge, evolve, expand, extend, fill out, flourish, flower, germinate, improve, increase, lengthen, live, make progress, mature, multiply, mushroom, progress, proliferate, prosper, ripen, rise, shoot up, spread, spring up, sprout, swell, thicken, thrive. 2 *grow roses.* cultivate, farm, nurture, produce, propagate, raise. 3 *grow older.* become, get, turn.

grown-up *adj* adult, fully-grown, mature, well-developed.

growth *n* 1 advance, augmentation, development, enlargement, evolution, expansion, extension, flowering, improvement, increase, maturation, maturing, progress, proliferation, prosperity, spread, success. 2 crop, harvest, plants, produce, vegetation, yield. 3 cancer, cyst, excrescence, lump, swelling, tumour.

grub *n* 1 caterpillar, larva, maggot. 2 [*inf*] ▷ FOOD.
• *v* ▷ DIG.

grudge *n* ▷ RESENTMENT.
• *v* begrudge, envy, resent.

grudging *adj* cautious, envious, guarded, half-hearted, jealous, reluctant, resentful, unenthusiastic, ungracious, unwilling. *Opp* ENTHUSIASTIC.

gruelling *adj* arduous, demanding, exhausting, laborious, severe, stiff, strenuous, tiring, tough, uphill, wearying. ▷ DIFFICULT. *Opp* EASY.

gruesome *adj* appalling, awful, dreadful, fearful, fearsome, frightful, ghastly, ghoulish, gory, grim, grisly, hair-raising, hideous, horrible, horrid, horrific, macabre, revolting, shocking, sickening, terrible.

gruff *adj* 1 guttural, harsh, hoarse, husky, rasping, rough, throaty. 2 ▷ BAD-TEMPERED.

grumble *v* fuss, *inf* gripe, *inf* grouch, *inf* grouse, make a fuss, object, protest, *inf* whinge. ▷ COMPLAIN.

guarantee *n* assurance, bond, oath, obligation, pledge, promise, surety, undertaking, warranty, word of honour.
• *v* 1 assure, certify, pledge, promise, swear, undertake, vouch, vow. 2 ensure, make sure of, reserve, secure.

guard *n* bodyguard, *inf* bouncer, custodian, escort, guardian, *sl* heavy, lookout, *sl* minder, patrol, picket, security guard, sentinel, sentry, warder, watchman.
• *v* care for, defend, keep safe, look after, mind, oversee, patrol, police, preserve, protect, safeguard, secure, shelter, shield, stand guard over, supervise, tend, watch, watch over. **on your guard** ▷ ALERT.

guardian *n* 1 adoptive parent, foster-parent. 2 defender, keeper, protector, trustee, warden. ▷ GUARD.

guess *n* assumption, conjecture, estimate, feeling, *sl* guesstimate, guesswork, hunch, hypothesis, intuition, opinion, prediction, *inf* shot in the dark, speculation, supposition, surmise, suspicion, theory.
• *v* assume, conjecture, divine, estimate, expect, fancy, feel, have a hunch, *inf* hazard a guess, hypothesize, imagine, judge, predict, *inf* reckon, speculate, suppose, surmise, suspect, think likely.

guest *n* 1 caller, visitor. 2 boarder, lodger, patron, resident.

guidance *n* advice, briefing, counselling, direction, guidelines, help, instruction, leadership, management, spoonfeeding, teaching, tips.

guide *n* 1 courier, escort, leader, navigator, pilot. 2 adviser, counsellor, director, guru, mentor. 3 atlas, directory, gazetteer, guidebook, handbook.
• *v* 1 conduct, direct, escort, lead, manœuvre, navigate, pilot, shepherd, show the way, steer, supervise, usher. 2 advise, brief, control, counsel, educate, govern, help along, influence, instruct, regulate, *inf* take by the hand, teach, train, tutor. *Opp* MISLEAD.

guilt *n* 1 blame, culpability, fault, guiltiness, liability, responsibility, sinfulness, wickedness, wrongdoing. 2 *look of guilt.* bad conscience, contrition, dishonour, penitence, regret, remorse, self-reproach, shame, sorrow. *Opp* INNOCENCE.

guiltless *adj* above suspicion, blameless,

clear, faultless, free, innocent, in the right, irreproachable, pure, sinless, untarnished, virtuous. *Opp* GUILTY.

guilty *adj* 1 at fault, culpable, in the wrong, liable, reprehensible, responsible. 2 *guilty look*. ashamed, conscience-stricken, contrite, penitent, *inf* red-faced, remorseful, repentant, rueful, shamefaced, sheepish, sorry. *Opp* GUILTLESS, SHAMELESS.

gullible *adj* credulous, easily taken in, *inf* green, impressionable, innocent, naive, trusting, unsuspecting. *Opp* SCEPTICAL.

gulp *n* mouthful, swallow, *inf* swig. • *v* 1 bolt down, gobble, *inf* wolf. ▷ EAT. 2 *inf* knock back, quaff, *inf* swig. ▷ DRINK. 3 *gulp back tears*. choke back, stifle, suppress.

gumption *n* cleverness, common sense, enterprise, initiative, judgement, *inf* nous, resourcefulness, sense, wisdom.

gun *n pl* artillery, firearm, weapon. **gun down** ▷ SHOOT.

gunfire *n* cannonade, crossfire, firing, gunshots, salvo.

gunman *n* assassin, fighter, gangster, killer, marksman, sniper, terrorist.

gurgle *v* babble, bubble, burble, ripple, purl, splash.

gush *n* burst, cascade, eruption, flood, flow, jet, outpouring, overflow, rush, spout, spurt, squirt, stream, tide, torrent. • *v* 1 cascade, flood, flow freely, overflow, pour, run, rush, spout, spurt, squirt, stream, well up. 2 be enthusiastic, be sentimental, fuss, prattle on, talk on. **gushing** ▷ EFFUSIVE, SENTIMENTAL.

gusto *n* delight, enjoyment, enthusiasm, excitement, liveliness, pleasure, relish, spirit, verve, vigour, zest.

gut *v* 1 clean, disembowel, eviscerate. 2 *gut a building*. clear, empty, loot, pillage, plunder, ransack, remove the contents of, sack, strip.

guts *pl n* 1 bowels, entrails, *inf* innards, insides, intestines, stomach, viscera. 2 ▷ COURAGE.

gutter *n* channel, conduit, ditch, drain, duct, guttering, sewer, sluice, trench, trough.

gypsy *n* nomad, Romany, traveller, wanderer.

gyrate *v* circle, revolve, rotate, spin, spiral, swivel, turn, twirl, wheel, whirl.

H

habit *n* 1 convention, custom, pattern, policy, practice, routine, rule, usage, wont. 2 bent, disposition, inclination, manner, mannerism, penchant, predisposition, propensity, quirk, tendency, way. 3 *bad habit.* addiction, compulsion, craving, dependence, fixation, obsession, vice.

habitable *adj* in good repair, inhabitable, usable.

habitual *adj* 1 accustomed, common, conventional, customary, expected, familiar, fixed, frequent, natural, normal, ordinary, predictable, regular, ritual, routine, set, settled, standard, traditional, typical, usual, wonted. 2 addictive, besetting, chronic, established, ingrained, obsessive, persistent, recurrent. 3 *habitual smoker.* addicted, confirmed, dependent, hardened, *inf* hooked, inveterate, persistent.

hack *v* carve, chop, gash, hew, mangle, mutilate, slash. ▷ CUT.

hackneyed *adj* banal, clichéd, commonplace, conventional, *inf* corny, familiar, feeble, obvious, overused, pedestrian, platitudinous, predictable, stale, stereotyped, stock, tired, trite, uninspired, unoriginal. *Opp* NEW.

haggard *adj* careworn, drawn, emaciated, exhausted, gaunt, hollow-eyed, pinched, run-down, scraggy, scrawny, shrunken, thin, tired out, wasted, weary, worn out, *inf* worried to death. *Opp* HEALTHY.

haggle *v* bargain, barter, negotiate, quibble. ▷ QUARREL.

hail *v* 1 accost, address, call to, greet, signal to. 2 ▷ ACCLAIM.

hair *n* 1 beard, bristles, curls, fleece, fur, locks, mane, *inf* mop, moustache, shock, tresses, whiskers. 2 coiffure, cut, haircut, *inf* hairdo, hairstyle.

hairdresser *n* barber, coiffeur, coiffeuse, hairstylist.

hairless *adj* bald, bare, clean-shaven, naked, shaved, shaven, smooth. *Opp* HAIRY.

hairy *adj* bearded, bristly, downy, fleecy, furry, fuzzy, hirsute, shaggy, stubbly, woolly. *Opp* HAIRLESS.

half-hearted *adj* apathetic, cool, feeble, indifferent, ineffective, lackadaisical, listless, lukewarm, passive, perfunctory, phlegmatic, uncommitted, unconcerned, unenthusiastic, wavering, weak, *inf* wishy-washy. *Opp* ENTHUSIASTIC.

hall *n* 1 auditorium, concert hall, lecture room, theatre. 2 corridor, entrance hall, foyer, hallway, lobby, passage, passageway, vestibule.

hallowed *adj* blessed, consecrated, holy, honoured, revered, sacred, sacrosanct.

hallucinate *v* daydream, dream, fantasize, *inf* see things.

hallucination *n* chimera, daydream, delusion, dream, fantasy, figment of the imagination, illusion, mirage. ▷ GHOST.

halt *n* break, close, end, interruption, pause, standstill, stop, stoppage, termination.
• *v* 1 block, break off, cease, check, curb, end, impede, obstruct, stop, terminate. 2 come to a halt, come to rest, discontinue, draw up, pull up, stop, wait. *Opp* START. **halting** ▷ HESITANT, IRREGULAR.

halve *v* bisect, cut by half, cut in half, decrease, lessen, share equally, split in two.

hammer *n* mallet, sledgehammer.
• *v* batter, beat, pound, strike. ▷ DEFEAT, HIT.

hamper *v* block, curb, delay, encumber, entangle, fetter, foil, frustrate, handicap, hinder, hold up, impede, inhibit, interfere with, obstruct, prevent, restrain, restrict, shackle, slow down, thwart. *Opp* HELP.

hand *n* 1 fist, *sl* mitt, palm, *inf* paw. 2 *hand on a dial.* indicator, pointer. 3 ▷ WORKER.
• *v* convey, deliver, give, offer, pass, present, submit. **at hand** ▷ HANDY. **give a hand** ▷ HELP. **hand down** ▷ BEQUEATH. **hand over** ▷ SURRENDER. **hand round** ▷ DISTRIBUTE. **lend a hand** ▷ HELP. **to hand** ▷ HANDY.

handicap *n* 1 barrier, disadvantage, difficulty, drawback, encumbrance, hindrance, impediment, inconvenience, *inf* minus, nuisance, obstacle, problem, restriction, shortcoming, stumbling block. *Opp* ADVANTAGE. 2 defect, disability, impairment.
• *v* burden, check, curb, disable, disadvantage, encumber, hamper, hinder, hold

back, impede, limit, restrain, restrict. *Opp* HELP.

handicapped *adj* 1 encumbered, hindered, impeded. 2 crippled, disabled, disadvantaged, paralysed.

handiwork *n* creation, doing, invention, production, responsibility, work.

handle *n* grip, haft, hilt, knob, stock (*of rifle*).
• *v* 1 feel, finger, fondle, grasp, hold, *inf* maul, *inf* paw, stroke, touch. 2 *handle situations, people.* contend with, control, cope with, deal with, direct, guide, look after, manage, manipulate, tackle, treat. ▷ ORGANIZE. 3 *car handles well.* manœuvre, operate, respond, steer, work. 4 *handle goods.* deal in, market, sell, stock, touch, traffic in.

handsome *adj* 1 attractive, beautiful, *old use* comely, *old use* fair, good-looking, personable, tasteful. *Opp* UGLY. 2 *handsome gift.* big, bountiful, generous, gracious, large, liberal, magnanimous, sizeable, unselfish, valuable. *Opp* MEAN.

handy *adj* 1 convenient, easy to use, helpful, manageable, practical, serviceable, useful, well-designed, worth having. 2 *handy with tools.* adept, capable, clever, competent, practical, proficient, skilful. 3 *keep tools handy.* accessible, available, close at hand, nearby, reachable, ready, to hand. *Opp* AWKWARD, INACCESSIBLE.

hang *v* 1 be suspended, dangle, droop, flap, flop, sway, swing, trail down. 2 attach, drape, fasten, fix, peg up, pin up. 3 *hang in the air.* drift, float, hover. **hang about** ▷ DAWDLE. **hang back** ▷ HESITATE. **hanging** ▷ PENDENT. **hangings** ▷ DRAPE. **hang on** ▷ WAIT. **hang on to** ▷ KEEP.

hank *n* coil, length, loop, skein.

hanker *v* **hanker after** crave, long for. ▷ DESIRE.

haphazard *adj* accidental, arbitrary, casual, chance, chaotic, confusing, disorderly, disorganized, fortuitous, *inf* higgledy-piggledy, *inf* hit-or-miss, illogical, irrational, random, unforeseen, unplanned, unstructured, unsystematic. *Opp* ORDERLY.

happen *v* arise, befall, chance, come about, *inf* crop up, emerge, follow, materialize, occur, result, take place, transpire. **happen on** ▷ FIND.

happening *n* accident, affair, chance, circumstance, episode, event, incident, occasion, occurrence, phenomenon.

happiness *n* bliss, cheerfulness, contentment, delight, ecstasy, elation, euphoria, exhilaration, exuberance, felicity, gaiety, gladness, glee, *inf* heaven, high spirits, joy, joyfulness, jubilation, light-heartedness, merriment, pleasure, rapture, well-being. *Opp* SADNESS.

happy *adj* 1 beatific, blessed, blissful, buoyant, cheerful, cheery, contented, delighted, ecstatic, elated, euphoric, exhilarated, exuberant, exultant, felicitous, festive, gay, glad, gleeful, good-humoured, halcyon (*days*), *inf* heavenly, high-spirited, idyllic, jocund, jolly, jovial, joyful, jubilant, laughing, light-hearted, lively, merry, *inf* on top of the world, overjoyed, *inf* over the moon, pleased, proud, radiant, rapturous, rejoicing, relaxed, satisfied, smiling, *inf* starry-eyed, sunny, thrilled. *Opp* SAD. 2 *happy accident.* advantageous, apt, auspicious, beneficial, convenient, favourable, fortuitous, fortunate, lucky, opportune, propitious, timely, welcome, well-timed.

harangue *n* diatribe, exhortation, *inf* pep talk. ▷ SPEECH.
• *v* exhort, *inf* hold forth, lecture, pontificate, preach, sermonize.

harass *v* annoy, attack, badger, bait, bother, disturb, *inf* hassle, hound, molest, nag, persecute, pester, *inf* pick on, plague, torment, trouble, vex, worry.

harassed *adj* *inf* at the end of your tether, careworn, distraught, distressed, exhausted, frayed, pressured, strained, stressed, tired, weary, worn out.

harbour *n* anchorage, dock, haven, jetty, landing stage, marina, mooring, pier, port, quay, safe haven, shelter, wharf.
• *v* 1 conceal, give asylum to, give refuge to, hide, protect, shelter, shield. 2 *harbour a grudge.* hold on to, keep in mind, maintain, nurse, nurture, retain.

hard *adj* 1 adamantine, compact, compressed, dense, firm, flinty, frozen, hardened, impenetrable, inflexible, rigid, rocky, solid, steely, stiff, stony, unyielding. 2 *hard labour.* arduous, back-breaking, exhausting, fatiguing, gruelling, harsh, heavy, laborious, onerous, rigorous, severe, strenuous, taxing, tiring, tough, uphill, wearying. 3 *hard problem.* baffling, complex, complicated, confusing, difficult, insoluble, intricate, involved, *inf* knotty, perplexing, puzzling, *inf* thorny. 4 *hard person.* callous, cold, cruel, harsh, heartless, hostile, inflexible, intolerant, merciless, obdurate, ruthless, severe, stern, strict, unbending, unfeeling, unkind. 5 *hard blow.* forceful, heavy, powerful, strong, violent. 6 *hard times.* austere, bad, calamitous, distressing, grim, intolerable, painful, unhappy, unpleasant. 7 *hard worker.* assiduous, conscientious, indefatigable, industrious, keen, unflagging, untiring, zealous. *Opp* EASY, SOFT. **hard-headed** ▷ BUSINESS-LIKE. **hard-hearted** ▷ CRUEL. **hard up** ▷ POOR. **hard-wearing** ▷ DURABLE.

harden *v* bake, cake, clot, congeal, freeze, reinforce, set, solidify, stiffen, strengthen, toughen. *Opp* SOFTEN.

hardly *adv* barely, faintly, only just, rarely, scarcely, seldom.

hardship *n* adversity, affliction, austerity, bad luck, deprivation, destitution, difficulty, distress, misery, misfortune, need, privation, suffering, trouble, unhappiness, want.

hardware *n* equipment, implements, instruments, ironmongery, machinery, tools.

hardy *adj* 1 durable, fit, healthy, resilient, robust, rugged, strong, sturdy, tough. *Opp* TENDER. 2 ▷ BOLD.

harm *n* abuse, damage, detriment, disadvantage, disservice, havoc, hurt, inconvenience, injury, loss, mischief, pain, unhappiness, *inf* upset. ▷ EVIL.
• *v* abuse, damage, hurt, ill-treat, impair, injure, maltreat, misuse, ruin, spoil, wound. *Opp* BENEFIT.

harmful *adj* bad, baleful, damaging, dangerous, deadly, deleterious, destructive, detrimental, evil, fatal, hurtful, injurious, lethal, malign, noxious, pernicious, poisonous, prejudicial, ruinous, unhealthy, unpleasant, unwholesome. *Opp* BENEFICIAL, HARMLESS.

harmless *adj* acceptable, benign, gentle, innocent, innocuous, inoffensive, mild, non-addictive, non-toxic, safe, tame, unobjectionable. *Opp* HARMFUL.

harmonious *adj* 1 concordant, consonant, *inf* easy on the ear, euphonious, harmonizing, melodious, musical, sweet-sounding, tuneful. *Opp* DISCORDANT. 2 *harmonious group.* amicable, compatible, congenial, cooperative, friendly, like-minded, sympathetic.

harmonize *v* agree, balance, be in harmony, blend, coordinate, correspond, go together, match, tally, tone in.

harmony *n* 1 assonance, consonance, euphony, tunefulness. 2 accord, agreement, amity, balance, compatibility, concord, conformity, cooperation, friendship, like-mindedness, peace, rapport, sympathy, understanding. *Opp* DISCORD.

harness *n* equipment, *inf* gear, straps, tackle.
• *v* control, domesticate, exploit, keep under control, make use of, mobilize, tame, use, utilize.

harsh *adj* 1 abrasive, bristly, coarse, hairy, rough, scratchy. 2 *harsh sounds.* cacophonous, croaking, disagreeable, discordant, dissonant, grating, gruff, guttural, hoarse, husky, irritating, jarring, rasping, raucous, rough, screeching, shrill, stertorous, strident, unpleasant. 3 *harsh colours, light.* bright, brilliant, dazzling, gaudy, glaring, lurid. 4 *harsh smell.* acrid, bitter, sour. 5 *harsh conditions.* arduous, austere, comfortless, difficult, hard, severe, tough. 6 *harsh criticism, treatment.* abusive, acerbic, bitter, blunt, brutal, cruel, draconian, frank, hard-hearted, hurtful, merciless, outspoken, pitiless, severe, sharp, stern, strict, unforgiving, unkind, unrelenting, unsympathetic. *Opp* GENTLE.

harvest *n* crop, gathering-in, produce, reaping, return, yield.
• *v* bring in, collect, garner, gather, glean, mow, pick, reap.

hash *n* 1 goulash, stew. 2 *inf* botch, confusion, *inf* hotchpotch, jumble, mess, *inf* mishmash, mixture, muddle. **make a hash of** ▷ BUNGLE.

hassle *n* argument, bother, confusion, difficulty, disagreement, disturbance, fuss, harassment, inconvenience, nuisance, problem, struggle, trouble, upset.
• *v* ▷ HARASS.

haste *n* impetuosity, precipitateness, rashness, recklessness, rush, urgency. ▷ SPEED.

hasty *adj* 1 abrupt, fast, foolhardy, headlong, hurried, ill-considered, impetuous, impulsive, incautious, *inf* pell-mell, precipitate, quick, rapid, rash, reckless, speedy, sudden, summary (*justice*), swift. 2 *hasty work.* brief, careless, cursory, perfunctory, rushed, slapdash, superficial, thoughtless, unthinking. *Opp* CAREFUL, SLOW.

hatch *v* 1 brood, incubate. 2 conceive, concoct, contrive, *inf* cook up, design, devise, dream up, formulate, invent, plan, plot, scheme, think up.

hate *n* 1 ▷ HATRED. 2 *pet hate.* abomination, aversion, *Fr* bête noire, dislike, loathing.
• *v* abhor, abominate, be hostile to, be revolted by, deplore, despise, detest,

dislike, execrate, fear, find intolerable, loathe, object to, recoil from, resent, scorn, shudder at. *Opp* LIKE, LOVE.

hateful *adj* abhorrent, abominable, awful, contemptible, cursed, *inf* damnable, despicable, detestable, disgusting, distasteful, execrable, foul, hated, horrible, horrid, loathsome, nasty, nauseating, obnoxious, odious, offensive, repellent, repugnant, repulsive, revolting, vile. ▷ EVIL. *Opp* LOVABLE.

hatred *n* abhorrence, animosity, antipathy, aversion, contempt, detestation, dislike, enmity, hate, hostility, ill will, loathing, misanthropy, odium, repugnance, revulsion. *Opp* LOVE.

haughty *adj* arrogant, bumptious, cavalier, *inf* cocky, conceited, condescending, disdainful, egotistical, *inf* high-and-mighty, *inf* hoity-toity, imperious, lofty, offhand, pompous, presumptuous, pretentious, proud, self-important, snobbish, *inf* snooty, *inf* stuck-up, supercilious, superior, vain. *Opp* MODEST.

haul *v* carry, cart, drag, draw, heave, lug, move, pull, tow, trail, tug.

haunt *v* 1 frequent, *inf* hang around, keep returning to, loiter about, patronize, visit regularly. 2 *haunt the mind.* beset, linger in, obsess, plague, prey on, torment.

have *v* 1 be in possession of, keep, maintain, own, possess, use, utilize. 2 *play has two themes.* comprise, consist of, contain, embody, hold, include, incorporate, involve. 3 *have fun, trouble.* endure, enjoy, experience, feel, go through, know, live through, put up with, suffer, tolerate, undergo. 4 *have a reward.* accept, acquire, be given, gain, get, obtain, receive. 5 *thieves had the lot. inf* get away with, remove, steal, take. 6 *have a snack.* consume, eat, drink, swallow. 7 *have a party.* arrange, hold, organize, prepare, set up. 8 *have guests.* be host to, cater for, entertain, put up. **have on** ▷ HOAX. **have to** be compelled to, be forced to, must, need to, ought to, should. **have up** ▷ ARREST.

haven *n* asylum, refuge, retreat, sanctuary. ▷ HARBOUR.

havoc *n* carnage, chaos, confusion, damage, destruction, devastation, disorder, disruption, *inf* mayhem, *inf* rack and ruin, ruin, *inf* shambles, waste, wreckage.

hazard *n* chance, danger, jeopardy, peril, risk, threat.
• *v* dare, gamble, jeopardize, risk, stake, venture.

hazardous *adj inf* chancy, dangerous, *inf* dicey, fraught with danger, perilous, precarious, risky, uncertain, unpredictable, unsafe. *Opp* SAFE.

haze *n* cloud, film, fog, mist, steam, vapour.

hazy *adj* 1 blurred, cloudy, dim, faint, foggy, fuzzy, indefinite, milky, misty, obscure, unclear. 2 ▷ VAGUE. *Opp* CLEAR.

head *adj* ▷ CHIEF.
• *n* 1 brain, cranium, skull. 2 *head for figures.* ability, brains, capacity, imagination, intelligence, intellect, mind, understanding. 3 *head of a mountain.* apex, crown, highest point, peak, summit, top. 4 director, leader, manager. ▷ CHIEF. 5 headmaster, headmistress, head teacher, principal. 6 *head of a river.* ▷ SOURCE.
• *v* 1 be in charge of, command, control, direct, govern, guide, lead, manage, rule, run, superintend, supervise. 2 *head for home.* aim, go, make, *inf* make a beeline, point, set out, start, steer, turn. **head off** ▷ DEFLECT. **lose your head** ▷ PANIC. **off your head** ▷ MAD.

heading *n* caption, headline, rubric, title.

headquarters *n* administration, base, depot, head office, *inf* HQ, main office, *inf* nerve-centre.

heal *v* 1 get better, improve, knit, mend, recover, recuperate. 2 cure, make better, minister to, nurse, rejuvenate, remedy, renew, restore, revitalize, tend, treat. 3 *heal differences.* patch up, put right, reconcile, repair, settle.

health *n* 1 condition, constitution, *inf* fettle, form, shape, trim. 2 *picture of health.* fitness, robustness, soundness, strength, vigour, well-being.

healthy *adj* 1 active, blooming, fine, fit, flourishing, good, hearty, *inf* in fine fettle, in good shape, lively, perky, robust, sound, strong, sturdy, vigorous, well. 2 bracing, hygienic, invigorating, salubrious, sanitary, wholesome. *Opp* ILL, UNHEALTHY.

heap *n* accumulation, assemblage, bank, collection, hill, hoard, mass, mound, mountain, pile, stack.
• *v* bank up, mass, pile, stack. ▷ COLLECT. **heaps** ▷ PLENTY.

hear *v* 1 attend to, catch, heed, listen to, overhear, pick up. 2 *hear evidence.* examine, investigate, judge, try. 3 *hear news.* discover, find out, gather, get, *inf* get wind of, learn, receive.

hearing *n* case, inquest, inquiry, trial.

heart *n* 1 *sl* ticker. 2 centre, core,

crux, essence, focus, hub, kernel, marrow, middle, *sl* nitty-gritty, nub, nucleus, pith. 3 affection, compassion, concern, courage, humanity, kindness, love, pity, sensitivity, sympathy, tenderness, understanding, warmth.

heartbreaking *adj* bitter, distressing, grievous, heart-rending, pitiful, tragic.

heartbroken *adj* desolate, despairing, grieved, inconsolable, miserable, *inf* shattered. ▷ SAD.

hearten *v* boost, cheer up, encourage, strengthen, uplift.

heartless *adj* callous, cold, icy, inhuman, ruthless, steely, stony, unemotional, unkind, unsympathetic. ▷ CRUEL.

hearty *adj* 1 enthusiastic, exuberant, friendly, genuine, healthy, lively, positive, robust, sincere, strong, vigorous, warm. *Opp* HALF-HEARTED. 2 *hearty meal.* ▷ BIG.

heat *n* 1 fever, fieriness, glow, incandescence, warmth. 2 closeness, hot weather, humidity, sultriness, warmth. 3 *heat of the moment.* anger, eagerness, excitement, feverishness, impetuosity, violence. ▷ PASSION. *Opp* COLD.
• *v* bake, blister, boil, burn, cook, fry, grill, inflame, melt, roast, scald, scorch, simmer, sizzle, smoulder, steam, stew, toast, warm. *Opp* COOL. **heated** ▷ FERVENT, HOT.

heath *n* common land, moor, moorland, open country, wasteland.

heathen *adj* atheistic, barbaric, godless, idolatrous, infidel, irreligious, pagan, philistine, savage, unenlightened.
• *n* atheist, barbarian, heretic, idolater, infidel, pagan, philistine, savage, unbeliever.

heave *v* 1 drag, haul, hoist, lift, lug, move, pull, raise, tow. 2 ▷ THROW. **heave into sight** ▷ APPEAR. **heave up** ▷ VOMIT.

heaven *n* 1 afterlife, eternal rest, the next world, nirvana, paradise. 2 bliss, contentment, delight, ecstasy, felicity, happiness, joy, perfection, pleasure, rapture, Utopia. *Opp* HELL.

heavenly *adj* angelic, beautiful, blissful, celestial, delightful, divine, exquisite, glorious, lovely, other-worldly, *inf* out of this world, saintly, spiritual, sublime, wonderful.

heavy *adj* 1 bulky, burdensome, dense, hefty, large, leaden, massive, ponderous, unwieldy, weighty. ▷ BIG, FAT. 2 *heavy work.* arduous, demanding, difficult, hard, exhausting, laborious, onerous, strenuous, tough. 3 *heavy rain.* severe, torrential. 4 *heavy with fruit.* abundant, copious, laden, loaded, profuse, thick. 5 *heavy heart.* burdened, gloomy, miserable, sorrowful. ▷ SAD. 6 *heavy conversation.* dull, intellectual, intense, serious, tedious, wearisome. *Opp* LIGHT. **heavy-handed** ▷ CLUMSY. **heavy-hearted** ▷ SAD.

hectic *adj* animated, brisk, bustling, busy, chaotic, excited, feverish, frantic, frenetic, frenzied, hurried, hyperactive, lively, mad, restless, riotous, turbulent, wild. *Opp* LEISURELY.

hedge *n* barrier, fence, hedgerow, screen.
• *v inf* beat about the bush, be evasive, equivocate, *inf* hum and haw, stall, temporize. **hedge in** ▷ ENCLOSE.

hedonistic *adj* epicurean, extravagant, intemperate, luxurious, pleasure-loving, self-indulgent, sensual, sybaritic, voluptuous. *Opp* PURITANICAL.

heed *v* attend to, bear in mind, consider, follow, keep to, listen to, mark, mind, note, notice, obey, observe, pay attention to, regard, take notice of. *Opp* DISREGARD.

heedful *adj* attentive, careful, concerned, considerate, mindful, observant, vigilant, watchful. *Opp* HEEDLESS.

heedless *adj* blind, careless, deaf, inattentive, inconsiderate, neglectful, oblivious, reckless, thoughtless, unconcerned, unobservant, unsympathetic. *Opp* HEEDFUL.

hefty *adj inf* beefy, brawny, bulky, heavy, heavyweight, muscular, powerful, robust, rugged, solid, *inf* strapping, strong, tough. ▷ BIG. *Opp* SLIGHT.

height *n* 1 altitude, elevation, level. 2 crag, fell, hill, mound, mountain, peak, prominence, ridge, summit, top. 3 *height of your career.* acme, climax, crest, culmination, high point, peak, pinnacle, zenith.

heighten *v* add to, amplify, augment, boost, build up, elevate, enhance, improve, increase, intensify, magnify, maximize, raise, reinforce, sharpen, strengthen. *Opp* LOWER, REDUCE.

hell *n* 1 Hades, inferno, nether world, *sl* the other place, underworld. 2 ▷ MISERY. *Opp* HEAVEN.

help *n* advice, aid, assistance, backing, benefit, boost, collaboration, contribution, cooperation, encouragement, friendship, guidance, moral support, relief, remedy, succour, support. *Opp* HINDRANCE.
• *v* 1 advise, aid, aid and abet, assist, back, befriend, boost, collaborate, contribute,

cooperate, encourage, facilitate, forward, further the interests of, *inf* give a hand, promote, prop up, *inf* rally round, serve, side with, spoonfeed, stand by, subsidize, succour, support, take pity on. *Opp* HINDER. 2 alleviate, benefit, cure, ease, improve, lessen, make easier, relieve, remedy. 3 *can't help it.* ▷ AVOID, PREVENT.

helper *n* accomplice, aide, ally, assistant, associate, collaborator, colleague, deputy, *inf* henchman, partner, *inf* right-hand man, second, supporter.

helpful *adj* 1 accommodating, benevolent, caring, considerate, constructive, cooperative, favourable, friendly, kind, neighbourly, obliging, practical, supportive, sympathetic, thoughtful, willing. 2 *helpful comment.* advantageous, beneficial, informative, instructive, profitable, valuable, useful, worthwhile. 3 *helpful tool.* ▷ HANDY. *Opp* UNHELPFUL, USELESS.

helping *adj* ▷ HELPFUL.
• *n* amount, *inf* dollop, plateful, portion, ration, serving, share.

helpless *adj* abandoned, defenceless, dependent, deserted, destitute, disabled, exposed, feeble, handicapped, impotent, incapable, in difficulties, infirm, lame, marooned, powerless, stranded, unprotected, vulnerable. *Opp* INDEPENDENT.

herald *n* 1 announcer, courier, messenger. 2 *herald of spring.* forerunner, harbinger, omen, precursor, sign.
• *v* advertise, announce, indicate, proclaim, promise. ▷ FORETELL.

herd *n* bunch, flock, mob, pack, swarm, throng. ▷ GROUP.
• *v* assemble, collect, congregate, drive, gather, group together, round up, shepherd.

hereditary *adj* 1 ancestral, bequeathed, family, handed down, inherited, passed on, willed. 2 congenital, constitutional, genetic, inborn, inherent, innate, native, natural, transmissible.

heresy *n* blasphemy, dissent, idolatry, nonconformity, unorthodoxy.

heretic *n* blasphemer, dissenter, free thinker, iconoclast, nonconformist, rebel, renegade, unorthodox thinker. *Opp* BELIEVER.

heretical *adj* atheistic, blasphemous, dissenting, freethinking, heathen, iconoclastic, idolatrous, impious, irreligious, nonconformist, pagan, rebellious, unorthodox. *Opp* ORTHODOX.

heritage *n* birthright, culture, history, inheritance, legacy, past, tradition.

hermit *n* monk, recluse, solitary.

hero, heroine *ns* champion, conqueror, exemplar, ideal, idol, luminary, protagonist, star, superman, *inf* superstar, superwoman, victor, winner.

heroic *adj* adventurous, bold, brave, chivalrous, courageous, daring, dauntless, epic, fearless, gallant, herculean, intrepid, noble, selfless, stout-hearted, superhuman, unafraid, valiant, valorous. *Opp* COWARDLY.

hesitant *adj* cautious, diffident, dithering, faltering, half-hearted, halting, hesitating, indecisive, irresolute, nervous, *inf* shilly-shallying, shy, stumbling, tentative, timid, uncertain, uncommitted, undecided, unsure, vacillating, wary, wavering. *Opp* DECISIVE, FLUENT.

hesitate *v* 1 be indecisive, *inf* be in two minds, delay, demur, *inf* dilly-dally, dither, equivocate, falter, halt, hang back, *inf* hum and haw, pause, *inf* shilly-shally, teeter, temporize, think twice, vacillate, wait, waver. 2 stammer, stumble, stutter.

hesitation *n* caution, delay, dithering, doubt, indecision, irresolution, nervousness, reluctance, *inf* shilly-shallying, uncertainty, vacillation.

hidden *adj* 1 concealed, covered, disguised, enclosed, invisible, obscured, out of sight, private, shrouded, *inf* under wraps, unseen, veiled. *Opp* VISIBLE. 2 *hidden meaning.* arcane, coded, covert, cryptic, dark, esoteric, implicit, mysterious, obscure, occult, recondite, secret, unclear. *Opp* OBVIOUS.

hide *n* fur, leather, pelt, skin.
• *v* 1 blot out, bury, camouflage, cloak, conceal, cover, disguise, eclipse, mantle, mask, obscure, put out of sight, screen, secrete, shelter, shroud, veil, wrap up. 2 *inf* go to ground, *inf* hole up, keep hidden, *inf* lie low, lurk, take cover. 3 *hide facts.* censor, *inf* hush up, repress, silence, suppress, withhold.

hideous *adj* appalling, beastly, disgusting, ghastly, grotesque, macabre, odious, repulsive, revolting, sickening, terrible. ▷ UGLY. *Opp* BEAUTIFUL.

hiding-place *n* den, haven, hideaway, *inf* hideout, lair, refuge, retreat, sanctuary.

hierarchy *n* ladder, pecking order, ranking, scale, sequence, series, social order.

high *adj* 1 elevated, high-rise, lofty, raised, soaring, tall, towering. 2 aristocratic, chief, distinguished, eminent, exalted, important, leading, powerful, prominent, royal, superior, top. 3 *high prices.* dear, excessive, exorbitant, expensive, outrageous, *inf* steep, unreasonable. 4 *high winds.* extreme, great, intense, *inf* stiff, stormy, strong. 5 *high reputation.* favourable, good, noble, respected, virtuous. 6 *high voice.* acute, high-pitched, penetrating, piercing, sharp, shrill, soprano, squeaky, treble. *Opp* LOW. **high-and-mighty** ▷ ARROGANT. **high-class** ▷ EXCELLENT. **high-handed** ▷ ARROGANT. **high-minded** ▷ MORAL. **high-powered** ▷ POWERFUL. **high-speed** ▷ FAST. **high-spirited** ▷ LIVELY.

highbrow *adj* 1 academic, bookish, *inf* brainy, cultured, intellectual, *derog* pretentious. 2 classical, cultural, deep, difficult, improving, serious. *Opp* LOWBROW.

highlight *n* best moment, climax, high spot, peak.

hilarious *adj* amusing, entertaining, jolly, *inf* side-splitting, uproarious. ▷ FUNNY.

hill *n* 1 elevation, eminence, foothill, height, hillock, knoll, mound, mount, mountain, peak, prominence, ridge, summit. 2 ascent, declivity, drop, gradient, incline, ramp, rise, slope.

hinder *v* arrest, bar, be a hindrance to, check, curb, delay, deter, frustrate, get in the way of, hamper, handicap, hold back, hold up, impede, limit, obstruct, oppose, prevent, restrain, restrict, retard, slow down, stand in the way of, stop, thwart. *Opp* HELP.

hindrance *n* bar, barrier, check, curb, deterrent, difficulty, disadvantage, drawback, encumbrance, handicap, impediment, inconvenience, limitation, obstacle, obstruction, restraint, restriction, snag, stumbling block. *Opp* HELP.

hinge *n* joint, pivot.
• *v* depend, hang, rest, turn.

hint *n* 1 allusion, clue, idea, implication, indication, inkling, innuendo, insinuation, pointer, sign, suggestion, tip, tip-off. 2 *hint of herbs.* dash, taste, tinge, touch, trace, undertone, whiff.
• *v* allude, imply, indicate, insinuate, intimate, mention, suggest, tip off.

hire *v* book, charter, employ, engage, lease, rent, take on. **hire out** lease out, let, rent out.

hiss *v* 1 buzz, fizz, sizzle, whizz. 2 ▷ JEER.

historic *adj* celebrated, eminent, epoch-making, famed, famous, important, momentous, notable, outstanding, remarkable, renowned, significant, well-known. *Opp* INSIGNIFICANT.

historical *adj* authentic, documented, factual, real, recorded, true, verifiable. *Opp* FICTITIOUS.

history *n* 1 antiquity, bygone days, heritage, historical events, the past. 2 annals, chronicles, memoirs, records.

histrionic *adj* actorish, dramatic, theatrical.

hit *n* 1 blow, bull's-eye, collision, impact, shot, stroke. 2 success, triumph, *inf* winner.
• *v* 1 bang, bash, batter, beat, *sl* belt, box, bludgeon, buffet, bump, butt, cane, cannon into, clip, *inf* clobber, clout, club, collide with, crack, crash into, cuff, deliver a blow, elbow, flog, hammer, head, head-butt, impact, jab, jar, kick, knee, knock, lash, pound, pummel, punch, punt, ram, rap, run into, slam, slap, slog, slug, smack, smash, *inf* sock, spank, strike, stub, swat, *sl* tan, tap, thrash, thump, *sl* wallop, *inf* whack, whip. 2 *The slump hit sales.* affect, attack, check, damage, harm, have an effect on, hinder, hurt, ruin. **hit back** ▷ RETALIATE. **hit on** ▷ DISCOVER.

hoard *n* cache, collection, fund, heap, pile, reserve, stockpile, store, supply, treasure trove.
• *v* accumulate, amass, assemble, collect, gather, keep, lay up, mass, pile up, put by, save, stockpile, store, treasure. *Opp* SQUANDER, USE.

hoarse *adj* croaking, grating, gravelly, gruff, harsh, husky, rasping, raucous, rough, throaty.

hoax *n* cheat, *inf* con, confidence trick, deception, fake, fraud, joke, *inf* leg-pull, practical joke, *inf* spoof, swindle, trick.
• *v* bluff, cheat, *inf* con, deceive, delude, dupe, fool, gull, *inf* have on, hoodwink, lead on, mislead, swindle, *inf* take for a ride, take in, trick. ▷ TEASE.

hoaxer *n inf* con-man, joker, practical joker, trickster. ▷ CHEAT.

hobble *v* falter, limp, shuffle, stagger, stumble, totter.

hobby *n* diversion, interest, pastime, pursuit, recreation, relaxation, sideline.

hoist *n* block-and-tackle, crane, jack, lift, pulley, tackle, winch, windlass.
• *v* elevate, heave, lift, pull up, raise, winch up.

hold *n* 1 clasp, clutch, foothold, grasp, grip, purchase. 2 *hold over someone.* authority, control, dominance, influence, leverage, mastery, power, sway.
• *v* 1 bear, carry, catch, clasp, cling to,

clutch, cradle, embrace, enfold, grasp, grip, hang on to, have, hug, keep, possess, retain, seize, support, take. 2 *hold a suspect.* arrest, confine, detain, imprison, keep in custody. 3 *hold an opinion.* believe in, stick to, subscribe to. 4 *hold a pose.* continue, keep up, maintain, occupy, preserve, retain, sustain. 5 *hold a party.* celebrate, conduct, convene, have, organize. 6 *jug holds a litre.* contain, enclose, have a capacity of, include. 7 *My offer holds.* continue, endure, hold out, keep on, last, persist, remain unchanged, stay. **hold back** ▷ RESTRAIN. **hold forth** ▷ SPEAK, TALK. **hold out** ▷ OFFER, PERSIST. **hold over**, **hold up** ▷ DELAY. **hold-up** ▷ ROBBERY.

hole *n* 1 abyss, burrow, cave, cavern, cavity, chamber, chasm, crater, dent, depression, excavation, fault, fissure, hollow, niche, pit, pot-hole, shaft, tunnel. 2 aperture, breach, break, chink, crack, cut, eyelet, fissure, gap, opening, orifice, perforation, puncture, rip, slot, split, tear, vent.

holiday *n* bank holiday, break, day off, furlough, half-term, leave, recess, respite, rest, sabbatical, time off, vacation.

holiness *n* devotion, divinity, faith, godliness, piety, *derog* religiosity, sacredness, saintliness, sanctity, venerability.

hollow *adj* 1 empty, unfilled, vacant, void. 2 cavernous, concave, deep, indented, recessed, sunken. 3 *hollow laugh, victory.* cynical, false, futile, insincere, meaningless, pointless, valueless, worthless.
• *n* cavern, cavity, concavity, crater, dent, depression, dimple, dip, excavation, furrow, hole, indentation, pit, trough. ▷ VALLEY. **hollow out** ▷ EXCAVATE.

holocaust *n* 1 ▷ FIRE. 2 annihilation, bloodbath, destruction, devastation, extermination, genocide, massacre, pogrom.

holy *adj* 1 blessed, consecrated, dedicated, devoted, divine, hallowed, heavenly, revered, sacred, sacrosanct, venerable. 2 *holy pilgrims.* devout, faithful, God-fearing, godly, pious, pure, religious, reverent, reverential, righteous, saintly, *derog* sanctimonious, sinless. *Opp* IRRELIGIOUS.

home *n* 1 abode, accommodation, base, domicile, dwelling, dwelling place, habitation, house, household, lodging, *inf* pad, quarters, residence. 2 birthplace, native land. 3 *derog* institution.

homeless *adj* abandoned, destitute, dispossessed, down-and-out, evicted, exiled, itinerant, outcast, rootless, vagrant.
•*pl n* beggars, refugees, tramps, vagrants.

homely *adj* comfortable, congenial, cosy, easygoing, friendly, informal, natural, relaxed, simple, unaffected, unassuming, unpretentious, unsophisticated. ▷ FAMILIAR. *Opp* FORMAL, SOPHISTICATED.

homogeneous *adj* alike, comparable, compatible, consistent, identical, matching, similar, uniform, unvarying. *Opp* DIFFERENT.

homosexual *adj inf* camp, gay, lesbian, *derog* queer.

honest *adj* above-board, blunt, candid, conscientious, direct, equitable, fair, forthright, frank, genuine, good, honourable, impartial, incorruptible, just, law-abiding, legitimate, moral, *inf* on the level, open, outspoken, plain, principled, pure, reliable, respectable, scrupulous, sincere, straight, straightforward, trustworthy, trusty, truthful, unbiased, unequivocal, unprejudiced, upright, veracious, virtuous. *Opp* DISHONEST.

honesty *n* 1 fairness, honour, integrity, morality, probity, rectitude, reliability, scrupulousness, trustworthiness, truthfulness, uprightness, veracity, virtue. *Opp* DECEIT. 2 bluntness, candour, directness, frankness, outspokenness, plainness, sincerity, straightforwardness.

honorary *adj* nominal, titular, unofficial, unpaid.

honour *n* 1 acclaim, accolade, compliment, credit, esteem, fame, good name, *inf* kudos, regard, renown, repute, respect, reverence, veneration. 2 distinction, duty, importance, privilege. 3 *sense of honour.* decency, dignity, honesty, integrity, loyalty, morality, nobility, principle, rectitude, righteousness, sincerity, uprightness, virtue.
• *v* acclaim, admire, applaud, celebrate, commemorate, commend, dignify, esteem, give credit to, glorify, pay homage to, pay tribute to, praise, remember, respect, revere, reverence, value, venerate, worship.

honourable *adj* admirable, chivalrous, creditable, decent, estimable, ethical, high-minded, irreproachable, loyal, moral, noble, proper, reputable, respected, righteous, sincere, trustworthy, upright, venerable, virtuous, worthy. ▷ HONEST. *Opp* DISHONOURABLE.

hoodwink *v* cheat, *inf* con, delude, dupe, fool, gull, *inf* have on, hoax, mislead, *inf* pull the wool over someone's eyes, swindle, take in, trick. ▷ DECEIVE.

hook *n* barb, catch, clasp, fastener, lock, peg.
▪*v* 1 ▷ FASTEN. 2 *hook a fish.* catch, take.

hooligan *n* delinquent, hoodlum, lout, ruffian, *inf* tearaway, thug, tough, troublemaker, vandal, *inf* yob.

hoop *n* band, circle, loop, ring.

hop *v* bound, caper, dance, jump, leap, skip, spring, vault.

hope *n* 1 ambition, aspiration, craving, desire, dream, longing, wish, yearning. 2 conviction, expectation, faith, likelihood, promise, prospect.
▪*v inf* anticipate, aspire, be hopeful, believe, count on, desire, expect, foresee, have faith, trust, wish. *Opp* DESPAIR.

hopeful *adj* 1 confident, expectant, optimistic, positive, sanguine. 2 *hopeful signs.* auspicious, cheering, encouraging, heartening, promising, propitious, reassuring. *Opp* HOPELESS.

hopefully *adv* 1 confidently, expectantly, optimistically, with hope. 2 [*inf*] *Hopefully I'll be better by then.* all being well, most likely, probably.

hopeless *adj* 1 defeatist, demoralized, despairing, desperate, disconsolate, pessimistic, wretched. 2 *hopeless situation.* impossible, incurable, irremediable, irreparable, irreversible. 3 [*inf*] *He's hopeless!* feeble, inadequate, incompetent, inefficient, useless. *Opp* HOPEFUL.

horde *n* crowd, gang, mob, swarm, tribe. ▷ GROUP.

horizontal *adj* even, flat, level, lying down, prone, prostrate, supine. *Opp* VERTICAL.

horrible *adj* awful, beastly, disagreeable, ghastly, hateful, loathsome, nasty, odious, offensive, revolting, terrible, unkind. ▷ HORRIFIC, UNPLEASANT. *Opp* PLEASANT.

horrific *adj* appalling, atrocious, blood-curdling, disgusting, dreadful, frightening, frightful, grisly, gruesome, hair-raising, harrowing, horrendous, horrifying, nauseating, shocking, sickening, spine-chilling, unnerving, unthinkable.

horrify *v* alarm, appal, disgust, frighten, outrage, scare, shock, sicken, stun, terrify, unnerve. **horrifying** ▷ HORRIFIC.

horror *n* 1 abhorrence, antipathy, aversion, detestation, disgust, dread, fear, hatred, loathing, repugnance, revulsion, terror. 2 awfulness, frightfulness, ghastliness, gruesomeness, hideousness.

horse *n* bronco, carthorse, cob, colt, dun, filly, foal, gelding, grey, hack, hunter, mare, mount, mule, mustang, *inf* nag, piebald, pony, racehorse, roan, skewbald, stallion, steed, warhorse.

horseman, horsewoman *ns* equestrian, jockey, rider.

hospitable *adj* courteous, generous, sociable, welcoming. ▷ FRIENDLY. *Opp* INHOSPITABLE.

hospital *n* clinic, health centre, hospice, infirmary, medical centre, nursing home, sanatorium, sick bay.

hospitality *n* 1 accommodation, entertainment. 2 cordiality, courtesy, friendliness, sociability, warmth, welcome.

host *n* 1 army, crowd, mob, multitude, swarm, throng, troop. ▷ GROUP. 2 ▷ COMPÈRE.

hostage *n* captive, pawn, prisoner, surety.

hostile *adj* 1 aggressive, antagonistic, antipathetic, attacking, averse, bellicose, belligerent, confrontational, ill-disposed, inhospitable, inimical, malevolent, pugnacious, resentful, rival, unfriendly, unsympathetic, unwelcoming, warlike, warring. ▷ ANGRY. *Opp* FRIENDLY. 2 *hostile conditions.* adverse, contrary, opposing, unfavourable, unhelpful, unpropitious. ▷ BAD. *Opp* FAVOURABLE.

hostility *n* aggression, animus, antagonism, bad feeling, belligerence, dissension, enmity, estrangement, friction, incompatibility, malevolence, malice, opposition, rancour, resentment, strife, unfriendliness. ▷ HATRED. *Opp* FRIENDSHIP. **hostilities** ▷ WAR.

hot *adj* 1 baking, blistering, boiling, burning, close, fiery, flaming, humid, oppressive, red-hot, roasting, scalding, scorching, searing, sizzling, steamy, stifling, sultry, sweltering, thermal, torrid, tropical, warm. 2 ardent, eager, emotional, excited, feverish, fierce, heated, hot-headed, impatient, impetuous, inflamed, intense, passionate, violent. 3 *hot taste.* gingery, peppery, piquant, pungent, spicy, strong. *Opp* COLD, COOL. **hot-tempered** ▷ BAD-TEMPERED. **hot under the collar** ▷ ANGRY.

hotel *n* guest house, hostel, inn, lodge, motel.

hound *n* ▷ DOG.
▪*v* annoy, chase, harass, harry, hunt, nag, persecute, pester, pursue.

house *n* 1 abode, domicile, dwelling, dwelling place, habitation, home, homestead, place, residence. 2 clan, dynasty, line, lineage. 3 business, company, firm.

▪ *v* accommodate, billet, board, harbour, keep, lodge, place, *inf* put up, quarter, shelter, take in.

household *n* establishment, family, home, ménage.

hovel *n* cottage, *inf* dump, hole, hut, shack, shanty, shed.

hover *v* 1 be suspended, drift, float, flutter, fly, hang. 2 dally, dither, hang about, hesitate, linger, loiter, pause, vacillate, wait about, waver.

howl *v* bay, bellow, cry, roar, scream, shout, wail, yowl.

hub *n* axis, centre, core, focal point, focus, heart, middle, nucleus, pivot.

huddle *n* ▷ GROUP.
▪ *v* 1 cluster, converge, crowd, flock, gather, group, heap, herd, jam, jumble, pile, press, squeeze, swarm, throng. 2 cuddle, curl up, hug, nestle, snuggle.

hue *n* cast, complexion, dye, nuance, shade, tone. ▷ COLOUR. **hue and cry** ▷ OUTCRY.

hug *v* clasp, cling to, crush, cuddle, embrace, enfold, fold in your arms, hold close, nurse, snuggle against, squeeze.

huge *adj* 1 colossal, elephantine, enormous, gargantuan, giant, gigantic, *inf* hulking, immense, imposing, mammoth, massive, mighty, *inf* monster, monstrous, monumental, mountainous, prodigious, stupendous, titanic, towering, *inf* tremendous, vast, *inf* whopping. ▷ BIG. 2 *huge number*. ▷ INFINITE. *Opp* SMALL.

hulk *n* 1 body, frame, shell, wreck. 2 lout, lump, oaf.

hulking *adj* awkward, bulky, cumbersome, heavy, ungainly, unwieldy. ▷ BIG, CLUMSY.

hull *n* body, frame, framework, skeleton.

hum *v* buzz, drone, murmur, purr, sing, thrum, vibrate, whirr. **hum and haw** ▷ HESITATE.

human *adj* 1 anthropoid, hominoid, mortal. 2 kind, rational, reasonable, sensible, sensitive, thoughtful. ▷ HUMANE. *Opp* INHUMAN. **human beings** folk, humanity, mankind, men and women, mortals, people.

humane *adj* altruistic, benevolent, charitable, civilized, compassionate, feeling, forgiving, good, human, humanitarian, kind-hearted, loving, magnanimous, merciful, pitying, sympathetic, tender, understanding, unselfish, warm-hearted. ▷ KIND. *Opp* INHUMANE.

humble *adj* 1 deferential, meek, modest, *derog* obsequious, respectful, self-effacing, *derog* servile, submissive, subservient, *derog* sycophantic, unassertive, unassuming, unpretentious. *Opp* PROUD. 2 *humble birth, lifestyle*. commonplace, insignificant, low, lowly, mean, obscure, ordinary, plebeian, poor, simple, undistinguished, unremarkable.
▪ *v* ▷ HUMILIATE.

humid *adj* clammy, close, damp, moist, muggy, steamy, sticky, sultry, sweaty.

humiliate *v* abase, abash, bring someone down, chasten, crush, deflate, degrade, demean, discredit, disgrace, embarrass, humble, make someone ashamed, *inf* make someone feel small, mortify, *inf* put someone in their place, shame, *inf* show someone up, *inf* take someone down a peg. **humiliating** ▷ SHAMEFUL.

humiliation *n* abasement, chagrin, degradation, discredit, disgrace, dishonour, embarrassment, ignominy, indignity, loss of face, mortification, shame.

humility *n* deference, humbleness, lowliness, meekness, modesty, self-abasement, self-effacement, *derog* servility. *Opp* PRIDE.

humorous *adj* absurd, amusing, comic, comical, diverting, droll, entertaining, facetious, farcical, funny, hilarious, *inf* hysterical, jocular, merry, *inf* priceless, satirical, *inf* side-splitting, slapstick, uproarious, whimsical, witty, zany. *opp* SERIOUS.

humour *n* 1 banter, comedy, facetiousness, fun, jesting, jocularity, jokes, joking, merriment, quips, raillery, repartee, satire, wit, witticism, wittiness. 2 *in a good humour*. disposition, frame of mind, mood, spirits, state of mind, temper.

hump *n* bulge, bump, curve, knob, lump, node, projection, protrusion, protuberance, swelling. 2 barrow, hillock, hummock, mound, rise.
▪ *v* 1 arch, bend, curl, curve, hunch, raise. 2 *hump a load*. drag, heave, hoist, lift, lug, raise, shoulder.

hunch *n* feeling, guess, idea, impression, inkling, intuition, premonition, presentiment, suspicion.
▪ *v* arch, bend, curl, curve, huddle, shrug.

hunger *n* 1 appetite, craving, greed, ravenousness, voracity. 2 famine, malnutrition, starvation, want.
▪ *v* ▷ DESIRE.

hungry *adj* avid, covetous, craving, eager, famished, greedy, longing, *inf* peckish, ravenous, starved, starving, undernourished, voracious.

hunt *n* chase, pursuit, quest, search. ▷ HUNTING.
• *v* 1 chase, course, ferret, hound, pursue, stalk, track, trail. 2 enquire after, *inf* ferret out, look for, rummage, search for, seek, trace, track down.

hunter *n* huntsman, huntswoman, predator, trapper.

hunting *n* blood sports, coursing, stalking, trapping.

hurdle *n* 1 barricade, barrier, fence, hedge, jump, obstacle, wall. 2 difficulty, handicap, hindrance, impediment, obstruction, problem, restraint, snag, stumbling block.

hurl *v* cast, catapult, *inf* chuck, dash, fire, fling, heave, launch, *inf* let fly, pitch, project, propel, send, shy, sling, throw, toss.

hurricane *n* cyclone, storm, tempest, tornado, typhoon, whirlwind.

hurry *n* ▷ HASTE.
• *v* 1 chase, dash, fly, *inf* get a move on, hasten, hurtle, hustle, make haste, rush, *inf* shift, speed, *inf* step on it. 2 *hurry a process.* accelerate, expedite, press on with, quicken, speed up. *Opp* DELAY. **hurried** ▷ HASTY.

hurt *v* 1 ache, be painful, burn, pinch, smart, sting, throb, tingle. 2 abuse, afflict, bruise, cripple, cut, disable, injure, maim, misuse, mutilate, torture, wound. 3 affect, aggrieve, be hurtful to, *inf* cut to the quick, distress, grieve, insult, offend, pain, sadden, torment, upset. 4 damage, harm, mar, ruin, sabotage, spoil.

hurtful *adj* cruel, cutting, damaging, derogatory, detrimental, distressing, hard to bear, harmful, injurious, malicious, nasty, painful, scathing, spiteful, uncharitable, unkind, upsetting, vicious, wounding. *Opp* KIND.

hurtle *v* charge, chase, dash, fly, plunge, race, rush, shoot, speed, *inf* tear.

hush *int* be quiet! *inf* hold your tongue! *inf* shut up!
• *v* ▷ SILENCE. **hush up** ▷ SUPPRESS.

hustle *v* 1 bustle, hasten, hurry, jostle. 2 *hustle along.* coerce, compel, force, push, shove, thrust.

hut *n* cabin, den, hovel, lean-to, shack, shanty, shed, shelter.

hybrid *n* combination, composite, compound, cross, cross-breed, mixture, mongrel.

hygiene *n* cleanliness, sanitariness, wholesomeness.

hygienic *adj* aseptic, clean, disinfected, germ-free, healthy, pure, salubrious, sanitary, sterile, sterilized, unpolluted, wholesome. *Opp* UNHEALTHY.

hypnotic *adj* fascinating, irresistible, magnetic, mesmerizing, soothing, soporific, spellbinding.

hypnotize *v* bewitch, captivate, cast a spell over, dominate, enchant, entrance, fascinate, magnetize, mesmerize, *inf* put to sleep.

hypocrisy *n* cant, deceit, deception, double-dealing, double standards, double-talk, duplicity, falsity, *inf* humbug, insincerity, pretence.

hypocritical *adj* deceptive, double-dealing, duplicitous, false, insincere, *inf* phoney, sanctimonious, *inf* two-faced.

hypothesis *n* conjecture, guess, premise, proposition, supposition, theory, thesis.

hypothetical *adj* academic, conjectural, imaginary, presumed, putative, speculative, supposed, theoretical, unreal.

hysteria *n* frenzy, hysterics, madness, mania, panic.

hysterical *adj* berserk, beside yourself, crazed, delirious, demented, distraught, frantic, frenzied, irrational, mad, over-emotional, raving, uncontrollable, wild.

I

ice *n* black ice, floe, frost, glacier, iceberg, icicle, rime.

icy *adj* 1 arctic, chilly, freezing, frosty, frozen, glacial, polar, Siberian. ▷ COLD. 2 *icy roads.* glassy, slippery.

idea *n* 1 attitude, belief, concept, conception, conjecture, conviction, doctrine, hypothesis, notion, opinion, principle, tenet, theory, view. 2 *bright idea.* brainwave, guess, inspiration, plan, proposal, scheme, suggestion. 3 aim, goal, intention, point, purpose. 4 *good idea of what to expect.* clue, guideline, impression, inkling, intimation, perception, suspicion.

ideal *adj* 1 best, classic, excellent, faultless, model, optimum, perfect, supreme, unsurpassable. 2 *ideal world.* dream, hypothetical, illusory, imaginary, unattainable, unreal, Utopian, visionary.
• *n* 1 acme, epitome, exemplar, model, paragon, pattern, standard. 2 ▷ PRINCIPLE.

idealistic *adj* high-minded, impractical, over-optimistic, quixotic, romantic, starry-eyed, unrealistic. *Opp* REALISTIC.

idealize *v* deify, exalt, glamorize, glorify, *inf* put on a pedestal, romanticize. ▷ IDOLIZE.

identical *adj* alike, corresponding, duplicate, equal, equivalent, indistinguishable, interchangeable, like, matching, the same, twin. *Opp* DIFFERENT.

identifiable *adj* detectable, discernible, distinctive, distinguishable, familiar, known, named, noticeable, perceptible, recognizable, unmistakable.

identify *v* 1 distinguish, label, mark, name, pick out, pinpoint, *inf* put a name to, recognize, single out, specify, spot. 2 *identify an illness.* diagnose. **identify with** empathize with, feel for, relate to, sympathize with.

identity *n* 1 *inf* ID, name. 2 character, distinctiveness, individuality, nature, particularity, personality, selfhood, singularity, uniqueness.

ideology *n* assumptions, beliefs, creed, convictions, ideas, philosophy, principles, tenets, theories, underlying attitudes.

idiom *n* dialect, expression, jargon, language, manner of speaking, parlance, phrase, phraseology, phrasing, turn of phrase, usage.

idiomatic *adj* colloquial, natural, vernacular.

idiosyncrasy *n* characteristic, eccentricity, feature, habit, individuality, mannerism, oddity, peculiarity, quirk, trait.

idiosyncratic *adj* characteristic, distinctive, eccentric, individual, odd, peculiar, personal, quirky, singular, unique. *Opp* COMMON.

idiot *n* [*most synonyms inf*] ass, blockhead, chump, clot, dimwit, dolt, dope, duffer, dummy, dunce, dunderhead, fool, half-wit, ignoramus, imbecile, moron, nincompoop, ninny, nitwit, simpleton, twerp, twit.

idiotic *adj* absurd, asinine, crazy, foolish, half-witted, insane, mad, nonsensical, ridiculous, senseless. ▷ STUPID. *Opp* SENSIBLE.

idle *adj* 1 dormant, inactive, inoperative, redundant, retired, unemployed, unoccupied, unproductive, unused. 2 good-for-nothing, indolent, lackadaisical, lazy, shiftless, slothful, work-shy. 3 *idle speculation.* casual, frivolous, futile, pointless. *Opp* BUSY.
• *v* be lazy, dawdle, do nothing, hang about, *inf* kill time, laze, loaf, loll, lounge about, potter, slack, take it easy. *Opp* WORK.

idler *n inf* good-for-nothing, *inf* layabout, *inf* lazybones, loafer, malingerer, shirker, *sl* skiver, slacker.

idol *n* 1 deity, effigy, god, graven image, icon, statue. 2 celebrity, *inf* darling, favourite, hero, *inf* pin-up, star, *inf* superstar.

idolize *v* adore, hero-worship, look up to, revere, venerate, worship. ▷ IDEALIZE.

idyllic *adj* charming, delightful, happy, idealized, lovely, pastoral, peaceful, perfect, picturesque, rustic, unspoiled.

ignite *v* burn, catch fire, fire, kindle, light, set alight, set on fire, spark off.

ignoble *adj* base, churlish, cowardly, despicable, disgraceful, dishonourable, infamous, low, mean, selfish, shabby, unworthy. *Opp* NOBLE.

ignorance *n* inexperience, innocence, unawareness, unconsciousness, unfamiliarity. ▷ STUPIDITY. *Opp* KNOWLEDGE.

ignorant *adj* 1 *inf* clueless, ill-informed, innocent, lacking knowledge, oblivious, unacquainted, unaware, unconscious, unfamiliar (with), uninformed, unwitting. 2 illiterate, uncultivated, uneducated, unenlightened. ▷ IMPOLITE, STUPID. *Opp* CLEVER, KNOWLEDGEABLE.

ignore *v* disobey, disregard, leave out, miss out, neglect, omit, overlook, pass over, reject, *inf* shut your eyes to, skip, slight, snub, take no notice of, *inf* turn a blind eye to.

ill *adj* 1 ailing, bad, bedridden, diseased, feeble, frail, *inf* groggy, indisposed, infirm, invalid, nauseated, nauseous, *inf* off-colour, *inf* out of sorts, pasty, poorly, queasy, *inf* seedy, sick, sickly, suffering, *inf* under the weather, unhealthy, unwell, weak. *Opp* HEALTHY. 2 *ill effects.* bad, damaging, detrimental, evil, harmful, injurious, unfavourable, unfortunate, unlucky. *Opp* GOOD.
• *pl n* the infirm, invalids, patients, the sick, sufferers. **be ill** ail, languish, sicken. **ill-advised** ▷ MISGUIDED. **ill-bred** ▷ RUDE. **ill-fated** ▷ UNLUCKY. **ill-humoured** ▷ BAD-TEMPERED. **ill-mannered** ▷ RUDE. **ill-natured** ▷ UNKIND. **ill-omened** ▷ UNLUCKY. **ill-tempered** ▷ BAD-TEMPERED. **ill-treat** ▷ MISTREAT.

illegal *adj* actionable, against the law, banned, black-market, criminal, felonious, forbidden, illicit, prohibited, proscribed, unlawful, unlicensed, wrong, wrongful. ▷ ILLEGITIMATE. *Opp* LEGAL.

illegible *adj* indecipherable, indistinct, obscure, unclear, unreadable. *Opp* LEGIBLE.

illegitimate *adj* 1 against the rules, improper, inadmissible, incorrect, invalid, irregular, spurious, unauthorized, unjustifiable, unreasonable, unwarranted. ▷ ILLEGAL. 2 bastard, natural. *Opp* LEGITIMATE.

illiterate *adj* unable to read. ▷ IGNORANT. *Opp* LITERATE.

illness *n* abnormality, affliction, ailment, allergy, attack, blight, *inf* bug, complaint, condition, disability, disease, disorder, epidemic, fever, health problem, indisposition, infection, infirmity, malady, malaise, pestilence, plague, sickness, *inf* trouble, *inf* upset.

illogical *adj* inconsequential, inconsistent, invalid, senseless, unreasonable. ▷ SILLY. *Opp* LOGICAL.

illuminate *v* 1 brighten, light up, make brighter, reveal. 2 clarify, clear up, elucidate, enlighten, explain, throw light on.

illusion *n* 1 apparition, conjuring trick, daydream, delusion, dream, fancy, fantasy, figment of the imagination, hallucination, mirage. 2 *under an illusion.* error, false impression, misapprehension, mistake.

illusory *adj* deceptive, deluding, fallacious, false, misleading, sham, unreal, untrue. ▷ IMAGINARY. *Opp* REAL.

illustrate *v* 1 demonstrate, elucidate, exemplify, explain, show. 2 adorn, decorate, depict, illuminate, picture, portray.

illustration *n* 1 case in point, demonstration, example, instance, sample, specimen. 2 depiction, diagram, drawing, figure, picture, sketch. ▷ IMAGE.

image *n* 1 imitation, likeness, reflection, representation. ▷ PICTURE. 2 carving, effigy, figure, icon, idol, statue. 3 *the image of her mother.* double, likeness, spitting image, twin.

imaginary *adj* fabulous, fanciful, fictional, fictitious, hypothetical, imagined, insubstantial, invented, legendary, made-up, mythical, mythological, non-existent, supposed, unreal, visionary. ▷ ILLUSORY. *Opp* REAL.

imagination *n* artistry, creativity, fancy, ingenuity, insight, inspiration, inventiveness, *inf* mind's eye, originality, sensitivity, thought, vision.

imaginative *adj* artistic, attractive, beautiful, clever, creative, fanciful, ingenious, innovative, inspired, inventive, original, poetic, resourceful, sensitive, thoughtful, visionary, vivid. *Opp* UNIMAGINATIVE.

imagine *v* 1 conceive, conjure up, create, dream up, envisage, fancy, fantasize, invent, make believe, picture, pretend, see, think of, think up, visualize. 2 assume, believe, guess, infer, judge, presume, suppose, surmise, suspect, think.

imitate *v* 1 ape, caricature, counterfeit, duplicate, echo, guy, mimic, parody, parrot, reproduce, satirize, *inf* send up, simulate, *inf* take off. ▷ IMPERSONATE. 2 copy, emulate, follow, match, model yourself on.

imitation *adj* artificial, copied, counterfeit, ersatz, man-made, mock, model, *inf* phoney, sham, simulated, synthetic. *Opp* REAL.
• *n* 1 copying, duplication, emulation, mimicry. 2 *inf* clone, copy, counterfeit, dummy, duplicate, fake, forgery, impersonation, impression, likeness, *inf* mock-

up, model, parody, replica, reproduction, sham, simulation, *inf* take-off, travesty.

immature *adj* adolescent, babyish, callow, childish, *inf* green, inexperienced, infantile, juvenile, new, puerile, undeveloped, young. *Opp* MATURE.

immediate *adj* 1 instant, instantaneous, prompt, quick, speedy, sudden, swift, unhesitating. 2 *immediate problem.* current, present, pressing, urgent. 3 *immediate neighbours.* adjacent, closest, direct, nearest, next.

immediately *adv* at once, directly, forthwith, instantly, now, promptly, *inf* right away, straight away, unhesitatingly.

immense *adj* colossal, elephantine, enormous, gargantuan, giant, gigantic, great, huge, *inf* hulking, immeasurable, imposing, impressive, incalculable, *inf* jumbo, large, mammoth, massive, mighty, *inf* monster, monstrous, monumental, mountainous, prodigious, stupendous, titanic, towering, *inf* tremendous, vast, *inf* whopping. ▷ BIG. *Opp* SMALL.

immerse *v* bathe, dip, drench, drown, duck, dunk, lower, plunge, sink, submerge. **immersed** ▷ BUSY, INTERESTED.

immersion *n* baptism, dipping, ducking, submersion.

immigrant *n* incomer, newcomer, outsider, settler.

imminent *adj* about to happen, approaching, close, coming, forthcoming, impending, looming, near, *inf* on the horizon, threatening.

immobile *adj* 1 ▷ IMMOVABLE. 2 frozen, inexpressive, inflexible, rigid. *Opp* MOBILE.

immobilize *v* cripple, damage, disable, paralyse, put out of action, sabotage, stop.

immoral *adj* base, corrupt, debauched, degenerate, depraved, dishonest, dissipated, dissolute, impure, indecent, licentious, loose, low, profligate, promiscuous, *inf* rotten, sinful, unchaste, unethical, unprincipled, wanton, wrong. ▷ WICKED. *Opp* MORAL. **immoral person** cheat, degenerate, liar, libertine, rake, reprobate, scoundrel, sinner, villain, wrongdoer.

immortal *adj* 1 ageless, deathless, endless, eternal, everlasting, incorruptible, indestructible, perpetual, timeless, unchanging, undying, unending, unfading. 2 *immortal beings.* divine, godlike, legendary, mythical. *Opp* MORTAL.

immortalize *v* commemorate, deify, enshrine, keep alive, make immortal, perpetuate.

immovable *adj* 1 anchored, fast, firm, fixed, immobile, immobilized, paralysed, riveted, rooted, secure, set, settled, solid, static, stationary, still, stuck. 2 ▷ IMMUTABLE.

immune *adj* exempt, free, immunized, invulnerable, protected, resistant, safe, unaffected. *Opp* VULNERABLE.

immunize *v* inoculate, vaccinate.

immutable *adj* constant, dependable, enduring, eternal, fixed, invariable, lasting, permanent, perpetual, reliable, settled, stable, unalterable, unchangeable, unvarying. ▷ RESOLUTE. *Opp* CHANGEABLE.

impact *n* 1 bang, blow, bump, collision, concussion, contact, crash, knock, smash. 2 consequence, effect, force, impression, influence, repercussions, reverberations, shock.
• *v* ▷ HIT.

impair *v* damage, harm, injure, mar, ruin, spoil, weaken.

impale *v* ▷ PIERCE.

impartial *adj* balanced, detached, disinterested, dispassionate, equitable, even-handed, fair, fair-minded, just, neutral, non-partisan, objective, open-minded, unbiased, uninvolved, unprejudiced. *Opp* BIASED.

impartiality *n* balance, detachment, disinterest, fairness, justice, neutrality, objectivity, open-mindedness. *Opp* BIAS.

impassable *adj* blocked, closed, obstructed, unusable.

impatient *adj* 1 anxious, eager, keen. 2 agitated, edgy, fidgety, fretful, irritable, nervous, restive, restless, uneasy. 3 *impatient manner.* abrupt, brusque, curt, hasty, intolerant, irascible, quick-tempered, short-tempered, snappish, snappy, testy. *Opp* APATHETIC, PATIENT.

impede *v* be an impediment to, obstruct. ▷ HINDER.

impediment *n* 1 bar, burden, check, curb, deterrent, *inf* drag, hindrance, inconvenience, limitation, obstacle, obstruction, restraint, snag, stumbling block. ▷ HANDICAP.

impending *adj* ▷ IMMINENT.

impenetrable *adj* 1 dense, resilient, solid, thick. ▷ IMPERVIOUS. 2 impregnable, invincible, inviolable, invulnerable, safe, secure, unassailable. *Opp* VULNERABLE. 3 *impenetrable language.* inaccessible, incomprehensible, inscrutable, unfathomable. *Opp* ACCESSIBLE.

imperceptible *adj* faint, gradual, inaudible, indistinguishable, insignificant, invisible, negligible, subtle, undetectable, unnoticeable. ▷ SMALL. *Opp* PERCEPTIBLE.

imperceptive *adj* undiscriminating, unobservant. ▷ STUPID. *Opp* PERCEPTIVE.

imperfect *adj* blemished, broken, damaged, defective, deficient, faulty, flawed, incomplete, marred, partial, shop-soiled, spoilt, unfinished, wanting. *Opp* PERFECT.

imperfection *n* blemish, defect, deficiency, error, failing, fault, flaw, frailty, inadequacy, shortcoming, weakness. *Opp* PERFECTION.

impermanent *adj* changing, ephemeral, evanescent, fleeting, momentary, passing, short-lived, temporary, transient, transitory. ▷ CHANGEABLE. *Opp* PERMANENT.

impersonal *adj* aloof, businesslike, cold, cool, detached, disinterested, dispassionate, distant, formal, mechanical, objective, official, remote, unemotional, unfriendly, unprejudiced, unsympathetic, wooden. *Opp* FRIENDLY.

impersonate *v* disguise yourself as, masquerade as, pass yourself off as, portray, pose as, pretend to be. ▷ IMITATE.

impertinent *adj* brazen, cheeky, disrespectful, forward, *inf* fresh, impudent, insolent, insulting, irreverent, pert. ▷ RUDE. *Opp* RESPECTFUL.

impervious *adj* 1 hermetic, impenetrable, impermeable, non-porous, solid, waterproof, water-repellent, watertight. *Opp* POROUS. 2 ▷ RESISTANT.

impetuous *adj* eager, hasty, headlong, hot-headed, impulsive, incautious, precipitate, quick, rash, reckless, speedy, spontaneous, *inf* spur-of-the-moment, thoughtless, unplanned, unpremeditated. *Opp* CAUTIOUS.

impetus *n* boost, drive, encouragement, energy, fillip, force, impulse, incentive, inspiration, momentum, motivation, power, push, spur, stimulus, thrust.

impiety *n* blasphemy, irreverence, profanity, sacrilege, sinfulness, ungodliness, unrighteousness, wickedness. *Opp* PIETY.

impious *adj* blasphemous, godless, irreligious, irreverent, profane, sacrilegious, sinful, unholy. ▷ WICKED. *Opp* PIOUS.

implausible *adj* doubtful, dubious, far-fetched, feeble, improbable, suspect, unconvincing, unlikely. *Opp* PLAUSIBLE.

implement *n* apparatus, appliance, device, gadget, instrument, tool, utensil. • *v* bring about, carry out, effect, enforce, execute, fulfil, perform, put into practice, realize, try out.

implicate *v* associate, connect, embroil, entangle, include, incriminate, involve.

implication *n* 1 hidden meaning, hint, innuendo, insinuation, overtone, significance. 2 association, connection, embroilment, entanglement, involvement.

implicit *adj* 1 hinted at, implied, indirect, tacit, undeclared, understood, unsaid, unspoken, unvoiced. *Opp* EXPLICIT. 2 *implicit faith*. ▷ ABSOLUTE.

imply *v* 1 hint, indicate, insinuate, intimate, mean, point to, suggest. 2 ▷ SIGNIFY.

impolite *adj* discourteous, disrespectful, ill-mannered. ▷ RUDE. *Opp* POLITE.

import *v* bring in, buy in, introduce, ship in. ▷ CONVEY.

important *adj* 1 basic, big, cardinal, central, chief, critical, epoch-making, essential, foremost, fundamental, grave, historic, key, main, major, momentous, noteworthy, once in a lifetime, outstanding, pressing, primary, principal, salient, serious, significant, urgent, vital, weighty. 2 celebrated, distinguished, eminent, famous, great, high-ranking, influential, leading, notable, noted, powerful, pre-eminent, prominent, renowned, well-known. *Opp* UNIMPORTANT. **be important** ▷ MATTER.

importunate *adj* demanding, insistent, persistent, pressing, relentless, urgent.

importune *v* harass, hound, pester, plague, plead with, press, solicit, urge. ▷ ASK.

impose *v* decree, dictate, enforce, exact, fix, foist, inflict, insist on, lay, levy, prescribe, set. **impose on** ▷ BURDEN, EXPLOIT. **imposing** ▷ IMPRESSIVE.

impossible *adj* hopeless, impracticable, impractical, inconceivable, insoluble, insurmountable, *inf* not on, out of the question, unattainable, unimaginable, unobtainable, unthinkable, unviable, unworkable. *Opp* POSSIBLE.

impotent *adj* emasculated, helpless, inadequate, incapable, ineffective, ineffectual, inept, infirm, powerless, unable. ▷ WEAK. *Opp* POTENT.

impracticable *adj* not feasible, useless. ▷ IMPOSSIBLE. *Opp* PRACTICABLE.

impractical *adj* idealistic, quixotic, romantic, unrealistic, visionary. *Opp* PRACTICAL.

imprecise *adj* ambiguous, approximate,

careless, estimated, fuzzy, guessed, hazy, ill-defined, inaccurate, inexact, loose, *inf* sloppy, undefined, vague, *inf* waffly. *Opp* PRECISE.

impregnable *adj* impenetrable, invincible, invulnerable, safe, secure, strong, unassailable. *Opp* VULNERABLE.

impress *v* 1 affect, excite, influence, inspire, leave its mark on, move, persuade, stir, touch. 2 emboss, engrave, imprint, mark, print, stamp.

impression *n* 1 effect, impact, influence, mark. 2 belief, fancy, feeling, hunch, idea, memory, notion, opinion, recollection, sense, suspicion, view. 3 dent, hollow, imprint, indentation, mark, print, stamp. 4 imitation, impersonation, parody, *inf* take-off. 5 edition, printing, reprint.

impressionable *adj* easily influenced, gullible, inexperienced, naive, receptive, suggestible, susceptible.

impressive *adj* affecting, awe-inspiring, awesome, commanding, formidable, grand, imposing, magnificent, majestic, memorable, moving, powerful, remarkable, splendid, stately, stirring, striking, touching. ▷ BIG. *Opp* INSIGNIFICANT.

imprison *v* cage, commit to prison, confine, detain, gaol, immure, incarcerate, intern, jail, keep in custody, *inf* keep under lock and key, lock up, *inf* put away, remand, *inf* send down, shut up. *Opp* FREE.

imprisonment *n* confinement, custody, detention, gaol, incarceration, internment, jail, remand.

improbable *adj* doubtful, dubious, far-fetched, *inf* hard to believe, implausible, incredible, unbelievable, unconvincing, unexpected, unlikely. *Opp* PROBABLE.

impromptu *adj inf* ad-lib, extempore, improvised, offhand, *inf* off the cuff, *inf* off the top of your head, spontaneous, unplanned, unpremeditated, unprepared, unrehearsed, unscripted. ▷ IMPULSIVE. *Opp* REHEARSED.

improper *adj* 1 inappropriate, irregular, mistaken, out of place, uncalled-for, unfit, unseemly, unsuitable, unwarranted. ▷ WRONG. 2 ▷ INDECENT. *Opp* PROPER.

impropriety *n* incorrectness, indecency, indelicacy, irregularity, rudeness, unseemliness. ▷ OBSCENITY. *Opp* PROPRIETY.

improve *v* 1 advance, develop, get better, grow, increase, *inf* look up, move on, progress. 2 *improve after illness.* convalesce, *inf* pick up, rally, recover, recuperate, revive, strengthen, *inf* turn the corner. 3 *improve your manners, finances.* ameliorate, amend, better, correct, enhance, mend, polish (up), rectify, refine, reform, revise. 4 *improve a home.* decorate, extend, modernize, rebuild, refurbish, renovate, repair, update. *Opp* WORSEN.

improvement *n* 1 advance, amelioration, correction, development, enhancement, gain, increase, progress, rally, recovery, reformation, upturn. 2 *home improvement.* alteration, extension, *inf* facelift, modernization, renovation.

improvise *v* 1 concoct, contrive, devise, invent, make do, make up, *inf* throw together. 2 *inf* ad-lib, extemporize, play by ear.

impudent *adj* bold, cheeky, disrespectful, forward, *inf* fresh, impertinent, insolent, pert, presumptuous, saucy. ▷ RUDE. *Opp* RESPECTFUL.

impulse *n* 1 drive, force, impetus, motive, pressure, push, stimulus, thrust. 2 caprice, desire, instinct, urge, whim.

impulsive *adj* emotional, hasty, headlong, hot-headed, impetuous, instinctive, intuitive, involuntary, madcap, precipitate, rash, reckless, spontaneous, *inf* spur-of-the-moment, sudden, thoughtless, unthinking, wild. ▷ IMPROMPTU. *Opp* DELIBERATE.

impure *adj* 1 adulterated, defiled, infected, polluted, tainted, unwholesome. ▷ DIRTY. 2 ▷ INDECENT.

impurity *n* contamination, defilement, taint. ▷ DIRT.

inaccessible *adj* cut off, desolate, godforsaken, impassable, impenetrable, isolated, lonely, outlying, out-of-the-way, private, remote, solitary, unattainable, unavailable, unfrequented, unobtainable. *Opp* ACCESSIBLE.

inaccurate *adj* erroneous, fallacious, false, faulty, imperfect, imprecise, incorrect, inexact, misleading, mistaken, unreliable, unsound, untrue, vague, wrong. *Opp* ACCURATE.

inactive *adj* asleep, dormant, hibernating, idle, immobile, inanimate, indolent, inert, languid, lazy, lethargic, passive, quiet, sedentary, sleepy, slothful, slow, sluggish, somnolent, torpid, unemployed, unoccupied. *Opp* ACTIVE.

inadequate *adj* deficient, imperfect, incompetent, incomplete, ineffective, insufficient, limited, meagre, niggardly, *inf* pathetic, scanty, scarce, skimpy, sparse, unsatisfactory. *Opp* ADEQUATE.

inadvisable *adj* misguided, unwise. ▷ SILLY. *Opp* WISE.

inanimate *adj* cold, dead, dormant, inactive, insentient, lifeless, motionless, unconscious. *Opp* ANIMATE.

inappropriate *adj* ill-judged, ill-timed, improper, inapplicable, inapposite, incongruous, incorrect, inopportune, irrelevant, out of place, tactless, tasteless, unbecoming, unfit, unseemly, unsuitable, untimely, wrong. *Opp* APPROPRIATE.

inarticulate *adj* dumb, faltering, halting, hesitant, mumbling, mute, shy, silent, speechless, stammering, stuttering, tongue-tied. ▷ INCOHERENT. *Opp* ARTICULATE.

inattentive *adj* absent-minded, abstracted, careless, daydreaming, distracted, dreaming, drifting, heedless, *inf* in a world of your own, negligent, preoccupied, unobservant, vague, wandering. *Opp* ATTENTIVE.

inaudible *adj* imperceptible, indistinct, quiet, silent, undistinguishable. ▷ FAINT. *Opp* AUDIBLE.

incapable *adj* 1 clumsy, helpless, impotent, incompetent, ineffective, ineffectual, inept, powerless, unable, unfit, unqualified, useless, weak. *Opp* CAPABLE. 2 ▷ DRUNK.

incentive *n* bait, *inf* carrot, encouragement, inducement, lure, motivation, reward, stimulus, *inf* sweetener.

incessant *adj* ceaseless, constant, continual, continuous, endless, eternal, everlasting, interminable, never-ending, non-stop, perennial, perpetual, persistent, relentless, unbroken, unending, unremitting. *Opp* INTERMITTENT, TEMPORARY.

incident *n* 1 affair, circumstance, episode, event, happening, occasion, occurrence. 2 accident, disturbance, scene, upset. ▷ COMMOTION.

incidental *adj* accidental, attendant, casual, chance, fortuitous, minor, odd, random, secondary, subordinate, subsidiary. *Opp* ESSENTIAL.

incipient *adj* beginning, developing, early, embryonic, growing, new, rudimentary.

incisive *adj* acute, clear, concise, cutting, decisive, direct, keen, penetrating, percipient, precise, sharp, telling, trenchant. *Opp* VAGUE.

incite *v* inflame, rouse, spur on, stir up, urge. ▷ PROVOKE.

inclination *n* affection, bent, bias, desire, disposition, fondness, habit, instinct, leaning, liking, partiality, penchant, predilection, predisposition, preference, proclivity, propensity, readiness, tendency, trend. ▷ DESIRE.

incline *n* ascent, declivity, descent, drop, gradient, hill, ramp, rise, slope.
• *v* angle, ascend, bend, descend, drop, lean, rise, slant, slope, tend, tilt, tip, veer.
inclined (to) ▷ LIABLE.

include *v* 1 add in, combine, comprehend, comprise, consist of, contain, embody, embrace, encompass, incorporate, involve, subsume, take in. 2 *The price includes VAT.* allow for, cover, take into account. *Opp* EXCLUDE.

incoherent *adj* confused, disconnected, disjointed, disordered, disorganized, garbled, illogical, incomprehensible, inconsistent, jumbled, mixed up, muddled, rambling, scrambled, unclear, unconnected, unintelligible. ▷ INARTICULATE. *Opp* COHERENT.

incombustible *adj* fireproof, fire-resistant, flameproof, non-flammable. *Opp* COMBUSTIBLE.

income *n* earnings, interest, pay, proceeds, profits, receipts, revenue, salary, takings, wages. *Opp* EXPENSE.

incoming *adj* 1 approaching, arriving, entering, landing, new, next. 2 *incoming tide.* flowing, rising. *Opp* OUTGOING.

incompatible *adj* at variance, clashing, conflicting, contradictory, contrasting, different, discordant, incongruous, inconsistent, irreconcilable, mismatched, opposed, unsuited. *Opp* COMPATIBLE.

incompetent *adj* 1 bungling, clumsy, feckless, gauche, helpless, *inf* hopeless, incapable, ineffective, ineffectual, inefficient, unfit, unprofessional, untrained. 2 bungled, inadequate, unsatisfactory, unskilful, useless. *Opp* COMPETENT.

incomplete *adj* abbreviated, abridged, *inf* bitty, deficient, edited, expurgated, faulty, fragmentary, imperfect, insufficient, partial, selective, sketchy, unfinished, wanting. *Opp* COMPLETE.

incomprehensible *adj* abstruse, arcane, baffling, beyond comprehension, cryptic, enigmatic, illegible, impenetrable, indecipherable, meaningless, mysterious, mystifying, obscure, opaque, perplexing, puzzling, recondite, strange, unclear, unfathomable, unintelligible. *Opp* COMPREHENSIBLE.

inconceivable *adj* implausible, incredible,

inf mind-boggling, staggering, unbelievable, undreamed-of, unimaginable, unthinkable. *Opp* CREDIBLE.

inconclusive *adj* ambiguous, equivocal, indefinite, open, open-ended, questionable, uncertain, unconvincing, unresolved, *inf* up in the air. *Opp* CONCLUSIVE.

incongruous *adj* clashing, conflicting, discordant, ill-matched, ill-suited, inappropriate, incompatible, inconsistent, irreconcilable, odd, out of place, surprising, uncoordinated, unsuited. ▷ ABSURD. *Opp* COMPATIBLE.

inconsiderate *adj* careless, heedless, insensitive, intolerant, negligent, rude, self-centred, selfish, tactless, thoughtless, uncaring, unconcerned, ungracious, unhelpful, unkind, unsympathetic, unthinking. *Opp* CONSIDERATE.

inconsistent *adj* capricious, changeable, erratic, fickle, patchy, unpredictable, unreliable, unstable, *inf* up-and-down, variable. ▷ INCOMPATIBLE. *Opp* CONSISTENT.

inconspicuous *adj* camouflaged, discreet, hidden, insignificant, in the background, invisible, modest, ordinary, out of sight, plain, retiring, unassuming, unobtrusive. *Opp* CONSPICUOUS.

inconvenience *n* annoyance, bother, discomfort, disruption, drawback, hindrance, impediment, irritation, nuisance, trouble.

• *v* annoy, bother, disturb, irk, irritate, put out, trouble.

inconvenient *adj* annoying, awkward, bothersome, difficult, embarrassing, ill-timed, inopportune, irksome, irritating, tiresome, troublesome, unsuitable, untimely, unwieldy. *Opp* CONVENIENT.

incorporate *v* ▷ INCLUDE.

incorrect *adj* erroneous, fallacious, false, faulty, imprecise, inaccurate, inexact, misinformed, misleading, mistaken, specious, untrue. *Opp* CORRECT.

incorrigible *adj* confirmed, *inf* dyed-in-the-wool, habitual, hardened, *inf* hopeless, impenitent, incurable, inveterate, irredeemable, obdurate, shameless, unalterable, unreformable, unrepentant. ▷ WICKED.

incorruptible *adj* 1 honest, just, moral, sound, *inf* straight, true, trustworthy, upright. *Opp* CORRUPT. 2 ▷ EVERLASTING.

increase *n* addition, amplification, boost, build-up, crescendo, development, enlargement, escalation, expansion, extension, gain, growth, increment, intensification, proliferation, rise, spread, upsurge, upturn.

• *v* 1 add to, advance, amplify, augment, boost, build up, develop, enlarge, expand, extend, lengthen, magnify, maximize, multiply, prolong, put up, raise, *inf* step up, strengthen, stretch, swell. 2 escalate, gain, grow, intensify, proliferate, *inf* snowball, spread. *Opp* DECREASE.

incredible *adj* beyond belief, far-fetched, implausible, impossible, improbable, inconceivable, unconvincing, unlikely, untenable, unthinkable. ▷ EXTRAORDINARY. *Opp* CREDIBLE.

incredulous *adj* disbelieving, distrustful, doubtful, dubious, questioning, sceptical, suspicious, uncertain, unconvinced. *Opp* CREDULOUS.

incriminate *v* accuse, blame, implicate, involve, *inf* point the finger at. *Opp* EXCUSE.

incur *v* earn, expose yourself to, get, lay yourself open to, provoke, run up, suffer.

incurable *adj* 1 fatal, hopeless, inoperable, irremediable, irreparable, terminal, untreatable. *Opp* CURABLE. 2 ▷ INCORRIGIBLE.

indebted *adj* beholden, bound, grateful, obliged, thankful.

indecent *adj* blue, coarse, crude, dirty, immodest, impolite, improper, impure, indelicate, *inf* naughty, obscene, offensive, risqué, rude, smutty, suggestive, unprintable, unrepeatable, vulgar. ▷ INDECOROUS. *Opp* DECENT.

indecisive *adj* doubtful, equivocal, *inf* in two minds, irresolute. ▷ HESITANT, INDEFINITE. *Opp* DECISIVE. **be indecisive** ▷ HESITATE.

indecorous *adj* ill-bred, inappropriate, *inf* in bad taste, tasteless, unbecoming, uncouth, undignified, unseemly. ▷ INDECENT. *Opp* DECOROUS.

indefensible *adj* insupportable, unjustifiable, unpardonable, untenable, vulnerable, weak. ▷ WRONG.

indefinite *adj* ambiguous, blurred, confused, dim, general, ill-defined, imprecise, indeterminate, inexact, obscure, uncertain, unclear, unsettled, unspecific, unsure, vague. ▷ INDECISIVE. *Opp* DEFINITE.

indelible *adj* ingrained, unfading, unforgettable. ▷ PERMANENT.

indentation *n* cut, dent, depression, dimple, dip, furrow, groove, hollow, nick, notch, pit.

independence *n* 1 autonomy, freedom, individualism, liberty, nonconformity, self-reliance, self-sufficiency. 2 home rule, self-determination, self-government, self-rule, sovereignty.

independent *adj* 1 carefree, *inf* footloose, free, freethinking, nonconformist, non-partisan, open-minded, private, self-reliant, separate, unbiased, unconventional, untrammelled, without ties. 2 autonomous, liberated, neutral, non-aligned, self-determining, self-governing, sovereign.

indescribable *adj* beyond words, indefinable, stunning, unspeakable, unutterable.

indestructible *adj* durable, enduring, eternal, everlasting, immortal, imperishable, lasting, permanent, solid, strong, tough, unbreakable.

index *n* 1 catalogue, directory, guide, key, register, table (*of contents*). 2 ▷ INDICATOR.

indicate *v* announce, communicate, convey, denote, describe, designate, display, express, give notice of, imply, intimate, make known, manifest, mean, notify, point out, register, reveal, say, show, signal, signify, specify, spell, stand for, suggest, warn.

indication *n* augury, clue, evidence, forewarning, hint, inkling, intimation, omen, portent, sign, signal, suggestion, symptom, token, warning.

indicator *n* clock, dial, display, gauge, marker, meter, needle, pointer, sign, signal.

indifferent *adj* 1 aloof, apathetic, blasé, bored, casual, cold, cool, distant, half-hearted, impassive, insouciant, nonchalant, uncaring, unconcerned, unemotional, unenthusiastic, unimpressed, uninterested, unmoved. ▷ IMPARTIAL. *Opp* ENTHUSIASTIC. 2 mediocre, *inf* nothing to write home about, undistinguished. ▷ ORDINARY. *Opp* EXCELLENT.

indigestion *n* dyspepsia, flatulence, heartburn.

indignant *adj* annoyed, disgruntled, exasperated, infuriated, irritated, *inf* miffed, *inf* peeved, piqued, put out, upset, vexed. ▷ ANGRY.

indirect *adj* 1 circuitous, devious, long, meandering, oblique, rambling, roundabout, tortuous, twisting, winding, zigzag. 2 ambiguous, backhanded, circumlocutory, disguised, equivocal, euphemistic, evasive, implicit, implied, oblique. *Opp* DIRECT.

indiscreet *adj* careless, foolish, ill-advised, ill-considered, ill-judged, incautious, injudicious, tactless, undiplomatic, unguarded, unthinking, unwise. *Opp* DISCREET.

indiscriminate *adj* aimless, careless, casual, desultory, general, haphazard, *inf* hit or miss, miscellaneous, mixed, random, uncritical, undifferentiated, undiscriminating, uninformed, unselective, unsystematic, wholesale. *Opp* SELECTIVE.

indispensable *adj* basic, central, compulsory, crucial, essential, imperative, key, necessary, needed, obligatory, required, requisite, vital. *Opp* UNNECESSARY.

indisputable *adj* absolute, accepted, acknowledged, axiomatic, beyond doubt, certain, clear, definite, evident, incontestable, incontrovertible, irrefutable, positive, proved, proven, self-evident, sure, unanswerable, undeniable, undoubted, unquestionable. *Opp* DEBATABLE.

indistinct *adj* 1 bleary, blurred, confused, dim, dull, faint, fuzzy, hazy, ill-defined, indefinite, misty, obscure, shadowy, unclear, vague. 2 muffled, mumbled, muted, slurred, unintelligible. *Opp* DISTINCT.

indistinguishable *adj* alike, identical, interchangeable, the same, twin. *Opp* DIFFERENT.

individual *adj* characteristic, different, distinct, distinctive, exclusive, idiosyncratic, particular, peculiar, personal, private, separate, singular, special, specific, unique. *Opp* COLLECTIVE, GENERAL.
•*n* ▷ PERSON.

indoctrinate *v* brainwash, re-educate. ▷ TEACH.

induce *v* 1 coax, encourage, incite, motivate, persuade, press, prevail on, sway, *inf* talk into, tempt, urge. *Opp* DISCOURAGE. 2 *induce a fever.* bring on, cause, engender, generate, give rise to, lead to, occasion, produce, provoke.

inducement *n* ▷ INCENTIVE.

indulge *v* be indulgent to, cosset, favour, give in to, gratify, humour, mollycoddle, pamper, pander to, spoil, treat. *Opp* DEPRIVE. **indulge in** ▷ ENJOY. **indulge yourself** be self-indulgent, give in to temptation, overdo it, spoil yourself, succumb, yield.

indulgent *adj* compliant, easygoing, fond, forbearing, forgiving, genial, kind, lenient, liberal, patient, permissive, tolerant. *Opp* STRICT.

industrious *adj* assiduous, busy, conscientious, diligent, earnest, energetic, enterprising, hard-working, keen, persistent, productive, sedulous, tireless, unflagging, untiring, zealous. *Opp* LAZY.

industry *n* 1 business, commerce, manufacturing, production, trade. 2 activity, application, commitment, determination, diligence, energy, enterprise, keenness, perseverance, persistence, zeal. ⊳ WORK. *Opp* LAZINESS.

inedible *adj* indigestible, nauseating, *inf* off, poisonous, rotten, tough, uneatable, unpalatable. *Opp* EDIBLE.

ineffective *adj* 1 fruitless, futile, *inf* hopeless, idle, inadequate, ineffectual, unproductive, unsuccessful, useless, vain, worthless. 2 feeble, incapable, incompetent, ineffectual, inefficient, powerless, shiftless, unenterprising, weak. *Opp* EFFECTIVE.

inefficient *adj* 1 uneconomic, wasteful. 2 ⊳ INEFFECTIVE. *Opp* EFFICIENT.

inelegant *adj* awkward, clumsy, crude, gauche, graceless, inartistic, rough, ungainly, unpolished, unskilful, unstylish. *Opp* ELEGANT.

ineligible *adj* disqualified, *inf* ruled out, unacceptable, unfit, unqualified, unsuitable. *Opp* ELIGIBLE.

inept *adj* 1 awkward, bumbling, bungling, clumsy, gauche, incompetent, inexpert, maladroit, unskilful, unskilled. 2 ⊳ INAPPROPRIATE.

inequality *n* contrast, difference, discrepancy, disparity, dissimilarity, imbalance, incongruity. *Opp* EQUALITY.

inert *adj* dormant, idle, immobile, inactive, inanimate, lifeless, passive, quiescent, quiet, sluggish, static, still, supine, torpid. *Opp* LIVELY.

inertia *n* apathy, idleness, immobility, inactivity, indolence, lassitude, laziness, lethargy, listlessness, numbness, passivity, sluggishness, torpor. *Opp* LIVELINESS.

inessential *adj* dispensable, expendable, minor, needless, optional, ornamental, spare, superfluous, unimportant, unnecessary. *Opp* ESSENTIAL.

inevitable *adj inf* bound to happen, certain, destined, fated, inescapable, inexorable, ordained, sure, unavoidable. ⊳ RELENTLESS.

inexcusable *adj* ⊳ UNFORGIVABLE.

inexpensive *adj* ⊳ CHEAP.

inexperienced *adj inf* born yesterday, callow, *inf* green, immature, inexpert, innocent, naive, new, probationary, raw, unskilled, unsophisticated, untried, *inf* wet behind the ears, young. *Opp* EXPERT.

inexplicable *adj* baffling, bewildering, enigmatic, incomprehensible, insoluble, mysterious, mystifying, perplexing, puzzling, strange, unaccountable, unfathomable, unsolvable. *Opp* STRAIGHTFORWARD.

infallible *adj* certain, dependable, faultless, foolproof, perfect, reliable, sound, sure, trustworthy, unerring, unfailing. *Opp* FALLIBLE.

infamous *adj* disgraceful, disreputable, notorious, outrageous, well-known. ⊳ WICKED.

infant *n* baby, *inf* tot. ⊳ CHILD.

infantile *adj* babyish, childish, immature, juvenile, puerile. ⊳ SILLY. *Opp* MATURE.

infatuated *adj* besotted, in love, obsessed, *inf* smitten.

infatuation *n inf* crush, obsession, passion. ⊳ LOVE.

infect *v* blight, contaminate, defile, poison, pollute, spoil, taint. **infected** ⊳ SEPTIC.

infection *n* contagion, contamination, epidemic, pollution, virus. ⊳ ILLNESS.

infectious *adj* ⊳ CONTAGIOUS.

infer *v* assume, conclude, deduce, derive, draw a conclusion, gather, guess, surmise, understand, work out.

inferior *adj* 1 junior, lesser, lower, menial, secondary, servile, subordinate, unimportant. 2 cheap, indifferent, mediocre, poor, second-class, shoddy, tawdry. *Opp* SUPERIOR.

•*n* ⊳ SUBORDINATE.

infertile *adj* barren, sterile, unfruitful, unproductive.

infest *v* **infested** alive, crawling, swarming, teeming, verminous.

infidelity *n* 1 adultery, unfaithfulness. 2 ⊳ DISLOYALTY.

infiltrate *v* enter secretly, intrude, penetrate.

infinite *adj* boundless, countless, endless, eternal, everlasting, immeasurable, immense, incalculable, inexhaustible, innumerable, interminable, limitless, never-ending, numberless, perpetual, uncountable, undefined, unending, unfathomable, unlimited, untold. ⊳ HUGE. *Opp* FINITE.

infinity *n* eternity, infinitude, perpetuity, space.

infirm *adj* feeble, frail, lame, old, poorly,

sickly, unwell. ▷ ILL, WEAK. *Opp* HEALTHY.

inflame *v* arouse, encourage, excite, fire, foment, ignite, incense, kindle, rouse, stimulate, stir up, work up. ▷ ANGER. *Opp* COOL. **inflamed** ▷ PASSIONATE, SEPTIC.

inflammable *adj* burnable, combustible, flammable, volatile. *Opp* INCOMBUSTIBLE.

inflammation *n* abscess, boil, infection, irritation, redness, sore, soreness, swelling.

inflate *v* 1 blow up, dilate, distend, enlarge, puff up, pump up, swell. 2 ▷ EXAGGERATE.

inflexible *adj* 1 firm, hard, hardened, immovable, rigid, solid, stiff, unbending, unyielding. 2 adamant, entrenched, fixed, immutable, intractable, intransigent, obdurate, obstinate, *inf* pig-headed, resolute, rigorous, strict, stubborn, unchangeable, uncompromising. *Opp* FLEXIBLE.

inflict *v* administer, apply, deal out, enforce, force, impose, mete out, perpetrate, wreak.

influence *n* authority, control, direction, dominance, effect, guidance, hold, impact, leverage, power, pressure, pull, sway.
• *v* 1 affect, change, control, direct, dominate, guide, impinge on, impress, manipulate, modify, motivate, move, persuade, prejudice, prompt, stir, sway. 2 bribe, corrupt, lead astray, suborn, tempt.

influential *adj* authoritative, compelling, convincing, dominant, effective, far-reaching, forceful, guiding, important, inspiring, leading, persuasive, powerful, significant, strong, telling, weighty. *Opp* UNIMPORTANT.

influx *n* flood, flow, inflow, inundation, invasion, rush, stream.

inform *v* advise, apprise, brief, enlighten, *inf* fill in, give information to, instruct, leak, notify, *inf* put in the picture, teach, tell, tip off. **inform against** ▷ BETRAY. **informed** ▷ KNOWLEDGEABLE.

informal *adj* 1 casual, comfortable, cosy, easy, easygoing, everyday, familiar, *inf* free and easy, friendly, homely, natural, ordinary, relaxed, simple, unceremonious, unofficial, unpretentious, unsophisticated. 2 *informal language*. chatty, colloquial, slangy, vernacular. *Opp* FORMAL.

information *n* 1 announcement, briefing, bulletin, communication, instruction, message, news, report, statement, tip-off, word. 2 data, evidence, facts, intelligence, knowledge, statistics.

informative *adj* communicative, edifying, educational, enlightening, factual, helpful, illuminating, instructive, meaningful, revealing, useful. *Opp* MEANINGLESS.

informer *n sl* grass, informant, spy, *inf* telltale, traitor.

infrequent *adj* exceptional, intermittent, irregular, occasional, *inf* once in a blue moon, rare, spasmodic, uncommon, unusual. *Opp* FREQUENT.

infringe *v* ▷ VIOLATE.

ingenious *adj* adroit, artful, astute, brilliant, clever, crafty, creative, cunning, deft, imaginative, inspired, intelligent, intricate, inventive, original, resourceful, shrewd, skilful, *inf* smart, subtle. *Opp* UNIMAGINATIVE.

ingenuous *adj* artless, childlike, frank, guileless, honest, innocent, naive, open, plain, simple, trusting, unaffected, unsophisticated. *Opp* SOPHISTICATED.

ingredient *n* component, constituent, element, factor, *pl* makings, part.

inhabit *v* colonize, dwell in, live in, occupy, people, populate, possess, reside in, settle in, set up home in.

inhabitable *adj* habitable, in good repair, usable.

inhabitant *n* citizen, denizen, dweller, inmate, native, occupant, occupier, *pl* population, resident, settler, tenant, *pl* townspeople.

inherent *adj* congenital, essential, fundamental, hereditary, inborn, ingrained, intrinsic, native, natural.

inherit *v* be left, *inf* come into, receive as an inheritance, succeed to. **inherited** ▷ HEREDITARY.

inheritance *n* bequest, birthright, estate, fortune, heritage, legacy, patrimony.

inhibit *v* check, curb, discourage, frustrate, hinder, hold back, prevent, repress, restrain. **inhibited** ▷ REPRESSED, SHY.

inhibition *n* 1 bar, barrier, check, constraint, curb, impediment, restraint. 2 diffidence, *inf* hang-up, repression, reserve, self-consciousness, shyness.

inhospitable *adj* standoffish, unsociable, unwelcoming. ▷ UNFRIENDLY. 2 bleak, cold, comfortless, desolate, hostile, lonely. *Opp* HOSPITABLE.

inhuman *adj* barbaric, bestial, bloodthirsty, brutish, diabolical, fiendish, merciless, pitiless, ruthless, savage, unnatural, vicious. ▷ INHUMANE. *Opp* HUMAN.

inhumane *adj* cruel, hard-hearted, heartless, inconsiderate, insensitive, uncaring, uncharitable, uncivilized, unfeeling, unkind, unsympathetic. ▷ INHUMAN. *Opp* HUMANE.

initial *adj* beginning, first, inaugural, introductory, opening, original, primary, starting. *Opp* FINAL.

initiate *v* ▷ BEGIN.

initiative *n* ambition, drive, dynamism, enterprise, *inf* get-up-and-go, inventiveness, lead, leadership, originality, resourcefulness. **take the initiative** ▷ INITIATE.

injection *n inf* fix, inoculation, *inf* jab, vaccination.

injure *v* break, crush, cut, damage, deface, disfigure, harm, hurt, ill-treat, mar, ruin, spoil. ▷ WOUND.

injurious *adj* 1 damaging, destructive, detrimental, harmful, ruinous. 2 ▷ ABUSIVE.

injury *n* damage, harm, hurt, mischief. ▷ WOUND.

injustice *n* bias, bigotry, discrimination, dishonesty, favouritism, inequality, inequity, one-sidedness, oppression, partiality, partisanship, prejudice, unfairness, unlawfulness, wrong. *Opp* JUSTICE.

inn *n* hostelry, hotel, *inf* local, pub, tavern.

inner *adj* central, hidden, innermost, inside, interior, internal, inward, middle, private, secret. *Opp* OUTER.

innocence *n* 1 goodness, honesty, purity, righteousness, virtue. 2 [*derog*] gullibility, inexperience, naivety.

innocent *adj* 1 above suspicion, blameless, faultless, free from blame, guiltless. *Opp* GUILTY. 2 pure, righteous, sinless, virtuous. *Opp* CORRUPT. 3 artless, childlike, credulous, *inf* green, guileless, gullible, inexperienced, ingenuous, naive, simple, trusting, unsophisticated.

innovation *n* change, departure, new feature, novelty, reform.

innovator *n* discoverer, inventor, pioneer, reformer.

innumerable *adj* countless, many, numberless, uncountable, untold. ▷ INFINITE.

inquest *n* hearing. ▷ INQUIRY.

inquire *v* investigate, probe, search, seek information, survey. ▷ ENQUIRE.

inquiry *n* cross-examination, examination, inquest, inquisition, interrogation, investigation, *inf* post-mortem, probe, review, study, survey.

inquisitive *adj* curious, inquiring, interfering, intrusive, investigative, meddlesome, meddling, *inf* nosy, probing, prying, questioning, *inf* snooping, spying. **be inquisitive** ▷ PRY.

insane *adj* crazy, deranged, lunatic, *inf* mental, psychotic, unhinged. ▷ MAD. *Opp* SANE.

inscription *n* dedication, engraving, writing.

insect *n inf* bug, *inf* creepy-crawly.

insecure *adj* 1 dangerous, flimsy, loose, precarious, rickety, rocky, shaky, unsafe, unstable, unsteady, unsupported, weak, wobbly. 2 *insecure feeling*. anxious, apprehensive, defenceless, exposed, open, uncertain, unconfident, vulnerable, worried. *Opp* SECURE.

insensible *adj* anaesthetized, *inf* dead to the world, inert, insentient, knocked out, numb, *inf* out, unaware, unconscious. *Opp* CONSCIOUS.

insensitive *adj* 1 dead, numb, unresponsive. 2 boorish, callous, crass, cruel, obtuse, tactless, *inf* thick-skinned, thoughtless, uncaring, unfeeling, unsympathetic. *Opp* SENSITIVE.

inseparable *adj* 1 indissoluble, indivisible, integral. 2 close, devoted, intimate.

insert *v* embed, implant, introduce, place in, *inf* pop in, push in, put in, tuck in.

inside *adj* central, indoor, inner, interior, internal.

• *n* centre, contents, core, heart, indoors, interior, middle. *Opp* OUTSIDE. **insides** ▷ ENTRAILS.

insidious *adj* creeping, furtive, stealthy, subtle, surreptitious, treacherous. ▷ CRAFTY.

insignificant *adj* forgettable, irrelevant, insubstantial, lightweight, meaningless, minor, negligible, paltry, small, trifling, trivial, unimpressive, valueless, worthless, unimportant. *Opp* SIGNIFICANT.

insincere *adj* deceitful, deceptive, devious, dishonest, false, feigned, flattering, disingenuous, hollow, hypocritical, lying, *inf* mealy-mouthed, *inf* phoney, pretended, *inf* put on, *inf* smarmy, sycophantic, *inf* two-faced, untrue, untruthful. *Opp* SINCERE.

insist *v* 1 assert, aver, declare, emphasize, hold, maintain, state, stress, swear, vow. 2 assert yourself, persist, *inf* put your foot down, stand firm. **insist on** ▷ DEMAND.

insistent *adj* assertive, demanding, dogged, emphatic, firm, forceful, importunate, persistent, relentless, repeated, unremitting, urgent.

insolence *n* arrogance, boldness, cheek, disrespect, effrontery, impertinence, impudence, insubordination, *inf* lip, presumptuousness, rudeness, *inf* sauce.

insolent *adj* arrogant, audacious, bold, brazen, cheeky, contemptuous, defiant, disdainful, forward, *inf* fresh, impertinent, impudent, insubordinate, insulting, pert, presumptuous, sneering. ▷ RUDE. *Opp* POLITE.

insoluble *adj* baffling, enigmatic, incomprehensible, inexplicable, mystifying, puzzling, strange, unaccountable, unfathomable. *Opp* SOLUBLE.

insolvent *adj* bankrupt, *inf* bust, failed, ruined. ▷ POOR.

inspect *v* check, examine, *sl* give it the once over, investigate, peruse, scan, scrutinize, study, survey, vet.

inspection *n* check, examination, *inf* going-over, investigation, review, scrutiny, survey.

inspector *n* controller, examiner, investigator, official, superintendent, supervisor.

inspiration *n* 1 creativity, genius, imagination, muse. 2 enthusiasm, impulse, incitement, spur, stimulation, stimulus. 3 *sudden inspiration.* brainwave, idea, insight, revelation, thought.

inspire *v* activate, animate, arouse, awaken, encourage, energize, enthuse, fire, galvanize, influence, inspirit, instigate, kindle, motivate, prompt, set off, spark off, spur, stimulate, stir, support.

instability *n* capriciousness, change, fickleness, fluctuation, flux, impermanence, inconstancy, insecurity, precariousness, shakiness, transience, uncertainty, unpredictability, unreliability, unsteadiness, *inf* ups-and-downs, variability, variations, weakness. *Opp* STABILITY.

install *v* ensconce, establish, fit, fix, introduce, place, plant, position, put in, settle, set up, station. *Opp* REMOVE.

instalment *n* 1 payment, rent, rental. 2 chapter, episode, part.

instance *n* ▷ EXAMPLE.

instant *adj* direct, fast, immediate, instantaneous, on-the-spot, prompt, quick, rapid, speedy, swift, unhesitating, urgent. • *n* ▷ MOMENT.

instigate *v* activate, begin, cause, encourage, foment, generate, incite, initiate, inspire, kindle, prompt, provoke, set up, start, stimulate, stir up, urge, *inf* whip up.

instigator *n* agitator, initiator, leader, mischief-maker, ringleader, troublemaker.

instil *v* *inf* din into, imbue, implant, inculcate, indoctrinate, introduce.

instinct *n* bent, faculty, feel, feeling, hunch, impulse, inclination, intuition, presentiment, sixth sense, tendency, urge.

instinctive *adj* automatic, *inf* gut, impulsive, inborn, inherent, innate, intuitive, involuntary, natural, reflex, spontaneous, unconscious, unreasoning, unthinking. *Opp* DELIBERATE.

institute *n* ▷ INSTITUTION.
• *v* begin, create, establish, found, inaugurate, initiate, introduce, launch, open, organize, originate, pioneer, set up, start.

institution *n* 1 creation, formation, inauguration, inception, initiation, introduction, setting-up. 2 academy, asylum, college, establishment, foundation, home, hospital, institute, organization, school, *inf* set-up. 3 convention, custom, habit, practice, ritual, routine, rule, tradition.

instruct *v* 1 ▷ TEACH. 2 authorize, command, direct, enjoin, order, tell.

instruction *n* 1 briefing, coaching, demonstration, drill, education, guidance, indoctrination, lecture, schooling, teaching, training, tuition. 2 authorization, command, direction, directive, order.

instructive *adj* didactic, edifying, educational, enlightening, helpful, illuminating, improving, informative, revealing.

instructor *n* coach, teacher, trainer, tutor.

instrument *n* apparatus, appliance, contraption, device, gadget, implement, machine, mechanism, tool, utensil.

instrumental *adj* active, advantageous, beneficial, contributory, helpful, influential, supportive, useful, valuable.

insubordinate *adj* defiant, disobedient, mutinous, rebellious, undisciplined, unruly. ▷ IMPERTINENT. *Opp* OBEDIENT.

insufficient *adj* deficient, inadequate, meagre, mean, niggardly, *inf* pathetic, poor, scanty, scarce, short, sparse, unsatisfactory. *Opp* EXCESSIVE, SUFFICIENT.

insular *adj* closed, limited, narrow, narrow-minded, parochial, provincial. *Opp* BROAD-MINDED, COSMOPOLITAN.

insulate *v* 1 cocoon, cover, cushion, enclose, lag, protect, shield, surround, wrap up. 2 ▷ ISOLATE.

insult *n* abuse, affront, aspersion, defamation, indignity, libel, *inf* put-down, slander, slight, slur, snub.
• *v* abuse, be rude to, *inf* call names, defame, dishonour, disparage, libel, mock, offend, patronize, revile, slander, slight, sneer at, snub, vilify. *Opp* COMPLIMENT.
insulting ▷ RUDE.

insuperable *adj* insurmountable, overwhelming, unconquerable. ▷ IMPOSSIBLE.

insurance *n* assurance, cover, guarantee, indemnity, protection, security.

insure *v* cover yourself, protect, take out insurance.

intact *adj* complete, unbroken, undamaged, whole. ▷ PERFECT.

intangible *adj* abstract, airy, disembodied, elusive, ethereal, impalpable, incorporeal, indefinite, insubstantial, invisible, shadowy, unreal, vague. *Opp* TANGIBLE.

integral *adj* 1 basic, essential, fundamental, indispensable, intrinsic, requisite. 2 complete, full, indivisible, whole. *Opp* SEPARATE.

integrate *v* amalgamate, blend, bring together, combine, consolidate, desegregate, fuse, harmonize, join, knit, merge, mix, unify, unite, weld. *Opp* SEPARATE.

integrity *n* 1 decency, fidelity, goodness, honesty, honour, incorruptibility, loyalty, morality, principle, probity, rectitude, righteousness, sincerity, trustworthiness, uprightness, virtue. 2 ▷ UNITY.

intellect *n* ▷ INTELLIGENCE.

intellectual *adj* 1 academic, *inf* bookish, cerebral, cultured, educated, scholarly, studious, thoughtful. ▷ INTELLIGENT. 2 cultural, deep, difficult, highbrow, improving.
• *n* academic, *inf* egghead, genius, highbrow, *inf* one of the intelligentsia, thinker.

intelligence *n* 1 ability, acumen, astuteness, brainpower, brains, brilliance, capacity, cleverness, discernment, genius, insight, intellect, judgement, mind, *inf* nous, perceptiveness, perspicacity, reason, sagacity, sense, sharpness, shrewdness, understanding, wisdom, wit, wits. 2 data, facts, information, knowledge, *inf* low-down, news, notification, report, tip-off, warning. 3 espionage, secret service, spying.

intelligent *adj* able, acute, alert, astute, *inf* brainy, bright, brilliant, canny, clever, discerning, intellectual, knowing, penetrating, perceptive, perspicacious, profound, quick, rational, sagacious, sharp, shrewd, *inf* smart, thoughtful, trenchant, wise, *inf* with it. *Opp* STUPID.

intelligible *adj* clear, comprehensible, decipherable, legible, logical, lucid, meaningful, plain, straightforward, unambiguous, understandable. *Opp* INCOMPREHENSIBLE.

intend *v* aim, contemplate, design, determine, have in mind, mean, plan, plot, propose, purpose, resolve, scheme.

intense *adj* 1 ardent, burning, consuming, deep, eager, earnest, fanatical, fervent, impassioned, passionate, powerful, profound, serious, strong, vehement, violent. *Opp* COOL, HALF-HEARTED. 2 *intense pain.* acute, agonizing, excruciating, extreme, fierce, great, harsh, keen, severe, sharp. *Opp* SLIGHT.

intensify *v* add to, aggravate, augment, boost, build up, deepen, emphasize, escalate, fire, fuel, heighten, *inf* hot up, increase, magnify, quicken, raise, redouble, reinforce, sharpen, *inf* step up, strengthen, whet. *Opp* REDUCE.

intensive *adj inf* all-out, concentrated, detailed, exhaustive, thorough, unremitting.

intent *adj* absorbed, attentive, committed, concentrating, determined, eager, engrossed, focused, keen, occupied, preoccupied, rapt, resolute, set, steadfast, watchful. *Opp* CASUAL.
• *n* ▷ INTENTION.

intention *n* aim, ambition, design, end, goal, intent, object, objective, plan, point, purpose.

intentional *adj* calculated, conscious, contrived, deliberate, designed, intended, planned, pre-arranged, premeditated, prepared, studied, wilful. *Opp* ACCIDENTAL.

intercept *v* ambush, arrest, block, catch, check, cut off, deflect, head off, impede, obstruct, stop, thwart, trap.

intercourse *n* 1 communication, conversation, dealings, interaction, traffic. 2 *sexual intercourse.* copulation, lovemaking. ▷ SEX.

interest *n* 1 attention, attentiveness, care, commitment, concern, curiosity, involvement, notice, regard. 2 *of no interest.* consequence, importance, note, significance, value. 3 *leisure interest.* activity, diversion, hobby, pastime, pursuit, relaxation.
• *v* absorb, appeal to, attract, captivate, capture the imagination of, concern, divert, enchant, engage, engross, entertain,

enthral, fascinate, intrigue, involve, preoccupy, *inf* turn on. ▷ EXCITE. *Opp* BORE.

interested *adj* 1 absorbed, attentive, curious, engrossed, enthusiastic, immersed, intent, keen, preoccupied, rapt, responsive, riveted. *Opp* UNINTERESTED. 2 concerned, involved. ▷ BIASED. *Opp* DISINTERESTED.

interesting *adj* absorbing, challenging, compelling, curious, engaging, engrossing, entertaining, enthralling, fascinating, gripping, intriguing, original, piquant, riveting, stimulating, unpredictable, unusual, varied. *Opp* BORING.

interfere *v* be a busybody, butt in, interrupt, intervene, intrude, meddle, *inf* poke your nose in, pry, tamper. **interfere with** ▷ OBSTRUCT. **interfering** ▷ NOSY.

interim *adj* half-time, provisional, stopgap, temporary.

interior *adj* ▷ INTERNAL.
• *n* centre, core, depths, heart, inside, middle, nucleus.

interlude *n* intermission. ▷ INTERVAL.

intermediary *n* go-between, spokesperson. ▷ MEDIATOR.

intermediate *adj* halfway, intermediary, intervening, middle, midway, transitional.

intermittent *adj* discontinuous, fitful, irregular, occasional, *inf* on and off, periodic, random, recurrent, spasmodic, sporadic. *Opp* CONTINUOUS.

internal *adj* 1 inner, inside, interior. *Opp* EXTERNAL. 2 confidential, personal, private, secret.

international *adj* cosmopolitan, global, universal, worldwide.

interpret *v* clarify, decipher, decode, define, elucidate, explain, expound, gloss, make sense of, paraphrase, rephrase, reword, simplify, sort out, translate, understand, unravel.

interpretation *n* clarification, definition, elucidation, explanation, gloss, paraphrase, reading, rendering, translation, understanding, version.

interrogation *n* cross-examination, debriefing, examination, grilling, inquisition, questioning, *inf* third degree.

interrupt *v* 1 break in, butt in, *inf* chip in, cut in, disrupt, disturb, heckle, hold up, interfere, intervene, intrude, obstruct, spoil. 2 break off, cut off, cut short, discontinue, halt, stop, suspend, terminate.

interruption *n* break, check, disruption, division, gap, halt, hiatus, interference, intrusion, stop, suspension. ▷ INTERVAL.

intersect *v* converge, criss-cross, cross, divide, meet.

interval *n* 1 adjournment, break, *inf* breather, breathing-space, delay, gap, hiatus, lapse, lull, opening, pause, recess, respite, rest, space, wait. 2 interlude, intermezzo, intermission.

intervene *v* 1 elapse, occur, pass. 2 arbitrate, butt in, intercede, interfere, interrupt, intrude, mediate, *inf* step in.

interview *n* appraisal, audience, meeting, selection procedure.
• *v* appraise, ask questions, evaluate, examine, interrogate, question, sound out, vet.

interweave *v* criss-cross, entwine, interlace, intertwine, knit, tangle, weave together.

intestines *pl n* bowels, entrails, *inf* innards, insides, offal.

intimate *adj* 1 close, familiar, informal, loving, sexual. ▷ FRIENDLY. 2 *intimate details.* confidential, detailed, personal, private, secret.
• *n* ▷ FRIEND.
• *v* ▷ INDICATE.

intimidate *v* browbeat, bully, coerce, cow, daunt, dismay, frighten, hector, menace, persecute, scare, terrify, terrorize, threaten, tyrannize.

intolerable *adj* impossible, insufferable, insupportable, unbearable, unendurable. *Opp* TOLERABLE.

intolerant *adj* biased, bigoted, chauvinistic, discriminatory, dogmatic, narrow-minded, opinionated, prejudiced, racist, sexist, xenophobic. *Opp* TOLERANT.

intonation *n* accent, inflection, modulation, pronunciation, sound, speech pattern, tone.

intoxicate *v* addle, inebriate, make drunk, stupefy. **intoxicated** ▷ DRUNK, EXCITED. **intoxicating** ▷ ALCOHOLIC, EXCITING.

intricate *adj* complex, complicated, convoluted, delicate, detailed, elaborate, *inf* fiddly, involved, *inf* knotty, labyrinthine, ornate, sophisticated, tangled, tortuous. *Opp* SIMPLE.

intrigue *n* ▷ PLOT.
• *v* 1 appeal to, arouse the curiosity of, attract, captivate, capture the interest of, engage, engross, fascinate, interest, stimulate. *Opp* BORE.

intrinsic *adj* basic, essential, fundamental,

inborn, inbuilt, inherent, native, natural, proper, real.

introduce *v* 1 acquaint, make known, present. 2 announce, lead into, preface. 3 add, advance, bring in, broach, create, establish, inaugurate, initiate, inject, insert, interpose, launch, offer, phase in, pioneer, put forward, set up, start, suggest, usher in. ▷ BEGIN.

introduction *n* foreword, *inf* intro, *inf* lead-in, overture, preamble, preface, prologue. ▷ BEGINNING.

introductory *adj* basic, early, first, inaugural, initial, opening, preliminary, preparatory, starting. *Opp* FINAL.

introverted *adj* introspective, inward-looking, pensive, quiet, reserved, retiring, self-contained, shy, unsociable, withdrawn. *Opp* EXTROVERTED.

intrude *v* break in, butt in, eavesdrop, encroach, gatecrash, interfere, interrupt, intervene, *inf* snoop.

intruder *n* burglar, gatecrasher, interloper, invader, prowler, raider, robber, *inf* snooper, thief, trespasser, *inf* uninvited guest.

intuition *n* insight. ▷ INSTINCT.

invade *v* descend on, encroach on, enter, impinge on, infest, infringe, march into, occupy, overrun, penetrate, raid, subdue, violate. ▷ ATTACK.

invalid *adj* 1 null and void, out-of-date, unacceptable, unusable, void, worthless. 2 false, illogical, incorrect, irrational, spurious, unfounded, unsound, untenable, untrue, wrong. *Opp* VALID. 3 ▷ ILL. •*n* patient, sufferer.

invaluable *adj* incalculable, precious, priceless, useful. ▷ VALUABLE. *Opp* WORTHLESS.

invariable *adj* certain, constant, eternal, even, immutable, inflexible, predictable, regular, reliable, rigid, stable, steady, unalterable, unchangeable, unchanging, unfailing, uniform, unvarying, unwavering. *Opp* VARIABLE.

invasion *n* 1 encroachment, incursion, infiltration, inroad, intrusion, raid, violation. ▷ ATTACK. 2 infestation, spate, swarm.

invasive *adj* increasing, mushrooming, proliferating, relentless, unstoppable.

invent *v* coin, conceive, concoct, contrive, *inf* cook up, create, design, devise, discover, *inf* dream up, fabricate, formulate, *inf* hit upon, imagine, improvise, make up, originate, plan, think up.

invention *n* 1 brainchild, contrivance, creation, design, discovery. 2 contraption, device, gadget. 3 fabrication, falsehood, fantasy, fiction, lie. 4 ▷ INVENTIVENESS.

inventive *adj* clever, creative, fertile, imaginative, ingenious, innovative, inspired, original, resourceful. *Opp* BANAL.

inventiveness *n* creativity, genius, imagination, ingenuity, originality, resourcefulness.

inventor *n* architect, author, creator, designer, discoverer, maker, originator.

inverse *adj* opposite, reversed.

invert *v* capsize, overturn, reverse, transpose, upset.

invest *v* 1 buy stocks and shares, speculate. 2 lay out, use profitably, venture. **invest in** ▷ BUY.

investigate *v* consider, examine, explore, follow up, gather evidence about, *inf* go into, inquire into, look into, probe, research, scrutinize, study.

investigation *n* enquiry, examination, inquiry, inquisition, inspection, *inf* post-mortem, probe, research, review, scrutiny, study, survey.

invidious *adj* discriminatory, offensive, unfair, unjust.

invigorating *adj* bracing, enlivening, exhilarating, fresh, refreshing, rejuvenating, revitalizing, stimulating, tonic, vitalizing. *Opp* EXHAUSTING.

invincible *adj* impregnable, indestructible, indomitable, invulnerable, strong, unassailable, unbeatable, unconquerable, unstoppable.

invisible *adj* camouflaged, concealed, covered, disguised, hidden, imperceptible, inconspicuous, out of sight, secret, undetectable, unnoticed, unseen. *Opp* VISIBLE.

invite *v* 1 ask, encourage, request, summon, urge. 2 attract, entice, solicit, tempt. **inviting** ▷ ATTRACTIVE.

invoice *n* account, bill, statement.

invoke *v* appeal to, call for, cry out for, entreat, implore, pray for, solicit, supplicate.

involuntary *adj* automatic, instinctive, mechanical, reflex, spontaneous, unconscious, uncontrollable, unintentional, unthinking. *Opp* DELIBERATE.

involve *v* 1 comprise, contain, entail, hold, include, incorporate, take in. 2 affect, concern, interest, touch. 3 *involve* *in crime*. embroil, implicate, include, incriminate, *inf* mix up. **involved** ▷ BUSY, COMPLEX.

involvement *n* 1 interest, participation. 2 association, complicity, entanglement, partnership.

ironic *adj* derisive, double-edged, ironical, sarcastic, satirical, wry.

irony *n* double meaning, paradox, sarcasm, satire.

irrational *adj* absurd, arbitrary, crazy, emotional, illogical, nonsensical, senseless, subjective, surreal, unconvincing, unreasonable, unreasoning, unsound, unthinking, wild. ▷ SILLY. *Opp* RATIONAL.

irregular *adj* 1 erratic, fitful, fluctuating, haphazard, intermittent, occasional, random, spasmodic, sporadic, unequal, unpredictable, variable, varying, wavering. 2 abnormal, anomalous, eccentric, exceptional, extraordinary, improper, odd, peculiar, quirky, unconventional, unofficial, unplanned, unusual. 3 *irregular surface*. broken, bumpy, jagged, lumpy, patchy, pitted, ragged, rough, uneven. *Opp* REGULAR.

irrelevant *adj inf* beside the point, extraneous, immaterial, inapplicable, inapposite, inappropriate, inessential, *inf* neither here nor there, unnecessary, unrelated. *Opp* RELEVANT.

irreligious *adj* agnostic, atheistic, godless, heathen, humanist, impious, irreverent, pagan, uncommitted, ungodly, wicked. *Opp* RELIGIOUS.

irreparable *adj* hopeless, incurable, irremediable, irretrievable, irreversible, permanent.

irreplaceable *adj* inimitable, priceless, unique. ▷ RARE.

irrepressible *adj* bouncy, *inf* bubbling, buoyant, ebullient, uncontrollable, uninhibited, unmanageable, unstoppable. ▷ LIVELY. *Opp* LETHARGIC.

irresistible *adj* compelling, inescapable, inexorable, not to be denied, overpowering, overriding, overwhelming, persuasive, powerful, relentless, seductive, strong, unavoidable. *Opp* WEAK.

irresolute *adj* doubtful, indecisive, tentative, uncertain, undecided, vacillating, wavering, weak, weak-willed. ▷ HESITANT. *Opp* RESOLUTE.

irresponsible *adj* careless, devil-may-care, feckless, immature, inconsiderate, negligent, rash, reckless, shiftless, thoughtless, unethical, unreliable, unthinking, untrustworthy, wild. *Opp* RESPONSIBLE.

irreverent *adj* disrespectful, mocking, profane, sacrilegious. ▷ RUDE. *Opp* REVERENT.

irrevocable *adj* binding, final, fixed, hard and fast, permanent, settled, unalterable, unchangeable.

irrigate *v* flood, inundate, supply water to, water.

irritable *adj* cantankerous, crabby, cross, crotchety, curmudgeonly, dyspeptic, edgy, fractious, grumpy, impatient, irascible, peevish, petulant, *inf* prickly, querulous, *inf* ratty, short-tempered, snappy, testy, tetchy, touchy, waspish. ▷ ANGRY. *Opp* EVEN-TEMPERED.

irritate *v* 1 chafe, itch, rub, tickle, tingle. 2 ▷ ANNOY.

island *n pl* archipelago, atoll, coral reef, isle, islet.

isolate *v* cordon off, cut off, detach, insulate, keep apart, quarantine, seclude, segregate, separate, set apart, shut off, shut out, single out. **isolated** ▷ SOLITARY.

issue *n* 1 affair, argument, controversy, dispute, matter, problem, question, subject, topic. 2 consequence, effect, end, impact, outcome, repercussions, result, upshot. 3 *issue of a magazine*. copy, edition, instalment, number, publication, version.
• *v* 1 appear, emerge, erupt, flow out, gush, leak, rise, spring. 2 bring out, broadcast, circulate, disseminate, distribute, give out, make public, print, produce, publish, put out, release, send out, supply.

itch *n* 1 irritation, prickling, tickle, tingling. 2 ache, craving, desire, hankering, hunger, impatience, impulse, longing, need, thirst, urge, wish, yearning, *inf* yen.
• *v* 1 prickle, tickle, tingle. 2 ▷ DESIRE.

item *n* 1 article, bit, component, entry, ingredient, lot, matter, object, particular, thing. 2 *item in a newspaper*. article, feature, notice, piece, report.

J

jab *v* dig, elbow, nudge, poke, prod, stab, thrust. ▷ HIT.

jacket *n* casing, cover, covering, envelope, folder, sheath, skin, wrapper, wrapping. ▷ COAT.

jaded *adj* 1 ▷ WEARY. 2 bored, fed up, gorged, listless, sated, satiated. *Opp* LIVELY.

jagged *adj* angular, barbed, broken, indented, irregular, ragged, rough, serrated, sharp, snagged, spiky, toothed, uneven, zigzag. *Opp* SMOOTH.

jail, jailer *ns* ▷ GAOL, GAOLER.

jam *n* 1 blockage, bottleneck, congestion, crush. ▷ CROWD. 2 difficulty, dilemma, *inf* fix, *inf* hole, *inf* pickle, plight, predicament, quandary, tight corner, trouble. 3 conserve, jelly, marmalade, preserve.
• *v* 1 block, *inf* bung up, clog, congest, cram, crowd, crush, force, pack, obstruct, ram, squash, squeeze, stop up, stuff. 2 prop, stick, wedge.

jar *n* carafe, crock, ewer, glass, jug, mug, pitcher, pot, receptacle, urn, vessel.
• *v* 1 jerk, jog, jolt, shake, shock. 2 *That noise jars on me.* grate. ▷ ANNOY. **jarring** ▷ HARSH.

jargon *n* dialect, idiom, language, patois, slang, vernacular.

jaunt *n* excursion, expedition, outing, tour, trip. ▷ JOURNEY.

jaunty *adj* breezy, buoyant, carefree, debonair, frisky, lively, perky, spirited, sprightly. ▷ HAPPY.

jazzy *adj* 1 ▷ LIVELY. *Opp* SEDATE. 2 *jazzy colours.* bold, clashing, contrasting, flashy, gaudy, loud.

jealous *adj* 1 bitter, covetous, envious, *inf* green-eyed, *inf* green with envy, grudging, resentful. 2 *jealous of your reputation.* careful, possessive, protective, vigilant, watchful.

jeer *v* boo, deride, gibe, heckle, hiss, laugh, make fun (of), mock, scoff, sneer, taunt. ▷ RIDICULE. *Opp* CHEER.

jeopardize *v* gamble, venture. ▷ ENDANGER.

jerk *v* jar, jiggle, jog, jolt, lurch, move suddenly, pluck, pull, rattle, shake, tug, tweak, twitch, wrench, *inf* yank.

jerky *adj* bouncy, bumpy, convulsive, erratic, fitful, jolting, jumpy, rough, shaky, spasmodic, twitchy, uncontrolled, uneven. *Opp* STEADY.

jest *n*, *v* ▷ JOKE.

jester *n* ▷ CLOWN.

jet *adj* ▷ BLACK.
• *n* 1 flow, fountain, gush, rush, spout, spray, spurt, stream. 2 nozzle, sprinkler.

jetty *n* breakwater, landing stage, pier, quay, wharf.

jewel *n* brilliant, gem, gemstone, ornament, precious stone, *inf* rock, *inf* sparkler.

jeweller *n* goldsmith, silversmith.

jewellery *n* gems, jewels, ornaments, treasure, *inf* sparklers.

jilt *v* abandon, desert, *inf* ditch, drop, *inf* dump, forsake, *inf* leave in the lurch, renounce, repudiate, *inf* throw over.

jingle *n* 1 doggerel, rhyme, song, tune, verse. 2 chinking, clinking, jangling, ringing, tinkling.
• *v* chime, chink, clink, jangle, ring, tinkle.

job *n* 1 activity, assignment, chore, duty, errand, function, mission, pursuit, responsibility, role, stint, task, undertaking, work. 2 appointment, calling, career, craft, employment, livelihood, métier, occupation, position, post, profession, situation, trade, vocation.

jobless *adj* out of work, redundant, unemployed, unwaged.

jocular *adj* cheerful, gay, glad, gleeful, happy, joking, jolly, jovial, merry, overjoyed. *Opp* SAD, SERIOUS.

jog *v* 1 bounce, jar, jerk, joggle, jolt, knock, nudge, shake. ▷ HIT. 2 *jog the memory.* prompt, refresh, remind, set off, stimulate, stir. 3 run, trot.

join *n* connection, joint, knot, link, seam.
• *v* 1 add, amalgamate, attach, combine, connect, couple, dovetail, fit, fix, knit, link, marry, merge, put together, splice, tack on, unite, yoke. ▷ FASTEN. *Opp* SEPARATE. 2 adjoin, border on, come together, converge, meet, touch. 3 *join a crowd.* accompany, follow, go with, *inf* latch on to, tag along with, team up with. 4 *join a*

club. become a member of, enlist in, enrol in, sign up for, subscribe to, volunteer for. *Opp* LEAVE.

joint *adj* collaborative, collective, combined, common, communal, concerted, cooperative, corporate, general, mutual, shared, united. *Opp* SEPARATE.
•*n* connection, hinge, junction, union.

joist *n* beam, girder, rafter.

joke *n inf* crack, funny story, *inf* gag, jest, laugh, pleasantry, pun, quip, wisecrack, witticism.
•*v* banter, be facetious, have a laugh, jest, quip, tease.

jolly *adj* cheerful, gay, gleeful, grinning, high-spirited, jocular, jovial, laughing, merry, playful, smiling, sportive. ▷ HAPPY. *Opp* SAD.

jolt *v* 1 bounce, bump, jar, jerk, jog, shake. ▷ HIT. 2 astonish, disturb, shake up, shock, startle, stun, surprise.

jostle *v* crowd in on, hustle, press, push, shove.

jot *v* **jot down** note, scribble, take down. ▷ WRITE.

journal *n* 1 daily, gazette, magazine, monthly, newsletter, newspaper, paper, periodical, review, weekly. 2 chronicle, diary, dossier, history, log, memoir, record, scrapbook.

journalist *n* broadcaster, columnist, contributor, correspondent, *derog* hack, *inf* newshound, reporter, writer.

journey *n* excursion, expedition, jaunt, mission, odyssey, outing, pilgrimage, progress, ride, route, tour, *pl* travels, trip, voyage, wandering.
•*v* ▷ TRAVEL.

joy *n* bliss, cheer, cheerfulness, delight, ecstasy, elation, euphoria, exhilaration, exultation, felicity, gaiety, gladness, glee, gratification, happiness, high spirits, joyfulness, jubilation, merriment, mirth, pleasure, rapture, rejoicing, triumph. *Opp* SORROW.

joyful *adj* cheerful, ecstatic, elated, euphoric, exhilarated, exultant, gay, glad, gleeful, joyous, jubilant, merry, overjoyed, pleased, rapturous, rejoicing, triumphant. ▷ HAPPY. *Opp* SAD.

jubilee *n* anniversary, celebration, commemoration, festival.

judge *n* 1 *sl* beak, justice, magistrate. 2 adjudicator, arbiter, arbitrator, moderator, referee, umpire. 3 authority, connoisseur, critic, expert.
•*v* 1 convict, examine, pass judgement on, sentence, try. 2 adjudicate, mediate, referee, umpire. 3 believe, conclude, consider, decide, decree, deem, determine, estimate, gauge, guess, reckon, rule, suppose. 4 appraise, assess, criticize, evaluate, rate, rebuke, scold, size up, weigh up.

judgement *n* 1 arbitration, conclusion, conviction, decision, decree, doom, finding, outcome, result, ruling, verdict. 2 *use your judgement.* common sense, discernment, discretion, discrimination, expertise, reason. ▷ INTELLIGENCE. 3 *in my judgement.* assessment, belief, estimation, evaluation, idea, impression, opinion, point of view.

judicial *adj* 1 forensic, legal, official. 2 ▷ JUDICIOUS.

judicious *adj* appropriate, astute, careful, circumspect, considered, diplomatic, discriminating, enlightened, expedient, judicial, politic, prudent, sensible, shrewd, well-judged. ▷ WISE.

jug *n* carafe, decanter, ewer, flagon, flask, jar, pitcher.

juggle *v* alter, falsify, *inf* fix, manipulate, move about, rearrange, rig.

juice *n* fluid, liquid, sap.

juicy *adj* lush, moist, soft, succulent, wet. *Opp* DRY.

jumble *n* chaos, clutter, confusion, disarray, disorder, *inf* hotchpotch, mess, muddle, tangle.
•*v* confuse, disarrange, disorganize, *inf* mess up, mingle, mix up, muddle, shuffle. *Opp* ARRANGE.

jump *n* 1 bounce, bound, hop, leap, pounce, skip, spring, vault. 2 ditch, fence, gap, gate, hurdle, obstacle. 3 *jump in prices.* ▷ RISE.
•*v* 1 bounce, bound, caper, dance, frisk, frolic, gambol, hop, leap, pounce, prance, skip, spring. 2 *jump a fence.* clear, hurdle, vault. 3 *jump in surprise.* flinch, recoil, start, wince. **jump on** ▷ ATTACK. **make someone jump** ▷ STARTLE.

junction *n* crossroads, interchange, intersection, joining, juncture, *inf* link-up, meeting, T-junction, union.

jungle *n* forest, rainforest, tangle, undergrowth, woods.

junior *adj* inferior, lesser, lower, secondary, subordinate, younger. *Opp* SENIOR.

junk *n* clutter, debris, flotsam and jetsam, garbage, litter, oddments, odds and ends, refuse, rubbish, scrap, trash, waste.

• *v* ▷ DISCARD.

just *adj* apt, deserved, equitable, even-handed, fair, fair-minded, impartial, justified, lawful, legal, legitimate, reasonable, rightful, unbiased, unprejudiced. ▷ MORAL. *Opp* UNJUST.

justice *n* 1 equity, even-handedness, fair play, impartiality, integrity, legality, neutrality, objectivity, right. ▷ MORALITY. 2 amends, reparation, redress.

justifiable *adj* acceptable, defensible, excusable, forgivable, justified, legitimate, pardonable, reasonable, understandable, warranted. *Opp* UNJUSTIFIABLE.

justify *v* condone, defend, excuse, exonerate, explain, explain away, forgive, pardon, rationalize, substantiate, support, sustain, uphold, validate, vindicate, warrant.

jut *v* extend, overhang, project, protrude. *Opp* RECEDE.

juvenile *adj* 1 babyish, childish, immature, infantile, puerile. 2 adolescent, *inf* teenage, underage, young. *Opp* MATURE.

K

keen *adj* 1 ambitious, ardent, assiduous, avid, bright, clever, committed, dedicated, diligent, eager, enthusiastic, fervent, industrious, intelligent, intent, interested, motivated, quick, zealous. 2 *keen knife*. piercing, razor-sharp, sharp, sharpened. 3 *keen wit*. acute, biting, clever, cutting, discerning, incisive, lively, mordant, rapier-like, sarcastic, satirical, scathing, shrewd, stinging. 4 *keen eyesight*. acute, clear, perceptive. 5 *keen wind*. bitter, cold, icy, intense, penetrating, severe. 6 *keen prices*. competitive, low, rock-bottom. *Opp* APATHETIC, DULL.

keep *v* 1 conserve, guard, hang on to, hoard, hold, preserve, protect, put aside, retain, safeguard, save, store, stow away, withhold. 2 *keep going*. carry on, continue, keep on, persevere in, persist in. 3 *keep left*. remain, stay. 4 *keep a family*. be responsible for, care for, cherish, feed, foster, guard, have charge of, look after, maintain, manage, mind, own, protect, provide for, support, tend, watch over. 5 *keep a birthday*. celebrate, commemorate, mark, observe. 6 *food keeps in the fridge*. last, stay fresh. 7 *won't keep you*. delay, detain, deter, get in the way of, hamper, hinder, hold up, impede, obstruct, prevent, restrain. **keep still** ▷ STAY. **keep to** ▷ FOLLOW, OBEY. **keep up** ▷ PROLONG, SUSTAIN.

keeper *n* caretaker, curator, custodian, gaoler, guard, guardian, warden, warder.

kernel *n* centre, core, essence, heart, middle, nub, pith.

key *n* 1 answer, clue, explanation, indicator, pointer, secret, solution. 2 *key to a map*. glossary, guide, index.

kick *v* boot, heel. ▷ HIT.

kidnap *v* abduct, carry off, run away with, seize, snatch.

kill *v* annihilate, assassinate, *sl* bump off, butcher, cull, decimate, destroy, *inf* dispatch, *inf* do away with, *sl* do in, execute, exterminate, *inf* finish off, *inf* knock off, massacre, murder, put down, put to death, put to sleep, slaughter, slay, *inf* snuff out.

killer *n* assassin, butcher, cut-throat, destroyer, executioner, exterminator, gunman, *sl* hit man, murderer, slayer.

killing *n* annihilation, assassination, bloodbath, bloodshed, butchery, carnage, decimation, destruction, elimination, eradication, euthanasia, execution, extermination, extinction, genocide, homicide, infanticide, manslaughter, massacre, murder, pogrom, regicide, slaughter, suicide, unlawful killing.

kin *n* clan, family, *inf* folks, kindred, kith and kin, relations, relatives.

kind *adj* accommodating, affable, affectionate, agreeable, altruistic, amenable, amiable, amicable, approachable, benevolent, benign, bountiful, caring, charitable, compassionate, considerate, cordial, courteous, favourable, friendly, generous, genial, gentle, good-natured, good-tempered, gracious, helpful, hospitable, humane, indulgent, kindly, lenient, loving, merciful, mild, neighbourly, nice, obliging, patient, philanthropic, pleasant, polite, public-spirited, soft-hearted, sweet, sympathetic, tactful, tender, thoughtful, tolerant, understanding, unselfish, warm, warm-hearted, well-intentioned, well-meaning. *Opp* UNKIND. ▪ *n* brand, breed, category, class, family, form, genre, genus, make, manner, nature, race, set, sort, species, style, type, variety.

kindle *v* 1 burn, fire, ignite, light, set alight, set fire to, spark off. 2 ▷ AROUSE.

king *n* 1 monarch, ruler, sovereign. 2 ▷ CHIEF.

kingdom *n* country, empire, land, monarchy, realm.

kink *n* 1 bend, coil, crimp, crinkle, curl, knot, loop, tangle, twist, wave. 2 ▷ QUIRK.

kiosk *n* booth, stall.

kiss *v* brush, caress, *sl* neck, peck, pet, *inf* smack.

kit *n* accoutrements, apparatus, baggage, effects, equipment, *inf* gear, implements, luggage, outfit, paraphernalia, rig, supplies, tackle, tools, utensils.

kitchen *n* cookhouse, galley, kitchenette, scullery.

knack *n* aptitude, art, dexterity, facility, flair, talent, trick, *inf* way. ▷ ABILITY.

knapsack *n* backpack, haversack, rucksack.

knead *v* massage, pound, press, pummel, squeeze, work.

kneel *v* bend, bow, crouch, fall to your knees, genuflect, stoop.

knickers *n* boxer-shorts, briefs, drawers, pants, shorts, trunks, underpants.

knife *n* blade.
•*v* cut, pierce, slash, stab, wound.

knit *v* 1 crochet, weave. 2 bind, combine, fasten, heal, interweave, join, knot, link, marry, mend, tie, unite. **knit your brow** ▷ FROWN.

knob *n* bulge, bump, handle, lump, projection, protuberance, protrusion, swelling.

knock *v* 1 bang, bump, pound, rap, strike, tap, thump. ▷ HIT. 2 ▷ CRITICIZE. **knock down** ▷ DEMOLISH. **knock off** ▷ CEASE. **knock out** ▷ STUN.

knot *n* 1 bow, tangle, tie. 2 ▷ GROUP.
•*v* entangle, entwine, tie, unite. ▷ FASTEN. *Opp* UNTIE.

know *v* 1 be certain, have no doubt. 2 *know facts.* be familiar with, comprehend, have experience of, remember, understand. 3 *know a person.* be acquainted with, be a friend of. 4 discern, distinguish, identify, make out, perceive, realize, recognize, see.

knowing *adj* astute, clever, conspiratorial, discerning, meaningful, perceptive, shrewd. ▷ CUNNING, KNOWLEDGEABLE. *Opp* INNOCENT.

knowledge *n* 1 data, facts, information. 2 acquaintance, awareness, consciousness, erudition, experience, expertise, familiarity, grasp, insight, *inf* know-how, learning, lore, scholarship, skill, training. *Opp* IGNORANCE.

knowledgeable *adj Fr* au fait, aware, conversant, educated, erudite, experienced, expert, familiar (with), learned, scholarly, versed (in), well-informed. *Opp* IGNORANT.

L

label *n* hallmark, identification, logo, marker, sticker, tag, ticket, trademark.
• *v* brand, call, categorize, class, classify, define, identify, mark, name, pigeonhole, stamp, tag.

laborious *adj* 1 arduous, back-breaking, difficult, exhausting, gruelling, hard, heavy, herculean, onerous, strenuous, taxing, tough, uphill, wearisome, wearying. *Opp* EASY. 2 *laborious style.* contrived, forced, laboured, overdone, overworked, ponderous, strained. *Opp* FLUENT.

labour *n* 1 *inf* donkey work, drudgery, effort, exertion, industry, *inf* pains, toil, work. 2 employees, *old use* hands, workers, workforce. 3 childbirth, contractions, delivery, labour pains.
• *v inf* slave, struggle, sweat, toil. ▷ WORK. **laboured** ▷ LABORIOUS.

labourer *n* employee, *old use* hand, manual worker, *inf* navvy, wage-earner, worker.

labour-saving *adj* convenient, handy, helpful, time-saving.

labyrinth *n* complex, jungle, maze, network, tangle.

lace *n* 1 filigree, mesh, net, openwork, web. 2 cord, shoelace, string, thong.
• *v* ▷ FASTEN.

lacerate *v* claw, gash, mangle, rip, scratch, slash, tear.

lack *n* absence, dearth, deficiency, insufficiency, need, paucity, privation, scarcity, shortage, want. *Opp* PLENTY.
• *v* be short of, be without, miss, need, require, want.

lacking *adj* defective, deficient, inadequate, short, wanting. ▷ STUPID.

laden *adj* burdened, full, hampered, loaded, piled high, weighed down.

lady *n* 1 wife, woman. 2 aristocrat, peeress.

ladylike *adj* aristocratic, cultured, elegant, genteel, refined, well-bred. ▷ POLITE.

lag *v* 1 be slow, dally, dawdle, delay, fall behind, go too slow, hang back, idle, linger, loiter, saunter, straggle, trail. 2 *lag pipes.* insulate, wrap up.

lair *n* den, hiding-place, refuge, retreat, shelter.

lake *n* lagoon, lido, loch, mere, pool, reservoir, sea.

lame *adj* 1 crippled, disabled, hobbling, incapacitated, limping, maimed. 2 *lame leg.* dragging, game, *inf* gammy, injured, stiff. 3 *lame excuse.* feeble, flimsy, inadequate, poor, tame, thin, unconvincing, weak.
• *v* cripple, disable, hobble, incapacitate, maim. **be lame** ▷ LIMP.

lament *n* dirge, elegy, lamentation, moaning, mourning, requiem.
• *v* bemoan, complain, cry, deplore, grieve, keen, mourn, regret, shed tears, sorrow, wail, weep.

lamentable *adj* deplorable, regrettable. ▷ SAD.

lamentation *n* crying, grief, grieving, moaning, mourning, regrets, tears, wailing, weeping.

lamp *n* headlamp, lantern, light, standard lamp, street light, torch.

land *n* 1 coast, ground, shore, *joc* terra firma. 2 *lie of the land.* geography, landscape, terrain, topography. 3 country, homeland, nation, region, state, territory. 4 earth, farmland, soil. 5 estate, grounds, property.
• *v* 1 alight, arrive, berth, come ashore, come to rest, disembark, dock, go ashore, settle, touch down. 2 *land a job.* ▷ GET.

landing *n* 1 docking, re-entry, return, touchdown. 2 alighting, arrival, disembarkation. 3 ▷ LANDING STAGE.

landing stage *n* berth, dock, jetty, pier, quay, wharf.

landlady, landlord *ns* 1 host, hostess, hotelier, *old use* innkeeper, licensee, publican, restaurateur. 2 landowner, letter, owner, proprietor.

landmark *n* 1 feature, high point. 2 milestone, turning point, watershed.

landscape *n* countryside, panorama, prospect, scene, scenery, terrain, view, vista.

language *n* 1 dialect, jargon, parlance, speech, tongue, vernacular. 2 linguistics. 3 *computer language.* code, system of signs.

languid *adj* apathetic, *inf* droopy, feeble, inactive, lazy, lethargic, slow, sluggish, torpid, unenthusiastic. *Opp* ENERGETIC.

languish *v* decline, flag, lose momentum, mope, pine, stagnate, suffer, waste away, wither. *Opp* FLOURISH.

lank *adj* 1 drooping, lifeless, limp. 2 ▷ LANKY.

lanky *adj* angular, bony, gaunt, lank, lean, long, scraggy, scrawny, skinny, tall, thin, weedy. *Opp* STURDY.

lap *n* circuit, course, orbit, revolution.
• *v* ▷ DRINK.

lapse *n* 1 blunder, error, failing, fault, mistake, omission, relapse, shortcoming, slip, *inf* slip-up, temporary failure. 2 break, gap, hiatus, *inf* hold-up, interruption, interval, lull, pause.
• *v* 1 decline, deteriorate, drop, fall, sink, slide, slip. 2 become invalid, expire, finish, run out.

large *adj* above average, abundant, ample, big, bold, broad, bulky, capacious, colossal, considerable, copious, enormous, extensive, fat, formidable, generous, giant, gigantic, great, heavy, hefty, high, huge, immense, impressive, *inf* jumbo, *inf* king-sized, lofty, long, mammoth, massive, mighty, monumental, outsize, overgrown, oversized, prodigious, roomy, sizeable, spacious, substantial, tall, thick, *inf* tidy (*sum*), titanic, towering, *inf* tremendous, vast, voluminous, weighty, *inf* whopping, wide. *Opp* SMALL.

larva *n* caterpillar, grub.

lash *n* ▷ WHIP.
• *v* 1 cane, flog, scourge, thrash, whip. ▷ HIT. 2 ▷ CRITICIZE.

last *adj* closing, concluding, final, furthest, hindmost, latest, most recent, rearmost, ultimate. *Opp* FIRST.
• *v* carry on, continue, endure, hold out, keep on, linger, live, persist, remain, stay, survive, *inf* wear well. *Opp* DIE, FINISH. **lasting** ▷ PERMANENT.

late *adj* 1 belated, delayed, overdue, slow, tardy, unpunctual. 2 *the late king.* dead, deceased, departed, ex-, former, past, previous.

latent *adj* dormant, hidden, invisible, potential, undeveloped, undiscovered.

latitude *n* freedom, leeway. ▷ SCOPE.

latter *adj* closing, concluding, last, last-mentioned, later, recent, second. *Opp* FORMER.

lattice *n* framework, grid, mesh, trellis.

laugh *v* chortle, chuckle, *sl* fall about, giggle, guffaw, roar with laughter, simper, smirk, sneer, snicker, snigger, titter. **laugh at** ▷ RIDICULE.

laughable *adj* derisory, ludicrous, ridiculous. ▷ FUNNY.

laughter *n* chuckling, giggling, guffawing, hilarity, *inf* hysterics, merriment, mirth, sniggering. ▷ RIDICULE.

launch *v* 1 begin, embark on, establish, found, inaugurate, initiate, open, set in motion, set up, start. 2 catapult, fire, propel, send off, set off, shoot.

lavatory *n* bathroom, cloakroom, convenience, *inf* Gents, *inf* Ladies, latrine, *inf* loo, *inf* men's room, public convenience, toilet, urinal, WC, *inf* women's room.

lavish *adj* 1 abundant, bountiful, copious, generous, liberal, luxuriant, munificent, opulent, plentiful, profuse, sumptuous, unselfish, unsparing, unstinting. 2 excessive, extravagant, prodigal, self-indulgent, wasteful. *Opp* ECONOMICAL.

law *n* 1 act, commandment, decree, directive, edict, injunction, mandate, measure, order, ordinance, regulation, rule, statute. 2 code, convention, practice. 3 *law of science.* formula, principle, proposition, theory.

law-abiding *adj* decent, good, honest, obedient, orderly, peaceable, peaceful, respectable, well-behaved. *Opp* LAWLESS.

lawful *adj* allowable, allowed, authorized, just, justifiable, legal, legitimate, permitted, proper, recognized, regular, right, rightful, valid. *Opp* ILLEGAL.

lawless *adj* anarchic, chaotic, disobedient, disorderly, insubordinate, mutinous, rebellious, rowdy, turbulent, uncontrolled, undisciplined, unrestrained, unruly, wild. ▷ WICKED. *Opp* LAW-ABIDING.

lawlessness *n* anarchy, chaos, disorder, mob-rule, rebellion, rioting. *Opp* ORDER.

lawyer *n* advocate, barrister, counsel, legal representative, solicitor.

lax *adj* careless, casual, easygoing, lenient, loose, negligent, permissive, remiss, slack, slipshod, unreliable, vague. *Opp* STRICT.

laxative *n* purgative, purge.

lay *v* 1 apply, arrange, deposit, leave, place, position, put down, rest, set down, set out, spread. 2 *lay foundations.* build, construct, establish. 3 *lay the blame on me.* assign, attribute, burden, plant, *inf* saddle. 4 *lay plans.* concoct, create, design, organize, plan, set up. **lay bare** ▷ REVEAL. **lay bets** ▷ GAMBLE. **lay by** ▷ STORE. **lay down the law** ▷ DICTATE. **lay in** ▷ STORE. **lay into** ▷ ATTACK. **lay low** ▷ DEFEAT. **lay off something** ▷ CEASE. **lay someone off** ▷ DISMISS.

lay to rest ▷ BURY. **lay up** ▷ STORE. **lay waste** ▷ DESTROY.

layer *n* 1 coat, coating, covering, film, sheet, skin, surface, thickness. 2 *layer of rock*. seam, stratum. **in layers** laminated, layered, sandwiched, stratified.

layman *n* 1 amateur, nonspecialist, untrained person. *Opp* PROFESSIONAL. 2 [*church*] layperson, member of the congregation, parishioner. *Opp* CLERGYMAN.

laze *v* do nothing, idle, lie about, loaf, lounge, relax, unwind.

laziness *n* idleness, inactivity, indolence, lethargy, sloth, sluggishness, torpor. *Opp* INDUSTRY.

lazy *adj* 1 idle, inactive, indolent, languid, lethargic, listless, shiftless, *sl* skiving, slack, slothful, slow, sluggish, torpid, work-shy. 2 peaceful, quiet, relaxing. *Opp* ENERGETIC, INDUSTRIOUS. **be lazy** ▷ LAZE. **lazy person** ▷ SLACKER.

lead *n* 1 direction, example, guidance, leadership. 2 *lead on a crime*. clue, hint, line, tip, tip-off. 3 *in the lead*. first place, front, vanguard. 4 *lead in a play*. chief part, hero, heroine, protagonist, starring role, title role. 5 cable, flex, wire. 6 *dog's lead*. chain, leash, strap.
• *v* 1 conduct, draw, escort, guide, influence, pilot, prompt, show the way, steer, usher. 2 be in charge of, captain, command, direct, govern, head, manage, preside over, rule, supervise. 3 be in front, excel, go first, head the field, outdo, outstrip, surpass. *Opp* FOLLOW. **lead astray** ▷ MISLEAD. **leading** ▷ CHIEF, INFLUENTIAL. **lead off** ▷ BEGIN.

leader *n* 1 ayatollah, captain, commander, conductor, director, figure-head, *inf* godfather, guide, head, patriarch, premier, prime minister, ringleader, superior. ▷ CHIEF, RULER. 2 *leader in a newspaper*. editorial, leading article.

leaf *n* 1 *pl* foliage, frond, *pl* greenery. 2 folio, page, sheet.

leaflet *n* advertisement, booklet, brochure, circular, flyer, handbill, notice, pamphlet.

league *n* alliance, association, coalition, confederation, guild, society, union. ▷ GROUP. **be in league with** ▷ CONSPIRE.

leak *n* 1 discharge, drip, emission, escape, leakage, oozing, seepage, trickle. 2 chink, crack, crevice, fissure, flaw, hole, opening, perforation, puncture. 3 *security leak*. disclosure, revelation.
• *v* 1 discharge, drip, escape, exude, ooze, seep, spill, trickle. 2 *leak secrets*. disclose, divulge, give away, let out, let slip, pass on, reveal, *inf* spill the beans.

leaky *adj* cracked, dripping, perforated, punctured.

lean *adj* angular, bony, emaciated, gaunt, lanky, long, rangy, skinny, slender, slim, spare, thin, wiry. *Opp* FAT.
• *v* 1 bank, incline, keel over, list, slant, slope, tilt, tip. 2 loll, recline, rest, support yourself.

leaning *n* bent, bias, inclination, instinct, liking, partiality, penchant, preference, propensity, taste, tendency, trend.

leap *v* 1 bound, hop over, hurdle, jump, skip over, spring, vault. 2 caper, dance, frolic, gambol, hop, prance. 3 *leap on someone*. ambush, attack, pounce.

learn *v* acquire, ascertain, become aware of, be taught, *inf* catch on, discover, find out, gain, gather, grasp, master, memorize, *inf* mug up, pick up, remember, study, *inf* swot up. **learned** ▷ ACADEMIC, EDUCATED.

learner *n* apprentice, beginner, cadet, novice, pupil, starter, student, trainee.

learning *n* culture, education, erudition, information, knowledge, lore, scholarship, wisdom.

lease *n* agreement, contract.
• *v* charter, hire out, let, rent out, sublet.

least *adj* fewest, lowest, minimum, negligible, slightest, smallest, tiniest.

leave *n* 1 authorization, consent, dispensation, liberty, permission, sanction. 2 *leave from work*. absence, free time, holiday, sabbatical, time off, vacation.
• *v* 1 *inf* be off, *inf* check out, decamp, depart, disappear, escape, go away, go out, *sl* hop it, *inf* pull out, retire, retreat, run away, say goodbye, set off, *inf* take off, take your leave, vacate, withdraw. 2 abandon, desert, forsake. 3 *leave your job*. *inf* chuck in, *inf* drop out, give up, quit, relinquish, resign from, retire from, *inf* walk out. 4 *leave it as it is*. *inf* let alone, let be. 5 *leave it here*. deposit, place, put down. 6 *I left my keys somewhere*. forget, lose, mislay. 7 *leave it to me*. consign, entrust, refer, relinquish. 8 *leave in a will*. bequeath, hand down, will. **leave off** ▷ STOP. **leave out** ▷ OMIT.

lecture *n* 1 address, discourse, lesson, paper, speech, talk, treatise. 2 *lecture on bad manners*. diatribe, harangue, sermon. ▷ REPRIMAND.
• *v* 1 discourse, harangue, *inf* hold forth, pontificate, preach, speak. 2 ▷ REPRIMAND.

lecturer *n* don, fellow, professor, speaker, teacher, tutor.

ledge *n* mantel, ridge, shelf, sill, step, window-sill.

left *adj, n* 1 left-hand, port [= *left facing bow of ship*]. 2 *left wing in politics.* communist, Labour, liberal, progressive, radical, *derog* red, revolutionary, socialist. *Opp* RIGHT.

leg *n* 1 limb, *inf* peg, *inf* pin, shank. 2 prop, support, upright. 3 *leg of a journey.* lap, part, section, stage, stretch. **pull someone's leg** ▷ HOAX.

legacy *n* bequest, endowment, estate, inheritance.

legal *adj* 1 above-board, admissible, allowable, allowed, authorized, just, lawful, licensed, permitted, permissible, proper, regular, rightful, valid. *Opp* ILLEGAL. 2 *legal proceedings.* judicial, judiciary.

legalize *v* allow, authorize, legitimize, license, permit, regularize, validate. *Opp* BAN.

legend *n* epic, folk tale, myth, saga, story, tradition.

legendary *adj* 1 apocryphal, fabled, fabulous, fictional, fictitious, imaginary, mythical, non-existent. 2 *legendary name.* ▷ FAMOUS.

legible *adj* clear, decipherable, distinct, neat, plain, readable. *Opp* ILLEGIBLE.

legitimate *adj* 1 authentic, genuine, proper, true. ▷ LEGAL. 2 ethical, just, justifiable, moral, proper, reasonable, right. *Opp* ILLEGITIMATE.

leisure *n* ease, freedom, holiday, liberty, quiet, recreation, relaxation, repose, respite, rest, spare time.

leisurely *adj* easy, gentle, lingering, peaceful, relaxed, relaxing, restful, unhurried. ▷ SLOW. *Opp* BRISK.

lend *v* advance, loan. *Opp* BORROW.

length *n* 1 distance, extent, measurement, mileage, reach, size. 2 duration, period, stretch, term.

lengthen *v* continue, drag out, draw out, elongate, expand, extend, increase, *inf* pad out, prolong, protract, pull out, stretch. *Opp* SHORTEN.

lenient *adj* easygoing, forbearing, forgiving, indulgent, merciful, mild, soft, soft-hearted, sparing, tolerant. ▷ KIND. *Opp* STRICT.

less *adj* fewer, reduced, shorter, smaller. *Opp* MORE.

lessen *v* 1 assuage, cut, deaden, decrease, ease, lighten, lower, minimize, mitigate, reduce, relieve, tone down. 2 abate, decline, die away, diminish, dwindle, ease off, let up, moderate, slacken, subside, tail off, weaken. *Opp* INCREASE.

lesson *n* 1 class, drill, instruction, lecture, practical, seminar, session, task, teaching, tutorial. 2 example, moral, warning.

let *v* 1 agree to, allow, consent to, give permission to, permit, sanction. 2 charter, contract out, hire, lease, rent. **let alone, let be** ▷ LEAVE. **let go, let loose** ▷ LIBERATE. **let off** ▷ FIRE. **let out** ▷ LIBERATE. **let someone off** ▷ ACQUIT. **let up** ▷ LESSEN.

letdown *n* anti-climax, disappointment, *inf* wash-out.

lethal *adj* deadly, fatal, mortal, poisonous.

lethargic *adj* apathetic, heavy, inactive, indolent, languid, lazy, listless, phlegmatic, sleepy, slow, sluggish, torpid. ▷ WEARY. *Opp* ENERGETIC.

lethargy *n* apathy, inactivity, indolence, inertia, laziness, listlessness, sluggishness, torpor, weariness. *Opp* ENERGY.

letter *n* 1 character, consonant, vowel. 2 card, communication, dispatch, epistle, message, missive, note, postcard. **letters** correspondence, mail, post.

level *adj* 1 even, flat, flush, horizontal, plane, regular, smooth, straight, true, uniform. 2 *level scores.* balanced, even, equal, *inf* neck-and-neck, the same. *Opp* UNEVEN.

• *n* 1 altitude, depth, elevation, height, value. 2 degree, echelon, grade, position, rank, *inf* rung on the ladder, stage, standard, standing, status. 3 *level in a building.* floor, storey.

• *v* 1 even out, flatten, rake, smooth. 2 bulldoze, demolish, destroy, devastate, knock down, lay low, raze, wreck. **level-headed** ▷ SENSIBLE.

lever *v* force, prise, wrench.

liable *adj* 1 accountable, answerable, responsible. 2 apt, disposed, inclined, in the habit of, likely, minded, predisposed, prone, ready, susceptible, tempted, willing.

liaison *n* 1 communication, contact, cooperation, mediation, tie. 2 ▷ AFFAIR.

liar *n* deceiver, *inf* fibber, perjurer, *inf* story-teller.

libel *n* defamation, insult, lie, misrepresentation, slander, slur, smear, vilification. • *v* defame, denigrate, disparage, malign, misrepresent, slander, slur, smear, write lies about, vilify.

libellous *adj* cruel, damaging, defamatory, disparaging, false, insulting, lying, malicious, scurrilous, slanderous, untrue, vicious.

liberal *adj* 1 abundant, ample, bounteous, bountiful, copious, free, generous, lavish, munificent, open-handed, plentiful, unstinting. 2 *liberal attitudes.* broad-minded, charitable, easygoing, enlightened, fair-minded, humanitarian, indulgent, lenient, magnanimous, open-minded, permissive, tolerant, unbiased, unprejudiced. *Opp* NARROW-MINDED. 3 *liberal politics.* progressive, radical, reformist. *Opp* CONSERVATIVE.

liberalize *v* ease, make more liberal, open up, relax, soften, widen.

liberate *v* discharge, emancipate, enfranchise, free, let go, let loose, let out, release, rescue, save, set free, untie. *Opp* CAPTURE, SUBJUGATE.

liberty *n* autonomy, emancipation, independence, liberation, release. ▷ FREEDOM. **at liberty** ▷ FREE.

licence *n* 1 certificate, document, papers, permit, warrant. 2 ▷ FREEDOM.

license *v* 1 allow, authorize, certify, entitle, give a licence to, permit, sanction. 2 buy a licence for, make legal.

lid *n* cap, cover, covering, top.

lie *n* deceit, dishonesty, disinformation, fabrication, falsehood, falsification, *inf* fib, fiction, invention, untruth, *inf* whopper. *Opp* TRUTH.
• *v* 1 *inf* be economical with the truth, bluff, falsify the facts, *inf* fib, perjure yourself, tell lies. 2 be recumbent, lean back, lounge, recline, repose, rest, sprawl, stretch out. 3 be, be found, be located, be situated. **lie low** ▷ HIDE.

life *n* 1 being, existence, living. 2 activity, animation, energy, enthusiasm, exuberance, *inf* go, liveliness, sparkle, spirit, verve, vigour, vitality, vivacity, zest. 3 autobiography, biography, memoir, story.

lifeless *adj* 1 comatose, dead, deceased, inanimate, inert, insensible, motionless, unconscious. 2 *lifeless desert.* arid, bare, barren, desolate, empty, sterile, waste. 3 *lifeless performance.* apathetic, boring, dull, flat, lacklustre, lethargic, slow, unexciting, wooden. *Opp* LIVELY, LIVING.

lifelike *adj* authentic, convincing, faithful, natural, photographic, realistic, true-to-life, vivid. *Opp* UNREALISTIC.

lift *n* elevator, hoist.
• *v* 1 buoy up, carry, elevate, hoist, pick up, pull up, raise, rear. 2 ascend, fly, lift off, rise, soar. 3 boost, cheer, enhance, improve. 4 ▷ STEAL.

light *adj* 1 lightweight, portable, weightless. *Opp* HEAVY. 2 bright, illuminated, lit-up, well-lit. *Opp* DARK. 3 *light work.* ▷ EASY. 4 *light wind.* ▷ GENTLE. 5 *light touch.* ▷ DELICATE. 6 *light colours.* ▷ PALE. 7 *light heart.* ▷ CHEERFUL. 8 *light traffic.* ▷ SPARSE.
• *n* 1 beam, blaze, brightness, brilliance, flare, flash, glare, gleam, glint, glitter, glow, halo, illumination, incandescence, luminosity, lustre, radiance, ray, reflection, shine, sparkle, twinkle. 2 beacon, candle, lamp, lantern, torch.
• *v* 1 fire, ignite, kindle, put a match to, set alight, set fire to, switch on. *Opp* EXTINGUISH. 2 ▷ LIGHTEN. **bring to light** ▷ DISCOVER. **give light, reflect light** be luminous, blaze, dazzle, flash, flicker, glare, gleam, glimmer, glint, glisten, glitter, glow, radiate, reflect, scintillate, shimmer, shine, spark, sparkle, twinkle. **light-headed** ▷ DIZZY. **light-hearted** ▷ CHEERFUL. **light up** ▷ LIGHTEN. **shed light on** ▷ EXPLAIN.

lighten *v* 1 cast light on, floodlight, illuminate, irradiate, light up, shed light on, shine on. 2 become lighter, brighten, cheer up, clear. 3 ▷ LESSEN.

lighthouse *n* beacon, light, lightship, warning-light.

like *adj* akin to, analogous to, close to, comparable to, corresponding to, equal to, equivalent to, identical to, parallel to, similar to.
• *v* admire, approve of, appreciate, be attracted to, be fond of, be interested in, be keen on, be partial to, delight in, enjoy, *sl* go for, *inf* go in for, *inf* have a weakness for, prefer, relish, revel in, take pleasure in, *inf* take to, welcome. ▷ LOVE. *Opp* HATE.

likeable *adj* admirable, attractive, charming, congenial, endearing, interesting, lovable, nice, personable, pleasant, pleasing. ▷ FRIENDLY. *Opp* HATEFUL.

likelihood *n* chance, hope, possibility, probability, prospect.

likely *adj* 1 anticipated, expected, feasible, foreseeable, plausible, possible, predictable, probable, unsurprising. 2 *likely candidate.* acceptable, appropriate, convincing, favourite, hopeful, promising, qualified, suitable. 3 *likely to help.* apt, disposed, inclined, liable, prone, ready, tempted, willing. *Opp* UNLIKELY.

liken *v* ▷ COMPARE.

likeness *n* 1 affinity, analogy, compatibility, correspondence, resemblance, similarity. *Opp* DIFFERENCE. 2 copy, drawing, duplicate, image, model, picture, portrait, replica, representation, reproduction.

liking *n* affection, affinity, appetite, eye, fondness, inclination, partiality, penchant, predilection, predisposition, preference, propensity, *inf* soft spot, taste, weakness. ▷ LOVE. *Opp* HATRED.

limb *n* appendage, member, offshoot, projection.

limber *v* **limber up** exercise, loosen up, prepare, warm up.

limbo *n* **in limbo** abandoned, forgotten, left out, neglected, neither one thing nor the other, *inf* on hold, unattached.

limit *n* 1 border, boundary, bounds, brink, confines, demarcation line, edge, end, extent, frontier, perimeter. 2 ceiling, check, curb, cut-off point, limitation, maximum, restraint, restriction, stop, threshold.
• *v* circumscribe, confine, control, curb, define, fix, hold in check, ration, restrain, restrict. **limited** ▷ FINITE, INADEQUATE.

limitation *n* 1 ▷ LIMIT. 2 defect, deficiency, fault, inadequacy, shortcoming, weakness.

limitless *adj* boundless, countless, endless, immeasurable, incalculable, inexhaustible, infinite, innumerable, never-ending, perpetual, renewable, unbounded, unconfined, unending, unimaginable, unlimited, unrestricted. ▷ VAST. *Opp* FINITE.

limp *adj inf* bendy, drooping, flaccid, *inf* floppy, loose, sagging, slack, soft, weak, wilting. ▷ WEARY. *Opp* RIGID.
• *v* be lame, hobble, hop.

line *n* 1 band, borderline, boundary, contour, mark, streak, strip, stripe, stroke, trail. 2 corrugation, crease, fold, furrow, groove, wrinkle. 3 cable, cord, flex, hawser, lead, rope, string, thread, wire. 4 chain, column, cordon, crocodile, file, procession, queue, rank, row, series. 5 *railway line*. route, service, track.
• *v* 1 rule, score, streak, underline. 2 *line the street*. border, edge, fringe. **line up** ▷ ALIGN, QUEUE.

linger *v* dally, dawdle, delay, dither, endure, hang about, hover, idle, lag, last, loiter, pause, persist, remain, *inf* shilly-shally, stay, stay behind, survive, wait about. *Opp* HURRY.

link *n* 1 bond, connection, coupling, join, joint, tie, yoke. ▷ FASTENER. 2 affiliation, alliance, association, communication, liaison, partnership, relationship, *inf* tie-up, union.
• *v* 1 amalgamate, associate, attach, compare, connect, couple, interlink, join, juxtapose, merge, relate, unite, yoke. ▷ FASTEN.

lip *n* brim, brink, edge, rim.

liquefy *v* become liquid, dissolve, liquidize, melt, run, thaw. *Opp* SOLIDIFY.

liquid *adj* aqueous, flowing, fluid, liquefied, molten, running, *inf* runny, sloppy, *inf* sloshy, thin, watery, wet, *Opp* SOLID.
• *n* fluid, juice, liquid, solution.

liquidate *v* annihilate, destroy, *inf* get rid of, remove, silence, wipe out. ▷ KILL.

liquor *n* 1 alcohol, *inf* booze, *sl* hard stuff, spirits, strong drink. 2 ▷ LIQUID.

list *n* catalogue, column, directory, file, index, inventory, register, roll, roster, rota, schedule.
• *v* 1 catalogue, enumerate, file, index, itemize, note, record, register, write down. 2 bank, incline, keel over, lean, slant, slope, tilt, tip.

listen *v* attend, concentrate, eavesdrop, hear, heed, *inf* keep your ears open, overhear, pay attention, take notice.

listless *adj* apathetic, enervated, feeble, heavy, languid, lazy, lethargic, lifeless, phlegmatic, sluggish, tired, torpid, unenthusiastic, uninterested, weak. ▷ WEARY. *Opp* LIVELY.

literal *adj* exact, faithful, matter of fact, strict, unimaginative, verbatim, word for word.

literary *adj* 1 cultured, educated, erudite, imaginative, learned, refined, scholarly, well-read. 2 *literary style*. ornate, poetic, polished, rhetorical, *derog* self-conscious.

literate *adj* cultured, educated, learned, well-read.

literature *n* books, brochures, circulars, creative writing, handbills, leaflets, pamphlets, papers, writings.

lithe *adj* agile, flexible, lissom, loose-jointed, pliable, pliant, supple. *Opp* STIFF.

litter *n* bits and pieces, clutter, debris, garbage, jumble, junk, mess, odds and ends, refuse, rubbish, trash, waste.
• *v* clutter, *inf* mess up, scatter, strew.

little *adj* 1 *inf* baby, bantam, diminutive, *inf* dinky, dwarf, infinitesimal, microscopic, midget, *inf* mini, miniature, minuscule, minute, petite, *inf* pint-sized, *inf* pocket-sized, *inf* poky, pygmy, short, slight, small, *inf* teeny, tiny, toy, undersized, *inf* wee, *inf* weeny. *Opp* BIG. 2 *little helping*. inadequate, insufficient, meagre, *inf* measly, miserly, modest, *inf* piddling, scanty, skimpy, stingy. 3 *of little importance*. inconsequential, insignificant, minor, negligible, slight, trifling, trivial, unimportant.

live *adj* 1 ▷ LIVING. 2 *live fire*. ▷ ALIGHT. 3 *live issue*. contemporary, current, important, pressing, relevant, topical, vital. *Opp* DEAD.
• *v* 1 breathe, continue, endure, exist, function, last, remain, stay alive, survive. *Opp* DIE. 2 dwell, lodge, reside, room, stay. 3 *live on £20 a week*. fare, *inf* get along, keep going, pay the bills, subsist. **live in** ▷ INHABIT. **live on** ▷ EAT.

liveliness *n* activity, animation, bustle, dynamism, energy, enthusiasm, exuberance, *inf* go, gusto, high spirits, spirit, verve, vigour, vitality, vivacity, zeal. *Opp* APATHY.

lively *adj* active, alert, animated, boisterous, bubbly, busy, cheerful, colourful, dashing, eager, energetic, enthusiastic, exciting, exuberant, frisky, gay, high-spirited, irrepressible, jaunty, jazzy, jolly, merry, *inf* perky, playful, quick, spirited, sprightly, stimulating, vigorous, vital, vivacious, vivid. ▷ HAPPY. *Opp* APATHETIC.

livestock *n* cattle, farm animals.

living *adj* active, actual, alive, animate, breathing, existing, extant, flourishing, functioning, live, *old use* quick, sentient, surviving. ▷ LIVELY. *Opp* DEAD, EXTINCT.
• *n* income, livelihood, occupation, subsistence, way of life.

load *n* 1 burden, cargo, consignment, freight, shipment. 2 anxiety, care, *inf* cross, millstone, onus, trouble, weight, worry.
• *v* 1 burden, encumber, fill, heap, pack, pile, saddle, stack, stow, weigh down. 2 *load a gun*. charge, prime. **loaded** ▷ BIASED, LADEN, WEALTHY.

loafer *n* idler, *inf* good-for-nothing, layabout, *inf* lazybones, shirker, *sl* skiver.

loan *n* advance, credit, mortgage.
• *v* advance, lend.

loathe *v* abhor, abominate, be revolted by, despise, detest, dislike, find intolerable, hate, recoil from, resent, scorn, shudder at. *Opp* LOVE.

lobby *n* 1 ante-room, entrance hall, entry, foyer, hall, hallway, porch, reception. 2 *environmental lobby*. campaign, campaigners, pressure group, supporters.
• *v* petition, pressurize, try to influence, urge.

local *adj* 1 adjacent, adjoining, nearby, neighbouring. 2 *local politics*. community, neighbourhood, parochial, particular, provincial, regional. *Opp* GENERAL, NATIONAL.
• *n* 1 inhabitant, resident. 2 [*inf*] ▷ PUB.

locality *n* area, community, district, location, neighbourhood, parish, region, town, vicinity, zone.

localize *v* concentrate, confine, contain, enclose, keep within bounds, limit, narrow down, pin down, restrict. *Opp* SPREAD.

locate *v* 1 detect, discover, find, identify, *inf* lay your hands on, track down, unearth. 2 build, establish, find a place for, place, position, put, set up, site, situate, station.

location *n* 1 locale, locality, place, point, position, site, situation, spot, venue, whereabouts. 2 *film location*. background, scene, setting.

lock *n* bar, bolt, catch, clasp, fastening, hasp, latch, padlock.
• *v* bolt, close, fasten, padlock, seal, secure, shut. **lock away** ▷ IMPRISON. **lock out** ▷ EXCLUDE. **lock up** ▷ IMPRISON.

lodge *n* cabin, chalet, cottage, house, hut, shelter.
• *v* 1 accommodate, billet, board, house, *inf* put up. 2 dwell, live, *inf* put up, reside, stay, stop. 3 *lodge a complaint*. enter, file, put on record, register, submit.

lodger *n* boarder, guest, inmate, paying guest, resident, tenant.

lodgings *n* accommodation, apartment, billet, boarding house, *inf* digs, *inf* pad, quarters, rooms, shelter.

lofty *adj* 1 elevated, high, imposing, majestic, noble, soaring, tall, towering. 2 ▷ ARROGANT.

log *n* 1 timber, wood. 2 account, diary, journal, record.

logic *n* clarity, logical thinking, rationality, reasoning, sense, validity.

logical *adj* clear, cogent, coherent, consistent, intelligent, methodical, rational, reasonable, sensible, sound, structured, systematic, valid, well-reasoned, well-thought-out, wise. *Opp* ILLOGICAL.

loiter *v* dally, dawdle, hang back, linger, loaf about, *inf* mess about, skulk, stand about, straggle.

lone *adj* isolated, separate, single, solitary, solo, unaccompanied. ▷ LONELY.

lonely *adj* 1 abandoned, alone, forlorn, forsaken, friendless, outcast, reclusive, retiring, solitary, withdrawn. ▷ SAD. 2 *inf* cut off, deserted, desolate, isolated, *inf* off the beaten track, out of the way, remote, secluded, unfrequented, uninhabited.

long *adj* drawn out, elongated, endless, extended, extensive, interminable, lasting, lengthy, prolonged, protracted, slow, stretched, sustained, time-consuming, unending.
• *v* crave, desire, hanker, have a longing (for), hunger, itch, pine, thirst, wish, yearn. **long-lasting, long-lived** ▷ PERMANENT. **long-standing** ▷ OLD. **long-suffering** ▷ PATIENT. **long-winded** ▷ TEDIOUS.

longing *n* appetite, craving, desire, hankering, hunger, itch, need, thirst, urge, wish, yearning, *inf* yen.

look *n* 1 gaze, glance, glimpse, peek, peep, *inf* squint, view. 2 air, appearance, aspect, bearing, complexion, countenance, demeanour, expression, face, looks, manner, mien.
• *v* 1 behold, *inf* cast your eye, consider, contemplate, examine, eye, gape, *inf* gawp, gaze, glance, glimpse, goggle, inspect, observe, ogle, peek, peep, peer, read, regard, scan, scrutinize, skim through, squint, stare, study, survey, view, watch. 2 *The windows look south.* face, overlook. 3 *look pleased.* appear, seem. **look after** ▷ TEND. **look down on** ▷ DESPISE. **look for** ▷ SEEK. **look into** ▷ INVESTIGATE. **look out** ▷ BEWARE. **look up to** ▷ ADMIRE.

lookout *n* guard, sentry.

loom *v* arise, appear, emerge, hover, materialize, menace, rise, stand out, take shape, threaten, tower.

loop *n* bend, bow, circle, coil, curl, eye, hoop, kink, noose, ring, turn, twist, whorl.
• *v* bend, coil, curl, entwine, make a loop, turn, twist, wind.

loophole *n* escape, *inf* get-out, *inf* let-out, outlet, way out.

loose *adj* 1 detached, disconnected, insecure, loosened, movable, scattered, shaky, unattached, unconnected, unfastened, unsteady, wobbly. 2 *loose animals.* at large, escaped, free, released, roaming, uncaged, unconfined, unrestricted, untied. 3 *loose hair.* hanging, spread out, straggling, trailing. 4 *loose clothing.* baggy, *inf* floppy, loose-fitting. 5 *loose agreement, translation.* broad, careless, casual, diffuse, general, ill-defined, imprecise, inexact, informal, lax, rambling, rough, *inf* sloppy, vague. *Opp* PRECISE, SECURE, TIGHT. 6 ▷ IMMORAL.
• *v* ▷ FREE, LOOSEN.

loosen *v* 1 free, let go, loose, relax, release, slacken, unfasten, untie. ▷ UNDO. 2 become loose, come adrift. *Opp* TIGHTEN.

loot *n* booty, contraband, haul, *inf* ill-gotten gains, plunder, prize, spoils, *inf* swag, takings.
• *v* pillage, plunder, raid, ransack, rob, steal from.

lopsided *adj* askew, asymmetrical, awry, crooked, tilting, uneven.

lord *n* aristocrat, noble, peer.

lose *v* 1 be deprived of, drop, forfeit, forget, leave (somewhere), mislay, misplace, miss, stray from. *Opp* FIND. 2 be defeated, capitulate, fail, succumb. *Opp* WIN. 3 *lose your chance.* let slip, squander, waste. 4 *lose pursuers.* escape from, evade, give the slip, leave behind, outrun, shake off, throw off. **losing** ▷ UNSUCCESSFUL.

loser *n* also-ran, *sl* no-hoper, runner-up, underdog. *Opp* WINNER.

loss *n* bereavement, defeat, deficit, depletion, deprivation, destruction, disappearance, erosion, failure, privation, reduction, sacrifice. *Opp* GAIN. **losses** casualties, deaths, death toll, fatalities.

lost *adj* 1 abandoned, disappeared, forgotten, gone, irretrievable, left behind, mislaid, misplaced, missing, strayed, untraceable, vanished. 2 absorbed, day-dreaming, distracted, engrossed, preoccupied, rapt. 3 corrupt, damned, fallen. ▷ WICKED.

lot *n lot in a sale.* ▷ ITEM. **a lot of, lots of** ▷ PLENTY. **draw lots** ▷ GAMBLE. **the lot** all (of), everything, the whole thing, *inf* the works.

lotion *n* balm, cream, liniment, ointment, salve.

lottery *n* 1 raffle, sweepstake. 2 gamble, speculation, venture.

loud *adj* 1 audible, blaring, booming, clamorous, deafening, ear-splitting, echoing, high, noisy, penetrating, piercing, raucous, resounding, reverberating, roaring, shrieking, shrill, sonorous, strident, thundering, thunderous, vociferous. 2 *loud colours.* ▷ GAUDY. *Opp* QUIET.

lounge *n* drawing room, living room, salon, sitting room.

• *v* be idle, be lazy, dawdle, hang about, idle, laze, loaf, lie around, loiter, *inf* loll about, *inf* mess about, relax, sprawl, stand about, take it easy, waste time.

lout *n* hooligan, oaf, *inf* yob.

lovable *adj* adorable, appealing, charming, cuddly, *inf* cute, *inf* darling, dear, enchanting, endearing, engaging, fetching, likeable, lovely, pleasing, winning. *Opp* HATEFUL.

love *n* 1 admiration, adoration, affection, ardour, attachment, desire, devotion, fervour, fondness, infatuation, passion, tenderness, warmth. ▷ FRIENDSHIP. 2 beloved, darling, dear, dearest, loved one. ▷ LOVER.
• *v* 1 admire, adore, be fond of, be infatuated with, be in love with, care for, cherish, desire, dote on, fancy, *inf* have a crush on, have a passion for, idolize, lose your heart to, lust after, treasure, value, worship. ▷ LIKE. *Opp* HATE. **in love** besotted, enamoured, fond, *inf* head over heels, infatuated. **love affair** courtship, liaison, relationship, romance. **make love** *inf* canoodle, caress, embrace, have sex, pet. ▷ SEX.

loved *adj* beloved, cherished, darling, dear, dearest, esteemed, favourite, precious, treasured, valued, wanted.

loveless *adj* cold, frigid, heartless, passionless, unfeeling, unloving. *Opp* LOVING. ▷ UNLOVED.

lovely *adj* appealing, charming, delightful, enjoyable, nice, pleasant, pretty, sweet. ▷ BEAUTIFUL. *Opp* NASTY.

lover *n* admirer, boyfriend, companion, fiancé(e), friend, gigolo, girlfriend, *inf* intended, mate, mistress, suitor, sweetheart, *sl* toy boy, valentine.

lovesick *adj* frustrated, languishing, lovelorn, pining.

loving *adj* admiring, adoring, affectionate, amorous, ardent, attached, brotherly, caring, close, concerned, dear, demonstrative, devoted, doting, fatherly, fond, inseparable, kind, maternal, motherly, passionate, paternal, sisterly, tender, warm. ▷ FRIENDLY. *Opp* LOVELESS.

low *adj* 1 flat, low-lying, sunken. 2 *low trees.* short, stumpy, stunted. 3 *low status.* abject, base, degraded, humble, inferior, junior, lesser, lower, lowly, menial, modest. 4 *low behaviour.* churlish, coarse, common, cowardly, crude, disreputable, ignoble, mean, nasty, vulgar, wicked. ▷ IMMORAL. 5 *low sounds.* gentle, indistinct, muffled, muted, quiet, soft, subdued, whispered. 6 *low notes.* bass, deep, reverberant. *Opp* HIGH. **in low spirits** ▷ SAD. **low point** ▷ NADIR.

lowbrow *adj* easy, pop, popular, *derog* rubbishy, simple, *derog* trashy, *derog* uncultured, undemanding, unsophisticated. *Opp* HIGHBROW.

lower *v* 1 dip, drop, let down, take down. 2 *lower prices.* bring down, cut, decrease, discount, lessen, reduce, *inf* slash. 3 *lower the volume.* diminish, quieten, turn down. 4 *lower yourself.* abase, degrade, demean, discredit, disgrace, humble, humiliate, stoop. *Opp* RAISE.

lowly *adj* base, humble, insignificant, meek, modest, obscure, unimportant. ▷ ORDINARY. *Opp* EMINENT.

loyal *adj* constant, dedicated, devoted, dutiful, faithful, honest, patriotic, reliable, staunch, steadfast, true, trustworthy, trusty, unswerving, unwavering. *Opp* DISLOYAL.

loyalty *n* allegiance, constancy, dedication, devotion, duty, faithfulness, fidelity, honesty, patriotism, reliability, steadfastness, trustworthiness. *Opp* DISLOYALTY.

lubricate *v* grease, oil.

luck *n* 1 accident, chance, coincidence, destiny, fate, fluke, fortune, serendipity. 2 *wish her luck.* good fortune, happiness, prosperity, success.

lucky *adj* 1 accidental, chance, *inf* fluky, fortuitous, opportune, providential, timely, unplanned, welcome. 2 blessed, favoured, fortunate, successful. ▷ HAPPY. 3 *lucky number.* auspicious. *Opp* UNLUCKY.

luggage *n* bags, baggage, belongings, cases, *inf* gear, paraphernalia, suitcases, *inf* things, trunks.

lukewarm *adj* 1 tepid, warm. 2 apathetic, cool, half-hearted, indifferent, unenthusiastic.

lull *n* break, calm, gap, hiatus, interlude, interval, lapse, *inf* let-up, pause, respite, rest, silence.
• *v* calm, hush, pacify, quell, quieten, soothe, subdue.

lumber *n* 1 planks, timber, wood. 2 clutter, junk, odds and ends, rubbish, *inf* white elephants.
• *v* 1 blunder, move clumsily, shamble, trudge. 2 ▷ BURDEN.

luminous *adj* bright, glowing, lustrous, phosphorescent, radiant, shining.

lump *n* 1 ball, bar, bit, block, cake, chunk, clod, clot, cube, *inf* dollop, gobbet, hunk, mass, nugget, piece, slab, wad, *inf* wodge.

2 boil, bulge, bump, cyst, excrescence, growth, hump, knob, node, nodule, protrusion, protuberance, spot, swelling, tumour.
• *v* **lump together** ▷ COMBINE.

lunacy *n* delirium, dementia, derangement, frenzy, hysteria, insanity, madness, mania, psychosis. ▷ STUPIDITY.

lunatic *adj* ▷ MAD.
• *n* ▷ MADMAN.

lunge *v* 1 jab, stab, strike, thrust. 2 charge, lurch, plunge, throw yourself.

lurch *v* list, lunge, pitch, plunge, reel, roll, stagger, stumble, sway, totter. **leave in the lurch** ▷ ABANDON.

lure *v* attract, coax, decoy, draw, entice, inveigle, lead on, persuade, seduce, tempt.

lurid *adj* 1 gaudy, glaring, striking, vivid. 2 ▷ SENSATIONAL.

lurk *v* crouch, hide, lie in wait, lie low, prowl, skulk, steal.

luscious *adj* delectable, delicious, juicy, mouth-watering, rich, succulent.

lust *n* 1 desire, lasciviousness, lechery, libido, passion, sensuality, sexuality. 2 appetite, craving, greed, hunger, itch, longing.

lustful *adj* carnal, lascivious, lecherous, lewd, libidinous, on heat, passionate, *sl* randy, sensual, *sl* turned on. ▷ SEXY.

lustrous *adj* burnished, gleaming, glossy, metallic, polished, reflective, shiny.

luxuriant *adj* 1 abundant, ample, copious, dense, exuberant, fertile, flourishing, green, lush, opulent, plentiful, profuse, prolific, rich, teeming, thick, thriving, verdant. 2 ▷ ORNATE. *Opp* SPARSE.

luxurious *adj* comfortable, costly, expensive, grand, hedonistic, lavish, lush, magnificent, palatial, opulent, *inf* plush, *inf* posh, rich, self-indulgent, splendid, sumptuous, voluptuous. *Opp* SPARTAN.

luxury *n* affluence, comfort, ease, enjoyment, extravagance, hedonism, high living, indulgence, opulence, pleasure, self-indulgence, splendour, sumptuousness, voluptuousness.

lying *adj* crooked, deceitful, deceptive, dishonest, double-dealing, duplicitous, false, hypocritical, insincere, mendacious, perfidious, untruthful. *Opp* TRUTHFUL.
• *n* deceit, deception, dishonesty, duplicity, falsehood, *inf* fibbing, hypocrisy, mendacity, perjury, prevarication.

lyrical *adj* emotional, impassioned, melodious, musical, poetic, rapturous, rhapsodic, song-like, tuneful. *Opp* PROSAIC.

M

macabre *adj* eerie, frightful, ghoulish, grim, grisly, gruesome, morbid, *inf* sick, weird.

machine *n* appliance, contraption, device, engine, gadget, instrument, mechanism, robot, tool. ▷ MACHINERY.

machinery *n* 1 apparatus, equipment, gear, machines, plant. 2 procedure, system.

mackintosh *n* anorak, cape, mac, sou'-wester, waterproof.

mad *adj* 1 berserk, *inf* bonkers, crazed, crazy, *inf* daft, delirious, demented, deranged, distracted, *inf* dotty, fanatical, frenzied, insane, lunatic, maniacal, manic, *inf* nutty, *inf* off your head, *inf* out of your mind, possessed, *inf* potty, psychotic, *inf* round the bend, *inf* touched, unbalanced, unhinged, unstable. *Opp* SANE. 2 *mad comedy.* ▷ ABSURD. 3 ▷ ANGRY. 4 ▷ ENTHUSIASTIC.

madden *v* anger, craze, derange, *inf* drive crazy, enrage, exasperate, incense, inflame, infuriate, irritate, *inf* make you see red, provoke, unhinge, vex.

madman, madwoman *ns* *inf* crackpot, lunatic, maniac, *inf* nutcase, *inf* nutter, psychopath.

madness *n* delirium, dementia, derangement, folly, frenzy, hysteria, insanity, lunacy, mania, mental illness, psychosis. ▷ STUPIDITY.

magazine *n* 1 comic, journal, monthly, paper, periodical, publication, quarterly, weekly. 2 *magazine of weapons.* armoury, arsenal, storehouse.

magic *adj* bewitching, charming, enchanting, entrancing, magical, miraculous, spellbinding, supernatural.
• *n* 1 black magic, enchantment, *inf* hocus-pocus, incantations, *inf* mumbo-jumbo, necromancy, the occult, sorcery, spells, voodoo, witchcraft, wizardry. 2 conjuring, illusion, sleight of hand, tricks.

magician *n* conjuror, magus, necromancer, sorcerer, witch, wizard.

magnetic *adj* alluring, attractive, bewitching, captivating, charismatic, charming, compelling, entrancing, fascinating, hypnotic, inviting, irresistible, seductive, spellbinding. *Opp* REPULSIVE.

magnetism *n* allure, appeal, attractiveness, charisma, charm, fascination, lure, power, pull, seductiveness.

magnificent *adj* awe-inspiring, beautiful, excellent, fine, glorious, gorgeous, grand, grandiose, imposing, impressive, majestic, marvellous, noble, opulent, *inf* posh, regal, rich, spectacular, splendid, stately, sumptuous, superb, wonderful. *Opp* ORDINARY.

magnify *v* 1 amplify, augment, *inf* blow up, enlarge, expand, increase, intensify, make larger. *Opp* SHRINK. 2 *magnify difficulties.* dramatize, exaggerate, heighten, inflate, make too much of, maximize, overdo, overestimate, overstate. *Opp* MINIMIZE.

magnitude *n* extent, immensity, importance, size.

mail *n* correspondence, letters, parcels, post.
• *v* dispatch, forward, post, send.

maim *v* cripple, disable, incapacitate, lame, mutilate.

main *adj* basic, cardinal, central, chief, critical, crucial, dominant, essential, first, foremost, fundamental, leading, major, most important, paramount, predominant, pre-eminent, primary, prime, principal, special, supreme, vital. *Opp* MINOR.

mainly *adv* above all, chiefly, especially, essentially, generally, largely, mostly, on the whole, predominantly, primarily, principally, usually.

maintain *v* 1 carry on, continue, hold to, keep going, keep up, perpetuate, preserve, retain, stick to, sustain. 2 *maintain a car.* keep in good condition, look after, service, take care of. 3 *maintain a family.* feed, keep, provide for, support. 4 *maintain your innocence.* affirm, allege, argue, assert, claim, contend, declare, defend, insist, proclaim, profess, uphold.

maintenance *n* 1 care, conservation, preservation, repairs, servicing, upkeep. 2 alimony, allowance, subsistence.

majestic *adj* august, awe-inspiring, dignified, distinguished, glorious, grand, imperial, imposing, impressive, kingly, lofty, magnificent, monumental, noble, pompous, princely, queenly, regal, royal, splendid, stately, sublime.

majesty *n* dignity, glory, grandeur, magnificence, nobility, pomp, royalty, splendour, stateliness, sublimity.

major *adj* bigger, extensive, greater, important, key, larger, leading, outstanding, serious, significant. ▷ MAIN. *Opp* MINOR.

majority *n* 1 *inf* best part, *inf* better part, bulk, greater number, mass, preponderance. 2 adulthood, coming of age, maturity. **be in the majority** ▷ DOMINATE.

make *n* brand, kind, model, sort, type, variety.
• *v* 1 assemble, beget, bring about, build, compose, constitute, construct, create, devise, do, engender, erect, execute, fabricate, fashion, forge, form, frame, generate, invent, make up, manufacture, originate, produce, put together. 2 *make dinner.* cook, *inf* fix, prepare. 3 *make clothes.* knit, *inf* run up, sew, weave. 4 *make an effigy.* carve, cast, model, mould, shape. 5 *make a speech.* deliver, pronounce, utter. ▷ SPEAK. 6 *make her director.* appoint, elect, nominate, ordain. 7 *make P into B.* alter, change, convert, transform, turn. 8 *make a fortune.* earn, gain, get, obtain. 9 *make a good employee.* become, grow into, turn into. 10 *make your objective.* accomplish, achieve, arrive at, attain, reach, win. 11 *2 and 2 make 4.* add up to, amount to, come to, total. 12 *make rules.* agree, arrange, establish, decide on, draw up, fix, write. 13 *make trouble.* cause, give rise to, provoke. 14 *make them obey.* coerce, compel, constrain, force, induce, oblige, order, pressurize, prevail on, require. **make amends** ▷ COMPENSATE. **make believe** ▷ IMAGINE. **make fun of** ▷ RIDICULE. **make good** ▷ PROSPER. **make love** ▷ LOVE. **make off** ▷ DEPART. **make off with** ▷ STEAL. **make out** ▷ UNDERSTAND. **make up** ▷ INVENT. **make up for** ▷ COMPENSATE. **make up your mind** ▷ DECIDE.

make-believe *adj* fanciful, imaginary, made-up, *inf* pretend, pretended, unreal.
• *n* dream, fantasy, play-acting, pretence, self-deception, unreality.

maker *n* architect, author, builder, creator, manufacturer, originator, producer.

makeshift *adj* provisional, stopgap, temporary.

maladjusted *adj* disturbed, muddled, neurotic, unbalanced.

male *adj* ▷ MASCULINE.
• *n* ▷ MAN. *Opp* FEMALE.

malefactor *n* ▷ WRONGDOER.

malice *n* animosity, *inf* bitchiness, bitterness, enmity, hatred, hostility, ill will, malevolence, maliciousness, rancour, spite, spitefulness, venom, viciousness, vindictiveness.

malicious *adj inf* bitchy, bitter, *inf* catty, evil, hateful, malevolent, malignant, nasty, rancorous, sly, spiteful, venomous, vicious, villainous, vindictive, wicked. *Opp* KIND.

malignant *adj* dangerous, deadly, destructive, fatal, harmful, injurious, life-threatening, *inf* terminal, virulent. ▷ MALICIOUS.

malleable *adj* ductile, plastic, pliable, soft, tractable, workable. *Opp* BRITTLE.

malnutrition *n* famine, hunger, starvation, undernourishment.

man *n* 1 ▷ MANKIND. 2 bachelor, boy, boyfriend, brother, chap, father, fellow, gentleman, groom, *inf* guy, husband, lad, son, *inf* squire, widower.
• *v* cover, crew, staff.

manage *v* 1 administer, be in charge of, conduct, control, direct, govern, head, lead, look after, mastermind, organize, oversee, preside over, regulate, rule, run, superintend, supervise, take care of. 2 *Can you manage that horse?* cope with, deal with, handle. 3 *I can manage 2 essays this week.* accomplish, achieve, carry out, do, finish, get through, perform, undertake. 4 *I can manage on my own.* cope, muddle through, scrape by, shift for yourself, succeed, survive. 4 *I can manage £10.* afford, spare.

manageable *adj* 1 convenient, handy, reasonable. *Opp* AWKWARD. 2 amenable, compliant, controllable, docile, submissive, tame, tractable. ▷ OBEDIENT. *Opp* DISOBEDIENT.

manager, manageress *ns* administrator, *inf* boss, chief, controller, director, executive, governor, head, organizer, overseer, proprietor, ruler, supervisor. ▷ CHIEF.

mandatory *adj* ▷ COMPULSORY.

mangle *v* crush, damage, deform, hack, injure, lacerate, maim, maul, mutilate, squash, tear, wound.

mangy *adj* moth-eaten, scabby, *inf* scruffy, shabby, squalid, *inf* tatty, unkempt, wretched.

manhandle *v* 1 haul, heave, hump, manœuvre, pull, push. 2 abuse, *inf* beat up, ill-treat, knock about, mistreat, misuse, *inf* rough up.

mania *n* craze, enthusiasm, fad, fetish, frenzy, infatuation, obsession, passion, rage. ▷ MADNESS.

maniac *n* ▷ MADMAN.

manifest *adj* apparent, clear, conspicuous, evident, explicit, glaring, noticeable, obvious, patent, plain, visible.
• *v* ▷ SHOW.

manifesto *n* declaration, policy statement.

manipulate *v* 1 feel, massage, rub. 2 *manipulate people, events.* control, direct, exploit, guide, handle, influence, manage, manoeuvre, steer.

mankind *n Lat* homo sapiens, human beings, humanity, the human race, man, men and women, people.

manly *adj* chivalrous, gallant, heroic, *inf* macho, male, masculine, strong, virile. ▷ BRAVE. *Opp* EFFEMINATE.

man-made *adj* artificial, imitation, manufactured, simulated, synthetic, unnatural. *Opp* NATURAL.

manner *n* 1 fashion, means, method, mode, procedure, process, style, technique, way. 2 air, aspect, attitude, bearing, behaviour, character, conduct, demeanour, disposition, look, mien. 3 *all manner of things.* kind, sort, type, variety.

manners *pl n* behaviour, conduct, courtesy, etiquette, politeness, protocol, refinement, social graces.

mannerism *n* characteristic, habit, peculiarity, quirk, trait.

manoeuvre *n* device, dodge, gambit, move, operation, plan, plot, ploy, ruse, scheme, stratagem, strategy, tactic, trick.
• *v* contrive, engineer, guide, jockey, manipulate, move, navigate, pilot, steer.

manoeuvres *pl n* army exercises, operations, training.

mansion *n* manor, manor house, palace, stately home.

mantle *n* cape, cloak, hood, shroud, wrap.
• *v* ▷ COVER.

manufacture *v* assemble, build, create, fabricate, make, mass-produce, process, *inf* turn out. **manufactured** ▷ MAN-MADE.

manufacturer *n* factory-owner, industrialist, maker, producer.

manure *n* compost, dung, fertilizer, *inf* muck.

manuscript *n* document, papers, script.

many *adj* abundant, copious, countless, diverse, frequent, innumerable, multifarious, myriad, numerous, profuse, *inf* umpteen, various. *Opp* FEW.

map *n* chart, diagram, plan.

mar *v* damage, hurt, impair, stain, tarnish. ▷ SPOIL.

marauder *n* bandit, invader, pirate, plunderer, raider.

march *n* demonstration, march-past, parade, procession, progress.
• *v* file, pace, parade, step, stride, troop.

margin *n* 1 border, boundary, brink, edge, frieze, perimeter, rim, side, verge. 2 latitude, leeway, room, scope, space.

marginal *adj* borderline, doubtful, minimal, negligible, peripheral.

marital *adj* conjugal, matrimonial, nuptial.

mark *n* 1 blemish, blot, blotch, dot, *pl* graffiti, line, pockmark, print, scar, scratch, scribble, smear, smudge, smut, *inf* splotch, spot, stain, *pl* stigmata, streak, trace, vestige. 2 *mark of breeding.* characteristic, feature, indication, token. 3 *identifying mark.* badge, brand, device, emblem, hallmark, label, seal, sign, stamp, standard, symbol, trademark.
• *v* 1 blemish, blot, brand, bruise, damage, deface, dirty, disfigure, draw on, mar, scar, scratch, smudge, spot, stain, stamp, streak, tattoo. 2 *mark pupils' work.* appraise, assess, correct, evaluate, grade. 3 *mark my words.* attend to, heed, listen to, mind, note, notice, observe, take note of, *inf* take to heart, watch.

market *n* auction, bazaar, exchange, fair, market place, sale. ▷ SHOP.
• *v* advertise, deal in, peddle, promote, put on the market, retail, sell, *inf* tout, trade, trade in, vend.

marksman *n* crack shot, gunman, sharpshooter, sniper.

maroon *v* abandon, cast away, desert, isolate, leave, strand.

marriage *n* 1 matrimony, partnership, union, wedlock. 2 nuptials, wedding.

marriageable *adj* adult, mature, nubile.

marry *v* espouse, *inf* get hitched, join in matrimony, *inf* tie the knot, unite, wed.

marsh *n* bog, fen, marshland, morass, mud, mudflats, quagmire, swamp, wetland.

marshal *v* arrange, assemble, deploy, gather, group, line up, muster, organize.

martial *adj* aggressive, belligerent, military, pugnacious, warlike. *Opp* PEACEABLE.

marvel *n* miracle, phenomenon, wonder. • *v* **marvel at** admire, be amazed by, gape at, wonder at.

marvellous *adj* amazing, astonishing, astounding, breathtaking, excellent, extraordinary, *inf* fabulous, *inf* fantastic, glorious, incredible, magnificent, miraculous, phenomenal, prodigious, remarkable, *inf* sensational, spectacular, splendid, stupendous, *inf* super, superb, *inf* terrific, unbelievable, wonderful. *Opp* ORDINARY.

masculine *adj* boyish, *inf* butch, gentlemanly, heroic, *inf* macho, male, manly, powerful, strong, virile. *Opp* FEMININE.

mash *v* beat, crush, grind, pound, pulp, pulverize, squash.

mask *n* camouflage, cloak, cover, cover-up, disguise, façade, front, guise, screen, shield, veil, visor.
• *v* blot out, camouflage, cloak, conceal, cover, disguise, hide, obscure, screen, shield, shroud, veil.

masonry *n* bricks, brickwork, stone, stonework.

mass *adj* general, popular, universal, wholesale, widespread.
• *n* 1 accumulation, body, bulk, collection, conglomeration, *inf* dollop, heap, hoard, *inf* load, lot, lump, mound, mountain, pile, profusion, quantity, stack, volume. 2 ▷ GROUP.
• *v* accumulate, amass, assemble, collect, congregate, convene, flock together, gather, marshal, meet, mobilize, muster, pile up, rally.

massacre *v* annihilate, slaughter. ▷ KILL.

massage *v* knead, manipulate, rub.

mast *n* aerial, flagpole, maypole, pylon, transmitter.

master *n* 1 keeper, owner, person in charge, proprietor. ▷ CHIEF. 2 captain, skipper. 3 *master of an art*. *inf* ace, authority, expert, genius, mastermind, maestro, virtuoso. 4 ▷ TEACHER.
• *v* 1 become expert in, *inf* get the hang of, grasp, learn, understand. 2 conquer, control, curb, defeat, dominate, *inf* get the better of, overcome, overpower, quell, repress, subdue, subjugate, suppress, tame, triumph over, vanquish.

masterly *adj* ▷ SKILFUL.

mastermind *n* architect, brains, creator, engineer, expert, genius, intellectual, inventor, manager, originator, prime mover.
• *v* carry through, conceive, devise, direct, engineer, execute, organize, originate, plan, plot. ▷ MANAGE.

masterpiece *n* best work, classic, magnum opus, masterwork, *Fr* pièce de résistance.

match *n* 1 bout, competition, contest, duel, game, tournament. 2 counterpart, double, equal, equivalent, twin. 3 *love match*. marriage, partnership, relationship, union.
• *v* 1 agree, accord, be compatible, be similar, blend, coincide, compare, coordinate, correspond, fit, *inf* go together, harmonize, suit, tally, tone in. *Opp* CONTRAST. 2 ally, combine, fit, join, link up, marry, mate, pair off, put together, team up. *Opp* SPLIT. **matching** ▷ SIMILAR.

mate *n* 1 *inf* better half, companion, consort, husband, partner, spouse, wife. ▷ FRIEND. 2 assistant, associate, colleague, helper.
• *v* copulate, couple, have intercourse, *inf* have sex, marry, *inf* pair up, unite.

material *adj* concrete, corporeal, palpable, physical, solid, substantial, tangible.
• *n* 1 cloth, fabric, stuff, textile. 2 content, data, facts, ideas, information, matter, statistics, subject matter, substance, supplies.

materialize *v* become visible, take shape. ▷ APPEAR.

mathematics *n* arithmetic, *inf* maths, number work.

matted *adj* knotted, tangled, uncombed, unkempt. ▷ DISHEVELLED.

matter *n* 1 body, material, stuff, substance. 2 discharge, pus, suppuration. 3 *matter of life and death*. affair, business, concern, incident, issue, occurrence, question, situation, subject, topic. 4 *What's the matter?* difficulty, problem, trouble, upset, worry.
• *v* be important, be significant, count, make a difference, signify. **matter-of-fact** ▷ PROSAIC.

mature *adj* 1 adult, experienced, full-grown, grown-up, nubile, of age. 2 mellow, ready, ripe. *Opp* IMMATURE.
• *v* age, develop, grow up, mellow, reach maturity, ripen.

maturity *n* adulthood, completion, majority, mellowness, perfection, readiness, ripeness.

maul *v* claw, lacerate, mangle, manhandle, mutilate, paw, savage, treat roughly, wound.

maximize *v* 1 build up, make the most of. ▷ INCREASE. 2 inflate, magnify, overdo, overstate. ▷ EXAGGERATE. *Opp* MINIMIZE.

maximum *adj* biggest, extreme, full, greatest, highest, largest, most, peak, supreme, top, topmost, utmost.
• *n* apex, ceiling, climax, highest point, peak, pinnacle, top, upper limit, zenith. *Opp* MINIMUM.

maybe *adv* conceivably, perhaps, possibly.

maze *n* complex, labyrinth, network, tangle, web.

meadow *n* field, paddock, pasture.

meagre *adj* deficient, inadequate, mean, paltry, poor, puny, scanty, slight, sparse, thin. ▷ SMALL. *Opp* GENEROUS.

meal *n* banquet, *inf* blow-out, breakfast, dinner, *inf* elevenses, feast, lunch, repast, snack, *inf* spread, supper, tea.

mean *adj* 1 close, close-fisted, *inf* mingy, miserly, niggardly, parsimonious, *inf* penny-pinching, selfish, sparing, stingy, *inf* tight, tight-fisted, ungenerous. 2 *mean disposition.* callous, contemptible, cruel, despicable, ignoble, malicious, nasty, spiteful, unkind, vicious. 3 *mean dwelling.* humble, inferior, lowly, miserable, poor, shabby, squalid, wretched. *Opp* GENEROUS, VALUABLE.
• *v* 1 betoken, connote, convey, denote, express, foretell, hint at, imply, indicate, intimate, portend, represent, say, signify, stand for, suggest, symbolize. 2 *I mean to succeed.* aim, desire, hope, intend, plan, propose, want, wish. 3 *The job means long hours.* entail, involve, necessitate.

meander *v* ramble, rove, snake, wander, wind, zigzag. **meandering** ▷ TWISTY.

meaning *n* connotation, definition, drift, explanation, force, gist, idea, implication, import, interpretation, message, point, purport, purpose, relevance, sense, significance, substance, thrust, value.

meaningful *adj* eloquent, expressive, pointed, positive, pregnant, serious, significant, suggestive, telling, weighty, worthwhile. *Opp* MEANINGLESS.

meaningless *adj* 1 absurd, incomprehensible, incoherent, nonsensical, pointless, senseless. 2 *meaningless compliments.* empty, flattering, hollow, insincere, shallow, sycophantic, worthless. *Opp* MEANINGFUL.

means *n* 1 ability, capacity, channel, course, medium, method, mode, process, way. 2 *private means.* ▷ WEALTH.

measurable *adj* appreciable, discernible, significant. *Opp* NEGLIGIBLE.

measure *n* 1 allocation, allowance, amount, extent, magnitude, portion, quantity, quota, ration, size, unit. ▷ MEASUREMENT. 2 criterion, *inf* litmus test, standard, test, yardstick. 3 course of action, expedient, means, procedure, step. 4 act, bill, law, statute.
• *v* assess, calculate, calibrate, compute, count, determine, estimate, gauge, judge, mark out, meter, plumb (*depth*), quantify, rate, reckon, survey. **measure out** ▷ DISPENSE.

measurement *n* assessment, calculation, dimension, evaluation, extent, size. ▷ MEASURE.

meat *n* flesh. ▷ FOOD.

mechanic *n* engineer, technician.

mechanical *adj* 1 automatic, machine-driven. 2 cold, habitual, impersonal, instinctive, lifeless, perfunctory, reflex, routine, soulless, unconscious, unemotional, unfeeling, unthinking. *Opp* HUMAN.

mechanize *v* automate, equip with machines, modernize.

medal *n* award, decoration, honour, medallion, prize, reward, trophy.

meddle *v* ▷ INTERFERE.

mediate *v* act as mediator, arbitrate, liaise, negotiate.

mediator *n* arbitrator, broker, go-between, intermediary, judge, liaison officer, middleman, moderator, negotiator, peacemaker, referee, umpire.

medicinal *adj* curative, healing, restorative, therapeutic.

medicine *n* 1 healing, surgery, therapy. 2 drug, medicament, medication, panacea, prescription, remedy, treatment.

mediocre *adj* average, commonplace, fair, indifferent, inferior, middling, moderate, ordinary, passable, pedestrian, *inf* run-of-the-mill, second-rate, *inf* so-so, undistinguished, unexceptional, uninspired, unremarkable. *Opp* OUTSTANDING.

meditate *v* be lost in thought, brood, cogitate, consider, contemplate, deliberate, mull things over, muse, ponder, pray, reflect, ruminate, think.

meditation *n* contemplation, deliberation, prayer, reflection, rumination, thought.

meditative *adj* ▷ THOUGHTFUL.

medium *adj* average, intermediate, mean, mid, middle, middling, moderate, normal, ordinary, standard, usual.
• *n* 1 average, compromise, mean, middle, midpoint. 2 agency, channel, form, means,

method, mode, vehicle, way. 3 clairvoyant, seer, spiritualist. **the media, mass media** ▷ COMMUNICATION.

meek *adj* acquiescent, compliant, deferential, docile, forbearing, gentle, humble, long-suffering, lowly, mild, modest, obedient, patient, quiet, resigned, retiring, self-effacing, shy, soft, spineless, submissive, tame, timid, tractable, unassuming, weak, *inf* wimpish. *Opp* AGGRESSIVE.

meet *v* 1 *inf* bump into, chance upon, come across, confront, encounter, face, happen on, run into, see. 2 be introduced to, make the acquaintance of. 3 greet, *inf* pick up, rendezvous with. 4 assemble, collect, come together, congregate, convene, gather, muster, rally, rendezvous. 5 *The roads don't meet.* come together, connect, converge, cross, intersect, join, link up, merge, touch, unite. 6 *meet a demand.* acquiesce in, agree to, answer, comply with, deal with, fulfil, *inf* measure up to, pay, satisfy, settle, take care of. 7 *meet difficulties.* endure, experience, suffer, undergo.

meeting *n* 1 assembly, audience, conference, congregation, convention, council, gathering, *inf* get-together, forum, rally. 2 appointment, assignation, date, engagement, rendezvous. 3 *chance meeting.* confrontation, encounter. 4 *meeting of lines, roads.* confluence (*of rivers*), convergence, crossing, crossroads, intersection, junction, union.

melancholy *adj* dejected, depressed, depressing, despondent, disconsolate, dismal, dispiriting, *inf* down, forlorn, gloomy, glum, low, lugubrious, miserable, mournful, sombre, sorrowful, unhappy, woebegone. ▷ SAD. *Opp* CHEERFUL.
• *n* ▷ SADNESS.

mellow *adj* 1 mature, rich, ripe, sweet. 2 *mellow mood.* agreeable, easygoing, genial, gentle, happy, mild, peaceful, pleasant, subdued, warm. *Opp* HARSH.
• *v* age, develop, improve with age, mature, ripen, soften, sweeten.

melodious *adj* dulcet, harmonious, lyrical, mellifluous, melodic, sweet, tuneful.

melodramatic *adj* emotional, exaggerated, histrionic, overdone, *inf* over the top, sensationalized, theatrical.

melody *n* air, song, strain, subject, theme, tune.

melt *v* dissolve, liquefy, soften, thaw, unfreeze. **melt away** ▷ DISAPPEAR.

member *n* 1 associate, colleague, fellow. 2 ▷ LIMB.

memorable *adj* catchy (*tune*), distinguished, extraordinary, haunting, impressive, indelible, outstanding, remarkable, striking, unforgettable.

memorial *n* cenotaph, gravestone, headstone, monument, plaque, statue, tablet, tomb.

memorize *n* commit to memory, learn, learn by heart, remember, retain.

memory *n* 1 recall, retention. 2 impression, recollection, reminder, reminiscence, souvenir. 3 *memory of the dead.* honour, remembrance.

menace *n* danger, peril, threat, warning.
• *v* intimidate, threaten. ▷ FRIGHTEN.

mend *v* 1 fix, patch up, put right, rectify, remedy, renew, renovate, repair, restore. 2 *mend your ways.* amend, correct, improve, reform, revise. 3 *mend after illness.* convalesce, heal, improve, recover, recuperate.

menial *adj* degrading, demeaning, humble, inferior, lowly, subservient, unskilled.
• *n* lackey, minion, slave, underling. ▷ SERVANT.

mental *adj* 1 abstract, cerebral, cognitive, conceptual, intellectual, rational, theoretical. 2 [*inf*] ▷ MAD. **mental illness** ▷ MADNESS.

mentality *n* attitude, bent, character, disposition, frame of mind, *inf* make-up, outlook, personality, predisposition, propensity, psychology, temperament.

mention *v* acknowledge, allude to, bring up, broach, cite, comment on, disclose, draw attention to, enumerate, hint at, *inf* let drop, make known, name, note, observe, pay tribute to, point out, refer to, remark, reveal, say, speak about, touch on.

mercenary *adj* acquisitive, avaricious, covetous, grasping, greedy.
• *n* fighter, soldier.

merchandise *n* commodities, goods, produce, products, stock.
• *v* ▷ ADVERTISE.

merchant *n* broker, dealer, distributor, retailer, seller, shopkeeper, stockist, supplier, trader, vendor, wholesaler.

merciful *adj* benevolent, charitable, clement, compassionate, forbearing, forgiving, generous, gracious, humane, humanitarian, kind, kindly, lenient, liberal, mild, pitying, *inf* soft, soft-hearted, sympathetic, tolerant. *Opp* MERCILESS.

merciless *adj* barbaric, brutal, callous, cruel, hard, hard-hearted, harsh, heartless, inexorable, inflexible, inhuman, intolerant, pitiless, relentless, remorseless, ruthless, savage, severe, stern, strict, tyrannical, unbending, unforgiving, unkind, unrelenting, unremitting, vicious. *Opp* MERCIFUL.

mercy *n* charity, clemency, compassion, feeling, forbearance, forgiveness, generosity, grace, humanity, kindness, leniency, love, pity, quarter, sympathy, understanding.

merge *v* 1 amalgamate, blend, coalesce, combine, consolidate, fuse, integrate, link up, mingle, mix, pool, put together, unite. 2 *motorways merge.* converge, join, meet. *Opp* SEPARATE.

merit *n* credit, distinction, excellence, importance, quality, strength, talent, value, virtue, worth, worthiness.
• *v* be entitled to, be worthy of, deserve, earn, justify, rate, warrant.

meritorious *adj* ▷ PRAISEWORTHY.

merriment *n* amusement, conviviality, gaiety, glee, high spirits, hilarity, jollity, joviality, laughter, levity, lightheartedness, liveliness, mirth, vivacity. ▷ MERRYMAKING.

merry *adj* bright, *inf* bubbly, carefree, cheerful, cheery, convivial, festive, fun-loving, gay, glad, jocular, jolly, jovial, joyful, light-hearted, lively, spirited, vivacious. ▷ HAPPY. *Opp* SERIOUS.

merrymaking *n* carousing, celebration, conviviality, festivity, frolic, fun, fun and games, merriment, revelry. ▷ PARTY.

mesh *n* grid, lace, lattice, net, netting, network, sieve, tangle, tracery, trellis, web, webbing.

mess *n* 1 chaos, clutter, disarray, disorder, *inf* hotchpotch, jumble, litter, *inf* mishmash, muddle, *inf* shambles, tangle, untidiness. ▷ CONFUSION, DIRT. 2 *got into a mess.* difficulty, dilemma, *inf* fix, *inf* jam, *inf* pickle, plight, predicament, trouble.
• *v* **mess about** amuse yourself, loaf, loiter, lounge about, *inf* play about. **make a mess of, mess up** ▷ BUNGLE, MUDDLE.

message *n* announcement, bulletin, cable, communication, communiqué, dispatch, information, letter, memo, memorandum, missive, news, note, notice, report, statement.

messenger *n* bearer, carrier, courier, dispatch-rider, emissary, envoy, go-between, herald, intermediary, runner.

messy *adj* careless, chaotic, cluttered, dirty, dishevelled, disorderly, grubby, mucky, muddled, *inf* shambolic, slapdash, *inf* sloppy, slovenly, unkempt, untidy. *Opp* NEAT.

metallic *adj* gleaming, lustrous, shiny.

metaphorical *adj* allegorical, figurative, symbolic. *Opp* LITERAL.

method *n* 1 approach, fashion, *inf* knack, manner, means, mode, plan, procedure, process, programme, recipe, scheme, style, technique, trick, way. 2 arrangement, design, discipline, order, orderliness, organization, pattern, routine, structure, system.

methodical *adj* businesslike, careful, deliberate, disciplined, logical, meticulous, neat, orderly, organized, painstaking, precise, regular, routine, structured, systematic, tidy. *Opp* DISORGANIZED.

meticulous *adj* accurate, careful, exact, fastidious, painstaking, particular, precise, punctilious, scrupulous, thorough. *Opp* CARELESS.

microbe *n* bacterium, *inf* bug, germ, micro-organism, virus.

middle *adj* central, centre, halfway, inner, inside, intermediate, intervening, mean, mid, midway, neutral.
• *n* bull's-eye, centre, core, focus, heart, hub, inside, midpoint, midst, nucleus.

middling *adj* average, fair, *inf* fair to middling, indifferent, mediocre, moderate, modest, ordinary, passable, *inf* run-of-the-mill, *inf* so-so, unremarkable. *Opp* OUTSTANDING.

might *n* energy, force, muscle, power, strength, vigour.

mighty *adj* forceful, great, hefty, muscular, potent, powerful, robust, *inf* strapping, strong, sturdy, vigorous, weighty. ▷ BIG. *Opp* WEAK.

migrate *v* move, relocate, resettle, settle, travel.

mild *adj* 1 affable, amiable, docile, easygoing, equable, forbearing, forgiving, gentle, good-tempered, harmless, indulgent, inoffensive, kind, kindly, lenient, meek, merciful, modest, peaceable, placid, quiet, *inf* soft, soft-hearted, submissive, tractable, unassuming. 2 *mild weather.* balmy, calm, clement, fair, peaceful, pleasant, serene, temperate, warm. 3 *mild illness.* insignificant, minor, slight, trivial, unimportant. 4 *mild flavour.* bland, delicate, faint, mellow, subtle. *Opp* SEVERE, STRONG.

mildness *n* affability, amiability, clemency, docility, forbearance, gentleness, kindness, leniency, placidity, softness, tenderness. *Opp* ASPERITY.

militant *adj* active, aggressive, assertive, attacking, combative, fierce, hostile. *Opp* PASSIVE.
• *n* activist, extremist, *inf* hawk, partisan.

militaristic *adj* ▷ WARLIKE. *Opp* PEACEABLE.

military *adj* armed, combatant, fighting, martial, uniformed, warlike.

militate *v* **militate against** cancel out, counteract, oppose, prevent, resist.

milk *v* bleed, drain, exploit, extract, tap, wring.

milky *adj* chalky, cloudy, misty, opaque, whitish. *Opp* CLEAR.

mill *n* 1 factory, foundry, plant, works. 2 crusher, grinder, watermill, windmill.
• *v* ▷ GRIND. **mill about** move aimlessly, seethe, swarm, throng.

mimic *n* impersonator, impressionist.
• *v* ape, caricature, copy, echo, imitate, impersonate, make fun of, mirror, mock, parody, parrot, pretend to be, reproduce, ridicule, satirize, simulate, *inf* take off.

mind *n* 1 astuteness, brain, brainpower, brains, *inf* grey matter, head, insight, intellect, intelligence, judgement, mental power, perception, psyche, reason, sense, shrewdness, wisdom, wit, wits. 2 attitude, belief, bias, disposition, humour, inclination, intention, opinion, outlook, point of view, position, viewpoint.
• *v* 1 attend to, guard, keep an eye on, look after, take care of, watch. 2 *mind the warning.* beware of, heed, listen to, look out for, mark, note, obey, pay attention to, remember, watch out for. 3 *won't mind if he's late.* be annoyed, bother, care, object, take offence, worry. **be in two minds** ▷ HESITATE. **make up your mind** ▷ DECIDE. **out of your mind** ▷ MAD.

mindful *adj* alert, attentive, aware, conscious, heedful, vigilant, watchful. ▷ CAREFUL. *Opp* CARELESS.

mindless *adj* fatuous, idiotic, senseless, thoughtless, unthinking, witless. ▷ STUPID. *Opp* INTELLIGENT.

mine *n* 1 coalfield, colliery, excavation, pit, quarry, shaft, tunnel, working. 2 *mine of information.* fund, repository, source, store, storehouse, supply, wealth.
• *v* dig, excavate, extract, quarry, remove.

mineral *n* metal, ore, rock.

mingle *v* amalgamate, associate, blend, circulate, combine, fraternize, *inf* hobnob, intermingle, merge, mix, *inf* rub shoulders, socialize.

miniature *adj inf* baby, diminutive, dwarf, pocket, pygmy, scaled-down, tiny, toy. ▷ SMALL.

minimal *adj* least, minimum, negligible, nominal, slightest, smallest, token.

minimize *v* 1 cut down, decrease, diminish, lessen, prune, reduce. 2 *minimize problems.* belittle, decry, gloss over, make light of, play down, underestimate, undervalue. *Opp* MAXIMIZE.

minimum *adj* bottom, least, lowest, minimal, minutest, nominal, *inf* rock bottom, slightest, smallest.
• *n* least, lowest, minimum amount. *Opp* MAXIMUM.

minister *n* ▷ CLERGYMAN, OFFICIAL.
• *v* **minister to** aid, assist, attend to, care for, help, look after, nurse, see to, support, wait on.

minor *adj* inconsequential, inferior, lesser, negligible, petty, secondary, subordinate, subsidiary, trivial, unimportant. ▷ SMALL. *Opp* MAJOR.
• *n* ▷ ADOLESCENT, CHILD.

minstrel *n* entertainer, musician, singer, troubadour.

mint *adj* brand-new, first-class, fresh, immaculate, new, perfect, unblemished, unmarked, unused.
• *n* fortune, heap, *inf* packet, pile, stack.
• *v* cast, coin, forge, make, manufacture, produce, stamp out, strike.

minute *adj* diminutive, dwarf, infinitesimal, insignificant, microscopic, *inf* mini, miniature, minuscule, *inf* pint-sized, pocket, pygmy, tiny. ▷ SMALL.

minutes *pl n* log, notes, proceedings, record, résumé, summary, transactions.

miracle *n* marvel, miraculous event, mystery, wonder.

miraculous *adj* extraordinary, incredible, inexplicable, magic, magical, mysterious, supernatural, unaccountable, unbelievable. ▷ MARVELLOUS.

mirage *n* delusion, hallucination, illusion, vision.

mire *n* bog, fen, marsh, morass, mud, ooze, quagmire, slime, swamp. ▷ DIRT.

mirror *n* glass, looking-glass, reflector.
• *v* ▷ REFLECT.

misadventure *n* accident, calamity, disaster, mischance, misfortune, mishap.

misanthropic *adj* antisocial, unfriendly, unpleasant, unsociable. *Opp* PHILANTHROPIC.

misappropriate *v* embezzle, expropriate. ▷ STEAL.

misbehave *v* behave badly, be mischievous, *inf* blot your copybook, disobey, do wrong, err, fool about, make mischief, *inf* play about, play up, sin, transgress.

misbehaviour *n* delinquency, disobedience, insubordination, mischief, mischief-making, misconduct, misdemeanour, naughtiness, rudeness, vandalism, wrongdoing.

miscalculate *v sl* boob, err, *inf* get it wrong, go wrong, make a mistake, misjudge, misread, overestimate, *inf* slip up, underestimate.

miscarriage *n* 1 abortion, premature birth, termination. 2 *miscarriage of justice*. breakdown, defeat, failure, perversion.

miscarry *v* 1 abort, *inf* lose a baby. 2 break down, *inf* come to grief, come to nothing, fail, fall through, go wrong, misfire. *Opp* SUCCEED.

miscellaneous *adj* assorted, different, diverse, heterogeneous, mixed, motley, multifarious, sundry, varied, various.

miscellany *n* jumble, *inf* mixed bag, variety. ▷ MIXTURE.

mischief *n* 1 devilry, misbehaviour, misconduct, naughtiness, playfulness, *inf* shenanigans, trouble. 2 damage, harm, hurt, injury, misfortune.

mischievous *adj* badly behaved, disobedient, full of mischief, impish, naughty, playful, roguish, *inf* up to no good, wayward. ▷ WICKED. *Opp* WELL-BEHAVED.

miser *n inf* Scrooge, *inf* skinflint. *Opp* SPENDTHRIFT.

miserable *adj* 1 crestfallen, dejected, depressed, desolate, despairing, despondent, disconsolate, dismayed, dispirited, distressed, doleful, *inf* down, downcast, forlorn, gloomy, glum, grief-stricken, heartbroken, hopeless, in low spirits, languishing, lonely, low, melancholy, moping, mournful, sad, sorrowful, tearful, unfortunate, unhappy, unlucky, woebegone, wretched. 2 churlish, cross, disagreeable, grumpy, mean, miserly, morose, pessimistic, sour, sulky, sullen, surly, unhelpful, unsociable. 3 *miserable living conditions*. abject, awful, deplorable, disgraceful, distressing, hopeless, impoverished, inadequate, inhuman, lamentable, pathetic, pitiful, poor, shameful, sordid, soul-destroying, squalid, vile, wretched. 4 *miserable weather*. damp, depressing, dismal, dreary, grey, unpleasant, wet. *Opp* HAPPY, PLEASANT.

miserly *adj* avaricious, *inf* cheese-paring, *inf* close, covetous, economical, grasping, greedy, mean, *inf* mingy, niggardly, parsimonious, penny-pinching, sparing, stingy, *inf* tight, *inf* tight-fisted. *Opp* GENEROUS.

misery *n* 1 angst, anguish, bitterness, despair, desperation, despondency, distress, gloom, grief, heartache, heartbreak, *inf* hell, hopelessness, melancholy, sadness, sorrow, suffering, unhappiness, woe, wretchedness. *Opp* HAPPINESS. 2 adversity, affliction, deprivation, destitution, hardship, misfortune, need, oppression, penury, poverty, privation, squalor, suffering, tribulation, trouble, want.

misfire *v* abort, fail, fall through, *inf* flop, founder, go wrong, miscarry. *Opp* SUCCEED.

misfortune *n* accident, adversity, affliction, bad luck, blow, calamity, catastrophe, curse, disappointment, disaster, evil, hardship, misadventure, mischance, mishap, reverse, set-back, tragedy, trouble, vicissitude.

misguided *adj* foolish, ill-advised, inappropriate, misinformed, misjudged, misled, mistaken, unfounded, unjust, unwise. ▷ WRONG.

misjudge *v* get wrong, guess wrongly, make a mistake, misinterpret, overestimate, underestimate. ▷ MISCALCULATE.

mislay *v* ▷ LOSE.

mislead *v* bluff, confuse, delude, fool, give a wrong impression to, lead astray, lie to, misguide, misinform, outwit, take in, *inf* throw off the scent, trick. ▷ DECEIVE.
misleading ▷ DECEPTIVE, PUZZLING.

miss *v* 1 avoid, be absent from, be too late for, dodge, escape, evade, forget, lose, play truant from, skip, *sl* skive off. 2 *miss a target*. be wide of, fail to hit, fall short of. 3 *miss absent friends*. grieve for, long for, need, pine for, want, yearn for. **miss out** ▷ OMIT.

misshapen *adj* bent, contorted, crooked, deformed, disfigured, distorted, gnarled, grotesque, knotted, malformed, monstrous, twisted, twisty, ugly, warped. *Opp* PERFECT.

missile *n* projectile, rocket, weapon.

missing *adj* absent, disappeared, lost, mislaid, straying, truant, unaccounted for. *Opp* PRESENT.

mission *n* 1 delegation, deputation, task-force. 2 *mission in life.* aim, assignment, calling, duty, goal, job, life's work, métier, objective, occupation, profession, purpose, quest, undertaking, vocation. 3 *evangelical mission.* campaign, crusade, holy war.

missionary *n* crusader, evangelist, minister, preacher.

mist *n* 1 cloud, drizzle, fog, haze, vapour. 2 condensation, film, steam.

mistake *n inf* bloomer, blunder, *sl* boob, error, fault, *Fr* faux pas, gaffe, *inf* howler, inaccuracy, indiscretion, lapse, misapprehension, miscalculation, misconception, misjudgement, misprint, misunderstanding, omission, oversight, slip, *inf* slip-up.
• *v* confuse, get wrong, misconstrue, misinterpret, misjudge, misread, misunderstand, mix up, *inf* take the wrong way.

mistaken *adj* erroneous, distorted, false, ill-judged, inappropriate, incorrect, misguided, misinformed, unfounded, unjust. ▷ WRONG. *Opp* CORRECT.

mistimed *adj* early, inconvenient, inopportune, late, untimely. *Opp* OPPORTUNE.

mistreat *v* abuse, damage, harm, hurt, ill-treat, injure, maltreat, manhandle, misuse, molest, treat roughly.

mistress *n* 1 keeper, owner, person in charge. 2 ▷ TEACHER. 3 ▷ LOVER.

mistrust *n* apprehension, distrust, doubt, misgiving, reservation, scepticism, suspicion, uncertainty, wariness.
• *v* be suspicious of, be wary of, disbelieve, distrust, doubt, fear, have misgivings about, question, suspect. *Opp* TRUST.

misty *adj* bleary, blurred, clouded, cloudy, dim, faint, foggy, fuzzy, hazy, indistinct, murky, obscure, opaque, shadowy, steamy, vague. *Opp* CLEAR.

misunderstand *v inf* get the wrong end of the stick, get wrong, misconstrue, mishear, misinterpret, misjudge, misread, mistake. *Opp* UNDERSTAND.

misunderstanding *n* 1 error, false impression, misapprehension, misconception, misinterpretation, misjudgement, misreading, mistake, *inf* mix up, wrong idea. 2 disagreement, dispute. ▷ QUARREL.

misuse *n* abuse, corruption, ill-treatment, maltreatment, misappropriation.
• *v* 1 damage, harm, mishandle, treat carelessly. 2 *misuse an animal.* ▷ MISTREAT. 3 *misuse funds.* fritter away, misappropriate, squander, waste.

mitigate *v* abate, allay, alleviate, decrease, ease, extenuate, lessen, lighten, moderate, qualify, reduce, relieve, soften, temper, tone down. *Opp* AGGRAVATE.

mix *n* amalgam, assortment, blend, combination, compound, range, variety.
• *v* 1 alloy, amalgamate, blend, coalesce, combine, compound, confuse, diffuse, fuse, integrate, intermingle, join, jumble up, merge, mingle, mix up, muddle, shuffle, stir together, unite. *Opp* SEPARATE. 2 *mix with people.* ▷ SOCIALIZE.

mixed *adj* 1 assorted, different, diverse, heterogeneous, miscellaneous, varied, various. 2 amalgamated, combined, composite, diluted, integrated, joint, united. 3 *mixed feelings.* ambiguous, ambivalent, confused, equivocal, muddled, uncertain.

mixture *n* 1 alloy, amalgam, amalgamation, assortment, blend, collection, combination, composite, compound, concoction, conglomeration, fusion, *inf* hotchpotch, intermingling, jumble, medley, miscellany, *inf* mishmash, mix, *inf* motley collection, pot-pourri, selection, synthesis, variety. 2 cross-breed, hybrid, mongrel.

moan *n* complaint, grievance, lament, lamentation.
• *v* 1 complain, *inf* grouse, grumble, whine. 2 cry, groan, keen, lament, sigh, ululate, wail, weep, whimper.

mob *n inf* bunch, crowd, gang, herd, horde, host, multitude, pack, press, rabble, riot, *inf* shower, swarm, throng. ▷ GROUP.
• *v* besiege, crowd round, hem in, jostle, surround.

mobile *adj* 1 itinerant, movable, portable, travelling. 2 able to move, active, *inf* up and about. 3 *mobile features.* animated, changeable, changing, expressive, flexible, fluid. *Opp* IMMOVABLE.

mobilize *v* activate, assemble, call up, enlist, enrol, gather, get together, marshal, muster, organize, rally, stir up, summon.

mock *adj* artificial, fake, false, *inf* pretend, substitute. ▷ IMITATION.
• *v* decry, deride, disparage, insult, jeer at, laugh at, make fun of, parody, poke fun at, ridicule, scoff at, scorn, *inf* send up, sneer at, taunt, tease. ▷ MIMIC.

mockery *n* 1 derision, insults, jeering, laughter, ridicule, scorn. 2 caricature, parody, *inf* send-up. travesty.

mocking *adj* contemptuous, derisive, disparaging, disrespectful, insulting, irreverent, jeering, rude, sarcastic, satirical, scornful, taunting, teasing, unkind. *Opp* RESPECTFUL.

mode *n* 1 approach, manner, medium, method, procedure, set-up, system, technique, way. 2 ▷ FASHION.

model *adj* 1 imitation, miniature, scaled-down, toy. 2 *model pupil.* exemplary, ideal, perfect, unequalled.
• *n* 1 archetype, copy, dummy, effigy, image, imitation, likeness, miniature, *inf* mock-up, prototype, replica, representation, toy. 2 *model of excellence.* byword, epitome, example, exemplar, ideal, paragon, pattern, standard, yardstick. 3 *artist's model.* sitter, subject. 4 *latest model.* brand, design, kind, type, version. 5 *fashion model.* mannequin.
• *v* carve, fashion, form, make, mould, *inf* sculpt, sculpture, shape. **model yourself on** ▷ IMITATE.

moderate *adj* 1 average, balanced, calm, cautious, fair, judicious, medium, middling, modest, ordinary, reasonable, respectable, sensible, sober, steady, temperate, unexceptional, usual. *Opp* EXTREME. 2 *moderate winds.* gentle, light, mild.
• *v* 1 abate, decline, decrease, die down, ease off, subside. 2 calm, check, keep down, lessen, mitigate, modify, modulate, reduce, regulate, restrain, slacken, subdue, temper, tone down.

moderately *adv* comparatively, fairly, passably, quite, rather, reasonably, somewhat.

moderation *n* balance, caution, common sense, fairness, reasonableness, restraint, reticence, sobriety, temperance.

modern *adj* advanced, avant-garde, contemporary, current, fashionable, forward-looking, fresh, futuristic, in vogue, latest, new, newfangled, novel, present, present-day, progressive, recent, stylish, *inf* trendy, up-to-date. *Opp* OLD.

modernize *v* bring up-to-date, *inf* do up, improve, rebuild, redesign, redo, refurbish, renovate, revamp, update.

modest *adj* 1 bashful, coy, diffident, discreet, humble, meek, quiet, reserved, restrained, reticent, retiring, self-conscious, self-effacing, shy, unassuming, unobtrusive, unpretentious. *Opp* CONCEITED. 2 *modest dress.* chaste, decent, demure, proper, simple. 3 *modest house.* inconspicuous, lowly, ordinary, plain, 4 *modest income.* moderate, ordinary, reasonable, unexceptional. *Opp* EXCESSIVE.

modesty *n* 1 bashfulness, coyness, discretion, humility, meekness, reserve, restraint, reticence, self-consciousness, shyness. *Opp* OSTENTATION. 2 decorum, decency, propriety, seemliness.

modify *v* adapt, adjust, alter, amend, change, improve, redesign, remake, remodel, reorganize, revise, reword, transform, vary. ▷ MODERATE.

modulate *v* adjust, balance, change key, change the tone, moderate, regulate, soften.

moist *adj* clammy, damp, dank, dewy, humid, muggy, rainy, steamy, watery. ▷ WET. *Opp* DRY.

moisten *v* dampen, soak, spray, wet. *Opp* DRY.

moisture *n* condensation, damp, dampness, dew, humidity, liquid, precipitation, spray, steam, vapour, water.

molest *v* abuse, accost, annoy, assault, badger, bother, disturb, harass, interfere with, manhandle, mistreat, persecute, pester, plague, torment, vex, worry.

molten *adj* fluid, liquid, liquefied, melted, soft.

moment *n* 1 flash, instant, *inf* jiffy, minute, second, split second, *inf* tick, *inf* twinkling of an eye. 2 *historic moment.* hour, juncture, occasion, opportunity, time.

momentary *adj* brief, ephemeral, evanescent, fleeting, fugitive, passing, short-lived, temporary, transient, transitory. *Opp* PERMANENT.

momentous *adj* critical, crucial, decisive, epoch-making, fateful, grave, historic, important, serious, significant, weighty. *Opp* UNIMPORTANT.

monarch *n* emperor, empress, king, queen, ruler, tsar.

monarchy *n* empire, domain, kingdom, realm.

money *n* affluence, assets, banknotes, *inf* bread, capital, cash, change, coins, currency, *inf* dough, earnings, finances, fortune, funds, legal tender, *inf* lolly, *old use* lucre, *inf* nest-egg, notes, pocket-money, proceeds, profit, *inf* the ready, resources, revenue, riches, savings, sterling, takings, wage, wealth, *inf* the wherewithal, winnings.

mongrel *n* cross-breed, hybrid.

monitor *n* 1 prefect, supervisor, watchdog. 2 *TV monitor.* screen, set, television, VDU, visual display unit.
• *v* check, *inf* keep an eye on, oversee, record, supervise, trace, track, watch.

monk *n* brother, friar, hermit.

monkey *n* ape, primate, simian.

monopolize *v* control, corner, dominate, *inf* hog, keep for yourself, take over. *Opp* SHARE.

monotonous *adj* boring, dreary, dull, featureless, flat, level, repetitive, soporific, tedious, tiresome, uneventful, uniform, uninteresting, unvarying, wearisome. *Opp* INTERESTING.

monster *n* beast, bogey-man, brute, demon, devil, fiend, giant, horror, monstrosity, mutant, ogre, troll.

monstrous *adj* 1 colossal, enormous, gargantuan, giant, gigantic, huge, *inf* hulking, immense, mammoth, mighty, prodigious, titanic, towering, tremendous, vast. ▷ BIG. 2 *monstrous crime*. abhorrent, atrocious, awful, beastly, brutal, cruel, dreadful, disgusting, evil, grisly, gross, gruesome, heinous, hideous, horrendous, horrible, horrific, inhuman, nightmarish, obscene, outrageous, repulsive, shocking, terrible, villainous, wicked. ▷ EVIL.

monument *n* cenotaph, cross, gravestone, headstone, mausoleum, memorial, obelisk, pillar, relic, reminder, shrine, tomb, tombstone.

monumental *adj* 1 awe-inspiring, awesome, enduring, epoch-making, grand, historic, impressive, lasting, major, memorable, unforgettable. ▷ BIG. 2 commemorative, memorial.

mood *n* 1 attitude, disposition, frame of mind, humour, spirit, state of mind, temper, vein. 2 atmosphere, feeling, tone. **in the mood** ▷ READY.

moody *adj* bad-tempered, cantankerous, capricious, changeable, crabby, cross, crotchety, depressed, disgruntled, erratic, gloomy, grumpy, irritable, melancholy, miserable, morose, peevish, petulant, short-tempered, snappy, sulky, sullen, temperamental, touchy, unpredictable, unstable, volatile. ▷ SAD.

moor *n* fell, heath, moorland.
• *v* anchor, berth, dock, make fast, secure, tie up. ▷ FASTEN.

mope *v* languish, *inf* moon, pine, sulk.

moral *adj* blameless, chaste, decent, ethical, good, high-minded, honest, honourable, incorruptible, innocent, irreproachable, just, moralistic, noble, principled, proper, pure, respectable, responsible, right, righteous, sinless, trustworthy, truthful, upright, virtuous. *Opp* IMMORAL.
• *n* lesson, maxim, meaning, message, point, precept, principle. **morals** ▷ MORALITY. **moral tale** allegory, cautionary tale, fable, parable.

morale *n* cheerfulness, confidence, *inf* heart, self-confidence, self-esteem, spirit, state of mind.

morality *n* decency, ethics, ethos, goodness, honesty, integrity, justice, morals, principles, rectitude, righteousness, scruples, standards, uprightness, virtue.

moralize *v* lecture, philosophize, pontificate, preach, sermonize.

morbid *adj* black (*humour*), brooding, ghoulish, gloomy, grim, lugubrious, macabre, pessimistic, *inf* sick, sombre, unhealthy, unpleasant, unwholesome. *Opp* CHEERFUL.

more *adj* added, additional, extra, further, increased, new, other, renewed, supplementary. *Opp* LESS.

moreover *adv* also, as well, besides, further, furthermore, in addition, too.

morose *adj* bad-tempered, depressed, gloomy, glum, grim, humourless, melancholy, moody, mournful, pessimistic, saturnine, sour, sulky, sullen, surly, taciturn, unhappy, unsociable. ▷ SAD. *Opp* CHEERFUL.

morsel *n* bite, crumb, fragment, mouthful, nibble, piece, sample, scrap, small amount, taste, titbit. ▷ BIT.

mortal *adj* 1 ephemeral, human, passing, transient. *Opp* IMMORTAL. 2 *mortal illness*. deadly, fatal, lethal, terminal. 3 *mortal enemies*. deadly, implacable, irreconcilable, sworn, unrelenting.
• *n* creature, human being, man, person, woman.

mortality *n* 1 humanity, impermanence, transience. 2 *infant mortality*. death rate, loss of life.

mortify *v* ▷ HUMILIATE.

mostly *adv* chiefly, generally, largely, mainly, predominantly, primarily, principally, typically, usually.

moth-eaten *adj* antiquated, decrepit, holey, mangy, ragged, shabby, *inf* tatty. ▷ OLD.

mother *n inf* ma, *inf* mamma, *old use* mater, *inf* mum, *inf* mummy, parent.
• *v* care for, cherish, comfort, cuddle, fuss over, indulge, look after, love, nurse, pamper, protect, take care of.

motherly *adj* caring, kind, maternal, protective. ▷ LOVING.

motif *n* decoration, design, device, figure, idea, ornament, pattern, symbol, theme.

motion *n* action, activity, agitation, change, commotion, movement, progress, rise and fall, shift, stir, travel, travelling.
• *v* ▷ GESTURE.

motionless *adj* at rest, calm, frozen, immobile, lifeless, paralysed, resting, stagnant, static, stationary, still, stock-still, unmoving. *Opp* MOVING.

motivate *v* activate, arouse, cause, drive, egg on, encourage, galvanize, goad, incite, induce, influence, inspire, instigate, move, persuade, prompt, provoke, push, rouse, spur, stimulate, stir, urge.

motive *n* aim, ambition, cause, drive, end, grounds, impulse, incentive, inducement, inspiration, instigation, intention, motivation, object, purpose, rationale, reason, spur, stimulus, thinking.

motor *n* engine, mechanism. ▷ CAR.
• *v* drive, go by car.

mottled *adj* blotchy, patchy, speckled, spotty. ▷ DAPPLED.

motto *n* ▷ SAYING.

mould *n* blight, fungus, growth, mildew.
• *v* cast, fashion, forge, form, model, *inf* sculpt, shape, stamp, work.

mouldy *adj* damp, decaying, fusty, mildewed, musty, rotten, stale.

mound *n* bank, dune, heap, hill, hillock, hummock, hump, knoll, pile, stack.

mount *n* ▷ MOUNTAIN.
• *v* 1 ascend, clamber up, climb, go up, rise, scale. *Opp* DESCEND. 2 *mount a horse.* get astride, jump onto. 3 *savings mount.* accumulate, build up, escalate, expand, grow, increase, intensify, multiply, pile up, swell. *Opp* DECREASE. 4 *mount a picture.* display, exhibit, frame, install, put in place, set up.

mountain *n* alp, eminence, height, mount, peak, prominence, range, ridge, sierra, summit, tor, volcano.

mountainous *adj* alpine, craggy, high, hilly, precipitous, rocky, rugged, steep, towering. ▷ BIG.

mourn *v* bemoan, bewail, grieve, keen, lament, pine, regret, wail, weep. *Opp* REJOICE.

mournful *adj* dismal, distressing, doleful, funereal, gloomy, grief-stricken, grieving, heartbreaking, lamenting, lugubrious, melancholy, plaintive, plangent, sad, sorrowful, tearful, tragic, unhappy, woeful. *Opp* CHEERFUL.

mouth *n* 1 *inf* chops, *sl* gob, jaws, lips, maw, muzzle. 2 *mouth of a cave.* aperture, door, entrance, exit, gateway, inlet, opening, orifice, outlet, way in. 3 *mouth of a river.* delta, estuary, outflow.
• *v* articulate, enunciate, form, pronounce. ▷ SAY.

mouthful *n* bite, gulp, morsel, sip, spoonful, swallow, taste.

movable *adj* adjustable, changeable, detachable, floating, mobile, portable, transferable, transportable, unfixed, variable. *Opp* IMMOVABLE.

move *n* 1 act, action, deed, device, dodge, gambit, manoeuvre, measure, movement, ploy, ruse, step, stratagem, *inf* tack, tactic. 2 *career move.* change, relocation, shift, transfer. 3 *your move.* chance, go, opportunity, turn.
• *v* 1 *move about.* be astir, budge, fidget, roll, shake, shift, stir, swing, toss, tremble, turn, twist, twitch, wag, wave. 2 *move along.* cruise, fly, jog, journey, make progress, march, pass, proceed, travel, walk. 3 *move quickly.* bolt, canter, career, dash, dart, flit, fly, gallop, hasten, hurry, hurtle, hustle, *inf* nip, race, run, rush, shoot, speed, stampede, streak, sweep along, *inf* tear, *inf* zip, zoom. 4 *move slowly.* amble, crawl, dawdle, drift, stroll. 5 *move gracefully.* dance, flow, glide, skate, skim, slide, sweep. 6 *move awkwardly.* falter, flounder, lumber, lurch, pitch, shuffle, stagger, stumble, totter, trip, trundle. 7 *move stealthily.* crawl, creep, edge, slink, slither. 8 *move things.* carry, export, import, shift, ship, relocate, transfer, transplant, transport, transpose. 9 *move him to action.* encourage, impel, influence, inspire, persuade, prompt, stimulate, urge. 10 *move one's feelings.* affect, arouse, fire, impassion, rouse, stir, touch. 11 *move on a problem.* act, make a move, take action. **move away** ▷ DEPART. **move back** ▷ RETREAT. **move down** ▷ DESCEND. **move in** ▷ ENTER. **move round** ▷ CIRCULATE, ROTATE. **move towards** ▷ APPROACH. **move up** ▷ ASCEND.

movement *n* 1 action, activity, migration, motion, shifting, stirring. ▷ GESTURE, MOVE. 2 *movement towards green issues.* change, development, drift, evolution, progress, shift, swing, tendency, trend. 3 *political movement.* campaign, crusade, faction, group, organization, party. 4 *military movements.* exercises, operations.

movie *n* film, *inf* flick, motion picture.

moving *adj* 1 active, alive, astir, dynamic, flowing, mobile, on the move, travelling, under way. *Opp* MOTIONLESS. 2 *moving tale.* affecting, emotional, emotive, heart-rending, heart-warming, inspiring, pathetic, poignant, stirring, *inf* tear-jerking, touching.

mow *v* clip, cut, scythe, shear.

muck *n* dirt, filth, grime, *inf* gunge, mess, mire, mud, ooze, ordure, rubbish, scum, sewage, slime, sludge. ▷ EXCRETA.

mucky *adj* dirty, filthy, foul, grimy, grubby, messy, muddy, scummy, slimy, soiled, sordid, squalid. *Opp* CLEAN.

mud *n* dirt, mire, muck, ooze, silt, slime, sludge, slurry, soil.

muddle *n* chaos, clutter, confusion, disorder, *inf* hotchpotch, jumble, mess, *inf* mishmash, *inf* mix up, *inf* shambles, tangle, untidiness.
• *v* 1 bemuse, bewilder, confound, confuse, disorientate, mislead, perplex, puzzle. *Opp* CLARIFY. 2 disarrange, disorder, entangle, *inf* foul up, jumble, make a mess of, *inf* mess up, mix up, shuffle, tangle. *Opp* TIDY.

muddy *adj* 1 caked, dirty, filthy, messy, soiled. 2 *muddy water.* cloudy, opaque. 3 *muddy ground.* boggy, marshy, sodden, soft, spongy, waterlogged, wet. *Opp* CLEAN, FIRM.

muffle *v* 1 cloak, conceal, cover, enclose, enfold, envelop, shroud, swathe, wrap up. 2 *muffle noise.* dampen, deaden, disguise, dull, hush, mask, mute, quieten, silence, soften, stifle, still, suppress.

muffled *adj* deadened, dull, fuzzy, indistinct, muted, silenced, stifled, suppressed, unclear. *Opp* CLEAR.

mug *n* beaker, cup, pot, tankard.
• *v* assault, rob, steal from. ▷ ATTACK.
mug up ▷ LEARN.

mugger *n* attacker, hooligan, robber, ruffian, thief, thug.

mugging *n* attack, robbery, street crime.

muggy *adj* clammy, close, damp, humid, moist, oppressive, steamy, sticky, stuffy, sultry.

multiple *adj* collective, compound, many, numerous, several, various.

multiplicity *n* abundance, array, number, profusion, variety.

multiply *v* 1 double, quadruple, triple. 2 breed, increase, proliferate, propagate, reproduce, spread.

multitude *n* crowd, host, mass, myriad, swarm, throng. ▷ GROUP.

mumble *v* murmur, mutter, speak indistinctly.

munch *v* bite, chew, champ, chomp, crunch, gnaw.

mundane *adj* banal, common, commonplace, dull, everyday, familiar, pedestrian, prosaic, routine, worldly. ▷ ORDINARY. *Opp* EXTRAORDINARY, SPIRITUAL.

municipal *adj* borough, city, civic, community, district, local, public, town, urban.

murder *n* assassination, genocide, homicide, infanticide, killing, manslaughter, regicide, unlawful killing.
• *v* ▷ KILL.

murderer *n* assassin, butcher, cut-throat, gunman, *sl* hit man, killer, slayer.

murderous *adj* barbarous, bloodthirsty, bloody, brutal, cruel, deadly, ferocious, fierce, homicidal, pitiless, ruthless, savage, vicious, violent.

murky *adj* clouded, cloudy, dark, dim, dull, foggy, funereal, gloomy, grey, misty, muddy, obscure, overcast, shadowy, sombre. *Opp* CLEAR.

murmur *n* background noise, buzz, drone, hum, mutter, rumble, undertone, whisper.
• *v* drone, hum, mumble, mutter, rumble, speak in an undertone, whisper.

muscular *adj* athletic, *inf* beefy, brawny, burly, hefty, powerful, robust, sinewy, *inf* strapping, strong, sturdy, tough, well-built, wiry. *Opp* WEAK.

muse *v* cogitate, consider, contemplate, deliberate, meditate, mull over, ponder, reflect, ruminate, study, think.

mushy *adj* pulpy, spongy, squashy. ▷ SOFT.

musical *adj* euphonious, harmonious, lyrical, melodious, pleasant, sweet-sounding, tuneful.

musician *n* composer, music-maker, performer, player, singer. **musicians** band, ensemble, group, orchestra.

muster *v* assemble, call together, collect, convene, convoke, gather, get together, group, marshal, mobilize, rally, round up, summon.

musty *adj* airless, damp, dank, fusty, mildewed, mouldy, stale, stuffy, unventilated.

mutant *n* deviant, freak, monster, monstrosity, variant.

mutation *n* alteration, evolution, metamorphosis, modification, transfiguration, transformation, variation. ▷ CHANGE.

mute *adj* dumb, quiet, silent, speechless, tongue-tied.
• *v* ▷ MUFFLE.

mutilate *v* cripple, damage, deface, disfigure, dismember, injure, lame, maim, mangle, mar, spoil, vandalize, wound.

mutinous *adj* defiant, disobedient, insubordinate, insurgent, rebellious, refractory, revolutionary, seditious, subversive, ungovernable, unmanageable, unruly. *Opp* OBEDIENT.

mutiny *n* defiance, disobedience, insubordination, insurrection, rebellion, revolt, revolution, sedition, subversion, uprising.
• *v* agitate, be mutinous, disobey, rebel, revolt, rise up, strike.

mutter *v* grumble, mumble, murmur, speak in an undertone, whisper.

mutual *adj* common, joint, reciprocal, requited, shared.

muzzle *n* jaws, mouth, nose, snout.
• *v* censor, gag, restrain, silence, stifle, suppress.

mysterious *adj* arcane, baffling, cryptic, curious, enigmatic, incomprehensible, inexplicable, inscrutable, magical, miraculous, mystical, mystifying, obscure, perplexing, puzzling, secret, strange, uncanny, unfathomable, unknown, weird. *Opp* STRAIGHTFORWARD.

mystery *n* conundrum, enigma, miracle, problem, puzzle, question, riddle, secret.

mystical *adj* arcane, mysterious, occult, other-worldly, religious, spiritual, supernatural. *Opp* MUNDANE.

mystify *v* baffle, *inf* bamboozle, bewilder, confound, confuse, *inf* flummox, perplex, puzzle.

myth *n* 1 allegory, fable, legend, mythology. 2 fabrication, fiction, invention, pretence, untruth.

mythical *adj* 1 allegorical, fabled, fabulous, legendary, mythological, symbolic. 2 fanciful, fictional, imaginary, invented, make-believe, non-existent, unreal. *Opp* REAL.

N

nadir *n* bottom, depths, low point, zero. *Opp* ZENITH.

nag *n* ▷ HORSE.
• *v* annoy, badger, chivvy, goad, harass, hector, *inf* henpeck, keep complaining, pester, *inf* plague, scold, worry.

nail *n* pin, spike, stud, tack.
• *v* ▷ FASTEN.

naive *adj* artless, *inf* born yesterday, childlike, credulous, *inf* green, guileless, gullible, inexperienced, ingenuous, innocent, simple, trustful, trusting, unsophisticated, unsuspecting. *Opp* ARTFUL.

naked *adj* bare, denuded, exposed, in the nude, nude, stark-naked, stripped, unclothed, uncovered, undressed.

name *n* 1 alias, Christian name, first name, forename, given name, *inf* handle, identity, nickname, pen name, pseudonym, surname, title. 2 designation, epithet, term.
• *v* 1 baptize, call, christen, dub, style. 2 *name a book*. entitle, label. 3 *name him man of the match*. appoint, choose, designate, elect, nominate, select, single out, specify. **named** ▷ SPECIFIC.

nameless *adj* 1 anonymous, incognito, unidentified, unnamed, unsung. 2 *nameless horrors*. dreadful, horrible. ▷ UNSPEAKABLE.

nap *n* catnap, doze, rest, siesta, sleep, snooze.

narrate *v* chronicle, describe, detail, recount, relate, report, tell, unfold.

narration *n* commentary, reading, recital, recitation, relation, storytelling, voice-over.

narrative *n* account, chronicle, description, history, report, story, tale, *inf* yarn.

narrator *n* author, reporter, storyteller.

narrow *adj* close, confined, cramped, enclosed, fine, limited, restricted, slender, slim, thin, tight. *Opp* WIDE.

narrow-minded *adj* biased, bigoted, conservative, conventional, hidebound, illiberal, inflexible, insular, intolerant, narrow, parochial, petty, prejudiced, prim, puritanical, reactionary, rigid, strait-laced, *inf* stuffy. *Opp* BROAD-MINDED.

nasty *adj* bad, beastly, dirty, disagreeable, disgusting, distasteful, foul, hateful, horrible, loathsome, objectionable, obnoxious, obscene, *inf* off-putting, repulsive, revolting, sickening, unkind, unpleasant. *Opp* NICE.

nation *n* civilization, community, country, domain, land, people, population, power, race, realm, society, state.

national *adj* 1 domestic, internal. 2 *national emergency*. countrywide, general, nationwide, widespread.
• *n* citizen, inhabitant, native, resident, subject.

nationalism *n* ▷ PATRIOTISM.

native *adj* 1 indigenous, local, original. 2 *native wit*. congenital, hereditary, inborn, inherent, inherited, innate, mother (*tongue*), natural.
• *n* citizen, local inhabitant.

natural *adj* 1 common, everyday, habitual, normal, ordinary, predictable, regular, routine, standard, typical, usual. 2 *natural feelings*. healthy, human, inborn, inherent, innate, instinctive, intuitive, maternal, paternal. 3 *natural smile*. artless, genuine, guileless, sincere, spontaneous, unaffected, unselfconscious. 4 *natural resources*. crude (*oil*), raw, unadulterated, unprocessed, unrefined. 5 *natural leader*. born, untaught. *Opp* UNNATURAL.

nature *n* 1 countryside, creation, environment, natural world. 2 attributes, character, constitution, disposition, essence, humour, *inf* make-up, manner, personality, properties, temperament, traits. 3 category, kind, sort, species, type, variety.

naughty *adj* 1 bad, badly-behaved, bad-mannered, contrary, delinquent, disobedient, disruptive, fractious, headstrong, impish, incorrigible, insubordinate, intractable, mischievous, obstinate, obstreperous, perverse, playful, rebellious, roguish, rude, self-willed, stubborn, troublesome, uncontrollable, undisciplined, unmanageable, unruly, wayward, wicked, wild, wilful. 2 [*inf*] cheeky, improper, ribald, risqué, smutty, vulgar. ▷ OBSCENE. *Opp* POLITE, WELL BEHAVED.

nauseate *v* disgust, offend, repel, revolt, sicken.

nauseating *adj* disgusting, offensive, repulsive, revolting, sickening.

nautical *adj* marine, maritime, naval, seafaring, seagoing.

navigate *v* direct, drive, guide, handle, manoeuvre, map-read, pilot, sail, steer.

navy *n* armada, convoy, fleet, flotilla.

near *adj* 1 adjacent, adjoining, bordering, close, connected, nearby, neighbouring. 2 *Christmas is near.* approaching, coming, forthcoming, imminent, impending, looming, *inf* round the corner. 3 *near friends.* close, dear, familiar, intimate. *Opp* DISTANT.

nearly *adv* about, all but, almost, approaching, approximately, around, as good as, close to, just about, not quite, practically, roughly, virtually.

neat *adj* 1 *neat room.* clean, orderly, shipshape, *inf* spick and span, tidy, uncluttered, well-kept. 2 *neat dress.* dainty, smart, spruce, trim. 3 *neat work.* accurate, deft, dexterous, methodical, meticulous, precise. 4 *neat alcohol.* pure, straight, unadulterated, undiluted. *Opp* CLUMSY, UNTIDY.

necessary *adj* compulsory, essential, imperative, important, indispensable, inescapable, inevitable, mandatory, needed, obligatory, required, requisite, unavoidable, vital. *Opp* UNNECESSARY.

necessity *n* 1 essential, inevitability, *inf* must, need, obligation, prerequisite, requirement, requisite. 2 destitution, hardship, need, penury, poverty, privation, shortage, suffering, want.

need *n* call, demand, lack, requirement, want. ▷ NECESSITY.
• *v* be short of, call for, demand, depend on, lack, miss, rely on, require, want.

needless *adj* excessive, gratuitous. ▷ UNNECESSARY.

needy *adj* destitute, *inf* hard up, impecunious, impoverished, indigent, penurious, poverty-stricken. ▷ POOR.

negate *v* deny, disprove. ▷ NULLIFY.

negative *adj inf* anti, contradictory, destructive, grudging, obstructive, pessimistic, uncooperative, unenthusiastic, unhelpful, unwilling.
• *n* denial, no, refusal, rejection, veto. *Opp* POSITIVE.

neglect *n* carelessness, inattention, indifference, negligence, oversight.
• *v* be remiss about, disregard, forget, ignore, let slide, omit, overlook, pay no attention to, shirk, skip. **neglected** ▷ DERELICT.

negligent *adj* careless, forgetful, heedless, inattentive, irresponsible, lax, offhand, reckless, remiss, slack, thoughtless, uncaring, unthinking. *Opp* CAREFUL.

negligible *adj* imperceptible, inconsequential, insignificant, paltry, petty, slight, small, tiny, trifling, trivial, unimportant. *Opp* CONSIDERABLE.

negotiate *v* arbitrate, bargain, confer, deal, discuss terms, haggle, make arrangements, mediate, parley.

negotiation *n* arbitration, bargaining, conciliation, debate, diplomacy, discussion, mediation, transaction.

negotiator *n* agent, ambassador, arbitrator, broker, conciliator, diplomat, go-between, intermediary, mediator, middleman.

neighbourhood *n* area, community, district, environs, locality, place, quarter, region, surroundings, vicinity, zone.

neighbouring *adj* adjacent, adjoining, attached, bordering, close, closest, connecting, near, nearby, nearest, next-door, surrounding.

neighbourly *adj* civil, considerate, friendly, helpful, kind, sociable, well-disposed.

nerve *n* coolness, resolution, resolve, willpower. ▷ COURAGE.

nervous *adj* afraid, agitated, anxious, apprehensive, edgy, excitable, fidgety, flustered, fretful, highly-strung, ill-at-ease, insecure, *inf* jittery, *inf* jumpy, neurotic, on edge, *inf* on tenterhooks, restless, shaky, shy, tense, timid, *inf* twitchy, uneasy, unnerved, unsettled, *inf* uptight, worried. ▷ FRIGHTENED. *Opp* CALM.

nestle *v* cuddle, curl up, huddle, nuzzle, snuggle.

net *n* lace, mesh, netting, network, web.
• *v* 1 catch, capture, ensnare, trap. 2 *net £40 a day.* bring in, clear, earn, get, make, realize, receive, *inf* take home.

network *n* 1 *inf* criss-cross, grid, labyrinth, lattice, maze, mesh, net, tracery, web. 2 complex, organization, system.

neurosis *n* anxiety, obsession, phobia.

neurotic *adj* anxious, distraught, irrational, nervous, obsessive, overwrought, unbalanced, unstable.

neuter *adj* asexual, sterile.
• *v* castrate, *inf* doctor, emasculate, geld, spay, sterilize.

neutral *adj* 1 detached, disinterested, dispassionate, fair, impartial, indifferent, non-aligned, non-partisan, objective, unbiased, uncommitted, uninvolved, unprejudiced. *Opp* BIASED. 2 *neutral colours.* colourless, dull, drab, indeterminate, intermediate, pale, vague. *Opp* DISTINCTIVE.

neutralize *v* cancel out, counteract, invalidate, make ineffective, negate, nullify, offset, wipe out.

new *adj* 1 brand-new, clean, fresh, mint, strange, unfamiliar, untried, unused. 2 *new ideas.* advanced, contemporary, current, different, fashionable, latest, modern, newfangled, novel, original, recent, revolutionary, *inf* trendy, up-to-date. 3 *new data.* additional, changed, extra, further, supplementary, unexpected. *Opp* OLD.

newcomer *n* arrival, immigrant, outsider, settler, stranger.

news *n* account, advice, announcement, bulletin, communication, communiqué, dispatch, headlines, information, intelligence, *inf* the latest, message, newsflash, notice, press release, report, rumour, statement, word.

newspaper *n inf* daily, gazette, journal, paper, periodical, *inf* rag, tabloid.

next *adj* 1 adjacent, adjoining, closest, nearest, neighbouring. 2 *the next moment.* following, subsequent, succeeding.

nice *adj* 1 accurate, careful, delicate, discriminating, exact, fine, hair-splitting, meticulous, precise, punctilious, scrupulous, subtle. 2 *nice manners.* dainty, elegant, fastidious, fussy, particular, *inf* pernickety, polished, refined. 3 [*inf*] acceptable, agreeable, amiable, attractive, beautiful, delicious, delightful, friendly, good, gratifying, kind, likeable, pleasant, satisfactory, welcome. *Opp* NASTY.

niche *n* alcove, corner, hollow, nook, recess.

nickname *n* alias, sobriquet.

niggardly *adj* mean, miserly, parsimonious, stingy.

nimble *adj* acrobatic, active, adroit, agile, brisk, deft, lithe, lively, *inf* nippy, sprightly, spry, swift. *Opp* CLUMSY.

nip *v* bite, clip, pinch, snap at, squeeze.

nobility *n* 1 dignity, grandeur, greatness, high-mindedness, integrity, magnanimity, morality, uprightness, virtue, worthiness. 2 *the nobility.* aristocracy, elite, peerage, the ruling classes, *inf* the upper crust.

noble *adj* 1 aristocratic, *inf* blue-blooded, courtly, distinguished, elite, gentle, patrician, princely, royal, thoroughbred, titled, upper-class. 2 *noble deeds.* brave, chivalrous, courageous, gallant, glorious, heroic. 3 *noble thoughts.* elevated, honourable, lofty, magnanimous, moral, upright, virtuous, worthy. 4 *noble edifice.* dignified, elegant, grand, great, imposing, magnificent, majestic, splendid, stately. *Opp* BASE, COMMON.
• *n* ▷ ARISTOCRAT.

nod *v* bend, bob, bow. **nod off** ▷ SLEEP.

noise *n* babel, babble, bedlam, blare, cacophony, caterwauling, clamour, clatter, commotion, din, discord, fracas, hubbub, hullabaloo, outcry, pandemonium, racket, *inf* row, *inf* rumpus, screaming, shouting, tumult, uproar. ▷ SOUND. *Opp* SILENCE.

noiseless *adj* inaudible, mute, muted, quiet, silent, soft, soundless, still. *Opp* NOISY.

noisy *adj* blaring, booming, cacophonous, clamorous, deafening, discordant, dissonant, ear-splitting, harsh, loud, raucous, resounding, reverberating, rowdy, screaming, screeching, shrieking, shrill, strident, talkative, thunderous, unmusical, uproarious, vociferous. *Opp* NOISELESS.

nomadic *adj* itinerant, roving, travelling, vagrant, wandering.

nominal *adj* 1 formal, in name only, ostensible, *inf* so-called, supposed, theoretical, titular. 2 *nominal sum.* insignificant, minimal, minor, small, token.

nominate *v* propose, put forward, recommend. ▷ NAME.

non-existent *adj* fictional, fictitious, hypothetical, imaginary, legendary, made-up, mythical, unreal. *Opp* REAL.

nonplus *v* amaze, baffle, disconcert, dumbfound, *inf* flummox, perplex, puzzle.

nonsense *n* 1 [Most synonyms *inf*] balderdash, bosh, bunkum, claptrap, codswallop, double Dutch, drivel, eyewash, foolishness, gibberish, gobbledegook, mumbo-jumbo, piffle, poppycock, rot, rubbish, silliness, trash, tripe, twaddle. 2 *The plan was a nonsense.* absurdity, mistake, nonsensical idea.

nonsensical *adj* absurd, crazy, *inf* daft, fatuous, foolish, idiotic, illogical, impractical, incomprehensible, irrational, laughable, ludicrous, mad, meaningless, ridiculous, senseless, stupid. ▷ SILLY. *Opp* SENSIBLE.

non-stop *adj* ceaseless, constant, continual, continuous, endless, eternal, incessant, interminable, perpetual, persistent, unbroken, unending, uninterrupted, unremitting.

norm *n* criterion, measure, model, pattern, rule, standard, type, yardstick.

normal *adj* 1 accustomed, average, common, commonplace, conventional, customary, established, everyday, familiar, general, habitual, natural, ordinary, orthodox, predictable, prosaic, regular, routine, *inf* run-of-the-mill, standard, typical, unsurprising, usual. 2 *normal person.* balanced, rational, reasonable, sane, stable, *inf* straight, well-adjusted. *Opp* ABNORMAL.

nose *n* 1 snout. 2 *nose of a boat.* bow, front, prow.
• *v* insinuate yourself, interfere, intrude, nudge your way, penetrate, probe, push, shove. **nose about** ▷ PRY.

nostalgia *n* longing, memory, pining, regret, reminiscence, sentimentality, yearning.

nostalgic *adj* emotional, maudlin, regretful, romantic, sentimental, wistful, yearning.

nosy *adj* curious, inquisitive, interfering, meddlesome, prying.

notable *adj* celebrated, conspicuous, distinguished, eminent, evident, extraordinary, famous, important, impressive, memorable, noted, noteworthy, noticeable, obvious, outstanding, pre-eminent, prominent, remarkable, renowned, striking, uncommon, unusual, well-known. *Opp* ORDINARY.

note *n* 1 chit, communication, correspondence, jotting, letter, *inf* memo, memorandum, message. 2 annotation, comment, explanation, footnote, jotting. 3 *note of frustration.* quality, sound, tone. 4 *£5 note.* banknote, bill, draft.
• *v* 1 enter, jot down, record, scribble, write down. 2 detect, discern, discover, feel, find, heed, mark, notice, observe, pay attention to, register, remark, see, spy. **noted** ▷ FAMOUS.

noteworthy *adj* exceptional, extraordinary, rare, remarkable, uncommon, unique, unusual. *Opp* ORDINARY.

nothing *n* nil, nought, zero, *sl* zilch.

notice *n* 1 advertisement, announcement, handbill, leaflet, message, note, notification, placard, poster, sign, warning. 2 attention, awareness, heed, note, regard.
• *v* be aware, detect, discern, discover, feel, find, heed, mark, note, observe, pay attention to, perceive, register, remark, see, spy, take note. **give notice** ▷ NOTIFY, WARN.

noticeable *adj* appreciable, audible, clear, conspicuous, detectable, discernible, distinct, distinguishable, manifest, marked, measurable, notable, obtrusive, obvious, overt, palpable, perceptible, plain, prominent, pronounced, salient, significant, striking, unconcealed, unmistakable, visible. *Opp* IMPERCEPTIBLE.

notify *v* acquaint, advise, alert, announce, give notice, inform, proclaim, report, tell, warn.

notion *n* belief, concept, conception, fancy, hypothesis, idea, impression, inkling, opinion, theory, thought, understanding, view.

notorious *adj* disgraceful, disreputable, flagrant, infamous, outrageous, scandalous, shocking, undisputed, well-known. ▷ FAMOUS.

nourish *v* feed, maintain, nurse, nurture, provide for, strengthen, support, sustain. **nourishing** ▷ NUTRITIOUS.

nourishment *n* diet, food, goodness, nutrient, nutriment, nutrition, sustenance.

novel *adj* different, fresh, imaginative, innovative, new, odd, original, singular, startling, strange, surprising, uncommon, unconventional, unfamiliar, unusual. *Opp* FAMILIAR.
• *n* best-seller, *inf* blockbuster, fiction, romance, story.

novelty *n* 1 freshness, oddity, originality, strangeness, surprise, unfamiliarity, uniqueness. 2 bauble, curiosity, knick-knack, souvenir, trifle, trinket.

novice *n* amateur, apprentice, beginner, initiate, learner, probationer, trainee.

now *adv* at once, at present, immediately, instantly, just now, nowadays, promptly, straight away, today.

noxious *adj* corrosive, foul, harmful, nasty, noisome, objectionable, poisonous, polluting, unwholesome.

nub *n* centre, core, crux, essence, gist, heart, kernel, nucleus, pith, point.

nucleus *n* centre, core, heart, kernel, middle.

nude *adj* bare, exposed, *inf* in the altogether, in the nude, naked, stark-naked, stripped, unclothed, uncovered, undressed.

nudge *v* bump, dig, elbow, jog, poke, prod, push, touch.

nuisance *n* annoyance, bother, inconvenience, irritation, *inf* pain, pest, trouble, worry.

nullify *v* abolish, annul, cancel, invalidate, negate, quash, repeal, rescind, revoke.

numb *adj* anaesthetized, *inf* asleep, cold, dead, deadened, frozen, insensible, insensitive, paralysed, senseless. *Opp* SENSITIVE.
• *v* anaesthetize, deaden, desensitize, drug, dull, freeze, paralyse, stun, stupefy.

number *n* 1 digit, figure, integer, numeral, unit. 2 aggregate, amount, collection, quantity, sum, total. ▷ GROUP. 3 *musical number*. item, piece, song. 4 *back number*. copy, edition, impression, issue, printing, publication.
•*v* add up to, total, work out at. ▷ COUNT.

numerous *adj* abundant, copious, countless, incalculable, infinite, innumerable, many, myriad, plentiful, several, untold. *Opp* FEW.

nun *n* abbess, mother superior, novice, prioress, sister.

nurse *n* 1 district nurse, sister. 2 nanny, nursemaid.
• *v* 1 care for, look after, minister to, nurture, tend, treat. 2 breast-feed, feed, suckle. 3 cherish, cradle, cuddle, hold, hug, mother, pamper.

nursery *n* 1 crèche, kindergarten, nursery school. 2 garden centre, market garden.

nurture *v* bring up, cultivate, educate, feed, look after, nourish, nurse, rear, tend, train.

nutriment *n* food, nourishment, nutrient, nutrition, sustenance.

nutritious *adj* beneficial, health-giving, healthy, nourishing, sustaining, wholesome.

O

oasis *n* 1 spring, well. 2 asylum, haven, refuge, retreat, safe harbour, sanctuary.

oath *n* 1 assurance, avowal, guarantee, pledge, promise, undertaking, vow, word of honour. 2 blasphemy, curse, expletive, *inf* four-letter word, imprecation, obscenity, profanity, swear word.

obedient *adj* acquiescent, amenable, biddable, compliant, deferential, disciplined, docile, dutiful, law-abiding, manageable, submissive, subservient, tractable, well-behaved. *Opp* DISOBEDIENT.

obese *adj* corpulent, gross, overweight. ▷ FAT.

obey *v* abide by, accept, acquiesce in, act in accordance with, adhere to, agree to, bow to, carry out, comply with, conform to, defer to, execute, follow, fulfil, give in to, heed, honour, keep to, mind, observe, perform, *inf* stick to, submit to. *Opp* DISOBEY.

object *n* 1 article, body, item, thing. 2 aim, end, goal, intention, objective, point, purpose, reason. 3 *object of ridicule*. butt, target.
• *v* argue, be opposed, carp, cavil, complain, demur, disapprove, dispute, dissent, expostulate, *inf* grouse, grumble, *inf* mind, oppose, protest, quibble, raise objections, remonstrate, take a stand, take exception. *Opp* ACCEPT, AGREE.

objection *n* argument, cavil, challenge, complaint, disapproval, opposition, outcry, protest, query, question, quibble, remonstration.

objectionable *adj* abhorrent, disagreeable, disgusting, distasteful, foul, hateful, insufferable, intolerable, loathsome, nasty, noisome, obnoxious, offensive, *inf* off-putting, repellent, repugnant, repulsive, revolting, sickening, unacceptable. ▷ UNPLEASANT. *Opp* ACCEPTABLE.

objective *adj* 1 detached, disinterested, dispassionate, factual, impartial, impersonal, neutral, open-minded, rational, scientific, unbiased, unemotional, unprejudiced. 2 *objective evidence*. empirical, existing, observable, real. *Opp* SUBJECTIVE.
• *n* ambition, aspiration, destination, goal, target. ▷ OBJECT.

obligation *n* commitment, compulsion, constraint, contract, duty, liability, need, requirement, responsibility. ▷ PROMISE. *Opp* OPTION.

obligatory *adj* essential, required. ▷ COMPULSORY. *Opp* OPTIONAL.

oblige *v* 1 coerce, compel, constrain, force, make, require. 2 *Please oblige me*. accommodate, gratify, indulge, please. **obliged** ▷ BOUND, GRATEFUL. **obliging** ▷ HELPFUL, POLITE.

oblique *adj* 1 angled, askew, diagonal, inclined, leaning, listing, slanted, slanting, sloping, tilted. 2 *oblique insult*. backhanded, implicit, implied, indirect. ▷ EVASIVE. *Opp* DIRECT.

obliterate *v* blot out, cancel, delete, destroy, efface, eliminate, eradicate, erase, expunge, leave no trace of, wipe out.

oblivion *n* 1 anonymity, darkness, disregard, extinction, obscurity. 2 forgetfulness, insensibility, unawareness, unconsciousness.

oblivious *adj* forgetful, heedless, ignorant, insensible, insensitive, unaware, unconscious, unfeeling, uninformed, unmindful. *Opp* AWARE.

obscene *adj* abominable, bawdy, blue, coarse, crude, debauched, degenerate, depraved, dirty, disgusting, filthy, foul, foul-mouthed, gross, immodest, immoral, improper, impure, indecent, indelicate, *inf* kinky, lecherous, lewd, offensive, outrageous, perverted, pornographic, prurient, ribald, risqué, rude, salacious, scurrilous, shameless, shocking, *inf* sick, smutty, suggestive, vile, vulgar. ▷ OBJECTIONABLE. *Opp* DECENT.

obscenity *n* abomination, blasphemy, coarseness, dirt, evil, filth, immorality, impropriety, indecency, licentiousness, offensiveness, outrage, perversion, pornography, profanity, vulgarity. ▷ SWEAR WORD.

obscure *adj* 1 blurred, clouded, dark, dim, faint, hazy, inconspicuous, indefinite, indistinct, misty, murky, nebulous, shadowy, shady, shrouded, unclear, unlit, unrecognizable, vague, veiled. *Opp* CLEAR. 2 *obscure subject*. arcane, baffling, complex, cryptic, enigmatic, esoteric, incomprehensible, mystifying, perplexing, puzzling, recondite, strange. *Opp* OBVIOUS. 3 *obscure poet*. forgotten, minor,

undistinguished, unimportant, unknown, unnoticed. *Opp* FAMOUS.
• *v* blur, cloak, cloud, conceal, cover, darken, disguise, eclipse, envelop, hide, mask, overshadow, screen, shade, shroud, veil. *Opp* CLARIFY.

obsequious *adj* abject, crawling, cringing, deferential, fawning, flattering, fulsome, *inf* greasy, grovelling, ingratiating, insincere, mealy-mouthed, *inf* oily, servile, *inf* smarmy, submissive, sycophantic, unctuous. **be obsequious** ▷ GROVEL.

observant *adj* alert, attentive, aware, careful, eagle-eyed, heedful, mindful, on the lookout, perceptive, percipient, quick, vigilant, watchful, with eyes peeled. *Opp* INATTENTIVE.

observation *n* 1 examination, inspection, monitoring, scrutiny, study, surveillance. 2 comment, reaction, reflection, remark, response, statement, thought, utterance.

observe *v* 1 contemplate, detect, discern, examine, *inf* keep an eye on, look at, monitor, note, notice, perceive, regard, scrutinize, see, spot, spy, study, view, watch, witness. 2 *observe rules.* abide by, adhere to, comply with, conform to, follow, heed, keep, obey, pay attention to, respect. 3 *observe Easter.* celebrate, commemorate, keep, mark, recognize, remember. 4 comment, declare, explain, make an observation, mention, reflect, remark, say, state.

observer *n* commentator, onlooker, witness. ▷ SPECTATOR.

obsess *v* consume, control, dominate, grip, haunt, monopolize, plague, possess, preoccupy, rule, take hold of.

obsession *n inf* bee in your bonnet, fetish, fixation, *inf* hang-up, *Fr* idée fixe, infatuation, mania, passion, phobia, preoccupation, *sl* thing.

obsessive *adj* addictive, compulsive, consuming, controlling, dominating, haunting.

obsolescent *adj* ageing, declining, dying out, fading, losing popularity, moribund, *inf* on the way out, waning.

obsolete *adj* anachronistic, antiquated, archaic, dated, discarded, disused, extinct, old-fashioned, *inf* old hat, out-of-date, outmoded, passé, superannuated, unfashionable. ▷ OLD. *Opp* CURRENT.

obstacle *n* bar, barricade, barrier, blockage, catch, difficulty, hindrance, hurdle, impediment, obstruction, problem, snag, stumbling block.

obstinate *adj* adamant, *inf* bloody-minded, defiant, determined, dogged, firm, headstrong, inflexible, intractable, intransigent, *inf* mulish, obdurate, persistent, pertinacious, *inf* pig-headed, refractory, resolute, rigid, self-willed, single-minded, stubborn, tenacious, uncooperative, unreasonable, unyielding, wilful. *Opp* AMENABLE.

obstreperous *adj* boisterous, disorderly, irrepressible, naughty, rowdy, turbulent, uncontrollable, undisciplined, unmanageable, unruly, wild. ▷ NOISY. *Opp* WELL-BEHAVED.

obstruct *v* arrest, bar, block, check, curb, delay, deter, frustrate, halt, hamper, hinder, hold up, impede, inhibit, interfere with, interrupt, prevent, restrict, retard, slow down, stand in the way of, stop, *inf* stymie, thwart. *Opp* HELP.

obtain *v* 1 acquire, attain, be given, buy, capture, come by, come into possession of, earn, enlist (*help*), extort, extract, find, gain, get, *inf* get hold of, *inf* lay your hands on, *inf* pick up, procure, purchase, receive, secure, seize, win. 2 *rules still obtain.* apply, be in force, be relevant, be valid, exist, prevail, stand.

obtrusive *adj* blatant, conspicuous, inescapable, intrusive, noticeable, out of place, prominent, unwanted, unwelcome. ▷ OBVIOUS. *Opp* INCONSPICUOUS.

obtuse *adj* dense, dull, slow, slow-witted. ▷ STUPID. *Opp* CLEVER.

obviate *v* make unnecessary, preclude, prevent, remove.

obvious *adj* apparent, blatant, clear, clear-cut, conspicuous, distinct, evident, eye-catching, flagrant, glaring, manifest, notable, noticeable, obtrusive, open, overt, palpable, patent, perceptible, plain, prominent, pronounced, recognizable, self-evident, self-explanatory, straightforward, unconcealed, undisguised, unmistakable, visible. *Opp* HIDDEN, OBSCURE.

occasion *n* 1 chance, moment, opportunity, time. 2 *no occasion for rudeness.* call, cause, excuse, grounds, justification, need, reason. 3 *happy occasion.* celebration, ceremony, event, function, *inf* get-together, happening, incident, occurrence, party.

occasional *adj* desultory, fitful, infrequent, intermittent, irregular, odd, *inf* once in a while, periodic, random, rare, spasmodic, sporadic, unpredictable. *Opp* FREQUENT, REGULAR.

occult *adj* ▷ SUPERNATURAL.

• *n* black arts, black magic, sorcery, the supernatural, witchcraft.

occupant *n* denizen, householder, inhabitant, occupier, owner, resident, tenant.

occupation *n* 1 lease, occupancy, possession, tenancy, tenure, use. 2 colonization, conquest, invasion, oppression, seizure, subjection, subjugation, *inf* takeover, usurpation. 3 business, calling, career, employment, job, *inf* line, métier, position, post, profession, situation, trade, vocation, work. 4 *leisure occupation.* activity, entertainment, hobby, interest, pastime, pursuit, recreation.

occupy *v* 1 dwell in, inhabit, live in, move into, reside in. 2 *occupy space.* fill, take up, use, utilize. 3 capture, colonize, conquer, invade, overrun, subjugate, take over, take possession of. 4 *occupy your time.* absorb, divert, engage, engross, involve, preoccupy. **occupied** ▷ BUSY.

occur *v* appear, arise, befall, be found, chance, come about, *inf* crop up, develop, exist, happen, materialize, *inf* show up, take place, transpire, *inf* turn out, *inf* turn up.

occurrence *n* affair, case, circumstance, development, event, happening, incident, manifestation, matter, occasion, phenomenon, proceeding.

odd *adj* 1 *odd numbers.* uneven. *Opp* EVEN. 2 *odd sock.* extra, left over, remaining, single, spare, superfluous, surplus. 3 *odd jobs.* casual, irregular, miscellaneous, occasional, random, sundry, varied, various. 4 *odd behaviour.* abnormal, anomalous, atypical, bizarre, curious, deviant, different, eccentric, extraordinary, freak, funny, incongruous, inexplicable, outlandish, out of the ordinary, peculiar, puzzling, queer, rare, singular, strange, uncharacteristic, uncommon, unconventional, unexpected, unusual, weird. *Opp* NORMAL.

oddments *pl n* bits, bits and pieces, fragments, junk, leftovers, litter, odds and ends, remnants, scraps, shreds.

odious *adj* detestable, execrable, loathsome, offensive, repugnant, repulsive. ▷ HATEFUL.

odorous *adj* fragrant, perfumed, scented. ▷ SMELLING.

odour *n* aroma, bouquet, fragrance, nose, redolence, scent, smell, stench, *inf* stink.

odourless *adj* deodorized, unscented. *Opp* ODOROUS.

offence *n* 1 crime, fault, infringement, lapse, misdeed, misdemeanour, outrage, peccadillo, sin, transgression, violation, wrong, wrongdoing. 2 anger, annoyance, disgust, displeasure, hard feelings, indignation, irritation, pique, resentment. **give offence** ▷ OFFEND.

offend *v* 1 affront, anger, annoy, disgust, displease, embarrass, give offence, insult, irritate, *inf* miff, outrage, provoke, *inf* put your back up, sicken, snub, upset, vex. 2 *offend against the law.* do wrong, transgress. **be offended** be annoyed, *inf* take umbrage.

offender *n* criminal, culprit, delinquent, guilty party, malefactor, miscreant, sinner, transgressor, wrongdoer.

offensive *adj* 1 abusive, annoying, antisocial, coarse, detestable, disagreeable, displeasing, disrespectful, embarrassing, impolite, indecent, insulting, loathsome, nasty, nauseating, noxious, objectionable, obnoxious, *inf* off-putting, repugnant, revolting, rude, sickening, unpleasant, unsavoury. ▷ OBSCENE. *Opp* PLEASANT. 2 *offensive action.* aggressive, antagonistic, hostile, threatening, warlike. *Opp* PEACEABLE.

• *n* ▷ ATTACK.

offer *n* bid, proposal, proposition, suggestion, tender.

• *v* 1 bid, extend, give the opportunity of, hold out, make an offer of, make available, proffer, put forward, put up, suggest. 2 *offer to help.* come forward, propose, *inf* show willing, volunteer.

offering *n* contribution, donation, gift, present, sacrifice.

offhand *adj* 1 abrupt, aloof, careless, cavalier, cool, curt, perfunctory, unceremonious, uninterested. ▷ CASUAL. 2 ▷ IMPROMPTU.

office *n* 1 bureau, workplace. 2 appointment, duty, function, job, occupation, place, position, post, responsibility, role, situation, work.

officer *n* 1 adjutant, aide-de-camp, CO, commanding officer. 2 constable, PC, policeman, policewoman, WPC. 3 ▷ OFFICIAL.

official *adj* accredited, approved, authentic, authoritative, authorized, bona fide, certified, formal, lawful, legal, legitimate, licensed, organized, recognized, valid. ▷ FORMAL.

• *n* administrator, agent, appointee, authorized person, bureaucrat, commissioner, dignitary, diplomat, executive, functionary, inspector, mandarin, minister, officer, organizer, representative, steward, umpire.

officiate *v* adjudicate, be in charge, be responsible, chair (*a meeting*), conduct, manage, preside, referee, umpire.

officious *adj inf* bossy, bumptious, dictatorial, forward, interfering, over-zealous, *inf* pushy, self-important.

offset *v* cancel out, compensate for, counteract, make amends for, make good, make up for, redress. ▷ BALANCE.

offshoot *n* branch, by-product, development, *inf* spin-off.

offspring *n* [*sing*] baby, child, descendant, heir, successor. [*pl*] brood, family, issue, litter, progeny, young.

often *adv* commonly, frequently, generally, habitually, regularly, repeatedly, time after time, time and again, usually.

oil *v* grease, lubricate.

oily *adj* 1 buttery, fatty, greasy. 2 *oily manner*. ▷ OBSEQUIOUS.

ointment *n* balm, cream, embrocation, liniment, lotion, salve.

old *adj* 1 ancient, antediluvian, antiquated, antique, crumbling, decaying, decrepit, dilapidated, early, historic, medieval, primitive, ruined, superannuated, time-worn, venerable, veteran, vintage. ▷ OLD-FASHIONED. 2 *old times*. bygone, former, (*time*) immemorial, olden (*days*), past, prehistoric, previous, remote. 3 *old people*. advanced in years, aged, *inf* doddery, elderly, geriatric, *inf* getting on, grey-haired, hoary, *inf* in your dotage, *inf* past it, senile. 4 *old customs*. age-old, established, lasting, long-standing, time-honoured, traditional. 5 *old clothes*. moth-eaten, ragged, *inf* scruffy, shabby, threadbare, worn, worn-out. 6 *old bread*. dry, stale. 7 *old tickets*. expired, invalid, used. 8 *old hand*. experienced, expert, familiar, practised, skilled, veteran. *Opp* NEW, YOUNG. **old age** *inf* declining years, decrepitude, dotage, senility.

old-fashioned *adj* anachronistic, antiquated, archaic, backward-looking, conventional, dated, narrow-minded, obsolete, old, *inf* old hat, out-of-date, out-of-touch, outmoded, passé, prudish, reactionary, time-honoured, traditional, unfashionable. *Opp* MODERN. **old-fashioned person** *inf* fogey, *inf* fuddy-duddy, reactionary, *inf* square.

omen *n* augury, foreboding, forewarning, harbinger, indication, portent, premonition, presage, sign, token, warning.

ominous *adj* baleful, dire, fateful, forbidding, foreboding, grim, ill-omened, ill-starred, inauspicious, menacing, portentous, prophetic, sinister, threatening, unfavourable, unlucky, unpromising, unpropitious. *Opp* AUSPICIOUS.

omission *n* 1 deletion, elimination, exclusion. 2 failure, oversight.

omit *v* 1 cut, dispense with, drop, eliminate, erase, exclude, ignore, jump, leave out, miss out, overlook, pass over, reject, skip. 2 fail, forget, neglect.

omnipotent *adj* all-powerful, almighty, invincible, supreme.

oncoming *adj* advancing, approaching, looming.

onerous *adj* burdensome, demanding, heavy, laborious, taxing. ▷ DIFFICULT.

one-sided *adj* 1 biased, bigoted, partial, partisan, prejudiced. 2 *one-sided game*. unbalanced, unequal, uneven.

onlooker *n* bystander, eyewitness, looker-on, observer, spectator, watcher, witness.

only *adj* lone, single, sole, solitary, unique. • *adv* just, merely, simply, solely.

ooze *v* bleed, discharge, emit, exude, leak, secrete, seep.

opaque *adj* cloudy, dark, dim, dull, filmy, muddy, murky, unclear. *Opp* CLEAR.

open *adj* 1 ajar, gaping, unfastened, unlocked, unsealed, wide-open, yawning. 2 accessible, available, exposed, free, public, revealed, unprotected, unrestricted. 3 *open space*. broad, clear, empty, extensive, spacious, treeless, uncrowded, undefended, vacant. 4 *open arms*. extended, outstretched. 5 *open nature*. artless, candid, communicative, frank, generous, guileless, honest, innocent, open-minded, sincere, straightforward, uninhibited. 6 *open defiance*. barefaced, blatant, conspicuous, downright, evident, flagrant, obvious, outspoken, overt, plain, unconcealed, undisguised, visible. 7 *open question*. arguable, debatable, moot, unanswered, undecided, unresolved. *Opp* CLOSED, HIDDEN.

• *v* 1 unblock, uncork, undo, unfasten, unfold, unfurl, unlatch, unlock, unseal, untie, unwrap. 2 *open proceedings*. begin, commence, establish, *inf* get going, inaugurate, initiate, *inf* kick off, launch, set in motion, set up, start. *Opp* CLOSE.

opening *adj* first, inaugural, initial, introductory. *Opp* FINAL.

• *n* 1 aperture, breach, break, chink, cleft, crack, crevice, doorway, fissure, gap, gateway, hatch, hole, leak, mouth, orifice, outlet, rift, slit, slot, space, split, tear, vent. 2 beginning, birth, dawn, inauguration, inception, initiation, launch, outset, start. 3 *business opening. inf* break, chance, opportunity, way in.

operate *v* 1 act, function, go, perform, run, work. 2 *operate a machine.* control, drive, handle, manage, use, work. 3 perform surgery.

operation *n* 1 control, direction, management. 2 action, activity, business, campaign, effort, enterprise, exercise, manoeuvre, movement, procedure, proceeding, process, transaction, undertaking, venture. 3 [*medical*] biopsy, surgery, transplant.

operational *adj* functioning, going, in operation, in working order, operating, *inf* up and running, usable, working.

operative *adj* ▷ OPERATIONAL.
• *n* ▷ WORKER.

opinion *n* assessment, belief, conclusion, conjecture, conviction, estimate, feeling, guess, idea, impression, judgement, notion, perception, point of view, sentiment, theory, thought, view, viewpoint.

opponent *n* adversary, antagonist, competitor, contender, contestant, enemy, foe, opposition, rival. *Opp* ALLY.

opportune *adj* advantageous, appropriate, auspicious, convenient, favourable, felicitous, fortunate, good, happy, lucky, propitious, suitable, timely, well-timed. *Opp* INCONVENIENT.

opportunity *n inf* break, chance, moment, occasion, opening, possibility, time.

oppose *v* argue with, attack, challenge, combat, compete against, confront, contend with, contest, contradict, counter, counter-attack, defy, disagree with, face, fight, object to, obstruct, quarrel with, resist, rival, stand up to, *inf* take a stand against, take issue with, withstand. *Opp* SUPPORT. **opposed** ▷ HOSTILE, OPPOSITE.

opposite *adj* 1 antithetical, conflicting, contradictory, contrasting, converse, different, hostile, incompatible, opposed, opposing, rival. 2 contrary, reverse. 3 *your opposite number.* corresponding, equivalent, facing, matching.
• *n* antithesis, contrary, converse, reverse.

opposition *n* antagonism, antipathy, competition, defiance, enmity, hostility, objection, resistance. ▷ OPPONENT. *Opp* SUPPORT.

oppress *v* abuse, afflict, burden, crush, depress, enslave, exploit, grind down, harass, intimidate, keep under, maltreat, persecute, subdue, subjugate, terrorize, *inf* trample on, tyrannize, weigh down.

oppressed *adj* browbeaten, downtrodden, enslaved, exploited, persecuted.

oppression *n* abuse, exploitation, harassment, injustice, maltreatment, persecution, pressure, repression, suppression, tyranny.

oppressive *adj* 1 brutal, cruel, despotic, harsh, repressive, tyrannical, unjust. 2 airless, close, heavy, hot, humid, muggy, stifling, stuffy, suffocating, sultry.

optimism *n* buoyancy, cheerfulness, confidence, hope, idealism, positiveness. *Opp* PESSIMISM.

optimistic *adj* buoyant, cheerful, confident, expectant, hopeful, idealistic, positive, sanguine. *Opp* PESSIMISTIC.

optimum *adj* highest, ideal, maximum, most favourable, perfect, prime. ▷ BEST.

option *n* alternative, chance, choice, possibility, selection.

optional *adj* discretionary, dispensable, inessential, possible, unforced, unnecessary, voluntary. *Opp* COMPULSORY.

oral *adj* by mouth, said, spoken, unwritten, verbal, vocal.

oratory *n* declamation, eloquence, fluency, *inf* gift of the gab, grandiloquence, rhetoric, speaking, speech making.

orbit *n* circuit, course, path, revolution, trajectory.
• *v* circle, travel round.

orchestrate *v* 1 arrange, compose. 2 ▷ ORGANIZE.

ordeal *n* difficulty, distress, hardship, misery, *inf* nightmare, suffering, test, torture, trial, tribulation, trouble.

order *n* 1 arrangement, array, classification, disposition, lay-out, *inf* line-up, neatness, organization, pattern, progression, sequence, series, succession, system, tidiness. 2 calm, control, discipline, government, harmony, law and order, obedience, orderliness, peace, quiet, rule. 3 *social order.* caste, category, class, degree, group, hierarchy, level, rank, status. 4 *in good order.* condition, repair, state. 5 command, decree, direction, directive, edict, fiat, injunction, instruction, law, mandate, ordinance, regulation, requirement, rule. 6 application, booking, commission, demand, request, requisition. 7 *religious order.* association, brotherhood, community, group, lodge, sect, sisterhood, society. *Opp* DISORDER.
• *v* 1 arrange, categorize, classify, codify,

lay out, organize, put in order, sort out, tidy up. 2 command, compel, decree, demand, direct, enjoin, instruct, require, tell. 3 book, reserve, requisition, send away for.

orderly *adj* 1 careful, methodical, neat, organized, regular, symmetrical, systematic, tidy, well-organized. *Opp* CONFUSED, DISORGANIZED. 2 civilized, controlled, decorous, disciplined, law-abiding, peaceable, restrained, well-behaved. *Opp* UNDISCIPLINED.

ordinary *adj* accustomed, average, common, *inf* common or garden, commonplace, conventional, customary, established, everyday, familiar, habitual, humble, humdrum, indifferent, mediocre, moderate, modest, mundane, nondescript, normal, orthodox, passable, pedestrian, plain, prosaic, regular, routine, *inf* run-of-the-mill, satisfactory, simple, *inf* so-so, standard, stock, typical, undistinguished, unexceptional, unexciting, unimpressive, uninteresting, unremarkable, unsurprising, usual, workaday. *Opp* EXTRAORDINARY.

organic *adj* 1 animate, biological, growing, live, living, natural. 2 *organic whole.* coherent, coordinated, evolving, integral, integrated, organized, structured, systematic.

organism *n* animal, being, cell, creature, living thing.

organization *n* 1 arrangement, categorization, classification, codification, composition, coordination, planning, *inf* running, structuring. 2 alliance, association, body, business, club, company, concern, confederation, consortium, corporation, federation, firm, group, institute, institution, league, network, *inf* outfit, party, society, syndicate, union.

organize *v* 1 arrange, catalogue, categorize, classify, codify, coordinate, group, order, pigeon-hole, put in order, rearrange, regiment, sort, sort out, structure, systematize, tidy up. 2 coordinate, deal with, establish, make arrangements for, manage, mobilize, orchestrate, plan, put together, run, *inf* see to, set up. **organized** ▷ OFFICIAL, SYSTEMATIC.

orgy *n inf* binge, *inf* fling, party, revel, revelry, *inf* splurge, *inf* spree.

orient *v* acclimatize, accustom, adapt, adjust, familiarize, orientate, position.

oriental *adj* Asiatic, eastern, far-eastern.

origin *n* 1 basis, beginning, birth, cause, commencement, cradle, creation, dawn, derivation, foundation, fount, genesis, inauguration, inception, provenance, root, source, start. *Opp* END. 2 *humble origin.* ancestry, background, descent, extraction, family, parentage, pedigree, start in life, stock.

original *adj* 1 archetypal, earliest, first, initial, native, primitive. 2 *original antiques.* authentic, genuine, real, true, unique. 3 *original ideas.* creative, fresh, imaginative, ingenious, innovative, inspired, inventive, new, novel, resourceful, unconventional, unfamiliar, unique, unusual. *Opp* HACKNEYED.

originate *v* 1 arise, be born, be derived, be descended, begin, commence, derive, emanate, emerge, issue, proceed, start, stem. 2 coin, conceive, create, design, discover, engender, found, give birth to, inaugurate, initiate, inspire, institute, introduce, invent, launch, pioneer, produce, think up.

ornament *n* accessory, adornment, bauble, decoration, embellishment, embroidery, filigree, frill, frippery, garnish, ornamentation, tracery, trimming, trinket. ▷ JEWELLERY.
• *v* adorn, beautify, deck, decorate, dress up, elaborate, embellish, embroider, festoon, garnish, prettify, trim.

ornamental *adj* attractive, decorative, fancy, pretty, showy.

ornate *adj* baroque, *inf* busy, decorated, elaborate, fancy, florid, flowery, fussy, luxuriant, overdone, pretentious, rococo. *Opp* PLAIN.

orphan *n* foundling, stray, waif.

orthodox *adj* accepted, approved, authorized, conservative, conventional, customary, established, mainstream, normal, official, ordinary, prevailing, recognized, regular, standard, traditional, usual. *Opp* UNCONVENTIONAL.

ostensible *adj* alleged, apparent, outward, pretended, professed, seeming, supposed. *Opp* REAL.

ostentation *n* affectation, display, exhibitionism, flamboyance, flaunting, parade, pretentiousness, show, showing-off, *inf* swank. *Opp* MODESTY.

ostentatious *adj* flamboyant, *inf* flashy, pretentious, showy, *inf* swanky, vulgar. ▷ BOASTFUL. *Opp* MODEST.

ostracize *v* avoid, banish, blacklist, boycott, cast out, cold-shoulder, *inf* cut, *inf* cut dead, exclude, expel, isolate, reject, *inf* send to Coventry, shun, shut out, snub.

oust *v* banish, drive out, eject, expel, *inf* kick out, remove, replace, supplant, unseat.

outbreak *n* epidemic, *inf* flare-up, plague, rash, upsurge.

outburst *n* attack, eruption, explosion, fit, flood, outbreak, outpouring, paroxysm, rush, spasm, surge, upsurge.

outcast *n* displaced person, exile, leper, outlaw, outsider, pariah, refugee.

outcome *n* ▷ RESULT.

outcry *n* clamour, complaint, hue and cry, objection, protest, protestation, uproar.

outdo *v* beat, defeat, exceed, excel, *inf* get the better of, outdistance, outshine, outstrip, overcome, surpass, top.

outdoor *adj* alfresco, open-air, out of doors, outside.

outer *adj* 1 exterior, external, outside, outward, superficial, surface. 2 distant, outlying, peripheral, remote. *Opp* INNER.

outfit *n* 1 accoutrements, clothes, costume, equipment, garb, *inf* gear, *inf* get-up, suit, trappings. 2 ▷ ORGANIZATION.

outgoing *adj* 1 *outgoing president.* departing, ex-, former, last, past, retiring. 2 *outgoing tide.* ebbing, falling, retreating. 3 ▷ SOCIABLE. *Opp* INCOMING. **outgoings** ▷ EXPENSE.

outing *n* excursion, expedition, jaunt, ride, tour, trip.

outlast *v* outlive, survive.

outlaw *n* bandit, brigand, criminal, deserter, desperado, fugitive, highwayman, marauder, outcast, renegade, robber.
• *v* ban, exclude, forbid, prohibit, proscribe. ▷ BANISH.

outlet *n* 1 channel, duct, exit, mouth, opening, orifice, safety valve, vent, way out. 2 ▷ SHOP.

outline *n* 1 *inf* bare bones, diagram, draft, framework, plan, précis, résumé, *inf* rough idea, scenario, skeleton, sketch, summary, synopsis. 2 contour, figure, form, profile, shadow, shape, silhouette.
• *v* delineate, draft, give the gist of, plan out, rough out, sketch out, summarize.

outlook *n* 1 ▷ VISTA. 2 *mental outlook.* attitude, frame of mind, opinion, perspective, point of view, position, slant, viewpoint. 3 *outlook for the future.* forecast, prediction, prognosis, prospect.

outlying *adj* distant, far-away, far-flung, far-off, outer, outermost, remote. *Opp* CENTRAL.

output *n* achievement, crop, harvest, production, yield.

outrage *n* 1 atrocity, crime, *inf* disgrace, enormity, indignity, scandal, *inf* sensation. 2 anger, disgust, fury, horror, indignation, resentment, revulsion, shock, wrath.
• *v* ▷ ANGER.

outrageous *adj* 1 abominable, atrocious, barbaric, beastly, cruel, disgraceful, disgusting, infamous, monstrous, nefarious, notorious, offensive, preposterous, scandalous, shocking, unspeakable, unthinkable, wicked. 2 *outrageous prices.* excessive, extortionate, extravagant, unreasonable. *Opp* REASONABLE.

outside *adj* 1 exterior, external, facing, outer, outward, superficial, surface, visible. 2 *outside interference.* extraneous, foreign. 3 *outside chance.* ▷ REMOTE.
• *n* casing, exterior, façade, face, front, shell, skin, surface.

outsider *n* alien, foreigner, gatecrasher, guest, immigrant, interloper, newcomer, non-resident, outcast, stranger, trespasser, visitor.

outskirts *pl n* borders, edge, fringe, margin, periphery, suburbs. *Opp* CENTRE.

outspoken *adj* blunt, candid, direct, explicit, forthright, frank, tactless, unambiguous, undiplomatic. ▷ HONEST. *Opp* EVASIVE.

outstanding *adj* 1 conspicuous, distinguished, dominant, eminent, excellent, exceptional, extraordinary, first-class, first-rate, important, impressive, memorable, noteworthy, noticeable, pre-eminent, remarkable, singular, special, striking, superior, unrivalled. ▷ FAMOUS. *Opp* ORDINARY. 2 ▷ OVERDUE.

outward *adj* apparent, evident, exterior, external, manifest, noticeable, observable, obvious, ostensible, outer, outside, superficial, surface, visible.

outwit *v* deceive, dupe, fool, *inf* get the better of, make a fool of, outmanoeuvre, *inf* outsmart, *inf* put one over on, trick. ▷ CHEAT.

oval *adj* egg-shaped, ovoid.

ovation *n* acclamation, applause, cheering, clapping, plaudits, praise.

overcast *adj* black, cloudy, dark, dismal, dull, gloomy, grey, leaden, lowering, murky, sombre, stormy, sunless, threatening. *Opp* CLOUDLESS.

overcoat *n* greatcoat, mackintosh, topcoat, trench coat.

overcome *adj* beaten, *inf* done in, exhausted, overwhelmed, prostrate, speechless.
• *v* ▷ OVERTHROW.

overcrowded *adj* congested, crammed, jammed, *inf* jam-packed, overloaded, packed.

overdue *adj* 1 belated, delayed, late, slow, unpunctual. *Opp* EARLY. 2 *overdue bills.* outstanding, owing, unpaid, unsettled.

overeat *v* be greedy, feast, gorge, guzzle, *inf* make a pig of yourself, overindulge, stuff yourself.

overflow *v* brim over, flood, pour over, run over, spill.

overgrown *adj* 1 outsize, oversized. ▷ BIG. 2 *overgrown garden.* overrun, rank, tangled, uncut, unkempt, untidy, unweeded, wild.

overhang *v* bulge, jut, project, protrude, stick out.

overhaul *v* check over, examine, *inf* fix, inspect, mend, recondition, renovate, repair, restore, service.

overhead *adj* aerial, elevated, overhanging, raised, upper.

overlook *v* 1 fail to notice, forget, miss, neglect, omit. 2 condone, disregard, excuse, gloss over, ignore, pardon, pass over, pay no attention to, *inf* shut your eyes to, *inf* turn a blind eye to, *inf* write off. 3 *overlook a lake.* face, front, have a view of, look on to.

overpower *v* ▷ OVERTHROW.

overpowering *adj* compelling, consuming, irresistible, overriding, overwhelming, powerful, strong, unbearable, uncontrollable, unendurable.

oversee *v* be in charge of, direct. ▷ SUPERVISE.

oversight *n* 1 carelessness, error, failure, fault, mistake, omission. 2 control, direction, management, supervision, surveillance.

overstate *v* *inf* blow up out of proportion, embroider, exaggerate, magnify, make too much of, maximize.

overt *adj* apparent, blatant, clear, evident, manifest, obvious, open, patent, plain, unconcealed, undisguised, visible. *Opp* SECRET.

overtake *v* catch up with, gain on, leave behind, outdistance, outpace, outstrip, pass.

overthrow *n* conquest, defeat, destruction, rout, subjugation, suppression.
• *v* beat, bring down, conquer, crush, deal with, defeat, depose, dethrone, get the better of, master, oust, overcome, overpower, overturn, overwhelm, rout, subdue, *inf* topple, triumph over, unseat, vanquish.

overtone *n* association, connotation, implication, suggestion, undertone.

overturn *v* 1 capsize, flip, invert, keel over, spill, tip over, topple, *inf* turn turtle, turn upside down, up-end, upset. 2 ▷ OVERTHROW.

overwhelm *v* 1 engulf, flood, immerse, inundate, submerge, swamp. 2 ▷ OVERTHROW. **overwhelming** ▷ OVERPOWERING.

owe *v* be in debt, be indebted to, have debts.

owing *adj* due, outstanding, overdue, owed, payable, unpaid, unsettled. **owing to** because of, caused by, resulting from, thanks to, through.

own *v* have, hold, keep, possess. **own up** ▷ CONFESS.

owner *n* holder, landlady, landlord, possessor, proprietor.

P

pace *n* 1 step, stride. 2 *fast pace.* gait, movement, rate, speed, tempo.
• *v* ▷ WALK.

pacify *v* appease, assuage, calm, conciliate, humour, mollify, placate, quell, quieten, soothe, subdue, tame. *Opp* ANGER.

pack *n* 1 bale, box, bundle, package, packet, parcel. 2 backpack, haversack, kitbag, knapsack, rucksack. 3 ▷ GROUP.
• *v* 1 bundle (up), fill, load, package, parcel up, put, put together, store, stow, wrap up. 2 compress, cram, crowd, jam, press, ram, squeeze, stuff, tamp down, wedge. **pack off** ▷ DISMISS. **pack up** ▷ FINISH.

pact *n* agreement, alliance, arrangement, bargain, concord, contract, covenant, deal, entente, league, peace, settlement, treaty, truce, understanding.

pad *n* 1 cushion, hassock, kneeler, padding, pillow, wad. 2 jotter, notebook, writing pad.
• *v* cushion, fill, pack, protect, stuff. **pad out** ▷ EXTEND.

padding *n* 1 filling, protection, stuffing, wadding. 2 verbiage, verbosity, *inf* waffle, wordiness.

paddle *n* oar, scull.
• *v* 1 propel, row, scull. 2 dabble, splash about, wade.

paddock *n* enclosure, field, meadow, pasture.

pagan *adj* atheistic, godless, heathen, idolatrous, infidel, irreligious, unchristian.
• *n* atheist, heathen, infidel, unbeliever.

page *n* 1 folio, leaf, sheet, side. 2 messenger, page-boy.

pageant *n* display, parade, procession, spectacle, tableau.

pageantry *n* ceremony, display, formality, grandeur, magnificence, pomp, ritual, show, spectacle, splendour.

pain *n* ache, affliction, agony, anguish, cramp, discomfort, distress, headache, hurt, irritation, ordeal, pang, smart, soreness, spasm, stab, sting, suffering, tenderness, throb, *pl* throes, toothache, torment, torture, twinge.
• *v* ▷ HURT.

painful *adj* 1 aching, *inf* achy, agonizing, burning, excruciating, hard to bear, hurting, inflamed, piercing, raw, severe, sharp, smarting, sore, *inf* splitting (*head*), stabbing, stinging, tender, throbbing. 2 distressing, harrowing, hurtful, traumatic, trying, unpleasant, upsetting. 3 *painful decision.* difficult, hard, troublesome. *Opp* PAINLESS. **be painful** ▷ HURT.

painkiller *n* anaesthetic, analgesic, anodyne, sedative.

painless *adj* comfortable, easy, effortless, simple, trouble-free. *Opp* PAINFUL.

paint *n* colour, colouring, dye, pigment, stain, tint.
• *v* 1 coat, colour, cover, daub, decorate, enamel, gild, lacquer, redecorate, stain, tint, touch up, varnish, whitewash. 2 delineate, depict, describe, picture, portray, represent.

painter *n* artist, decorator, illustrator, miniaturist.

painting *n* fresco, landscape, miniature, mural, oil painting, portrait, still life, water colour.

pair *n* brace, couple, duet, duo, set of two, twins, twosome.
• *v* **pair off, pair up** find a partner, get together, *inf* make a twosome, match up, mate, *inf* pal up, team up.

palace *n* castle, chateau, mansion, official residence, stately home.

palatable *adj* acceptable, agreeable, appetizing, easy to take, eatable, edible, pleasant, tasty. *Opp* UNPALATABLE.

palatial *adj* aristocratic, grand, luxurious, majestic, opulent, *inf* posh, splendid, stately, up-market.

pale *adj* 1 anaemic, ashen, blanched, bloodless, colourless, *inf* deathly, drained, etiolated, ghastly, ghostly, pallid, pasty, *inf* peaky, sallow, sickly, unhealthy, wan, *inf* washed-out, *inf* whey-faced, white, whitish. 2 *pale colours.* bleached, faded, faint, light, pastel, subtle, weak. *Opp* BRIGHT.
• *v* blanch, fade, lighten, lose colour, whiten.

pall *n* cloth, mantle, shroud, veil. ▷ COVERING.
• *v* become boring, cloy, irritate, jade, sate, satiate, weary.

palliative *adj* calming, reassuring, sedative, soothing.
• *n* sedative, tranquillizer.

palpable *adj* apparent, corporeal, evident, manifest, obvious, patent, physical, real, solid, substantial, tangible, visible. *Opp* INTANGIBLE.

palpitate *v* beat, flutter, pound, pulsate, quiver, throb, vibrate.

paltry *adj* contemptible, inconsequential, insignificant, petty, *inf* piddling, pitiful, puny, trifling, unimportant, worthless. ▷ SMALL. *Opp* IMPORTANT.

pamper *v* cosset, indulge, mollycoddle, overindulge, pet, spoil, spoonfeed.

pamphlet *n* booklet, brochure, bulletin, catalogue, circular, flyer, folder, handbill, leaflet, notice, tract.

pan *n* container, pan, saucepan, utensil. • *v* ▷ CRITICIZE.

panache *n* confidence, dash, élan, flair, flamboyance, flourish, *Fr* savoir faire, self-assurance, spirit, style, verve, zest.

pandemonium *n* babel, bedlam, chaos, hubbub, *inf* rumpus, turmoil, uproar. ▷ COMMOTION.

pander *n* go-between, *inf* pimp. • *v* **pander to** cater for, fulfil, gratify, humour, indulge, please, satisfy.

pane *n* glass, panel, sheet of glass, window-pane.

panel *n* 1 insert, pane, panelling, rectangular piece. 2 committee, group, jury, team.

panic *n* alarm, consternation, *inf* flap, horror, hysteria, stampede, terror. ▷ FEAR. • *v* become panic-stricken, *inf* flap, *inf* go to pieces, *inf* lose your head, overreact, stampede.

panic-stricken *adj* alarmed, *inf* beside yourself, frantic, frenzied, horrified, hysterical, *inf* in a cold sweat, *inf* in a tizzy, jumpy, panicky, terror-stricken, unnerved, worked up. ▷ FRIGHTENED. *Opp* CALM.

panorama *n* landscape, prospect, scene, view, vista.

panoramic *adj* extensive, scenic, sweeping, wide.

pant *v* breathe quickly, gasp, *inf* huff and puff, puff, wheeze. **panting** ▷ BREATHLESS.

pants *n* 1 boxer shorts, briefs, cami-knickers, drawers, knickers, shorts, *inf* smalls, underpants, *inf* undies, Y-fronts. 2 [*Amer*] trousers.

paper *n* 1 folio, leaf, sheet. 2 [often *pl*] certificate, deed, document, form, licence, record. 3 *daily paper*. *inf* daily, journal, newspaper, *inf* rag, tabloid. 4 *academic paper*. article, discourse, dissertation, essay thesis, treatise.

parable *n* allegory, fable, moral tale.

parade *n* cavalcade, ceremony, column, cortège, display, file, march-past, motorcade, pageant, procession, show, spectacle. • *v* 1 assemble, file past, form up, line up, march past, process. 2 ▷ DISPLAY.

paradise *n* bliss, Eden, heaven, nirvana, Utopia.

paradox *n* absurdity, anomaly, contradiction, incongruity, inconsistency.

paradoxical *adj* absurd, anomalous, conflicting, contradictory, illogical, incongruous.

parallel *adj* 1 equidistant. 2 *parallel events*. analogous, contemporary, corresponding, equivalent, like, matching, similar. • *n* 1 counterpart, equal, likeness, match. 2 analogy, comparison, correspondence, equivalence, resemblance, similarity. • *v* be parallel with, correspond to, equate with, keep pace with, match, run alongside.

paralyse *v* 1 cripple, disable, incapacitate. 2 anaesthetize, deaden, desensitize, freeze, halt, immobilize, numb, stop, stun.

paralysed *adj* 1 crippled, disabled, incapacitated, palsied. 2 dead, desensitized, frozen, immobile, numb, unusable, useless.

paralysis *n* 1 immobility, numbness, palsy. 2 breakdown, halt, standstill.

paraphernalia *pl n* accessories, baggage, belongings, effects, equipment, materials, *inf* odds and ends, possessions, property, stuff, tackle, things, trappings.

paraphrase *v* explain, interpret, put into other words, rephrase, translate.

parcel *n* bale, box, bundle, carton, case, pack, package, packet. **parcel out** ▷ DIVIDE. **parcel up** ▷ PACK.

parch *v* bake, burn, dehydrate, desiccate, dry, scorch, shrivel, wither. **parched** ▷ DRY, THIRSTY.

pardon *n* absolution, amnesty, discharge, exoneration, forgiveness, indulgence, mercy, release, reprieve. • *v* absolve, condone, exculpate, excuse, exonerate, forgive, free, let off, overlook, release, reprieve, set free, spare.

pardonable *adj* allowable, excusable,

forgivable, justifiable, minor, negligible, petty, understandable, venial (*sin*). *Opp* UNFORGIVABLE.

parent *n* begetter, father, guardian, mother, procreator.

parentage *n* ancestry, birth, descent, extraction, family, line, lineage, pedigree, stock.

park *n* common, estate, gardens, grounds, nature reserve, parkland, recreation ground.
• *v* deposit, leave, place, position, put, station, store. **park yourself** ▷ SETTLE.

parliament *n* assembly, congress, convocation, council, government, legislature, lower house, upper house.

parody *n* burlesque, caricature, imitation, lampoon, mimicry, satire, *inf* send-up, *inf* spoof, *inf* take-off, travesty.
• *v* ape, burlesque, caricature, imitate, lampoon, mimic, satirize, *inf* send up, *inf* take off. ▷ RIDICULE.

parry *v* avert, block, deflect, evade, fend off, push away, repel, stave off, ward off.

part *n* 1 bit, branch, component, constituent, division, element, fraction, fragment, ingredient, particle, percentage, piece, portion, ramification, scrap, section, segment, shard, share, single item, subdivision, unit. 2 department, faction, party. 3 *part of a book.* chapter, episode. 4 *part of a town.* area, district, neighbourhood, quarter, region, sector. 5 *part of the body.* limb, member, organ. 6 *part in a play.* cameo, character, role.
• *v* 1 detach, disconnect, divide, pull apart, separate, sever, split, sunder. *Opp* JOIN. 2 depart, go away, leave, part company, quit, say goodbye, separate, split up, take leave. *Opp* MEET. **part with** ▷ RELINQUISH. **take part** ▷ PARTICIPATE.

partial *adj* 1 incomplete, limited, qualified. *Opp* COMPLETE. 2 *partial judge.* biased, one-sided, partisan, prejudiced, unfair. *Opp* IMPARTIAL. **be partial to** ▷ LIKE.

participate *v* assist, be involved, contribute, cooperate, engage, enter, help, join in, share, take part.

participation *n* assistance, complicity, contribution, cooperation, engagement, involvement, partnership, sharing.

particle *n* 1 bit, crumb, dot, drop, fragment, grain, hint, iota, jot, mite, morsel, piece, scrap, shred, sliver, *inf* smidgen, speck, trace. 2 atom, molecule.

particular *adj* 1 distinct, idiosyncratic, individual, personal, singular, specific, unique, unmistakable. 2 *particular with detail.* exact, meticulous, nice, painstaking, precise, rigorous, scrupulous, thorough. 3 *gave particular pleasure.* especial, exceptional, marked, notable, outstanding, significant, special, unusual. 4 *particular about food. inf* choosy, discriminating, fastidious, finicky, fussy, *inf* pernickety, selective. *Opp* GENERAL, EASYGOING. **particulars** circumstances, details, facts, information, *inf* low-down.

parting *n* departure, farewell, leave-taking, leaving, saying goodbye, separation.

partisan *adj* biased, bigoted, blinkered, devoted, factional, fanatical, narrow-minded, one-sided, partial, prejudiced, sectarian, unfair. *Opp* IMPARTIAL.
• *n* adherent, devotee, fanatic, freedom fighter, guerrilla, zealot.

partition *n* 1 break-up, division, separation, splitting up. 2 barrier, panel, room-divider, screen, wall.
• *v* cut up, divide, parcel out, separate off, share out, split up, subdivide.

partner *n* 1 accomplice, ally, assistant, associate, *inf* bedfellow, collaborator, colleague, companion, comrade, confederate, helper, *inf* mate. 2 consort, husband, mate, spouse, wife.

partnership *n* 1 affiliation, alliance, association, combination, company, confederation, syndicate. 2 collaboration, complicity, cooperation. 3 marriage, relationship, union.

party *n* 1 celebration, dance, *inf* do, festivity, function, gathering, *inf* get-together, *inf* jollification, *inf* knees-up, merrymaking, *inf* rave-up, reception, *inf* shindig, social gathering. 2 *political party.* alliance, association, *inf* camp, caucus, clique, coalition, faction, league, sect, side. ▷ GROUP.

pass *n* 1 canyon, cut, gap, gorge, gully, opening, passage, ravine, valley, way through. 2 *identity pass.* authorization, clearance, *inf* ID, licence, passport, permission, permit, ticket, warrant.
• *v* 1 go beyond, go by, move on, move past, outstrip, overtake, overshoot, proceed, progress. 2 disappear, elapse, fade, go away, tick by, vanish. 3 *pass drinks.* circulate, deliver, give, hand round, offer, present, share, supply. 4 *pass a resolution.* agree, approve, authorize, confirm, decree, enact, establish, ratify. 5 *pass exams* get through, qualify, succeed. **pass away** ▷ DIE. **pass on** ▷ TRANSFER. **pass out** ▷ FAINT. **pass over** ▷ IGNORE.

passable *adj* 1 acceptable, adequate,

allowable, all right, fair, indifferent, mediocre, middling, moderate, ordinary, satisfactory, *inf* so-so, tolerable. *Opp* UNACCEPTABLE. 2 clear, navigable, open, unobstructed, usable. *Opp* IMPASSABLE.

passage *n* 1 corridor, entrance, hall, hallway, lobby, passageway, vestibule. 2 *passage of time.* advance, flow, lapse, march, movement, passing, progress, transition. 3 *sea passage.* crossing, cruise, journey, voyage. 4 *through passage.* pass, route, thoroughfare, tunnel, way through. 5 *passage from a book.* citation, episode, excerpt, extract, paragraph, piece, quotation, scene, section, selection.

passenger *n* commuter, rider, traveller, voyager.

passer-by *n* bystander, onlooker, witness.

passion *n* appetite, ardour, craving, craze, desire, drive, eagerness, emotion, enthusiasm, fervour, fire, flame, frenzy, greed, heat, hunger, infatuation, intensity, keenness, love, lust, mania, obsession, strong feeling, thirst, urge, vehemence, warmth, zeal, zest.

passionate *adj* ardent, aroused, avid, burning, eager, emotional, enthusiastic, excited, fervent, fiery, frenzied, greedy, heated, hot, hungry, impassioned, infatuated, inflamed, intense, lustful, obsessive, sexy, strong, urgent, vehement, warm, worked up, zealous. *Opp* APATHETIC.

passive *adj* apathetic, complaisant, compliant, docile, inert, inactive, long-suffering, malleable, non-violent, patient, phlegmatic, pliable, quiescent, resigned, submissive, supine, tame, tractable, unassertive, unmoved, yielding. ▷ CALM. *Opp* ACTIVE.

past *adj* bygone, *inf* dead and buried, earlier, ended, finished, forgotten, former, historical, late, *inf* over and done with, previous, recent, sometime.
• *n* antiquity, days gone by, days of yore, former times, history, old days, olden days. *Opp* FUTURE.

paste *n* 1 adhesive, fixative, glue, gum. 2 pâté, spread.
• *v* fix, glue, stick. ▷ FASTEN.

pastiche *n* blend, *inf* hotchpotch, miscellany, mixture, *inf* motley collection, patchwork, selection.

pastime *n* activity, amusement, diversion, entertainment, fun, game, hobby, leisure activity, occupation, play, recreation, relaxation, sport.

pastoral *adj* 1 bucolic, country, idyllic, outdoor, provincial, rural, rustic. ▷ PEACEFUL. *Opp* URBAN. 2 *pastoral duties.* clerical, ecclesiastical, parochial, priestly.

pasture *n* field, grassland, grazing, mead, meadow, paddock.

pat *v* caress, stroke, tap. ▷ TOUCH.

patch *n* 1 darn, mend, repair. 2 area, garden, plot.
• *v* cover, darn, fix, mend, reinforce, repair, sew up, stitch up.

patchy *adj inf* bitty, blotchy, changing, dappled, erratic, inconsistent, irregular, speckled, spotty, uneven, unpredictable, variable, varied, varying. *Opp* UNIFORM.

patent *adj* apparent, evident, manifest, plain, transparent. ▷ OBVIOUS.

path *n* 1 alley, bridle path, footpath, pathway, pavement, road, *Amer* sidewalk, towpath, track, trail, walkway. 2 approach, course, direction, flight path, orbit, route, trajectory, way.

pathetic *adj* 1 affecting, emotional, emotive, heartbreaking, heart-rending, moving, piteous, pitiful, plaintive, poignant, stirring, touching, tragic. ▷ SAD. 2 ▷ INADEQUATE.

pathos *n* pity, poignancy, sadness, tragedy.

patience *n* 1 calmness, composure, endurance, equanimity, forbearance, fortitude, resignation, restraint, self-control, serenity, stoicism, toleration, *inf* unflappability. 2 determination, diligence, doggedness, endurance, firmness, perseverance, persistence, tenacity.

patient *adj* 1 accommodating, acquiescent, calm, composed, docile, easygoing, even-tempered, forbearing, forgiving, lenient, long-suffering, mild, philosophical, quiet, resigned, serene, stoical, tolerant, uncomplaining. 2 *patient worker.* determined, diligent, dogged, persevering, persistent, steady, tenacious, untiring. *Opp* IMPATIENT.
• *n* case, invalid, outpatient, sufferer.

patriot *n derog* chauvinist, loyalist, nationalist, *derog* xenophobe.

patriotic *adj derog* chauvinistic, *derog* jingoistic, loyal, nationalistic, *derog* xenophobic.

patriotism *n derog* chauvinism, *derog* jingoism, loyalty, nationalism, *derog* xenophobia.

patrol *n* 1 beat, guard, policing, sentry duty, surveillance, watch. 2 guard, lookout, patrolman, sentinel, sentry, watchman.

• *v* be on patrol, defend, guard, keep a lookout, make the rounds, police, protect, tour.

patron *n* 1 *inf* angel, backer, benefactor, champion, defender, helper, philanthropist, promoter, sponsor, subscriber, supporter. 2 *patron of a shop.* client, customer, frequenter, *inf* regular.

patronage *n* backing, custom, sponsorship, support, trade.

patronize *v* 1 back, be a patron of, buy from, deal with, encourage, frequent, shop at, support. 2 *Don't patronize me!* *inf* put down, talk down to. **patronizing** ⊳ SUPERIOR.

pattern *n* 1 arrangement, decoration, design, device, figure, motif, ornamentation, sequence, shape. 2 archetype, criterion, example, exemplar, guide, ideal, model, norm, original, precedent, prototype, sample, specimen, standard.

pause *n* break, *inf* breather, breathing-space, delay, gap, halt, hesitation, hiatus, hold-up, interlude, intermission, interruption, interval, *inf* let-up, lull, respite, rest, standstill, stop, suspension, wait.
• *v* break off, delay, falter, halt, hang back, hesitate, mark time, rest, stop, *inf* take a breather, wait.

pave *v* asphalt, concrete, surface, tarmac, tile. **pave the way** ⊳ PREPARE.

pavement *n* footpath, *Amer* sidewalk. ⊳ PATH.

pay *n* dividend, earnings, fee, income, money, payment, profit, recompense, reimbursement, remittance, return, salary, settlement, stipend, take-home pay, wages.
• *v* 1 *inf* cough up, *inf* fork out, give, grant, hand over, recompense, remunerate, spend, *inf* stump up. 2 *pay debts.* bear the cost of, clear, compensate, *inf* foot, honour, meet, pay back, pay off, refund, reimburse, repay, settle. 3 *crime doesn't pay.* be profitable, pay off, produce results. 4 *pay for mistakes.* be punished, suffer. ⊳ ATONE. **pay back** ⊳ RETALIATE.

payment *n* advance, alimony, allowance, charge, commission, compensation, contribution, cost, deposit, donation, expenditure, fare, fee, fine, instalment, loan, outgoings, outlay, premium, price, rate, remittance, reward, royalty, *inf* sub, subscription, surcharge, tip, toll, wage. *Opp* INCOME.

peace *n* 1 accord, agreement, amity, conciliation, concord, friendliness, harmony, order. *Opp* CONFLICT. 2 alliance, armistice, ceasefire, pact, treaty, truce. *Opp* WAR. 3 calmness, peace and quiet, peacefulness, placidity, quiet, repose, serenity, silence, stillness, tranquillity. *Opp* ANXIETY.

peaceable *adj* amicable, civil, conciliatory, cooperative, easygoing, friendly, gentle, harmonious, inoffensive, mild, non-violent, placid, temperate, understanding. *Opp* QUARRELSOME.

peaceful *adj* balmy, calm, easy, gentle, pacific, placid, pleasant, quiet, relaxing, restful, serene, soothing, still, tranquil, undisturbed, unruffled, untroubled. *Opp* NOISY, STORMY.

peacemaker *n* adjudicator, arbitrator, conciliator, diplomat, intermediary, mediator, referee, umpire.

peak *n* 1 apex, brow, cap, crest, crown, eminence, hill, mountain, pinnacle, point, summit, tip, top. 2 *peak of your career.* acme, climax, crisis, crown, culmination, height, highest point, zenith.

peal *n* chime, chiming, knell, reverberation, ringing, tintinnabulation, toll.
• *v* chime, clang, resonate, ring, sound, toll.

peasant *n* bumpkin, countryman, rustic, yokel.

pebbles *pl n* cobbles, gravel, stones.

peculiar *adj* 1 aberrant, abnormal, anomalous, atypical, bizarre, curious, deviant, eccentric, exceptional, funny, odd, offbeat, outlandish, out of the ordinary, queer, quirky, surprising, strange, uncommon, unconventional, unusual, weird. 2 *a style peculiar to her.* characteristic, distinctive, identifiable, idiosyncratic, individual, particular, personal, singular, special, unique, unmistakable. *Opp* COMMON, ORDINARY.

peculiarity *n* abnormality, characteristic, distinctiveness, eccentricity, foible, idiosyncrasy, individuality, mannerism, oddity, quirk, singularity, speciality, trait, uniqueness.

pedantic *adj* 1 academic, bookish, dry, formal, learned, old-fashioned, pompous, scholarly, stiff, stilted, *inf* stuffy. 2 *inf* by the book, exact, fastidious, fussy, inflexible, *inf* nit-picking, precise, punctilious, strict, unimaginative. *Opp* INFORMAL, LAX.

peddle *v* *inf* flog, hawk, market, *inf* push, sell, traffic in, vend.

pedestrian *adj* 1 pedestrianized, traffic-free. 2 banal, boring, dull, commonplace,

flat-footed, mundane, prosaic, *inf* run-of-the-mill, tedious, unimaginative. ▷ ORDINARY.
• *n* foot-traveller, walker.

pedigree *adj* pure-bred, thoroughbred.
• *n* ancestry, blood, descent, extraction, family history, genealogy, line, lineage, parentage, roots, stock, strain.

pedlar *n* door-to-door salesman, hawker, *inf* pusher, seller, street trader, trafficker, vendor.

peel *n* coating, rind, skin.
• *v* denude, flay, pare, skin, strip. ▷ UNDRESS.

peep *v* glance, have a look, peek, squint.

peer *n* aristocrat, countess, duchess, duke, earl, grandee, lady, lord, marquis, nobleman, noblewoman, viscount.
• *v* look earnestly, spy, squint. ▷ LOOK.
peers 1 aristocracy, nobility, peerage. 2 colleagues, equals, fellows, peer-group.

peevish *adj* cantankerous, crabby, grumpy, irritable, petulant, querulous, testy, touchy, waspish. ▷ BAD-TEMPERED.

peg *n* bolt, dowel, pin, rod, stick.
• *v* ▷ FASTEN.

pelt *n* coat, fur, hide, skin.
• *v* bombard, shower. ▷ THROW.

pen *n* 1 coop, corral, enclosure, fold, hutch, pound. 2 ballpoint, biro, felt-tip, fountain pen.

penalize *v* discipline, fine, impose a penalty on, punish.

penalty *n* fine, forfeit, price, punishment.
pay the penalty ▷ ATONE.

penance *n* amends, atonement, reparation.
do penance ▷ ATONE.

pendent *adj* dangling, hanging, loose, pendulous, suspended, swaying, swinging, trailing.

pending *adj* about to happen, imminent, impending, *inf* in the offing, undecided, waiting.

penetrate *v* 1 bore through, break through, drill into, enter, get into, get through, infiltrate, lance, perforate, pierce, puncture, stab. 2 *damp penetrates.* filter through, impregnate, permeate, pervade, seep into, suffuse.

penitent *adj* apologetic, conscience-stricken, contrite, regretful, remorseful, repentant, rueful, shamefaced, sorry. *Opp* UNREPENTANT.

pennon *n* ▷ FLAG.

pension *n* annuity, benefit, old age pension, superannuation.

pensive *adj* brooding, contemplative, daydreaming, *inf* far-away, lost in thought, meditative, reflective, ruminative, thoughtful.

penury *n* destitution, impoverishment, lack, need, poverty, scarcity, want.

people *n* 1 folk, human beings, humanity, humans, individuals, mankind, men and women, mortals, persons. 2 citizens, community, electorate, *inf* grass roots, nation, populace, population, the public, society, subjects. 3 *your own people.* clan, family, kinsmen, kith and kin, race, relations, relatives, tribe.
• *v* colonize, fill, inhabit, occupy, overrun, populate, settle.

perceive *v* 1 become aware of, catch sight of, detect, discern, distinguish, glimpse, identify, make out, notice, note, observe, recognize, see, spot. 2 appreciate, apprehend, comprehend, deduce, feel, figure out, gather, grasp, infer, realize, sense, understand.

perceptible *adj* appreciable, audible, detectable, discernible, distinct, distinguishable, evident, identifiable, manifest, marked, notable, noticeable, obvious, palpable, plain, recognizable, unmistakable, visible. *Opp* IMPERCEPTIBLE.

perception *n* appreciation, awareness, comprehension, consciousness, discernment, insight, instinct, intuition, observation, recognition, sensation, sense, understanding, view.

perceptive *adj* acute, alert, astute, attentive, aware, clever, discerning, discriminating, observant, percipient, quick, responsive, sensitive, sharp, sharp-eyed, shrewd, sympathetic, understanding. ▷ INTELLIGENT.

perch *n* rest, resting place, roost.
• *v* balance, rest, settle, sit.

perdition *n* ▷ DAMNATION.

perfect *adj* 1 absolute, complete, consummate, excellent, exemplary, faultless, flawless, ideal, immaculate, incomparable, matchless, mint, superlative, unbeatable, undamaged, unqualified, whole. 2 blameless, irreproachable, pure, sinless, spotless, unimpeachable. 3 accurate, authentic, correct, exact, faithful, impeccable, precise, true. *Opp* IMPERFECT.
• *v* bring to fruition, carry through, complete, consummate, effect, execute, finish, fulfil, realize.

perfection *n* 1 beauty, completeness, excellence, flawlessness, ideal, precision, purity, wholeness. *Opp* IMPERFECTION.

2 *the perfection of a plan.* achievement, completion, consummation, end, fruition, fulfilment, realization.

perforate *v* bore through, drill, penetrate, pierce, prick, punch, puncture, riddle.

perform *v* 1 accomplish, achieve, bring about, carry out, commit, complete, discharge, dispatch, do, effect, execute, finish, fulfil. 2 behave, function, go, operate, run, work. 3 *perform on stage.* act, appear, dance, feature, figure, take part. 4 *perform a play, song.* enact, mount, present, produce, put on, render, represent, sing, stage.

performance *n* 1 accomplishment, achievement, carrying out, completion, execution, fulfilment. 2 behaviour, conduct, exhibition, exploit, feat, play-acting, pretence. 3 *stage performance.* acting, debut, interpretation, play, playing, portrayal, presentation, production, rendition, representation, show, turn.

performer *n* actor, actress, artist, artiste, entertainer, player, singer, star, *inf* superstar.

perfume *n* 1 aroma, bouquet, fragrance, odour, scent, smell. 2 aftershave, eau de Cologne, scent, toilet water.

perfunctory *adj* apathetic, brief, cursory, dutiful, fleeting, half-hearted, hurried, indifferent, mechanical, offhand, routine, superficial, unenthusiastic. *Opp* ENTHUSIASTIC.

perhaps *adv* conceivably, maybe, possibly.

peril *n* danger, hazard, insecurity, jeopardy, risk, threat.

perilous *adj* dangerous, hazardous, insecure, risky, uncertain, unsafe. *Opp* SAFE.

perimeter *n* border, borderline, boundary, bounds, circumference, confines, edge, fringe, frontier, limit, margin, periphery, verge.

period *n* 1 duration, interval, phase, season, session, span, spell, stage, stint, stretch, term, while. 2 age, epoch, era, time.

periodic *adj* recurrent, repeated. ▷ OCCASIONAL.

peripheral *adj* 1 distant, on the perimeter, outer, outermost, outlying. 2 borderline, incidental, inessential, irrelevant, marginal, nonessential, unimportant. *Opp* CENTRAL.

perish *v* 1 be destroyed, be killed, die, expire. 2 decay, decompose, disintegrate, go bad, rot.

perjury *n* ▷ LYING.

permanent *adj* abiding, changeless, chronic, constant, continual, continuous, durable, enduring, eternal, everlasting, fixed, immutable, incessant, incurable, indestructible, ineradicable, invariable, irreparable, irreversible, lasting, lifelong, long-lasting, never-ending, non-stop, ongoing, perennial, perpetual, persistent, stable, steady, unalterable, unchanging, undying, unending. *Opp* TEMPORARY.

permeate *v* diffuse, filter through, impregnate, infiltrate, penetrate, pervade, saturate, spread through.

permissible *adj* acceptable, admissible, allowed, lawful, legal, legitimate, permitted, proper, right, sanctioned, tolerable, valid, venial (*sin*). *Opp* UNACCEPTABLE.

permission *n* agreement, approbation, approval, assent, consent, dispensation, franchise, *inf* go-ahead, *inf* green light, leave, licence, *inf* rubber stamp, sanction, seal of approval, support. ▷ PERMIT.

permissive *adj* easygoing, indulgent, lenient, liberal, libertarian, tolerant.

permit *n* authority, authorization, charter, licence, order, pass, passport, ticket, visa, warrant.
• *v* admit, agree to, allow, approve of, authorize, consent to, endorse, give permission for, give your blessing to, legalize, license, sanction, support, tolerate.

perpendicular *adj* at right angles, upright, vertical.

perpetual *adj* abiding, ceaseless, chronic, constant, continual, continuous, endless, enduring, eternal, everlasting, immutable, incessant, incurable, indestructible, interminable, lasting, long-lasting, never-ending, non-stop, ongoing, perennial, permanent, persistent, protracted, recurrent, repeated, timeless, unceasing, unchanging, undying, unending, unremitting. *Opp* TEMPORARY.

perpetuate *v* extend, immortalize, keep going, maintain, preserve.

perplex *v* baffle, *inf* bamboozle, bewilder, confound, confuse, disconcert, dumbfound, muddle, mystify, nonplus, puzzle, *inf* stump, worry.

perquisite *n* benefit, bonus, extra, fringe benefit, gratuity, *inf* perk, tip.

persecute *v* annoy, badger, bother, bully, discriminate against, harass, ill-treat, intimidate, maltreat, molest, oppress, pester, *inf* put the screws on, suppress, terrorize, torment, torture, tyrannize, victimize, worry.

persist *v* carry on, continue, endure, go on, *inf* hang on, hold out, keep going, keep on, last, linger, persevere, remain, *inf* soldier on, stand firm, stay, *inf* stick at it. *Opp* CEASE.

persistent *adj* 1 ceaseless, chronic, constant, continual, continuous, endless, eternal, everlasting, incessant, interminable, lasting, long-lasting, never-ending, permanent, perpetual, recurrent, recurring, unending, unrelenting, unrelieved, unremitting. *Opp* BRIEF, INTERMITTENT. 2 assiduous, determined, dogged, hard-working, indefatigable, patient, persevering, relentless, resolute, steadfast, steady, stubborn, tenacious, tireless, unflagging, untiring, unwavering, zealous.

person *n* adolescent, adult, being, *inf* body, character, child, figure, human, human being, individual, infant, mortal, personage, *inf* soul, *inf* type. ▷ MAN, PEOPLE, WOMAN.

persona *n* character, façade, guise, identity, image, personality, role, self-image.

personal *adj* 1 distinct, distinctive, exclusive, idiosyncratic, individual, inimitable, particular, peculiar, private, special, unique, your own. *Opp* GENERAL. 2 *personal appearance.* in person, in the flesh, live, physical. 3 *personal letters.* confidential, informal, intimate, private, secret. *Opp* PUBLIC. 4 *personal friends.* close, dear, familiar, intimate. 5 *personal remarks.* belittling, critical, derogatory, disparaging, insulting, offensive, pejorative, rude, slighting. 6 *personal knowledge.* direct, empirical, experiential.

personality *n* 1 character, disposition, identity, individuality, *inf* make-up, nature, persona, temperament. 2 *inf* big name, celebrity, idol, luminary, name, public figure, star, *inf* superstar.

personification *n* embodiment, epitome, incarnation, living image, manifestation.

personify *v* embody, epitomize, exemplify, incarnate, manifest, represent, stand for, symbolize, typify.

personnel *n* employees, people, staff, workforce, workers.

perspective *n* angle, approach, attitude, outlook, point of view, position, slant, standpoint, view, viewpoint.

persuade *v* bring round, cajole, coax, convert, convince, entice, induce, influence, inveigle, press, prevail upon, talk into, tempt, urge, use persuasion, wheedle (into), win over. *Opp* DISSUADE.

persuasion *n* 1 argument, blandishment, cajolery, coaxing, enticement, inducement, persuading. 2 affiliation, belief, conviction, creed, denomination, faith, religion, sect.

persuasive *adj* cogent, compelling, convincing, credible, effective, eloquent, forceful, influential, logical, plausible, potent, reasonable, sound, strong, telling, valid. *Opp* UNCONVINCING.

pertain *v* apply, be relevant, have bearing, relate, refer. **pertain to** affect, concern.

pertinent *adj* ▷ RELEVANT.

perturb *v* agitate, bother, confuse, discomfit, disconcert, disquiet, distress, disturb, fluster, make anxious, ruffle, shake, trouble, unnerve, unsettle, upset, worry. *Opp* REASSURE.

peruse *v* inspect, look over, read, scan, scrutinize, study.

pervade *v* diffuse, fill, filter through, flow through, penetrate, permeate, saturate, spread through, suffuse.

pervasive *adj* general, pervading, prevalent, rife, ubiquitous, universal, widespread.

perverse *adj* contradictory, contrary, disobedient, illogical, intractable, intransigent, obdurate, obstinate, *inf* pig-headed, rebellious, refractory, self-willed, stubborn, tiresome, uncooperative, unreasonable, wayward, wilful, wrong-headed. *Opp* REASONABLE.

perversion *n* 1 corruption, distortion, falsification, misrepresentation, misuse, twisting. 2 abnormality, depravity, deviance, immorality, impropriety, vice, wickedness.

pervert *n* degenerate, deviant.
• *v* 1 bend, distort, falsify, misrepresent, perjure, subvert, twist, undermine. 2 *pervert a witness.* bribe, corrupt.

perverted *adj* abnormal, amoral, bad, corrupt, degenerate, depraved, deviant, evil, immoral, profligate, twisted, unnatural, warped, wicked, wrong. ▷ OBSCENE. *Opp* NATURAL.

pessimism *n* cynicism, despair, despondency, gloom, hopelessness, resignation, unhappiness. *Opp* OPTIMISM.

pessimistic *adj* bleak, cynical, defeatist, despairing, fatalistic, gloomy, hopeless, morbid, negative, resigned. ▷ SAD. *Opp* OPTIMISTIC.

pest *n* 1 annoyance, bane, bother, curse, irritation, nuisance, *inf* pain in the neck. 2 *inf* bug, insect, parasite, *pl* vermin.

pester *v* annoy, badger, bait, besiege, bother, harass, *inf* hassle, irritate, molest, nag, plague, torment, trouble, worry.

pestilence *n* blight, epidemic, illness, plague, scourge.

pet *n inf* apple of your eye, darling, favourite, idol.
• *v* caress, cuddle, fondle, kiss, nuzzle, pat, stroke. ⊳ TOUCH.

petition *n* appeal, entreaty, list of signatures, plea, request, supplication.
• *v* appeal to, call upon, entreat, importune, supplicate. ⊳ ASK.

petty *adj* 1 insignificant, minor, niggling, small, trivial, trifling. ⊳ UNIMPORTANT. *Opp* IMPORTANT. 2 *petty complaints.* grudging, *inf* nit-picking, small-minded. *Opp* GENEROUS.

phase *n* development, period, season, spell, stage, state, step. ⊳ TIME. **phase in** ⊳ INTRODUCE. **phase out** ⊳ FINISH.

phenomenal *adj* amazing, astonishing, astounding, exceptional, extraordinary, *inf* fantastic, incredible, marvellous, *inf* mind-boggling, outstanding, prodigious, rare, remarkable, *inf* sensational, singular, staggering, unbelievable, wonderful. *Opp* ORDINARY.

phenomenon *n* 1 circumstance, event, fact, happening, incident, occasion, occurrence, sight. 2 curiosity, marvel, miracle, prodigy, rarity.

philanthropic *adj* altruistic, beneficent, bountiful, charitable, generous, humanitarian, magnanimous, munificent, public-spirited. ⊳ KIND. *Opp* MISANTHROPIC.

philanthropist *n* altruist, benefactor, donor, giver, *inf* Good Samaritan, humanitarian, patron, provider, sponsor.

philistine *adj* ignorant, lowbrow, uncivilized, uncultured, unenlightened.

philosopher *n* sage, thinker.

philosophical *adj* 1 abstract, analytical, erudite, ideological, intellectual, learned, logical, metaphysical, rational, reasoned, theoretical, thoughtful, wise. 2 calm, collected, composed, patient, reasonable, resigned, serene, sober, stoical, unemotional, unruffled. *Opp* EMOTIONAL.

philosophize *v* analyse, moralize, pontificate, preach, reason, theorize, think things out.

philosophy *n* 1 ideology, logic, metaphysics, thinking, thought. 2 *philosophy of life.* convictions, outlook, set of beliefs, tenets, values, viewpoint, wisdom.

phlegmatic *adj* apathetic, impassive, imperturbable, lethargic, passive, placid, slow, sluggish, stolid, torpid, undemonstrative, unemotional, unenthusiastic, unresponsive. *Opp* EXCITABLE.

phobia *n* anxiety, aversion, dislike, dread, *inf* hang-up, hatred, horror, loathing, neurosis, obsession, repugnance, revulsion. ⊳ FEAR.

phone *v* ⊳ TELEPHONE.

phoney *adj* affected, artificial, assumed, bogus, cheating, contrived, counterfeit, deceitful, ersatz, fake, faked, false, fraudulent, hypocritical, imitation, insincere, mock, pretended, *inf* pseudo, *inf* put-on, sham, spurious, synthetic, trick. *Opp* REAL.

photograph *n* enlargement, exposure, negative, *inf* photo, picture, plate, print, shot, slide, *inf* snap, snapshot, transparency.
• *v* film, shoot, snap.

photographic *adj* 1 accurate, exact, faithful, graphic, lifelike, realistic, true to life. 2 *photographic memory.* pictorial, retentive, visual.

phrase *n* clause, expression. ⊳ SAYING.
• *v* ⊳ SAY.

phraseology *n* expression, idiom, language, parlance, phrasing, turn of phrase, wording.

physical *adj* actual, bodily, carnal, concrete, corporeal, earthly, fleshly, material, palpable, physiological, real, solid, substantial, tangible. *Opp* INTANGIBLE, SPIRITUAL.

physician *n* consultant, general practitioner, *inf* GP, specialist. ⊳ DOCTOR.

physiological *adj* anatomical, bodily, physical. *Opp* PSYCHOLOGICAL.

physique *n* body, build, figure, form, frame, shape.

pick *n* 1 choice, election, option, preference, selection. 2 best, cream, elite, favourite, flower, pride.
• *v* 1 choose, decide on, elect, fix on, name, nominate, opt for, prefer, select, settle on, single out, vote for. 2 *pick flowers.* collect, cut, gather, harvest, pluck, pull off. **pick on** ⊳ BULLY. **pick up** ⊳ GET, IMPROVE.

pictorial *adj* diagrammatic, graphic, illustrated, representational.

picture *n* 1 delineation, depiction, design, drawing, engraving, illustration, image, likeness, outline, painting, portrait, print,

portrayal, profile, representation, reproduction, sketch. 2 film, movie, video.
• *v* 1 delineate, depict, display, draw, engrave, illustrate, outline, paint, portray, represent, show, sketch. 2 *picture the future.* conceive, describe, envisage, fancy, imagine, see in your mind's eye, think up, visualize.

picturesque *adj* 1 charming, idyllic, lovely, pleasant, pretty, quaint, scenic, *inf* story-book. ▷ BEAUTIFUL. *Opp* UNATTRACTIVE. 2 *picturesque language.* colourful, descriptive, expressive, graphic, poetic, vivid.

pie *n* flan, pasty, quiche, tart, turnover.

piece *n* 1 bar, bit, bite, block, chip, chunk, crumb, *inf* dollop, fraction, fragment, grain, helping, hunk, length, lump, morsel, part, particle, portion, quantity, sample, scrap, section, segment, shard, share, shred, slab, slice, sliver, snippet, speck, stick, *inf* titbit, wedge. 2 component, constituent, element, spare part, unit. 3 *piece of music, writing.* article, composition, example, item, passage, specimen, work. **piece together** ▷ ASSEMBLE.

pied *adj* dappled, flecked, piebald, spotted, variegated.

pier *n* 1 breakwater, jetty, landing stage, quay, wharf. ▷ DOCK. 2 buttress, column, pile, pillar, post, support, upright.

pierce *v* bore through, cut, drill, enter, go through, impale, jab, lance, make a hole in, penetrate, perforate, prick, punch, puncture, skewer, spear, spike, spit, stab, stick into, transfix, wound. **piercing** ▷ SHARP.

piety *n* devotion, devoutness, faith, godliness, holiness, piousness, religion, *derog* religiosity, saintliness, sanctity. *Opp* IMPIETY.

pig *n* boar, hog, piglet, runt, sow, swine.

pile *n* 1 abundance, accumulation, collection, conglomeration, deposit, heap, hoard, mass, mound, *inf* mountain, plethora, quantity, stack, stockpile, *inf* tons. 2 column, post, support, upright.
• *v* accumulate, amass, assemble, build up, collect, concentrate, gather, heap, hoard, load, mass, stack up, stockpile, store.

pilfer *v* *inf* filch, *inf* pinch, rob, shoplift. ▷ STEAL.

pilgrim *n* ▷ TRAVELLER.

pill *n* capsule, lozenge, tablet.

pillage *n* depredation, devastation, looting, marauding, piracy, plunder, ransacking, rape, robbery, robbing, stealing.
• *v* devastate, raid, ransack. ▷ PLUNDER.

pillar *n* baluster, column, pilaster, pile, post, prop, shaft, support, upright.

pilot *n* 1 airman, *old use* aviator, captain, flier. 2 helmsman, leader, navigator.
• *v* conduct, direct, drive, fly, guide, lead, navigate, shepherd, steer.

pimple *n* blackhead, boil, eruption, pustule, spot, swelling, *sl* zit. **pimples** acne, rash.

pin *n* brooch, clip, drawing-pin, nail, peg, rivet, safety pin, spike, staple.
• *v* clip, nail, pierce, staple, tack, transfix. ▷ FASTEN.

pinch *v* 1 crush, hurt, nip, squeeze. 2 ▷ STEAL.

pine *v* mope, mourn, sicken, waste away. **pine for** ▷ WANT.

pinnacle *n* 1 acme, apex, cap, climax, crest, crown, height, highest point, peak, summit, top, zenith. 2 spire, steeple, turret.

pioneer *n* 1 colonist, discoverer, explorer, pathfinder, settler, trail-blazer. 2 innovator, inventor, originator, trend-setter.
• *v* begin, *inf* bring out, create, develop, discover, establish, found, inaugurate, initiate, institute, introduce, invent, launch, originate, set up, start.

pious *adj* 1 devout, faithful, God-fearing, godly, holy, moral, religious, reverent, reverential, saintly, sincere, spiritual, virtuous. *Opp* IMPIOUS. 2 [*derog*] *inf* goody-goody, *inf* holier-than-thou, hypocritical, mealy-mouthed, sanctimonious, self-righteous, self-satisfied, unctuous. *Opp* SINCERE.

pip *n* 1 pit, seed, stone. 2 spot, star. 3 bleep, sound, stroke.

pipe *n* conduit, channel, duct, hose, hydrant, line, main, pipeline, tube.
• *v* 1 carry along a pipe, channel, convey, supply, transmit. 2 *pipe a tune.* blow, play, sound, whistle. **pipe up** ▷ SPEAK. **piping** ▷ HOT, SHRILL.

piquant *adj* 1 appetizing, pungent, salty, sharp, spicy, tangy, tart, tasty. *Opp* BLAND. 2 *piquant notion.* exciting, provocative, stimulating. *Opp* BANAL.

pirate *n* buccaneer, marauder, privateer, raider. ▷ THIEF.
• *v* ▷ PLAGIARIZE.

pit *n* 1 abyss, chasm, crater, depression, excavation, hole, hollow, pothole, well.

2 coal mine, colliery, mine, quarry, shaft, working.

pitch *n* 1 bitumen, tar. 2 angle, gradient, incline, slope, tilt. 3 *musical pitch*. sound, timbre, tone. 4 *soccer pitch*. arena, ground, playing field.
• *v* 1 erect, put up, raise, set up. 2 *pitch stones*. bowl, *inf* bung, cast, *inf* chuck, fling, heave, hurl, lob, sling, throw, toss. 3 *pitch into the water*. dive, drop, fall headlong, plunge, plummet, topple. **pitch about** ▷ TOSS. **pitch in** ▷ COOPERATE. **pitch into** ▷ ATTACK.

piteous *adj* affecting, distressing, heart-breaking, heart-rending, lamentable, moving, pathetic, pitiable, pitiful, plaintive, poignant, wretched. ▷ SAD.

pitfall *n* catch, danger, difficulty, hazard, peril, snag, trap.

pitiful *adj* 1 abject, contemptible, hopeless, inadequate, incompetent, laughable, *inf* miserable, *inf* pathetic, ridiculous, sorry, trifling, useless, worthless. *Opp* ADMIRABLE. 2 ▷ PITEOUS.

pitiless *adj* bloodthirsty, brutal, cruel, ferocious, heartless, inhuman, merciless, relentless, ruthless, sadistic, unrelenting, unremitting, unsympathetic. *Opp* MERCIFUL.

pitted *adj* dented, *inf* holey, pock-marked, rough, scarred, uneven. *Opp* SMOOTH.

pity *n* charity, clemency, commiseration, compassion, condolence, forbearance, forgiveness, grace, humanity, kindness, mercy, sympathy, tenderness, understanding. *Opp* CRUELTY.
• *v* commiserate with, *inf* feel for, feel sorry for, sympathize with.

pivot *n* axis, axle, centre, fulcrum, hinge, hub, pin, point of balance, swivel.
• *v* hinge, revolve, rotate, spin, swivel, turn, whirl.

placard *n* advert, advertisement, bill, notice, poster, sign.

placate *v* ▷ PACIFY.

place *n* 1 area, country, district, location, locality, neighbourhood, part, point, position, region, scene, setting, site, situation, *inf* spot, town, venue, whereabouts. 2 *place in society*. function, niche, office, position, rank, role, standing, station, status. 3 *place to live*. accommodation, *inf* digs, room, home, house.
• *v* 1 deposit, *inf* dump, lay, leave, locate, pinpoint, plant, position, put down, rest, set down, settle, situate, stand, station. 2 categorize, class, classify, grade, order, position, put in order, rank, sort. 3 *can't place it*. identify, put a name to, recognize, remember.

placid *adj* 1 collected, composed, cool, equable, even-tempered, imperturbable, mild, phlegmatic, stable, unexcitable. 2 calm, motionless, peaceful, quiet, tranquil, unruffled. *Opp* EXCITABLE, STORMY.

plagiarize *v* borrow, copy, *inf* crib, imitate, *inf* lift, pirate, reproduce, steal.

plague *n* 1 affliction, bane, blight, calamity, contagion, epidemic, illness, infection, outbreak, pestilence, scourge. 2 infestation, invasion, swarm.
• *v* afflict, annoy, be a nuisance to, bother, disturb, harass, hound, irritate, molest, nag, persecute, pester, torment, torture, trouble, vex, worry.

plain *adj* 1 apparent, audible, clear, comprehensible, definite, distinct, evident, intelligible, legible, lucid, manifest, obvious, patent, transparent, unambiguous, understandable, unmistakable, visible, well-defined. *Opp* OBSCURE. 2 *plain speech*. blunt, candid, direct, explicit, forthright, frank, honest, outspoken, prosaic, sincere, straightforward, unequivocal, unvarnished. 3 *plain dress, food*. austere, everyday, frugal, homely, modest, ordinary, simple, spartan, unattractive, unexciting, unprepossessing, unremarkable, workaday. *Opp* SOPHISTICATED.
• *n* grassland, pasture, pampas, prairie, savannah, steppe, tundra, veld.

plaintive *adj* doleful, melancholy, mournful, plangent, sorrowful, wistful. ▷ SAD.

plan *n* 1 blueprint, chart, design, diagram, drawing, layout, map, representation, sketch-map. 2 *plan of action*. design, formula, idea, intention, method, plot, policy, procedure, programme, project, proposal, scheme, strategy, system.
• *v* 1 arrange, concoct, contrive, design, devise, formulate, invent, map out, organize, outline, plot, prepare, think out, work out. 2 *I plan to leave*. aim, contemplate, envisage, expect, intend, mean, propose. **planned** ▷ DELIBERATE.

plane *adj* even, flat, flush, level, smooth, uniform.
• *n* 1 flat surface, level surface. 2 aeroplane, aircraft, glider.

planet *n* globe, orb, satellite, sphere, world.

plank *n* beam, board, timber.

planning *n* arrangement, design, drafting, forethought, organization, preparation, setting up, thinking out.

plant *n* [*sing*] flower, herb, shrub, tree, weed. [*pl*] greenery, growth, undergrowth, vegetation. 2 *manufacturing plant.* factory, foundry, mill, shop, works. 3 *industrial plant.* apparatus, equipment, machinery.
• *v* 1 bed out, sow, transplant. 2 locate, place, position, put, situate, station.

plaster *n* 1 mortar, stucco. 2 dressing, sticking plaster.
• *v* coat, cover, daub, smear, spread.

plastic *adj* ductile, flexible, malleable, pliable, shapable, soft, supple, workable.

plate *n* 1 dinner-plate, dish, platter, salver, side-plate. 2 lamina, layer, leaf, pane, panel, sheet, slab, stratum. 3 illustration, *inf* photo, photograph, picture, print. 4 *dental plate.* dentures, false teeth.
• *v* coat, cover, electroplate, gild (*with gold*).

platform *n* 1 dais, podium, rostrum, stage, stand. 2 *political platform.* ▷ POLICY.

platitude *n* banality, cliché, commonplace, truism.

plausible *adj* acceptable, believable, conceivable, credible, feasible, glib, likely, logical, persuasive, possible, probable, reasonable, *derog* specious, tenable. *Opp* IMPLAUSIBLE.

play *n* 1 amusement, diversion, entertainment, frivolity, fun, fun and games, horseplay, joking, make-believe, merrymaking, recreation, revelry, *inf* skylarking, sport. 2 flexibility, freedom, *inf* give, leeway, looseness, movement. 3 ▷ DRAMA.
• *v* 1 caper, enjoy yourself, fool about, frisk, frolic, gambol, have fun, *inf* mess about, romp, sport. 2 *play a game.* join in, participate, take part. 3 *play an opponent.* challenge, compete against, take on. 4 *play a role.* act, depict, perform, portray, pretend to be, represent, take the part of. **play along, play ball** ▷ COOPERATE. **play down** ▷ MINIMIZE. **play for time** ▷ DELAY. **play it by ear** ▷ IMPROVISE. **play up** ▷ MISBEHAVE. **play up to** ▷ FLATTER.

player *n* 1 competitor, contestant, participant, sportsman, sportswoman. 2 actor, actress, artiste, entertainer, instrumentalist, musician, performer, soloist.

playful *adj* cheerful, flirtatious, frisky, frolicsome, fun-loving, high-spirited, humorous, impish, *inf* jokey, joking, lighthearted, lively, mischievous, roguish, skittish, spirited, sportive, sprightly, *inf* tongue-in-cheek, vivacious. *Opp* SERIOUS.

plea *n* 1 appeal, entreaty, invocation, petition, prayer, request, suit, supplication. 2 excuse, explanation, justification, reason.

plead *v* 1 appeal, ask, beg, beseech, entreat, implore, importune, petition, request, seek, solicit, supplicate. 2 argue, maintain. ▷ ALLEGE.

pleasant *adj* acceptable, affable, agreeable, amiable, attractive, balmy, beautiful, charming, cheerful, congenial, delightful, enjoyable, entertaining, fine, friendly, genial, gentle, good, gratifying, hospitable, kind, likeable, lovely, mellow, mild, nice, palatable, pleasing, pleasurable, relaxed, satisfying, soothing, sympathetic, warm, welcome, welcoming. *Opp* UNPLEASANT.

please *v* 1 amuse, content, delight, divert, entertain, give pleasure to, gladden, gratify, make happy, satisfy, suit. 2 *Do what you please.* ▷ WANT. **pleasing** ▷ PLEASANT.

pleased *adj inf* chuffed, contented, delighted, elated, euphoric, glad, gratified, satisfied, thankful, thrilled. ▷ HAPPY. *Opp* ANNOYED.

pleasure *n* 1 bliss, comfort, contentment, delight, ecstasy, enjoyment, euphoria, fulfilment, gratification, happiness, joy, rapture, satisfaction. 2 amusement, diversion, entertainment, fun, luxury, recreation, self-indulgence.

pleat *n* crease, fold, gather, tuck.

plebiscite *n* ballot, poll, referendum, vote.

pledge *n* 1 assurance, covenant, guarantee, oath, pact, promise, undertaking, vow, warranty, word. 2 bail, bond, collateral, deposit, pawn, security, surety.
• *v* agree, commit yourself, contract, give your word, guarantee, promise, swear, undertake, vow.

plenary *adj* full, general, open.

plentiful *adj* abundant, ample, bountiful, bristling, bumper (*crop*), copious, generous, lavish, liberal, overflowing, profuse. *Opp* SCARCE. **be plentiful** ▷ ABOUND.

plenty *n* abundance, affluence, cornucopia, excess, fertility, fruitfulness, glut, *inf* heaps, *inf* loads, *inf* lots, *inf* masses, much, more than enough, *inf* oodles, *inf* piles, plethora, profusion, prosperity, quantities, *inf* stacks, surfeit, surplus, *inf* tons, wealth. *Opp* SCARCITY.

pliable *adj* 1 bendable, *inf* bendy, ductile, flexible, plastic, pliant, springy, supple. 2 *pliable character.* adaptable, compliant, easily led, impressionable, manageable, persuadable, responsive, suggestible, susceptible, tractable, yielding.

plod *v* 1 slog, tramp, trudge. 2 grind on, labour, persevere, *inf* plug away, toil. ▷ WORK.

plot *n* 1 acreage, allotment, area, estate, garden, lot, patch, smallholding, tract. 2 *plot of a novel.* chain of events, narrative, outline, scenario, story, storyline, thread. 3 *subversive plot.* conspiracy, intrigue, machination, plan, scheme.
• *v* 1 chart, draw, map out, mark, outline, plan, project. 2 collude, conspire, intrigue, scheme. 3 *inf* brew, concoct, *inf* cook up, design, devise, dream up, hatch.

pluck *n* ▷ COURAGE.
• *v* 1 collect, gather, harvest, pick, pull off, remove. 2 grab, pull, seize, snatch, tweak, yank. 3 *pluck a guitar.* strum, twang.

plug *n* 1 bung, cork, stopper. 2 ▷ ADVERTISEMENT.
• *v* 1 block up, *inf* bung up, close, cork, fill, jam, seal, stop up. 2 advertise, mention frequently, promote, publicize. **plug away** ▷ WORK.

plumb *adv* 1 *inf* dead, exactly, precisely, *inf* slap. 2 vertically.
• *v* fathom, measure, probe, sound.

plume *n* feather, *pl* plumage, quill.

plump *adj* ample, buxom, chubby, dumpy, podgy, pudgy, *inf* roly-poly, rotund, round, tubby, *inf* well-upholstered. ▷ FAT. *Opp* THIN. **plump for** ▷ CHOOSE.

plunder *n* booty, contraband, loot, pickings, pillage, prize, spoils, *inf* swag, takings.
• *v* devastate, lay waste, loot, maraud, pillage, raid, ransack, ravage, rifle, rob, seize, spoil, strip, vandalize.

plunge *v* 1 dive, drop, fall, fall headlong, hurtle, immerse, jump, leap, nosedive, pitch, plummet, sink, submerge, swoop, tumble. 2 force, push, thrust.

poach *v* 1 hunt, steal, trap. 2 boil, cook, steam.

pocket *n* bag, container, pouch, receptacle.
• *v* ▷ TAKE.

pod *n* case, hull, shell.

poem *n* ballad, *inf* ditty, limerick, lyric, ode, piece of poetry, rhyme, sonnet, verse.

poet *n* bard, lyricist, minstrel, rhymer, versifier, writer.

poetic *adj* emotive, *derog* flowery, imaginative, lyrical, metrical, poetical. *Opp* PROSAIC.

poignant *adj* affecting, distressing, heartbreaking, heart-rending, moving, pathetic, pitiful, tender, touching, upsetting. ▷ SAD.

point *n* 1 apex, peak, prong, spike, spur, tip. 2 *point on a map.* location, place, position, site, situation, spot. 3 *point in time.* instant, juncture, moment, second, stage, time. 4 *decimal point.* dot, full stop. 5 *point of an argument.* aim, crux, drift, end, essence, gist, goal, heart, import, intention, meaning, motive, nub, object, pith, purpose, relevance, significance, subject, substance, theme, thrust, use. 6 *points to raise.* detail, idea, item, matter, particular, question, thought, topic. 7 *She has many good points.* attribute, characteristic, facet, feature, property, quality, trait.
• *v* 1 draw attention to, indicate, point out, show, signal. 2 aim, direct, guide, lead, steer. **pointed** ▷ SHARP. **to the point** ▷ RELEVANT.

pointer *n* arrow, hand (*of clock*), indicator.

pointless *adj* aimless, fruitless, futile, ineffective, senseless, unproductive, useless, vain, worthless. ▷ STUPID.

poise *n* aplomb, assurance, balance, calmness, composure, coolness, dignity, equanimity, equilibrium, equipoise, imperturbability, presence, sang-froid, self-confidence, self-control, self-possession, serenity, steadiness.
• *v* balance, be poised, hover, keep in balance, support, suspend.

poised *adj* 1 balanced, hovering, in equilibrium, standing, steady, teetering, wavering. 2 *poised to begin.* keyed up, prepared, ready, set, standing by, waiting. 3 *poised performer.* assured, calm, composed, cool, cool-headed, dignified, self-confident, self-possessed, serene, suave, *inf* unflappable, unruffled, urbane.

poison *n* toxin, venom.
• *v* 1 adulterate, contaminate, infect, pollute, taint. 2 *poison the mind.* corrupt, defile, deprave, pervert, prejudice, subvert, warp. **poisoned** ▷ DIRTY, POISONOUS.

poisonous *adj* deadly, fatal, lethal, noxious, poisoned, toxic, venomous, virulent.

poke *v* butt, dig, elbow, jab, jog, nudge, prod, stab, thrust. **poke about** ▷ SEARCH. **poke fun at** ▷ RIDICULE. **poke out** ▷ PROTRUDE.

poky *adj* confined, cramped, restrictive, small, uncomfortable. *Opp* SPACIOUS.

polar *adj* arctic, freezing, glacial, icy, Siberian. ▷ COLD.

polarize *v* divide, move to opposite positions, split.

pole *n* 1 bar, column, flagpole, mast, post, rod, shaft, spar, staff, stake, standard, stick, stilt, upright. 2 *opposite poles.* end, extreme, limit. **poles apart** ▷ DIFFERENT.

police *n sl* the Bill, *sl* the fuzz, constabulary, *inf* the law, police force.
• *v* control, guard, keep in order, patrol, protect, supervise, watch over.

policeman, **policewoman** *ns inf* bobby, constable, *sl* cop, *sl* copper, detective, inspector, officer, (W)PC, (woman) police constable.

policy *n* 1 approach, code of conduct, custom, guidelines, *inf* line, method, practice, procedure, protocol, rules, stance, strategy, tactics. 2 manifesto, plan of action, platform, programme, proposals.

polish *n* 1 brightness, brilliance, finish, glaze, gleam, gloss, lustre, sheen, shine, sparkle. 2 beeswax, varnish, wax. 3 *His manners show polish. inf* class, elegance, finesse, grace, refinement, sophistication, style, urbanity.
• *v* brighten, brush up, buff up, burnish, gloss, rub up, shine, smooth, wax. **polish off** ▷ FINISH. **polish up** ▷ IMPROVE.

polished *adj* 1 bright, burnished, gleaming, glossy, lustrous, shining, shiny. 2 *polished manners.* civilized, *inf* classy, cultured, elegant, faultless, fine, flawless, genteel, gracious, impeccable, perfect, polite, *inf* posh, refined, sophisticated, suave, urbane. *Opp* ROUGH.

polite *adj* agreeable, attentive, chivalrous, civil, considerate, correct, courteous, deferential, diplomatic, formal, gallant, genteel, gentlemanly, gracious, ladylike, obliging, polished, proper, respectful, tactful, thoughtful, well-bred, well-mannered, well-spoken. *Opp* RUDE.

political *adj* 1 administrative, diplomatic, governmental, legislative, parliamentary, state. 2 factional, partisan, party-political.

politics *n* diplomacy, government, political affairs, public affairs, statesmanship.

poll *n* 1 *go to the polls.* ballot, election, vote. 2 *opinion poll.* plebiscite, referendum, survey.
• *v* ballot, canvass, question, sample, survey.

pollute *v* adulterate, blight, contaminate, corrupt, defile, dirty, foul, infect, poison, taint.

pomp *n* ceremony, display, formality, grandeur, magnificence, ostentation, pageantry, ritual, show, solemnity, spectacle, splendour.

pompous *adj* affected, arrogant, bombastic, grandiose, haughty, imperious, long-winded, ostentatious, pedantic, pretentious, self-important, sententious, showy, snobbish, *inf* snooty, *inf* stuck-up, *inf* stuffy, supercilious, turgid, vain. ▷ PROUD. *Opp* MODEST.

ponderous *adj* 1 awkward, clumsy, cumbersome, heavy, hefty, huge, massive, unwieldy, weighty. *Opp* LIGHT. 2 *ponderous style.* dull, heavy-handed, humourless, laboured, lifeless, long-winded, pedestrian, plodding, slow, stilted, stodgy, tedious, tiresome, verbose. *Opp* LIVELY.

pool *n* lagoon, lake, mere, pond, puddle, swimming pool.
• *v* ▷ COMBINE.

poor *adj* 1 badly off, bankrupt, *inf* broke, deprived, destitute, disadvantaged, *inf* down-and-out, *inf* hard up, impecunious, impoverished, in debt, indigent, insolvent, needy, *inf* on your uppers, penniless, penurious, poverty-stricken, *sl* skint, underprivileged. 2 *poor soil.* barren, exhausted, infertile, unfruitful, unproductive. 3 *poor salary.* inadequate, insufficient, low, meagre, mean, small. 4 *poor in health. inf* below par, poorly. ▷ ILL. 5 *poor quality.* bad, cheap, defective, disappointing, faulty, imperfect, inferior, low-grade, mediocre, second-rate, shoddy, substandard, unacceptable, unsatisfactory, useless, worthless. 6 *poor child!* hapless, luckless, miserable, pathetic, pitiable, unfortunate, unlucky, wretched. *Opp* GOOD, LARGE, LUCKY, RICH.
• *pl n* beggars, the destitute, down-and-outs, the homeless, tramps, the underprivileged, vagrants.

populace *n* masses, people, public, *derog* rabble, *derog* riff-raff.

popular *adj* 1 accepted, *inf* all the rage, approved, celebrated, famous, fashionable, favoured, favourite, *inf* in, in demand, liked, loved, renowned, sought-after, *inf* trendy, well-known, well-liked. *Opp* UNPOPULAR. 2 *popular opinion.* common, conventional, current, general, predominant, prevailing, representative, standard, universal.

popularize *v* 1 make popular, promote, spread. 2 *popularize classics.* make easy, simplify.

populate *v* colonize, dwell in, inhabit, live in, occupy, people, reside in, settle.

population *n* citizens, community, denizens, inhabitants, natives, occupants, people, populace, public, residents.

populous *adj* crowded, full, heavily populated, jammed, packed, swarming, teeming.

porch *n* doorway, entrance, lobby, portico.

pore *v* **pore over** examine, peruse, read, scrutinize, study.

pornographic *adj* arousing, blue, erotic, explicit, exploitative, titillating. ▷ OBSCENE.

porous *adj* absorbent, penetrable, permeable, pervious, spongy. *Opp* IMPERVIOUS.

port *n* anchorage, dock, harbour, haven, marina, mooring.

portable *adj* compact, convenient, easy to carry, handy, light, lightweight, manageable, mobile, pocket, pocket-sized, small, transportable. *Opp* UNWIELDY.

porter *n* 1 caretaker, concierge, doorman, gatekeeper, janitor, security guard. 2 baggage-handler, bearer, carrier.

portion *n* allocation, allowance, bit, division, fraction, fragment, helping, measure, part, percentage, piece, quantity, quota, ration, section, segment, serving, share, slice, wedge. **portion out** ▷ SHARE.

portrait *n* depiction, image, likeness, picture, portrayal, profile, representation, self-portrait.

portray *v* delineate, depict, describe, evoke, illustrate, paint, picture, represent, show.

pose *n* 1 attitude, position, posture, stance. 2 act, affectation, façade, masquerade, pretence.
• *v* 1 model, sit, strike a pose. 2 posture, *inf* put on airs, show off. 3 *pose a question.* advance, ask, posit, postulate, put forward, submit, suggest. **pose as** ▷ IMPERSONATE.

poser *n* 1 dilemma, enigma, problem, puzzle, question, riddle. 2 ▷ POSEUR.

poseur *n* exhibitionist, fraud, impostor, masquerader, *inf* phoney, *inf* poser, *inf* show-off.

posh *adj inf* classy, elegant, formal, grand, luxurious, showy, smart, stylish, sumptuous, *inf* swanky, *inf* swish.

position *n* 1 locality, location, place, point, site, situation, spot, whereabouts. 2 *awkward position.* circumstances, condition, predicament, state. 3 *position of the body.* posture, stance. 4 *intellectual position.* attitude, contention, hypothesis, opinion, outlook, perspective, proposition, standpoint, view, viewpoint. 5 *position in a firm.* appointment, employment, function, grade, job, level, niche, occupation, place, post, rank, role, standing, station, status.
• *v* arrange, deploy, fix, locate, place, put, settle, site, situate, stand, station.

positive *adj* 1 affirmative, categorical, certain, clear, conclusive, confident, convinced, decided, definite, emphatic, explicit, firm, incontestable, incontrovertible, irrefutable, sure. 2 *positive advice.* beneficial, constructive, helpful, practical, useful, worthwhile. *Opp* NEGATIVE.

possess *v* 1 enjoy, have, hold, own. 2 *possess territory.* acquire, control, dominate, invade, occupy, seize, take over. 3 *possess a person.* bewitch, captivate, cast a spell over, charm, enthral, haunt, obsess.

possessions *pl n* assets, belongings, chattels, effects, estate, fortune, goods, property, riches, things, wealth, worldly goods.

possessive *adj* clinging, domineering, jealous, proprietorial, protective, selfish.

possibility *n* chance, danger, feasibility, likelihood, odds, opportunity, potential, practicality, probability, risk.

possible *adj* achievable, attainable, conceivable, credible, feasible, imaginable, likely, obtainable, *inf* on, plausible, potential, practicable, practical, probable, prospective, thinkable, viable, workable. *Opp* IMPOSSIBLE.

possibly *adv* God willing, *inf* hopefully, if possible, maybe, perhaps.

post *n* 1 baluster, column, leg, paling, picket, pile, pillar, pole, prop, pylon, shaft, stake, standard, starting post, strut, support, upright, winning post. 2 *He returned to his usual post.* location, position, station. 3 appointment, assignment, employment, job, occupation, office, place, position, situation, work. 4 airmail, cards, junk mail, letters, mail, parcels, postcards.
• *v* 1 advertise, announce, display, pin up, proclaim, put up, stick up. 2 dispatch, mail, send. 3 *A guard was posted at the gate.* assign, place, postion, set, situate, station.

poster *n* advertisement, announcement, bill, display, flyer, notice, placard, sign.

posterity *n* descendants, future generations, heirs, issue, offspring, progeny, successors.

postpone *v* adjourn, defer, delay, hold over, put back, put off, *inf* put on ice, *inf* shelve, suspend.

postscript *n* addendum, addition, afterthought, codicil (*to will*), epilogue, *inf* PS.

postulate *v* assume, posit. ▷ SUPPOSE.

posture *n* 1 bearing, carriage, deportment, pose, position, stance. 2 ▷ ATTITUDE.

posy *n* bouquet, bunch of flowers, buttonhole, corsage, nosegay, spray.

pot *n* basin, bowl, casserole, container, dish, jar, pan, saucepan, vessel.

potent *adj* 1 effective, forceful, formidable, influential, intoxicating (*drink*), mighty, overpowering, overwhelming, powerful, puissant, strong, vigorous. ▷ STRONG. 2 *potent argument*. ▷ PERSUASIVE. *Opp* WEAK.

potential *adj* aspiring, budding, embryonic, future, imminent, latent, likely, possible, probable, prospective, *inf* would-be. • *n* aptitude, capability, capacity, possibility, power, resources.

potion *n* brew, concoction, dose, draught, drink, drug, elixir, liquid, medicine, mixture, tonic.

potter *v* dabble, fiddle about, *inf* mess about, tinker.

pottery *n* ceramics, china, crockery, earthenware, porcelain, stoneware.

pouch *n* bag, pocket, purse, sack, wallet.

pounce *v* ambush, attack, jump on, leap on, spring at, swoop down on, take by surprise.

pound *n* compound, corral, enclosure, pen.
• *v* batter, beat, crush, grind, hammer, knead, mash, pulp, pulverize, smash. ▷ HIT.

pour *v* 1 cascade, course, flood, flow, gush, run, spill, spout, spurt, stream. 2 *pour wine*. decant, serve, tip.

poverty *n* 1 beggary, bankruptcy, destitution, hardship, indigence, insolvency, necessity, need, penury, privation, want. 2 *poverty of talent*. absence, dearth, insufficiency, lack, paucity, scarcity, shortage. *Opp* WEALTH.

powder *n* dust, particles, talc.
• *v* 1 crush, granulate, grind, pound, pulverize, reduce to powder. 2 dredge, dust, sprinkle.

powdered *adj* 1 ▷ POWDERY. 2 dehydrated, dried.

powdery *adj* chalky, crumbly, disintegrating, dry, dusty, fine, friable, granular, granulated, ground, loose, powdered, pulverized, sandy.

power *n* 1 ability, capability, capacity, competence, faculty, force, might, muscle, potential, vigour. 2 *power to arrest*. authority, privilege, right. 3 *power of a tyrant*. *inf* clout, command, control, dominance, dominion, influence, omnipotence, potency, rule, sovereignty, supremacy, sway. ▷ STRENGTH. *Opp* WEAKNESS.

powerful *adj* authoritative, cogent, commanding, compelling, convincing, dominant, dynamic, effective, energetic, forceful, high-powered, influential, invincible, irresistible, mighty, omnipotent, overpowering, overwhelming, persuasive, potent, vigorous, weighty. ▷ STRONG. *Opp* POWERLESS.

powerless *adj* defenceless, helpless, impotent, incapable, incapacitated, ineffective, paralysed, unable, unfit. ▷ WEAK. *Opp* POWERFUL.

practicable *adj* achievable, attainable, feasible, possible, practical, realistic, sensible, viable, workable. *Opp* IMPRACTICABLE.

practical *adj* 1 applied, empirical, experimental. 2 businesslike, capable, competent, down-to-earth, efficient, expert, hard-headed, matter-of-fact, *inf* no-nonsense, pragmatic, realistic, sensible. 3 convenient, functional, handy, useful. 4 ▷ PRACTICABLE. *Opp* IMPRACTICAL, THEORETICAL. **practical joke** ▷ TRICK.

practically *adv* almost, close to, just about, nearly, to all intents and purposes, virtually.

practice *n* 1 action, actuality, application, effect, operation, reality, use. 2 *inf* dummy-run, exercise, preparation, rehearsal, *inf* run-through, training, *inf* try-out. 3 *common practice*. convention, custom, habit, routine, tradition, way, wont. 4 *doctor's practice*. business, office, work.

practise *v* 1 drill, exercise, prepare, rehearse, train, *inf* work out. 2 *practise what you preach*. carry out, do, follow, make a practice of, perform, put into practice.

praise *n* 1 acclaim, accolade, admiration, applause, approbation, approval, commendation, compliments, congratulations, encomium, eulogy, homage, honour, ovation, panegyric, plaudits, tribute. 2 *praise to God*. adoration, devotion, glorification, worship.
• *v* 1 acclaim, admire, applaud, cheer,

commend, compliment, congratulate, eulogize, extol, give a good review of, pay tribute to, *inf* rave about, recommend, sing the praises of. *Opp* CRITICIZE. 2 *praise God*. exalt, glorify, honour, worship. *Opp* CURSE.

praiseworthy *adj* admirable, commendable, creditable, deserving, laudable, meritorious, worthy. ▷ GOOD. *Opp* BAD.

prance *v* bound, caper, cavort, dance, frisk, frolic, gambol, hop, jig about, jump, leap, play, romp, skip, spring.

prattle *v* babble, chatter, gabble, *inf* rattle on, *inf* witter on.

pray *v* beseech, say prayers, supplicate. ▷ ASK.

prayer *n* entreaty, invocation, litany, meditation, petition, supplication.

preach *v* 1 deliver a sermon, evangelize. 2 give moral advice, *inf* lay down the law, lecture, moralize, pontificate, sermonize.

preacher *n* divine, ecclesiastic, evangelist, minister, missionary, moralist, pastor. ▷ CLERGYMAN.

pre-arranged *adj* arranged beforehand, planned, predetermined, prepared. *Opp* SPONTANEOUS.

precarious *adj* dangerous, *inf* dicey, *inf* dodgy, hazardous, insecure, perilous, risky, treacherous, uncertain, unreliable, unsafe, unstable, unsteady, vulnerable. *Opp* SAFE.

precaution *n* preventive measure, provision, safeguard, safety measure.

precede *v* come before, go in front, herald, introduce, lead, lead into, pave the way for, preface, start. *Opp* FOLLOW.

precious *adj* 1 expensive, irreplaceable, priceless, valuable. *Opp* WORTHLESS. 2 adored, beloved, darling, dear, loved, prized, treasured, valued.

precipice *n* bluff, cliff, crag, drop, height, escarpment.

precipitate *adj* hasty, headlong, meteoric, premature. ▷ QUICK.
• *v* accelerate, bring on, cause, encourage, hasten, hurry, induce, instigate, occasion, provoke, spark off, trigger off.

precipitation *n* condensation, moisture, rain.

precipitous *adj* abrupt, perpendicular, sharp, sheer, steep.

precise *adj* 1 accurate, clear-cut, correct, defined, definite, distinct, exact, explicit, fixed, measured, right, specific, unambiguous, well-defined. *Opp* IMPRECISE. 2 *precise work*. careful, fastidious, faultless, flawless, meticulous, perfect, punctilious, rigorous, scrupulous. *Opp* CARELESS.

preclude *v* avert, debar, exclude, forestall, make impossible, obviate, pre-empt, prevent, prohibit, rule out.

precocious *adj* advanced, forward, gifted, mature, quick. ▷ CLEVER. *Opp* BACKWARD.

preconception *n* assumption, expectation, preconceived idea, predisposition.

predatory *adj* avaricious, greedy, hunting, marauding, plundering, preying, rapacious, ravenous, voracious.

predecessor *n* ancestor, antecedent, forebear, forefather, forerunner, precursor.

predetermined *adj* 1 ▷ FATED. 2 agreed, pre-arranged, preplanned, recognized, *inf* set up.

predicament *n* crisis, difficulty, dilemma, emergency, *inf* fix, *inf* jam, *inf* mess, *inf* pickle, plight, problem, quandary, situation.

predict *v* augur, forebode, forecast, foreshadow, foretell, forewarn, intimate, presage, prophesy.

predictable *adj* anticipated, expected, foreseeable, foreseen, likely, *inf* on the cards, probable, unsurprising. *Opp* UNPREDICTABLE.

predominant *adj* chief, dominating, leading, main, prevalent, primary, ruling.

predominate *v* be in the majority, dominate, hold sway, lead, outnumber, outweigh, prevail.

pre-eminent *adj* distinguished, excellent, matchless, unsurpassed. ▷ OUTSTANDING.

pre-empt *v* anticipate, forestall.

preface *n* foreword, introduction, *inf* lead-in, overture, preamble, prelude, prologue.
• *v* begin, introduce, lead into, open, precede, start.

prefer *v* *inf* back, be partial to, choose, fancy, favour, *inf* go for, incline towards, like, like better, opt for, pick out, *inf* plump for, recommend, select, single out, vote for, want.

preferable *adj* better, desirable, favoured, likely, preferred, recommended, right. *Opp* OBJECTIONABLE.

preference *n* 1 choice, fancy, favourite, liking, option, pick, selection, wish.

2 favouritism, inclination, partiality, predilection, prejudice, proclivity.

preferential *adj* advantageous, better, biased, favourable, privileged, special, superior.

pregnant *adj* 1 carrying a child, expectant, *inf* expecting, *inf* in the club, *inf* in the family way, *old use* with child. 2 *pregnant remark*. ▷ MEANINGFUL.

prejudice *n* bias, bigotry, chauvinism, discrimination, favouritism, intolerance, leaning, partiality, partisanship, predisposition, racism, sexism, unfairness, xenophobia. *Opp* TOLERANCE.
• *v* 1 bias, colour, incline, influence, make prejudiced, predispose, sway. 2 *prejudice your chances*. damage, harm, injure, ruin, spoil, undermine.

prejudiced *adj* biased, bigoted, chauvinist, discriminatory, illiberal, intolerant, narrow-minded, one-sided, parochial, partial, partisan, racist, sexist, unfair, xenophobic. *Opp* IMPARTIAL. **prejudiced person** bigot, chauvinist, fanatic, racist, sexist, zealot.

prejudicial *adj* damaging, detrimental, harmful, injurious, unfavourable.

preliminary *adj* advance, early, experimental, exploratory, first, inaugural, initial, introductory, opening, preparatory, tentative, trial.
• *n* ▷ PRELUDE.

prelude *n* beginning, *inf* curtain-raiser, introduction, opener, opening, overture, preamble, precursor, preface, preliminary, preparation, prologue, start, starter. *Opp* CONCLUSION.

premature *adj* before time, early, hasty, precipitate, *inf* previous, too soon, undeveloped, untimely. *Opp* LATE.

premeditated *adj* calculated, conscious, considered, deliberate, intended, intentional, planned, pre-arranged, preconceived, wilful. *Opp* SPONTANEOUS.

premiss *n* assertion, assumption, basis, grounds, hypothesis, proposition, supposition.

premonition *n* fear, foreboding, forewarning, *inf* hunch, intuition, misgiving, omen, portent, presentiment, suspicion, warning.

preoccupied *adj* 1 absorbed, engrossed, immersed, involved, intent, wrapped up. 2 absent-minded, abstracted, daydreaming, distracted, inattentive, lost in thought, musing, pensive, rapt, thoughtful.

preparation *n* arrangements, briefing, getting ready, groundwork, organization, plans, practice, preparing, setting up, spadework, training.

prepare *v* 1 arrange, *inf* fix up, get ready, make arrangements, make ready, organize, pave the way, plan, set up. ▷ MAKE. 2 *prepare for exams*. *inf* cram, practise, revise, study, *inf* swot. 3 *prepare pupils for exams*. coach, educate, equip, groom, instruct, teach, train, tutor. **prepared** ▷ PRE-ARRANGED, READY. **prepare yourself** be prepared, be ready, brace yourself, steel yourself.

preposterous *adj* bizarre, excessive, extreme, monstrous, outrageous, unthinkable. ▷ ABSURD.

prerequisite *adj* compulsory, essential, indispensable, mandatory, necessary, obligatory, prescribed, required, requisite, specified, stipulated. *Opp* OPTIONAL.
• *n* condition, necessity, precondition, proviso, qualification, requirement, stipulation.

prescribe *n* assign, command, dictate, direct, fix, impose, lay down, ordain, order, recommend, require, specify, stipulate.

presence *n* 1 attendance, closeness, companionship, company, proximity, society. 2 air, appearance, aura, bearing, demeanour, mien, personality, poise, self-assurance, self-possession.

present *adj* 1 adjacent, at hand, close, here, in attendance. 2 contemporary, current, existing, extant.
• *n* 1 *inf* here and now, today. 2 bonus, contribution, donation, endowment, gift, grant, gratuity, handout, offering, tip.
• *v* 1 award, bestow, confer, donate, give, hand over, offer. 2 *present evidence*. demonstrate, display, exhibit, furnish, proffer, put forward, reveal, set out, show, submit. 3 *present a guest*. announce, introduce. 4 *present a play*. perform, put on, stage. **present yourself** ▷ ATTEND, REPORT.

presentable *adj* acceptable, clean, decent, good enough, neat, passable, proper, respectable, satisfactory, tidy, tolerable, *inf* up to scratch.

presently *adv old use* anon, before long, by and by, *inf* in a jiffy, shortly, soon.

preserve *n* 1 conserve, jam, jelly, marmalade. 2 *wildlife preserve*. reservation, reserve, sanctuary.
• *v* conserve, defend, guard, keep, look after, maintain, perpetuate, protect, retain, safeguard, save, secure, stockpile, store, sustain, uphold. *Opp* DESTROY. 2 *preserve*

food. can, cure, freeze, irradiate, pickle, refrigerate, salt. 3 *preserve a corpse.* embalm, mummify.

preside *v* be in charge, chair, officiate, take charge, take the chair. **preside over** ▷ GOVERN.

press *n* newspapers, magazines, the media.
▪ *v* 1 apply pressure to, compress, condense, crowd, crush, force, *inf* jam, push, shove, squash, squeeze. 2 *press laundry.* iron. 3 *press someone to stay.* ask, beg, bully, coerce, constrain, entreat, implore, importune, induce, *inf* lean on, persuade, pressure, pressurize, put pressure on, request, urge. **pressing** ▷ URGENT.

pressure *n* 1 force, heaviness, load, power, strength, weight. 2 *pressure of modern life.* constraints, demands, difficulties, exigencies, *inf* hassle, hurry, strain, stress.
▪ *v* coerce, entreat, implore, persuade. ▷ PRESS.

prestige *n* cachet, credit, distinction, esteem, fame, glory, good name, honour, importance, influence, *inf* kudos, renown, reputation, respect, standing, status.

prestigious *adj* acclaimed, celebrated, distinguished, eminent, esteemed, famed, famous, highly regarded, honourable, honoured, important, influential, preeminent, renowned, reputable, respected. *Opp* INSIGNIFICANT.

presume *v* 1 assume, believe, conjecture, gather, guess, imagine, infer, suppose, surmise, suspect, *inf* take it, think. 2 *He presumed to correct me.* be presumptuous enough, dare, have the effrontery, take the liberty, venture.

presumptuous *adj* arrogant, bold, cheeky, forward, impertinent, impudent, overconfident, *inf* pushy. ▷ PROUD.

pretence *n* act, acting, affectation, artifice, charade, deception, disguise, display, dissembling, dissimulation, fabrication, façade, front, guise, hoax, *inf* humbug, hypocrisy, invention, make-believe, masquerade, pretext, pose, posturing, ruse, sham, show, simulation, trickery.

pretend *v* 1 act, affect, bluff, dissemble, fake, feign, imitate, impersonate, *inf* kid, *inf* make out, play-act, play a part, pose, put on an act, sham, simulate. 2 imagine, make believe, suppose.

pretender *n* aspirant, claimant.

pretentious *adj* affected, conceited, exaggerated, extravagant, grandiose, immodest, inflated, ostentatious, *inf* over the top, pompous, showy, *inf* snobbish. *Opp* UNPRETENTIOUS.

pretext *n* cover, disguise, excuse, pretence.

pretty *adj* appealing, attractive, charming, *inf* cute, dainty, *inf* easy on the eye, fetching, good-looking, lovely, nice, pleasing. ▷ BEAUTIFUL. *Opp* UGLY.
▪ *adv* [*inf*] fairly, moderately, quite, rather, somewhat. *Opp* VERY.

prevail *v* be prevalent, hold sway, predominate, triumph, *inf* win the day. ▷ WIN. **prevailing** ▷ PREVALENT.

prevalent *adj* accepted, common, current, customary, dominant, established, extensive, fashionable, general, governing, ordinary, pervasive, popular, predominant, prevailing, ubiquitous, universal, usual, widespread. *Opp* UNUSUAL.

prevaricate *v inf* beat about the bush, be evasive, equivocate, *inf* hum and haw, hedge, mislead, temporize.

prevent *v* anticipate, avert, avoid, curb, deter, foil, forestall, frustrate, hamper, *inf* head off, *inf* help (*can't help it*), hinder, impede, inhibit, intercept, *inf* nip in the bud, obstruct, obviate, preclude, pre-empt, restrain, stave off, stop, take precautions against, thwart. ▷ FORBID. *Opp* ENCOURAGE.

preventive *adj* obstructive, precautionary, pre-emptive, preventative.

previous *adj* 1 above-mentioned, aforementioned, earlier, erstwhile, former, past, preceding, prior. *Opp* SUBSEQUENT. 2 ▷ PREMATURE.

prey *n* kill, quarry, victim.
▪ *v* **prey on** eat, feed on, hunt, kill, live off. ▷ EXPLOIT.

price *n* 1 amount, charge, cost, *inf* damage, expenditure, expense, fare, fee, figure, outlay, payment, rate, sum, terms, toll, value, worth. 2 *Give me a price.* estimate, offer, quotation, valuation. **pay the price for** ▷ ATONE.

priceless *adj* 1 costly, dear, expensive, incalculable, invaluable, irreplaceable, precious, rare, valuable. *Opp* WORTHLESS. 2 ▷ FUNNY.

prick *v* 1 bore into, jab, perforate, pierce, puncture, stab, sting. 2 ▷ SPUR.

prickle *n* 1 barb, bristle, needle, spike, spine, thorn. 2 irritation, itch, prickling, tingle, tingling.
▪ *v* irritate, itch, make your skin crawl, scratch, sting, tingle.

prickly *adj* 1 bristly, rough, scratchy, spiky, spiny, stubbly, thorny, unshaven. *Opp* SMOOTH. 2 ▷ IRRITABLE.

pride *n* 1 honour, self-esteem. self-respect. ▷ DIGNITY. 2 *her pride and joy*. jewel, treasure, treasured possession. 3 *pride before a fall*. arrogance, conceit, egotism, haughtiness, narcissism, overconfidence, presumption, self-admiration, self-importance, self-love, smugness, snobbishness, vanity. *Opp* HUMILITY.

priest *n* confessor, minister, preacher. ▷ CLERGYMAN.

priggish *adj inf* goody-goody, moralistic, prudish, self-righteous, sententious, stiff-necked, *inf* stuffy. ▷ PRIM.

prim *adj* demure, fastidious, formal, inhibited, precise, *inf* prissy, proper, prudish, *inf* starchy, strait-laced. *Opp* BROAD-MINDED.

primal *adj* early, earliest, first, original, primeval, primordial.

primarily *adv* basically, chiefly, especially, essentially, firstly, fundamentally, generally, mainly, mostly, predominantly, principally.

primary *adj* basic, cardinal, chief, dominant, first, foremost, fundamental, leading, main, major, paramount, predominant, pre-eminent, prime, principal, supreme, top.

prime *adj* 1 best, first-class, first-rate, foremost, select, superior, top, top-quality. ▷ EXCELLENT. 2 ▷ PRIMARY.
• *v* get ready, prepare.

primitive *adj* 1 ancient, early, prehistoric, primeval, savage, uncivilized, uncultivated. 2 *primitive technology*. basic, *inf* behind the times, crude, elementary, obsolete, rough, rudimentary, simple, undeveloped. ▷ OLD. 3 *primitive art*. childlike, crude, naive, unsophisticated. *Opp* ADVANCED, SOPHISTICATED.

principal *adj* cardinal, chief, dominant, first, foremost, fundamental, highest, important, key, leading, main, major, outstanding, paramount, pre-eminent, predominant, prevailing, primary, prime, starring, supreme, top.
• *n* 1 ▷ CHIEF. 2 *principal in a play*. diva, hero, heroine, lead, leading role, prima ballerina, star.

principle *n* 1 axiom, belief, creed, criterion, doctrine, dogma, ethic, idea, ideal, maxim, notion, precept, proposition, rule, standard, teaching, tenet, truth, value. 2 *person of principle*. conscience, high-mindedness, honesty, honour, ideals, integrity, morality, probity, scruples, standards, uprightness, virtue.

print *n* 1 impression, imprint, indentation, mark, stamp. 2 characters, lettering, letters, printing, text, type, typeface. 3 copy, duplicate, engraving, etching, facsimile, photograph, picture, reproduction, woodcut.
• *v* 1 copy, issue, publish, run off, stamp. 2 ▷ WRITE.

prior *adj* ▷ PREVIOUS.

priority *n* first place, greater importance, precedence, preference, right-of-way, seniority.

prise *v* force, lever, wrench.

prison *n* cell, *sl* clink, custody, detention centre, dungeon, gaol, house of correction, jail, *inf* lock-up, *Amer* penitentiary, reformatory, *sl* slammer. ▷ CAPTIVITY.

prisoner *n* captive, convict, detainee, *inf* gaolbird, hostage, inmate, *sl* lifer.

privacy *n* isolation, quietness, retirement, retreat, seclusion, secrecy, solitude.

private *adj* 1 exclusive, individual, particular, personal, reserved. 2 classified, confidential, *inf* hush-hush, *inf* off the record, secret, top secret. 3 *private meeting*. clandestine, covert, intimate, surreptitious. 4 *private hideaway*. concealed, hidden, isolated, little-known, quiet, secluded, solitary, unknown. *Opp* PUBLIC.

privilege *n* advantage, benefit, concession, entitlement, exemption, freedom, immunity, licence, prerogative, right.

privileged *adj* 1 authorized, elite, entitled, favoured, honoured, immune, licensed, protected, sanctioned, special. 2 ▷ WEALTHY.

prize *n* award, jackpot, *inf* purse, reward, trophy, winnings.
• *v* appreciate, cherish, esteem, hold dear, like, rate highly, revere, treasure, value.

probable *adj* believable, convincing, credible, expected, feasible, likely, *inf* odds-on, plausible, possible, predictable. *Opp* IMPROBABLE.

probationer *n* learner, novice. ▷ APPRENTICE.

probe *n* examination, exploration, inquiry, investigation, research, scrutiny, study.
• *v* 1 feel around, poke, prod. 2 examine, explore, go into, investigate, look into, scrutinize, study.

problem *n* 1 *inf* brain-teaser, conundrum, enigma, mystery, *inf* poser, puzzle, question, riddle. 2 complication, difficulty; dilemma, dispute, *inf* headache, *inf* hornet's nest, predicament, quandary, set-back, snag, trouble, worry.

problematic *adj* complicated, controversial, debatable, difficult, enigmatic, hard to deal with, *inf* iffy, intractable, problematical, puzzling, questionable, taxing, tricky, worrying. *Opp* STRAIGHTFORWARD.

procedure *n* approach, course of action, *inf* drill, formula, method, plan of action, policy, practice, process, routine, scheme, strategy, system, technique, way.

proceed *v* 1 advance, carry on, continue, follow, go ahead, make headway, make progress, move forward, press on, progress. 2 arise, be derived, begin, develop, emerge, grow, originate, spring up, start. ▷ RESULT.

proceedings *pl n* 1 events, *inf* goings-on, happenings. 2 *legal proceedings.* action, lawsuit, procedure, process. 3 *proceedings of a meeting.* business, matters, minutes, records, report, transactions.

proceeds *pl n* earnings, gain, income, profit, receipts, returns, revenue, takings.

process *n* 1 method, operation, procedure, proceeding, system, technique. 2 *process of ageing.* course, development, evolution, progression.
• *v* 1 alter, change, convert, deal with, make usable, modify, prepare, refine, transform, treat. 2 ▷ PARADE.

procession *n* cavalcade, chain, column, cortège, file, line, march, march-past, motorcade, pageant, parade, sequence, string, succession, train.

proclaim *v* 1 announce, assert, declare, give out, make known, profess, pronounce. 2 ▷ DECREE.

procrastinate *v* be indecisive, dally, delay, *inf* dilly-dally, dither, *inf* drag your feet, equivocate, evade the issue, hesitate, *inf* hum and haw, pause, *inf* play for time, prevaricate, *inf* shilly-shally, stall, temporize.

procure *v* acquire, buy, come by, find, get, *inf* get hold of, *inf* lay your hands on, obtain, purchase.

prod *v* dig, elbow, goad, jab, nudge, poke, push. ▷ URGE.

prodigal *adj* extravagant, improvident, irresponsible, lavish, profligate, reckless, self-indulgent, wasteful. *Opp* THRIFTY.

prodigy *n* genius, marvel, miracle, phenomenon, rarity, sensation, talent, virtuoso, *inf* whizz kid, wonder.

produce *n* crop, harvest, output, yield. ▷ PRODUCT.
• *v* 1 assemble, bring out, cause, compose, conjure up, construct, create, cultivate, develop, fabricate, form, generate, give rise to, grow, invent, make, manufacture, originate, provoke, result in, supply, turn out, yield. 2 *produce evidence.* advance, bring out, disclose, display, exhibit, furnish, introduce, offer, present, provide, put forward, reveal, show, supply. 3 *produce children.* bear, breed, give birth to. 4 *produce a play.* mount, present, put on, stage.

product *n* 1 artefact, by-product, commodity, end-product, goods, merchandise, output, produce. 2 consequence, fruit, issue, outcome, result, upshot.

productive *adj* 1 beneficial, constructive, creative, effective, efficient, gainful (*employment*), profitable, remunerative, rewarding, useful, valuable, worthwhile. 2 *productive garden.* abundant, fecund, fertile, fruitful, lush, prolific. *Opp* UNPRODUCTIVE.

profess *v* 1 affirm, announce, assert, declare, maintain, state, vow. 2 *profess to be an expert.* allege, claim, make out, pretend, purport.

profession *n* 1 business, calling, career, craft, employment, job, line of work, métier, occupation, trade, vocation, work. 2 *profession of love.* affirmation, assertion, avowal, confession, declaration, statement, testimony.

professional *adj* 1 educated, experienced, expert, knowledgeable, licensed, official, proficient, qualified, skilled, trained. *Opp* AMATEUR. 2 *professional work.* businesslike, competent, conscientious, efficient, skilful, thorough, well-done. *Opp* UNPROFESSIONAL.
• *n* ▷ EXPERT.

proficient *adj* able, accomplished, adept, capable, competent, efficient, expert, gifted, professional, skilled, talented. *Opp* INCOMPETENT.

profile *n* 1 outline, shape, side view, silhouette. 2 *personal profile.* account, biography, *inf* CV, sketch, study.

profit *n* advantage, benefit, excess, gain, interest, proceeds, return, revenue, surplus, yield.
• *v* 1 avail, benefit, pay, serve. ▷ HELP. 2 *profit from a sale.* capitalize (on), *inf* cash in on, gain, make a profit, make money. **profit by, profit from** ▷ EXPLOIT.

profitable *adj* advantageous, beneficial, commercial, fruitful, gainful, lucrative, money-making, paying, productive, profit-making, remunerative, rewarding, useful, valuable, well-paid, worthwhile. *Opp* UNPROFITABLE.

profiteer *n* black-marketeer, extortioner, racketeer.
• *v* exploit, extort, overcharge.

profligate *adj* 1 debauched, degenerate, depraved, dissolute, immoral, licentious, perverted, promiscuous, sinful, unprincipled, wanton. ▷ WICKED. 2 ▷ PRODIGAL.

profound *adj* 1 deep, extreme, heartfelt, intense, sincere. 2 *profound ideas.* abstruse, erudite, esoteric, informed, intellectual, knowledgeable, learned, penetrating, philosophical, recondite, sagacious, scholarly, serious, thoughtful, wise. 3 *profound silence.* absolute, complete, perfect, thorough, total, unqualified. *Opp* SUPERFICIAL.

profuse *adj* abundant, ample, bountiful, copious, extravagant, exuberant, generous, lavish, luxuriant, plentiful, productive, prolific. *Opp* MEAN, SPARSE.

programme *n* 1 agenda, curriculum, *inf* line-up, listing, plan, prospectus, schedule, scheme, syllabus, timetable. 2 *TV programme.* broadcast, performance, presentation, production, show, transmission.

progress *n* 1 advance, breakthrough, development, evolution, gain, growth, headway, improvement, march (*of time*), progression, *inf* step forward. 2 journey, route, travels, way. 3 *progress in a career.* advancement, elevation, promotion, rise, *inf* step up.
• *v* advance, *inf* come on, develop, forge ahead, make headway, make progress, move forward, press on, proceed, prosper. ▷ IMPROVE. *Opp* REGRESS, STAGNATE.

progression *n* 1 ▷ PROGRESS. 2 chain, course, flow, order, row, sequence, series, string, succession.

progressive *adj* 1 advancing, continuing, continuous, developing, escalating, gradual, growing, increasing, ongoing, steady. 2 *progressive ideas.* advanced, avant-garde, dynamic, enterprising, forward-looking, *inf* go-ahead, radical, reformist, revolutionary. *Opp* CONSERVATIVE.

prohibit *v* ban, bar, block, censor, debar, disallow, exclude, forbid, impede, inhibit, make illegal, outlaw, place an embargo on, preclude, prevent, proscribe, restrict, rule out, shut out, stop, veto. *Opp* ALLOW.

prohibitive *adj* excessive, exorbitant, impossible, *inf* out of reach, out of the question, unreasonable.

project *n* activity, assignment, design, enterprise, idea, job, piece of research, plan, programme, proposal, scheme, task, undertaking, venture.
• *v* 1 concoct, contrive, design, devise, scheme, think up. 2 bulge, extend, jut out, overhang, protrude, stand out, stick out. 3 *project into space.* fling, launch, shoot. ▷ HURL. 4 *project light.* cast, shine, throw out. 5 *project future profits.* estimate, forecast, predict.

proliferate *v* burgeon, flourish, grow, increase, multiply, mushroom, reproduce, thrive.

prolific *adj* 1 abundant, bountiful, copious, fruitful, numerous, plenteous, profuse, rich. 2 *prolific writer.* fertile, productive. *Opp* UNPRODUCTIVE.

prolong *v inf* drag out, draw out, extend, lengthen, *inf* pad out, protract, *inf* spin out, stretch out. *Opp* SHORTEN.

prominent *adj* 1 conspicuous, discernible, distinguishable, evident, eye-catching, large, noticeable, obtrusive, obvious, pronounced, recognizable, salient, significant, striking. *Opp* INCONSPICUOUS. 2 jutting out, projecting, protruding, protuberant, sticking out. 3 celebrated, distinguished, eminent, familiar, foremost, important, leading, major, outstanding, public, renowned. ▷ FAMOUS. *Opp* UNKNOWN.

promiscuous *adj* 1 casual, haphazard, indiscriminate, irresponsible, random. 2 ▷ IMMORAL.

promise *n* 1 assurance, commitment, contract, covenant, guarantee, oath, pledge, undertaking, vow, word, word of honour. 2 *actor with promise.* capability, potential, promising qualities, talent.
• *v* 1 agree, assure, commit yourself, consent, contract, engage, give your word, guarantee, pledge, swear, take an oath, undertake, vow. 2 *The clouds promise rain.* augur, forebode, foretell, hint at, indicate, presage, prophesy, show signs of, suggest.

promising *adj* auspicious, encouraging, favourable, hopeful, likely, optimistic, propitious, talented, *inf* up-and-coming.

promontory *n* cape, headland, point, projection, spit, spur.

promote *v* 1 advance, elevate, give promotion, move up, prefer, raise, upgrade. 2 *promote a product.* advertise, back, boost, champion, encourage, endorse, further, market, *inf* plug, popularize, publicize, *inf* push, recommend, sell, speak for, sponsor, support. ▷ HELP.

promoter *n* backer, champion, patron, sponsor, supporter.

promotion *n* 1 advancement, elevation,

preferment, rise, upgrading. 2 *promotion of a product.* advertising, backing, marketing, publicity, recommendation, selling, sponsorship.

prompt *adj* eager, immediate, instantaneous, on time, punctual, timely, unhesitating, willing. ▷ QUICK. *Opp* UNPUNCTUAL.
• *n* cue, line, reminder.
• *v* egg on, encourage, help, incite, influence, inspire, jog the memory, motivate, nudge, persuade, prod, provoke, remind, spur, stimulate, urge.

prone *adj* 1 face down, horizontal, on your front, prostrate, stretched out. *Opp* SUPINE. 2 *prone to colds.* apt, disposed, given, inclined, liable, likely, predisposed, susceptible, vulnerable. *Opp* IMMUNE.

prong *n* point, spike, spur, tine.

pronounce *v* 1 articulate, enunciate, express, put into words, say, sound, speak, utter, voice. 2 *pronounce judgement.* announce, assert, declare, decree, proclaim, state.

pronounced *adj* clear, conspicuous, decided, definite, distinct, evident, marked, noticeable, obvious, prominent, recognizable, striking, unmistakable.

pronunciation *n* accent, articulation, delivery, diction, elocution, enunciation, inflection, intonation, modulation, speech.

proof *n* 1 confirmation, corroboration, demonstration, evidence, facts, grounds, substantiation, testimony, validation, verification. 2 *the proof of the pudding.* criterion, measure, test, trial.

prop *n* buttress, crutch, post, stay, strut, support, truss, upright.
• *v* 1 bolster, buttress, hold up, reinforce, shore up, support, sustain. 2 lean, rest, stand.

propaganda *n* advertising, *sl* hype, promotion, publicity.

propagate *v* 1 breed, generate, increase, multiply, produce, proliferate, reproduce. 2 *propagate ideas.* circulate, disseminate, publish, spread, transmit. 3 *propagate plants.* grow from seed, sow, take cuttings.

propel *v* drive, force, impel, launch, push, send, shoot, spur, thrust, urge.

proper *adj* 1 becoming, conventional, decent, decorous, delicate, dignified, formal, genteel, gentlemanly, in good taste, ladylike, modest, polite, *derog* prim, respectable, sedate, seemly, tactful, tasteful. 2 acceptable, accepted, advisable, apposite, appropriate, apt, deserved, fair, fitting, just, lawful, legal, normal, orthodox, sensible, suitable, usual, valid. 3 *the proper time.* accurate, correct, exact, precise, right. 4 *the proper place.* individual, own, particular, reserved, separate, special, unique. *Opp* IMPROPER.

property *n* 1 assets, belongings, capital, chattels, effects, fortune, goods, holdings, patrimony, possessions, resources, riches, wealth. 2 buildings, estate, land, premises. 3 attribute, characteristic, feature, hallmark, idiosyncrasy, peculiarity, quality, quirk, trait.

prophecy *n* augury, divination, forecast, foretelling, fortune-telling, prediction, prognosis.

prophesy *v* augur, bode, divine, forecast, foresee, foreshadow, foretell, portend, predict, presage, promise.

prophet *n* clairvoyant, forecaster, fortune-teller, oracle, seer, sibyl, soothsayer.

prophetic *adj* inspired, oracular, predictive, prescient, visionary.

propitious *adj* advantageous, auspicious, favourable, fortunate, happy, lucky, opportune, promising, timely, well-timed.

proportion *n* 1 balance, correlation, correspondence, ratio, symmetry. 2 allocation, fraction, part, percentage, piece, quota, ration, section, share. ▷ NUMBER, QUANTITY. **proportions** dimensions, extent, magnitude, measurements, size, volume.

proportional *adj* balanced, commensurate, comparable, corresponding, in proportion, proportionate, relative, symmetrical. *Opp* DISPROPORTIONATE.

proposal *n* bid, motion, offer, plan, project, proposition, recommendation, scheme, suggestion, tender.

propose *v* 1 advance, *inf* come up with, present, propound, put forward, recommend, submit, suggest. 2 aim, have in mind, intend, mean, offer, plan. 3 *propose a candidate.* nominate, put up, sponsor.

propriety *n* aptness, correctness, courtesy, decency, decorum, delicacy, dignity, etiquette, fairness, fitness, formality, gentility, good manners, modesty, politeness, *derog* prudishness, refinement, respectability, seemliness, sensitivity, suitability, tact, tastefulness. *Opp* IMPROPRIETY.

prosaic *adj* 1 clear, direct, down to earth, factual, matter-of-fact, plain, simple, straightforward, to the point, unadorned, unvarnished. 2 [*derog*] characterless, clichéd, commonplace, dry, dull, flat, hackneyed, lifeless, mundane, pedestrian, routine, stereotyped, trite, unimaginative, uninspired, uninspiring. ▷ ORDINARY. *Opp* POETIC.

prosecute *v* 1 accuse, bring an action against, bring to trial, charge, indict, prefer charges against, put on trial, sue, take to court. 2 ▷ PURSUE.

prospect *n* 1 aspect, landscape, outlook, panorama, perspective, scene, sight, spectacle, view, vista. 2 *prospect of fine weather.* chance, expectation, hope, likelihood, possibility, probability, promise.
• *v* explore, search, survey.

prospective *adj* anticipated, awaited, expected, forthcoming, future, imminent, impending, intended, likely, pending, possible, potential, probable.

prospectus *n* brochure, catalogue, leaflet, manifesto, pamphlet, programme, syllabus.

prosper *v* become prosperous, be successful, *inf* boom, burgeon, do well, flourish, *inf* get ahead, *inf* get on, *inf* go from strength to strength, grow, *inf* make good, profit, progress, succeed, thrive. *Opp* FAIL.

prosperity *n* affluence, *inf* boom, good fortune, growth, plenty, profitability, riches, success, wealth.

prosperous *adj* affluent, *inf* blooming, *inf* booming, buoyant, expanding, flourishing, healthy, moneyed, productive, profitable, rich, successful, thriving, vigorous, wealthy, *inf* well-heeled, well-off, well-to-do. *Opp* UNSUCCESSFUL.

prostitute *n* call girl, *old use* courtesan, *old use* harlot, *inf* hooker, streetwalker, *inf* tart, whore.
• *v* cheapen, debase, degrade, demean, devalue, misuse.

prostrate *adj* ▷ OVERCOME, PRONE.
• *v* *prostrate yourself* abase yourself, bow, kowtow, lie flat. ▷ GROVEL.

protagonist *n* chief actor, contender, contestant, hero, heroine, lead, leading figure, principal.

protect *v* care for, cherish, conserve, defend, guard, insulate, keep, keep safe, look after, mind, preserve, safeguard, screen, secure, shield, stand up for, support, take care of, tend, watch over. *Opp* ENDANGER, NEGLECT.

protection *n* 1 care, conservation, custody, defence, guardianship, safekeeping, safety, security. 2 barrier, buffer, bulwark, cloak, cover, guard, insulation, screen, shelter, shield.

protective *adj* 1 fireproof, insulating, protecting, sheltering, shielding, waterproof. 2 *protective parents.* careful, defensive, heedful, possessive, solicitous, vigilant, watchful.

protector *n* benefactor, bodyguard, champion, defender, guard, guardian, *sl* minder, patron.

protest *n* 1 complaint, cry of disapproval, exception, grievance, *inf* gripe, *inf* grouse, grumble, objection, opposition, outcry, protestation, remonstrance. 2 *inf* demo, demonstration, march, rally.
• *v* 1 appeal, argue, challenge a decision, complain, cry out, expostulate, express disapproval, *inf* gripe, *inf* grouse, grumble, *inf* moan, object, remonstrate, take exception. 2 demonstrate, march. 3 *protest your innocence.* affirm, assert, declare, insist on, profess, swear.

protracted *adj* endless, extended, interminable, long-winded, never-ending, prolonged. ▷ LONG. *Opp* SHORT.

protrude *v* bulge, extend, overhang, poke out, project, stand out, stick out, stick up.

protruding *adj* bulbous, bulging, jutting, overhanging, projecting, prominent, protuberant, swollen.

proud *adj* 1 content, glad, gratified, happy, honoured, pleased, satisfied. 2 *a proud history.* august, dignified, distinguished, glorious, great, honourable, illustrious, noble, reputable, respected, splendid, worthy. 3 [*derog*] arrogant, *inf* big-headed, boastful, bumptious, *inf* cocksure, *inf* cocky, conceited, disdainful, egotistical, haughty, *inf* high and mighty, narcissistic, self-centred, self-important, self-satisfied, smug, snobbish, *inf* snooty, *inf* stuck-up, supercilious, *inf* swollen-headed, *inf* toffee-nosed, vain. *Opp* MODEST.

provable *adj* demonstrable, verifiable.

prove *v* ascertain, attest, authenticate, *inf* bear out, certify, check, confirm, corroborate, demonstrate, establish, explain, justify, show to be true, substantiate, verify. *Opp* DISPROVE.

proven *adj* accepted, proved, reliable, tried and tested, trustworthy, undoubted, unquestionable, valid, verified. *Opp* DOUBTFUL, THEORETICAL.

proverb *n* adage, maxim, *old use* saw. ▷ SAYING.

proverbial *adj* axiomatic, conventional, famous, legendary, time-honoured, traditional, well-known.

provide *v* afford, allot, allow, arrange for,

cater, contribute, donate, endow, equip, *inf* fix up with, *inf* fork out, furnish, give, grant, lay on, lend, offer, produce, spare, stock, supply, yield.

providence *n* ▷ FATE.

provident *adj* careful, economical, far-sighted, frugal, judicious, prudent, thrifty.

providential *adj* fortunate, happy, lucky, opportune, timely.

provincial *adj* 1 local, regional. *Opp* NATIONAL. 2 [*derog*] insular, narrow-minded, parochial, small-minded, uncultured, unsophisticated. *Opp* COSMOPOLITAN.

provisional *adj* conditional, interim, stop-gap, temporary, tentative, transitional. *Opp* DEFINITIVE, PERMANENT.

provisions *pl n* food, foodstuffs, groceries, rations, requirements, stocks, stores, subsistence, supplies.

proviso *n* condition, exception, limitation, qualification, requirement, restriction, stipulation.

provocation *n inf* aggravation, cause, challenge, grievance, grounds, incitement, motivation, motive, reason, stimulus, taunts, teasing.

provocative *adj* 1 alluring, arousing, erotic, exciting, *inf* raunchy, seductive, sexy, tantalizing, tempting. 2 *inf* aggravating, annoying, infuriating, irksome, irritating, maddening, vexing.

provoke *v* 1 arouse, awaken, bring about, call forth, cause, elicit, encourage, excite, foment, generate, give rise to, induce, inspire, instigate, kindle, motivate, prompt, spark off, start, stimulate, stir up. 2 *inf* aggravate, anger, annoy, enrage, exasperate, *inf* get on your nerves, goad, incense, incite, inflame, infuriate, irk, irritate, madden, offend, outrage, pique, rouse, tease, torment, upset, vex, *inf* wind up, worry. *Opp* PACIFY.

prowess *n* 1 ability, adroitness, aptitude, cleverness, competence, dexterity, excellence, expertise, flair, genius, proficiency, skill, talent. 2 *prowess in battle.* boldness, bravery, courage, daring, gallantry, heroism, mettle, spirit, valour.

prowl *v* creep, lurk, roam, rove, skulk, slink, sneak.

proximity *n* 1 closeness, propinquity. 2 locality, neighbourhood, vicinity.

prudent *adj* advisable, careful, cautious, circumspect, discreet, economical, far-sighted, frugal, judicious, politic, proper, provident, sagacious, sage, sensible, shrewd, thrifty, vigilant, watchful, wise. *Opp* UNWISE.

prudish *adj* easily shocked, intolerant, narrow-minded, old-fashioned, priggish, prim, *inf* prissy, proper, puritanical, rigid, strait-laced, strict. *Opp* BROAD-MINDED.

prune *v* clip, cut back, lop, pare down, trim. ▷ CUT.

pry *v inf* be nosy, delve, *inf* ferret, interfere, intrude, meddle, nose about, peer, poke about, *inf* poke your nose in, search, *inf* snoop. **prying** ▷ INQUISITIVE.

pseudonym *n* alias, assumed name, false name, nickname, pen-name, sobriquet, stage name.

psychic *adj* clairvoyant, extrasensory, mystic, occult, preternatural, spiritual, supernatural, telepathic.
• *n* astrologer, clairvoyant, crystal-gazer, fortune-teller, medium, mind-reader, spiritualist, telepathist.

psychological *adj* emotional, mental, subconscious, subjective, unconscious. *Opp* PHYSIOLOGICAL.

pub *n* bar, *inf* boozer, hostelry, inn, *inf* local, public house, saloon, tavern, wine bar.

puberty *n* adolescence, growing-up, pubescence, *inf* teens.

public *adj* 1 accessible, available, common, familiar, known, open, shared, unrestricted, visible, well-known. 2 *public support.* collective, communal, democratic, general, majority, national, popular, social, universal. 3 *public figure.* ▷ PROMINENT. *Opp* PRIVATE.
• *n* citizens, the community, the country, the nation, people, the populace, society, voters.

publication *n* 1 appearance, issuing, printing, production. ▷ BOOK, MAGAZINE. 2 announcement, broadcasting, disclosure, dissemination, proclamation, reporting.

publicity *n* 1 attention, fame, limelight, notoriety. 2 advertising, *sl* hype, marketing, promotion.

publicize *v* advertise, *sl* hype, *inf* plug, promote. ▷ PUBLISH.

publish *v* 1 bring out, circulate, issue, print, produce, release. 2 *publish secrets.* advertise, announce, broadcast, communicate, declare, disclose, divulge, *inf* leak, make known, make public, proclaim, publicize, *inf* put about, report, reveal, spread.

pucker *v* contract, crease, crinkle, draw together, purse, screw up, tighten, wrinkle.

puerile *adj* babyish, boyish, childish, immature, infantile, juvenile. ▷ SILLY.

puff *n* 1 blast, breath, draught, flurry, gust, whiff, wind. 2 *puff of smoke.* cloud, wisp.
• *v* 1 blow, breathe heavily, gasp, pant, wheeze. 2 *puff at a cigar. inf* drag, draw, inhale, pull, smoke. 3 *sails puffed by the wind.* balloon, billow, distend, enlarge, inflate, swell.

pugnacious *adj* aggressive, antagonistic, argumentative, bellicose, belligerent, combative, contentious, hostile, hot-tempered, militant, unfriendly, warlike. ▷ QUARRELSOME. *Opp* PEACEABLE.

pull *v* 1 drag, draw, haul, lug, tow, trail. *Opp* PUSH. 2 jerk, tug, pluck, wrench, *inf* yank. 3 *pull a tooth.* extract, pull out, remove. **pull off** ▷ DETACH. **pull out** ▷ WITHDRAW. **pull round** ▷ RECOVER. **pull someone's leg** ▷ TEASE. **pull through** ▷ RECOVER. **pull together** ▷ COOPERATE. **pull up** ▷ HALT.

pulp *n* mash, pap, paste, purée.
• *v* crush, liquidize, mash, pound, pulverize, purée, squash.

pulsate *v* beat, drum, palpitate, pound, quiver, reverberate, throb, tick, vibrate.

pulse *n* beat, drumming, pounding, pulsation, rhythm, throb, ticking, vibration.

pump *v* drain, draw off, empty, force, raise, siphon. **pump up** blow up, fill, inflate.

punch *v* 1 beat, *sl* biff, box, clout, cuff, pummel, slog, slug, *inf* sock, strike, thump. ▷ HIT. 2 ▷ PIERCE.

punctual *adj* in good time, *inf* on the dot, on time, prompt. *Opp* UNPUNCTUAL.

punctuate *v* 1 accentuate, emphasize, stress. 2 *punctuated by applause.* break, interrupt, intersperse, *inf* pepper.

puncture *n* blow-out, *inf* flat, flat tyre, hole, leak, perforation, pinprick, rupture.
• *v* deflate, go through, let down, penetrate, perforate, pierce, prick, rupture.

pungent *adj* 1 aromatic, hot, peppery, piquant, sharp, spicy, strong, tangy. 2 acid, acrid, astringent, caustic, harsh, sour, stinging. 3 *pungent criticism.* biting, incisive, mordant, sarcastic, scathing, trenchant.

punish *v* castigate, chastise, discipline, exact retribution from, *inf* make an example of, pay back, penalize, *inf* rap over the knuckles, scold, *inf* teach someone a lesson.

punishment *n* 1 chastisement, correction, discipline, *inf* just deserts, penalty, punitive measure, retribution, revenge, sentence. 2 abuse, battering, beating, maltreatment, torture.

punitive *adj* disciplinary, retaliatory, severe, stiff.

puny *adj* diminutive, feeble, frail, sickly, undernourished, weak. ▷ SMALL. *Opp* LARGE, STRONG.

pupil *n* apprentice, disciple, follower, learner, novice, protégé(e), scholar, schoolboy, schoolgirl, student.

puppet *n* doll, dummy, finger puppet, glove puppet, marionette.

purchase *n* 1 acquisition, *inf* buy (*a good buy*). 2 grasp, grip, hold, leverage.
• *v* acquire, buy, get, obtain, pay for, procure, secure.

pure *adj* 1 genuine, neat, real, solid, sterling, straight, unadulterated, unalloyed, undiluted. 2 *pure food.* hygienic, uncontaminated, untainted, wholesome. 3 *pure water.* clean, clear, distilled, drinkable, fresh, sterile, unpolluted. 4 *pure in morals.* blameless, chaste, decent, good, impeccable, innocent, irreproachable, modest, moral, proper, sinless, virginal, virtuous. 5 *pure genius.* absolute, complete, downright, out and out, perfect, sheer, total, true, unmitigated, unqualified, utter. 6 *pure science.* abstract, conceptual, hypothetical, speculative, theoretical. *Opp* IMPURE, PRACTICAL.

purgative *n* enema, laxative, purge.

purge *v* 1 clean out, cleanse, clear, empty, purify, wash out. 2 eject, eliminate, eradicate, expel, get rid of, oust, remove, root out.

purify *v* clean, cleanse, decontaminate, disinfect, distil, filter, make pure, purge, refine, sterilize.

puritan *n* fanatic, killjoy, moralist, prig, prude, zealot.

puritanical *adj* ascetic, austere, moralistic, narrow-minded, pietistic, priggish, prim, proper, prudish, rigid, self-denying, self-disciplined, severe, stern, stiff-necked, strait-laced, strict. *Opp* HEDONISTIC.

purpose *n* 1 aim, ambition, aspiration, design, end, goal, hope, intention, motive, object, objective, outcome, plan, result, target, wish. 2 determination, devotion, drive, firmness, persistence, resolution, resolve, steadfastness, tenacity, will, zeal. 3 *purpose of a tool.* application, benefit,

good (*what's the good of it?*), point, use, usefulness, utility, value.
▪ *v* ▷ INTEND.

purposeful *adj* decided, decisive, deliberate, determined, firm, persistent, positive, resolute, steadfast, unfaltering, unwavering. ▷ INTENTIONAL. *Opp* HESITANT.

purposeless *adj* aimless, empty, gratuitous, meaningless, pointless, senseless, unnecessary, useless, wanton. *Opp* MEANINGFUL, USEFUL.

purposely *adv* deliberately, intentionally, knowingly, on purpose, wilfully.

purse *n* bag, handbag, pocketbook, pouch, wallet.

pursue *v* 1 chase, follow, go in pursuit of, hound, hunt, run after, shadow, stalk, *inf* tail, trace, track down, trail. 2 aim for, aspire to, be committed to, carry on, conduct, continue, engage in, follow up, *inf* go for, persevere in, persist in, proceed with, prosecute, *inf* stick with, strive for, try for. 3 *pursue truth.* inquire into, investigate, search for, seek.

pursuit *n* 1 chase, chasing, following, *inf* hue and cry, hunt, hunting, shadowing, stalking, tracking down. 2 *leisure pursuit.* activity, employment, enthusiasm, hobby, interest, occupation, pastime, pleasure.

push *v* 1 drive, force, impel, jostle, move, nudge, poke, press, prod, propel, set in motion, shove, thrust. 2 *push a button.* depress, press. 3 *push into a space.* compress, cram, crowd, crush, insert, jam, pack, ram, squash, squeeze. 4 *push someone to act.* bully, coerce, compel, constrain, encourage, force, hurry, incite, induce, influence, *inf* lean on, motivate, nag, persuade, pressurize, prompt, put pressure on, spur, urge. 5 *push a new product.* advertise, boost, market, *inf* plug, promote, publicize. *Opp* PULL. **push around** ▷ BULLY. **push off** ▷ DEPART. **push on** ▷ ADVANCE.

put *v* 1 arrange, assign, consign, deploy, deposit, dispose, fix, lay, leave, locate, park, place, *inf* plonk, position, rest, set down, settle, situate, stand, station. 2 *put a question.* express, frame, phrase, say, state, utter, voice, word, write. 3 *put a proposal.* advance, bring forward, offer, outline, present, propose, submit, suggest, tender. 4 *put blame on someone.* attach, attribute, cast, fix, impose, inflict, lay, *inf* pin. **put across** ▷ COMMUNICATE. **put back** ▷ RETURN. **put by** ▷ SAVE. **put down** ▷ KILL, SUPPRESS. **put in** ▷ INSERT, INSTALL. **put off** ▷ POSTPONE. **put out** ▷ EJECT, EXTINGUISH. **put over** ▷ COMMUNICATE. **put right** ▷ REPAIR. **put someone up** ▷ ACCOMMODATE. **put up** ▷ RAISE. **put your foot down** ▷ INSIST. **put your foot in it** ▷ BLUNDER.

putative *adj* alleged, conjectural, hypothetical, presumed, reputed, rumoured, supposed.

putrefy *v* decay, decompose, *inf* go off, moulder, rot, spoil.

putrid *adj* bad, decaying, decomposing, fetid, foul, mouldy, putrefying, rotten, rotting.

puzzle *n* *inf* brain-teaser, conundrum, difficulty, dilemma, enigma, mystery, paradox, *inf* poser, problem, quandary, question, riddle.
▪ *v* baffle, bewilder, confound, confuse, *inf* floor, *inf* flummox, mystify, perplex, *inf* stump, worry. **puzzle out** ▷ SOLVE. **puzzle over** ▷ CONSIDER.

puzzling *adj* baffling, bewildering, confusing, cryptic, enigmatic, impenetrable, inexplicable, insoluble, *inf* mind-boggling, mysterious, mystifying, perplexing, strange, unaccountable, unfathomable. *Opp* STRAIGHTFORWARD.

pygmy *adj* dwarf, midget, tiny. ▷ SMALL.

Q

quadrangle *n* cloisters, courtyard, enclosure, *inf* quad.

quagmire *n* bog, fen, marsh, mire, morass, mud, quicksand, swamp.

quail *v* back away, blench, cower, cringe, falter, flinch, quake, recoil, shrink, tremble, wince.

quaint *adj* antiquated, charming, curious, eccentric, fanciful, fantastic, odd, offbeat, old-fashioned, outlandish, peculiar, picturesque, strange, *inf* twee, unusual, whimsical.

quake *v* convulse, heave, move, quaver, quiver, rock, shake, shiver, shudder, sway, tremble, vibrate, wobble.

qualification *n* 1 ability, aptitude, capability, capacity, competence, eligibility, experience, fitness, *inf* know-how, knowledge, proficiency, skill, suitability. 2 certificate, degree, diploma, doctorate. 3 *agree without qualification.* condition, exception, limitation, modification, proviso, reservation, restriction.

qualified *adj* 1 able, capable, competent, eligible, equipped, experienced, expert, fit, practised, professional, proficient, skilled, suitable, trained, well-informed. *Opp* UNSKILLED. 2 *qualified praise.* cautious, conditional, equivocal, guarded, half-hearted, limited, modified, provisional, restricted. *Opp* UNCONDITIONAL.

qualify *v* 1 authorize, entitle, equip, fit, make eligible, permit, sanction. 2 be eligible, get through, *inf* make the grade, meet requirements, pass. 3 *qualify your praise.* lessen, limit, mitigate, moderate, modify, restrict, temper.

quality *n* 1 calibre, class, condition, grade, rank, sort, standard, status, value, worth. 2 *personal quality.* attribute, characteristic, feature, mark, peculiarity, property, trait.

quandary *n inf* catch-22, *inf* cleft stick, confusion, difficulty, dilemma, plight, predicament, uncertainty.

quantity *n* aggregate, amount, bulk, consignment, dosage, dose, extent, length, load, lot, magnitude, mass, measurement, number, part, portion, proportion, sum, total, volume, weight. ▷ MEASURE.

quarrel *n* altercation, argument, bickering, clash, conflict, confrontation, controversy, debate, difference, disagreement, discord, disharmony, dispute, dissension, division, feud, *inf* hassle, misunderstanding, *inf* row, *inf* ructions, *inf* scene, *inf* slanging match, split, squabble, strife, *inf* tiff, vendetta, wrangle.
• *v* argue, *inf* be at loggerheads, bicker, clash, conflict, contend, *inf* cross swords, differ, disagree, dissent, *inf* fall out, feud, haggle, *inf* row, squabble, wrangle. ▷ FIGHT. **quarrel with** ▷ DISPUTE.

quarrelsome *adj* aggressive, argumentative, bad-tempered, cantankerous, contrary, defiant, disagreeable, dyspeptic, fractious, impatient, irascible, irritable, petulant, peevish, querulous, quick-tempered, *inf* stroppy, testy, truculent, unfriendly, volatile. ▷ PUGNACIOUS. *Opp* PEACEABLE.

quarry *n* 1 game, kill, object, prey, victim. 2 excavation, mine, pit, working.
• *v* dig out, excavate, extract, mine.

quarter *n* area, district, locality, neighbourhood, part, region, section, sector, territory, vicinity, zone.
• *v* accommodate, billet, board, house, lodge, *inf* put up. **quarters** accommodation, barracks, dwelling place, home, housing, living quarters, lodgings, residence, rooms.

quash *v* 1 abolish, annul, cancel, invalidate, overrule, overthrow, reject, rescind, reverse, revoke. 2 ▷ QUELL.

quaver *v* falter, quake, quiver, shake, shiver, shudder, tremble, vibrate, waver.

quay *n* berth, dock, harbour, jetty, landing stage, pier, wharf.

queasy *adj* bilious, *inf* green, nauseated, nauseous, poorly, *inf* queer, sick. ▷ ILL.

queer *adj* 1 abnormal, anomalous, atypical, bizarre, curious, different, eerie, exceptional, extraordinary, *inf* fishy, freakish, *inf* funny, incongruous, inexplicable, irrational, mysterious, odd, offbeat, outlandish, peculiar, puzzling, quaint, *inf* rum, singular, strange, uncanny, uncommon, unnatural, unorthodox, unusual, weird. 2 *inf* cranky, eccentric, *inf* shady (*customer*), *inf* shifty, suspect, suspicious. *Opp* NORMAL. 3 ▷ ILL. 4 ▷ HOMOSEXUAL.

quell *v* 1 crush, overcome, put down, quash, repress, subdue, suppress. 2 *quell* *fears.* allay, alleviate, calm, mitigate, mollify, pacify, soothe.

quench 1 allay, appease, sate, satisfy, slake. 2 *quench a fire.* damp down, douse, extinguish, put out, smother, snuff out.

quest *n* crusade, expedition, hunt, mission, pilgrimage, search, voyage of discovery.
• *v* **quest after** ▷ SEEK.

question *n* 1 demand, enquiry, inquiry, *inf* poser, query. 2 argument, controversy, debate, difficulty, dispute, doubt, misgiving, mystery, problem, puzzle, uncertainty.
• *v* 1 ask, catechize, cross-examine, cross-question, examine, *inf* grill, inquire of, interrogate, interview, probe, *inf* pump, quiz. 2 *question a decision.* be sceptical about, call into question, cast doubt upon, challenge, dispute, inquire about, object to, oppose, quarrel with, query.

questionable *adj* arguable, borderline, debatable, disputable, doubtful, dubious, *inf* iffy, moot, suspect, suspicious, uncertain, unclear, unprovable, unreliable.

questionnaire *n* opinion poll, quiz, survey, test.

queue *n* chain, column, *inf* crocodile, file, line, line-up, procession, row, string, tailback, train.
• *v* fall in, form a queue, line up.

quibble *n* ▷ OBJECTION.
• *v* be evasive, carp, cavil, equivocate, *inf* nit-pick, object, *inf* split hairs, wrangle.

quick *adj* 1 breakneck, brisk, fast, headlong, high-speed, *inf* nippy, rapid, *inf* smart (*pace*), *inf* spanking, speedy, swift. 2 *quick steps.* agile, animated, brisk, deft, dexterous, energetic, lively, nimble, spirited, spry, vivacious. 3 *quick response.* abrupt, hasty, hurried, immediate, instant, instantaneous, perfunctory, precipitate, prompt, punctual, ready, sudden, summary, unhesitating. 4 *quick mind.* acute, alert, astute, bright, clever, intelligent, perceptive, quick-witted, sharp, shrewd, smart. *Opp* SLOW. 5 *quick visit.* brief, fleeting, momentary, passing, short, temporary, transitory. 6 [*old use*] *the quick and the dead.* ▷ ALIVE. *Opp* SLOW.

quicken *v* 1 accelerate, expedite, hasten, hurry, go faster, speed up. 2 ▷ AROUSE.

quiet *adj* 1 inaudible, noiseless, silent, soundless. 2 *quiet music.* hushed, low, soft. 3 *quiet person.* contemplative, gentle, introverted, meditative, meek, mild, modest, peaceable, placid, reserved, retiring, shy, taciturn, thoughtful, uncommunicative, unforthcoming, unsociable, withdrawn. 4 *quiet life.* cloistered, sheltered, tranquil, unadventurous, untroubled. 5 *quiet place.* isolated, lonely, peaceful, private, secluded, undisturbed, unfrequented. 6 *quiet sea.* calm, motionless, serene, still. *Opp* BUSY, NOISY, RESTLESS.

quieten *v* 1 calm, compose, hush, lull, pacify, sedate, soothe, subdue. 2 deaden, dull, muffle, mute, silence, soften, stifle, suppress, tone down.

quirk *n* aberration, caprice, eccentricity, idiosyncrasy, kink, oddity, peculiarity, whim.

quit *v* 1 abandon, decamp from, depart from, desert, forsake, leave, walk out (on), withdraw. 2 abdicate, discontinue, drop, give up, leave, *inf* pack in, relinquish, renounce, resign from, retire from, withdraw from. 3 [*inf*] *Quit pushing!* cease, desist from, leave off, stop.

quite *adv* [NB: senses are almost opposite.] 1 *I've quite finished.* absolutely, altogether, completely, entirely, perfectly, thoroughly, totally, utterly, wholly. 2 *quite good.* comparatively, fairly, moderately, *inf* pretty, rather, relatively, somewhat.

quits *adj* equal, even, level, repaid, revenged, square.

quiver *v* flicker, fluctuate, flutter, palpitate, pulsate, quake, quaver, shake, shiver, shudder, tremble, vibrate, wobble.

quixotic *adj* fanciful, idealistic, impracticable, impractical, romantic, *inf* starry-eyed, unrealistic, Utopian, visionary. *Opp* REALISTIC.

quiz *n* competition, exam, questioning, questionnaire, test.
• *v* ▷ QUESTION.

quizzical *adj* amused, curious, perplexed, puzzled, questioning.

quota *n* allocation, allowance, *inf* cut, part, portion, proportion, ration, share.

quotation *n* 1 allusion, citation, excerpt, extract, passage, piece, reference, selection. 2 estimate, price, tender, valuation.

quote *v* 1 cite, instance, mention, refer to, repeat, reproduce. 2 *quote a price.* estimate, tender.

R

rabble *n* crowd, gang, herd, horde, mob, *inf* riff-raff, swarm, throng. ▷ GROUP.

race *n* 1 breed, ethnic group, family, folk, genus, kind, lineage, nation, people, species, stock, tribe, variety. 2 chase, competition, contest, heat, marathon, rally, rivalry.
• *v* 1 compete with, have a race with, try to beat. 2 *race along.* career, dash, fly, gallop, hasten, hurry, run, rush, speed, sprint, *inf* tear, *inf* zip, zoom.

racial *adj* ethnic, folk, genetic, national, tribal.

racism *n* anti-Semitism, apartheid, bias, bigotry, chauvinism, discrimination, prejudice, xenophobia.

racist *adj* biased, bigoted, chauvinist, discriminatory, intolerant, prejudiced, xenophobic.

rack *n* frame, framework, holder, shelf, stand, support.
• *v* ▷ TORTURE.

radiant *adj* 1 bright, brilliant, gleaming, glorious, glowing, incandescent, luminous, phosphorescent, shining. 2 *The bride was radiant.* ▷ HAPPY.

radiate *v* beam, diffuse, emanate, emit, give off, gleam, glow, send out, shed, shine, spread, transmit.

radical *adj* 1 basic, deep-seated, elementary, essential, fundamental, primary, principal, profound. 2 complete, comprehensive, drastic, entire, exhaustive, thorough, thoroughgoing. 3 *radical politics.* extremist, fanatical, revolutionary, subversive. *Opp* MODERATE, SUPERFICIAL.

radio *n* CB, *sl* ghettoblaster, receiver, set, transistor, transmitter, walkie-talkie, *old use* wireless.
• *v* broadcast, send out, transmit.

rafter *n* beam, girder, joist.

rage *n* ▷ ANGER.
• *v* fume, go berserk, lose control, rave, *inf* see red, seethe, storm.

ragged *adj* 1 frayed, in ribbons, old, patched, patchy, ripped, rough, rough-edged, shabby, tattered, *inf* tatty, threadbare, torn, unkempt, unravelled, untidy, worn out. 2 *ragged line.* erratic, irregular, jagged, serrated, uneven, zigzag.

rags *pl n* bits and pieces, fragments, old clothes, remnants, scraps, shreds, tatters.

raid *n* assault, attack, blitz, foray, incursion, inroad, invasion, onslaught, sortie, strike, surprise attack, swoop.
• *v* 1 assault, attack, descend on, invade, rush, storm, swoop down on. 2 loot, pillage, plunder, ransack, rifle, rob, sack, steal from, strip.

raider *n* attacker, invader, looter, marauder, outlaw, pirate, ransacker, robber, rustler, thief.

railway *n* branch line, line, main line, metro, monorail, overground, *Amer* railroad, rails, track, tramway, tube, underground.

rain *n* cloudburst, deluge, downpour, drizzle, precipitation, raindrops, rainfall, shower, squall.
• *v* *inf* bucket down, drizzle, pelt, pour, *inf* rain cats and dogs, spit, teem.

rainy *adj* damp, drizzly, showery, wet.

raise *v* 1 elevate, hoist, hold up, jack up, lift, pick up, put up, rear. 2 *raise prices.* augment, increase, put up, *inf* up. 3 *raise to a higher rank.* exalt, promote, upgrade. 4 *raise a monument.* build, construct, create, erect, set up. 5 *raise hopes.* arouse, awaken, build up, buoy up, encourage, engender, excite, foment, foster, heighten, incite, kindle, provoke, rouse, stimulate, uplift. 6 *raise animals, children, crops.* breed, bring up, care for, cultivate, educate, farm, grow, look after, nurture, produce, propagate, rear. 7 *raise money.* collect, get, make, receive. 8 *raise questions.* advance, bring up, broach, express, instigate, introduce, mention, moot, pose, present, put forward, suggest. *Opp* LOWER, REDUCE. **raise from the dead** ▷ RESURRECT. **raise the alarm** ▷ WARN.

rally *n* 1 assembly, *inf* demo, demonstration, gathering, march, mass meeting. 2 ▷ COMPETITION.
• *v* 1 assemble, congregate, convene, get together, group, marshal, muster, organize, round up, summon. 2 *rally after illness.* ▷ RECOVER.

ram *v* 1 bump, butt, collide with, crash into, slam into, strike. ▷ HIT. 2 compress, cram, crowd, crush, drive, force, jam, pack, press, push, squash, squeeze, wedge.

ramble *n* hike, tramp, trek, walk.
• *v* 1 hike, range, roam, rove, stroll, tramp, trek, walk, wander. 2 digress,

drift, *inf* lose the thread, *inf* rattle on, talk aimlessly, wander, *inf* witter on.

rambling *adj* 1 circuitous, indirect, labyrinthine, meandering, roundabout, tortuous, twisting, wandering, winding, zigzag. *Opp* DIRECT. 2 aimless, circumlocutory, confused, digressive, disconnected, discursive, disjointed, illogical, incoherent, jumbled, muddled, periphrastic, verbose, wordy. *Opp* COHERENT. 3 *rambling house.* irregular, large, sprawling, straggling. *Opp* COMPACT.

ramification *n* branch, by-product, complication, consequence, division, effect, extension, implication, offshoot, result, subdivision, upshot.

ramp *n* gradient, incline, rise, slope.

rampage *n* frenzy, riot, tumult, uproar, violence.
• *v* go berserk, go wild, lose control, run amok, run riot, storm about. **on the rampage** ▷ WILD.

ramshackle *adj* broken-down, crumbling, decrepit, derelict, dilapidated, rickety, ruined, run-down, shaky, tottering, tumbledown, unsafe, unstable, unsteady. *Opp* SOLID.

random *adj* accidental, aimless, arbitrary, casual, chance, fortuitous, haphazard, *inf* hit-or-miss, indiscriminate, irregular, stray, unplanned, unpremeditated, unsystematic. *Opp* DELIBERATE, SYSTEMATIC.

range *n* 1 area, compass, distance, extent, field, limit, orbit, radius, reach, scope, span, spectrum, sphere, spread, sweep. 2 *wide range of goods.* diversity, selection, variety. 3 *range of mountains.* chain, file, line, rank, row, series, string.
• *v* 1 differ, extend, fluctuate, reach, run the gamut, spread, stretch, vary. 2 ▷ RANK. 3 ▷ ROAM.

rank *adj* 1 *rank growth.* ▷ ABUNDANT. 2 *rank odour.* ▷ SMELLING.
• *n* 1 column, file, formation, line, order, queue, row, series, tier. 2 caste, class, condition, degree, echelon, estate, grade, level, position, standing, station, status, title.
• *v* arrange, array, categorize, class, classify, grade, line up, order, organize, range, rate, set out in order, sort.

ransack *v* 1 go through, rummage through, scour, search, *inf* turn upside down. 2 *ransack a shop.* despoil, loot, pillage, plunder, raid, rob, sack, strip, wreck.

ransom *n* payment, *inf* pay-off, price, redemption.
• *v* deliver, redeem, rescue.

rap *v* 1 knock, strike, tap. ▷ HIT. 2 ▷ CRITICIZE.

rape *n* 1 assault, sexual attack. 2 ▷ PILLAGE.
• *v* assault, defile, force yourself on, ravish, violate.

rapid *adj* breakneck, brisk, express, fast, hasty, headlong, high-speed, hurried, immediate, impetuous, instant, instantaneous, *inf* lightning, *inf* nippy, precipitate, prompt, quick, smooth, speedy, swift. *Opp* SLOW.

rapids *pl n* cataract, current, waterfall, white water.

rapture *n* bliss, delight, ecstasy, elation, euphoria, exaltation, happiness, joy, pleasure.

rare *adj* abnormal, atypical, exceptional, extraordinary, *inf* few and far between, infrequent, irreplaceable, occasional, out of the ordinary, peculiar, scarce, singular, special, strange, surprising, uncommon, unfamiliar, unusual. *Opp* COMMON.

rascal *n* good-for-nothing, knave, mischief-maker, miscreant, ne'er-do-well, rogue, scallywag, scamp, scoundrel, troublemaker, villain, wretch.

rash *adj* careless, foolhardy, hare-brained, hasty, heedless, hot-headed, ill-advised, ill-considered, impetuous, imprudent, impulsive, incautious, indiscreet, injudicious, madcap, precipitate, reckless, risky, thoughtless, unthinking, wild. *Opp* CAREFUL.
• *n* 1 eruption, spots. 2 *rash of thefts.* ▷ OUTBREAK.

rasp *v* 1 file, grate, rub, scrape. 2 *rasp orders.* croak, screech, speak hoarsely. **rasping** ▷ HARSH.

rate *n* 1 gait, pace, speed, tempo, velocity. 2 amount, charge, cost, fare, fee, figure, payment, price, tariff, wage.
• *v* 1 appraise, assess, consider, estimate, evaluate, gauge, grade, judge, measure, put a price on, rank, reckon, regard, value, weigh. 2 be worthy of, deserve, merit. 3 ▷ REPRIMAND.

rather *adv* 1 fairly, moderately, *inf* pretty, quite, relatively, slightly, somewhat. 2 *I'd rather have coffee.* preferably, sooner.

ratify *v* approve, authorize, confirm, endorse, sanction, sign, validate, verify.

rating *n* classification, evaluation, grade, grading, mark, order, placing, ranking.

ratio *n* balance, correlation, fraction, percentage, proportion, relationship.

ration *n* allocation, allotment, allowance, amount, helping, measure, percentage, portion, quota, share.
• *v* allocate, allot, apportion, conserve, control, distribute fairly, limit, restrict, share equally. **rations** food, necessities, provisions, stores, supplies.

rational *adj* balanced, clear-headed, enlightened, intelligent, judicious, logical, lucid, normal, reasonable, reasoned, sane, sensible, sound, thoughtful, wise. *Opp* IRRATIONAL.

rationale *n* argument, case, cause, excuse, explanation, grounds, justification, logical basis, principle, reason, reasoning, theory.

rationalize *v* 1 account for, be rational about, excuse, explain, justify, make rational, think through, vindicate. 2 ▷ REORGANIZE.

rattle *v* 1 clatter, vibrate. 2 agitate, jar, joggle, jiggle about, jolt, shake about. 3 [*inf*] discomfit, discompose, disconcert, disturb, fluster, frighten, make nervous, put off, unnerve, upset, worry. **rattle off** ▷ RECITE. **rattle on** ▷ RAMBLE.

raucous *adj* ear-splitting, grating, harsh, jarring, noisy, rasping, rough, screeching, shrill, squawking, strident.

ravage *v* damage, despoil, destroy, devastate, lay waste, loot, pillage, plunder, raid, ransack, ruin, sack, spoil, wreak havoc on, wreck.

rave *v* 1 be angry, fulminate, fume, rage, rant, roar, storm, thunder. 2 be enthusiastic, enthuse, *inf* go into raptures, *inf* gush, rhapsodize.

ravenous *adj* famished, hungry, insatiable, ravening, starved, starving, voracious. ▷ GREEDY.

ravish *v* 1 bewitch, captivate, charm, delight, enchant, entrance, transport. 2 ▷ RAPE. **ravishing** ▷ BEAUTIFUL.

raw *adj* 1 fresh, uncooked, underdone, unprepared. 2 *raw materials*. crude, natural, unprocessed, unrefined, untreated. 3 *raw recruits*. *inf* green, ignorant, immature, inexperienced, innocent, new, untrained. 4 *raw skin*. bloody, chafed, grazed, inflamed, painful, red, rough, scraped, scratched, sensitive, sore, tender. 5 *raw wind*. ▷ COLD.

ray *n* 1 bar, beam, laser, shaft, streak, stream. 2 *ray of hope*. flicker, gleam, glimmer, hint, indication, sign, trace.

raze *v* bulldoze, demolish, destroy, flatten, tear down.

reach *n* compass, distance, orbit, range, scope, sphere.
• *v* 1 arrive at, come to, get to, go as far as. 2 *reach the semifinals*. achieve, attain, *inf* make. 3 *reach me by phone*. contact, *inf* get hold of, get in touch with. **reach out** ▷ EXTEND.

react *v* act, answer, behave, reciprocate, reply, respond, retaliate, retort. **react to** ▷ COUNTER.

reaction *n* answer, backlash, *inf* comeback, effect, feedback, reflex, rejoinder, reply, reprisal, response, retaliation, retort, revenge, riposte.

reactionary *adj* conservative, die-hard, old-fashioned, right-wing, *inf* stick-in-the-mud, traditionalist. *Opp* PROGRESSIVE.

read *v* 1 devour, *inf* dip into, glance at, look over, peruse, pore over, scan, skim, study. 2 *can't read his writing*. decipher, decode, interpret, make out, understand.

readable *adj* 1 absorbing, compulsive, easy, enjoyable, entertaining, gripping, interesting, well-written. *Opp* BORING. 2 clear, decipherable, distinct, intelligible, legible, neat, plain. *Opp* ILLEGIBLE.

readily *adv* cheerfully, eagerly, easily, freely, gladly, happily, promptly, quickly, voluntarily, willingly.

ready *adj* 1 *inf* all set, arranged, at hand, available, complete, convenient, done, finalized, finished, obtainable, prepared, ripe, set, set up, waiting. 2 *ready to help*. agreeable, content, disposed, eager, equipped, *inf* game, glad, inclined, in the mood, keen, keyed up, likely, minded, open, organized, pleased, poised, predisposed, primed, *inf* psyched up, raring (*to go*), trained, willing. 3 *ready reply, wit*. acute, alert, apt, immediate, prompt, quick, quick-witted, rapid, sharp, smart, speedy. *Opp* SLOW, UNPREPARED.

real *adj* 1 actual, authentic, certain, everyday, existing, factual, genuine, material, natural, ordinary, palpable, physical, pure, realistic, tangible, visible. 2 authenticated, legal, legitimate, official, valid, verifiable. 3 *real friends*. dependable, reliable, sound, true, trustworthy, worthy. 4 *real grief*. earnest, heartfelt, honest, sincere, undoubted, unfeigned. *Opp* FALSE.

realism *n* 1 authenticity, fidelity, verisimilitude. 2 clear-sightedness, common sense, objectivity, practicality, pragmatism.

realistic *adj* 1 businesslike, clear-sighted,

commonsense, down-to-earth, feasible, level-headed, logical, matter-of-fact, *inf* no-nonsense, objective, possible, practicable, practical, pragmatic, rational, sensible, tough, unemotional, unsentimental, viable, workable. 2 *realistic pictures*. authentic, convincing, faithful, lifelike, natural, recognizable, true-to-life, truthful, vivid. 3 *realistic prices*. acceptable, fair, justifiable, moderate, reasonable. *Opp* UNREALISTIC.

reality *n* actuality, authenticity, certainty, experience, *sl* nitty-gritty, real life, the real world, truth, verity. *Opp* FANTASY.

realize *v* 1 accept, appreciate, be aware of, become conscious of, *inf* catch on to, comprehend, conceive of, *inf* cotton on to, grasp, know, perceive, recognize, see, sense, understand, *inf* wake up to. 2 *realize an ambition*. accomplish, achieve, bring about, complete, effect, fulfil, implement, obtain, perform, put into effect. 3 *realize a price*. *inf* clear, earn, fetch, make, net, obtain, produce.

realm *n* country, domain, empire, kingdom, monarchy.

reap *v* 1 cut, garner, gather in, glean, harvest, mow. 2 *reap a reward*. acquire, collect, get, obtain, receive, win.

rear *adj* back, end, hind, hindmost, last, rearmost. *Opp* FRONT.*n* 1 back, end, stern (*of ship*), tail-end. 2 ▷ BUTTOCKS.
• *v* 1 breed, bring up, care for, educate, feed, look after, nurse, nurture, produce, raise, train. 2 *rear your head*. hold up, lift, raise. 3 ▷ BUILD.

rearrange *v* change round, regroup, reorganize, switch round, transpose. ▷ CHANGE.

rearrangement *n* reorganization. ▷ CHANGE.

reason *n* 1 apology, argument, case, cause, defence, excuse, explanation, grounds, incentive, justification, motive, occasion, pretext, rationale, vindication. 2 brains, common sense, *inf* gumption, intelligence, judgement, logic, mind, *inf* nous, sanity, sense, understanding, wisdom, wit. ▷ REASONING. 3 *reason for living*. aim, motivation, motive, object, objective, point, purpose, stimulus.
• *v* 1 calculate, conclude, consider, deduce, estimate, figure out, hypothesize, infer, judge, *inf* put two and two together, theorize, think, use your head, work out. 2 *I reasoned with her*. argue, debate, discuss, remonstrate.

reasonable *adj* 1 calm, honest, intelligent, rational, realistic, sane, sensible, sober, thinking, thoughtful, unemotional, wise. 2 *reasonable argument*. arguable, believable, credible, defensible, justifiable, logical, plausible, practical, reasoned, sound, tenable, viable. 3 *reasonable prices*. acceptable, appropriate, average, cheap, competitive, fair, inexpensive, moderate, ordinary, proper, right, suitable, tolerable. *Opp* IRRATIONAL.

reasoning *n* analysis, argument, case, deduction, hypothesis, line of thought, logic, proof, *derog* sophistry, theorizing, thinking.

reassure *v* assure, bolster, buoy up, calm, cheer, comfort, encourage, give confidence to, hearten, *inf* set someone's mind at rest, support, uplift. *Opp* ALARM, THREATEN. **reassuring** ▷ SOOTHING, SUPPORTIVE.

rebel *adj* ▷ REBELLIOUS.
• *n* anarchist, dissenter, freedom fighter, heretic, iconoclast, insurgent, malcontent, maverick, mutineer, nonconformist, revolutionary.
• *v* disobey, dissent, fight, *inf* kick over the traces, mutiny, refuse to obey, revolt, rise up, *inf* run riot, *inf* take a stand. *Opp* CONFORM. **rebel against** ▷ DEFY.

rebellion *n* defiance, disobedience, insubordination, insurrection, mutiny, rebelliousness, resistance, revolt, revolution, rising, sedition, uprising.

rebellious *adj inf* bolshie, breakaway, defiant, difficult, disaffected, disloyal, disobedient, insubordinate, insurgent, intractable, malcontent, mutinous, obstinate, quarrelsome, rebel, recalcitrant, refractory, resistant, revolutionary, seditious, uncontrollable, unmanageable, unruly, wild. *Opp* OBEDIENT.

rebirth *n* reawakening, regeneration, renaissance, renewal, resurgence, resurrection, return, revival.

rebound *v inf* backfire, bounce, misfire, ricochet, spring back.

rebuff *n inf* brush-off, discouragement, refusal, rejection, slight, snub.
• *v* cold-shoulder, discourage, refuse, reject, repulse, slight, snub, spurn, turn down.

rebuild *n* reassemble, reconstruct, recreate, redevelop, remake. ▷ RECONDITION.

rebuke *v* admonish, castigate, censure, reprehend, reproach, reprove, scold, upbraid. ▷ REPRIMAND.

recall *v* 1 bring back, call in, summon, withdraw. 2 ▷ REMEMBER.

recede *v* decline, dwindle, ebb, fall back, go back, lessen, retire, retreat, sink, subside, wane, withdraw.

receipt *n* 1 account, acknowledgement, bill, proof of purchase, ticket. 2 *receipt of goods.* acceptance, delivery. **receipts** gains, income, proceeds, profits, return, takings.

receive *v* 1 accept, acquire, be given, be sent, collect, come by, come into, derive, earn, gain, get, gross, inherit, make, net, obtain, take. 2 *receive an injury.* be subjected to, endure, experience, meet with, suffer, sustain, undergo. 3 *receive visitors.* admit, entertain, greet, meet, show in, welcome. *Opp* GIVE.

recent *adj* contemporary, current, fresh, just out, latest, modern, new, novel, present-day, up-to-date. *Opp* OLD.

reception *n* 1 greeting, response, welcome. 2 ▷ PARTY.

receptive *adj* amenable, favourable, interested, open, open-minded, responsive, susceptible, sympathetic, welcoming, well-disposed. *Opp* RESISTANT.

recess *n* 1 alcove, bay, corner, cranny, hollow, niche, nook. 2 adjournment, break, *inf* breather, breathing-space, interlude, interval, respite, rest, time off.

recession *n* decline, depression, downturn, slump.

recipe *n* directions, formula, instructions, method, procedure, technique.

reciprocal *adj* corresponding, exchanged, joint, mutual, requited, returned, shared.

reciprocate *v* exchange, match, repay, requite, return.

recital *n* 1 concert, performance, programme. 2 *recital of events.* account, description, narrative, recounting, relation, story, telling. ▷ RECITATION.

recitation *n* declamation, delivery, monologue, narration, performance, presentation, reading, speaking, telling.

recite *v* articulate, declaim, deliver, narrate, perform, present, quote, *inf* rattle off, recount, reel off, rehearse, relate, repeat, speak, tell.

reckless *adj* 1 careless, crazy, daredevil, devil-may-care, foolhardy, harebrained, hasty, heedless, impetuous, imprudent, impulsive, incautious, indiscreet, injudicious, irresponsible, *inf* mad, madcap, negligent, rash, thoughtless, unconsidered, unwise, wild. *Opp* CAREFUL. 2 *reckless criminals.* dangerous, desperate, violent.

reckon *v* 1 add up, assess, calculate, count, enumerate, estimate, evaluate, figure out, gauge, tally, total, value, work out. 2 ▷ THINK.

reclaim *v* 1 get back, recapture, recover, regain. 2 *reclaim land.* make usable, regenerate, rescue, restore, salvage, save.

recline *v* lean back, lie, lounge, rest, sprawl, stretch out.

recluse *n* hermit, loner, monk, nun, solitary.

recognizable *adj* detectable, distinctive, distinguishable, identifiable, known, noticeable, perceptible, undisguised, unmistakable, visible.

recognize *v* 1 detect, diagnose, discern, distinguish, identify, know, name, notice, perceive, pick out, place (*can't place him*), *inf* put a name to, recall, recollect, remember, see, spot. 2 *recognize your faults.* accept, acknowledge, admit to, appreciate, be aware of, concede, confess, grant, realize, understand. 3 *recognize someone's rights.* endorse, ratify, sanction, support.

recoil *v* blench, draw back, falter, flinch, jump, quail, shrink, shy away, start, wince.

recollect *v* recall, think back to. ▷ REMEMBER.

recommend *v* 1 advise, advocate, counsel, prescribe, propose, put forward, suggest, urge. 2 approve of, *inf* back, commend, favour, praise, *inf* push, *inf* put in a good word for, speak well of, support, vouch for. ▷ ADVERTISE.

recommendation *n* advice, advocacy, approbation, approval, *inf* backing, commendation, counsel, favourable mention, reference, seal of approval, support, testimonial.

reconcile *v* bring together, harmonize, placate, reunite, settle differences between. **be reconciled to** accept, adjust to, resign yourself to, submit to.

recondition *v* make good, overhaul, rebuild, renew, renovate, repair, restore.

reconnaissance *n* examination, exploration, inspection, investigation, observation, *inf* recce, reconnoitring, survey.

reconnoitre *v* *inf* check out, examine, explore, gather intelligence (about), inspect, investigate, patrol, scout, scrutinize, spy, survey.

reconsider *v* be converted, change your mind, come round, reappraise, reassess, re-examine, rethink, review your position, think better of.

reconstruct *v* act out, mock up, recreate, rerun. ⊳ REBUILD.

record *n* 1 account, annals, archives, catalogue, chronicle, diary, documentation, dossier, file, journal, log, minutes, narrative, note, register, report, transactions. 2 best performance, best time. 3 ⊳ RECORDING.
• *v* 1 chronicle, document, enter, inscribe, list, log, note, register, set down, transcribe, write down. 2 keep, tape, tape-record, video.

recording *n* album, cassette, CD, compact disc, disc, performance, record, release, single, tape, video, videotape.

record player *n* CD player, gramophone, midi system, record deck, turntable.

recount *v* communicate, describe, impart, narrate, recite, relate, report, tell, unfold.

recover *v* 1 find, get back, make good, recapture, reclaim, recoup, regain, repossess, restore, retrieve, salvage, trace, track down, win back. 2 *inf* be on the mend, come round, convalesce, get better, heal, improve, mend, *inf* pull round, *inf* pull through, rally, recuperate, regain your strength, revive, survive, *inf* take a turn for the better.

recovery *n* 1 recapture, reclamation, repossession, restoration, retrieval, salvage, salvaging. 2 *recovery from illness.* convalescence, cure, healing, improvement, rally, recuperation, revival, upturn.

recreation *n* amusement, diversion, enjoyment, entertainment, fun, games, hobby, leisure, pastime, play, pleasure, relaxation, sport.

recrimination *n* accusation, *inf* comeback, reprisal, retaliation, retort.

recruit *n* apprentice, beginner, conscript, initiate, learner, new boy *or* girl, novice, trainee. *Opp* VETERAN.
• *v* advertise for, conscript, draft in, engage, enlist, enrol, mobilize, muster, register, sign on, sign up, take on.

rectify *v* amend, correct, cure, *inf* fix, make good, put right, repair, revise.

recumbent *adj* flat, flat on your back, horizontal, lying down, prone, reclining, stretched out, supine. *Opp* UPRIGHT.

recuperate *v* convalesce, get better, heal, mend, rally, regain strength. ⊳ RECOVER.

recur *v* be repeated, happen again, persist, reappear, return.

recurrent *adj* chronic, frequent, intermittent, periodic, persistent, recurring, regular, repeated. ⊳ CONTINUAL.

recycle *v* retrieve, reuse, salvage, use again.

red *adj* 1 bloodshot, blushing, embarrassed, fiery, flaming, florid, flushed, glowing, inflamed, rosy, ruddy. 2 auburn, crimson, magenta, maroon, ruby, scarlet, vermilion, wine-coloured. **red herring** ⊳ DECOY.

redden *v* blush, colour, flush, glow.

redeem *v* buy back, cash in, reclaim, recover, trade in, win back. ⊳ LIBERATE. **redeem yourself** ⊳ ATONE.

redolent *adj* 1 aromatic, fragrant, perfumed, scented, smelling. 2 *redolent of the past.* reminiscent, suggestive.

reduce *v* 1 abbreviate, abridge, clip, compress, curtail, cut, cut back, decimate, decrease, detract from, devalue, dilute, diminish, *inf* dock (*wages*), *inf* ease up on, halve, lessen, limit, lower, minimize, moderate, narrow, prune, shorten, shrink, simplify, *inf* slash, slim down, trim, truncate, weaken, whittle. 2 contract, dwindle, shrink. 3 *reduce a liquid.* concentrate, condense, thicken. 4 *reduce to rubble.* break up, destroy, grind, pulp, pulverize. 5 *reduce to poverty.* degrade, humble, impoverish, ruin. *Opp* INCREASE, RAISE.

reduction *n* 1 contraction, curtailment, cutback, decimation, decline, decrease, diminution, drop, lessening, limitation, loss, moderation, narrowing, remission, shortening, shrinkage, weakening. 2 *reduction in price.* concession, cut, depreciation, devaluation, discount, rebate, refund. *Opp* INCREASE.

redundant *adj* excessive, inessential, non-essential, superfluous, surplus, unnecessary, unneeded, unwanted. *Opp* NECESSARY.

reek *n* stench, stink. ⊳ SMELL.

reel *n* bobbin, spool.
• *v* lurch, pitch, rock, roll, spin, stagger, stumble, sway, totter, whirl, wobble. **reel off** ⊳ RECITE.

refer *v* **refer to** 1 allude to, bring up, cite, comment on, draw attention to, mention, name, point to, quote, speak of, touch on. 2 *refer one person to another.* direct to, hand over to, pass on to, recommend to, send to. 3 *refer to the dictionary.* consult, resort to, study, turn to.

referee *n* arbiter, arbitrator, judge, mediator, umpire.

reference *n* 1 allusion, citation, example, illustration, instance, mention, note, quotation, referral, remark. 2 recommendation, testimonial.

refill *v* fill up, refuel, renew, replenish, top up.

refine *v* 1 clarify, cleanse, clear, decontaminate, distil, process, purify, treat. 2 *refine manners.* civilize, improve, perfect, polish.

refined *adj* 1 aristocratic, civilized, courteous, courtly, cultured, delicate, dignified, discriminating, elegant, fastidious, genteel, gentlemanly, gracious, ladylike, polished, polite, *inf* posh, *derog* pretentious, *derog* prissy, sensitive, sophisticated, subtle, tasteful, *inf* upper-crust, urbane, well-bred, well brought-up. *Opp* RUDE. 2 *refined oil.* distilled, processed, purified, treated. *Opp* CRUDE.

refinement *n* 1 breeding, *inf* class, courtesy, cultivation, delicacy, discrimination, elegance, finesse, gentility, graciousness, polish, *derog* pretentiousness, sophistication, style, subtlety, taste, urbanity. 2 *refinement in design.* enhancement, improvement, modification.

reflect *v* 1 echo, mirror, return, shine back, throw back. 2 brood, *inf* chew things over, consider, contemplate, deliberate, meditate, ponder, reminisce, ruminate. ▷ THINK. 3 *Her success reflects her hard work.* bear witness to, demonstrate, illustrate, indicate, match, point to, reveal, show.

reflection *n* 1 echo, image, likeness. 2 *reflection of hard work.* demonstration, evidence, indication, result. 3 *no reflection on you.* criticism, discredit, reproach, shame, slur. 4 *time for reflection.* cogitation, contemplation, deliberation, meditation, pondering, rumination, self-examination, study, thinking, thought.

reflective *adj* 1 glittering, lustrous, reflecting, shiny, silvery. 2 ▷ THOUGHTFUL.

reform *v* 1 ameliorate, amend, better, change, convert, correct, improve, mend, put right, rectify. 2 *reform a system.* reconstruct, regenerate, remodel, reorganize, revolutionize.

refrain *v* **refrain from** abstain from, avoid, cease, desist from, do without, eschew, forbear, leave off, *inf* quit, renounce, stop.

refresh *v* 1 cool, energize, enliven, freshen, invigorate, *inf* perk up, quench the thirst of, rejuvenate, renew, restore, resuscitate, revitalize, revive, slake (*thirst*). 2 *refresh the memory.* awaken, jog, remind, prod, prompt, stimulate.

refreshing *adj* 1 bracing, cool, enlivening, exhilarating, invigorating, restorative, reviving, stimulating, thirst-quenching, tonic. *Opp* EXHAUSTING. 2 *refreshing change.* fresh, interesting, new, novel, original, unexpected, unfamiliar, unforeseen, welcome. *Opp* BORING.

refreshments *n* drinks, *inf* eats, *inf* nibbles, snacks.

refrigerate *v* chill, cool, freeze, ice, keep cold.

refuge *n* asylum, *inf* bolt-hole, cover, harbour, haven, hideaway, *inf* hideout, hiding-place, protection, retreat, safety, sanctuary, security, shelter, stronghold.

refugee *n* displaced person, exile, fugitive, outcast.

refund *n* rebate, repayment.
• *v* give back, pay back, reimburse, repay, return.

refusal *n inf* brush-off, denial, rebuff, rejection, veto. *Opp* ACCEPTANCE.

refuse *n* detritus, dirt, garbage, junk, litter, rubbish, trash, waste.
• *v* baulk at, decline, disallow, *inf* pass up, rebuff, reject, repudiate, spurn, turn down, veto, withhold. *Opp* ACCEPT, GRANT.

refute *v* counter, discredit, disprove, negate, prove wrong.

regain *v* be reunited with, find, get back, recapture, reclaim, recoup, recover, retake, retrieve, win back.

regal *adj derog* haughty, imperial, kingly, lordly, majestic, noble, palatial, princely, queenly, royal, stately. ▷ SPLENDID.

regard *n* 1 gaze, look, scrutiny, stare. 2 attention, care, concern, consideration, deference, heed, notice, reference, thought. 3 admiration, affection, appreciation, approval, esteem, favour, honour, love, respect, reverence, veneration.
• *v* 1 behold, contemplate, eye, gaze at, keep an eye on, look at, note, observe, scrutinize, view, watch. 2 *regarded me as a liability.* consider, deem, esteem, judge, look upon, perceive, rate, reckon, respect, think of, value, view.

regarding *prep* about, apropos, concerning, connected with, involving, on the subject of, with reference to, with regard to.

regardless *adj* **regardless of** despite, heedless of, indifferent to, neglectful of, notwithstanding, unmindful of.

regime *n* administration, government,

leadership, management, order, reign, rule, system.

regiment *v* arrange, control, discipline, organize, regulate.

region *n* area, country, department, district, division, expanse, land, locality, neighbourhood, part, place, province, quarter, sector, territory, tract, vicinity, zone.

register *n* catalogue, diary, directory, file, index, inventory, journal, ledger, list, record, roll.
• *v* 1 enlist, enrol, enter your name, join, sign on. 2 *register a complaint.* enter, list, log, make official, present, record, set down, submit, write down. 3 *register emotion.* display, express, indicate, manifest, reflect, reveal, show. 4 *register in a hotel.* *inf* check in, sign in. 5 *register what someone says.* make a note of, mark, notice, take account of.

regress *v* backslide, degenerate, deteriorate, go back, retreat, retrogress, revert, slip back. *Opp* PROGRESS.

regret *n* 1 compunction, contrition, guilt, penitence, pang of conscience, remorse, repentance, self-reproach, shame. 2 disappointment, grief, sadness, sorrow, sympathy.
• *v* bemoan, deplore, deprecate, feel remorse, grieve (about), lament, mourn, repent (of), reproach yourself, rue, weep (over).

regretful *adj* apologetic, ashamed, conscience-stricken, contrite, disappointed, penitent, remorseful, repentant, rueful, sorry. ▷ SAD. *Opp* UNREPENTANT.

regrettable *adj* deplorable, disappointing, distressing, lamentable, reprehensible, sad, shameful, undesirable, unfortunate, unlucky, upsetting, woeful, wrong.

regular *adj* 1 consistent, constant, daily, equal, even, fixed, hourly, measured, monthly, ordered, predictable, recurring, repeated, rhythmic, steady, systematic, weekly, yearly. 2 *regular procedure.* accustomed, common, conventional, customary, established, everyday, familiar, frequent, habitual, normal, ordinary, proper, routine, scheduled, standard, traditional, typical, usual. 3 *regular supporter.* dependable, faithful, reliable. *Opp* IRREGULAR.
• *n* habitué, regular customer, patron.

regulate *v* 1 administer, control, direct, manage, order, organize, oversee, restrict, supervise. 2 *regulate temperature.* adjust, alter, change, get right, moderate, set, vary.

regulation *n* by-law, decree, dictate, directive, edict, law, order, ordinance, requirement, rule, ruling, statute.

rehearsal *n* dress rehearsal, *inf* dry run, practice, *inf* run-through, trial, *inf* try-out.

rehearse *v* drill, go over, practise, prepare, *inf* run over, *inf* run through, try out.

rehearsed *adj* practised, pre-arranged, prepared, scripted, studied, thought out. *Opp* IMPROMPTU.

reign *n* ascendancy, command, empire, jurisdiction, monarchy, power, rule, sovereignty.
• *v* be on the throne, command, govern, have power, hold sway, rule, *inf* wear the crown.

reincarnation *n* rebirth, return to life.

reinforce *v* 1 back up, bolster, buttress, fortify, give strength to, hold up, prop up, stiffen, strengthen, support, toughen. 2 *reinforce an army.* add to, augment, help, provide reinforcements for, supplement.

reinforcements *pl n* additional troops, auxiliaries, backup, help, reserves, support.

reinstate *v* recall, rehabilitate, restore, take back, welcome back. *Opp* DISMISS.

reject *v* 1 discard, discount, dismiss, eliminate, exclude, jettison, *inf* junk, put aside, scrap, throw away, throw out. 2 *reject friends.* disown, *inf* drop, *inf* give (someone) the cold shoulder, jilt, rebuff, renounce, repel, repudiate, repulse, shun, spurn, turn your back on. 3 *reject an invitation.* decline, refuse, turn down, veto. *Opp* ACCEPT, ADOPT.

rejoice *v* be happy, celebrate, delight, exult, glory, revel, triumph. *Opp* GRIEVE.

relapse *n* degeneration, deterioration, recurrence (*of illness*), regression, *inf* setback, worsening.
• *v* backslide, degenerate, deteriorate, lapse, regress, revert, sink back, slip back, weaken.

relate *v* 1 communicate, describe, detail, divulge, impart, narrate, present, recite, recount, report, reveal, tell. 2 ally, associate, compare, connect, consider together, correlate, couple, join, link. **relate to** 1 apply to, be relevant to, concern, pertain to, refer to. 2 *relate to other people.* empathize with, handle, identify with, socialize with, understand.

related *adj* affiliated, akin, allied, associated, comparable, connected, interdependent, interrelated, joined, joint, linked, mutual, parallel, reciprocal, relative, similar. ▷ RELEVANT. *Opp* UNRELATED.

relation *n* 1 *pl* kith and kin, member of the family, relative. ▷ FAMILY. 2 *relation of a story*. ▷ NARRATION.

relationship *n* 1 affiliation, affinity, association, attachment, bond, closeness, connection, correlation, correspondence, interdependence, kinship, link, parallel, rapport, ratio, tie, understanding. ▷ SIMILARITY. *Opp* CONTRAST. 2 affair, *inf* intrigue, *inf* liaison, love affair, romance. ▷ FRIENDSHIP.

relative *adj* ▷ RELATED, RELEVANT. **relative to** commensurate (with), comparative, proportional, proportionate. *Opp* UNRELATED.
• *n* ▷ RELATION.

relax *v* 1 be relaxed, calm down, feel at home, *inf* let go, *inf* put your feet up, rest, *inf* slow down, *inf* take it easy, unbend, unwind. *Opp* TENSION. 2 decrease, diminish, ease off, lessen, loosen, mitigate, moderate, reduce, release, relieve, slacken, soften, temper, *inf* tone down, unclench, unfasten, weaken. *Opp* INCREASE.

relaxation *n* 1 ease, informality, loosening up, relaxing, rest, unwinding. ▷ RECREATION. *Opp* TENSION. 2 alleviation, diminution, lessening, *inf* let-up, moderation, remission, slackening. *Opp* INCREASE.

relaxed *adj derog* blasé, calm, carefree, casual, comfortable, contented, cool, easygoing, *inf* free and easy, friendly, good-humoured, happy, *inf* happy-go-lucky, informal, *inf* laid-back, leisurely, nonchalant, peaceful, restful, serene, *derog* slack, tranquil, unconcerned, unhurried, untroubled. *Opp* TENSE.

relay *n* 1 shift, turn. 2 *live relay*. broadcast, programme, transmission.
•*v* broadcast, communicate, pass on, send out, spread, televise, transmit.

release *v* 1 acquit, allow out, discharge, dismiss, emancipate, excuse, exonerate, free, let go, liberate, loose, pardon, rescue, save, set free, set loose, unfasten, unfetter, unleash, untie. *Opp* DETAIN. 2 fire off, launch, let off. 3 *release information*. circulate, disseminate, distribute, issue, make available, present, publish, send out.

relegate *v* consign to a lower position, demote, downgrade.

relent *v* acquiesce, be merciful, capitulate, give in, give way, relax, show pity, soften, weaken, yield.

relentless *adj* 1 dogged, fierce, hard-hearted, implacable, inexorable, intransigent, merciless, obdurate, obstinate, pitiless, remorseless, ruthless, uncompromising, unforgiving, unmerciful, unyielding. ▷ CRUEL. 2 unceasing, unrelieved, unstoppable. ▷ CONTINUAL.

relevant *adj* applicable, apposite, appropriate, apt, connected, essential, fitting, linked, material, pertinent, proper, related, relative, significant, suitable, suited, to the point. *Opp* IRRELEVANT.

reliable *adj* certain, consistent, constant, dependable, devoted, efficient, faithful, honest, loyal, predictable, proven, punctilious, regular, reputable, responsible, safe, solid, sound, stable, staunch, steady, sure, trusted, trustworthy, unchanging, unfailing. *Opp* UNRELIABLE.

relic *n* heirloom, keepsake, memento, remains, reminder, remnant, souvenir, token, vestige.

relief *n* abatement, aid, alleviation, assistance, comfort, cure, deliverance, diversion, ease, help, *inf* let-up, mitigation, relaxation, release, remedy, remission, respite, rest.

relieve *v* abate, alleviate, anaesthetize, assuage, bring relief to, calm, comfort, console, cure, diminish, dull, ease, lessen, lift, lighten, mitigate, moderate, palliate, reduce, relax, release, soften, soothe, unburden. ▷ HELP. *Opp* INTENSIFY.

religion *n* 1 belief, creed, divinity, doctrine, dogma, theology. 2 creed, cult, denomination, faith, persuasion, sect.

religious *adj* 1 devotional, divine, holy, sacramental, sacred, scriptural, theological. *Opp* SECULAR. 2 church-going, committed, dedicated, devout, God-fearing, godly, *derog* pietistic, pious, reverent, righteous, saintly, *derog* sanctimonious, spiritual. *Opp* IRRELIGIOUS. 3 *religious wars*. doctrinal, sectarian.

relinquish *v* concede, hand over, part with, surrender, yield.

relish *n* 1 appetite, delight, enjoyment, enthusiasm, gusto, pleasure, zest. 2 flavour, piquancy, savour, tang, taste.
•*v* appreciate, delight in, enjoy, like, love, revel in, savour, take pleasure in.

reluctant *adj* averse, disinclined, grudging, hesitant, loath, unenthusiastic, unwilling. *Opp* EAGER.

rely *v* **rely on** *inf* bank on, count

on, depend on, have confidence in, lean on, put your faith in, *inf* swear by, trust.

remain *v* be left, carry on, continue, endure, keep on, linger, live on, persist, stay, *inf* stay put, survive, wait. **remaining** ▷ RESIDUAL.

remainder *n* balance, excess, extra, remnant, rest, surplus. ▷ REMAINS.

remains *pl n* 1 crumbs, debris, detritus, dregs, fragments, leftovers, oddments, *inf* odds and ends, remainder, remnants, residue, rubble, ruins, scraps, traces, vestiges, wreckage. 2 *historic remains*. heirloom, keepsake, memento, monument, relic, reminder, souvenir. 3 *human remains*. ashes, body, bones, carcass, corpse.

remake *v* piece together, rebuild, reconstitute, reconstruct, redo. ▷ RENEW.

remark *n* comment, mention, observation, reflection, statement, thought, utterance, word.
• *v* 1 assert, comment, declare, mention, note, observe, reflect, say, state. 2 perceive, see. ▷ NOTICE.

remarkable *adj* amazing, astonishing, astounding, curious, different, distinguished, exceptional, extraordinary, impressive, marvellous, memorable, notable, noteworthy, odd, out of the ordinary, outstanding, peculiar, phenomenal, prominent, signal, significant, singular, special, strange, striking, surprising, *inf* terrific, tremendous, uncommon, unusual, wonderful. *Opp* ORDINARY.

remedy *n inf* answer, antidote, corrective, countermeasure, cure, drug, elixir, medicament, medication, medicine, palliative, panacea, prescription, redress, relief, restorative, solution, therapy, treatment.
• *v* alleviate, correct, counteract, *inf* fix, heal, help, mend, mitigate, palliate, put right, rectify, redress, relieve, repair, solve, treat. ▷ CURE.

remember *v* 1 be mindful of, have in mind, keep in mind, recognize. 2 learn, memorize, retain. 3 *remember old times*. be nostalgic about, hark back to, recall, recollect, reminisce about, review, summon up, think back to. 4 *remember an anniversary*. celebrate, commemorate, observe. *Opp* FORGET.

remind *v* cause to remember, jog the memory, prompt.

reminder *n* 1 cue, hint, *inf* memo, memorandum, note, *inf* nudge, prompt, *inf* shopping list. 2 keepsake, memento, relic, souvenir.

reminisce *v* be nostalgic, hark back, look back, recall, remember, review, think back.

reminiscence *n* account, anecdote, memoir, memory, recollection, remembrance.

reminiscent *adj* evocative, nostalgic, redolent, suggestive.

remiss *adj* careless, dilatory, forgetful, irresponsible, lax, negligent, slack, thoughtless. *Opp* CAREFUL.

remit *v* 1 *remit a debt*. cancel, let off, pay, settle. 2 decrease, ease off, lessen, relax, slacken. 3 dispatch, forward, send.

remittance *n* allowance, fee, payment.

remnants *pl n* bits, fragments, leftovers, oddments, offcuts, residue, scraps, traces, vestiges. ▷ REMAINS.

remodel *v* ▷ RENEW.

remorse *n* compunction, contrition, grief, guilt, mortification, pangs of conscience, penitence, regret, repentance, sadness, self-reproach, shame, sorrow.

remorseful *adj* ashamed, conscience-stricken, contrite, guilt-ridden, penitent, regretful, repentant, rueful, sorry. *Opp* UNREPENTANT.

remorseless *adj* dogged, implacable, inexorable, merciless, obdurate, pitiless, relentless, ruthless, unkind, unmerciful, unremitting. ▷ CRUEL.

remote *adj* 1 cut off, desolate, distant, faraway, foreign, godforsaken, hard to find, inaccessible, isolated, lonely, outlying, out of reach, out of the way, secluded, solitary, unfamiliar, unfrequented, unreachable. *Opp* CLOSE. 2 *remote chance*. doubtful, improbable, outside, poor, slender, slight, small, unlikely. *Opp* SURE. 3 *remote manner*. abstracted, aloof, cold, cool, detached, haughty, preoccupied, reserved, standoffish, withdrawn. *Opp* FRIENDLY.

removal *n* 1 relocation, transfer, transportation. 2 elimination, eradication, extermination, liquidation, purge. ▷ KILLING. 3 *removal from a position*. deposition, dethronement, dislodgement, dismissal, displacement, ejection, expulsion, *inf* firing, *inf* sacking, transference, unseating. 4 *removal of teeth*. drawing, extraction, pulling, taking out.

remove *v* 1 abolish, amputate (*limb*), banish, clear away, cut off, cut out, delete, depose, detach, disconnect, dismiss, dispense with, displace, dispose of, do away with, eject, eliminate, eradicate, erase, evict, exile, expel, *inf* fire, *inf* get rid of, *inf* kick out, kill, oust, purge, root out, *inf* sack, sweep away, take out, throw out, turn out, uproot, wash off, wipe out. 2 *remove furniture*. carry away, convey, move, transfer, transport. 3 *remove a tooth*. draw out, extract, pull out. 4 *remove clothes*. doff (*a hat*), peel off, strip off, take off.

rend *v* cleave, pull apart, rip, rupture, shred, split, tear.

render *v* 1 cede, deliver, furnish, give, hand over, offer, present, proffer, provide, tender, yield. 2 *render a song*. ⊳ PERFORM. 3 *render speechless*. cause to be, make.

rendezvous *n* appointment, assignation, date, engagement, meeting, meeting place.

renegade *n* backslider, defector, deserter, fugitive, heretic, mutineer, outlaw, rebel, runaway, traitor, turncoat.

renege *v* **renege on** *inf* back out of, break, default on, fail to keep, go back on, repudiate.

renew *v* 1 bring up to date, *inf* do up, *inf* give a facelift to, improve, mend, modernize, overhaul, recondition, reconstitute, recreate, redecorate, redesign, redevelop, redo, refit, refresh, refurbish, reintroduce, remake, remodel, renovate, repaint, repair, replace, replenish, restore, resurrect, revamp, revive, transform, update. 2 *renew an activity*. come back to, pick up again, restart, resume, return to. 3 *renew vows*. confirm, reaffirm, repeat, restate.

renounce *v* 1 abandon, abstain from, deny, discard, disown, eschew, forgo, forsake, forswear, give up, reject, repudiate, spurn. 2 *renounce the throne*. abdicate, quit, relinquish, resign, surrender.

renovate *v* ⊳ RENEW.

renovation *n* improvement, modernization, overhaul, redevelopment, refit, refurbishment, renewal, repair, restoration, transformation, updating.

renowned *adj* celebrated, eminent, illustrious, prominent, well-known. ⊳ FAMOUS.

rent *n* 1 fee, instalment, payment, rental. 2 *rent in a garment*. ⊳ SPLIT.
• *v* charter, hire, lease, let.

reorganize *v* rationalize, rearrange, reshuffle, restructure.

repair *v* 1 *inf* fix, mend, overhaul, patch up, put right, rectify, service. ⊳ RENEW. 2 darn, patch, sew up.

repay *v* 1 compensate, pay back, recompense, refund, reimburse, remunerate, settle. 2 avenge, get even, *inf* get your own back, requite, retaliate, return, revenge.

repeal *v* abolish, annul, cancel, nullify, rescind, reverse, revoke.

repeat *v* 1 do again, duplicate, redo, rehearse, replicate, reproduce, re-run. 2 echo, quote, recapitulate, re-echo, reiterate, restate, retell, say again.

repel *v* 1 drive away, fend off, fight off, *inf* keep at bay, parry, push away, rebuff, repulse, ward off. 2 *repel water*. be impermeable to, exclude, keep out. 3 *cruelty repels us*. alienate, be repellent to, disgust, nauseate, offend, *inf* put off, revolt, sicken, *inf* turn off. *Opp* ATTRACT.

repellent *adj* 1 impermeable, impervious, resistant. 2 ⊳ REPULSIVE.

repent *v* bemoan, be repentant about, bewail, feel repentance for, lament, regret, rue.

repentance *n* contrition, guilt, penitence, regret, remorse, self-reproach, shame, sorrow.

repentant *adj* apologetic, ashamed, conscience-stricken, contrite, guilt-ridden, penitent, regretful, remorseful, rueful, sorry. *Opp* UNREPENTANT.

repertory *n* collection, repertoire, stock, store, supply.

repetitive *adj* boring, monotonous, recurrent, repeated, repetitious, tautologous, tedious, unvaried. ⊳ CONTINUAL.

replace *v* 1 put back, reinstate, restore, return. 2 come after, follow, oust, succeed, supersede, supplant, take over from, take the place of. ⊳ DEPUTIZE. 3 *replace worn parts*. change, renew, substitute.

replacement *n* *inf* fill-in, proxy, stand-in, substitute, successor, understudy.

replenish *v* fill up, refill, renew, restock, top up.

replete *adj* *inf* bursting, gorged, *inf* jam-packed, sated, stuffed. ⊳ FULL.

replica *n* *inf* carbon copy, clone, copy, duplicate, facsimile, imitation, likeness, model, reproduction.

reply *n* acknowledgement, answer, *inf* comeback, reaction, rejoinder, response, retort, riposte.

• *v* answer, react, rejoin, respond. **reply to** ▷ ACKNOWLEDGE, COUNTER.

report *n* 1 account, announcement, article, communication, communiqué, description, dispatch, narrative, news, record, statement, story, *inf* write-up. 2 bang, blast, boom, crack, detonation, explosion, noise.
• *v* 1 announce, broadcast, circulate, communicate, declare, describe, document, give an account of, notify, proclaim, publish, put out, record, recount, reveal, state, tell. 2 *report for duty*. check in, clock in, introduce yourself, present yourself, sign in. 3 *report someone to the police*. complain about, denounce, inform against, *inf* tell on.

reporter *n* columnist, commentator, correspondent, *inf* hack, journalist, news presenter, newsreader, photojournalist, writer.

repose *n* calm, calmness, comfort, ease, inactivity, peace, peacefulness, quiet, quietness, relaxation, respite, rest, serenity, tranquillity. ▷ SLEEP. *Opp* ACTIVITY.

reprehensible *adj* culpable, deplorable, disgraceful, immoral, objectionable, regrettable, shameful, unworthy, wicked. ▷ GUILTY. *Opp* INNOCENT.

represent *v* 1 act out, be an example of, embody, enact, epitomize, exemplify, exhibit, illustrate, impersonate, masquerade as, personify, pose as, present, stand for, symbolize, typify. 2 characterize, define, delineate, depict, describe, draw, paint, picture, portray, reflect, show, sketch. 3 act for, speak for, stand up for.

representation *n* depiction, figure, image, imitation, likeness, model, picture, portrait, portrayal, semblance, statue.

representative *adj* 1 archetypal, average, characteristic, illustrative, normal, typical. *Opp* ABNORMAL. 2 *representative government*. chosen, democratic, elected.
• *n* 1 delegate, deputy, proxy, spokesman, spokeswoman, stand-in, substitute. 2 agent, *inf* rep, salesman, saleswoman. 3 ambassador, consul, diplomat, emissary, envoy. 4 *Amer* congressman, councillor, MP, ombudsman.

repress *v* 1 control, crush, curb, keep down, put down, quell, restrain, subdue, subjugate. 2 *repress emotion*. *inf* bottle up, inhibit, stifle, suppress.

repressed *adj* 1 cold, frustrated, inhibited, neurotic, *inf* prim and proper, tense, undemonstrative, *inf* uptight. *Opp* UNINHIBITED. 2 *repressed emotion*. *inf* bottled up, hidden, latent, subconscious, suppressed, unconscious.

repression *n* 1 censorship, coercion, control, dictatorship, oppression, restraint, subjugation, tyranny. 2 *repression of emotion*. *inf* bottling up, inhibition, suffocation, suppression.

repressive *adj* authoritarian, autocratic, brutal, cruel, despotic, dictatorial, harsh, oppressive, restricting, severe, totalitarian, tyrannical, undemocratic. *Opp* LIBERAL.

reprieve *n* amnesty, pardon, respite, stay of execution.
• *v* forgive, let off, pardon, postpone execution, set free, spare.

reprimand *n* admonition, castigation, censure, condemnation, criticism, *inf* dressing-down, lecture, lesson, *inf* rap on the knuckles, rebuke, remonstration, reproach, reproof, scolding, *inf* slap on the wrist, *inf* slating, *inf* talking-to, *inf* telling-off, *inf* ticking-off.
• *v* admonish, berate, blame, *inf* carpet, castigate, censure, condemn, criticize, find fault with, *inf* haul over the coals, lecture, *inf* rap, rate, rebuke, reprehend, reproach, reprove, scold, *inf* slate, take to task, *inf* teach a lesson, *inf* tell off, *inf* tick off, upbraid. *Opp* PRAISE.

reprisal *n* counter-attack, redress, repayment, retaliation, retribution, revenge, vengeance.

reproach *n* blame, disapproval, disgrace, scorn.
• *v* censure, criticize, scold, upbraid. ▷ REPRIMAND. *Opp* PRAISE.

reproachful *adj* censorious, critical, disapproving, disparaging, reproving, withering.

reproduce *v* 1 copy, counterfeit, duplicate, forge, imitate, mimic, photocopy, print, reissue, reprint. ▷ REPEAT. 2 breed, increase, multiply, procreate, produce offspring, propagate, regenerate, spawn.

reproduction *n* 1 breeding, cloning, increase, multiplying, procreation, proliferation, propagation, spawning. 2 *inf* carbon copy, clone, copy, duplicate, facsimile, fake, forgery, imitation, likeness, print, replica.

repudiate *v* 1 deny, dispute, rebuff, refute, reject, scorn, turn down. *Opp* ACKNOWLEDGE. 2 *repudiate an agreement*. discard, go back on, recant, renounce, rescind, retract, reverse, revoke.

repugnant *adj* ▷ REPULSIVE.

repulsive *adj* abhorrent, abominable, beastly, disagreeable, disgusting, distasteful, foul, gross, hateful, hideous, loathsome, nasty, nauseating, obnoxious, odious, offensive, *inf* off-putting, repellent, repugnant, revolting, *inf* sick, sickening, unpalatable, unpleasant, unsavoury, unsightly, vile. ▷ UGLY. *Opp* ATTRACTIVE.

reputable *adj* creditable, dependable, good, highly regarded, honourable, prestigious, reliable, respectable, respected, trustworthy, up-market, well-thought-of, worthy. *Opp* DISREPUTABLE.

reputation *n* character, fame, name, prestige, renown, repute, standing, stature, status.

reputed *adj* alleged, believed, considered, deemed, judged, reckoned, regarded, rumoured, said, supposed, thought.

request *n* appeal, application, call, demand, entreaty, petition, plea, prayer, requisition, solicitation, suit, supplication.
• *v* appeal, apply (for), ask, beg, beseech, call for, claim, demand, entreat, implore, importune, invite, petition, pray for, require, requisition, seek, solicit, supplicate.

require *v* 1 be short of, lack, need, want. 2 *require a response.* call for, command, compel, direct, force, insist, instruct, make, oblige, order, put pressure on. ▷ REQUEST. **required** ▷ REQUISITE.

requirement *n* condition, demand, necessity, need, precondition, prerequisite, provision, proviso, qualification, stipulation.

requisite *adj* compulsory, essential, mandatory, necessary, needed, obligatory, prescribed, required, set, stipulated. *Opp* OPTIONAL.

requisition *n* application, authorization, demand, order, request.
• *v* 1 demand, order, *inf* put in for, request. 2 appropriate, commandeer, confiscate, occupy, seize, take over, take possession of.

rescue *n* deliverance, emancipation, freeing, liberation, recovery, release, relief, salvage.
• *v* 1 deliver, emancipate, extricate, free, let go, liberate, loose, ransom, release, save, set free. 2 get back, recover, retrieve, salvage.

research *n* analysis, examination, experimentation, exploration, fact-finding, investigation, probe, scrutiny, study.
• *v inf* check out, experiment, investigate, probe, search, study.

resemblance *n* affinity, closeness, coincidence, comparison, conformity, congruity, correspondence, equivalence, likeness, similarity.

resemble *v* approximate to, bear resemblance to, be similar to, compare with, look like, mirror, *inf* take after.

resent *v* begrudge, be resentful about, envy, feel bitter about, grudge, object to, take exception to, *inf* take umbrage at.

resentful *adj* aggrieved, annoyed, begrudging, bitter, disgruntled, displeased, embittered, envious, grudging, irked, jaundiced, jealous, offended, *inf* peeved, put out, spiteful, unfriendly, vexed, vindictive. ▷ ANGRY.

resentment *n* animosity, bitterness, discontent, envy, grudge, hatred, hurt, ill will, irritation, jealousy, pique, rancour, spite, unfriendliness, vexation, vindictiveness. ▷ ANGER.

reservation *n* 1 condition, doubt, hesitation, misgiving, proviso, qualification, qualm, reluctance, reticence, scruple. 2 *hotel reservation.* booking. 3 *wildlife reservation.* ▷ RESERVE.

reserve *n* 1 cache, fund, hoard, *inf* nest-egg, reservoir, savings, stock, stockpile, store, supply. 2 backup, deputy, *pl* reinforcements, replacement, standby, stand-in, substitute, understudy. 3 *wildlife reserve.* game park, preserve, protected area, reservation, safari park, sanctuary. 4 aloofness, caution, modesty, quietness, reluctance, reticence, self-consciousness, self-effacement, shyness, timidity.
• *v* 1 earmark, hoard, hold back, keep, keep back, preserve, put aside, retain, save, set aside, stockpile, store up. 2 *reserve seats. inf* bag, book, order. **reserved** ▷ RETICENT.

reside *v* **reside in** dwell in, inhabit, live in, lodge in, occupy, settle in.

residence *n* abode, address, domicile, dwelling, dwelling place, habitation, home, house, quarters, seat.

resident *adj* in residence, living in, permanent, staying.
• *n* citizen, denizen, householder, inhabitant, *inf* local, native.

residual *adj* continuing, left over, persisting, remaining, spare, surplus.

resign *v* abandon, abdicate, *inf* chuck in, forsake, give up, leave, quit, relinquish, renounce, retire, stand down, step down, surrender, vacate. **resigned** ▷ PATIENT. **resign yourself to** ▷ ACCEPT.

resilient *adj* 1 bouncy, elastic, firm, plastic, pliable, rubbery, springy, supple. *Opp* BRITTLE. 2 *resilient person*. adaptable, buoyant, irrepressible, strong, tough. *Opp* VULNERABLE.

resist *v* avoid, be resistant to, confront, counteract, defy, face up to, hinder, hold out against, impede, inhibit, keep at bay, oppose, prevent, rebuff, refuse, stand up to, withstand. ▷ FIGHT. *Opp* ASSIST, YIELD.

resistant *adj* defiant, hostile, intransigent, obstinate, opposed, stubborn, uncooperative, unresponsive, unyielding. **resistant to** impervious to, invulnerable to, opposed to, proof against, unaffected by, unsusceptible to. *Opp* SUSCEPTIBLE.

resolute *adj* adamant, bold, committed, constant, courageous, decided, decisive, determined, dogged, firm, immovable, immutable, indefatigable, *derog* inflexible, *derog* obstinate, persevering, persistent, relentless, resolved, single-minded, staunch, steadfast, strong-willed, *derog* stubborn, tireless, unbending, undaunted, unflinching, unswerving, untiring, unwavering. *Opp* IRRESOLUTE.

resolution *n* 1 boldness, constancy, determination, devotion, doggedness, firmness, *derog* obstinacy, perseverance, persistence, purposefulness, resolve, single-mindedness, steadfastness, *derog* stubbornness, tenacity, will-power. ▷ COURAGE. 2 commitment, oath, pledge, promise, undertaking, vow. 3 *resolution at a meeting*. decision, motion, proposal, statement. 4 *resolution of a problem*. answer, settlement, solution, sorting out.

resolve *n* ▷ RESOLUTION.
• *v* 1 agree, conclude, decide, determine, elect, fix, make a decision, opt, pass a resolution, settle, undertake, vote. 2 *resolve a problem*. answer, clear up, figure out, settle, solve, sort out, work out.

resonant *adj* booming, resounding, reverberant, reverberating, rich, ringing, sonorous, vibrant, vibrating.

resort *n* 1 alternative, course of action, expedient, option, recourse. 2 *seaside resort*. holiday town, retreat, spot.
• *v* **resort to** adopt, *inf* fall back on, have recourse to, make use of, turn to, use.

resound *v* boom, echo, resonate, reverberate, ring, rumble, vibrate. **resounding** ▷ RESONANT.

resourceful *adj* clever, creative, enterprising, imaginative, ingenious, innovative, inspired, inventive, original, *inf* smart, talented. *Opp* SHIFTLESS.

resources *pl n* 1 assets, capital, funds, money, possessions, property, reserves, riches, wealth. 2 *natural resources*. materials, raw materials.

respect *n* 1 admiration, appreciation, consideration, courtesy, deference, esteem, honour, liking, love, regard, reverence, tribute, veneration. 2 *perfect in every respect*. aspect, attribute, characteristic, detail, element, facet, feature, particular, point, property, quality, trait, way.
• *v* admire, appreciate, esteem, have high regard for, honour, look up to, revere, show respect to, think well of, value, venerate. *Opp* DESPISE.

respectable *adj* 1 decent, genteel, honest, honourable, law-abiding, respected, upright, virtuous, worthy. 2 *respectable clothes*. clean, decorous, modest, presentable, proper, seemly. *Opp* DISREPUTABLE. 3 *respectable sum*. ▷ CONSIDERABLE.

respectful *adj* admiring, civil, considerate, cordial, courteous, deferential, dutiful, gracious, humble, obliging, polite, proper, reverent, *derog* servile, thoughtful, well-mannered. *Opp* DISRESPECTFUL.

respective *adj* individual, own, particular, personal, separate, specific.

respite *n* break, *inf* breather, delay, hiatus, holiday, interval, *inf* let-up, lull, pause, recess, relaxation, relief, remission, rest, time off, vacation.

resplendent *adj* brilliant, dazzling, glittering, shining, splendid. ▷ BRIGHT.

respond *v* 1 answer, come back, counter, react, reciprocate, reply, retort. 2 *respond to a need*. ▷ SYMPATHIZE.

response *n* acknowledgement, answer, *inf* comeback, feedback, reaction, rejoinder, reply, retort, riposte.

responsible *adj* 1 at fault, culpable, guilty, liable, to blame. 2 *responsible person*. accountable, answerable, concerned, conscientious, dependable, diligent, dutiful, ethical, honest, in charge, law-abiding, loyal, mature, moral, reliable, sensible, sober, steady, thinking, trustworthy. *Opp* IRRESPONSIBLE. 3 *responsible job*. executive, *inf* front-line, important, managerial, *inf* top. *Opp* MENIAL.

responsive *adj* alert, alive, aware, interested, open, perceptive, receptive, sensitive, sharp, sympathetic, willing. *Opp* UNINTERESTED.

rest *n* 1 break, *inf* breather, breathing-space, ease, hiatus, holiday, inactivity, interlude, intermission, interval, leisure, *inf* let-up, *inf* lie-down, lull, *inf* nap, pause, recess, relaxation, relief, remission, repose, respite, siesta, tea-break, time off, vacation. ⊳ SLEEP. 2 base, holder, prop, stand, support, trestle, tripod. 3 ⊳ REMAINDER.
• *v* 1 doze, have a rest, idle, laze, lie back, lie down, lounge, nod off, *inf* put your feet up, recline, relax, snooze, *inf* take it easy, unwind. ⊳ SLEEP. 2 lean, place, position, prop, set, stand, support. 3 *It rests on the weather.* depend, hang, hinge, rely, turn. **come to rest** ⊳ HALT.

restaurant *n* bistro, brasserie, buffet, café, cafeteria, canteen, carvery, diner, dining room, refectory, snack bar.

restful *adj* calm, calming, comfortable, leisurely, peaceful, quiet, relaxed, relaxing, soothing, still, tranquil, undisturbed, unhurried, untroubled. *Opp* EXHAUSTING.

restless *adj* 1 agitated, anxious, edgy, excitable, fidgety, highly-strung, impatient, *inf* jittery, jumpy, nervous, *inf* on tenterhooks, uneasy, worried. ⊳ ACTIVE. 2 *restless night.* disturbed, interrupted, sleepless, *inf* tossing and turning, troubled, uncomfortable, unsettled. *Opp* RESTFUL.

restore *v* 1 bring back, give back, put back, reinstate, replace, return. 2 *restore antiques.* clean, *inf* do up, fix, *inf* make good, mend, rebuild, recondition, refurbish, renew, renovate, repair, touch up. 3 *restore good relations.* re-establish, reinstate, reintroduce, rekindle, revive. 4 *restore to health.* cure, nurse, rejuvenate, resuscitate, revitalize.

restrain *v* 1 check, control, curb, govern, hold back, inhibit, keep under control, limit, regulate, rein in, repress, restrict, stifle, stop, subdue, suppress. 2 arrest, confine, detain, handcuff, harness, imprison, incarcerate, jail, *inf* keep under lock and key, lock up, muzzle, pinion, tie up. **restrained** ⊳ CALM, DISCREET.

restrict *v* circumscribe, confine, control, cramp, enclose, impede, imprison, inhibit, keep within bounds, limit, regulate, shut. ⊳ RESTRAIN. *Opp* FREE.

restriction *n* ban, constraint, control, curb, curfew, inhibition, limit, limitation, proviso, qualification, regulation, restraint, rule, stipulation.

result *n* 1 conclusion, consequence, effect, end-product, fruit, issue, outcome, repercussion, sequel, upshot. 2 *result of a trial.* decision, judgement, verdict. 3 *result of a game, sum.* answer, score, total.
• *v* arise, be produced, come about, develop, emerge, ensue, follow, happen, issue, occur, proceed, spring, stem, turn out. **result in** ⊳ CAUSE.

resume *v* begin again, carry on, continue, *inf* pick up the threads, proceed, recommence, reconvene, re-open, restart.

resumption *n* continuation, re-opening, restart.

resurrect *v* breathe new life into, bring back, raise (from the dead), reawaken, restore, resuscitate, revive. ⊳ RENEW.

retain *v* 1 *inf* hang on to, hold, hold back, keep, maintain, preserve, reserve, save. *Opp* LOSE. 2 *retain moisture.* absorb, soak up. 3 *retain facts.* keep in mind, learn, memorize, remember. *Opp* FORGET.

retaliate *v* avenge yourself, be revenged, counter-attack, exact retribution, *inf* get even, *inf* get your own back, *inf* give tit for tat, hit back, pay back, repay, *inf* settle a score, strike back, take revenge, wreak vengeance.

retaliation *n* counter-attack, reprisal, retribution, revenge, vengeance.

retard *v* hold back, obstruct, slow down. ⊳ DELAY. **retarded** ⊳ BACKWARD.

reticent *adj* aloof, bashful, cautious, *derog* cold, cool, demure, diffident, distant, modest, quiet, remote, reserved, restrained, retiring, secretive, self-effacing, shy, silent, *derog* standoffish, taciturn, timid, uncommunicative, undemonstrative, unforthcoming, unsociable, withdrawn. *Opp* DEMONSTRATIVE.

retinue *n* attendants, company, entourage, followers, *inf* hangers-on, servants.

retire *v* 1 give up, leave, quit, resign. 2 *retire from society.* become reclusive, go away, go into retreat, withdraw. 3 go to bed. ⊳ SLEEP.

retort *n* answer, *inf* comeback, rejoinder, reply, response, retaliation, riposte.
• *v* answer, counter, react, rejoin, reply, respond, retaliate, return.

retract *v* 1 draw in, pull back, pull

in. 2 cancel, disclaim, *inf* have second thoughts about, recant, renounce, repeal, rescind, reverse, revoke, withdraw.

retreat *n* 1 departure, escape, evacuation, exit, flight, withdrawal. 2 *secluded retreat.* asylum, den, haven, hideaway, *inf* hideout, hiding-place, refuge, resort, sanctuary, shelter.
• *v* 1 back away, back down, decamp, depart, fall back, flee, give ground, leave, move back, pull back, retire, run away, take flight, *inf* take to your heels, *inf* turn tail, withdraw. 2 *the floods retreated.* ebb, flow back, recede, shrink back. *Opp* ADVANCE.

retribution *n* compensation, recompense, redress, reprisal, retaliation, revenge, vengeance. *Opp* FORGIVENESS.

retrieve *v* bring back, find, get back, recapture, recoup, recover, regain, repossess, rescue, restore, return, salvage, save, take back, trace, track down.

retrograde *adj* backward, regressive, retreating, reverse.

retrospective *adj* backward-looking, looking back, nostalgic, with hindsight.

return *n* 1 arrival, homecoming, reappearance, re-entry. 2 *return to normality.* re-establishment (of), reversion. 3 *return of a problem.* recurrence, re-emergence, repetition. 4 *return of stolen goods.* replacing, restitution, restoration. 5 *return on an investment.* earnings, gain, income, interest, proceeds, profit, yield.
• *v* 1 backtrack, come back, do a U-turn, double back, go back, reassemble, reconvene, re-enter, retrace your steps, revert, turn back. 2 put back, readdress, replace, restore, send back. 3 *return money.* give back, refund, reimburse, repay. 4 *return a verdict. inf* come up with, deliver, give, report. 5 *The problem returned. inf* crop up again, happen again, reappear, recur, resurface.

reveal *v* announce, bare, betray, bring to light, confess, declare, dig up, disclose, display, divulge, exhibit, expose, *inf* give the game away, lay bare, leak, let out, let slip, make known, proclaim, produce, publish, show, show up, *inf* spill the beans, tell, uncover, unearth, unfold, unmask, unveil. *Opp* HIDE.

revel *n* carnival, festival, fête, *inf* jamboree, *inf* rave-up, *inf* spree. ▷ REVELRY.
• *v* carouse, celebrate, have fun, *inf* live it up, make merry, *inf* paint the town red.
revel in ▷ ENJOY.

revelation *n* admission, announcement, confession, declaration, disclosure, discovery, exposé, exposure, *inf* leak, news, publication, unmasking, unveiling.

revelry *n* carousing, celebration, conviviality, festivity, fun, gaiety, *inf* high jinks, *inf* jollification, jollity, *inf* living it up, party, merrymaking, revelling, revels, *inf* spree.

revenge *n* reprisal, retaliation, retribution, vengeance.
• *v* avenge, repay. **be revenged** ▷ RETALIATE.

revenue *n* gain, income, interest, money, proceeds, profits, receipts, returns, takings, yield.

reverberate *v* boom, echo, pulsate, resonate, resound, ring, rumble, thunder, vibrate.

revere *v* admire, adore, esteem, feel reverence for, glorify, honour, idolize, pay homage to, praise, respect, venerate, worship. *Opp* DESPISE.

reverence *n* admiration, adoration, awe, deference, devotion, esteem, glorification, homage, honour, praise, respect, veneration, worship.

reverent *adj* adoring, awed, deferential, devoted, devout, pious, religious, respectful, reverential, solemn. *Opp* IRREVERENT.

reverie *n inf* brown study, daydream, dream, fantasy, thought.

reverse *adj* back, backward, contrary, inverse, inverted, opposite, rear.
• *n* 1 antithesis, contrary, converse, opposite. 2 back, rear, underside, wrong side. 3 defeat, difficulty, disaster, failure, mishap, misfortune, problem, reversal, set-back, *inf* upset, vicissitude.
• *v* 1 change, invert, overturn, transpose, turn upside down. 2 *reverse a car.* back, drive backwards, go into reverse. 3 *reverse a decision.* annul, cancel, countermand, invalidate, negate, nullify, overturn, quash, repeal, rescind, retract, revoke, undo.

review *n* 1 *inf* post-mortem, reappraisal, reassessment, recapitulation, reconsideration, re-examination, report, retrospective, study, survey. 2 *book review.* appreciation, assessment, commentary, criticism, critique, evaluation, notice, *inf* write-up.
• *v* 1 appraise, assess, consider, evaluate, *inf* go over, inspect, reassess, recapitulate, reconsider, re-examine, scrutinize, study, survey, take stock, *inf* weigh up. 2 *review a book.* criticize, write a review of.

revise *v* 1 adapt, alter, change, correct, edit, improve, modify, overhaul, *inf* polish up, reconsider, rectify, *inf* redo, rephrase, revamp, reword, rewrite, update. 2 *revise for exams.* brush up, *inf* cram, study, *inf* swot.

revival *n* reawakening, rebirth, recovery, renaissance, renewal, restoration, resurgence, resurrection, return, revitalization, upsurge.

revive *v* 1 awaken, *inf* come round, *inf* come to, rally, reawaken, recover, rouse, waken. *Opp* RELAPSE. 2 bring back to life, *inf* cheer up, freshen, invigorate, refresh, renew, restore, resurrect, resuscitate, revitalize, strengthen.

revolt *n* civil war, coup, coup d'état, insurrection, mutiny, rebellion, revolution, rising, *inf* takeover, uprising.
• *v* 1 disobey, mutiny, rebel, riot, rise up. 2 appal, disgust, nauseate, offend, outrage, repel, sicken. **revolting** ▷ OFFENSIVE.

revolution *n* 1 ▷ REVOLT. 2 circuit, cycle, orbit, rotation, spin, turn. 3 change, reorganization, shift, transformation, *inf* turn-about, upheaval, U-turn.

revolutionary *adj* 1 insurgent, mutinous, rebel, rebellious, seditious, subversive. 2 *revolutionary ideas.* avant-garde, different, experimental, extremist, innovative, new, novel, progressive, radical, unheard-of. *Opp* CONSERVATIVE.
• *n* anarchist, extremist, freedom fighter, insurgent, mutineer, rebel, terrorist.

revolve *v* circle, go round, gyrate, orbit, pirouette, pivot, reel, rotate, spin, swivel, turn, twirl, wheel, whirl.

revulsion *n* abhorrence, aversion, disgust, hatred, loathing, nausea, outrage, repugnance.

reward *n* award, bonus, compensation, decoration, favour, honour, medal, payment, prize, recompense, remuneration, tribute. *Opp* PUNISHMENT.
• *v* compensate, decorate, honour, recompense, remunerate, repay. *Opp* PENALIZE, PUNISH. **rewarding** ▷ PROFITABLE, WORTHWHILE.

rhapsodize *v* be expansive, effuse, enthuse, *inf* go into raptures.

rhetoric *n* eloquence, expressiveness, *inf* gift of the gab, grandiloquence, oratory, rhetorical language, *derog* speechifying.

rhetorical *adj* [*most synonyms derog*] bombastic, florid, *inf* flowery, grandiloquent, grandiose, high-flown, oratorical, ornate, pretentious, verbose, wordy.

rhyme *n* doggerel, jingle. ▷ POEM.

rhythm *n* accent, beat, metre, movement, pattern, pulse, stress, tempo, time.

rhythmic *adj* beating, measured, metrical, regular, repeated, steady. *Opp* IRREGULAR.

ribald *adj* bawdy, coarse, earthy, *inf* naughty, racy, rude, smutty, vulgar. ▷ OBSCENE.

ribbon *n* band, braid, line, strip, stripe, tape, trimming. **in ribbons** ▷ RAGGED.

rich *adj* 1 affluent, *inf* flush, *inf* loaded, moneyed, prosperous, wealthy, *inf* well-heeled, well-off, well-to-do. *Opp* POOR. 2 *rich furnishings.* costly, elaborate, expensive, lavish, luxurious, opulent, priceless, splendid, sumptuous, valuable. 3 *rich land.* fecund, fertile, fruitful, lush, productive. 4 *rich harvest.* abundant, ample, bountiful, copious, plentiful, profuse, prolific, teeming. 5 *rich colours.* deep, full, intense, strong, vibrant, vivid, warm. 6 *rich food.* cloying, creamy, fat, fattening, fatty, heavy, luscious, sweet. **rich person** billionaire, capitalist, millionaire, plutocrat, tycoon.

riches *pl n* affluence, fortune, resources. ▷ WEALTH.

rickety *adj* dilapidated, flimsy, frail, insecure, ramshackle, shaky, tottering, tumbledown, unsteady, wobbly. ▷ WEAK.

rid *v* clear, deliver (from), free, purge. **get rid of** ▷ DESTROY, REMOVE.

riddle *n* 1 *inf* brain-teaser, conundrum, enigma, mystery, *inf* poser, problem, puzzle, question. 2 filter, sieve.
• *v* 1 filter, sieve, sift, strain. 2 *riddle with holes. inf* pepper, perforate, pierce, puncture.

ride *n* ▷ JOURNEY.
• *v* 1 *ride a bike.* control, freewheel, handle, pedal, sit on, steer. 2 *ride a horse.* canter, gallop, trot.

ridge *n* bank, crest, edge, embankment. ▷ HILL.

ridicule *n* badinage, banter, caricature, derision, jeering, laughter, mockery, parody, raillery, *inf* ribbing, sarcasm, satire, scorn, sneers, taunts, teasing.
• *v* be sarcastic, caricature, chaff, deride, guy, hold up to ridicule, jeer at, joke about, lampoon, laugh at, make fun of, mimic, mock, parody, pillory, *inf* poke fun at, *inf* rib, satirize, scoff at, *inf* send up, *inf* take the mickey, taunt, tease.

ridiculous *adj* absurd, amusing, comic, comical, crazy, *inf* daft, farcical, foolish, idiotic, illogical, irrational, laughable, ludicrous, mad, nonsensical, preposterous, senseless, silly, unbelievable. ▷ FUNNY, STUPID. *Opp* SENSIBLE.

rife *adj* abundant, common, endemic, prevalent, widespread.

rift *n* 1 break, chink, cleft, crack, fracture, gap, gulf, opening, split. 2 *rift between friends.* alienation, breach, difference, disagreement, separation.

rig 1 *oil rig.* platform. 2 *sporting rig.* clothes, equipment, *inf* gear, kit, outfit, tackle.
• *v* **rig out** equip, fit out, kit out, supply.

right *adj* 1 decent, ethical, fair, good, honest, honourable, just, law-abiding, lawful, moral, principled, responsible, righteous, right-minded, upright, virtuous. 2 *right answers.* accurate, appropriate, correct, exact, faultless, fitting, perfect, precise, proper, suitable, true, truthful, valid, veracious. 3 *the right way.* best, convenient, normal, preferable, preferred, recommended, sensible, usual. 4 *your right side.* right-hand, starboard [= *right facing bow of ship*]. 5 *right wing in politics.* conservative, fascist, reactionary, Tory. *Opp* LEFT, WRONG.
• *n* 1 decency, equity, fairness, goodness, honesty, integrity, justice, morality, propriety, reason, truth, virtue. 2 *right to free speech.* entitlement, freedom, liberty, prerogative, privilege. 3 *right to give orders.* authority, licence, position, power, title.
• *v* 1 correct, make amends for, put right, rectify, redress, remedy, repair, set right. 2 set upright, stand upright, straighten up.

righteous *adj* blameless, God-fearing, good, guiltless, *derog* holier-than-thou, just, law-abiding, moral, pious, *derog* sanctimonious, upright, virtuous. *Opp* SINFUL.

rightful *adj* authorized, bona fide, correct, just, lawful, legal, legitimate, licensed, proper, real, true, valid. *Opp* ILLEGAL.

rigid *adj* 1 adamantine, firm, hard, inelastic, inflexible, set, solid, steely, stiff, strong, unbending, wooden. 2 *rigid discipline.* austere, harsh, intransigent, stern, strict, unkind, unrelenting, unyielding. ▷ RIGOROUS. *Opp* FLEXIBLE.

rigorous *adj* 1 conscientious, demanding, exact, exacting, meticulous, painstaking, precise, punctilious, rigid, scrupulous, strict, stringent, thorough, tough, uncompromising, undeviating, unsparing, unswerving. *Opp* LAX. 2 *rigorous climate.* extreme, hard, harsh, inhospitable, severe, unfriendly, unpleasant. *Opp* MILD.

rim *n* brim, brink, circumference, edge, lip, perimeter.

rind *n* crust, husk, peel, skin.

ring *n* 1 band, bracelet, circle, circlet, collar, corona, eyelet, girdle, halo, hoop, loop, ringlet. 2 *boxing ring.* arena, enclosure, rink. 3 *drugs ring.* association, band, gang, organization, syndicate. ▷ GROUP. 4 *ring of a bell.* buzz, chime, clang, clink, jangle, jingle, knell, peal, ping, reverberation, tinkle, tintinnabulation, tolling. 5 *give me a ring. inf* bell, *inf* buzz, call.
• *v* 1 circle, encircle, enclose, encompass, surround. 2 boom, buzz, chime, clang, clink, jangle, jingle, peal, ping, resound, reverberate, sound (the knell), tinkle, toll. 3 call, *inf* give someone a buzz, phone, ring up, telephone.

rinse *v* bathe, clean, flush, sluice, swill, wash.

riot *n* affray, anarchy, brawl, chaos, commotion, disorder, disturbance, fracas, fray, hubbub, insurrection, lawlessness, mass protest, mêlée, mutiny, pandemonium, *inf* punch-up, revolt, rioting, rising, *inf* rumpus, strife, tumult, turmoil, unrest, uproar, violence.
• *v* brawl, *inf* go on the rampage, *inf* go wild, mutiny, rampage, rebel, revolt, rise up, run riot, *inf* take to the streets. ▷ FIGHT.

riotous *adj* anarchic, boisterous, chaotic, disorderly, lawless, mutinous, noisy, obstreperous, rebellious, rowdy, uncivilized, uncontrollable, undisciplined, unrestrained, unruly, uproarious, violent, wild. *Opp* ORDERLY.

rip *v* gash, lacerate, pull apart, rend, shred, slit, split, tear.

ripe *adj* mature, mellow, ready to eat, seasoned.

ripen *v* age, come to maturity, develop, mature, mellow.

ripple *n* ▷ WAVE.
• *v* agitate, disturb, make waves, purl, ruffle, stir.

rise *n* 1 ascent, bank, climb, elevation, hill, hump, incline, ramp, ridge, slope. 2 *rise in prices.* escalation, gain, increase, increment, jump, leap, upsurge, upturn, upward movement.
• *v* 1 arise, ascend, climb, fly up, jump, leap, lift, lift off, mount, soar, spring, take off. 2 get to your feet, get up, stand up. 3 *prices rise each year.* escalate,

grow, increase, spiral. 4 *cliffs rise above us.* loom, stand out, tower. **rise up** ▷ REBEL.

risk *n* 1 chance, likelihood, possibility. 2 danger, gamble, hazard, peril, speculation, uncertainty.
• *v* 1 chance, dare, endanger, hazard, jeopardize. 2 *risk money.* gamble, speculate, venture.

risky *adj inf* chancy, *inf* dicey, hazardous, *inf* iffy, perilous, precarious, unsafe. ▷ DANGEROUS. *Opp* SAFE.

ritual *n* ceremonial, ceremony, custom, formality, observance, practice, rite, routine, service, set procedure, tradition.

rival *n* adversary, antagonist, challenger, competitor, contender, contestant, enemy, opponent.
• *v* 1 challenge, compete with, contend with, contest, emulate, oppose, struggle with, undercut, vie with. *Opp* COOPERATE. 2 compare with, equal, match, measure up to.

rivalry *n* antagonism, competition, conflict, contention, feuding, opposition, strife. *Opp* COOPERATION.

river *n* brook, channel, rivulet, stream, tributary, watercourse, waterway.

road *n* alley, avenue, boulevard, bypass, crescent, dual carriageway, *Amer* freeway, highway, lane, motorway, path, ring road, roadway, route, side-street, slip-road, street, thoroughfare, trunk road, way.

roam *v* amble, drift, meander, prowl, ramble, range, rove, saunter, stray, stroll, traipse, travel, walk, wander.

roar *v* bellow, cry out, growl, howl, shout, snarl, thunder, yell, yowl.

rob *v* burgle, *inf* con, defraud, hold up, loot, mug, pilfer from, plunder, ransack, rifle, steal from. ▷ STEAL.

robber *n* bandit, brigand, burglar, *inf* con-man, defrauder, embezzler, housebreaker, looter, mugger, pickpocket, raider, shoplifter, swindler, thief.

robbery *n* breaking and entering, burglary, *inf* con, confidence trick, embezzlement, fraud, *inf* hold-up, larceny, looting, mugging, pilfering, plunder, shoplifting, stealing, theft, thieving.

robe *n* bathrobe, caftan, cassock, cloak, dress, dressing gown, frock, gown, habit, kimono, surplice, vestment.
• *v* ▷ DRESS.

robust *adj* 1 athletic, brawny, fit, *inf* hale and hearty, hardy, healthy, hearty, muscular, powerful, rugged, sound, strong, sturdy, tough, vigorous. 2 durable, serviceable, well-made. *Opp* WEAK.

rock *n* boulder, crag, flint, granite, limestone, marble, ore, outcrop, quartz, sandstone, scree, shale, slate, stone.
• *v* 1 lurch, move to and fro, pitch, reel, roll, shake, sway, swing, totter, wobble. 2 ▷ SHOCK.

rocky *adj* 1 barren, craggy, pebbly, rough, rugged, stony. 2 ▷ UNSTEADY.

rod *n* bar, baton, cane, pole, rail, shaft, spoke, staff, stick, strut, wand.

rogue *n* blackguard, charlatan, cheat, *inf* con-man, fraud, mischief-maker, rascal, ruffian, scoundrel, swindler, trickster, villain, wretch.

role *n* 1 character, impersonation, part, portrayal. 2 *role in a business.* contribution, duty, function, job, position, post, task.

roll *n* 1 cylinder, drum, reel, scroll, spool, tube. 2 catalogue, directory, index, inventory, list, listing, record, register.
• *v* 1 gyrate, move round, revolve, rotate, spin, turn, twirl, whirl. 2 coil, curl, furl, twist, wind, wrap. 3 *roll the lawn.* flatten, level out, smooth. 4 *roll in a storm.* lumber, lurch, pitch, reel, rock, stagger, sway, toss, totter, wallow, welter. **rolling** ▷ WAVY. **roll in, roll up** ▷ ARRIVE.

romance *n* 1 fantasy, legend, story, tale. 2 adventure, excitement, fascination, glamour, mystery. 3 amour, attachment, intrigue, liaison, love affair, relationship.

romantic *adj* 1 exotic, fairy-tale, glamorous, idealized, idyllic, imaginary, picturesque. 2 *romantic feelings.* affectionate, amorous, loving, passionate, tender. 3 *romantic fiction.* emotional, escapist, heart-warming, nostalgic, sentimental, *inf* soppy. 4 *romantic ideals. inf* head in the clouds, idealistic, illusory, impractical, quixotic, starry-eyed, unrealistic, Utopian, visionary. *Opp* REALISTIC.

room *n* 1 *inf* elbow-room, freedom, latitude, leeway, margin, scope, space. 2 apartment, cell, chamber, cubicle, office. **rooms** accommodation, dwelling, lodgings, quarters.

roomy *adj* capacious, commodious, large, sizeable, spacious, voluminous. ▷ BIG. *Opp* SMALL.

root *n* 1 rhizome, rootlet, tuber. 2 *root of a problem.* base, basis, bottom, cause,

foundation, origin, seat, source, starting point.
• *v* **root out** ▷ REMOVE.

rope *n* cable, cord, hawser, lasso, line, strand, string, tether.
• *v* bind, hitch, lash, moor, tether, tie. ▷ FASTEN.

rot *n* 1 corrosion, decay, decomposition, deterioration, disintegration, dry rot, mould, putrefaction, wet rot. 2 *What rot!* ▷ NONSENSE.
• *v* become rotten, corrode, decay, decompose, degenerate, deteriorate, disintegrate, fester, go bad, *inf* go off, perish, putrefy, spoil.

rota *n* list, roster, schedule, timetable.

rotary *adj* revolving, rotating, spinning, turning.

rotate *v* 1 gyrate, move round, pirouette, pivot, reel, revolve, roll, spin, swivel, turn, turn anticlockwise *or* clockwise, twiddle, twirl, twist, wheel, whirl. 2 *rotate duties.* alternate, take in turn, take turns.

rotten *adj* 1 bad, corroded, crumbling, decayed, decaying, decomposed, disintegrating, foul, mouldering, mouldy, *inf* off, overripe, putrid, tainted, unfit for consumption. 2 ▷ IMMORAL.

rough *adj* 1 broken, bumpy, coarse, craggy, irregular, knobbly, jagged, lumpy, pitted, ragged, rocky, rugged, rutted, stony, uneven. 2 *rough skin.* bristly, callused, chapped, coarse, leathery, scratchy, unshaven. 3 *rough sea.* agitated, choppy, stormy, tempestuous, turbulent, violent, wild. 4 *rough voice.* discordant, grating, gruff, harsh, hoarse, husky, rasping, raucous, strident. 5 *rough crowd, manners.* badly-behaved, blunt, brusque, churlish, ill-bred, impolite, loutish, rowdy, rude, surly, *inf* ugly, uncivil, uncivilized, undisciplined, unfriendly. 6 *rough treatment.* brutal, cruel, painful, violent. 7 *rough work.* amateurish, careless, crude, hasty, imperfect, inept, *inf* rough and ready, unfinished, unpolished, unskilful. 8 *rough estimate.* approximate, general, imprecise, inexact, sketchy, vague. *Opp* EXACT, GENTLE, SMOOTH.

roughly *adv* about, approximately, around, close to, nearly.

round *adj* 1 [*two-dimensional*] circular, curved, disc-shaped, ring-shaped. 2 [*three-dimensional*] bulbous, cylindrical, globe-shaped, globular, spherical. 3 *round stomach.* ample, full, plump, rotund, rounded, well-padded. ▷ FAT.
• *n* bout, contest, game, heat, stage.
• *v* skirt, travel round, turn. **round off** ▷ COMPLETE. **round on** ▷ ATTACK. **round the bend** ▷ MAD. **round the clock** ▷ CONTINUOUS. **round up** ▷ ASSEMBLE.

roundabout *adj* circuitous, circular, devious, indirect, long, meandering, oblique, rambling, tortuous, twisting, winding. *Opp* DIRECT.
• *n* 1 carousel, merry-go-round. 2 traffic island.

rouse *v* 1 arouse, awaken, call, get up, wake up. 2 *rouse to a frenzy.* animate, excite, galvanize, goad, incite, inflame, provoke, stimulate, stir up, *inf* wind up, work up.

rout *v* conquer, crush, overwhelm, put to flight, *inf* send packing. ▷ DEFEAT.

route *n* course, direction, itinerary, journey, path, road, way.

routine *adj* accustomed, commonplace, customary, everyday, familiar, habitual, normal, ordinary, planned, *inf* run-of-the-mill, scheduled, uneventful, well-rehearsed.
• *n* 1 course of action, custom, *inf* drill, habit, method, pattern, practice, procedure, schedule, system, way. 2 *comedy routine.* act, number, performance, programme, set piece.

row *n* 1 chain, column, cordon, file, line, queue, rank, sequence, series, string, tier. 2 ado, commotion, fracas, hubbub, hullabaloo, racket, *inf* rumpus, tumult, uproar. ▷ NOISE. 3 altercation, argument, disagreement, dispute, fight, *inf* ructions, *inf* slanging match, squabble. ▷ QUARREL.
• *v* 1 *row a boat.* move, propel, scull. 2 ▷ QUARREL.

rowdy *adj* badly-behaved, boisterous, disorderly, irrepressible, obstreperous, riotous, rough, turbulent, undisciplined, unruly, violent, wild. ▷ NOISY. *Opp* QUIET.

royal *adj* imperial, kingly, majestic, princely, queenly, regal, stately, sovereign.
• *n* [*inf*] member of royal family.

rub *v* 1 knead, massage, smooth, stroke. 2 chafe, graze, scrape, wear away. 3 *rub clean.* buff, burnish, polish, scour, scrub, shine, wipe. **rub it in** ▷ EMPHASIZE. **rub out** ▷ ERASE. **rub up the wrong way** ▷ ANNOY.

rubbish *n* 1 debris, detritus, dregs, dross, filth, flotsam and jetsam, garbage, junk, leavings, leftovers, litter, lumber, *inf* odds and ends, refuse, rubble, scrap, sweepings, trash, waste. 2 ▷ NONSENSE.

rubble *n* broken bricks, debris, fragments, remains, ruins, wreckage.

ruddy *adj* fresh, flushed, glowing, healthy, red, sunburnt.

rude *adj* 1 abrupt, abusive, bad-mannered, blunt, boorish, brusque, cheeky, churlish, coarse, contemptuous, curt, discourteous, disparaging, disrespectful, graceless, ill-bred, ill-mannered, impertinent, impolite, improper, impudent, in bad taste, inconsiderate, indecent, insolent, insulting, mocking, *inf* naughty, oafish, offensive, offhand, peremptory, personal (*remarks*), saucy, scurrilous, shameless, tactless, unchivalrous, uncivil, uncomplimentary, uncouth, ungracious, unprintable, vulgar. ▷ OBSCENE. *Opp* POLITE. 2 *rude workmanship*. basic, clumsy, crude, inartistic, primitive, rough, rough-hewn, simple, unpolished, unskilful, unsophisticated. *Opp* SOPHISTICATED. **be rude to** ▷ INSULT.

rudeness *n* abuse, *inf* backchat, bad manners, cheek, contempt, discourtesy, disrespect, ill-breeding, impertinence, impudence, incivility, insolence, insults, oafishness, tactlessness, vulgarity.

rudiments *pl n* basic principles, basics, elements, essentials, first principles, foundations, fundamentals.

rudimentary *adj* basic, crude, elementary, embryonic, initial, preliminary, primitive, provisional, undeveloped. *Opp* ADVANCED.

ruffian *n inf* brute, bully, hoodlum, hooligan, lout, rogue, scoundrel, thug, *inf* tough, villain, *inf* yob.

ruffle *v* 1 disturb, ripple, stir. 2 *ruffle your hair*. disarrange, dishevel, disorder, *inf* mess up, rumple, tangle, tousle. 3 *ruffle your composure*. agitate, confuse, disconcert, disquiet, fluster, irritate, *inf* nettle, *inf* rattle, *inf* throw, unnerve, unsettle, upset, worry. *Opp* SMOOTH.

rug *n* blanket, coverlet, mat, matting.

rugged *adj* 1 bumpy, craggy, irregular, jagged, pitted, rocky, rough, stony, uneven. 2 *rugged conditions*. arduous, difficult, hard, harsh, rough, severe, tough. 3 *rugged good looks*. burly, hardy, muscular, robust, rough, strong, sturdy, weather-beaten.

ruin *n* bankruptcy, collapse, *inf* crash, destruction, downfall, end, failure, fall, ruination, undoing, wreck.

• *v* damage, demolish, destroy, devastate, flatten, overthrow, shatter, spoil, wreck. **ruins** debris, remains, rubble, wreckage.

ruined *adj* crumbling, derelict, dilapidated, fallen down, in ruins, ramshackle, tumbledown, uninhabitable, wrecked.

ruinous *adj* calamitous, cataclysmic, catastrophic, crushing, destructive, devastating, dire, disastrous, fatal, harmful, injurious, pernicious, shattering.

rule *n* 1 code, decree, *pl* guidelines, law, ordinance, precept, principle, regulation, ruling, statute. 2 administration, ascendancy, authority, command, control, domination, dominion, empire, government, influence, jurisdiction, management, mastery, power, regime, reign, sovereignty, supervision, supremacy, sway. 3 *as a general rule*. convention, custom, norm, standard.

• *v* 1 administer, command, control, direct, dominate, govern, hold sway, lead, manage, predominate, reign, run, superintend. 2 decide, decree, deem, determine, find, judge, pronounce, resolve. **rule out** ▷ EXCLUDE.

ruler *n* administrator, despot, dictator, emir, emperor, empress, governor, king, leader, lord, leader, manager, monarch, potentate, president, prince, princess, queen, regent, sovereign, sultan, tsar, viceroy. ▷ CHIEF.

rumour *n* gossip, hearsay, *inf* low-down, news, report, scandal, *inf* tittle-tattle, whisper.

run *n* 1 dash, gallop, jog, marathon, race, sprint, trot. 2 *run in the car*. drive, excursion, jaunt, journey, ride, *inf* spin, trip. 3 *run of bad luck*. chain, sequence, series, stretch. 4 *chicken run*. compound, coop, enclosure, pen.

• *v* 1 bolt, career, dash, gallop, hare, hurry, jog, race, rush, scamper, scurry, scuttle, speed, sprint, tear, trot. 2 *buses run hourly*. go, operate, provide a service, travel. 3 *car runs well*. function, perform, work. 4 *water runs downhill*. cascade, dribble, flow, gush, leak, pour, spill, stream, trickle. 5 *run a business* administer, conduct, control, direct, govern, look after, manage, rule, supervise. **run across** ▷ MEET. **run after** ▷ PURSUE. **run away** ▷ ESCAPE. **run into** ▷ MEET.

runner *n* 1 athlete, competitor, entrant, hurdler, jogger, participant, sprinter. 2 courier, dispatch-rider, messenger. 3 shoot, sprout, sucker, tendril.

runny *adj* fluid, free-flowing, liquid, thin, watery. *Opp* SOLID, VISCOUS.

rupture *n* 1 breach, break, burst, fracture, puncture, rift, split. 2 *rupture between friends.* break-up, separation. 3 [*medical*] hernia.
• *v* break, burst, fracture, part, separate, split.

rural *adj* agrarian, agricultural, bucolic, countrified, pastoral, rustic. *Opp* URBAN.

rush *n* 1 bustle, dash, haste, hurry, panic, race, scramble, speed, urgency. 2 *rush of water.* flood, gush, spate, surge. 3 *rush of people.* charge, onslaught, stampede.
• *v* bolt, burst, bustle, canter, career, charge, dash, fly, gallop, *inf* get a move on, hare, hasten, hurry, make haste, race, run, scamper, *inf* scoot, scramble, scurry, scuttle, shoot, speed, sprint, stampede, *inf* step on it, *inf* tear, zoom.

rust *v* become rusty, corrode, crumble away, oxidize, rot.

rustic *adj* 1 ▷ RURAL. 2 *rustic simplicity.* artless, naive, plain, rough, simple, uncomplicated, unsophisticated.

rusty *adj* 1 corroded, oxidized, tarnished. 2 [*inf*] *My French is rusty.* out of practice, unused, unpractised.

rut *n* 1 channel, furrow, groove, indentation, pothole, track, trough. 2 *in a rut.* dead end, pattern, routine, treadmill.

ruthless *adj* bloodthirsty, brutal, callous, cruel, fierce, hard, heartless, inhuman, merciless, pitiless, relentless, sadistic, unfeeling, unrelenting, unsympathetic, vicious, violent. *Opp* MERCIFUL.

S

sabotage *n* vandalism, wilful damage, wrecking.
• *v* cripple, damage, destroy, disable, disrupt, incapacitate, put out of action, vandalize, wreck.

sack *n* 1 bag, pouch. 2 *inf* the boot, *inf* the chop, dismissal, *inf* your cards.
• *v* 1 *inf* axe, discharge, dismiss, *inf* fire, give someone notice, *inf* give someone the boot, lay off, make redundant. 2 ▷ DESTROY, PLUNDER. **get the sack** be dismissed, be sacked, *inf* get your cards, get your marching orders, lose your job.

sacred *adj* blessed, consecrated, dedicated, divine, godly, hallowed, holy, religious, revered, sacrosanct, sanctified, venerable, venerated. *Opp* SECULAR.

sacrifice *n* offering, propitiation, votive offering.
• *v* 1 kill, offer up, slaughter. 2 abandon, forfeit, forgo, give up, lose, relinquish, renounce, surrender.

sacrilege *n* blasphemy, desecration, heresy, impiety, irreverence.

sacrilegious *adj* blasphemous, disrespectful, heretical, impious, irreligious, irreverent, profane, ungodly. ▷ WICKED.

sacrosanct *adj* inviolable, inviolate, protected, untouchable. ▷ SACRED.

sad *adj* 1 abject, blue, broken-hearted, cheerless, crestfallen, dejected, depressed, desolate, despairing, despondent, disappointed, disconsolate, disheartened, dismal, dispirited, distressed, doleful, *inf* down, downcast, downhearted, dreary, forlorn, friendless, funereal, gloomy, glum, grave, grief-stricken, grieving, grim, heartbroken, *inf* heavy, heavy-hearted, homesick, in low spirits, *inf* in the doldrums, joyless, lachrymose, lonely, *inf* long-faced, *inf* low, lugubrious, melancholy, miserable, moody, moping, morose, mournful, pathetic, pessimistic, piteous, pitiable, pitiful, plaintive, poignant, regretful, rueful, saddened, sombre, sorrowful, sorry, tearful, troubled, unhappy, upset, wistful, woebegone, woeful, wretched. 2 *sad news.* calamitous, depressing, dispiriting, distressing, grievous, heartbreaking, heart-rending, lamentable, moving, painful, regrettable, *inf* tear-jerking, touching, tragic, unfortunate, unwelcome, upsetting. 3 *sad state of disrepair.* ▷ UNSATISFACTORY. *Opp* HAPPY.

sadden *v inf* break someone's heart, depress, disappoint, discourage, dishearten, dismay, dispirit, distress, grieve, upset. *Opp* CHEER.

sadistic *adj* brutal, inhuman, monstrous, perverted, ruthless, vicious. ▷ CRUEL.

sadness *n* dejection, depression, desolation, despair, despondency, disappointment, disillusionment, distress, gloom, grief, heartbreak, heaviness, homesickness, hopelessness, loneliness, melancholy, misery, mournfulness, pessimism, poignancy, regret, sorrow, tearfulness, unhappiness, wistfulness, woe. *Opp* HAPPINESS.

safe *adj* 1 defended, foolproof, guarded, immune, impregnable, invulnerable, protected, secured, shielded. ▷ SECURE. *Opp* VULNERABLE. 2 *inf* alive and well, *inf* in one piece, intact, sound, undamaged, unharmed, unhurt, uninjured, unscathed. 3 *safe drivers.* cautious, circumspect, reliable, trustworthy. 4 *safe pets.* docile, friendly, harmless, tame. 5 *safe to drink.* drinkable, eatable, fit for human consumption, fresh, good, innocuous, non-toxic, pure, purified, uncontaminated, unpolluted, wholesome. 6 *safe vehicle.* airworthy, roadworthy, seaworthy, tried and tested. *Opp* DANGEROUS. **make safe** ▷ SECURE. **safe keeping** care, charge, custody, guardianship, protection.

safeguard *v* defend, look after, protect, shelter, shield.

safety *n* 1 cover, immunity, protection, refuge, sanctuary, security, shelter. 2 *safety of air travel.* dependability, reliability.

sag *v* be limp, bend, dip, droop, fall, flop, hang down, sink, slump. ▷ DROP.

sail *n* 1 canvas, mainsail, mizzen, spinnaker. 2 cruise, sea-passage, voyage.
• *v* 1 navigate, paddle, pilot, punt, row, skipper, steer. 2 cruise, go sailing, put to sea, set sail, steam.

sailor *n* boatman, captain, *pl* crew, helmsman, mariner, navigator, pilot, seafarer, seaman, skipper, yachtsman, yachtswoman.

saintly *adj* angelic, blessed, godly, holy,

innocent, moral, pious, pure, religious, righteous, sinless, virtuous. ▷ GOOD. *Opp* SATANIC.

sake *n* account, advantage, behalf, benefit, gain, good, interest, welfare.

salary *n* earnings, income, pay, payment, remuneration, stipend, wages.

sale *n* 1 marketing, selling, trade, traffic, transaction, vending. 2 auction, bazaar, car-boot sale, jumble sale, mark-down.

salesperson *n* assistant, representative, salesman, saleswoman, shopkeeper.

saliva *n inf* dribble, *inf* spit, spittle, sputum.

sallow *adj* anaemic, colourless, pale, pallid, pasty, unhealthy, wan, yellowish.

salt *adj* brackish, briny, saline, salted, salty, savoury.

salubrious *adj* health-giving, healthy, hygienic, nice, pleasant, sanitary, wholesome.

salute *n* acknowledgement, gesture, greeting, salutation, wave.
• *v* 1 address, greet, hail. 2 honour, pay respects to, recognize.

salvage *n* 1 reclamation, recovery, rescue, retrieval, salvation, saving. 2 recyclable material, waste.
• *v* conserve, preserve, reclaim, recover, recycle, rescue, retrieve, reuse, save.

salvation *n* deliverance, escape, redemption, rescue, saving, way out. *Opp* DAMNATION.

salve *n* balm, cream, embrocation, liniment, lotion, ointment.
• *v* appease, comfort, ease, mitigate, mollify. ▷ SOOTHE.

same *adj* 1 actual, identical, selfsame. 2 comparable, consistent, corresponding, duplicate, equal, equivalent, indistinguishable, interchangeable, matching, parallel, similar, synonymous [= *having same meaning*], twin, unaltered, unchanged, uniform, unvaried. *Opp* DIFFERENT.

sample *n* bit, demonstration, example, foretaste, illustration, indication, model, selection, snippet, specimen, taste, trailer (*of film*), trial offer.
• *v* experience, inspect, taste, test, try.

sanatorium *n* clinic, convalescent home, hospital, nursing home, rest-home.

sanctify *v* beatify, bless, consecrate, hallow, purify.

sanctimonious *adj* holier-than-thou, hypocritical, moralizing, pietistic, pious, self-righteous, smug, superior, unctuous.

sanction *n* agreement, approval, authorization, *inf* blessing, confirmation, consent, endorsement, licence, permission, ratification, support, validation.
• *v* agree to, allow, approve, authorize, confirm, consent to, endorse, *inf* give your blessing to, give permission for, licence, permit, ratify, support, validate.

sanctity *n* godliness, piety. ▷ HOLINESS.

sanctuary *n* 1 asylum, haven, protection, refuge, retreat, safety, shelter. 2 *wildlife sanctuary.* conservation area, park, preserve, reservation, reserve. 3 *holy sanctuary.* chapel, church, holy place, sanctum, shrine, temple.

sands *pl n* beach, seaside, shore.

sane *adj* balanced, compos mentis, level-headed, lucid, normal, of sound mind, rational, reasonable, sensible, sound, stable, well-balanced. *Opp* MAD.

sanguine *adj* buoyant, cheerful, confident, hopeful, *inf* looking on the bright side, optimistic, positive. *Opp* PESSIMISTIC.

sanitary *adj* aseptic, clean, disinfected, germfree, healthy, hygienic, pure, salubrious, sterile, sterilized, uncontaminated, unpolluted, wholesome. *Opp* UNHEALTHY.

sanitation *n* drains, lavatories, sewage disposal, sewers.

sap *n* fluid, life-blood, moisture, vigour, vitality, vital juices.
• *v* bleed, drain. ▷ EXHAUST.

sarcasm *n* derision, irony, mockery, ridicule, satire, scorn.

sarcastic *adj* biting, caustic, contemptuous, cutting, cynical, derisive, disparaging, ironic, mocking, sardonic, satirical, scathing, scornful, sharp, taunting.

sardonic *adj* bitter, black (*comedy*), cruel, cynical, malicious, mordant, sarcastic, wry.

sash *n* band, belt, cummerbund, girdle, waistband.

satanic *adj* demonic, devilish, diabolical, fiendish, infernal. ▷ WICKED. *Opp* SAINTLY.

satellite *n* 1 moon, planet, spacecraft, sputnik. 2 attendant, follower, *inf* hanger-on.

satire *n* burlesque, caricature, irony, lampoon, mockery, parody, ridicule, sarcasm, *inf* send-up, *inf* spoof, *inf* take-off, travesty.

satirical *adj* critical, derisive, disparaging, ironic, irreverent, mocking, scornful. ▷ SARCASTIC.

satirize *v* caricature, criticize, deride, hold up to ridicule, lampoon, laugh at, make fun of, mimic, mock, parody, pillory, *inf* send up, *inf* take off. ▷ RIDICULE.

satisfaction *n* comfort, content, contentment, delight, enjoyment, fulfilment, gratification, happiness, joy, pleasure, pride. *Opp* DISSATISFACTION.

satisfactory *adj* acceptable, adequate, *inf* all right, competent, fair, good enough, passable, satisfying, sufficient, suitable, tolerable, *inf* up to scratch. *Opp* UNSATISFACTORY.

satisfy *v* appease, assuage, comfort, comply with, content, fill, fulfil, gratify, meet, pacify, placate, please, quench, sate, satiate, serve (*a need*), settle, slake (*thirst*). *Opp* FRUSTRATE. **satisfied** ▷ CONTENT.

saturate *v* drench, permeate, soak, souse, steep, suffuse, waterlog, wet.

sauce *n* 1 gravy, ketchup, relish. 2 ▷ INSOLENCE.

saucepan *n* cauldron, pan, pot, skillet, stockpot.

savage *adj* 1 barbarian, heathen, pagan, primitive, uncivilized, uneducated. *Opp* CIVILIZED. 2 *savage beasts.* feral, fierce, undomesticated, untamed, wild. *Opp* TAME. 3 *savage attack.* atrocious, barbarous, beastly, bestial, blistering, bloodthirsty, bloody, brutal, callous, cold-blooded, cruel, ferocious, fierce, heartless, inhuman, merciless, murderous, pitiless, ruthless, sadistic, unfeeling, vicious, violent.
• *n* barbarian, brute, heathen, wild man *or* woman.
• *v* attack, bite, claw, lacerate, maul, mutilate.

save *v* 1 be sparing with, collect, conserve, economize, hoard, hold back, keep, lay aside, put by, put in a safe place, reserve, retain, scrape together, set aside, *inf* stash away, store up. *Opp* WASTE. 2 bail out, deliver, free, liberate, ransom, recover, redeem, release, rescue, retrieve, salvage, set free. 3 *save from danger.* defend, deliver, guard, keep safe, preserve, protect, safeguard, screen, shelter, shield. 4 *saved me from looking a fool.* prevent, spare, stop. *Opp* ABANDON.

saving *n* economizing, frugality, parsimony, prudence, *inf* scrimping and scraping, thrift. **savings** funds, investments, *inf* nest-egg, reserves, resources, riches, wealth.

saviour *n* champion, defender, deliverer, *inf* friend in need, guardian, liberator, rescuer.

savour *n* flavour, piquancy, smell, tang, taste, zest.
• *v* appreciate, delight in, enjoy, relish, smell, taste.

savoury *adj* appetizing, delicious, flavoursome, piquant, salty. ▷ TASTY. *Opp* SWEET.

saw *n* 1 chainsaw, hacksaw. 2 [*old use*] *just an old saw.* ▷ SAYING.
• *v* ▷ CUT.

say *v* affirm, allege, announce, answer, articulate, *inf* come out with, comment, communicate, convey, declare, disclose, divulge, enunciate, exclaim, express, intimate, maintain, mention, mouth, phrase, pronounce, read out, recite, rejoin, remark, repeat, reply, report, respond, retort, reveal, signify, state, suggest, tell, utter. ▷ SPEAK, TALK.

saying *n* adage, aphorism, axiom, catchphrase, catchword, cliché, epigram, expression, formula, maxim, motto, phrase, precept, proverb, quotation, remark, *old use* saw, slogan, statement, tag, truism, watchword.

scale *n* 1 *scale forms in a kettle.* caking, coating, crust, deposit, encrustation, *inf* fur. 2 *scale on a thermometer.* calibration, gradation, graduation. 3 *the social scale.* hierarchy, ladder, order, ranking, spectrum. 4 *scale of a map.* proportion, ratio. ▷ SIZE. 5 *musical scale.* sequence, series.
• *v* ascend, clamber up, climb, go up, mount. **scales** balance, weighing machine.

scamper *v* dash, frisk, frolic, gambol, hasten, hurry, play, romp, run, rush, scuttle.

scan *v* 1 check, examine, eye, gaze at, investigate, look at, pore over, search, stare at, study, survey, view, watch. 2 *scan the papers.* flip through, glance at, read quickly, skim.

scandal *n* 1 discredit, disgrace, dishonour, disrepute, embarrassment, ignominy, infamy, notoriety, outrage, shame. 2 defamation, innuendo, libel, slander, slur, smear.

scandalize *v* affront, appal, disgust, horrify, offend, outrage, shock, upset.

scandalous *adj* 1 disgraceful, disgusting, dishonourable, disreputable, ignominious, immoral, indecent, infamous, licentious, notorious, outrageous, shameful, shocking, sinful, sordid, unmentionable, unspeakable, wicked. 2 *scandalous lie*. defamatory, libellous, scurrilous, slanderous, untrue.

scanty *adj* 1 inadequate, insufficient, meagre, mean, *inf* measly, minimal, scant, scarce, sparing, sparse, stingy. ▷ SMALL. *Opp* PLENTIFUL. 2 *scanty clothes*. revealing, *inf* see-through, skimpy, thin.

scapegoat *n* dupe, *sl* fall guy, *inf* front, whipping-boy, victim.

scar *n* blemish, brand, burn, cut, disfigurement, injury, mark, scab, scratch, wound.
• *v* brand, burn, damage, deface, disfigure, injure, leave a scar on, mark, scratch, spoil.

scarce *adj inf* few and far between, inadequate, infrequent, in short supply, insufficient, lacking, meagre, rare, scant, scanty, sparse, *inf* thin on the ground, uncommon. *Opp* PLENTIFUL.

scarcely *adv* barely, hardly, only just.

scarcity *n* dearth, famine, insufficiency, lack, paucity, poverty, rarity, shortage, want. *Opp* PLENTY.

scare *n* alarm, jolt, shock, start. ▷ FRIGHT.
• *v* alarm, intimidate, make someone afraid, *inf* make someone jump, panic, shock, startle, terrorize, threaten, unnerve. ▷ FRIGHTEN. *Opp* REASSURE.

scarf *n* headscarf, muffler, shawl, stole.

scary *adj* [*inf*] creepy, eerie, hair-raising, unnerving. ▷ FRIGHTENING.

scathing *adj* biting, caustic, critical, mordant, satirical, savage, scornful, tart, withering. *Opp* COMPLIMENTARY.

scatter *v* 1 break up, disband, disintegrate, disperse, divide, send in all directions, separate. 2 *scatter seeds*. disseminate, shed, shower, sow, spread, sprinkle, strew, throw about. *Opp* GATHER.

scatterbrained *adj* absent-minded, careless, disorganized, forgetful, muddled, *inf* not with it, *inf* scatty, thoughtless, unreliable, unsystematic, vague. ▷ SILLY.

scavenge *v* forage, rummage, scrounge, search.

scenario *n* framework, outline, plan, scheme, storyline, summary.

scene *n* 1 area, background, context, locality, location, place, position, setting, site, situation, spot, whereabouts. 2 *beautiful scene*. picture, sight, spectacle. ▷ SCENERY. 3 *scene from a film*. *inf* clip, episode, part, section, sequence. 4 *nasty scene*. altercation, argument, *inf* carry-on, commotion, disturbance, furore, fuss, quarrel, *inf* row, tantrum, *inf* to-do.

scenery *n* 1 landscape, outlook, panorama, prospect, scene, terrain, view, vista. 2 *stage scenery*. backdrop, flats, set.

scenic *adj* attractive, beautiful, breathtaking, grand, impressive, lovely, panoramic, picturesque, pretty, spectacular.

scent *n* 1 aroma, bouquet, fragrance, nose, odour, perfume, redolence, smell. 2 eau de cologne, toilet water, perfume. 3 *animal's scent*. spoor, track, trail.
• *v* ▷ SMELL. **scented** ▷ SMELLING.

sceptic *n* agnostic, cynic, doubter, *inf* doubting Thomas, unbeliever. *Opp* BELIEVER.

sceptical *adj* agnostic, cynical, disbelieving, distrustful, dubious, incredulous, mistrustful, questioning, suspicious, uncertain, unconvinced, unsure. *Opp* CONFIDENT.

scepticism *n* agnosticism, cynicism, disbelief, distrust, doubt, incredulity, mistrust, suspicion. *Opp* FAITH.

schedule *n* agenda, calendar, diary, itinerary, list, plan, programme, scheme, timetable.
• *v* appoint, arrange, book, earmark, fix a time, organize, plan, programme, time.

scheme *n* 1 blueprint, design, draft, idea, method, plan, procedure, programme, project, proposal, strategy, system. 2 *dishonest scheme*. conspiracy, intrigue, machinations, manoeuvre, plot, ploy, *inf* racket, ruse, stratagem, subterfuge, tactic. 3 *colour scheme*. arrangement, design.
• *v* collude, connive, conspire, *inf* cook up, hatch a plot, intrigue, manoeuvre, plan, plot.

scholar *n* academic, *inf* egghead, highbrow, intellectual, professor. ▷ PUPIL.

scholarly *adj* 1 academic, bookish, *inf* brainy, erudite, highbrow, intellectual, knowledgeable, learned, widely-read. 2 *scholarly treatise*. scientific, well-argued, well-informed.

scholarship *n* 1 academic achievement, education, erudition, intellectual attainment, knowledge, learning, research, wisdom. 2 *scholarship to Oxford*. award, bursary, endowment, grant.

school *n* 1 academy, boarding school, college, comprehensive, educational institution, high school, infant school,

institute, junior school, kindergarten, nursery school, primary school, public school, secondary school, seminary. 2 adherents, circle, disciples, group, set.
• *v* ▷ EDUCATE.

science *n* (body of) knowledge, discipline, field, subject, systematic study.

scientific *adj* analytical, methodical, orderly, organized, precise, rational, systematic.

scientist *n inf* boffin, researcher, scientific expert, technologist.

scintillating *adj* brilliant, clever, dazzling, lively, sparkling, vivacious, witty. *Opp* DULL.

scoff *v* 1 belittle, be scornful, deride, disparage, gibe, jeer, laugh, mock, *inf* poke fun, ridicule, sneer, taunt. 2 ▷ EAT.

scold *v* admonish, berate, blame, *inf* carpet, castigate, censure, criticize, find fault with, lecture, nag, rate, rebuke, reprehend, reprimand, reproach, reprove, *inf* slate, *inf* tell off, *inf* tick off, upbraid.

scoop *n* 1 bailer, ladle, shovel, spoon. 2 *news scoop*. exclusive, inside story, *inf* latest, revelation.
• *v* dig, gouge, hollow, scrape, shovel, spoon.

scope *n* 1 area, capacity, compass, competence, extent, field, limit, range, reach, span, sphere, terms of reference. 2 *scope for expansion*. *inf* elbow-room, freedom, latitude, leeway, liberty, opportunity, outlet, room, space.

scorch *v* blacken, burn, char, heat, roast, sear, singe.

score *n* 1 amount, count, marks, points, reckoning, result, sum, tally, total. 2 cut, groove, incision, line, mark, nick, scrape, scratch.
• *v* 1 achieve, add up, *inf* chalk up, earn, gain, *inf* knock up, make, tally, win. 2 *score a groove*. engrave, scrape, scratch. ▷ CUT. 3 *score music*. orchestrate, write out. **settle a score** ▷ RETALIATE.

scorn *n* contempt, derision, detestation, disdain, disgust, dislike, disparagement, disrespect, mockery, rejection, ridicule, scoffing, taunting. *Opp* ADMIRATION.
• *v* be scornful about, deride, despise, disdain, dislike, dismiss, disparage, insult, jeer at, laugh at, look down on, make fun of, mock, reject, ridicule, scoff at, sneer at, spurn, *inf* turn up your nose at. *Opp* ADMIRE.

scornful *adj* condescending, contemptuous, derisive, disdainful, dismissive, disparaging, disrespectful, insulting, jeering, mocking, patronizing, sarcastic, satirical, scathing, sneering, *inf* snide, *inf* snooty, supercilious, superior, taunting, withering. *Opp* RESPECTFUL.

scoundrel *n* blackguard, good-for-nothing, knave, rascal, rogue, ruffian, scallywag, scamp, villain, wretch.

scour *v* 1 clean, polish, rub, scrape, scrub, shine, wash. 2 *scour the house*. comb, hunt through, ransack, rummage through, search, *inf* turn upside down.

scourge *n* 1 affliction, bane, curse, evil, misery, misfortune, plague, torment, woe. 2 ▷ WHIP.
• *v* beat, *sl* belt, flog, lash, whip.

scout *n* lookout, spy.
• *v* explore, hunt around, investigate, look about, reconnoitre, search, spy.

scowl *v* frown, glower, grimace, *inf* look daggers.

scraggy *adj* bony, emaciated, gaunt, scrawny, skinny, starved, thin. *Opp* PLUMP.

scramble *n* commotion, confusion, *inf* free-for-all, hurry, mêlée, race, rush, scrimmage, struggle.
• *v* 1 clamber, climb, crawl, grope, scrabble. 2 *scramble for gold*. compete, dash, fight, hasten, hurry, jostle, push, run, rush, scuffle, struggle, tussle, vie. 3 *scramble a message*. confuse, jumble, mix up.

scrap *n* 1 atom, bit, crumb, fraction, fragment, grain, iota, jot, mite, molecule, morsel, particle, piece, rag, shard, shred, sliver, snippet, speck, trace. 2 junk, leavings, litter, odds and ends, offcuts, refuse, remains, remnants, residue, rubbish, salvage, waste. 3 argument, quarrel, scuffle, *inf* set-to, squabble, tiff, tussle, wrangle. ▷ FIGHT.
• *v* 1 abandon, cancel, discard, *inf* ditch, drop, give up, jettison, throw away, write off. 2 argue, bicker, flare up, quarrel, spar, squabble, tussle, wrangle. ▷ FIGHT.

scrape *n* 1 abrasion, graze, injury, laceration, scratch, scuff, wound. 2 *awkward scrape*. difficulty, escapade, mischief, plight, prank, predicament, trouble.
• *v* 1 bark, bruise, damage, graze, injure, lacerate, scratch, scuff, skin, wound. 2 *scrape clean*. file, rasp, rub, scour, scrub. **scrape together** ▷ COLLECT.

scrappy *adj inf* bitty, careless, disjointed, fragmentary, imperfect, incomplete, inconclusive, sketchy, slipshod, unfinished, unsatisfactory. *Opp* PERFECT.

scratch *n* abrasion, dent, gash, gouge, graze, groove, indentation, injury, laceration, line, mark, score, scoring, scrape, scuff, wound.
• *v* claw at, cut, damage the surface of, dent, gash, gouge, graze, groove, injure, lacerate, mark, score, scrape, scuff, wound. **up to scratch** ▷ SATISFACTORY.

scrawl *v* doodle, scribble, write hurriedly. ▷ WRITE.

scream *n* & *vb* bawl, caterwaul, cry, howl, roar, screech, shout, shriek, squeal, wail, yell, yowl.

screen *n* 1 blind, curtain, divider, partition. 2 camouflage, concealment, cover, disguise, protection, shelter, shield, smokescreen. 3 *sift through a screen.* filter, mesh, riddle, sieve, strainer.
• *v* 1 divide, partition off. 2 camouflage, cloak, conceal, cover, disguise, guard, hide, mask, protect, safeguard, shade, shelter, shield, shroud, veil. 3 *screen employees. inf* check out, examine, investigate, vet.

screw *n* 1 bolt, screw-bolt. 2 rotation, spiral, turn, twist.
• *v* rotate, turn, twist. **screw down** ▷ FASTEN. **screw up** ▷ BUNGLE, TIGHTEN.

scribble *v* ▷ SCRAWL.

scribe *n* clerk, copyist, secretary, writer.

script *n* 1 calligraphy, handwriting. 2 *script of a play.* libretto, screenplay, text, words.

scripture *n* bible, holy writ, sacred writings.

scrounge *v* beg, cadge, sponge on.

scrub *v* 1 brush, clean, rub, scour, wash. 2 ▷ CANCEL.

scruffy *adj* bedraggled, dirty, dishevelled, disordered, messy, ragged, scrappy, shabby, slovenly, *inf* tatty, unkempt, untidy, worn out. *Opp* SMART.

scruple *n* compunction, conscience, doubt, misgiving, qualm, reluctance, *inf* second thought.
• *v He didn't scruple about taking the money.* be reluctant, have a conscience (about), have scruples (about), hesitate, *inf* think twice (about).

scrupulous *adj* 1 careful, conscientious, diligent, exacting, fastidious, finicky, meticulous, neat, painstaking, precise, punctilious, rigorous, strict, systematic, thorough. 2 *scrupulous honesty.* ethical, fair-minded, honest, honourable, just, moral, principled, proper, upright. *Opp* UNSCRUPULOUS.

scrutinize *v* analyse, check, examine, inspect, investigate, look closely at, observe, probe, sift, study, survey.

scrutiny *n* analysis, examination, inspection, investigation, probing, search, study.

sculpture *n* bust, carving, cast, effigy, figure, figurine, moulding, statue, statuette.
• *v* carve, cast, chisel, fashion, form, hew, model, mould, *inf* sculpt, shape.

scum *n* dirt, film, foam, froth, muck, suds.

scurrilous *adj* abusive, coarse, defamatory, derogatory, disparaging, indecent, insulting, libellous, low, obscene, offensive, shameful, slanderous, vile, vulgar.

sea *adj* marine, maritime, nautical, naval, ocean-going, oceanic, salt-water, seafaring, seagoing.
• *n inf* briny, *poet* deep, lake, ocean.

seal *n* 1 sea lion, walrus. 2 *royal seal.* badge, coat of arms, crest, emblem, impression, imprint, mark, monogram, sign, stamp, symbol.
• *v* 1 close, fasten, lock, make airtight, make watertight, plug, secure, shut, stick down, stop up. 2 *seal an agreement.* clinch, conclude, confirm, decide, endorse, finalize, guarantee, ratify, settle, sign, validate.

seam *n* 1 join, stitching. 2 *seam of coal.* bed, layer, lode, stratum, thickness, vein.

seamy *adj* disreputable, distasteful, sordid, squalid, unpleasant, unsavoury, unwholesome.

search *n* check, enquiry, examination, hunt, inspection, investigation, look, probe, quest, scrutiny.
• *v* 1 explore, ferret about, hunt, investigate, *inf* leave no stone unturned, look, nose about, poke about, pry, seek. 2 *search suspects.* check, examine, *inf* frisk, inspect, scrutinize. 3 *search a house.* comb, go through, ransack, rifle, rummage through, scour. **searching** ▷ INQUISITIVE, THOROUGH.

seaside *n* beach, coast, coastal resort, sands, seashore, shore.

season *n* period, phase, time.
• *v* 1 add seasoning to, flavour, *inf* pep up, salt, spice. 2 age, mature, ripen.

seasonable *adj* convenient, favourable, opportune, suitable, timely. ▷ APPROPRIATE.

seasoning *n* condiments, dressing, flavouring, relish, spice.

seat *n* 1 armchair, bench, chair, couch, deckchair, easy chair, form, pew, place, rocking-chair, saddle, settee, sofa, stool, throne. 2 *country seat.* ▷ RESIDENCE. 3 ▷ BUTTOCKS. **seat yourself** ▷ SIT.

secluded *adj* cloistered, concealed, cut off, hidden, isolated, lonely, *inf* off the beaten track, private, remote, screened, sheltered, solitary, unfrequented, unvisited. *Opp* PUBLIC.

seclusion *n* concealment, hiding, isolation, privacy, remoteness, retirement, separation, solitude.

second *adj* added, additional, alternative, another, duplicate, extra, following, further, later, next, other, repeated, subsequent, twin.
• *n* 1 flash, instant, *inf* jiffy, moment, *inf* tick, *inf* twinkling. 2 *second in a fight.* assistant, deputy, helper, *inf* right-hand man *or* woman, second-in-command, stand-in, subordinate, supporter, understudy.
• *v* 1 aid, assist, back, encourage, give approval to, help, promote, side with, sponsor, support. 2 *second to another job.* move, reassign, relocate, transfer.

secondary *adj* 1 alternative, auxiliary, backup, extra, inessential, inferior, lesser, lower, minor, non-essential, reserve, second, spare, subordinate, subsidiary, supplementary, supporting, unimportant. 2 *secondary sources.* derivative, second-hand, unoriginal.

second-hand *adj* 1 *inf* hand-me-down, old, used, worn. *Opp* NEW. 2 *second-hand experience.* indirect, vicarious. *Opp* DIRECT.

second-rate *adj* indifferent, inferior, low-grade, mediocre, middling, ordinary, poor, second-best, second-class, undistinguished.

secret *adj* 1 clandestine, concealed, covert, disguised, hidden, *inf* hush-hush, invisible, private, secluded, shrouded, stealthy, undercover, underground, unknown. 2 *secret papers.* classified, confidential, intimate, personal, restricted, sensitive, top secret, undisclosed, unpublished. 3 *secret meanings.* arcane, cryptic, esoteric, incomprehensible, mysterious, recondite. 4 *secret about his private life.* ▷ SECRETIVE. *Opp* OPEN, PUBLIC.

secretary *n* clerk, personal assistant, scribe, typist, word-processor operator.

secrete *v* 1 cloak, conceal, cover up, disguise, hide, mask, put away. 2 *secrete fluid.* emit, excrete, exude, leak, ooze. ▷ DISCHARGE.

secretion *n* discharge, emission, leakage.

secretive *adj* enigmatic, furtive, mysterious, quiet, reserved, reticent, secret, *inf* shifty, tight-lipped, uncommunicative, unforthcoming, withdrawn. *Opp* COMMUNICATIVE.

sect *n* cult, denomination, faction, party. ▷ GROUP.

sectarian *adj* bigoted, clannish, dogmatic, factional, inflexible, narrow, narrow-minded, partial, partisan, prejudiced.

section *n* bit, branch, chapter, compartment, component, department, division, element, fraction, fragment, group, instalment, part, passage, piece, portion, quarter, sample, sector, segment, slice, stage, subdivision, subsection.

sector *n* area, district, division, part, quarter, region, zone. ▷ SECTION.

secular *adj* earthly, lay, non-religious, temporal, worldly. *Opp* RELIGIOUS.

secure *adj* 1 cosy, defended, guarded, immune, impregnable, invulnerable, protected, safe, sheltered, shielded, snug, unharmed, unhurt, unscathed. 2 *the doors are secure.* bolted, burglar-proof, closed, fast, fastened, fixed, locked, shut, solid, tight, unyielding. 3 *secure faith.* certain, confident, firm, stable, steady, strong, sure.
• *v* 1 defend, guard, make safe, preserve, protect, shelter, shield. 2 anchor, attach, bolt, close, fix, lock, make fast. ▷ FASTEN. 3 *secure a loan.* acquire, gain, get, obtain, procure, win.

sedate *adj* calm, collected, composed, cool, decorous, deliberate, dignified, grave, level-headed, peaceful, proper, quiet, sensible, serene, serious, slow, sober, solemn, staid, tranquil, unruffled. *Opp* LIVELY.
• *v* calm, put to sleep, tranquillize, treat with sedatives.

sedative *adj* calming, narcotic, relaxing, soothing, soporific, tranquillizing.
• *n* anodyne, barbiturate, narcotic, opiate, sleeping-pill, tranquillizer.

sedentary *adj* desk-bound, inactive, seated, sitting down. *Opp* ACTIVE.

sediment *n* deposit, dregs, grounds, lees, precipitate, remains, residue, *inf* sludge.

sedition *n* agitation, incitement, rabble-rousing. ▷ REBELLION.

seduce *v* 1 allure, beguile, charm, deceive,

ensnare, entice, inveigle, lure, mislead, tempt. 2 corrupt, deflower, dishonour, lead astray, ravish.

seduction *n* captivation, enticement, lure, temptation.

seductive *adj* alluring, appealing, attractive, bewitching, captivating, charming, enchanting, enticing, inviting, irresistible, persuasive, provocative, tantalizing, tempting, sexy. *Opp* REPULSIVE.

see *v* 1 behold, catch sight of, discern, discover, distinguish, espy, glimpse, identify, look at, make out, mark, note, notice, observe, perceive, recognize, regard, sight, spot, spy, view, watch, witness. 2 *I see what you mean.* appreciate, comprehend, fathom, follow, *inf* get the hang of, grasp, know, realize, take in, understand. 3 *see problems ahead.* anticipate, envisage, foresee, foretell, imagine, picture, visualize. 4 *see what can be done.* consider, decide, mull over, think about, weigh up. 5 *see a play.* attend, watch. 6 *Are you still seeing him?* court, go out with, *inf* date, socialize with. 7 *see you home.* accompany, conduct, escort. 8 *saw fighting in the war.* endure, experience, go through, undergo. 9 *I saw Joe today.* encounter, meet, run into, talk to, visit. **see to** ▷ ORGANIZE.

seed *n* 1 egg, embryo, germ, ovule, ovum, semen, spawn, sperm, spore. 2 *seed in fruit.* pip, pit, stone.
• *v* ▷ SOW.

seek *v* aim at, ask for, aspire to, beg for, desire, go after, hunt for, inquire after, look for, pursue, request, search for, solicit, strive after, try for, want, wish for.

seem *v* appear, feel, give an impression of being, look, pretend to be, sound.

seep *v* dribble, drip, exude, flow, leak, ooze, percolate, run, soak, trickle.

seer *n* clairvoyant, fortune-teller, oracle, prophet, prophetess, psychic, sibyl, soothsayer.

seethe *v* 1 boil, bubble, foam, simmer. 2 be angry, fume, rage.

segment *n* bit, division, fragment, part, piece, portion, slice, wedge. ▷ SECTION.

segregate *v* compartmentalize, cut off, isolate, keep apart, put apart, separate, set apart.

segregation *n* 1 apartheid, discrimination. 2 isolation, quarantine, separation.

seize *v* 1 abduct, apprehend, arrest, capture, catch, clutch, *inf* collar, detain, grab, grasp, grip, hold, *inf* nab, snatch, take, take prisoner. 2 *seize a country.* annex, invade. 3 *seize property.* appropriate, commandeer, confiscate, hijack, impound, steal. *Opp* RELEASE. **seize up** ▷ STICK.

seizure *n* 1 abduction, annexation, appropriation, arrest, capture, confiscation, hijacking, theft, usurpation. 2 [*medical*] attack, convulsion, epileptic fit, fit, paroxysm, spasm, stroke.

seldom *adv* infrequently, occasionally, rarely.

select *adj* choice, chosen, elite, exceptional, exclusive, favoured, finest, first-class, *inf* hand-picked, prime, privileged, rare, selected, special, top-quality. *Opp* ORDINARY.
• *v* appoint, cast (*an actor*), choose, decide on, elect, nominate, opt for, pick, prefer, settle on, single out, vote for.

selection *n* 1 choice, option, pick, preference. 2 *selection of goods.* assortment, range, variety. 3 *selection from the classics.* excerpts, extracts, passages.

selective *adj* careful, *inf* choosy, discerning, discriminating, particular, specialized. *Opp* INDISCRIMINATE.

self-confident *adj* assertive, assured, collected, cool, outgoing, poised, positive, self-assured, self-possessed, sure of yourself. ▷ BOLD. *Opp* SELF-CONSCIOUS.

self-conscious *adj* awkward, bashful, blushing, diffident, embarrassed, ill at ease, insecure, nervous, self-effacing, shy, uncomfortable. ▷ TIMID. *Opp* SELF-CONFIDENT.

self-contained *adj* 1 complete, independent, separate. 2 aloof, cold, reserved, self-reliant, undemonstrative, unemotional.

self-control *n* calmness, composure, coolness, patience, restraint, self-discipline, self-possession, will-power.

self-denial *n* abstemiousness, fasting, moderation, self-sacrifice, temperance, unselfishness. *Opp* SELF-INDULGENCE.

self-employed *adj* freelance, independent.

self-esteem *n* 1 ▷ SELF-RESPECT. 2 arrogance, conceit, egotism, self-importance, self-love, smugness, vanity.

self-explanatory *adj* apparent, clear, patent, plain, self-evident. ▷ OBVIOUS.

self-governing *adj* autonomous, free, independent, sovereign.

self-important *adj* arrogant, bombastic, conceited, haughty, officious, pompous, pretentious, smug, *inf* snooty, *inf* stuck-up, supercilious, superior.

self-indulgence *n* extravagance, gluttony, greed, hedonism, pleasure, profligacy, self-gratification. ▷ SELFISHNESS. *Opp* SELF-DENIAL.

self-indulgent *adj* dissipated, extravagant, gluttonous, greedy, hedonistic, immoderate, pleasure-loving, profligate. ▷ HEDONISTIC. *Opp* ABSTEMIOUS.

selfish *adj* acquisitive, avaricious, covetous, demanding, egocentric, egotistical, grasping, greedy, inconsiderate, mean, mercenary, miserly, self-centred, self-indulgent, self-interested, self-seeking, thoughtless, ungenerous. *Opp* UNSELFISH.

selfishness *n* avarice, covetousness, egotism, greed, meanness, miserliness, self-indulgence, self-interest, self-love, thoughtlessness.

self-reliant *adj* ▷ SELF-SUF CIENT

self-respect *n* dignity, honour, integrity, morale, pride, self-esteem.

self-righteous *adj* complacent, *inf* goody-goody, *inf* holier-than-thou, mealy-mouthed, pietistic, pious, pompous, priggish, sanctimonious, self-satisfied, smug, superior.

self-sufficient *adj* autonomous, independent, self-contained, self-reliant, self-supporting.

self-willed *adj* determined, dogged, forceful, headstrong, inflexible, intractable, intransigent, *inf* mulish, obstinate, *inf* pig-headed, stubborn, uncontrollable, uncooperative, wilful.

sell *v* 1 auction, barter, deal in, *inf* keep, offer for sale, peddle, *inf* put under the hammer, retail, sell off, stock, tout, trade, *inf* trade in, traffic in, vend. 2 advertise, market, promote, *inf* push.

seller *n* agent, dealer, merchant, pedlar, purveyor, *inf* rep, representative, retailer, salesman, saleswoman, shop assistant, shopkeeper, stockist, supplier, trader, tradesman, vendor, wholesaler.

seminal *adj* basic, creative, formative, important, influential, innovative, new, original, primary.

send *v* 1 address, consign, convey, deliver, direct, dispatch, fax, forward, mail, post, remit, ship, transmit. 2 fire, launch, project, release, shoot. **send away** ▷ DISMISS. **send down** ▷ IMPRISON. **send for** ▷ SUMMON. **send-off** ▷ GOODBYE. **send out** ▷ EMIT. **send round** ▷ CIRCULATE. **send up** ▷ PARODY.

senile *adj inf* in your dotage, old, *derog* past it.

senior *adj* chief, elder, higher, major, older, principal, revered, superior, well-established. *Opp* JUNIOR.

sensation *n* 1 awareness, feeling, perception, sense. 2 *She caused a sensation.* commotion, excitement, furore, outrage, scandal, stir, thrill.

sensational *adj* 1 electrifying, exciting, hair-raising, lurid, melodramatic, shocking, spine-tingling, startling, thrilling. 2 [*inf*] *sensational result.* amazing, astonishing, astounding, breathtaking, electrifying, exciting, extraordinary, *inf* fabulous, *inf* fantastic, *inf* great, incredible, marvellous, remarkable, spectacular, superb, surprising, unbelievable, unexpected, wonderful.

sense *n* 1 awareness, consciousness, faculty, feeling, sensation. 2 hearing, sight, smell, taste, touch. 3 gumption, intelligence, intuition, judgement, logic, *inf* nous, perception, reason, reasoning, understanding, wisdom, wit. 4 *the sense of a message.* coherence, connotations, *inf* drift, gist, import, intelligibility, meaning, message, point, purport, significance, substance.
• *v* be aware (of), detect, discern, divine, feel, guess, *inf* have a hunch, hear, notice, perceive, *inf* pick up vibes, realize, respond to, see, suspect, understand. **make sense of** ▷ UNDERSTAND.

senseless *adj* 1 anaesthetized, comatose, numb, stunned, unconscious. 2 absurd, crazy, fatuous, meaningless, pointless, purposeless, silly. ▷ STUPID.

sensible *adj* 1 calm, commonsense, cool, discriminating, intelligent, judicious, level-headed, logical, prudent, rational, realistic, reasonable, sage, sane, serious-minded, sound, straightforward, thoughtful, wise. *Opp* STUPID. 2 *sensible phenomena.* ▷ TANGIBLE. 3 *sensible clothes.* comfortable, functional, *inf* no-nonsense, practical, useful. *Opp* IMPRACTICAL. **sensible of** alert to, alive to, appreciative of, aware of, in touch with, mindful of, responsive to, *inf* wise to.

sensitive *adj* 1 considerate, perceptive, receptive, responsive, susceptible, sympathetic, tactful, thoughtful, understanding. 2 *sensitive temperament.* emotional, hypersensitive, thin-skinned, touchy. 3 *sensitive skin.* delicate, fine, fragile, painful, soft, sore, tender. 4 *sensitive topic.* confidential, controversial, delicate, secret, tricky. *Opp* INSENSITIVE. **sensitive to** affected by, aware of, considerate of, perceptive about, receptive to, responsive to.

sensual *adj* animal, bodily, carnal, fleshly, physical, pleasure-loving, self-indulgent, voluptuous. ▷ SEXY. *Opp* ASCETIC.

sensuous *adj* hedonistic, luxurious, rich, sumptuous. ▷ SENSUAL.

sentence *n* decision, judgement, pronouncement, punishment, ruling.
• *v* condemn, pass judgement on, pronounce sentence on.

sentiment *n* 1 attitude, belief, idea, judgement, opinion, outlook, thought, view. 2 *sentiment of a poem.* emotion, feeling.

sentimental *adj* 1 emotional, nostalgic, romantic, soft-hearted, sympathetic, tearful, tender, warm-hearted, *inf* weepy. 2 [*derog*] gushing, insincere, maudlin, mawkish, *inf* mushy, over-emotional, *inf* sloppy, *inf* soppy, *inf* sugary, treacly, unrealistic. *Opp* CYNICAL.

sentimentality *n* emotionalism, insincerity, mawkishness, nostalgia, *inf* slush.

sentry *n* guard, lookout, patrol, sentinel, watch, watchman.

separable *adj* detachable, distinguishable, removable.

separate *adj* apart, autonomous, cut off, detached, different, disjoined, distinct, divided, divorced, fenced off, free-standing, independent, individual, isolated, particular, secluded, segregated, separated, shut off, unattached, unconnected, unique, unrelated, withdrawn.
• *v* 1 break up, cut off, detach, disconnect, disengage, disentangle, dismember, dissociate, divide, fence off, hive off, isolate, keep apart, part, pull apart, segregate, sever, split, sunder, take apart, unfasten, unhook, unravel. 2 *The paths separate here.* branch, diverge, fork. 3 *separate the men from the boys.* distinguish, filter out, remove, single out, sort out. 4 *His parents separated.* become estranged, divorce, part company, *inf* split up. *Opp* COMBINE, UNITE.

separation *n* 1 cutting off, detachment, disconnection, dissociation, division, fragmentation, parting, rift, severance, splitting. *Opp* CONNECTION. 2 *separation of partners.* break, *inf* break-up, divorce, estrangement, rift, split. *Opp* UNION.

septic *adj* festering, infected, inflamed, poisoned, putrefying, putrid, suppurating.

sequel *n* consequence, continuation, development, *inf* follow-up, issue, outcome, result, upshot.

sequence *n* 1 chain, concatenation, course, cycle, line, order, procession, progression, range, row, run, series, set, string, succession, train. 2 *sequence from a film. inf* clip, episode, excerpt, extract, scene.

serene *adj* 1 calm, idyllic, peaceful, placid, quiet, restful, still, tranquil, undisturbed, unperturbed, unruffled, untroubled. 2 *serene temperament.* composed, contented, cool, easygoing, equable, even-tempered, imperturbable, peaceable, poised, self-possessed, *inf* unflappable. *Opp* BOISTEROUS, EXCITABLE.

series *n* 1 chain, concatenation, course, cycle, line, order, procession, programme, progression, range, row, run, sequence, set, string, succession, train. 2 *TV series.* mini-series, serial, *inf* soap, soap opera.

serious *adj* 1 dignified, earnest, grave, grim, humourless, long-faced, pensive, sedate, sober, solemn, sombre, staid, stern, straight-faced, thoughtful, unsmiling. *Opp* CHEERFUL. 2 grave, important, *inf* life-and-death, momentous, significant, urgent, weighty. 3 *serious illness.* acute, alarming, awful, calamitous, critical, dangerous, dreadful, ghastly, grievous, life-threatening, nasty, severe, terrible, unfortunate, unpleasant, violent. *Opp* TRIVIAL. 4 *Is she being serious?* genuine, honest, in earnest, sincere.

sermon *n* address, discourse, homily, lecture, lesson, talk.

serpentine *adj* labyrinthine, meandering, roundabout, sinuous, tortuous, twisting, winding. *Opp* STRAIGHT.

serrated *adj* indented, jagged, notched, saw-like, toothed, zigzag. *Opp* STRAIGHT.

servant *n* assistant, attendant, *derog* dogsbody, *inf* domestic, *derog* drudge, *derog* flunkey, helper, *derog* hireling, *derog* lackey, *derog* menial, *pl* retinue, *inf* skivvy, slave.

serve *v* 1 aid, assist, *inf* be at someone's beck and call, further, help, look after, minister to, wait upon, work for. 2 *serve in the forces.* be employed, do your duty, fight. 3 *serve goods.* distribute, dole out, give out, provide, sell, supply. 4 *serve at table.* carve, *inf* dish up, wait.

5 *serve a sentence*. complete, go through, pass, spend.

service *n* 1 aid, assistance, benefit, favour, help, kindness. 2 *service of the community*. attendance (on), employment (by), ministering (to), work (for). 3 *bus service*. organization, provision, system, timetable. 4 *My car needs a service*. check-over, maintenance, overhaul, repair, servicing. 5 *church service*. ceremony, meeting, rite, ritual, worship.
• *v* check, maintain, mend, overhaul, repair, tune.

serviceable *adj* dependable, durable, functional, hard-wearing, lasting, practical, strong, tough, usable.

servile *adj* abject, *inf* boot-licking, cringing, fawning, flattering, grovelling, humble, ingratiating, menial, obsequious, slavish, submissive, subservient, sycophantic, toadying, unctuous. *Opp* BOSSY. **be servile** ▷ GROVEL.

serving *n* helping, plateful, portion, ration.

session *n* 1 assembly, conference, hearing, meeting, sitting. 2 period, term, time.

set *adj* 1 *set price*. advertised, agreed, arranged, definite, fixed, pre-arranged, scheduled, standard. 2 *set in your ways*. predictable, regular, unchanging, unvarying. ▷ STUBBORN.
• *n* 1 batch, category, class, clique, collection, kind, series, sort. ▷ GROUP. 2 *TV set*. apparatus, receiver. 3 *set for a play*. scene, scenery, setting, stage.
• *v* 1 arrange, deploy, deposit, lay, leave, locate, lodge, park, place, plant, *inf* plonk, put, position, rest, set down, set out, settle, situate, stand, station. 2 *set a clock*. adjust, correct, put right, regulate. 3 *set a post in concrete*. embed, fasten, fix. 4 *set like concrete*. congeal, harden, *inf* jell, stiffen. 5 *set a question*. ask, formulate, frame, phrase, pose, present, put forward, suggest. 6 *set a date*. allocate, allot, appoint, decide, designate, determine, establish, name, prescribe, settle. **set about** ▷ ATTACK, BEGIN. **set free** ▷ LIBERATE. **set off** ▷ DEPART, EXPLODE. **set on** ▷ ATTACK. **set on fire** ▷ IGNITE. **set out** ▷ DEPART. **set up** ▷ ESTABLISH.

set-back *n inf* blow, complication, delay, difficulty, disappointment, *inf* hitch, hold-up, impediment, misfortune, obstacle, problem, reverse, snag, upset.

settee *n* chaise longue, couch, sofa.

setting *n* 1 background, context, environment, frame, habitat, location, place, position, site, surroundings. 2 *setting for a play*. backdrop, scene, scenery, set.

settle *v* 1 arrange, conclude, deal with, organize, put in order, straighten out. 2 alight, come to rest, land, *inf* make yourself comfortable, *inf* park yourself, pause, rest, sit down. 3 *settle things in place*. deploy, deposit, lay, lodge, park, place, position, put, rest, set, situate. ▷ SET. 4 *the dust settled*. calm down, clear, sink, subside. 5 *settle what to do*. agree, decide, establish, fix. 6 *settle differences*. end, put an end to, reconcile, resolve, sort out, square. 7 *settle debts*. clear, discharge, pay, pay off. 8 *settle new territory*. colonize, occupy, populate, set up home in, stay in.

settlement *n* 1 camp, colony, community, kibbutz, outpost, town, village. 2 agreement, arrangement, contract, payment.

settler *n* colonist, immigrant, newcomer, pioneer.

sever *v* 1 amputate, break, cut off, detach, disconnect, part, separate, split. ▷ CUT. 2 *sever a relationship*. abandon, break off, discontinue, end, put an end to, terminate.

several *adj* assorted, different, a few, a handful of, many, miscellaneous, a number of, some, sundry, various.

severe *adj* 1 brutal, cold, cold-hearted, cruel, dour, exacting, forbidding, glowering, grave, grim, hard, harsh, inexorable, merciless, obdurate, relentless, rigorous, stern, stony, strict, unbending, uncompromising, unkind, unsympathetic, unyielding. 2 *severe illness*. acute, critical, dangerous, drastic, fatal, great, intense, keen, life-threatening, mortal, nasty, serious, sharp, terminal. 3 *severe penalties*. draconian, extreme, maximum, stringent. 4 *severe weather*. adverse, bad, inclement, violent. ▷ COLD, STORMY. 5 *severe challenge*. arduous, demanding, difficult, onerous, punishing, taxing, tough. 6 *severe style*. austere, bare, chaste, plain, simple, spartan, stark, unadorned. *Opp* FRIENDLY, MILD, ORNATE.

sew *v* darn, hem, mend, repair, stitch.

sewer *n* drain, drainage, *pl* sanitation, septic tank.

sewing *n* dressmaking, embroidery, mending, needlepoint, needlework, tapestry.

sex *n* 1 gender. 2 carnal knowledge, coitus, copulation, coupling, fornication, *inf* going to bed, intercourse, intimacy, love-making, mating, seduction, sexual intercourse, sexual relations, union. **have sex (with)** be intimate (with), copulate (with), fornicate (with), have sexual intercourse (with), make love (to), mate (with), *sl* screw, seduce.

sexism *n inf* chauvinism, discrimination, prejudice.

sexual *adj* arousing, earthy, erotic, physical, sensual, sexy, voluptuous.

sexy *adj* 1 arousing, desirable, erotic, flirtatious, provocative, seductive, sensual, sensuous, suggestive, sultry, tempting, voluptuous. 2 aroused, lecherous, lustful, passionate, *sl* randy. 3 dirty, indecent, *inf* naughty, obscene, pornographic, *inf* raunchy, risqué, rude, smutty, *inf* steamy, titillating, vulgar.

shabby *adj* 1 dilapidated, dingy, dirty, dowdy, drab, faded, frayed, grubby, mangy, *inf* moth-eaten, ragged, run-down, *inf* scruffy, seedy, tattered, *inf* tatty, threadbare, worn, worn-out. *Opp* SMART. 2 *shabby behaviour.* contemptible, despicable, discreditable, dishonest, dishonourable, disreputable, ignoble, mean, shameful, shoddy, unfair, unkind, unworthy. *Opp* HONOURABLE.

shack *n* cabin, hovel, hut, lean-to, shanty, shed.

shade *n* 1 ▷ SHADOW. 2 awning, blind, canopy, covering, curtain, parasol, screen, shelter, shield, umbrella. 3 colour, hue, tinge, tint, tone. 4 *shades of meaning.* degree, nicety, nuance, variation.
▪ *v* 1 camouflage, conceal, cover, hide, mask, obscure, protect, screen, shield, shroud, veil. 2 *shade with pencil.* block in, darken, fill in.

shadow *n* 1 darkness, dimness, dusk, gloom, obscurity, semi-darkness, shade. 2 *The sun casts shadows.* outline, silhouette. 3 *shadow of doubt.* ▷ HINT.
▪ *v* follow, *inf* keep tabs on, keep watch on, pursue, stalk, *inf* tail, track, trail, watch.

shadowy *adj* 1 faint, hazy, indistinct, nebulous, obscure, unrecognizable, vague. ▷ GHOSTLY. 2 ▷ SHADY.

shady *adj* 1 cool, dark, dim, dusky, gloomy, leafy, shaded, shadowy, sheltered, sunless. *Opp* SUNNY. 2 *shady character.* dishonest, disreputable, dubious, *inf* fishy, *inf* shifty, suspicious, untrustworthy. *Opp* HONEST.

shaft *n* 1 arrow, column, handle, pillar, pole, post, rod, stem, stick, upright. 2 mine, pit, tunnel, well, working. 3 *shaft of light.* beam, gleam, ray, streak.

shaggy *adj* bushy, dishevelled, fleecy, hairy, hirsute, rough, tousled, unkempt, untidy, woolly. *Opp* SMOOTH.

shake *v* 1 convulse, heave, jump, quake, quiver, rattle, rock, shiver, shudder, sway, totter, tremble, vibrate, waver, wobble. 2 agitate, flourish, gyrate, jerk, jiggle, joggle, sway, swing, twirl, twitch, vibrate, wag, *inf* waggle, wave, *inf* wiggle. 3 distress, disturb, frighten, perturb, *inf* rattle, shock, startle, *inf* throw, unnerve, unsettle, upset. ▷ SURPRISE.

shaky *adj* 1 decrepit, dilapidated, feeble, flimsy, frail, insecure, precarious, ramshackle, rickety, rocky, unsteady, weak, wobbly. 2 *shaky voice.* faltering, quavering, quivering, trembling, tremulous. 3 *shaky start.* nervous, tentative, uncertain, unimpressive, unpromising. *Opp* STEADY, STRONG.

shallow *adj* empty, facile, foolish, frivolous, glib, insincere, puerile, silly, skin-deep, slight, superficial, trivial, unconvincing. *Opp* DEEP.

sham *adj* artificial, bogus, counterfeit, ersatz, fake, false, fraudulent, imitation, mock, *inf* pretend, pretended, simulated, synthetic.
▪ *n* counterfeit, fake, fraud, hoax, imitation, pretence, *inf* put-up job, simulation.
▪ *v* counterfeit, fake, feign, imitate, pretend, simulate.

shambles *pl n* [*inf*] chaos, confusion, devastation, disorder, mess, muddle, *inf* pigsty, *inf* tip.

shame *n* 1 chagrin, degradation, discredit, disgrace, dishonour, distress, embarrassment, guilt, humiliation, ignominy, infamy, loss of face, mortification, opprobrium, remorse, stain, stigma. 2 *What a shame!* outrage, pity, scandal.
▪ *v* abash, chagrin, chasten, disgrace, embarrass, humble, humiliate, make someone ashamed, mortify, *inf* put someone in their place, *inf* show someone up.

shamefaced *adj* 1 ashamed, chagrined, *inf* hang-dog, humiliated, mortified, penitent, *inf* red-faced, remorseful, repentant, sorry. 2 modest, self-conscious, sheepish, shy. ▷ BASHFUL. *Opp* SHAMELESS.

shameful *adj* base, contemptible, degrading, demeaning, deplorable, discreditable, disgraceful, dishonourable, embarrassing, humiliating, ignominious, infamous, inglorious, low, mean, mortifying, outrageous, scandalous, unworthy. *Opp* HONOURABLE.

shameless *adj* barefaced, bold, brazen, flagrant, immodest, impudent, insolent, rude, shocking, unabashed, unashamed, unblushing, unrepentant, unselfconscious, wanton. *Opp* SHAMEFACED.

shape *n* 1 body, build, figure, physique, profile, silhouette. 2 *geometrical shape*. configuration, figure, form, model, mould, outline, pattern.
• *v* adapt, adjust, carve, cast, cut, fashion, form, frame, give shape to, model, mould, *inf* sculpt, sculpture, whittle.

shapeless *adj* 1 amorphous, formless, indeterminate, nebulous, undefined, unformed, unstructured, vague. 2 *shapeless figure*. dumpy, misshapen, unattractive. *Opp* SHAPELY.

shapely *adj* attractive, *inf* curvaceous, good-looking, graceful, neat, voluptuous, well-proportioned. *Opp* SHAPELESS.

share *n* allocation, allowance, bit, cut, division, due, fraction, helping, part, percentage, piece, portion, proportion, quota, ration, serving.
• *v* 1 allocate, allot, apportion, deal out, distribute, divide, dole out, *inf* go halves or shares (with), halve, portion out, ration out, split. 2 cooperate, join, participate, take part. **shared** ▷ JOINT.

sharp *adj* 1 cutting, fine, jagged, keen, knife-edged, needle-sharp, pointed, razor-sharp, sharpened, spiky. 2 *sharp bend, drop*. abrupt, acute, angular, hairpin, precipitous, sheer, steep, sudden, surprising, unexpected. 3 *sharp focus*. clear, distinct, well-defined. 4 *sharp storm*. heavy, intense, severe, sudden, violent. 5 *sharp frost*. biting, bitter, keen. ▷ COLD. 6 *sharp pain*. acute, excruciating, stabbing, stinging. 7 *sharp reply*. acerbic, acid, barbed, biting, caustic, critical, cutting, hurtful, mocking, mordant, sarcastic, sardonic, scathing, tart, trenchant, unkind, vitriolic. 8 *sharp mind*. acute, agile, alert, astute, bright, clever, crafty, *inf* cute, discerning, incisive, intelligent, penetrating, perceptive, probing, quick-witted, shrewd, *inf* smart. 9 *sharp eyes*. observant, *inf* peeled (*keep your eyes peeled*), watchful, wide-open. 10 *sharp taste, smell*. acid, acrid, bitter, piquant, pungent, sour, spicy, tangy, tart. 11 *sharp sound*. clear, ear-splitting, high, high-pitched, penetrating, piercing, shrill, staccato, strident. *Opp* BLUNT, DULL, SLIGHT.

sharpen *v* file, grind, hone, make sharp, whet. *Opp* BLUNT.

shatter *v* blast, break, break up, burst, crack, dash to pieces, destroy, disintegrate, explode, pulverize, smash, *inf* smash to smithereens, splinter, wreck. **shattered** ▷ SURPRISED, WEARY.

sheaf *n* bunch, bundle, file, ream.

shear *v* clip, strip, trim. ▷ CUT.

sheath *n* casing, covering, scabbard, sleeve.

sheathe *v* cocoon, cover, encase, enclose, put away, wrap.

shed *n* hut, lean-to, outhouse, potting-shed, shack, shelter, storehouse.
• *v* abandon, cast off, discard, drop, let fall, moult, scatter, shower, spill. **shed light** ▷ SHINE.

sheen *n* brightness, burnish, glaze, gleam, gloss, lustre, patina, polish, radiance, shine.

sheep *n* ewe, lamb, ram.

sheepish *adj* abashed, ashamed, bashful, coy, embarrassed, guilty, meek, shamefaced, shy, timid. *Opp* SHAMELESS.

sheer *adj* 1 absolute, complete, downright, out and out, pure, thoroughgoing, total, unadulterated, unmitigated, unqualified, utter. 2 *sheer cliff*. perpendicular, precipitous, steep, vertical. 3 *sheer silk*. diaphanous, filmy, fine, flimsy, gauzy, gossamer, *inf* see-through, thin, translucent, transparent.

sheet *n* 1 [*paper*] folio, leaf, page. 2 [*glass, etc*] pane, panel, plate. 3 [*ice, etc*] area, blanket, coating, covering, expanse, film, layer, skin, stretch, surface, veneer. 4 [*rock*] lamina, stratum.

shell *n* 1 carapace (*of tortoise*), case, casing, covering, crust, exterior, façade, hull, husk, outside, pod. 2 cartridge, projectile.
• *v* attack, blitz, bomb, bombard, fire at, shoot at, strafe.

shellfish *n* bivalve, crustacean, mollusc.

shelter *n* 1 asylum, cover, haven, lee, protection, refuge, safety, sanctuary, security. 2 barrier, cover, fence, hut, roof, screen, shield. 3 accommodation, lodging, home, housing, resting place. 4 *air-raid shelter*. bunker.
• *v* 1 defend, guard, keep safe, protect, safeguard, screen, shade, shield. 2 *shelter a runaway*. give shelter to, harbour, hide, *inf* put up. **sheltered** ▷ QUIET.

shelve *v* 1 defer, lay aside, postpone, put off, put on ice. 2 ▷ SLOPE.

shield *n* barrier, defence, guard, protection, safeguard, screen, shelter.

• *v* cover, defend, guard, keep safe, protect, safeguard, screen, shade, shelter.

shift *n* 1 adjustment, alteration, change, move, switch, transfer. 2 *night shift.* crew, gang, group, *inf* stint, team.
• *v* adjust, alter, budge, change, reposition, switch, transfer, transpose. ▷ MOVE.
shift for yourself ▷ MANAGE.

shiftless *adj* idle, indolent, inefficient, irresponsible, lazy, unenterprising. *Opp* RESOURCEFUL.

shifty *adj* crafty, cunning, deceitful, devious, dishonest, evasive, *inf* foxy, furtive, scheming, secretive, *inf* shady, slippery, sly, tricky, untrustworthy, wily. *Opp* STRAIGHTFORWARD.

shimmer *v* flicker, glimmer, glisten, ripple. ▷ SHINE.

shine *n* brightness, burnish, glaze, gleam, glint, gloss, lustre, patina, phosphorescence, polish, radiance, reflection, sheen, shimmer, sparkle.
• *v* 1 beam, be luminous, blaze, dazzle, flare, flash, glare, gleam, glint, glisten, glitter, radiate, reflect, scintillate, shed light, shimmer, sparkle, twinkle. 2 *shine at maths.* be clever, do well, excel, stand out. 3 *shine your shoes.* brush, buff up, clean, polish, rub up. **shining** ▷ BRIGHT, CONSPICUOUS.

shingle *n* gravel, pebbles, stones.

shiny *adj* bright, brilliant, burnished, gleaming, glistening, glossy, luminous, lustrous, phosphorescent, polished, reflective, shining, sleek, smooth. *Opp* DULL.

ship *n* boat, craft, vessel.
• *v* carry, convey, deliver, ferry, move, send, transport.

shirk *v* avoid, dodge, duck, evade, get out of, neglect, shun, *sl* skive, sidestep.

shiver *n* flutter, frisson, quiver, rattle, shake, shudder, tremor, vibration.
• *v* chatter, flap, flutter, quake, quaver, quiver, rattle, shake, shudder, tremble, twitch, vibrate.

shock *n* 1 blow, collision, impact, jolt, thud. 2 *came as a shock. inf* bombshell, surprise, *inf* thunderbolt. 3 *state of shock.* dismay, distress, fright, trauma, upset.
• *v* 1 alarm, amaze, astonish, astound, daze, dismay, distress, dumbfound, frighten, *inf* give someone a turn, jolt, numb, paralyse, rock, scare, shake, stagger, startle, stun, stupefy, surprise, *inf* throw, traumatize, unnerve. 2 *Cruelty shocks us.* appal, disgust, horrify, offend, outrage, revolt, scandalize, sicken.

shoddy *adj* 1 cheap, flimsy, gimcrack, inferior, poor quality, *inf* rubbishy, second-rate, *sl* tacky, *inf* tatty, tawdry, *inf* trashy. 2 *shoddy work.* careless, messy, slipshod, *inf* sloppy, slovenly, untidy. *Opp* SUPERIOR, CAREFUL.

shoe *n* boot, clog, *pl* footwear, moccasin, plimsoll, sandal, slipper, trainer, wellington.

shoemaker *n* bootmaker, cobbler.

shoot *n* branch, bud, new growth, offshoot, sucker, twig.
• *v* 1 *shoot a gun.* discharge, fire. 2 *shoot someone.* bombard, fire at, gun down, hit, kill, *inf* let fly at, open fire on, shell, strafe, *inf* take pot-shots at. 3 *shoot out of bed.* bolt, dart, dash, fly, hurtle, leap, race, run, rush, speed, spring, streak. 4 *plants shoot in the spring.* bud, burgeon, flourish, grow, put out shoots, spring up, sprout.

shop *n* boutique, cash-and-carry, department store, emporium, establishment, hypermarket, market, minimarket, outlet, store, supermarket.

shopkeeper *n* dealer, merchant, retailer, salesman, saleswoman, storekeeper, tradesman, tradeswoman.

shopper *n* buyer, customer, patron.

shopping *n* 1 buying, *inf* spending-spree. 2 goods, purchases.

shopping centre *n* arcade, complex, hypermarket, mall, precinct.

shore *n* beach, coast, sands, seashore, seaside, shingle, strand.
• *v* **shore up** ▷ SUPPORT.

short *adj* 1 diminutive, dumpy, little, midget, petite, *inf* pint-sized, slight, small, squat, stubby, stumpy, stunted, tiny, *inf* wee. 2 *short visit.* brief, cursory, curtailed, fleeting, momentary, passing, quick, short-lived, temporary, transient. 3 *short book.* abbreviated, abridged, compact, concise, shortened, succinct. 4 *in short supply.* deficient, inadequate, insufficient, lacking, limited, low, meagre, scanty, scarce, sparse, wanting. 5 *a short manner.* abrupt, bad-tempered, blunt, brusque, cross, curt, gruff, grumpy, impolite, irritable, sharp, snappy, taciturn, terse, testy, unfriendly, unkind. *Opp* EXPANSIVE, LONG, PLENTIFUL, TALL. **cut short** ▷ SHORTEN.

shortage *n* absence, dearth, deficiency, deficit, insufficiency, lack, paucity, poverty, scarcity, shortfall, want. *Opp* PLENTY.

shortcoming *n* bad habit, defect, drawback, failing, fault, foible, imperfection, vice, weakness, weak point.

shorten *v* abbreviate, abridge, compress, condense, curtail, cut, cut down, cut short, précis, prune, reduce, summarize, take up (*clothes*), trim, truncate. *Opp* LENGTHEN.

shortly *adv old use* anon, before long, by and by, presently, soon.

short-sighted *adj* 1 myopic, near-sighted. 2 unadventurous, unimaginative, without vision.

short-tempered *adj* abrupt, crabby, cross, crusty, curt, gruff, irascible, irritable, peevish, shrewish, snappy, testy, touchy, waspish.

shot *n* 1 ball, bullet, missile, pellet, projectile, round, slug. 2 *heard a shot.* bang, blast, crack, explosion, report. 3 *first-class shot.* marksman, markswoman, sharpshooter. 4 *give it a shot.* attempt, chance, *inf* crack, endeavour, *inf* go, *inf* stab, try. 5 *photographic shot.* photograph, picture, scene, snap, snapshot.

shout *v* bawl, bellow, call, cheer, clamour, cry out, exclaim, howl, rant, roar, scream, screech, shriek, whoop, yell. *Opp* WHISPER.

shove *v inf* barge, crowd, drive, elbow, hustle, jostle, press, push, shoulder, thrust.

shovel *v* clear, dig, scoop, shift.

show *n* 1 drama, entertainment, performance, play, presentation, production. 2 *flower show.* competition, demonstration, display, exhibition, *inf* expo. 3 *show of strength.* appearance, demonstration, illusion, impression, pose, pretence, threat. 4 *just for show.* affectation, exhibitionism, flamboyance, ostentation, showing off.
• *v* 1 bare, demonstrate, display, divulge, exhibit, expose, make public, make visible, manifest, present, produce, reveal, uncover. 2 appear, be seen, be visible, catch the eye, come out, emerge, materialize, *inf* peep through, stand out, stick out. 3 *show the way.* conduct, direct, escort, guide, indicate, lead, point out. 4 *show kindness.* bestow, confer, grant, treat with. 5 *The graph shows the results of the survey.* depict, illustrate, picture, portray, represent. 6 *Show me how.* describe, explain, instruct, make clear, teach, tell. 7 *Tests show I was right.* attest, bear out, confirm, demonstrate, evince, manifest, prove, substantiate, verify, witness. **show off** ▷ BOAST. **show up** ▷ ARRIVE, HUMILIATE.

showdown *n* confrontation, crisis, *inf* decider, *inf* moment of truth.

shower *n* cloudburst, downpour, sprinkling. ▷ RAIN.
• *v* 1 rain, spatter, splash, spray, sprinkle. 2 *shower with gifts.* heap, inundate, load, overwhelm.

show-off *n inf* big-head, boaster, conceited person, egotist, exhibitionist, *inf* poser, poseur, swaggerer.

showy *adj* bright, conspicuous, elaborate, fancy, flamboyant, *inf* flashy, fussy, garish, gaudy, loud, lurid, ornate, ostentatious, *inf* over the top, pretentious, vulgar. *Opp* DISCREET.

shred *n* atom, bit, fragment, grain, hint, iota, jot, piece, scrap, sliver, snippet, speck, trace.
• *v* cut to shreds, destroy, grate, rip up. **shreds** rags, ribbons, tatters.

shrewd *adj* acute, artful, astute, calculating, canny, clever, crafty, cunning, discerning, discriminating, intelligent, knowing, observant, perceptive, perspicacious, quick-witted, sharp, sly, smart, wily, wise. *Opp* STUPID.

shriek *v* cry, scream, screech, squawk, squeal.

shrill *adj* ear-splitting, harsh, high, high-pitched, jarring, piercing, raucous, screaming, screeching, sharp, shrieking, strident, treble. *Opp* GENTLE, SONOROUS.

shrine *n* altar, chapel, holy of holies, holy place, place of worship, sanctum, tomb.

shrink *v* 1 contract, decrease, diminish, dwindle, lessen, narrow, reduce, shorten. ▷ SHRIVEL. *Opp* EXPAND. 2 *shrink with fear.* cower, cringe, flinch, quail, recoil, retire, shy away, wince, withdraw. *Opp* ADVANCE.

shrivel *v* become parched, dehydrate, droop, dry out, dry up, wilt, wither, wrinkle. ▷ SHRINK.

shroud *n* blanket, cloak, cover, mantle, mask, pall, veil.
• *v* camouflage, cloak, conceal, cover, enshroud, envelop, hide, mask, screen, swathe, veil.

shrub *n* bush, plant, tree.

shudder *v* be horrified, quake, quiver, shake, shiver, squirm, tremble, vibrate.

shuffle *v* 1 disorganize, jumble, mix, mix

up, rearrange, reorganize. 2 *shuffle along.* drag your feet, limp, shamble.

shun *v* avoid, disdain, flee, give (someone) the cold shoulder, rebuff, reject, shy away from, spurn, steer clear of. *Opp* SEEK.

shut *v* bolt, close, fasten, latch, lock, seal, secure, slam. **shut in** ▷ CONFINE, IMPRISON. **shut off** ▷ ISOLATE. **shut out** ▷ EXCLUDE. **shut up** ▷ CONFINE, IMPRISON, SILENCE.

shutter *n* blind, louvre, screen.

shy *adj* apprehensive, bashful, cautious, coy, diffident, hesitant, inhibited, introverted, modest, *inf* mousy, nervous, reserved, reticent, retiring, self-conscious, self-effacing, sheepish, timid, timorous, withdrawn. *Opp* ASSERTIVE, UNINHIBITED.
• *v* ▷ THROW.

sibling *n* brother, sister, twin.

sick *adj* 1 afflicted, ailing, bedridden, diseased, indisposed, infirm, *inf* laid up, poorly, sickly, *inf* under the weather, unwell. ▷ ILL. 2 airsick, bilious, carsick, nauseated, nauseous, queasy, seasick. 3 *sick of rudeness.* annoyed (by), bored (with), disgusted (by), *inf* fed up (with), nauseated (by), sickened (by), tired, weary. 4 [*inf*] *sick joke.* ▷ MORBID. **be sick** ▷ VOMIT.

sicken *v* 1 fall ill, take sick. 2 appal, disgust, nauseate, offend, repel, revolt, *inf* turn someone off, *inf* turn someone's stomach. **sickening** ▷ REPULSIVE.

sickly *adj* 1 ailing, anaemic, delicate, feeble, frail, pale, pallid, *inf* peaky, unhealthy, wan, weak. ▷ ILL. *Opp* HEALTHY. 2 *sickly sentiment.* cloying, maudlin, mawkish, nauseating, obnoxious, syrupy, treacly, unpleasant. *Opp* REFRESHING.

sickness *n* nausea, queasiness, vomiting. ▷ ILLNESS.

side *n* 1 *sides of a cube.* face, facet, flank, surface. 2 *side of the road.* border, boundary, brim, brink, edge, fringe, margin, perimeter, rim, verge. 3 *sides in a debate.* angle, aspect, attitude, perspective, point of view, position, slant, standpoint, view, viewpoint. 4 *sides in a quarrel.* army, camp, faction, interest, party, team.
• *v* **side with** ally with, favour, *inf* go along with, join up with, prefer, support, team up with. ▷ HELP.

sidestep *v* avoid, dodge, *inf* duck, evade, skirt round.

sidetrack *v* deflect, distract, divert.

sideways *adj* 1 indirect, oblique. 2 *sideways glance.* covert, sidelong, sly, sneaky, unobtrusive.

siege *n* blockade.
• *v* ▷ BESIEGE.

sieve *n* colander, riddle, screen, strainer.
• *v* ▷ SIFT.

sift *v* 1 filter, riddle, separate, sieve, strain. 2 *sift evidence.* analyse, examine, investigate, review, select, sort out, weed out.

sigh *n* breath, exhalation, moan, murmur.

sight *n* 1 eyesight, seeing, vision. 2 *within sight.* field of vision, gaze, range, view, visibility. 3 *brief sight of it.* glimpse, look. 4 *impressive sight.* display, exhibition, scene, show, spectacle.
• *v* behold, discern, distinguish, glimpse, make out, notice, observe, perceive, recognize, see, spot. **catch sight of** ▷ SEE.

sightseer *n* globe-trotter, holidaymaker, tourist, tripper, visitor.

sign *n* 1 augury, forewarning, hint, indicator, intimation, omen, pointer, portent, presage, warning. ▷ SIGNAL. 2 *sign of his presence.* clue, *inf* give-away, indication, manifestation, marker, proof, reminder, spoor (*of animal*), symptom, token, trace, vestige. 3 *put up a sign.* advertisement, notice, placard, poster. 4 *identifying sign.* badge, cipher, device, emblem, flag, insignia, logo, mark, monogram, symbol, trademark.
• *v* 1 autograph, countersign, endorse, inscribe, write. 2 ▷ SIGNAL. **sign off** ▷ FINISH. **sign on** ▷ ENLIST. **sign over** ▷ TRANSFER.

signal *n* 1 communication, cue, gesticulation, gesture, *inf* go-ahead, indication, sign, signal, tip-off, warning. 2 beacon, bell, buoy, flag, flare, siren, whistle.
• *v* beckon, communicate, flag, gesticulate, gesture, indicate, motion, notify, sign, wave.

signature *n* autograph, endorsement, mark, name.

signet *n* seal, stamp.

significance *n* force, idea, implication, import, importance, message, point, purport, relevance, sense, value, weight. ▷ MEANING.

significant *adj* 1 eloquent, expressive, indicative, informative, knowing, meaningful, pregnant, revealing, suggestive, symbolic, *inf* tell-tale. 2 *significant event.* consequential, considerable, influential, memorable, relevant, serious, valuable, worthwhile. *Opp* INSIGNIFICANT.

signify *v* 1 announce, be a sign of, connote, convey, denote, express, imply, indicate, intimate, make known, reflect, reveal, signal, suggest, symbolize, tell, transmit. 2 *It doesn't signify.* be significant, count, matter.

signpost *n* pointer, road sign, sign.

silence *n* 1 calm, calmness, hush, peace, quiet, quietness, stillness, tranquillity. *Opp* NOISE. 2 *Her silence puzzled us.* reticence, speechlessness, taciturnity.
• *v* 1 gag, hush, keep quiet, make silent, muzzle, shut up, suppress. 2 *silence engine noise.* deaden, muffle, mute, quieten, smother, stifle. **Silence!** Be quiet! *inf* Hold your tongue! Hush! *inf* Pipe down! Shut up! Stop talking!

silent *adj* 1 inaudible, muffled, muted, noiseless, quiet, soundless. 2 dumb, *inf* mum, reticent, speechless, taciturn, tight-lipped, tongue-tied, uncommunicative, unforthcoming, voiceless. 3 *silent listeners.* attentive, rapt, restrained, still. 4 *silent agreement.* implicit, implied, mute, tacit, understood, unspoken. *Opp* EXPLICIT, NOISY, TALKATIVE. **be silent** keep quiet, *inf* pipe down, say nothing, *inf* shut up.

silhouette *n* contour, form, outline, profile, shadow, shape.

silky *adj* fine, glossy, lustrous, satiny, silken, sleek, smooth, soft, velvety.

silly *adj* 1 absurd, asinine, brainless, childish, crazy, *inf* daft, *inf* dopey, *inf* dotty, fatuous, feather-brained, foolish, frivolous, *inf* half-baked, hare-brained, idiotic, ill-advised, illogical, immature, inane, infantile, irrational, laughable, light-hearted, ludicrous, mad, meaningless, mindless, misguided, nonsensical, playful, pointless, ridiculous, scatter-brained, *inf* scatty, senseless, simple-minded, simplistic, *inf* soppy, stupid, thoughtless, unintelligent, unwise, witless. *Opp* SERIOUS, WISE. 2 [*inf*] *knocked silly.* ▷ UNCONSCIOUS.

silt *n* deposit, mud, ooze, sediment, slime, sludge.

similar *adj* akin, alike, analogous, comparable, compatible, congruous, corresponding, equal, equivalent, harmonious, homogeneous, identical, indistinguishable, like, matching, parallel, related, resembling, the same, uniform, well-matched. *Opp* DIFFERENT.

similarity *n* affinity, closeness, congruity, correspondence, kinship, likeness, match, relationship, resemblance, sameness. *Opp* DIFFERENCE.

simmer *v* boil, bubble, cook, seethe, stew.

simple *adj* 1 artless, basic, candid, childlike, elementary, frank, guileless, homely, humble, ingenuous, innocent, lowly, modest, *derog* naive, natural, *derog* silly, simple-minded, unaffected, unassuming, unpretentious, unsophisticated. *Opp* SOPHISTICATED. 2 *simple instructions.* clear, comprehensible, direct, easy, foolproof, intelligible, lucid, straightforward, uncomplicated, understandable. *Opp* COMPLEX. 3 *simple dress.* austere, classical, plain, severe, stark, unadorned. *Opp* ORNATE.

simplify *v* clarify, explain, paraphrase, *inf* put in words of one syllable, streamline, untangle. *Opp* COMPLICATE.

simplistic *adj* [*derog*] facile, naive, oversimplified, shallow, silly, superficial.

simulate *v* act, counterfeit, fake, feign, imitate, *inf* mock up, pretend, reproduce, sham.

simultaneous *adj* coinciding, concurrent, contemporary, synchronous.

sin *n* blasphemy, corruption, depravity, desecration, error, evil, fault, guilt, immorality, impiety, iniquity, irreverence, misdeed, offence, peccadillo, sacrilege, sinfulness, transgression, ungodliness, vice, wickedness, wrong, wrongdoing.
• *v* blaspheme, do wrong, err, fall from grace, go astray, lapse, misbehave, offend, transgress.

sincere *adj* candid, direct, earnest, frank, genuine, guileless, heartfelt, honest, open, real, serious, straight, straightforward, true, truthful, unaffected, unfeigned, upright, wholehearted. *Opp* INSINCERE.

sincerity *n* candour, directness, earnestness, frankness, honesty, honour, integrity, openness, straightforwardness, truthfulness.

sinewy *adj* brawny, muscular, tough, wiry. ▷ STRONG.

sinful *adj* bad, blasphemous, corrupt, depraved, erring, evil, fallen, guilty, immoral, impious, iniquitous, irreligious, irreverent, profane, sacrilegious, ungodly, unholy, unrighteous, wicked, wrong. *Opp* RIGHTEOUS.

sing *v* carol, chant, chirp, chorus, croon, hum, serenade, trill, warble, yodel.

singe *v* blacken, burn, char, scorch, sear.

singer *n pl* choir, chorister, *pl* chorus, entertainer, minstrel, performer, soloist, songster, vocalist.

single *adj* 1 exclusive, individual, isolated, lone, odd, one, only, personal, separate, singular, sole, solitary, unique. 2 *single person.* *inf* free, unattached, unmarried.
▪ *v* **single out** ▷ CHOOSE.

single-handed *adj* alone, independent, solitary, unaided, unassisted, without help.

single-minded *adj* dedicated, devoted, dogged, *derog* fanatical, *derog* obsessive, persevering, resolute, tireless. ▷ DETERMINED.

singular *adj* 1 ▷ SINGLE. 2 abnormal, curious, exceptional, extraordinary, odd, outstanding, rare, remarkable, strange, unusual. ▷ DISTINCTIVE. *Opp* COMMON.

sinister *adj* 1 dark, disquieting, disturbing, evil, forbidding, frightening, gloomy, inauspicious, malevolent, menacing, ominous, threatening, upsetting. 2 *sinister motives.* bad, corrupt, criminal, dishonest, illegal, nefarious, questionable, *inf* shady, suspect, treacherous, villainous.

sink *v* 1 collapse, decline, descend, diminish, disappear, drop, dwindle, ebb, fade, fail, fall, plunge, set (*sun sets*), slip down, subside. 2 be engulfed, be submerged, founder, go down, go under. 3 *sink a ship.* scupper, scuttle. 4 *sink a well.* bore, dig, drill, excavate.

sinner *n* evil-doer, malefactor, miscreant, offender, reprobate, transgressor, wrongdoer.

sip *v* drink, lap, sample, taste.

sit *v* 1 be seated, perch, rest, seat (yourself), settle, take a seat, *inf* take the weight off your feet. 2 *sit for a portrait.* pose. 3 *sit an exam.* take, write. 4 *Parliament sat for 12 hours.* assemble, be in session, convene, gather, meet.

site *n* area, campus, ground, location, place, plot, position, setting, situation, spot.
▪ *v* ▷ SITUATE.

sitting room *n* drawing room, living room, lounge.

situate *v* build, establish, locate, place, position, put, set up, site, station.

situation *n* 1 area, locale, locality, location, place, position, setting, site, spot. 2 *awkward situation.* circumstances, condition, *inf* kettle of fish, plight, position, predicament, state of affairs. 3 *situations vacant.* job, place, position, post.

size *n* amount, area, breadth, bulk, capacity, depth, dimensions, extent, height, immensity, length, magnitude, mass, measurement, proportions, scale, scope, volume, weight, width. ▷ MEASURE.
▪ *v* **size up** ▷ ASSESS.

sizeable *adj* considerable, decent, generous, significant, worthwhile. ▷ BIG.

skate *v* glide, skim, slide.

skeleton *n* bones, frame, framework, structure.

sketch *n* 1 description, design, diagram, draft, drawing, outline, picture, plan, *inf* rough, skeleton. 2 *comic sketch.* performance, scene, skit, turn.
▪ *v* depict, draw, indicate, portray, represent. **sketch out** ▷ OUTLINE.

sketchy *adj* cursory, hasty, hurried, imperfect, incomplete, perfunctory, rough, scrappy, unfinished, unpolished. *Opp* DETAILED, PERFECT.

skid *v* aquaplane, glide, go out of control, slide, slip.

skilful *adj* able, accomplished, adept, adroit, apt, capable, competent, crafty, cunning, deft, dexterous, expert, handy, ingenious, masterly, practised, professional, proficient, talented, trained, versatile, workmanlike. ▷ CLEVER. *Opp* UNSKILFUL.

skill *n* ability, accomplishment, adroitness, aptitude, art, artistry, capability, cleverness, competence, craft, cunning, dexterity, expertise, facility, flair, gift, ingenuity, knack, mastery, professionalism, proficiency, prowess, talent, technique, versatility, workmanship.

skilled *adj* experienced, expert, qualified, trained, versed. ▷ SKILFUL.

skim *v* 1 coast, glide, sail, skate, skid, slide, slip. 2 *skim through a book.* dip into, leaf through, look through, read quickly, scan, skip.

skin *n* casing, coat, coating, complexion, covering, epidermis, exterior, film, fur, hide, husk, membrane, outside, peel, pelt, rind, shell, surface.
▪ *v* flay, pare, peel, shell, strip.

skin-deep *adj* ▷ SUPERFICIAL.

skinny *adj* bony, gaunt, lanky, scraggy. ▷ THIN.

skip *v* 1 bound, caper, cavort, dance, frisk, gambol, hop, jump, leap, prance, romp, spring. 2 *skip the boring bits.* forget, ignore, leave out, miss out, omit, pass over, skim through. 3 *skip lessons.* cut, miss, play truant from.

skirmish *n* brush, fight, *inf* set-to, tussle.
▪ *v* ▷ FIGHT.

skirt *v* avoid, border, bypass, circle, go round, *inf* steer clear of, surround.

skit *n* burlesque, parody, satire, sketch, *inf* spoof, *inf* take-off.

sky *n* air, atmosphere, *poet* firmament, *poet* heavens, stratosphere.

slab *n* block, chunk, hunk, lump, piece, slice, wedge, *inf* wodge.

slack *adj* 1 limp, loose, sagging, soft. *Opp* TIGHT. 2 *slack attitude.* careless, dilatory, disorganized, easygoing, idle, inattentive, indolent, lax, lazy, neglectful, negligent, relaxed, remiss, slothful, unbusinesslike, undisciplined. *Opp* RIGOROUS. 3 *slack trade.* quiet, slow, slow-moving, sluggish. *Opp* BUSY.
• *v* be lazy, idle, malinger, neglect your duty, shirk, *sl* skive.

slacken *v* 1 loosen, relax, release. 2 *slacken speed.* abate, decrease, ease, lessen, lower, moderate, reduce, slow down.

slacker *n inf* good-for-nothing, lazy person, *sl* skiver. ⊳ IDLER.

slake *v* allay, assuage, cool, ease, quench, relieve, satisfy.

slam *v* 1 bang, shut. 2 [*inf*] ⊳ CRITICIZE.

slander *n* backbiting, calumny, defamation, denigration, insult, libel, lie, misrepresentation, slur, smear, vilification.
• *v* blacken the name of, defame, denigrate, disparage, libel, malign, misrepresent, slur, smear, tell lies about, vilify.

slanderous *adj* abusive, damaging, defamatory, disparaging, false, libellous, lying, mendacious, scurrilous, untrue, vicious.

slang *n* argot, cant, jargon.
• *v* ⊳ INSULT. **slanging match** ⊳ QUARREL.

slant *n* 1 angle, diagonal, gradient, incline, list, pitch, ramp, slope, tilt. 2 *slant on a problem.* approach, attitude, perspective, point of view, standpoint, view, viewpoint. 3 *slant to the news.* bias, distortion, emphasis, imbalance, one-sidedness.
• *v* 1 be at an angle, incline, lean, slope, tilt. 2 *slant the news.* bias, colour, distort, twist, weight. **slanting** ⊳ OBLIQUE.

slap *v* smack, spank. ⊳ HIT.

slash *v* gash, slit. ⊳ CUT.

slaughter *n* carnage, massacre, murder. ⊳ KILLING.
• *v* butcher, massacre, murder, slay. ⊳ KILL.

slave *n* drudge, serf, servant, vassal.
• *v* drudge, grind away, labour, sweat, toil, *inf* work your fingers to the bone. ⊳ WORK.

slave-driver *n* despot, hard taskmaster, tyrant.

slaver *v* dribble, drool, foam at the mouth, salivate, slobber.

slavery *n* bondage, captivity, enslavement, servitude, subjugation. *Opp* FREEDOM.

slavish *adj* 1 abject, cringing, fawning, grovelling, humiliating, menial, obsequious, servile, submissive. 2 *slavish imitation.* close, flattering, strict, sycophantic, unimaginative, unoriginal. *Opp* INDEPENDENT.

slay *v* assassinate, butcher, destroy, execute, exterminate, martyr, massacre, murder, put to death, slaughter. ⊳ KILL.

sleazy *adj* dirty, disreputable, mean, rundown, seedy, slovenly, sordid, squalid, unprepossessing.

sledge *n* bob-sleigh, sled, sleigh, toboggan.

sleek *adj* 1 brushed, glossy, graceful, lustrous, shining, shiny, silken, silky, smooth, soft, trim, velvety, well-groomed. 2 complacent, contented, fawning, self-satisfied, *inf* smarmy, smug, suave, unctuous, well-fed.

sleep *n inf* beauty sleep, catnap, doze, *inf* forty winks, hibernation, *sl* kip, *inf* nap, repose, rest, *inf* shut-eye, siesta, slumber, snooze.
• *v* catnap, *inf* doss down, doze, *inf* drop off, drowse, fall asleep, *inf* have forty winks, hibernate, *sl* kip, *inf* nod off, rest, slumber, snooze, *inf* take a nap. **sleeping** ⊳ ASLEEP.

sleepiness *n* drowsiness, lassitude, lethargy, somnolence, tiredness, torpor.

sleepless *adj* awake, conscious, restless, *inf* tossing and turning, wakeful, watchful, wide awake. *Opp* ASLEEP.

sleepy *adj* 1 *inf* dopey, drowsy, heavy, lethargic, sluggish, somnolent, tired, weary. 2 *sleepy village.* boring, dull, inactive, quiet, restful, torpid, unexciting. *Opp* LIVELY.

slender *adj* 1 graceful, lean, narrow, slender, slight, svelte, sylphlike, thin, trim. 2 *slender thread.* fragile, tenuous. 3 *slender means.* inadequate, meagre, scanty, small. *Opp* FAT, LARGE.

slice *n* carving, layer, piece, rasher, shaving, sliver, wedge.
• *v* carve, sever, split. ⊳ CUT.

slick *adj* 1 adroit, artful, clever, cunning,

deft, dexterous, quick, skilful, smart. 2 *slick talker*. glib, plausible, *inf* smarmy, smooth, smug, suave, superficial, unctuous, urbane, wily. 3 *slick hair*. glossy, oiled, plastered down, shiny, sleek, smooth.

slide *n* 1 avalanche, landslide, landslip. 2 *photographic slide*. transparency.
• *v* coast, glide, skate, skid, skim, slip, slither, toboggan.

slight *adj* 1 imperceptible, inconsequential, inconsiderable, insignificant, little, minor, negligible, scanty, slim (*chance*), small, superficial, trifling, trivial, unimportant. 2 *slight build*. delicate, diminutive, fragile, frail, petite, slender, slim, svelte, sylphlike, thin, weak. *Opp* BIG.
• *n*, *v* ▷ INSULT.

slightly *adv* hardly, moderately, only just, scarcely. *Opp* VERY.

slim *adj* 1 graceful, lean, narrow, slender, svelte, sylphlike, trim. ▷ THIN. 2 *slim chance*. little, negligible, remote, slight, unlikely.
• *v* diet, lose weight, reduce.

slime *n* muck, mucus, mud, ooze, sludge.

slimy *adj* clammy, greasy, oily, oozy, slippery, *inf* slippy, slithery, wet.

sling *v* cast, *inf* chuck, fling, heave, hurl, launch, *inf* let fly, lob, pelt, pitch, propel, shoot, shy, throw, toss.

slink *v* creep, edge, move guiltily, prowl, skulk, slither, sneak, steal.

slinky *adj* [*inf*] clinging, close-fitting, sexy, sinuous, sleek.

slip *n* 1 accident, *inf* bloomer, blunder, error, fault, *Fr* faux pas, inaccuracy, indiscretion, lapse, miscalculation, mistake, oversight, *inf* slip of the tongue, *inf* slip-up. 2 *slip of paper*. note, piece, sheet, strip.
• *v* 1 coast, glide, skate, skid, skim, slide, slither, stumble, trip. 2 *slip into the room*. creep, edge, slink, sneak, steal. **give someone the slip** ▷ ESCAPE. **let slip** ▷ REVEAL. **slip away**, **slip the net** ▷ ESCAPE. **slip up** ▷ BLUNDER.

slippery *adj* 1 glassy, greasy, icy, lubricated, oily, slimy, *inf* slippy, slithery, smooth, wet. 2 *slippery customer*. crafty, cunning, devious, evasive, *inf* hard to pin down, *inf* shifty, sly, specious, tricky, unreliable, untrustworthy, wily.

slipshod *adj* careless, disorganized, lax, messy, slapdash, *inf* sloppy, slovenly, untidy.

slit *n* aperture, breach, break, chink, cleft, crack, cut, fissure, gap, gash, hole, incision, opening, rift, slot, split, tear, vent.
• *v* cut, gash, slice, split, tear.

slither *v* creep, glide, slide, slip, snake, worm.

sliver *n* flake, shard, shaving, snippet, splinter. ▷ PIECE.

slobber *v* ▷ SLAVER.

slogan *n* catchphrase, catchword, jingle, motto, watchword. ▷ SAYING.

slope *n* angle, ascent, bank, descent, dip, drop, gradient, fall, hill, incline, pitch, ramp, rise, slant, tilt.
• *v* ascend, bank, decline, descend, dip, fall, incline, lean, pitch, rise, shelve, slant, tilt, tip. **sloping** ▷ OBLIQUE.

sloppy *adj* 1 liquid, runny, *inf* sloshy, slushy, squelchy, watery, wet. 2 *sloppy work*. careless, disorganized, lax, messy, slapdash, slipshod, slovenly, unsystematic, untidy. 3 ▷ SENTIMENTAL.

slot *n* 1 aperture, breach, break, chink, cleft, crack, cut, gap, gash, groove, hole, incision, opening, rift, slit, split, vent. 2 *slot on a schedule*. place, space, spot, time.

sloth *n* apathy, idleness, indolence, inertia, laziness, lethargy, sluggishness, torpor.

slouch *v* droop, hunch, loaf, loll, lounge, sag, shamble, slump, stoop.

slovenly *adj* careless, *inf* couldn't-care-less, disorganized, messy, shoddy, slapdash, sleazy, *inf* sloppy, untidy. *Opp* CAREFUL.

slow *adj* 1 careful, cautious, crawling, delayed, deliberate, dilatory, gradual, lazy, leisurely, lingering, loitering, measured, moderate, painstaking, plodding, protracted, slow-moving, sluggish, steady, unhurried. 2 *slow learner*. dense, dim, dull, obtuse, *inf* thick. ▷ STUPID. 3 *slow worker*. reluctant, unenthusiastic, unwilling. ▷ SLUGGISH. *Opp* FAST.
• *v* **slow down** brake, decelerate, *inf* ease up, hold back, reduce speed. **be slow** ▷ DAWDLE, DELAY.

sludge *n* mire, muck, mud, ooze, precipitate, sediment, silt, slime, slurry, slush.

sluggish *adj* apathetic, dull, idle, inactive, lazy, lethargic, lifeless, listless, phlegmatic, slothful, torpid, unresponsive. ▷ SLOW. *Opp* LIVELY.

sluice *v* flush, rinse, swill, wash.

slumber *n*, *v* ▷ SLEEP.

slump *n* collapse, crash, decline, dip, downturn, drop, fall, falling-off, recession, trough. *Opp* BOOM.

• *v* 1 collapse, crash, decline, dive, drop, fall off, plummet, plunge, sink, slip, *inf* take a nosedive, worsen. *Opp* PROSPER. 2 *slump in a chair.* collapse, droop, flop, hunch, loll, lounge, sag, slouch, subside.

slur *n* affront, aspersion, innuendo, insinuation, insult, libel, slander, smear.
• *v* garble, mumble.

sly *adj* artful, canny, conniving, crafty, cunning, deceitful, designing, devious, *inf* foxy, furtive, guileful, insidious, knowing, scheming, secretive, *inf* shifty, shrewd, sneaky, stealthy, surreptitious, tricky, underhand, wily. *Opp* CANDID, OPEN.

smack *v* pat, slap, spank. ▷ HIT.

small *adj* 1 *inf* baby, compact, concise, cramped, diminutive, *inf* dinky, dwarf, infinitesimal, little, microscopic, midget, *inf* mini, miniature, minuscule, minute, narrow, petite, *inf* pint-sized, *inf* pocket-sized, *inf* poky, portable, pygmy, short, slight, *inf* teeny, tiny, toy, undersized, *inf* wee, *inf* weeny. 2 *small helpings.* inadequate, insufficient, meagre, mean, *inf* measly, miserly, modest, *inf* piddling, scanty, skimpy, stingy, ungenerous. 3 *small problem.* inconsequential, insignificant, minor, negligible, slight, trifling, trivial, unimportant. *Opp* BIG.
small arms ▷ WEAPON.

small-minded *adj* bigoted, hidebound, intolerant, narrowminded, parochial, petty, prejudiced, rigid, unimaginative. ▷ MEAN. *Opp* BROAD-MINDED.

smart *adj* 1 acute, artful, astute, bright, clever, crafty, *inf* cute, discerning, ingenious, intelligent, perceptive, perspicacious, quick, quick-witted, shrewd, *sl* streetwise. *Opp* DULL. 2 *smart appearance.* bright, chic, clean, dapper, *inf* dashing, elegant, fashionable, fresh, *inf* natty, neat, *inf* snazzy, spruce, stylish, tidy, trim, well-dressed, well-groomed. *Opp* SCRUFFY. 3 *smart pace.* brisk, *inf* cracking, fast, quick, rapid, *inf* rattling, speedy, swift. 4 *smart blow.* painful, sharp, stinging.
• *v* ▷ HURT.

smash *v* 1 crumple, crush, demolish, destroy, shatter, wreck. ▷ BREAK. 2 bang, bash, batter, bump, collide, crash, hammer, knock, pound, ram, slam, strike, thump. ▷ HIT.

smear *n* 1 blot, daub, mark, smudge, stain, streak. 2 *smear on your name.* aspersion, imputation, innuendo, insinuation, libel, slander, slur, vilification.
• *v* 1 dab, daub, plaster, rub, smudge, spread, wipe. 2 *smear a reputation.* blacken, defame, discredit, libel, malign, slander, stigmatize, tarnish, vilify.

smell *n* aroma, bouquet, fragrance, miasma, nose, odour, *inf* pong, redolence, reek, scent, stench, stink.
• *v* 1 *inf* get a whiff of, scent, sniff. 2 *onions smell. inf* hum, *inf* pong, reek, stink.

smelling *adj* 1 *pleasant-smelling.* aromatic, fragrant, musky, odorous, perfumed, redolent, scented. 2 *unpleasant-smelling.* fetid, foul, gamy, *inf* high, miasmic, musty, noisome, *inf* off, *inf* pongy, pungent, rank, reeking, smelly, stinking, *inf* whiffy. *Opp* ODOURLESS.

smelly *adj* ▷ SMELLING.

smile *n*, *v* beam, grin, simper, smirk.

smoke *n* 1 exhaust, fog, fumes, gas, smog, vapour. 2 cigar, cigarette, *inf* fag, pipe.
• *v* 1 fume, smoulder. 2 *smoke cigars.* inhale, puff at.

smoky *adj* clouded, foggy, hazy, sooty. *Opp* CLEAR.

smooth *adj* 1 even, flat, horizontal, level, plane, unbroken. 2 *smooth sea.* calm, peaceful, placid, quiet. 3 *smooth finish.* glassy, glossy, polished, satiny, shiny, silken, silky, sleek, soft, velvety. 4 *smooth progress.* comfortable, easy, effortless, steady, uneventful, uninterrupted, unobstructed. 5 *smooth taste.* agreeable, bland, mellow, mild, pleasant. 6 *smooth mixture.* creamy, runny. 7 *smooth talker.* convincing, facile, glib, plausible, polite, self-assured, self-satisfied, slick, smug, sophisticated, suave, urbane. *Opp* ROUGH.
• *v* even out, file, flatten, iron, level, level off, plane, polish, press, roll out, sand down.

smother *v* 1 asphyxiate, choke, cover, kill, snuff out, stifle, strangle, suffocate, throttle. 2 ▷ SUPPRESS.

smoulder *v* burn, smoke. **smouldering** ▷ ANGRY.

smudge *v* blot, blur, dirty, mark, smear, stain, streak.

smug *adj* complacent, conceited, *inf* holier-than-thou, self-righteous, self-satisfied, sleek, superior. *Opp* HUMBLE.

snack *n* bite, *inf* elevenses, light meal, *inf* nibble, refreshments.

snack bar *n* buffet, café, cafeteria, fast-food restaurant.

snag *n* catch, complication, difficulty, drawback, hindrance, hitch, obstacle, problem, stumbling block.

• *v* catch, jag, rip, tear.

snake *n* serpent.
• *v* crawl, creep, meander, twist and turn, wander, worm, zigzag. **snaking** ▷ TWISTY.

snap *adj* ▷ SUDDEN.
• *v* 1 crack, fracture, split. ▷ BREAK. 2 *snap your fingers.* click, crack. 3 *The dog snapped at his heels.* bite, gnash, nip. 4 *Don't snap at me!* bark, growl, *inf* jump down someone's throat, snarl, speak angrily.

snare *n* ambush, booby-trap, noose, trap.
• *v* capture, catch, ensnare, entrap, net, trap.

snarl *v* 1 bare the teeth, growl. 2 *snarl up rope.* confuse, knot, tangle, twist.

snatch *v* 1 catch, clutch, grab, grasp, lay hold of, pluck, seize, take. 2 abduct, kidnap, steal.

sneak *v* 1 creep, move stealthily, prowl, skulk, slink, stalk, steal. 2 [*inf*] *sl* grass, inform (against), report, *sl* snitch, *inf* tell tales (about).

sneaking *adj* half-formed, intuitive, nagging, *inf* niggling, private, uncomfortable, worrying.

sneaky *adj* cheating, contemptible, crafty, deceitful, despicable, devious, dishonest, furtive, nasty, *inf* shady, *inf* shifty, sly, treacherous, underhand, unscrupulous, untrustworthy. *Opp* STRAIGHTFORWARD.

sneer *v* be contemptuous, be scornful, hiss, jeer, scoff. **sneer at** ▷ DENIGRATE, RIDICULE.

sniff *v* 1 *inf* get a whiff of, scent, smell. 2 ▷ SNIVEL. 3 ▷ SNEER.

snigger *v* chuckle, giggle, laugh, snicker, titter.

snip *v* clip, nick, nip. ▷ CUT.

snipe *v* fire, shoot, *inf* take pot-shots. **snipe at** ▷ CRITICIZE.

snippet *n* fragment, morsel, scrap, shred, snatch. ▷ PIECE.

snivel *v* *inf* grizzle, sniff, sniffle, snuffle, whimper, whine, *inf* whinge. ▷ WEEP.

snobbish *adj* affected, condescending, disdainful, highfalutin, *inf* hoity-toity, patronizing, pompous, *inf* posh, pretentious, *inf* snooty, *inf* stuck-up, supercilious, superior, *inf* toffee-nosed. ▷ CONCEITED. *Opp* UNPRETENTIOUS.

snoop *v* be inquisitive, interfere, intrude, investigate, meddle, nose about, pry, sneak, spy, *inf* stick your nose in.

snooper *n* busybody, detective, investigator, meddler, spy.

snout *n* face, muzzle, nose, nozzle, proboscis, trunk.

snub *v* be rude to, brush off, cold-shoulder, disdain, humiliate, insult, offend, *inf* put someone down, rebuff, reject, scorn, *inf* squash.

snuff *v* extinguish, put out. **snuff it** ▷ DIE. **snuff out** ▷ KILL.

snug *adj* 1 comfortable, *inf* comfy, cosy, enclosed, friendly, intimate, protected, reassuring, relaxed, relaxing, restful, safe, secure, sheltered, soft, warm. 2 *snug fit.* close-fitting, exact, well-tailored.

soak *v* bathe, drench, dunk, immerse, marinate, permeate, saturate, souse, steep, submerge, wet thoroughly. **soaked, soaking** ▷ WET. **soak up** ▷ ABSORB.

soar *v* 1 ascend, climb, float, fly, glide, rise, tower. 2 *prices soared.* escalate, increase, rise, rocket, shoot up, spiral.

sob *v* cry, howl, snivel, *inf* sob your heart out. ▷ WEEP.

sober *adj* 1 calm, clear-headed, composed, dignified, grave, in control, level-headed, quiet, rational, sedate, sensible, serious, solemn, steady, subdued, unexciting. *Opp* SILLY. 2 *sober habits.* abstemious, moderate, restrained, self-controlled, staid, teetotal, temperate. *Opp* DRUNK. 3 *sober dress.* drab, dull, plain, sombre.

sociable *adj* affable, approachable, companionable, convivial, extroverted, friendly, gregarious, hospitable, neighbourly, outgoing, warm, welcoming. *Opp* UNFRIENDLY, WITHDRAWN.

social *adj* 1 *social events.* collective, communal, community, group, popular, public. 2 *social person.* ▷ SOCIABLE. *Opp* SOLITARY.
• *n* dance, disco, *inf* do, gathering, *inf* get-together, party, reception, reunion, soirée.

socialize *v* associate, be sociable, entertain, fraternize, get together, *inf* go out together, mix.

society *n* 1 civilization, the community, culture, mankind, nation, people, the public. 2 *the society of our friends.* camaraderie, companionship, company, fellowship, friendship. 3 *secret society.* alliance, association, circle, club, group, guild, league, organization, union.

sofa *n* chaise longue, couch, seat, settee.

soft *adj* 1 crumbly, cushiony, flexible, floppy, limp, malleable, mushy, plastic, pliable, pliant, pulpy, spongy, springy, squashy, supple, yielding. 2 *soft ground.* boggy, marshy, muddy, sodden, waterlogged. 3 *soft bed.* comfortable, cosy. 4 *soft texture.* downy, feathery, fleecy, fluffy, furry, satiny, silky, sleek, smooth, velvety. 5 *soft music, light.* dim, faint, low, muted, quiet, relaxing, restful, soothing, subdued. 6 *soft breeze.* balmy, delicate, gentle, light, mild, pleasant. 7 [*inf*] *soft option.* easy, undemanding. 8 *soft feelings.* ▷ SOFT-HEARTED. *Opp* HARD, HARSH, VIOLENT.

soften *v* 1 *soften the blow.* abate, alleviate, cushion, moderate, mitigate, reduce, temper. 2 *soften the high notes* deaden, lower, muffle, quell, quieten, tone down, turn down. 3 *soften in attitude.* concur, ease up, give in, give way, *inf* let up, relax, succumb, weaken, yield. 4 *soften him up.* appease, mellow, mollify, pacify. *Opp* HARDEN, INTENSIFY.

soft-hearted *adj* compassionate, easygoing, generous, gentle, indulgent, *derog* lax, lenient, mild, sentimental, *inf* soft, sympathetic, tender, tender-hearted, understanding. ▷ KIND. *Opp* CRUEL.

soggy *adj* drenched, dripping, heavy (*soil*), saturated, soaked, sodden, sopping, wet through. ▷ WET. *Opp* DRY.

soil *n* clay, dirt, earth, ground, humus, land, loam, topsoil.
• *v* blacken, contaminate, defile, dirty, pollute, smear, stain, sully, tarnish.

solace *n* comfort, consolation, reassurance.
• *v* ▷ CONSOLE.

soldier *n* fighter, mercenary, serviceman, servicewoman, trooper, *pl* troops, veteran, warrior.
• *v* **soldier on** ▷ PERSIST.

sole *adj* exclusive, individual, lone, one, only, single, singular, solitary, unique.

solemn *adj* 1 earnest, gloomy, glum, grave, grim, long-faced, reserved, sedate, serious, sober, sombre, staid, thoughtful, unsmiling. *Opp* CHEERFUL. 2 *solemn occasion.* august, awe-inspiring, ceremonial, ceremonious, dignified, formal, grand, important, imposing, impressive, momentous, ritualistic, stately. *Opp* FRIVOLOUS.

solicit *v* appeal for, ask for, beg, entreat, importune, petition, seek.

solicitous *adj* 1 attentive, caring, concerned, considerate, sympathetic. 2 ▷ ANXIOUS.

solid *adj* 1 *solid ground.* compact, concrete, hard, impenetrable, impermeable. 2 *solid with people.* crammed, crowded, jammed, packed. 3 *solid gold.* authentic, genuine, pure, real, unadulterated, unalloyed. 4 *ten solid hours.* continuous, unbroken, uninterrupted, unrelieved, whole. 5 *solid foundations.* firm, fixed, robust, sound, stable, steady, stout, strong, sturdy, substantial, well-made. 6 *solid shape.* cubic, rounded, spherical, three-dimensional. 7 *solid evidence.* authoritative, cogent, coherent, convincing, genuine, indisputable, irrefutable, proven, real, sound, tangible, weighty. 8 *solid support.* dependable, reliable, stalwart, strong, trustworthy, unanimous, united, unwavering, vigorous. *Opp* FLUID, FRAGMENTARY, WEAK.

solidarity *n* accord, agreement, coherence, concord, harmony, like-mindedness, unanimity, unity. *Opp* DISUNITY.

solidify *v* cake, clot, coagulate, congeal, crystallize, freeze, harden, *inf* jell, set, thicken. *Opp* LIQUEFY.

soliloquy *n* monologue, speech.

solitary *adj* 1 alone, friendless, isolated, lonely, reclusive, unsociable, withdrawn. 2 *solitary survivor.* individual, one, only, single, sole. 3 *solitary place.* desolate, distant, hidden, isolated, out-of-the-way, private, remote, secluded, unfrequented. *Opp* NUMEROUS, PUBLIC, SOCIAL.
• *n* anchorite, hermit, *inf* loner, recluse.

solitude *n* isolation, loneliness, privacy, remoteness, retirement, seclusion.

solo *adv* alone, individually, on your own, unaccompanied.

soloist *n* musician, performer, player, singer.

soluble *adj* explicable, solvable, understandable. *Opp* INSOLUBLE.

solution *n* 1 answer, conclusion, elucidation, explanation, key, resolution, solving, unravelling, working out. 2 *chemical solution.* compound, mixture, suspension.

solve *v* answer, clear up, *inf* crack, explain, figure out, find the solution to, puzzle out, resolve, unravel, work out.

solvent *adj* creditworthy, in credit, profitable, solid, sound, viable. *Opp* BANKRUPT.

sombre *adj* bleak, cheerless, dark, dim, dismal, doleful, drab, dull, funereal, gloomy, grave, grey, lugubrious, melancholy, morose, mournful, serious, sober. ▷ SAD. *Opp* CHEERFUL.

somewhat *adv* fairly, moderately, *inf* pretty, quite, rather.

song *n* air, anthem, ballad, carol, chant, *inf* ditty, folk song, *inf* hit, hymn, jingle, lullaby, lyric, number, psalm, serenade, tune.

sonorous *adj* deep, full, loud, powerful, resonant, resounding, reverberant, rich, ringing. *Opp* SHRILL.

soon *adv old use* anon, *inf* any minute now, before long, *inf* in a minute, presently, quickly, shortly.

sooner *adv* 1 before, earlier. 2 preferably, rather.

soothe *v* allay, appease, assuage, calm, comfort, ease, mollify, pacify, quiet, relieve, salve, settle, still.

soothing *adj* 1 *soothing lotion.* comforting, emollient, healing, mild, palliative. 2 *soothing music.* calming, gentle, peaceful, pleasant, reassuring, relaxing, restful.

sophisticated *adj* 1 adult, *sl* cool, cosmopolitan, cultivated, cultured, elegant, fashionable, *inf* grown-up, mature, polished, *inf* posh, refined, stylish, urbane, worldly. *Opp* UNSOPHISTICATED. 2 *sophisticated ideas.* advanced, clever, complex, complicated, elaborate, ingenious, intricate, involved, subtle. *Opp* PRIMITIVE, SIMPLE.

soporific *adj* boring, hypnotic, sleep-inducing, tedious. *Opp* LIVELY.

sorcerer *n* enchanter, enchantress, magician, magus, medicine man, necromancer, sorceress, *old use* warlock, witch, witch-doctor, wizard.

sorcery *n* black magic, charms, incantations, magic, *inf* mumbo-jumbo, necromancy, the occult, spells, voodoo, witchcraft, wizardry.

sordid *adj* 1 dingy, dirty, disreputable, filthy, foul, miserable, nasty, seamy, seedy, sleazy, *inf* slummy, squalid, ugly, unclean, undignified, unpleasant, unsanitary, wretched. *Opp* CLEAN. 2 *sordid dealings.* base, corrupt, despicable, dishonourable, ignoble, ignominious, immoral, mean, mercenary, selfish, shabby, shameful, unethical, unscrupulous. *Opp* HONOURABLE.

sore *adj* 1 aching, burning, chafing, hurting, inflamed, painful, raw, red, sensitive, smarting, stinging, tender. 2 aggrieved, hurt, irked, *inf* peeved, *inf* put out, resentful, upset. ▷ ANNOYED.
▪ *n* abrasion, abscess, boil, bruise, burn, graze, inflammation, injury, laceration, rawness, scrape, spot, swelling, ulcer, wound. **make sore** burn, bruise, chafe, graze, hurt, inflame, redden, rub.

sorrow *n* 1 anguish, dejection, depression, desolation, despair, despondency, disappointment, dissatisfaction, distress, gloom, glumness, grief, heartache, heartbreak, heaviness, homesickness, hopelessness, loneliness, melancholy, misery, misfortune, mourning, sadness, suffering, tearfulness, trouble, unhappiness, wistfulness, woe, wretchedness. *Opp* HAPPINESS. 2 guilt, penitence, regret, remorse, repentance.
▪ *v* agonize, be sorrowful, bewail, grieve, lament, mourn, weep. *Opp* REJOICE.

sorrowful *adj* broken-hearted, dejected, disconsolate, doleful, grief-stricken, heartbroken, lugubrious, melancholy, miserable, mournful, rueful, saddened, sombre, tearful, unhappy, upset, woebegone, woeful, wretched. ▷ SAD, SORRY. *Opp* HAPPY.

sorry *adj* 1 apologetic, ashamed, conscience-stricken, contrite, guilt-ridden, penitent, regretful, remorseful, repentant, shamefaced. 2 *sorry for the homeless.* compassionate, concerned, pitying, sympathetic.

sort *n* 1 brand, category, class, classification, description, form, genre, group, kind, make, mark, nature, quality, set, type, variety. 2 breed, class, family, genus, race, species, stock, strain, variety.
▪ *v* arrange, catalogue, categorize, classify, divide, file, grade, group, order, organize, put in order, rank, systematize, tidy. *Opp* MIX. **sort out** 1 choose, *inf* put on one side, select, separate, set aside. 2 *sort out a problem.* attend to, clear up, cope with, deal with, handle, manage, organize, put right, resolve, solve, straighten out, tackle.

soul *n* 1 psyche, spirit. 2 [*inf*] *poor soul!* ▷ PERSON.

soulful *adj* deeply felt, emotional, expressive, fervent, inspiring, moving, passionate, profound, sincere, uplifting, warm.

soulless *adj* cold, inhuman, mechanical, perfunctory, routine, superficial, trite, unemotional, unfeeling, uninspiring.

sound *adj* 1 durable, fit, healthy, hearty, *inf* in good shape, robust, secure, solid, strong, sturdy, tough, undamaged, uninjured, unscathed, vigorous, well, whole. 2 *sound food.* eatable, edible, fit for human consumption, good,

wholesome. 3 *sound ideas.* balanced, coherent, commonsense, convincing, correct, judicious, logical, prudent, rational, reasonable, reasoned, sane, sensible, well-founded, wise. 4 *a sound business.* dependable, established, profitable, recognized, reliable, reputable, safe, secure, trustworthy, viable. *Opp* BAD, WEAK.
• *n* bang, clamour, clatter, din, echo, murmur, noise, resonance, reverberation, ring, rumble, thunder, timbre, tone.
• *v* 1 become audible, be heard, echo, make a noise, resonate, resound, reverberate. 2 *sound an alarm.* activate, make, produce, set off. **sound out** check, examine, investigate, measure, plumb, probe, research, survey, test, try.

soup *n* broth, consommé, stock.

sour *adj* 1 acid, acidic, bitter, citrus, lemony, sharp, tangy, tart, unripe, vinegary. 2 *sour milk.* bad, curdled, *inf* off, rancid, stale, turned. 3 *sour remarks.* acerbic, bad-tempered, bitter, caustic, curmudgeonly, cynical, disaffected, disagreeable, grudging, grumpy, ill-natured, irritable, jaundiced, peevish, snappy, testy, unpleasant.

source *n* 1 author, cause, creator, derivation, informant, initiator, originator, root, starting point. 2 *source of river.* head, origin, spring, start, well-spring. ▷ BEGINNING.

souvenir *n* heirloom, keepsake, memento, relic, reminder.

sovereign *adj* 1 absolute, all-powerful, dominant, highest, royal, supreme. 2 *sovereign state.* autonomous, independent, self-governing.
• *n* emperor, empress, king, monarch, prince, princess, queen. ▷ RULER.

sow *v* broadcast, disseminate, plant, scatter, seed, spread.

space *adj* extraterrestrial, interplanetary, interstellar.
• *n* 1 emptiness, infinity, ionosphere, stratosphere, the universe. 2 *space to move. inf* elbow-room, expanse, freedom, latitude, leeway, margin, room, scope, spaciousness. 3 *an empty space.* area, blank, break, distance, duration, gap, hiatus, intermission, interval, lacuna, lapse, opening, place, spell, stretch, time, vacuum, wait.
• *v space things out.* ▷ ARRANGE.

spacious *adj* ample, broad, capacious, commodious, extensive, large, open, roomy, sizeable, vast, wide. ▷ BIG. *Opp* SMALL.

span *n* breadth, compass, distance, duration, extent, interval, length, period, reach, scope, stretch, term, width.
• *v* arch over, bridge, cross, extend across, reach over, straddle, stretch over, traverse.

spank *v* slap, slipper, smack. ▷ HIT, PUNISH.

spar *v* box, exchange blows, scrap. ▷ FIGHT.

spare *adj* 1 additional, auxiliary, extra, free, inessential, in reserve, leftover, odd, remaining, superfluous, supplementary, surplus, unnecessary, unneeded, unused, unwanted. *Opp* NECESSARY. 2 *a spare figure.* ▷ THIN.
• *v* 1 be merciful to, forgive, free, have mercy on, let go, let off, pardon, release, reprieve, save. 2 *spare money, time.* afford, allow, donate, give, give up, manage, part with, provide, sacrifice. **sparing** ▷ ECONOMICAL, MISERLY.

spark *n* flash, flicker, gleam, glint, sparkle.
• *v* **spark off** ignite, kindle. ▷ PROVOKE.

sparkle *v* flash, flicker, gleam, glint, glitter, reflect, scintillate, shine, spark, twinkle, wink.

sparkling *adj* 1 brilliant, flashing, glinting, glittering, scintillating, shining, shiny, twinkling. ▷ BRIGHT. *Opp* DULL. 2 bubbling, bubbly, carbonated, effervescent, fizzy, foaming.

sparse *adj inf* few and far between, inadequate, light, little, meagre, scanty, scarce, scattered, thin, *inf* thin on the ground. *Opp* PLENTIFUL.

spartan *adj* abstemious, ascetic, austere, bare, bleak, frugal, hard, harsh, plain, rigorous, severe, simple, stern, strict. *Opp* LUXURIOUS.

spasm *n* attack, convulsion, eruption, fit, jerk, paroxysm, seizure, *pl* throes, twitch.

spasmodic *adj* erratic, fitful, intermittent, irregular, jerky, occasional, *inf* on and off, periodic, sporadic. *Opp* CONTINUOUS, REGULAR.

spate *n* cataract, flood, flow, gush, inundation, outpouring, rush, torrent.

spatter *v* bespatter, daub, pepper, scatter, shower, slop, speckle, splash, splatter, spray, sprinkle.

speak *v* answer, articulate, communicate, converse, declaim, declare, deliver a speech, discourse, enunciate, express yourself, harangue, hold a conversation, *inf* hold forth, *inf* pipe up, recite, say something, soliloquize, tell, utter, verbalize, vocalize, voice. ▷ SAY, TALK. **speak about** ▷ MENTION. **speak to** ▷ ADDRESS. **speak your mind** be honest, say what you think, speak honestly, speak out, state your opinion, voice your thoughts.

speaker *n* lecturer, orator, spokesperson.

spear *n* assegai, harpoon, javelin, lance, pike.

special *adj* 1 distinguished, exceptional, extraordinary, important, memorable, momentous, notable, noteworthy, out of the ordinary, rare, red-letter (*day*), remarkable, significant, uncommon, unconventional, unusual. *Opp* ORDINARY. 2 *She has a special style.* characteristic, distinctive, idiosyncratic, peculiar, singular, unique, unmistakable. 3 *my special chair.* especial, individual, particular, personal. 4 *He's a special friend of mine.* close, dear, intimate, particular, valued.

specialist *n* 1 authority, connoisseur, expert, master, professional, pundit. 2 [*medical*] consultant.

speciality *n* expertise, field, forte, genius, *inf* line, specialization, special skill, strength, strong point, talent.

specialize *v* **specialize in** be a specialist in, concentrate on, devote yourself to, have a reputation for.

specialized *adj* esoteric, expert, specialist, technical.

species *n* breed, class, genus, kind, race, sort, type, variety.

specific *adj* clear-cut, defined, definite, detailed, exact, explicit, express, individual, named, particular, peculiar, precise, predetermined, special, specified, unequivocal. *Opp* GENERAL.

specify *v* be specific about, define, detail, enumerate, identify, itemize, list, name, spell out, stipulate.

specimen *n* example, illustration, instance, model, pattern, representative, sample.

specious *adj* deceptive, misleading, plausible.

speck *n* bit, crumb, dot, fleck, grain, mark, mite, mote, particle, speckle, spot, trace.

speckled *adj* brindled, dappled, dotted, flecked, freckled, mottled, patchy, spattered (with), spotted, spotty, sprinkled (with), stippled.

spectacle *n* ceremony, display, exhibition, extravaganza, grandeur, magnificence, ostentation, pageantry, parade, pomp, show, sight, splendour. **spectacles** glasses, *inf* specs.

spectacular *adj* breathtaking, colourful, dramatic, eye-catching, impressive, magnificent, sensational, showy, splendid, stunning.

spectator *n pl* audience, bystander, *pl* crowd, eye-witness, looker-on, observer, onlooker, viewer, watcher, witness.

spectre *n* apparition, ghost, phantom, spirit, vision, wraith.

spectrum *n* scale, scope, variety. ▷ RANGE.

speculate *v* 1 conjecture, consider, hypothesize, meditate, ponder, reflect, ruminate, surmise, theorize, wonder. ▷ THINK. 2 *speculate in shares.* gamble, invest speculatively, *inf* play the market, take a chance, wager.

speculative *adj* 1 abstract, based on guesswork, conjectural, doubtful, hypothetical, notional, theoretical, unfounded, unproven, untested. *Opp* PROVEN. 2 *speculative investments. inf* chancy, *inf* dicey, *inf* dodgy, hazardous, *inf* iffy, risky, uncertain, unpredictable, unreliable. *Opp* SAFE.

speech *n* 1 articulation, communication, delivery, diction, elocution, enunciation, expression, pronunciation, speaking, talking, utterance. 2 dialect, idiom, jargon, language, parlance, register, tongue. 3 *public speech.* address, discourse, disquisition, harangue, homily, lecture, oration, paper, presentation, sermon, *sl* spiel, talk, tirade. 4 *speech in a play.* dialogue, lines, monologue, soliloquy.

speechless *adj* dumb, dumbfounded, dumbstruck, mute, silent, thunderstruck, tongue-tied, voiceless. *Opp* TALKATIVE.

speed *n* 1 pace, rate, tempo, velocity. 2 alacrity, briskness, haste, hurry, quickness, rapidity, speediness, swiftness.
• *v* 1 bolt, *inf* bowl along, career, dash, dart, flash, fly, gallop, *inf* go like the wind, hasten, hurry, hurtle, make haste, *inf* nip, *inf* put your foot down, race, run, rush, shoot, sprint, stampede, streak, tear, *inf* zoom. 2 break the speed limit, go too fast. **speed up** ▷ ACCELERATE.

speedy *adj* 1 fast, nimble, quick, rapid, swift. 2 *speedy exit.* hasty, hurried, immediate, precipitate, prompt. *Opp* SLOW.

spell *n* 1 bewitchment, charm, enchantment, incantation, magic formula,

sorcery, witchcraft. 2 *I fell under his spell.* allure, captivation, charm, fascination, glamour, magic. 3 *spell of rain.* interval, period, phase, season. 4 *spell at the wheel.* session, stint, stretch, term, time, turn, watch.
• *v* augur, bode, foretell, indicate, mean, portend, presage, signal, signify. **spell out** ▷ CLARIFY.

spellbound *adj* bewitched, captivated, charmed, enchanted, enthralled, entranced, fascinated, hypnotized, mesmerized.

spend *v* 1 *sl* blue, consume, *inf* cough up, exhaust, expend, *inf* fork out, fritter, *inf* get through, pay out, *inf* shell out, *inf* splash out, *inf* splurge, squander. 2 *spend time.* devote, fill, occupy, pass, use up, waste.

spendthrift *n inf* big spender, wasteful person. *Opp* MISER.
• *adj* extravagant, prodical, profligate.

sphere *n* 1 ball, globe, globule, orb. 2 *sphere of influence.* area, department, domain, field, province, range, scope, speciality, subject, territory. 3 *social sphere.* caste, class, domain, milieu, position, rank, society, station, stratum, walk of life.

spherical *adj* globe-shaped, globular, rotund, round.

spice *n* 1 flavouring, piquancy, relish, seasoning. 2 *add spice to life.* colour, excitement, gusto, interest, *inf* lift, *inf* pep, vigour, zest.

spicy *adj* aromatic, fragrant, gingery, hot, peppery, piquant, seasoned, spiced, tangy, zestful. *Opp* BLAND.

spike *n* barb, nail, pin, point, prong, skewer, spine, stake, tine.
• *v* impale, perforate, pierce, skewer, spear, stab.

spill *v* 1 overturn, slop, tip over, upset. 2 brim, flow, overflow, run, pour. 3 *lorry spilled its load.* discharge, drop, shed, tip.

spin *v* 1 gyrate, pirouette, revolve, rotate, swirl, turn, twirl, twist, wheel, whirl. 2 be giddy, reel, swim. **spin out** ▷ PROLONG.

spindle *n* axle, pin, rod, shaft.

spine *n* 1 backbone, spinal column, vertebrae. 2 barb, bristle, needle, point, prickle, quill, spike, thorn.

spineless *adj* cowardly, craven, faint-hearted, feeble, irresolute, *inf* lily-livered, pusillanimous, timid, *inf* wimpish. ▷ WEAK. *Opp* BRAVE.

spiral *adj* coiled, corkscrew, turning, whorled.
• *n* coil, curl, helix, whorl.
• *v* 1 turn, twist. 2 *spiralling prices.* ▷ FALL, RISE.

spire *n* pinnacle, steeple, tower.

spirit *n* 1 mind, psyche, soul. 2 *supernatural spirits.* apparition, demon, devil, genie, ghost, ghoul, gremlin, hobgoblin, imp, phantasm, phantom, poltergeist, *poet* shade, spectre, *inf* spook, vision, visitant, wraith, zombie. 3 *spirit of the times.* atmosphere, feeling, mood. 4 *spirit of the law.* aim, essence, heart, intention, meaning, sense. 5 *fighting spirit.* bravery, cheerfulness, confidence, courage, daring, determination, dynamism, energy, enthusiasm, *inf* get-up-and-go, *inf* go, *inf* guts, heroism, liveliness, mettle, morale, motivation, optimism, pluck, valour, will-power, zest. 6 ▷ ALCOHOL.

spirited *adj* active, animated, assertive, brave, buoyant, courageous, daring, determined, dynamic, energetic, enterprising, enthusiastic, gallant, *inf* gutsy, intrepid, lively, plucky, positive, sparkling, sprightly, vigorous, vivacious. *Opp* SPIRITLESS.

spiritless *adj* apathetic, despondent, dispirited, dull, lacklustre, lethargic, lifeless, listless, negative, passive, slow, unenthusiastic. *Opp* SPIRITED.

spiritual *adj* devotional, divine, eternal, heavenly, holy, incorporeal, inspired, other-worldly, religious, sacred, unworldly, visionary. *Opp* TEMPORAL.

spit *n* 1 dribble, saliva, spittle, sputum.
• *v* dribble, expectorate, salivate, splutter. **spit out** ▷ DISCHARGE. **spitting image** ▷ TWIN.

spite *n* animosity, animus, *inf* bitchiness, bitterness, grudge, hate, hatred, hostility, ill feeling, ill will, malevolence, malice, maliciousness, rancour, resentment, venom, vindictiveness.
• *v* ▷ ANNOY.

spiteful *adj* acid, acrimonious, *inf* bitchy, bitter, *inf* catty, cruel, cutting, hateful, hostile, hurtful, ill-natured, malevolent, malicious, nasty, poisonous, rancorous, resentful, sharp, *inf* snide, sour, venomous, vicious, vindictive. *Opp* KIND.

splash *v* 1 bespatter, shower, slop, *inf* slosh, spatter, spill, splatter, spray, sprinkle, squirt, wash. 2 bathe, dabble, paddle, wade. 3 *splash across the front page.* blazon, display, flaunt, *inf* plaster, show, spread. **splash out** ▷ SPEND.

splendid *adj* admirable, awe-inspiring, beautiful, brilliant, costly, dazzling, dignified, elegant, fine, first-class, glittering, glorious, gorgeous, grand, great, handsome, imposing, impressive, lavish, luxurious, magnificent, majestic, marvellous, noble, ornate, palatial, *inf* posh, regal, resplendent, rich, royal, spectacular, stately, sublime, sumptuous, *inf* super, superb, supreme, wonderful. ▷ EXCELLENT.

splendour *n* beauty, brilliance, ceremony, display, elegance, *inf* glitter, glory, grandeur, luxury, magnificence, majesty, nobility, pomp and circumstance, richness, show, spectacle, stateliness, sumptuousness.

splice *v* bind, entwine, join, knit, marry, tie together, unite.

splinter *n* chip, flake, fragment, shard, shaving, sliver.
▪ *v* chip, crack, fracture, shatter, smash, split. ▷ BREAK.

split *n* 1 break, chink, cleavage, cleft, crack, cranny, crevice, fissure, gash, leak, opening, rent, rift, rip, rupture, slash, slit, tear. 2 breach, difference, dissension, divergence of opinion, division, divorce, estrangement, schism, separation. ▷ QUARREL.
▪ *v* 1 break up, disintegrate, divide, divorce, go separate ways, separate. 2 burst, chop, cleave, crack, rend, rip apart, rip open, slash, slice, slit, splinter, tear. ▷ CUT. 3 *split profits.* distribute, divide, halve, share. 4 *road splits.* branch, diverge, fork. **split on** ▷ INFORM.

spoil *v* 1 blight, blot, bungle, damage, deface, destroy, disfigure, harm, injure, *inf* make a mess of, mar, *inf* mess up, ruin, stain, undermine, undo, upset, vitiate, wreck. *Opp* IMPROVE. 2 curdle, decay, decompose, go bad, *inf* go off, moulder, perish, putrefy, rot, *inf* turn. 3 *spoil children.* cosset, dote on, indulge, make a fuss of, mollycoddle, overindulge, pamper.

spoken *adj* oral, unwritten, verbal. *Opp* WRITTEN.

spokesperson *n* mouthpiece, representative, spokesman, spokeswoman.

sponge *v* 1 clean, mop, rinse, wash, wipe. 2 *sponge on friends.* cadge (from), scrounge (from).

spongy *adj* absorbent, elastic, porous, soft, springy, yielding. *Opp* SOLID.

sponsor *n inf* angel, backer, benefactor, donor, patron, promoter, supporter.
▪ *v* back, finance, fund, help, promote, subsidize, support, underwrite.

sponsorship *n* auspices, backing, funding, guarantee, patronage, promotion, support.

spontaneous *adj* 1 *inf* ad lib, extempore, impromptu, impulsive, *inf* off-the-cuff, unplanned, unpremeditated, unprepared, unrehearsed, voluntary. 2 *spontaneous reaction.* automatic, instinctive, involuntary, natural, reflex, unconscious, unthinking. *Opp* PREMEDITATED.

spooky *adj* creepy, eerie, frightening, ghostly, haunted, mysterious, *inf* scary, uncanny, unearthly, weird.

spool *n* bobbin, reel.

spoon *n* dessertspoon, ladle, tablespoon, teaspoon.

spoonfeed *v* cosset, help, mollycoddle, pamper, spoil.

spoor *n* footprints, scent, traces, track, trail.

sporadic *adj* erratic, fitful, intermittent, irregular, occasional, periodic, scattered, unpredictable.

sport *n* 1 activity, amusement, diversion, entertainment, exercise, fun, games, pastime, play, pleasure, recreation. 2 badinage, banter, humour, jesting, joking, merriment, raillery, teasing.
▪ *v* 1 caper, cavort, frisk about, frolic, gambol, lark about, romp, skip about. 2 *sport new clothes.* display, exhibit, flaunt, show off, wear.

sporting *adj* considerate, fair, generous, good-humoured, honourable, sportsmanlike.

sportive *adj* coltish, frisky, light-hearted. ▷ PLAYFUL.

sportsperson *n* contestant, participant, player, sportsman, sportswoman.

sporty *adj* 1 active, athletic, energetic, fit, vigorous. 2 *sporty clothes.* casual, informal, *inf* snazzy.

spot *n* 1 blemish, blot, blotch, discoloration, dot, fleck, mark, patch, smudge, speck, speckle, stain. 2 *spot on the skin.* birthmark, boil, freckle, mole, pimple, pock-mark, *pl* rash, sty, *sl* zit. 3 *spots of rain.* bead, blob, drop. 4 *spot for a picnic.* locality, location, place, point, position, setting, site, situation. 5 *awkward spot.* difficulty, dilemma, embarrassment, mess, predicament, quandary, situation. 6 *spot of bother.* bit, small amount, *inf* smidgen.

• *v* 1 blot, fleck, mark, mottle, smudge, spatter, speckle, splash, spray, stain. 2 ▷ SEE.

spotless *adj* 1 clean, fresh, immaculate, laundered, unmarked. 2 *spotless reputation.* blameless, flawless, immaculate, innocent, irreproachable, pure, unblemished, unsullied, untarnished, *inf* whiter than white.

spotty *adj* blotchy, flecked, freckled, mottled, pimply, pock-marked, spattered, speckled, speckly, *inf* splodgy.

spouse *n inf* better half, husband, partner, wife.

spout *n* duct, fountain, geyser, jet, lip, nozzle, outlet, spray, waterspout.
• *v* 1 emit, erupt, flow, gush, jet, pour, shoot, spew, spit, spurt, squirt, stream. 2 *inf* hold forth, ramble on, rave, talk.

sprawl *v* 1 flop, lean back, lie, loll, lounge, recline, relax, slouch, slump, spread out, stretch out. 2 be scattered, spread, straggle.

spray *n* 1 droplets, fountain, mist, shower, splash, sprinkling. 2 *spray of flowers.* arrangement, bouquet, bunch, corsage, posy, sprig. 3 *paint spray.* aerosol, atomizer, spray-gun, sprinkler.
• *v* diffuse, disperse, scatter, shower, spatter, splash, sprinkle.

spread *n* 1 broadcasting, broadening, development, diffusion, dispensing, dispersal, dissemination, distribution, expansion, extension, growth, increase, passing on, proliferation. 2 *spread of a bird's wings.* breadth, compass, extent, size, span, stretch, sweep. 3 ▷ MEAL.
• *v* 1 arrange, display, lay out, open out, unfold. 2 broaden, enlarge, expand, extend, fan out, lengthen, mushroom, proliferate, straggle, widen. 3 *spread news.* broadcast, circulate, diffuse, dispense, disperse, disseminate, distribute, divulge, give out, make known, pass on, proclaim, promote, promulgate, publicize, publish, scatter, transmit. 4 *spread butter.* apply, cover with, smear, smooth.

spree *n inf* binge, escapade, *inf* fling, *inf* orgy, outing, *inf* splurge. ▷ REVELRY.

sprightly *adj* active, agile, animated, brisk, energetic, jaunty, lively, nimble, *inf* perky, playful, spirited, sportive, spry, vivacious. *Opp* LETHARGIC.

spring *n* 1 bounce, buoyancy, elasticity, give, liveliness, resilience. 2 bound, jump, leap, skip. 3 *spring of water.* fount, fountain, source (*of river*), spa, well-spring.
• *v* bounce, bound, hop, jump, leap, pounce, vault. **spring from** derive from, proceed from, stem from. **spring up** appear, develop, emerge, germinate, grow, shoot up, sprout.

springy *adj inf* bendy, elastic, flexible, pliable, resilient, spongy, stretchy, supple. *Opp* RIGID.

sprinkle *v* drip, dust, pepper, scatter, shower, spatter, splash, spray, strew.

sprint *v* dash, *inf* hare, race, speed, *inf* tear. ▷ RUN.

sprout *n* bud, shoot.
• *v* bud, develop, germinate, grow, shoot up, spring up.

spruce *adj* clean, dapper, elegant, *inf* natty, neat, smart, tidy, trim, well-dressed, well-groomed, *inf* well-turned-out. *Opp* SCRUFFY.
• *v* **spruce up** ▷ TIDY.

spur *n* encouragement, goad, impetus, incentive, incitement, inducement, motivation, motive, prod, prompting, stimulus, urging.
• *v* egg on, encourage, impel, incite, motivate, pressure, pressurize, prick, prod, prompt, stimulate, urge.

spurn *v* disown, give (someone) the cold shoulder, jilt, rebuff, reject, shun, snub, turn your back on.

spy *n* contact, double agent, *sl* grass, infiltrator, informant, informer, *inf* mole, private detective, secret agent, *inf* snooper, undercover agent.
• *v* 1 be a spy, eavesdrop, gather intelligence, inform, *inf* snoop. 2 ▷ SEE. **spy on** keep under surveillance, *inf* tail, trail, watch.

spying *n* counter-espionage, detective work, eavesdropping, espionage, intelligence, *inf* snooping, surveillance.

squabble *v* argue, bicker, *inf* row, wrangle. ▷ QUARREL.

squalid *adj* 1 dingy, dirty, disgusting, filthy, foul, insalubrious, mean, mucky, nasty, repulsive, run-down, sleazy, *inf* slummy, sordid, ugly, unpleasant, wretched. *Opp* CLEAN. 2 *squalid behaviour.* degrading, dishonest, dishonourable, disreputable, immoral, scandalous, shabby, shameful, unethical, unworthy. *Opp* HONOURABLE.

squander *v inf* blow, *sl* blue, dissipate, fritter, misuse, spend unwisely, *inf* splurge, use up, waste. *Opp* SAVE.

square *adj* 1 *square deal. inf* above-board, decent, equitable, ethical, fair, honest,

honourable, proper, *inf* straight. 2 [*inf*] *Don't be so square!* conservative, conventional, old-fashioned, *inf* stuffy.
• *n* 1 piazza, plaza. 2 [*inf*] *He's an old square.* die-hard, *inf* fuddy-duddy, *inf* old fogey, *inf* stick-in-the-mud, traditionalist.
• *v square an account.* ▷ SETTLE. **squared** chequered, criss-crossed.

squash *v* 1 compress, crumple, crush, flatten, mangle, mash, pound, press, pulp, stamp on, tread on. 2 *squash into a room.* cram, crowd, pack, push, shove, squeeze, wedge. 3 *squash an uprising.* control, put down, quash, quell, repress, suppress. 4 *squash with a look.* humiliate, *inf* put down, silence.

squashy *adj* mushy, pulpy, shapeless, soft, spongy, squelchy, yielding. *Opp* FIRM.

squat *adj* dumpy, short, stocky, thick, thickset. *Opp* TALL.
• *v* crouch, sit.

squeamish *adj inf* choosy, fastidious, finicky, particular, *inf* pernickety, prim, *inf* prissy, prudish.

squeeze *v* 1 clasp, compress, crush, embrace, enfold, exert pressure on, grip, hug, mangle, pinch, press, squash, wring. 2 cram, crowd, pack, push, ram, shove, squash, stuff, thrust, wedge. 3 *squeeze money out of someone.* extort, extract, wrest.

squirm *v* twist, wriggle, writhe.

squirt *v* gush, jet, send out, shoot, spit, splash, spout, spray, spurt.

stab *n* 1 blow, cut, jab, prick, thrust, wound. 2 *stab of pain.* pang, sting, throb, twinge.
• *v* cut, injure, jab, perforate, pierce, puncture, skewer, spike, thrust, wound. **have a stab at** ▷ TRY.

stability *n* balance, durability, equilibrium, firmness, permanence, reliability, solidity, steadiness, strength. *Opp* INSTABILITY.

stabilize *v* balance, become stable, give stability to, make stable, settle. *Opp* UPSET.

stable *adj* 1 balanced, firm, fixed, solid, steady, strong. 2 constant, continuing, durable, established, lasting, long-lasting, permanent, predictable, reliable, steadfast, unchanging, unwavering. 3 *stable personality.* balanced, even-tempered, sane, sensible. *Opp* UNSTABLE.

stack *n* 1 accumulation, heap, hoard, mound, mountain, pile, quantity, stockpile, store. 2 chimney, pillar, smokestack. 3 *stack of hay.* haystack, rick, stook.
• *v* accumulate, amass, assemble, collect, gather, heap, load, mass, pile, *inf* stash away, stockpile.

stadium *n* amphitheatre, arena, ground, sports ground.

staff *n* 1 baton, crook, crosier, flagstaff, pole, rod, sceptre, shaft, stake, standard, stick, wand. 2 assistants, crew, employees, *old use* hands, personnel, team, workers, workforce.
• *v* man, provide with staff, run.

stage *n* 1 dais, performing area, platform, podium, rostrum. 2 *stage of a journey.* juncture, leg, phase, point, time.
• *v* arrange, *inf* get up, mount, organize, perform, present, produce, put on, set up, stage-manage.

stagger *v* 1 falter, lurch, reel, rock, stumble, sway, teeter, totter, walk unsteadily, waver, wobble. 2 *price staggered us.* amaze, astonish, astound, dismay, dumbfound, flabbergast, shake, shock, startle, stun, stupefy, surprise.

stagnant *adj* motionless, sluggish, stale, standing, static, still. *Opp* MOVING.

stagnate *v* become stale, be stagnant, degenerate, deteriorate, idle, languish, vegetate. *Opp* PROGRESS.

stain *n* 1 blemish, blot, blotch, discoloration, mark, smear, speck, spot. 2 *wood stain.* colouring, dye, paint, pigment, tinge, tint, varnish.
• *v* 1 blacken, blemish, blot, contaminate, dirty, discolour, mark, smudge, soil, tarnish. 2 *stain your reputation.* damage, defile, disgrace, shame, spoil, sully, taint. 3 *stain wood.* colour, dye, paint, tinge, tint, varnish.

stair *n* riser, step, tread. **stairs** escalator, flight of stairs, staircase, stairway, steps.

stake *n* 1 paling, pole, post, rod, shaft, stick. 2 bet, pledge, wager.
• *v* 1 fasten, hitch, tether, tie up. 2 *stake a claim.* establish, put on record, state. 3 *stake my life on it.* bet, chance, gamble, hazard, risk, venture, wager. **stake out** define, demarcate, enclose, fence in, mark off, outline.

stale *adj* 1 dry, hard, mouldy, musty, *inf* off, old, *inf* past its best, tasteless. 2 *stale ideas.* banal, clichéd, hackneyed, old-fashioned, overused, stock, *inf* tired, trite, uninteresting, unoriginal, worn out. *Opp* FRESH.

stalemate *n* deadlock, impasse, standstill.

stalk *n* branch, shoot, stem, trunk, twig.
• *v* 1 follow, hunt, pursue, shadow, *inf* tail, track, trail. 2 *stalk about.* prowl, rove, stride, strut.

stall *n* booth, compartment, kiosk, stand, table.
• *v* delay, hang back, hesitate, pause, *inf* play for time, postpone, prevaricate, procrastinate, put off, stop, temporize, waste time.

stalwart *adj* dependable, determined, faithful, indomitable, intrepid, reliable, resolute, robust, staunch, steadfast, sturdy, tough, trustworthy, valiant. ▷ BRAVE, STRONG. *Opp* WEAK.

stamina *n* endurance, energy, *inf* grit, resilience, staying power, strength.

stammer *v* falter, hesitate, splutter, stumble, stutter.

stamp *n* 1 brand, hallmark, impression, imprint, print, seal. 2 franking, postage stamp. 3 *stamp of genius.* characteristic, mark, sign.
• *v* 1 squash, *inf* stomp, trample, tread. 2 *stamp a mark.* brand, emboss, engrave, impress, imprint, label, mark, print. **stamp on** ▷ SUPPRESS. **stamp out** ▷ ELIMINATE.

stampede *n* charge, dash, rout, rush, sprint.
• *v* 1 bolt, career, charge, dash, gallop, run, rush, sprint, *inf* take to your heels, *inf* tear. 2 *stampede cattle.* frighten, panic, scatter.

stand *n* 1 base, pedestal, rack, support, tripod. 2 booth, kiosk, stall. 3 grandstand, terraces.
• *v* 1 arise, get to your feet, get up, rise. 2 *Stand it on the floor.* arrange, deposit, locate, place, position, put up, set up, situate, station. 3 *My offer stands.* be unchanged, continue, remain valid, stay. 4 *I can't stand it any longer.* abide, bear, endure, put up with, suffer, tolerate, *inf* wear. **stand by** ▷ SUPPORT. **stand for** ▷ SYMBOLIZE. **stand in for** ▷ DEPUTIZE. **stand out** ▷ SHOW. **stand up for** ▷ PROTECT, SUPPORT. **stand up to** ▷ RESIST.

standard *adj* accepted, accustomed, approved, average, basic, classic, common, conventional, customary, definitive, established, everyday, familiar, habitual, normal, official, ordinary, orthodox, popular, prevailing, prevalent, recognized, regular, routine, set, staple (*diet*), stock, traditional, typical, universal, usual. *Opp* UNUSUAL.
• *n* 1 archetype, benchmark, criterion, example, gauge, grade, guide, guideline, ideal, level of achievement, measure, model, paradigm, pattern, requirement, rule, sample, touchstone, yardstick. 2 average, level, mean, norm. 3 *standard of a regiment.* ▷ FLAG. 4 *lamp standard.* column, pillar, pole, post, support, upright. **standards** ▷ MORALITY.

standardize *v* average out standard, equalize, normalize, stereotype, systematize.

standoffish *adj* aloof, antisocial, cold, cool, distant, frosty, haughty, remote, reserved, reticent, secretive, *inf* snooty, taciturn, unapproachable, unforthcoming, unfriendly, unsociable, withdrawn. *Opp* FRIENDLY.

standpoint *n* angle, attitude, belief, opinion, perspective, point of view, position, stance, vantage point, view, viewpoint.

standstill *n inf* dead end, deadlock, halt, impasse, stalemate, stop, stoppage.

staple *adj* basic, chief, important, main, principal. ▷ STANDARD.

star *n* 1 celestial body, comet, evening star, falling star, morning star, shooting star. 2 asterisk, pentagram. 3 *TV star.* attraction, big name, celebrity, diva, *inf* draw, idol, leading lady, leading man, personage, starlet, *inf* superstar. ▷ PERFORMER.

starchy *adj* conventional, formal, prim, stiff. ▷ UNFRIENDLY.

stare *v* gape, *inf* gawp, gaze, glare, goggle, look fixedly, peer. **stare at** contemplate, examine, eye, scrutinize, study, watch.

stark *adj* 1 austere, bare, bleak, depressing, desolate, dreary, gloomy, grim. 2 *stark contrast.* absolute, clear, complete, perfect, plain, sharp, sheer, total, unqualified, utter.

start *n* 1 beginning, birth, commencement, creation, dawn, establishment, founding, inauguration, inception, initiation, institution, introduction, launch, onset, opening, origin, outset, point of departure, setting out. *Opp* FINISH. 2 *unfair start.* advantage, edge, head start, opportunity. 3 *The loan gave me a start.* assistance, backing, *inf* break, financing, help, sponsorship. 4 *I woke with a start.* jump, shock, surprise.
• *v* 1 depart, *inf* get going, get under way, *sl* hit the road, leave, move off, proceed, set off, set out. 2 activate, begin, commence, create, embark on, engender, establish, found, *inf* get off the ground, *inf* get the ball rolling,

inaugurate, initiate, instigate, institute, introduce, launch, open, originate, pioneer, set in motion, set up. *Opp* FINISH. 3 blench, draw back, flinch, jerk, jump, quail, recoil, shy, twitch, wince. **make someone start** ▷ STARTLE.

startle *v* alarm, catch unawares, disturb, frighten, jolt, make you jump, scare, shake, shock, surprise, take aback, take by surprise, upset. **startling** ▷ SURPRISING.

starvation *n* deprivation, famine, hunger, malnutrition, undernourishment, want.

starve *v* die of starvation, go hungry, go without, perish. **starve yourself** diet, fast, go on hunger strike, refuse food. **starving** ▷ HUNGRY.

state *n* 1 *pl* circumstances, condition, health, mood, *inf* shape, situation. 2 agitation, excitement, *inf* flap, panic, plight, predicament, *inf* tizzy. 3 *sovereign state.* land, nation. ▷ COUNTRY.
• *v* affirm, announce, assert, communicate, declare, express, formulate, proclaim, put into words, report, submit, testify, voice. ▷ SAY, SPEAK.

stately *adj* august, dignified, distinguished, formal, grand, imperial, imposing, impressive, lofty, majestic, noble, regal, royal, solemn, splendid. *Opp* INFORMAL. **stately home** ▷ MANSION.

statement *n* account, affirmation, announcement, assertion, bulletin, comment, communiqué, declaration, disclosure, explanation, message, notice, proclamation, proposition, report, testimony, utterance.

statesman *n* diplomat, politician.

static *adj* fixed, immobile, immovable, inert, invariable, motionless, passive, stable, stagnant, stationary, still, unchanging, unmoving. *Opp* MOBILE, VARIABLE.

station *n* 1 calling, class, level, location, occupation, place, position, post, rank, situation, standing, status. 2 *fire station.* base, depot, headquarters, office. 3 *radio station.* channel, company, wavelength. 4 *railway station.* halt, platform, terminus, train station.
• *v* assign, garrison, locate, place, position, put, site, situate, spot, stand.

stationary *adj* at a standstill, halted, immobile, motionless, parked, standing, static, still, stock-still, unmoving. *Opp* MOVING.

stationery *n* paper, office supplies, writing materials.

statistics *n* data, figures, information, numbers.

statue *n* carving, figure, statuette. ▷ SCULPTURE.

statuesque *adj* dignified, imposing, impressive, stately.

stature *n* 1 build, height, size. 2 *artist of international stature.* importance, reputation, standing. ▷ STATUS.

status *n* class, degree, eminence, grade, importance, level, position, prestige, prominence, rank, reputation, significance, standing, station, stature, title.

staunch *adj* ▷ STEADFAST.

stay *n* 1 holiday, stop, stopover, visit. 2 *stay of execution.* ▷ DELAY. 3 ▷ SUPPORT.
• *v* 1 carry on, continue, endure, hang about, hold out, keep on, last, linger, live on, loiter, persist, remain, survive, wait. 2 *stay in a hotel.* abide, be a guest, be housed, board, dwell, live, lodge, reside, stop, visit. 3 *stay judgement.* ▷ DELAY.

steadfast *adj* committed, constant, dedicated, dependable, devoted, faithful, firm, loyal, patient, persevering, reliable, resolute, single-minded, sound, stalwart, staunch, steady, true, trustworthy, trusty, unchanging, unflinching, unswerving, unwavering. ▷ STRONG. *Opp* UNRELIABLE.

steady *adj* 1 balanced, fast, firm, poised, safe, secure, settled, solid, stable. 2 *steady flow.* ceaseless, consistent, constant, continuous, endless, even, incessant, invariable, never-ending, non-stop, persistent, regular, reliable, repeated, rhythmic, *inf* round-the-clock, unbroken, unchanging, unhurried, uniform, uninterrupted, unrelieved, unremitting, unvarying. *Opp* UNSTEADY. 3 ▷ STEADFAST.
• *v* 1 balance, brace, keep still, secure, stabilize, support. 2 *steady your nerves.* calm, control, soothe.

steal *v* 1 appropriate, burgle, commandeer, confiscate, embezzle, expropriate, *inf* filch, hijack, *inf* lift, loot, *inf* make off with, misappropriate, *inf* nick, pick pockets, pilfer, pillage, *inf* pinch, pirate, plagiarize, plunder, poach, purloin, *inf* rip off, rob, seize, shoplift, *sl* snitch, *inf* swipe, take, thieve, walk off with. 2 *steal quietly upstairs.* creep, move stealthily, slink, slip, sneak, tiptoe.

stealing *n* pilfering, *inf* pinching, robbery, thieving. ▷ THEFT.

stealthy *adj* clandestine, covert, disguised, furtive, inconspicuous, quiet, secret, secretive, sly, sneaky, surreptitious, underhand, unobtrusive. *Opp* BLATANT.

steam *n* condensation, haze, mist, moisture, vapour.

steamy *adj* 1 blurred, clouded, cloudy, fogged over, foggy, hazy, misted over, misty. 2 close, damp, humid, moist, muggy, *inf* sticky, sultry, sweaty, sweltering. 3 [*inf*] *steamy sex scenes.* ▷ SEXY.

steep *adj* 1 abrupt, headlong, perpendicular, precipitous, sharp, sheer, sudden, vertical. *Opp* GRADUAL. 2 *steep prices.* ▷ EXPENSIVE.
• *v* ▷ SOAK.

steeple *n* pinnacle, point, spire.

steer *v* be at the wheel, control, direct, drive, guide, navigate, pilot. **steer clear of** ▷ AVOID.

stem *n*, shoot, stalk, trunk, twig.
• *v* arise, derive, develop, flow, issue, originate, proceed, result, spring, sprout. 2 *stem the flow.* ▷ CHECK.

stench *n inf* pong, reek, stink. ▷ SMELL.

step *n* 1 footfall, footstep, pace, stride, tread. 2 doorstep, rung, stair, tread. 3 advance, move, movement, progress, progression. 4 *step in a process.* action, initiative, measure, phase, procedure, stage.
• *v* move, pace, stride, tread, walk. **steps** ladder, stairs, staircase, stairway, stepladder. **step down** ▷ RESIGN. **step in** ▷ ENTER, INTERVENE. **step on it** ▷ HURRY. **step up** ▷ INCREASE. **take steps** ▷ BEGIN.

stereotype *n* formula, model, pattern, stereotyped idea.

stereotyped *adj* clichéd, conventional, hackneyed, predictable, standard, stock, typecast, unoriginal.

sterile *adj* 1 arid, barren, childless, fruitless, infertile, lifeless, unfruitful, unproductive. 2 *sterile bandage.* antiseptic, aseptic, clean, disinfected, germ-free, hygienic, pure, sterilized, uncontaminated, uninfected, unpolluted. *Opp* FERTILE, FRUITFUL, SEPTIC.

sterilize *v* 1 clean, cleanse, decontaminate, disinfect, fumigate, make sterile, purify. 2 *sterilize animals.* castrate, emasculate, geld, neuter, spay.

stern *adj* austere, authoritarian, dour, forbidding, frowning, grim, hard, harsh, inflexible, obdurate, rigid, rigorous, severe, strict, tough, unbending, uncompromising, unrelenting, unremitting. ▷ SERIOUS. *Opp* LENIENT.
• *n stern of ship.* aft, back, rear end.

stew *n* casserole, goulash, hotpot.
• *v* braise, casserole, simmer.

steward, **stewardess** *ns* 1 attendant, waiter. 2 marshal, officer, official.

stick *n* baton, cane, pole, stake, stalk, twig, walking stick, wand.
• *v* 1 dig, jab, pierce, pin, poke, prick, prod, puncture, stab, thrust. 2 *stick with glue.* adhere, affix, bind, bond, cement, fasten, glue, gum, paste, solder, weld. 3 *stick in your mind.* be fixed, continue, endure, last, linger, persist, remain, stay. 4 *the gears stuck.* seize up, jam, freeze. 5 ▷ TOLERATE. **stick at** ▷ PERSIST. **stick out** ▷ PROTRUDE. **stick together** ▷ UNITE. **stick up** ▷ PROTRUDE. **stick up for** ▷ DEFEND. **stick with** ▷ SUPPORT.

sticky *adj* 1 adhesive, gummed, self-adhesive. 2 *sticky paint.* gluey, glutinous, *inf* gooey, gummy, tacky, viscous. 3 *sticky weather.* clammy, close, damp, humid, muggy, steamy, sultry, sweaty. *Opp* DRY.

stiff *adj* 1 firm, hard, inelastic, inflexible, rigid, solid, solidified, stiffened, taut, thick, tough, unbendable. 2 *stiff joints.* arthritic, painful, rheumatic, tight. 3 *stiff task.* arduous, challenging, difficult, exacting, exhausting, hard, laborious, tiring, tough, uphill. 4 *stiff opposition.* determined, dogged, resolute, stubborn, unyielding, vigorous. 5 *stiff manner.* artificial, awkward, cold, forced, formal, graceless, haughty, inelegant, laboured, mannered, pedantic, self-conscious, standoffish, starchy, stilted, *inf* stuffy, tense, turgid, unnatural, wooden. 6 *stiff penalties.* cruel, drastic, excessive, harsh, merciless, pitiless, punitive, rigorous, severe, strict. 7 *stiff wind.* brisk, fresh, strong. 8 *stiff drink.* alcoholic, potent, strong. *Opp* EASY, RELAXED, SOFT.

stiffen *v* become stiff, clot, coagulate, congeal, dry out, harden, *inf* jell, set, solidify, thicken, tighten, toughen.

stifle *v* 1 asphyxiate, choke, smother, strangle, suffocate, throttle. 2 *stifle laughter.* check, control, curb, dampen, muffle, restrain, suppress, withhold. 3 *stifle free speech.* destroy, extinguish, quash, repress, silence, stamp out, stop.

stigma *n* blot, disgrace, dishonour, mark, shame, slur, stain, taint.

stigmatize *v* brand, condemn, denounce, label, mark, slander, vilify.

still *adj* at rest, calm, even, flat, hushed, immobile, inert, lifeless, motionless,

noiseless, peaceful, placid, quiet, restful, serene, silent, smooth, soundless, static, stationary, tranquil, unmoving, unruffled, untroubled, windless. *Opp* ACTIVE, NOISY.
▪ *v* allay, appease, assuage, calm, lull, pacify, quieten, settle, silence, soothe, subdue. *Opp* AGITATE.

stimulant *n* antidepressant, drug, *inf* pick-me-up, restorative, *inf* reviver, *inf* shot in the arm, tonic. ▷ STIMULUS.

stimulate *v* activate, arouse, awaken, encourage, excite, fan, fire, foment, galvanize, goad, incite, inflame, inspire, instigate, invigorate, kindle, motivate, prompt, provoke, quicken, rouse, spur, stir up, urge, whet. *Opp* DISCOURAGE.

stimulating *adj* arousing, challenging, exciting, exhilarating, inspiring, interesting, intoxicating, invigorating, provocative, rousing, stirring, thought-provoking. *Opp* UNINTERESTING.

stimulus *n* encouragement, fillip, goad, incentive, inducement, inspiration, provocation, spur, stimulant. *Opp* DISCOURAGEMENT.

sting *n* bite, prick, stab. ▷ PAIN.
▪ *v* 1 bite, nip, prick, wound. 2 smart, tingle. ▷ HURT.

stingy *adj* 1 *inf* cheese-paring, close, close-fisted, mean, *inf* mingy, miserly, niggardly, parsimonious, penny-pinching, tight-fisted, ungenerous. 2 *stingy helpings*. insufficient, meagre, *inf* measly, scanty. ▷ SMALL. *Opp* GENEROUS.

stink *n*, *v* ▷ SMELL.

stipulate *v* demand, insist on, require, specify.

stipulation *n* condition, demand, prerequisite, proviso, requirement, specification.

stir *n* ▷ COMMOTION.
▪ *v* 1 beat, blend, churn, mingle, mix, scramble, whisk. 2 *stir from sleep*. arise, bestir yourself, *inf* get a move on, *inf* get going, get up, move, rise, *inf* show signs of life. 3 *stir emotions*. activate, affect, arouse, awaken, electrify, excite, exhilarate, fire, impress, inspire, kindle, move, revive, rouse, stimulate, touch, upset.

stirring *adj* affecting, arousing, dramatic, electrifying, emotional, emotive, exciting, exhilarating, heady, impassioned, inspiring, interesting, intoxicating, invigorating, moving, provocative, rousing, spirited, stimulating, thought-provoking, thrilling. *Opp* UNEXCITING.

stitch *v* darn, mend, repair, sew, tack.

stock *adj* banal, clichéd, commonplace, conventional, customary, expected, hackneyed, ordinary, predictable, regular, routine, *inf* run-of-the-mill, set, standard, staple, stereotyped, *inf* tired, traditional, trite, usual. *Opp* UNEXPECTED.
▪ *n* 1 cache, hoard, reserve, reservoir, stockpile, store, supply. 2 goods, merchandise, range, wares. 3 *farm stock*. animals, beasts, cattle, livestock. 4 *ancient stock*. ancestry, blood, breeding, descent, extraction, family, forebears, genealogy, line, lineage, parentage, pedigree. 5 *treasury stock*. ▷ CAPITAL.
▪ *v* carry, deal in, handle, have available, *inf* keep, keep in stock, offer, provide, sell, supply, trade in. **out of stock** sold out, unavailable. **take stock** ▷ REVIEW.

stockade *n* fence, paling, palisade, wall.

stockist *n* merchant, retailer, seller, shopkeeper, supplier.

stocky *adj* burly, dumpy, short, solid, stubby, sturdy, thickset. *Opp* TALL, THIN.

stodgy *adj* 1 filling, heavy, indigestible, solid, starchy. 2 *stodgy book*. boring, dull, ponderous, *inf* stuffy, tedious, tiresome, turgid, uninteresting. *Opp* LIVELY.

stoical *adj* calm, cool, impassive, imperturbable, long-suffering, patient, philosophical, phlegmatic, resigned, stolid, uncomplaining. *Opp* EXCITABLE.

stoke *v* fuel, keep burning, put fuel on, tend.

stole *n* cape, shawl, wrap.

stolid *adj* bovine, dull, heavy, impassive, phlegmatic, unemotional, unimaginative, wooden. ▷ STOICAL. *Opp* LIVELY.

stomach *n* abdomen, belly, *inf* guts, *inf* insides, *derog* paunch, *derog* pot, *inf* tummy.
▪ *v* ▷ TOLERATE.

stomach-ache *n* colic, *inf* gripes, *inf* tummy-ache.

stone *n* 1 boulder, cobble, *pl* gravel, pebble, *pl* scree. ▷ ROCK. 2 block, flagstone, slab. 3 *memorial stone*. gravestone, headstone, obelisk, tablet. 4 *precious stone*. ▷ JEWEL. 5 *peach stone*. pip, pit, seed.

stony *adj* 1 pebbly, rocky, rough, shingly. 2 *stony silence*. callous, chilly, cold, expressionless, hard, heartless, hostile, icy, indifferent, merciless, obdurate, pitiless, steely, unfeeling, unforgiving, unresponsive, unsympathetic.

stooge *n* butt, dupe, *inf* fall-guy, lackey, puppet.

stoop *v* 1 bend, bow, crouch, duck, hunch

your shoulders, kneel, lean, squat. 2 condescend, degrade yourself, deign, humble yourself, lower yourself, sink.

stop *n* 1 ban, cessation, close, conclusion, end, finish, halt, pause, shut-down, standstill, stoppage, termination. 2 *bus stop.* station, stopping place, terminus. 3 *a stop at a hotel.* break, holiday, stay, vacation, visit.
• *v* 1 break off, call a halt to, cease, conclude, cut off, desist from, discontinue, end, finish, halt, *inf* knock off, leave off, *inf* pack in, pause, *inf* quit, refrain from, terminate. 2 bar, block, check, curb, delay, frustrate, halt, hamper, hinder, impede, intercept, interrupt, *inf* nip in the bud, obstruct, put a stop to, stanch, stem, suppress, thwart. 3 *stop in a hotel.* be a guest, have a holiday, spend time, stay, visit. 4 *stop a gap.* close, fill in, plug, seal. 5 *stop a thief.* arrest, capture, catch, detain, hold, seize. 6 *the rain stopped.* cease, come to an end, finish, peter out. 7 *the bus stopped.* come to rest, draw up, halt, pull up.

stopper *n* bung, cork, plug.

store *n* 1 accumulation, cache, fund, hoard, quantity, reserve, reservoir, stock, stockpile, supply. ▷ STOREHOUSE. 2 *grocery store.* ▷ SHOP.
• *v* accumulate, deposit, hoard, keep, lay by, lay in, lay up, preserve, put away, reserve, save, set aside, *inf* stash away, stockpile, stock up, stow away.

storehouse *n* armoury, arsenal, depository, depot, repository, store, storeroom, warehouse.

storey *n* deck, floor, level, stage, tier.

storm *n* 1 blizzard, cloudburst, cyclone, deluge, disturbance, dust-storm, electrical storm, gale, hailstorm, hurricane, monsoon, rainstorm, sandstorm, snowstorm, squall, tempest, thunderstorm, tornado, typhoon, turbulence, whirlwind. 2 *storm of protest.* ▷ CLAMOUR.
• *v* ▷ ATTACK.

stormy *adj* angry, blustery, choppy, fierce, furious, gusty, raging, rough, squally, tempestuous, thundery, tumultuous, turbulent, vehement, violent, wild, windy. *Opp* CALM.

story *n* 1 account, anecdote, chronicle, detective story, epic, fable, fairy tale, fiction, history, legend, myth, narrative, parable, plot, recital, romance, saga, tale, thriller, *inf* whodunit, yarn. 2 *story in newspaper.* article, exclusive, feature, news item, piece, report, scoop. 3 falsehood, *inf* fib, lie, tall story, untruth.

storyteller *n* author, narrator, raconteur, teller.

stout *adj* 1 *inf* beefy, chubby, corpulent, fleshy, heavy, *inf* hulking, overweight, plump, portly, solid, stocky, *inf* strapping, thickset, tubby, well-built. ▷ FAT. *Opp* THIN. 2 *stout rope.* durable, robust, sound, strong, sturdy, substantial, thick, tough. 3 *stout fighter.* bold, brave, courageous, fearless, gallant, heroic, intrepid, plucky, resolute, spirited, valiant. *Opp* WEAK.

stove *n* boiler, cooker, fire, furnace, heater, oven, range.

stow *v* load, pack, put away, *inf* stash away, store.

straggle *v* be scattered, dawdle, drift, fall behind, lag, loiter, meander, ramble, scatter, spread out, stray, trail, wander. **straggling** ▷ DISORGANIZED, LOOSE.

straight *adj* 1 direct, even, flat, horizontal, level, regular, smooth, true, unbending, undeviating, unswerving, vertical. 2 neat, orderly, organized, right, shipshape, spruce, tidy. 3 *straight sequence.* consecutive, continuous, non-stop, perfect, sustained, unbroken, uninterrupted. 4 ▷ STRAIGHTFORWARD. *Opp* CROOKED, INDIRECT, UNTIDY. **straight away** at once, directly, immediately, instantly, now, without delay.

straighten *v* disentangle, put straight, rearrange, sort out, tidy, unravel, untangle.

straightforward *adj* blunt, candid, direct, easy, forthright, frank, genuine, honest, intelligible, lucid, open, plain, simple, sincere, straight, truthful, uncomplicated. *Opp* DEVIOUS.

strain *n* 1 anxiety, difficulty, effort, exertion, hardship, pressure, stress, tension, worry. 2 *genetic strain.* ▷ ANCESTRY.
• *v* 1 haul, heave, pull, stretch, tug. 2 *strain to succeed.* endeavour, exert yourself, labour, make an effort, strive, struggle, toil, try. 3 *strain yourself.* exhaust, overtax, *inf* push to the limit, stretch, tax, tire out, weaken, wear out. 4 *strain a muscle.* damage, hurt, injure, pull, sprain, tear, twist, wrench, 5 *strain liquid.* drain, draw off, filter, percolate, purify, riddle, separate, sieve, sift.

strained *adj* 1 artificial, awkward, false, forced, insincere, self-conscious, stiff, tense, uncomfortable, uneasy, unnatural. 2 *strained look.* drawn, tired, weary. 3 *strained interpretation.* far-fetched, incredible, laboured, unlikely. *Opp* NATURAL, RELAXED.

strainer *n* colander, filter, riddle, sieve.

strand *n* fibre, filament, string, thread, wire.
• *v* 1 abandon, desert, forsake, maroon. 2 *strand a ship.* beach, ground, run aground, wreck. **stranded** ▷ AGROUND, HELPLESS.

strange *adj* 1 abnormal, astonishing, atypical, bizarre, curious, eerie, exceptional, extraordinary, fantastic, *inf* funny, irregular, odd, out of the ordinary, peculiar, quaint, queer, rare, remarkable, singular, surprising, surreal, uncommon, unexpected, unheard-of, unique, unnatural, untypical, unusual. 2 *strange neighbours. inf* cranky, eccentric, unconventional, weird. 3 *strange problem.* baffling, bewildering, inexplicable, mysterious, mystifying, perplexing, puzzling, unaccountable. 4 *strange places.* exotic, foreign, little-known, off the beaten track, outlandish, out-of-the-way, remote, unexplored. 5 *strange experience.* different, fresh, new, novel, unaccustomed, unfamiliar. *Opp* FAMILIAR, ORDINARY.

strangeness *n* abnormality, bizarreness, eccentricity, eeriness, irregularity, mysteriousness, novelty, oddity, peculiarity, rarity, singularity, unfamiliarity.

stranger *n* alien, foreigner, newcomer, outsider, visitor.

strangle *v* 1 asphyxiate, choke, garrotte, smother, stifle, suffocate, throttle. 2 *strangle a cry.* ▷ SUPPRESS.

strangulation *n* asphyxiation, garrotting, suffocation.

strap *n* band, belt, thong, webbing.
• *v* ▷ FASTEN.

stratagem *n* device, *inf* dodge, manoeuvre, plan, ploy, ruse, scheme, subterfuge, tactic, trick.

strategic *adj* advantageous, critical, crucial, deliberate, key, politic, tactical, vital.

strategy *n* approach, design, manoeuvre, method, plan, plot, policy, procedure, programme, scheme, tactics.

stratum *n* layer, seam, sheet, thickness, vein.

stray *adj* 1 abandoned, homeless, lost, roaming, wandering. 2 *stray bullets.* accidental, chance, haphazard, occasional, odd, random.
• *v* 1 get lost, get separated, go astray, meander, ramble, range, roam, rove, straggle, wander. 2 *stray from the point.* deviate, digress, diverge, drift, get off the subject, go off at a tangent, veer.

streak *n* 1 band, bar, dash, line, mark, smear, stain, strip, stripe, vein. 2 *selfish streak.* element, strain, touch, trace. 3 *streak of good luck.* period, run, series, spate, spell, stretch, time.
• *v* 1 smear, smudge, stain. 2 *streak past.* dart, dash, flash, fly, gallop, hurtle, move at speed, rush, *inf* scoot, speed, sprint, *inf* tear, *inf* whip, zoom.

streaky *adj* barred, lined, smeary, smudged, streaked, stripy, veined.

stream *n* 1 beck, brook, burn, channel, *poet* rill, river, rivulet, watercourse. 2 cascade, cataract, current, deluge, flood, flow, fountain, gush, jet, outpouring, rush, spate, spurt, surge, tide, torrent.
• *v* cascade, course, deluge, flood, flow, gush, issue, pour, run, spill, spout, spurt, squirt, surge, well.

streamer *n* banner, flag, pennant, pennon, ribbon.

streamlined *adj* 1 aerodynamic, elegant, graceful, sleek, smooth. 2 ▷ EFFICIENT.

street *n* avenue, roadway, terrace. ▷ ROAD.

strength *n* 1 brawn, capacity, energy, fitness, force, health, might, muscle, power, resilience, robustness, sinew, stamina, toughness, vigour. 2 *strength of purpose.* backbone, commitment, courage, determination, firmness, *inf* grit, perseverance, persistence, resolution, resolve, spirit, tenacity. *Opp* WEAKNESS.

strengthen *v* 1 bolster, boost, brace, build up, buttress, encourage, fortify, harden, hearten, increase, make stronger, prop up, reinforce, stiffen, support, tone up, toughen. 2 *strengthen an argument.* back up, consolidate, corroborate, enhance, justify, substantiate. *Opp* WEAKEN.

strenuous *adj* 1 arduous, back-breaking, burdensome, demanding, difficult, exhausting, gruelling, hard, laborious, punishing, stiff, taxing, tough, uphill. *Opp* EASY. 2 *strenuous efforts.* active, determined, dogged, dynamic, eager, energetic, herculean, indefatigable, spirited, strong, tenacious, tireless, unremitting, vigorous, zealous. *Opp* CASUAL.

stress *n* 1 anxiety, difficulty, distress, hardship, pressure, strain, tension, trauma, worry. 2 accent, accentuation, beat, emphasis, importance, urgency, weight.
• *v* 1 accent, accentuate, assert, draw attention to, emphasize, feature, highlight, insist on, lay stress on, mark, repeat, spotlight, underline, underscore. 2 *stressed by work.* burden, overstretch, pressure, pressurize, *inf* push to the limit, tax, weigh down.

stressful *adj* anxious, difficult, taxing, tense, traumatic, worrying. *Opp* RELAXED.

stretch *n* 1 period, spell, stint, term, time, tour of duty. 2 *stretch of country.* area, distance, expanse, length, span, spread, sweep, tract.
• *v* 1 crane (*your neck*), dilate, distend, draw out, elongate, expand, extend, inflate, lengthen, open out, pull out, spread out, swell, tauten, tighten, widen. 2 *stretch into the distance.* continue, disappear, extend, go, reach out, spread. 3 *stretch resources.* overextend, overtax, *inf* push to the limit, strain, tax.

strew *v* disperse, distribute, scatter, spread, sprinkle.

strict *adj* 1 austere, authoritarian, autocratic, firm, harsh, merciless, *inf* no-nonsense, rigorous, severe, stern, stringent, tyrannical, uncompromising. *Opp* EASYGOING. 2 *strict rules.* absolute, binding, *inf* hard and fast, inflexible, precise, rigid, stringent, tight. *Opp* FLEXIBLE. 3 *strict truthfulness.* accurate, complete, correct, exact, perfect, precise, right, scrupulous.

stride *n* pace, step.
• *v* ▷ WALK.

strident *adj* clamorous, discordant, grating, harsh, jarring, loud, noisy, raucous, screeching, shrill, unmusical. *Opp* SOFT.

strife *n* animosity, arguing, bickering, competition, discord, disharmony, dissention, enmity, friction, hostility, quarrelling, rivalry, unfriendliness. ▷ FIGHT. *Opp* COOPERATION.

strike *n* 1 go-slow, industrial action, stoppage, walk-out, withdrawal of labour. 2 assault, attack, bombardment.
• *v* 1 bang against, bang into, beat, collide with, hammer, knock, rap, run into, smack, smash into, thump, whack. ▷ ATTACK, HIT. 2 *strike a match.* ignite, light. 3 *The tragedy struck us deeply.* affect, afflict, *inf* come home to, *inf* impress. 4 *clock struck one.* chime, ring, sound. 5 *strike for more pay. inf* come out, *inf* down tools, stop work, take industrial action, withdraw labour, work to rule. 6 *strike a flag, tent.* dismantle, lower, pull down, remove, take down.

striking *adj* arresting, conspicuous, distinctive, extraordinary, glaring, impressive, memorable, noticeable, obvious, out of the ordinary, outstanding, prominent, showy, stunning, telling, unmistakable, unusual. *Opp* INCONSPICUOUS.

string *n* 1 cable, cord, fibre, line, rope, twine. 2 chain, file, line, procession, progression, queue, row, sequence, series, stream, succession, train.
• *v string together* connect, join, line up, link, thread.

stringy *adj* chewy, fibrous, gristly, sinewy, tough. *Opp* TENDER.

strip *n* band, belt, fillet, line, narrow piece, ribbon, shred, slat, sliver, stripe, swathe.
• *v* 1 bare, clear, defoliate, denude, divest, flay, lay bare, peel, remove the covering, remove the paint, remove the skin, skin, uncover. *Opp* COVER. 2 *strip to the waist.* bare yourself, disrobe, get undressed, uncover yourself. *Opp* DRESS. **strip down** ▷ DISMANTLE. **strip off** ▷ UNDRESS.

stripe *n* band, bar, chevron, line, ribbon, streak, strip.

striped *adj* banded, barred, lined, streaky, stripy.

strive *v* attempt, *inf* do your best, endeavour, make an effort, strain, struggle, try.

stroke *n* 1 blow, knock, move, swipe. ▷ HIT. 2 *stroke of the pen.* flourish, gesture, line, mark, movement, sweep. 3 [*medical*] attack, embolism, fit, seizure, spasm, thrombosis.
• *v* caress, fondle, massage, pat, pet, rub, soothe, touch.

stroll *n*, *v* amble, meander, saunter, wander. ▷ WALK.

strong *adj* 1 durable, hard, hard-wearing, heavy-duty, impregnable, indestructible, permanent, reinforced, resilient, robust, sound, stout, substantial, thick, unbreakable, well-made. 2 *strong physique.* athletic, *inf* beefy, brawny, burly, fit, *inf* hale and hearty, hardy, *inf* hefty, mighty, muscular, powerful, robust, sinewy, stalwart, *inf* strapping, sturdy, tough, well-built, wiry. 3 *strong personality.* assertive, determined, dogmatic, domineering, dynamic, energetic, forceful, independent, reliable, resolute, stalwart, steadfast, strong-minded, strong-willed, tenacious, vigorous. ▷ STUBBORN. 4 *strong commitment.* active, assiduous, deep-rooted, deep-seated, eager, earnest, enthusiastic, fervent, fierce, firm, genuine, intense, keen, loyal, passionate, positive, sedulous, staunch, true, vehement, zealous. 5 *strong government.* decisive, dependable, *derog* dictatorial, *derog* doctrinaire, firm, unswerving. 6 *strong measures.* aggressive, draconian, drastic, extreme, harsh, high-handed, ruthless, severe, tough, unflinching, violent. 7 *strong army.* formidable, invincible, large, numerous, powerful, unconquerable, well-equipped, well-trained. 8 *strong colour, light.* bright, brilliant, clear, dazzling, garish, glaring, vivid. 9 *strong taste, smell.* highly-flavoured, hot, intense, noticeable, obvious, overpowering, prominent, pronounced, pungent, sharp, spicy, unmistakable. 10 *strong evidence.* clear-cut, cogent, compelling, convincing, persuasive, plain, solid, telling, undisputed. 11 *strong drink.* alcoholic, concentrated, intoxicating, potent, undiluted. *Opp* WEAK.

stronghold *n* bastion, bulwark, castle, citadel, fort, fortification, fortress, garrison.

structure *n* 1 arrangement, composition, configuration, constitution, design, form, *inf* make-up, order, organization, plan, shape, system. 2 building, construction, edifice, fabric, framework, pile, superstructure.
• *v* arrange, build, construct, design, form, frame, give structure to, organize, shape, systematize.

struggle *n* 1 challenge, difficulty, effort, endeavour, exertion, labour, problem. 2 ▷ FIGHT.
• *v* 1 endeavour, exert yourself, labour, make an effort, strain, strive, toil, try, work hard, wrestle. 2 *struggle through mud.* flail, flounder, stumble, wallow. 3 ▷ FIGHT.

stub *n* butt, end, remains, remnant, stump.
• *v* ▷ HIT.

stubble *n* 1 stalks, straw. 2 beard, bristles, *inf* five-o'clock shadow, hair, roughness.

stubbly *adj* bristly, prickly, rough, unshaven.

stubborn *adj* defiant, determined, difficult, dogged, headstrong, inflexible, intractable, intransigent, *inf* mulish, obdurate, obstinate, persistent, pertinacious, *inf* pig-headed, recalcitrant, refractory, rigid, self-willed, tenacious, uncompromising, uncooperative, unmanageable, unreasonable, unyielding, wayward, wilful. *Opp* AMENABLE.

stuck *adj* 1 bogged down, cemented, fast, fastened, firm, fixed, glued, immovable. 2 baffled, beaten, *inf* stumped, *inf* stymied.

stuck-up *adj* arrogant, *inf* big-headed, bumptious, *inf* cocky, conceited, condescending, *inf* high-and-mighty, patronizing, proud, self-important, snobbish, *inf* snooty, supercilious, *inf* toffee-nosed. *Opp* MODEST.

student *n* apprentice, disciple, learner, postgraduate, pupil, scholar, schoolchild, trainee, undergraduate.

studied *adj* calculated, conscious, contrived, deliberate, intentional, planned, premeditated.

studious *adj* academic, assiduous, attentive, bookish, *inf* brainy, earnest, hard-working, intellectual, scholarly, serious-minded, thoughtful.

study *v* 1 analyse, consider, contemplate, enquire into, examine, give attention to, investigate, look closely at, peruse, pore over, read carefully, research, scrutinize, survey, think about. 2 *study for exams.* *inf* cram, learn, *inf* mug up, read, *inf* swot, work.

stuff *n* 1 ingredients, matter, substance. 2 cloth, fabric, material, textile. 3 *all sorts of stuff.* accoutrements, articles, belongings, *inf* bits and pieces, *inf* clobber, effects, *inf* gear, junk, objects, paraphernalia, possessions, *inf* tackle, things.
• *v* 1 compress, cram, crowd, force, jam, pack, press, push, ram, shove, squeeze, stow, thrust. 2 *stuff a cushion.* fill, pad. **stuff yourself** ▷ EAT.

stuffing *n* 1 filling, padding, quilting, wadding. 2 *stuffing in poultry.* forcemeat, seasoning.

stuffy *adj* 1 airless, close, fetid, fuggy, fusty, heavy, humid, muggy, musty, oppressive, stale, steamy, stifling, suffocating, sultry, unventilated, warm. *Opp* AIRY. 2 [*inf*] *stuffy old bore.* boring, conventional, dreary, dull, formal, humourless, narrow-minded, old-fashioned, pompous, prim, staid, *inf* stodgy, strait-laced. *Opp* LIVELY.

stumble *v* 1 blunder, flounder, lurch, miss your footing, reel, slip, stagger, totter, trip, tumble. 2 *stumble through a speech.* become tongue-tied, falter, hesitate, stammer, stutter.

stumbling block *n* difficulty, hindrance, hurdle, impediment, obstacle, snag.

stump *v* baffle, bewilder, *inf* catch out, confound, confuse, defeat, *inf* flummox, mystify, outwit, perplex, puzzle, *inf* stymie. **stump up** ▷ PAY.

stun *v* 1 daze, knock out, knock senseless. 2 amaze, astonish, astound, bewilder, confound, confuse, dumbfound, flabbergast, numb, shock, stagger, stupefy. **stunning** ▷ BEAUTIFUL, STUPENDOUS.

stunt *n* exploit, feat, trick.
• *v* *stunt growth.* ▷ CHECK.

stupendous *adj* amazing, colossal, enormous, exceptional, extraordinary, huge, incredible, marvellous, miraculous, phenomenal, prodigious, remarkable, *inf* sensational, singular, special, staggering, stunning, tremendous, unbelievable, wonderful. *Opp* ORDINARY.

stupid *adj* [*Most synonyms derog*] 1 addled, bird-brained, bone-headed, bovine, brainless, clueless, dense, dim, doltish, dopey, drippy, dull, dumb, empty-headed, feather-brained, feeble-minded, foolish, gormless, half-witted, idiotic, ignorant, imbecilic, lacking, mindless, moronic, naive, obtuse, puerile, senseless, silly, simple, simple-minded, slow, slow in the uptake, thick, thickheaded, thick-skulled, unintelligent, unthinking, unwise, vacuous, weak in the head, witless. 2 *It was a stupid thing to do.* absurd, asinine, barmy, crack-brained, crass, crazy, fatuous, futile, half-baked, hare-brained, ill-advised, inane, irrational, irresponsible, laughable, ludicrous, lunatic, mad, nonsensical, pointless, rash, reckless, ridiculous, scatterbrained, thoughtless. 3 *I had to read a pile of stupid books.* boring, dreary, dull, monotonous, tedious, tiresome, uninteresting. *Opp* INTELLIGENT. **stupid person** ▷ FOOL.

stupidity *n* absurdity, crassness, *inf* dumbness, fatuousness, folly, foolishness, futility, idiocy, ignorance, imbecility, lack of intelligence, lunacy, madness, mindlessness, naivety, pointlessness, recklessness, silliness, thoughtlessness. *Opp* INTELLIGENCE.

stupor *n* coma, daze, inertia, lassitude, lethargy, numbness, shock, state of insensibility, torpor, trance, unconsciousness.

sturdy *adj* 1 athletic, brawny, burly, hardy, healthy, hefty, muscular, powerful, robust, stalwart, stocky, *inf* strapping, vigorous, well-built. 2 *sturdy shoes.* durable, solid, substantial, tough, well-made. 3 *sturdy opposition.* determined, firm, indomitable, resolute, staunch, steadfast, vigorous. ▷ STRONG. *Opp* WEAK.

stutter *v* falter, hesitate, stammer, stumble.

style *n* 1 chic, dash, dress-sense, elegance, flair, flamboyance, panache, polish, refinement, smartness, sophistication, stylishness, taste. 2 *the latest style.* craze, fad, fashion, mode, look, trend, vogue. 3 *style of writing.* approach, manner, mode of expression, phraseology, phrasing, sentence structure, tenor, tone, wording. 4 *style of clothes.* cut, design, fashion, make, pattern, shape, type.

stylish *adj* chic, *inf* classy, contemporary, dapper, elegant, fashionable, modern, *inf* natty, *inf* posh, smart, *inf* snazzy, sophisticated, *inf* trendy, up-to-date. *Opp* OLD-FASHIONED.

subconscious *adj* deep-rooted, hidden, inner, intuitive, latent, repressed, subliminal, suppressed, unacknowledged, unconscious. *Opp* CONSCIOUS.

subdue *v* check, curb, hold back, moderate, quieten, repress, restrain, suppress, temper. ▷ SUBJUGATE.

subdued *adj* 1 chastened, crestfallen, depressed, downcast, grave, reflective, restrained, serious, silent, sober, solemn, thoughtful. ▷ SAD. *Opp* EXCITED. 2 *subdued music.* hushed, low, mellow, muted, peaceful, placid, quiet, soft, soothing, tranquil, unobtrusive.

subject *adj* 1 captive, dependent, enslaved, oppressed, ruled, subjugated. 2 *subject to interference.* exposed, liable, prone, susceptible, vulnerable. *Opp* FREE.
• *n* 1 citizen, dependant, national, passport-holder, taxpayer, voter. 2 *subject for discussion.* affair, business, issue, matter, point, proposition, question, theme, thesis, topic. 3 *subject of study.* area, branch of knowledge, course, discipline, field.
• *v* 1 *subject a thing to scrutiny.* expose, lay open, submit. 2 ▷ SUBJUGATE.

subjective *adj* biased, emotional, *inf* gut (*reaction*), individual, instinctive, intuitive, personal, prejudiced. *Opp* OBJECTIVE.

subjugate *v* beat, conquer, control, crush, defeat, dominate, enslave, *inf* get the better of, master, oppress, overcome, overpower, put down, quash, quell, subdue, subject, tame, triumph over, vanquish.

sublimate *v* divert, idealize, purify, redirect, refine.

sublime *adj* ecstatic, elevated, exalted, heavenly, inspiring, lofty, noble, spiritual, splendid, transcendent. *Opp* BASE.

submerge *v* 1 cover with water, dip, drench, drown, dunk, engulf, flood, immerse, inundate, overwhelm, soak, swamp. 2 dive, go under, plummet, sink, subside.

submission *n* 1 acquiescence, capitulation, compliance, giving in, surrender, yielding. ▷ SUBMISSIVENESS. 2 contribution, entry, offering, presentation, tender. 3 *legal submission.* argument, claim, contention, idea, proposal, suggestion, theory.

submissive *adj* accommodating, acquiescent, amenable, biddable, *derog* bootlicking, compliant, deferential, docile, humble, meek, obedient, obsequious, passive, resigned, servile, sycophantic, tame, tractable, unassertive, uncomplaining, weak, yielding. *Opp* ASSERTIVE.

submissiveness *n* acquiescence, compliance, deference, docility, humility, meekness, obedience, passivity, resignation, submission, subservience, tameness.

submit *v* 1 accede, bow, capitulate, concede, give in, *inf* knuckle under, succumb, surrender, yield. 2 *submit a proposal.* advance, enter, give in, hand in, offer, present, proffer, propose, propound, put forward, state, suggest. **submit to** ▷ ACCEPT, OBEY.

subordinate *adj* inferior, junior, lesser, lower, menial, minor, secondary, subservient, subsidiary.
• *n* aide, assistant, dependant, employee, inferior, junior, menial, *inf* underling.

subscribe *v* **subscribe to** 1 contribute to, donate to, give to, patronize, sponsor, support. 2 *subscribe to a magazine.* buy regularly, pay a subscription to. 3 *subscribe to a theory.* advocate, agree with, approve of, *inf* back, believe in, condone, endorse, *inf* give your blessing to.

subscriber *n* patron, regular customer, sponsor, supporter.

subscription *n* fee, due, payment, regular contribution, remittance.

subsequent *adj* consequent, ensuing, following, future, later, next, resultant, resulting, succeeding. *Opp* PREVIOUS.

subside *v* 1 abate, decline, decrease, die down, diminish, dwindle, ebb, fall, lessen, melt away, moderate, quieten, recede, shrink, slacken, wear off. 2 *subside into a chair.* collapse, descend, lower yourself, settle, sink. *Opp* RISE.

subsidiary *adj* additional, ancillary, auxiliary, complementary, contributory, lesser, minor, secondary, subordinate.

subsidize *v* aid, back, finance, fund, maintain, promote, sponsor, support, underwrite.

subsidy *n* aid, backing, financial help, funding, grant, sponsorship, support.

substance *n* 1 actuality, body, corporeality, reality, solidity. 2 chemical, fabric, material, matter, stuff. 3 *substance of an argument.* core, essence, gist, import, meaning, significance, subject-matter, theme. 4 [*old use*] *person of substance.* ▷ WEALTH.

substandard *adj inf* below par, disappointing, inadequate, inferior, poor, shoddy.

substantial *adj* 1 durable, hefty, massive, solid, stout, strong, sturdy, well-built, well-made. 2 big, considerable, generous, great, large, significant, sizeable, worthwhile. *Opp* FLIMSY, SMALL.

substitute *adj* 1 acting, deputy, relief, reserve, stand-by, surrogate, temporary. 2 alternative, ersatz, imitation.
• *n* alternative, deputy, locum, proxy, relief, replacement, reserve, stand-in, stopgap, substitution, supply, surrogate, understudy.
• *v* 1 change, exchange, interchange, replace, *inf* swop, *inf* switch. 2 *substitute for an absentee.* cover, deputize, double, stand in, supplant, take the place of, understudy.

subtle *adj* 1 delicate, elusive, faint, fine, gentle, mild, slight, unobtrusive. 2 *subtle argument.* clever, indirect, ingenious, refined, shrewd, sophisticated, tactful, understated. ▷ CUNNING. *Opp* OBVIOUS.

subtract *v* debit, deduct, remove, take away. *Opp* ADD.

suburban *adj* residential, outer, outlying.

suburbs *n* fringes, outer areas, outskirts, residential areas, suburbia.

subversive *adj* challenging, disruptive, questioning, radical, seditious, treacherous, unsettling. ▷ REVOLUTIONARY. *Opp* CONSERVATIVE, ORTHODOX.

subvert *v* challenge, corrupt, destroy, disrupt, overthrow, overturn, pervert, ruin, undermine, upset, wreck.

subway *n* tunnel, underpass.

succeed *v* 1 *inf* arrive, be a success, do well, flourish, *inf* get on, *inf* get to the top, *inf* make it, prosper, thrive. 2 be effective, *inf* catch on, produce results, work. 3 be successor to, come after, follow, inherit from, replace, take over from. *Opp* FAIL. **succeeding** ▷ SUBSEQUENT.

success *n* 1 fame, good fortune, prosperity, wealth. 2 *success of a plan.* accomplishment, achievement, attainment, completion, effectiveness, successful outcome. 3 *a great success. inf* hit, *inf* sensation, triumph, victory, *inf* winner. *Opp* FAILURE.

successful *adj* 1 booming, effective, flourishing, fruitful, lucrative, money-making, productive, profitable, profit-making, prosperous, thriving, useful, well-off. 2 best-selling, celebrated, famed, famous, leading, popular, top, unbeaten, victorious, well-known, winning. *Opp* UNSUCCESSFUL.

succession *n* chain, flow, line, procession, progression, run, sequence, series, string.

successive *adj* consecutive, continuous, in succession, uninterrupted.

successor *n* heir, inheritor, replacement.

succinct *adj* brief, compact, concise, condensed, epigrammatic, pithy, short, terse, to the point. *Opp* WORDY.

succulent *adj* fleshy, juicy, luscious, moist, mouthwatering, rich, tender.

succumb *v* accede, be overcome, capitulate, give in, give up, give way, submit, surrender, yield. *Opp* RESIST.

suck *v* **suck up** absorb, soak up. **suck up to** ▷ FLATTER.

sudden *adj* 1 abrupt, hasty, hurried, impetuous, impulsive, precipitate, quick, rash, *inf* snap, swift, unconsidered, unplanned, unpremeditated. *Opp* SLOW. 2 *sudden shock.* sharp, startling, surprising, unexpected, unforeseeable, unforeseen, unlooked-for. *Opp* PREDICTABLE.

suds *n* bubbles, foam, froth, lather, soapsuds.

sue *v* 1 indict, proceed against, prosecute, summons, take legal action against. 2 *sue for peace.* ▷ ENTREAT.

suffer *v* 1 bear, cope with, endure, experience, feel, go through, live through, put up with, stand, tolerate, undergo, withstand. 2 *suffer from a wound.* ache, agonize, hurt, smart. 3 *suffer for a crime.* be punished, make amends, pay.

suffice *v* answer, be sufficient, *inf* do, satisfy, serve.

sufficient *adj* adequate, enough, satisfactory. *Opp* INSUFFICIENT.

suffocate *v* asphyxiate, choke, smother, stifle, stop breathing, strangle, throttle.

sugary *adj* 1 glazed, iced, sugared, sweetened. ▷ SWEET. 2 *sugary sentiments.* cloying, sickly. ▷ SENTIMENTAL.

suggest *v* 1 advise, advocate, counsel, moot, move, propose, propound, put forward, raise, recommend, urge. 2 call to mind, evoke, hint, imply, indicate, insinuate, intimate, mean, signal.

suggestion *n* 1 advice, counsel, offer, plan, prompting, proposal, recommendation, urging. 2 breath, hint, idea, indication, intimation, notion, suspicion, touch, trace.

suggestive *adj* 1 evocative, expressive, indicative, reminiscent, thought-provoking. 2 ▷ INDECENT.

suicidal *adj* 1 hopeless, *inf* kamikaze, self-destructive. 2 ▷ DESOLATE.

suit *n* costume, dress, ensemble, outfit.
• *v* 1 accommodate, be suitable for, conform to, fit in with, gratify, match, please, satisfy, tally with. *Opp* DISPLEASE. 2 *That colour suits you.* become, fit, look good on.

suitable *adj* acceptable, applicable, apposite, appropriate, apt, becoming, befitting, congenial, convenient, decorous, fit, fitting, handy, opportune, pertinent, proper, relevant, right, satisfactory, seemly, tasteful, timely, well-chosen, well-judged, well-timed. *Opp* UNSUITABLE.

sulk *v* be sullen, brood, mope.

sullen *adj* 1 antisocial, bad-tempered, brooding, crabby, cross, disgruntled, dour, glum, grudging, ill-humoured, lugubrious, moody, morose, *inf* out of sorts, pouting, resentful, silent, sour, stubborn, sulking, sulky, surly, uncommunicative, unforgiving, unfriendly, unhappy, unsociable. 2 *sullen sky.* dark, dismal, dull, gloomy, grey, leaden, sombre. *Opp* CHEERFUL.

sultry *adj* 1 close, hot, humid, muggy, oppressive, steamy, stifling, stuffy, warm. *Opp* COLD. 2 *sultry beauty.* erotic, provocative, seductive, sensual, sexy, voluptuous.

sum *n* aggregate, amount, number, quantity, reckoning, result, score, tally, total, whole.
• *v* **sum up** ▷ SUMMARIZE.

summarize *v* abridge, condense, encapsulate, give the gist, outline, précis, *inf* recap, recapitulate, reduce, review, shorten, simplify, sum up. *Opp* ELABORATE.

summary *n* abridgement, abstract, digest, gist, outline, précis, recapitulation, reduction, résumé, review, summation, summing-up, synopsis.

summery *adj* bright, sunny, warm. *Opp* WINTRY.

summit *n* 1 apex, crown, height, peak, pinnacle, point, top. *Opp* BASE. 2 *summit of success.* acme, climax, culmination, high point, zenith. *Opp* NADIR.

summon *v* 1 command, demand, invite, order, send for. 2 assemble, call, convene, convoke, gather together, muster, rally.

sunbathe *v* bake, bask, get a tan, sun yourself, tan.

sunburnt *adj* blistered, bronzed, brown, peeling, tanned, weather-beaten.

sundry *adj* assorted, different, miscellaneous, mixed, various.

sunken *adj* 1 submerged, underwater. 2 *sunken cheeks.* concave, haggard, drawn, hollow, hollowed.

sunless *adj* cheerless, cloudy, dark, dismal, dreary, dull, gloomy, grey, overcast, sombre. *Opp* SUNNY.

sunlight *n* daylight, sun, sunbeams, sunshine.

sunny *adj* 1 bright, clear, cloudless, fair, fine, summery, sunlit, sunshiny, unclouded. *Opp* SUNLESS. 2 ▷ CHEERFUL.

sunrise *n* dawn, daybreak.

sunset *n* dusk, evening, nightfall, sundown, twilight.

superannuated *adj* 1 discharged, *inf* pensioned off, *inf* put out to grass, old, retired. 2 discarded, disused, obsolete, thrown out, worn out. ▷ OLD.

superb *adj* admirable, excellent, fine, first-class, first-rate, impressive, marvellous, superior. ▷ SPLENDID. *Opp* INFERIOR.

superficial *adj* 1 cosmetic, external, exterior, on the surface, outward, shallow, skin-deep, slight, surface, unimportant. 2 careless, casual, cursory, desultory, facile, frivolous, hasty, hurried, lightweight, *inf* nodding (*acquaintance*), oversimplified, passing, perfunctory, simplistic, sweeping (*generalization*), trivial, unconvincing, uncritical, undiscriminating, unquestioning, unscholarly. *Opp* ANALYTICAL, DEEP.

superfluous *adj* excess, excessive, extra, needless, redundant, spare, surplus, unnecessary, unneeded, unwanted. *Opp* NECESSARY.

superhuman *adj* 1 herculean, heroic, phenomenal, prodigious. 2 *superhuman powers.* divine, higher, supernatural.

superimpose *v* overlay, place on top of.

superintend *v* administer, be in charge of, control, direct, look after, manage, organize, oversee, preside over, run, supervise, watch over.

superior *adj* 1 better, *inf* classier, greater, higher, loftier, more important, nobler, senior, up-market. 2 *superior quality.* choice, exclusive, fine, first-class, first-choice, first-rate, select, top, unrivalled. 3 *superior attitude.* arrogant, condescending, contemptuous, disdainful, elitist, haughty, *inf* high-and-mighty, lofty, patronizing, self-important, smug, snobbish, *inf* snooty, *inf* stuck-up, supercilious. *Opp* INFERIOR.

superlative *adj* best, choicest, consummate, excellent, finest, first-rate, incomparable, matchless, peerless, *inf* tip-top, *inf* top-notch, unrivalled, unsurpassed. ▷ SUPREME.

supernatural *adj* abnormal, ghostly, inexplicable, magical, miraculous, mysterious, mystic, occult, other-worldly, paranormal, preternatural, psychic, spiritual, unearthly, unnatural, weird.

superstition *n* myth, *inf* old wives' tale, superstitious belief.

superstitious *adj* credulous, illusory, irrational, mythical, traditional, unfounded.

supervise *v* administer, be in charge of, conduct, control, direct, govern, invigilate (*an exam*), *inf* keep an eye on, lead, look after, manage, organize, oversee, preside over, run, superintend, watch over.

supervision *n* administration, conduct, control, direction, government, invigilation, management, organization, oversight, surveillance.

supervisor *n* administrator, chief, controller, director, foreman, *inf* gaffer, head, inspector, invigilator, leader, manager, organizer, overseer, superintendent.

supine *adj* 1 face upwards, flat on your back, prostrate, recumbent. *Opp* PRONE. 2 ▷ PASSIVE.

supplant *v* displace, dispossess, eject, expel, oust, replace, supersede, *inf* step into the shoes of, *inf* topple, unseat.

supple *adj* bending, *inf* bendy, elastic, flexible, graceful, limber, lithe, pliable, pliant, resilient, soft. *Opp* RIGID.

supplement *n* 1 additional payment, excess, surcharge. 2 *newspaper supplement, etc.* addendum, addition, appendix, codicil, continuation, endpiece, extra, insert, postscript, sequel.
• *v* add to, augment, boost, complement, extend, reinforce, *inf* top up.

supplementary *adj* accompanying, added, additional, ancillary, auxiliary, complementary, extra, further, new, spare.

supplication *n* appeal, entreaty, petition, plea, prayer, request, solicitation.

supplier *n* dealer, provider, purveyor, retailer, seller, shopkeeper, vendor, wholesaler.

supply *n* cache, hoard, quantity, reserve, reservoir, stock, stockpile, store. 2 [*pl*] equipment, food, necessities, provisions, rations, shopping. 3 *regular supply*. delivery, distribution, provision.
• *v* cater to, contribute, deliver, distribute, donate, endow, equip, feed, furnish, give, produce, provide, purvey, sell, stock.

support *n* 1 aid, approval, assistance, backing, backup, contribution, cooperation, donation, encouragement, friendship, help, interest, loyalty, patronage, protection, reassurance, reinforcement, sponsorship, succour. 2 brace, bracket, buttress, crutch, foundation, frame, pillar, post, prop, sling, stay, strut, substructure, trestle, truss, underpinning. 3 *financial support*. funding, keep, maintenance, subsistence, upkeep.
• *v* 1 bear, bolster, buoy up, buttress, carry, give strength to, hold up, keep up, prop up, provide a support for, reinforce, shore up, strengthen, underlie, underpin. 2 *support someone in trouble*. aid, assist, back, be faithful to, champion, comfort, defend, encourage, fight for, give support to, help, rally round, reassure, side with, speak up for, stand by, stand up for, *inf* stick up for, take someone's part. 3 *support a family*. bring up, feed, finance, fund, keep, look after, maintain, provide for, sustain. 4 *support a charity*. be a supporter of, contribute to, espouse (*a cause*), follow, give to, patronize, sponsor, subsidize, work for. 5 *support a point of view*. adhere to, advocate, agree with, argue for, confirm, corroborate, defend, endorse, justify, promote, ratify, substantiate, uphold, validate, verify. *Opp* SUBVERT, WEAKEN. **support yourself** lean, rest.

supporter *n* 1 adherent, admirer, advocate, aficionado, apologist, champion, defender, devotee, enthusiast, *inf* fan, fanatic, follower, seconder, upholder, voter. 2 ally, assistant, collaborator, helper, *inf* henchman, second.

supportive *adj* caring, concerned, encouraging, helpful, favourable, heartening, interested, kind, loyal, positive, reassuring, sustaining, sympathetic, understanding. *Opp* UNSYMPATHETIC.

suppose *v* 1 accept, assume, believe, conclude, conjecture, expect, guess, infer, judge, postulate, presume, presuppose, speculate, surmise, suspect, take for granted, think. 2 daydream, fancy, fantasize, hypothesize, imagine, pretend, theorize. **supposed** ▷ HYPOTHETICAL, PUTATIVE. **supposed to** expected to, meant to, required to.

supposition *n* assumption, belief, conjecture, fancy, guess, hypothesis, inference, notion, opinion, speculation, surmise, theory, thought.

suppress *v* 1 conquer, *inf* crack down on, crush, overcome, overthrow, put an end to, put down, quash, quell, stamp out, stop, subdue. 2 *suppress emotion, the facts*. bottle up, censor, choke back, conceal, cover up, hide, hush up, keep quiet about, keep secret, muffle, repress, restrain, silence, smother, stamp on, stifle, strangle.

supremacy *n* ascendancy, dominance, domination, dominion, lead, mastery, predominance, pre-eminence, sovereignty, superiority.

supreme *adj* best, choicest, consummate, crowning, culminating, finest, greatest, highest, incomparable, matchless, outstanding, paramount, peerless, predominant, pre-eminent, prime, principal, superlative, surpassing, *inf* tip-top, top, *inf* top-notch, ultimate, unbeatable, unbeaten, unparalleled, unrivalled unsurpassable, unsurpassed.

sure *adj* 1 assured, certain, confident, convinced, definite, persuaded, positive. 2 *sure to come*. bound, certain, obliged, required. 3 *sure fact*. accurate, clear, convincing, guaranteed, indisputable, inescapable, inevitable, infallible, proven, reliable, true, unchallenged, undeniable, undisputed, undoubted, verifiable. 4 *sure ally*. dependable, established, faithful, firm, infallible, loyal, reliable, resolute, safe, secure, solid, steadfast, steady, trustworthy, trusty, unerring, unfailing, unfaltering, unflinching, unswerving, unwavering. *Opp* UNCERTAIN.

surface *n* 1 coat, coating, covering, crust, exterior, façade, outside, shell, skin, veneer. 2 *cube has six surfaces*. face, facet, plane, side. 3 *working surface*. bench, table, top, worktop.
• *v* 1 appear, arise, *inf* come to light, come up, *inf* crop up, emerge, materialize, rise, *inf* pop up. 2 coat, cover, laminate.

surfeit *n* excess, flood, glut, overabundance, oversupply, plethora, superfluity, surplus.

surge *n* burst, gush, increase, onrush, outpouring, rush, upsurge. ▷ WAVE.
• *v* billow, eddy, flow, gush, heave, move irresistibly, push, roll, rush, stampede, stream, sweep, swirl, well up.

surgery *n* 1 biopsy, operation. 2 *doctor's surgery.* clinic, consulting room, health centre, infirmary, medical centre.

surly *adj* bad-tempered, boorish, cantankerous, churlish, crabby, cross, crotchety, crusty, curmudgeonly, dyspeptic, gruff, grumpy, ill-natured, irascible, miserable, morose, peevish, rude, sulky, sullen, testy, touchy, unfriendly, ungracious, unpleasant. *Opp* FRIENDLY.

surmise *v* assume, believe, conjecture, expect, fancy, gather, guess, hypothesize, imagine, infer, judge, postulate, presume, presuppose, sense, speculate, suppose, suspect, take for granted, think.

surpass *v* beat, better, eclipse, exceed, excel, go beyond, leave behind, *inf* leave standing, outclass, outdo, outshine, outstrip, overshadow, top, transcend, worst.

surplus *n* balance, excess, extra, glut, oversupply, remainder, residue, superfluity, surfeit.

surprise *n* 1 alarm, amazement, astonishment, consternation, incredulity, stupefaction, wonder. 2 *complete surprise.* blow, *inf* bolt from the blue, *inf* bombshell, *inf* eye-opener, jolt, shock.
• *v* 1 alarm, amaze, astonish, astound, disconcert, dumbfound, flabbergast, nonplus, rock, shock, stagger, startle, stun, stupefy, take aback, take by surprise, *inf* throw. 2 capture, catch out, *inf* catch red-handed, come upon, detect, discover, take unawares.

surprised *adj* alarmed, amazed, astonished, astounded, disconcerted, dumbfounded, flabbergasted, incredulous, *inf* knocked for six, nonplussed, *inf* shattered, shocked, speechless, staggered, startled, struck dumb, stunned, taken aback, *inf* thrown, thunderstruck.

surprising *adj* alarming, amazing, astonishing, astounding, disconcerting, extraordinary, frightening, incredible, shocking, staggering, startling, stunning, sudden, unexpected, unforeseen, unlooked-for, unplanned, unpredictable. *Opp* PREDICTABLE.

surrender *n* capitulation, giving in, resignation, submission.
• *v* 1 acquiesce, capitulate, *inf* cave in, collapse, concede, fall, *inf* give in, give up, give way, give yourself up, resign, submit, succumb, *inf* throw in the towel, yield. 2 *surrender your ticket.* give up, hand over, part with, relinquish. 3 *surrender your rights.* abandon, cede, renounce, waive.

surreptitious *adj* clandestine, concealed, covert, crafty, disguised, furtive, hidden, private, secret, secretive, *inf* shifty, sly, sneaky, stealthy, underhand. *Opp* BLATANT.

surround *v* besiege, beset, cocoon, cordon off, encircle, enclose, encompass, engulf, hedge in, hem in, ring, skirt, trap, wrap.

surrounding *adj* adjacent, adjoining, bordering, local, nearby, neighbouring.

surroundings *n* area, background, context, environment, location, milieu, neighbourhood, setting, vicinity.

surveillance *n* check, observation, reconnaissance, scrutiny, supervision, vigilance, watch.

survey *n* appraisal, assessment, census, count, evaluation, examination, inquiry, inspection, investigation, review, scrutiny, study.
• *v* 1 appraise, assess, estimate, evaluate, examine, inspect, investigate, look over, review, scrutinize, study, view, weigh up. 2 do a survey of, map out, measure, plan out, plot, reconnoitre.

survival *n* continuance, continued existence, persistence.

survive *v* 1 *inf* bear up, carry on, continue, endure, keep going, last, live, persist, remain. 2 *survive disaster.* come through, live through, outlast, outlive, pull through, weather, withstand. *Opp* SUCCUMB.

susceptible *adj* affected (by), disposed, given, inclined, liable, open, predisposed, prone, responsive, sensitive, vulnerable. *Opp* RESISTANT.

suspect *adj* doubtful, dubious, questionable, *inf* shady, suspicious, unconvincing, unreliable, unsatisfactory, untrustworthy.
• *v* 1 call into question, disbelieve, distrust, doubt, have suspicions about, mistrust. 2 *suspect that she's lying.* believe, conjecture, consider, guess, imagine, infer, presume, speculate, suppose, surmise, think.

suspend *v* 1 dangle, hang, swing. 2 *suspend work.* adjourn, break off, defer, delay, discontinue, hold in abeyance, interrupt, postpone, put off, *inf* put on ice, shelve. 3 *suspend from duty.* debar, dismiss, exclude, expel, lay off, lock out.

suspense *n* anticipation, anxiety, apprehension, doubt, excitement, expectancy, expectation, insecurity, nervousness, not knowing, tension, uncertainty, waiting.

suspicion *n* 1 apprehension, caution, distrust, doubt, dubiousness, *inf* funny feeling, guess, hesitation, *inf* hunch, impression, misgiving, mistrust, presentiment, qualm, scepticism, uncertainty, wariness. 2 *suspicion of a smile*. glimmer, hint, inkling, shadow, suggestion, tinge, touch, trace.

suspicious *adj* 1 apprehensive, chary, disbelieving, distrustful, doubtful, dubious, incredulous, mistrustful, sceptical, uncertain, unconvinced, uneasy, wary. *Opp* TRUSTFUL. 2 *suspicious character*. disreputable, dubious, *inf* fishy, peculiar, questionable, *inf* shady, suspect, unreliable, untrustworthy. *Opp* TRUSTWORTHY.

sustain *v* 1 continue, develop, extend, keep alive, keep going, keep up, maintain, prolong. 2 ▷ SUPPORT.

sustenance *n* eatables, food, foodstuffs, nourishment, provisions, rations, *old use* victuals.

swag *n* booty, loot, plunder.

swagger *v* boast, brag, parade, strut.

swallow *v* consume, *inf* down, gulp down, guzzle, ingest. ▷ DRINK, EAT. **swallow up** absorb, assimilate, enclose, enfold. ▷ SWAMP.

swamp *n* bog, fen, marsh, marshland, morass, mud, mudflats, quagmire, quicksand, wetlands.
• *v* deluge, drench, engulf, envelop, flood, immerse, inundate, overcome, overwhelm, sink, submerge, swallow up.

swampy *adj* boggy, marshy, muddy, soft, soggy, waterlogged, wet. *Opp* DRY, FIRM.

swarm *n* cloud, crowd, horde, host, multitude. ▷ GROUP.
• *v* cluster, congregate, crowd, flock, gather, mass, throng. **swarm up** ▷ CLIMB. **swarm with** ▷ TEEM.

swarthy *adj* brown, dark, dark-skinned, dusky, tanned.

swashbuckling *adj* adventurous, bold, daredevil, daring, dashing, *inf* macho, swaggering. *Opp* TIMID.

sway *v* 1 bend, lean, lurch, oscillate, reel, rock, roll, swing, undulate, wave, wobble. 2 affect, bias, bring round, change (someone's mind), convert, convince, influence, persuade, win over. 3 *sway from a chosen path*. divert, go off course, swerve, veer, waver.

swear *v* 1 affirm, attest, avow, declare, give your word, insist, pledge, promise, state on oath, take an oath, testify, vouchsafe, vow. 2 blaspheme, curse, utter profanities.

swear word *n* curse, expletive, *inf* four-letter word, imprecation, oath, obscenity, profanity, swearing.

sweat *v* 1 *inf* glow, perspire, swelter. 2 ▷ WORK.

sweaty *adj* clammy, damp, humid, moist, perspiring, steamy, sticky, sweating.

sweep *v* brush, clean, clear, dust, tidy up. **sweep along** ▷ MOVE. **sweep away** ▷ REMOVE. **sweeping** ▷ GENERAL, SUPERFICIAL.

sweet *adj* 1 aromatic, fragrant, honeyed, luscious, mellow, perfumed, sweetened, sweet-smelling. 2 [*derog*] cloying, saccharine, sentimental, sickening, sickly, sugary, syrupy, treacly. 3 *sweet sounds*. dulcet, euphonious, harmonious, heavenly, mellifluous, melodious, musical, pleasant, silvery, soothing, tuneful. 4 *sweet nature*. affectionate, amiable, attractive, charming, dear, endearing, engaging, friendly, genial, gentle, gracious, lovable, lovely, nice, pretty, unselfish, winning. *Opp* ACID, BITTER, NASTY, SAVOURY.
• *n* 1 *inf* afters, dessert, pudding. 2 [*pl*] *Amer* candy, confectionery, *inf* sweeties.

sweeten *v* 1 make sweeter, sugar. 2 *sweeten your temper*. appease, assuage, calm, mellow, mollify, pacify, soothe.

swell *v* 1 balloon, billow, blow up, bulge, dilate, distend, enlarge, expand, fatten, fill out, grow, increase, inflate, mushroom, puff up, rise. 2 *swell numbers*. augment, boost, build up, increase, raise, step up. *Opp* SHRINK.

swelling *n* blister, boil, bulge, bump, distension, enlargement, excrescence, hump, inflammation, knob, lump, protuberance, protrusion, tumescence, tumour.

sweltering *adj* humid, muggy, oppressive, steamy, sticky, stifling, sultry. ▷ HOT.

swerve *v* change direction, deviate, dodge about, sheer off, swing, take avoiding action, turn aside, veer, wheel.

swift *adj* agile, brisk, fast, fleet-footed, hasty, hurried, nimble, *inf* nippy, prompt, quick, rapid, speedy, sudden. *Opp* SLOW.

swill *v* 1 bathe, clean, rinse, sponge down, wash. 2 ▷ DRINK.

swim *v* bathe, float, go swimming, *inf* take a dip.

swimming pool *n* baths, lido, swimming bath.

swimsuit *n* bathing costume, bathing suit, bikini, swimwear, trunks.

swindle *n* cheat, chicanery, *inf* con, confidence trick, deception, double-dealing, fraud, *inf* racket, *inf* rip-off, *inf* sharp practice, *inf* swizz, trickery.
• *v inf* bamboozle, cheat, *inf* con, deceive, defraud, *inf* diddle, *inf* do, double-cross, dupe, exploit, *inf* fiddle, fleece, fool, hoax, hoodwink, *inf* pull a fast one, *inf* take for a ride, trick, welsh (*on a bet*).

swindler *n* charlatan, cheat, *inf* con-man, counterfeiter, double-crosser, extortioner, forger, fraud, hoaxer, impostor, quack, racketeer, *inf* shark, trickster.

swing *n* change, fluctuation, movement, oscillation, shift, variation.
• *v* 1 be suspended, dangle, flap, fluctuate, move to and fro, oscillate, revolve, rock, sway, swivel, turn, twirl, wave about. 2 *swing opinion.* affect, bias, bring round, change (someone's mind), convert, convince, influence, persuade, win over. 3 *support swung to the opposition.* change, move across, shift, transfer. 4 *swing from a path.* deviate, divert, go off course, swerve, veer, waver, zigzag.

swipe *v* 1 lash out at, strike, swing at. ▷ HIT. 2 ▷ STEAL.

swirl *v* boil, churn, curl, eddy, move in circles, seethe, spin, surge, twirl, twist, whirl.

switch *n* light-switch, power-point.
• *v* change, divert, exchange, replace, reverse, shift, substitute, swap, transfer, turn.

swivel *v* gyrate, pirouette, pivot, revolve, rotate, spin, swing, turn, twirl, wheel.

swoop *v* descend, dive, drop, fall, fly down, lunge, plunge, pounce. **swoop on** ▷ RAID.

sword *n* blade, broadsword, cutlass, dagger, rapier, sabre, scimitar.

sycophantic *adj* flattering, insincere, obsequious, servile, *inf* smarmy, unctuous.

syllabus *n* course, curriculum, outline, programme of study.

sylvan *adj* arboreal, leafy, tree-covered, wooded.

symbol *n* badge, character, cipher, crest, device, emblem, figure, insignia, logo, mark, motif, representation, sign, token, trademark.

symbolic *adj* allegorical, emblematic, figurative, meaningful, metaphorical, representative, symptomatic, token (*gesture*).

symbolize *v* be a sign of, betoken, connote, denote, epitomize, imply, indicate, mean, represent, signify, stand for, suggest.

symmetrical *adj* balanced, even, proportional, regular. *Opp* ASYMMETRICAL.

sympathetic *adj* benevolent, caring, charitable, comforting, compassionate, concerned, consoling, friendly, humane, interested, kind-hearted, kindly, merciful, soft-hearted, sorry, supportive, tender, tolerant, understanding, warm. *Opp* UNSYMPATHETIC.

sympathize *v inf* be on the same wavelength, be sorry, be sympathetic, comfort, commiserate, condole, console, empathize, feel for, identify (with), pity, respond, show sympathy, understand.

sympathy *n* affinity, commiseration, compassion, concern, condolence, consideration, empathy, feeling, fellow-feeling, kindness, mercy, pity, rapport, tenderness, understanding.

symptom *n* characteristic, evidence, feature, indication, manifestation, mark, marker, sign, warning, warning-sign.

symptomatic *adj* characteristic, indicative, representative, suggestive, typical.

synopsis *n* ▷ SUMMARY.

synthesis *n* amalgamation, blend, combination, composite, compound, fusion, integration, union.

synthetic *adj* artificial, bogus, concocted, counterfeit, ersatz, fabricated, fake, *inf* made-up, man-made, manufactured, mock, *inf* phoney, simulated, spurious, unnatural. *Opp* GENUINE, NATURAL.

syringe *n* hypodermic, needle.

system *n* 1 network, organization, *inf* set-up, structure. 2 approach, arrangement, method, methodology, order, plan, practice, procedure, process, routine, rules, scheme, technique. 3 *system of government.* constitution, regime. 4 *system of knowledge.* classification, code, discipline, philosophy, science, set of principles, theory.

systematic *adj* businesslike, classified, coordinated, logical, methodical, neat, ordered, orderly, organized, planned, rational, routine, scientific, structured, tidy, well-arranged, well-organized, well-rehearsed, well-run. *Opp* UNSYSTEMATIC.

systematize *v* arrange, catalogue, categorize, classify, codify, organize, rationalize, standardize, tabulate.

T

table *n* 1 bench, board, counter, desk, worktop. 2 *table of information.* catalogue, chart, diagram, graph, index, inventory, list, register, schedule, tabulation, timetable.
• *v* lay on the table, offer, proffer, propose, submit.

tablet *n* 1 capsule, lozenge, medicine, pellet, pill. 2 *tablet of soap.* bar, block, chunk, piece, slab. 3 *tablet of stone.* gravestone, headstone, memorial, plaque, plate, tombstone.

taboo *adj* banned, censored, forbidden, off limits, out of bounds, prohibited, proscribed, rude, unacceptable, unmentionable, unthinkable.
• *n* anathema, ban, prohibition, proscription, taboo subject.

tabulate *v* arrange as a table, catalogue, list, set out in columns, systematize.

tacit *adj* implicit, implied, silent, undeclared, understood, unsaid, unspoken, unvoiced.

taciturn *adj* quiet, reserved, reticent, silent, tight-lipped, uncommunicative, unforthcoming. *Opp* TALKATIVE.

tack *n* 1 drawing-pin, nail, pin, tintack. 2 *the wrong tack.* approach, bearing, course, direction, line, policy, procedure, technique.
• *v* 1 nail, pin. ⊳ FASTEN. 2 sew, stitch. 3 *tack in a yacht.* beat against the wind, change course, zigzag. **tack on** ⊳ ADD.

tackle *n* 1 accoutrements, apparatus, *inf* clobber, equipment, *inf* gear, implements, kit, outfit, paraphernalia, rig, tools. 2 *football tackle.* attack, block, challenge, interception, intervention.
• *v* 1 address (yourself to), apply yourself to, attempt, attend to, concentrate on, confront, cope with, deal with, face up to, focus on, get involved in, *inf* get to grips with, grapple with, handle, *inf* have a go at, manage, settle down to, sort out, take on, undertake. 2 *tackle an opponent.* attack, challenge, intercept, stop, take on.

tacky *adj* adhesive, gluey, *inf* gooey, gummy, sticky, viscous, wet. *Opp* DRY.

tact *n* adroitness, consideration, delicacy, diplomacy, discernment, discretion, finesse, judgement, perceptiveness, politeness, *Fr* savoir faire, sensitivity, tactfulness, thoughtfulness, understanding. *Opp* TACTLESSNESS.

tactful *adj* adroit, appropriate, considerate, courteous, delicate, diplomatic, discreet, judicious, perceptive, polite, politic, sensitive, thoughtful, understanding. *Opp* TACTLESS.

tactical *adj* artful, calculated, clever, deliberate, planned, politic, prudent, shrewd, skilful, strategic.

tactics *n* approach, campaign, course of action, design, device, manoeuvre, manoeuvring, plan, ploy, policy, procedure, ruse, scheme, stratagem, strategy.

tactless *adj* blundering, blunt, clumsy, discourteous, gauche, heavy-handed, hurtful, impolite, impolitic, inappropriate, inconsiderate, indelicate, indiscreet, inept, insensitive, maladroit, misjudged, thoughtless, undiplomatic, unkind. ⊳ RUDE. *Opp* TACTFUL.

tactlessness *n* clumsiness, gaucherie, indelicacy, indiscretion, ineptitude, insensitivity, lack of diplomacy, misjudgement, thoughtlessness. ⊳ RUDENESS. *Opp* TACT.

tag *n* 1 docket, label, marker, name tag, price tag, slip, sticker, tab, ticket. 2 *a Latin tag.* ⊳ SAYING.
• *v* identify, label, mark, ticket. **tag along with** ⊳ FOLLOW.

tail *n* appendage, back, brush (*of fox*), buttocks, end, extremity, rear, rump, scut (*of rabbit*), tail-end.
• *v* dog, follow, hunt, pursue, shadow, stalk, track, trail. **tail off** ⊳ DECLINE.

taint *v* 1 adulterate, contaminate, defile, dirty, infect, poison, pollute, soil. 2 *taint a reputation.* blacken, damage, dishonour, harm, ruin, smear, spoil, stain, tarnish.

take *v* 1 acquire, bring, carry away, *inf* cart off, clasp, fetch, gain, get, grab, grasp, grip, hold, pick up, pluck, seize, snatch. 2 *take prisoners.* abduct, arrest, capture, catch, detain, ensnare, secure. 3 *take property.* appropriate, pocket, remove. ⊳ STEAL. 4 *take 2 from 4.* deduct, subtract, take away. 5 *I can take two passengers.* accommodate, carry, have room for, hold. 6 *I'll take you home.* accompany, conduct, convey, escort, ferry, guide, lead. 7 *take a taxi.* engage, hire, travel by, use. 8 *take a subject.* have lessons in, read, study. 9 *He can't take it any longer.* abide, bear, brook, endure, stand, stomach, suffer, tolerate, undergo, withstand. 10 *take food, drink.* consume, drink, eat, have, swallow. 11 *It takes courage to own up.* necessitate, need, require. 12 *take a new name.* adopt, assume, choose, select. **take aback** ▷ SURPRISE. **take after** ▷ RESEMBLE. **take against** ▷ DISLIKE. **take back** ▷ WITHDRAW. **take in** ▷ ACCOMMODATE, DECEIVE, UNDERSTAND. **take life** ▷ KILL. **take off** ▷ IMITATE. **take off, take out** ▷ REMOVE. **take on, take up** ▷ UNDERTAKE. **take over** ▷ USURP. **take part** ▷ PARTICIPATE. **take place** ▷ HAPPEN. **take to task** ▷ REPRIMAND. **take up** ▷ BEGIN, OCCUPY.

takeover *n* amalgamation, incorporation, merger.

takings *n* earnings, gains, gate, income, proceeds, profits, receipts, revenue.

tale *n* account, anecdote, chronicle, fable, legend, narration, narrative, report, saga, *sl* spiel, story, yarn.

talent *n* ability, accomplishment, aptitude, brilliance, capacity, expertise, facility, faculty, flair, genius, gift, knack, *inf* know-how, prowess, skill, versatility.

talented *adj* able, accomplished, artistic, brilliant, distinguished, expert, gifted, inspired, proficient, skilful, skilled, versatile. ▷ CLEVER. *Opp* UNSKILFUL.

talisman *n* amulet, charm, mascot.

talk *n* 1 baby-talk, *inf* blarney, *inf* chat, *inf* chin-wag, *inf* chit-chat, conference, conversation, dialogue, discourse, discussion, gossip, language, palaver, *inf* powwow, *inf* tattle, *inf* tittle-tattle, words. 2 *a public talk.* address, diatribe, exhortation, harangue, lecture, oration, *inf* pep talk, presentation, sermon, speech, tirade.
▪ *v* 1 address one another, commune, communicate, confer, converse, discourse, discuss, exchange views, have a conversation, *inf* hold forth, negotiate, *inf* pipe up, pontificate, speak, use your voice, utter, verbalize, vocalize. 2 *She never stops talking!* babble, *inf* chat, chatter, gabble, gossip, jabber, jaw, mumble, mutter, *inf* natter, prattle, *inf* rabbit on, *inf* rattle on, spout, whisper, *inf* witter. 3 *talk French.* communicate in, converse in, express yourself in, speak. 4 *get someone to talk.* confess, give information, *sl* grass, inform, *inf* spill the beans, *inf* squeal, *inf* tell tales. 5 *talk to an audience.* deliver a speech, give an address, lecture, preach, sermonize. ▷ SAY, SPEAK. **talk about** ▷ DISCUSS. **talk to** ▷ ADDRESS.

talkative *adj* articulate, chatty, communicative, effusive, eloquent, expansive, garrulous, glib, gossipy, long-winded, loquacious, open, prolix, unstoppable, verbose, vocal, voluble, wordy. *Opp* TACITURN. **talkative person** chatterbox, *sl* gasbag, gossip, *inf* windbag.

tall *adj* colossal, giant, gigantic, high, lofty, soaring, towering. ▷ BIG. *Opp* SHORT.

tally *n* addition, count, reckoning, record, sum, total.
▪ *v* 1 accord, agree, coincide, concur, correspond, match up, square. 2 *tally up the bill.* add, calculate, compute, count, reckon, total, work out.

tame *adj* 1 amenable, biddable, compliant, docile, gentle, ineffectual, meek, mild, obedient, passive, subdued, submissive, tractable, unassertive. 2 *tame animals.* approachable, broken in, domesticated, fearless, friendly, harmless, house-trained, manageable, safe, sociable, tamed, trained, unafraid. 3 *Her life was very tame.* bland, boring, colourless, dull, feeble, flat, insipid, prosaic, tedious, unadventurous, unexciting, uninspiring, uninteresting, vapid, *inf* wishy-washy. *Opp* EXCITING, WILD.
▪ *v* break in, conquer, curb, discipline, domesticate, house-train, make tame, master, pacify, quell, repress, subdue, subjugate, suppress, temper, tone down, train.

tamper *v* **tamper with** alter, fiddle about with, interfere with, make adjustments to, meddle with, tinker with.

tan *n* sunburn, suntan.
▪ *v* bronze, brown, burn, colour, darken, get tanned.

tang *n* acidity, *inf* bite, *inf* nip, piquancy, pungency, savour, sharpness, spiciness, zest.

tangible *adj* actual, concrete, corporeal, definite, material, palpable, perceptible, physical, real, solid, substantial, tactile, touchable. *Opp* INTANGIBLE.

tangle *n* coil, complication, confusion, jumble, jungle, knot, labyrinth, mass, maze, mesh, mess, muddle, scramble, web.
▪ *v* 1 complicate, confuse, entangle, entwine, *inf* foul up, intertwine, interweave, muddle, scramble, *inf* snarl up, twist. 2 *tangle fish in a net.* catch, enmesh, ensnare, trap. *Opp* DISENTANGLE, FREE. 3 *tangle with criminals.* become involved

with, confront, cross. **tangled** ▷ DISHEVELLED, INTRICATE.

tangy *adj* acid, appetizing, bitter, fresh, piquant, pungent, refreshing, sharp, spicy, strong, tart. *Opp* BLAND.

tank *n* 1 aquarium, basin, cistern, reservoir. 2 *army tank.* armoured vehicle.

tanned *adj* brown, sunburnt, suntanned, weather-beaten.

tantalize *v* entice, frustrate, *inf* keep on tenterhooks, lead on, provoke, taunt, tease, tempt, titillate, torment.

tap *n* 1 *Amer* faucet, spigot, stopcock, valve. 2 knock, rap.
• *v* 1 knock, rap, strike. ▷ HIT. 2 *tap a savings account.* drain, draw on, exploit, milk, utilize.

tape *n* 1 band, binding, braid, ribbon, strip. 2 audiotape, cassette, magnetic tape, tape recording, videotape.
• *v* 1 *tape up a package.* ▷ FASTEN. 2 *tape a programme.* record, tape-record, video.

taper *n* candle, lighter, spill.
• *v* attenuate, become narrower, narrow, thin. **taper off** ▷ DECLINE.

target *n* 1 aim, ambition, end, goal, hope, intention, objective, purpose. 2 *target of attack.* butt, object, quarry, victim.

tariff *n* 1 charges, menu, pricelist, schedule. 2 *tariff on imports.* customs, duty, excise, impost, levy, tax, toll.

tarnish *v* 1 blacken, corrode, dirty, discolour, soil, taint. 2 *tarnish a reputation.* blemish, blot, defame, denigrate, disgrace, dishonour, mar, ruin, spoil, stain, sully.

tarry *v* dawdle, hang about, linger, wait. ▷ DELAY.

tart *adj* 1 acid, acidic, astringent, biting, citrus, lemony, piquant, pungent, sharp, sour, tangy. 2 *tart rejoinder.* ▷ SHARP. *Opp* BLAND, SWEET.
• *n* 1 flan, pastry, pie, quiche, tartlet, turnover. 2 ▷ PROSTITUTE.

task *n* activity, assignment, business, charge, chore, duty, employment, enterprise, errand, job, mission, requirement, test, undertaking, work. **take to task** ▷ REPRIMAND.

taste *n* 1 character, flavour, relish, savour. 2 bit, bite, morsel, mouthful, nibble, piece, sample, titbit. 3 *acquired taste.* appetite, appreciation, choice, fondness, inclination, judgement, leaning, liking, partiality, preference. 4 *person of taste.* breeding, cultivation, culture, discernment, discretion, discrimination, education, elegance, fashion sense, finesse, good judgement, perception, polish, refinement, sensitivity, style.
• *v* nibble, relish, sample, savour, sip, test, try. **in bad taste** ▷ TASTELESS. **in good taste** ▷ TASTEFUL.

tasteful *adj* aesthetic, artistic, attractive, charming, cultivated, decorous, dignified, discerning, discreet, discriminating, elegant, fashionable, in good taste, judicious, *inf* nice, proper, refined, restrained, sensitive, smart, stylish, well-judged. *Opp* TASTELESS.

tasteless *adj* 1 cheap, coarse, crude, *inf* flashy, garish, gaudy, graceless, improper, in bad taste, indecorous, indelicate, inelegant, injudicious, in poor taste, *inf* kitsch, loud, ugly, unattractive, uncouth, undiscriminating, unfashionable, unimaginative, unpleasant, unrefined, unseemly, unstylish, vulgar. *Opp* TASTEFUL. 2 *tasteless food.* bland, flavourless, insipid, mild, watered-down, watery, weak, *inf* wishy-washy. *Opp* TASTY.

tasty *adj* appetizing, delectable, delicious, flavoursome, luscious, *inf* mouth-watering, *inf* nice, palatable, piquant, savoury, *inf* scrumptious, spicy, tangy, *sl* yummy. *Opp* TASTELESS.

tattered *adj* frayed, ragged, ripped, shredded, *inf* tatty, threadbare, torn, worn out. *Opp* SMART.

tatters *pl n* bits, pieces, rags, ribbons, shreds, torn pieces.

tatty *adj* 1 frayed, old, patched, ragged, ripped, *inf* scruffy, shabby, tattered, torn, threadbare, untidy, worn out. 2 ▷ TAWDRY. *Opp* SMART.

taunt *v* annoy, goad, insult, jeer at, mock, tease, torment. ▷ RIDICULE.

taut *adj* firm, rigid, stiff, strained, stretched, tense, tight. *Opp* SLACK.

tautological *adj* long-winded, prolix, redundant, repetitious, repetitive, superfluous, tautologous, verbose, wordy. *Opp* CONCISE.

tautology *n* longwindedness, prolixity, repetition, verbiage, verbosity, wordiness.

tavern *n old use* alehouse, bar, hostelry, inn, *inf* local, pub, public house.

tawdry *adj* cheap, common, fancy, *inf* flashy, garish, gaudy, inferior, meretricious, poor quality, showy, tasteless, *inf* tatty, tinny, vulgar, worthless. *Opp* TASTEFUL.

tax *n* charge, customs, due, duty, excise, impost, income tax, levy, tariff, toll.
• *v* 1 assess, exact, impose a tax on, levy a tax on. 2 *tax someone's patience.* burden, exhaust, make heavy demands on, overwork, strain, try. ▷ TIRE. **tax with** accuse of, blame for, charge with, reproach for, reprove for.

taxi *n* cab, minicab, taxicab.

taxing *adj* arduous, demanding, exhausting, onerous, stressful, tiring. ▷ DIFFICULT.

teach *v* advise, coach, counsel, demonstrate to, discipline, drill, edify, educate, enlighten, familiarize with, give lessons in, ground in, guide, impart knowledge to, indoctrinate, inform, instruct, lecture, school, train, tutor.

teacher *n* adviser, coach, don, educator, governess, guide, guru, headteacher, instructor, lecturer, master, mentor, mistress, professor, schoolteacher, trainer, tutor.

teaching *n* 1 coaching, education, grounding, guidance, indoctrination, instruction, schooling, training, tuition. 2 *religious teaching.* doctrine, dogma, gospel, precept, principle, tenet.

team *n* club, crew, gang, *inf* line up, side. ▷ GROUP.

tear *n* 1 droplet, tear-drop. [*pl*] *inf* blubbering, crying, sobs, weeping. 2 cut, fissure, gash, hole, laceration, opening, rent, rip, slit, split.
• *v* 1 claw, gash, lacerate, mangle, rend, rip, rupture, scratch, sever, shred, slit, snag, split. 2 [*inf*] ▷ RUSH. **shed tears** ▷ WEEP.

tearful *adj inf* blubbering, crying, emotional, in tears, lachrymose, snivelling, sobbing, weeping, *inf* weepy, whimpering. ▷ SAD.

tease *v inf* aggravate, annoy, bait, chaff, goad, irritate, laugh at, make fun of, mock, *inf* needle, pester, plague, provoke, *inf* pull someone's leg, *inf* rib, tantalize, taunt, torment. ▷ RIDICULE.

teasing *n* badinage, banter, chaffing, joking, mockery, provocation, raillery, *inf* ribbing, ridicule, taunts.

technical *adj* 1 complicated, detailed, expert, professional, specialized. 2 *technical skill.* mechanical, scientific, technological.

technician *n* engineer, mechanic, skilled worker.

technique *n* 1 approach, knack, manner, means, method, mode, procedure, routine, system, trick, way. 2 *artist's technique.* art, artistry, craft, craftsmanship, expertise, facility, *inf* know-how, proficiency, skill, talent, workmanship.

technological *adj* automated, computerized, electronic, scientific.

tedious *adj* boring, dreary, *inf* dry as dust, dull, endless, humdrum, irksome, laborious, long-drawn-out, long-winded, monotonous, prolonged, repetitive, slow, soporific, tiresome, tiring, unexciting, uninteresting, wearing, wearisome, wearying. *Opp* INTERESTING.

tedium *n* boredom, dreariness, dullness, ennui, monotony, slowness, tediousness.

teem *v* 1 abound (in), be alive (with), be full (of), be infested, be overrun (by), *inf* bristle, *inf* crawl, proliferate, seethe, swarm with. 2 ▷ RAIN.

teenager *n* adolescent, boy, girl, juvenile, minor, youngster, youth.

teetotal *adj* abstemious, abstinent, *sl* on the wagon, self-disciplined, sober.

teetotaller *n* abstainer, nondrinker.

telegram *n* cable, cablegram, fax, telemessage, telex, wire.

telepathic *adj* clairvoyant, psychic.

telephone *n inf* blower, carphone, handset, phone.
• *v inf* buzz, call, dial, *inf* give someone a buzz, *inf* give someone a call, phone, ring, ring up.

televise *v* broadcast, relay, send out, transmit.

television *n inf* the box, receiver, *inf* small screen, *inf* telly, *inf* TV, video.

tell *v* 1 acquaint with, advise, announce, assure, communicate, describe, disclose, divulge, explain, impart, inform, make known, narrate, notify, portray, promise, recite, recount, rehearse, relate, reveal, utter. ▷ SPEAK, TALK. 2 *tell the difference.* comprehend, discover, discriminate, distinguish, identify, notice, recognize, see. 3 *tell me what to do.* command, direct, instruct, order. **tell off** ▷ REPRIMAND.

teller *n* 1 author, narrator, raconteur, storyteller. 2 *teller in a bank.* bank clerk, cashier.

telling *adj* effective, influential, potent, powerful, significant, striking, weighty.

temper *n* 1 attitude, character, disposition, frame of mind, humour, *inf* make-up, mood, personality, state of mind, temperament. 2 *Beware of his temper.* anger, churlishness, fury, ill-humour, irascibility, irritability, peevishness, petulance,

surliness, volatility, wrath. 3 *She flew into a temper.* fit of pique, *inf* paddy, passion, rage, tantrum. 4 *Try to keep your temper.* calmness, composure, *sl* cool, coolness, equanimity, sang-froid, self-control, self-possession.
• *v* 1 assuage, lessen, mitigate, moderate, modify, reduce, soften, soothe, tone down. 2 *temper steel.* harden, strengthen, toughen.

temperament *n* attitude, character, disposition, frame of mind, humour, *inf* make-up, mood, nature, personality, spirit, state of mind, temper.

temperamental *adj* 1 characteristic, constitutional, inherent, innate, natural. 2 *temperamental moods.* capricious, changeable, emotional, erratic, excitable, explosive, fickle, highly-strung, impatient, inconsistent, inconstant, irascible, irritable, mercurial, moody, neurotic, passionate, touchy, unpredictable, unreliable, *inf* up and down, variable, volatile.

temperance *n* abstemiousness, moderation, self-denial, self-discipline, self-restraint, sobriety, teetotalism.

temperate *adj* calm, mild, moderate, reasonable, restrained, self-possessed, sensible, sober, stable, steady. *Opp* EXTREME.

tempest *n* cyclone, gale, hurricane, tornado, tumult, typhoon, whirlwind. ▷ STORM.

tempestuous *adj* fierce, furious, tumultuous, turbulent, violent, wild. ▷ STORMY. *Opp* CALM.

temple *n* church, house of God, mosque, pagoda, place of worship, shrine, synagogue.

tempo *n* beat, pace, rate, rhythm, pulse, speed.

temporal *adj* earthly, fleshly, impermanent, material, mortal, mundane, non-religious, secular, terrestrial, transient, transitory, worldly. *Opp* SPIRITUAL.

temporary *adj* 1 brief, ephemeral, evanescent, fleeting, fugitive, impermanent, interim, makeshift, momentary, passing, provisional, short, short-lived, short-term, stopgap, transient, transitory. 2 *temporary captain.* acting. *Opp* PERMANENT.

tempt *v* allure, attract, bait, bribe, coax, decoy, entice, fascinate, inveigle, lure, offer incentives, persuade, seduce, tantalize, woo. **tempting** ▷ APPETIZING, ATTRACTIVE.

temptation *n* allure, appeal, attraction, cajolery, coaxing, draw, enticement, fascination, inducement, lure, persuasion, pull, seduction.

tenable *adj* believable, conceivable, credible, defensible, feasible, justifiable, legitimate, logical, plausible, rational, reasonable, sensible, sound, supportable, understandable, viable. *Opp* INDEFENSIBLE.

tenacious *adj* determined, dogged, firm, intransigent, obdurate, obstinate, persistent, pertinacious, resolute, single-minded, steadfast, strong, stubborn, tight, uncompromising, unfaltering, unshakeable, unswerving, unwavering, unyielding. *Opp* WEAK.

tenant *n* inhabitant, leaseholder, lodger, occupant, occupier, resident.

tend *v* 1 attend to, care for, cherish, cultivate, guard, keep, *inf* keep an eye on, look after, manage, mind, minister to, protect, take care of, watch. 2 *tend the sick.* nurse, treat. 3 *tend to fall asleep.* be disposed, be inclined, be liable, be prone, have a tendency, incline.

tendency *n* bias, disposition, drift, inclination, instinct, leaning, liability, partiality, penchant, predilection, predisposition, proclivity, propensity, readiness, susceptibility, trend.

tender *adj* 1 dainty, delicate, fragile, frail, vulnerable, weak. 2 *tender meat.* chewable, eatable, edible, soft. 3 *tender place.* aching, inflamed, painful, sensitive, smarting, sore. 4 *tender love-song.* emotional, heartfelt, moving, poignant, romantic, sentimental, touching. 5 *tender care.* affectionate, amorous, caring, compassionate, concerned, considerate, fond, gentle, humane, kind, loving, merciful, pitying, soft-hearted, sympathetic, warm-hearted. 6 *tender age.* immature, inexperienced, young, youthful. *Opp* TOUGH, UNSYMPATHETIC.

tense *adj* 1 rigid, strained, stretched, taut, tight. 2 *tense person.* anxious, apprehensive, edgy, excited, fidgety, highly-strung, intense, *inf* jittery, jumpy, keyed up, nervous, on edge, *inf* on tenterhooks, overwrought, restless, strained, stressed, *inf* strung up, touchy, uneasy, *inf* uptight, worried. 3 *tense situation.* exciting, fraught, *inf* nail-biting, nerve-racking, stressful, worrying. *Opp* RELAXED.

tension *n* 1 pull, strain, tautness, tightness. 2 *the tension of waiting.* anxiety, apprehension, edginess, excitement, nervousness, stress, suspense, unease, worry. *Opp* RELAXATION.

tent *n* big-top, marquee, tepee, wigwam.

tentative *adj* cautious, diffident, doubtful, experimental, exploratory, half-hearted, hesitant, inconclusive, indecisive, indefinite, nervous, preliminary, provisional, shy, speculative, timid, uncertain, unsure. *Opp* DECISIVE.

tenuous *adj* attenuated, fine, flimsy, fragile, insubstantial, slender, slight, weak. ▷ THIN. *Opp* STRONG.

tepid *adj* 1 lukewarm, warm. 2 *tepid response*. ▷ APATHETIC.

term *n* 1 duration, period, season, span, spell, stretch, time. 2 *school term. Amer* semester, session. 3 *technical terms*. designation, expression, name, phrase, saying, title, word. **terms** 1 conditions, particulars, provisions, specifications, stipulations. 2 *hotel's terms*. charges, fees, prices, rates, tariff.

terminal *adj* deadly, fatal, final, incurable, killing, lethal, mortal.
▪ *n* 1 keyboard, VDU, workstation. 2 *passenger terminal*. destination, terminus. 3 *electric terminal*. connection, connector, coupling.

terminate *v* bring to an end, cease, come to an end, discontinue, end, finish, *inf* pack in, phase out, stop, *inf* wind up. ▷ END. *Opp* BEGIN.

terminology *n* choice of words, jargon, language, nomenclature, phraseology, special terms, vocabulary.

terminus *n* destination, last stop, station, terminal.

terrain *n* country, ground, land, landscape, territory.

terrestrial *adj* earthly, mundane, ordinary.

terrible *adj* 1 acute, appalling, awful, beastly, distressing, dreadful, fearful, fearsome, formidable, frightening, frightful, ghastly, grave, gruesome, harrowing, hideous, horrendous, horrible, horrific, horrifying, intolerable, loathsome, nasty, nauseating, outrageous, revolting, shocking, terrifying, unbearable, vile. 2 ▷ BAD.

terrific *adj Terrific* may mean *causing terror* (▷ TERRIBLE). It is more often used *informally* of anything which is *extreme* in its own way: *a terrific problem* ▷ EXTREME; *terrific size* ▷ BIG; *a terrific party* ▷ EXCELLENT; *a terrific storm* ▷ VIOLENT.

terrify *v* appal, dismay, horrify, *inf* make your blood run cold, petrify, shock, terrorize. ▷ FRIGHTEN. **terrified** ▷ FRIGHTENED. **terrifying** ▷ FRIGHTENING.

territory *n* area, colony, district, domain, dominion, enclave, jurisdiction, land, neighbourhood, precinct, preserve, province, region, sector, sphere, state, terrain, tract, zone. ▷ COUNTRY.

terror *n* alarm, awe, dismay, dread, fright, horror, panic, shock, trepidation. ▷ FEAR.

terrorist *n* assassin, bomber, guerilla, gunman, hijacker, revolutionary.

terrorize *v* browbeat, bully, coerce, cow, intimidate, menace, persecute, terrify, threaten, torment, tyrannize. ▷ FRIGHTEN.

terse *adj* abrupt, brief, brusque, concise, crisp, curt, epigrammatic, incisive, laconic, pithy, short, *inf* short and sweet, *inf* snappy, succinct, to the point. *Opp* VERBOSE.

test *n* analysis, appraisal, assessment, audition, *inf* check-over, *inf* check-up, evaluation, examination, inspection, interrogation, investigation, quiz, screen-test, trial, *inf* try-out.
▪ *v* analyse, appraise, assess, audition, check, evaluate, examine, experiment with, inspect, interrogate, investigate, probe, *inf* put someone through their paces, put to the test, question, quiz, screen, try out.

testify *v* affirm, attest, bear witness, declare, give evidence, proclaim, state on oath, swear, vouch, witness.

testimonial *n* character reference, commendation, recommendation, reference.

testimony *n* assertion, declaration, deposition, evidence, statement, submission.

tether *n* chain, cord, halter, lead, leash, restraint, rope.
▪ *v* chain up, fetter, keep on a tether, leash, restrain, rope, secure, tie up. ▷ FASTEN.

text *n* 1 argument, content, contents, matter, subject matter, wording. 2 *literary text*. book, textbook, work. 3 *text from scripture*. line, passage, quotation, sentence, theme, topic, verse.

textile *n* cloth, fabric, material, stuff.

texture *n* composition, consistency, feel, finish, grain, quality, surface, touch, weave.

thank *v* acknowledge, express thanks, say thank you, show gratitude.

thankful *adj* appreciative, contented, glad,

grateful, happy, indebted, pleased, relieved. *Opp* UNGRATEFUL.

thankless *adj* bootless, futile, profitless, unappreciated, unrecognized, unrewarded, unrewarding. *Opp* PROFITABLE.

thanks *pl n* acknowledgement, appreciation, gratitude, recognition, thanksgiving. **thanks to** as a result of, because of, owing to, through.

thaw *v* defrost, de-ice, heat up, melt, soften, unfreeze, warm up. *Opp* FREEZE.

theatre *n* 1 amphitheatre, auditorium, hall, opera house, playhouse. 2 acting, stagecraft. ▷ DRAMA. **the theatre** entertainment, show business, *inf* showbiz, the stage.

theatrical *adj* 1 *theatrical company.* dramatic, repertory, stage. 2 [*derog*] *theatrical behaviour.* affected, artificial, exaggerated, forced, *inf* hammy, melodramatic, ostentatious, overacted, overdone, *inf* over the top, showy, stagy, unnatural. *Opp* NATURAL.

theft *n* burglary, embezzlement, fraud, housebreaking, larceny, looting, pilfering, *inf* pinching, poaching, purloining, robbery, shoplifting, stealing, swindling, thieving.

theme *n* 1 argument, essence, gist, idea, issue, keynote, matter, subject, text, thesis, thread, topic. 2 *musical theme.* air, melody, motif, subject, tune.

theology *n* divinity, religion, religious studies.

theoretical *adj* abstract, academic, conjectural, doctrinaire, hypothetical, ideal, notional, pure (*science*), putative, speculative, suppositious, unproven, untested. *Opp* PRACTICAL, PROVEN.

theorize *v* conjecture, form a theory, guess, hypothesize, reason, speculate.

theory *n* 1 argument, assumption, belief, conjecture, explanation, guess, hypothesis, idea, notion, speculation, supposition, surmise, thesis, view. 2 *theory of a subject.* laws, principles, rules, science. *Opp* PRACTICE.

therapeutic *adj* beneficial, corrective, curative, healing, healthy, helpful, medicinal, remedial, restorative, salubrious. *Opp* HARMFUL.

therapist *n* analyst, counsellor, healer, physiotherapist, psychoanalyst, psychotherapist.

therapy *n* 1 cure, healing, remedy, tonic, treatment. 2 *therapy sessions.* analysis, group therapy, psychotherapy, psychoanalysis.

therefore *adv* accordingly, consequently, hence, so, thus.

thesis *n* 1 argument, assertion, contention, hypothesis, idea, opinion, postulate, premise, premiss, proposition, theory, view. 2 *research thesis.* dissertation, essay, paper, tract, treatise.

thick *adj* 1 broad, *inf* bulky, chunky, stout, sturdy, wide. ▷ FAT. 2 *thick layer, sweater.* deep, heavy, substantial, woolly. 3 *thick crowd.* dense, impenetrable, numerous, packed, solid. 4 *thick liquid.* clotted, coagulated, concentrated, condensed, firm, glutinous, heavy, sticky, stiff, viscous. 5 *thick growth.* abundant, bushy, luxuriant, plentiful. 6 *thick with visitors.* alive, bristling, *inf* chock-full, choked, covered, crammed, crawling, crowded, filled, full, jammed, swarming, teeming. *Opp* THIN.

thicken *v* clot, coagulate, concentrate, condense, congeal, firm up, *inf* jell, reduce, solidify, stiffen.

thickness *n* 1 breadth, density, depth, viscosity, width. 2 *thickness of paint, rock.* coating, layer, seam, stratum.

thief *n* bandit, brigand, burglar, criminal, *inf* crook, embezzler, highwayman, housebreaker, kleptomaniac, looter, mugger, pickpocket, pilferer, pirate, plagiarist, poacher, purloiner, robber, safe-cracker, shoplifter, stealer, swindler.

thieving *adj* dishonest, light-fingered, rapacious.
▪ *n* ▷ THEFT.

thin *adj* 1 anorexic, attenuated, bony, cadaverous, emaciated, fine, gangling, gaunt, lanky, lean, narrow, pinched, rangy, scraggy, scrawny, skeletal, skinny, slender, slight, slim, small, spare, spindly, underfed, undernourished, underweight, wiry. *Opp* FAT. 2 *thin layer.* delicate, diaphanous, filmy, fine, flimsy, gauzy, insubstantial, light, *inf* see-through, shallow, sheer (*silk*), superficial, translucent, wispy. 3 *thin crowd.* meagre, scanty, scarce, scattered, sparse. 4 *thin liquid.* dilute, fluid, runny, sloppy, watery, weak. 5 *thin atmosphere.* rarefied. 6 *thin excuse.* feeble, implausible, tenuous, transparent, unconvincing. *Opp* DENSE, STRONG, THICK.
▪ *v* dilute, water down, weaken. **thin out** 1 decrease, diminish, disperse. 2 prune, reduce, trim, weed out.

thing *n* 1 apparatus, artefact, article, device, entity, gadget, implement, item, object, utensil. 2 affair, circumstance, deed, event, eventuality, happening, incident, occurrence, phenomenon. 3 *I need to mention one thing.* detail, fact, factor, feature, point, statement, subject, thought. 4 *the first thing to do.* act, action, chore, deed, job, responsibility, task. 5 [*inf*] *thing about snakes.* aversion, fixation, *inf* hang-up, mania, neurosis, obsession, passion, phobia, preoccupation. **things** 1 baggage, belongings, clothing, equipment, *inf* gear, luggage, possessions, *inf* stuff. 2 *How are things?* circumstances, conditions, life.

think *v* 1 attend, brood, chew things over, cogitate, concentrate, consider, contemplate, daydream, deliberate, dream, dwell (on), expect, fantasize, give thought (to), imagine, meditate, mull over, muse, ponder, *inf* rack your brains, reason, reflect, remind yourself of, reminisce, ruminate, work things out. 2 *Do you think it's true?* accept, admit, assume, believe, be under the impression, conclude, deem, estimate, feel, guess, imagine, judge, presume, reckon, suppose, surmise. **think better of** ▷ RECONSIDER. **thinking** ▷ INTELLIGENT, THOUGHTFUL. **think up** ▷ DEVISE.

thinker *n inf* brain, innovator, intellect, inventor, philosopher, sage, scholar.

thirst *n* 1 drought, dryness, thirstiness. 2 *thirst for knowledge.* appetite, craving, desire, eagerness, hunger, itch, longing, love (of), lust, passion, urge, wish, yearning, *inf* yen.
• *v* be thirsty, crave, have a thirst, hunger, long, strive (after), wish, yearn. **thirst for** ▷ WANT.

thirsty *adj* 1 arid, dehydrated, dry, *inf* gasping, panting, parched. 2 *thirsty for news.* avid, craving, desirous, eager, greedy, hankering, itching, longing, voracious, yearning.

thorn *n* barb, bristle, needle, prickle, spike, spine.

thorny *adj* 1 barbed, bristly, prickly, scratchy, sharp, spiky, spiny. 2 ▷ DIFFICULT.

thorough *adj* 1 assiduous, attentive, careful, comprehensive, conscientious, deep, detailed, diligent, efficient, exhaustive, extensive, full, *inf* in-depth, methodical, meticulous, minute, observant, orderly, organized, painstaking, scrupulous, searching, systematic, thoughtful, watchful. *Opp* SUPERFICIAL. 2 *thorough rascal.* absolute, complete, downright, out and out, perfect, proper, sheer, thoroughgoing, total, unmitigated, unmixed, unqualified, utter.

thought *n* 1 *inf* brainwork, brooding, *inf* brown study, cogitation, concentration, consideration, contemplation, daydreaming, deliberation, intelligence, introspection, meditation, musing, pensiveness, reason, reasoning, reflection, reverie, rumination, study, thinking, worrying. 2 *clever thought.* belief, concept, conception, conclusion, conjecture, conviction, idea, notion, observation, opinion. 3 *no thought of gain.* aim, design, dream, expectation, hope, intention, plan, prospect, purpose. 4 *kind thought.* compassion, concern, consideration, kindness, solicitude, thoughtfulness.

thoughtful *adj* 1 absorbed, abstracted, attentive, brooding, contemplative, dreamy, engrossed, grave, introspective, meditative, pensive, rapt, reflective, serious, solemn, studious, thinking, watchful. 2 *thoughtful work.* careful, conscientious, diligent, exhaustive, intelligent, methodical, meticulous, observant, orderly, organized, painstaking, rational, scrupulous, sensible, systematic, thorough. 3 *thoughtful behaviour.* caring, compassionate, concerned, considerate, good-natured, helpful, obliging, public-spirited, solicitous, unselfish. ▷ KIND. *Opp* THOUGHTLESS.

thoughtless *adj* 1 absent-minded, careless, hasty, heedless, ill-considered, impetuous, inadvertent, inattentive, injudicious, irresponsible, mindless, negligent, rash, reckless, scatterbrained, unobservant, unthinking. ▷ STUPID. 2 *thoughtless insult.* cruel, heartless, inconsiderate, insensitive, rude, selfish, tactless, undiplomatic, unfeeling. ▷ UNKIND. *Opp* THOUGHTFUL.

thrash *v* beat, birch, cane, flay, flog, lash, scourge, whip. ▷ DEFEAT, HIT.

thread *n* 1 fibre, filament, hair, strand, string, twine, yarn. 2 *thread of a story.* argument, course, direction, drift, line of thought, plot, story line, theme.
• *v* put on a thread, string together. **thread your way** file, pass, pick your way, wind.

threadbare *adj* frayed, old, ragged, shabby, tattered, *inf* tatty, worn, worn-out.

threat *n* 1 danger, intimidation, menace, risk, warning. 2 *threat of rain.* foreboding, forewarning, intimation, omen, portent, presage.

threaten *v* 1 browbeat, bully, cow, intimidate, menace, pressurize, terrorize. ▷ FRIGHTEN. *Opp* REASSURE. 2 *clouds threaten rain.* forebode, foreshadow, portend, presage, warn of. 3 *the recession threatens jobs.* endanger, imperil, jeopardize, put at risk.

threatening *adj* forbidding, grim, impending, looming, menacing, ominous, portentous, sinister, stern, *inf* ugly, unfriendly, worrying.

three *n* threesome, triad, trio, triplet, triumvirate.

threshold *n* 1 doorstep, doorway, entrance, sill. 2 *threshold of a new era.* ▷ BEGINNING.

thrifty *adj* careful, *derog* close-fisted, economical, frugal, *derog* mean, *derog* niggardly, parsimonious, provident, prudent, skimping, sparing. *Opp* EXTRAVAGANT.

thrill *n* adventure, *inf* buzz, excitement, frisson, *inf* kick, pleasure, sensation, shiver, suspense, tingle, titillation, tremor.
• *v* arouse, delight, electrify, excite, rouse, stimulate, stir, titillate. **thrilling** ▷ EXCITING.

thriller *n* crime story, detective story, mystery, *inf* whodunit.

thrive *v* be vigorous, bloom, boom, burgeon, *inf* come on, do well, expand, flourish, grow, increase, *inf* make strides, prosper, succeed. *Opp* DIE. **thriving** ▷ PROSPEROUS, VIGOROUS.

throat *n* gullet, neck, oesophagus, windpipe.

throaty *adj* deep, gravelly, gruff, guttural, hoarse, husky, rasping, rough, thick.

throb *v* beat, palpitate, pound, pulsate, pulse, vibrate.

throe *n* convulsion, fit, *pl* labour-pains, pang, paroxysm, spasm. ▷ PAIN.

thrombosis *n* blood-clot, embolism, stroke.

throng *n* crowd, gathering, horde, mass, mob, multitude, swarm. ▷ GROUP.
• *v* ▷ GATHER.

throttle *v* asphyxiate, choke, smother, stifle, strangle, suffocate.

throw *v* 1 bowl, *inf* bung, cast, *inf* chuck, fling, heave, hurl, launch, lob, pelt, pitch, propel, put (*the shot*), send, *inf* shy, sling, toss. 2 *throw light.* cast, project, shed. 3 *throw a rider.* dislodge, floor, shake off, throw down, throw off, unseat, upset. 4 ▷ DISCONCERT. **throw away** ▷ DISCARD. **throw out** ▷ EXPEL. **throw up** ▷ PRODUCE, VOMIT.

throw-away *adj* 1 cheap, disposable. 2 *throw-away remark.* casual, offhand, passing, unimportant.

thrust *v* butt, drive, elbow, force, impel, jab, lunge, plunge, poke, press, prod, propel, push, ram, send, shoulder, shove, stab, stick, urge.

thug *n* assassin, *inf* bully-boy, delinquent, gangster, hoodlum, hooligan, mugger, *inf* rough, ruffian, *inf* tough, troublemaker, vandal, *inf* yob. ▷ CRIMINAL.

thunder *n* clap, crack, peal, reverberation, roll, rumble.
• *v* ▷ REVERBERATE.

thunderous *adj* booming, deafening, reverberant, reverberating, roaring, rumbling. ▷ LOUD.

thus *adv* accordingly, consequently, for this reason, hence, so, therefore.

thwart *v* baffle, foil, frustrate, hinder, impede, obstruct, prevent, stand in the way of, stop, *inf* stump.

ticket *n* 1 coupon, pass, permit, token, voucher. 2 *price ticket.* docket, label, marker, tab, tag.

ticklish *adj* 1 hypersensitive, *inf* prickly, sensitive, touchy. 2 *ticklish situation.* awkward, delicate, difficult, precarious, risky, tricky, uncertain.

tide *n* current, drift, ebb and flow, movement, rise and fall.

tidiness *n* meticulousness, neatness, order, orderliness, organization, smartness, system. *Opp* DISORDER.

tidy *adj* 1 neat, orderly, presentable, shipshape, smart, *inf* spick and span, spruce, straight, trim, uncluttered, well-groomed, well-kept. 2 *tidy habits.* businesslike, careful, house-proud, methodical, meticulous, organized, systematic, well-organized. *Opp* UNTIDY.
• *v* arrange, clean up, groom, neaten, put in order, rearrange, reorganize, set straight, smarten, spruce up, straighten. *Opp* MUDDLE.

tie *v* 1 bind, do up, hitch, join, knot, lash, moor, rope, secure, splice, tether, truss up. ▷ FASTEN. *Opp* UNTIE. 2 *tie in a race.* be equal, be level, be neck and neck, draw.

tier *n* layer, level, line, order, range, rank, row, stage, storey, stratum, terrace.

tight *adj* 1 close, fast, firm, fixed, immovable, secure, snug. 2 *tight lid.* airtight, close-fitting, hermetic, impermeable, impervious, leak-proof, sealed, waterproof, watertight. 3 *tight supervision*. inflexible, rigorous, severe, strict, stringent. 4 *tight ropes*. rigid, stiff, stretched, taut. 5 *tight space*. compact, constricted, crammed, cramped, crowded, inadequate, limited, packed, small. 6 ▷ DRUNK. 7 ▷ MISERLY. *Opp* FREE, LOOSE.

tighten *v* 1 clamp down, close, close up, constrict, harden, make tighter, squeeze, stiffen, tense. ▷ FASTEN. 2 *tighten ropes*. pull tighter, stretch, tauten. 3 *tighten screws*. give another turn to, screw up, secure. *Opp* LOOSEN.

till *v* cultivate, dig, farm, plough, work.

tilt *v* 1 angle, bank, incline, keel over, lean, list, slant, slope, tip. 2 *tilt with lances*. joust, thrust. ▷ FIGHT.

timber *n* 1 trees, forest, woodland. 2 beams, boards, hardwood, logs, lumber, planks, softwood. ▷ WOOD.

time *n* 1 date, hour, instant, juncture, moment, occasion, opportunity, point. 2 duration, interval, period, phase, season, *Amer* semester, session, spell, stretch, term, while. 3 *time of Queen Victoria*. age, days, epoch, era, period. 4 *time in music*. beat, measure, rhythm, tempo. • *v* 1 choose a time for, estimate, fix a time for, judge, organize, plan, schedule, timetable. 2 *time a race*. clock, measure the time of.

timeless *adj* ageless, deathless, eternal, everlasting, immortal, immutable, unchanging, undying, unending.

timely *adj* appropriate, apt, fitting, suitable.

timepiece *n* chronometer, clock, hourglass, stopwatch, sundial, timer, watch, wrist-watch.

timetable *n* agenda, calendar, curriculum, diary, list, programme, rota, schedule.

timid *adj* afraid, apprehensive, bashful, cowardly, diffident, faint-hearted, fearful, modest, *inf* mousy, nervous, pusillanimous, reserved, retiring, scared, shrinking, shy, spineless, tentative, timorous, unadventurous, unheroic, *inf* wimpish. ▷ FRIGHTENED. *Opp* BOLD.

tingle *n* 1 itch, itching, pins and needles, prickling, stinging, throb, throbbing, tickle, tickling. 2 *tingle of excitement*. quiver, shiver, thrill.
• *v* itch, prickle, sting, tickle.

tinker *v* dabble, fiddle, fool about, interfere, meddle, *inf* mess about, *inf* play about, tamper, try to mend.

tinny *adj* cheap, flimsy, inferior, insubstantial, poor-quality, shoddy, tawdry.

tinsel *n* decoration, glitter, gloss, show, sparkle.

tint *n* colour, colouring, dye, hue, shade, stain, tincture, tinge, tone, wash.

tiny *adj* diminutive, dwarf, imperceptible, infinitesimal, insignificant, microscopic, *inf* mini, miniature, minuscule, minute, negligible, pygmy, *inf* teeny, unimportant, *inf* wee, *inf* weeny. ▷ SMALL. *Opp* BIG.

tip *n* 1 apex, cap, crown, end, extremity, head, nib, peak, pinnacle, point, sharp end, summit, top, vertex. 2 *tip for a waiter*. gift, gratuity, money, present, reward, service charge. 3 *useful tip*. advice, clue, forecast, hint, information, pointer, prediction, suggestion, tip-off, warning. 4 *rubbish tip*. dump, rubbish-heap.
• *v* 1 incline, keel, lean, list, slant, slope, tilt. 2 drop off, dump, empty, pour out, spill, unload, upset. 3 *tip a waiter*. give a tip to, reward. **tip over** ▷ OVERTURN.

tire *v* 1 become bored, become tired, flag, grow weary. 2 debilitate, drain, enervate, exhaust, fatigue, *inf* finish, *sl* knacker, overtire, sap, *inf* shatter, *inf* take it out of, tax, wear out, weary. *Opp* REFRESH. **tired** ▷ WEARY. **tired of** bored with, *inf* fed up with, sick of. **tiring** ▷ EXHAUSTING.

tiredness *n* drowsiness, exhaustion, fatigue, inertia, jet-lag, lassitude, lethargy, listlessness, sleepiness, weariness.

tireless *adj* determined, diligent, dogged, dynamic, energetic, hard-working, indefatigable, persistent, pertinacious, resolute, sedulous, unceasing, unfaltering, unflagging, untiring, unwavering, vigorous. *Opp* LAZY.

tiresome *adj* 1 boring, dull, monotonous, tedious, tiring, unexciting, uninteresting, wearisome, wearying. *Opp* EXCITING. 2 *tiresome delays*. annoying, bothersome, exasperating, inconvenient, infuriating, irksome, irritating, maddening, troublesome, trying, unwelcome, upsetting, vexing.

tiring *adj* debilitating, demanding, difficult, exhausting, fatiguing, hard, laborious, strenuous, taxing, wearying. *Opp* REFRESHING.

tissue *n* 1 fabric, material, stuff, substance. 2 napkin, paper handkerchief, serviette.

title *n* 1 caption, heading, headline, inscription, name, rubric. 2 appellation, designation, form of address, office, position, rank, status. ▷ RANK. 3 *title to an inheritance*. claim, deed, entitlement, ownership, possession, prerogative, right. • *v* call, designate, entitle, give a title to, label, name, tag.

titled *adj* aristocratic, noble, upper-class.

titter *v* chortle, chuckle, giggle, laugh, snicker, snigger.

titular *adj* formal, nominal, official, *inf* so-called, theoretical, token. *Opp* ACTUAL.

toast *v* 1 brown, cook, grill. 2 *toast a guest*. drink a toast to, drink the health of, drink to, honour, pay tribute to, raise your glass to.

together *adv* all at once, at the same time, collectively, concurrently, hand in hand, in chorus, in unison, jointly, shoulder to shoulder, side by side, simultaneously.

toil *n inf* donkey work, drudgery, effort, exertion, industry, labour, work.
• *v* drudge, exert yourself, grind away, *inf* keep at it, labour, *inf* plug away, *inf* slave away, struggle, sweat. ▷ WORK.

toilet *n* 1 convenience, ladies' room, latrine, lavatory, *inf* loo, men's room, urinal, WC. 2 [*old use*] *make your toilet*. dressing, grooming, making up.

token *adj* cosmetic, emblematic, nominal, notional, perfunctory, representative, superficial, symbolic. *Opp* GENUINE.
• *n* 1 badge, emblem, evidence, indication, mark, marker, proof, reminder, sign, symbol. 2 *token of affection*. keepsake, memento, reminder, souvenir. 3 *bus token*. coin, counter, coupon, disc, voucher.

tolerable *adj* 1 acceptable, bearable, endurable, sufferable. 2 *tolerable food*. adequate, all right, average, fair, mediocre, middling, *inf* OK, ordinary, passable, satisfactory. *Opp* INTOLERABLE.

tolerance *n* 1 broad-mindedness, charity, fairness, forbearance, forgiveness, lenience, open-mindedness, openness, patience, permissiveness. 2 *tolerance of others*. acceptance, sympathy (towards), toleration, understanding. 3 *tolerance in moving parts*. allowance, clearance, play, variation.

tolerant *adj* big-hearted, broad-minded, charitable, easygoing, fair, forbearing, forgiving, generous, indulgent, lenient, liberal, magnanimous, open-minded, patient, permissive, *derog* soft, sympathetic, understanding. *Opp* INTOLERANT.

tolerate *v* abide, accept, admit, bear, brook, condone, countenance, endure, *inf* lump (*I'll have to lump it!*), make allowances for, permit, put up with, sanction, *inf* stick, stand, stomach, suffer, *inf* take, undergo, *inf* wear, weather.

toll *n* charge, dues, duty, fee, levy, payment, tariff, tax.
• *v* chime, peal, ring, sound.

tomb *n* burial chamber, burial place, catacomb, crypt, grave, last resting place, mausoleum, memorial, monument, sepulchre, vault.

tone *n* 1 accent, expression, inflection, intonation, manner, modulation, note, phrasing, pitch, quality, sound, timbre. 2 air, atmosphere, character, effect, feel, mood, spirit, style, temper, vein. 3 *colour tone*. colour, hue, shade, tinge, tint. **tone down** ▷ SOFTEN. **tone in** ▷ HARMONIZE. **tone up** ▷ STRENGTHEN.

tongue *n* dialect, idiom, language, parlance, patois, speech, talk, vernacular.

tongue-tied *adj* dumbfounded, inarticulate, *inf* lost for words, mute, silent, speechless, struck dumb.

tonic *n* boost, fillip, *inf* pick-me-up, refresher, restorative, stimulant.

tool *n* 1 apparatus, appliance, contraption, contrivance, device, gadget, hardware, implement, instrument, invention, machine, mechanism, utensil, weapon. 2 *He was used as a tool*. dupe, puppet, stooge.

tooth *n* canine, eye-tooth, fang, incisor, molar, tusk, wisdom tooth. **false teeth** bridge, denture, dentures, plate.

toothed *adj* jagged, ragged, rough, serrated. *Opp* SMOOTH.

top *adj inf* ace, best, choicest, finest, first, foremost, greatest, highest, leading, maximum, most, pre-eminent, prime, principal, supreme, topmost, unequalled, winning.
• *n* 1 acme, apex, crest, crown, culmination, head, height, high point, peak, pinnacle, summit, tip, vertex, zenith. 2 *top of a table*. surface. 3 *top of a jar*. cap, cover, covering, lid, stopper. *Opp* BOTTOM.
• *v* 1 complete, cover, decorate, finish off, garnish. 2 beat, better, cap, exceed, excel, outdo, outstrip, surpass, transcend.

topic *n* issue, matter, point, question, subject, talking point, text, theme, thesis.

topical *adj* contemporary, current, recent, timely, up-to-date.

topography *n* features, geography, *inf* lie of the land.

topple *v* 1 bring down, fell, knock down,

overturn, tip over, upset. 2 collapse, fall, overbalance, totter, tumble. 3 *topple a rival.* overthrow, unseat. ▷ DEFEAT.

torment *n* affliction, agony, anguish, distress, harassment, misery, ordeal, persecution, plague, scourge, suffering, torture, vexation, woe, worry, wretchedness. ▷ PAIN.
• *v* afflict, annoy, bait, bedevil, bother, bully, distress, harass, intimidate, nag, persecute, pester, plague, tease, torture, vex, victimize, worry. ▷ HURT.

torpid *adj* apathetic, dull, inactive, indolent, inert, languid, lethargic, lifeless, listless, passive, phlegmatic, slothful, slow, slow-moving, sluggish, somnolent, spiritless. *Opp* LIVELY.

torrent *n* cascade, cataract, deluge, downpour, flood, flow, gush, inundation, outpouring, overflow, rush, spate, stream, tide.

torrential *adj* copious, heavy, relentless, soaking, teeming, violent.

tortuous *adj* bent, circuitous, complicated, contorted, convoluted, corkscrew, crooked, curling, curvy, devious, indirect, involved, labyrinthine, meandering, roundabout, serpentine, sinuous, turning, twisted, twisting, twisty, wandering, winding, zigzag. *Opp* DIRECT, STRAIGHT.

torture *n* 1 cruelty, degradation, humiliation, persecution, punishment, torment. 2 affliction, agony, anguish, distress, misery, pain, suffering.
• *v* 1 be cruel to, brainwash, bully, degrade, dehumanize, humiliate, hurt, inflict pain on, intimidate, persecute, rack, torment, victimize. 2 *tortured by doubts.* afflict, agonize, bedevil, bother, distress, harass, pester, plague, vex, worry.

toss *v* 1 bowl, cast, *inf* chuck, fling, flip, heave, hurl, lob, pitch, shy, sling, throw. 2 *toss about in a storm.* bob, dip, flounder, lurch, pitch, plunge, reel, rock, roll, twist and turn, wallow, welter, writhe.

total *adj* 1 complete, comprehensive, entire, full, gross, overall, whole. 2 *total disaster.* absolute, downright, out and out, outright, perfect, sheer, thorough, thoroughgoing, unalloyed, unmitigated, unqualified, utter.
• *n* aggregate, amount, answer, lot, sum, whole.
• *v* 1 add up to, amount to, come to, make. 2 add up, calculate, compute, count, reckon up, *inf* tot up, work out.

totalitarian *adj* absolute, authoritarian, autocratic, despotic, dictatorial, fascist, one-party, oppressive, tyrannous, undemocratic. *Opp* DEMOCRATIC.

totter *v* dodder, falter, reel, rock, stagger, stumble, teeter, topple, tremble, waver, wobble.

touch *n* 1 feel, feeling, texture. 2 brush, caress, contact, pat, stroke, tap. 3 *expert's touch.* ability, capability, experience, expertise, facility, flair, gift, knack, manner, sensitivity, skill, style, technique, understanding, way. 4 *touch of salt.* bit, dash, drop, hint, intimation, suggestion, suspicion, taste, tinge, trace.
• *v* 1 be in contact with, brush, caress, embrace, feel, finger, fondle, graze, handle, kiss, lay a hand on, lean against, nuzzle, pat, paw, pet, push, rub, stroke, tap. 2 *touch the emotions.* affect, arouse, awaken, disturb, impress, influence, inspire, move, stimulate, stir, upset. 3 *touch 100 m.p.h.* attain, reach, rise to. 4 *No-one can touch him.* be in the same league as, come near, *inf* come up to, compare with, equal, match, parallel, rival. **touched** ▷ EMOTIONAL, MAD. **touching** ▷ EMOTIONAL. **touch off** ▷ BEGIN, IGNITE. **touch on** ▷ MENTION. **touch up** ▷ IMPROVE.

touchy *adj* edgy, highly-strung, hypersensitive, irascible, irritable, *inf* jittery, jumpy, over-sensitive, peevish, querulous, quick-tempered, sensitive, short-tempered, snappy, temperamental, testy, tetchy, thin-skinned, waspish.

tough *adj* 1 durable, hard-wearing, indestructible, lasting, rugged, stout, strong, substantial, unbreakable, well-built, well-made. 2 *tough physique. inf* beefy, brawny, burly, hardy, muscular, robust, stalwart, strong, sturdy. 3 *tough man to work for.* cold, cool, hard, *inf* hard-boiled, *inf* hard-nosed, obstinate, resolute, ruthless, severe, stern, stony, stubborn, unsentimental, unsympathetic, unyielding. 4 *tough meat.* chewy, hard, gristly, inedible, leathery, rubbery. 5 *tough job.* arduous, demanding, difficult, exacting, exhausting, gruelling, hard, laborious, strenuous, taxing, troublesome. 6 *tough questions.* baffling, *inf* knotty, mystifying, perplexing, puzzling, *inf* thorny. *Opp* EASY, TENDER, WEAK.

toughen *v* harden, make tougher, reinforce, strengthen.

tour *n* drive, excursion, expedition, jaunt, journey, outing, ride, trip.
• *v* do the rounds of, go round, make a tour of, visit. ▷ TRAVEL.

tourist *n* day-tripper, holidaymaker, sightseer, traveller, tripper, visitor.

tournament *n* championship, competition, contest, event, match, meeting, series.

tow *v* drag, draw, haul, lug, pull, trail, tug.

tower *n* belfry, bell-tower, minaret, skyscraper, spire, steeple, turret.
• *v* loom, rear, rise, soar, stand out, stick up.

towering *adj* 1 colossal, gigantic, high, huge, imposing, lofty, mighty, soaring. ▷ TALL. 2 *towering rage.* extreme, fiery, intense, overpowering, passionate, unrestrained, vehement, violent.

town *n* borough, city, community, conurbation, municipality, settlement, township, village.

toxic *adj* dangerous, deadly, harmful, lethal, noxious, poisonous. *Opp* HARMLESS.

trace *n* 1 clue, evidence, footprint, *inf* give-away, hint, indication, intimation, mark, remains, sign, spoor, token, track, trail, vestige. 2 ▷ BIT.
• *v* 1 detect, discover, find, recover, retrieve, seek out, track down. 2 chart, copy, draw, map, mark out, outline, sketch. **kick over the traces** ▷ REBEL.

track *n* 1 footmark, footprint, mark, scent, spoor, trace, trail, wake (*of ship*). 2 *farm track.* bridle path, bridleway, footpath, path, road, route, trail, way. 3 *racing track.* circuit, course, dirt track, racetrack. 4 *railway track.* branch, branch line, line, rails, railway, route, tramway.
• *v* chase, dog, follow, hound, hunt, pursue, shadow, stalk, *inf* tail, trace, trail. **make tracks** ▷ DEPART. **track down** ▷ TRACE.

tract *n* 1 *tract of land.* area, expanse, region, stretch, territory. 2 *political tract.* ▷ TREATISE.

trade *n* 1 barter, business, buying and selling, commerce, dealing, exchange, marketing, merchandising, trading, traffic, transactions. 2 *skilled trade.* calling, career, craft, employment, job, *inf* line, occupation, profession, pursuit, work.
• *v* buy and sell, do business, have dealings, market goods, merchandise, retail, sell, traffic (in). **trade in** ▷ EXCHANGE. **trade on** ▷ EXPLOIT.

trader *n* broker, buyer, dealer, merchant, retailer, salesman, seller, shopkeeper, stockist, supplier, tradesman, trafficker (*in illegal goods*), vendor.

tradition *n* 1 convention, custom, habit, institution, practice, ritual, routine, usage. 2 *popular tradition.* belief, folklore.

traditional *adj* 1 accustomed, conventional, customary, established, familiar, habitual, historic, normal, orthodox, regular, time-honoured, typical, usual. *Opp* UNCONVENTIONAL. 2 *traditional stories.* folk, handed down, old, oral, popular, unwritten. *Opp* MODERN.

traffic *n* conveyance, movements, shipping, trade, transport, transportation.
• *v* ▷ TRADE.

tragedy *n* adversity, affliction, *inf* blow, calamity, catastrophe, disaster, misfortune.

tragic *adj* 1 appalling, awful, calamitous, catastrophic, dire, disastrous, dreadful, fatal, fearful, hapless, ill-fated, ill-omened, ill-starred, inauspicious, lamentable, terrible, unfortunate, unlucky. 2 *tragic expression.* bereft, distressed, grief-stricken, hurt, pathetic, piteous, pitiful, sorrowful, woeful, wretched. *Opp* COMIC.

trail *n* 1 evidence, footmarks, footprints, marks, scent, signs, spoor, traces, wake (*of ship*). 2 path, pathway, route, track.
• *v* 1 dangle, drag, draw, pull, tow. 2 chase, follow, hunt, pursue, shadow, stalk, *inf* tail, trace, track. 3 ▷ DAWDLE.

train *n* 1 carriage, coach, diesel, electric train, express, intercity, local train, railcar, steam train. 2 *train of servants.* cortège, entourage, escort, followers, retainers, retinue, staff, suite. 3 *train of events.* ▷ SEQUENCE.
• *v* 1 coach, discipline, drill, educate, instruct, prepare, school, teach, tutor. 2 exercise, *inf* get fit, practise, prepare yourself, rehearse, *inf* work out. 3 *train a gun.* ▷ AIM.

trainee *n* apprentice, beginner, cadet, learner, *inf* L-driver, novice, pupil, starter, student.

trainer *n* coach, instructor, teacher, tutor.

training *n* discipline, education, instruction, practice, teaching, tuition.

trait *n* attribute, characteristic, feature, idiosyncrasy, peculiarity, property, quality, quirk.

traitor *n* betrayer, blackleg, collaborator, defector, deserter, double-crosser, informer, *inf* Judas, quisling, renegade, turncoat.

tramp *n* 1 hike, march, trek, trudge, walk. 2 beggar, destitute person, *inf* dosser,

inf down and out, drifter, homeless person, rover, traveller, vagabond, vagrant, wanderer.
• *v inf* footslog, hike, march, plod, stride, toil, traipse, trek, trudge.

trample *v* crush, flatten, squash, *inf* squish, stamp on, step on, tread on, walk over.

trance *n inf* brown study, daydream, daze, dream, hypnotic state, reverie, semi-consciousness, spell, stupor.

tranquil *adj* 1 calm, halcyon (*days*), peaceful, placid, quiet, restful, serene, still, undisturbed, unruffled. *Opp* STORMY. 2 *tranquil mood.* collected, composed, dispassionate, *inf* laid-back, sedate, sober, untroubled. *Opp* EXCITED.

tranquillizer *n* barbiturate, narcotic, opiate, sedative.

transaction *n* agreement, bargain, business, contract, deal, negotiation, proceeding.

transcend *v* beat, exceed, excel, outdo, outstrip, rise above, surpass, top.

transcribe *v* copy out, render, reproduce, take down, translate, write out.

transfer *v* bring, carry, change, convey, deliver, displace, ferry, hand over, make over, move, pass on, relocate, remove, shift, sign over, take, transplant, transport, transpose.

transform *v* adapt, alter, change, convert, improve, metamorphose, modify, rebuild, reconstruct, remodel, revolutionize, transfigure, translate, transmute, turn.

transformation *n* adaptation, alteration, change, conversion, improvement, metamorphosis, modification, mutation, reconstruction, revolution, transfiguration, transition, *inf* turn-about.

transgression *n* crime, error, fault, lapse, misdeed, misdemeanour, offence, sin, wickedness, wrongdoing.

transient *adj* brief, ephemeral, evanescent, fleeting, fugitive, impermanent, momentary, passing, quick, short, short-lived, temporary, transitory. *Opp* PERMANENT.

transit *n* conveyance, journey, movement, moving, passage, progress, shipment, transfer, transportation, travel.

transition *n* alteration, change, changeover, conversion, development, evolution, modification, progression, shift, transformation, transit.

translate *v* change, convert, decode, elucidate, explain, interpret, paraphrase, render, reword, transcribe. ▷ TRANSFORM.

translation *n* interpretation, paraphrase, rendering, transcription, version.

translator *n* interpreter, linguist.

transmission *n* 1 broadcast, communication, diffusion, dissemination, relaying, sending out. 2 *transmission of goods.* carriage, conveyance, dispatch, shipment, transfer, transport, transportation.

transmit *v* 1 convey, dispatch, disseminate, forward, pass on, post, send, transfer, transport. 2 *transmit a message.* broadcast, cable, communicate, emit, fax, phone, radio, relay, telephone, telex, wire. *Opp* RECEIVE.

transparent *adj* 1 clear, crystalline, diaphanous, filmy, gauzy, limpid, pellucid, *inf* see-through, sheer, translucent. 2 *transparent honesty.* ▷ CANDID.

transpire *v* ▷ HAPPEN.

transplant *v* displace, move, relocate, reposition, resettle, shift, transfer, uproot.

transport *n* 1 carrier, conveyance, haulage, removal, shipment, shipping, transportation. 2 *Do you have any means of transport?* ▷ VEHICLE.
• *v* 1 bear, carry, convey, fetch, haul, move, remove, send, shift, ship, take, transfer. 2 ▷ DEPORT.

transpose *v* change, exchange, interchange, move round, rearrange, reverse, substitute, swap, switch, transfer.

transverse *adj* crosswise, diagonal, oblique.

trap *n* ambush, booby-trap, net, noose, pitfall, ploy, snare, trick.
• *v* ambush, capture, catch, catch out, corner, deceive, dupe, ensnare, entrap, inveigle, net, snare, trick.

trappings *pl n* accessories, accoutrements, adornments, decorations, equipment, finery, fittings, furnishings, *inf* gear, ornaments, paraphernalia, *inf* things, trimmings.

trash *n* 1 debris, garbage, junk, litter, refuse, rubbish, sweepings, waste. 2 ▷ NONSENSE.

trauma *n* ▷ SHOCK.

travel *n* globe-trotting, moving around, touring, tourism, travelling. **travels** excursions, expeditions, holidays, journeys, outings, pilgrimages, tours, treks, trips, voyages, wanderings.
• *v* 1 *inf* gad about, *inf* gallivant, journey, make a trip, proceed, progress, roam,

rove, voyage, wander. 2 commute, cruise, cycle, drive, fly, hitchhike, navigate, ride, sail, tour, trek. ▷ GO.

traveller *n* 1 astronaut, aviator, commuter, cosmonaut, cyclist, driver, flyer, motorcyclist, motorist, passenger, pedestrian, sailor, voyager, walker. 2 *company traveller. inf* rep, representative, salesman, saleswoman. 3 *overseas traveller.* explorer, globe-trotter, hiker, hitchhiker, holidaymaker, pilgrim, rambler, stowaway, tourist, tripper, wanderer, wayfarer. 4 *live as a traveller.* gypsy, itinerant, nomad, tramp.

travelling *adj* itinerant, migrant, migratory, nomadic, peripatetic, restless, roaming, roving, touring, wandering.

treacherous *adj* 1 deceitful, disloyal, double-crossing, double-dealing, duplicitous, faithless, false, perfidious, sneaky, unfaithful, untrustworthy. 2 *treacherous conditions.* dangerous, deceptive, hazardous, perilous, risky, unreliable, unsafe, unstable. *Opp* LOYAL, RELIABLE.

treachery *n* betrayal, dishonesty, disloyalty, double-dealing, duplicity, faithlessness, infidelity, perfidy. ▷ TREASON. *Opp* LOYALTY.

tread *v* **tread on** crush, squash underfoot, stamp on, step on, trample, walk on.

treason *n* betrayal, high treason, mutiny, rebellion, sedition. ▷ TREACHERY.

treasure *n* cache, fortune, gold, hoard, jewels, riches, treasure trove, valuables, wealth.
• *v* adore, appreciate, cherish, esteem, guard, keep safe, love, prize, rate highly, value, worship.

treasury *n* bank, exchequer, treasure-house, vault.

treat *n* entertainment, gift, outing, pleasure, surprise.
• *v* 1 attend to, behave towards, care for, look after, use. 2 *treat a topic.* consider, deal with, discuss, tackle. 3 *treat a patient, wound.* cure, dress, give treatment to, heal, nurse, prescribe medicine for, tend. 4 *treat food.* process. 5 *I'll treat you to lunch.* entertain, pay for, regale.

treatise *n* dissertation, essay, monograph, pamphlet, paper, thesis, tract.

treatment *n* 1 care, conduct, dealing (with), handling, management, organization, reception, usage, use. 2 *treatment of illness.* cure, first aid, healing, medicine, nursing, remedy, therapy.

treaty *n* agreement, alliance, armistice, concordat, contract, convention, covenant, *inf* deal, entente, pact, peace, settlement, truce, understanding.

tree *n* bush, deciduous tree, conifer, evergreen, sapling.

tremble *v* quail, quake, quaver, quiver, shake, shiver, shudder, vibrate, waver.

tremendous *adj* alarming, appalling, awe-inspiring, fearsome, frightening, horrifying, overpowering, terrible. ▷ BIG, EXCELLENT, REMARKABLE.

tremor *n* 1 quiver, shaking, trembling, vibration. 2 earthquake.

tremulous *adj* 1 agitated, anxious, excited, frightened, *inf* jittery, jumpy, nervous, timid. *Opp* CALM. 2 quivering, shaking, shivering, trembling. *Opp* STEADY.

trend *n* 1 direction, drift, inclination, leaning, movement, shift, tendency. 2 *latest trend.* craze, fad, fashion, style, *inf* thing, vogue.

trendy *adj inf* all the rage, fashionable, *inf* in, latest, modern, stylish, up-to-date. *Opp* OLD-FASHIONED.

trespass *v* encroach, enter illegally, intrude, invade.

trial *n* 1 case, court martial, enquiry, examination, hearing, judicial proceeding, tribunal. 2 attempt, *inf* dry run, experiment, rehearsal, test, trial run, *inf* try-out. 3 affliction, difficulty, hardship, nuisance, ordeal, *sl* pain in the neck, *inf* pest, tribulation, trouble, worry.

triangular *adj* three-cornered, three-sided.

tribe *n* clan, dynasty, family, group, people, race, stock, strain.

tribute *n* accolade, commendation, compliment, eulogy, homage, honour, panegyric, praise, respect. **pay tribute to** ▷ HONOUR.

trick *n* 1 illusion, magic, sleight of hand. 2 *deceitful trick.* cheat, *inf* con, deceit, deception, fraud, hoax, joke, *inf* leg-pull, ploy, practical joke, prank, pretence, ruse, scheme, stratagem, stunt, subterfuge, swindle, trap, trickery, wile. 3 *useful trick.* art, craft, knack, *inf* know-how, secret, skill, technique. 4 *trick of speech.* characteristic, habit, idiosyncrasy, mannerism, peculiarity, way.
• *v inf* bamboozle, catch out, cheat, *inf* con, deceive, *inf* diddle, dupe, fool, hoax, hoodwink, *inf* kid, mislead, outwit, *inf* pull your leg, swindle, take in.

trickery *n* bluffing, cheating, deceit, deception, dishonesty, double-dealing, duplicity, fraud, *inf* funny business, guile, *inf* hocus-pocus, *inf* skulduggery, swindling, trick.

trickle *v* dribble, drip, drizzle, drop, exude, leak, ooze, run, seep. *Opp* GUSH.

trifle *v* dabble, fiddle, play about. **trifling** ▷ TRIVIAL.

trill *v* sing, warble, whistle.

trim *adj* compact, neat, orderly, shipshape, smart, spruce, tidy, well-groomed, well-kept. *Opp* UNTIDY.
▪ *v* clip, crop, cut, pare down, prune, shape, shear, shorten, snip, tidy.

trip *n* day out, drive, excursion, expedition, holiday, jaunt, journey, outing, ride, tour, visit, voyage.
▪ *v* 1 fall, stumble, totter, tumble. 2 *trip along.* caper, dance, frisk, gambol, run, skip. **make a trip** ▷ TRAVEL.

trite *adj* banal, commonplace, ordinary, pedestrian, predictable, uninspired, uninteresting.

triumph *n* 1 accomplishment, achievement, conquest, coup, *inf* hit, knockout, master-stroke, success, victory, *inf* walk-over, win. 2 *return in triumph.* elation, exultation, joy, jubilation.
▪ *v* be victorious, carry the day, prevail, succeed, win. **triumph over** ▷ DEFEAT.

triumphant *adj* 1 conquering, dominant, successful, victorious, winning. *Opp* UNSUCCESSFUL. 2 *inf* cocky, elated, exultant, gleeful, gloating, joyful, jubilant, proud.

trivial *adj* frivolous, inconsequential, inconsiderable, inessential, insignificant, little, meaningless, minor, negligible, paltry, petty, *inf* piddling, *inf* piffling, slight, small, superficial, trifling, trite, unimportant, worthless. *Opp* IMPORTANT.

trophy *n* 1 [*pl*] booty, loot, souvenirs, spoils. 2 *sporting trophy.* award, cup, medal, prize.

trouble *n* 1 adversity, affliction, anxiety, burden, difficulty, distress, grief, hardship, inconvenience, misfortune, problem, sadness, sorrow, suffering, trial, tribulation, unhappiness, vexation, worry. 2 *crowd trouble.* commotion, conflict, discontent, disorder, dissatisfaction, disturbance, fighting, fuss, misconduct, *inf* row, strife, turmoil, unpleasantness, unrest, violence. 3 *stomach trouble.* ▷ ILLNESS. 4 *took the trouble to get it right.* care, concern, effort, exertion, pains, struggle.
▪ *v* afflict, agitate, alarm, annoy, bother, concern, distress, disturb, exasperate, harass, *inf* hassle, impose on, inconvenience, interfere with, irk, irritate, molest, nag, pain, perturb, pester, plague, put out, ruffle, threaten, torment, upset, vex, worry. **troubled** ▷ WORRIED.

troublemaker *n* agitator, culprit, delinquent, hooligan, mischief-maker, offender, rabble-rouser, rascal, ringleader, *inf* stirrer, vandal.

troublesome *adj* annoying, bothersome, disobedient, disorderly, distressing, inconvenient, irksome, irritating, naughty, tiresome, trying, uncooperative, unruly, upsetting, vexatious, vexing, wearisome, worrying. *Opp* HELPFUL.

truancy *n* absenteeism, malingering, *sl* skiving.

truant *n* absentee, malingerer, runaway, shirker, *sl* skiver. **play truant** be absent, malinger, *sl* skive, stay away.

truce *n* armistice, ceasefire, pact, peace, suspension of hostilities, treaty.

true *adj* 1 accurate, actual, authentic, correct, exact, factual, faithful, genuine, literal, proper, real, realistic, right, veracious, verified. *Opp* FALSE. 2 *true friend.* constant, dependable, devoted, faithful, firm, honest, honourable, loyal, reliable, sincere, staunch, steadfast, trustworthy. 3 *the true owner.* authorized, legitimate, rightful, valid. 4 *true aim.* accurate, exact, perfect, precise, *inf* spot-on, unerring. *Opp* INACCURATE.

truncheon *n* ▷ BATON.

trunk *n* 1 shaft, stalk, stem. 2 body, frame, torso. 3 proboscis, snout. 4 box, case, casket, chest, coffer, crate, suitcase.

trust *n* 1 belief, certainty, confidence, conviction, credence, faith, reliance. 2 *position of trust.* duty, responsibility.
▪ *v* 1 *inf* bank on, believe in, be sure of, confide in, count on, depend on, have confidence in, have faith in, rely on. 2 assume, expect, hope, imagine, presume, suppose. *Opp* DOUBT.

trustful *adj* credulous, gullible, innocent, trusting, unquestioning, unsuspecting. *Opp* DISTRUSTFUL.

trustworthy *adj* constant, dependable, ethical, faithful, honest, honourable, loyal, moral, *inf* on the level, reliable, responsible, *inf* safe, sincere, steadfast, true, truthful, upright. *Opp* DECEITFUL.

truth *n* 1 facts, reality. *Opp* LIE. 2 accuracy, authenticity, correctness, exactness, integrity, reliability, truthfulness, validity, veracity. 3 *an accepted truth.* axiom, fact, maxim, truism.

truthful *adj* accurate, candid, correct, credible, factual, faithful, forthright, frank, honest, realistic, reliable, right, sincere, straight, true, trustworthy, veracious, unvarnished. *Opp* DISHONEST.

try *n* attempt, *inf* bash, effort, endeavour, *inf* go, *inf* shot, *inf* stab, test, trial.
• *v* 1 aim, attempt, endeavour, make an effort, strain, strive, struggle. 2 *try something new.* *inf* check out, evaluate, examine, experiment with, *inf* have a go at, *inf* have a stab at, investigate, test, try out. **trying** ▷ ANNOYING, TIRESOME. **try someone's patience** ▷ ANNOY.

tub *n* barrel, bath, butt, cask, drum, keg, pot, vat.

tube *n* capillary, cylinder, duct, hose, pipe, tubing.

tuck *v* insert, push, shove, stuff. **tuck in** ▷ EAT.

tuft *n* bunch, clump, tussock.

tug *v* drag, draw, haul, heave, jerk, lug, pluck, pull, tow, twitch, wrench, *inf* yank.

tumble *v* collapse, drop, fall, flop, pitch, roll, stumble, topple, trip up.

tumbledown *adj* broken down, crumbling, decrepit, derelict, dilapidated, ramshackle, rickety.

tumult *n* ado, agitation, commotion, excitement, fracas, hubbub, upheaval. ▷ UPROAR.

tumultuous *adj* agitated, confused, excited, frenzied, hectic, passionate, stormy, tempestuous, turbulent, unruly, violent, wild. *Opp* CALM.

tune *n* air, melody, song, strain.
• *v* adjust, regulate, set.

tuneful *adj* *inf* catchy, euphonious, mellifluous, melodious, musical, pleasant, sweet-sounding. *Opp* TUNELESS.

tuneless *adj* cacophonous, discordant, dissonant, harsh, unmusical. *Opp* TUNEFUL.

tunnel *n* burrow, gallery, hole, mine, passage, passageway, shaft, subway.
• *v* burrow, dig, excavate, mine.

turbulent *adj* 1 agitated, confused, disordered, excited, hectic, passionate, restless, seething, violent, volatile, wild. 2 *turbulent crowd.* disorderly, lawless, obstreperous, riotous, rowdy, undisciplined, unruly. 3 *turbulent weather.* blustery, choppy (*sea*), rough, stormy, tempestuous, violent, wild, windy. *Opp* CALM.

turf *n* grass, green, lawn.
• *v* **turf out** ▷ EVICT.

turgid *adj* bombastic, grandiose, high-flown, pompous, stilted, wordy.

turmoil *n* bedlam, chaos, commotion, confusion, disturbance, ferment, hubbub, hullabaloo, riot, *inf* row, *inf* rumpus, tumult, unrest, upheaval, uproar. *Opp* CALM.

turn *n* 1 coil, cycle, loop, pirouette, revolution, rotation, spin, twirl, twist, whirl. 2 angle, bend, change of direction, corner, curve, detour, dogleg, hairpin bend, junction, shift, turning point, U-turn, zigzag. 3 *It's my turn.* chance, *inf* go, innings, opportunity, shot. 4 *comic turn.* ▷ PERFORMANCE. 5 *gave me a turn.* ▷ SHOCK.
• *v* 1 circle, gyrate, loop, orbit, pivot, revolve, roll, rotate, spin, spiral, swivel, twirl, twist, whirl, wind. 2 bend, change direction, go round a corner, swerve, veer, wheel. 3 *turn a book into a film.* adapt, alter, change, convert, make, modify, transform. 4 *turn to and fro.* squirm, twist, wriggle, writhe. **turn aside** ▷ DEVIATE. **turn down** ▷ REJECT. **turn into** ▷ BECOME. **turn off** ▷ DEVIATE, DISCONNECT, REPEL. **turn on** ▷ ATTRACT, CONNECT. **turn out** ▷ EXPEL, HAPPEN, PRODUCE. **turn over** ▷ CONSIDER, OVERTURN. **turn tail** ▷ ESCAPE. **turn up** ▷ ARRIVE, DISCOVER.

turning point *n* crisis, crossroads, new direction, watershed.

turnover *n* efficiency, output, production, productivity, profits, yield.

twiddle *v* fiddle with, fidget with, twirl, twist.

twig *n* branch, offshoot, shoot, spray, sprig, stalk, stem, stick, tendril.

twilight *n* dusk, evening, gloaming, gloom, nightfall, sundown, sunset.

twin *adj* corresponding, duplicate, identical, indistinguishable, matching, paired, similar, symmetrical.
• *n* clone, double, duplicate, *inf* look-alike, match, pair, *inf* spitting image.

twirl *v* gyrate, pirouette, revolve, rotate, spin, turn, twist, wheel, whirl.

twist *n* 1 bend, coil, curl, kink, knot, loop, tangle, turn, zigzag. 2 *twist to a story.* revelation, surprise ending.
• *v* 1 bend, coil, corkscrew, curl, curve, loop, rotate, spin, spiral, turn, weave, wind, wreathe, wriggle, writhe, zigzag. 2 *twist ropes.* entangle, entwine, tangle. 3 *twist a lid.* turn, wrench. 4 *twist out of shape.* buckle, contort, crumple, distort, warp. 5 *twist meaning.*

alter, change, falsify, misquote, misrepresent. **twisted** ▷ CONFUSED, PERVERTED, TWISTY.

twisty *adj* bending, *inf* bendy, crooked, curving, *inf* in and out, indirect, meandering, rambling, roundabout, serpentine, twisted, twisting, *inf* twisting and turning, winding, zigzag. *Opp* STRAIGHT.

twitch *n* blink, convulsion, flutter, jerk, jump, spasm, tic, tremor.
• *v* fidget, flutter, jerk, jump, start, tremble.

type *n* 1 category, class, classification, designation, form, genre, group, kind, sort, species, variety. 2 *the very type of evil.* embodiment, epitome, model, pattern, personification. 3 *large type.* characters, lettering, letters, print, typeface.

typical *adj* 1 characteristic, distinctive, particular, representative. 2 *typical day.* average, conventional, normal, ordinary, standard, stock, unsurprising, usual. *Opp* UNUSUAL.

tyrannical *adj* authoritarian, autocratic, *inf* bossy, cruel, despotic, dictatorial, domineering, harsh, high-handed, imperious, oppressive, overbearing, ruthless, severe, totalitarian, undemocratic, unjust. *Opp* DEMOCRATIC.

tyrant *n* autocrat, despot, dictator, *inf* hard taskmaster, slave-driver.

U

ugly *adj* 1 deformed, disfigured, disgusting, frightful, ghastly, grisly, grotesque, gruesome, hideous, horrible, misshapen, monstrous, offensive, repulsive, revolting, shocking, sickening, terrible, vile. 2 *ugly furniture*. inelegant, plain, tasteless, unattractive, unprepossessing, unsightly. 3 *ugly mood, weather*. angry, dangerous, hostile, menacing, ominous, sinister, unfriendly. *Opp* BEAUTIFUL.

ulterior *adj* concealed, covert, hidden, secret, undeclared, undisclosed. *Opp* OVERT.

ultimate *adj* 1 closing, concluding, eventual, extreme, final, last. 2 *ultimate truth*. basic, fundamental.

umpire *n* arbiter, arbitrator, judge, official, *inf* ref, referee.

unable *adj* impotent, incapable, powerless, unfit, unprepared, unqualified. *Opp* ABLE.

unacceptable *adj* distasteful, inadmissible, inappropriate, inexcusable, invalid, objectionable, unpalatable, unsatisfactory. *Opp* ACCEPTABLE.

unaccompanied *adj* alone, lone, single-handed, unaided.

unadventurous *adj* cautious, conventional, diffident, quiet, tame, timid, unimaginative. *Opp* ADVENTUROUS.

unalterable *adj* ⊳ IMMUTABLE.

unambiguous *adj* ⊳ DEFINITE.

unanimous *adj* ⊳ UNITED.

unassuming *adj* ⊳ MODEST.

unattached *adj inf* available, free, independent, separate, single, uncommitted, unmarried.

unattractive *adj* colourless, dowdy, dull, nasty, objectionable, *inf* off-putting, plain, repulsive, tasteless, uninviting, unpleasant, unprepossessing, unsightly. ⊳ UGLY. *Opp* ATTRACTIVE.

unauthorized *adj* illegal, illicit, irregular, unlawful, unofficial. *Opp* OFFICIAL.

unavoidable *adj* certain, compulsory, destined, fated, fixed, inescapable, inevitable, inexorable, mandatory, necessary, obligatory, required, unalterable.

unaware *adj* ⊳ IGNORANT.

unbalanced *adj* 1 asymmetrical, irregular, lopsided, off-centre, shaky, uneven, unstable, wobbly. 2 *unbalanced mind*. ⊳ MAD.

unbearable *adj* insufferable, insupportable, intolerable, unacceptable, unendurable. *Opp* TOLERABLE.

unbeatable *adj* ⊳ INVINCIBLE.

unbecoming *adj* inappropriate, indecorous, indelicate, offensive, tasteless, unattractive, undignified, ungentlemanly, unladylike, unseemly, unsuitable. *Opp* DECOROUS.

unbelievable *adj* ⊳ INCREDIBLE.

unbend *v* 1 straighten. 2 [*inf*] loosen up, relax, rest, unwind.

unbending *adj* ⊳ INFLEXIBLE.

unbiased *adj* balanced, disinterested, even-handed, fair, impartial, independent, just, neutral, non-partisan, objective, open-minded, reasonable, straight, unprejudiced. *Opp* BIASED.

unbroken *adj* ⊳ CONTINUOUS, WHOLE.

uncalled-for *adj* ⊳ UNNECESSARY.

uncaring *adj* ⊳ CALLOUS.

unceasing *adj* ⊳ CONTINUOUS.

uncertain *adj* 1 ambiguous, arguable, *inf* chancy, conjectural, *inf* iffy, inconclusive, indefinite, indeterminate, questionable, risky, speculative, *inf* touch and go, unclear, unconvincing, undetermined, unforeseeable, unknown, unresolved, woolly. 2 *uncertain what to believe*. ambivalent, doubtful, dubious, equivocal, *inf* in two minds, unconvinced, undecided, unsure, vague, wavering. 3 *uncertain climate*. changeable, erratic, precarious, unpredictable, unreliable, unsettled, variable. *Opp* CERTAIN.

unchanging *adj* ⊳ CONSTANT.

uncharitable *adj* ⊳ UNKIND.

uncivilized *adj* 1 primitive, savage, wild. 2 antisocial, coarse, crude, philistine, rough, uncultured, uneducated, unsophisticated. *Opp* CIVILIZED.

unclean *adj* ⊳ DIRTY.

unclear *adj* ⊳ UNCERTAIN.

uncomfortable *adj* 1 cramped, formal, hard, lumpy, painful, restrictive, tight, tight-fitting. 2 *uncomfortable silence*. awkward, distressing, embarrassing, nervous, restless, troubled, uneasy, worried. *Opp* COMFORTABLE.

uncommon *adj* ▷ UNUSUAL.

uncommunicative *adj* ▷ TACITURN.

uncomplimentary *adj* censorious, critical, derogatory, disparaging, pejorative, scathing, slighting, unfavourable, unflattering. ▷ RUDE. *Opp* COMPLIMENTARY.

uncompromising *adj* ▷ INFLEXIBLE.

unconcealed *adj* ▷ OBVIOUS.

unconditional *adj* absolute, categorical, complete, full, outright, total, unequivocal, unlimited, unqualified, unreserved, unrestricted, wholehearted, *inf* with no strings attached. *Opp* CONDITIONAL.

uncongenial *adj* disagreeable, incompatible, unfriendly, unpleasant, unsympathetic. *Opp* CONGENIAL.

unconscious *adj* 1 anaesthetized, comatose, concussed, *inf* dead to the world, insensible, *inf* out for the count, sleeping. 2 ignorant, oblivious, unaware. 3 *unconscious humour*. accidental, inadvertent, unintentional, unwitting. 4 *unconscious reaction*. automatic, instinctive, involuntary, reflex, unthinking. 5 *unconscious desire*. repressed, subconscious, subliminal, suppressed. *Opp* CONSCIOUS.

unconsciousness *n* blackout, coma, faint, oblivion, sleep.

uncontrollable *adj* ▷ UNDISCIPLINED.

unconventional *adj* abnormal, different, eccentric, exotic, independent, odd, off-beat, original, peculiar, strange, surprising, unorthodox, unusual, *inf* way-out, weird. *Opp* CONVENTIONAL.

unconvincing *adj* implausible, improbable, incredible, unbelievable, unlikely. *Opp* PERSUASIVE.

uncooperative *adj* awkward, difficult, obstructive, stubborn, unhelpful. *Opp* COOPERATIVE.

uncover *v* bare, come across, detect, dig up, disclose, discover, expose, reveal, strip, unearth, unmask, unveil, unwrap. *Opp* COVER.

undamaged *adj* ▷ PERFECT.

undefended *adj* defenceless, exposed, insecure, unprotected, vulnerable.

undemanding *adj* ▷ EASY.

undemonstrative *adj* ▷ ALOOF.

underclothes *pl n* lingerie, *inf* smalls, underwear, *inf* undies.

undercurrent *n* atmosphere, feeling, hint, sense, suggestion, trace, undertone.

underestimate *v* belittle, minimize, miscalculate, misjudge, underrate, undervalue. *Opp* EXAGGERATE.

undergo *v* bear, endure, experience, go through, put up with, stand, suffer, withstand.

underground *adj* 1 buried, subterranean. 2 clandestine, hidden, revolutionary, secret, subversive, unofficial.

undergrowth *n* brush, bushes, ground cover, vegetation.

undermine *v* 1 erode, excavate, mine under, tunnel under. 2 destroy, ruin, sap, spoil, subvert, weaken.

underprivileged *adj* deprived, disadvantaged, impoverished, needy. ▷ POOR. *Opp* PRIVILEGED.

understand *v* 1 appreciate, be conversant with, *inf* catch on, comprehend, decipher, fathom, figure out, follow, gather, *inf* get, grasp, know, learn, make out, make sense of, master, perceive, realize, recognize, see, take in, *inf* twig. 2 be in sympathy with, empathize with, sympathize with.

understanding *n* 1 ability, acumen, brains, cleverness, discernment, insight, intellect, intelligence, judgement, penetration, perceptiveness, sense, wisdom. 2 *understanding of a problem*. appreciation, awareness, comprehension, grasp, knowledge. 3 *understanding between people*. accord, agreement, consensus, empathy, fellow feeling, harmony, sympathy, tolerance. 4 *formal understanding*. arrangement, bargain, contract, deal, pact, settlement, treaty.

understate *v* belittle, *inf* make light of, minimize, *inf* play down. *Opp* EXAGGERATE.

undertake *v* 1 agree, consent, guarantee, pledge, promise, try. 2 *undertake a task*. accept responsibility for, address, approach, attend to, begin, commence, commit yourself to, embark on, manage, tackle, take on.

undertaking *n* 1 affair, business, enterprise, project, task, venture. 2 ▷ PROMISE.

undervalue *v* ▷ UNDERESTIMATE.

underwater *adj* submarine, sunken, undersea.

undeserved *adj* unfair, unjustified, unwarranted.

undesirable *adj* ▷ OBJECTIONABLE.

undisciplined *adj* anarchic, chaotic, disobedient, disorderly, disorganized, intractable, rebellious, uncontrollable, unmanageable, unruly, wild, wilful. *Opp* OBEDIENT.

undisguised *adj* ▷ OBVIOUS.

undistinguished *adj* ▷ ORDINARY.

undo *v* 1 detach, disconnect, loosen, open, unchain, unfasten, unhook, unleash, unlock, unpick, unscrew, untie, unwrap, unzip. 2 *undo someone's good work.* cancel out, destroy, nullify, reverse, ruin, spoil, undermine, vitiate, wipe out, wreck.

undoubted *adj* ▷ INDISPUTABLE.

undoubtedly *adv* certainly, definitely, of course, surely, undeniably, unquestionably.

undress *v* disrobe, *inf* peel off, shed your clothes, strip off. **undressed** ▷ NAKED.

undue *adj* ▷ EXCESSIVE.

undying *adj* ▷ ETERNAL.

uneasy *adj* anxious, apprehensive, awkward, distressed, disturbed, edgy, fearful, insecure, *inf* jittery, nervous, restless, tense, troubled, uncomfortable, unsettled, worried.

uneducated *adj* ▷ IGNORANT.

unemotional *adj* apathetic, clinical, cold, cool, dispassionate, frigid, hard-hearted, heartless, impassive, indifferent, objective, unfeeling, unmoved, unresponsive. *Opp* EMOTIONAL.

unemployed *adj* jobless, laid off, on the dole, out of work, redundant, unwaged. ▷ IDLE.

unenthusiastic *adj* ▷ APATHETIC, UNINTERESTED.

unequal *adj* 1 different, differing, disparate, dissimilar, varying. 2 *unequal treatment.* biased, prejudiced, unjust. 3 *unequal contest.* one-sided, unbalanced, uneven, unfair. *Opp* EQUAL, FAIR.

unequalled *adj* incomparable, inimitable, matchless, peerless, supreme, unparalleled, unsurpassed.

unethical *adj* ▷ IMMORAL.

uneven *adj* 1 broken, bumpy, irregular, jagged, pitted, rough, rutted. 2 *uneven rhythm.* erratic, fitful, fluctuating, inconsistent, jerky, spasmodic, unpredictable. 3 *uneven load.* lopsided, unsteady. 4 *uneven contest.* one-sided, unbalanced, unequal, unfair. *Opp* EVEN.

uneventful *adj* ▷ UNEXCITING.

unexciting *adj* boring, dull, monotonous, predictable, routine, tedious, trite, uneventful, uninspiring, vapid, wearisome. ▷ ORDINARY. *Opp* EXCITING.

unexpected *adj* accidental, chance, fortuitous, sudden, surprising, unforeseen, unlooked-for, unplanned, unpredictable, unusual. *Opp* PREDICTABLE.

unfair *adj* ▷ UNJUST.

unfaithful *adj* disloyal, duplicitous, faithless, false, fickle, inconstant, perfidious, traitorous, treacherous, untrustworthy. *Opp* FAITHFUL.

unfaithfulness *n* 1 duplicity, perfidy, treachery. 2 adultery, infidelity.

unfamiliar *adj* ▷ STRANGE.

unfashionable *adj* dated, old-fashioned, *inf* out, passé, unstylish. *Opp* FASHIONABLE.

unfasten *v* ▷ UNDO.

unfavourable *adj* 1 adverse, bad, critical, disapproving, discouraging, hostile, ill-disposed, negative, uncomplimentary, unfriendly, unkind. 2 *unfavourable conditions.* inauspicious, unpromising, unpropitious. *Opp* FAVOURABLE.

unfeeling *adj* ▷ CALLOUS.

unfinished *adj* imperfect, incomplete, rough, sketchy. *Opp* PERFECT.

unfit *adj* 1 inadequate, incapable, incompetent, unsatisfactory, useless. 2 *unfit for family viewing.* inappropriate, unsuitable, unsuited. 3 out of condition, unhealthy. ▷ ILL. *Opp* FIT.

unflagging *adj* ▷ TIRELESS.

unforeseen *adj* ▷ UNEXPECTED.

unforgettable *adj* ▷ MEMORABLE.

unforgivable *adj* inexcusable, mortal (*sin*), shameful, unjustifiable, unpardonable. *Opp* FORGIVABLE.

unfortunate *adj* ▷ UNLUCKY.

unfriendly *adj* aloof, antagonistic, antisocial, cold, cool, detached, disagreeable, distant, forbidding, hostile, ill-disposed, impersonal, inhospitable, quarrelsome, remote, reserved, rude, sour, standoffish, *inf* starchy, sullen, threatening, unapproachable, uncivil, uncongenial, unforthcoming, unkind, unresponsive, unsociable, unsympathetic, unwelcoming. *Opp* FRIENDLY.

ungainly *adj* ▷ AWKWARD.

ungodly *adj* ▷ IRRELIGIOUS.

ungrateful *adj* ill-mannered, rude, unappreciative. *Opp* GRATEFUL.

unhappy *adj* 1 dejected, depressed, dispirited, discontented, disgruntled, dissatisfied, down, downcast, gloomy, fed up, miserable, mournful, sorrowful. ▷ SAD. 2 *unhappy coincidence*. ill-fated, unlucky. 3 *unhappy choice*. inappropriate, unfortunate, unsuitable.

unhealthy *adj* 1 ailing, delicate, diseased, feeble, frail, infected, infirm, *inf* poorly, sick, sickly, unwell, weak. ▷ ILL. 2 *unhealthy conditions*. dirty, harmful, insalubrious, insanitary, noxious, polluted, unhygienic, unwholesome. *Opp* HEALTHY.

unheard-of *adj* ▷ UNUSUAL.

unhelpful *adj* difficult, disobliging, inconsiderate, uncooperative. *Opp* HELPFUL.

unidentifiable *adj* camouflaged, disguised, hidden, unknown, unrecognizable. *Opp* IDENTIFIABLE.

unidentified *adj* anonymous, incognito, nameless, unknown, unmarked, unnamed, unrecognized, unspecified. *Opp* SPECIFIC.

uniform *adj* consistent, even, homogeneous, invariable, regular, same, similar, smooth, steady, unbroken, unvarying. *Opp* DIFFERENT.
• *n* costume, livery, outfit.

unify *v* amalgamate, bring together, combine, consolidate, fuse, integrate, join, merge, unite. *Opp* SEPARATE.

unimaginative *adj* banal, boring, conventional, derivative, dull, hackneyed, obvious, ordinary, prosaic, stale, trite, uninspired, uninteresting, unoriginal. *Opp* IMAGINATIVE.

unimportant *adj* forgettable, immaterial, inessential, insignificant, irrelevant, minor, negligible, peripheral, petty, secondary, slight, trifling, trivial, worthless. ▷ SMALL. *Opp* IMPORTANT.

uninhabited *adj* abandoned, deserted, desolate, empty, unoccupied, vacant.

uninhibited *adj* candid, easygoing, frank, natural, open, outgoing, outspoken, relaxed, spontaneous, unconstrained, unreserved, unrestrained, unselfconscious, wild. *Opp* REPRESSED.

unintelligent *adj* ▷ STUPID.

unintelligible *adj* ▷ INCOMPREHENSIBLE.

unintentional *adj* accidental, fortuitous, inadvertent, involuntary, unconscious, unwitting. *Opp* INTENTIONAL.

uninterested *adj* apathetic, bored, indifferent, passive, phlegmatic, unconcerned, unenthusiastic, uninvolved, unresponsive. *Opp* INTERESTED.

uninteresting *adj* boring, dreary, dry, dull, flat, monotonous, predictable, tedious, uninspiring. ▷ ORDINARY. *Opp* INTERESTING.

uninterrupted *adj* ▷ CONTINUOUS.

uninvited *adj* unasked, unbidden, unwelcome.

uninviting *adj* ▷ UNATTRACTIVE.

union *n* 1 alliance, amalgamation, association, coalition, confederation, federation, integration, joining together, merger, unification, unity. 2 blend, combination, compound, fusion, mixture, synthesis. 3 marriage, matrimony, partnership, wedlock.

unique *adj* distinctive, incomparable, *inf* one-off, peerless, *inf* second to none, single, singular, unequalled, unparalleled, unrepeatable.

unit *n* component, constituent, element, entity, item, module, part, piece, portion, section, segment, whole.

unite *v* ally, amalgamate, associate, blend, bring together, collaborate, combine, connect, consolidate, cooperate, couple, fuse, go into partnership, incorporate, integrate, join, join forces, link, merge, mingle, mix, tie up, unify. *Opp* SEPARATE.

united *adj* agreed, allied, collective, common, concerted, corporate, harmonious, integrated, joint, like-minded, *inf* of one mind, shared, unanimous, undivided. *Opp* DISUNITED. **be united** ▷ AGREE.

unity *n* accord, agreement, concord, consensus, harmony, integrity, oneness, rapport, solidarity, unanimity, wholeness. *Opp* DISUNITY.

universal *adj* all-embracing, all-round, common, comprehensive, general, global, international, prevailing, prevalent, total, ubiquitous, unlimited, widespread, worldwide.

universe *n* cosmos, creation, the heavens.

unjust *adj* biased, bigoted, indefensible, one-sided, partisan, prejudiced, undeserved, unfair, unreasonable, unwarranted, wrong, wrongful. *Opp* JUST.

unjustifiable *adj* excessive, indefensible, inexcusable, unacceptable, unforgivable, unwarranted. *Opp* JUSTIFIABLE.

unkind *adj* abrasive, *inf* beastly, callous, hard, hard-hearted, harsh, heartless, hurtful, ill-natured, inconsiderate, inhumane, insensitive, malicious, mean, nasty, rough, ruthless, selfish, severe, sharp, spiteful, tactless, thoughtless, uncaring, uncharitable, unfeeling, unfriendly, unpleasant, unsympathetic. ▷ CRITICAL, CRUEL. *Opp* KIND.

unknown *adj* 1 anonymous, disguised, incognito, mysterious, strange, unidentified, unnamed, unrecognized. 2 *unknown country*. alien, foreign, uncharted, unexplored, unfamiliar. 3 *unknown actor*. little-known, obscure, undistinguished. *Opp* FAMOUS.

unlawful *adj* ▷ ILLEGAL.

unlikely *adj* 1 doubtful, dubious, faint, improbable, remote, slight. 2 far-fetched, implausible, incredible, unconvincing. *Opp* LIKELY.

unlimited *adj* ▷ BOUNDLESS.

unload *v* discharge, drop off, *inf* dump, empty, offload, unpack. *Opp* LOAD.

unloved *adj* abandoned, forsaken, loveless, neglected, rejected, spurned, uncared-for, unwanted. *Opp* LOVED.

unlucky *adj* 1 accidental, calamitous, chance, tragic, unfortunate, untimely. 2 *unlucky person*. *inf* accident-prone, hapless, luckless, unhappy, unsuccessful. 3 *unlucky number*. cursed, ill-fated, ill-omened, ill-starred, inauspicious, jinxed, unfavourable. *Opp* LUCKY.

unmanageable *adj* ▷ UNDISCIPLINED.

unmarried *adj* *inf* available, *inf* free, single, unwed. **unmarried person** bachelor, spinster.

unmentionable *adj* ▷ TABOO.

unmistakable *adj* ▷ DEFINITE, OBVIOUS.

unnamed *adj* ▷ UNIDENTIFIED.

unnatural *adj* 1 abnormal, bizarre, eerie, extraordinary, fantastic, freak, freakish, inexplicable, magic, magical, odd, outlandish, queer, strange, supernatural, unaccountable, uncanny, unusual, weird. 2 *unnatural feelings*. callous, cold-blooded, heartless, inhuman, inhumane, monstrous, perverse, perverted, sadistic. 3 *unnatural behaviour*. affected, contrived, fake, feigned, forced, insincere, laboured, mannered, *inf* out of character, *inf* phoney, pretended, *inf* pseudo, *inf* put on, self-conscious, stagey, stiff, stilted, theatrical, uncharacteristic. 4 *unnatural materials*. ▷ MAN-MADE. *Opp* NATURAL.

unnecessary *adj* dispensable, excessive, expendable, extra, inessential, needless, non-essential, redundant, superfluous, surplus, uncalled-for, unjustified, useless. *Opp* NECESSARY.

unobtrusive *adj* ▷ INCONSPICUOUS.

unofficial *adj* informal, *inf* off the record, unconfirmed. *Opp* OFFICIAL.

unorthodox *adj* ▷ UNCONVENTIONAL.

unpaid *adj* due, outstanding, owing, payable, unsettled.

unpalatable *adj* disgusting, inedible, nauseating, *inf* off, rancid, sour, unacceptable, unappetizing, uneatable, unpleasant. *Opp* PALATABLE.

unparalleled *adj* ▷ UNEQUALLED.

unplanned *adj* ▷ SPONTANEOUS.

unpleasant *adj* disagreeable, disgusting, displeasing, distasteful, foul, ghastly, grim, hateful, horrible, *inf* horrid, nasty, objectionable, obnoxious, offensive, *inf* off-putting, repulsive, sordid, squalid, unattractive, undesirable, unfriendly, unkind, unsavoury, unwelcome, upsetting. ▷ BAD. *Opp* PLEASANT.

unpopular *adj* disliked, friendless, ignored, out of favour, rejected, shunned, unfashionable, unloved, unwanted. *Opp* POPULAR.

unpredictable *adj* changeable, erratic, uncertain, unexpected, unforeseeable, variable. *Opp* PREDICTABLE.

unprejudiced *adj* ▷ UNBIASED.

unprepared *adj* caught napping, caught out, ill-equipped, taken off-guard, unready.

unpretentious *adj* humble, modest, plain, simple, unaffected, unassuming, unsophisticated. *Opp* PRETENTIOUS.

unproductive *adj* 1 ineffective, fruitless, futile, pointless, unprofitable, unrewarding, useless, worthless. 2 *unproductive land*. arid, barren, infertile, sterile, unfruitful. *Opp* PRODUCTIVE.

unprofessional *adj* amateurish, incompetent, inefficient, negligent, shoddy, *inf* sloppy, unethical, unseemly, unskilful, unskilled. *Opp* PROFESSIONAL.

unprofitable *adj* futile, loss-making, uneconomic, unproductive, unremunerative, unrewarding, worthless. *Opp* PROFITABLE.

unpunctual *adj* belated, delayed, late, overdue, tardy, unreliable. *Opp* PUNCTUAL.

unravel *v* disentangle, solve, straighten out, undo, untangle.

unreal *adj* false, fanciful, illusory, imaginary, imagined, make-believe, non-existent, *inf* pretend, *inf* pseudo, sham. *Opp* REAL.

unrealistic *adj* 1 inaccurate, unconvincing, unnatural, unrecognizable. 2 *unrealistic* *ideas.* fanciful, idealistic, impossible, impracticable, impractical, over-ambitious, quixotic, romantic, silly, visionary, unworkable. 3 *unrealistic prices.* ▷ EXCESSIVE. *Opp* REALISTIC.

unreasonable *adj* ▷ IRRATIONAL.

unrelated *adj* 1 different, independent, unconnected. 2 ▷ IRRELEVANT. *Opp* RELATED.

unreliable *adj* 1 deceptive, false, flimsy, inaccurate, misleading, suspect, unconvincing. 2 *unreliable friends.* changeable, fallible, fickle, inconsistent, irresponsible, unpredictable, unstable, untrustworthy. *Opp* RELIABLE.

unrepentant *adj* brazen, confirmed, hardened, impenitent, incorrigible, incurable, inveterate, irredeemable, shameless, unashamed. *Opp* REPENTANT.

unripe *adj* green, immature, sour, unready. *Opp* RIPE.

unrivalled *adj* ▷ UNEQUALLED.

unruly *adj* ▷ UNDISCIPLINED.

unsafe *adj* ▷ DANGEROUS.

unsatisfactory *adj* defective, deficient, disappointing, displeasing, faulty, frustrating, imperfect, inadequate, incompetent, inefficient, inferior, insufficient, lacking, poor, *inf* sad, unacceptable, unhappy, *inf* wretched. *Opp* SATISFACTORY.

unscrupulous *adj* amoral, corrupt, *inf* crooked, cunning, dishonest, dishonourable, immoral, improper, shameless, slippery, unethical, untrustworthy. *Opp* SCRUPULOUS.

unseemly *adj* ▷ UNBECOMING.

unselfish *adj* altruistic, caring, charitable, considerate, generous, humanitarian, kind, magnanimous, open-handed, philanthropic, public-spirited, self-effacing, selfless, self-sacrificing, thoughtful. *Opp* SELFISH.

unsightly *adj* ▷ UGLY.

unskilful *adj* amateurish, bungled, clumsy, crude, incompetent, inept, inexpert, maladroit, shoddy, unprofessional. *Opp* SKILFUL.

unskilled *adj* inexperienced, unqualified, untrained. *Opp* SKILLED.

unsociable *adj* ▷ UNFRIENDLY.

unsophisticated *adj* artless, childlike, guileless, ingenuous, innocent, lowbrow, naive, plain, simple, straightforward, unaffected, unpretentious, unrefined, unworldly. *Opp* SOPHISTICATED.

unspeakable *adj* dreadful, indescribable, inexpressible, nameless, unutterable.

unstable *adj* ▷ CHANGEABLE, UNSTEADY.

unsteady *adj* 1 flimsy, frail, insecure, precarious, rickety, *inf* rocky, shaky, tottering, unbalanced, unsafe, unstable, wobbly. 2 erratic, inconstant, intermittent, irregular, variable. 3 *unsteady light.* flickering, fluctuating, quivering. *Opp* STEADY.

unsuccessful *adj* 1 abortive, failed, fruitless, futile, ill-fated, ineffective, loss-making, unavailing, unlucky, unproducttive, unprofitable, unsatisfactory, useless, vain, worthless. 2 *unsuccessful contestants.* beaten, defeated, losing, vanquished. *Opp* SUCCESSFUL.

unsuitable *adj* ill-chosen, ill-judged, ill-timed, inapposite, inappropriate, inapt, unbecoming, unfitting, unhappy, unsatisfactory, unseemly, untimely. *Opp* SUITABLE.

unsure *adj* ▷ UNCERTAIN.

unsurpassed *adj* ▷ UNEQUALLED.

unsuspecting *adj* ▷ CREDULOUS.

unsympathetic *adj* callous, dispassionate, hard-hearted, heartless, indifferent, insensitive, pitiless, ruthless, stony, unaffected, uncaring, uncharitable, unconcerned, unfeeling, unkind, unmoved, unresponsive. *Opp* SYMPATHETIC.

unsystematic *adj* chaotic, confused, disorganized, haphazard, jumbled, muddled, random, *inf* shambolic, *inf* sloppy, unmethodical, unstructured, untidy. *Opp* SYSTEMATIC.

unthinkable *adj* ▷ INCONCEIVABLE.

unthinking *adj* ▷ THOUGHTLESS.

untidy *adj* 1 careless, chaotic, cluttered, disorderly, disorganized, haphazard, *inf* higgledy-piggledy, in disarray, jumbled, messy, muddled, *inf* shambolic, slapdash, *inf* sloppy, slovenly, *inf* topsy-turvy, unsystematic, upside-down. 2 bedraggled, dishevelled, disordered, rumpled, *inf* scruffy, shabby, tangled, tousled, uncombed, unkempt. *Opp* TIDY.

untie *v* cast off (*boat*), disentangle, free, loosen, release, undo, unfasten.

untried *adj* experimental, innovatory, new, novel, unproved, untested. *Opp* ESTABLISHED.

untroubled *adj* carefree, peaceful, quiet, relaxed, undisturbed, unruffled.

untrue *adj* ▷ FALSE.

untrustworthy *adj* ▷ DISHONEST.

untruthful *adj* ▷ LYING.

unused *adj* blank, clean, fresh, intact, mint (*condition*), new, pristine, untouched. *Opp* USED.

unusual *adj* abnormal, atypical, curious, different, exceptional, extraordinary, *inf* funny, irregular, odd, out of the ordinary, peculiar, queer, rare, remarkable, singular, strange, surprising, uncommon, unconventional, unexpected, unfamiliar, unheard-of, *inf* unique, unnatural, untypical. *Opp* USUAL.

unwanted *adj* ▷ UNNECESSARY.

unwarranted *adj* ▷ UNJUSTIFIABLE.

unwavering *adj* ▷ RESOLUTE.

unwelcome *adj* disagreeable, undesirable, uninvited, unwanted. *Opp* WELCOME.

unwell *adj* ▷ ILL.

unwholesome *adj* ▷ UNHEALTHY.

unwieldy *adj* awkward, bulky, cumbersome, unmanageable. *Opp* HANDY, PORTABLE.

unwilling *adj* averse, disinclined, grudging, half-hearted, hesitant, lazy, loath, reluctant, uncooperative, unenthusiastic, unhelpful. *Opp* WILLING.

unwise *adj inf* daft, foolhardy, foolish, ill-advised, ill-judged, imprudent, inadvisable, indiscreet, injudicious, irresponsible, misguided, rash, reckless, senseless, short-sighted, silly, stupid, thoughtless. *Opp* WISE.

unworthy *adj* contemptible, despicable, discreditable, dishonourable, disreputable, ignoble, shameful, substandard, undeserving, unsuitable. *Opp* WORTHY.

unwritten *adj* oral, spoken, verbal. *Opp* WRITTEN.

unyielding *adj* ▷ INFLEXIBLE.

upbringing *n* care, education, instruction, nurture, raising, rearing, teaching, training.

update *v* bring up to date, correct, modernize, revise.

upgrade *v* enhance, expand, improve, promote.

upheaval *n* chaos, commotion, confusion, disruption, disturbance, *inf* to-do, turmoil.

uphill *adj* arduous, difficult, exhausting, gruelling, hard, laborious, strenuous, taxing, tough.

uphold *v* back, champion, defend, endorse, maintain, preserve, promote, stand by, support, sustain.

upkeep *n* care, conservation, keep, maintenance, operation, preservation, running, support.

uplifting *adj* edifying, enlightening, enriching, exhilarating, spiritual.

upper *adj* elevated, higher, raised, superior, upstairs.

uppermost *adj* dominant, highest, supreme, top.

upright *adj* 1 erect, on end, perpendicular, vertical. 2 conscientious, fair, high-minded, honest, honourable, incorruptible, just, moral, principled, righteous, *inf* straight, true, upstanding, virtuous.
• *n* column, pole, post, vertical.

uproar *n* bedlam, chaos, clamour, commotion, confusion, din, disorder, disturbance, furore, hubbub, hullabaloo, noise, outcry, pandemonium, racket, riot, *inf* row, *inf* ructions, *inf* rumpus, tumult, turmoil.

uproot *v* eliminate, eradicate, get rid of, pull up, remove, tear up, weed out.

upset *v* 1 capsize, overturn, spill, tip over, topple. 2 *upset a plan.* alter, change, disrupt, hinder, interfere with, interrupt, jeopardize, spoil. 3 *upset someone's feelings.* agitate, annoy, disconcert, dismay, distress, disturb, fluster, grieve, irritate, offend, perturb, *inf* rub up the wrong way, ruffle.

upside-down *adj inf* topsy-turvy, upturned, wrong way up.

upstart *n* arriviste, nobody, *Fr* nouveau riche, social climber.

up-to-date *adj* contemporary, current, fashionable, *inf* in, modern, new, *inf* trendy. *Opp* OLD-FASHIONED.

upward *adj* ascending, going up, rising, uphill. *Opp* DOWNWARD.

urban *adj* built-up, metropolitan, suburban. *Opp* RURAL.

urge *n* compulsion, craving, desire, drive, hunger, impetus, impulse, itch, longing, pressure, thirst, yearning, *inf* yen.
• *v* advise, advocate, appeal to, beg, beseech, chivvy, compel, counsel, drive, egg on, encourage, entreat, exhort, goad, impel, implore, importune, incite, induce, nag, persuade, plead with, press, prod, prompt, propel, push, recommend, spur. *Opp* DISCOURAGE.

urgent *adj* 1 acute, compelling, essential, high-priority, immediate, imperative, important, necessary, pressing, top-priority, unavoidable. 2 *urgent request.* earnest, importunate, insistent, persistent.

usable *adj* fit to use, functioning, operational, serviceable, valid, working.

use *n* advantage, application, benefit, employment, *inf* point, purpose, usefulness, utility, value, worth.
• *v* 1 administer, apply, employ, exercise, exploit, handle, make use of, manage, operate, put to use, utilize, work. 2 consume, exhaust, expend, spend, use up, waste.

used *adj* cast-off, *inf* hand-me-down, second-hand.

useful *adj* 1 advantageous, beneficial, constructive, good, helpful, invaluable, positive, profitable, salutary, valuable, worthwhile. 2 *useful tool.* convenient, effective, efficient, handy, practical, utilitarian. 3 *useful player.* capable, competent, proficient, skilful, talented. *Opp* USELESS.

useless *adj* 1 fruitless, futile, hopeless, pointless, unavailing, unprofitable, unsuccessful, vain, worthless. 2 *inf* broken down, faulty, unusable. 3 *useless player.* incapable, incompetent, unhelpful, unskilful, untalented. *Opp* USEFUL.

usual *adj* accustomed, average, common, conventional, customary, everyday, expected, familiar, general, habitual, natural, normal, ordinary, orthodox, predictable, prevalent, recognized, regular, routine, standard, stock, traditional, typical, unsurprising, well-known, widespread, wonted. *Opp* UNUSUAL.

usurp *v* appropriate, commandeer, seize, take over.

utensil *n* ▷ TOOL.

utter *v* articulate, *inf* come out with, express, pronounce, voice. ▷ SPEAK, TALK.

V

vacancy *n* job, opening, place, position, post, situation.

vacant *adj* 1 available, clear, empty, free, open, unfilled, void. 2 abandoned, deserted, uninhabited, unoccupied. 3 *vacant look.* absent-minded, abstracted, blank, dreamy, expressionless, far-away, inattentive, vacuous. *Opp* BUSY.

vacate *v* abandon, desert, evacuate, get out of, give up, leave, quit.

vacuous *adj* blank, empty-headed, inane, mindless, uncomprehending, vacant. ▷ STUPID. *Opp* ALERT.

vacuum *n* emptiness, space, void.

vagary *n* caprice, fluctuation, quirk, uncertainty, whim.

vagrant *n* beggar, *inf* down-and-out, homeless person, itinerant, tramp, traveller.

vague *adj* 1 ambiguous, diffuse, equivocal, evasive, general, generalized, imprecise, indefinite, inexact, loose, nebulous, uncertain, unclear, undefined, unspecific, unsure, *inf* woolly. 2 amorphous, blurred, dim, hazy, ill-defined, indistinct, misty, shadowy, unrecognizable. 3 absent-minded, disorganized, forgetful, inattentive, scatterbrained. *Opp* DEFINITE.

vain *adj* 1 arrogant, *inf* big-headed, boastful, *inf* cocky, conceited, egotistical, narcissistic, proud, self-important, self-satisfied. *Opp* MODEST. 2 *vain attempt.* abortive, fruitless, futile, ineffective, pointless, senseless, unproductive, unsuccessful, useless. *Opp* SUCCESSFUL.

valiant *adj* courageous, gallant, heroic. ▷ BRAVE. *Opp* COWARDLY.

valid *adj* authentic, authorized, bona fide, current, genuine, lawful, legal, legitimate, official, permissible, ratified, rightful, usable. *Opp* INVALID.

validate *v* authenticate, authorize, certify, endorse, legalize, legitimize, ratify.

valley *n* canyon, dale, dell, dingle, glen, gorge, gully, hollow, pass, ravine, vale.

valour *n* bravery, courage.

valuable *adj* 1 expensive, irreplaceable, precious, priceless, prized, treasured. 2 *valuable advice.* advantageous, beneficial, constructive, helpful, invaluable, profitable, useful, worthwhile. *Opp* WORTHLESS.

value *n* 1 cost, price, worth. 2 advantage, benefit, importance, merit, significance, use, usefulness.
• *v* 1 assess, evaluate, price, *inf* put a figure on. 2 appreciate, care for, cherish, esteem, *inf* hold dear, love, prize, respect, treasure.

vandal *n* delinquent, hooligan, thug, troublemaker.

vanish *v* disappear, disperse, dissolve, evaporate, fade, melt away, pass. *Opp* APPEAR.

vanity *n* arrogance, conceit, egotism, narcissism, pride, self-esteem.

vapour *n* fog, fumes, gas, haze, miasma, mist, smoke, steam.

variable *adj* capricious, changeable, erratic, fitful, fluctuating, fluid, inconsistent, inconstant, mercurial, mutable, protean, shifting, uncertain, unpredictable, unreliable, unstable, unsteady, *inf* up-and-down, varying, volatile. *Opp* INVARIABLE.

variation *n* alteration, change, deviation, difference, discrepancy, elaboration, modification, permutation.

variety *n* 1 change, difference, diversity, variation. 2 array, assortment, blend, collection, combination, medley, miscellany, mixture, multiplicity. 3 brand, breed, category, class, kind, make, sort, species, strain, type.

various *adj* assorted, different, differing, dissimilar, diverse, heterogeneous, miscellaneous, mixed, *inf* motley, multifarious, several, sundry, varied, varying.

vary *v* 1 change, deviate, differ, fluctuate. 2 *vary your speed.* adapt, adjust, alter, modify, regulate. *Opp* STABILIZE. **varied, varying** ▷ VARIOUS.

vast *adj* boundless, broad, colossal, enormous, extensive, gigantic, great, huge, immeasurable, immense, infinite, limitless, massive, monumental, sweeping, tremendous, unbounded, unlimited, voluminous, wide. ▷ BIG. *Opp* SMALL.

vault *n* basement, cavern, cellar, crypt, strongroom.
• *v* bound over, clear, hurdle, jump, leap, spring over.

veer *v* change direction, dodge, swerve, turn, wheel.

vegetable *adj* growing, organic.

vegetate *v* do nothing, *inf* go to seed, idle, stagnate.

vegetation *n* foliage, greenery, plants, undergrowth, weeds.

vehement *adj* ardent, eager, emphatic, enthusiastic, fervent, fierce, forceful, heated, impassioned, intense, passionate, strong, urgent, vigorous, violent. *Opp* APATHETIC.

vehicle *n* bus, car, coach, conveyance, lorry, means of transport, minibus, taxi, van, *inf* wheels.

veil *v* cloak, conceal, cover, disguise, hide, mask, shroud.

vein *n* 1 artery, blood vessel, capillary. 2 *mineral vein.* bed, course, deposit, line, lode, seam, stratum. 3 ▷ MOOD.

veneer *n* covering, layer, surface.
• *v* ▷ COVER.

venerable *adj* august, esteemed, estimable, honourable, honoured, old, respectable, respected, revered, sedate.

venerate *v* esteem, hero-worship, honour, idolize, look up to, pay homage to, respect, revere, worship.

vengeance *n* reprisal, retaliation, retribution, revenge.

vengeful *adj* avenging, bitter, spiteful, unforgiving, vindictive. *Opp* FORGIVING.

venom *n* poison, toxin.

venomous *adj* deadly, lethal, poisonous, toxic.

vent *n* aperture, duct, gap, hole, opening, outlet, passage, slit.
• *v* articulate, express, give vent to, voice. ▷ SPEAK.

ventilate *v* aerate, air, freshen.

venture *n* ▷ ENTERPRISE.
• *v* 1 bet, chance, gamble, put forward, risk, speculate, stake, wager. 2 *venture out.* dare to go, risk going.

venturesome *adj* ▷ ADVENTUROUS.

venue *n* meeting place, location.

verbal *adj* oral, spoken, unwritten, vocal, word-of-mouth. *Opp* WRITTEN.

verbatim *adj* exact, faithful, literal, precise, word for word.

verbose *adj* long-winded, rambling, repetitious. ▷ WORDY. *Opp* CONCISE.

verbosity *n* long-windedness, prolixity, verbiage, wordiness.

verdict *n* assessment, conclusion, decision, finding, judgement, opinion, sentence.

verge *n* bank, brim, brink, edge, hard shoulder, kerb, lip, margin, roadside, side.

verifiable *adj* demonstrable, provable.

verify *v* affirm, ascertain, attest to, authenticate, *inf* check out, confirm, corroborate, establish, prove, show the truth of, substantiate, support, uphold, validate, vouch for.

verisimilitude *n* authenticity, realism.

vermin *pl n* parasites, pests.

vernacular *adj* indigenous, local, native, ordinary, popular.

versatile *adj* adaptable, all-round, multipurpose, resourceful, skilful, talented.

verse *n* lines, metre, poem, rhyme, stanza.

versed *adj* accomplished, competent, experienced, expert, practised, proficient, skilled, trained.

version *n* 1 account, description, portrayal, report, story. 2 adaptation, interpretation, rendering, translation. 3 design, kind, model, style, type, variant.

vertical *adj* erect, perpendicular, sheer, upright. *Opp* HORIZONTAL.

vertigo *n* dizziness, giddiness.

very *adv* acutely, enormously, especially, exceedingly, extremely, greatly, highly, noticeably, outstandingly, particularly, really, remarkably, *inf* terribly, unusually.

vessel *n* 1 ▷ CONTAINER. 2 boat, craft, ship.

vet *v inf* check out, examine, investigate, review, scrutinize.

veteran *adj* experienced, mature, old, practised.
• *n* experienced soldier, old hand, old soldier, survivor, *inf* vet.

veto *n* ban, embargo, prohibition, refusal, rejection, *inf* thumbs down.
• *v* ban, bar, block, disallow, forbid, prohibit, quash, refuse, reject, rule out, say no to, turn down, vote against. *Opp* APPROVE.

vex *v inf* aggravate, annoy, bother, displease, exasperate, harass, irritate, provoke, put out, trouble, upset, worry. ▷ ANGER.

viable *adj* achievable, feasible, possible, practicable, practical, realistic, reasonable, workable. *Opp* IMPRACTICAL.

vibrant *adj* alive, animated, dynamic, electric, energetic, lively, pulsating, quivering, resonant, spirited, vivacious. *Opp* LIFELESS.

vibrate *v* judder, pulsate, quiver, rattle, reverberate, shake, shiver, shudder, throb, wobble.

vibration *n* juddering, pulsation, quivering, rattling, reverberation, shaking, shivering, shuddering, throbbing, tremor.

vicarious *adj* indirect, second-hand, surrogate.

vice *n* 1 corruption, depravity, evil, immorality, iniquity, sin, villainy, wickedness, wrongdoing. 2 bad habit, defect, failing, fault, flaw, foible, imperfection, shortcoming, weakness.

vicinity *n* area, district, environs, locale, locality, neighbourhood, proximity, region, surroundings, zone.

vicious *adj* 1 atrocious, barbaric, bloodthirsty, brutal, callous, cruel, diabolical, fiendish, heinous, hurtful, inhuman, merciless, monstrous, murderous, pitiless, ruthless, sadistic, savage, violent. 2 *vicious character*. depraved, evil, heartless, immoral, malicious, mean, perverted, rancorous, sinful, spiteful, venomous, villainous, vindictive, vitriolic, wicked. 3 *vicious animals*. aggressive, dangerous, ferocious, fierce. 4 *vicious wind*. cutting, severe, sharp. *Opp* GENTLE.

vicissitude *n* change, flux, mutability, unpredictability.

victim *n* casualty, fatality, injured person, martyr, scapegoat, sufferer.

victimize *v* bully, discriminate against, exploit, intimidate, oppress, persecute, *inf* pick on, take advantage of, terrorize, torment. ▷ CHEAT.

victor *n* champion, conqueror, winner. *Opp* LOSER.

victorious *adj* champion, conquering, first, leading, successful, top, triumphant, winning. *Opp* UNSUCCESSFUL.

victory *n* conquest, success, superiority, supremacy, triumph, *inf* walk-over, win. *Opp* DEFEAT.

vie *v* compete, contend, strive.

view *n* 1 aspect, outlook, panorama, picture, prospect, scene, scenery, vista. 2 perspective, sight, vision. 3 *political views*. attitude, belief, conviction, idea, notion, opinion, perception, position, thought.
• *v* 1 behold, contemplate, examine, eye, gaze at, inspect, observe, regard, scan, survey, witness. 2 *view TV*. look at, watch.

viewer *n pl* audience, observer, onlooker, spectator, watcher.

viewpoint *n* angle, perspective, point of view, position, slant, standpoint.

vigilant *adj* alert, attentive, awake, careful, eagle-eyed, observant, on your guard, *inf* on your toes, wary, watchful, wide awake. *Opp* NEGLIGENT.

vigorous *adj* active, alive, animated, brisk, dynamic, energetic, flourishing, forceful, *inf* full of beans, healthy, lively, potent, robust, spirited, strenuous, strong, thriving, virile, vivacious, zestful. *Opp* FEEBLE.

vigour *n* animation, dynamism, energy, force, gusto, health, life, liveliness, might, potency, power, robustness, spirit, stamina, strength, verve, virility, vitality, zeal, zest.

vile *adj* base, contemptible, degenerate, depraved, despicable, disgusting, evil, execrable, filthy, foul, hateful, horrible, loathsome, nauseating, obnoxious, odious, offensive, perverted, repellent, repugnant, repulsive, revolting, sickening, ugly, vicious, wicked.

vilify *v* abuse, denigrate, insult. ▷ SLANDER.

villain *n* criminal, evil-doer, malefactor, mischief-maker, miscreant, reprobate, rogue, scoundrel, sinner.

villainous *adj* bad, corrupt, criminal, dishonest, evil, sinful, treacherous, vile. ▷ WICKED.

vindictive *adj* malicious, nasty, rancorous, spiteful, unforgiving, vengeful, vicious. *Opp* FORGIVING.

vintage *adj* choice, classic, fine, good, high-quality, mature, mellowed, old, seasoned.

violate *v* 1 breach, break, contravene, defy, disobey, disregard, flout, ignore, infringe, transgress. 2 *violate someone's privacy*. abuse, disturb, invade. 3 [*of men*] *violate a woman*. assault, attack, force yourself on, rape.

violation *n* breach, contravention, defiance, flouting, infringement, invasion, offence (against), transgression.

violent *adj* 1 acute, damaging, dangerous, destructive, devastating, explosive, ferocious, fierce, furious, hard, intense, powerful, rough, savage, severe, strong, swingeing, tempestuous, turbulent, uncontrollable, vehement. 2 *violent behaviour*. brutal, cruel, desperate, frenzied, homicidal, murderous, riotous, rowdy, ruthless, uncontrolled, unruly, vehement, vicious, wild. *Opp* GENTLE.

VIP *n* celebrity, dignitary, important person.

virile *adj derog* macho, manly, masculine, potent, vigorous.

virtue *n* 1 decency, fairness, goodness, high-mindedness, honesty, honour, integrity, morality, nobility, principle, rectitude, respectability, righteousness, sincerity, uprightness, worthiness. 2 advantage, asset, good point, merit, *inf* redeeming feature, strength. 3 *sexual virtue.* chastity, innocence, purity, virginity. *Opp* VICE.

virtuoso *n* expert, genius, maestro, prodigy, *inf* wizard.

virtuous *adj* blameless, chaste, decent, ethical, exemplary, fair, God-fearing, good, high-minded, honest, honourable, innocent, irreproachable, just, law-abiding, moral, noble, principled, praiseworthy, pure, respectable, righteous, sincere, *derog* smug, spotless, uncorrupted, unsullied, upright, virginal, worthy. *Opp* WICKED.

virulent *adj* 1 deadly, lethal, life-threatening, noxious, poisonous, toxic. 2 *virulent abuse.* acrimonious, bitter, hostile, malicious, nasty, spiteful, vicious, vitriolic.

viscous *adj* gluey, sticky, syrupy, thick. *Opp* RUNNY.

visible *adj* apparent, clear, conspicuous, detectable, discernible, distinct, evident, manifest, noticeable, obvious, open, perceptible, plain, recognizable, unconcealed, undisguised, unmistakable. *Opp* INVISIBLE.

vision *n* 1 eyesight, perception, sight. 2 apparition, chimera, daydream, delusion, fantasy, ghost, hallucination, mirage, phantasm, phantom, spectre, spirit. 3 *man of vision.* foresight, imagination, insight, understanding.

visionary *adj* dreamy, fanciful, far-sighted, idealistic, imaginative, mystical, prophetic, quixotic, romantic, speculative, unrealistic, Utopian.
• *n* dreamer, idealist, mystic, prophet, seer.

visit *n* 1 call, stay, stop, visitation. 2 excursion, outing, trip.
• *v* call on, *inf* descend on, *inf* drop in on, *inf* look up, pay a call on, stay with. **visit regularly** ⊳ HAUNT.

visitor *n* 1 caller, *pl* company, guest. 2 foreigner, holidaymaker, sightseer, tourist, traveller, tripper.

vista *n* landscape, outlook, panorama, prospect, scene, scenery, seascape, view.

visualize *v* conceive, dream up, envisage, imagine, picture.

vital *adj* 1 alive, animate, animated, dynamic, energetic, exuberant, life-giving, live, lively, living, spirited, vigorous, vivacious, zestful. *Opp* LIFELESS. 2 crucial, essential, fundamental, imperative, important, indispensable, mandatory, necessary, relevant, requisite. *Opp* INESSENTIAL.

vitality *n* animation, dynamism, energy, exuberance, *inf* go, life, liveliness, *inf* sparkle, spirit, stamina, strength, vigour, vivacity, zest.

vitriolic *adj* biting, bitter, caustic, cruel, hostile, hurtful, malicious, savage, scathing, vicious, virulent.

vituperate *v* ⊳ ABUSE.

vivacious *adj* animated, bubbly, cheerful, ebullient, energetic, high-spirited, light-hearted, lively, merry, spirited, sprightly. *Opp* LETHARGIC.

vivid *adj* 1 bright, brilliant, colourful, dazzling, fresh, *derog* gaudy, glowing, intense, rich, shining, strong, vibrant. 2 *vivid description.* clear, detailed, graphic, imaginative, lifelike, memorable, powerful, realistic, striking. *Opp* LIFELESS.

vocabulary *n* 1 diction, words. 2 dictionary, glossary, lexicon, word-list.

vocal *adj* 1 oral, said, spoken, sung, voiced. 2 communicative, loquacious, outspoken, talkative, vociferous. *Opp* TACITURN.

vocation *n* ⊳ CALLING.

vogue *n* craze, fad, fashion, *inf* latest thing, rage, style, taste, trend. **in vogue** ⊳ FASHIONABLE.

voice *n* articulation, expression, speech, utterance, words.
• *v* ⊳ SPEAK.

void *adj* 1 blank, empty, unoccupied, vacant. 2 cancelled, invalid, not binding, useless.
• *n* emptiness, nothingness, space, vacancy, vacuum.

volatile *adj* 1 explosive, unstable. 2 *volatile moods.* changeable, erratic, fickle, flighty, inconstant, mercurial, temperamental, unpredictable, *inf* up and down. *Opp* STABLE.

volley *n* barrage, bombardment, burst, cannonade, fusillade, salvo, shower.

voluble *adj* chatty, fluent, garrulous, glib, loquacious, talkative. ▷ WORDY.

volume *n* 1 book, publication, tome. 2 amount, bulk, capacity, dimensions, mass, quantity, size.

voluminous *adj* ample, billowing, bulky, capacious, enormous, extensive, immense, large, roomy, spacious, vast. ▷ BIG. *Opp* SMALL.

voluntary *adj* 1 free, gratuitous, optional, spontaneous, unpaid, willing. *Opp* COMPULSORY. 2 *voluntary act.* ▷ CONSCIOUS. *Opp* INVOLUNTARY.

volunteer *v* 1 be willing, offer, put yourself forward. 2 ▷ ENLIST.

voluptuous *adj* 1 *voluptuous pleasures.* ▷ HEDONISTIC. 2 *voluptuous figure.* buxom, *inf* curvaceous, desirable, erotic, sensual, sexy, shapely, *inf* well-endowed.

vomit *v* be sick, *inf* bring up, disgorge, *inf* heave up, regurgitate, retch, *inf* throw up.

voracious *adj* avid, eager, gluttonous, greedy, hungry, insatiable, ravenous.

vortex *n* eddy, spiral, whirlpool, whirlwind.

vote *n* ballot, election, plebiscite, poll, referendum, show of hands.
• *v* cast your vote. **vote for** choose, nominate, opt for, pick, return, select.

vouch *v* **vouch for** answer for, guarantee, speak for, sponsor, support.

voucher *n* coupon, ticket, token.

vow *n* assurance, guarantee, oath, pledge, promise, undertaking, word of honour.
• *v* declare, give your word, guarantee, pledge, promise, swear, take an oath.

voyage *n* cruise, journey, passage.
• *v* cruise, sail, travel.

vulgar *adj* 1 coarse, common, crude, foul, gross, ill-bred, impolite, improper, indecent, indecorous, offensive, rude, uncouth. ▷ OBSCENE. *Opp* POLITE. 2 *vulgar colour scheme.* crude, gaudy, in bad taste, tasteless, tawdry, unsophisticated. *Opp* TASTEFUL.

vulnerable *adj* 1 at risk, defenceless, exposed, helpless, unguarded, unprotected, weak, wide open. 2 sensitive, thin-skinned. *Opp* RESILIENT.

W

wad *n* bundle, lump, mass, pack, pad, plug, roll.

wadding *n* filling, lining, packing, padding, stuffing.

wade *v* ford, paddle, splash.

waffle *n* evasiveness, padding, verbiage, wordiness.
▪ *v inf* beat about the bush, hedge, prattle.

waft *v* 1 drift, float, travel. 2 bear, carry, convey, transport.

wag *v* bob, flap, move to and fro, nod, oscillate, rock, shake, sway, undulate, *inf* waggle, wave, *inf* wiggle.

wage *n* earnings, income, pay, pay packet, remuneration, reward, salary, stipend.
▪ *v* carry on, conduct, engage in, undertake.

wager *n*, *v* ⊳ BET.

wail *v* caterwaul, complain, cry, howl, lament, moan, shriek, weep, *inf* yowl.

waist *n* middle, waistline.

wait *n* delay, halt, hesitation, hiatus, *inf* hold-up, interval, pause, postponement, rest, stay, stop, stoppage.
▪ *v* 1 delay, halt, *inf* hang on, hesitate, hold back, keep still, linger, mark time, pause, remain, rest, stand by, stay, stop. 2 *wait at table*. serve.

waive *v* abandon, disclaim, dispense with, forgo, give up, relinquish, renounce, resign, sign away, surrender.

wake *n* 1 funeral, vigil, watch. 2 *ship's wake*. path, track, trail, wash.
▪ *v* 1 awaken, call, disturb, rouse, stimulate, stir, waken. 2 bestir yourself, *inf* come to life, get up, rise, *inf* stir, wake up. **wake up to** ⊳ REALIZE. **waking** ⊳ CONSCIOUS.

wakeful *adj* alert, awake, insomniac, restless, sleepless.

walk *n* 1 carriage, gait, stride. 2 constitutional, hike, promenade, ramble, saunter, stroll, traipse, tramp, trek, trudge, *inf* turn. 3 *paved walk*. aisle, alley, path, pathway, pavement.
▪ *v* advance, amble, go, march, move, pace, promenade, ramble, saunter, step, stride, stroll, tramp, traipse, trek, trudge. **walk away with** ⊳ WIN. **walk off with** ⊳ STEAL. **walk out** ⊳ QUIT. **walk out on** ⊳ DESERT.

walker *n* hiker, pedestrian, rambler.

wall *n* barricade, barrier, dam, divider, embankment, fence, obstacle, parapet, partition, rampart, screen, stockade. **wall in** ⊳ ENCLOSE.

wallet *n* notecase, pocketbook, pouch, purse.

wallow *v* 1 flounder, roll about, stagger about, tumble. 2 *wallow in luxury*. glory, indulge yourself, luxuriate, revel, take delight.

wan *adj* anaemic, ashen, colourless, feeble, livid, pale, pallid, pasty, sickly.

wand *n* baton, rod, staff, stick.

wander *v* 1 drift, meander, ramble, range, roam, rove, stray, stroll, travel about, walk. 2 *wander off course*. deviate, digress, drift, go off at a tangent, stray, swerve, turn, twist, veer, zigzag. **wandering** ⊳ INATTENTIVE, NOMADIC.

wane *v* decline, decrease, dim, diminish, dwindle, ebb, fade, fail, *inf* fall off, lessen, peter out, shrink, subside, taper off, weaken. *Opp* STRENGTHEN.

want *n* 1 demand, desire, need, requirement, wish. 2 *want of ready cash*. absence, lack, shortage. 3 *war against want*. famine, hunger, penury, poverty, privation.
▪ *v* 1 aspire to, covet, crave, demand, desire, fancy, hanker after, *inf* have a yen for, hunger for, itch for, long for, miss, pine for, *inf* set your heart on, thirst for, wish for, yearn for. 2 *want manners*. be short of, lack, need, require.

war *n* battle, campaign, conflict, crusade, fighting, hostilities, military action, strife, warfare. **wage war** ⊳ FIGHT.

ward *n* charge, dependant, minor.
▪ *v* **ward off** avert, beat off, chase away, deflect, fend off, forestall, parry, repel, repulse, stave off, thwart.

warder *n* gaoler, guard, jailer, keeper, prison officer.

warehouse *n* depository, depot, store, storehouse.

wares *pl n* commodities, goods, merchandise, produce, stock, supplies.

warlike *adj* aggressive, bellicose, belligerent, hawkish, hostile, militant, militaristic, pugnacious, warmongering.

warm *adj* 1 close, hot, subtropical, sultry, summery, temperate, tepid. 2 *warm clothes.* cosy, thick, woolly. 3 *warm welcome.* affable, affectionate, cordial, emotional, enthusiastic, fervent, friendly, genial, kind, loving, sympathetic, warm-hearted. *Opp* COLD, UNFRIENDLY.
• *v* heat, melt, thaw, thaw out. *Opp* COOL.

warn *v* advise, alert, caution, counsel, give notice, inform, notify, raise the alarm, remind, tip off.

warning *n* 1 advance notice, augury, forewarning, hint, indication, notice, notification, omen, portent, premonition, presage, prophecy, reminder, sign, signal, threat, tip-off, *inf* word to the wise. 2 *let off with a warning.* admonition, reprimand. ▷ CAUTION.

warp *v* bend, buckle, contort, deform, distort, kink, twist.

warrant *n* authority, authorization, guarantee, licence, permit, pledge, sanction, search-warrant, warranty.
• *v* ▷ JUSTIFY.

wary *adj* alert, apprehensive, careful, chary, cautious, circumspect, distrustful, heedful, observant, on your guard, suspicious, vigilant, watchful. *Opp* RECKLESS.

wash *n joc* ablutions, bath, rinse, shampoo, shower.
• *v* 1 clean, cleanse, flush, launder, mop, rinse, scrub, shampoo, sluice, sponge down, swill, wipe. 2 bath, bathe, *joc* perform your ablutions, shower. 3 *The sea washes against the cliff.* dash, flow, pound, roll, splash. **wash your hands of** ▷ ABANDON.

washout *n* debacle, disappointment, disaster, failure, *inf* flop.

waste *adj* 1 discarded, extra, superfluous, unusable, unused, unwanted, worthless. 2 *waste land.* bare, barren, derelict, empty, overgrown, run-down, undeveloped.
• *n* 1 debris, dregs, effluent, excess, garbage, junk, leavings, leftovers, litter, offcuts, refuse, remnants, rubbish, scrap, scraps, trash, wastage. 2 extravagance, prodigality, wastefulness.
• *v* be wasteful with, dissipate, fritter, misspend, misuse, *inf* splurge, squander, use up. *Opp* CONSERVE. **waste away** become thin, mope, pine, weaken.

wasteful *adj* excessive, extravagant, improvident, imprudent, lavish, needless, prodigal, profligate, reckless, spendthrift, uneconomical. *Opp* ECONOMICAL. **wasteful person** ▷ SPENDTHRIFT.

watch *n* chronometer, clock, digital watch, stopwatch, timepiece, timer, wrist-watch.
• *v* 1 attend, concentrate, contemplate, eye, gaze, heed, keep your eyes on, look at, mark, note, observe, pay attention, regard, see, stare, take notice, view. 2 care for, chaperon, defend, guard, keep an eye on, look after, mind, protect, superintend, supervise, take charge of, tend. **keep watch** ▷ GUARD. **on the watch** ▷ WATCHFUL. **watch your step** ▷ BEWARE.

watcher *n pl* audience, observer, onlooker, spectator, viewer, witness.

watchful *adj* attentive, eagle-eyed, heedful, observant, *inf* on the lookout, sharp-eyed, vigilant. ▷ ALERT. *Opp* INATTENTIVE.

watchman *n* caretaker, custodian, night-watchman, security guard. ▷ GUARD.

water *n* 1 brine, distilled water, drinking water, mineral water, rainwater, sea water, spring water, tap water. 2 lake, lido, ocean, pond, pool, river, sea. ▷ STREAM.
• *v* dampen, douse, drench, flood, hose, irrigate, moisten, saturate, soak, spray, sprinkle, wet. **water down** ▷ DILUTE.

waterfall *n* cascade, cataract, chute, rapids, torrent.

waterlogged *adj* full of water, saturated, soaked.

waterproof *adj* damp-proof, impermeable, impervious, water-resistant, watertight, weatherproof. *Opp* LEAKY.
• *n* cape, *inf* mac, mackintosh, sou'wester.

watertight *adj* hermetic, sealed, sound. ▷ WATERPROOF.

watery *adj* 1 aqueous, diluted, fluid, liquid, *inf* runny, *inf* sloppy, tasteless, thin, watered-down, weak, *inf* wishy-washy. 2 *watery eyes.* damp, moist, tearful, *inf* weepy.

wave *n* 1 billow, breaker, crest, ridge, ripple, roller, surf, swell, tidal wave, undulation, wavelet, *inf* white horse. 2 flourish, gesticulation, gesture, shake, sign, signal. 3 *wave of enthusiasm.* current, flood, ground swell, outbreak, surge, tide, upsurge. 4 *a new wave.* advance, tendency, trend.
• *v* 1 billow, brandish, flap, flourish, fluctuate, flutter, move to and fro, ripple, shake, sway, swing, twirl, undulate, waft, wag, zigzag. 2 gesticulate, gesture, indicate, sign, signal. **wave aside** ▷ DISMISS.

wavelength *n* channel, station.

waver *v inf* be in two minds, dither, falter, flicker, hesitate, quaver, quiver, shake, sway, teeter, totter, tremble, vacillate, wobble.

wavy *adj* curly, curving, rippling, rolling, sinuous, undulating, up and down, winding, zigzag. *Opp* STRAIGHT.

way *n* 1 course, direction, journey, path, progress, road, route. 2 distance, length, stretch. 3 *way to do something.* approach, fashion, knack, manner, means, method, mode, procedure, process, system, technique. 4 *foreign ways.* custom, fashion, habit, practice, routine, style, tradition. 5 *funny ways.* characteristic, idiosyncrasy, peculiarity. 6 *in some ways.* aspect, detail, feature, particular, respect.

waylay *v* accost, ambush, buttonhole, detain, intercept, lie in wait for, surprise.

wayward *adj* disobedient, headstrong, obstinate, self-willed, stubborn, wilful. ▷ NAUGHTY. *Opp* COOPERATIVE.

weak *adj* 1 breakable, brittle, flimsy, fragile, frail, frangible, inadequate, insubstantial, rickety, shaky, slight, substandard, unsafe, unsound, unsteady. 2 *weak in health.* anaemic, debilitated, delicate, exhausted, feeble, frail, helpless, ill, infirm, listless, *inf* low, poorly, puny, sickly, *derog* weedy. 3 *weak character.* cowardly, fearful, impotent, indecisive, ineffective, ineffectual, powerless, pusillanimous, spineless, timid, unassertive, *inf* wimpish. 4 *weak position.* ▷ DEFENCELESS. 5 *weak excuses.* hollow, lame, *inf* pathetic, shallow, unconvincing. 6 *weak light.* dim, fading, faint, indistinct, pale, poor. 7 *weak tea.* diluted, tasteless, thin, watery. *Opp* STRONG.

weaken *v* 1 debilitate, destroy, dilute, diminish, emasculate, enervate, erode, exhaust, impair, lessen, lower, reduce, ruin, sap, soften, thin down, undermine, *inf* water down. 2 abate, decline, decrease, dwindle, ebb, fade, flag, give in, give way, sag, wane, yield. *Opp* STRENGTHEN.

weakling *n* coward, *inf* pushover, *inf* runt, weak person, *inf* weed, *inf* wimp.

weakness *n* 1 *inf* Achilles' heel, defect, failing, fault, flaw, flimsiness, fragility, frailty, imperfection, inadequacy, instability, shortcoming, *inf* weak spot. 2 debility, decrepitude, delicacy, feebleness, impotence, incapacity, infirmity, lassitude, vulnerability. ▷ ILLNESS. 3 affection, fancy, fondness, inclination, liking, partiality, penchant, predilection, *inf* soft spot, taste. *Opp* STRENGTH.

wealth *n* 1 affluence, assets, capital, fortune, means, money, opulence, possessions, property, prosperity, riches, *old use* substance. *Opp* POVERTY. 2 *wealth of information.* abundance, copiousness, cornucopia, mine, plenty, profusion, store. *Opp* SCARCITY.

wealthy *adj* affluent, *inf* flush, *inf* loaded, moneyed, opulent, privileged, prosperous, rich, *inf* well-heeled, well-off, well-to-do. *Opp* POOR. **wealthy person** billionaire, capitalist, millionaire, tycoon.

weapon *n* bomb, gun, missile. **weapons** armaments, armoury, arms, arsenal, magazine, munitions, ordnance, small arms, weaponry.

wear *v* 1 be dressed in, clothe yourself in, don, dress in, have on, put on, wrap up in. 2 *wear a smile.* adopt, assume, display. 3 *wears the carpet.* damage, fray, wear away, weaken. 4 *wear well.* endure, last, *inf* stand the test of time, survive. **wear away** ▷ ERODE. **wear off** ▷ SUBSIDE. **wear out** ▷ WEARY.

wearisome *adj* boring, dreary, exhausting, monotonous, repetitive, tedious, tiring, wearying. ▷ TROUBLESOME. *Opp* STIMULATING.

weary *adj inf* dead beat, *inf* dog-tired, *inf* done in, drained, enervated, exhausted, fatigued, fed up, flagging, foot-sore, jaded, *inf* jet-lagged, listless, *inf* shattered, *inf* sick (of), sleepy, spent, tired out, *inf* whacked, worn out. *Opp* FRESH, LIVELY.
• *v* 1 debilitate, drain, enervate, exhaust, fatigue, sap, *inf* shatter, tax, tire, wear out. *Opp* REFRESH. 2 become bored, become tired, flag, grow weary.

weather *n* climate, the elements, meteorological conditions.
• *v* ▷ SURVIVE. **under the weather** ▷ ILL.

weave *v* 1 braid, criss-cross, entwine, interlace, intertwine, interweave, knit, plait. 2 *weave a story.* compose, create, put together. 3 *weave your way.* dodge, *inf* twist and turn, wind, zigzag.

web *n* criss-cross, lattice, mesh, net, network.

wedding *n* marriage, nuptials, union.

wedge *v* cram, force, jam, pack, squeeze, stick.

weep *v* bawl, *inf* blub, blubber, cry, *inf* grizzle, lament, mewl, moan, shed tears, snivel, sob, wail, whimper, whine.

weigh *v* 1 measure the weight of. 2 assess, consider, contemplate, evaluate, judge, ponder, reflect on, think about, weigh up. 3 be important, carry weight, *inf* cut ice, count, matter. **weigh down** ▷ BURDEN. **weigh up** ▷ EVALUATE.

weight *n* 1 avoirdupois, burden, heaviness, load, mass, pressure, strain, tonnage. 2 *His voice had some weight.* authority, emphasis, force, gravity, importance, power, seriousness, substance.
• *v* hold down, load, make heavy, weigh down.

weird *adj* 1 creepy, eerie, ghostly, mysterious, *inf* scary, *inf* spooky, supernatural, uncanny, unearthly, unnatural. 2 *weird clothes.* abnormal, bizarre, curious, eccentric, *inf* funny, grotesque, odd, outlandish, peculiar, queer, strange, unconventional, unusual, *inf* way-out. *Opp* CONVENTIONAL, NATURAL.

welcome *adj* acceptable, accepted, agreeable, appreciated, gratifying, much-needed, *inf* nice, pleasant, pleasing, pleasurable. *Opp* UNWELCOME.
• *n* greeting, hospitality, reception, salutation.
• *v* 1 greet, hail, receive. 2 *They welcome comments.* accept, appreciate, delight in, like, want.

weld *v* bond, cement, fuse, join, solder, unite.

welfare *n* advantage, benefit, felicity, good, happiness, health, interest, prosperity, well-being.

well *adj* 1 fit, healthy, hearty, *inf* in fine fettle, lively, robust, sound, strong, thriving, vigorous. 2 *All is well.* fine, *inf* OK, satisfactory.
• *n* fountain, source, spring, waterhole.

well-behaved *adj* cooperative, dutiful, good, law-abiding, manageable, polite, quiet, well-trained. ▷ OBEDIENT. *Opp* NAUGHTY.

well-bred *adj* courteous, cultured, genteel, polite, proper, refined, sophisticated, urbane, well-mannered. *Opp* RUDE.

well-built *adj* athletic, burly, muscular, powerful, stocky, *inf* strapping, strong, sturdy.

well-known *adj* celebrated, eminent, familiar, famous, illustrious, noted, *derog* notorious, prominent, renowned. *Opp* UNKNOWN.

well-meaning *adj* good-natured, obliging, sincere, well-intentioned, well-meant. ▷ KIND. *Opp* UNKIND.

well-off *adj* affluent, comfortable, moneyed, prosperous, rich, *inf* well-heeled, well-to-do. *Opp* POOR.

well-spoken *adj* articulate, educated, polite, *inf* posh, refined.

wet *adj* 1 awash, bedraggled, clammy, damp, dank, dewy, drenched, dripping, moist, saturated, soaked, soaking, sodden, soggy, sopping, waterlogged, wringing. 2 *wet weather.* drizzly, misty, pouring, rainy, showery, teeming. 3 *wet paint.* runny, sticky, tacky.
• *n* dampness, dew, drizzle, humidity, moisture, rain.
• *v* dampen, douse, drench, irrigate, moisten, saturate, soak, spray, sprinkle, steep, water. *Opp* DRY.

wheel *n* circle, disc, hoop, ring.
• *v* change direction, circle, gyrate, pivot, spin, swerve, swing round, swivel, turn, veer, whirl.

wheeze *v* breathe noisily, cough, gasp, pant, puff.

whereabouts *n* ▷ LOCATION.

whiff *n* breath, hint, puff, smell.

whim *n* caprice, desire, fancy, impulse, quirk, urge.

whine *v* complain, cry, *inf* grizzle, moan, wail, whimper, *inf* whinge.

whip *n* birch, cane, cat-o'-nine-tails, crop, lash, scourge, switch.
• *v* 1 beat, birch, cane, flog, lash, scourge, *sl* tan, thrash. ▷ HIT. 2 beat, stir vigorously, whisk.

whirl *v* circle, gyrate, pirouette, reel, revolve, rotate, spin, swivel, turn, twirl, wheel.

whirlpool *n* eddy, maelstrom, swirl, vortex, whirl.

whirlwind *n* cyclone, hurricane, tornado, typhoon, vortex.

whisk *n* beater, mixer.
• *v* beat, mix, stir, whip.

whiskers *pl n* bristles, hairs, moustache.

whisper *n* 1 murmur, undertone. 2 *whisper of scandal.* hint, rumour, suspicion, whiff.
• *v* breathe, hiss, murmur, mutter. ▷ TALK.

whistle *n* hooter, pipe, siren.
• *v* blow, pipe.

white *adj* chalky, ivory, milky, off-white, snow-white, snowy, spotless. ▷ PALE.

whiten *v* blanch, bleach, fade, lighten, pale.

whole *adj* coherent, complete, entire, full, in one piece, intact, perfect, sound, total, unabridged, unbroken, uncut, undamaged, undivided, unedited, unexpurgated, unscathed. *Opp* FRAGMENTARY, INCOMPLETE.

wholesale *adj* comprehensive, extensive,

general, global, indiscriminate, mass, total, universal, widespread. *Opp* LIMITED.

wholesome *adj* beneficial, good, health-giving, healthy, hygienic, nourishing, nutritious, salubrious. *Opp* UNHEALTHY.

wicked *adj* abominable, *inf* awful, bad, base, beastly, corrupt, criminal, depraved, diabolical, dissolute, evil, foul, guilty, heinous, immoral, impious, incorrigible, indefensible, iniquitous, insupportable, intolerable, irresponsible, lawless, lost (*soul*), machiavellian, malevolent, malicious, mischievous, murderous, naughty, nefarious, offensive, perverted, scandalous, shameful, sinful, sinister, spiteful, *inf* terrible, ungodly, unprincipled, unrighteous, unscrupulous, vicious, vile, villainous, wrong. *Opp* MORAL. **wicked person** ▷ VILLAIN.

wickedness *n* depravity, guilt, immorality, infamy, iniquity, malice, misconduct, sin, sinfulness, spite, turpitude, vice, villainy, wrongdoing. ▷ EVIL.

wide *adj* 1 ample, broad, expansive, extensive, large, panoramic, spacious, vast, yawning. 2 *wide sympathies.* all-embracing, broad-minded, catholic, comprehensive, eclectic, inclusive, wide-ranging. 3 *arms open wide.* extended, outspread, outstretched. 4 *a wide shot.* off-course, off-target. *Opp* NARROW.

widen *v* augment, broaden, dilate, distend, enlarge, expand, extend, flare, increase, open out, spread, stretch.

widespread *adj* common, extensive, far-reaching, general, global, pervasive, prevalent, rife, universal, wholesale. *Opp* RARE.

width *n* beam (*of ship*), breadth, compass, diameter, distance across, extent, girth, range, scope, span, thickness.

wield *v* 1 brandish, flourish, handle, hold, ply, wave. 2 *wield power.* exercise, exert, possess, use.

wild *adj* 1 *wild animals.* free, undomesticated, untamed. 2 *wild country.* deserted, desolate, godforsaken, overgrown, remote, rough, rugged, uncultivated, uninhabited, waste. 3 *wild people.* ferocious, fierce, savage, uncivilized. 4 *wild behaviour.* aggressive, boisterous, disorderly, hysterical, noisy, obstreperous, on the rampage, out of control, reckless, riotous, rowdy, uncontrollable, uncontrolled, undisciplined, unmanageable, unrestrained, unruly, uproarious, violent. 4 *wild weather.* blustery, stormy, tempestuous, turbulent, violent, windy. 5 *wild enthusiasm.* eager, excited, passionate, unrestrained. 6 *wild notions.* crazy, fantastic, irrational, silly, unreasonable. 7 *wild guess.* impetuous, inaccurate, random. *Opp* CALM, CULTIVATED, TAME.

wilderness *n* desert, jungle, waste, wasteland, wilds.

wile *n* artifice, machination, manoeuvre, plot, ploy, ruse, stratagem, subterfuge, trick.

wilful *adj* 1 calculated, conscious, deliberate, intended, intentional, premeditated, purposeful, voluntary. *Opp* ACCIDENTAL. 2 *wilful child. inf* bloody-minded, determined, headstrong, obstinate, perverse, refractory, self-willed, stubborn, unyielding, wayward. *Opp* AMENABLE.

will *n* aim, commitment, desire, determination, disposition, inclination, intention, purpose, resolution, resolve, volition, will-power, wish.
• *v* 1 encourage, influence, inspire, persuade. 2 bequeath, hand down, leave, pass on, settle on.

willing *adj* acquiescent, agreeable, amenable, complaisant, compliant, cooperative, disposed, docile, *inf* game, happy, helpful, inclined, pleased, prepared, obliging, ready, well-disposed. ▷ EAGER. *Opp* UNWILLING.

wilt *v* become limp, droop, fade, flag, flop, languish, sag, shrivel, weaken, wither. *Opp* THRIVE.

wily *adj* artful, astute, canny, clever, crafty, cunning, deceptive, designing, devious, disingenuous, guileful, scheming, *inf* shifty, shrewd, sly, underhand. ▷ DISHONEST. *Opp* STRAIGHTFORWARD.

win *v* 1 be victorious, carry the day, come first, conquer, overcome, prevail, succeed, triumph. 2 *win a prize.* achieve, *inf* carry off, collect, earn, gain, get, obtain, *inf* pick up, receive, secure, *inf* walk away with. *Opp* LOSE.

wind *n* 1 air current, blast, breath, breeze, current of air, cyclone, draught, gale, gust, hurricane, puff, tornado, whirlwind. 2 *wind in the stomach.* flatulence, gas.
• *v* bend, coil, curl, curve, furl, loop, meander, ramble, roll, snake, spiral, turn, twine, twist, *inf* twist and turn, veer, wreathe, zigzag. **winding** ▷ TORTUOUS. **wind up** ▷ FINISH.

windswept *adj* bare, bleak, desolate, exposed. ▷ WINDY.

windy *adj* blowy, blustery, breezy, draughty, fresh, gusty, squally, stormy, tempestuous, windswept. *Opp* CALM.

wink *v* 1 bat (*eyelid*), blink, flutter. 2 flash, flicker, sparkle, twinkle.

winner *n inf* champ, champion, conqueror, medallist, prizewinner, title-holder, victor. *Opp* LOSER.

winning *adj* 1 champion, conquering, first, successful, top, top-scoring, triumphant, undefeated, victorious. *Opp* UNSUCCESSFUL. 2 *winning smile*. ▷ ATTRACTIVE.

wintry *adj* arctic, icy, snowy. ▷ COLD. *Opp* SUMMERY.

wipe *v* clean, cleanse, dry, mop, polish, rub, scour, sponge, swab, wash. **wipe out** ▷ DESTROY.

wire *n* 1 cable, flex, lead, wiring. 2 cablegram, telegram.

wiry *adj* lean, muscular, sinewy, strong, thin, tough.

wisdom *n* astuteness, common sense, discernment, discrimination, good sense, insight, judgement, penetration, perceptiveness, perspicacity, prudence, reason, sagacity, sense, understanding. ▷ INTELLIGENCE.

wise *adj* 1 astute, discerning, enlightened, erudite, fair, just, knowledgeable, perceptive, philosophical, sagacious, sage, sensible, shrewd, sound, thoughtful, understanding, well-informed. ▷ INTELLIGENT. 2 *wise decision*. advisable, considered, diplomatic, expedient, informed, judicious, politic, proper, prudent, rational, reasonable, right. *Opp* UNWISE. **wise person** philosopher, pundit, sage.

wish *n* aim, ambition, appetite, aspiration, craving, desire, fancy, hankering, hope, inclination, itch, keenness, longing, request, urge, want, yearning, *inf* yen.
• *v* ask, bid, desire, request, want. **wish for** ▷ WANT.

wisp *n* shred, strand, streak.

wispy *adj* flimsy, fragile, gossamer, insubstantial, light, thin. *Opp* SUBSTANTIAL.

wistful *adj* disconsolate, forlorn, melancholy, mournful, nostalgic, regretful, yearning. ▷ SAD.

wit *n* 1 banter, cleverness, comedy, facetiousness, humour, ingenuity, repartee, witticisms, wordplay. ▷ INTELLIGENCE. 2 comedian, comic, humorist, joker, wag.

witch *n* enchantress, gorgon, hag, sibyl, sorceress, *pl* weird sisters.

witchcraft *n* black magic, charms, enchantment, magic, *inf* mumbo-jumbo, necromancy, the occult, sorcery, spells, voodoo, wizardry.

withdraw *v* 1 call back, cancel, *inf* go back on, recall, rescind, retract, take back. 2 *withdraw from the fight*. back away, back out, *inf* chicken out, *inf* cry off, draw back, drop out, move back, pull out, quit, recoil, retire, retreat, run away. ▷ LEAVE. *Opp* ADVANCE, ENTER. 3 *withdraw teeth*. extract, pull out, remove, take out.

withdrawn *adj* bashful, diffident, distant, introverted, private, quiet, reclusive, remote, reserved, retiring, shy, silent, solitary, taciturn, timid, uncommunicative. *Opp* SOCIABLE.

wither *v* become limp, dehydrate, droop, dry up, fail, flag, flop, sag, shrink, shrivel, waste away, wilt. *Opp* THRIVE.

withhold *v* conceal, hide, hold back, keep secret, repress, retain, suppress. *Opp* GIVE.

withstand *v* bear, confront, cope with, defy, endure, fight, grapple with, hold out against, oppose, put up with, resist, stand up to, *inf* stick, survive, take, weather (*storm*). *Opp* SURRENDER.

witness *n* bystander, eyewitness, looker-on, observer, onlooker, spectator, viewer, watcher.
• *v* be present at, notice, observe, see, view, watch. **bear witness** ▷ TESTIFY.

witty *adj* amusing, clever, comic, droll, facetious, funny, humorous, ingenious, intelligent, jocular, waggish.

wizard *n* enchanter, magician, magus, sorcerer, *old use* warlock, witch-doctor.

wobble *v* be unsteady, move unsteadily, quake, quiver, rock, shake, sway, teeter, totter, vibrate, waver.

wobbly *adj* loose, rickety, rocky, shaky, teetering, tottering, unsafe, unstable, unsteady. *Opp* STEADY.

woe *n* affliction, anguish, dejection, despair, distress, grief, heartache, melancholy, misery, misfortune, sadness, suffering, trouble, unhappiness, wretchedness. ▷ SORROW. *Opp* HAPPINESS.

woebegone *adj* crestfallen, dejected, downhearted, forlorn, gloomy, melancholy, miserable, woeful, wretched. ▷ SAD. *Opp* CHEERFUL.

woman *n* bird, bride, daughter, dowager, female, girl, girlfriend, housewife, lady, lass, madam, maid, *old use* maiden, matriarch, matron, mistress, mother, virgin, widow, wife.

wonder *n* 1 admiration, amazement, astonishment, awe, bewilderment, curiosity,

fascination, respect, reverence, stupefaction, surprise. 2 *wonder of science.* marvel, miracle, phenomenon.
• *v* ask yourself, be curious, conjecture, marvel, ponder, speculate. ▷ THINK. **wonder at** ▷ ADMIRE.

wonderful *adj* amazing, astonishing, astounding, awe-inspiring, extraordinary, impressive, incredible, marvellous, miraculous, phenomenal, remarkable, surprising, unexpected. *Opp* ORDINARY.

woo *v* 1 *sl* chat up, court. 2 *woo custom.* attract, cultivate, persuade, pursue, seek, tempt.

wood *n* 1 afforestation, coppice, copse, forest, grove, jungle, orchard, plantation, spinney, thicket, trees, woodland, woods. 2 chipboard, deal, hardwood, lumber, planks, plywood, softwood, timber.

wooded *adj* afforested, *poet* bosky, forested, sylvan, timbered, tree-covered, woody.

wooden *adj* 1 timber, wood. 2 *wooden acting.* dead, emotionless, expressionless, lifeless, rigid, stiff, stilted, unnatural. *Opp* LIVELY.

woodwork *n* carpentry, joinery.

woody *adj* fibrous, hard, tough, wooden.

woolly *adj* 1 wool, woollen. 2 *woolly toy.* cuddly, fleecy, furry, fuzzy, shaggy, soft. 3 *woolly ideas.* confused, hazy, ill-defined, indefinite, uncertain, unclear, unfocused, vague.

word *n* 1 expression, name, term. 2 ▷ NEWS. 3 ▷ PROMISE.
• *v* articulate, express, phrase. **word for word** ▷ VERBATIM.

wording *n* choice of words, expression, language, phraseology, phrasing, style, terminology.

wordy *adj* diffuse, digressive, discursive, garrulous, long-winded, loquacious, prolix, rambling, repetitious, talkative, unstoppable, verbose, voluble. *Opp* CONCISE.

work *n* 1 *inf* donkey work, drudgery, effort, exertion, *inf* fag, *inf* graft, *inf* grind, industry, labour, *inf* slog, *inf* spadework, strain, struggle, *inf* sweat, toil. 2 *work to be done.* assignment, chore, commission, duty, errand, job, mission, project, responsibility, task, undertaking. 3 *regular work.* business, calling, career, employment, job, livelihood, living, métier, occupation, post, profession, situation, trade.
• *v* 1 *inf* beaver away, drudge, exert yourself, *inf* grind away, *inf* keep your nose to the grindstone, labour, *inf* plug away, *inf* slave, *inf* slog away, strain, strive, struggle, sweat, toil. 2 be effective, function, go, operate, perform, run, succeed, thrive. 3 *work employees hard.* drive, use, utilize. **working** ▷ EMPLOYED, OPERATIONAL. **work out** ▷ CALCULATE. **work up** ▷ DEVELOP, EXCITE.

worker *n* artisan, breadwinner, craftsman, employee, *old use* hand, labourer, member of staff, navvy, operative, operator, tradesman, wage-earner, workman.

workforce *n* employees, staff, workers.

workmanship *n* art, artistry, craft, craftsmanship, expertise, handiwork, skill, technique.

workshop *n* factory, mill, studio, workroom.

world *n* 1 earth, globe, planet. 2 *the art world.* domain, field, milieu, sphere.

worldly *adj* 1 earthly, human, mundane, physical, secular, temporal. 2 cosmopolitan, urbane, sophisticated. 3 covetous, greedy, materialistic, selfish.

worm *v* crawl, creep, slither, squirm, wriggle. writhe.

worn *adj* 1 frayed, moth-eaten, old, ragged, *inf* scruffy, shabby, tattered, *inf* tatty, thin, threadbare. 2 *worn out.* ▷ WEARY.

worried *adj* afraid, agitated, alarmed, anxious, apprehensive, bothered, concerned, distraught, distressed, disturbed, edgy, fearful, *inf* fraught, fretful, insecure, nervous, obsessed (by), on edge, overwrought, perplexed, perturbed, tense, troubled, uncertain, uneasy, unhappy, upset.

worry *n* 1 agitation, anxiety, apprehension, disquiet, distress, fear, perplexity, tension, unease, uneasiness. 2 affliction, bother, burden, care, concern, misgiving, problem, *pl* trials and tribulations, trouble.
• *v* 1 agitate, annoy, badger, bother, disquiet, distress, disturb, *inf* hassle, irritate, nag, perplex, perturb, pester, plague, torment, trouble, upset. *Opp* REASSURE. 2 *worry about money.* agonize, be anxious, brood, exercise yourself, feel uneasy, fret.

worsen *v* 1 aggravate, exacerbate, intensify, make worse. 2 *His health worsened.* decline, degenerate, deteriorate, get worse, *inf* go downhill. *Opp* IMPROVE.

worship *n* adoration, devotion, glorification, homage, love, praise, reverence, veneration.

• *v* admire, adore, be devoted to, dote on, exalt, glorify, hero-worship, idolize, lionize, laud, look up to, love, pay homage to, praise, pray to, *inf* put on a pedestal, revere, venerate.

worth *n* benefit, cost, good, importance, merit, quality, significance, use, usefulness, utility, value. **be worth** be priced at, cost, have a value of.

worthless *adj* dispensable, disposable, futile, *inf* good-for-nothing, hollow, insignificant, meaningless, meretricious, paltry, pointless, poor, *inf* rubbishy, *inf* trashy, trifling, trivial, unimportant, unprofitable, useless, vain, valueless. *Opp* WORTHWHILE.

worthwhile *adj* advantageous, beneficial, considerable, fruitful, gratifying, helpful, important, invaluable, meaningful, noticeable, productive, profitable, remunerative, rewarding, satisfying, significant, sizeable, substantial, useful, valuable. ▷ WORTHY. *Opp* WORTHLESS.

worthy *adj* admirable, commendable, creditable, decent, deserving, estimable, good, honest, honourable, laudable, meritorious, praiseworthy, reputable, respectable, worthwhile. *Opp* UNWORTHY.

wound *n* 1 bite, bruise, burn, contusion, cut, damage, gash, graze, injury, laceration, scar, scratch. 2 distress, grief, hurt, insult, pain, trauma.
• *v* 1 bite, bruise, cut, damage, harm, hurt, gore, graze, injure, lacerate, lash, maul, scratch, shoot, stab. 2 cause pain to, distress, grieve, offend, shock, traumatize. *Opp* HEAL, MEND.

wrap *n* cape, cloak, mantle, poncho, shawl, stole.
• *v* bundle up, cloak, cocoon, conceal, cover, encase, enclose, enfold, envelop, hide, insulate, lag, muffle, pack, package, shroud, surround, swathe.

wreathe *v* adorn, decorate, encircle, festoon, intertwine, interweave, twist, weave.

wreck *n* 1 hulk, shipwreck. ▷ WRECKAGE. 2 *wreck of all my hopes.* demolition, destruction, devastation, loss, obliteration, overthrow, ruin, undoing.
• *v* 1 annihilate, break up, crush, dash to pieces, demolish, destroy, devastate, ruin, shatter, smash, spoil, *inf* write off. 2 *wreck a ship.* capsize, founder, scuttle, sink, shipwreck.

wreckage *n* debris, flotsam and jetsam, fragments, pieces, remains, rubble, ruins.

wrench *v* force, jerk, lever, prize, pull, rip, strain, tear, tug, twist, wrest, wring, *inf* yank.

wrestle *v* grapple, strive, struggle, tussle. ▷ FIGHT.

wretch *n* 1 miserable person, poor devil, unfortunate. 2 rascal, rogue, scoundrel, villain.

wretched *adj* 1 dejected, depressed, dispirited, downhearted, hapless, melancholy, miserable, pitiful, unfortunate. ▷ SAD. 2 ▷ UNSATISFACTORY.

wriggle *v* crawl, snake, squirm, twist, worm, writhe.

wring *v* 1 clasp, crush, grip, shake, squeeze, twist, wrench, wrest. 2 coerce, extort, extract, force.

wrinkle *n* corrugation, crease, crinkle, *pl* crow's feet, fold, furrow, gather, line, pleat, pucker, ridge, ripple.
• *v* corrugate, crease, crinkle, crumple, fold, furrow, gather, pleat, pucker up, ridge, ripple, rumple, screw up.

wrinkled *adj* corrugated, creased, crinkly, crumpled, furrowed, lined, pleated, ridged, rumpled, screwed up, shrivelled, wizened, wrinkly. *Opp* SMOOTH.

write *v* compile, compose, copy, correspond, draft, draw up, inscribe, jot, note, pen, print, put in writing, record, scrawl, scribble, take down, transcribe. **write off** ▷ CANCEL, DESTROY.

writer *n* author, columnist, composer, contributor, correspondent, dramatist, essayist, *derog* hack, journalist, novelist, *derog* pen-pusher, playwright, poet, reporter, scribe, scriptwriter,

writhe *v* coil, contort, squirm, struggle, thrash about, twist, wriggle.

writing *n* 1 calligraphy, characters, copperplate, handwriting, hieroglyphics, inscription, longhand, penmanship, scrawl, screed, scribble, script. 2 literature, letters. 3 [sometimes *pl*] article, book, column, composition, correspondence, diary, document, editorial, essay, fiction, manuscript, non-fiction, novel, play, poem, poetry, prose, opus, publication, review, text, treatise, typescript, work.

written *adj* documentary, *inf* in black and white, inscribed, in writing, set down, transcribed, typewritten. *Opp* SPOKEN.

wrong *adj* 1 base, corrupt, criminal, *inf* crooked, deceitful, dishonest, dishonourable, evil, illegal, illegitimate, illicit, immoral, iniquitous, irresponsible, misleading, reprehensible, sinful, specious, unethical, unjustifiable, unlawful, unprincipled, unscrupulous, vicious, villainous, wicked. 2 *wrong answers.* erroneous, false, imprecise, inaccurate, incorrect, misleading, mistaken, wide of the mark. 3 *wrong decision, idea.* ill-advised, ill-considered, ill-judged, impolitic, imprudent, injudicious, misguided, misjudged, unfair, unfounded, unjust, untrue, unwise, wrongful. 4 *He saw nothing wrong in his behaviour.* improper, inappropriate, incongruous, unacceptable, undesirable, unseemly, unsuitable, 5 *Something's wrong.* amiss, defective, faulty, out of order, the matter. *Opp* RIGHT.

• *v* abuse, chear, do an injustice to, harm, hurt, injure, malign, misrepresent, mistreat, treat unfairly. **do wrong** ▷ MISBEHAVE.

wrongdoer *n* convict, criminal, *inf* crook, culprit, delinquent, evil-doer, lawbreaker, malefactor, mischief-maker, miscreant, offender, sinner, transgressor.

wrongdoing *n* crime, delinquency, disobedience, evil, iniquity, malpractice, misbehaviour, mischief, naughtiness, offence, sin, wickedness.

wry *adj* 1 askew, awry, crooked, lopsided, twisted, uneven. 2 *wry sense of humour.* droll, dry, ironic, mocking, sardonic.

Y Z

yard *n* court, courtyard, enclosure, garden.

yarn *n* 1 fibre, thread. 2 anecdote, narrative, story, tale.

yawning *adj* gaping, open, wide.

yearly *adj* annual, perennial.

yearn *v* ache, hanker, hunger, itch, long, pine. ▷ WANT.

yellow *adj* blond(e), gold, golden, tawny.

yield *n* 1 crop, harvest, output, product. 2 earnings, gain, income, interest, proceeds, profit, return, revenue.
• *v* 1 acquiesce, assent, bow, capitulate, *inf* cave in, comply, concede, defer, give in, give way, submit, succumb, surrender, *inf* throw in the towel. 2 *yield interest.* bear, earn, generate, pay out, produce, provide, return, supply. **yielding** ▷ FLEXIBLE, SUBMISSIVE.

young *adj* 1 baby, early, growing, immature, new-born, undeveloped. 2 *young people.* adolescent, juvenile, pubescent, teenage, underage, youthful. 3 *young for your age.* babyish, boyish, childish, girlish, *inf* green, immature, infantile, juvenile, naive, puerile.
• *n* brood, family, issue, litter, offspring, progeny.

youth *n* 1 adolescence, boyhood, childhood, girlhood, infancy, minority, puberty, *inf* salad days, *inf* teens. 2 adolescent, boy, juvenile, *inf* kid, lad, minor, teenager, youngster.

youthful *adj* fresh, lively, sprightly, vigorous, well-preserved. ▷ YOUNG.

zany *adj* absurd, eccentric, *inf* mad, madcap, ridiculous.

zeal *n derog* bigotry, enthusiasm, fanaticism, fervour, partisanship.

zealot *n* bigot, extremist, fanatic, radical.

zealous *adj* eager, earnest, enthusiastic, fanatical, fervent, keen, militant, obsessive, partisan, passionate. *Opp* APATHETIC.

zenith *n* acme, apex, height, highest point, peak, pinnacle, summit, top. *Opp* NADIR.

zero *n* nil, nothing, nought, *sl* zilch. **zero in on** ▷ AIM.

zest *n* appetite, eagerness, energy, enjoyment, enthusiasm, gusto, passion, relish, zeal.

zigzag *adj inf* bendy, *inf* in and out, indirect, meandering, serpentine, twisting, winding.
• *v* bend, curve, meander, snake, tack, twist, wind.

zone *n* area, belt, district, locality, neighbourhood, quarter, region, sector, sphere, territory, vicinity.

zoom *v* career, dart, dash, hurry, hurtle, race, rush, shoot, speed, *inf* whiz, *inf* zip.